Body Psychotherapy

Body Psychotherapy: History, Concepts, and Methods

Michael C. Heller

W. W. Norton & Company
New York • London

For information about permission to reproduce selections from this book, write to
Permissions, W. W. Norton & Company, Inc., 500 Fifth Avenue, New York, NY 10110

For information about special discounts for bulk purchases, please contact
W. W. Norton Special Sales at specialsales@wwnorton.com or 800-233-4830

Manufacturing by Courier, Kendallville
Production manager: Leeann Graham

Library of Congress Cataloging-in-Publication Data
Heller, Michael, 1949–
    [Psychotherapies corporelles. English]
    Body psychotherapy : history, concepts, and methods / Michael C. Heller.
        p. cm. — (A Norton professional book)
    Includes bibliographical references and index.
    ISBN 978-0-393-70669-7 (hardcover)
1. Mind and body therapies.   I. Title.
    RC489.M53H4513 2012
    615.5—dc23   2011042668

W. W. Norton & Company, Inc., 500 Fifth Avenue, New York, N.Y. 10110
www.wwnorton.com

W. W. Norton & Company, Ltd., Castle House, 75/76 Wells Street, London W1T 3QT

1 2 3 4 5 6 7 8 9 0

Contents

PART VII. NONVERBAL COMMUNICATION RESEARCH
AND PSYCHOTHERAPY

Foreword
Resisting Reductionism

Philippe Rochat

It is not unusual to hear that psychology is dead, or dying, gasping for air under the tidal wave in the neurosciences. It reminds us of Hegel and Marx announcing the end of history, with the establishment of the modern democratic state for one, the crowning of socialism for the other. Two hundred years later, look where we stand! History continues with plentiful blood and injustice. The fundamentals remain the same despite the goodwill of all the bloody French and other red revolutions. By analogy, exciting progress in current neurosciences do not eliminate the fundamental questions that drove centuries of psychological inquiries, from Heraclitus in ancient Greece to great Eastern thinkers like Lao Tzu, all trying to capture human experience: what it means to be alive in this world.

I often see my colleagues reassured by their vision of a dying psychology, agonizing under the new lights of the brain sciences. But are we really on the edge of reducing human experience to its brain substance? Are we truly at the threshold of an absolute deterministic understanding of what it means to be alive, in this world, and more important, alive among other embodied and sentient entities? Nothing of the sort since the stuff of basic science is, as always and in an infinite regress, opening doors leading to more, never able to get absolute closure on anything. We are just getting better at *approximating* psychic phenomena. My neuroscience colleagues tend to get ahead of themselves in their renewed enthusiasm, and psychology resists reductionism in all its classic dimensions, be they clinical, cognitive, social, or developmental. Michael Heller's book is a masterful demonstration of psychology resisting brain reductionism.

It is not a secret that part of the enthusiasm around the neurosciences is dictated by the exponential technological progress in imaging and recording brain activities, notwithstanding the enormous financial investment in brain imaging laboratories that put much pressure on the kind of psychological research questions addressed by neuroscientists: questions and psychological phenomena that have the potential of being reduced and redescribed in neurochemical, biological terms. But the new brain enthusiasm comes at a cost and at a loss. Because of its necessary reductionist and mechanistic undertone, it eludes the meaning of human experience in all its complexity and all its basic nondeterministic "messiness." It is an experience that in essence cannot be captured by the study of a brain "in a vat" or a contextual vacuum (see Thompson, 2008). Our brain is just part of a whole that includes the rest of the body, but also other bodies and other interacting brains.

When we think of it, in the end, the fundamental problem of psychology (i.e., the meanings of being alive in this world and what can be deduced from such meanings to capture the human experience) is not reducible to an individual bodily and brain system, a system that would be completely isolatable to be "decorticated" to its marrow, in the same way that one now decodes and describes the human genome with one long string combining a small ensemble of constitutive DNA elements. No.

The rapid progress in our understanding of brain structure and functioning certainly forces us to reformulate ancient questions about human experience: the mind–body question, the interplay between the physical and the mental, intersubjectivity in general. It does not however resolve questions raised for at least twenty centuries, from the Greeks in the West and the philosophies and meditation practices in the East, particularly those that flourished in India. This textbook is a brilliant demonstration of the importance of anchoring historically the relation of the psyche to the organism, and eventually to the body within traditions and conceptions that have evolved and continue to evolve. Heller reminds us of the importance of positing issues within a diachronic, historical perspective.

In our rich era made of exponential technological inventions and scientific discoveries, we should not get blinded of the fact that the problems of the relation between the body, the organism, and the psyche are *eternal problems*. They take roots in a long Western and Eastern tradition. If the current neurosciences provide a decisive jolt to reflections about these problems, they are far from offering decisive answers, particularly when limiting its foray to an isolated, individual brain in a vat, be it a bony scull.

In his book, Heller demonstrates painstakingly and cogently that psychological phenomena cannot be captured only inside the individual but rather emerge at the interface of individual bodies, organisms, and brains. The meanings of psychological phenomena can be only captured in the process of an interaction between these systems. Heller makes the demonstration in ways that are reminiscent of the eighteenth-century encyclopedic tradition, not shying away from a large harvest, with broad connections from Western philosophy to Eastern traditions and other Eastern and Western ancestral intuitions and practices.

Heller reminds us that psychic experience is the integration of all these levels with processes that operate within and outside the individual, in interaction
with other individuals, like patients interacting with therapists.

Psychotherapy of any kind, whether it focuses primarily on the body or
not, does not just pertain to a body, an organism, or a psyche organization that
is more or less well functioning. It always pertains to a relation between bodies,
organisms, and psychic entities.

There is developmental proof of such general assertion in the fact that from
around two years of age, all children (except probably those showing symptoms
of autism) start to conceptualize themselves as perceived and judged through
the evaluative eyes of others. From this age children start to express unambigu-
ous embarrassment and the first signs of shame and guilt, presumably the trade-
marks of our species (see Darwin, 1872, on blushing). All these self-conscious
emotions are eminently social, determined by the interplay and integration of
mutual self and others' feelings and mental representations, a major source of
typical psychological ills that eventually lead patients to seek therapeutic help.

These psychological ills are not just circumscribed and contained within the
patient's head and body. Such ills are revealed in interaction of the patient with
others, with the therapist in particular, who become aware *with* the patient of
his or her suffering. In interaction, patient and therapist become co-conscious of
ills and sufferings that become objectified to both. In the therapeutic relation or
alliance, both parties reactualize such ills so they can be objectified and treated
together, rendering them public for the duration of the therapy.

This point is not as trivial as it might sound. In the case of body therapies,
when patients allow the therapist to touch them or to be guided in breathing
exercises, they surrender to the therapist providing intimate access and the possibility for the therapist to share the experience of the patients, particularly the
experience that led them to seek therapy, whether it is an acute pain, an obsessive rumination, a simple curiosity, or a need for social attention and recognition on the part of the patient.

No matter what, therapeutic effects rest on a basic phenomenon of co-
consciousness. They cannot be attributed to either the patient or the therapist. It
is, rather, at the interface of their encounter, and this is why there is something
fundamentally wrong in thinking that the comprehension of the individual
brain will exhaust what is conceived by some as "prehistorical" psychological
problems. Current leaps in individual brain understanding are only one decisive, yet not exhaustive progress in a traditional questioning, namely, the interplay between body, organism, and psyche. This a major point brilliantly made
by Heller in his book, using a vast array of cogent details and analogies that
cross over clinical and experimental psychology, the neurosciences, and also history: the history of sciences as well as the history of Eastern and Western philosophies. It is a masterful contribution.

Heller's book provides an indispensable tool of reflection on what is at the
core of any clinical work: the relation and interplay between body, organism,

and the psyche. Heller provides here a broad, encyclopedic synthesis on an issue that is at the core of clinical psychology and allied disciplines. He offers us the gift of his insatiable curiosity, enormous knowledge, and, more important, an untamed enthusiasm that permeates this monumental contribution. The enthusiasm is not just intellectual or academic. It is also clinical. Heller's effort is primarily aimed at therapists who will benefit from his knowledge by becoming more cogent of their own practices and theoretical intuitions. Heller's bet is that they will become better therapists. Not too farfetched, really.

By its clarity and enormous intellectual breadth, this book can only broaden the clinical grasp of practitioners, whether or not they are well versed in the practice of body psychotherapies.

Preface to the English Edition

THE BASIC AIM OF THIS TEXTBOOK

This book has been written for all those who wish to study a form of body psychotherapy or who wish to discover the basic issues that have structured this field. The notion of body psychotherapy includes a discussion of any form of psychotherapy that explicitly includes body dynamics in its way of thinking about *psychological* dynamics. This option is different from (although related to) other forms of body–mind approaches that explicitly include psychological dynamics in their way of thinking about body dynamics but do not focus on psychological dynamics as their main object of attention.

The structure of this volume is that of a textbook, because it contains what I think people should know about the field of body psychotherapy, rather than an essay that publicizes my personal thoughts on the matter. Had I wanted to write an essay or a history of the field, I would have detailed each chapter in a different way. Writing a textbook forced me to be as clear as possible, leave out some of my personal positions, and use summarization and simplification when required by sound pedagogy.

Some people have voiced their appreciation of the way this book presents the practice of body psychotherapy. However, they complained that its content did not help them know how to work therapeutically with patients. For the moment, such knowledge is taught by schools of psychotherapy. Each movement has its own set of coherent concepts and methods, which require several years of apprenticeship before they can be used in the treatment of patients. This book does not replace the manuals that describe what specific schools of body psychotherapy teach their students. It focuses on a description of the field as a whole, so that students can situate what they learn in a particular school within a wider context. I focus on the issues and methods that have structured the field as it develops new ways of approaching the psyche for therapeutic purposes. Once a student becomes aware of these issues and methods, he can forge his own vision of body psychotherapy with greater precision and can identify his interests, all while being aware of the different options that exist in the field.

THE FIELD OF BODY PSYCHOTHERAPY AS COVERED IN THIS BOOK

The field of psychotherapy is made up of different schools. Each school distinguishes itself from the others by its vocabulary, methods, and practices and a particular vision. Sometimes, the same word used by several schools covers different concepts and methods, or different words yield understandings that are similar.

A first way to approach the idea of a book about body psychotherapy is to propose a work that describes a school's concepts and methods. A good example of such a book in French is the School of Psycho-Organic Analysis's own training handbook, edited in several volumes by Jacqueline Besson since 1991. This handbook defines the vocabulary, the models, the practices, and the modes of intervention taught in the school's training program. It also describes the clinical perspective of this approach—that is, how a therapist trained in this school perceives his patients and their problems, how he envisions the psychotherapeutic process, and the goals that can be linked to a treatment that uses the methods of Psycho-Organic Analysis. The manual also demonstrates how this school conceptualizes the rapport between its clinical approach and that of other schools. It attempts to define the compatibility between its clinical approach and the diagnostics used in psychiatry, psychoanalysis, cognitive and behavioral therapy, and so on.

This book has another goal. It wants to complement other texts like the one I just mentioned. Its usefulness has been the object of discussions in several committees in which I have taken part in the European Association of Body Psychotherapy (EABP). To the extent that each school's training manual covers a selection of different practices and concepts, it is also useful to put together a manual that would allow students to situate what they learn in a particular school in the larger field of body psychotherapy. Most of the people trained in psychotherapy often have a limited view of the history of their discipline, the big issues that animate their approach, and the place their school occupies in the history of human thought. Thus, many practitioners have both an exaggerated regard for the knowledge bestowed on them by those who trained them and too little regard for the knowledge they obtained through their own broader education and in their own clinical practice. Their inability to evaluate what they know relative to the sciences, philosophy, and other psychotherapeutic approaches creates feelings of insecurity. This manual presents the entire field to those who would like to understand the full scope of body psychotherapy and what it can contribute to other disciplines.

The perspective of a textbook is to summarize some basic concepts that must be developed in courses, seminars, internships, and workshops that tackle practical problems like case analyses. I have followed this customary procedure. Although this text can be understood by many without additional help, as I have tried to be as clear and simple as possible, it remains relatively dense because I had to cover an immense number of issues that are regularly brought up in conversations between body psychotherapists. Those discussions can become complex, and this book defends the necessity that psychotherapists must be capable of understanding difficult questions. Our patients consider with us the meaning of life and death; they question pleasure and life itself, as well as how difficult it is to love. None of these topics yields easy answers. It seems to me that a body psychotherapist must learn to follow the complexities of their patients' thoughts, physiology, and behaviors. By understanding the myriad byways of the questions that haunt a patient, a practitioner reaches that moment when a simple response permits a patient's thought to crystallize around a useful metaphor. I have only developed complex theoretical issues when they can help a practitioner understand connected practical issues. Sometimes a difficult chapter will become easier to understand once other chapters have been read. I have not attempted to describe body exercises in detail, because I do not recommend working on one's body or the body of another person without having first worked with a teacher.

THE LIMITS OF THE BOOK

I have focused the discussions in this book on the psychotherapeutic treatment of patients in individual adult psychotherapy. This choice does not exclude interest in other approaches or other patient populations, but it permits me to stay relatively focused. I will not speak at all about group therapy, although it is often used by body psychotherapists, and I only discuss a few methods used in child psychotherapy.

Although I mention important theories about the body and the psyche, I do not really propose a new one. The plan of this textbook was inspired by many discussions with my colleagues. This permitted me to cover a maximum number of existing options in body psychotherapy. It is more or less inevitable that my own journey has permitted me to more easily understand and appreciate some propositions more than others.[1] It is thus inevitable that I would write this book in the first person. However, this "I" is a "pedagogical I" who attempts to describe a discipline that needs to synthesize numerous points of view. The topics developed in these pages are rarely issues about which it is possible or even desirable to have a fixed position. Each reader will inevitably have positions that are his own as they relate to the topics.

Practitioners rarely know the history of the notions they frequently use. Furthermore, having been trained in developmental psychology, I am used to situating ideas in their historical context. This strategy often helps one understand the connections between different concepts. So I decided to organize the material herein in a historical narrative envelope. Those who already know certain schools or certain personalities that I mention will notice that it is the relevance of a model for today's practitioner that is favored, rather than an exact description of what happened. These movements and personalities serve as historical reference points. It seems useful to me to show how these reference points, like magnets attracting iron filings, gather a multitude of topics that can call out to contemporary psychotherapists. The reader may use these reference points as a way to organize important ideas in body psychotherapy and consult more specialized works if, per chance, he wants to explore the formulations of a school of thought, or recent developments in that discipline.

As an individual, I can develop a wide variety of themes in a relatively coherent way. However such a procedure is inevitably influenced by my personal biases. It complements the method used by Gustl Marlock and Halko Weiss (2006) that covers similar models by asking experts from a number of different schools to describe their vision of basic notions of body psychotherapy.

HOW TO USE THE BOOK

It is best to read this book from the first chapter to the last. It seems important to me to get an idea of the whole range of a domain before becoming a specialist. Nonetheless, a textbook is hardly ever used in that manner. Certain chapters are more relevant to adherents of one school than to those of another, and it can be read more easily by some because they resonate to a particular training. To allow the reader to read only a chapter of interest, I developed certain important themes several times in the course of the book. These themes run through the text as in a musical variation or fugue. These repetitions permit the reader to learn how to reconstruct a concept in different contexts.

I have tried to gather most of the topics that a body psychotherapist ought to have thoughtfully considered. The majority of the schools of psychotherapy require written work during each year of study or at least at the end of the training. This book can be useful as a basis for these assignments because it contains a detailed bibliography for each topic. The more recent texts also contain bibliographies that can help you find the writings you need.

If you are seeking possible ways to read this book, I propose an exercise that I have often found useful. For each chapter, you can ask yourself the following questions: If the content of this chapter served as the basis of a psychotherapeutic approach, in what ways would I engage with a patient, a person I am trying to understand? What characteristics of this individual does this approach help me explore? For example, you can ask yourself how a psychotherapist would work were he inspired by Taoism, by Descartes, or by Hume.[2] Also, do not hesitate to use online search engines to find complementary information. For the subject matter covered by this manual, Wikipedia often gives exact and pertinent information, although often incomplete. This type of site cannot be used for reference purposes, to support a treatment, or to support an academic or professional paper; but it does refer to serious works, proposes useful links, and indicates texts that can be downloaded.

In the references, I have identified texts that can be found online. A glossary, at the end of the book, defines certain key terms. At the end of the volume, an appendix develops some technical points of postural anatomy.

Because some of my references exist in several editions, I have often indicated them in function of the system of the chapters and the sections proper to the work. The page number is insufficient if you want to find out what I am referring to in another edition than the one I used. If you consult a work in another language or in another translation, the difficulty will even be greater.

For the English translation, I tried to improve the text that had first been published in French with some clarifications. I added a chapter on gymnastics and psychotherapy at the request of several colleagues. This is, therefore, a second edition of the original work.

Acknowledgments

If this book is able to present a wide vision of the domain of body psycho-therapy, it is because my project has been sustained by the discussions with many trainers, colleagues, friends, and patients to whom I want to express my gratitude. The meetings within the European Association of Body Psychotherapy (EABP) permitted me not only to meet individuals that represent many diverse approaches but also to discuss with colleagues the types of trainings that would be beneficial to develop in the future. Courtney Young, when president of the association, had even used the term *Academy* to designate a form of general instruction that would complement the more specific knowledge taught in each psychotherapy school. I also thank all those who have inspired me throughout my life. I would like to give thanks here particularly to those who have helped me write and publish this book.

Above all, I discussed the ideas in this book with Claire Colliard, George Downing, and Philippe Rochat. Even though we were not always in agreement, they insisted that I detail the themes I wanted to elaborate here with as much precision and clarity as possible. I thank them for their important intellectual support and friendship. George Downing also provided me with crucial references. Claire Colliard initiated the project in conversation with De Boeck Publishing. I thank Frederic Jongen and Julie Sansdrap from De Boeck Publishing for having made this project possible.

Maud Struchen, Claire Colliard, and Jean-Marie Baron helped me improve the French version.

For the English project, I must first thank the translator, Marcel A. Duclos, who first supported the book in a warm review (Duclos, 2008), and then coura-geously took up the project of translating it. Our collaboration was extremely comfortable, efficient, collegial, and friendly. Jacqueline A. Carleton, board member of the United States Association for Body Psychotherapy (USABP) and editor of the journal of this association, has also supported the translation project, helping and rereading it as it developed. As Marcel A. Duclos is also a board member of the USABP, it can be said that the present translation was strongly supported by members of that group. Professor Ed Tronick helped me present the translation project to W. W. Norton and then convinced them to accept the project. The EABP and the Swiss section supported the translation project and sponsored most of the translation costs.

Deborah Malmud and her team at W.W. Norton publishers have supported this project in a supportive and efficient way. Jean Blackburn and her editorial team at Bytheway Publishing Services have also brought useful corrections and remarks that helped Marcel Duclos and myself to improve the original translation.

Many colleagues helped me with different parts of this book: Maartin Aalberse, Béatrice Bajetta, Jean-Marie Baron, Beatrice Beebe, Angela Belz-Knöferl, Lucio Bizzini, Bjørn Blumenthal, Berit Heir Bunkan, Yves Brault, Urs Daendliker, Alison Duguid, Ernst Falzeder, Anne Fraise, Siegfried Frey, François Fleury, Peter Geissler, Ulf Geuter, Marulla Hauswirth, André Haynal, Véronique Haynal-Reymond, Rubens Kignel, Sander Kirsch, Michel Meignant, Nic Minden, Maryvonne Nicolet-Gognalons, Kaj Noschis, Bjørn Skar Ødegaard, Cédric Papazian, Claudia Passos, Alain Ringger, Magalie Rochat, Florin Roulet, Georgette Salveson-Delvaux, Michael Salveson, Roger Tellenbach, Ed Tronick, Joop Valstar, Judyth O. Weaver, and Courtenay Young. They helped me be as precise as possible, and often inspired me by discussing some aspects of the book. They also helped me improve the content after the French edition came out.

I also thank my wife, Nicole, for having so well protected the space and time that I needed to write this book.

It is extremely rewarding to write a textbook for a field that has so often and so kindly helped me become as creative as possible.

Body Psychotherapy

Introduction

BODY PSYCHOTHERAPY

Classical psychotherapy preoccupies itself with the psychological functions, that is, with the ways a person perceives and experiences what is happening. The first psychotherapeutic approaches, like Freudian psychoanalysis and Jungian analysis, mostly used two approaches to access the patient's psyche:

1. An explicit access that uses verbal communication to construct a shared representation of the patient's experience.
2. An implicit access composed of impressions about what is happening during a psychotherapy session. For psychoanalysts, this type of access led to discussions on transference and countertransference. The boundaries of this form of communication remain imprecise, even when one accepts that information can be transferred from one person to another and influences how each person experiences what is going on. This mode of communication is often considered preverbal. It is explicitly present in all forms of psychotherapy and may become central in child psychotherapy and in the treatment of psychotic patients.

A first characterization of body psychotherapy is to include in this category all forms of psychotherapy that explicitly use body techniques to strengthen the developing dialogue between patient and psychotherapist about what is being experienced and perceived. In most schools of body psychotherapy, the body is considered a means of communication and exploration just as complex and rich as verbal communication: "The body is no longer experienced as an object of awareness but as an aspect of awareness" (Salveson, 1997, p. 35). It is often a shared understanding among the schools of body psychotherapy that language and body became increasingly complex within the same developmental process, and language is a subsystem of the organism's capacity to communicate.[1] Initially, the body psychotherapeutic approaches integrated two dimensions associated with the body:

1. An explicit exploration of behavior. The psychotherapist serves as a mirror and describes the way he perceives the patient's behavior. He also asks the patient to explore what is happening when he tries to behave differently.
2. The utilization of body techniques developed in the fields of physical therapy, dance, and sports. The focus is first on the interaction between muscle tone, respiration, the coordination of movements, and the psyche.

More recently, certain body psychotherapists integrate a larger scope of body-related phenomena, like the analysis of nonverbal communication. These visible and spontaneous activities are situated at the intersection of social norms, behavior, the body, and habitual movements.[2]

Psychotherapy that systematically explores behavior is not referred to as body psychotherapy but as behavior therapy. The integration in psychotherapy of what the anthropologist Marcel Mauss (1934) called the "techniques of the body" characterizes the field of body psychotherapy. To create a model that integrates bodily and psychological dynamics, body psychotherapists found it necessary to modify classical theories, which had been developed to explain what happens in one of these two domains: "When we take into account the impact of body phenomena on relational dynamics, we quickly notice to what extent the current theoretical constructs relative to interaction need to be radically reformulated" (Rispoli, 1995; translated by Marcel Duclos). In this book, I elected to discuss that which essentially establishes the domain of body psychotherapy. There exist age-old practices and discussions that permit us to affirm that the body–mind approaches carry with them robust experience and robust[3] expertise. Because scientific researchers have not yet studied this domain in a systematic way, we count mostly on phenomena that have often been observed over time in a great variety of cultural contexts. The relevance of integrating body techniques in psychotherapeutic approaches is supported by extensive clinical research and numerous collegial interactions. It is, above all, these robust models that merit learning by body psychotherapists in training and by those who would like to reflect on what these approaches are discovering and proposing.

The following section is a theoretical summary of the reference model used for this volume. Some may prefer to read the concrete examples in the chapters of this book and then read this section later.

THE DIMENSIONS OF THE ORGANISM

While writing this book, I discovered that I could group most of the models I was describing in a *system of the dimensions of the organism* (SDO), or *system of organismic dimensions*. This systemic model claims a pedagogical status but not a scientific one. Its purpose is to allow a clinician to situate the types of interventions he might use in psychotherapy sessions and situate those used by colleagues. No single approach corresponds to the model of reference provided herein, but it allows a relatively accurate description of the different modes of intervention used in psychotherapy. This system of organismic dimensions is used to situate the various topics presented in this book with greater ease. I therefore describe this system in the following sections.

An Individual Is an Organism

Galileo (1630) and Newton (1686) use the term *body* to designate any material object that can be perceived and weighted and has a clear contour. Thus, a star seen from far way, a stone, or a plant is a "body." Mechanics is the science that attempts to describe and predict the behavior of inanimate bodies.

The term *body* was also used to designate animated entities. Any individual plant or animal is a body. For William James,[4] the brain, hormones, and veins are parts of the human body. This meaning is still used today. For example, Antonio Damasio (1999) wrote a book with the subtitle *Body and Emotion in the Making of Consciousness*. In this title, the term *body* designates all the physiological dynamics of an organism—the nervous system, hormones, muscles, and breathing—in an undifferentiated way. This remains the most familiar usage of the term *body*. Body psychotherapeutic approaches that use this vocabulary are sometimes called *somatic psychotherapy*.

This meaning of the term *body* is equivalent to the term *organism* used by most biologists. In seventeenth-century France, the term *organism* designated "a living being endowed with organs whose totality constitutes a living being." The term *organism* thus replaced the term *living body* used by Lamarck. This French term entered the English language in the eighteenth century to designate "an individual animal, plant, or single-celled life form" (*The New Oxford Dictionary of English*, 1999, p. 1307). In this volume, I use the term *organism* to designate an individual system. For example, Darwin writes that "The relation of organism to organism . . . [is] the most important of all relations."[5]

All the mechanisms contained in an organism participate in several regulatory systems. They may thus have several functions simultaneously. One of these functions may be to belong to a particular dense network that organizes itself around a particular adaptive function of the organism. The principal functions of adaptation form what I call the *dimensions* of the organism. There are no clear limits between one dimension and the other mechanisms of regulation of an organism, but it is useful for treatment to consider the dimensions like relatively well-differentiated subsystems. As the SDO is a systemic model, I first summarize certain general features of system theory.[6]

Some Basic Systemic Assumptions Used for the SDO Model

My main frame of reference is a systemic developmental theory,[7] close to the genetic and constructivist structuralism of Jean Piaget (1967, 1985). As system theory can become complex, I focus on a few points that are often useful during psychotherapy sessions:

1. A system is a dynamic organization of subsystems that allow for the conservation of a collection of dynamic connections over time. This organization can evolve over time. All the substances contained in the system can be renewed without destroying the system. A biological system is in interaction with its environment, and is susceptible to internal regulations for its adaptation to its environment in order to maximize its chances of survival. The psychotherapist generally centers his attention on a human organism, that is, an individual person.

2. The genetic approach to a system[8] supposes that an organism shapes, constitutes, and develops itself in the course of its entire life. The universe, nature, and organisms are systems "in becoming" that transform themselves according to historical rhythms that can be more or less rapid. For psychotherapy, it is useful to distinguish biological and individual histories. Biological genesis (phylogenesis) is described by Lamarck's (1802) theory of evolution. In that history, some species took millions of years to evolve. As for the genesis of a human organism (ontogenesis), it uses the units of months and years as a frame of reference. A detailed view of the history of our planet and its species demonstrates that each phenomenon has its particular time frame.

The functioning of a system is regulated by *mechanisms* that participate in the continuing interactions between the system and its subsystems. To the extent that in psychotherapy, the mechanisms observed are often too complex to be situated with precision, it is wise to analyze a mechanism following the advice of Jon Elster: "Roughly speaking, mechanisms are frequently occurring and easily recognizable causal patterns that are triggered under generally unknown conditions or with indeterminate conditions" (Elster, 1998, I.I.1, p. 1).

One of the fundamental ideas of system theory is that each entity is a system onto itself and systems are hierarchically organized. The molecule is a system made up of atoms that organize themselves in a particular fashion; the cell is a system composed of molecules that also organize themselves in a particular fashion. In a similar way, the organism is an organization of organs; a group is an organization of organisms in interactions.[9] This hierarchical organization is known as the levels of organization of matter. Each subsystem follows a particular set of rules, even when they are included in the same system:

1. Subsystems can be composed of different elements.
2. The elements can be organized differently.

This implies that an organism consists of a heterogeneous set of mechanisms. The dimensions of an organism are *open* systems. Each subsystem has an internal cohesion in which it is grounded, but it also has roots that dig into the external regulators of its ecological environment. There is, for example, a set of mental procedures that allows one to think that 2 + 2 = 4,[10] but at the same time this capacity is rooted in neurological and cultural (e.g., mathematics) dynamics. It is important to understand that the dynamics of a particular system typically has such multiple sources. This is well illustrated by the following quote on the meaning of gestures, written by anthropologist Edward Sapir:

> Gestures are hard to classify and it is difficult to make a conscious separation between that in gesture which is of merely individual origin and that which is referable to the habits of the group as a whole. In spite of these difficulties of conscious analysis, we respond to gestures with an extreme alertness and, one might almost say, in accordance with an elaborate and secret code that is written nowhere, known by none, and understood by all. Like everything else in human conduct, gestures roots in the reactive necessities of the organism, but the laws of gestures, the unwritten code of gestured messages and responses, is the anonymous work of an elaborate social tradition. (Sapir, 1927, p. 556)

Similarly, on a more cognitive level, a thought is rooted in several environments. This flexibility is possible because there is not one coherent psyche; but instead, a multitude of heterogeneous mechanisms that can generate different ways of thinking. We will see in this volume that these multiple forms of psychic mechanisms root themselves differently in the diverse environments that shape their ecology. This explains why there are many different ways to perceive and to think, many different aspects to memory and consciousness, and so on. Thus, certain events stored in the hippocampus of the brain's limbic system when we are young can be recalled, later on, in the temporal cortex when we are more than fifty years old.[11]

The Dynamic Relationship between a System and Its Parts: Elements, Organization, and Emergence

Classical *materialism* supposes that the properties of a system are the sum of the properties of the elements that it contains, whereas a system model postulates that an organization can have *emerging* properties, that is, properties that are not part of the elements contained in the system.[12] Elements, organization, and emerging systems mutually influence one other. This dynamic often leads to expressions such as these: *a system is structured by what it structures, or a system structures itself by structuring that which structures it.* These expressions sometimes appear obscure to those who do not know system theory. It is my hope that by the end of the book these notions will have become easily understandable. These formulations point to the fact that subsystems allow an organism to auto-regulate and participate in the regulation of the systems that contain it (e.g., nature, culture).

One of the first psychologists to distinguish between the elements and the organization is soviet psychologist Lev Vygotsky.[13] He wanted to show that certain human faculties, such as intelligence, emerge from the combination of information processes produced by the brain and the languages taught in societies. To illustrate what he means by *emergence*, he reminds us what transpires when water arises from the association of oxygen and hydrogen. These atoms, alone, embolden flames. Once they are associated in an H_2O molecule, their combination acquires a property that is not contained in either oxygen or hydrogen: that of being able to put out a fire, or to transform itself into steam if we were to put water in contact with a flame. This property *emerged* from the organization of the three atoms. The *organization* of matter is thus as important as its particles. In this example, we have identified three aspects of matter:

1. The *elemental* atoms.
2. The *organization* of the atoms that make up a chemical chain. At every level of matter, the nature of the links that form the organization of the elements are different.
3. An *emergent* entity (the molecule) that has properties that are not those of its elements.

Introduction to Jean Piaget's Notions of Adaptation, Assimilation, and Accommodation

The adaptability of a living system is in its capacity to find connections with its environment that promotes its survival. According to Piaget,[14] this adaptive capacity can follow two types of mechanisms:

1. *Assimilation* allows a system to react to stimulation in at least a relatively appropriate fashion with the available means at a given moment. A baby can assimilate milk during the first year of life, but not pieces of meat. Psychoanalysts like Otto Fenichel (1931) used the terms *introjection* and *identification* to designate a primitive form of the mechanisms of assimilation that are felt as a need to totally or partially incorporate objects, persons, or experiences.
2. *Accommodation* occurs when an organism modifies an existing mechanism to adapt to stimulation that it cannot otherwise assimilate. An infant accommodates his gestures with objects that surround him, to make use of them more adequately.

A baby discovers that it can take a rubber ball and make it bounce by letting it fall. If he then assimilates a doll into the schema[15] that he used with the ball, the baby risks being surprised by the fact that the doll does not bounce. He also risks making the discovery that he might be scolded if he uses the same schema with a glass because it will break. Therefore, the baby will accommodate the schema developed with the ball into three sensorimotor schemata: one for that which bounces, one for that which falls but does not bounce, and one for that which falls and breaks. This differentiation of the initial schema permits him to discover particular ways to use these three objects. The child might then discover that it is pleasant to sleep with a doll and drink delicious juice out of a glass. Accommodation is thus an adaptation by innovation, whereas assimilation allows a schema to stabilize and refine itself in becoming more particularized.

A way to define therapy is to present illnesses as an adaptation disorder that activates forms of assimilation that are destructive to the organism.[16] An example that many travelers will recognize is that of the tourist who is traveling in an area where it is inadvisable to eat the local raw produce, because they do not have the antibodies the local population has developed. The desire to eat the wonderful salads that are presented is a form of destructive assimilation for their own organism. The accommodations activated by the appropriate vaccines would allow for the pleasure of eating salads without harm to the organism. Psychotherapy proposes analogous changes, but the targeted accommodations are not situated at the level of antibodies. Instead, they consist of activating the processes of mental and behavioral know-how that permit a process of social integration that is constructive for an individual organism.

Social System, Individual System, and Psyche

Just as we walk without thinking, we think without thinking! We do not know how our muscles make us walk—nor do we know much about the agencies that do our mental work.

If we could really sense the working of our minds, we couldn't act so often in accord with motives we don't suspect. We wouldn't have such varied and conflicting theories for psychology.

No doubt, a mind that wants to change itself could benefit from knowing how it works. But such knowledge might as easily encourage us to wreck ourselves—if we were to poke our clumsy fingers into the tricky circuits of the mind's machinery. (Minsky,[17] 1985, *The Society of Mind*, 6.8. and 6.13, pp. 63 and 68)

The Properties of an Organism

Let us come back to the concept of the organism.[18] Every individual biological system capable of reproduction is referred to by the term *organism* in biology. This term designates a plant or a particular animal as a total entity. The caterpillar is apparently a different system than the butterfly, but it is nonetheless the same creature. Certain fundamental properties, like the genetic code contained in the cells of the system, remain constant; and the dynamic profile of these changes is one of the characteristics of the species.

The concept of organism is ultimately stable in the biological disciplines, but its functioning remains difficult to study. The majority of biological studies achieve a description of the many small mechanisms that make up the general dynamics of an organism, but there is not yet an approach that describes the way they coordinate with each other, especially the physiological coordinations that include the phenomena of consciousness. This explains why so many body workers use *energetic* models, in somewhat of a metaphorical sense, to work with the large movements of the organism that are always present.[19] Some practitioners succumb to the temptation, which is rampant in the human species, to believe that a metaphor is *a real mechanism*.

The Identity, Flexibility, and Coherence in a Heteroclite System

An organism is a system that has an identity, flexibility, and coherence:

1. There is *identity* to the extent that we suppose that, from fertilization to death, the organism is a unique system.
2. There is *flexibility* to the extent that, from fertilization to death, a considerable number of elements and characteristics of the organism have changed.
3. There is *coherence* to the extent that all the dynamics that occur within the organism are part of what an organism becomes.

Each one of these terms is relative:

1. The *identity* of the organism is a partial identity, given that an organism can change its shape (a caterpillar becomes a butterfly) and its cells renew themselves many times over the course of a lifetime. Even if a person is seventy years old and has the impression of always having been the same person, some psychologists[20] ask themselves the question: Up to what point does a person define herself in the same way at the age of six and at the age of sixty?
2. The *flexibility* of the organism is a partial flexibility to the extent that it is counterbalanced by the *constraints* that ensure the identity and coherence of the organism.
3. The *coherence* of the organism is relative to the extent that it can become physically and psychologically diseased.

The subsystems of an organism are called *heteroclite* to the extent that they do not all function the same way. The liver does not function like the lungs, the muscles, and the bones. They are subsystems of the same organism, but they are not constituted the same way, nor do they have the same cells (bones have more calcium than the liver), and they do not react the same way (the liver has a local action that influences numerous parts, whereas the musculature is active here and there throughout the organism). To understand how these heteroclite subsystems can function in a relatively complementary fashion to maintain the coherence of the system, we must postulate not only a hierarchy of subsystems but also an organization that regulates the coordination of these subsystems. In each case, there exist *interfaces* that permit one system to interact with another that functions differently. For example, in the brain there are receptors that are sensitive to the presence of neurotransmitters such as serotonin and dopamine. The nervous system has interfaces that can activate a muscle, and others that are responsive to the activity of a muscle.

These systems are part of the regulatory mechanisms of the organism. Because there is no such thing as a "super" regulator of the organism (a regulator of regulators of the organism[21]), a moment arrives when an organism is regulated by the manner in which it interacts with its surroundings. That which an organism needs to receive from the exterior to regulate itself is also heteroclite (light, nourishment, affection, recognition, weather, etc.). The coherence of a system is therefore maintained by four groups of forces:

1. The regulation of that which is within.
2. The regulation of that which contains it (e.g., society).
3. The regulations maintained by an organism with its environment.
4. The regulations maintained by the environment with an organism.

The organismic processes that generate various forms of awareness are inaccessible to self-exploration by introspection. Introspection is a central tool in psychotherapy because it consists in observing as explicitly as possible, and in a detailed manner, inner impressions: how we think, our body sensations, the feelings that animate us, the thinking that creates our beliefs, interior conflicts, the way we love and/or hate ourselves, and so on. The mechanisms of the organism that are inaccessible to consciousness are *nonconscious*.[22] It is impossible for a human to grasp the functioning of the organism's physiological mechanisms in which thoughts arise by *introspection*, or the system of social interactions in which an organism constitutes itself. Introspection cannot even allow a person to explore the *structure* of the psyche. Conscious thoughts can perceive certain effects of these dynamics, and are almost blind to the ways its perceptions are organized. *A person consciously and explicitly perceives a mental phenomenon, but not that which structures it.*

Where Do We Situate the Psychological?

Psychology is defined as the "the scientific study of the human mind and its functions, especially those affecting behavior in a given context" (*New English Oxford Dictionary*, 1998, p. 1497). Europeans often use the term *psyche* to designate the object of psychology and stress the notion that representations are only part of the mind. This terminology is coherent, as it is the root of the term *psychology*. In English, the term *psyche* (or *psychic*) is avoided because it is often associated with magical powers. *Mind* is not an adequate term to designate what psychotherapists work with because it reduces the psyche to its computational modalities. The dictionary recommends the use of *psychology* as a noun to designate the object of psychology, as when one speaks of the psychology of a person. I sometimes follow this recommendation, but because this book is strongly influenced by European literature, I also use the term *psyche* as it is used by European psychologists and psychiatrists,[23] which is as a way of designating all the mechanisms studied by psychologists. To summarize, *psychic* is too close to magical disciplines, and *mind* too close to artificial intelligence. These remarks do not intend to disqualify these disciplines but to defend a choice of words that is appropriate in psychotherapy.

With the current systems model, the difficulty for psychologists is that however easy it is to situate physiological systems in an organism, it is not so easy with regard to the mind or behaviors. Thoughts are inevitably part of the mechanisms of the organism's regulation, but their relationship with the organization of the organs is vague. The only thing that can be affirmed is that psychological and behavioral dynamics are situated somewhere at the intersection between (a) the mechanisms of regulation of an organism, and (b) the mechanisms that regulate the interaction between several organisms. The organismic models in psychology are mostly interested in how the psyche participates in the dynamics of organisms.[24]

The System of the Dimensions of the Organism (SDO)

The Topographic SDO

The system of organismic dimensions is a topographic model, designed to *situate* a set of phenomena. This type of model was notably proposed by Freud. In his first topographic model,[25] he situates the conscious, the preconscious, and the unconscious and the defense mechanisms that regulate the flow of thoughts between these regions of the mind. In his second topographic model,[26] Freud distinguishes the id, the ego, and the superego. These two reference models have remained useful, although the psychological mechanisms associated with these categories have evolved considerably, even in psychoanalysis, with regard to the development of clinical and experimental research (see, for example, Roussillon, 2007).

If Freud's first topography was centered on the geography of the mind, the SDO is an attempt to furnish a diagram of the internal dynamics of the organism. With it, a practitioner can easily describe what happens when different forms of intervention are used in a psychotherapy process, which is often the case today; for example, when a psychiatrist uses a psychodynamic approach and prescribes antidepressants. This model can also facilitate communication between psychotherapists, especially when they want to describe their particular way of working with patients.

The Notion of Dimension

Every dimension of the human organism has:

1. *A basic adaptive function*: gravity, equilibrium of the internal milieu, adaptation to surrounding objects and organisms, and the capacity to insert oneself into institutional dynamics.
2. *Basic tools* to accomplish this adaptation: the body, metabolic regulators, behavior, and the mind (see fig. I.1).
3. Each dimension forms a sufficiently coherent system to become the target of a therapeutic discipline (psychotherapy for the mind, physical therapy for the body, medicine for the metabolism and physiology, etc.).

The *organismic dimensions* (metabolism, body, behavior, and the mind) are coordinated by *organismic regulation mechanisms*. The connections between dimensions (between the body and the mind, for example) are mostly indirect. The mobilization of the organism's regulation mechanisms activates affects (moods, emotions, drives, addictions, etc.) in the conscious dynamics of the mind.

A dimension is thus a subsystem of the organism that support a certain form of global adaptive activity. Each one has a particular way to mobilize the organism's regulatory mechanisms. Each dimension is approached by particular

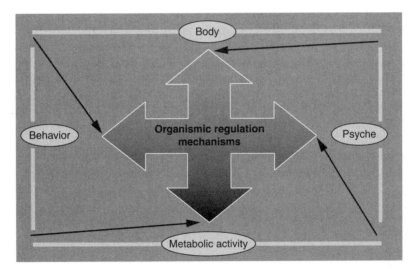

FIGURE I.1. The relations between the dimensions and the global regulation system of the organism. The *global organismic regulation mechanisms* connect the *dimensions of the organism* (metabolism, body, behavior, and psyche). They organize the communication between dimensions and are organized by these dimensions. The relations between dimensions are thus mainly indirect. Affective dynamics (instincts, drives, moods, emotions, etc.) are rooted in the organismic regulation system.

set of therapeutic disciplines. The dimensions of the organism distinguished in the system of organismic dimensions are the following:[27]

1. *Body and gravity:* The postural dynamics of the body[28] regulate the relationship between the organism and the gravity field. Standing on one's head or on one's feet creates different relations between gravity and blood circulation, gravity and respiration, and so on. The study of the body dimension includes the analysis of how the segments of the body coordinate within the Earth's gravity field. This activity necessitates particular organizations of the musculature and the skeleton, for example. Their dynamics are central aspects of the theories used by orthopedists, physical therapists, athletes, dancers, gymnasts, and in some methods of relaxation.

2. *Metabolic regulation:* The physiological variables of the organism's fluids (the internal milieu) must vary according to certain strict constraints to permit the cells of the organism to live and communicate. These variables are regulated by the mechanisms situated at the level of the organs and tissues (mostly kidneys, lungs, and bowels).[29] These phenomena are mostly studied in biological and medical laboratories.

3. *Behavior and interaction:* Behavior allows an organism to interact with the objects and the organisms in its environment *in present time.* This dimension is especially studied by ethologists, psychologists, behaviorists, and in research on nonverbal communication.

4. *The psyche and social integration:* The psyche is the dimension that allows an organism to insert itself in social rituals and social institutions. This form of adaptation requires the capacity to use various forms of communication media, such as tools, writing, means of transportation, cinema, and so on.[30]

Let us now consider each dimension in more detail.

THE BODY

Body dynamics are mostly composed of mechanisms that permit the organism to adapt to the constraints of gravity. Gravity influences every aspect of an organism, but the organism contains a series of devices that are specialized in the management of gravity: the skeleton, the muscles and the sensorimotor nervous system. Figure I.2 demonstrates a basic method taught by almost all the body centered approaches called the "plumb line." It consists in taking a mason's plumb line to evaluate the alignment of the body's segments within the field of gravity when a person is standing up. By default, there is an expected alignment when the articulations of the ankle, the hips, and the shoulder are aligned with the ear. When this alignment cannot be easily maintained, at least one of the following problems is usually present:

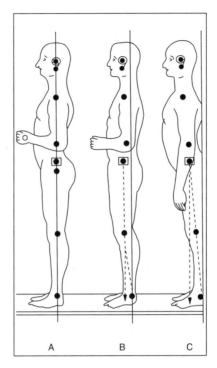

FIGURE I.2. The body.

1. An erroneous conscious representation and perception of the body.
2. A deviation of the spine (lordosis or scoliosis).
3. A hypo- or hyper-muscle tone in the muscular chains.

BEHAVIOR

Behavior is generally discussed by behaviorists or in studies concerning nonverbal communication. It is the capacity to manipulate objects—sometimes with fine movements, as when one plays the violin—and to communicate with others. This occurs necessarily in the here-and-now, as behavior is an attempt to respond immediately to what is happening. Behavior mobilizes several mechanisms of the body, but its aims are different. Using identical mechanisms for several purposes can become problematic. It is well known, for example, that a profession that requires sitting for long hours can create muscular tensions that twist the spine and cause blood circulation problems.[31] The objectives that behavioral demands impose on the body sometimes conflict with the needs of the body as defined in the disciplines like hatha yoga, gymnastics, and orthopedics.

In studies on nonverbal communication, the researchers analyze the postures, gestures, and facial expressions that permit two organisms to communicate and mutually influence one another. The behavior of one person has an automatic impact on the physiology of those who are around. The gesture of person A influences the senses of person B. The sensory system of B can subsequently activate physiological, affective, and cognitive mechanisms, as well as modes of automatic reactivity. Most of these activations unfold nonconsciously, outside of the conscious intentions of the interacting organisms. A person is able, for example, to drive a car while thinking of something else. His behavior is obviously guided by habits. The behaviorist often misunderstands the body of gymnasts, and the orthopedist does not always know how to understand interactive behaviors.

The photographic example in figure I.3 was one of the points of departure

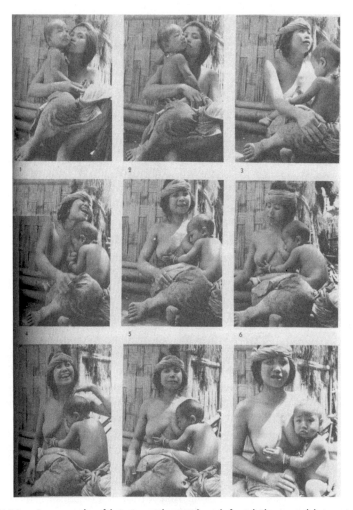

FIGURE I.3.   An example of how a mother and an infant behave and interact in Bali (Bateson and Mead, 1947, plate 47, p. 149).

for the study of nonverbal behavior during the 1950s. According to Margaret Mead and Gregory Bateson, it demonstrates a typical automatic dynamic of the mother–child relationship in the traditional culture of Bali. We see in each subsequent frame how the mother goes from a stimulating and joyful expression to a negative or off-putting one. This alternating behavior organizes itself spontaneously when a mother interacts with her infant in this culture.

METABOLISM

Metabolism regulation manages the energy of the organism at the level of the internal milieu and the cells. Metabolism also has importance in therapeutic practices, for example, when individuals handle an extra supply of oxygen poorly, as when their head turns as soon as they perform a breathing exercise, or when the metabolism of an anorexic patient adapts itself to the condition. Here we are at the heart of physiological auto-regulation.

THE PSYCHE

An important aspect of the psyche is to allow an organism to integrate itself into the dynamics of social institutions, thanks to its ability to manage tools and media. It can interact *beyond* the immediate here-and-now. Corrections are thus possible, as when one corrects a text. A reader cannot be aware of the many corrections made by the author of a book. Even if the mind has other important functions, this one distinguishes humans from other species. Neither art, nor law, nor economics, nor religion, nor science could exist without the human capacity to construct a body of knowledge that inscribes itself in a media accessible to all. This understanding is close to the concepts of present-day psychologists and sociologists, like Ed Tronick's notion of co-construction, Philippe Rochat's co-consciousness, Pierre Bourdieu's analysis of distinction, or the coordinating function of the rituals described by Claude Lévi-Strauss.

This aspect of psychological dynamics has been explored in the past by psychologists at least since Vygotsky. Even if this definition of the mind still needs to be refined, it allows us to differentiate it from the other dimensions and to specify the therapeutic aims of psychotherapy. To ask someone to describe, using words or gestures, what one is aware of implies a clear distinction between behavioral expressive dynamics and psychological impressions. One can then distinguish in a more explicit way (a) problems in thinking, (b) problems in expression, and (c) problematic connections between thoughts and behavior.

It is difficult to demonstrate that the interpersonal regulatory system of humans is more evolved than that of monkeys (Waal, 1998, 2002). We could not easily show, for example, that the relationship between parents and infants are more developed among the citizens of Geneva than among chimpanzees in the wild. For example, I doubt that abusive parents are as numerous in a tribe of chimpanzees as they are in human families. On the other hand, the difference between the two species becomes intuitively obvious when we observe how mind and *institutional organizations* interact (Boyd and Richerson, 1996, 2005;

Moessinger, 2008). To study the interaction between socially constructed beliefs and individual minds, it is also useful to distinguish between (a) the psychological means used by the organism to integrate itself in a social network (intelligence, imagination, etc.), and (b) the socially constructed ways of helping (or forcing) the organism of a citizen to integrate itself in an institutional environment. This relative differentiation between psychological mechanisms (representations, reasoning, perception, etc.) and social mechanisms (tools, rituals, etc.) explains the human capacity to exist in a great variety of cultural environments.

The organism can become relatively independent from the constraints imposed by the here and now when it uses its psychological capacity to use tools, which is not the case when it uses its behavioral resources. When I read a passage written by Homer, I have the impression that his thoughts meet mine, even though he has been dead for more than 2,000 years. The communication strategies used by a society to facilitate the inclusion of citizens in institutional dynamics influences the manner in which the mechanisms of the mind develop. Alfred Russel Wallace[32] describes the case of the girl he adopted who was born in a jungle. In London, she became a renowned classical pianist. For Wallace, it was evident the psychological and behavioral skills that made it possible for this girl to become a pianist would never have developed in the jungle. Her original environment would have mobilized other capacities. In other words, an organism can develop in different ways, which are all potentially available.

THE REGULATORY MECHANISMS OF THE ORGANISM

To interact with each other, the dimensions need to interact with the mechanisms that connect them: the *organismic regulation systems* (see fig. I.1). The activity of these organismic mechanisms is often partially perceived as an *affect* (mood, emotion, drive, addiction, internal atmosphere, etc.) by consciousness. Because the organismic mechanisms of regulation function as a system, they are equally influenced by what occurs in each subsystem—that is, in the dimensions. Here are examples of the most important organismic regulation systems:

1. The autonomous, central, and peripheral nervous systems.
2. The cardiovascular system.
3. The internal and external respiratory system.
4. The hormonal system, which includes the action of neurotransmitters.
5. The immune system, which is notably set in action in a state of stress.

The *homeostatic* mechanisms prolong the metabolic dynamics by mobilizing the resources of the organism to regulate the vital variables of the extracellular fluids. These are already complex organismic mechanisms because they coordinate metabolic dynamics with the other dimensions and guide the interaction between the organism and its environment. A typical example is that of the construction of houses, clothing, and the heating systems used to maintain the body's metabolic temperature at around 36°C.

The activity of a dimension of the organism requires the support of the organismic regulation and of other dimensions to be able to accomplish its tasks. A thought needs the logistic support of the nervous system and a supply of oxygen delivered through the bloodstream. The more important the recruiting of the organism's logistic support becomes, the more the activity of a dimension becomes organismic. A nervous movement of the foot necessarily recruits all the resources of the organism, but in a peripheral way. When a soccer player kicks a ball with his eye on the goal guarded by the other team, the movement of the foot mobilizes the other organismic dimensions in a much more important fashion.

The Architecture of Matter and Information Processing in a Computer

The way I use the notion of dimension may seem strange to some readers, but it has an equivalent in engineers who build computers. They aptly identify two dimensions in a computer when they speak of *hardware* (the electromechanical functioning of the computer) and the *software* (a series of operations written in the program that manages particular information in circulation within the circuits). These two dimensions are found in the functioning of almost every part of the computer.

Yet the activity of the electric circuits is not directly organized by a program, because the rapport between the program (thought) and the electric circuits (activities of the central nervous system) is managed by the *architecture* (or *design*) of the computer: that which corresponds (in this metaphor) to the organismic regulations. When engineers conceptualize a computer, they decide in advance how circuits and programs will interact. These a priori decisions determine the architecture of the computer. The architecture coordinates not only the circuits and the programs but also their way of interacting with diverse interfaces like a screen, a hard disk, or a printer. All these elements are heteroclites and have certain independence. For example, a computer's memory and its screen function differently. A similar memory can be associated with a great diversity of screens and hard disks. A typical expression used to describe this type of system is to say that it is *modular*. Every individual part of a computer functions in a relatively independent manner, all the while making it possible to fulfill functions that allow the system to work as a whole. Many people can buy the same computer but use different programs; or they can use identical programs (a word processing program) to achieve different tasks (write a book or organize email). Nevertheless, architecture imposes constraints. It can be connected to a great variety of screens, but not all of them. It can operate a great number of programs, but not all of them.

In the case of a malfunction, certain mechanisms of the computer can be affected and others not:

1. If the hard disk no longer functions, nothing works. If certain parts of the disk are damaged, some information is lost. There are individuals who can fix this type of problem without knowing how to program. These are the people, for example, who know how to replace a faulty disk with one that works.

2. In other cases, the computer works well, but a program does not. This requires either a reinstallation of the program or a modification of the lines (the logic) in one or more of the parts of the program by a programmer.

3. Finally, some problems are caused by the user. The user makes a spelling error, clicks on the wrong icon, has not read the manual, and so on. These problems resolve themselves by advising the user to read the manual and take a course.

These three cases can be related to one computer, but the mechanisms involved and the solutions are almost independent of one another. Some cases are more complex. One then needs to understand how these dimensions interact with each other (for example, when engineers design a computer). An interesting aspect for the psychophysiology of perception is the way that computer engineers take to transform information managed by electric circuits into information that a user can understand (by reading what appears on the screen) or activate (by hitting letters on the keyboard). This transformation, this *reformatting* of information, is notably possible because identical electrical information is transformed by several layers of programming languages. The routines that register the "e" that I hit on my keyboard are not the same that produce an "e" on my screen.

In the SDO, the program corresponds to the mind, the parts that make up the computer to my physiology, and the design to the organism.

Information Processing and Psychological Dynamics
The psychological dimension can be divided into three principal layers that can each be broken down into a multitude of subsystems or modules:

1. *Dealing with physiological information.* Every physiological reaction is activated by a series of stimulations that often automatically activate physiological responses. This is how an antibody from the immune system reacts selectively to certain substances that are characterized by the simple fact that they are the only substances that activate an immunizing reaction. In its development, the nervous system allows for an increasingly complex coordination of the reactions of the organism that fan out to include an ever larger number of internal and external stimuli. The human brain can thereby distinguish a great variety of stimuli and ecological characteristics. A computer can propose a variety of different reactions for a similar stimulus.[33] So can the brain. A mammalian brain

can generate a large repertoire of coordinations between stimuli and responses because the brain has developed *intermediary zones* between the sensory and motor systems. Everything that happens in these intermediary zones is already a form of analysis and synthesis about what is going on. Having said that, these dynamics are systems of information management that are not part of the dynamics habitually found in the mind.

2. *Psychology and consciousness.* The notion that humans have a psyche imposed itself because humans experience conscious impressions. Consciousness is a "virtual" domain of perception and the management of perceptions that refines the way an organism perceives what is going on around it and how it acts. We cannot presently determine with precision the status of our conscious thoughts. Consciousness is something that is part of everyone's experience. For the moment it can only be defined by making reference to this experience. Consciousness is therefore the core around which psychology has become a meaningful science. One of Freud's greatest contributions to psychology was to oblige us to admit that there are unconscious thoughts that can influence how we think and behave. Freud only includes in the unconscious perceptions that can become conscious, that may have subsequently been repressed, and that can rise to consciousness again (after a psychoanalytical treatment, for example). These unconscious psychic dynamics are psychological (in the traditional sense of the term) to the extent that they function like conscious perceptions. Trained in neurology, Freud makes a clear distinction between how mind and brain manage information. His first topography describes the circulation of information in the psyche. What he calls the defense mechanisms show us that even if the psyche has conscious dynamics for its center, the psychic dimension also contains *nonconscious* regulators and mechanisms that regulate how a mind is organized and how conscious impressions are produced.

3. *The editing mechanisms.* Between the management of information performed by the nervous and hormonal systems on one hand and the mind on the other, we must postulate an interface that edits neurological information in psychological data. It is possible that the organizational systems of consciousness are mostly anchored in such an interface, but there exists no research on the subject at the moment. Its function would be close to that of the editor in making a film. It consists, in effect, in reformatting (translating) information circulating in the brain in virtual thoughts that can be perceived consciously. Every computer or television station has such a system. These machines transform electrical impulses into sounds and images that can be perceived[34] by human senses. Even if one assumes that there really is a system of repression of unconscious material, as described by Freud, there are certainly other, even more powerful forms of information-sorting at the level of the editing interface. Thus, a social censure can demand the suppression of particular

images in a film. This form of censure is different from the one that manifests itself when the team making the film sorts through the images to keep a limited percentage that will be used to create the final product. It consists here in creating the sequence of images, the duration of each sequence, and drawing the attention of the viewers to particular elements gathered during the filming.

These different layers (psychological, editing devices, neurological management of information), often referred to in neuropsychology, are all part of the organism's systems of regulation. We can see that the further away we are from the dynamics of the brain to get closer to the virtual world that we perceive consciously, the more we can speak of the psychological dimension. We also see, in this analysis, how it is impossible to define a precise border between one dimension and the global regulatory mechanism of the organism.

The Practices of the Organism

I will present theories that can support discussions on the coordination between the mind and the organism from diverse points of view—all of them instructive and representative of the human imagination in this domain. None of these models uses the system of organismic dimensions. Yet all can be reread, in large part, with this model in mind to create an ensemble of views useful to a psychotherapist and even an experimental psychologist. In other words, this system is sufficiently flexible to be used by different approaches: all the while creating a common language permitting different schools to communicate with each other. A key term to describe the aspects of the organism that are explored in psychotherapy is the word *practice*.[35] A practice has two dimensions:

1. A set of goals.
2. A way of functioning.

To differentiate different practices, it is useful to distinguish between identical behaviors (to lift a glass) that mobilize different underlying mechanisms and identical underlying mechanisms that can generate different behaviors. A body psychotherapist works with physiological, bodily, behavioral, and mental practices and with practices that coordinate each dimension in a certain way. *A practice is, by definition, a habit, a propensity, a tendency to act in a particular way.* These practices activate without asking the individual's permission. Often, the individual does not have the means to understand the *implications* of the practices that were acquired by his organism.[36] Furthermore, to the extent that an individual's thoughts are generally practices themselves, they do not always have to the capacity to evaluate a practice. These practices are not always beneficial to the individual or to one's entourage. They construct and calibrate themselves depending on multiple factors so complex that even researchers are not able to account for the dynamics that favor certain practices, nor evaluate the advantages and dangers of a group of practices. That explains why it is so difficult to understand, evaluate and modify the practices that are perceived as detrimental or constructive by an individual and by those who know the person well. A psychotherapist's central interest is the system of conscious psychological practices, but these are so intrinsically linked to other dimensions of the organism that it is often difficult to analyze mental practices without situating them in their organismic ecology. Such an approach to the mind is typical of body psychotherapies.

The complaints of our patients usually refer to their *habitual* ways of functioning: often depressed, anxious, angry, sad, afraid, and so on. By differentiating metabolism, body, behavior, and the mind, I define four ways to approach an individual that corresponds to four great originators of organismic practices that have an impact on the mechanisms that generate these symptomatic complaints. It is possible to associate many practices to each dimension. The general medical practitioner is evidently attentive to the metabolic phenomena above all else; the psychotherapist of an anorexic patient must also take into account how the patient's organism has accommodated to a diet. The athletic coach cannot avoid taking into account the metabolic and psychological factors when he tries to develop a more sustained respiratory effort. In these three cases, the practitioner needs metaphors to support the motivations of a patient and establish a rapport of mutual confidence. Even when one focuses on mental practices, one needs to situate them in their organismic, multidimensional environment.

THE EPISTEMOLOGICAL AND ETHICAL FRAMEWORK OF PSYCHOTHERAPEUTIC KNOWLEDGE

Psychotherapy is a form of therapeutic practice that is inspired from the sciences as much as is possible. It hopes to become at least as scientific as allopathic medicine some day. The influence of science manifests itself in two ways:

1. Psychotherapists accommodate their way of thinking to scientific discoveries, to the extent that these are relevant for their practice. When the scientific approaches cannot offer a relevant option, the therapist seeks useful propositions from other approaches. This entire book illustrates this point of view.
2. Psychotherapy adopts a strategy to develop knowledge compatible with the ethics of science.

The second point interests me at this moment. It consists of giving a frame to the psychotherapist's ethics in the face of what he presents as knowledge. The butcher guarantees wholesome meats that correspond to what is written on the label. The effectiveness of therapy is more difficult to evaluate, but the propositions of a method obey the same laws of ethics. The therapist is expected to propose a course of treatment that is relevant to a patient's particular need for support. This ethical stance is based on the following basic principles:

1. *A scientific enterprise is a collective enterprise.* Science is an institutional construct that inscribes itself in a time period far longer than a lifetime. The idea of an institution implies not only a collective construction but also the necessity to communicate via the intermediary of the tools of communication. In effect, to admit a collegial construction is to admit the need to be informed about the activities of colleagues. Once this view is accepted, it becomes necessary for the individual to recognize one's obligation to communicate knowledge in a comprehensible manner to colleagues. Personal impressions do not have the capacity to evaluate what is important and useful from an institutional point of view, or from the perspective of a society that emerges from these institutions. Personal views may be relevant and sometime innovative, but they often need to be calibrated through discussions with colleagues. This is why peer reviews of each other's work are essential to scientific ethics.

2. *The economy of hypotheses.*[37] Every observation awakens in us a multitude of associations, some of which we hold dear more than others. To maintain a useful collegial collaboration, the rule of the game is to try to find the most economical hypothesis possible—that is, one that stays closer to the existing accepted knowledge. The root *hypo* is the opposite of *hyper*. Hypo is by definition something weak, as in the word *hypotonic*. A hypothesis is therefore a "weak thesis." This rule does not imply that the most economical hypothesis is the one that is the closest to what is really happening. Rather, in the short term, colleagues as a group can agree that it is the smallest common denominator they can use, given a set of published observations. An important issue in such discussions is to be able to separate belief from knowledge. The distinction will never be clear because even a collectivity is subject to the influence of belief systems and ideologies. But this procedure forces all involved to advance prudently and take the greatest precautions. Another advantage of working with hypotheses is that it is easier to demonstrate if they are true or false in a given methodology. This allows one to sort out, in a first pass, what can be immediately included in collegial discussions and what can be left for the future. When discoveries permit the construction of a new methodology, this sorting out must often be repeated and may lead to a different set of hypothesis. What was before a "hyperthesis" can now be included in the realm of a hypothesis. An example of a hyperthesis is the assumption that God or cosmic energy created the human species. One cannot know if such hypertheses are true, but we know that they cannot be assimilated in current psychotherapeutic theories and research systems. These domains remain the province of beliefs. We speak

of a powerful hypothesis when a hypothesis, containing a minimum of presuppositions, accounts for a maximum number of phenomena. Widely known examples are Newton's law of gravity and Wallace's law of the survival of the fittest.

3. *An explanation is never a truth.* When one observes a phenomenon, one has the tendency to want to give it an explanation. An observation is necessarily fuzzy, because it is always subject to the limits of the perceptual mechanisms. But it can at least be experienced by many others, in many situations. An observation can often be replicated. Imagined explanations are even more fragile to the extent that they are limited by the mechanisms of thinking that build themselves in the intimate regions of the individual's psychic system. In psychotherapy, by default, the fundamental rule is: *Never deny an experience, but never accept an explanation.* This default rule must then be calibrated according to the available material. If someone claims to have spoken to the Virgin Mary, the psychotherapist accepts that such was the individual's experience, or at least one of the experiences that so constructed itself at a certain moment. Once we admit this, all speculations are possible for the therapist and for the patient. Both may try to explain how this experienced emerged.[38]

The Organism in the Far East: In Search of the Universe that Manifests in the Organism

In the following chapters, I gather some discussions around Hindu and Chinese teachings like yoga, acupuncture, and tai chi chuan.[1] These practices are thousands of years old and still timely today. They are part of cultural systems that have assimilated European technology and science without losing their creativity. Today, they are taught in every country. Many medical, physical, and psychological therapist trained in universities have learned how useful these approaches can be for their personal development and their practice with patients. A steadily increasing number of empirical studies are showing that certain yoga exercises and meditation techniques can become useful as a psychotherapeutic mode of intervention for depression[2] and schizophrenia.[3]

A characteristic of the methods developed in the Far East is that a person can only change or be cured if she becomes actively involved in a process that influences most dimensions of the organism: posture, breathing, ways of thinking, beliefs, diet, and so on. These modes of intervention become efficient if they can influence the dynamics of deep organismic processes that are associated with such terms as *prana* in India, and *chi* in China.

1

Asana and Pranayama of Hatha Yoga

THE EIGHT LIMBS OF YOGA

The Yoga technique places central emphasis upon controlled breathing and related means of inducing apathetic ecstasy. In this connection it concentrates the conscious psychic and mental functions upon the partly meaningful, partly meaningless flow of inner experiences. They may be endowed with an indefinite emotional and devotional character, but are always controlled through self-observation to the point of completely emptying consciousness of anything expressible in rational words, by gaining deliberate control over the inner motions of heart and lungs, and finally, auto-hypnosis. (Weber, 1913, p. 164)

A Search that Involves the Totality of the Organism

There are many reasons to include yoga in this book:

1. It is the oldest known discipline that combines the psychological, physiological, and complex body dynamics.
2. The system created by the yogis remains the most complete practice that promotes the engagement of the organism and its dimensions. Its way to engage the postures remain a reference point for many specialists oriented toward the body (physical therapists, orthopedists, etc.).
3. It remains one of the most popular body–mind disciplines in the world.

Expressed differently, body and mind are activated in resonance with each other, in a way that allows certain particular soulful states to emerge. For the yogis,[1] posture, gesture, breathing, physiology, relaxation, mental concentration, and intellectual knowledge are dimensions that constitute an individual. The yogi of old knew all of these distinctions. For him, an individual cannot transform himself deeply without mobilizing these dimensions of human experience.

Ecstasy Is Born through the Mastery of the Multiplicity that Flourishes in Each One of Us

Indian philosophers have explored nearly every imaginable avenue of speculation.[2] Although Yoga is already a particular trend of thought, it nevertheless includes a great variety of schools. Their common ground is a form of self-development that aims to commune with the dynamics of the universe.

The first known book dedicated to yoga is the *Yoga Sutra of Patanjali*, which appeared 2,300 years ago. The word *yoga* comes from the root word *yuj*, which peasants use to harness two buffaloes to a plow. Yoga is that mix of methods that permits an individual's spirit to experience what links him to the Great All (Paramatma or Supreme Spirit) of which he is a part.[3] These methods help an individual slow down the rush of thoughts and feelings that habitually distracts him, to create a space of tranquility and thus an experience of the winds of the universe that penetrate his organism and enliven him. Consequently, the individual experiences the welling up of a form of bliss that by far surpasses what reason can comprehend: "The aim was to harness 'the powers of the human person (intelligence, activities of the senses, etc.) so as to master them and to access, beyond consciousness, spiritual states susceptible to rescue the soul (atman or purusa) from the "prison of the body"'" (Varenne, 1970, pp. 621–622, translated by Marcel Duclos).

I discuss, in the following sections, the hatha yoga that is known worldwide. Although the use of posture is only a part of that approach, its expertise on postural dynamics remains without rival, even today. Yogis assume that one needs a set of highly differentiated approaches to grasp and master the complexity of an individual human system. Thus, Iyengar identifies eight limbs of yoga[4] that promote an individual's quest:

1. *Yama.* Ethical disciplines: nonviolence, truth, no stealing, continence, no coveting, and love.
2. *Niyama.* Rules of conduct for individuals: purity of the tissues of the organism, emotional tranquility, joyful austerity, understanding how one functions, dedication to the sacred.
3. *Asana.* The mastery of the organism's repertoire of postures. The asana are the postures explored by the yogis. The term *asana* designates both the methods of self-exploration based on the use of the postures and particular postures. A person practices each posture in a way that is firm and comfortable (Patanjali, 2007, 2.46). This politeness toward oneself,

which is also stressed in point 6, is pedagogically crucial, and should always be stressed when yoga is used in a psychotherapeutic context. The aims are (a) not to create tension in other parts of the body when one works on specific muscles (see the section on Bülow-Hansen in chapter 19 for more on this point, p. 543), (b) supporting the need to practice regularly, (c) not to use yoga to strengthen the superego (as defined in the section on Freud's Second Topography in chapter 15, p. 400f). *It is best to meditate with a real teacher in a real group.* The teacher can then provide feedback on the beneficial use of meditation and yoga exercises. This feedback is essential. I have met several people who have attempted such a process alone, with the help of a book or a DVD. The result was always counterproductive, not only because essential external feedback was missing but also because it led to an overdeveloped will, which is often associated with an overly powerful superego in psychodynamic clinical discussions.

4. *Pranayama.* The mastery of the breath. Soft breathing exercises are essential when yoga is used with depressive patients. The softness and gentleness is crucial, as mentioned in the previous paragraph (see the section on Gindler's Berlin in chapter 12, p. 302ff for more on this point).

5. *Pratyahara.* To free oneself from the needs imposed by the senses.

6. *Dharana.* The development of attention by learning to concentrate on one task and one point alone with gentleness, serenity, and patience (Patanjali, 2007, 3.1.).

7. *Dhyana.* The capacity to integrate that which goes on in meditation. This implies the capacity to observe what is happening with benevolence, without desire for money and power.

8. *Samadhi.* The goal of this quest is the state of illumination.[5]

For Bellur Krishnamachar Sundararaja Iyengar,[6] these limbs are the pillars of a coherent method. If the practicing individual has not acquired an ethics that leads to yoga (1 and 2), he has a lesser chance to find the inner strength and enthusiasm to travel the arduous paths that lead to illumination (8). The practice of postures allows a yogi to train his body to hold a posture without moving for hours and without disturbing his attention (3). Once a posture can be sustained, it can become a bowl capable of containing the pulsations of life: the respiratory movements and the beating of the heart (4). The practicing yogi must then be able to contain in his spirit the forces that grow in him and further be able to enter into contact with the essence of the forces that animate him (5, 6, and 7).

Each limb designates a method that relates to a dimension of the human being. It is not only the combination of these methods that fosters an existential quest; it is also a certain internal alchemy that cannot crystallize unless the quest occurs in a specific spirit.

The yogis are aware of the unbelievable adventure that they propose and of the complexity of the task. For them, this total transformation of one's being is not possible unless it is in a process that lasts millions of lifetimes. A psychotherapist can be inspired by yoga but his goals are clearly other. The psychotherapist aims at goals that are achievable within a few years at the most.

We can find this kind of vision in a number of Far Eastern schools, as in the writings attributed to the Buddha, such as in *The Sutra on the Full Awareness of Breathing*.[7] It supposes that each dimension has its particularities and demands an approach adapted to these particularities. Gradually the devotee will learn to recognize the functioning of the dimensions within; he will find creative ways of living while sensing the heteroclite dynamics that animate him.

Yogis thus assume that there are many dimensions of the human being and that each has need of a different pedagogy. We can imagine that the individual is a house of many stories. Entering a school of yoga, the individual can participate in different courses that seek to develop a particular level. These courses are like scaffolding erected around an individual. Each level of the scaffolding is constructed in such a way as to be able to support the particularities of each story of the house. The scaffolding allows the individual to rearrange his structure, all the while following a number of developmental constraints (the function of the cellar is not like that of the roof). Similarly, a school acquires the experience relative to a type of scaffolding that sustains a certain type of transformation of the whole individual. This teaching thus acquires a relative coherence that corresponds to its own way of conceptualizing how the different activities necessary for the development of an individual (morality, compassion, body, physiology, meditation, etc.) can be coordinated.

The Yogi's Knowledge of the Body

There are a great number of religious and mystical movements that profess to liberate an individual's essence from the body. Theories on "essence" vary from one movement to another. However, we do not need to enter into the multiple Hindu theories on this topic.

Yoga subscribes to this enterprise. Its originality is to have explored, in a particularly exhaustive way, the tools the body places at the disposal of those who attempt to influence the soul by *voluntarily* manipulating the bodily dimension.

The bodily methods of hatha yoga are centered on the notion of the postures, designated in the yogi's vocabulary by the term *asana*. I do not know of another movement that has gathered such an extensive knowledge of what posture and respiration allow in terms of the transformation of a human being. Physical therapists, sports trainers, martial arts instructors, orthopedic surgeons, and psychotherapists continue to have confidence in this approach. They often recommend the postural and respiratory exercises of hatha yoga and of pranayama, independently from their original context (the eight pillars).

Clinical Research and Its Inventory

Hatha yoga does not use postures as they are used in everyday life. The yogis select postures that have an *orthopedic* relevance. These postures, like the gestures proposed today by a physical therapist, have nothing spontaneous about them. They are defined by criteria appropriate to their approach and theoretical principles.

When a researcher attempts to study the postural repertoire of daily life, he is confronted by an immense repertoire.[8] The utilization of posture responds to such a varied mix of causes that today's researcher is rapidly drowned by more data than he can manage. It is possible to propose a list of relatively stable postures observed in a given situation. To define the postural repertoire of a population would require so much work that the task has not yet been undertaken. The yogi's solution to this dilemma, thousands of years before the invention of the camera and automatic data processing, was to focus on a restricted repertoire of postures. These postures can be held long enough to be observed and analyzed in detail. A practicing yogi can inwardly experience (through introspection) what is going on and can observe what happens when others use the same posture. The research then divides itself between the pupils and the masters. A pupil can learn to observe how he reacts to a posture, and thus form a personal clinical profile of how he functions. He notices that certain postures are more or less comfortable, more or less stimulating, provoke certain types of dreams, help when he has a headache, and so on. Given that a posture is static and that its configuration is consciously and explicitly observable, they can examine what a posture induces during long periods in their life and can find related constants. Pupils are also able to discuss among each other and compare their experiences. They can notice that a detail renders a posture more comfortable for everyone or interacts with respiration in a certain way. Some of these followers are also masters who discuss the results of their observations relative to a posture with their colleagues. Thereby, they attempt to understand general mechanisms that are not necessarily part of their personal experience, and also incorporate other forms of available knowledge into their discussions.

Hardly anyone takes a posture in exactly the same way, even one as simple as the "cross-legged position" (tailor's position).[9] A person tilts her head or keeps it straight, place hands on knees or on the thighs, may experience pain between the shoulder blades or in the hollow of the lower back, places his bottom more or less on the coccyx, and places the feet more or less near the genitals, and so on. Once we have observed the subtleties of a posture, the enormous number of variations is quickly evident, and the possible combinations reach astronomical numbers. Through the discussions with colleagues who gather the same type of data, the yogis slowly create a precise clinical approach relative to the links that can exist between one posture and the physical and mental dimensions of an organism, and on particular ways of constructing a posture.

Hatha yoga is both inspiring in its simplicity and powerful in its exploratory possibilities. Today, it is common in psychotherapy to build a knowledge base in this way from a practice. It is what we refer to as *clinical research*. This practical clinical knowledge is often included in theoretical speculations. Like psychotherapists, yogis have always tried to relate their practical knowledge to all the available information about the human organism. Yogis accommodate their knowledge to include what science discovers as much as possible; even if the practitioner does not always have the necessary expertise to integrate the most recent discoveries. It often occurs that yogis observe phenomena that the sciences have not yet studied or maintain a position with the assumption that further research will be needed. Scientists themselves know that their present formulations may be revised by future research.

In Meditation

I will now describe a typical meditation session, the way it is taught in the initial stages of meditation, by focusing on postural variables. I assume, here, that the person meditating is comfortably using the lotus (padmasana) posture. Most of my remarks also apply to someone who, because of a lack of flexibility, prefers to meditate sitting on a chair.

1. The person meditating first properly organizes the *situation*[10] in which he finds himself. He does not want to be disturbed during the following half-hour. The organism wants to protect itself from the stimulations of ordinary life so that its attention can concentrate on what is going on in the confines of the body. Nothing is cooking in the kitchen. The phone is silenced. The computer is turned off.

2. The person meditating then structures his *basic posture*.[11] He sits on a clean rug and places the back of each foot on the opposite upper thigh near the groin.[12] The triangle formed on the ground by the knees and ischia[13] feels like an immense and solid pedestal that firmly maintains the base of the spine. He bends forward and backward and senses his spinal column rise like a tree trunk toward the sky. The articulation that links the head and the spine is stretched and made supple by some movements of the head up to the point when the individual himself, aligned from the perineum[14] to the anterior fontanel, feels as if a string tied to an immobile star above the body axis was pulling the fontanel. This metaphor is used by many body–mind methods today. I have heard it in dance, in the methods of Moshe Feldenkrais and Mathias Alexander, in yoga and tai chi chuan courses in Europe, and so on.

3. Having regulated the basic posture, the one meditating now passes through a phase of *auto-regulation*. There is a need of some time before the heartbeat, the thoughts of the day, and the respiration calms down. A fish swims near the bottom of a pond, disturbs the silt with its tail. The water loses its transparency. Once the fish moves away, it takes a certain amount of time before the silt falls to the bottom and the water becomes

transparent again. Such is the type of metaphor that inspires someone in meditation at such moments. To calm his respiration, for example, he breathes alternately with each nostril. He bends an elbow and blocks his right nostril with a finger. He breathes in through the left nostril; then he blocks that nostril and breathes out through the right one. He breathes in this manner for a few minutes, blocking one nostril and then the other until his respiration becomes noiseless.[15] He will then let his arm rest. A variation would be to bend the arms so that the back of the wrists can rest on each knee; or he will place the back of the left hand on the feet in front of the navel, and then the back of the right hand on the palm of the left hand.[16]

4. The *meditative state* can finally emerge. The individual slides into the oceanic depths of his being, practices his attention exercises, and sometimes senses rising within, like a giant ray fish, the very life that animates him.

Sometimes, a moment will come when, like a deep-sea diver, the individual in meditation finally returns to the surface of his awareness. His legs are becoming numb, the blood circulates poorly, the tissues need more oxygen, and the joints need to move. To resurface, the individual follows a procedure quite like the diver who must return to the surface in stages so that the body can progressively re-accommodate to breathing like before, for his eyes to tolerate the surrounding light, and for his ears to be able to comprehend the words that someone will soon enough speak to him. One possibility is to bend an elbow again, move a few fingers, and then use them to repeat the alternating breathing exercises so that his physiology gradually accustoms itself to handling more oxygen. The individual is now able to auto-regulate to become active again. He opens and closes his eyelids repeatedly. At first, everything is blurred. He unfolds his arms and legs and stretches them. He also shakes them a bit to help restore the flow of blood to the extremities. To enter the meditative state, he paid attention to the setting and to himself. Now he retraces his steps as he rises, walks about, drinks something, and then gradually returns to his ordinary life.

Muscular Tensions as the Chains of the Soul
In discussions with colleagues who regularly practice yoga, I came to realize that for them every *chronic muscular tension* is experienced as a chain that binds them to their passions and to those close to them. They assume that a chronic muscular tension that makes up the daily structure of the body is associated to affects that have become rigidly habitual. Hate directed at one's parents becomes, for them, a tension maintained toward others, and consequently, a tie that the person tends to perpetuate. A person cannot relax his muscles without first having accepted to renounce an affective link to someone in his life. For the yogis, to relax the muscles is to liberate oneself from the emotional chains that bind a person to this earthly life and to others who hold him in a

network of dependence and mutual demands. It is also to liberate his postural repertoire, and consequently to become capable of exploring all the postures a skeleton can adopt. To have access to all the postural repertoire of one's skeleton is required to disinhibit all of the dimensions of the organism.[17]

This idea is taken up in almost all schools of body psychotherapy in the twentieth century.[18] However, this notion has a different theoretical framework, because in psychotherapy, emotional ties are often valued. To paraphrase a famous distinction between Corneille and Racine, taught in most French schools: the yoga talks about man such as he ought to be; the psychotherapist talks of man such as he is. For Iyengar,[19] a yogi renounces all that distances him from God or from the spirit of the universe. He renounces everything personal, especially his desires. Only the universe should animate an organism. The emotions create activations that block the influence of the "Great All" by linking the dynamics of the organism to interests that are mostly tied to human and social aims. While the yogi seeks a regular respiration, the emotions upset this equilibrium.[20]

Vignette on the turtle posture *(kurmasana)*.[21] *The posture can be taken only by someone who has a highly flexible body. When a person gains the ability to hold this posture with comfort, and can maintain it for some time while breathing comfortably, the spirit calms itself and distances itself from all manner of sadness or joy. A person frees himself of anxieties caused by the fear and anger that controls his thoughts.[22] The turtle posture creates an organismic context incompatible with emotional dynamics. The idea here is not that the yogis cut themselves off from their emotions, but that the emotions become useless, that they lose their relevance.[23]*

To be able to take a posture like that of the turtle requires having gone beyond those thoughts that activate passions. This notion implies that the yogi no longer has thoughts and affects repressed into the Freudian unconscious. This point is often important for the psychotherapist who has a patient in front of him who has used hatha yoga to repress certain impulses more effectively.

THE PRANAYAMA AS THE FOUNDATIONAL LINK
BETWEEN MIND AND BODY

It is customary to divide respiration into two series of mechanisms:

1. The *external* respiration is the route traveled by oxygen (O_2) and carbon dioxide (CO_2) in the air circulation that is created between the nostrils, the mouth, and the lungs.
2. The *internal* respiration is the route traveled by oxygen (O_2) and carbon dioxide (CO_2) in the physiological channels of the organism outside of the lungs.

In body psychotherapy, the external respiration is mostly the focus of attention because it can be changed by the voluntary movement of the muscles. The body psychotherapist cannot directly affect the internal respiration, but he is mindful of it, for it has a great impact on the vegetative and affective dynamics. However, these internal interactions are for the moment not well understood, or more specifically, not sufficiently understood to allow an explicit handling in body psychotherapy.

The breathing exercises in yoga form the discipline of pranayama. They use hatha yoga to modulate the external respiration and call the effects of internal respiration on the organism, prana. Prana designates metabolic operations that remain difficult to explain as long as we do not have a full description of the impact of internal breathing on the organism, on affects, and on the vitality of the mind. The body psychotherapist of today has but a simplistic vision of what is described by the Hindu theories of prana, which has been associated with magical and alchemical properties. It is probable that some of these magical properties will be "revisited" by tomorrow's scientists.

The Phases of Respiration

Spontaneous and Anxious Respiration

In *spontaneous* respiration, from being at rest, inspiration stretches the muscles of the torso in a way that can be likened to an elastic that we stretch. It is therefore an *active* movement. Breathing out is the *passive* reaction of this elastic once we release it. The muscles that are mobilized for respiration thus return to their initial tone.

In a breathing exercise that is found in most body–mind methods, the therapist asks the patient to let the thoracic cage and the abdomen drop during exhalation as if one were letting go of a stone. This letting go during exhalation is impossible for someone who is tense or anxious. Chronic muscular tension raises the level of the basic muscle tone. As the muscles are less elastic, the variations in respiratory volume are limited.

The relationship between anxiety and the inhibition of respiratory activity is a good example of what I mean when I speak of a robust ancient knowledge about mind-body phenomena. I do not know if all anxious people have a troubled respiratory function, but the correlation is frequently observed. It has since been confirmed by most practitioners who have not waited for scientific research to use breathing exercises to reduce anxiety. The important point for body psychotherapy is the observation that an emotion is, among other things, a breathing pattern.

It is only recently that researchers confirmed the existence of a correlation between respiratory problems and anxiety.[24] The detailed descriptions provided by these researchers confirm the descriptions given by yogis and acupuncturists, as well as the impact of respiratory problems on almost all of the functions influenced by the vegetative regulatory mechanisms (circulation of the blood, sudden weaknesses, etc.). It is interesting to note that respiratory exercises can relieve anxiety for a moment, but only rarely provide a lasting modification of the connection between anxiety and the respiratory constriction. Yogis and Buddhists knew that anxiety is also caused by a way of thinking, a way of managing one's affects. We still need more information on the complex mechanisms that influence the link between anxiety and breathing so that we can improve our way of working with respiration in the treatment of affective disorders. The difficulty is that once a physiological mode of functioning embeds itself in a stable organismic dynamic, it becomes difficult to change it. Body psychotherapists developed new methods to work on the emotional mechanisms that connect anxiety and breathing.

The Big Respiratory Circle Shows the Importance of Apneas

> Try this: at the end of the next out-breath, just *wait* for the following in-breath to occur—as though you were a cat waiting for a mouse to emerge from its hole. You know that the next in-breath will come, but you have no idea precisely when. So while your attention remains as alert and as poised in the present as that of a cat's, it is free from any intention to control what will happen next. Without expectation, just wait. Then suddenly it happens and you catch "it" breathing. (Batchelor, 1997, p. 95f.)

Besides exhalation and inhalation, yogis are very attentive to the *apneas* that separate breathing out from breathing in, and breathing in from breathing out. Finally, it is customary to distinguish *thoracic* respiration from *ventral* respiration. The first relates to the impact of the movements of the lungs on the rib cage, whereas the second relates to the impact of the movement of the *diaphragm* on the viscera of the abdomen. This leads to the basic schema shown in figure 1.1, which is utilized in many cultures.

THE TOPOGRAPHIC DIAGNOSIS OF RESPIRATION
The topographic diagnosis of respiration, based on the schema in figure 1.1, presents an analysis of respiration according to the degree of utilization at each phase. Certain diagrams are more refined, distinguishing, for example, the top and bottom of the thorax. Few persons utilize these six phases all the time. To propose a relevant respiratory diagnosis, the therapist takes note of the duration and the amplitude of each phase. This analysis sometimes changes when a person is either lying down or standing, or engaged in different kinds of activities. This type of diagnostic distinguishes above all between individuals who breathe mostly with their abdomen from those who breathe mostly from the thorax. It is generally recognized that the persons who breathe only from the thorax easily become affectively labile and overstimulated. The explanations of this relationship are rarely convincing, but the correlation is sufficiently robust. Most of the approaches to respiration recommend, above all, verifying that there exists a good ventral respiration that expresses a minimum functioning of

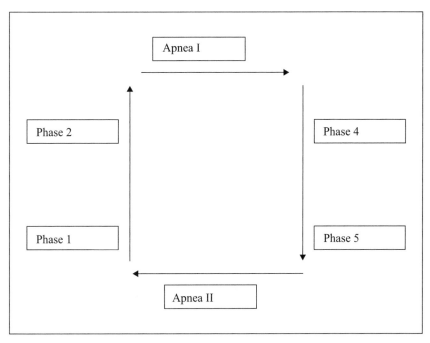

FIGURE 1.1. The moments of respiration. Phase 1: Inhalation by the ventral segment. Phase 2: Inhalation by the thoracic segment. Phase 3, Apnea I: The duration between inhalation and exhalation. Phase 4: Exhalation of the thoracic segment. Phase 5: Exhalation of the ventral segment. Phase 6, Apnea II: The duration between exhalation and inhalation.

the horizontal respiration (top ↔ bottom when a person is standing) of the lungs and a flexibility of the diaphragm. Typically, a citizen[25] has a diaphragm that is only relatively mobile, to which voice teachers will attest. These deviations from the ideal norm are not necessarily pathological. *Full* breathing exercises demand that a person attempt to take in and let out as much air as possible. They make it possible to evaluate the degree of adaptability of the respiratory schema to demanding situations on the organism. The therapist, for example, asks a person who breathes mostly from the abdomen what is going on when he also breathes from the thorax.

Another important element of a topographic diagnostic is the distinction between ventral, dorsal, and lateral respiration. Respiration that is visible on the front of the body is common to everyone. Fewer people have a respiration that visibly mobilizes the back. Still fewer have a respiration that mobilizes the sides of the rib cage other than in moments of breathlessness.

Most of the body psychotherapists who work with breathing make these distinctions. Typically, the mobilization of the dorsal respiration permits the patient to regain contact with an impression of strength, whereas the mobilization of the lateral respiration can help a person experience containment and calm.

DYNAMIC RESPIRATORY DIAGNOSTIC

The term *dynamic* refers to the unfolding of a mechanism in time. A dynamic analysis of respiration is based principally on the observation of the following two dimensions:[26]

1. The temporal unfolding of each element distinguished by a topographic model of respiration. Thus, certain individuals inhale first with the abdomen and others first with the thorax. Some have a longer apnea I than an apnea II.
2. The way each phase is coordinated with the next one. Let us take as an example an exercise in which one asks a patient with no experience in breathing techniques to exhale slowly and deeply. Typically, this person will not succeed in exhaling harmoniously from the top to the bottom. There is often a kind of awkward jump that occurs at the level of the diaphragm that tells the therapist that his patient holds tension in his diaphragm. Most techniques encourage people to harmonize how body segments participate in a respiratory pattern. For example, one can ask a person if he can breathe out deeply in such a way that the body movements form a wave that gradually spreads from the throat to the pelvis.

It is useful for this kind of analysis, and especially for the observation of the diaphragm, to distinguish between *spontaneous* and *voluntary* respiration.

APNEAS AND RESPIRATION RHYTHM

One of the well-known characteristics of yoga is its work on the apneas. These moments of transition are often set aside in the body practices based on the information from anatomy and physiology, as if they were without importance. For a yogi, these moments are crucial. It is mostly at those moments that the mind can introduce a lever to master not only the rhythm and the volume of the external respiration but also the vegetative coordination that exists between the emotions and the internal respiration. By concentrating on these phases of transition, yoga facilitates the acquisition of a certain voluntary mastery of affect. It is at that moment that a yoga exercise becomes effectively a *yoke* that can master the body–mind connection.

> Vignette on the mastery of the breath. *In the Ujjyayi Pranayama, Iyengar*[27] *proposes to explore what goes on when we breathe in as deeply as possible with the thorax, while pulling the abdomen back as close as possible to the spinal column. Once inspiration is complete, the pupil explores what is going on while holding his breath, keeping the air in the organism for a few seconds.*

This is an example of respiratory *retention*, currently utilized in the practice of pranayama. Those who are following yoga classes in Europe will notice that they work mostly on the retention after inspiration. By contrast, those who practice tai chi chuan may spend more time exploring what is going on between exhalation and inhalation.

If we observe someone's spontaneous respiration, we notice that these moments of transition take more or less time, varying from person to person and in function of circumstances. In a state of relaxation, my patients have the tendency to move rapidly from inhalation to exhalation (the release of the elastic), while the move from exhalation to inhalation spontaneously lasts longer. This moment of transition can be experienced as an end of respiration by a person who is not familiar with this kind of work. But the very reason that yogis work on these transitions is that these are moments of intense physiological and psychological activity.

One of the aims of pranayama is to slow down the rhythm of respiration by lengthening the four phases of the respiratory rhythm. According to Iyengar,[28] a person has about fifteen respirations per minute.[29] This rhythm accelerates in the case of indigestion, fever, a cold or a cough, or in conditions such as fear, anger, or desire. Anxious people often have a restrained but rapid respiration. Certain yogis think that the number of respirations a person can have in a lifetime is determined; consequently, the slower the rhythm, the longer the person will live. Sensory and instinctual activity activates the respiratory rhythm, while detachment diminishes it. Finding a lifestyle that is in synergy with the requirements of metabolic dynamics allows one to live with an even slower respiratory rhythm. This analysis is compatible with those proposed in a text on physiology (Bonnet and Millet, 1971, pp. 305–306) for adults. For children, the younger a child the more rapid the respiration (forty-four breaths per minute on an average for newborns).

In my practice, persons who observe their respiration think spontaneously like yogis. When they lie down for a relaxation session, they sense that something is not well when their breathing is rapid, superficial, and brief. When the exercise begins to have effect, they sense that their breathing is spontaneously deepening and slowing down. At that moment the diaphragm relaxes and the person yawns, and sometimes stretches.[30] In general, the people who come to see me have never found it useful to think about their apneas. To become attentive to what is going on within them during spontaneous apneas is often, for them, an amusing, even intriguing, discovery. Once they have learned to observe this aspect of the respiratory rhythm, they notice that during their relaxation, these moments also lengthen. For certain individuals, the slowing down is mostly marked during one of the two apneas; for others, it is during both.

Internal Respiration or the Dynamics of Prana

Internal respiration begins when air leaves the lungs to enter the arteries. The red blood cells carry the oxygen to nourish cellular activity in the whole organism, and bring back the carbon dioxide to the lungs. Somehow this dynamic also influences affects in a multitude of ways. The impact of internal breathing on moods and needs was already known by yogis centuries ago.

Basic Physiology

Three gases are inhaled and exhaled (average values):

1. Nitrogen (N): 80 percent.
2. Oxygen (O_2): 20 percent at inhalation, 16 percent at exhalation.
3. Carbon dioxide (CO_2): 1 percent at inhalation, 4 percent at exhalation.

The composition of the air inhaled and exhaled is thus grossly the same. Everything turns on an exchange of about 4 percent oxygen and 3 percent carbon dioxide.

The inhaled oxygen bonds to the iron atoms contained in the hemoglobin molecules that circulate in the arteries. Oxygen makes up about 20 percent of the volume of the arterial blood and 12 percent of the venous blood. The capacity of the blood to contain oxygen can easily double, but that happens very rarely. Carbon dioxide, transported mostly by blood plasma, makes up 50 percent of the plasma's volume. Four percent of CO_2 in circulation is freed through exhalation. The remaining amount is indispensable for the functioning of the internal respiration.

The issues linked to the ratio of iron in the blood introduce the concept of *intermediary mechanisms*. The more iron atoms in the blood, the more the blood can transport oxygen molecules. When the ratio of iron in the blood diminishes, the ratio of oxygen also inevitably diminishes. Respiration can then no longer respond to the demands of an increase in physiological activity, even when there is an increase of respiration and cardiac activity. Because the problem is not caused by the lungs or the heart but by a lack of iron, the organism soon finds itself in a crisis. If a physician gives a supplemental iron injection, and if the iron attaches well to the hemoglobin, the problem resolves immediately. The main causes of iron deficiency are poor absorption of iron by the body, inadequate daily intake of iron, pregnancy, blood loss due to heavy menstrual bleeding, or internal bleeding. Too much iron in the blood causes other problems.[31]

The equilibrium I have just described is important for the *metabolic* activity of the organism. For example, it is influenced by the energy sources utilized by the activity of the organism (sugars, proteins, or fats). This is an example of interaction between respiratory behavior and the dynamics of metabolism. The fatigue experienced by individuals who lack iron is an example of conscious awareness activated by physiological regulatory mechanisms of the organism.

Internal Respiration and Prana

Physiologists know that internal respiration is not a globally structured phenomenon but a multitude of operations that can be analyzed in many different ways. These operations take in oxygen and release carbon dioxide. They participate in the process through which these two molecules are distributed in the organism. These mechanisms are consumers of energy more than organismic regulators. They do not consume oxygen to produce carbon dioxide. They are content to carry out their mission utilizing their environment as a source of supply and as a means of waste disposal. Some global physiological mechanisms, like venous circulation, then gather the excess amount of carbon dioxide to expel it from the organism, notably through external respiration (exhalation) but also by other avenues like perspiration.

This introduction to internal respiration is also an introduction to the notion of prana. I do not know what the Hindus knew relative to internal respiration,[32] but the yogis had observed, clinically at least, that respiration intimately influenced all of the physiological mechanisms of the organism. Prana is this dynamic interaction between respiration and the physiological mechanisms. Their theories were based on whatever knowledge and philosophical speculations were fashionable at a given moment. This explains why they sometimes appear folkloric and magical to some physiologists. What is astonishing with regard to the theories about prana is the extent to which the intuition of the yogis is fundamentally correct, in the measure in which they perceived how breathing had a profound impact on the dynamics of the organisms, moods, and thoughts. The yogis developed, in the course of the centuries, an impressive number of explicit techniques, capable of having foreseeable effect on this nebulous group of mechanisms that they called prana.

The Handling of Prana

Yogis have developed refined ways of influencing the dynamics of the prana; yet most body psychotherapists who want to influence internal breathing tend to use only simplistic and rudimentary methods. Here are some points of reflection that highlight the minimum knowledge that a body psychotherapist ought to have on this topic. He will rarely find more information than this in the various textbooks dedicated to his profession.

THE EXPERIENCE OF RELAXATION

When a breathing exercise is correctly prescribed and well accepted, all those who practice it speak spontaneously of an intensification of *body sensations* (tingling, pins and needles sensations, warmth diffused throughout the body), a feeling of relaxation, and an impression of having become denser, more coherent, and more together. The power of this impression explains the importance accorded to internal respiration that has, as its first function, the maintenance of the vitality of the cells of the organism.

HYPERVENTILATION AND THE CRISIS OF TETANY

Hyperventilation occurs when the organism stores more oxygen than it spends. At that moment, the ratio between oxygen and carbon dioxide is not what the organism expects. At a weak level, this imbalance can activate an agreeable euphoric state. When it becomes stronger, it leads to a crisis of hyperventilation. During such a crisis, people complain of rapid and superficial respiration, an oppressive thoracic sensation, and suffocation.[33] Some people experience a muscular tetany, with a sharp flexion of the wrist and ankle joints. Such a crisis accelerates the pulse and abruptly lowers arterial pressure. It can provoke buzzing and hissing in the ears and cramps (typically in the hands). Tetany is probably due to some modifications in the dynamics of the acids in the blood and the muscles.

One reason some therapists propose exercises that lead to hyperventilation is that it can sometimes provoke states of regression during which a person's psychological defenses are weakened and unconscious content activated. When this happens, the patient becomes aware of past experiences that were repressed. Those regressions can be powerful and lead to an intense experience. In reliving such experiences, a person sometimes learns to no longer fear profound emotional experiences.

When an individual voluntarily hyperventilates for two to three minutes, we observe an automatic sequence (that cannot be controlled voluntarily) that William Francis Ganong calls *periodic respiration*.[34] While holding her breath, the person experiences prolonged apnea. This moment can be experienced as an ecstasy by some, as panic by others, and as a mixture of both by the majority of people. When the person breathes spontaneously again, it is at first in a rapid and superficial fashion. One can then observe an oscillation between a phase of rapid breathing and apnea repeating itself several times, for not more than ten minutes:

> If body activity stays the same, an increase in breathing will increase the rate of CO_2 diffusing from the blood into the lungs. This can cause the CO_2 concentration in the blood to fall, which will cause the acid level of the blood to drop, and its pH will become alkalotic (too alkaline). . . . When the pH exceeds 7.60, hyperventilation tetany takes place. If breathing is depressed, CO_2 concentrations in blood will rise, causing the acid level to rise and the pH of the blood will become acidic. (Caldwell and Victoria, 2011)

Gradually, the respiration returns to its habitual dynamic.

The drawbacks of such a method of self-exploration are important. First, the euphoria resulting from such exercises often renders individuals dependent on the therapist with whom this experience was triggered and on the method he used. Then, with the momentary lowering of the defense system, individuals can become aware of affects and memories that they are unable to integrate, especially if they are intensely relived. Such an experience can be traumatizing, and generate a form of retraumatization during therapy. Finally, in the case of impulsive personalities, the experience of boundaries diminishes dramatically. They no longer fear that expressing what they experience can become dangerous for them and their entourage. For these reasons, most schools of body psychotherapy avoid using these methods or use them only in specific cases.[35]

It is difficult, in such instances, to sort out memories from fantasy, delusions, and hallucinations. They are often intermingled. Some psychotherapists have an excessive confidence in the material imagined in such states and may even suggest to the patient that all that is perceived is true. This attitude has proven itself dangerous, because the patient is inclined to reorganize himself on the bases of an unfounded belief.[36] The case in point is that of individuals who reconstruct their self-understanding on the belief that they suffered from abuse in their early childhood or in a past life when nothing of the sort existed.[37] The proper manner to use this material, sometimes available in abundance with this method, is to explore if the same material can be found through other methods (e.g., dream analysis) and take it up anew. Therapist and patient can then separate out what is remembered, what is delusional, what is a blend of both, and what is impossible to evaluate.

When a patient hyperventilates, it is better for the psychotherapist not to worry about it. Such crises tend to subside. It is essential to stay present with the patient in a reassuring and containing manner while he is going through it. There is usually no hyperventilation if the patient spends the energy taken in through inhalation by moving and speaking. If the patient's hands take on the characteristic position that announces a crisis of tetany (fingers are hyperextended and touch each other while getting closer to the interior of the wrists), the therapist can encourage still more movements and more vocalizations to use up the excess oxygen.

PEOPLE WHO ARE EASILY IN A STATE OF OVER-OXYGENATION

Each organism has a particular way of associating metabolism and respiration. This association also varies in function of one's lifestyle. Certain individuals therefore hyperventilate more easily than others. The hypothesis is that the more an organism can utilize a large quantity of oxygen, the more active it can become. This notion suggests that breathing exercises influences physiological resiliency. The neo-Reichian psychotherapists have also observed that, at least in some cases, reducing the quantity of oxygen one lives with is a way of reducing not only one's vitality but also the intensity of one's needs and affects.

In my practice, I have observed that some patients who breathe poorly grew up in an early environment that could not integrate the activities and demands of infants and little children.[38] In the two schools (psychotherapy and yoga), for different reasons, practitioners work with the assumption that such individuals should learn to tolerate more oxygen to reinforce their physiological and affective vitality. Modifying the balance between a vast numbers of heterogeneous mechanisms without creating undesirable secondary effects is a complex business. Therefore, a process that wants to support the accommodation of physiological processes to a greater quantity of oxygen requires time and regularity. Time is necessary not only because regular practice is required to change the dynamics of organs but also because the therapist needs to *calibrate* the exercises he proposes in function of the patients particularities.

Some Dynamics of Prana Known Today

Certain ways to measure out overoxygenation via exercises can have complex implications for psychophysiology, notably in the modulation of the concentration of the neurotransmitters in the organism,[39] the composition of the blood (the diaphragm is also a pump for the venous blood of the legs), and the nervous system. The rapport between the hormones and the respiration is so rich that Tarja Saaresranta and Olli Polo (2002) have even proposed that the studies of this topic form the discipline of *respiratory endocrinology*. For the moment, this research mostly shows how the hormones influence respiration, but—cybernetics duly noted—this implies that respiration is included in the regulatory systems of the hormones, which is also responsive to the functioning of respiration.[40] It is therefore possible to relate effects of respiration to a cascade of chemical implications that diffuse themselves throughout the body.

Having said this, the recent knowledge on the influence of oxygen on the metabolic activity does not explain all of the phenomena associated with prana. Expressed differently, the clinical *impression* of the Hindus, concerning the relationship between their way of handling respiration and certain physiological phenomena, can be empirically sound. But that does not imply that their *explanation* is sound.

TANTRIC TECHNIQUES OF TRANCES

The yoga based on the sequence of static postures, taught by masters such as Iyengar, is the one the world knows best. There are other types of yoga. One of them is tantric or *bhakti* yoga, developed in the Himalayas.[41] One of its particularities is a way to "let oneself go" (*prapatti*), which allows one to free oneself from all imaginable ties that an individual might establish with what surrounds him. In this way of thinking, sexuality and emotions are those human forces that permit an individual to experience the other, to abandon oneself to the forces that surround us all, and to submit oneself (seva) to the divine forces to be able to join with it.[42] This school often uses techniques in which chant, dance, and trance allow the individual to feel enlivened by divine forces and unite to them. The tantric exercises sometimes utilize sexual intercourse. Men must become capable of refraining from ejaculating even during orgasm. The mastery of the breath that characterizes *pranayama* is also part of these practices.

The fact that there are tantric schools in many parts of the world indicates that it is almost as easy to be in a trance as to be hypnotized. A trance can be induced by a series of exercises that one can learn in a few days during a course or workshop. It often suffices to approach these exercises with curiosity, without becoming irritated by what is proposed. The fact that such states can be reached so easily demystifies the impression that a trance is a bizarre phenomenon. Just as there are persons who resist hypnosis, there are some who resist a trance.

Kundalini

Hindus gave a lot importance to the spine. The spine links the segments of the body and makes it possible for the central nervous system to coordinate gestures with thought. The spine is the axis of all the postures. A yogi's spinal column can be as strong as a tree trunk and as flexible as a snake. They have developed highly effective massages of the spinal column, and hatha yoga always takes into account the interests of the spinal column. Because of its key function, yogis have situated the power that can animate the body and coordinate its segments at the base of the spine. They call this force the *kundalini*. It is an affirmative and sexual force, which leads to a form of sexual arousal mobilized by tantric yoga. To feel one's kundalini is to feel a powerful, warm, and agreeable current rise up the spinal column from the coccyx to the crown of the head. This form of arousal is deemed so powerful that it can activate an involuntary movement of the spinal column that undulates like a snake. This movement of the spine engages the entire body in a global movement that goes from the feet to the head and activates a trance state. The body acquires an autonomic dynamic that mobilizes the resources of the organism independent of volition. The follower needs the containment of a group and a master to maintain a certain mastery over what is happening. At the beginning of a tantric process, the kundalini is like a sleeping serpent, wrapped around itself in the coccyx.[43] This notion is included today in a more or less central fashion in the teachings of the majority of the schools of yoga.

Body psychotherapists know well the sensation of warmth that rises up the back when a patient rocks back and forth many times on his bottom, sensing the movement of the spine. This phenomenon is close to Wilhelm Reich's Vegetotherapy method to elicit an orgasmic reflex. One's gaze becomes clearer and one's back more tonic while more relaxed. Thus, body psychotherapies often use the term *kundalini* to describe this phenomenon because they do not have a better one.

The Chakras

The model of the chakras is also used by many schools of body psychotherapy.[44] It is a model built on the centers of every segment of the body coordinated by the kundalini. The flow of the kundalini must pass through a number of psycho-organic "doors" before being able to freely circulate the length of the spine and set the organism in an ecstatic trance. These doors, which are often closed when a student begins his yoga practice, are called chakras. According to many authors, these chakras are represented by wheels or flowers situated on the back, superimposed on the spinal column, or on the front of the body, parallel to the spine. We are thus very much in a segmental approach to the body because the front and the back of the body are linked to a chakra. The number of these wheels and their symbolism varies. Iyengar prudently mentions ten principal chakras.[45] The most often mentioned are the following:

1. The *muladhara* chakra, situated above the anus for the pelvis, associated to the idea of rootedness and source of the kundalini.
2. The *svadhisthana* chakra, situated above the genitals, associated with the vital energy and the soul.
3. The *mana* chakra, situated above the navel, associated with thought.
4. The *surya* chakra, situated at the solar plexus, associated with the sun.
5. The *anahata* chakra, situated in the region of the heart, associated with the heart (as organ and as openness to others).
6. The *visuddha* chakra, situated in the larynx, associated with purity.
7. The ajana chakra, situated between the eyes (the famous third eye), associated with mastery.
8. The *sahasraha* chakra, also called the lotus of a million leaves, is situated in the cerebral cavity.

I present this list only as an example, because the literature on the segments is extremely varied. Iyengar wonders whether these zones might correspond to the endocrine glandular system that regulates the major movements of the organism.

To awaken a chakra, the devotee must be able to move the designated area of the body in coordination with the respiration, associated affective mechanisms and mental representations. When all of these can be vividly integrated, the disciple moves on the next door. Once two doorways have been opened, the metaphor of the snake is there to remind us that each door refers to a psycho-organic whole, and that the *coordination* of the segments must acquire the same continuous grace as that of a cobra that dances vertically to the sound of a flute.

You may try and see how difficult it is to get the spinal column to move like a serpent while you breathe comfortably for ten minutes. We often find this type of movement in dances from around the world.

2

Chinese and Taoist Refinements

The Metaphysics of the Tao Are Associated to the Notions of the Chi, the Yin, and the Yang

Metaphysical Taoism, or ontological Taoism for some, is known to us today through the book of divination, called the *I Ching*,[1] and the theory of acupuncture. To introduce these domains, I will discuss three terms that are often used by Chinese authors:

1. The *Tao*. The universe was at its origin an immense chaos. Gradually, a *process* that the Chinese call the Tao came to be. This process became the structuring dynamic of the known universe. The Tao is a force that no one can understand, but its impact on our organism can be experienced.[2]

2. The *yin* and the *yang*. The Tao has two component forces called the yin and the yang. Their combinations form various systems that we humans can perceive. To sense how these forces balance each other in one's organism and around oneself and then sense in which direction they flow is to accommodate oneself to the Tao. This Tao is thus a way, a path. It is not a state that produces movement and multiplicity but a dynamic that is organized by all that it produces. The yin is the energy that stabilizes, and the yang is the energy that sets things in motion. Thus, all the systems of the universe contain stabilizing and creative dynamics.

3. The *chi*. The chi is a force linked to respiration that diffuses its influence throughout the organism. This notion is close to that of prana in India because it can be related to the impact of the internal respiration on the

dynamics of the organism. However, the chi is more independent of respiration than the prana, because it relates to all the forces that influences
the metabolism of an organism. Thus, the chi is activated not only by
breathing techniques but also by gestures, by the mind, and by acupuncture needles.

This model served as a reference point around which Chinese culture has woven
thousands of variations.

The *I Ching*

Confucianism is the art of living for a civil servant. Imperial China was an extremely structured country, with an important and powerful administration at
the service of the emperor, capable of representing the central administration
throughout the immense territory of the country. Confucianism is the theory
that organizes the principles of the imperial administration, one that remains a
model of strict and precise social organization. It freely incorporates elements of
Taoism, and then of Buddhism when it arrived in China around AD 200. It situates the social hierarchy in the order of the world and the individual in the social order. This movement was founded by Confucius (c. 551–497 BC) and
Mencius (c. 380–289 BC) in the same era as the first Taoists.[3] A way to summarize Confucianism is to conceptualize the universe as a piece of furniture in
which everything has its own drawer. There is the world, the Chinese empire,
the regions, the towns, the individuals, and the organs. The details of this first
systemic vision of the world are found in the *I Ching*. This is a book of divination that is also the first manual that proposes a formal language[4] capable of
describing the systemic dynamics of all phenomena and their capacity to change.
Confucianism, like other Chinese schools of thought, not only utilized the *I
Ching* but also contributed to its elaboration. Certain commentaries on the *I
Ching* are attributed to Confucius.

The Systemic Dimension of the Hexagrams in the I Ching
According to the *I Ching*, all that exists is a system. Each system can pass
through sixty-four states. Each of these states is a particular balance of yin and
yang forces. In certain circumstances, each state can transform itself and become another state. The universe is a system that contains subsystems like the
planets and the living creatures. The universe does not function like an organism, but it is organized by the same principles. The universe, the society, the individual, and the organs are bound to take up the sixty-four states described by
the *I Ching*.

I will not attempt to summarize this system, but I would like to highlight
certain characteristics of the *I Ching* that can be found in most Chinese approaches to the body. The states described by the *I Ching* are represented by the

symbols called *hexagrams*. These symbols are generated by the combination of six lines that can be either yin or yang. These combinations make up the sixty-four systems. A basic rule is to analyze hexagrams by going from bottom to top. This practice can be related to the Chinese practice of reading a body from the feet to the head, from the anchor points to fine motor skills.

> An example of how to use the *I Ching* when one analyzes the behavior of a person. *One of the hexagrams describes how a system can influence another system.[5] In a passage dedicated to this system, the authors of the* I Ching *take as an example a marriage proposal. They discuss two extreme situations:*
>
> 1. *The feelings of love are so deep that they are* activated in the feet. *From there they rise in the direction of the face and the voice. These feelings are deeply felt but are not always capable of finding an adequate expression.*
> 2. *Love that expresses itself* through the jaw, cheeks, and tongue *is "the most superficial way of trying to influence others." "The influence produced by mere tongue wagging must necessarily remain insignificant." (Wilhelm 1924, p. 125)*

This example introduces a metaphor that is regularly mentioned by body psychotherapists:

1. A thought or a feeling is not necessarily localized in the brain. Here, the feelings of love can be part of dynamics that build up from the feet up to the face, or from the throat to the face.
2. The more a way of thinking is anchored in the feet, the more it is profound. The body psychotherapist, Alexander Lowen[6] takes up this idea when he speaks of a way to think and to feel that is more or less *grounded*.

In these two cases, the mind depends on mechanisms that distribute themselves throughout the organism. We also find this perspective in the philosophical writings of the Taoists: "The True Man breathes with his heels; the mass of men breathe with their throats. Crushed and bound down, they gasp out their words as though they were retching" (Chuang Tzu, 1968, IV, p. 78).

When one uses such a theoretical frame, one can easily conceive that a hand gesture can, at the same time, participate in a fine equilibrium of the body in the gravity field, express a thought (it is springtime), betray a feeling (I am anxious), handle an object (to pass a cup of tea in a particular manner), and communicate something quite explicit (encourage a father to accept my marriage proposal to his daughter). This state may create another. Perhaps the fiancé is overly respectful (his feet are immobilized) and the father feels ill at ease and distant. Most hexagrams are associated with a metaphor linked to the movements of the elements. Here, it is the one of the sun distancing itself from the mountain. If the fiancé has an overly easygoing attitude, the father may not want to welcome someone who irritates him (like water on fire) into the family.

The Dialectical Turnarounds of the I Ching

Many specialists in bodywork know the *I Ching* well because it is a formalized way that can be used to understand and describe certain observable complex dynamics used by organisms. An example of the intellectual comfort offered by the dialectical system of the *I Ching* is the following:

> Walking analyzed using the principles of the *I Ching*. *Every extreme state (whether yin or yang) is considered unstable. The stability of a system demands a blend of yin and yang energies. If I am standing with all of my weight (a yang function) on my right foot, my left foot carries no weight (a yin function). This absolutely unbalanced distribution of yin and yang on my feet makes for an unstable posture. A more stable manner to stand up is to distribute my weight equally on both feet. There will therefore be an equal amount of yin and yang in each foot. This position is totally static. If I want to walk, I will shift the yang from one foot to the other while the yin distributes itself in a complementary fashion. The distribution of my body weight changes in such a rhythm that it permits me to move about. There is then in place a stable activity that establishes a balance between the feet that alternatively become yin and yang.*

This type of discussion concerning the dynamics of the body can be found in the majority of the Chinese and Japanese martial arts.

Acupuncture: Influencing the Deep Dynamics of the Organism through Touch and Movement

Acupuncture is a second group of practices and theories that illustrate how Taoist metaphysics can be used. It is one of the main branches of Chinese medicine. The theory of acupuncture is close to that of the *I Ching*, but it develops themes that are born out of a detailed exploration of the dynamics of chi.

Chinese Medicine and Western Medicine

A way to situate the particular alternatives of Chinese medicine is to contrast its origins with those of the medicine of the ancient Egyptians.[7] The Egyptians and Chinese of old felt an immense respect for their dead. However, this respect expressed itself in opposite ways that lead to two different types of medicine.

The Egyptians embalmed the cadaver so that it might protect the soul of the deceased and buried it near the family home (in a pyramid if the deceased were a pharaoh). To accomplish that, they developed an immense surgical and physiological competence that allowed them to preserve the body for thousands of years. The art of embalming seems to have been particularly developed between c. 1738 and 1102 BC. This is how the Egyptians established one of the bases of allopathic medicine that is characterized in this discussion by the necessity to *penetrate* the body to gain understanding and provide treatment. The traditional Chinese belief is that an individual's body belongs to the family. Therefore, the body must be delivered intact to the family before its incineration. That is why the eunuchs of the imperial court preserved and kept their sexual organs in formalin, so that these could be burned with the rest of the body at the end of their life. The Chinese were thus horrified by any attempt to dissect a body, dead or alive. Their physicians also believed that an organ lost what characterized it on dying, and consequently, they would learn very little by dissecting a cadaver.

In the nineteenth century, European colonial powers and the United States were occupying some of the main cities of China. Their power was terrifying, their rule sometimes cruel. Their allopathic medicine was a standard-bearer of their civilizing mission. For the Europeans, "scientific" medicine was the only valid approach to cure disease. They constructed schools of medicine and asked the Chinese government for cadavers for their courses on anatomy. The Chinese authorities did not dare ignore what was presented to them as a requirement. At the same time, these authorities could not authorize the dissection of Chinese citizens. The compromise was to send to the European medical schools the cadavers of criminals put to death as soon as the executioner had severed their head. This solution posed a problem for the professors of anatomy when they wanted to teach the anatomy of the neck, for it had been damaged by the ax used for the execution. They wanted, for courses on head and neck anatomy, to receive the cadavers of individuals who had been killed in other ways. The Chinese authorities proposed sending those who were condemned to death to the medical schools, so that the physicians could kill them any way they wanted.[8]

In spite of their fear of dissection, the Chinese nonetheless possessed important knowledge about the body. Chinese physicians could observe cadavers on the battlefield or accompany the executioner during torture sessions. They would ask the executioner to torture the part of the body they wanted to study and documented it. The advantage was to be able to observe a living anatomy.[9] On the battlefield, Chinese physicians measured the length of the principal blood vessels. In the torture chambers, they studied the circulation of the blood in the organs 2,000 years before European physicians. Having said this, Chinese anatomy leaves a lot to be desired. The Taoist Zhao Bichen (1933) published anatomical drawings based on what can be known by touching and through meditation. Even if it was influenced by the anatomy charts produced by Western medical schools, this anatomy is not precise and is simplistic. One of the reasons this book is interesting is that it shows the limits of introspection to explore anatomy, even when it is used by great masters of meditation.

The cult of the ancestors is a foundation of Chinese culture. It explains the enormous investment in nonsurgical therapeutic methods, and consequently the institutional efforts dedicated to the development of therapeutic methods using massage, movement, and medication. This effort opened up to the therapeutic approach that is acupuncture. Like the *I Ching*, this method has only recently integrated scientific procedures, but its principles are explicit and intelligible, and therefore teachable.

The Chi of Acupuncture

Before the arrival of Buddhism, chi was conceived as a sort of undifferentiated matter that serves as the basis for all other matter.[10] The idea is close to the one of stem cells that can transform themselves into any other kind of particular tissue (bone, blood, nerves, etc.). Chi is the prime matter of the universe, undifferentiated but rich, that transforms itself and particularizes itself as it differentiates itself. For the Chinese, matter is dynamic. It transforms itself and contains the forces that render it dynamic. The yin characterizes one type of force, a particular type of dynamic.

Chinese theories on the relationship between chi and Tao varied. For certain schools of acupuncture, chi is a derivative of the Tao; for others, it is a sort of twin of Tao, and the Tao is not even mentioned. Chi and Tao are not phenomena that the senses can detect. A wise person can only observe what modifies itself on the surface of things and then deduce, from these observations, what forces such as the chi are being activated. Hot and cold, heavy and light, bright and dark, mobile and static, solid and liquid, and so on, allow us to know if it is the aspect of yang or yin that is at play. In other words, chi particularizes itself in creating a particular material dynamic whose contour and properties it is possible to identify.

Some dynamics of chi pass through the meridians, sort of arteries and veins of the chi. As the blood is just one of the fluids of the body, the chi that circulates in the meridians is but one part of the chi of the organism.

The Intervention Methods of Acupuncture

Acupuncture assembles a large number of interesting methods. The basic method consists in exciting specific points situated on the surface of the body, in or on the skin, with needles, moxibustion, massage, and movement.[11] These interventions often have a remarkable power to influence the deep physiological dynamics of the human organism. Legend contends that acupuncture was discovered by a hunter, accidentally wounded by an arrow. It had penetrated the external face of the foot behind the ankle. When the arrow was removed, the hunter began to dance and exhibited a strange and joyous behavior. He explained to those who were providing care that he had been suffering for some days from a sharp pain that extended from his kidneys to his feet. He was saying to himself that the arrow must be magical because the pain had suddenly disappeared. A physician, witness to these events, would have subsequently stuck an arrow in the same place on persons who were complaining of a similar pain and thereby cured them.[12] Analogous legends allow us to suppose that others found, by trial and error, various "miraculous" points that they pierced with needles, with the intent to intervene in the least painful way possible. They discovered that various ways to stimulate a point could have different effects. Sometimes applying pressure with a finger sufficed; sometimes turning the needle one way had one effect and turning it another way had another effect (yin for left or yang for right). It would seem that Chinese physicians noticed that the points organized themselves in the form of lines, which are the meridians.

Each line could be associated to a group of particular set of psychophysiological dynamics and the circulation of chi in the body. The acupuncture points are thus handled as if they were like doors that can regulate the flow of the chi in a meridian, like the valves in the veins of the legs.

According to George Soulié de Morant,[13] we find a therapy using 120 points around the year 500; but it wasn't until 1027 that a physician made a statue showing all of the known points, and 1102 until we had a definite chart relating the points to organs: something established after a particularly systematic research on prisoners condemned to death (pierced with needles before death and then dissected). This medicine "of the points" established correlations between the state of the inner organs and the cutaneous sensations (hot/cold, irritation/comfort, red/pale, etc.). A clinical teaching method based on such observations was developed over more than a thousand years. Every meridian is associated with a yin or a yang value, to an organ, and sometimes to affects. The meridian of the liver is associated with certain headaches and anger, whereas the meridian of the kidneys is associated to clammy and cold hands and fear.

Acupuncture and Massage

Chinese massage techniques are extremely varied. In the courses given by Hiroshi Nozaki in Lausanne, I learned to massage with fingers, hands, elbows, head, and feet and by walking on the back. Some massages are gentle, and some are painful. We massaged the muscles, the bones, the skin, the organs, the acupuncture points, the scalp, and sometime the space surrounding the body. Some massages follow the theory of acupuncture[14] and require a solid understanding of the points and the meridians.

A Chinese masseur only rarely works directly with the emotions that express themselves during a session. If an individual begins to cry, to let sexual movements occur, or to erupt in anger, the therapist typically places a blanket on the person and waits for the crisis to subside by itself. These affects are known and included in the clinical teachings of acupuncture. Often in China, a physician treats several patients at the same time. He moves from one to another, adjusting the needles of one and massaging another. Once a patient's emotional outburst has subsided, the therapist talks with the patient while he is preparing to leave, sometimes discussing recent events that might be related to the emotional experience. It can happen that at the following session, the physician focuses on the points associated with the emotions previously expressed, but the emotional content is not verbally discussed. There is thus no psychotherapy born out of acupuncture. We are here manifestly in the treatment system of the mechanisms of organismic regulation. The mind is part of these mechanisms without being the center.

PHILOSOPHICAL TAOISM

Imperial China is without doubt the first lay state in the world. Classically, the historians distinguish a philosophical Taoism and Confucianism born around

500 BC and more religious versions that developed during the Middle Ages under the conjoint influence of Buddhism and Christianity.[15] For body psychotherapists, frequenting the philosophical Taoism of Lao Tzu (c. 570–490 BC), Chuang Tzu (c. 370–301 BC), and Lie Tzu (c. 400 BC) is often perceived as useful.[16] It is not certain that these personages ever existed or that they are the only authors of the books attributed to them, but these writings remain classics in the history of human thought. Two themes developed by this philosophical movement remain relevant for today's psychotherapists:

1. Their understanding of how conscious and nonconscious dynamics of the organism can learn to collaborate in a synergistic way.
2. An original way of approaching the rapport between the ideal body and the real body.

The choice of these themes does not imply that they consist of the essential of what Taoism has to teach, only that these are Taoist themes that contribute to some of the discussions in this textbook.

The Sage Acts in Accord with Nature

> I have heard of letting the world be, of leaving it alone; I have never heard of governing the world. You let it be for fear of corrupting the inborn nature of the world; you leave it alone for fear of distracting the Virtue of the world. You let it be for fear of corrupting the inborn nature of the world; you leave it alone for fear of distracting the Virtue of the world. If the nature of the world is corrupted, if the Virtue of the world is not distracted, why should there be any governing of the world? (Chuang Tzu, 1968, XI, p. 114)

Philosophical Taoism may have begun as a movement for retired functionaries, who had been followers of Confucianism while they were working for the state.[17] Because their retirement pay is low, they want to learn to live as serenely as possible in such conditions. They think this is feasible only if they acquire a better ability to listen to the dynamics of nature that course through them. The Taoist helps nature help him because he supposes that nature has a restorative energy often inhibited by an attitude that prefers to accommodate to the current mores rather than to nature. Humans are not capable of comprehending or voluntarily mastering this restorative power. But an individual can benefit from it if his attitude and his way of acting create a space within him to permit these forces to express themselves more freely: by meditating, for example. This is the famous "let be" or "let go" of the Taoists that oppose the more voluntary initiatives of yoga.

Consciousness and the Reactions of the Organism

To create this space in which nature can express itself for the good of the individual, the Taoist elaborated a practice of awareness that permitted him to forge an alliance with the energies that enliven him but that he cannot comprehend. The theoretical frame of philosophical Taoism is minimalist but sufficiently powerful to combat the propensity of consciousness to want to understand and master everything. It consists in learning how to *perceive* as precisely as possible without interfering. The Taoist sage actively listens to ever-changing atmospheres produced by his organism and his environment like someone who listens to music without telling the musicians how they should play. Once the mind of a Taoist has established a lasting and constructive form of contact between consciousness and the dynamics of chi in the organism, it can finally make informed decisions and use its will to influence the dynamics it perceives with tact. Such voluntary actions are applied in interaction with what is being influenced. The aim is synergic improvement, not an attempt to impose a theory, a desire, or the opinion of others.

The psychotherapist who reads this probably immediately grasps how this way of conceptualizing the dynamics of consciousness can enrich models like Freud's *free association* proposed in 1912. "He [the doctor] should withhold all conscious influences from his capacity to attend, and give himself over completely to his 'unconscious memory'" (Freud, 1912a, pp. 111–112). The psychoanalyst lets himself be permeated by what is going on. The nonconscious regulation systems of the therapist thus have the time to integrate the complexities of the regulatory systems that develop between the therapist and the patient. The flow of conscious thoughts and impressions that inevitably emerge within the therapist can thus stabilize around an emerging theme, which he can explore when he has the impression that it may help him understand the patient. This "letting go" is not a spontaneous property of the mind. It gradually develops by constantly listening to what happens when explicit thoughts interact with implicit impressions. These implicit impressions allow explicit thinking to contact atmospheres that float in the organism and in the space that surrounds the therapist and the patient. We are much closer to the apprenticeship of a musician who sharpens his ear and his virtuosity through practice than to what can be acquired by rigidly applying a set of rules. These Taoists live in nature, are supported by nature, respect nature, and integrate themselves in nature.[18] From the point of view of a Taoist, an individual may learn to know oneself better, but he will never be able to comprehend how he functions.

Gradually, awareness and the rest of the organism learn to interact with each other. The Taoist learns to tame brute willfulness, which can often become so violent that it tends to destroy everything the moment it penetrates the subtleties of the being.

The same principle applies for the rapport between willfulness and nature. This attitude is well summarized by the following metaphor.

Vignette on how consciousness relates to nature. *The image is that of a boat captain who is traveling on one of the great rivers that nourish the Chinese countryside. The advice is as follows: if the captain thinks he can change the course of the river on which he is navigating, he risks becoming a victim of the whirlpools and*

*currents of the river. If he learns to pilot his boat only as well as is possible, he will
know when it is time to draw alongside of or to bypass a reef.*[19]

One of the great contributions of philosophical Taoism for the techniques
of body psychotherapy is to have made explicit a way to ally consciousness and
body reactions without one drowning the other. By stepping away from the
world, the wise one does not cut himself off from what is going on in society.
Instead, he creates for himself an environment sufficiently simple that his project becomes possible. In the little tales that make up the writings of Chuang Tzu
and of Lie Tzu, the wise persons are often consulted by "powerful people." The
dialogue between a retired person and social life is thus maintained.

The Taoist is as wary of the directives given by the emotions as those given
by rationalizations. Nevertheless, his search for moderation never leads to the
repression of the spontaneous reactions of the organism. The wise person could
have "fragile bones and weak muscles," and have his penis erect "so full is his
vitality," without necessarily being with a woman or trying to intensify his vitality with stimulating exercises.[20] If he avoids women, it is because he is in a process of energy conservation. He does not want to waste his aging resources by
distributing them to others. To lose his semen wastes what the body contains. I
suppose that the Taoist also avoids masturbation. Conforming to the mores of
the time, this discourse addresses itself only to men.

Consciousness and Respiration

The breathing exercises of the philosophical Taoists are only known through
indirect sources. I am not aware of works showing how these exercises were
practiced before the arrival of Buddhism,[21] but the majority of them were taken
up by Chi-Kong, in a similar spirit. In these techniques, each movement is associated with a precise respiratory schema to appropriately mobilize the chi and
the meridians. Chinese teachers generally avoid teaching how to breathe until
the student has learned the movements. The learning of the movements already
mobilizes a spontaneous respiration, one that accommodates to the movements
without any conscious or voluntary intervention. Thus, the association between
movements and breathing occurs at the level of the reflexes and the habits. Only
later does the student learn the usefulness of harmonizing respiration and gesture in a more explicit manner. This pedagogy protects students from the damage that the will can do to the deep muscles of respiration.

The student begins by listening to his breathing following a teaching system
close to the one already described in the sections on pranayama. He observes
whether he is breathing from the abdomen or from the chest. He is asked not to
change anything if he notices that his respiration does not correspond to his
personal theories about respiration. Spontaneous respiration follows rules that
reason does not know. The student is asked to explore his breathing, to become
acquainted with it—for example, to evaluate, by counting, whether he breathes
in longer than he breathes out, how long each apnea lasts, and so on.

While learning to analyze his breathing and the impact each phase has on the organism, a person realizes that the very act of observation modifies the spontaneous respiration. That must also be observed. Slowly, a student discovers that when his awareness focuses on his breathing, he contacts deep layers of his psyche. By repeating such forms of exploration, he notices how his respiration changes as a function of the seasons, of his inner well-being, or of an illness.

> Push far enough towards the Void,
> Hold fast enough to Quietness,
> And of the ten thousand things none but can be worked on by you.
> (Lao Tzu, 1949, XVI)

As the first writings about yoga recommended, this gradual contact with the dynamics of chi is to learn how to make contact with self in a gentle, kind, and tolerant way. If a person does not gradually acquire a softer form of awareness, this type of approach should be left aside. I have already mentioned that the more fragile parts of a person should be protected from anxious forms of psychic intrusion.

Gymnastics for the Elderly

To slow down the aging process, the first Taoists took good care of their bodies, and probably made use of acupuncture. The fundamentals of aging wisely consist of conserving, for as long as possible, a large postural and respiratory repertoire. They also cultivated intelligence and memory to preserve the agility of their spirit. This search for longevity drove them to become obsessed about their health and their physique. Health care was not as publicly formalized as it is today and remained costly. It was wiser to seek prevention than a cure.

A large part of an apprenticeship consisted in living with a master and in trying to understand his attitude. These old masters accepted but a few students at a time[22] and only became authoritarian during the period of Lie Tzu.[23]

The Old Twisted Trees of the Immortals

> When the twisted tree at last shall be my body
> Then I shall begin to live out my natural span.
> (Meng Chiao, *Song of the Old Man of the Hills*, 814, p. 64)

If the old wise Taoist takes care of his body and the circulation of chi in his organism, it is because he is preoccupied with the *te* of the *Tao Te Ching*. This te points to a path, a way to live, a way to perceive the world, a mental attitude, and an ability to accommodate to what is. For Taoists, it does not consist in spending a thousand lives to straighten the spine but to plan an aging process that lasts but a lifetime. Moreover, for them, to attempt to render one's body perfectly balanced does not necessarily make for a serene and durable aging. To impose on oneself schemata that seduce one to think one way about the body demands less work than to try to appreciate how the laws of nature evolve bodies so different from one another. This diversity may well have useful functions that conscious understanding is unable to grasp. If we observe individuals who live more than 100 years while maintaining their mental health, we notice that is not necessarily those individuals with particularly supple or well-balanced bodies. The following anecdote illustrates the Taoist point of view.

> Tzu-ch'i of Nan-po was wandering around the Hill of Shang when he saw a huge tree there, different from all the rest. A thousand teams of horses could have taken shelter under it and its shade would have covered them all. Tzu-ch'i said, "What tree is this? It must certainly have some extraordinary usefulness!" But, looking up, he saw that the smaller limbs were gnarled and twisted, unfit for beams or rafters, and looking down, he saw that the trunk was pitted and rotten and could not be used for coffins. He licked one of the leaves and it blistered his mouth and made it sore. He sniffed the odor and it was enough to make a man drunk for three days. "It turns out to be a completely unusable tree," said Tzu-ch'i, "and so it has been able to grow this big. Aha!—it is this unusableness that the Holy Man makes use of!" (Chuang Tzu, 1968, IV, p. 65)

In the same way that a knotted tree survives the others because the carpenter cannot saw boards out of it, a deformed and bent man survives the others because he is never recruited for war or hard labor.[24] Lao Tzu approaches this appreciation of biomechanics from another angle, when he declares:

> What is most straight seems crooked;
> The greatest skill seems like clumsiness;
> The greatest eloquence like stuttering.
>   (Lao Tzu, 1949, XLV)

Windmill Motions

The wise old Taoists developed a sophisticated gymnastics for the elderly. This sophistication reconciled two necessities:

1. An exercise must be easy as possible to execute.
2. An exercise must be as effective as possible.

The yogi tries to open up every joint and mode of respiration directly. He can do it through skillful instructions, with gentleness, but the intention is still to use a direct approach. The population of those days had a healthier postural repertoire than the Westerners of today. In their daily lives, they used the lotus position, the tailor's position, squatted feet flat on the floor and bottom on top of the heels, sat on their heels, sat T-square (legs extended, back straight up). Using these postures was therefore not considered acrobatic. Most exercises can be performed squatting, sitting in a chair, or standing. Taoist gymnasts prefer to concentrate on the gestures that will have an impact on the respiration without the involvement of consciousness. For example, a number of writings speak of windmill motions. The gymnast rapidly turns his arms clockwise then counter-clockwise. The faster the arms turn, the faster the ribs and the diaphragm move and consequently, the more activated the respiration. The choice of the gesture decides what will be stimulated, but the attention does not direct itself necessarily at that moment on the thoracic breathing or on the coordination of abdominal and thoracic respiration. If the exercise is done standing, which is easiest, the attention focuses mostly on keeping the feet well anchored, without violently turning the arms, and counting the number of windmill motions.[25]

At first glance, this exercise seems too easy; nonetheless, it is very effective. More than that, the Chinese compensate for the lack of mechanical difficulty with length of the practice. If you turn your arms as fast as you can 100 times, you will see that the exercise tones up the postural and respiratory muscles quite well. The idea here is that it is better to exercise regularly in an easy, well-targeted way than to become discouraged by a difficult exercise. We are far from the daily two-minute stretching exercises to solve all of our problems; but we must not forget that these exercises are designed for the retired.

Breathing from the Lower Belly

In this section, I detail certain particularities in the Chinese approach from a concrete example. The technical problem is to facilitate the respiration to "go down" to the lower abdomen in a person who breathes mostly from the chest. I describe two effective ways to attain this result. The first is often used by a number of body psychotherapists inspired by Alexander Lowen (see fig. 2.1), whereas the second one probably comes to us from China (see fig. 2.2). It is so discretely effective that, although it is well known by physical therapists, it goes unnoticed in body psychotherapy.

IN BIOENERGETIC ANALYSIS

When Alexander Lowen,[26] one of the founders of bioenergetic analysis, gave a demonstration, it was often spectacular and impressive for those who had no knowledge of body psychotherapy. However, even students of bioenergetics could be shocked by the intrusive, sometimes violent, and direct style of these

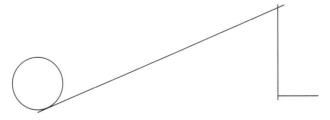

FIGURE 2.1.   The bioenergetic exercise to activate respiration in the lower abdomen.

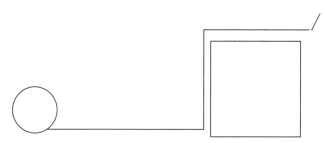

FIGURE 2.2. The Chinese exercise of the stool to activate breathing in the lower abdomen.

interventions. Here is a description of the way Lowen demonstrates how to bring the breath down to the lower belly.[27]

> A vignette on Lowen's method. *Lowen asks a male patient to undress down to his underwear, then to lie down on a mattress. Lowen notices that the patient is not breathing spontaneously from the abdomen. He asks the patient to breath from the lower abdomen. The patient cannot do this. He then asks the patient to keep his feet flat on the mat, knees bent, and to lift his bottom as high as possible;[28] and then to hold this position, at all cost, as long as possible while letting the respiration develop.[29] He recommends to the patient to breathe deeply with an open mouth; for this way to breath mobilizes the vegetative and emotional reactions. Typically, within five minutes, the participant complains of painful stress. Lowen proposes that the individual face the pain of the stress by expressing the pain and rage that is being experienced by screaming "No!" while hitting the mat with the fists, and by shaking the head from side to side without losing the basic position. At the end of ten minutes, in a rather spectacular way, the respiration of the lower abdomen releases itself and memories of childhood trauma rise to the surface.*

This way of doing things is sometimes useful, but if the goal is to liberate the abdominal respiration, then this method is uselessly shocking and sometimes retraumatizing.

THE STOOL EXERCISE

I have found this particularly easy and useful exercise in a book on tai chi chuan by Dominique de Wespin (1973), and have used it with many patients. It generally does not activate the emotional and unconscious dimensions; but this work can be done with other techniques available to the body psychotherapist:

> Lie down on the floor. Place the legs up to the knees on a bed.[30] Let yourself breathe and just leisurely observe the respiration. It will, little by little, descend to the abdomen. (de Wespin, 1973, p. 137)

It is important that there be a right angle between the thighs and the spine and between the thighs and the calves. As breathing expands, "fanning" the lower belly, it extends itself gradually from the pelvis to the rib cage, thus making more space for the diaphragm to move.

When I have an anxious patient who does not breathe with his belly, I often ask him to try this exercise during the session and then at home. If the chair or stool is too low, one can place a cushion under the calves. This position relaxes and elongates the lower back while relaxing the abdominal muscles. This exercise can easily be done repeatedly in the course of many weeks. This often brings about a lasting relaxation, less fear, and in the end, sometimes, the advent of dreams that provide contact with repressed material. The difficult part of this exercise is to ensure that the patient does not voluntarily direct his breathing. The ideal is that he simply observes what happens. If the patient does not have this capacity, it is better to distract him with a mental placebo, such as asking him to observe what is going on in his feet. When an individual is compulsively self-controlling, we can suggest that he listen to some calm music that he likes during the exercise. This exercise is also useful to detect certain muscle tone problems linked to the way the muscles of the back, abdomen, and psoas influence the position of the pelvis.

I have rarely met someone who does not relax in this position. The respiration gradually relaxes and finishes—in less than ten minutes most of the time—by settling comfortably in the lower belly. Like all exercises, it does not work for everyone. The psychotherapist then tries to understand why it does not work. That leads inevitably to something interesting.

I do not know if this universally known exercise was really invented by Taoists, but it is a good example of how they approach the body. They try to find methods whose simplicity and efficacy are the result of a profound comprehension of the mechanics of the body.

RELIGIOUS TAOISM AND THE DEVELOPMENT OF THE MARTIAL ARTS

The Arrival of Buddhism in China

> To bring about the awakening of students of all temperaments, the Buddha taught a wonderful variety of spiritual practices. There are foundation practices for the development of loving-kindness, generosity, and moral integrity, the universal ground of spiritual life. Then there is a vast array of meditation practices to train the mind and open the heart. These practices include awareness of the breath and body, mindfulness of feelings and thoughts, practices of *mantra* and devotion, visualization and contemplative reflection, and practices leading to a refined and profoundly expanded state of consciousness. (Kornfield and Fronsdal, 1993, p. xiii)

Buddhism was developed by Prince Siddhartha Gautama, born in India around 500 BC. When Siddhartha attained a state of illumination, he became a Buddha who founded a movement that is relatively independent from yoga. It maintained the notion that consciousness is a regulator of the organism. Thus only a global transformation of all the dimensions of the organism, and of how the mind perceives the organism, can support the development of consciousness. The Buddhist notion of mindfulness has recently had a strong impact on cognitive and body psychotherapies.[31]

There is a China before and after Buddhism. Buddhism arrives in homeopathic doses from the third century CE onward and solidly implants itself by the seventh century.[32] It brings along not only a philosophy but also knowledge mastered by the Hindus. The Chinese incorporated this immense cultural legacy so well that today it is impossible to distinguish the contributions of yoga from that of the Chinese tradition in the domain of the body techniques. The Chinese martial arts, for example, owe a huge debt to the monks of the Chao Lin temple. These Buddhist monks founded a monastery around 500 CE in the region of Ho-Nan. They created a synthesis out of the Hindu martial arts and the Chinese body techniques that became one of the foundations of most of the body, martial, and therapeutic techniques in China and Japan.

The Alchemy of the Taoists

The Taoist Monasteries: A Kitsch Mystical Movement

The translators of Taoist books on meditation who introduced the notion of Chinese alchemy were probably influenced by Jung's alchemical considerations (1953). He supported the translation and the distribution of an eighteenth-century Taoist treatise titled *The Secret of the Golden Flower* (*Tai Yi Jin Hua Zong Zhi*).[33] The Chinese use the term *mei-tan* to designate an exploration that transforms the organism into a psychophysiological laboratory. Influenced by spiritual movements, Jung used the word *alchemy* in its large sense, to designate a process that seeks to ameliorate the dynamics of the vital energy in a body and thus transform the human organism. The basic European metaphor, the operations used by the alchemists to transform a stone or lead into gold, is similar to those used to reach illumination. For alchemists, one cannot understand how to create gold without becoming illuminated. The alchemical transformation of the organism seeks immortality.

From Lao Tzu to Lie Tzu, the Taoist movement is suspicious of all forms of institutional organizations. At the arrival of Buddhism, some Taoists, inspired by the way the Buddhist monks live an organized monastic life, created similar communities of their own.[34] These Taoist monks are the ones who associated the term *Taoism* to the meticulous pursuit of the mastery of chi. They claimed to be able to circulate chi in multiple ways throughout their entire body. These monks integrated the old Chinese religions, the Taoist philosophy, the *I Ching*, diverse forms of Buddhism, yoga, and gradually even ideas from European "alchemical" movements. The chi thus acquired magical properties, an extraordinary power, something akin to what certain esoteric movements referred to as vital energy. In their development, they created a "jungle" of schools. Some of them took on the form of sects using black magic and supporting violent political movements. These movements promised health, eternal youth, immortality, joy, and sexual prowess.[35] Some sought money and power by using every means at their disposal, such as blackmail, manipulation, prostitution for the wealthy, and deceit. The similarity between the definitions of chi and of the vital energy of Christian cultures intensified during the occupation of China's maritime regions by Europeans and the United States. This "synthesis" influenced and was influenced by movements such as that of the theosophists.

These Taoist movements had an important influence on the development of Chinese thought as well as on the new body–mind methods. They created theories full of flashy and seductive concepts. They nonetheless deserve credit for having passed on useful ancient knowledge and for having proposed some important ideas like the notion of *tan tien* (*hara* in Japan) taken up by the martial arts.[36] It is often this movement that represents the Chinese thought in the writings of and courses given by body psychotherapists.

The Wheel of Chi[37]

A CHI THAT DIFFERENTIATES ITSELF FROM MATTER

A number of Chinese practitioners divide the dynamics of the organism into passive/active, soft/hard, active/receptive—parts that correspond somewhat to a chart of the yin/yang of the organism. This chart has different nuances from one school to another, but it is often read in the following way:[38]

1. The back, the right side, and the head are yang.
2. The front, the feet, and the left side are yin.

At the heart of these great classifications, we find the sophistications of the *I Ching*. The female sexual organs are yin, but contain important yang modules that are needed when the matrix produces an embryo.

The alchemists take up the respiratory circuit that I already described in the sections dedicated to the pranayama and coordinate it with the wheel of the chi (fig. 2.3) that they also associate with the cycle of the seasons. Everything happens as if chi was some sort of fluid made up of a subtle but powerful substance. This fluid should go up the back during inhalation, having a yang quality, and return yin on the front of the body during exhalation.[39] To get everybody to agree, Taoists also speak of an underlying current that moves in the opposite direction. These two directions are well described in the bottle exercise, already practiced by the yogis.

THE BOTTLE EXERCISE

The bottle exercise is a simple exercise, used in a number of schools of bodywork, that facilitates observing the coordination of the segments at the occasion

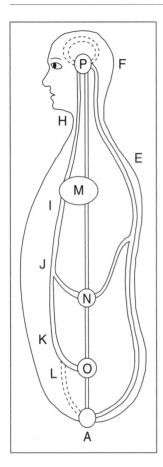

FIGURE 2.3. The circulation of chi during meditation according to the Taoist alchemists. The points A-E-F-H-I-J-K-L indicate the peripheral circulation of chi. This circulation generally passes from K to O to A, but sometimes passes by L, as during sexual intercourse. The axis P-M-O is the central axis. The point O is the tan tien or hara; point A is the perineum (Yü, 1970, p. 124).

of a complete respiration. When you pour water into a bottle, the water falls to the bottom, then gradually rises up to the rim. You can center your attention on two separate movements:

1. The *descending* movement of the water entering into the bottle.
2. The *ascending* movement of the water that is filling the bottle.

In the bottle breathing exercise, one invites an individual to breathe as if the air is water and the body a bottle. Thus, in exhaling, the air at the top of the lungs comes out first; the air at the bottom of the lungs, linked to a respiratory movement from the lower abdomen, comes out last. This respiration creates a movement from the top to the bottom during exhalation and from the lower abdomen toward the top of the chest during inhalation. In this example, we see that we can pay equal attention to the descending air current as well as to the ascending muscular effort.

THE CENTRAL CIRCUIT: THE THREE FIELDS OF THE CINNABAR

Question. Will you please teach me the proper method of swallowing saliva?

Answer. This is the quickest way to produce the generative force; it consists of touching the palate with the tongue to increase the flow of saliva more than usual. When the mouth is so full you can hold no more and you are about to spurt it out, straighten your neck and swallow it. It will then enter the channel of function (jen mo) to reach the cavity of vitality (below the navel) where it will change into negative and positive generative force. (Lu K'uan Yü, 1970, 2, p. 10f)

Other than the wheel of chi that moves around the body, there exists a central circuit (chung mo or jen mo), an axis, that comes down from the head, passes through the respiratory pathways and the intestines, and ends up in the perineum at the bottom of the pelvis (see fig. 2.3). Like the peripheral circuit, this circuit corresponds approximately only to the acupuncture meridians. This central circuit links together three centers[40] that form the "three fields of the cinnabar" (Baldrian-Hussein, 1984, p. 156):

1. The center of the head, situated in the brain,
2. The center of the heart,
3. The center of the belly (lower tan tien or hara) that corresponds to the source and to the foundation of chi. It also corresponds to the center of gravity of the standing body, situated a little below the navel; it is lower in women than in men (which is anatomically correct).

This lower tan tien is the part most often mentioned in the study of the martial arts around the world. When we are standing, it corresponds to the center of gravity, and is thus associated with weight, stability, and the source of the organism's power. All gestures originate from this center. At the end of an exercise, it becomes the place where the chi gathers for rest. The expression "to be centered" makes reference to these practices.

The Techniques of the Martial Arts: Paradoxical Respiration, Punch, and Grounding

The Paradoxical Respiration

The tan tien is so important for the Taoists that they developed *paradoxical respiration*. Habitually, the abdomen expands with inhalation and then flattens with exhalation when the diaphragm ascends to push up the lungs. There is an instance when respiration does not follow this schema: when an individual has a bowel movement. In that instance, the diaphragm descends during exhalation to massage the intestines and push their content downward. The Taoist alchemists and the masters of the martial arts took up this reflex to make chi descend toward the tan tien. This exhalation extends the abdominal segment and lowers the center of gravity to ensure greater stability.[41] This apparently insignificant

detail corresponds to some important concerns to the martial arts. They associate the notion of being grounded (to lower the center of gravity) to that of cen-
tering (to concentrate on the center of gravity).

The Anti-Emotional Punch

To better indicate the specifics of the Chinese method, I will contrast, as before,
the Chinese point of view to that of Lowen. The concrete example here is a punch.

THE PUNCH AS AN EMOTIONAL EXPRESSION

According to Lowen,[42] exhalation accompanies an emotional expression. One
reason is that an expression is often accompanied by vocalizations. The entire
energy of the body is expended in this action. During inhalation, the organism
is rebuilding its reserves to prepare for the next wave of expressions. The punch
also needs the support of proper posture, that is, stable feet. The more a person
stands solidly on his feet, the more he can use this base to build an attack that
adds the weight of the back to the force of the arms. From this point of view,
every emotional expression made while inhaling reveals a restraint, a lack of
confidence on the part of the person relative to the expression. If we add to that
a weak anchoring of the feet, the punch often leads to an aggressive expression
that can have harmful consequences for the person throwing the punch. That is
often the case with impulsive children when they have a temper tantrum. They
hit and scream a lot, but they can get hurt.

A typical way to understand how an individual expressed his aggression in
bioenergetic analysis is to explore what is going on when, under the guise of an
exercise, he hits a cushion numerous times while yelling as loud as possible. The
exercise works particularly well if the individual can imagine that the cushion is
someone against whom he feels anger. Typically, the examination conducted
during this exercise will be done according to two levels of analysis:

1. *At the level of body movement and expression.* Lowen analyzes with the
   patient how the body elements (coordination of the feet, pelvis, back,
   face, arms, voice, eyes, and respiration) are coordinated during the exercise. This permits him to help the patient understand how he manages
   his emotions and how he could express himself more effectively.
2. *At the psychological level based on a psychodynamic model.* The patient
   explores with Lowen what he has felt while doing this exercise, what
   images were activated, what memories eventually came to the surface,
   and so on. This phase of the analysis takes into account not only what
   went on during the exercise but also the way the patient subsequently
   integrates it (dreams, emotional reactions in everyday life, etc.).

The coordination of the body elements utilized by an emotional reaction is
not the same for all the emotions. In grief, for example, the foundation of the
feet is often lost because a sad individual would like to be able to lay his head

on another's shoulder and be held. This conceptualization is close enough to that of the Chinese.

The chi-kong of the animals is composed of exercises in which participants imitate different animals in particular ways to reveal certain negative emotions. In the version that I learned with the master Dee Chow,[43] one of the exercises integrates in a march movements of crooked fingers that evoke bear claws and possessiveness. In the monkey exercise, associated with indecision, the student walks looking to the right while the hands move to the left, then looking to the left while the hands move to the right. By doing this exercise, one learns precise gestures and emotional associations. Within this containing framework, someone can explore what is happening within while meditating on what these movements activate in his organism.

THE WARRIOR'S PUNCH

If the system of analysis of a master of tai chi chuan is close to the one I attributed to Lowen, the goals are different. A warrior has no intention of being possessed by his emotions. He intends to become effective. He wants to give a punch that is correctly supported by his legs, pelvis, and back. The force comes from the back of the body, not from the arms and the hands. The entire mass of the body brings weight to the punch. Moreover, the thrust of the punch must never go beyond the postural base, defined by the feet, to maintain the mastery of the equilibrium. For as soon as the fist is too far advanced, the weight of the body tips toward the front of the feet and the equilibrium of the body "loses its footing." The individual is thus no longer centered because of the off-balanced forward thrust in the attempt to hit another; consequently he is now vulnerable to a counterattack. That is why, instead of breathing out in hitting, as the innate physiological mechanisms linked to aggression would have it, the warrior often hits while using the paradoxical expiration and sometimes while breathing in. The message is no longer "I am going to smash your jaw," but mostly, "you will not make me lose my equilibrium."

I do not believe the Chinese are "masters of their emotions." The option developed by Chinese martial arts requires a lengthy and regular training to establish itself. To impose on the organism a way to be and act other than the one put in place by innate biological mechanisms requires an immense effort, a discipline that must be reinforced almost every day through hours of practice. In the face of emotions, knowing never suffices.

Tai Chi Chuan: The Mobility of Grounding

Tai chi chuan is a martial art that came of age in the eighteenth century. It incorporates almost all of the Hindu and Chinese knowledge and understanding that I mentioned earlier. Its current form dates from the middle of the nineteenth century.[44] This martial art developed a version that is so slow that it makes it possible to differentiate every articulation of every part of the body for a movement that is then executed as fast as lightning. I want to speak about this unending *adagio*. Millions of students, in China and in the rest of the world, practice this gymnastics. It is related to chi-kong, composed of a few movements that are associated more specifically to health problems and to mobilizations of the meridians. There are numerous manuals and websites that explicitly detail the existence of a link between gesture, the circulation of chi in the meridians, respiration, and the particular work of the joints and of mental images.

Many tai chi chuan manuals describe a series of standardized postures that can be drawn or photographed. Learning the form of these postures is a first part of this discipline's apprenticeship. In some manuals, the position of the feet and the placement of the body's weight on each foot are specified. The weight of the body can be divided equally on both feet, in a position (the *chi shih*) that will be, with a few differences, also a position of reference in bioenergetic analysis (grounding); or the weight of the body can be distributed all on one foot and on the tip of the other, like in the grasping the sparrow's tail (*lan chiao wei*).[45] Each of these postures is the most clearly defined part of a movement that has a beginning and an end and is to be carried out in a particular mindset. The spirit of a movement that situates a posture in between two others defines itself according to a number of criteria. For example:

1. *A movement has a function in combat.* Movement must be carried out according to its function.
2. *A movement is established from the bottom up.* The feet must be placed where they belong, the weight well distributed. The action is supported by a position of the feet that allows one to position the pelvis in a relevant way. The position of the pelvis serves as a foundation to establish the position of the trunk, the arms, and the head. If this construction is appropriate, the neurological coordination of these elements creates a unified action that coordinates the dynamics of the gaze and of the fingers in a relevant way.[46]

When a person takes the chi shih position, he checks that his feet are exactly parallel, equidistant, and even with the width of the shoulders. The knees are unlocked, slightly bent. The arms are relaxed alongside the body. Then slowly, "the individual lifts the wrists forward up to the height of the shoulders, the arms remaining parallel, the elbows pulled downward" (Despeux, 1981, p. 143; translated by Marcel Duclos). When an individual is relaxed, this movement inevitably engages a slight flexing of the knees. The arm rises during an inbreath, and the eyes follow the wrists.

If you try to make this gesture, you will see that to coordinate the movements of the arms with breathing is a task that requires an apprenticeship. To do that in coordination with one's breath is one thing; but to let the knees flex is yet another! A central notion of tai chi chuan is that when a movement is executed correctly, movement and consciousness follow the laws of biomechanics[47] and the circulation of the chi. Consciousness has learned to follow movements that are in harmony with the properties of the organism.

Like the dots of a line, these postures first insert themselves into a series of movements and finish by becoming one long movement where all of the dimensions of the organism move in harmony with each other. The movements are defined by an empirical study of what transitions are the most economical (in terms of physical effort) and the most effective (in terms of combat) to go from one posture to another. The fighter must, for example, deflect a blow, then another, and attack. The sequence from one posture to another follows the rules of the *I Ching* on the manner in which a structure (or hexagram) transforms itself into another: how to pass from one position of the feet to another, how to change the distribution of the weight on the feet, how to rebuild the position of the pelvis that will sustain a new action (to block a punch and then give one). Only after years of practice can each position and each transition be in such alignment that an observer can have the impression of a continuous, fluid, and harmonious motion that lasts for twenty minutes. Yoga had already worked on how to go from an asana to another. However, the coordination between posture and movement proposed by tai chi chuan is, for me, one of the seven marvels of our present world.

Discussion

OBSERVE THE FEET MOSTLY, THE FACE A LITTLE
I will now emphasize two implications of what I described in the preceding sections:

1. *It is always useful to observe what is going on at the level of the feet, at the level of the anchor points of a posture.*[48] In the last analysis, this information is often more useful than that furnished by the face and hands. The brain has the tendency to direct the conscious attention to the upper part of the body because that is where the explicit actions of the fine motor functions originate (speech, professional gestures, emotional expressions, etc.). However, the mechanics of a global body movement tend to be constructed from feet to head. A person who wants to kill you can very well approach you with a smile, but the important thing is that he is close enough to you to be able to strike you with his knife, and he must do it from a position of the feet that allows his arm to have the force to accomplish the deed.

2. *Spontaneous postural dynamics are only partially organized.* It takes years of regular training to be able to move in a coherent manner. The Far East teaches us that the body has its logic, but that it can only partially establish itself in a lifetime. The utilization of the potential of the mechanisms of the organism is something that develops over time. Everybody can sing, but to sing well requires much assiduous work. It is the same for dance and fighting, for love and cooking. Even the behaviors the most closely associated to the instincts are given to us as raw material that needs to be shaped by cultural know-how. In terms of ad-

aptation and survival, this basic incompletion is essential for a species that proliferates in extremely different natural milieus (from the desert to the North Pole), and which, to do that, has developed cultures just as varied. This makes it possible for an individual to calibrate how his organism adapts to the demands of the milieu that surrounds him and to at least partially modify his adaptive procedures when he changes environment. The temptation to believe that a healthy individual moves spontaneously in a harmonious way is a temptation that exists in the mind-body professions, but it does not correspond to reality. The methods from the Far East show us that the citizen never moves harmoniously, and he is not ill for all of that. The one who undertakes a discipline such as tai chi chuan or yoga develops a potential that ordinary life does not promote. Such a project is marvelous, but it is not the project of a psychotherapy.

THE TWO RESPIRATIONS
We have made the distinction between physiological and paradoxical respiration. This distinction overlaps approximately with two ways to coordinate gestures and breathing.[49]

1. *Biomechanical coordination.* During inhalation, the thorax expands. When all of the muscles are relaxed, the arms and the legs follow this movement to create more space for the expansion of the thorax. Similarly, when the thorax contracts during exhalation, arms and thighs get closer to the thorax to support the respiratory movement.
2. *Emotional coordination.* Here, what is important is the coordination between the expenditure of metabolic energy and the function of the gesture. This coordination no longer follows the laws of relaxation and biomechanics but those of the affects. In-breath absorbs energy that will be spent when out-breath supports expressive activities. This implies, from this point of view, that we have, in this instance, a paradoxical coordination. The hands distance themselves from the thorax while it contracts during the exhalation, and get closer to the thorax when it expands in inhalation. These two logical contradictions (on the biomechanical plane) help the organism tense up and mobilize the vegetative sympathetic system.

By default, the proper breathing for any form of relaxation is the one that conforms to the biomechanical respiratory movement. Every movement that crushes the thorax is associated with exhalation, and every movement that favors the expansion of the thorax is associated with inhalation. In the case of movements that have a contradictory effect on the volume of the thorax, a detailed biomechanical analysis is recommended. An example of this would be when the arms close in on the thorax while the knees move away from the abdomen. In the case of doubt, always let the patient move any way he wants. When a "correct" respiration comes into conflict with the patient's spontaneity, respect the mechanisms of the patient first and analyze what is happening before confronting the patient's defense system.

FINAL COMMENTS ON PRANA AND CHI

The notions of prana and of chi were developed in a world where the dualities such as body and soul, psyche and soma, or energy and matter did not exist.

The Chinese chi is initially an undifferentiated dynamic *matter* that serves as the basis for the production of differentiated elements such as fire, earth, metal, water, and wood. Each represents a certain relationship between yin and yang. The immense variety of the dynamics of matter managed by human practices derives from these fundamental forces. The notion of *active matter* does not have an equivalent in a physics that separates matter and energy.

When we spoke of prana, we saw that all activity that influences attention and breathing (such as the postures) has an impact on prana. Chi is a similar substance but more differentiated. It is influenced by what enters and leaves the body through respiration, but also by gestures and acupuncture needles. Most of the Chinese masters realize that they understand chi only by their ability to influence it, but it would be difficult to define it positively, to explain its constituents.

PART II

Starting with the Certitudes of the Soul and Ending with the Ambivalences of the Mind

In the following chapters I highlight philosophical speculations that are still influential in the psychotherapeutic literature. Their impact is often camouflaged by recent refinements, but it remains timely as witnessed by the renowned personalities I discuss and the frequency with which they are referenced in specialized works currently under publication.

3

About Plato: Idealism and Body Psychotherapy

Idealist theories[1] assume that immaterial structures animate and organize all that exists. These structures can be Plato's "Ideas." In other forms of Idealism, like the ones that enlivened Galileo's and Newton's scientific discoveries, scientists mostly hypothesize that all the mechanisms of the universe structure themselves according to a "natural logic"[2] that mathematicians attempt to express formally.

IDEALISM, BODY, AND SOUL AT THE DAWN OF SCIENCE

> For soul is so entwined through the veins,
> The flesh, the thews, the bones, that even the teeth
> Share in sensation, as proven by dull ache,
> By twinge from icy water, or grating crunch
> Upon a stone that got in mouth with bread.
> Wherefore, again, again, souls must be thought
> Nor void of birth, nor free from law of death;
> Nor, if, from outward, in they wound their way,
> Could they be thought as able so to cleave
> To these our frames, nor, since so interwove,
> Appears it that they're able to go forth
> Unhurt and whole and loose themselves unscathed
> From all the thews, articulations, bones.
>   (Lucretius, *On the Nature of Things*, 1998, Book III,
>   691–697, translated by William Ellery Leonard[3])

Philosophical Idealism attempts to provide a foundation to the conscious impression that there exists an absolute Truth, Beauty, and Goodness. It is useful to have a clear vision of what Idealism proposes because this trend permeates all forms of European thought; it influences all the cultures that integrate the lifestyles proposed by the Europeans, such as the United States. We find Idealistic trends from Judaism and from Islam. This mode of thought is found in many schools of psychotherapy. For example, the schools of Carl Gustav Jung and of Wilhelm Reich often use an Idealistic frame of mind. Given the importance of Reich in body psychotherapy, it may be helpful to outline this way of thinking.

It is sometimes difficult to detect Idealism explicitly. After Plato, many philosophers presented themselves as being opposed to Idealism. Yet most of their propositions were subsequently classified as variations of omnipresent Idealism in Judeo-Christian cultures. It is therefore interesting to understand why so many brilliant intellectuals, like Marx and Nietzsche, present themselves as an alternative to an Idealism that they detest, and why they nevertheless ended up proposing convictions tainted with Idealism. This chapter presents a few reasons for the popularity of these ideas, as well as some arguments to explain the hatred evoked by Idealism.

My impression is that explicit conscious procedures can only function if they can assume that, at a given moment, there exists but one truth. A person needs to have the intimate conviction that the words she uses have but the sense she attributes to them, even though her intellect knows that terms are always polysemous. As a philologist, Nietzsche was an expert in the analysis of words.[4] He insists on the fact that human functioning is such that it is impossible for words not to have many meanings: they are *polysemous*. This is especially true when they designate abstracts entities like good and evil. For Nietzsche, the idea that such terms could only have one meaning, one signifier, as the Idealists propose, can only be imposed on a human population by tyrannies. Nietzsche's position, strengthened by research that I will discuss, demonstrates that there exist many ways of thinking inscribed in the architecture of the mind,[5] and consequently, it is impossible to associate one style of mental practice and knowledge to a term (or signifier).

It is useful to begin this discussion on philosophy with Plato, for the following reasons:

1. He is the founder of academic philosophy.
2. He is the founder of an explicit Idealism. The Idealism of certain Asiatic schools of thought does exist, but it is often more diffused.
3. His theory serves as a reference point for those who have wanted to make of the opposition the between soul and body a dogma of European and religious thought.

Idealist schools have presented a variety of theories on how body and mind associate. Here are a few examples that are discussed in this volume:

1. For *Plato*, the life of the soul is independent from that of the body. The mind is situated in the body.
2. *Aristotle*'s Idealism is particularly complex. Even though he was Plato's student, his doctrine is different. For him, "the affections of soul are inseparable from the material substratum of animal life" (Aristotle, *Of the Soul*, I.1). The mind is now situated in the soul.
3. *Descartes*'s Idealism also situates the mind in the soul. Like Aristotle, he wanted to find a theory of the organism that could support the development of a Science. Descartes can be considered as one of the founders of a scientific psychology. He adopted a particularly nuanced and tolerant Idealistic position due to the influence of Montaigne's *Essays*.
4. The Idealism that *Reich* introduced into body psychotherapy is above all intuitive and ideological. His knowledge of Plato and Spinoza is probably superficial. The Ideas are, for Reich, as with Spinoza (whom I discuss after Descartes), not concepts but the dynamics that an omnipotent nature breathes into each one of us. These dynamics are close to the Ideas in the way that nature is conceived by these authors as being totally good, coherent, and omnipresent.

The general plan of the following sections on the philosophers begins with a divine soul, capable of flying like a god in a heavenly and pure world. It then takes us finally to Hume's materialism where thoughts are managed like a computer or a prayer wheel that generate ideas arbitrarily.

THE IDEALISM OF PLATO

But if the self-moving is proved to be immortal, he who affirms that self-motion is the very idea and essence of the soul will not be put in confusion. For the body which is moved from without is soulless; but that which is moved from within has a soul, for such is the nature of the soul. But if this be true, must not the soul be the self-moving, and therefore of necessity unbegotten and immortal? (Plato, 1937, *Phaedrus*, 245a, p. 250)[6]

The Soul and the Body

> . . .
> And besides,
> If soul immortal is, and winds its way
> Into the body at the birth of man,
> Why can we not remember something, then,
> Of life-time spent before? Why keep we not
> Some footprints of the things we did of, old?
> (Lucretius, *Of the Nature of Things*, 1998, III.
> 670–674, translated by William Ellery Leonard[7])

It Is More Comfortable to Think with Fables than with Baseless Speculations

> To describe what the soul actually is would require a very long account, altogether
> a task for a god in every way; but to say what it is like is humanly possible and
> takes less time. (Introduction to Plato, 1937, by Cooper, *Phaedrus*, 246a, p. 524)

To present his version of Idealism, Plato (Athens, 427–348 BC) uses stories halfway between the fables and myths that he invented.[8] A theory is generally a
succession of formulations that constitute a logical and coherent development.
In antiquity, many writers preferred to use a parable that allowed the reader to
acquire an intuitive sense of the general outline of a way of thinking. It permitted the expression of an intimate conviction on a subject without having already acquired the means to refine the details of what one understands. On the
other hand, it makes it difficult to differentiate between reasoning and an emotional commitment. That partly explains the confusion between forms of thinking (knowledge, ideology, belief, etc.) that characterizes Idealism.[9]

   Aristotle, Plato's student, tried to transform Idealism into an explicit system.[10] That obliged him to make pronouncements on a number of questions
that could not yield any useful answers at that time. His way of thinking became one of the bases of the debates as vain as the ones by Byzantine theolo-
gians as to the sex of angels.

From the Death of Socrates to the Rapture of the Soul

When Socrates (Athens, ca. 469–399 BC), Plato's master, was condemned to
death by the Athenian populace, Plato was manifestly shocked.[11] This shock
permitted him to take a leap and imagine his Idealistic theory. His theory is a
mixture of the thoughts of Socrates and Pythagoras added to his own thoughts.
He wrote three dialogues on the death of Socrates. In the first, the *Apology of
Socrates*, respectful of his master, he puts forth what his master probably said at
his trial. Socrates ends his defense by envisioning two forms of death.[12] He does
not know which one awaits him, but both seem liberating to him:

1. The first type of death is a death where only one thing happens: the fact
   of no longer existing, no longer thinking, no longer feeling. This way to
   die is already perceived as a relief for Socrates.
2. The second type of death is a death where the soul goes to the kingdom
   of Hades. There, Socrates will be judged by a god much more competent
   in the matter than an assembly of citizens who cast their votes according
   to political opinions. Socrates sees himself on the way to rejoin Homer
   and Ulysses and a host of people that he has long admired. This perspective also pleases him.

In the last of the dialogues concerning the death of Socrates, the *Phaedo*,
Plato shows him in prison at the moment when he is about to drink the hemlock

in front of his students. He puts words in his teacher's mouth and has him tell the fable that establishes his own Idealism.[13] This fable could let one think that Plato knows what happens after death. But it is more probable that this vision, inspired by Pythagoras, was proposed for pedagogical purposes and not to describe what really happens:

> At the death of a body, the soul which it contained, flies toward a mysterious region, perfect and pure, and enters into contact with the *Ideas*. These Ideas make it possible to experience what is True, Beautiful, Good, and Just. Liberated from the constraints imposed by the body, the soul can gather nectar in this garden of truths. Finally, at long last, sadly, it must be "enshrined" again in a body, where it is imprisoned like an oyster in its shell.[14] However, the soul retains the memory of the voyage and of what she has learned.[15]

Soul and Thoughts

> Any meaning given to what happens comes from *us*. We are facing the difficult task of translating natural processes into psychological language. (Jung, 1940, *Children's dreams*, seminar 1, p. 2)

Learning to Define the Emanations of the Soul

Plato does not define the soul. He seems to refer to a myth that is known to his readers. The soul can enter and leave the body, which she animates; but she remains distinct from the body. Thereby, Plato does not propose a psychology, as he supposed that everybody assumes that the part of us that feels and thinks is part of the body and not the soul.

With Plato, the relationship between the soul and thoughts is complex. The soul animates the body and the thoughts; but she does not transmit her content to consciousness. Most humans do not consciously know that they have a soul, or they suppose it without really knowing it. On the other hand, the soul can be apprehended by our thoughts in dreams and intuitions that are sort of emanations of the soul. There is no such thing as direct messages from the soul that reformulate themselves into thoughts. In the Idealistic writings of Plato, Socrates becomes a mouthpiece for Plato. His teaching consists in learning how to self-explore to apprehend the shape of the emanations of the soul, so as to reconstruct in consciousness ideas as identical as possible to the ones contained in the soul. This model implies three stages of knowing:

1. Perfect knowledge as contained in the world of Ideas.
2. The soul absorbs a little more of this knowledge every time that she visits the world of Ideas.
3. Conscious processes can acquire, at its own pace, in a more or less elaborate manner, a sketch of what is contained in the soul.

Even though Plato does not broach this problem explicitly, he probably thinks that the soul does not have as many resources as the world of Ideas, and that the mind does not have as many resources as the soul. This implies that no philosopher has the means to formulate what emanates from the world of Ideas. The human faculty to think does not have the tools to really comprehend the Truths of the soul and give them expression. Explicit theories (philosophical, religious, scientific, etc.) are constructed by a consciousness that does not have the capacity to apprehend and express eternal Truths. However, metaphors and fables can at least convey an intuitive sense of these truths.

We thus had, in the Athens of those days, two kinds of theories:

1. *Plato*'s theories often use *metaphors*.[16] Their pedagogical purpose is to help and instruct citizens who want to acquire meaningful intellectual representations on human dynamics.
2. *Aristotle*'s academic and scientific theories. They propose general laws that attempt to integrate all the known facts.

In psychotherapy, even Freud's theory can be situated halfway between the strategies of Plato and Aristotle. That is why I refer to them as *metaphorical theories*. They consist of "metaphorical models" of observable phenomena that are not close enough to the data to be considered laws, but are useful to guide the therapist's interventions and the patient's representations. "The unconscious," "defense systems," and "muscular armoring" are examples of what I call metaphorical notions.

The Socratic Therapist

The greatest difficulty that we have in writing about Socrates is that he did not write anything. We only know of him by what others have said.[17] Our main source on what Socrates was like is Plato. A first myth about Socrates is that Plato's first writings give us a more faithful image of Socrates than his later writings. The "Socratic" dialogues were written while Socrates was alive, before Plato became an Idealist and before he began to speak of the soul and body. That platonic Socrates gradually became an emblematic figure in psychotherapy, a sort of precursor of and model for many psychotherapists.[18] This Socrates is presented to us like a sort of hygienist of the mind, like a hunter of false truths, a demand to think as honestly as possible. This Socrates takes up the message of the wise men from the Orient and founds a philosophy based on the proposition that all theories contain a fragment of truth, and consequently, the pretense to have the truth is false. This type of skepticism is a foundation stone for philosophers such as Hume and Kant. It does not consist in teaching a thought but in acquiring the courage to not believe that we know when we do not know. Socrates claimed that he was more intelligent than most because he knew that he knows nothing.[19]

Francois Roustang, a French psychotherapist, isolates the following factors in Plato's Socratic dialogues:[20]

1. There is a *dialogue* between individuals who must take responsibility for what they think.
2. Socrates "requires that his counterpart use brief phrases and often that he only content himself with an assent. That puts the interlocutor in a position of dependence or submission. He is definitely manipulated by the first speaker. If there were the possibility to hold a longer dialogue with the first speaker, the counterpart would find his proper ground. Thus, *the intent, before anything else, is to disconcert.*" (Roustang, 2009, Avant-propos, translated by Marcel Duclos)

In psychotherapy, reference is made mostly to that vision of Socrates. For many people, he is the icon of the honest philosopher who is persecuted because he annihilates all manipulation of knowledge, and because people are afraid of someone who brings their imposture to the light of day. As a young man and not yet an Idealist, Plato perhaps imagined that the search for truth was this aspect of Socrates that he describes in his first works. Later on, he develops an Idealism that was probably also part of Socrates's teaching. People change. Certainly Plato greatly changed in the course of his life. It is probable that Socrates also evolved, and that he developed a varied set of approaches.

We know that Socrates was not only an individual who liked to ask questions of those he encountered on the street. He was also a master and the head of a school. For Plato, his teacher had as his mission to help his students better understand the messages of the soul, messages that appeared to consciousness in the form of vague intuitions, by trying to make them more explicit in a form the human spirit could more easily employ. Contemporary psychotherapists, like Roustang (2009), admire a Socrates who is mainly a hygienist of the mind; but it is probable that the real Socrates was more complex and more ambiguous than that.

The Socrates of the psychotherapists addresses himself uniquely to individuals without proposing socially constructed enterprises (political, theoretical, moral, etc.). The Socrates of psychotherapists, like Roustang, distinguishes a Socratic therapy from a Platonic therapy in the following manner. Plato wants to treat the being (or the subject or the soul), whereas Socrates is content to reach that in which a person "excels, his quality, his particular virtue, where his activity attains it perfection, its fullness" (Roustang, 2009, 2, p. 50, translated by Marcel Duclos).

For this, he uses a pedagogy that has served as a model for numerous psychotherapists. In the writings of Plato, Socrates's strategy can be broken down into three phases:

1. *The torpedo.* This is probably Socrates's most well-known technique. The Socrates who asks questions lays bare the ready-made thoughts of the other. Socrates the torpedo chooses to use irony and skepticism to

unmask the falsehood of certain forms of reasoning and fashionable beliefs. Often irritating, Socrates does not disqualify a logical argument
and always attempts to demonstrate the relevance of his questions. In
psychotherapy, the torpedo technique is often used to analyze defense
systems and rigid mental practices.

2. *The midwife.* Socrates, whose mother is thought to have been a midwife,
perceives his work as the midwifery of the Truths in an individual's soul
when these are born in the mind. In psychotherapy, this function is often
taken up in what Jung calls a "process of individuation"; that is, "the
process by which a person becomes a psychological 'individual,' that is a
separate, indivisible unity or 'whole'" (Jung, 1939, p. 275). This notion
does not presuppose some general truths but an idea that an individual
can be more or less himself, more or less conformed to his essence. We
often find these types of concepts in the "humanistic" psychotherapies,
such as the Gestalt therapy of Fritz Perls or the Biodynamic psychology
of Gerda Boyesen. One of Socrates's principal tools as a midwife is *Socratic questioning,* of which I previously spoke.

3. *Self-knowledge.* Socrates's "know thyself" is mostly defined by Plato as
a necessity of self-exploration to discover the Truths contained in one's
soul. The imperative to know oneself has little to do with what psychotherapists ask their patients to discover relative to the history of their
drives.[21]

Only the first strategy—that of the torpedo—can be associated with the Socrates
who hunts down prejudice (that which is judged even before the start of the
conversation). The second strategy is taken up by the psychotherapists who are
idealists, who assume that there exists a fundamental self, a human being's authentic center.

This first portrait of Socrates was the first great philosophical myth that
Plato proposed to humanity. What Plato offers us is a representation of the
philosophical inquiry, of the searching philosopher. There is nonetheless a com-
monality between psychotherapists and young Plato's Socrates: the necessity to
destabilize and cleanse the mind of its prejudices so that it can perceive with
enlightened clarity what is really happening around and within oneself. This
fundamental overture remains young Plato's essential message. To then decide
that this overture ought to focus on the messages of the unconscious mind, of
the soul's hidden wisdom, is already the beginning of a closure. Such closure is
sometimes necessary. An individual cannot open himself up to everything and
assimilate it. Thus there is a necessity to choose what is important at a given
moment: a choice that differentiates the exploration in psychotherapy, the exploration in philosophy, or the exploration in meditation. If an individual goes
from the exploration of his mind to that of his soul, he must first clean his mental glasses, because each form of self-exploration implies a well-established
habit that fosters a focus on certain inner dynamics of the self. Thus, being able

to free associate, as Freud would propose 2,400 years later, is to try to eliminate all forms of mental prejudices and let spring forth in word all that takes shape in the mind. I notice that often those who subject themselves to this discipline rarely become sensitive to what opens up in meditation; the inverse is equally true. To open oneself by following one method inevitably leads to the establishment of a way of thinking and perceiving. The mind becomes particularly sensitive to certain inner dynamics and develops intellectual structures better able to appreciate them. All of this is put in place, thanks to a regular practice. Plato, who believes in only one kind of true thought, does not pay attention to the formation of these mental habits. All the same, his Socrates is a startling example that is it impossible to not become, with experience, a heap of mannerisms that sometimes resemble tics. There is a Socratic style, a Socratic irony,[22] a Socratic way to perplex the other, and a Socratic form of inquiry that is found in almost all of Plato's early dialogues. Only later does Plato present a Socrates who will sometimes have a healing and hospitable voice. However, this version, we are told, would be more Plato than Socrates.

The Socratic Inquiry

In the Greek language, the psyche is that force of the soul that generates thoughts, behaviors, and a personality.[23] Plato situates these dynamics outside of the soul. It disappears when the organism dies.

In the *Meno,* Socrates demonstrates that he can help a young, uneducated slave discover in himself the rules of geometry and mathematics.[24] At first, the questions reveal the young adolescent's vague intuition of the properties of a triangle and the square root. The adolescent is able to intuitively respond correctly with a yes or a no to Socrates's questions without any explicit understanding of the rules of mathematics known to Meno and to Socrates. Yet gradually, these rules begin to rise up out of the haze like a volcano out of the ocean to create an island. With this demonstration, Socrates wants to suggest that after an advanced education, it is not one or two islands that break the surface of consciousness but entire continents of truths. This is labeled a process of *reminiscence.*[25] I remember what my soul acquired in the world of Ideas.

This strategy is used in psychotherapy to help a person become conscious of what is within, what is repressed, or one's intimate wishes. Socrates serves as a model that inspires certain psychotherapists to question a patient in great detail until he becomes more conscious, more explicit with regard to one of his organismic practices. The psychotherapist proposes to the patient that he comprehend, in as a detailed a manner as possible, an aspect of his negative impulses, his needs, and his resources.

Differences between Mind and Soul

In this section,[26] I summarize certain aspects of Plato's thinking that influenced many school of psychotherapy. It will consist of showing that the mind is different from the content of the soul because the mind can only digest truths in small doses. In psychotherapy, we often notice that an individual can handle just a limited amount of truth at one time. Every time I try to move at a faster pace, often at the request of the patient, he is soon overwhelmed and disoriented. What Freud called the defense system brings any acceleration of information to a screeching halt. The patient experiences strong dis-ease and may want to end psychotherapy. It is not necessarily that the individual no longer wants to gain self-knowledge. He just cannot integrate a powerful dose of new information.[27] A schoolchild has the same difficulty at school, as does a new employee who is bombarded with instructions by the employer.

Idealists often think not only that the mind has quantitative limits but also that the Ideas are of another nature than what the mind can manage. The mind must transform itself before it can integrate this type of information. The ordinary citizen who accidently perceives a Truth may not notice the value of what he has just experienced. If, on the other hand, the defenses are too weak, the mind risks blowing a fuse when it perceives a dose of truth that it cannot manage. In subsequent pages, we shall see that Plato used his myth of the cave to show the importance of avoiding becoming blind when the mind enters into contact with the Truths of the soul.

The Signifier of an Idea

> A text is a text only if it hides at first view, for any one, the law of its composition and the rules of its game. Besides, a text always remains imperceptible. The law and the rule do not shelter themselves in the inaccessibility of a secret. They simply never reveal themselves, in the present, to anything that we can rigorously call a perception. (Jacques Derrida, 1972, *Plato's Pharmacy*, p. 79; translated by Marcel Duclos)

The recourse to fables shows that Plato does not have the intellectual means to explicitly define Beauty, but he trusts that he has an adequate intuition about what is beautiful and ugly. He has a difficult time translating what he feels into a structured discourse. I think his difficulty is part and parcel of the human condition. Plato experiences a celebratory inner itch every time someone says something that seems just and an almost hateful inner irritation when someone preaches something that seems manifestly false. With his theory of the Ideas, he tries to show that it is possible to gain understanding and that consequently, the human daring to invest in the scientific endeavor defines an attempt to construct a social knowledge of the mechanisms that animate the universe. The theory of the Ideas is there to tell us that in the human there is a capacity to reflect on what is perceived. Plato wanted, in this way, to support people like Aristotle, who was building the bases of an emerging science by battling against a skepticism that discourages those who would have the hubris to understand that which makes them alive. Plato made this audacious challenge by discovering a plausible theory for his day which affirms that each human has the means to know something, to construct an understanding that corresponds to a reality. He could not have done better to express this intimate conviction than to invent this fable, according to which, between two lives, our souls float in the world of the Ideas.

THE DANGERS OF SOCIAL PROCEDURES

Plato imagines that there exist kernels of innate knowledge, but any one of these kernels are of little worth if not animated by a sharp, intuitive awareness of ideas. The difficulty lies in that the support brought forth by the society for such an enterprise must be managed with precaution, because it can also falsify (to support political, ideological, and economic projects, for example) the psychic perception of the Truths of the soul. The ability to listen to one's intuitions presumes a refined apprenticeship. This is why "know thyself" is so important to Plato. Without it we could not develop our capacity to evaluate the relevance of what is presented to us as a truth. Becoming aware of what ideas we would like to support is, for Plato, the key to knowledge; this key only turns in the lock if the subject experiences pleasure when a Truth is perceived. In the *Meno*, Plato allows an adolescent to confront the representations brought about by lazy conscious thinking and helps him feel a celebratory pleasure each time he can correct what is represented in function of what is rightly experienced. This dialogue between conscious thought and profound intuition is the constant preoccupation of philosophers.

Plato defended, as a high stake, the *social construction* of knowledge.[28] Even if the nuclei of consciousness are principally regulated by the nonconscious mechanisms of regulation that coordinate the social, psychological, and biological dimensions, only through individual thought and explicit interactions between citizens can knowledge be actualized. This form of co-constructed intelligence permits today's reader to refine the questions and answers raised by Plato.

CONSCIOUSNESS AND WRITING

> With the evolution of language, this faith in culturally transmitted information became vulnerable to exploitation by individuals. (Scott Atran, 2010, "The Evolution of Religion")

One of the examples that Plato gives about the acquisition of a consciousness that allows for the creation of explicit transmissible content is that of writing. He proposes a fable on the origin of writing in *Timaeus* (21–26). This fable would have been passed on from father to son in his family since the time when the great Athenian politician Solon related it to one of Plato's ancestors:

> One day in Egypt, Solon enters a city allied to Athens. He tells the Greek legend about the origin of the world to an assembled group. A listener politely laughs. He is one of the Egyptian High Priests. He explains that one of the traumas of Greece

is to have been often devastated by natural catastrophes and by war that, each time, destroyed everything that they wrote. In contrast, peaceful Egypt possesses manuscripts that exist since the origin of writing. According to the priest, the Egyptian texts recount events that the Greeks ignore, like the history of the city Atlantis, founded 9,000 years before Athens. When this city was destroyed by ocean waves, some survivors fled to Greece and founded Athens.

In this fable, Plato shows that writing adds capacities to individual memory that do not exist in the brain.

Plato expresses in *Phaedrus* his distrust of writing that can just as easily transmit fables, the reasoning of the sophists, lies, or truths. Writing and speech are therefore tools that can be used, with more or less reliability, to support propaganda or by the seekers of truth. The French philosopher Jacques Derrida (1972) points out that for Plato, writing and medication have the same status, in that they both have an undeniable utility but can also inhibit the desire to explore and use the forces of the soul. During the same period in China, Chuang Tzu expressed an analogous distrust:

> But until the sage is dead, great thieves will never cease to appear, and if you pile on more sages in hopes of bringing the world to order, you will only be pilling up more profit for Robber Chih. Fashion pecks and bushels for people to measure by and they will steal by peck and bushel.[29] Fashion scales and balances for people to weigh by and they will steal by scales and balance. Fashion tallies and seals to insure trustworthiness and people will steal with tallies and seals. Fashion benevolence and righteousness to reform people and they will steal with benevolence and righteousness. How do I know this is so? He who steals a belt buckle pays with his life; he who steals a state gets to be the feudal lord—and we all know that benevolence and righteousness are to be found at the gates of the feudal lords. (Chuang Tzu, 1968, X, p. 109f)

The relationship between these two nearly contemporary points of view makes me think that in China as well as in Greece, the introduction of new technologies posed the same kind of philosophical problems, even if the cultures were profoundly different. Indeed, the Taoist argument states that people knew how to estimate the weight of a commodity by holding it in their hands. After the invention of weights, people had such confidence in the system of measures that they no longer bothered to develop their capacity to estimate weight with their hands. It then became easy to steal by falsifying the instruments of measure. It is the same with written laws. People end up not learning how to evaluate for themselves what is good and just. This is what makes it possible for villains who take over a state to manage the justice system at will and for dishonest religious authorities to use the few saints that exist to justify doubtful religious practices. When people lose contact with their own profound resources, they become subject to manipulation because they easily notice the existence of petty thieves but they are not capable of experiencing as pernicious and dangerous those who rob them blind through the manipulation of social rituals and political power.

The Myth of the Cave: Blinding Truths and the
Creative Shadows of the Psyche

Plato's Socrates, in *The Republic,* teaches that most citizens, even those who are educated, do not achieve an integration of their intuition of what is Good; but they are often responsive to examples of what is Good.[30] It is the same for Truth and knowledge. Socrates uses the myth of the cave[31] (see the following summary) to illustrate the difficulty that most citizens experience when they try to contact the Ideas:

> Socrates describes persons facing the inner far wall of a cave like spectators facing the screen in a cinema. On that wall, they see moving shadows. As at the cinema, the citizen quickly forgets that what is happening comes from a projector situated behind him. He forgets that what he perceives is produced by mechanisms situated outside of his consciousness. Plato describes a scene in which the projector is in fact the sun that casts as a shadow that which is happening behind the spectators. If a spectator suddenly turns around to see what is going on at the entrance of the cave, he is immediately blinded by the sun. This explains why the spectators content themselves with what they see on the screen, and end up believing that what they perceive is the reality. Occasionally, passers-by enter the cave and explain to the spectators, who are prisoners of their fears, that once outside, the sun becomes less blinding, and reality directly perceptible. A spectator cannot directly go from the obscurity of the cave to the light of day without definitively blinding oneself. However, proceeding with a method, he can gradually get accustomed to the increasing intensity of the light. He will first perceive the real starry night, then the dawn and the sunrise, and finally everything that exists.

In the first part of the myth of the cave, Plato explains why he cannot be more explicit when he communicates with persons who have not learned how to get out of the cave, and he presents himself as one of those who knows how to get out. Having said that, he admits that we can only perceive a fraction of what is.

A psychotherapist does not hold such a black and white Manichaean view of the dynamics of human nature. Jung suggests that the shadows projected on the cave's rock wall are more than a simple reflection of reality,[32] because they form another reality that merits as much consideration—that is, the psyche and the impressions it produces. The portrait proposed by a painter is never the exact copy of a face because it is also a creative act that seeks to produce a vision. Art is a domain unto itself. It has its own relevance. So do the shadows on Plato's cave! For Jung, the fact that the psychic elaborations are not conforming copies of what is perceived takes nothing away from the wonder he feels when he studies the extraordinary construction that is the human capacity to think. To hope that the mind can capture Ideas, such as they exist, is to expect of the human spirit that it be transparent and neutral: a kind of leech that has, as its only task, that of stuffing itself with celestial nourishment. If an organism develops systems of defense and of protection, like the immune system, it is because it wants to survive. To seek to know whether one's life is good or bad, useful or not, pertinent or not, is a luxury that is not one of the priorities of the dynamics of life, notably of human organisms.

Religious people would like it if God became each person's highest goal; a philosopher like Plato would like it if Truth became the highest goal of every human organism. The psychotherapist is content to support a person for whom life is far too uncomfortable and help him find the type of understanding that he needs to improve his life. The Jungian psychotherapist has a deep respect for all of the productions of the mind. He understands the necessity that humans have to transform their environment into digestible shadows, projected onto the screen of the interior cinema. To seek to modify a person's internal cinema inevitably passes through a deconstruction that aims at a reconstruction: one that is more able to defend what is at stake in one's life. He would like to transform the black and white film of a depressed patient into one containing the full array of colors and the saturated colors of neurotic thoughts into vivid film full of contrasts. The psychotherapist is endlessly confronted by individuals who are blinded by their unshakable faith in the perception they have about what happened to them.

IDEALISM AND ABSOLUTE TRUTHS
IN BODY PSYCHOTHERAPY

Some people, to whom we always feel strangely attracted, seem to live out of a greater inner richness. Basically everyone has it; the problem is that most of us don't know about it. The practical work of gradually discovering this inner richness is the substance of our teaching. (Charlotte Selver & Charles V. W. Brooks, 1980, "Sensory Awareness," p. 117)

The Neo-Reichian Idealism

One must note the widespread practice of interrupting children's play as though it were of no importance. Through this, children come to feel that there is no natural rhythm in things, and that it is right for activities to be cut off in mid-air. . . . When children have been interrupted often enough, their innate sense of rhythm becomes confused; as well as their sense of the social value of their own experience. (Selver & Brooks, 1980, "Sensory Awareness," p. 117)

Idealism admits only one form of relativism: that an individual consciousness can be more or less intensely in contact with the truths of the soul, and consequently be more or less rational and have more or less good taste. The diverse forms of Idealism that we encounter in body psychotherapy are often related to diverse forms of spirituality. Biosynthesis, Biodynamic psychology, and Core energetics are influential examples.[33] Their brand of Idealism leads them to propose expressions such as "the unconscious knows," "the body never lies," or "the body knows." The body, the organism, and the unconscious are then equivalent terms to designate the nonconscious dynamics that animate our thoughts.

These authors (notably David Boadella, Gerda Boyesen, and John Pierrakos) postulate that each organism contains a soul, defined here as a nucleus of natural forces, of cosmic vitality. According to them, there exists in everyone a part of their being that knows, that is true, that is good, that is incapable of lying, and that would allow an individual to act in harmony with his real and profound needs and with those in his intimate circle and of nature.[34] The universe is conceived as a perfect entity, without any malice, seeking a coherence that harmonizes everything it contains. The soul is thus this part of nature that animates the organism. These authors then develop their arguments to show that a being's center is often inhibited by social factors that pervert the rapport that an individual entertains with the depth of his nature. Psychotherapy would then have the goal of restoring this profound link with the primary nature of the organism. What is difficult to understand in the writings of these authors, as well as in Plato, is how this nature could have brought about this destructive influence of societies. We find, in this, the same questions that children ask themselves about why an all-powerful God authorized the existence of the devil and of so much pain.

A Passionate and Profoundly Emotional Experience Is a Way to Taste the World of Ideas

> Now of all motions that is the best which is produced in a thing by itself, for it is most akin to the motion of thought and of the universe; but that motion which is caused by others is not so good, and worst of all is that which moves the body, when at rest, in parts only and by some external agency. Wherefore of all modes of purifying and re-uniting the body the best is gymnastic; the next best is a surging motion, as in sailing or any other mode of conveyance which is not fatiguing; the third sort of motion may be of use in a case of extreme necessity, but in any other will be adopted by no man of sense: I mean the purgative treatment of physicians; for diseases unless they are very dangerous should not be irritated by medicines, since every form of disease is in a manner akin to the living being, whose complex frame has an appointed term of life.... And this holds also of the constitution of diseases; if any one regardless of the appointed time tries to subdue them by medicine, he only aggravates and multiplies them. Wherefore we ought always to manage them by regimen, as far as a man can spare the time, and not provoke a disagreeable enemy by medicines. (Plato, 1937, *Timaeus, III,* 89a, p. 65)

Idealism places in the depths of the world of Ideas, not only Truths but also a power to heal. We could find the quote from *Timaeus* in a number of texts on natural medicine or homeopathy. There would be in each one of us a restorative given that knows what we ought to do to get better. This vision is close to that of Jung, for whom "the general function of dreams is to attempt to reestablish our psychological equilibrium with the help of an oneiric material that, in a subtle way, reconstitutes the total equilibrium of our psyche" (Jung, 1961, p. 75, my translation).

This way of thinking, which we find in the writings of Reich in his last years, has often activated in the psychotherapeutic community a reaction akin to that of the Athenians in the face of Socrates: a mixture of admiration for an undeniable gift and a refusal to accept that such a power really exists. Some psychotherapists think that when a person renders the unconscious conscious, not only the psyche functions better, but so do all the other dynamics of the organism. The body psychotherapists who adopt this point of view sometimes have the ability to lead persons into near trance-like states that mobilize the total organism and that have an immense intensity of astoundingly intermingled joy and sorrow. These experiences have a hypnotic impact. Patients who live these experiences subsequently have a clear impression of having made contact with their depth, that they are no longer alone, and to have found within themselves a serene vitality that will accompany them for the rest of their lives.

The Transpersonal Dimension

The platonic soul brings to the mind organizing principles elaborated during her voyages to the land of Ideas. She conveys a body of knowledge developed beyond the human species that cannot be created by individuals. These Truths have been set before an individual's birth, and the individual's thoughts have no impact on their content. For a number of psychotherapists who are Idealists, Plato's interpretation of the soul is a metaphor that has permitted humans to become more conscious of the fact that their mind has *transpersonal*[35] or *supra-ordinate*[36] content. This is the content that led Jung to the notion of the *collective unconscious*.[37] Ervin Laszlo[38] even goes so far as to speak of a *pan-mind, or pan-psyche*, that is, a global knowledge that is rooted in every cell.

A more academic vision of the transpersonal mechanisms defines them as elaborations that influence an individual psyche but have not been created or elaborated by it. At most, a person can only add a nuance to the general structure. Once this definition is accepted, one can distinguish several forms of "transpersonal" contents:

1. The *innate* mechanisms, like the way that the eyes transform light to create the perception of the color red.
2. The systems created by *culture* (language, ethical systems, morality, religions, etc.).
3. The academic disciplines suggest the *construction* of transpersonal truths. Scientific research is perhaps influenced in a prominent way by particular personalities (like Aristotle and Newton), but it is built on the themes studied by thousands of research teams over the centuries.[39]

4. These days, the term *transpersonal* is mostly used by authors like Ken Wilber[40] in a *spiritual* context to designate the forces that enliven an individual without his understanding of it, and that are deeply felt as an experience of transcendence, such as the Buddhist state of illumination.

Plato's fable has the benefit of not proposing a plausible explanation on the origin and the functioning of transpersonal forces. It contents itself to make people attentive to the phenomenon by making them aware that these impressions have a massive impact on how an individual thinks. Those that use the term *transpersonal* often have the tendency to suggest "explanations" of this phenomenon that are finally more fanciful than Plato's fables.

What I retain from the term *transpersonal* is the idea that an individual feels forces within himself that he has not built in the course of his life that also enliven most of the people that surround him. That sentiment is active from birth, and is encouraged by almost all educators worldwide. It is also active in the sense that an individual has the impression of participating in the animation of what animates him. For example, I am formed by the social world that surrounds me, but I also actively participate in what this social life becomes. It is therefore possible to distinguish two types of transpersonal thoughts:

1. The *anthropological dimension*. There would be transpersonal regulation systems and mechanisms brought about by biological and social history that motivate each individual in multiple ways. These mechanisms generate forms of universal regulation, but they are not necessarily mechanisms that contain a truth. They only allow for the reproduction of a know-how. The term *transpersonal* gathers a multitude of causal systems that activate the impression that there exist universal mechanisms that are beyond us.[41]
2. The *anthropological and spiritual dimension*. There would be transpersonal systems of regulation and mechanisms brought about by biological and social history, which motivate each individual in multiple ways. Among these systems, some are in contact with some absolute Truths, capable of engendering self-healing. These theories often postulate a total coherence of the universe, a coherent relationship between the elements and the system that contain them (as in the phrase "everything is linked to everything").[42] The term *transpersonal* does not only designate a psychological impression but also a unique force that structures the multiple mechanisms enlivening human history.

Must a Treatment Create Harmony in the Organism?

Eros Heals

Plato's *Symposium* describes a banquet that is the second in a series of celebrations organized by the very rich Athenian poet Agathon to celebrate the literary prize that he recently won. What is at hand is a prestigious prize given for the best tragedy of the year 416 BC. This banquet gathers illustrious Athenians, such as Socrates, the general Alcibiades, and the author Aristophanes. The first banquet has been so sumptuous that this time the guests prefer to drink and eat less and spend more time presenting their homage to the god of love, Eros:

> Vignette on *The Symposium. The first orator is called Phaedrus. He presents Eros as one of the most ancient and powerful gods. Eros gives humans the possibility to love each other, and thus to live in a paradisiacal and reparative emotional state in a world often difficult to handle.*
>
> *The second orator, Pausanias, distinguishes two form of love. The first is a love between two souls, without doubt what Phaedrus was speaking about. The second is an attraction between bodies that often lead to a moral decline of the soul.*

The homage delivered by the third orator, the physician Eryximachus, is the one that interests us here. Phaedrus had presented Eros as one of the most ancient and powerful gods of the universe. To believe that he only occupies himself with the amorous sentiments of individual humans is not, consequently, doing him justice. The amorous sentiments are but a human expression of the fundamental forces that regulate the relations between all that exists in the universe: galaxies, stars, plants, animals, organs, atoms, and so on. Eros is therefore a force of the universe. As Pausanias has shown, Eros creates intense and creative links between the elements of the cosmos, whereas Chaos, born just before Eros, creates destructive links between all that exist. Phaedrus has already showed how the birth of Eros repaired the damage caused by his older brother. In medicine, Eros is the force that regulates a constructive attraction between the elements of a body and what allows for a healthy life; whereas Chaos deregulates the attractions and the pleasures of the body and renders everything unwell. This perspective shows that the constructive and destructive forces of human love are animated by such powerful universal forces that we can now understand the importance of Eros, who is one of the principal gods of medicine.[43] Eros is therefore not only the god of love, of the attraction between atoms, but also of healing.

Eryximachus thus describes the therapeutic act as a way of supporting the influence of Eros. This proposition has had a considerable influence on all of the therapists influenced by Idealism. The duty of the physician is to reinforce the harmony between the elements of the body and foster the birth of a state of love and harmony in an organism torn apart by discordant forces. This task is difficult to the extent that there exist numerous elements that have contradictory functions in an organism, like cold and hot, bitter and sweet, wet and dry. It is not possible to contemplate that blood would become dry like a bone or bones fluid like blood. That is why it requires enormous experience before a physician can become able to restore all of the dissimilar elements of the organism into lovers of one another.

The Rite of Spring

> Harmony needs low and high, as progeny needs man and woman. (43)
> From the strain of binding opposites comes harmony. (46)
> The cosmos works by harmony of tensions, like the lyre and bow. Therefore, good
>   and ill are one. (56)
>   (Heraclitus, 2001, *Fragments*)

For Eryximachus, the power of Eros manifests itself in the same manner in music and medicine. According to him, the composer has the mission to harmonize the high and low notes. The harmony established between the high and the low notes creates the musical event by overcoming an initial opposition.[44] The creation of a musical chord is thus another way to honor Eros. Eryximachus is so intent on finding harmony between all things that he attempts to include Heraclitus's thought into his own:

> For he says that The One is united by disunion, like the harmony of the bow and the lyre. Now there is an absurdity in saying that harmony is discord or is composed of elements which are still in a state of discord. But what he probably meant was, that harmony is composed of differing notes of higher and lower pitch which disagreed once, but are now reconciled by the art of music; for if the higher and lower notes still disagreed, there could be no harmony. (Plato, *The Symposium*, 187a and b, p. 314)

Heraclitus also uses a dialectical approach toward reality (thesis, antithesis, synthesis) and thinks that man is but a pale reflection of the potential that animates the universe. However, for Heraclitus, managing disharmony is often even more creative (even more healthy) than reaching a harmonious state. He could also have said that conflicts can become a particularly creative form of harmony. He thus rather announces a form of reasoning that we will find when we will speak of Hume and Darwin. For Heraclitus, Chaos's work (the antithesis) is as important and crucial for the evolution of the universe (the synthesis) than that of Eros (the thesis). The conflicting dialectic dynamic between Eros and Chaos allows for the emergence of the emotion of love, desire, creativity, and music. This unceasing battle structures the organism and reinforces it. Briefly, if Heraclitus had been a therapist, he sometimes would have put oil on the inner conflicts of a soul, so that she might strengthen herself and learn to manage the conflicts of existence with greater ease.

Before becoming a student of Socrates, Plato had studied with Cratylus, a student of Heraclitus. Later, Plato wrote a dialogue in which he imagines Socrates trying to explain to Cratylus why Heraclitus is wrong and he, Socrates, is right. In this dialogue, titled *Cratylus* or *Of the Uprightness of Words,* Socrates and Cratylus discuss the meaning of words. Socrates thinks that words have a meaning, or that at least certain words like *goodness* or *beauty* have a precise meaning, that is not immediately accessible to comprehension but can be discovered. Plato's Socrates attacks the idea that Heraclitus expresses when he writes that we can never bathe twice in the same river. If everything changes and is in a perpetual flux, it is impossible to have words that have a meaning:

> Socrates: Nor can we reasonably say, Cratylus, that there is knowledge at all, if everything is in a state of transition and there is nothing abiding; for knowledge too cannot continue to be knowledge unless continuing always to abide and exist. But if the very nature of knowledge changes, at the time when the change occurs there will be no knowledge; and if the transition is always going on, there will always be no knowledge, and, according to this view, there will be no one to know and nothing to be known. (Plato, 1937, *Cratylus*, 440a and b, p. 229)

This is the dilemma. Eryximachus certainly speaks of dialectics, but of dialectics that envisage only two types of organizations: harmonious and disharmonious. Harmonious organizations favor the emergence of a state of health, happiness, pleasure, and love that leads to the most sacred dimensions of life. Disharmonious organizations lead to hatred, illness, chaos, and the destruction of all that humans have tried to create. In other words, Eryximachus relates harmony to "good" and discord to "evil." Heraclitus, on the other hand, supposes that the same elements can be organized in multiple ways, notably harmonious and conflicted, and that from each type of organization can emerge creative and destructive dialectics:

1. A conflicting organization can be creative.
2. A creative organization is not necessarily constructive (an illness also constructs itself).
3. This implies that a harmonious and creative organization can be destructive.

Even though by temperament I find myself more at ease with the thinking of Heraclitus than that of Plato, my experience does not permit me to eliminate an approach to the detriment of another. They both have their utility and their limits. In music, for example, I adore the seeking for harmony that I hear in Johann Sebastian Bach's *The Art of the Fugue*, and I am fascinated by Igor Stravinsky's *Rite of Spring* that contains nothing other than dissonance.

Patients That Suffer from Too Much Harmony
Eryximachus's discourse also raises a long list of questions for psychotherapists, notably these:

1. Does a healthy spirit function coherently?
2. Must we harmonize the conflicting elements of an experience?
3. Must we live like La Fontaine's cicada or his ant?
4. Does the clarification of a conflict aim at the harmonization of the elements in conflict?

On these questions, it is possible for me to sketch the outlines of a few responses that have accompanied me over the years and have been useful in my practice of psychotherapy.

THE DIFFERENCE OF POTENTIAL AND INTERACTION

Paul Boyesen (1993) taught the following model when I was studying with him in the 1970s. I am reconstructing it for you as I remember it and in the way I use it in my work. Because I mention it here in a section on Plato's *Symposium*, it evidently consists of some aspects of the love relationship.

The basic idea is as follows. An electric current exist only if there is a difference of potential between two poles of opposite charges (+ and –). If the two poles have an identical charge, no current exists between them. If the two poles are too strongly opposed, an explosion can possible destroy them both and consequently cancel the difference of potential that created the energy. If two individuals fall madly in love with each other, something very powerful has happened between them. Something facilitated the emergence of this love. In the case of love at first sight, two people fall in love with each other without really knowing each other. From what they were at this moment, love emerged.

This model is particularly relevant with regard to enmeshed couples,[45] where each one would like it if there were no conflicts, no disagreements, and no disillusions. They both try to change each other to render their relationship increasingly harmonious. One of the problems with such a couple is that the more they manipulate each other, the less they look like who they were when they fell in love. They progressively move away from who they really are to obtain a relationship that they imagine to be harmonious. The difference in the potential energy of their original identity lessens as they fashion themselves to look more alike, as they develop a common ideology and affect and begin to become a caricature of each other. The first evidence of this leveling of differences is often the loss of sexual activity. The moral of this story is that to want to blend water and soil is to transform a region into an ocean of mud. To create harmony between water and fire is a difficult art, according to Eryximachus, because it requires the creation of an entity that maintains the nature of both water and fire. Such a harmonious accord can only exist if the identity of each remains intact. This is what an enmeshed couple who consults with me has to learn if they want to extract themselves from the muddy emotional, aesthetic, and identity crisis in which they are drowning.

RELAXATION AS A HAVEN

In the course of my training, I learned a great many massage, meditation, and relaxation techniques that intend to create a sense of inner harmony. I have myself been able to appreciate the restorative pleasure that these states can bring about. They often relate to a sense of profound psychophysiological relaxation, like being cleansed from the inside, like being at peace with oneself and with what surrounds us, and finally offer a powerful impression of inner unity.

When I practice one of these exercises, I am like a ship's pilot navigating out of life's storms and finding a quiet port where I can rest and regain strength. I try to help my patients discover such havens in the course of therapy; not only because such peaceful moments are pleasant but also because they have a powerful healing effect on the soul's wounds, and they sometimes foster the rediscovery of the will to live, and to feel anew, from within, the flowing vigor of life.

For most people, a port is a stopover and not a goal. It is a place to load and unload merchandise. These states of inner harmony nurse consciousness and calm psychological turbulence, but they are not states that satisfactorily support the confrontation of life's complexities. People who would like to spend their life in such a state protect themselves not only from anxiety but also from all of the creative impulses that promote their existence.[46]

In general, a psychotherapist chooses a type of psychotherapy with which his conscious and nonconscious potential finds resonance and that may have a beneficial effect on most of his patients. This criterion is not one of truth but of convenience. Some work well when they seek a harmony between the elements presented, as Eryximachus suggests; others are more effective when they support the tensions that keep an organism alive, according to Heraclitus. Some patients sometimes have the need of one style of therapy more than another; for others, in other situations, this distinction is irrelevant.

This type of dialectical way of thinking had already been developed in China and in Japan, for example, by acupuncturists. My teacher of Chinese massage during the 1980s, Hiroshi Nozaki, taught us the theory of the elements used in Japanese medicine. He gave us the following example:

> Vignette on metal in acupuncture. *If you place metal between water and fire, the antagonism between the two elements can be mastered usefully. The metal permits the regulation of the tension that naturally exists between fire and water. Through the mastery of this possibility, humans have been able to develop, for example, the culinary arts or the steam engine.*

For Hiroshi Nozaki, a medicine like metal does not harmonize fire and water but creates new constructive possibilities between elements that remain antagonists.

THE DANGERS OF IDEALISM

Now I want to prophesy to those who convicted me, for I am at the point when men prophesy most, when they are about to die. I say gentlemen, to those who voted to kill me, that vengeance will come upon you immediately after my death, a vengeance much harder to bear than that which you took in killing me. You did this in the belief that you would avoid giving an account of your life, but I maintain that quite the opposite will happen to you. There will be people to test you, whom I now held back, but you did not notice it. They will be more difficult to deal with as they will be younger and you will resent them more. (Plato, 1997, *Apology*, III.39c, p. 421)

In the preceding chapters, I have described Idealistic propositions that are often considered good reasons to become an Idealist. I now discuss some implications of this stance that may explain the violent reactions that Idealism has aroused. I limit myself in situating those implications in the life of Plato; in speaking of Wilhelm Reich, we will see that these implications are always present.

The Political, Moral, and Sexual Implications of Idealism

Bodily delight is a sensory experience, not any different from pure looking or the pure feeling with which a beautiful fruit fills the tongue; it is a great, an infinite learning that is given to us, a knowledge of the world, the fullness and the splendor of all knowledge. (Rainer-Marie Rilke, 1908, *Letters to a Young Poet*, IV, p. 36f)

Idealism has never been a pure speculation. It opens almost automatically on a global and militant vision. Those who have the impression of having entered into contact with the Truth often think that they are authorized to make pronouncements on everything that goes on in the world. They assume that their deep intuition about what is Just and False gives them permission to judge everything.

But when the souls we call immortal reach the top, they move outward and take their stand on the high ridge of heaven, where its circular motion carries them around as they stand while they gaze upon what is outside heaven. (Plato, 1997, *Phaedrus*, 247–248, p. 525)

They have the impression that their wisdom guarantees the relevance of their delusions and their thirst for power. In their way of thinking, their judgment necessarily trumps the examination of those who have not learned to integrate the Truths of the soul into their consciousness.

Let us take the case of an Idealist chemist who discovers a new and important fact in the course of his research. He becomes convinced that his capacity to find a scientific truth is a sign that he also has access to global Truth. This position is coherent with the supposition that there exist but one Truth. He then believes that he knows more about politics than the politician or more about morality than the moralist. It is thus that a school that extolls an Idealist theory often does not limit the propagation of its teaching to the expertise it acquired. It will use its reputation for a particular expertise as a platform to diffuse a much larger understanding. Students that come to such a school to acquire a professional competence will be submitted to requirements relative to what they think about beauty, love, justice, and so on.

A curious but frequent aspect of this way of thinking that I cannot explain to my satisfaction is that it often leads to a form of sexual militancy: a militant homosexuality with Plato;[47] chastity with some Christians, or at least an absolute separation of sexual pleasure and the necessity to procreate; and the insistence on heterosexual orgasm with Reich. In all of these theories, sexuality is part of the world of Ideas or can give access to it. A wrong use of sexuality leads necessarily to an impoverished contact with the Ideas, God, or Nature. There are many ethical problems in this contagion from one truth to another:

1. The one who knows is critical only of others.
2. An Idealist teacher (or therapist) wants to influence his students in domains other than those that define his expertise.
3. This teaching is necessarily disrespectful of all forms of collective decisions, because collective decisions are often taken by people who do not have real knowledge. Collegiality is therefore not possible, or even hoped for, between a group of Idealists and other colleagues and citizens.

If I am right when I assume that Idealism describes a functioning of consciousness, the following developments can be useful to clinicians who treat a patient in whom Idealism has become omnipresent. A psychotherapist who is unaware of this can find it difficult to come face to face with a series of mental mechanisms that exist in his own mind. The student or the patient who faces an authority that believes it rises above any limits often does not have a sufficient education to defend himself against this type of intrusion. Such a person will often adhere to what is presented or will drown in a revolt against something he does not understand.

Are Those Who Condemn Socrates Necessarily Ignorant and Wicked Citizens?

> Socrates, whose piety, continence and obedience to the laws has no equal, is presented to us at the same time as one who criticizes the rules instituted by the State, who insults the governing class and ridicules them in public. (Roustang, 2009, *Le secret de Socrate pour changer la vie*, 9, p. 173; translated by Marcel Duclos)

Over the centuries, the myth of Socrates has been the myth of the Christ of the philosophers who died for having tried to improve the way other citizens think by asking disturbing questions. Having had enough of being continuingly brought up short, they wanted to assassinate the very one who showed them how lazy they were in their thinking. According to Plato, Socrates's worst enemies were the sophists, those who know how to make convincing arguments in favor of any opinion to influence those who cast votes within a democracy. Only since the postmodern philosophers do we attend to a criticism of this myth and a rehabilitation of the sophists in relationship to the media. Indeed, improving how minorities present their opinions is an important element of the dynamics of a democracy, even if this function eventually favors the most powerful movements. The problem for the Idealists is that the media publicize points of view that are distant from all manner of Truths.

In continuing this reflection, I propose an ethical analysis of what I understand to be the notion of a master and of a school, basing myself on what was at stake at Socrates's trial. This discussion seems pertinent to me to support the students of Idealistic schools of psychotherapy. They can therefore profit from the knowledge of an often useful Idealistic instruction and protect themselves from the disrespect that these teaching often have toward the free will of others.

Political Context

To understand the trial of Socrates, it is useful to situate it in its political context. Half a century earlier, Athens was a powerful republic in which every adult male citizen had the right to vote. Women and the numerous slaves in the city did not have the same right. Athens had become powerful in creating an empire that the city governed in a tyrannical manner. It is nonetheless the custom to consider Athens the first republic and the first attempt to create a democratic government.

THE PELOPONNESIAN WAR (CA. 431–404 BC)

The golden age of Athens occurred while the city was governed by Pericles. The republic was extremely rich, and it attracted a number of particularly important artists and brilliant thinkers. The beginning of its decadence also occurred during this epoch. The royal city of Sparta and her allies decided to support the revolt of those kingdoms previously conquered by Athens. This unleashed the interminable Peloponnesian War that ended with victory for Sparta. The royalists created a government composed of thirty members of the old Athenian aristocracy. This government of "thirty oligarchs" persecuted the republicans. Greatly unpopular, they were toppled within a few months by the republicans, who then persecuted those who had supported the oligarchy. Socrates's trial is one of the last and most well-known reprisals carried out by the citizens of Athens.

SOCRATES, PLATO, AND THE OLIGARCHS

Plato's parents were from some illustrious Athenian families. Certain branches of the family were close to the oligarchs, and other branches had supported Pericles. Pericles and Plato's father had died not long after Plato's birth.

In *The Symposium*, Plato shows us Socrates about to carry out a philosophical discussion with Athenian personalities close to the oligarchs, especially Alcibiades. This dignitary had been a brilliant Athenian politician. Having led the Athenian army in a disastrous campaign, he had gone over to the enemy and given the Spartans precious information that helped them capture the port of

Athens. This dialogue, redacted after Socrates's trial, demonstrates that Socrates and Plato were members of an "intelligentsia" relatively indifferent to the interests of the republic.

Socrates was, at that time, the head of a renowned school that educated the golden youth of Athens. Among the students were many sons of families who had close ties to the oligarchy. The school had a questionable reputation because it seemed to be, in the eyes of some (like Aristophanes), what we would today call a sect: "It is a Thinkery for intellectual souls. That's where people live who try to prove that the sky is like a baking-pot all round us, and we're the charcoal inside it. And if you pay them well, they can teach you how to win a case whether you're right or not"[48] (Aristophanes, 2002, *The Clouds*, p. 78).

The Socrates of Plato's first dialogues can sometimes be perceived as a master who exercises a kind of gentle but insidious hammering that finally leaves the other confused and without a voice. Even today, one finds authors for whom Plato's early dialogues show a Socrates "backed up by yes-men and opposed by the philosophically naïve who are doomed to confusion" (Gaskin, 1993, p. xxiii).

ENLIGHTENED TYRANNY
The students of Socrates came from the milieu of the grand families who were often not at ease with the democratic management of Athens. This antidemocratic sentiment was exacerbated when the republic of Athens was drawn into the Peloponnesian War: a war it mismanaged with disastrous results. Alcibiades was not the only one of Socrates's students to go over to the enemy. Xenophanes, who wrote several works in the defense of Socrates, was also one of them.

When the republicans regained power, Socrates and his friends publicly advocated an enlightened tyranny. For them, the only thing wrong with the oligarchy was that it was formed by incompetent people selected by Sparta. An oligarchy of philosophers and experts would have governed better than a republic.

After the death of Socrates, Plato details, in *The Republic*, a political proposition that still influences various forms of totalitarian power. His first argument against democratic regimes is that a citizen rarely has the expertise to evaluate the implications at stake in a vote.[49] Only a philosopher—that is to say, only a person in contact with the Ideas contained in his soul—has the capacity to know what has to be undertaken for the common good. The philosopher may have to lie, rig the votes, and manipulate the opinions of the citizens, if he does so to defend a position necessary for the survival of the city. In other words, he is the expert who decides what others ought to know, think, and do. This discussion also takes place in the therapeutic milieus of the twenty-first century. An Idealist therapist believes that he is in a position to decide what a patient has the right to know concerning his own health. The actual position, clearly in opposition to Idealistic propositions, is that the patient always has the right to know what one knows about him. Yet the Idealist stance is still employed in all of the world's democracies,[50] if only in their way of carrying out secret services. Some people sometimes relate the government of the European common market to a platonic oligarchy of experts instead of a democracy such as it is defined and practiced in countries such as Switzerland.

Plato touches on practices that are even more difficult to accept when, always for the good of the state, he proposes eugenics procedures. He would like the government to make it such that the most gifted would mate with each other and that individuals who are gifted for particular professions would marry each other:[51]

> The offspring of the inferior, or of the better when they chance to be deformed, will be put away in some mysterious, unknown place, as they should be.
>   Yes, he said, that must be done if the breed of the guardians is to be kept pure.
> (Plato, 1937, *The Republic*, V 460c, p. 722)

While waiting for the development of philosophers able to govern in an oligarchy, united by the one and only Truth, Plato and Aristotle tried to promote enlightened tyrants.

The Ethical Context

MORALITY

The force of Idealism is to give hope that humanity will be able to discover not only how to govern the world but also how to establish a morality. For Plato, it is not possible to vote, even in a democracy, on what is Advantageous, Beautiful, Good, Just, and True, because these Ideas are defined in a dimension other than the one in which humans think. Scientific truth demands more than a vote among the scholars, because it depends on systems of validation produced by an experimental method that only the experts know how to apply. In such a system, the individual spontaneously grants himself the right to be beyond social directives as soon as a rule is defined in an interpersonal dimension. At the end of World War II, it became evident that following the laws instituted by the Nazis and the Communists were incompatible with moral behavior. An individual saw fit to protect Jewish refugees who were pursued by the state. In France, although the government had signed a peace treaty with the invading Germans, many people decided, in the name of an individual and interpersonal (religious, existentialist, humanistic, etc.) conviction to form pockets of resistance against the invader. For these people, it was moral to disobey the law. The difficulty in such a situation is to determine what is moral and who decides what is moral.

The seductive side of the Idealist analysis of moral responsibility is that it allows one to foresee the possibility of explaining a pertinent morality for everybody; that is, as soon as we designate an instance capable of "translating" what is inscribed in the transpersonal dimension. Once we accept this act of faith, it becomes possible to be convinced that we are able to discern good from evil. This approach remains, in the final analysis, the only one that the conscious mind of individual humans can assume. It is difficult to solicit the responsibility of citizens without having the impression that each one can have a sense of responsibility, an intuition about what is just.

AN EXTREME HOMOSEXUAL MILITANCY

> Those who are inspired by this love turn to the male, and delight in him who is the more valiant and intelligent nature; any one may recognize the pure enthusiasts in the very character of their attachments. For they love not boys, but intelligent beings whose reason is beginning to be developed, much about the time at which their beards begin to grow. (Plato, 1937, *The Symposium*, 181c–d, p. 309)

> But when it [the soul of an initiate] looks upon the beauty of the boy and takes the stream of particles flowing into it from his beauty (that is what is called "desire"), when it is watered and warmed by this, then all its pain subsides and is replaced by joy.[52] (Plato, 1997, *Phaedrus*, 251c–d, p. 528f)

In *The Symposium,* it is not only a milieu close to the oligarchs that is described, but also a milieu in which homosexuality is considered the only way love can become so intense and profound that it can allow one to enter into contact with the world of Ideas. There is no platonic love unless two united bodies permit two souls to love each other.[53] Men are the only persons capable of enough maturity to love this way. "The love who is the offspring of the common Aphrodite is essentially common, and has no discrimination, being such as the meaner sort of men feel and is apt to be of woman as well as of youths, and is of the body rather than of the soul" (Plato, 1937, *The Symposium*, 181 a–b, p. 309).

In this milieu, homosexuality was only part-time, as even Socrates was married. He had also had as a teacher a woman named Aspasia. She was no ordinary woman: she was a foreigner and a courtesan. Exceptionally beautiful and intelligent, she initiated Socrates to the pleasures of the soul by introducing him to sexuality.[54] Plato also admitted that a relatively strong love could exist between women and men, like Alcestis who accepted dying in the place of her husband.[55] There are two texts on *The Symposium*: one by Plato and one by Xenophon. Both agree that (1) Socrates did not make love with his students, and (2) homosexual eroticism did play a role in his pedagogical strategy. He used the eroticism that could exist in his relationship with his students to help them sense the Truth and Beauty that surpasses what the majority of citizens could experience. In Phaedrus, an aging Plato dares to describe, in one of his most beautiful texts, the orgasmic pleasure of an adolescent who loses his virginity to a philosopher. This ecstasy is depicted as a moment of extreme intensity during which the adolescent is initiated not only to Love but also to Poetry, to the most absolute Beauty, and to the Truth that he holds in the depths of his being.[56]

These texts are often presented as hardly reprehensible, to the extent that homosexuality would have been common in ancient Greece,[57] and the age of marriage was then that of puberty. Such arguments are only partially relevant. It suffices to read Homer to see the importance of heterosexual relations in Greece, as is evident in the rapport of Hector and Ulysses with their wives. Nicole Loraux[58] shows that the Athenians at the time of *The Symposium* spoke mostly of the virility of the warrior. Warriors were becoming rare, because many died at war. The homosexual militancy of Socrates's school far surpasses the homosexuality such as it was lived habitually in Greece. Later we discuss Reich, who develops similar arguments when he speaks of heterosexual orgasm. Reich's idealized heterosexuality was as far removed from the heterosexual practices of his time as the homosexuality of Plato was from the homosexual practices of his epoch.

The Trial of a Great Master

Sometime around 399 BC, Socrates was accused of "corrupting the young and of not believing in the gods to whom the City believes and to be substituting new divinities" (Plato, 1937, *Apology of Socrates*, 24b, p. 407). The trial judges had functions similar to those of judges in contemporary courts of law in Europe; the jury was composed of all of the citizens of Athens who were asked to vote on the verdict and the sentence.[59] The trial unfolded in two phases:

Phase I. Decide whether Socrates was innocent or guilty.

Phase II. Decide the punishment.

This distinction is also relevant when I shall discuss the trial of Wilhelm Reich.

IS SOCRATES GUILTY?

We now know enough to understand that Socrates's behavior corresponded to the wording of the accusation.

1. *Socrates does not believe in the gods in whom the City believes and he replaces them with new divinities.* As a good Idealist, he had a personal understanding of the Gods and the relationship he can have with them. He claimed to be in a personal relationship with some secondary gods and ignored most of the ritual that were not required out of politeness, such as invoking the appropriate god when pouring a small amount of wine in sacrifice. Plato went even further, for at the end of his life he invented gods for the needs of a fable.

2. *He corrupts the youth.* This is the most serious accusation. We have seen that Socrates could have been accused of (a) having an excessive hold on students that he seemed to mesmerize into an admiring attitude; (b) teaching his students an ideology dangerous to the republic; (c) teaching

a morality that led them to disdain other citizens and the authorities; (d) teaching them a morality that encouraged them to prefer their own interest in philosophy to their responsibilities toward their families; and (e) holding homosexual love as sacred at the expense of heterosexual love.

The impression that Socrates represented a danger to the republic by being an activist in political movements that threatened its existence was well founded. Aristotle, Plato's student, became the tutor of the boy who became Alexander the Great. As a symbol of enlightened tyranny (and probably homosexual), Alexander represents Plato's hopes and dreams. He destroyed the republic of Athens and subjugated Greece before conquering the Asia of his time.

Having arrived at the end of the first phase of the trial, the majority of the citizens thought Socrates guilty as charged; however, they waited for him to present his defense before deciding on his punishment. None of them were thinking of condemning him to death.

HOW TO CONDEMN SOCRATES?

The death sentence is suggested and promoted by Socrates. He accuses his fellow citizens of incompetence and stupidity. He absolves himself of any and all error. Only the gods have the competence to judge a man as righteous as he. Socrates is now seventy years old; he deems himself ill-equipped to suffer the disapproval of his co-citizens or even a gilded exile.

In the discussions he has with his students while in prison awaiting the day of his execution, Socrates speaks to them of the grief and sorrow he feels having been condemned for a life that he totally claims as his own—he had wanted it to be as close to his personal convictions as possible. For him and for those who admire him, this condemnation is also a condemnation of all attempts to develop and publicly display personal convictions. For this, Socrates is often held up as the martyr of free thinkers.

It is for his disdain of the court, and not for what he did, that his Athenian co-citizens condemned Socrates to death, obliging him to drink poisonous hemlock. We will find the same chain of events when we speak of Reich's trial. He was condemned to prison for contempt of court, not because of his treatments based on his orgone theory, judged as quackery or a delusion.

DISCUSSION: THE LAST OF THE GREAT TEACHERS CREATES THE ACADEMY OF MASTERS

In his works, Plato presents Socrates to us as the greatest of all teachers; in his institutional work, he also tells us that Socrates is not an example to emulate. It is only in contrasting Plato's institutional work with his writings that his salient originality and his importance can be fully appreciated.

Even though Plato spent his life defending Socrates's reputation, he founded in 387 BC the antidote to the omnipotence of the great masters by creating an Academy (the name of the gardens that surround a building). The structure of the Academy indicates that from the time of the judgment on the fate of Socrates, Plato had intensely questioned his former beliefs. It contains a library, lecture halls, and rooms for particularly gifted students.[60] This Academy gathers authorities in many disciplines to establish an education that cannot be associated with one sect or one school of thought. In this way, students can learn from masters who represent different approaches. Nothing will stop them from specializing after having followed different ways of thinking. This Academy is recognized as the foundation of the academic institutions (wherein lies the etymological link).

Socrates's teaching addressed itself to the elite students who frequented his school. To discover the Ideas in a school like his, engaging in intense reflection is a luxury that very few people could afford. Plato and then Aristotle proceeded from the conviction that we all have the same truths within us. They can be made explicit, together or individually. A public knowledge could thus complement the unavoidable self-exploration every citizen must undertake.

The Academy founded science, to the extent that it initiated a collective search for the truth. Aristotle was a student and then a teaching member of this institution. We attribute to him the foundation of the scientific movement. *Science is then conceived as coordination between rigorous observations and reflections undertaken collectively to be able to enter into resonance with the intuitions of the soul.* Therein lies the potential to foresee the possibility of creating a kind of human knowledge able to bring about the true functioning of the world and the way humans should participate in the future of this world. The scientific movement has the task of producing irrefutable truths, close to the visions inspired by the Truth of the world of Ideas.

The different psychotherapies constitute a domain that has not yet developed enough to be considered academic. The question here is not to know up to what point the formulations produced by psychotherapists are "scientific" but up to what point they are produced by an ethics of knowledge compatible with science. This implies the capacity to leave behind the structure of particular schools, masters, and teachings that constitute themselves in a conceptual frame that is limited to a specific endeavor. The inability of the schools of psychotherapy to produce concepts and terms common to the whole of their discipline and debates on the different ways to understand these common notions keep them in an intellectual status that predates Plato.

4

René Descartes: The Body and the Soul of Scientists

AN EPISTEMOLOGICAL UNDERTAKING

From Plato to Descartes

After the extraordinary creativity that reigned at the early beginnings of the Academy, the scientific and philosophical disciplines of Europe fossilized themselves around the work of Plato and Aristotle. The existence of the soul, like so many other notions, became dogma. The fable was transformed into belief. The Renaissance is called renaissance precisely because some European intellectuals want the spirit of Plato's Academy to be reborn: the desire to seek and develop, with all of the material that is available, a better knowledge of self and what surrounds us.

I am going to follow a common practice in epistemology. Having discussed Plato's Idealism, I will leap right over 2,000 years of discussions to land alongside René Descartes (1596–1650). This practice was already recommended by Descartes, as he thought that those that came after Plato and Aristotle "laid more store on following their opinions than on seeking something better" (Descartes, 1644, p. 177). Descartes's message is not that he is the greatest intellectual since Plato, but that, the science developing in Europe since the sixteenth century finally permits one to go further than what had been written in Europe about human nature up until then.

From Athens to Amsterdam: One Maritime City to Another

> The true mirror of our thoughts is the conduct of our lives. (Montaigne, 1592, *Essais, I*, XXVI, p. 247)

Descartes was born in France in 1596, in The Hague, a city of Touraine. He attended the Jesuit College of La Fleche, on the banks of the Loire, where he studied law, mathematics, and philosophy. He remained in contact with certain Jesuit priests all of his life.[1] This did not prevent him from taking Galileo's side at the occasion of his trial in 1633. Nonetheless, he had too much fear of the Church to publish his writings on astronomy, which adopt the theses of Galileo and Kepler.

Descartes became a soldier. Having traveled in Germany and France, he established himself in the Netherlands, where it was possible to think with relative freedom. He felt close to Montaigne's humanism. The latter was frightened by the bloody and cruel religious wars that tore Europe apart for a century. These wars were notably caused by individuals who were convinced they were right and unable to value those who thought otherwise. The Catholics and their inquisition massacred the Protestants, the Gnostics, and the free thinkers. After having had to defend themselves, the Protestants also become all too often intolerant. Montaigne proposed a humanism that questions all forms of idealism. He therefore rejects the possibility that a human being might know what is true and false. Only God is thus able. Idealism is thereby not rejected but relativized. The god of the humanists is the smallest common denominator to that of the Catholics, the Protestants, the Muslims, and the Jews.

In this spirit Descartes thought that the scientific method is a good way to help human beings seek the truth together, instead of looking for it by killing each other. The choice of Amsterdam was not insignificant for Descartes. Amsterdam has much in common with Athens. Holland was part of the very Catholic and very tyrannical Holy Roman Empire of Charles V and was annexed to Spain, which was close to the Catholic Inquisition under Philip II. In liberating itself from Spain, Holland became a relatively tolerant Calvinist republic.[2] The Netherlands rapidly built a colonial empire for themselves in diverse continents and became one of the richest European nations.[3] Just like Athens, she partially democratized her internal institutions without renouncing her sometimes cruel domination of her colonies. And like Athens, the Netherlands became a center for art and philosophy that was characterized as a golden age of human thought.

Descartes finished his days in Sweden, guest of the Swedish Queen Elizabeth, where he died of pneumonia in 1650.

The Body in the Renaissance: From Empiricism to Science

The battleground of the Renaissance, among other things, manifested itself in the need to know how a human body was really constituted: a curiosity shared by artists, learned people, and physicians alike. The Church required that people accept that all that could be known about the body had been written by Aristotle, Galen, and the Bible. Those who only referred to Aristotle were called Peripaticians. All the same, most physicians knew to what extent this knowledge was limited and that it did not allow for the care of the suffering that confronted them. Artists, physicians, and philosophers had organized a large clandestine network to make anatomical observation of stolen cadavers and the mutual exchange of their observations possible. Galileo recounts an anecdote about the debate between a Humanist and Peripatetic physicians:

> It happened on this day that he [an anatomist from Venice] was investigating the source and origin of the nerves, about which there exists a notorious controversy between the Galenist and Peripatetic doctors. The anatomist showed that the great trunk of nerves, leaving the brain and passing through the nape, extended on down the spine and then branched out through the whole body, and that only a single strand as fine as a thread arrived at the heart. Turning to a gentleman whom he knew to be a peripatetic philosopher, and on whose account he had been exhibiting and demonstrating everything with unusual care, he asked this man whether he was at last satisfied and convinced that the nerves originated in the brain and not in the heart. The philosopher, after considering for a while, answered: "You have made me see this matter so plainly and palpably that if Aristotle's text were not contrary to it, stating clearly that the nerves originate in the heart, I should be forced to admit it to be true." (Galileo, *Dialogue Concerning the Two Chief World Systems*, 1630, II, p. 108)

The Peripatetic teachers of the day defended the theory that diverse organs were the seat of various psychic propensities: the liver for passions, the brain for judgments, and the heart for affects.[4] Peripatetic physicians assumed that there are connections between the mind and the organs that do not pass through the soul.

The idea that knowledge must be compatible with what is observable is referred to as empiricism. If that is all there had been to their endeavors, Galileo and his colleagues would have met the criterion of empiricists but not that of scientists. This generation of thinkers searches for rigorous observations and most of all for *laws*; that is, a theoretical construct that describes the mechanisms that organize what is observed. This combination makes Galilean physics a science. He postulates that the entire universe organizes itself coherently by following a logic that is close to what mathematics and geometry describe. This logic can be used to analyze all observed phenomena and all phenomena that will be observed. This idea could have been a theory only as interesting as all of the others, if it had not revealed itself particularly fruitful, easy to teach, and easy to disseminate. Furthermore this theory could be improved upon by constant research.

From the Causal System to Parallelism

> These principles gave me a natural way of explaining the union of the soul with the organic body, or rather their conformity with one another. Soul and body each follow their own laws; and are in agreement in virtue of the fact that, since they all represent the same universe. There is a pre-established harmony among all substances. (Leibniz, 1714, *Monadology*, 78, p. 10)

According to the philosopher Edmund Husserl,[5] Galileo's generation also postulated that each event of the universe can be defined in function of fundamental properties that are applicable everywhere: location, space and time, weight, size, and so on. The calculations become possible when the object studied is reduced to an "idealized" form (sphere, cube, etc.) associated to the properties of the real object (location, weight, size, etc.). Once these properties have been isolated, the physicist can compute how an object can be situated in a causal chain. This type of procedure permits scholars to construct an explanatory scientific system. This vision is monistic and materialistic: the universe is composed of one basic material substance. The relationship between the properties and mathematics makes it possible to sort out the great laws of a causal system that allows one to understand the functioning of the universe. Science would henceforth associate empiricism (e.g., experimental physics) and mathematical theory (e.g., theoretical physics). If one accepts that every particle of the universe obeys these laws, then one also assumes that the thoughts of the mind follow these same principles. Even today, no one knows what the properties of the mind really are. But if we follow this vision, the day when psychologists will be able to isolate the properties of a thought or a sentiment will be the day when it becomes possible to foresee, mathematically, the way these phenomena relate to each other.

Galileo's absolute formulation leaves little place for God. Some philosophers of the subsequent generation, like Descartes, distinguished a dimension of the universe that effectively follows the scientific laws (matter) and a parallel dimension whose dynamics are distinct, near to those that actuate God (soul):[6]

1. Matter is everything that the senses can perceive: planets, objects, particles, air, fluids, and light.
2. The soul can perceive and think.

The parallelist argumentation is still used today. There cannot be more than one object at the same time in the same space; but there can be several thoughts at the same time in the same space (in an individual). I cannot extend both arms, as on a cross, and touch my chest at the same time; but I can have the desire to do both gestures at the same time. The parallelists of the seventeenth century think that matter acts on matter and reacts only to matter. In similar fashion, the mind can only act on the mind, not on matter. According to Husserl, such a clear distinction between the substance of the mind and that of matter is a creation of the seventeenth century. In the preceding centuries, the differences between body and soul were more fluid.

A physical event is necessarily caused by an event that precedes it, whereas two thoughts that follow one another are not necessarily related and can be part of two independent causal systems. The soul and the body cannot interact directly because their functioning is so different. They are therefore part of two distinct dimensions.

Descartes had, at one moment, put forth the idea that the soul is "the assembly of the organs,"[7] that is, the organization of the organs that constitutes an organism. But he did not have the means to explore this hypothesis. It is nonetheless so tempting that the subsequent generation of philosophers like Spinoza found ways to tease something out of this analysis.

This argumentation is different from that of Aristotle, for whom affects and logical thoughts emerge in a soul that is a dimension of the individual system:

> It therefore seems that all the affections of soul involve a body-passion, gentleness, fear, pity, courage, joy, loving, and hating; in all these there is a concurrent affection of the body. In support of this we may point to the fact that, while sometimes on the occasion of violent and striking occurrences there is no excitement or fear felt, on others faint and feeble stimulations produce these emotions, viz. when the body is already in a state of tension resembling its condition when we are angry. . . . From all this it is obvious that the affections of soul are enmattered formulable essences. (Aristotle, *Of the Soul*, I.1)

Aristotle also quotes Democritus, for whom breath is the medium through which the soul animates the organism.[8]

Spinoza proposed a compromise between the positions of Descartes and Aristotle. He maintains the distinction of the parallelistic dimensions, but he introduces three restrictions to the independence between soul and body:

1. There is but one universe and it obeys integrally to the laws of logic, geometry, and mathematics.
2. This implies that although the objects of the mind and the objects themselves have different properties, they both follow the same causal laws.
3. As thoughts and objects are part of the same nature, the events that unfold in each dimension are influenced by the dynamics of the universe and by its architecture.

Thus, a thought cannot influence the body; a gesture cannot influence the unfolding of ideas. However, these two independent causal systems are part of an individual system (or organism) that has an architecture. This architecture can influence and is sensitive to what goes on in each dimension. Therefore, there exist regulators between each dimension.[9] These regulators have different properties, of a third type, that Spinoza will not be able to specify.

Rules for the Direction of the Mind of Scientific Philosophers

In his first great works, The Rules for the Direction of the Mind (1628) and The Discourse on Method (1637), Descartes observes how scholars think when they want to develop a scientific theory. He derives from their intellectual methods a set of rules that can be used by all those who want to become rigorous observers of the dynamics that animate the universe. These rules form a method of thinking composed of the following elements:

1. The rules of scientific thinking are the ones that are being implemented in mathematics, logic, and geometry.
2. These rules are capable of organizing, in an optimal fashion, all of the empirical data observed with enough precision to be described in the form of empirically validated properties.
3. It is essential to create such rules to frame the discussion among scholars so that scientific research can become a common enterprise.

Descartes is convinced that this method can be applied to all domains, even the study of the soul. He wants to explain it, make it public, put it at the disposition of all those who want to think correctly.

The Protestants had showed that by printing the Bible and learning how to read, each Christian could do without religious hierarchies. He no longer had the need of intermediaries between himself and God's message. Descartes follows an analogous reasoning. He begins with the Idealist's conclusion that the soul of each individual knows how to think and possesses an intuition about what is True or False, Good or Evil. Any individual who can read a book that describes the scientific method of thinking has the inner capacity to use it. Once he knows these rules, he can learn to develop his inner potential in a way that will allow him to study the phenomena that interest him.

THE REALM OF THOUGHTS

No objective science, no psychology—which, after all, sought to become the universal science of the subjective—and no philosophy has ever made thematic and thereby actually discovered the realm of the subjective. . . . It is a realm of something subjective which is completely closed off within itself, existing in its own way, functioning in all experiencing, all thinking, all life, thus everywhere inseparably involved; yet it has never been held in view, never been grasped and understood. (Husserl, 1936, *The Crisis*, III.A.29, p. 112)[10]

Thoughts Are the Source of Science

I always did and still do accept the innate idea of God, which Descartes upheld, and thus accept other innate ideas that couldn't come to us from the senses. Now the new system takes me even further. As you'll see later on, I think that all the thoughts and actions of our soul come from its own depths and couldn't be given to it by the senses! But in the meantime I'll set that aside and conform to accepted ways of speaking which purport to distinguish mental content that does come through the senses from mental content that doesn't. These ways of speaking are sound and justifiable: the outer senses can be said to be, in a certain sense, partial causes of our thoughts. So I'll work within the common framework, speaking of "how the body acts on the soul" . . . ; and I shall look into why, even within this framework, one should say that there are some ideas and principles that we find ourselves to have though we didn't form them, and that didn't reach us through the senses though the senses bring them to our awareness. Descartes' famous "cogito ergo sum" (I think, therefore I am) anchors all of the knowledge that God puts at the disposal of humans in the soul of each individual. It is in the interior of each soul that Descartes situates the intuitions of truth, the capacity to reflect and to know what one is thinking. Conscious thoughts are like soap bubbles floating about in the soul. In other words, contrary to Plato, Descartes situates the mind in the soul. (Leibniz, 1705, *New Essays*, I, p. 15)

Thought According to Descartes

When he has a feeling inside, how is he to know whether he is the only person on earth to have felt it, or even something like it? (Daniel Stern, 1990, *Diary of a Baby*, p. 106f)

To designate human explicit inner impressions, Descartes speaks not of consciousness but of thoughts. Thoughts are interior phenomena about which "we have immediate knowledge."[11] A thought is a reflexive mental activity, that is to say, a mental activity that perceives what is happening. This is the first explicit definition of the psychic system, or of the psyche of the Greeks: "By the term to think, I understand all that happens within us in such a way that we perceive it immediately by ourselves; that is why not only to hear, to want, to imagine, but also to feel is the same thing here as to think" (Descartes, 1644, The Principles of Philosophy, I, p. 574; translated by Marcel Duclos). There is a fine point here. Descartes does not tell us what thoughts are, only that we can have immediate knowledge of them. He does say that we are necessarily aware of them.

Certain thoughts are perceptions of events situated in the organism, like bodily sensations and sensory data. Other thoughts perceive what is going on outside of the organism. Other forms of thought have the task of organizing what has been detected by the senses. These "meta-perceptions" enable reasoning and reflection. This vocabulary was quite customary at that time. For example, the English philosopher Thomas Hobbes gives an analogous definition: "The secret thoughts of a man run over all things, holy, profane, clean, obscene, grave, and light, without shame, or blame; which verbal discourse cannot do, farther than the Judgement shall approve of the Time, Place, and Persons" (Hobbes, 1651, I.8.34, p. 55). Hobbes also insists on the fact that only the individual has access to his thoughts. A thought cannot be censured by another unless it is communicated by behaviors such as speech, gestures, or messages (books, performances, etc.).

At the end of his life, in *The Passions of the Soul*,[12] Descartes makes the distinction between some thoughts as "our will" that come from the soul and go toward the body and "the passions" that are intrusions of the body into the dynamics of the soul. Body sensations are part of thoughts because they are part of what is perceived.

Consciousness and Co-consciousness

> Our mind is nothing else than the sum of our inner experiences, than our ideation, feeling and willing collected to a unity in consciousness. . . . Conscious experience is immediate experience. . . . Our mental experiences are as they are presented to us. The distinction between appearance and reality necessary for the apprehension of the world without . . . ceases to have any meaning when applied to the apprehension of the thinking subject by himself. (Wilhelm Wundt, 1892, *Lectures on Human and Animal Psychology*, 30.V, p. 451f)

The term *consciousness* is today generally used to designate the human capacity to have impressions that one can explicitly perceive. This choice of term is problematic, as we shall now see. Some readers, for example, may have asked themselves why I did not just write that for Descartes thoughts are any conscious psychological phenomena. This definition is indeed adequate if one follows the twentieth-century English used in psychology. Yet taking this custom for granted would prevent us from perceiving several important issues and distinctions concerning conscious dynamics. For example, Descartes is often quoted as being the one who introduced the notion of consciousness in philosophy.[13] To check this intellectual tradition, I downloaded all of Descartes's work and searched for the term conscious. I thus discovered that Descartes uses the word only twice, in a particular way I discuss later on. Another important and related example is Freud's work. He never uses the term consciousness because this word has no direct equivalent in German. The familiar association between Freud and the term unconscious has been introduced by English and French translators. Descartes and Freud use the same terminology: there are psychological events we "know of" (in German, *bewusst*) and others we do "not know of" (*unbewusst*). Yet as we shall see, in French, the term conscience exists. The first interesting point pertaining to this linguistic observation is that the general psychological vocabulary used in Freud's day was probably more influenced by Descartes's theory than is usually assumed. I am not talking of a direct influence, but of one that has implicitly engraved itself in cultural know-how. In the next sections, I show what theoretical issues can be highlighted by reconsidering how the term consciousness has been used and by differentiating the word from the phenomena that are presently labeled as conscious.

Conscious as "Cum-scio" or as Co-conscious

> Conscience. *Noun.* An inner feeling or voice viewed as acting as a guide to the rightness or wrongness of one's behavior: *he had a guilty conscience about his de-*

sires. —origin. Middle English (also in the sense "inner thoughts or knowledge").
(*The New Oxford Dictionary of English,* 1999)

> And this was capable from then on of freeing me from all repentance and remorse
> which habitually agitate the consciences of those weak and wavering minds which
> allow themselves to proceed with vacillation to practice as being good things
> which they judge afterwards to be bad. (Descartes, 1637, *Discourse on Method,*
> Discourse, 3, p. 47)

In the seventeenth century, the word conscious had another meaning, closer to
its Latin etymology. The first meaning of the word conscious in Latin, such as it
evolved in ancient Rome, is that of a shared knowledge (*cum-scio,* "knowledge
with"). This term was originally used in court proceedings. A fact became conscious for the ancient Romans when the court could establish, with the testimony of witnesses, a version of the facts that could be accepted by all. Hobbes[14]
perfectly summarizes the meaning of this term at that time: "When two, or
more men, know of one and the same fact, they are said to be conscious of it
one to another; which is as much as know it together" (Hobbes, 1651, I.7.31,
p. 50).

The Latin word *conscientia* means complicity, confidence, intimate knowledge, conviction.[15] This brings us back to the transpersonal dimension of the
mind; but this dimension is examined from another angle than the one I brought
up in the sections dedicated to platonic Idealism. For Descartes and Hobbes,
there is consciousness when many people think that others have a thought similar to theirs. Consciousness is like a kind of electric plug of the mind that allows
it to branch out on a network of social communication. The distinction is important. In one case, we have individual thoughts that influence only the individual who has them. In the other case, we have thoughts that circulate from
soul to soul and form the support of the social networks, like justice, ideologies,
art, or science. To know that we are many who follow a law or accept that the
Earth turns around the sun is consciousness. In that sense, according to Hobbes,
animals would not have consciousness.

Recently, several psychologists have become interested in phenomena that
are close to the notion that consciousness is a form of shared thinking. They
study how a psychological impression often emerges out of a co-construction
between several persons.[16] Thus, to designate the appearance of the conscious
thoughts that an infant constructs while interacting with his parents, Philippe
Rochat speaks of co-consciousness.[17] Given the first meaning of the word conscious, the notion of co-consciousness, such as Rochat uses it, is a pleonasm.
However, the pleonasm is necessary today as soon as we speak of something
that is explicitly known by many people.

In psychotherapy, it is essential to distinguish between what an individual is
conscious of and the conscious construction that is built between the psychotherapist and the patient. In analyzing a dream, the psychotherapist constructs,
with the patient, a series of images that are associated to the way the patient

experiences what is going on within and outside of himself. Experiencing in his own body the impact of the patient's respiration, the body psychotherapist facilitates a dialogue that builds a representation of what the patient does to himself and others when he breathes in a particular fashion. In this type of discussion, which is central in psychotherapy, it is essential to differentiate sharply the thoughts of the patient, the thoughts of the therapist, and the co-construction that is created thanks to the dialogue between the therapist and the patient. This co-construction emerges out of an attempt to coordinate the elements contained in the two individual organisms.[18]

The second common meaning of the French word conscience in the seventeenth century connotes having a good or bad conscience. It consists of a type of thought strongly influenced by the moral and religious value system of the culture in which a person lives. That is the meaning Descartes associates with the term consciousness the two times where he uses the word conscience.

Conscious Thoughts

Aware. *Adjective.* Having knowledge or perception of a situation or fact. (*The New Oxford Dictionary of English,* 1999)

Men think themselves free, because they are conscious of their volitions and their appetite. (Spinoza, *Ethics,* 1677a, I. Appendix, p. 26)

All the perceptions of the human mind resolve themselves into two distinct kinds, which I shall call impressions and ideas. The difference betwixt these consists in the degrees of force and liveliness, which they strike upon the mind, and make their way into our thought or consciousness. (David Hume, 1737, *Treatise of Human Nature,* I.1.1, p. 7)

The most sophisticated meaning of the word conscious, in a dictionary of the English language,[19] designates the capacity to have reflective thoughts, that is, to be able to perceive the existence of a thought. In this case, the dictionaries recommend the use of the term awareness. This meaning of the word conscious, in the sense of an intimate psychological capacity, appears around 1676, with some of Descartes's students like Malebranche and Spinoza. Hobbes had announced this tendency when he writes that the French word conscience is about to lose its usual meaning: "Afterwards, men made use of the same word metaphorically, for the knowledge of their own secret facts, and secret thoughts" (Hobbes, 1651, I.7.31, p. 50). The idea of an "intimate consciousness" becomes generalized in the eighteenth century in the writings of popular authors like Jean-Jacques Rousseau and David Hume, to designate immediate knowledge, more or less intuitive, of a thing inside or outside of oneself.[20] Today, this meaning derived from the French word conscience dominates to the point that we have forgotten its original meaning. In the psychotherapeutic literature, there is yet another complication: Freud's opposition between the conscious and the unconscious on the one hand, and the use of the term awareness in schools such as Gestalt therapy on the other hand.[21] Awareness is then used to designate what Freud would call preconscious dynamics. One cannot be conscious, at a given moment, of more than a few items, but we are surrounded by events we could become aware of if we paid attention to them. I may not realize that my fingers are taping rapidly on one of my knees, but if a person asks why I am moving my fingers in this way, I will immediately become aware of it. Or I may meet someone and not notice the color of this person's eyes, as I was focusing on others aspects of his appearance. If somebody asks me if I noticed this person's beautiful green eyes, I can then look again and notice them. One can also learn to develop a finer perception by using awareness exercises.

After this semantic digression, I use, like everybody, the word conscious to designate the thoughts of Descartes and the *bewusst* of Freud; but I maintain a clear theoretical distinction between the inner consciousness of an individual and the communication between the consciousness of more than one individual. The relevance of this distinction is evident as soon as we take into account the fact that a thought constructed by two organisms is not of the same nature as a thought constructed in one.

THE SOUL AS A BOAT THAT TRIES TO SURVIVE AN ENDLESS STORM

An "instinct" appears to us as a concept on the frontier between the mental and the somatic as the psychical representative of the stimuli originating from within the organism and reaching the mind as a measure of the demand made upon the mind for work in consequence of its connection with the body. (Freud, 1915b, *Instincts and Their Vicissitudes,* 214, p. 122).

The Psychologist Is Not Competent in Biology and the Biologist Is Not Competent in Psychology

The Descartes, Spinoza, and Leibniz trio gave precision to the framework still in effect: neurologists know how to study the nervous system, and psychologists know how to study the mind. In their discussions, psychologists and neurologists can notice that there exists connections between their respective domains, because a cervical lesion modifies specific capacities of the mind (even the Greeks and the yogis of antiquity knew this); however, they remain unable to describe the nature and the functioning of these connections. Neurologists are not able to explain the dynamics of the mind by observing the brain, and psychologists are not able to explain the dynamics of the brain by observing the mind. The more that the scientists go into details, the less they see solutions. On the other hand, that which psychologists observe can permit the elaboration of suppositions (of hypotheses) that can encourage a neurologist to observe the far reaches of an organism that one hitherto had the tendency to ignore, and vice versa.

The data from psychophysiology is closer to the imaginations of the Hindus and the Chinese who presuppose a series of complex links between many dimensions of the mind and the body. The Europeans, boxed in by the soul/body polarity of the Idealists, can only envision one body and one mind per person. Everything happens a bit as if a laboratory were to use ever more powerful microscopes to seek out, between two points, what allows them to draw a line on a sheet of paper. The more detailed the enlargement, the more powerful the microscope that explores the space between the points in the line formed by the ink from the pen, showing the detail of the cells of the paper's cellulose, consequently finding nothing that could resemble what links the points in the line.

Crouching down into the world of his thoughts, Descartes hoped to be able to observe the junction between the soul and the body. However, because his thoughts observed but his thoughts, he found nothing. By incessantly fixing his sights on the space between the two points, he ended up seeing double. His imagination took over, as it does with all those who tried to clearly think about the juncture between body and thoughts. Descartes invented a gadget for himself that allowed him to express the ideas that have formed within him relative to this connection without being able to do so coherently. This gadget, which he names the H gland,[22] has somewhat of the same function as Plato's fables. I do not know why all those who try to define the junction between the soul and the body end up imagining an instructive but delusional mechanism like in the following examples:

1. The philosopher and mathematician Gottfried Wilhelm Leibniz: *The Monadology* (1714), where everything is linked to everything.
2. The medical sexologist and psychoanalyst Wilhelm Reich: *The Cosmic Superposition* (1951), where everything is regulated by the cosmic energy.
3. The neurologist and Nobel Prize laureate Gerald M. Edelman, in *On the Matter of the Mind* (1992), claims that he can explain everything with his mysterious qualia, which has some hints of the pineal gland and the monad.

These are all members of the intellectual aristocracy! On the other hand, persons who have maintained a classical and academic approach to the issue[23] abandon us as soon as we look at the space that separates the two points of a line: the structure of the brain and the structure of a thought. They have one foot in psychology, the other foot in neurology, and remain unable to find a bridge.

The Body as an Infernal Prison

Descartes and Leibniz both thought that God made the body and the soul separately, but in such a way that they could cooperate. It is only because God exists that Descartes lets himself think that the senses bring relevant information to the soul about what is happening around the organism. The I who thinks about the resources that God deigned to place in the soul is terribly dependent on the body and the senses to obtain information about what surrounds him. The flesh is made up of organic systems that we can begin to detail in a reliable way in the seventeenth century; it functions without the I's ability to feel (by introspection) what is at play. The soul is indeed a reflexive system, but it is also a kind of impasse. Some information produced by the body is swallowed up by the soul and then emerges transformed. The body, according to Descartes, is the space from whence information leaves and returns.

The body has the capacity to react automatically to its environment via mechanisms like the reflexes that are observable in all animals. These reactions, often effective, have no need of the soul and seek her out only occasionally. The soul tries to influence these sensorimotor reactions so that the body and the soul can together create forms of behaviors that cannot be produced by the reflexes of the body. Descartes situates the affects (passions) at the heart of this to and fro:

1. The affects are thoughts that form in the soul under the influence of some tumultuous dynamics of the body.
2. Their intrusion is always problematic for the soul because they are regulated according to automatic reflexes that influence the soul without being able to manage what is already happening in the mind.
3. The affects are nonetheless useful, even crucial, because they allow a thought to move the body.

This analysis is not so far from certain approaches in body psychotherapy like the one described by Jane R. Wheatley-Crosbie (2006) in an article that describes a cure during which "psyche's return from soma's underworld." From the point of view of philosophers like Descartes and Spinoza, the individual cannot truly become himself without learning how to understand his passions and the way they impose the logic of the body on the dynamics of the mind. Consequently, a therapy of the soul is necessarily a form of body psychotherapy that focuses on how body and mind interact with each other.

The Vitality of the Body

William Harvey had described the circulation of the blood[24] when Descartes was thirty years old. This discovery struck Descartes's imagination, and he then set about using Harvey's theory to describe the link between the soul and the body. He therefore devised a vision of the impassioned body, animated by wild dynamics, that is everything save what we ordinarily refer to as Cartesian. Descartes proposes a precise and detailed vision that takes into account all that is known, but one that invents connections where there is no evidence to allow for a view of the whole.

Descartes's concept of the body is of a sort of hydraulic robot that is animated by great physiological systems that interact with each other like dancers at a ball. It appears as a precise choreography, probably foreseen by God; in practice, the dancers sometimes let themselves be carried away by their enthusiasm and bang into each other.

The body is composed of distinct systems such as the skeleton, the muscles, the nervous system, the circulation of the blood and the heart, the lungs, as well as the deeper organs (liver, spleen, kidneys, etc.). These systems are already relatively well known. Things become more difficult when Descartes tries to understand how these systems interact. He knows that certain organs discharge products into the bloodstream, that oxygen is transported by the blood—in short, that the blood links all of the tissues of the body. The arterial blood nourishes the tissues. Venous blood, as a sewage system, takes their toxins and distributes these waste products in diverse organs, principally the kidneys and the lungs. The second system that strongly participates in the organization of the human organism is the nervous system because it coordinates what the senses bring to the body, what certain nerves detect in the body, and the orders given to the muscles. For Descartes, matter is by nature living and dynamic without the soul having any role in it. The flesh has its own sensual and juicy dynamics, whereas the soul has its capacity for wisdom. After all, like the soul, the flesh was created by God. Where Descartes's imagination becomes both stimulating and whimsical is when he sets about to describe, in *The Passions of the Soul*, the interactions between the circulation of the blood and the nervous system to try to define the dynamics between the soul and the body. This work is always full of learning if we read it attentively, trying to bring to mind the details of Descartes's imaginative device.

Descartes knows that blood must fight gravity on the way to the head. He imagines that the heavier particles of blood stay at the bottom, and only the lighter and smaller particles irrigate the brain. The most refined ones are retained by the nerve tissues to become a "spirit" that will flow in the nerves and form the nerve impulses. The word spirit is to be taken here in the chemical sense, like a state between liquid and gas that breathes agreeably in a glass of cognac or brandy. Once it is admitted that the nervous fluids are refined blood, it becomes possible to think that (a) the dynamics of the heart can influence the nervous system, and (b) all that influences the nervous system can indirectly influence the circulation of blood. Thus, a muscle is a kind of bag that is treated in two ways by the blood:

1. The blood fills the muscle like a wineskin, hardens it, and then retires.
2. The nervous fluids that contract the muscles are also a derivative of blood.

The sensory organs provoke the movement of fluids in the nerves that can directly animate the muscles. This is the way Descartes explains the activity of the reflexes, or the habits that make a body move without the intervention of thoughts. Instincts,[25] like hunger and thirst, are also mechanisms that arise from the body and make the fluids move toward the muscles and the soul.

The Connections between the Soul and the Body

For Descartes, there are three links between the soul and the body:

1. The soul is "jointly" linked to all the parts of the body via the mechanisms that regulate "the assembling of organs" (Descartes, 1649, *Passions of the Soul*, I.30). He specifies that there is no spatial connection between the body and the soul, probably to dispel the theoretical tradition that professes that each part of the body corresponds to a property of the soul.
2. The cerebral nerves have a privileged connection to the soul. In reading *The Passions of the Soul,* I sometimes have the impression that the cavities in the brain are grottos in sea cliffs in which the tides exercise more or less strong fluctuations at the convenience of bodily events. These fluctuations also influence the soul.
3. Finally, there is the famous H gland. This gland would have a particularly important blood pathway, and therefore would be the power station that transforms the blood into nerve impulses. Suspended in a void, it can be moved from the inside by the soul or from the outside by the fluids of the body. Descartes uses this theoretical "gadget" with the same enthusiasm as a child who learns to use a joystick to play a video game, or a person who enjoys changing the speed of a race car.

The important point that the H gland introduces into future psychology is that the link between the psyche and the soma is full of unforeseeable events that are therefore difficult to master and understand. The connections between the body and the psyche that are made via the H gland are subject to a great variability quite close to random. The large number of variables that can influence this gland at a given moment make it such that a stimulus (an animal approaches) can provoke different reactions (fear, courage, indifference) in different persons or in a person at a different moment or even arouse the three passions at the same time.

Descartes also shows the enormous physiological mobilization that accompanies the slightest reflex, the slightest stimulation, and the fact that a stimulus can, in the same instance, introduce a quick behavioral reaction and slowly become a thought in the soul. In this system, there can easily be conflict between several drives, between drives and the desires of the soul, or between the will and the drives.[26] The soul can also influence a drive to regulate another drive. A passion is in general a high stake for the body (what does the body good and what does the body ill) that transforms itself into a thought to recruit the help of the soul. At the same time, a passion recruits the resources of the organism so that the will of the soul might have the logistic support necessary to act.

No one believes that the H gland could be the connection between body and thoughts. The current theories lean more favorably toward the first point on Descartes's list (the connection between the psyche and the organization of the organism). However, in showing all of the forces and stakes at play that could move this gland, Descartes finds a metaphor that makes it possible to show the extraordinary power of the interactions between the realm of thoughts, the sensorimotor circuits, and the affective dynamics. He also shows that these interactions mobilize, in a massive way, the collection of physiological mechanisms—in other words, "the assembling of the organs." Today, the organization of the organs is on the verge of being detailed by research; it serves as a foundation for the idea that psychological dynamics inevitably interact with the powerful currents of the organism.

A last important point in the mind of Descartes that will be taken up by Spinoza and in particular by Hume is that the domain of the passions play a crucial role in sorting out physiological mobilization, behavior, and thought.

Descartes shows how these systems are both heterogeneous and connected (linked notably by the blood). They are heterogeneous to the extent that they are constituted of materials so different that they do not have the same properties. The substances that link these systems (blood and nerve impulse) have properties that are their own. Finally, even in the soul, we find thoughts that have a different logistic support. The sensory data, the passions, and the instincts have distinct physiological mechanics that have different impacts on the soul and manifest differently thereon. The intellectual intuitions come from the soul, and they have an impact on the body that is not that of the perceptions, the passions, and the instincts.

5

Spinoza's Parallelist Systemics Situates the Mind in a Lay Universe

SPINOZA'S THEORY ON NATURE, SOCIETY, AND THE INDIVIDUAL

A Project for Democracy

In the seventeenth century, there were many different kinds of republics in Europe, like the Swiss Confederation, the Italian republics (Venice and Florence), and the "free cities" of the German empire. But Europe was mostly governed by kings and lords supported by the Catholic Church. Baruch de Spinoza (1632–1677) grew up in the Republic of the United Provinces (The Netherlands). Like the Swiss Confederation, the Netherlands were formed while getting rid of the Habsburgs. However, this time, it was the Spanish Catholic Habsburgs that were chased away by the Flemish Protestants. Certain movements within this republic had hoped to distribute the power to a greater number of citizens. They wanted to form a democracy in the image of the Athenian republic at the time of Pericles. They held power from 1653 to 1672. They installed Johan de Witt as the Grand Pensionary of Holland.

Spinoza felt this project needed the support of an appropriate global vision of the world. He decided to elaborate a proposition in that direction. He detailed his new vision of the place of humans in nature in his *Ethics* and in *A Political Treatise,* published the year of his death, 1677. These works are evidently a response to Plato's *Republic.* They attempt to demonstrate that a democracy is a regime that conforms to nature's functioning, and consequently is more creative than an enlightened tyranny that served as the model for most of the nobility, kings, and emperors of the Europe of his day, and even in most of the former republics.

Spinoza Takes Us from a Universe Created by Superior Forces to a World that Spontaneously Organizes Itself

> That eternal and infinite being we call God *or* nature, acts from the same necessity from which he exists. (Spinoza, 1677a, *Ethics* IV, preface, II/207, p. 114)

> As soon as we intend to know all the variety of causes and conditions influencing, directly or indirectly, a given event, causation appears so complicated that it practically becomes unrecognizable. No one short of an Omniscient Being could cognize the infinite variety of all circumstances that can influence the production of an event. (Stcherbatsky, 1930, *Buddhist logic*, II.II.6, p. 129)[1]

In the first part of his *Ethics,* Spinoza indicates that the notion of democracy is incompatible with that of a universe created by God. A creator God leads us to the concept of a universe that exists only by the grace of an exterior almighty force. Applied to human history, this metaphor suggests that a society is incapable of organizing itself without the intervention of an exterior almighty being, that is, a king. The more a sovereign is powerful, the more he lives beyond the rules that govern the citizens, and the more he has the capacity to impose the politics that structure his kingdom. On the contrary, if we conceive of a universe that created itself, it becomes possible to imagine that a population can govern itself. For Spinoza, this second conceptualization is the most probable. The fact that a creator God could exist is as extraordinary, inexplicable, and improbable as a universe capable of creating itself. It is therefore more economical[2] and more rational to imagine a universe that created itself.

The terms *God, nature,* or *universe*[3] are interchangeable in Spinoza's mind. Nature has almost all of the properties previously attributed to God. It is infinitely vast and powerful. It is composed of an infinite number of elements, dimensions, and attributes. Because the universe has all of the properties of God, it has the power to create itself in a coherent fashion. The only one of God's properties that the universe does not possess is that of being a spirit—a spiritual force that has a center, a will, a plan, and a goal that elaborates itself outside of the universe. Spinoza replaces an imaginary entity that fills fables and myths by an *intellection*[4] of what exists and whose shape is about to be clarified by scientific research (Galileo, Newton, etc.). Spinoza breaks down this global universe into subsystems (galaxies, planets, societies, individuals, organs, etc.). Each system participates in the formation of its subsystems, all the while being structured by them. They emerge out of a coordination of subsystems that constitute themselves in function of what contains them. Nature is what emerges out of the interactions between all the existing systems. A human organism is a totality that emerges out of the interactions that combines all of its organs; it is also structured by the cultural systems (family, government, beliefs, knowledge, etc.) that contain it. The complexity of all of these connections is such that it is out of the question that a single subsystem, such as the mind, could apprehend everything that regulates it.[5]

The Notion of Complexity in Spinoza's System

In the following sections, I detail the three aspects of a system distinguished by Spinoza: the *dimensions,* the *coordination of parts,* and *power.* This analysis is used to introduce the notion of complexity in *systemics.* The complexity of an individual human system is necessarily nonconscious. Introspection and perception can only discover some *manifestations* of this complexity that organizes the mind of an individual. An individual system of representation does not have the capacity to apprehend an organization that follows rules more complicated than what the human mind can imagine. On the other hand, it happens that discoveries achieved by institutions, like institutes of scientific research, produce data that can enrich the imagination of those who have heard of their work. Therefore, all those who have seen cells or constellations in movies have an imagination capable of conceiving that these entities exist. Their mind, if it is taken up by these images, can then research supplementary sources of information by questioning those who study these phenomena, by reading, or by becoming capable of using certain optical tools. This metaphor is pertinent in this chapter because Spinoza was an optician.

The Notion of a Dimension Introduces That of an Organism

The term *dimension* designates, in Spinoza as in Descartes, entities that have different basic modes of functioning. Spinoza supposes that there exist an infinite number of dimensions in the universe; he admits that the human spirit can conceive of only two: matter and thought. The limits of the human mind make it impossible to know if the human organism has more than two dimensions, but Spinoza supposes that it is probably the case.

For Descartes, the notion of an organism exists only in as much as there is an H gland. Spinoza[6] ridicules this reductionism and shows that the organism is a global system[7] that has at least the two following functions:

1. The organism structures the dynamics of the body and of the spirit, while at the same time being influenced by them.
2. The organism coordinates what goes on in the two dimensions, for the dynamics of these two dimensions cannot interact *directly* because they function differently.

In modern terms, the organism is an *architecture* that permits the hardware of a computer to support the exigencies of the software. This architecture has properties that are neither those of matter nor those of thoughts: they coordinate the dimensions and are sensitive to the dynamics of each dimension. These coordinating interfaces belong to that part of nature that can coordinate an infinite number of dimensions.

With Spinoza, the more dimensions a system contains, the more the coordination of the dimensions demands a powerful global architecture. At this point, it is useful to identify two criteria of complexity:

1. It is possible that two systems would each have two dimensions, but these two dimensions would not be necessarily the same.
2. A subsystem cannot have more dimensions than the system that contains it. Thus, a cell possesses two dimensions at the maximum, whereas a society has two dimensions at the minimum. This evaluation is calculated on the basis of the two dimensions in the human being that contains cells and is also part of a society.

The Multiplicity of Connections in a System

> The human mind is capable of perceiving a great many things, and is the more capable, the more its body can be disposed in a great many ways. (Spinoza, 1677a, *Ethics*, II proposition XIV, p. 44)

> In proportion as a body is more capable than others of doing many things at once, or being acted on in many ways at once, so its mind is more capable than others of perceiving many things at once. (Spinoza, 1677a, *Ethics*, II, Proposition XIII, scholium, p. 40)

The more subsystems that a system contains, the more complex it is because the possibility to organize the parts in different ways is greater. This argument allows one to distinguish between two types of complexity:

1. If all of the parts of a system are identical, only *qualitatively* different forms of organization can generate distinct organizations.
2. If all of the parts are different (heterogeneous), a single combining rule can create different organizations.

In an alphabet made up of two letters (A and B), it is possible to generate four basic combinations (words): A, B, AB, and BA. On the other hand, by adding the following two rules, I can generate an infinite number of words with two letters:

1. A *quantitative rule* allows me to include as many letters "A" and "B" that I want in a word.
2. A *qualitative rule* distinguishes the order of the words (AB is not equal to BA).

These are the basic rules of binary language, developed a little later by Leibniz, which is used today by computer programmers. The greater the number of elements in a system (for example, twenty-six letters instead of two), and the greater the number of different rules (like grammatical rules), the greater the possibility of generating a vast variety of combinations. The more these elements and rules are qualitatively heterogeneous, the greater the potential complexity of an organization.

A subsystem can be more or less active, that is, it can participate more or less actively in the organization of the relationships that it entertains with other subsystems. One of the implications of this way of thinking is that the more complex a system, the more it has the capacity to rearrange its organization locally and globally. The mind of an individual, for example, is capable of important rearrangements if society affords it new information. A society can rearrange the relationship between citizens if the citizens can be convinced to do so. For Spinoza, these changes are only *improvements* if the complexity of social dynamics becomes closer to the dynamics of nature.[8] At this level the philosopher and the scientist can enrich the social system in which they are a part.

To the extent that a system perceives and masters its capacity to change, in a similar manner, it can adapt itself profoundly to the laws of nature. For Spinoza, to understand the laws of nature (he does not believe it is possible to function outside of these laws) is to accept the inevitable. It is also to be able to learn to better use available resources. For example, democracy would be superior to tyranny for at least two reasons:

1. Individuals in a democratic society can more easily become active, and thus complex. This permits them to have a greater variety of relationships between them which makes possible a greater social complexity.
2. The greater complexity of democratic societies more easily promotes the activity of the citizens. It is therefore closer to the dynamics of nature.

A society that is maintained under the yoke of a tyranny allows for fewer combinations between citizens; therefore, it allows only for a restricted exploitation of the possibilities contained in a social system and within each of its citizens. In summary, tyranny has the tendency to reduce the functioning of a society to what the leaders have been able to imagine and conceptualize. On the other hand, democracy allows for a greater number of nonconscious regulations to be established, and it mobilizes a greater variety of individual forms of imagination.

The Power of a System

ORGANISM, THOUGHTS, AFFECTS, PASSIONS, AND BODY

> Mistake the false for the true,
> And the true for the false,
> You overlook the heart
> And fill yourself with desire

. . . .
An unreflecting mind is a poor roof.
Passion, like the rain, floods the house,
But if the roof is strong, there is shelter.
(Byron, 1993, *Dhammapada: The Sayings of the Buddha*, I, p. 4)

At this moment, we have considered two notions that permit us to characterize the mechanisms of the functioning of an organism:

1. The *dimensions* of the body and of the mind.
2. The *organization* of the parts of the organism.

Like Descartes, Spinoza situates the affects in the organismic mechanisms that coordinate the mind and the body. To put this operation into effect in a manner coherent with his system, Spinoza introduces the notion of *power*. An organism has a basic *power* that can express itself more or less fully. This power is at its maximum when all of the possibilities of a system are immediately accessible (as in an ideal democracy), and at its minimum when many possibilities are inhibited, consider frozen (as in an unjust tyranny, or a body hampered by multiple chronic muscular tensions). This power gives an organism the force "to do something" and "to persevere in its own being" to attain a goal.[9] The affects are part of the mechanisms that regulate this power. They are therefore neither part of the body nor of the mind,[10] but of the architecture that connects them.

The quality of these organismic regulators modifies the power of the organism and depends on the adequacy of the thoughts. An *inadequate* thought is one that creates a partial or false representation of an event.[11] When a person fully understands what is going on around him, the impact of the thoughts on the organism permits him to organize himself adequately and, consequently, to organize an adequate behavior. When a situation is perceived inadequately, the system of affective regulation becomes a *passion*—that is, a form of inadequate regulation of the organism that will diminish its power and the relevance of the behaviors that an individual system activates.[12] Misunderstanding what is happening in one's family automatically engenders passions that deregulate the organism.

A thought is, by its very nature, inadequate to the extent that a thought is built on a partial perception of what is happening and is managed only by the tools of the mind. It is therefore predictable that from time to time the passions will take over the power in an organism. But there are moments, situations, and persons (e.g., trauma and abuse) who engender particularly inadequate thoughts. These deregulations inhibit the power of the organism, engender depressive moods, and increase the error of the initial capacity to understand. To the extent that organismic regulations influence behavior, there will also be dysfunction in the way the organism participates in the interactions of a group and influences the functioning of the group and the organisms that constitute the group. Thus, vicious circles can come about that increase the potential of a person's passions within a group or even all the individuals in the group. If a psychotherapist can help someone better understand what happened and what is happening, not only will the mind be helped but the remainder of the entire system will be helped as well.

SPINOZA AND ANTIDEPRESSANTS

> *Clinical observation n. 5.* A young family man is struck with a fast spreading melanoma already in multiple locations thus creating a serious risk of a brutal death caused by hemorrhaging. He refused to see his wife and children, and maintains a hostile attitude toward the staff because he deems his room unacceptable and his roommate disagreeable. Clearly, this man is extremely traumatized and in anguish. He is totally disconnected from his situation. He cannot reflect and adopt a mood to make better use of the time he has left. (Patrice Guex, 1989, *An Introduction to Psycho-Oncology,* p. 128; translated by Marcel Duclos)

Patrick Guex's case illustrates the topic of this section if we admit that in this instance, the reactions of the patient were really irrational and were caused by an extreme dread, not only because of his reaction to having cancer but also by the impact of the disease on his psychophysiology. The example would be trivial if the extreme anxiety of the patient were caused only by a disagreeable roommate and the fears that cancer inevitably activates. We have here an example of the difficulty of evaluating clinical data. We must have confidence in Patrick Guex, who was at the time already a skilled clinician, and that what we have here is really anxiety amplified by the impact of the melanoma on the power of the organism.

Even if Spinoza does not envision an intervention that rises up from the body to influence thoughts, his theory allows for it. If the body functions inadequately, the organism will become dysfunctional, and it will engender inadequate reasoning such that renders the dysfunction of the organism even more severe. This is the reciprocal of the cognitive reasoning developed in the previous section. This is what psychiatrists observe and report when they study the impact of cancer on the mind, of neurotransmitters on depression, or of a thyroid disease on mood.

Spinoza's systemic model allows one to understand how something as insignificant as a pill may improve the functioning of the affects and, through this, the dimensions of mind and body. Contemporary biological research demonstrates that depression is notably caused by the production of insufficient neurotransmitters like serotonin and/or by an underdevelopment of neurotransmitter receptor sites. Depression is generally characterized as a weakening of the power of the organism, a turning of aggression against this power, and repetitively devaluing thoughts. These thoughts are part of what Spinoza calls a *passive spirit.*[13] Depressive feelings are typically a passion that turns aggression against self and engenders dark thoughts—sometimes suicidal ones. A classical cognitive treatment begins with work on the inadequate thoughts. A classical biological treat-ment starts by compensating for the lack of serotonin. Taken regularly for at least a year, the antidepressant "teaches" the mechanisms of the organism to live with a stronger dose of serotonin.[14]

It would therefore seem that the depressive affect is related to the organis-mic regulators that generate dark thoughts, which reinforce destructive vicious circles that install themselves in the dynamics of the organism. It is often impos-sible to know if depression is mostly created by inadequate thoughts or by a lack of serotonin. What is certain is that once a depression is established, these two dynamics mutually reinforce each other. It would seem that a therapy that acts on one of the dimensions can have an impact on the other. Sometimes, both modes of intervention must be used together.

Patients who take antidepressants and the patients whose depression is lifted through psychotherapy often report that they now react less violently to what is happening, that they no longer take every word or every phrase like a personal attack, or perceive every single tragedy in the world showed on televi-sion as a personal crisis. Something of the order of the regulation of the mind and the affects creates a personal space in which a patient can relax and redis-cover his immediate needs. He takes anew the time to reflect on his personal preoccupations, without being distressed by everything that is going on around him. It is not so much a distancing oneself from others but the taking of one's own personal space.

Therefore, I can also use Spinoza's model to define certain outlines of mind-body interventions, even if this did not enter into his objectives. This is because he includes a parallelist constraint in the face of the "everything influences ev-erything" that renders comprehensible the interaction between the mind and the body.

MENTAL STRUCTURE, SPONTANEOUS ILLUSIONS, AND PROJECTIONS

Men think of themselves as free because they are conscious of their volitions and their appetite, and do not think, even in their dreams, of the causes by which they are disposed to wanting and willing, because they are ignorant of those causes. (Spinoza, 1677a, *Ethics*, I, appendix I, II/79, p. 26)

The Inherent Perversions of the Mind

This doctrine concerning the end turns nature completely upside down. For what is really a cause, it considers as an effect, and conversely (what is an effect it con-siders as a cause). (Spinoza, 1677a, *Ethics*, I, appendix II, II/81, p. 28)

To reflect with ease, the thinking individual needs to have the *impression* that he is reasoning on all of the existing data. The mind has difficulty including in its reasoning the fact that it is influenced by the very forces it wants to control. Humans automatically have the impression that the functioning of nature is so simple that they can easily understand it.[15] This impression creates a form of the reversal that characterizes perversion. The human being believes to be the cause of what is going on around him, whereas very often this perception is organized by an environment that thoughts perceive only in a partial way.

Imagination, Reason, and Intuition

> Primates are visual animals, and we think best in pictorial or geometric terms. Words are an evolutionary afterthought. The power of pictures, as epitomes or encapsulators of central concepts in our culture, may best be appreciated in studying what I like to call "canonical icons," or standard images that automatically trigger a body of associations connected with an important theory. (Stephen Jay Gould, 1996, *Dinosaur in a Haystack*, p. 249)

Spinoza distinguishes among three subsystems of the mind:

1. The *imagination*: Spinoza's imagination receives the material that the senses and the memory continually pour into the mind.[16] It also contains certain mechanisms that permit the rapid organization of this mass of thoughts, like the mechanisms that associate all of the events that arrive in consciousness at the same time. This level is important to the extent that it brings forth the psychic materials that can be elaborated later.
2. *Reason* allows for the relatively logical organization of the material produced in the imagination.
3. *Intuition* is nourished by those aspects of the human mind that contain more of the aspects of nature. These are no longer the fully formed Ideas of Plato and Descartes, but a "know-how" inspired by this complexity of which humans are a part. To be alert to our intuitions is to admit that there exist forces that regulate thoughts.

These three subsystems are part of the psychic system, from which the mind emerges. They do not necessarily act on the same materials at a given moment. Identical perceptions are not organized in the same way in these three levels of the mind.

To illustrate this analysis, Spinoza takes the example of the impact of a sunset on a person's thoughts. A first series of information about the sun comes from the way it is integrated in the physiological dynamics[17] that are activated when the solar rays reach the retina. This activity unfolds automatically in a nonconscious way. The organism will then create in the mind representations derived from the activity of the sensory nervous system. The mechanisms that translate nervous impulses into thoughts are unknown. However, once these representations enter the mind, they first follow psychological laws such as those of Spinoza's imagination. Given that these first mechanisms are primitive, they will create a kind of illusion that inspires poets but not the astronomer:[18]

> When we look at the sun, we imagine it as about two hundred feet away from us,
> an error which does not consist simply in his imagining, but in the fact that while
> we imagine it in this way, we are ignorant of its true distance and of the cause of
> this imagining. For even if we later come to know that it is more than six hundred
> diameters of the earth away from us, we nevertheless imagine it as near. For we
> imagine the sun near not because we do not know its true distance, but because an
> affection of our body involves the essence of the sun insofar as our body is affected
> by the sun. (Spinoza, 1677a, *Ethics*, II, proposition XXXV, scholium, p. 53f)

Given that thoughts are not conscious of being fabricated by the nervous
system, the individual has the impression that his perceptions correspond to reality. Siegfried Frey has recently indicated, with research to back it up, that this
impression is not negotiable, even when various lectures and trainings indicate
that these impressions are illusions. In this way, Frey and Masters explain the
incredible impact of the visual media (especially television) on citizens.[19] Spinoza's imagination is thus a type of thinking that perceives the sun as a sphere that
descends behind the horizon, and reacts as if what is perceived is what is. Imagination has no more critical sense than a camera.

Spinoza's reason takes up this perception of the sun in a parallel fashion,
without annulling the impression furnished by the imagination, and associates
it to the understanding proposed by astronomers.[20] Reason creates verbal and
mathematical representations that can be combined in logical fashion. As far as
an experience created in the nervous system, this second layer of information
and reflection is of a different nature than those produced by the impact of the
sun on the retina. Thoughts can distinguish between these two types of information, which explains why they do not match up. To the extent that information
taught to people is often unreliable, it is probably useful that the human mind
spontaneously distinguishes between information that comes from qualitatively
different sources and uses different procedures to assimilate them. That is how
Spinoza explains the fact that even astronomers like him love to look at the setting sun as it seems to slip below the horizon.

We therefore notice a parallel functioning of the mind that is made explicit
by philosophers and some psychologists. Once this point is recognized by an
individual, there are two different ethical positions that can be developed:

1. A *fatalistic* option. This is how our spirit is made, and our consciousness
   has nothing else to do but to suffer the storms that our physiology and
   environment impose.
2. A *constructivist*[21] option. This analysis is enlightening because it allows
   us to find new ways of coordinating these two dynamics of the mind.

These are the types of issues that daily arise during a psychotherapeutic
practice. We know that asking too much from oneself can bring about anxiety
and depression (it is often one of the main causes of depression), whereas on the
other hand, having too few expectations hinders the mobilization of a person's
resources or those of his environment. This way of distinguishing the relatively

independent layers of the mind is useful for getting a handle on a delicate point for the psychotherapeutic profession: how to measure out personal authenticity and professionalism. To be able to experience the poetry of a sunset without forgetting one's astronomy is to be on the road to becoming a therapist.

The Regulation of the Organism by Social Dynamics

Spinoza also uses affects as an organismic regulator to show: (1) how the human organism defends a functioning that is its own; and (2) how it is regulated by social systems that direct it toward political, theological, economic, and military goals. This theme is developed in *A Political Treatise*,[22] in a section where Spinoza discusses the relationship between *individual* and *social rights*.

Spinoza takes the example of a person who has given his word that he would accomplish a particular action. From the point of view of this person, his promise "remains valid so long as the will of him that gave his word remains unchanged" (Spinoza, 1677b, II.12, p. 296). At this point, the individual has not engaged the power of his organism, only his words.

Spinoza continues by taking the case of two persons who have gone into a partnership based on this given word. They gather the power of the two organisms. The greater the number of partner organisms, the greater the power of the group, and "the more right they all collectively possess" (Spinoza, 1677b, 13, p. 296). The functioning of the group can help or hinder the power mobilized in each organism and consequently, the power of the group. This implies that a system can influence the way a subsystem (the organism) self-regulates. Because the affects are regulators of the power of the organism, the impact of the group influences the functioning of the affects. All of this occurs automatically and in a nonconscious way.

Let us take a secret, as an example.[23] The group hides something from the person who gave his word. Without knowing why, things do not unfold as this person had expected. The group has taken control of some information; the mind of the individual now functions with an inadequate data base, which will transform the affective regulation into a passion. The individual in question will necessarily (according to Spinoza) become dysfunctional. For example, he will spend restless nights asking himself if he ought to take back his word while feeling guilty about it.

The other problem that Spinoza brings up for this person is that the part of the group that holds the secret has greater power. Because they lie, they may also have mobilized other forms of trickery and dangerous intentions that render the individual, who gave his word based on false information, even more vulnerable:

> But inasmuch as in the state of nature each is so long independent, as he can guard against oppression by another, and it is in vain for one man alone to try and guard against all, it follows hence that so long as the natural right of man is determined

by the power of every individual, and belongs to everyone, so long it is a nonentity, existing in opinion rather than fact, as there is no assurance of making it good. And it is certain the greater cause of fear every individual has, the less power, and consequently the less right, he possesses. To this must be added, that without mutual help men can hardly support life and cultivate the mind. (Spinoza, 1677b, II.15, p. 296)

This individual will not find salvation unless he forges a new alliance that will serve him better. In a state with reliable rights, he would be able to file a complaint, that is, make an alliance with another group, which in this case would be the judicial system. An individual can only survive if he accepts becoming part of a group and seeks, as much as possible, constructive alliances for himself.

If this person consults a psychotherapist, the psychotherapist has at least three options:

1. The psychotherapist can concentrate on the *organism of the patient*. The discussion will focus on the patient's tendency to become anxious when he takes his word back. This type of analysis often makes him feel even more guilty because he then believes he is neurotic, mentally disordered. The body psychotherapist will remark, for example, that when the patient feels increasingly guilty, his loss of power is accompanied by a respiratory restriction and a weakening of the organism's grounding.
2. The false information the patient receives from his environment may weaken his confidence in his spontaneous reactions and gut feelings. When he has been surrounded by secrets for many years, he may develop an unsecure relation with reality, which can sometimes lead to a psychotic cleavage and psychotic episodes, with delusional beliefs.[24]
3. The psychotherapist can also work on the *relationship* between the organism of the patient and the situation in which he lives. The therapist uses the therapeutic alliance to give the patient the force to question his network of alliances. They are now two to accomplish this task instead of only one. If the psychotherapist also has the means to discover that those who manipulated his patient hid certain information from him, his task will be greatly facilitated, because the patient's passions will be able to return to appropriate emotions.

The "Spinozan" psychotherapist has a systemic approach not only to the individual organism but also to the situation in which this individual is a part. This is a constant theme in body[25] and systemic[26] psychotherapy.

TOO MUCH COHERENCE

We see then, that every citizen depends not on himself, but on the commonwealth, all whose commands he is bound to execute, and has no right to decide, what is equitable or iniquitous, just or unjust. . . . And so, however iniquitous the subject

may think the commonwealth's decisions, he is none the less bound to execute
them. (Spinoza, 1677b, III.5, p. 302f)

The flaws in Plato's Idealism become particularly apparent in its political implications. It is the same with Spinoza. The quotes at the beginning of this section
indicate how Spinoza's thought can be used to justify the power of the masses
on an individual, which can be as frightening as the power of the elite. Robespierre referred explicitly to Spinoza when he installed the reign of terror and the
guillotine during the first French Revolution (1792–1794). He replaced the
Christian religion with a religion proclaimed by the state: *The Cult of the Supreme Being that is Nature and Reason*. Robespierre also refers to Spinoza to
insist that each citizen appreciate studies, solitary labor, temperance, incorrupt-
ibility, and the cult of virtue. He persecutes and condemns the aristocrats, the
Freemasons, the bachelor (that is against nature) to the guillotine: requiring of
each citizen the abdication of individual freedoms to the benefit of the supreme
common good.

If Plato advocated the taking over of power by the elite, Spinoza did not
wish to see the totalitarianism of the majority come about. But it appeared to
him to be one of the risks implied in a democracy based on his principles. The
trap that this risk affords us to unveil is that Spinoza's system wants to be totally coherent, and it extolls a society that adopts this need to be coherent.

With Plato we discussed the danger of believing that only *harmony* is constructive. Now, with Spinoza, we have discussed the danger of believing that
only *coherence* is creative. I shall not discuss Leibniz, who hoped that the world
could be a harmonious and coherent system. None of these philosophers could
explain in a satisfactory way why our world only had pockets of harmony and
coherence. However, this bias did not prevent them from developing other
themes in a particularly interesting way.

6

Hume and Kant: A Mind without a Soul, without a Body, and without Direction

The cause or causes of order in the universe probably bear some remote analogy to human intelligence. (Hume, 1776, *Dialogues Concerning Natural Religion*, XII, p. 129)

So far from admitting . . . that the operations of a part can afford us any just conclusion concerning the origin of the whole, I will not allow any one part to form a rule for another part. . . . The narrow views of a peasant, who makes his domestic economy the rule for the government of kingdoms, is in comparison a pardonable sophism. (Hume, 1776, *Dialogues Concerning Natural Religion*, II, p. 51)

In the preceding chapters, I have described the creativity with which the philosophers of the seventeenth century integrated the new propositions of physicists like Galileo and Newton. They identified (1) a world of matter about which physicists and physiologists accumulated impressive data, and (2) a world of ideas on which scientists did not dare to pronounce themselves, because they had the impression that it has different properties. They believed that once they could isolate these properties, it would suffice to apply appropriate mathematical formulae to unlock their causal dynamics. This ideal has not been achieved to this day.

The skeptic philosophers of the eighteenth century, especially the Britons George Berkley and David Hume, go even further in demonstrating the absolute necessity of understanding the mind to validate scientific undertakings. Descartes had initiated this meditation; but he forestalled the power of his questions by invoking the existence of God to validate the relevance of the data gathered through the senses. Using God as proof became invalid in a world that presumes that the mind, even if it has particular properties, is part of the dynamics of nature. If we are not able to validate the pertinence of sensory data, then every construction based on these data could be simply a delusion. The same reasoning can be applied to the logical systems produced by the human mind. Thus, science must be validated not only by the technology whose construction it promotes but also by demonstrating that the mind is capable, at least sometimes, of observing and thinking in an adequate and appropriate manner. We know that false reasoning can lead to useful technologies. Berkley and Hume radicalized this critique by exposing it in a more systematic way:

Thus world-enigmas now enter the stage, of a sort previously never imagined, and they bring about a completely new manner of philosophizing, the "epistemological" philosophy, that of the "theory of reason." Soon they also give rise to systematic philosophies with completely novel goals and methods. (Husserl, 1936, II.13, p. 68)

It is necessary to understand how thinking works to understand what the mind can do and the value of its products. If Descartes's "I think, therefore I am" shows the necessity of having a psychology, Kant's *Critique of Pure Reason* demonstrates that it is possible to begin to propose realistic and pertinent models concerning the functioning of the mind and its creativity.

DAVID HUME: A STUDENT IN CRISIS

The Treatise of a Tumultuous Youth

He [Hume] threw no light on this species of knowledge, but he certainly struck a spark from which light might have been obtained, had it caught some inflammable substance and had its smoldering fire been carefully nursed and developed. (Kant, 1783, *Prolegomena*, Preface)

Everyone who is acquainted either with the Philosophers or Critics knows that there is nothing yet established in either of these two Sciences, & that they contain little more than endless Disputes, even in the most fundamental Articles. Upon Examination of these, I found a certain Boldness of temper, growing in me, which was not enclin'd to submit to any Authority in these Subjects. (Hume, quoted in Mossner, 1980, I.5, p. 62)

David Hume (1711–1776) was raised as a Scot Presbyterian Protestant. He was manifestly gifted since his early childhood. His parents wanted him to pursue a career in law, which he studied at the University of Edinburgh. However, his real ambition was to become a writer. To fulfill this ambition, and to cure a recurring depression, he decided to continue his studies in France.[1] He departed for England, and then for France, where he lived close to the Jesuit College of La Fleche, where Descartes had studied a century earlier. In spite of a difficult emotional life, Hume was adept at managing the meager funds provided by his family, read abundantly, was mostly self-taught, and organized himself by writing *A Treatise of Human Nature*.

Hume was twenty-six years old when he published the first part of the treatise in 1737. This edition was "stillborn": it did not sell, and it received few reviews. The entire treatise was finished in 1740. In contrast, his *Essays Moral and Political*, published in 1742, was a resounding success. He then wrote a monumental history of England, which immediately became a best-seller and a reference for the philosophers of the Age of Enlightenment. Instead of focusing on the epic story of kings and the nobility, he used historical inquiry to improve his understanding of human nature. It is therefore as an essayist and a historian that Hume became one of the principal representatives of the Age of Enlightenment in Great Britain and then in Europe.

His *Essays* popularized certain themes of the treatise that, nevertheless, remained rarely read and never understood. In 1748 Hume tried to reformulate the first part of his treatise related to the mind by retaining only the least provocative formulations. He titled it *An Enquiry Concerning Human Understanding*. The inquiry leaves aside his analysis of the passions. This work also had little success. Hume subsequently abandoned philosophy. He and his friend, Adam Smith, became leading figures of a British economic liberalism that played a central role in the Industrial Revolution. His works, except for the *Treatise*, were on every bookshelf in every respectable home in Europe. Hume became one of the first writers to become rich thanks to the sale of his books. His *Treatise* is what we discuss here.

That Which Makes Me Comfortable Is True

> If we were to ask the dispassionate *David Hume*—a philosopher endowed, in a degree that few are, with a well-balanced judgement: What motive induced you to spend so much labour and thought in undermining the consoling and beneficial persuasion that reason is capable of assuring us of the existence, and presenting us with a determinate conception of a Supreme Being?—his answer would be: Nothing but the desire of teaching reason to know its own powers better, and, at the same time, a dislike of the procedure by which that faculty was compelled to support foregone conclusions, and prevented from confessing the internal weaknesses which it cannot but feel when it enters upon a rigid self-examination. (Kant, 1787, *Critique of Pure Reason*, Transcendental Doctrine of Method, I.2, p. 426)

Like Descartes, Hume had enclosed himself in the realm of his thoughts like a gardener who ignores what goes on in the rest of the world. Although he loves to meet people and has an active social life, his garden is a secret realm. He can speak of what he experiences in it, but he wants to be alone when he gardens. He can thus freely lay out his garden as he pleases, experiment in a way that enlivens his intelligence and mood, and ignore the counsels of his elders whom he has read but toward whom he holds the disdain of a young man:

> At the time, therefore, that I am tir'd with amusement and company, and have indulg'd a *reverie* in my chamber, or in a solitary walk by the river-side, I feel my mind all collected within itself, and am naturally *inclin'd* to carry my view into all those subjects, about which I have met with so many disputes in the course of my reading and conversation. (Hume, 1737, 1, 4, 7, p. 176)

Hume's method is apparently simple, because it is common sense wedded to a maximum of intelligence, imagination, and humor. Every notion that is not manifestly evident when it is considered with common sense is considered false.

It is not false in an absolute sense, only useless. Hume takes each great philosophical idea, plays with it as would an infant who shakes his toys, and throws everything that breaks into the garbage. After this dazzling critique, which is simple to understand, Hume keeps only a few relative notions in his garden that he cultivates with great care.

A Mind that Follows Rules without Worrying about Relevance

> In Newton this island may boast of having produced the greatest and rarest genius that ever rose for the ornament and instruction of the species. Cautious in admitting no principles but such as were founded on experiment; but resolute to adopt every such principle, however new and unusual. (Hume, 1792, *History of England*, VI, p. 542)[2]

Hume was still a student when Newton died in 1727. Influenced by the great physicist, Hume assumes that even the affects and thoughts follow laws of causality. Meteorology describes coherent laws that manage the winds, humidity, and seasons. This system acts without taking into account the fact that farmers would like to have sun on such a day, rain during a particular week, and so on. This vision is well summarized by Carl Gustav Jung when he describes the dynamics of dreams:

> We are dealing with a particular way of functioning independent of the human ego's will and wishes, intention or aim. It is an unintentional occurrence, just like everything occurring in nature. So we also cannot assume that the sky gets clouded only to annoy us; it simply is as it is. The difficulty is, however, to get a *handle* on that natural occurrence. (Jung, 1940, p. 2)

For Hume, the mind functions like the climate. It is also a system subject to laws that are particular to it, that act without knowing the workings of all that surrounds it. The mind is a system of algorithms that can manage certain data in a certain way and other data in another way; it excludes the data for which it does not have a procedure. What each individual takes as knowledge is a certain number of thoughts created by psychological algorithms. Society itself follows procedures that coordinate individual productions, thus creating common myths, pretenses to know that are sometimes constructive and often destructive. The human mind can only engender "fictions"[3] created by the algorithms of the mind and the information produced by more or less relevant means through the senses. To pretend to be able to make pronouncements on the existence of God or on the functioning of the universe with such means is, for Hume, a form of omnipotence.[4]   .

This notion of fiction starts with the idea that before Newton, philosophers thought the universe worked the way they imagined it to work, or the way a culture conceived it to be. It became impossible for Hume to think like that anymore, because science had just taken a decisive step showing that the derivatives of the mind are speculative when they are not supported by solid empirical data and interrelated with sound common sense and rational laws like those of mathematics.

Intensity, Thoughts, and Affects

As Hume noted in The Natural History of Religion, the greater the impact of events on our lives, the greater is our drive to impose purpose and coherence on those events. (Scott Atran, 2010, *The Evolution of Religion*, p. 19)

There are some philosophers who imagine we are every moment intimately conscious of what we call our self. . . . For my part, when I enter most intimately into what I call myself, I always stumble on some particular perception or other, of heat or cold, light or shade, love or hatred, pain or pleasure. I never can catch myself at any time without a perception, and never can observe anything but the perception. When my perceptions are removed for any time, as by sound sleep, so long am I insensible of myself, and may truly be said not to exist. . . . I may venture to affirm of the rest of mankind, that they are nothing but a bundle or collection of different perceptions, which succeed each other with an inconceivable rapidity, and are in a perpetual flux and movement. (Hume, 1737, *Treatise*, 1.6.4, 1–4, pp. 251–253)[5]

THE NATURE OF CONCEPTS

The "associationist" schools of Herbart in Germany, and of Hume, the Mills and Bain in Britain, have thus constructed a psychology without a soul by taking discrete "ideas", faint or vivid, and showing how, by their cohesions, repulsions, and forms of succession, such things as reminiscences, perceptions, emotions, volitions, passions, theories, and all the other furnishings of an individual's mind may be engendered. (William James, 1890, *Principles of Psychology*, I, The scope of psychology, p. 15)

The Rules that Organize the Mind. Hume's psychological theory is a radical *associationism* inspired by the theories of Berkley and Locke.[6] Thoughts are constructed from sensory impressions that are associated and then organized by simple algorithms. Two perceptions that arrive at the same time, or that define a same space, are automatically associated together. Beyond the rules of *contiguity* (in time and space), Hume observes that in the world of representations, everything that looks alike has the tendency to group together. These rules are applied whatever their relevance. Certain laws are a bit more complex, like those of cause and effect. If I perceive two objects that touch each other and two actions that succeed each other in time, I automatically suppose that the first action is the cause of the other, that the first object moved the second one.[7] This correlation is often useful, but sometimes deceptive.

The notions of time and space can be defined operationally. First, one sensation enters into the mind and then another. A subroutine of the mind that perceives two successive sensations creates a sensation of time passing. This does not mean that time exists in reality. A similar reasoning is used to explain the impression that space exists. In this system, there does not exist any Idea of time or of space, but these notions are nonetheless transpersonal to the extent that the algorithms construct them in every human being without any neurological damage because nature so conceived these rules. On the other hand, the interrelated elements form mental entities that are more complex than the content of sensory data.[8] The rules of association are, in effect, exterior to the content that is associated. There is then, with Hume, already a distinction between the perceptions and an organization of perceptions. What characterizes human thought "is never this or that idea as a term, but only ways of passing from one particular idea to another" (Deleuze, 1972, p. 229, translated by Marcel Duclos).

Do We Have a Need for Meaning?   Many psychotherapists have the tendency to propose a pursuit of meaning, for they suppose that life is tolerable only if we can give it a meaning.

For Hume, the search for meaning is a kind of antidepressant that leads to the opiate of the people that is religion. The philosopher is strong enough to be able to live comfortably with the idea that life has no meaning and that all of the meanings that we attribute to it are confabulations that blind the mind. One of the characteristics of a sect is to propose to psychically weak people a search for meaning that strengthen them while making them dependent.

THE AFFECT OF A THOUGHT

The multiple associations generated by the algorithms of the mind often have a short life when they are not reinforced by the forces that intensify and stabilize them. Hume suggests, in the first page of his *Treatise*, that we can distinguish between impressions and ideas:

1. An *impression* is a perception that enters into the mind, such as "sensations, passions and emotions, as they make their first appearance in the soul" (Hume, 1737, 1, 1, 1, p. 7).
2. *Ideas* are "faint images" of impressions used "in thinking and reasoning" (Hume, 1737, 1, 1, 1, p. 7). In this case, the word idea is not capitalized.

When an impression associates itself with an idea, this idea becomes more intense. *The more intense an idea is, the more it is experienced as true.*[9] When I feel a strong anger rise up in me while I take hold of a teapot, the teapot will enter my memory associated to my anger, even if no link exist between the two. For Hume, God is but a word. However, this word is sometimes associated to marvelously conceived and touching images, moving and stimulating words and songs, and ceremonies that integrate us into a community and with people we love. This word, through its associations, gradually becomes so intense that persons who have participated in religious rituals have the impression that God exists.

I point out this construction because it already announces Darwin and Freud. Two aspects of this model are found in the one that Freud proposes:

1. The observation that ideas and emotions can be associated independently of what is going on in reality points to the *mechanism* that notably explains lapses.
2. The notion that an idea can become more or less *intense*.[10]

BODY AND THOUGHTS

Hume includes behavior and the movements of the body among the regulators of thoughts and their intensity. He goes even as far as to think that an individual changes his way of thinking by changing his behavior. This shows that the mind is part of the organization of the organism. The reasoning is as follows. From the point of view of consciousness, a bodily position is nothing but a bodily position. The mind has the *impression* that it unfolds independently of the body's activity. However, if we analyze this impression carefully, we have to admit that there exists a relationship between the body and the mind; otherwise, it becomes impossible to explain how a thought can activate a movement of the hand. If the activity of the body is manifestly one of the regulators of the intensity of an idea, it can also be one of the regulators of its content. Hume concludes his reasoning by affirming that even though we do not have any conscious impression of this phenomenon, the movements of the body are often the causes of thought and perception.[11]

Propensities, Instincts, and Passions

> Our memory presents us with a vast number of instances of perceptions perfectly resembling each other that return at different distances of time, and after considerable interruptions. This resemblance gives us a propension to consider these interrupted perceptions as the same; and also a propension to connect them by a continued existence, in order to justify this identity, and avoid the contradiction, in which the interrupted appearance of these perceptions seems necessarily to involve us. Here then we have a propensity to feign the continued existence of all sensible objects; and as this propensity arises from some lively impressions of the memory, it bestows a vivacity on that fiction: or in other words, makes us believe the continued existence of body. (Hume, 1737, *The Treatise*, 1.4.2.42, p. 138f)

> Every duration in time consists of point-instants following one another, every extension in space consists of point-instants arising in contiguity and simultaneously, every motion consists of these point-instants arising in contiguity and in succession. There is therefore no Time, no Space and no Motion over and above the point-instants of which these imagined entities are constructed by our imagination. (Stcherbatsky, 1930, *Buddhist Logic*, II.I.3, p. 84)

In the first volume of his *Treatise*, Hume develops his theory about the cognitive functioning of humans. At the end of this section, he shows that reasoning only leads to *ambivalence*. In effect, a thought allows for the evaluation of a situation in many different ways, which can all be equally convincing. Reason thus proposes a *repertoire* of more or less plausible arguments that often lead to different solutions:

> Most fortunately it happens, that since reason is incapable of dispelling these clouds, nature herself suffices to that purpose, and cures me of this philosophical melancholy and delirium, either by relaxing this bent of mind, or by some avocation, and lively impressions of my senses, which obliterate all these chimeras. I dine, I play a game of back-gammon, I converse, and am merry with my friends. (Hume, 1737, 1.4.7, p. 175)

The passions, according to Hume, as with Descartes, are intense emotional propensities. They are not, as with Spinoza, the negative aspect of the affects. What motivates someone to act are not his reflections but his passions. The passions are therefore that part of the mind that *impulsively* adopts an option in a sufficiently intense and durable manner to create a behavior. Passions want to attain a goal associated with an object, and they have difficulty integrating the results of reflection into their project. Passions prefer to ally themselves to other passions that augment their intensity than to rational thoughts that often put a brake on a propensity to act by reducing their intensity and the pleasure associated to this intensity.[12] The pleasure that is associated with the intensity of the passions is independent of their content. Therefore, there would be pleasure in intense hate.

To designate this stubbornness of intense ideas, Hume sometimes uses the terms *propension* or *propensity*, as in the quote at the beginning of this section. I use the term *propensity* to designate, in a broad fashion, all the forces of an organism that repeatedly aim at the attainment of a goal. A propensity is an automatic tendency. These automatic tendencies coordinate the heteroclite mechanisms of the organism.

Hume perceives the mind as a republic within which diverse entities are united by reciprocal subordinate relationships to a government. They propagate themselves in this republic by unceasingly exchanging their riches.[13] This metaphor is close to the one proposed in 1985 by Marvin Minsky in *The Society of Mind*. This was one of the first works that made the models of artificial intelligence accessible to a large public. It is possible to distinguish two types of propensities:

1. *Internal* propensities coordinate the heteroclite mechanisms situated within an organism (ideas, impressions, body movements, etc.) to accomplish a task.
2. *External* propensities relate social rituals to internal propensities. Thus, an urge to eat stimulated by a commercial is an example of an external propensity.

Instincts and emotions are examples of internal propensities.[14] A feeling of discomfort is activated as soon as an event impedes its propensity to express itself.

Whether this resistance comes from the inside or from the outside, the feeling of frustration is the same. The idea here is that the *representation* of an internal or external event has the power to inhibit a propensity that creates the same affective impression. Likewise, an interior image or a beautiful painting hung on a wall can produce a similar feeling of satisfaction.[15] An external event does not become active in the mind until the moment it is perceived. Thus, the origin of a representation can be multiple (social activity, memory, etc.), but its effects obey the laws of the mind. Every event that is experienced as enhancing one's self-image is experienced as pleasure and pride, whereas any event that is experienced as harmful for one's self-image is experienced as pain and shame.

An example of external propensity is Hume's analysis of the appreciation of beauty. According to Hume, the impression that a woman is beautiful is a natural stimulation of sexual excitement in a man. This impression, therefore, depends as much on internal as on external factors, because the characteristics of beauty vary from culture to culture or from one epoch to another. The male organism would have a natural propensity to seek out beautiful women to satisfy his sexual needs (an example of internal propensity). However, this propensity is conceived in such a way by nature as to be calibrated by the social environment (an example of external propensity). In the case of an external propensity, a man mostly seeks the love of a woman who corresponds to socially constructed clichés, instead of a woman who corresponds to his profound instinctive and affective needs. Thus, the particularities of a person's representations have a greater impact on passions than what is often thought. For psychotherapy, this implies that working on the way a person tends to imagine the object of his propensities allows one to improve one's understanding of how a person associates his habitual mental propensities with his habitual ways of behaving.[16]

In this theory of instincts, there exists an internal propensity ("I need a beautiful woman") that cannot function until and unless it grafts itself onto a system of aesthetic social values. This model is close to the one of the laptop computer that must be connected to the Internet to receive emails. In both these cases, it is possible to speak of internal mechanisms, but these mechanisms calibrate themselves according to the network to which they are connected. The development of muscles and nerve connections adapts to the activities of the organism. Similarly, once a laptop is linked to an Internet connection, it is able receive updates that can modify the way its programs behave. Not only do the external propensities come to coordinate the dynamics of the organism to social rituals, but these same rituals, by influencing behavior, can have an impact on the way an organism thinks.[17]

The Basic Ethics of All Intellectual Inquiries:
Socrates, Spinoza, Hume, Kant

We have just seen that Hume is the antithesis of Socrates and Spinoza when he pretends that the universe can function without global coherence, and that a thinker can propose pertinent ideas without having access to Ideas constructed by forces other than human activity. However, there is a domain where these three personalities defend exactly the same cause: the ethics of philosophers.

These philosophers organized their thoughts in similar environments. The relationship between the republic of Athens and the Republic of the United Provinces is easily evident; whereas the British Empire is inspired much more by the Roman Empire at the time of Julius Cesar. However, Hume was part of an important movement in Great Britain that pressed toward more democracy, greater freedom of thought, more justice for all, and an Industrial Revolution directed by merchants and industrialists. They preferred the Roman Republic of Cicero.

The ethics of a philosopher has been summarized by Kant (1784) as a refusal to accept any form of tutelage on his thoughts, be it internal (the passions) or external (censorship). Socrates, Spinoza, and Hume all refused to integrate the gods of their society into their philosophy while remaining models of independent, dignified, ethical, and moral behavior. They are icons for all the atheistic and lay movements that fashioned democratic thought. Socrates and Hume, above all, are also personalities who made public their capacity to die with dignity, without having recourse to the folklore of religious rituals.[18]

For these philosophers, an enlightened freedom of thought is a shared phenomenon. It refers not only to the notions but also to the methods used in an inquiry. It consists of making one's speculations accessible to everyone, appreciating a dialogue with all who criticize (positively or negatively) these thoughts, and communicating how we react to the thoughts of others. Only in this way does following our intimate convictions lead to an enlightened social construction of ideas instead of a sectarian derivative. In the domain of collegiality, Hume was an example of generosity during his lifetime.[19]

This ethical stance was taken up by the scientific movements. It distinguishes the scientists from those who used science to advocate a dogmatic materialism.

KANT DECREES THE IMPOSSIBILITY OF MAKING PRONOUNCEMENTS ABOUT THE GREAT DOGMATIC METAPHYSICAL PREOCCUPATIONS

The *Critique of Pure Reason* Resonates with *An Inquiry Concerning Human Understanding*

I openly confess, the suggestion of David Hume was the very thing, which many years ago first interrupted my dogmatic slumber, and gave my investigations in the field of speculative philosophy quite a new direction. (Kant, 1783, *Prolegomena*, Preface)

That sensation is a momentary flash is proved by introspection. But a momentary sensation is but the reflex of a momentary thing. It can seize neither what preceded nor what follows. (Stcherbatsky, 1930, *Buddhist Logic*, II.I.5, p. 87)

When Hume died in 1776, Immanuel Kant (1724–1804) was already one of the great philosophers of the Age of Enlightenment.[20] Like most of the philosophers before him, Kant tried to propose the most accurate vision possible of the way in which the universe and humans function. That is what, in his *Critique of Pure Reason,* he calls "a *dogmatic* thought." A dogmatic thought is the belief that the mind has the capacity to know how the world works by just thinking, through speculation.

At the occasion of Hume's death in 1776, many people read and reread the works of this great man. This was also the case with Kant, who reread some of Hume's earlier writings as well. That is how he discovered, at the age of fifty-four, *An Inquiry Concerning Human Understanding*, which is a watered-down version of the *Treatise of Human Nature*. In reading this work, Kant was profoundly shocked and unsettled. He had the impression of having walked on a land mine. He immediately understood that Hume had perceived something powerful that nevertheless required some editing. The questioning of reason and knowledge carried out by Hume had manifestly solid foundations for Kant.

Kant was then in a crisis. He had published nothing since 1760. In an implicit and confused way, he felt that all dogmatic thoughts led to an impasse. But he could not put his finger on what bothered him.[21] He was trying to understand the rapport between two psychic phenomena:

1. What type of information enters the brain.
2. How this information is analyzed, categorized, and synthesized.

In this state of inner wandering, Kant discovered Hume's *Inquiry*. He spontaneously took what he appreciated in Hume's thought, while trying to circumvent the skepticism and the atheism of the great English thinker. Kant feared that the analysis of Hume could cause all that the philosophers of the Enlightenment had constructed to falter. As far as the workings of the mind, what Kant developed went much further than what the young Hume had succeeded in imagining. Kant then conceived of an immense project that breaks down into two phases:

1. Develop the themes initiated by Hume to give them an intellectual structure that Hume had not taken the time to specify.
2. Give to Hume's thinking a structure that would allow Kant to support philosophy and science, while criticizing it.

Even if the critique of Hume is irrefutable, Kant refused to admit that the work of philosophers and of scientists was nothing more than a series of delusions. This is how the *Critique of Pure Reason* came to the light of day and was published in 1781, then revised for the second edition in 1787. Without this work, almost no one would speak of Kant today. During the entire nineteenth century, intellectuals believed that Kant had integrated the few interesting points developed by the young Hume in his philosophical writings.

Almost a century later, Edmund Husserl[22] presented Hume's *Treatise of Human Nature* as one of the great classics in philosophy. Husserl shows that Kant had only been shocked by Hume's 1748 *Inquiry,* which was less explosive than the *Treatise.*[23] Husserl did not try to contain Hume's radical analysis; on the contrary, he highlighted the value of what was the most radical in the *Treatise.* Later, the philosopher Ludwig Wittgenstein also found "important" remarks in Hume's *Treatise.* For example, he agreed with Hume that thoughts are not capable of following a strict logical causality. One thought does not necessarily lead to another thought, to a way of feeling, or to a way of acting (Wittgenstein, 1967, p. 42). The *Treatise* is the only book by Hume that is found in most bookstores today. It has become one of the bibles of psychology and artificial intelligence at the beginning of the twenty-first century.[24]

The New Metaphysics

Kant admits with Hume that a dogmatic metaphysic is, in the end, but a human propensity to create for oneself a virtual representation of the universe. Humans have the capacity to generate an infinite number of plausible representations of the universe. He also agrees with Hume that thoughts are organized by rules independent of the thoughts' content, but he proposes a more complex vision of these mechanisms. He qualifies them as *a priori,* to state more saliently the fact that they exist before an idea (a perception, a memory, a feeling) appears in the mind. The core statement is that humans need to realize that the way people think is not how nature works. The mind is a small part of nature. It can therefore only use a few of the available natural procedures. It is only once they have become aware of this issue that humans can improve their intellectual tools in a constructive way.[25]

The *Critique of Pure Reason* is read today as the first textbook about artificial intelligence because Kant proposes a description of the architecture of the human mind. He details the way a perception is formed and evaluated, how it is integrated to form representations, and how thoughts produce generalizations and theories. He also includes in his model of the mind regulators that make it possible to verify the appropriateness of a mental construct and prevent it from forming theories that are not founded on observations. These regulators are part of rational thinking but not of emotions. Beliefs, as Hume indicated, are caused by the influence of the affects on ideas. Contrary to Hume, Kant rejoins Spinoza and Leibniz in the hope that the purely intellectual mechanisms can follow laws other than those that the passions impose to sustain the formation of beliefs. This hope justifies the notion of "pure reason."

The "antinomies"[26] are an example of a priori mental procedures that permit reason to detect which theories cannot be supported by sensory data. This mechanism automatically proposes options that are impossible to choose rationally. The antinomies automatically set up a competition between complementary explanations when the sensory data are insufficient so as to avoid unnecessary conclusions. Here is an example:

1. The human spirit can imagine that *everything has a beginning*. It consists here of an a priori disposition that is automatically activated as soon as an event is perceived. This tool is useful in ordinary life to understand the perceived events; but it becomes problematic when it is applied to an imaginary situation or a theoretical concept, relatively independent of the data from the senses, like an "intellection."[27] These mechanisms, for example, force the mind to imagine that there is a beginning to the history of the universe. These a priori mechanisms do not allow us to know if God truly exists, but it inevitably leads the human spirit to imagine a moment of creation in which something like a creator god could have existed.

2. The second a priori argument that arises as soon as the mind brutally lacks information to come to a conclusion about the origin of things is that *there is always a moment that comes before and after a given moment*; and there is always a space around a given space. Once again, this tool is altogether pertinent for practical everyday life; it becomes more difficult to handle in contexts when the mind functions with insufficient data. It does allow for the construction of the notion of infinity and shows that there will always be a moment before the creation of the universe. This leads to the conclusion that there has never been a creation, and it therefore eliminates the possibility that a god could have created the universe.

As soon as one of these two arguments appears, the other is automatically activated—either in the person who is thinking or in those with whom the person is debating. Reason is therefore unable to prove or disprove the existence of God. These antinomies also explain why believers and atheists always have the same valuable theoretical arguments and have the impression that their argument is correct.[28] This capacity to generate concepts independently of what exists allows for the clarification of categories, judgments, and a priori concepts.[29] Consequently, the spirit spontaneously tries to situate a perception in space and time in an a priori fashion, using mental reflexes that are applied to all perceptions:

> It is therefore from the human point of view only that we can speak of space, extended objects, etc. If we depart from the subjective condition, under which alone we can obtain external intuition,[30] or, in other words, by means of which we are affected by objects, the representation of space has no meaning whatsoever. (Kant, 1787, I.1.4, p. 46)

This manner of situating a perception exists before it enters into the brain. On the other hand, the fact that the Earth turns around the sun is not an a priori judgment because there was a need of empirical data to establish this truth.

These a priori mechanisms guarantee a constant activity of the mind. They push the sense organs to seek the elements that they can manage in the environment. In that way, the human spirit expects to be able to break down their environment into independent entities that can be distinguished from others in the visual space perceived by visual organs. If the perceptual system did not have this expectation, the mind would not know how to deal with the *continuum* of information that ceaselessly bombards the retina. As it expects to be able to extract shapes in space, the perceptual system has various tools at its disposal that can isolate these forms and associate them to other properties like color, the direction of a movement, and so on. The mind is thus structured in such a way that sensory data can be analyzed, evaluated, judged, and then cataloged according to certain innate categories. An object can thus be categorized as belonging to me or another person, dangerous or useful, and so on. This is how human psychological activity gradually includes sensory data in increasingly complex forms of analysis. Having understood how the mind operates, it becomes evident that the perception of an object depends not only on its situation in its environment but also on the psychological algorithms that categorize sensory data. Consequently, we can only have approaches, points of view concerning who we are and what surrounds us.[31]

The Necessary Illusions

A transcendental paralogism has a transcendental foundation, and concludes falsely, while the form is correct and unexceptionable. In this manner the paralogisms has its foundation in the nature of human reason, and is the parent of unavoidable, though not insoluble, mental illusion. (Kant, 1787, *Critique of Pure Reason*, Transcendental dialectic II.1, p. 43)

Using a particular set of definitions and terms, Kant describes a mind that has a structure that follows procedures. With these procedures, the mind actively constructs representations on sensory data that has been extracted from the reality it explores. These procedures have limits that generate illusions. Consequently, the antinomy of time makes it possible to conceive (a) that there is always a beginning, (b) that there can always be a moment before the beginning, and (c) nothing else. The human spirit is not able to imagine other possibilities, even if the other possibilities could be relevant.

The constraints of theses algorithms necessarily lead to a constructed reduction[32] of what is perceived. The reality is filtered through the structure of the senses, the nervous system, and the mind. Reality is then re-created. This creativity necessarily generates illusions. In some cases, illusions falsify reality without pertinence, whereas in other cases they are a construction that differs from reality to facilitate the adaptation of the organism. This second mechanism is what I call *necessary illusions*. The following is an example. "By means of the external sense (a property of the mind), we represent to ourselves objects as without us, and these all in space" (Kant, 1787, I.1.2, p. 43). This illusion functions in two different steps:

1. Our organism is part of the physical, biological, and social world, and the mind has the impression that it "understands and contains" the world. In certain moments, it dissociates from the sensation of its existence to be able to concentrate on what is perceived.
2. Our perceptions are constructed within the cranium, but we have the spontaneous impression that what we perceive is situated outside of the organism, in the place where the perceived object is. This capacity follows from the preceding point.

It goes without saying that having the impression that objects are outside of the confines of the body does allow us to act *as if* we see things such as they are. In practical, ordinary daily life, this makes our life so much easier.

As I mention in the Glossary, the Kantian notion of "subject," highly valued by French psychoanalysts since Lacan, is an example of an inevitable impression that does not necessarily correspond to an existing psychological entity. In the sections dedicated to Darwin we will see that the organism is replete with innate tools that are of little use or even counterproductive. The notion of subject is associated to the impression of being a coherent person who thinks, feels, and acts. The reinforcement of this impression can serve as a protection against anxiety, but also reinforces the illusion that the center of our being is situated in the mind. In this book, I give examples that show (1) that the organism probably has no center, and (2) that if such a center existed, it would not necessarily be conscious. The same analysis can be used for the current impression of having a "self."

Visions and Reason

Kant also defined the ethics of knowledge that is appropriate for a rationalist like himself when confronted by the discourse of a person who describes spiritual visions. Descartes had imposed the necessity of taking into consideration, for a scientific study, only weak hypotheses and problems that the available methodologies can tackle. For Kant, this necessity remains relevant for scientific research, but his preoccupation is to create a model that situates all of the existing phenomena of the mind. The mind does not follow scientific procedures. An example of an apparently irrational mechanism of the mind discussed by Kant (1776) is that of the *visions* describes by a Swedish "spirit-seer" named Emanuel Swedenborg. Like Rudolf Steiner in the twentieth century, Swedenborg recounts that he perceives other dimensions of reality that most humans are unable to perceive. He describes landscapes and creatures that exist around us, that influence us and are affected by what we do without us having any awareness of this.

Kant cannot evaluate the status of such visions because he does not have that kind of perceptual ability. However, the fact that he does not perceive something does not demonstrate that others cannot perceive it. It would be flagrant stupidity to deny the existence of Swedenborg's landscapes or consider them to be hallucinations, until researchers could prove, in a pertinent manner, that these other dimensions do not exist. The psychology that Kant wants to establish must be able to account for these phenomena. Either the theory admits that certain forms of perception exist only in some individuals, or it admits that certain persons have a rare capacity to extract data that the senses of all people receive but do not usually perceive, or it admits that the complexity of the mind generates virtual realities, or it is content to trivialize these visions by calling them hallucinations. All of these possibilities demand an extensive investigation. What is at stake is to know whether all minds have the same repertoire of a priori psychological mechanisms.

What is still important for today's psychotherapist, in this analysis, is the ethical stance that others can perceive phenomena of which a therapist cannot become aware. The therapist's default position, in this instance, is that of an open inquiry into the cause or origin of these visions (blood poisoning, hallucinations, poorly interpreted perceptual illusions, bizarre phenomena, individual particularities of a mental system, etc.). It is as dangerous to immediately associate all of the above phenomena to psychological hallucinations as to hastily dismiss the possibility. The technical, ethical, and clinical recommendation adopted in this book is to *always accept the experience* of what is perceived but always investigate how a patient or a therapist explains what is perceived. This recommendation is found in many schools of psychotherapy.[33]

I developed this issue because I have known colleagues who claim to be able to perceive an aura, the force-field of an organism, or the malevolent waves that subjugate the life forces. These individuals are sometime as renowned as Wilhelm Reich, Gerda Boyesen, and Alexander Lowen. Some are colleagues, friends, or patients. These are respectable people whom I admire, even if I do not perceive what they do. Kant's ethical proposition is useful to me every time I meet them or read their works, as it also implies that I do not need to believe that what they perceive necessarily exits.

Conscious Thoughts as Virtual Organismic Phenomena and Unconscious Memories of Abuse

Conscious thoughts are the only organismic dynamics that are clearly mental. Some even think that thoughts and perceptions are necessarily conscious. It is evident that an organism can manage information in complex ways that are not conscious. However, the idea that the mind can think and perceive without using conscious dynamics is an intellectual stance that cannot be demonstrated in a convincing and robust way. It is easy to show that the brain manages nonconscious information that can influence conscious representations, but it is more difficult to demonstrate that there exist nonconscious psychological processes. For example, in artificial intelligence, there exists endless discussion on whether the data management of a computer can be considered a form of thinking.[34] Between conscious representations and neural data management, there is an immense realm of phenomena that is difficult to situate. Since Kant, it is assumed that the organization of conscious perceptions and representations is mostly nonconscious.

As an ensemble of fuzzy virtual phenomena, conscious dynamics are incapable of appreciating in an explicit way the contours of the dimension of which it is a part, the insertion of the psychological dimension in the organism, and especially the pertinence of what is perceived. Everything happens as if conscious thinking assumes that what is perceived is relatively close to what happens. The elusive and ephemeral substance of thoughts has fascinated wise men in every culture (Hindus, Buddhists, Taoists, Sufis, Descartes, etc.). Conscious dynamics were thus considered useful illusions until the theory of evolution showed how they could have acquired at least a form of relevance. At the same time, conscious thoughts evidently play a crucial function in the development of the human species. This function is not an illusion, even if it is difficult to grasp. That is why it is more suitable to talk of necessary illusions than of "right" or "wrong" ideas.

In talking about psychotherapy, we shall see that it is more useful to help a consciousness define the limits of what is going on than to affirm that a thought corresponds to a reality. This is particularly obvious when a person talks to us about a dream or presents a drawing that we interpret to be a representation of an unconscious memory. For instance, some psychotherapists have interpreted certain representations as the proof that there is an unconscious memory of childhood abuse that was perpetrated by the parents. By such an assertion, these psychotherapists have sometimes brought about an investigation that showed that it was in fact the case; but in affirming that this interpretation was "true," other psychotherapists have created a destructive doubt for everyone concerned when the abusive behaviors did not happen or could not be proven. It is important, here as elsewhere, to distinguish clearly between what is a thought and what is a fact. The relationship between a thought and some acts can only be established after an investigation that clearly defines the mental and behavioral dimension.

Plasticity and Constraints of the Mental System

In the days when the mind was situated in the soul, conscious thoughts were approached as living entities, independent of organic dynamics. They could be true or false, but their power was manifest, even if they were still associated to the shadows in Plato's cave.[35] Since Descartes's *The Passions of the Soul* (1649), it became evident that the mechanisms that link thoughts and physiology give power to the mind.

It is because the mind is a virtual and fuzzy entity that the understanding of the necessary illusions and the knowledge of the rules of the mind are so important. Thus, Kant's analysis continues to be important today. Reacting to Hume's flexible and imaginative mind, Kant admits that this flexibility is real; he adds that happily there exist a certain number of rules that allow the mental system to function by putting limits to this flexibility.

This global vision is still found in the works of numerous psychologists like Vygotsky and Piaget, who are inspired by systemic and structuralist theories. It is not so common in the psychotherapeutic literature, because in this domain one seldom finds explicit psychological models. Freud, who had read Kant, attempted to propose a rough theory of the mind at the end of his book on dreams, known as the first topic.[36] Later, he realized that his model was too simplistic, and he abandoned it. Since then, neither Freud nor any other psychotherapist has found a way to associate clinical observations with an explicit psychological model. They prefer to leave to the cognitive neurosciences (neurologists and psychologists) the care of putting the finishing touches on a model of the mind.[37] These models follow Kant to the extent that they support the necessity of describing the mind as a fuzzy system structured by constraints. These constraints, like the body's skeleton, provide a structure that is used to create boundaries within which the complexity of the system can operate.

PART III

The Organism of the Biologists

7

From Evolutionary Theory to Artificial Intelligence

THE GRADUAL DIFFERENTIATION OF ORGANISMS HAS GENERATED PSYCHOLOGICAL DIMENSIONS

What is most at play in these sections dedicated to the theory of evolution is to show how the notion of organism came to be and the issues it has raised. As we will see, the organism is an entity that evolves over time through self-differentiation. Only gradually did mental and body mechanisms differentiate themselves more and more from each other. The new organisms gained the capacity to integrate, in a more or less coherent way, the diversity of emerging mechanisms. In this way of thinking, the opposition of body and soul disappears, but it becomes more difficult for the psychologists to defend the specificity of the mental mechanisms. Most of the models of psychotherapy situate their reflections within the framework of the theories of evolution, which were formulated during the past two centuries. I concentrate on the first formulations by Lamarck, Darwin, and Wallace. It seems to me that when the high stakes raised in their discussions are well understood, it is possible to approach recent developments with greater acuity.

The Mind Is a Constituent of the Development of the Organism's Complexity

Our senses, you say, are fallacious, our understanding erroneous, our ideas even of the most familiar objects, extension, duration, motion, full of absurdities and contradictions. You defy me to solve the difficulties, or reconcile the repugnancies, which you discover in them. . . . Your own conduct, in every circumstance, refutes your principles; and shows the firmest reliance on all the received maxims of science, morals, prudence, and behaviour. (Hume, 1776, *Dialogues Concerning Natural Religion*, I, p. 39)

In the preceding chapters, I have indicated that philosophers did not succeed in explaining the following points:

1. The conscious perceptions seem to correspond to what is going on in the organism's environment.
2. This correspondence is partial, inexplicable, and sometimes leads to delirious representations (for example, that the Earth is flat).

Kant is one who reflected the most on these issues. He died in 1804, two years after Lamarck's first book on the theory of evolution. Yet Kant never envisioned, even in passing, a single solution that resembles the solutions brought forth by Lamarck's theory. This theory is an example of the ability that certain individuals have to facilitate the emergence of a theory that no one had ever thought about before and without which no one can henceforth think. Lamarck's theory gathers a whole series of formulations that were already in circulation. The synthesis that emerged in his thoughts is so new, so useful, so relevant, and so simple that one can only be astonished that no one had thought about it before. Humanity had already known this type of discovery with the invention of the wheel, the mastery of fire, as well as the physics of Galileo and Newton. The mechanisms that foster the emergence of this type of key pivotal idea are poorly understood.[1]

If we admit, like Descartes and Leibniz, that God did "preset" the appropriateness between the perceptions and the stimulations of the organism, it is difficult to understand why he did not construct it any better. The philosophers who assume that this appropriateness was constructed by nature (as do Lucretius and Hume) have a difficult time explaining how material dynamics were able to build a perceptual system that seems to work relatively well. Ever since the formulations of Lamarck, Wallace, and Darwin, the evolutionists can provide an explanation that answers these questions in a plausible and empirically robust way. For them, the evolution of the organism includes the exploration of different forms of perception that correlate better and better with what is going on in their environment, all of this without implying that perceptions are identical to what exists in their surroundings. For example, the fact that the eye makes grass green does not mean that grass is not red. But as the choice of colors made by the eyes correlates well with what surrounds us, this type of question does not impose itself for ordinary human practices or for the survival of the species. This answer confirms that what is perceived is not necessarily what exists, but it also shows that a partial appropriateness is inevitable when the criteria of survival are taken into consideration.

Time Is a Factor that Allows the Essence of Beings to Change: The Multiple Layers of a Slow History

> Thus, nature, always active, always impassible, renewing and changing all sorts of bodies, preserving none from destruction, offers to us an imposing never ending scene, and shows to us that in her lies a particular power which only acts out of necessity. (Lamarck, 1820, *Système Analytique des Connaissances Positives de l'Homme*, I.II.2, p. 58; translated by Michael C. Heller)

An outstanding aspect of this revolution in the history of human theories is the introduction of a time scale in the analysis of the structure of living beings. Before Lamarck, a system (the universe, a planet, an animal) has a fundamental structure (its essence) that can only suffer "surface" modifications during its life (an amputation, for example). These changes are often referred to as "accidental." They do not influence the structure of the soul, which shapes the essence of an individual. From Lamarck onward, the fundamental structure of a system constitutes itself progressively on a time scale that varies according to systems. A few seconds for a cell can correspond to thousands of years for the human species, millions of years for a planet, and billions of years for the universe.

It is only after Lamarck's death that Hegel integrated time into a philosophical conception of human nature[2] and created a philosophy of human history.[3] This history describes the way the human mind developed by creating increasing complex civilizations across the centuries.[4] Time thus becomes a part of the mechanisms that generate the human mind, because the capacity to structure oneself in time—to be in becoming—is now part of the properties of the human mind. It was then only a matter of time before scientists would discover that there had been humanoids who, in the prehistoric period,[5] did not walk and did not think like a human being of the nineteenth century. Finally, in 1830, Scottish geologist Charles Lyell began to publish a series of volumes that demonstrated that the Earth has been shaped for millions of years by forces that are still presently active.[6] Before the nineteenth century, the Europeans, inspired by the Bible, imagined a history of only some thousands of years. Today, we think that the first humans appeared several million years ago.

Lamarck[7] remarks that thoughts not only grasp the organismic system of which they are a part with difficulty but that they also poorly evaluate the impact of time on what is happening and on the way they function. From the point of view of the mind, to include time as a variable is experienced as a complication that requires much attention. Psychologists know that it is equally true when they want to organize a developmental research study. An experimental design that wants to study the unfolding of a behavior at different moments in a lifetime exponentially multiplies the costs, work time, quantity of data to consider, and complexity of the statistical methods. It is not for nothing that theories integrating the notion of time are rare and recent. Even today, it is difficult to integrate the implications of a developmental and historical approach in psychological theories.

LAMARCK ESTABLISHES BIOLOGY BY SHOWING
THAT THE ESSENCE OF NATURE IS DYNAMIC

Situating Biology: From Buffon to Lamarck

The Botanical Gardens of Buffon

Count George-Louis Leclerc Buffon (1707–1788) was one of the great French botanists. He published a marvelously illustrated reference catalog of plants: *Natural History, General and Particular*, from 1749 to 1788. He is also known because he transformed the King's Gardens in Paris into an immense Museum of Natural History. The Botanical Gardens that surround the museum contain a great variety of plants. In the same spirit, the museum preserves examples of most of the inventoried animal species on the planet. Buffon died in time to avoid witnessing the torments of the first French Revolution. During this period, the different succeeding governments maintained the operation of this museum.

Jean-Baptiste Pierre Antoine de Monet, Chevalier de Lamarck (1744–1829), a botanist trained by Buffon, participated in the establishment of the Museum of Natural History, where he became in charge of the section on invertebrates (insects, mostly). His major work is the *Natural History of Animals without Vertebra*, made up of seven volumes published between 1815 and 1822. This work quickly became a reference for many biologists.

The Theory of Evolution from Humans to Polyps

At least since Aristotle, many authors had proposed refined classifications of animals. Anatomical studies had showed physiological similarities between species and had confirmed the animal status of the human body. Nonetheless, it was the common belief that God had conceived of each species and each creature. The similarities observed in different species demonstrate that God had used the similar organs to create different creatures. The idea eventually emerged that certain creatures, like the monkey, were closer to God (and humans) than others, like the amoeba,[8] for instance.

The theory of evolution began to take form in Lamarck's thoughts while he walked the corridors of the Museum of Natural History and wondered how the countless samples of species should be placed. He also benefited from the many projects undertaken by his colleagues at the museum and from the scientists with whom he was in contact, like Charles Bonnet of Geneva. Yet he is the only member of this community of brilliant biologists to have conceived of the possibility that there might be a *history* of the species. This required not only a great imagination and intelligence but also the courage of a warrior who jumps across a precipice. The difficulty was not only to imagine that such a history could have generated the human species, but also to accompany this hypothesis with arguments capable of making a theory of it that could be acceptable to his colleagues. He detailed this view in 1802 in *Research on the Organism of Living Bodies*. This volume presented the theory of evolution to the ordinary citizen. Beautifully written, it is still pleasing and surprising to read.

Lamarck's pedagogy, developed in the first part of his work, is stimulating and effective. He starts from what is particular to humans and shows that it is possible to classify the species of animals according to what they do *not* possess. He conjectures that the simpler the organism, the more it is constitutionally distant from humans, the more it is ancient. The creatures lose their limbs, lay eggs instead of giving live birth. The regulation of the body temperature becomes less efficient when the animal is "cold-blooded." Insects do not have vertebrae. In moving backward, Lamarck helps the reader feel how life progressed in its development from matter, by becoming plants and then ever more complex creatures. This complexity *gradually* builds itself up, differentiating itself from what existed previously, by creating a growing variety of mechanisms. This progressive differentiation allows for the creation of the capacity to have a social life (ants and bees already have such a life), an affective life (manifest in mammals), and intellectual capacities (developed particularly in humans). The differentiation of organs, sensorimotor actions, and the capacity to think all make up the history of organisms. The organism, or the individual system, thus becomes the basic building block of the theory of evolution in the nineteenth century.

Lamarck's theory follows, in its broad lines, the coherent and systemic vision of the universe proposed by Spinoza. Time does not alter this coherence, because nature did not, in its history, jump from the mollusks to humans to end up with crocodiles. This development is nonetheless not linear. For example, the dog's keen sense of smell is more developed than that of humans.

Lamarck's Second Law

If Lamarck described the course of evolution in a convincing fashion, he was not able, with the data available to him, to understand the *mechanisms* of this evolution in a convincing way. The mechanisms he imagined are expressed in two laws that we must consider because they are still often discussed:

1. "In every animal which has not passed the limit of its development, a more frequent and continuous use of any organ gradually strengthens, develops and enlarges that organ, and gives it a power proportional to the length of time it has been so used; while the permanent disuse of any organ imperceptibly weakens and deteriorates it, and progressively diminishes its functional capacity, until it finally disappears" (Lamarck, 1809, I.VII, p. 113).
2. "All the acquisitions or losses wrought by nature on individuals, through the influence of the environment in which their race has long been

placed, and hence through the influence of the predominant use or permanent disuse of any organ: all these are preserved by reproduction to the new individuals which arise, provided that the acquired modifications are common to both sexes, or at least to the individuals which produce the young" (Lamarck, 1809, I.VII, p. 113).

The best-known example is that of the giraffe:

> It is interesting to observe the result of habit in the peculiar shape and size of the giraffe (Camelo-pardalis): this animal, the largest of the mammals, is known to live in the interior of Africa in places where the soil is nearly always arid and barren, so that it is obliged to browse on the leaves on the trees and to make constant efforts to reach them. From this habit long maintained in all its race, it has resulted that the animal's fore-legs have become longer than its hind legs, and that its neck is lengthened to such a degree that the giraffe, without standing up on its hind legs, attains a height of six meters (nearly 20 feet). (Lamarck, 1809, I.VII, p. 122)

Expressed in this fashion, after a century and a half of debate, it is admitted that these two laws do not adequately explain what is happening. The laws of natural selection, genetics, and the function of DNA permitted biologists to propose different and considerably more refined models.[9] Yet Lamarck had reason to think that behavior is one of the great levers of the mechanisms of evolution. Both he and Darwin believed that a habitual behavior could be part of what a parent transmits *directly* to its descendants. Ever since the discovery of the genetic code by Mendel,[10] it seems that the relationship between habitual behavior and lineage is indirect. The relationship exists to the extent that the new behavior is associated to a mutation of the genes and that it favors survival. The *survival of a mutation* has become the determining aspect of what is biologically transmitted to its progeny. Modern genetics often assume that mutations are random. However, I have some difficulty with this assumption, as I do not see why genetic dynamics should be the only dynamics of the universe that are guided by pure randomness. Associating the core of biological dynamics to the notion of pure randomness may have been useful to free the human mind from religious thinking during the first half of the twentieth century, but only ideological preoccupations can guarantee that pure randomness can exist.

The Science of the Living

The theory of evolution is presented by Lamarck as one of the branches of a new science of the living that he calls *biology*. The need to gather all of the knowledge about life was felt by several scientists. Karl Friedrich Burdach and Gottfried Reinhold Treviranus also simultaneously and independently proposed this term. The term *biology* can be understood in two ways:

1. *The science of life*. Biology as the science of life is the science that studies the forces that animate all living things, and that is qualitatively differ-

ent from the forces that created matter. This hypothesis is often referred to as *vitalism*. Lamarck speaks of a *vital orgasm,* which he defines as "a particular tension in all of the points of the soft tissue of living bodies which hold their molecules at a certain distance from one another: a distance that they are susceptible to lose, by the simple fact of attraction, when the cause that maintains this space ceases to act"[11] (Lamarck, 1802, II.2, p. 61f), translated by Marcel Duclos). This vital orgasm is related to the fluids in which all the cells of the organism float, and which circulate in the cardiovascular system and in the nerves. These theories attempt to explain what causes living creatures to exist. The notion of orgasm is not necessarily associated, in the French of the period, to the sexual act. Although this type of orgasm is at the root of the power of life, it can become destructive when it causes an excess of heat in an organ.[12]

2. *The science of the living.* The study of living creatures (plants and animals) does not necessarily imply a "vitalistic" approach. Most of the biological theories, since Claude Bernard and Charles Darwin, take this option.

The curriculum for biology is detailed by Lamarck in his *Zoological Philosophy* (1809):

1. The description of *natural history,* that is, the history of organs and of their organization.
2. The description of the *physiological* phenomena that maintain the life of the organism.
3. A *psychophysiology* that explains the mechanisms that give rise to the movements that an organism executes and to the feelings and the intelligence that motivate it.

The second part of this curriculum is the testimony to what was considered physiology at the time, but the advances in this domain are so formidable that that has all been surpassed. I therefore concentrate on the third part, which presents the beginnings of an evolutionary psychophysiology. This psychophysiology is developed in the first volume of the *Natural History of Invertebrates.*

The Psychophysiology of the Organism

A First Draft of an Evolutionary Psychology

The decade of the 1990s saw the appearance of a series of books, often written by philosophers, who presented a psychology inspired by Darwin's theory of evolution.[13] It is in this context that it was discovered that Lamarck, now blind at the end of his life, had dictated a first draft of the implications of the theory of evolution for psychology to his eldest daughter. It is *The Analytical System of the Positive Knowledge about Man* (my translation of his French title, *Système analytique des connaissances positives de l'homme*), which was published in 1820.

The Burial of the Soul

Lamarck's basic finding is that evolutionary biology points to a parallel evolution of the organism,[14] the nervous system, the mind, behavior, and socialization. These different dimensions participate in building up the organism. In other words, the mind would be a biological phenomenon like the other dimensions. The irrational and destructive behavior of humans demonstrates that they are not animated by forces superior to those that bring life to animals.[15] It is almost as if Lamarck avoids writing that the complexity of humans is beyond their resources and that this is what renders them more dangerous than the other creatures. The last species to appear is probably the most complex, but certainly the least complete. Its complexity makes the integration of its heterogeneity particularly difficult.

For Lamarck, everything that will be said about the soul "is baseless and purely imaginary" (1809, III.I, p. 294). This paragraph is, for scientific thought, the tomb in which he buried the soul such as it existed from Plato to Descartes.

The Structure of the Nervous System

> All animals, whose brains are provided with two wrinkled hemispheres, possess the power of muscular movement and of feeling, the faculty of experiencing inner emotions, and, in addition, that of forming ideas, making comparisons and judgments and, in short, of carrying out various acts of intelligence, corresponding to the degrees of development of the hypocephalon.[16] (Lamarck, 1809, *Zoological Philosophy*, III.I, p. 310)

Lamarck divides the human nervous system into five principal parts:

1. Sensorimotor *medullar masses* situated in each vertebra. Each center sends information via the nerves to stimulate certain muscles and receives information from the nerves that are sensitive to the activity of these same muscles.
2. A *spinal cord* in which the activity of each medullar mass is transmitted to other medullar masses. This system already exists in insects.
3. The *brainstem*: The part of the brain that receives the information from the spinal cord. It can therefore centralize information from the body. This primitive brain that provides for vision exists already in insects, spiders, crustaceans, and mollusks.[17]
4. The *limbic system*:[18] A part of the brain that creates a first centralized coordination of the sensory data to produce some coordinated motor responses of the organism. This form of reaction is that of the *sentiments*,[19] the affects, the instincts, and the emotions. Observable in crus-

taceans and mollusks, the limbic system can be related to the appearance of hearing and then smell.

5. The two lobes of the *neocortex,* in which an even more complex coordination can take place. It is in this network that Lamarck grounds *intelligence*. These lobes exist in all of the superior mammals.

This division, inspired by the neurology of the period and by the evolution of the species, remains pertinent for some present-day authors.[20] In Lamarck's conception, there is no relationship between a zone and a mental function,[21] but there are more complex forms of the organization of the neurological activity that open into various modes of treating information that are *experienced* as sensations (in the brainstem), as feelings (in the limbic system), or as thinking (in the neocortex). I find it important to insist on the fact that intelligence *is not situated* in the neocortex, but that the neocortex allows for a more complex *organization*[22] of the entire neurological activity that unfolds into the capacity to think. This explains that the intelligence of mammals is more or less developed according to the advanced degree of the organization permitted by the neocortex of a species.[23] The notion that each structure of the brain permits the creation of more complex organizations of the whole nervous system already announces some of the present neurological models.[24] An essential point is that consciousness requires a simultaneous coordination of many parts of the nervous system, but not necessarily of the entire system.

The relevance of this division is justified by the fact that these five parts of the nervous system correspond to its evolution and to the development of mental capacities. There exist animals with a neocortex (down to the rat), others without a neocortex, others without a brainstem, some without a spinal cord, and finally some that do not even have isolated sensorimotor centers. However the neurological hierarchy is not as strict as Lamarck and Darwinians of the first half of the century had assumed. For example, the highly intelligent and skillful octopus has a nervous system that cannot easily be fitted in the classical evolutionary frame.

This model was taken up in the 1950s by MacLean. His formulation, presented in Darwinian language, became fashionable with "psys" (see the Glossary) and philosophers.[25] However useful it might be, when used as a metaphor or a shortcut, this model does not take into account the complexity of the connections in the brain.[26]

From Propensity to Inclination[27]

> Instinct is, in all sensitive beings, the production of an inner sentiment which it possesses, a very obscure sentiment which, in certain circumstances, leads it to execute actions without knowing it, without previous cause, and without the use of an idea, and then, without the participation of will. (Lamarck, 1820, *Système Analytique*, II.II.2, p. 228f; translated by Michael C. Heller and Marcel Duclos)

As man thrived in different regions of the globe, he increased in number, established himself in society with fellow creatures, and finally progressed and became civilized. His delights and his needs increased and became more and more diversified. He developed increasingly varied ways of relating to the society in which he lived; which, among other things, generated increasingly complex personal interests. His inclinations subdivided endlessly, generated new needs that activated themselves beyond the scope of his awareness. These grew into a huge mass of connections that control, outside of his perception, nearly every part of him. (Lamarck, 1815, *Natural History,* p. 278; translated by Michael C. Heller and Marcel Duclos)

A natural propensity can be calibrated either with the help of "reason," either thanks to different forms of education, or by entering in competition with other innate or acquired propensities.[28] There is passion, according to Lamarck, when a propensity manifests itself without being contained by reason, education, or acquired propensities.[29] The innate central purpose of these propensities renders them recognizable as independent from the modifications brought about through education. To drink at a spring demands a different series of coordinations than to ask a dinner companion to pass the carafe of water at a banquet. In this example a common core instinctual procedure is included in two different propensions.[30] This flexibility of the behavioral organization of the organism has had a profound impact on the development of human social behavior.

According to Lamarck, it was always thus that the initial human propensities developed and differentiated gradually as more complex social systems made the social exploitation of the propensities' flexibility possible. This complexity is such that its organization is necessarily nonconscious. This is why the diverse developments of the natural propensities form today, in every human being, a web of activities "unbeknown to him" and that continuously "govern him" (Lamarck, 1820, II.II.1, p. 207; translated by Marcel Duclos).[31] As a good systemic thinker, Lamarck does not defend a linear development that would have first occurred in one's imagination, then at the level of the propensities, and then in social organization.[32] All these factors structure each other continuously.

Lamarck already introduces the idea, exploited by Darwin, that this network of influences is not necessarily coherent and leads to conflicts of interests between the different heteroclite constituents of a propensity. The propensities, such as they exist today in humans, connect a network of natural and acquired propensities that calibrate every behavior. Even when it consists in being thirsty, the natural stakes can be associated to other interests like those of manipulating a speaker by the way one holds a cup of tea: "Therefore, for those who know how to study humans, it is curious to observe the diversity of masks under which one can disguise a personal interest according to their status, their social ranking, their power, etc." (Lamarck, 1820, II.II.1, p. 209; translated by Marcel Duclos). The relevance of this analysis for the psychotherapist is that we must advance prudently when we try to reduce behavior to a unique biological constituent. For example, asking for more tea to protect oneself by controlling others and the need to drink enough water for self-preservation both activate different mechanisms, which are nevertheless associated to the core of the same instinct. These two ways of using thirst are so intermingled that any attempt to understand them by a cause that might be "more basic" than others could lead to an error in understanding.

Lamarck seems to center his psychology on schema,[33] skills, or action systems[34] that inevitably lead the psychotherapist to approach the human being as if it were but a combination of gestures and thoughts. Thoughts move the body, and gestures create thoughts. To analyze a representation without taking into account the behaviors associated to it often leads to an incomplete analysis of a person's propension.[35]

Lamarck is fascinated by the power with which an instinct mobilizes the resources of the organism needed to accomplish a task. From the point of view of consciousness, all that is perceived is an imperative feeling experienced as a rational desire. It shows that the study of the evolution of the mind is possible only by studying how physiology and behavior are coordinated.[36] His knowledge of evolution allows Lamarck to understand how certain biological dynamics become active components of the psychological development of individuals.

WALLACE

A Self-Taught Gentleman

Alfred Russel Wallace (1823–1913) is an exceptional version of a familiar personage in the landscape of the body psychotherapies.[37] He was a self-taught individual who was brilliant, curious, and learned as he practiced without any follow-up studies. He read everything with the same passion, the same curiosity, without preoccupying himself with any academic prejudice. Brilliant and honest, he adhered to whatever interested him. This is how he came to be passionate about the classification of vegetable and animal species, cartography, mesmerism, and phrenology. In all of these domains, he mostly read the books written for the layman. He discovered the theory of evolution in books that are often more moralistic than scientific. These British authors only mention Lamarck to disqualify his studies because he worked during the French Revolution and Napoleonic Wars.[38] For an English person of this period, these political involvements are unacceptable. Such an out-of-hand rejection is similar to that of past disqualifications of any theory elaborated in the Soviet Union or in fascist regimes. All that Wallace knew of Lamarck was that his theory would be simplistic and based on an unprovable "second law."

In this vast landscape that makes up Wallace's reading, certain works influenced him so profoundly that they guided his career. While reading Darwin's book on his voyage to the Galápagos, written in 1839,[39] he discovered his desire to become an explorer. Wallace, like Darwin ten years earlier, was also taken by the *Essay on the Principle of Population* by Thomas Robert Malthus (1826).[40] Wallace and Darwin were both astonished by the fact that it only takes ten generations for a pair of birds to produce 100,000 offspring *on condition* that the creatures were able to survive the dangers in their environment (predators, variations in the climate, sickness, famine, etc.) before reproducing.

The Jungle: A Particularly Inspiring Museum of Natural History

Wallace became an explorer and traveled into the jungles of South America and Indonesia, where he gathered plant and animal specimens for collectors. Darwin was one of his clients. Wallace also amassed numerous observations of the indigenous peoples who inhabited these jungles, for whom he had a profound respect.

If Lamarck was able to conceive of the theory of evolution thanks to his Museum of Natural History, Wallace had an even more stimulating environment. He had, in his head, the theories developed by Lamarck's students and Malthus's theory; all the while, the jungles of South America and Asia seethed around him. He observed animals in their own environments and could note how the species varied from one landscape to another. As he needed to satisfy a demanding clientele, he quickly learned to distinguish the subspecies of plants and animals, to observe the details that change from one part of the jungle to another.[41] Lamarck had had the opportunity to reflect on a variety of creatures already classified, without having to observe their environment.

Nature Selects Nothing, but Survival Rules All

In 1855, while in Borneo, Wallace wrote his first article on the theory of evolution. At first glance, this article does not seem to contain anything new. Nonetheless, in it he presented a first version of what became the principal law of the theory of evolution: "Every species has come into existence coincidentally both in time and space with a pre-existing closely allied species." Wallace was flattered to learn that well-known personalities, like geologist Charles Lyell[42] and Charles Darwin, had discussed his article.

In 1558, Wallace sent Darwin his second article, written in Indonesia. This time, Wallace's great law has taken a definitive form. The idea developed in this text is so simple that it appears almost absurd at first. How is one to pretend to explain so many things with what is a sort of "nonlaw?"

On one hand, we have this nature as prolific and dynamic as the lava of an erupting volcano. On the other hand, we have an environment that exists quite contentedly. And that is it! Wallace merely observes that certain products of nature survive, and others do not. If a family survives, it can proliferate at an astonishing pace.[43] According to Wallace's law, there is no *force* that selects and sorts. It is not even the strongest or the most intelligent who survives. It is the one that reproduces the most easily in a given environment. The one that can reproduce in many regions propagates more easily than one that can survive in only one region. This vision is close to the laws that Hume describes in *A Treatise of Human Nature*. There is no logic, no criteria for validation, or even rules of the game. To survive and reproduce without knowing why suffices.

Another brilliant idea, which Wallace had already sketched in his previous article, is that everything changes, and certain changes "take hold" and others do not. These changes are always small, as those that differentiate one brother from the other, and nothing more.[44] However, if these changes have characteristics that are genetically transmitted, and if they help an organism reproduce over many generations, their impact may modify the chances of the survival of a progeny. It is, therefore, step by step that the species would have modified themselves over millions of years, which explains the variety that exists today.

According to Wallace, there is no necessity for any other law to explain the evolution of the species. Lamarck's two laws are therefore useless.

The Survival of the Fittest and Natural Selection

> As the preservation of incapables is habitually secured by our social arrangements; and as very few except criminals are prevented by their inferiorities from leaving the average number of offspring (indeed the balance of fertility is probably in favour of the inferior); it results that survival of the fittest, can scarcely at all act in such a way as to produce specialities of nature, either bodily or mental. (Herbert Spencer, 1864, *The Principles of Biology*, p. 469)[45]

Wallace uses the expression *survival of the fittest*, which is often understood as the survival of the strongest.[46] Survival, according to Wallace, depends mostly on health and behavior. These two dimensions of the organism can integrate themselves more or less easily with the resources of an environment. For Wallace, fitness is a way of doing things that is particularly well adapted to an environment, like a shoe in which a foot is comfortable. A piece of a puzzle fits with another piece when they can fit together and form the part of the design that is sought. This has nothing to do with the notion, driven by certain neo-Darwinian movements, that only the *strongest* survive. Not all tyrants and geniuses had children; those that did, did not necessarily beget particularly powerful or brilliant offspring.[47]

Health is the *assimilating* factor that rules survival. If an organism cannot withstand the temperature or the available food in an environment, it becomes ill and dies. The *accommodating* factor is the capacity to calibrate behavior. This behavior can be motivated by many types of thoughts and physiological mechanisms. Without knowing it, Wallace thus confirmed the importance that Lamarck gave to behavior, even if the framework of their thinking was different:

> It is not the organs, which is to say the nature and shape of the parts of the body of an animal, which have created its habits and particular faculties. On the contrary, it is his habits, the way he lives, and the circumstances in which its parents

met that have with time created the shape of his body, the number and the structure of his organs, and finally the faculties he possesses. (Lamarck, 1802, p. 44;
translated by Marcel Duclos)

The Mind: Somewhere between Unknown Forces and Biology

The principal disagreement between Darwin and the positions of Wallace concern the mind. Wallace was attracted not only by mesmerism and phrenology
but by the spiritualism that was developing in the United States.[48] He talks
about ghosts, telepathy, and the communication between the dead and the living. He is not speaking of belief, but from a conviction based on numerous experiences that he evaluated critically. He identifies two levels of the mind:[49]

1. A level of the mind *that is intimately linked to the shape of the body* and
   to behavior as described by German neurologist Franz Josef Gall. This
   level corresponds to the instinctive and emotional innate behaviors and
   to some know-how, like the use of tools. This type of behavior is subject
   to the rules of the theory of evolution.
2. *Other mental forces are not directly linked to the shape of the body.*
   These are *potential* resources that will not develop outside of particular
   social contexts, like the spiritual resources activated by religious instruction. To the extent that evolution only selects activated behaviors, it is
   therefore not possible to explain the potential resources of the human
   mind with a biological theory.

For Wallace, evolution advances in small increments. The changes in mental
capacity between humans and monkeys are so important that they cannot be
explained by the small steps of biological evolution.[50] Some mental capacities
are more developed in one culture than in another. These are referred to as *potential* capacities. An individual born in the wild can go to London and become
a pianist who plays classical music.[51] If such a person had stayed in the wild,
this potential capacity would have never expressed itself. Therefore, it cannot
have been selected by biological processes. It is probably because of this argument that scientists eliminated Wallace from the current references related to
the theory of evolution. On that point (mind and evolution), Lamarck remains
the reference.

DARWIN

Darwin's Passion for the Evolution of the Species

Charles Darwin (1809–1882)[52] is halfway between Lamarck and Wallace. He is
a rich man who pursued university studies in theology and became an enlight-

ened amateur biologist. He does not defend a theory or a coherent vision of nature. He felt an inner urge to observe animals in a detailed way and improve Lamarck's theory of evolution. This passion increased with age. He was one of those explorers for whom an obsessive interest for details leads to the emergence of global theoretical issues. For example, because he would record every minute detail of each individual animal, he became keenly aware of the infinite variety that is generated by nature.

Erasmus Darwin

Darwin's family acquired their wealth during the English Industrial Revolution. They were profoundly influenced by the philosophers of the Age of Enlightenment, especially Voltaire.

Charles Darwin's paternal great-grandfather, Erasmus Darwin, was a renowned physician who introduced Lamarck's theory in Great Britain during the Napoleonic Wars. As Lamarck was perceived as a French revolutionary and an enemy of Great Britain, this interest was followed with ambivalence: British intellectuals could not repress a fascination for the general frame of the theory of evolution, but they refused to integrate a theory produced by the guillotines of the revolution and the horrible wars undertaken by Napoleon. A passionate defense of Lamarck's theory was part of the intellectual world in which Charles Darwin grew up.

The Biologist Pastor

Darwin studied theology at Cambridge. His family hoped that he could then become a minister in the Anglican Church. Influenced by his grandfather, he followed the discussions of the biologists concerning the works of Lamarck. One of his professors in Cambridge put him in contact with Captain Fitzroy,[53] who was looking for a companion for a research trip to the Pacific Ocean. That is how Darwin reached the Galápagos Islands, where he transformed himself into a passionate observer of nature. The material he gathered during this trip provided him with what he needed to write the book that made his reputation: *The Voyage of the Beagle.* This work tells of a journey full of interesting observations, but it does not develop any theoretical theme, and it does not mention the theory of evolution.

Darwin became a renowned intellectual who frequented the greatest scientists of his time, like geologist Sir Charles Lyell. Darwin set himself the task of improving Lamarck's theory, which was still severely criticized. This was a private pastime about which he said very little. But with the aid of his obsessive tendencies, he became, in his time, one of the greatest specialists on the details and the potential still hidden in the theory of evolution.[54]

He wrote in his notebooks of his attempts at formulating laws that would *complete* Lamarck's two laws. While reading Malthus's *Essay,* he sensed vaguely that the notion of survival is important, but he did not find an explicit formulation.

A Small Detour via Wallace

When Alfred Russel Wallace sent him his article of 1858, Darwin sensed that he has just read the formulation that was on the tip of his tongue. He used his influence to ensure that both of them would be recognized as the originators of the theory of natural selection. If Wallace had the genius to make explicit the law of natural selection, Darwin had all the examples necessary to support this hypothesis in his copious notes. He was then able to publish a convincing argument for a theory of evolution based on Wallace's nonlaw in one year, *The Origin of Species*. In this book, where Darwin must demonstrate that Wallace and he discovered the same thing, he describes all the aspects of the theory of evolution that can be explained by the principle of survival of the fittest. However, those among you who read Darwin's other books will soon see that for him, this mechanism may be the principal tool of evolution, but it is not the only one. Darwin still uses Lamarck's two laws to explain a number of observations.

Darwin and the Emotions

Ethologists, like Konrad Lorenz and Desmond Morris, have tried to present a kind and coherent Darwin. Every element of nature seems to have a clear function, like Lamarck's example of the giraffe. This view allows for the appearance, like in the films of Walt Disney (I am thinking of Perry the squirrel), of a cruel world in which everyone must learn how to survive but where everything has a cause, everything is explainable.[55] The tears of sadness and the wide eyes of astonishment have a function adapted to the expressed emotion. When someone attacks me, I show my teeth to scare him, to show him that I could bite him. These would be the functions that allow for survival. These signals were selected and related to a behavior because they give an individual a greater chance at survival. Thus, to frown and wrinkle one's nose, as often happens when a person cries, protects the eyes against an eventual blow.[56] This view may be relevant, but those who hold it are wrong when they associate it with Darwin. Wilhelm Reich caricatures this type of thinking when he speaks of biologist Oscar Hertwig:

> What disturbed particularly in biology was the application of the teleological principle. The cell was supposed to have to have a membrane *in order to* better protect itself against external stimuli; the male sperm cell was so agile *in order to* better get to the ovum. The male animals were bigger and stronger than the females, or more beautifully colored, *in order to* be more attractive to the females; or they had horns *in order to* beat off their rivals. (Reich, 1940, I, p. 5)

In an article on Reich's bioenergy, David Boadella[57] manages to find a quote from Darwin where he writes that to express our emotions is good for our health and to inhibit their expression represses emotional sentiments.[58] This quote illustrates two aspects of Darwin's thought:

1. It is possible to find citations in which Darwin asserts that the expression of emotion is necessary for the equilibrium of the individual. Boadella quotes him justifiably because this paragraph is found at the end of the conclusion in Darwin's book, *The Expression of the Emotions in Man and Animals* (1872). The sentence is presented as a summary of Darwin's thought. It is therefore plausible to think that this is the opinion of Darwin . . . unless we read the rest of the text.

2. The preceding remark shows how Darwin ceaselessly attempts to find new formulations, and that he does not mind if his compulsive search leads to contradictions. In this precise case, he probably tries to end his book on a positive note.

The Raw Realism of the English Mind

Darwin's intelligence makes me think of a rat in a maze. The rat I have in mind does not really think. He does not elaborate a strategy, does not synthesize things in any relevant manner, remembers poorly the route traveled, and often ends up in the same impasses. However, he persists! He ceaselessly advances in every which way and eventually finds the exit by chance. Wallace certainly proceeds with more elegance. He reflects, reasons, and finds the exit more quickly. But Darwin's way of proceeding has an advantage. By rushing all around before thinking, he covered all of the nooks and crannies of the maze that he has gotten to know by heart. With his bullet-proof skepticism, Darwin's way of proceeding prevents him from drawing conclusions that others too easily adopt.

Wallace and Darwin thought that only a few details changed from one generation to another. Therefore, these details distinguish one individual from another and can influence the chances of survival. Let us imagine that cats that were able to see at night had a greater chance of survival than those who ran faster but could not see at night. The first species will survive better than the second, and the capacities of the second will be lost. Not all of the capacities of an organism favor its survival. An animal is a complex coordination of inherited traits. Only some of them influence the chances of survival in a particular way. However, if a cat survives, the totality of his traits is transmitted.

This is how Wallace and Darwin explained that a creature often possesses traits that enhance his capacity to survive and others that diminish this capacity.[59] Thus, humans may have been favored by the fact that their hands and feet were different. The advantage brought about by this trait in terms of survival allowed them to reproduce even if they also had other traits that were useless or even self-destructive. To confirm this analysis, Darwin (1872) undertook a study of the emotional expressions in man and in animals.

Emotional Expressions Often Create Obnoxious Forms of Interaction

Darwin's idea was that the domain of emotional expressions was an ideal terrain to find (1) psychological reactions inherited from other species, (2) which had a functional value for the survival of certain species, and (3) which had no useful function for humans.[60] If a trait is of no use for the survival of a species and is innate, it is highly probable that it was produced by evolution. The coccyx is a well-known example in the human species of all that remains of the tails of our ancestors, the monkeys. Thus Darwin chose to study emotions *because* they were an example of "purposeless"[61] psychological mechanisms that are "not at all useful."[62] His research led to such powerful and abrasive considerations that he tried to soften his analysis at the end of his work on the human and animal expressions with the famous phrase quoted by David Boadella. Darwin's idea was that once he had proven with this research that some psychological mechanisms had been produced by evolution, biologists could then tackle more complex psychological mechanisms influenced by evolution but still have a constructive function for the human species (e.g., some psychological dimensions of the instincts).

Consequently, for Darwin, to tremble with fear is not necessarily a useful reaction, and can even be "of no service."[63] It is not possible, for him, that this reaction was preserved by human organisms because it positively influenced their survival. He remarks that the angry vocalizations that we inherited from some animals are often less expressive and powerful than some musical melodies.[64] Tears often reveal "pitiful" thoughts (Darwin, 1872, VI, p. 173). They are not even advantageous when we are with our loved ones. Darwin[65] thinks that to cry is as useless as the tears that flow after a blow near the eyes, a sneeze, or too bright a light projected into the eye. The fact remains that the same tears, for totally incidental[66] reasons, can alleviate some suffering. In the first chapter of his book on the expressions, Darwin insists on the idea that all the practical habits of a human organism activate themselves independently of conscious thoughts.

To the extent that Darwin thinks that these inherited reflexes have no relevance, it becomes reasonable to imagine that the same reflex acquired some useful and useless functions on the way. Darwin even notices that the more violent or "hysteric" the crying (Darwin, 1872, VI, p. 175), the more they bring a sense of relief. It is the same when someone who is suffering turns every which way, clenches his teeth, and makes ear-splitting screams. He observes these reactions in children and concludes that they are innate. But as a fine English gentleman of the Victorian period, he does not see the usefulness of these "simian" behaviors in a salon or in a meeting of scientists. In other words, the human emotional expressions sometimes procure a certain momentary relief, but they sabotage the survival of an individual in a socialized environment more than they help.

The Emotional Repertoire
Darwin so liked to describe what he observed in minute detail that he could never have been content to reduce the emotional expressions to a few traits or a few basic emotions. What he includes in his list of emotional expressions is, at the same time, varied to the extreme and heterogeneous. Here is the list of the

expressive traits and the emotions identified in the chapter headings of Darwin's book (the numbers correspond to the chapters):[67]

<EXT>(III) General principles of expression. The principle of the direct action of the excited nervous system on the body, independently of the will and in part of habit—Change of colour in the hair—Trembling of the muscles—Modified secretions—Perspiration—Expression of extreme pain—Of rage, great joy, and terror—Contrast between the emotions which cause and do not cause expressive movements—Exciting and depressing states of the mind.

(IV) Means of expression in animals. The emission of sounds—Vocal sounds—Sounds otherwise produced—Erection of the dermal appendages, hairs, feathers, &c., under the emotions of anger and terror—The drawing back of the ears as a preparation for fighting, and as an expression of anger—Erection of the ears and raising the head, a sign of attention.

(V) Special expressions of animals. The Dog, various expressive movements of—Cats—Horses—Ruminants—Monkeys, their expression of joy and affection—Of Pain—Anger—Astonishment and Terror

(VI) The screaming and weeping of infants—Form of features—Age at which weeping commences—The effects of habitual restraint on weeping—Sobbing—Cause of the contraction of the muscles round the eyes during screaming—Cause of the secretion of tears.

(VII) General effect of grief on the system—Obliquity of the eyebrows under suffering—On the cause of the obliquity of the eyebrows—On the depression of the corners of the mouth.

(VIII) Laughter primarily the expression of joy—Ludicrous ideas—Movements of the features during laughter—Nature of the sound produced—The secretion of tears during loud laughter—Gradation from loud laughter to gentle smiling—High spirits—The expression of love—Tender feelings—Devotion.

(IX) The act of frowning—Reflection with an effort or with the perception of something difficult or disagreeable—Abstracted meditation—Ill-temper—Moroseness—Obstinacy—Sulkiness and pouting—Decision or determination—The firm closure of the mouth.

(X) Hatred—Rage, effects of, on the system—Uncovering of the teeth—Rage in the insane—Anger and indignation—As expressed by the various races of man—Sneering and defiance—The uncovering of the canine tooth on one side of the face.

(XI) Contempt, scorn and disdain, variously expressed—Derisive smile—Gestures expressive of contempt—Disgust—Guilt, deceit, pride, &c.—Helplessness or impotence—Patience—Obstinacy—Shrugging the shoulders common to most of the races of man—Signs of affirmation and negation.

(XII) Surprise, astonishment—Elevation of the eyebrows—Opening the mouth—Protrusion of the lips—Gestures accompanying surprise—Admiration—Fear—Terror—Erection of the hair—Contraction of the platysma muscle[68]—Dilatation of the pupils—Horror.

(XIII) Nature of a blush—Inheritance—The parts of the body most affected—Blushing in the various races of man—Accompanying gestures—Confusion of mind—Causes of blushing—Self-attention, the fundamental element—Shyness—Shame, from broken moral laws and conventional rules—Modesty.

In the text, Darwin mentions an even greater variety of mental and bodily traits. In the lists for chapters IV and XI, he included the sign "&c." to indicate that in his mind, the emotional domain includes a greater number of traits.

Instincts and Emotions

AN INSTINCTIVE BEHAVIOR ARISES IN ASSOCIATION TO SOME
FUNCTIONAL COVARIATIONS OF THE DIMENSIONS OF THE ORGANISM
We find in Darwin's thinking examples of external propensities (the milieu participates in their calibration) that reorganize the heteroclite mechanisms. A species that survives especially because of a series of characteristics of the organism conserves other traits that do not influence its survival. It is possible that afterward, another detail that has nothing to do with the precedent becomes pertinent and would be "selected." It is thus the association of these two details that favors survival while the rest of the body varies independently. If such is how evolution functions, the organism is nothing other than a heap of disparate mechanisms that more or less hold together just enough to ensure survival. Regulating such messy architectures could explain why evolution is so slow. A mutation does not generate a global reconstruction of the organism. Only the changes that do not destabilize the totality of the organism too much can perpetuate themselves.

It is eventually possible for Darwin that there exists a kind of functionally coordinated *covariation* of mental and bodily traits in the domain of the instincts.[69] An herbivore (a cow) does not have an anatomy and physiology that permit it to become, on a daily basis, a carnivore; the large cats do not have the capacity to become exclusively herbivores. The anatomy and physiology of these species correspond to a certain type of food resource, and the organism of these species (the digestive tract, the teeth, the shape of their feet, etc.) little by little adjusted itself to be more effective at exploiting such resources in the environment. If we adopt Darwin's way of thinking, this adaptation can only have a relative, fuzzy coherence. It is nonetheless possible to define an instinct as being what associates certain mental and anatomical traits. *This relative coherence disappears in the construction of the emotions that mostly exploit and connect the parts of the body that no longer have any function.*[70]

Darwin distinguishes between several types of emotional schemata:

1. *The serviceable actions:* a useful action that is related to states of mind which are at play at the same time as the action, independent of their relevance. This definition is close to Hume's associationism, because it is the co-occurrence and not its relevance that creates the association.[71]
2. *The principle of antithesis:* "Certain states of the mind lead, as we have seen, . . . to certain habitual movements which were primarily, or may still be, of service; and we shall find that when a directly opposite state of mind is induced, there is a strong and involuntary tendency to the

performance of movements of a directly opposite nature, through these have never been of service" (Darwin, 1872, II, p. 50).[72]

This type of flexibility follows rules that are activated by default. Body psychotherapists know of many cases of persons who cry every time they are angry, who get angry when they are sad, who stimulate the two forms of expressions when they are sad or angry, or who cannot get angry without becoming sad. Here, we again find Descartes's idea, as expressed in *The Passions of the Soul*. He observed that an emotion can modify another emotion by amplifying or attenuating its intensity or even by concealing it. This kind of flexibility of the emotional schemata is often perceived today in psychotherapy as a manifestation of the defense systems. This type of interpretation sometimes forgets a little too quickly that this flexibility exists in any case. In some instances, defense systems exploit this flexibility to fulfill the regulation of an unconscious agenda. In other words, flexibility in the expressivity of the emotions can sometimes be the sign that a defense system is activated, but not always. I can only repeat that before concluding that crying instead of yelling is certainly brought about by a defense system, the therapist must also consider other alternatives.

DO WE HAVE TO CRY WHEN WE ARE SAD?

For Darwin, the emotions relate mostly to the parts of the body and the physiological mechanisms that have been conserved for reasons of general equilibrium, like serving as a counterweight for a segment of the body in the gravity field. This position is particularly well illustrated by the analysis of the expressions of sadness that Darwin develops in chapter 6 of his book on emotional expressions. This discussion remains a reference in the literature on emotions.

The basis for Darwin's analysis is the idea that a too rapid flow of blood to the eyes can raise the blood pressure at the back of the eyes, which can become dangerous.[73] Every time that a person exhales violently while laughing, crying, or sneezing, there is an acceleration of blood flow to the face, which risks modifying the ocular tension abruptly. The dilation of the retro-ocular arteries sometime pushes the eyes forward and makes them appear as if they are bulging. A rapid increase in vascular blood activity in the eye unleashes a reflex that contracts the muscles around the eyes to diminish the flow of blood in the eyes. This reflex often produces tears.

For Darwin, the reflex that produces tears is not unleashed by exhalation but by the activity of the muscles that provoke the exhalation. If a person contracts the muscles of the thorax and the abdomen while holding his breath, the reflex around the eyes is automatically unleashed. There is also a risk that the eyes will become engorged when a person vomits or when the muscles of the belly are suddenly contracted to expulse a bowel movement. Releasing fluids can then help lower that pressure. This reflex is therefore useful for the health of the eyes.

In this discussion,[74] Darwin indicates that many causes can activate the muscles used by a person who cries without it being necessarily related to sadness. It only consists, for the moment, of a reflexive sequence linked to the contraction of the muscles of the thorax and the belly. The first function of this reflex is to protect the eye when this type of respiration raises the pressure in it.

TEARS

To support his analysis of emotional expression, Darwin quotes several authors who presume that tears are part of the mechanisms that participate in the regulation of eye pressure. They can be associated to a variety of emotions (Darwin mentions laughter) and can sometimes be provoked by nonemotional reactions like violent coughs and yawning.[75] It is possible that this "nucleus" could have been associated with sadness for generations and could have finally become genetically transmissible. It is even possible that the attitude of parents could have participated in the construction of this association. For example, if they perceive tears as an expression of sadness, the infant may discover that tears are useful to convey his sentiment of sadness. In this example, Darwin describes an association between body and emotions that is constructed in two stages:

1. There exists a reflex that still has or had a function that has nothing to do with the emotions.
2. An emotion ties itself to available body reactions without any necessary functional links between the two.

Contrary to the instincts, there is therefore no covariation between the history of one part of the body and the affect that associates itself to it.

Today, physicians clearly distinguish between tears and the aqueous humor that rinses the interior of the eye socket. Only the aqueous humor has an influence on the ocular tension. Tears would therefore not have the function of protecting the eye from changes in pressure but only that of keeping the surface of the eye clean. On the other hand, physicians still think that respiration influences both the tears and the ocular pressure.[76] This complicates Darwin's analysis a bit. But it also confirms it because, finally, the inclusion of tears in the expression of sadness, distress, joy, and anger touches functions still less central than Darwin thought. Whatever are the underlying mechanisms of tears, it is undeniable that a profound activation of respiration stimulates tears. Emotions also often activate such deep breathing. Therefore by grouping existing heterogeneous mechanisms, emotions produce a series of impacts on self and on those around us.[77]

Idealism and Variety

> You know that Darwin based his hypothesis of the origin of species by "natural selection" upon two principles—the principle of variability and the principle of inheritance of individual characteristics. (Wilhelm Wundt, 1892, *Lectures on Human and Animal Psychology*, 26.II, p. 385)

Hegel and Marx were Idealists because they believed that history was taking us to a transpersonal goal. For them, humans build themselves through improvements and will eventually become perfect. We find this point of view in some research carried out in industry; for example, in those enterprises that want to find the perfect apple, the perfect computer, the perfect medicine, the product that meets a maximum of needs (lowest cost and indestructible), and so on.

For Darwin, more than for Wallace, nature's strategy is altogether different. It does not aim for perfection but for *variety*.[78] It does not consist in producing a hero capable of vanquishing all situations but a multitude of keys with the hope that there will always be one that will be fit into the keyhole of a door that blocks our passage. As a whole, this is the strategy of the immune system when it generates antibodies. The more a species produces varied organisms, the more it has a chance to beget offspring that will survive. Wilhelm Reich summarizes the relevance of this point of view for psychotherapy in this way:

> Darwin's theory of natural selection, also, corresponded to the reasonable expectation that, although life is governed by certain fundamental laws, there is, nevertheless, ample room for the influence of environmental factors. In this theory, nothing was considered eternally immutable, nothing was explained on the basis of invisible hereditary factors; everything was *capable of development*. (Reich, 1940, I, p. 7)

Darwin includes his cult of variety in his theoretical constructs. Contrary to Wallace, he does not believe that all evolutionary mechanisms could be explained by a single law or by a coherent assembly of laws. In his way of thinking, there is no problem including (1) Wallace's law of survival and (b) Lamarck's second law, according to which acquired habits can become hereditary. It is not only in his early writings, influence by his grandfather Erasmus, but also in his last works that Darwin defends the second law. Thus, in his 1872 book on emotional expressions, he repeatedly defends the position without making any reference to Lamarck.

Darwin assumes that habits can influence the material structure of the nervous system, because without this argument, he cannot explain how acquired habits can enter into the domain of what can be inherited.[79] He states, in several places in his book, that habits acquired in a culture can "become permanent and inheritable."[80] For me, one of the bases of the ethic conveyed by psychotherapists is this respect (1) of the variety and heterogeneity of what exists and (2) of the variety and heterogeneity of the mechanisms that regulate the living.

Wallace's Darwinism

> A wild population of any species consists always of individuals whose genetic constitution varies widely. In other words, potentiality and readiness for change is already built into the survival unit. The heterogeneity of the wild population is already one-half of the trial-and-error system which is necessary for dealing with the environment.

> The artificially homogenized populations of man's domestic animals and plants are scarcely fit for survival. (Gregory Bateson, 1972, *Steps to an Ecology of Mind*, II.V.5, p. 451)

For some, the founder of the theory of evolution is Alfred Russel Wallace. Charles Darwin used his influence to be recognized as co-discoverer and then quickly published the *The Origin of Species* while Wallace was still in the jungle. For others, Darwin is the only one who could have produced a convincing theory of evolution. His book was an immediate best-seller. This was recognized by Wallace, who was content to be co-inventor of Darwinism. His social position became much more comfortable than he had expected. Apparently, he and Darwin became great friends and respected each other.

However, there is a twist to this story. In 1889, seven years after Darwin's death, Wallace published a volume that summarized their theory, titled *Darwinism*. This book influenced several generations of intellectuals, who believed it was the best summary of the Darwinian theory and therefore mostly referred to this book and Darwin's *The Origin of Species* when they wanted to clarify the particularities of Darwinism. This strategy helped academics avoid endless discussions on the respective contributions of each man. It was more urgent to accumulate additional data on the subject, which would inevitably lead to constant reformulations. Darwinism became the part of the theory on which the two pioneers agreed. The particularities of each thinker were thus soon forgotten. Keeping "the best of both worlds" is a typical English attitude when one wants to be on the safe side. It is this "averaged" vision of Darwinism that has been used when Darwinism was associated to Mendel's genetics to form the current vision of Darwinism taught in schools and universities.[81] Only a few thinkers found it interesting to discuss the particular options that Darwin or Wallace could have supported.[82]

It is only recently that a careful reading of all of Darwin's publications has highlighted the less conventional ideas that Darwin developed on the fuzziness, variety, and lack of coherence of biological dynamics. The impact of this rereading of Darwin's theory on contemporary psychology is what I now summarize. It is possible than an equally thorough reading of Wallace could inspire other new developments.

THE NEO-DARWINISM OF TODAY

> Is there any reasonable ground to conclude, that the inhabitants of other planets possess thought, intelligence, reason, or anything similar to these faculties in men? When nature has so extremely diversified her manner of operation in this small globe; can we imagine, that she incessantly copies herself throughout so immense a universe? (Hume, 1776, "Dialogues Concerning Natural Religion," II, p. 50)

The preceding sections permit us to distinguish between at least three neo-Darwinian trends:

1. *Wallace-Mendel*: The Darwinism of molecular biology is mostly influenced by a synthesis between the last formulations of Wallace on Darwinism and the genetics of Mendel. In these theories, chance ends up creating, of necessity, a wonderfully coherent world (Jacob 2000). This proposition was incorporated into the utopia of economic liberalism and academic biology.

2. *Lamarck-Darwin*: The ethologists avoid talking about Lamarck, but they finally present a form of Darwinism in which chance necessarily leads to functional forms of coherence. This position leads to conclusions that are close to Lamarck's observations.

3. *Darwin*: The theoretical issues raised by artificial intelligence and the postmodern philosophers seem to have favored a rereading of Darwin that associates the meanderings of his thought to a nature that modifies things without any necessity, as if it continuously tinkered with everything that exists.

I only discuss the third trend in the following sections because it allows for a synthesis of the themes that I initiated, while talking about Hume and Darwin, about a world and a mind that makes no sense, save for the meaning the human imagination attributes to it. Even the enlightened Darwinians have a difficult time integrating such a radical analysis. Australian philosopher Paul E. Griffiths[83] mentions Darwin's remarks on the uselessness of the emotional expressions, and he is ready to admit that they have lost the functions they had for other species. However, he assumes that if they are always present in the genetic repertoire, they have acquired new functions. Like most of the scientists and philosophers, he reluctantly accepts the notion that nature selects useless behaviors, even self-destructive ones.

There is in this a difficulty given the tools that reason uses. Consciousness likes beautiful and grand edifices that architects refer to as "classical." Each element is in harmony with the others; their organization is coherent and their structure contains no useless elements. Spinoza's theory is one of the most beautiful examples of a classical theory. Reason has difficulty appreciating more baroque and less functional architecture. The rococo style is an example of this kind of architecture. The facades follow the associations of the imagination. The walls change shape at every turn; they are decorated and then plain, all without any necessity for the solidity of the building. In the discussions at the end of the twentieth century, philosophers contrasted a classical or modern style to the rococo or postmodern style.[84] In Darwin's theory, the bricks are stacked on top of each other without any architect ensuring the coherence of the whole. The only criterion is that some constructions survive better than others, even when the makeshift arrangement that constitutes them contains weak and poorly constructed elements.

This discussion has a profound influence on the theories of today. To understand what is at stake, I begin by going back over the way this discussion was expressed, a short time after Lamarck's death, in the debate that occurred between Saint-Hilaire and Cuvier.

Saint-Hilaire against Cuvier: On the Degree of Coherence of Biological Architectures

Etienne Geoffroy Saint-Hilaire (1772–1844) and Georges Cuvier (1769–1832) are two great biologists who worked at the Museum of Natural History of Paris. Saint-Hilaire pursued the reflection begun by Lamarck by studying the unfolding of the anatomy of animals, as if all the species were partial manifestations of the same underlying structure. There would be on one side—in the world of Ideas or God's plan—a perfect architecture, and on the other side, species that incarnate this plan in a more or less complete way. For him, the theory of evolution shows how the forces of life gradually approach the Ideal architecture.[85] In his research, Saint-Hilaire attempted to define the anatomy of each species and the links that can exist between each organ. He was one of those who reinforced the evolutionary theory that anatomical links exist between all of the species. He demonstrated, among other things, that the anatomical similarities between species of mammals are particularly salient when biologists study their respective fetuses.

On a theoretical plane, Saint-Hilaire presents three laws that characterize the relationship between anatomy and evolution:[86]

1. The *law of development* is illustrated by the observation that in the history of the species, no organ abruptly appears or disappears. Wallace and Darwin would often refer to this law.
2. The *law of compensation* postulates that no organ can grow disproportionately unless other organs reduce their size and mass.
3. The *law of relative position* states that the parts of all animals maintain the same positions relative to each other.

Cuvier was one of the principal adversaries against the theory of evolution. He was especially well known for his ability to reconstruct the overall anatomy of a fossil starting with mere fragments. This skill made it possible for him to become the first great specialist of the vanished species, such as prehistoric animals. He explains these disappearances with the theory of geological catastrophe proposed by certain geologists of his time.

It was his thesis that each animal has a coherent anatomy and no element of this architecture can be modified without deeply upsetting the general equilibrium. There would not have been any survival possible if things had come about as Lamarck and Saint-Hilaire claimed. This led Cuvier to propose a law of the necessary correlation of the parts. Darwin often used Cuvier's law to demonstrate the opposite of what Cuvier wanted to prove. For Darwin, the need to maintain a minimum of general equilibrium can explain the maintenance of the parts of organs that had a precise function but that are then maintained uniquely to guarantee the equilibrium of the whole in the gravity field. It would be mostly these remnants, kept for architectural reasons, to which the emotions are related.

The discussion between Cuvier and Saint-Hilaire became one of the great popular debates of the 1820s. Cuvier represented a scientific vision compatible with the views of the aristocracy and the Catholic Church. Saint-Hilaire's evolutionary vision was associated with the progressive forces that were about to take power in Western Europe. The following anecdote demonstrates to what extent this debate had become a major high-profile stake:[87]

> Anecdote about Goethe at breakfast. *The debates that were the rage concerning Cuvier and Saint-Hilaire were temporarily interrupted by the second French Revolution which erupted in July 1830. On the afternoon of the second of August, the elderly Goethe was reading the newspaper while eating breakfast. He asked his secretary, Johann Peter Eckermann, what he thought about the events in France: "The volcano has come to an eruption, everything is in flames, and we have no longer a transaction with closed doors!" Eckermann thought that Goethe was referring to the upheaval in the streets and to the abdication of King Charles X. But in fact he was referring to the debate between Cuvier and Saint-Hilaire that was heating up now that the present government supported Saint-Hilaire. (Based on Eckermann, 1848, p. 290f)*

The following sections are a tightly written theoretical summary of neo-Darwinian models. Some readers may prefer to read this material once they have a general vision of the content of this manual.

A Few Key Concepts from Artificial Intelligence and the Neurosciences

In the previous sections, we have seen Darwin's propensity to catalog all of the small variations of nature, as well as his aversion to those theories that, like Wallace's, try to explain everything with a single model.[88] Still more deeply anchored is his aversion to those grand theories that try to render everything coherent and functional, like those of Spinoza and Cuvier.

An admirer of Lamarck, Darwin freely accepted a systemic vision that situates the details in the elaboration of the great movements of history. However, he mostly admired how Lamarck had begun to undermine theories based on the notion that the world was a coherent entity. For Darwin, nature is an unbelievably imaginative makeshift of small mechanisms. That aspect of his thought rejoins the thought of the young Hume and was taken up in the 1970s to establish a movement that blends neurology, artificial intelligence, and psychology. This movement is called, according to its components, *evolutionary psychology*, the *neurosciences*, or the *neuro-cognitive sciences*. The best synthesis of these movements that I know remains the book of philosopher Andy Clark (1997): *Being*

There: Putting Brain, Body, and World Together Again.[89] I quote the title of his book in full because it aptly gives the impression of a tinkering nature.

In the following sections, I summarize concepts without which the recent developments inspired by Darwin in psychology, and consequently in psychotherapy, remain greatly unintelligible. It consists of the global/local distinction and the notions of modular and parallel activity.

I employ the procedures used to write software programs as a basic metaphor for the contemporary discussions on the mind. Building machines that can automatically reproduce certain performances of the mind have forced engineers to invent practical ways of accomplishing psychological tasks for which no one has a convincing explanation. The "tricks" they discovered are efficient enough, but are often "messy." The term *messy* is used for a set of procedures that are not necessarily coherent, logical, or satisfying from a purely intellectual point of view but that are good enough to satisfy those who use computers. These messy procedures have what one sometimes calls bugs. A bug, in this context, is usually a few lines of a program that do not accomplish what one expects them to do. The problem is that huge software is composed of millions of instructions, written for decades by sometimes thousands of engineers. Some of these engineers may have left the company, died, or changed profession. Even if one can still contact an engineer who wrote an old routine, he often cannot remember all that he did when he worked on that program.

Detecting where bugs are can sometimes take more time than rewriting a part of the program. Given the financial pressure of the software industry, this second strategy is often used. The problem is that there may be a few lines in another routine that still need to use some parts of the old program that functions. Such big programs, like the operating systems of computers,[90] are typically composed of old routines and new routines, forming an incredibly messy entity that has no coherence. Given the size of the program and the teams that participated in its construction, there probably is no single engineer who knows how such large software really operates. They have a general idea of the particularities of the program they work with, of the general rules used by all the engineers that developed that program, and a more intimate understanding of those parts of the program they have worked on. But they cannot know how each individual procedure (also called a subroutine) operates and associates with a web of other procedures. The present situation is even more complicated when one considers that the set of general rules used to coordinate all the engineers that work on a program today may not always be exactly the same ones that were used 10 years ago.

An increasing number of psychologists and neurologist observe that the brain and the mind have the same sort of messy architecture. No one knows the exact biological history of each mechanism, how each mechanism is influenced by other mechanisms, and what changed when the organism that contained this mechanism had a mutation and developed new forms of habitual behavior. I use the term *messy* to designate this type of loose organization that somehow manages to survive and reproduce because it is often used in the contemporary literature. This type of approach to the mind is becoming increasingly popular. In the chapters on philosophers, I opposed schools that assume a coherent organization of the mind and schools that had an intuition about the messiness of the mind. In artificial intelligence these two trends may describe forms of organization that exist in parallel, as illustrated in the following quotation:

> Over the years, I've written a number of books in praise of the Computational Theory of Mind. . . . It is, in my view, by far the best theory of cognition that we've got; indeed, the only one we've got that's worth the bother of a serious discussion. . . . But it hadn't occurred to me that anyone could think that it's a very *large* part of the truth; still less that it's within miles of being the whole story about how the mind works. (Fodor, 2000, p. 1)

Global/Local

If I describe respiration *globally*, I must first describe the large meteorological and social movements that in their interaction regulate the quality of the air. Gradually, I arrive at a global description of the physiology of respiration. At the interior of these large movements of the environment and of the organism, the scientist will study some *local* events. For example, he can study the interaction between the nostrils and the air. This is a local interaction if we think that the nostrils automatically inhale the air that is near the nose. As soon as a local environment is situated in a global mechanism, the question of the organization that relates one global mechanism to a local mechanism becomes relevant.

MODULES

The notion of module is an example of a local mechanism. A modular mechanism attends to a number of events. When these events occur, it extracts a certain amount of information, treats this information in a standard way, and produces a behavior that varies according to the information received in a standardized way. Here are three domains that illustrate different ways of using the concept of a module.

1. *Modules and the neurology of vision.*[91] The concept of modules was mostly introduced in psychology by the researchers who studied the visual cortex.[92] For example, Hubel and Wiesel observed that the stimulation of the retina creates a neurological activity that starts at the eyes and ends up in the visual cortex above the nape of the neck. There, small "pillars" of neurons extract particular information from this flow of neurological activity and produces distinctions that did not hitherto exist in the brain. Each pillar is a module,[93] to the extent that it extracts a certain type of information and deduces a certain number of properties that produce a chemical behavior that correlates with the analyzed data. This behavior is information that will be used to create a perception.

Each module will produce, in independent fashion, data on the shape, color, contrasts, degree of mobility, direction of movement, and so on. Not only does each module work independently of the others, in addition, its analysis does not take into account the operations that were previously performed in the brain by other modules.

2. *The subroutines of a computer program.* We find a similar organization in most computer programs. One program is composed of one or more programs; and each one coordinates a series of subprograms or subroutines that can be used in many different ways by each program. In addition, each subroutine can coordinate many other subroutines. The more we descend in the hierarchy of the organization of a software program, the more the hierarchy becomes fuzzy. A subroutine can activate another subroutine; it can activate or deactivate a program; it can shut down the computer. Some subroutines are used more often than others. Thus, the majority of existing programs contain a series of subroutines that make it possible to save data on an external data storage device (a CD, a USB drive, etc.). Each time a program is used by someone who does not use such a device, this series of subroutines will not be used.

3. *Modularity and philosophy.* Models on modular brains and machines appeared in U.S. research institutes during the 1960s. One of these was the Massachusetts Institute of Technology (MIT). MIT is one of the centers of artificial intelligence. It created this discipline by recruiting the help of not only engineers but also researchers in other disciplines and philosophers. They set about to elaborate a theoretical model that allowed for the fabrication of machinery, the study of how nature manages modular information, and to find the concepts necessary to create the relationship between the formulations of the engineers and what is observable. The work of U.S. philosopher Jerry Alan Fodor (1983), *Modularity of Mind,* is often quoted; I suspect that it is mostly due to his title, because the content is focused on the rapport between modularity and theories concerning the localization of the psychic functions in the brain, like phrenology. Somewhat like Kant with regard to Hume, Fodor (1998, 2000) tries to show that modularity is a form of the organization of information that makes it possible to describe relatively simple neurological mechanisms, but that it is improbable that the functioning of human reasoning could be understood with a model of this type.

PARALLEL AND SEQUENTIAL PROCESS OF INFORMATION[94]

When I described the pillars that analyze the visual information entering the visual cortex, I spoke not only of modularity, but also of the *parallel* activity of the modules. From the moment that each module works independently at the same time on the same flow of information, the management of the information is considered parallel. As the activity of each module occurs simultaneously, each module acts without waiting for the results of the analysis of the other modules. Imagine a patient who arrives at the emergency room of a hospital. Medical personnel will take blood and urine samples, for example. They will send what they have obtained to different laboratories, which will each analyze a specific aspect of those samples without waiting for the results of the other tests. During this time, the patient will be sent to radiology for more tests. The synthesis will be done later. Only at the moment of determining the diagnosis and the sequence of care will the attending physician know what test results are pertinent. That form of analysis is different from a sequential analysis procedure. *Sequential* analysis requires that each analysis is undertaken one after the other and only once the result of the previous analysis is known. This procedure is used in traditional causal models and logic.[97] Take, for example, a laboratory that runs tests on blood samples:

1. *Sequential analysis:* In sequential analysis, one begins with what seems to be the most important analysis required for a certain diagnostic. Once this analysis has been carried out, the clinician may need a second analysis to specify his intuitive diagnostic. He will then carry out this second analysis and continue with this procedure until he can propose the best diagnostic possible. He may, for example, begin by analyzing the cholesterol, then the sugars, then the antibodies, then the concentration of red blood cells, then iron. He may find that the sudden weakness of a person is due to a lack of iron in the blood.
2. *Modular and parallel analysis:* To carry out these five tests, blood is placed into five separate test tubes. Each tube is placed in a different machine that analyzes a pertinent property (one for sugars, one for lipids, one for iron, etc.). A switch activates these five machines that carry out their test at the same time in parallel fashion. In general, a complete blood test measures about 20 variables of this type. The physician will receive, on paper or on a screen, the list of the results of these tests. He will subsequently evaluate which variables can be considered relevant. Sometimes, analytical software will also indicate if some combinations (low iron and low red blood cell count) require his attention.

The syllogism is an example of sequential reasoning:

If A = B,
And B = C,
Then A = C.

A parallel analysis of the syllogism made by the subroutines of a program runs according to the following procedure:

Module 1: Question: A = B? Answer: yes or no.

Module 2: Question: B = C? Answer: yes or no.

Module 3: If answer 1 and answer 2 = yes, then A = C; if answer 1 and 2 are not equal, then A and C are not equal.

In fact, in modular thinking, it is often simpler to have a routine that directly compares A and C without needing the answers from the two other modules. There is therefore no longer a logical linear thought, even if the empirical result is the same.

Fodor, Johnson-Laird, and Crick[95] think that conscious reasoning follows a sequential logic, whereas the rustling of imagination[96] and the nonconscious mechanisms function mostly in a modular and parallel fashion. This type of model implies that the organism is capable of generating independent responses to each stimulus that is perceived by an organism at a given moment.

When one talks of modular analysis, the term *parallel* is not used the same way as when one talks of the parallelism of Descartes, Spinoza, and Leibniz. Even if there exists some relationship between these two ways to use the term *parallel*, it is important not to confuse them.

HILL CLIMBING

The limits of a mind functioning only with parallel modular procedures became apparent as soon as engineers tried to construct robots that could move on the surface of the moon. For example, they could not build a robot that was capable of climbing a hill.

When an officer orders a soldier to climb to the top of a hill, the soldier executes the order and climbs to the top with relative ease. When programmers have to detail what the soldier actually did to climb the hill, they suddenly discover the millions of small automatic skills that were accomplished in a relatively smooth way. As we have already seen, most of these activities are nonconscious, whereas others require the support of conscious dynamics. Before engineers began to write such programs, no philosopher or psychologist could have imagined the complexity involved to accomplish such a banal task.

At first, the engineers assumed that all they had to do was to give instructions to put one foot after the other on the ground ahead that was a bit higher and to stop when no higher ground could be found.[97] What happened was that the machine would end up on top of a rock that was miles away from the top of the hill. The soldier that climbs a hill would have automatically realized that the top of a mound is not the top of the hill. He would also know that one must sometimes go downhill for a while before resuming the climb, as a hill does not necessarily rise in a straight line. This is how, slowly but surely, engineers began to explore all the procedures that are required to climb a hill. Allen Newell and Herbert A. Simon[98] worked on similar problems from 1956 onward for more than 20 years, "introducing fundamental ideas that are still the core of *problem solving theory*" (Newell, 1990). The crux of the analysis is that the robots need to define long-term goals (e.g., where is the top of the hill?) and short-term goals (the next step). Long-term goals require a different kind of thinking than what is needed for the next step. Indeed, the next step requires not only finding what is the most relevant next step but also the capacity to avoid falling into holes or bumping into a tree when one can walk around it. A poor analysis of such tasks would slow down the machine's progress and could even cause its destruction. The machine must also analyze the geography that separates it from the top of the hill to find a manageable route. A manageable route goes to the top of the hill rather than to the top of a mound and will ensure the machine's integrity.

The number of variables involved in such a task, from the point of view of an engineer, is staggering. Engineers found that an intellectual analysis (e.g., where is the top of the hill?) requires relatively small programs, whereas a machine that acts requires an immense amount of work. One needs software programs that coordinate hardware and environmental factors. Traditionally, it was thought that intellectual performances are the most complex accomplishments of evolution. Engineers are now showing that the coordination between mental acts and relevant behavior is the really remarkable achievement. This has led to a series of theories that differentiate computing skills from *embodied intelligence*:[99]

> Processing is involved in routine behaviours such as driving, cooking, taking a walk, or manipulating everyday objects. These abilities, simple for humans, remain distant goals for robotics and seem to impose hard real-time requirements on an agent. . . . A local subsystem integrating sensory data or generating potential actions may have incomplete, uncertain, or erroneous information about what is happening in the environment or what should be done. But if there are many such local nodes, the information may in fact be present, in the aggregate, to assess a situation correctly or select an appropriate global action policy. (Rosenschein, 1999, pp. 410–412)

This quotation[100] shows the compatibility between artificial intelligence and an evolutionary approach to the mind. It allows one to describe forms of mental computation that could have evolved into increasingly efficient dynamics that became capable of producing symbolic thought and conscious activity. Once again, if such mechanisms were used by human nature, consciousness does not have the means to grasp such complex dynamics. They are actually sufficiently simple to be implemented in a robot, but too complex to be perceived through individual conscious perception.

The Fuzziness of the Architecture of Nonconscious Procedures

RITUALS SELECT A REPERTOIRE OF SCHEMA

Guy Cellérier is mostly known for his attempt to combine the theories of Kant, Darwin, and Piaget with the development of artificial intelligence.[101] Cellérier's reasoning appears simple, but it has multiple and complex implications. He takes up Wallace's nonlaw while insisting that in fact the interaction between the dynamics of an environment and the repertoire of available schema in each individual structure each other. A way of thinking or a way of behaving can be more or less adapted to the needs of the environment at a given moment, but this equilibrium can change with time, as an environment can also be experienced as more or less comfortable by individuals. With humans, the survival of a practice often depends more on the social environment than on geographical constraints. Cellérier's proposal, therefore, can be related to a form of social Darwinism he now calls "pluri-constructivism."[102] This coordination of practices is especially put in place by three types of mechanisms:

1. A practice necessarily depends on certain *innate structures of the organism*. It goes without saying that the behavior of speaking a language and the skill to write a novel are only observed (on our planet) in humans. On the other hand, a practice does not depend on all of the innate structures of an organism because language can be used by physically handicapped persons.
2. A practice also depends on the fine-tuning of physiological mechanisms that are *calibrated by the practices of a lifetime*. These diverse refined calibrations then influence the way the dimensions of the organism are built and reciprocally influence one another.
3. One form of such fine-tuning is *the capacity to learn how to manage particular forms of moving and thinking*. We have already seen, for example, that the learning of the martial arts such as tai chi chuan requires not only learning gestures but also learning how thoughts and respiration coordinate with the postural dynamics. This learning usually requires the support of an institution (a school, for example).

Cellérier's originality lies in showing how social and mental practices are already part of the selection systems of behaviors. Certain accentuations of the voice, modulations of the movements of the arm, or ways of thinking create individual practices that will be automatically evaluated from different points of view:

1. A behavior is more or less compatible with other existing behaviors within an organism.
2. A person can more or less appreciate the behaviors that are built within her.
3. A behavior has an impact on another who may appreciate it more or less.
4. A behavior can be more or less compatible with the behaviors of other members of the social environment.
5. An individual can value one of his behaviors, but not the impact that it has on his intimate ones.

Sometimes an individual likes a way of doing things, his environment also likes it, and the individual refuses to do it to express his resistance to the environment. This is the case of the anorexic who refuses to eat to oppose one of the parents.[103] Let us consider the following typical situation:

> Vignette on a typical form of anorexia. *A child has an intrusive mother, who absolutely wants her to eat large quantities of food. Although the child needs to eat, when she refuses to eat her mother becomes frustrated and angry. So the child, as vengeance and a defense against a continuously intrusive mother, refuses to eat. This anorexic behavior tends to increase when the parents, at last, start to panic and worry about what their child feels.*

The dynamic described by Cellérier lacks coherence because each option is a local choice that activates itself independently from other choices. Consciousness does not have a sufficiently powerful memory to remember all of the small choices made in a lifetime. The majority of the habits produced by these choices have not even gone through a psychological stage of learning. There are only functional accommodations of the body (nerve connections, muscle development, etc.) that have built up at the physiological level. As an individual, I have the conscious impression of being a coherent identity, but I cannot become aware of the millions of small habits that make up this impression. I am not able to achieve a conscious inventory of all of these built-up habits; I am even less able to perceive how they are coordinated. Thus, without my understanding how, one of my propensities can acquire a predominant role. I may suddenly discover that I am alcoholic, addicted to gambling, or so talented as a writer that editors and readers want me to write more books. Even when they have become public, such a propension is like an iceberg. Its mass and roots remain below the conscious surface of the mind. For example, alcoholism can have unconscious roots that may be elucidated in psychotherapy, but it has also created a form of equilibrium with metabolic dynamics that are more difficult to understand and integrate.

This implies that each little calibration develops almost independently of each other, sometimes in parallel fashion, that is, at the same time. The word *almost* makes reference to the constraints imposed by a choice. For example, once a connection between two neurons is fixed, these neurons are no longer available for other connections. Only constraints of this type can limit the number of physiological and psychological calibrations possible at any given moment.

AGENDAS AND PRIMING

I will now detail two models derived from this type of point of view that are often useful in psychotherapy: planning and priming.

The Agenda According to Cellérier.   For Guy Cellérier, to the extent that a human organism is a heap of disorganized know-how, its needs necessarily impose an impossible agenda. This is unavoidable if we consider the following points:

1. The propensities are multiple and poorly coordinated.
2. Their calibration depends on the context.
3. The modalities by which a propensity obtains satisfaction are not entirely prewired.

To satisfy their need for food, the Chinese use an assortment of practices manifestly different than those used by Europeans. To become a couple, to have children, and to educate them corresponds to an instinctive and innate parental propensity, but the modalities vary in each social milieu, even for each couple. We are far from the standardized ritual behavior of fish like the stickleback, observed by Tinbergen (1951).

The calibration of each propensity therefore requires such complex learning procedures that it is not possible to adequately develop all of its components. Take some of an individual's few essential activities and try to discover a plausible agenda for them. You will soon discover that it is an impossible task. Every expert will explain that it suffices to accomplish a certain number of simple acts to achieve the proper unfolding of the propensity he finds to be central for human well-being. Once you have made the round of the specialists (sexologist, nutritionist, body worker, physician, professional coach, artist, priest, etc.), you will find yourself faced with the necessity to make choices, each of which will have their advantages and their dangers.

This argument assumes that the selection of behavioral skills comes about through practice. The more a propensity is practiced, the better it functions in this particular way. Behaviors that are seldom used become inefficient and lose contact with the know-how that could support its insertion into social practices. It takes time to become a good lover, a good parent, to work well, to maintain a constructive social network, to have a mindset that gives us the desire to continue to live, and so on. But to properly develop all of these practices demands an amount of time (100-hour days) that is available to no one. Furthermore, this calibration depends not only on the number of times that the practice is carried out but also on the way it is done, and on how it is supported by the organismic dimensions.

Priming According to Michal Hoey.

Hoey suggests that, as a word is acquired through encounters, it becomes accumulatively loaded with the contexts and co-texts in which it is encountered and we are primed with certain expectations about its collocations, colligations, semantic and pragmatic associations among other things. Our knowledge, use and expectations about words are determined by our exposure to words in context. (Alison Duguid, 2008, *Men at Work*)

The theory of "priming," proposed by linguist Michael Hoey (2005), goes in the same direction.[104] It shows that each individual's ways of thinking are affected by a complex network of influences. Priming is at the same time "what is highlighted" and "what prepares." Hoey analyzes how key words or key sentences used by an individual and their associated thoughts depend on the number of times such a formulation appears in his life and on the intensity of how these stimuli relate to a listener's habitual practices. Priming activates a network of associations that links several dimensions:

1. A formulation is associated to other formulations that often appear in a same discourse.
2. A formulation is associated to some grammatical contexts, to some ways of speaking, all while avoiding other ways of talking and other grammatical contexts.
3. When a word is polysemous, some of its meanings can be associated to certain formulations, and some others to other formulations.

For Alison Duguid (2008), everything happens as if these associations formed sediments that mass together around certain habits already in place in the organism. These old habits are then recalibrated—perhaps even modified—without the person concerned being aware of it. These practices are gradually associated to expectations, to habits that link the individual to formulations. These processes are nonconscious and consequently difficult to master by introspection.

Researchers have observed that this process is sometimes consciously activated by institutions. Duguid studied specifically how Tony Blair's group, while he was prime minister of England, suggested key words that were to be used every time a collaborator faced a journalist from the press, radio, or television. Her study shows how this strategy was established in a conscious and systematic way to orient the opinion of the English citizens in a moment of crisis, without them being aware of it. In this, we see a form of soft but profound manipulation utilized in our democracies—one that is transmitted virally, thanks to the media and publicity spots. This phenomenon is a good example of the power of association that links the mind and institutions to each other.

What I am describing here is a form of mental manipulation carried out deliberately and lucidly, using the media as the intermediary. The strategy is close to that of computer viruses, which spread through the Internet and manage data on hard disks in an invisible way. Computer users and the media become at least passive accomplices of such strategies if they do not actively install procedures that detect viruses or priming to protect not only themselves but also all those with whom they communicate.

There is no reason that nonverbal, postural, and even sometimes respiratory habits would escape this type of mechanism while following dynamics a bit different than those of language.

Fuzzy Causality and Logic.   Philosopher Andy Clark (1997) describes a nature that can appear disorganized for someone who expects a coherence defined by the rules of logic and the mathematics of Leibniz's time, but perhaps less so for an individual born in the twenty-first century. What is at stake is to find a formulation that tolerates not only the heterogeneity of the elements but also the heterogeneity of the mechanisms and the goals of a system.[105] This heterogeneity can lead to competing contradictory mechanisms that are sometimes automatically and simultaneously activated in the same system. In this new vision of systems, there can be a blend of direct and indirect relations and many ways of accomplishing an apparently identical action.[106] A gesture can be mobilized by a series of regulatory systems; then, during its execution, it can activate another series of regulatory systems that do not necessarily have the same goals and functioning as the systems that initiated the gesture. Recent theories are looking for ways of describing this mode of functioning by using expressions such as "fuzzy logic" and "soft causal matrices." Here are a few examples of such notions:

1. A *fuzzy logic*[107] is a form of reasoning composed of written instructions in a software program.[108] Because it is a procedure, it can be applied as often as we want, like a mathematical formula. But the logic the programmer uses is often more intuitive than that used by an engineer, who bases his approach on classical logic and mathematics.[109] This type of procedure, for example, permits one to regulate the lenses of a camera so that two distinct areas of a space appear with maximum clarity. Fuzzy logic is probably closer to mental procedures than other forms of logic.

2. A *messy* architecture: English-speaking authors use the term *messy* to designate the architecture of the regulatory mechanisms of an organism or most of the great data-processing programs. Engineers use this term when they do a makeshift repair. To the extent that each part of an organism has its own particular biological history, and the selection of each composite is carried out according to global advantages (of survival), the relationship between local mechanisms and global functioning is weak and relatively independent from the history of the organism. That is why an organism as complex as a human needs more than 20 years to calibrate itself in an approximately functional fashion, and this regulation is then often put into question by the events of a lifetime. One of the problems raised by this hodgepodge architecture is that each mechanism can have a perfectly predictable causal behavior, but their combination leads to various forms of blending that are difficult to foresee (if one mechanism is more active than another, then the probability that the combination will lead to such a behavior is stronger).[110]

3. A *fuzzy causality* is a system that organizes itself from the bottom and the top, by the effect of an element on another, and by the impact of the organism on the causal chain set in place between the elements. Here is

an example given by Andy Clark.[111] Imagine that you place oil in a frying pan. The more the oil heats up, the more it moves in an apparently coordinated fashion. A horizontal movement forms patterns that we might observe with pleasure and curiosity. The source of this movement is the difference in temperature between the surface of the oil (in contact with the air) and the bottom of the oil (in contact with the frying pan). The hot and lighter oil rises, and the cooler and heavier oil goes to the bottom. This cycle repeats itself as the cooler oil, now at the bottom, heats up, and the hot oil, now at the top, cools down. This movement has a definite cause: the source that heats up the frying pan. This cause acts on each oil molecule. The movement of each oil molecule will act on each adjacent molecule and on no other. Nothing in this system is trying to create the beautiful global movement of the oil that you might enjoy seeing. "Such spontaneous pattern formation is exactly what we mean by self-organization: the system organized itself, but there is no 'self', no agent inside the system doing the organizing. . . . These systems are such that it is simultaneously true to say that the actions of the parts cause the overall behavior and that the overall behavior guides the actions of the parts" (Clark, 1997, p. 107).

Like the movements of the oil, an organism can give the impression to its mind and to the mind of others that it acts with coherence, while in fact what is going on is often an accumulation of small mechanisms that interact locally. In sociology, the same type of model can, for example, be used to analyze the traffic patterns of vehicles and predict when and where the traffic jams will occur in a city.

It sometimes happens that the functioning of a family generates schizophrenia in a child, as it also happens that the innate schizophrenia of a child traumatizes the family. In most of the cases, the factors that reinforce a tendency toward schizophrenia are multiple and hardly coordinated. Possibly the organization of these factors would be close to the organization that I summarized with regard to heating oil, but the underlying mechanisms are probably more complex. There would be, once again, a combination of dynamics that are activated in parallel on many levels, but that lead to the formation of an apparently global emerging movement that then coordinates all of the dynamics involved (notably genetic, neurological, organismic, familial, institutional). This type of model makes it possible to understand what is going on at the occasion of a treatment that combines neuroleptics, psychotherapy, and psychiatric support.[112]

Arteriosclerosis is a good example. In a population of people who consume foods that contain little cholesterol and who have a varied postural repertoire, arteriosclerosis is a rare occurrence. In the United States, there is a significant population that consumes a large amount of cholesterol and uses a restricted postural repertoire. Some of these people will develop arteriosclerosis, and some will not. For this illness, there are no direct cause-and-effect relationships, but there are lifestyles that have a higher probability of producing arteriosclerosis.

Implications for the Psychotherapist

This type of fuzzy engineering posits a number of questions for the psycho-therapeutic practitioner. For example, if we accept this point of view, it becomes difficult to use the notion of psychopathology. In all populations, there will be immense variations of every imaginable trait: bodily (height, width, regularity of the traits, etc.), mental (intelligence, feelings, imagination, type of memory, etc.), and behavioral (endurance, ability, frigidity or impotence, impulsivity, violence, etc.).[113] This variation is inevitable as soon as we accept that the randomness of genetic mechanisms have a profound influence on each human being.[114] All that a Darwinian psychotherapist can evaluate is a pile of mechanisms and practices that more or less hold the course, that more or less have the chance of mental as well as bodily survival in a given environment. That is what a Darwinian neuropsychiatrist like Boris Cyrulnik (2004) designates in the way he uses the term *resilience*: close to the word *fitness* as used by Wallace.

A therapist must therefore be able to evaluate the resources contained in a mass of mechanisms that have been agglomerated by nature as well as their capacity to survive more or less comfortably in an environment where human traits (physiological health, the performance of the body, behavioral skills, and mental flexibility) are stressed by constant competition (within and between each organism).[115] The finesse of a psychotherapist who uses a conception that combines the models of Clark and Cellérier is to perceive—with the patient—which interventions allow for the calibration of a detail (a way of thinking, a postural readjustment, a change in the style of communication), which allows for a slight realignment of an organismic system within the social system. Having observed the effect of the first calibration, it becomes possible to proceed to a following calibration that will permit consolidation of the one first acquired, and so on. We are following here—in fast forward speed—the process of evolution such as it was defined by Wallace and Darwin. After more than 100 years of psychology and psychotherapy, clinical research allows us to identify some causal chains that are particularly pertinent for certain types of individuals. This clinical research can help a therapist perceive and more precisely use forms of intervention to help a patient better understand himself and survive in a more comfortable way.

8

Homeostasis, Hormones, Vegetative Functions, and the Brain: Somatic Autoregulation of the Affects and the Organism

In the sections dedicated to the theory of evolution, we have mostly discussed the interaction that constructs itself between behavior and environment. Lamarck had also foreseen, in his syllabus for biology, a study of the interaction between behavior and the internal environment of the organism. This second portion of Lamarck's project is what I now want to address. It is a pivotal theme for body and somatic psychotherapists, because it describes how the interaction influences not only the psyche but also other regulators of the organism.

INTRODUCTION: PHYSIOLOGY AND PSYCHOTHERAPY

To fully understand psychophysiology requires the study of physiology and biology. Even if he has not undertaken such studies, a psychotherapist—especially if he works with the body and the soma—cannot avoid being interested in what is known in these domains. The mixture of a psychological clinical model and physiological models is nonetheless problematic for several reasons:

1. Typically, a clinician selects, from the body of literature in which he is interested, scientific models that confirm the psychotherapeutic approach he has developed. He cannot, given his education and training, situate what interests him in the dynamics of the field of research in psychophysiology. In this discipline, as in psychotherapy, many theories are in competition with each other. They all have some strong points and important limitations. Therefore, to adopt one of these theories because it is appealing and confirms the stance one has adopted does not mean that this choice is pertinent.

2. In neurophysiology, certain studies are surpassed after only a few decades. To want to associate a psychological clinical model to one approach in the neurosciences is to court disaster, for the clinical model
   will consequently be surpassed as rapidly as the physiological model
   that supports it, even if the psychological information used for this perspective is still valid.

As Philippe Rochat repeats tirelessly in his presentations and writings:[1] even an
academic psychologist is unable to find his way in the unbelievably complex
mazes in the area of psychophysiological research. There is nothing scientific in
wanting to act "as if" one understands. It is more honest and often more rewarding if you are a psychologist to defend a *psychological* model that corresponds to a practice, a familiar know-how, and to articulate its theory without
using data from other fields. The clinician can then present his model to experts
in psychophysiology, who may not only find some relationships with what they
are doing, but will perhaps be inspired by some aspect of the clinical model.
However much psychophysiological models may inspire you, they must not be
utilized as a scientific guarantee, but as a source of inspiration that allows you
to take up your clinical observations and reformulate your models without
using the physiological models that caught your attention to validate your point
of view. A psychological model only has value if it is based on the observations
and notions of psychologists and psychotherapists.

Being both a psychologist and a psychotherapist, I do not have the education
that would allow me to summarize the status of the research in contemporary
psychophysiology. In the sections that follow, I highlight psychophysiological
models that are often discussed by body psychotherapists and must be known
to understand the literature in this domain. These models have been selected, a
bit haphazardly, by psychotherapists who often ignored a large part of the literature and who do not always have enough knowledge in psychophysiology to
know the implications of their choice of model. This is also true for a number of
psychiatrists who have a sound initial foundation in psychophysiology and have
sometimes conducted fine research as students (like Freud), but who ended up
focusing on a particular clinical dimension in which they were interested. Having said that, these accidental choices are useful, as they allow us to perceive
what sort of psychophysiology is compatible to what body psychotherapists
imagine when they develop a form of intervention. If scientific rigor is not always present in the choice of physiological theories adopted by psychotherapists, the choice is at least pertinent as a metaphor of what is conceptualized in
a practice, just as Plato's fables are often more relevant than they appear at first
glance. Research is in effect not only an attempt to understand but also a stimulus of humanity's imagination that can conceive of realities it could not previously picture.[2] In the Middle Ages, no one could have imagined, even in dreams,
the images that we now have of the galaxies and cellular life.

The following sections allow today's starting psychotherapists to acquire a minimum of basic concepts they may then have to shore up by taking courses designed to introduce them to recent refinements. I hope the notions I discuss will help and encourage everyone to more easily consult recent textbooks in psychophysiology.

THE INTERNAL ENVIRONMENT, HOMEOSTASIS,
AND THE SOCIAL REGULATION OF CELLS

One of the implications of Lamarck's theory is that there probably exists in all of the species common mechanisms susceptible to reconstruction in function of their organismic, social, and geographic context.[3] Today, the most obvious example of such modifications is the mutations of the genes. In the nineteenth and beginning of the twentieth century, the common mechanisms between the species was the metabolic functioning of the aqueous milieu contained in each organism and the homeostatic mechanisms, which coordinate the requirements of the internal environment and the exigencies of the social and geographic environment.

The Internal Environment According to Bernard

Two themes developed by the French physiologist Claude Bernard[4] (1813–1878) are still discussed in the literature:

1. *The experimental method.* His *Introduction to the Study of Experimental Medicine*[5] (1865) (the French title refers to biology not to medicine) is always consulted by students in biology, medicine, and psychology in French-speaking universities. This work remains a model of clarity on the subject.
2. *The internal environment.* Bernard proposed the first consistent theory of *the systems of organismic regulation,* by discussing the way an organism protects the equilibrium of its internal environment.

This second theme will permit us to situate the notion of the auto-regulation of the organism. This notion had been taken up by those body psychotherapists[6] for whom one of the functions of body psychotherapy is to facilitate an organism's capacity to self-regulate constructively.

In his evolutionary physiology, Lamarck demonstrates that organisms are, before anything else, membranes containing fluids. A way to describe the evolution of anatomy and physiology is to show how the regulatory mechanisms of the fluids evolved.[7] The development of the organs relate to a differentiation of the body fluids (venous and arterial blood, lymph, urine, saliva, sweat, tears, etc.). When the nervous system finally appears, it participates not only in the regulation of the fluids but also in the interaction between body movements and body fluids. Thus, the muscular activity that animates a gesture is structured by the nervous system but must also have a pertinent logistic support from the cardiovascular system.

The Internal Environment as the Basic Dimension of the Organism

> Little by little the idea that the internal environment was nothing other than a part of the ocean that our distant ancestors had taken with them when they passed from an aquatic to an aerial life established itself within me; but that which needed to be revived above all else was the cell. (Laborit, 1989, *La Vie Antérieure*, 7.3, p. 102; translated by Marcel Duclos)

Claude Bernard has called the water contained in living organism the "internal environment." A large percentage of the weight of each organism is made up of fluids in which the cells can live and communicate with each other. These fluids have a certain number of particularities that make it possible to distinguish between biological water and the water from a brook. To be able to sustain the ongoing activity of the cells, these fluids must maintain the stability of a number of properties, such as temperature (between 36°C and 37°C in humans) and a neutral *hydrogen potential* (or pH[8]). This fluid must be able to nourish the cells and evacuate their waste, and furnish enough free ions (+ and –) to guarantee various forms of exchanges between the cells and the milieu that surrounds them. These exchanges are at the basis of *metabolic activity*. The maintenance of the properties of the internal environment is the first and main task of a living organism. Claude Bernard found convincing ways of demonstrating that cellular activity can be entirely described and explained by physical and chemical conditions.[9] He is one of the scientists who actively sought to exclude vitalism[10] from mainstream biology.

The properties of the internal environment cannot stray from their central values without endangering the survival of the organism. It is mostly the warm-blooded species that can sustain changes in the ambient climate, for they have the physiological means to maintain a constant internal temperature in conditions that sometimes vary considerably. Yet even humans have difficulty handling changes of more than 60°F in ambient temperature.

Fluids and Vegetative Pulsation of the Organism

In an amoeba, the fluids are hardly differentiated. Their dynamics regulate the solidification of the membranes in the constriction phase, and the softening of the membranes that allows various forms of mobility. This mechanism is a first kind of passage between a form of protection against aggression and displacement as a predator. The amoeba can modify the consistency of its tissues by oscillating between several states:[11]

1. *Contraction.* By contracting, the amoeba can reduce its volume to take up less space, be less visible, and consume less metabolic energy. This

reaction is one of the fundamental phylogenetic reactions of hibernation and various forms of immobilization associated with fear.

1a. *Hardening.* The quantity of fluids contained in the organism diminishes and the tissues harden. Perhaps here we have the first version of what will become the chronic tension of the muscles, which leads to the restriction of mobility, respiration, and the pleasure in moving.

1b. Hardening is often associated to a *disengagement from peripheral activity.*

2. The *expansion phase* is associated with the softening of the tissues, mobility, appetite, an increase of peripheral activity, and the capacity to reproduce.

For many physicians, like Wilhelm Reich, some of these functions are found in the more differentiated functioning of the human vegetative system:[12]

1. A phase of contraction is associated with anxiety, the loss of contact with the environment, muscular tension, the diminution of the vitality of the organism, and the parasympathetic system.

2. A phase of expansion that is associated with pleasure, the need to express oneself and to communicate, the release in the sexual act, and the sympathetic activation of the resources of the organism.

In the same period, the ethologist Konrad Lorenz proposed a complementary analysis concerning the relationship between the mobility of unicellular organisms and human motricity.[13] The pulsation of the amoeba is the basis of the construction of the affects of withdrawal (the 3 Fs: flight, fear, and freeze) and attack. Fight and flight are just two of the many behaviors associated with aggression, anxiety, and fear. If I base myself on the current observations of body psychotherapists who work with anxious individuals, we can distinguish two types of fear:[14]

1. The amoebic reaction oscillates between periods of *contraction and expansion*, permitting the amoeba to move and feed itself by creating pseudopods. This dynamic is due to the interplay between the fluids of the cell and its membrane. The internal environment becomes fluid in the expansion phase (it is then sol) and becomes dense in contact with the exterior (it then becomes gel). The contraction reaction is accentuated in dangerous situations, as when the pool in which the amoeba lives dries up. Its pseudopods retract, its protoplasm becomes less fluid and takes less space by expulsing fluids, which provoke a hardening of the external membrane.

2. There is also in other unicellular organisms a physical reaction of fear, which is to *move in all directions.* As soon as a protozoan senses a pain-

ful sensation, it increases its mobility. Not having the possibility to situate the danger, it moves without knowing where it is going. If the pain continues, it moves again and again until the pain is diminished. This strategy has refined itself in the course of evolution, as when a rat that is in a panic state explores every nook and cranny of a cage. We observe that anxious humans also have a tendency to move without stopping. They become restless. Psychiatrists often refer to the *agitation* of their patients.

Another behavior associated with danger that is often observed in a psychotherapy practice is an abrupt immobilization.[15] This reaction is used by some herbivores on the savanna when they can no longer escape a big cat. They become immobile and hold their breath to trick the predator into believing they are dead. If the predator is distracted, the zebra can suddenly stand, run, and escape. In humans, we sometimes observe some variations of this reaction, which would be a variation on the theme under way in the evolution of the species by the amoebic contraction.

This attempt to have everything start from the mechanisms of the amoeba is sometimes useful,[16] but a bit too simplistic for the clinician:

1. In isolating oneself from others and in opening up to oneself, as in meditation, there can be a particular form of pleasure. *Therefore, the turning in on oneself and the parasympathetic activity are not only manifestations of anxiety.* Similarly, the dispersion in communication, aggression, sympathetic activity, and even sexual contact can also be manifestations of anxiety. *Expansion is not only pleasure.*
2. The two phases of the amoeba differentiated themselves to form a *larger repertoire* of reactions. Hibernation, relaxation, and immobilization are three forms of withdrawal from surrounding activity that have different functions, even if they all require an activation of the parasympathetic system. Thus, sleep allows the parasympathetic functions to repair certain psychophysiological functions to restore the forces of the organism, whereas nothing is repaired when the organism withdraws all that it can from the periphery of the body to protect itself from a predator.

This discussion indicates how Bernard's approach made it possible to coordinate apparently purely physiological mechanisms with global behavioral dynamics that mobilize the organism almost in its entirety.

Cannon and Homeostasis

Walter B. Cannon (1871–1945) completed his medical studies at Harvard University, where he then became a physician, a researcher, and a professor.[17] The first body psychotherapists hardly ever quote him,[18] but they often propose formulations that were manifestly influenced, at least indirectly, by his theories. Most of Cannon's models were taught in the biology classes of secondary schools. In other words, for many, Cannon = Physiology.[19] His model of homeostasis is the first medical model that describes the capacity of the organism to auto-regulate. It also became a reference for European psychologists of the 1930s.[20]

An Organism Submissive to the Metabolic Needs

At the end of World War I, Cannon was a military physician in France. In Paris, he discovered the work of Claude Bernard and his idea that every organism has, at its disposal, strategies to regulate its internal environment in a changing environment. Cannon then undertook research on the strategies that permit an organism to regulate the internal environment. He refers to these regulatory systems as homeostasis.[21]

The concept of homeostasis is a precursor of the systemic and cybernetic theories. Like Lamarck and Bernard, Cannon situates the mind in the mechanisms created to enhance the regulatory systems of the internal environment of the organism. This approach does not prohibit other functions from having grafted themselves to the regulatory mechanisms of the internal environment. This point of view is compatible with Darwin's hypothesis on the emotions, which, like parasites, latch on to the regulatory systems that were not originally conceived for them. Cannon mentions, for example, the observation of Bernard quoted by Darwin:[22] that there exists a spontaneous link between certain emotional expressions and cardiac activity. Having demonstrated, in detailed fashion for certain mechanisms, that the affects are associated to diverse physiological mechanisms, Cannon concluded that the mechanisms *of internal homeostatic regulation* are composed of physiological, mental, and behavioral mechanisms. Other researchers, like Wilhelm Reich (1940) and Henri Laborit (1971), studied how these mechanisms insert themselves into social and political strategies.

Homeostasis and Social Behavior

> I went from the idea that an oyster can only make an oyster shell; a snail, a snail shell; and that a city is nothing other than a shell constructed by a living organism: a human society. (Laborit, 1989, *La vie antérieure*, 10.1, p. 187; translated by Marcel Duclos)

In humans, the mechanisms of homeostatic regulation often function in association with the mechanisms of relational and social regulation. The regulation of an infant's temperature cannot be maintained without the help of the parents.[23] In a land as cold as Scandinavia, parents would not be able to help their children maintain an adequate temperature if they did not have the proper clothing, housing, and heating systems. It is therefore possible to think that the homeostatic systems of socialized species, like ants and humans, are carried out in social dynamics.

The homeostatic mechanisms of humans only function if they receive a constant social support. Physicians allow themselves to have social requirements (in the matter of hygiene, of nutrition, etc.), which go far beyond the care dispensed to particular organisms. The interpenetration of all of these mechanisms is of an unheard-of complexity that Cannon could not study with the limited means of a laboratory. He contented himself to study the homeostatic mechanisms situated in an organism, that is, the mechanisms that coordinate behavior and the demands of the internal environment. He analyzes, for example, what motivates an organism to seek out the shade, sweat, and drink when the temperature of the ambient air increases. Like most of the authors I have already mentioned, Cannon situates the affects in the center of what coordinates behavior and physiology. The affects would be one of the tools that permit the organism to coordinate mind, behavior, and physiological needs.

Physiology, Homeostasis, and Mood

Affects and Mood

Taking up the language of the System of the Dimensions of the Organism (SDO) that serves as the reference point for this textbook, *the affects are propensities organized by the mechanisms of organismic regulation to coordinate the dimensions of the organism in function of a goal structured by one of the dimensions.* There are several types of affects.

The homeostatic *instincts* form at least two types of propensities:[24]

1. The *instincts of auto-regulation* (hunger, thirst, thermoregulation, etc.) have as the first goal the regulation of the internal environment. Having said this, the propensities of this type can be managed in many ways as soon as they are associated to the mental and the behavioral dimensions. These instincts can also serve as a basis for diverse forms of conditioning.
2. The *instinctive reactions* of flight and fight, above all, are behaviors unleashed by sensorimotor bundles that go through the central nervous system. They preserve the survival of the organism in a hostile environment. Only when the mechanisms of regulation of the organism have mobilized the other dimensions of the organism do the behaviors become effective.

The instinctive affects have as their first goal the mobilization of the *power*[25] of the organism for a task linked to survival.

Other types of affect, well known to psychiatrists, are the *moods,* like depression and euphoric mania. Some practitioners have a tendency to place *depression* and *anxiety* on the same plane. They consequently use the word *mood* to designate these two affects. Psychiatric and psychotherapeutic practice often compares and contrasts depression and anxiety on an axis different than the contrast between depressive and manic states.[26] For Andre Haynal,[27] for example, *depression is often the regret for a past that never existed, and anxiety, the fear of a future that will not come about.* This formula was often useful to me in my practice.

In psychiatry, the term mood designates all the affective systems that can be easily influenced by medications because their organization depends largely on the physiological mechanisms that are structured around the vegetative, cerebral, and hormonal mechanisms. The positive moods are those that participate in the constructive regulations for the integrity of the organism; the negative moods are linked to the regulations that accelerate the deterioration of the organism. This usage rejoins the meaning the term has when someone says they woke up in a good or bad mood.

Like depression, a mood can be triggered by a specific event; the length of time during which it lasts is greater than the status of a simple response or reaction to a stimulus. A mood often presents a cyclical face, independent of circumstances, that makes one think of a genetic factor. The formula that prevails, since Freud, is that of a genetic predisposition that can be modulated by events. A predominant mood in a patient is often found markedly[28] in the family history. In psychotherapy, by default, I propose that the patient learn to live with his moods rather than desire to master the moods.[29] The disappearance of a significant tendency toward cyclical depression or anxiety is rare, although it can sometimes be observed. The reason for the stability of these moods becomes apparent as soon as we admit that there is a link between mood and particular forms of homeostatic auto-regulation which engenders a lifestyle and a style of communication. Therefore, to reduce the rhythm and the intensity of the mood swings requires taking into account the coordination between a lifestyle, a way to behave and think, and the modulation of the mechanisms of homeostatic regulation. Sometimes, changes on all these levels are necessary; sometimes a well-localized change modifies the entire system. The prognosis is better when the patient lives in a supportive environment.

Metabolism and Nutrition

All the passing moods have a constructive value for the organism, if we admit that they are a type of homeostatic regulation (anxiety before an exam can be useful) to a situation whose contours are relatively clear. As soon as a mood becomes habitual, it associates with a multitude of regulatory mechanisms of the organism. If this mood inserts itself in a person's character, it ends up becoming a permanent form of regulation for the organism. By associating itself so profoundly with a particular mood, it makes them less available to other moods. The organism therefore loses its flexibility and diminishes its capacity to adapt.

I take the case of the depressive affect in a person who suffers from obesity[30] to detail the deep-rooted nature of a mood in the physiological dynamics of an organism. To do so, I detail a part of the connections between depression and the consumption of carbohydrates:

1. For example, consider an obese person who must often follow a diet to fight against cardiovascular problems, an excess of bad cholesterol, a reduction of respiratory capacity, or joint pains.

2. Most of the proposed diets require lowering the consumption of carbohydrates, like pasta, bread, and potatoes.[31] This change in eating habits can favor the onset of depressive feelings brought about by the sadness that the loss of rituals or the loss of the dishes that define a way of life to which a person is identified.

3. One of the reasons the human senses appreciate carbohydrates is that the consumption of "slow sugars" is vital in an environment that produces little food, where there is the need of exhausting activity to supply the organism. The valuing of carbohydrates causes very little damage in the cultures in which people eat little of them or eat them moderately. In industrialized cultures where food is in abundance, this tendency to assimilate carbohydrates becomes noxious for every organism that (a) expends little physical energy and (b) has a metabolism that consumes few substances activated by the carbohydrates. The fact that the food industry discourages the production of fruits and vegetables that have taste and assaults the people with advertising that encourages the consumption of products full of unhealthy sugars, fat, and carbohydrates accentuates the health problems associated with the overconsumption of carbohydrates. This is an example of the negative impact of a social aspect of an instinctive propensity on the organism.

4. Physicians often recommend reducing carb consumption because they stimulate the production of insulin. This increase can favor the advent of diabetes. The increase of insulin facilitates the storage of what is eaten, and consequently the formation of lipids that promote the advent of obesity.

5. On the other hand, lowering the intake of carbohydrates and lowering cholesterol[32] can together provoke a reduction in the amount of serotonin[33] produced by the organism and induce suicidal tendencies. Because there is often a link between depression and serotonin, in this mechanism we have yet another possible cause of the way that a diet can increase a depressive mood.

6. In the case of anorexia and obesity, the metabolic activity accommodates to the eating habits of the organism.[34] If a person decides to change diet, the metabolism will not change its demands unless the change lasts at least for months. Therapy therefore demands a long-term strategy to resolve the physiological, mental, and behavioral vicious circle that rules the organism.[35]

As we can see in these examples, the link between carbohydrates, serotonin, insulin, depression, and obesity is almost unsolvable without a profound change in the social functioning that participates in the formation of the eating habits.

This explains the failure of most of the interventions related to obesity. In the elements I have summarized, we can see that each variable has a series of implications and branch lines that can activate mobilizations with contradictory effects. As it happens, the rapport between a change of diet and depression can be caused (a) by the psychological difficulty to accept a change of habits, and (b) by lowering serotonin production. In this model, there are two distinct causal systems that reinforce a depressive mood.

Metabolism and Respiration

As soon as a practitioner attends to the respiration of his patients, he notices that some people can be considered "oxygen anorexics." When he asks his patients to breathe deeply, many feel "dizzy." They need to reduce the volume of their respiration or reduce the increase of metabolic energy by moving, or by hyperventilating. The reeducation of the metabolism of respiration cannot be accomplished only in the context of psychotherapy, because such a change requires the regular practice of breathing exercises, as this is done in pranayama training, in the Pilates method, in sports, and so on. Thus certain forms of hyperactivity (constant chatter, the need to move incessantly, etc.) can be explained by a physiological incapacity to "digest" an increase of the metabolic activity.

The following is a way to explain "anorexic" respiration, that is presently taught in several body psychotherapy schools (e.g., in Bioenergetics analysis):

1. The capacity to metabolize more oxygen allows the organism to produce more metabolic energy.
2. Energy is stored with difficulty, or sometimes in a harmful way for the physiological dynamics (storage of lipids, for example). It must be expended, discharged through action.
3. The increase of metabolic activity due to an increase of oxygen creates an increase in the feeling of vitality and a reinforcement of affective dynamics.
4. If the environment does not tolerate this vitality, the organism learns to reduce its metabolic activity to avoid a sense of frustration that it cannot manage and to protect the organism from painful reprisals.

I have observed this vicious circle, for example, in patients whose parents needed to be protected from the intensity of their children's needs.[36] Other persons act before having the need to (eat as soon as they are aware of the slightest hunger, masturbate as soon as there is the slightest sexual desire, etc.). In this group, we often find individuals who have little tolerance for frustration and who act impulsively. They prefer many small frustrations to intense ones.

As we can see in these examples, metabolism is a dimension the psychotherapist has not learned to understand in a detailed manner, but which could be useful to him to keep in mind. Reducing the intake of oxygen reduces the metabolic activity and consequently the energetic charge that all the dimensions of the organism need to have available to them. The relationship between the dimensions and metabolism is evidently cybernetic: the influence is asymmetrical (not of the same type) but reciprocal. Thus, the metabolic activity depends on breathing and eating behaviors. The available energy can then be dispensed in many ways: by moving, by thinking, by storing lipids, and so on. This domain is what the biochemists often call "bioenergy."[37] In my point of view, it is mostly these chemical dynamics that make it possible to give an account of the whole of the energetic dynamics of an organism.

In the domain of body psychotherapy, Alexander Lowen proposed the term bioenergy to designate what Wilhelm Reich called the orgone. Charles Kelley followed a similar reasoning when he called Reich's[38] cosmic energy "radix" (root). The use of a scientific term to designate a notion considered unscientific in academia did reveal itself to be lucrative in terms of clients, but it reinforced the rupture that developed between academia and Reichian therapies. Even Reich would probably have objected to a procedure that is manifestly a mystification. To justify this approach, the neo-Reichians discredited the chemistry of the chemists as an inanimate mechanic; on the other hand, their Reichian energy was presented as being full of the vitality that generates the universe. Yet an inverse argument could be directed at these Reichians who reduce the chemical dynamics to something foolishly mechanical. They know so little about chemistry that they fail to grasp the unbelievable creativity that is activated thanks to the chemical and atomic operations. Enhancing the value of theories like that of the orgone often covers up ignorance of the chemical dynamics and their creativity, all the while wanting to give the impression of being omniscient.

THE SYSTEM OF VEGETATIVE REGULATION AND AFFECTS

The Vegetative Neurohormonal Regulatory System of the Organs and Affects

The Autonomic or Vegetative Nervous System

The first observations of the vegetative or autonomic nervous system goes back to Claudius Galen of ancient Rome; but John Newport Langley (1899) is generally recognized[39] as the first to have proposed a correct vision of the structure and the function of this system. Cannon uses the term *autonomic,* which prevailed in the Anglo-Saxon literature, whereas Reich follows the Germanic tradition in using the term *vegetative:*

1. The term *autonomic* underscores the relative independence of this system in relation to the *central nervous system.*[40] It would probably be more accurate to say that the autonomic nervous system is a very well-differentiated *intermediary* between the central nervous system and the other great physiological functions of the organism. The notion of autonomy is too ambiguous to be retained in present-day physiology.

2. The term *vegetative* designates the domain regulated by this neurological structure, that is, the world of the organs, the glands, the circulation of the blood, the maintenance of the vital properties of the internal environment, and so on. I mostly use the term vegetative in this text, because it is the term that Reich used to identify his *Vegetotherapy*.[41] Given his influence on body psychotherapy, it is the term that most body psychotherapists use, unless they have adopted the current medical vocabulary.

Cannon's research on the vegetative system tries to demonstrate that it is one of the central mechanisms of the homeostatic system. An increasing number of researchers indicate that the vegetative system is also associated to the emotions. Levensen (2003), for example, showed that it is possible to associate some emotions to some types of activation of the autonomic nervous system. He is able to associate the basic emotions, as distinguished by Ekman[42] to distinct vegetative activities. Thus, happiness reduces the electric activity of the skin, and this activity is elevated when the emotion is negative (anger, fear, sadness, disgust), or the cardiac activity is particularly low when a person feels disgusted.

The Sympathetic and Parasympathetic Systems

Cannon was the first to give as much weight to the chemical as well as to the neurological dimension of the vegetative system:

1. The dimension of the vegetative nervous system is classically divided into the *sympathetic and parasympathetic nervous system*. These two systems are organized outside of the vertebral column and parallel to the spinal cord, with which it has numerous interactions.
2. Each of these two nervous systems relate to the activity of the *hormones* used as *neurotransmitters* that influence other parts of the nervous system through the blood.

Therefore, there is not only a sympathetic and parasympathetic *nervous* system but also sympathetic and parasympathetic *functions*:

1. The *sympathetic* function supports activity. It stimulates the circulation of substances like *adrenaline* and *calcium*.[43]
2. The *parasympathetic* function supports an auto-reparatory function of the organism during sleep. It activates the secretion of substances like *acetylcholine* and *potassium*.[44]

Certain organs, like the heart and the digestive system, are influenced by these two systems. Thus, the sympathetic system accelerates the cardiac rhythm and slows down the peristaltic activity of the digestive tract, while the parasympathetic system slows down the heart and accelerates the peristaltic activity. The more active the body, the greater the mobilization of the sympathetic system, which can be qualified as the vegetative support system of the action. The less active the body, the greater the mobilization of the parasympathetic system, which actively contributes to the state of relaxation and sleep.

In certain cases, the nerve and hormone pathways have the same effect on an organ.[45] The vegetative regulations coordinate the moods and the overall condition of the organism. The vegetative coordination is mostly nonconscious but sensitive to the impact of the central nervous system (especially on the striated muscles). This explains why individuals can influence these systems by indirect modalities (breathing exercises, relaxation, yoga exercises, etc.). The vegetative system is part of the mechanisms of organismic regulation. It is consequently used in most of the interactions between the dimensions of the psyche and the body.

Recent research shows that vegetative dynamics are more complex than what Cannon's generation of physiologists thought. For example, there is more chemical vegetative activity than what was previously assumed by Cannon and Reich.[46]

In the subsequent sections, I illustrate Cannon's general understanding by quoting more recent works. They show how the affective and vegetative systems insert themselves into both the fundamental physiological functioning, like the peristaltic activity, and the activity of the central nervous system.

Anxiety and the Peristaltic Movement of the Digestive Tract

ANXIETY INHIBITS THE PERISTALTIC ACTIVITY

At the end of the nineteenth century, while he was still a student, Cannon worked with X-rays, which had recently been made operational, to explore the physiological functioning of the digestive system. He accidentally discovered that an emotional disturbance blocks the motor activity of the stomach, and the return to a more serene state promptly restores the peristaltic movements of the digestive tract.[47] This research confirmed the observations that a general practitioner, William Beaumont, had made on one of his patients.[48] Edmund Jacobson, who had been a student of Cannon, undertook research in psychophysiology in Chicago, and he established that anxiety influences not only the stomach but also the motility of the duodenum, the esophagus, and the colon.[49]

Between the two world wars, most physicians and psychologists thought that the emotions influenced the behavior of the digestive tract.[50] Like the rest of Cannon's work, this theme disappeared from serious discussions during the 1960s without being invalidated.[51] It was considered trivial and without influence on the evolution of psychosomatic practice and theory. Trygve Braatøy,[52] for example, mentions as if it were self-evident that the releasing of the stretching reflexes and of yawning, as well as peristaltic gurgling, are an evident sign of relaxation that often accompanies—in a spontaneous way—a postural and muscular release.

THE PSYCHOPERISTALISM OF GERDA BOYESEN

In the 1960s, going against the general trend, Gerda Boyesen, a Norwegian clinical psychologist and physical therapist, developed forms of intervention in body psychotherapy that were based on listening to the peristaltic sounds of the sigmoid colon[53] with a stethoscope. The basic principle is that any intervention that returns movement to the peristaltic activity is pertinent to the restoration of the organism's systems of physiological auto-regulation. This work is founded on the hypothesis that the peristaltic process can be activated by digestion or mechanisms linked to the release of stress. In the case where the mobility of the digestive tract is associated to affective dynamics, Boyesen speaks of *psychoperistalism.*[54]

Currently, psychotherapists who practice this method use electric stethoscopes with loud speakers to detect rapid changes in the motility of the colon:

1. Everything that occurred at the moment when *the peristaltic activity quiets down* is likely to be an event associated to an anxiety that has a negative impact on the mechanism of auto-reparation of the organism. Boyesen assumed that something *knots up* at the vegetative level when something knots up at the affective level.

2. Everything that occurred at the moment when *the peristaltic activity gets going again* in a noticeable fashion is likely to be an event that is associated to something that unknots itself at the vegetative, the affective, and the cognitive level.

The event associated with the change of peristaltic activity can be a gesture, a mental association of the patient, a smile of the therapist, a particular way to massage, a change of light in the room, and so on. The therapist and the patient therefore inquire together about what happened at the crucial moment and give a particular importance to these events. The method used for this inquiry is free association. Having said that, it is impossible to know with certainty what event is really associated to each change of peristaltic activity. The relevance of a series of thoughts, conceived at a particular moment, can be confirmed by its impact on the therapeutic process, or if its association with a peristaltic change repeats itself. This method is useful to distinguish two types of utterances:

1. *The relevance of the content from the point of view of the thoughts:* a phrase can be used to express an idea, a feeling, or a memory. Here, the patient and the therapist closely follow the validity and the cognitive relevance of the content—for example, the exactness of a memory and its link with what has effectively happened. There is therefore no reason to listen to the peristaltic noises because the relevance of an utterance is based on criteria that have nothing to do with the physiological reactions.

2. *The relevance of the content for the vegetative system:* a phrase can unleash a peristaltic activity that was previously blocked. A patient is thus
able to discover that to speak about God, about the love of his parents,
about his need to succeed in life does him some good, although this person intellectually refused to accord any value to these notions. The idea
here is not to transform an atheist into a believer but to help a person
sense that a phrase can be logically false but positively resonate at one
level of his being. A patient who believes himself to be independent of
religion or of his parents can thus discover that his detachment is not as
absolute as he believed. An identical argument can be made to bring to
the light of day contents that block the peristaltic activity of the patient.
Sometimes there are truths that hurt, or ways to experience a truth that
hurts.

One of Gerda Boyesen's hypotheses is that any topic accompanied by a return of peristaltic activity is susceptible to being integrated by the patient,
whereas any subject that provokes a slowing down of the peristaltic activity can
be indigestible for the patient's psyche. In any case, Boyesen recommends to her
students that they consider this method only as a tool whose relevance depends
on the context of the therapeutic process. We are in a world where a bodily
event can have many causes. The peristaltic motility is, above all, regulated by
the sympathetic (reduction in the activity of the intestines) and parasympathetic
(increase in the noises), each of which have multiple functions. Anxiety keeps an
organism in a sympathetic state even during a relaxation exercise.

An example that demonstrates the danger of thinking that there is a direct
link between relaxation, the parasympathetic system, and gastric motility is the
observation that during some states of relaxation, peristaltic noises often cease.
We can then evoke a number of hypotheses:

1. Even when the patient is in a manifest state of relaxation, *the relaxation
can be a way to repress affects and drives.* The patient thus uses the state
of relaxation to dissociate by falling asleep, for example. In this case, the
relaxation can increase a state of profound tension, which can be detected when the therapist hears a reduction in the peristaltic activity.
2. It is probable that certain states of sleep or relaxation lead to a slowing
down of all of the functions of the organism: sympathetic and parasympathetic. In this case, the slowdown of the peristaltic activity is also explainable. There is no manifestation of the unconscious defense systems.
Instead, there is a state of fundamental openness on the part of the organism that cannot establish itself until the functions of the parasympathetic auto-reparation have done their work.

When such questions arise, the therapist needs to use other forms of inquiry
before he can find the correct interpretation. This approach is useful in that it

helps the therapist narrow the range of questions that are relevant at a particular moment in the therapeutic process.

THE "SECOND BRAIN" ACCORDING TO GERSHON

Michael D. Gershon's book (1998), titled *The Second Brain*, announces a new approach relative to the rapport between the intestines and the brain. He demonstrates that the *enteric nervous system*, situated around and in the digestive tract, is an immense mass of nerves that function parallel to the brain. Traditionally, this system is considered as the part of the vegetative nervous system which is the most autonomic part with regard to the central nervous system. This immense mass of nerves also supports the production of many neurotransmitters made in the intestines. Notably, three-fourths of the serotonin available in a human organism is produced in the intestines. This substance is used in most of the antidepressant medications. The synthesis of serotonin may depend on the quantity of carbohydrates contained in food.

Gershon's model[55] on the connection between depression and the gastrointestinal system is an example of multiple and indirect links between the psyche and soma. The nerve connections that link the intestinal system and the spinal column are rare, and none of these connections has a direct access to the central nervous system.

This area of research has not verified the link between peristaltic noise and moods because it is probable that the link expresses a weak positive correlation, given the multiplicity of implied variables. For the practitioner who uses methods like those of Gerda Boyesen, this means that when the practitioner hears a definite effect, it is probable that Cannon's model remains relevant. But as soon as we enter into an attempt to explain difficult clinical complexities, Cannon's model becomes less pertinent. The studies on the intestinal system allow us to refine two ways to approach psychoperistaltism that clinicians had identified with regard to the diverse forms of relaxation mentioned earlier:

1. *The apparent direct correlations between two behaviors for the observer.* Cannon describes a correlation between the noises in the belly and a state of anxiety. He provides no clear hypothesis on the mechanisms that link the phenomena. The relation between anxiety and peristaltic activity is perceived as direct by the researcher's consciousness. I suspect research did not pursue this path because, in looking at it more closely, there are an immense variety of belly noises and an immense variety of states of mind that could be called anxious. The variety of peristaltic noises is well known by individuals trained by Gerda Boyesen. Medical and paramedical personnel who hear the sounds of their own gut on a loud speaker for the first time are often amazed by their variety. Clinicians will try to create a series of labels for each distinguishable noise and then try to correlate them with mental experiences. They work as if there were a direct link between certain moods and certain noises. Every

time they spot a repeated correlation between peristaltic and mental activities, they have the impression that they are working on a direct link.[56] The hope of the therapist is that when eventually the researchers will know how to manipulate all of these variables, they will be able to refine the direct rapport that seems to exist between certain forms of peristaltic activity and certain psychological dynamics and will finally complete Boyesen's model.

2. *Manifestly indirect connections from the point of view of the mechanisms between two systems of behavior.* Scientists are close to demonstrating that there effectively exists a multitude of connections between the affective and digestive systems and that these links are at least as complex as foreseen by clinicians. But the scientists approach the problem from another angle, which demonstrates that the correlation between affective dynamics and peristaltism is necessarily indirect, complex and multiple.[57]

It is altogether possible, from there, to take up a dialogue between the body psychotherapist and the researcher; but this dialogue will necessarily take some directions that the psychotherapists had not necessarily anticipated. The correlation is not, after all, between a behavior of the gastrointestinal system and a mental behavior but between a *functioning* of the digestive system and a functioning of the affective system. At first, the clinician works with a simple labeling system; as the research progresses, this strategy must often be replaced by one that is more complex.

The Psychophysiology of Stress

The basic thesis defended in the subsequent sections is that the mechanisms which lead to stress are useful in situations that spontaneously occur in a natural setting; but that they lose their relevance in situations that have been recently produced by civilization. They can then become dangerous for the survival of the organism.

War, Trauma, and Auto-Destruction

The survivors wanted to erase from their memory the ten million victims who died uselessly and to forget themselves and their tragically wasted and lost years. (Manes Sperber, 1976, "Malraux and Politics," p. 201; translated by Marcel Duclos)

World War I was particularly traumatic for Europe for at least three reasons:[58]

1. The soldiers could not understand why they were fighting. Even today, historians have a difficult time understanding why there was a first world war. The only result was to plunge Europe into horror: communism, anticommunism, World War II, and the loss of its power in the world.

2. The soldiers of each nation were maltreated, not by the enemy but by their own government that transformed them into "cannon fodder," made them live in dehumanizing fashion in poorly constructed trenches, and shot them if they refused to fight. It was especially true of the "democratic" countries like France and England.

3. The major countries explored the use of chemical warfare, which often caused as much harm to their own soldiers as those of the enemy. These weapons created illnesses even more terrible and insidious than anything that the soldiers regularly suffered.

The result of this situation was that a number of soldiers were profoundly and permanently traumatized. Their hospitalization mobilized the resources and research of countless physicians because no theoretical framework existed to understand the disastrous psychophysiological state in which these soldiers found themselves. The theories of stress I summarize in the following sections are based on attempts (often only partially beneficial) to support the soldiers traumatized by the war. The limits of these modes of intervention illustrate that it is not possible to heal all ills with a medical perspective. Other solutions, more political, are certainly necessary.

EROS AND THANATOS

Several military hospitals consulted the psychoanalysts who had built their reputation on the treatment of certain forms of trauma. Because the treatments they developed were useful in certain cases, more and more psychoanalytic psychiatrists were hired by hospitals, where they sometimes assumed important positions.[59]

Nonetheless, traumatized war veterans responded only moderately well to the psychoanalytic treatment. The psychoanalysts had particular difficulty understanding why certain horrible nightmares regularly invaded the soldiers mind after the war, when the organism was no longer under threat. Freud had grown weary of the incessant slaughter and the lies,of the politicians of the time. He (1915d) viewed humanity with an increasing bitterness. The only way he had to make sense about what was going on was to postulate the existence of a destructive instinct (Thanatos) aimed at self and others that was at least as powerful as the pursuit of pleasure (Eros).[60]

Freud's first theory attempts to construct itself, like Wallace's theory, around a single principle that is almost a "nonlaw." Therefore, Freud proposed that the psyche structures itself around the pursuit of sexualized pleasure. He advanced in this direction, in spite of the severe critical opposition of psychiatrists like Carl Gustav Jung who were willing, if need be, to admit to a basic life force (élan vital) that was not necessarily sexual. It is difficult for someone who works with individuals who suffer from schizophrenia to admit that their problem reduces itself to a fear of sexuality. In analyzing the descriptions of the behaviors of those traumatized by war with his colleagues, Freud had to admit that the psyche cannot be explained by only one principle. He nevertheless had confidence in his analysis about the relationship between libido and neurosis. He therefore took up, in part, Jung's argument; he postulated that the impulses of life are differentiated into survival forces through violence and survival forces through sexual pleasure. In these two cases, he notes an autoerotic component (masturbation and self-destruction) and a component directed toward the exterior (copulation and combat).[61]

THE ORGANISM ACCORDING TO GOLDSTEIN

Kurt Goldstein (1878–1965) was a German neurologist who is known for having studied the lesions that cause aphasia from a perspective influenced by Gestalt psychology (see the Glossary). This influence led him to demonstrate how a local lesion inscribes itself into the global dynamics of the brain and then of the entire organism. This position was original and courageous at a time when most neurologists associated psychological functions to specific areas of the brain. He had been trained by preeminent figures who defended the cerebral localization approach, like Carl Wernicke, who, with Paul Broca, discovered the areas of the brain linked to language.

Goldstein had participated in the medical care of German soldiers traumatized by World War I. He had noticed that it was impossible to find a precise organic locus to be treated by a specific medicine that could alleviate the suffering of these soldiers. Independently of Cannon, he was probably the first neurologist to propose a neurological model that situates the nervous system as a global subsystem in the organism.

Persecuted by the Nazis, he fled first to Amsterdam, where he wrote *The Organism* (1939). When he immigrated to the United States, this work was published with an introduction by psychologist Karl S. Lashley, who was renowned for his studies on the cortical basis of motor activities. *The Organism* is the first scientific book that explicitly associates the entity that is a human being to a holistic notion of the organism. Kurt Goldstein's organism is as coherent as Spinoza's systems. This vision created such a salutary contrast to the neurological literature of the day that it filled the intellectual world with enthusiasm. The work was read by an entire generation of body psychotherapists like Gerda Boyesen (2001, p. 33) and Malcolm Brown (2001) who called his school *Organismic Psychotherapy* in honor of Goldstein.[62] He also had an important influence on neurology (Lashley, Luria, and more recently Edelman) and philosophy (Ludwig Binswanger, George Canguilhem, Ernst Cassirer, and Maurice Merleau-Ponty).

Kurt Goldstein[63] details, in an explicit way, the methodological obstacles that make the analysis of the global organismic system difficult. He supposes that a living organ does not function the same way in its natural environment as it does in a laboratory.[64] It is also probable that certain functions of the brain are not highlighted unless we can understand how the brain integrates itself into the organismic system. Forty years later, this methodological remark received the support of specialists in animal behavior. They had noticed that the observations of animals in captivity only partially resemble those of the animals living in their natural environment.[65] Today, neurologists who use magnetic resonance imaging (MRI) confirm this analysis when they observe how a brain functions while a person performs a specific psychological task.[66]

In his studies of traumatized individuals, Goldstein distinguishes the feelings that are associated to an explicit cause from those that do not seem to have a cause. It is mostly the second type of affects which haunts the traumatized persons. Goldstein noticed that the individuals who do not succeed in relating their fears to an identified aggressor also often lose their sense of identity. Many psychotherapists follow this distinction when they distinguish between emotions with or without "an object." For a great number of psychoanalysts, an emotion without an object, of necessity, has a repressed unconscious object. Today, certain psychotherapists who specialize in the disorders caused by trauma recommend, on the contrary, that the emotions without an associated cause be addressed at the start of therapy. I single out this discussion because *it seems important to me to become particularly attentive as soon as a person speaks of affects without objects;* however, the status of these affects remain a topic of research for which no satisfactory answers have yet been proposed. When a patient speaks to me of affects without objects, I know I must explore what is going on with him when he has this sort of experience.

Selye and Stress

FLIGHT AND FIGHT ACCORDING TO CANNON:
THE DANGER OF LOCAL SOLUTIONS THAT GLOBALIZE

A military physician for the U.S. Army during both world wars, Cannon developed other means of support for traumatized soldiers. One of the approaches he proposed (1915) to deal with the organismic dysfunctional state observed in traumatized persons, is to focus on the two basic reactions in the face of aggression: flight and fight. These two forms of reaction mobilize all the resources of the organism for a goal that is relatively clear. This mobilization only ceases once this instinctive reaction is inactivated.

To understand the nature of stress, Cannon takes up the Darwinian idea that certain pertinent adaptive mechanisms of the species can become dangerous for survival when they are inherited by another species. The mechanisms mobilized by traumatized humans would be based on the reactions of flight and fight elaborated by other mammals. This system of adaptation remains relevant for humans when they undergo a manifest aggression of short duration, as when a person is physically threatened by another at the occasion of an attempted robbery. The contour of the aggression is fuzzier during a war, or when one is being harassed by colleagues. In such cases it is difficult to know when the danger begins and ends and how to find a form of flight or fight that is relevant. Often, there is no precise predator, as the danger can come from several sources in unpredictable ways. These forms of aggression are generated by institutions. It is then difficult to know against which predator to direct a flight-or-fight response.[67] When the reactions of flight or fight are mobilized to react against an aggression such as war, their activation is often automatic. They instantly mobilize all the resources of the organism. During a war, an individual attacks and is being attacked, but the aims are defined institutionally. A soldier may not only be afraid of enemies. He can also find it difficult to accept that he has to kill others. An individual who is being mobbed often does not know why he is being persecuted or who organizes the mobbing. He just feels disempowered. He cannot prevent the activation of a flight or attack response that automatically activates itself in his organism, even when it is counterproductive.

Once in place, the response mobilizes the affective and intellectual resources to react in a particular fashion. They are monopolized by the need to flee or attack. There is no energy to look for other options. To resolve this difficulty, researchers like Lazarus and Folkman (1984) propose methods that facilitate change in the cognitive behavior of traumatized persons to help them construct other forms of adjustment (coping skills) in the face of a real or imaginary danger. The traumatized person *needs external help* to cope with the flight-or-attack response that has been activated by their organism. Yet he is often too proud and too ashamed to look for help.

To understand the mobilization of a fight-or-flight response, Cannon focused on the association between the activity of the sympathetic nervous system and the increase in the rate of adrenaline in the blood. This hormone is secreted by the central part of the adrenal glands (the medulla) situated on the top of the kidneys. In a cat, the increase in the rate of adrenaline in the blood, set in motion by the sympathetic nervous system, brings about an increase in respiration, cardiac rhythm, and goose bumps. Adrenaline also creates increased irrigation of the muscles and the brain, enlarges the diameter of the pupils, and facilitates access to the energy resources such as sugar.

Since Cannon's time, Levine and Frederick (1997) have described how, in the animal that survives an attack, this kind of mobilization is followed by vegetative reactions that permit the organism to recover its strength and energy. The animal trembles and evacuates everything that was accumulated at the occasion of the slowing down of the visceral and renal functioning. Going from a sympathetic functioning to a parasympathetic functioning is only possible once the predator is clearly absent. If the hunted animal is caught, he is killed and eaten. In that case, there is no need for a mechanism to shut down the stress reaction. This is a flaw that humans have inherited. In our case, when there is no clear ending to a stressful situation, the mobilization of stress can be activated until the stressed person dies.

THE GENERAL SYNDROME OF ADAPTATION

Hans Selye (1907–1982) was one of the researchers who pursued the work of Cannon on trauma during World War II.[68] This Canadian of Austro-Hungarian origin introduced the term *stress* in 1946.

One of Selye's basic hypotheses is that when a person must suddenly accommodate to a particularly shocking situation, he often finds a way to function that allows for survival by developing powerful modes of *accommodation* in very short time.[69] But then something is blocked, and flexibility is lost. As I have often indicated, the organism needs time to structure itself. In traumatizing situations, a sudden reconstruction of certain modes of functioning can save the life of the organism, but then the organism has difficulty getting out of this state. Everything that happens after that is *assimilated* by the new mode of functioning. The organism thus loses its capacity *to reaccommodate* itself[70] to an environment that no longer has a traumatizing dimension. The frozen accommodation does not include the entire organism but focuses only on some organismic systems.

Different than traumatic situations (such as being arrested and then tortured), stress designates more progressive changes. Selye (1936) then talks about the *general adaptation syndrome.* This syndrome is unleashed by an accommodation in three phases:

1. Placing on alert all of the functions of the organism, unleashed by a stimulus the receptors of the organism categorize as potentially dangerous. This system resembles the one described by Cannon at the occasion of a mobilization for a reaction of flight or fight. *During this phase, the organism lacks defenses* because it blocks its mechanisms of parasympathetic auto-regulation to focus all of its resources on survival.

2. Putting in place a *system of fight against the assault,* organized by the vegetative systems and the secretion of cortisol by the adrenal glands. This secretion is unleashed by the hypothalamus. Cortisol especially increases muscular strength and intervenes in diverse regulatory mechanisms of the organism. A mobilization of the resources of the organism organizes around the sympathetic system. The cardiac rhythm and respiration, perspiration, worries, and sleep problems become more intense. Therefore, the individual experiences a persistent impression that he does not have the means to face what is going on. Finally, he panics.

3. The *exhaustion* phase comes about if the stress factor continues to arouse the organism. The resources of the defense system are exhausted and exhaust the organism. Then we notice the modifications of the organs that sometimes lead to death. Wilhelm Reich[71] speaks here of the effect of *constriction* on the organism. He observes an excessive contraction of the tissues, a loss of energetic resources, and a mind that perceives fewer options. Selye notices, above all, a reduction in the size of the thymus, the spleen, and the lymphatic ganglions; gastrointestinal ulcerations; an increase in size of the suprarenal cortex; a reduction in the number of lymphocytes in the blood; as well as the total disappearance of the eosinophils (cells of the immune system). This state of exhaustion, sometimes called "burnout," can lead to the death of the affected cells.

The Activation of the Organism by Stress.   Selye isolated an axis *of stress* that is organized around a reciprocal influence between the *hypothalamus* in the brain and the median part of the suprarenal endocrine glands, situated at the upper extremity of the kidneys (see figure 8.1). The hypothalamus activates the suprarenal glands through the neurovegetative system. The suprarenal glands secrete catecholamines, like adrenaline and noradrenaline, into the blood. These hormones unleash a classic sympathetic mobilization. This process, shown in figure 8.1, forms a loop of negative retroaction where the excess of cortisol activates the glucocorticoids receptors of the brain and suppresses the production of CRH. In depressed patients, however, this loop no longer functions, hence an excessive production of CDR and thus of cortisol. This system is known as the *hypothalamic-pituitary-adrenal (HPA) axis.*

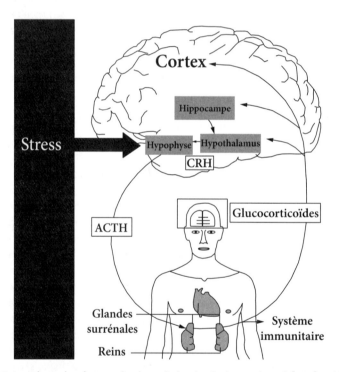

FIGURE 8.1.   The axis of stress (or hypothalamic-pituitary-adrenal [HPA] axis). When someone suffers a stressful event, his rate of glucocorticoids in the blood increases. This brings about, via specific receptors situated in the hippocampus, an activation of the hypothalamus, which then secretes corticotrophin-releasing hormone (CRH). This hormone, in turn, activates the pituitary gland (or hypophysis) to produce ATHC (adrenocorticotropine), which circulates in the blood system and reaches the suprarenal glands, where they provoke the release of cortisol. *Source:* Retrieved on September 29, 2007, from a site dedicated to Henri Laborit: http://lecerveau.mcgill.ca/flash/a/a_08/a_08_m/a_08_m_dep/a_08_m_dep.html

The activity unleashed by the catecholamines allows all of the reactions produced by the axis of stress to draw from energetic resources of the body by metabolizing lipids and sugars. In activating the hypothalamus, this circuit makes it possible to draw more deeply from the organism's reserves.

Other layers of the central nervous system, situated underneath the hypothalamus, can also activate the adrenal glands. These regions are situated in the medulla, the marrow, and some reflex pathways. A lack of adrenaline in the blood can also activate the adrenal glands via the mechanisms of homeostatic regulation. The hypothalamus can be influenced by other centers of the brains, especially those that govern perceptive and cognitive analysis or the emotions.

This phase of stress is considered to be constructive because it predisposes the organism to become creative. If a resting phase (a small cup of tea) ensues, the organism restores its forces.

The Stress Reaction.   The stress reaction varies in *intensity* according to (a) the danger and (b) the way the stress is felt by the mechanisms that regulate the reaction. Richard S. Lazarus (1991) analyzed how certain mental reactions could activate or deactivate a stress. He sought to define the means with which to cope with stress. Selye thought that the axis of stress, once it was activated by a mechanism that is still not well understood, reacted in an undifferentiated manner. Since research has shown that the vegetative system is less "autonomous" than was believed, this statement has been marginalized.

THE ORGANIZATION OF THE DEFENSES AGAINST EXHAUSTION.   If the organism is repeatedly placed under stress, the axis of stress runs out of easily available resources. To continue to function, it sets about to draw from those resources that are more difficult to use and activates mechanisms that slow down the reactions of exhaustion. The organism sets itself up in a state of *accommodation to the shock*. The HPA axis is reinforced by an increase of chemical activity that doubles the activity of the sympathetic nervous system. The activation often begins with the *hypothalamus*, which recruits the help of the pituitary gland this time. The pituitary then secretes *corticoliberin*, which will produce a hormone called *adrenocorticotrophic hormone* (ACTH), also known as corticotropin. ACTH activates yet a greater number of the adrenals, which in turn, among others, will activate the corticoadrenal hormones, which are released by the paraventricular nucleus (PVN) of the hypothalamus. It then activates the adrenal gland, which will release hormones such as the *glucocorticoids*, like *cortisol* and *cortisone*. These hormones mobilize the reserves available in the form of carbohydrates and add "slow" sugars into the blood. They inhibit the antiallergic and antiinflammatory manifestations caused by the damage to the tissues during the stress reaction by diminishing the activity of the immune system (especially eosinophils).

At the moment when this system becomes established and can no longer be curbed, there will be permanent vasodilation in the organs necessary for a reaction of fight or flight and a permanent vasoconstriction in the organs dependent on the parasympathetic circuit. This vasoconstriction is in part noxious to the tissues that depend on it and impedes the disposal of the metabolic waste produced by the muscles in permanent tension:[72]

> We were brought to consider the shock syndromes no longer as an exhaustion of the means of defense; but, to the contrary, as a consequence of their activation and of the persistence of their action in the case of the ineffectiveness of flight or fight. (Laborit, 1994, 2.2.2, p. 236; translated by Marcel Duclos)

THE EXHAUSTION REACTION. The large consumption of carbohydrates reduces the production of other substances that depend on it, like serotonin. As we have seen, a reduction of serotonin can produce depressive and suicidal tendencies. These tendencies sometimes are linked to bulimic crises which seek to compensate for the lack of production of substances like serotonin. Stress can manifest through two distinct mechanisms:

1. A *mental* stress, associated to negative and biased representations of the situation.
2. A *vegetative stress* that exhausts the physiological resources of the organism.

These two mechanisms are activated in *parallel* fashion. They mutually influence each other, but follow a different causal pathway. The feelings of disempowerment and depression that follow the exhaustion phase are thus accompanied by depressive affects like anger at oneself and one's powerlessness. The organism has fewer and fewer resources. The waste products in the muscles are not eliminated, breathlessness sets in, the arteries and the heart function poorly.

An excess of cortisol lowers the immune defenses, but it also attacks tissues of the central nervous system, which it saturates via the bloodstream. At the beginning, this effect is stimulating because it allows the ions of the nerve membranes to circulate more rapidly (it consists especially of the circulation of calcium in the membranes). Once this chemical reaction has been exploited, the neurons are in turn exhausted, and sometimes die, due especially to depolarization. Several studies describe a reduction in the volume of the hippocampus in persons who have lived through this form of sudden accommodation.[73] The hippocampus, situated in the limbic system, is especially implied in the management of memory and spatial relations. The attack on this neurological structure causes uncontrollable psychological reactions of disorientation. The glucocorticoids also excite other regions of the brain. They modify the functioning of the frontal lobe, which can explain why persons under stress often make poor decisions. They also excite the amygdala, which increases the feeling of fear. The amygdala reinforces the activity of the pituitary while the hippocampus can inhibit it.[74]

Certain attacks to the hippocampus can be repaired by taking antidepressants, which is one of the reasons they are prescribed. This implies taking these medications during a prescribed time (at least a year) to restructure zones of the hippocampus that were destroyed by stress.[75]

Laborit: From the Cell to Politics, from Spinoza to Reich

Henri-Marie Laborit[76] (1914–1995) was also influenced by the study of the shock that unsettles soldiers at war. He was a surgeon in the French navy during World War II and during the last French colonial wars (Indochina and Algeria). In the latter part of his life, he became a kind of Spinoza of biology who shows how each system actively influences the system that contains it. Laborit[77] arrives at similar conclusions as Spinoza with regard to human beings when he shows that the mental system cannot be conscious of the nonconscious mechanisms by which it is regulated. One of his principal preoccupations seems to have been to find a way to understand how an individual, entangled in systems of regulations that go through many levels (atoms, cells, organisms, institutions, ecology), can actively and lucidly participate in what animates him. This theme gradually became a form of individual and social engagement.

Laborit's research observes mechanisms that enrich the models of Bernard, Cannon, and Selye. He describes in greater detail how the regulatory mechanisms of the organism are like a bridge that links the cellular and social dynamics. Like a bridge, the homeostatic mechanisms are rooted in two shores. Thus, the food industry makes it possible for human organisms to feed themselves, but it uses this support to render individuals dependent on a system that exploits them. He describes in a detailed way the chain of mechanisms that connect cellular, organismic and social dynamics. This allows him to provide an enlarged panoramic view of the heterogeneity of the mechanisms involved in the homeostatic regulation of the human species.

THE INDIVIDUAL AND HIS SOCIAL ENVIRONMENT

Henri Laborit[78] knew and admired Selye.[79] For both of them, one could only alleviate the destruction of the cells by seeing to the equilibrium of the internal environment and by keeping its values as balanced as possible. His first model on the biology of stress is close to the one Selye was developing. They were using different but complementary research strategies to analyze how stress could destroy some of the organism's tissues. Laborit's first original contribution to that area of research was based on his observation that an amelioration of the ecology of the cells was only useful if the cell modified its behavior in function of this amelioration. Because of this finding, Laborit and his French colleagues focused on the "pumps" in the cell membrane that facilitate the exit and entry of substances. You will find detailed descriptions in textbooks on physiology that show how the cell membrane polarizes and depolarizes by passing ions from both side of the membrane:

> When a cell depolarizes itself, the sodium, whose concentration outside of the cell is greater than in the interior of the cell, penetrates within. Conversely, the potas-

sium, whose intracellular concentration is elevated, in the course of the depolarization, exits the cell toward the extracellular milieu. (Laborit, 1989, 7.3, p. 102;
translated by Marcel Duclos)

This exchange requires that there is enough sodium and potassium in the internal environment of the organism. However, Laborit observes, in certain circumstances, the sodium and potassium pumps become inactive. The restoration of
equilibrium in the internal environment does not suffice to restore the activity
of the pumps.[80] Therefore, Laborit sought to find those substances that would
restore not only the internal environment but also the activity of cellular pumps.
Here, the action is doubled:

1. On the *environment* of the cell.
2. On the *functioning* of the cell.

Without this dual action, not only do the individual cells waste away but also
their participation in the maintenance of the equilibrium of the internal environment becomes defective. A negative vicious circle is then established in which
the disequilibrium of the internal environment renders the cells inactive, and the
inactivity of the cells destabilizes its immediate environment. At the beginning,
this disequilibrium is local; but if it persists, it can invade the organism. Indeed,
the exchange of potassium and sodium between the internal environment and
the cell adjusts the equilibrium of the substances in the organism's internal environment. If some cells retain one of these, there is a possible disequilibrium in the
internal environment that can create a lack of supply in other well-functioning
cells. Moreover, the death of some cells can set toxic wastes like lactic acid in
circulation in the internal environment of the organism. This can create a metabolic acidosis. It can also modify the equilibrium of the internal environment.[81]

Laborit goes from this model between the cell and its immediate milieu
when he wants to show how the social environment of an individual and the
activity of the individuals who are part of it can become synergistic or destructive. We have already seen that an individual under stress can no longer make
sound decisions, and he wastes his metabolic resources. To treat this individual,
his environment must also be restabilized, or he must be assisted in finding a
more supportive environment. In *"L'homme imaginant"* (1970) (literally: *"man
while he imagines"*), Laborit's wording is close to the analysis of Stalin's regime
by Reich.[82] Both think that a stressful environment can pollute its subsystems
and the systems that contain them. It can go both ways. Thus human societies
can pollute nature and the tissues of individual organisms, and this pollution is
then maintained by these polluted subsystems. This idea is often developed in
systems theory when it assumes that to repair a system one needs to coordinate
top-down strategies (working on the globality of the system to repair local damage) with *bottom-up* strategies (working on a local mechanisms that can influence global dynamics).[83]

CYBERNETICS AND THE SYSTEM OF REGULATION

Systems thinking was defined when thinkers like Ludwig von Bertalanffy (1950, 1968a, 1968b) and Norbert Wiener (1948) created a rigorous model for the notions of system and of regulation. Laborit is one of those who introduced this way of thinking in France.

Ascending and Descending Causal Chains. In the example of the rapport between the membrane's pump and the internal environment, there is a constant oscillation between the concentration of sodium around the cell and in the cell. These variations are due to three factors at least:[84]

1. The variations induced by the cycles of the organism (the biorhythms).
2. The variations induced by the environment in which the organism finds itself.
3. The organism/environment interaction produces a chain of modifications at each level (organs, cells, etc.) of the organism. This cascading action, which influences each level of the organism, is referred to as "descending" and "ascending." For Laborit, stress is produced by mechanisms embedded in cascading dynamics.

The environment imposes some conditions on the organism; the organism has its own proper conditions for its existence. These two types of conditions create a vital dialogue between the metabolic demands and what the environment has to offer. Take the example of temperature. If the basal milieu of the human organism is not 36°C (98.6°F), the organism can die. The environment of the planet follows dynamics that do not take this exigency into account.

Temperature activates a "descending" causal chain that has influenced the mechanisms of evolution (only that which can live in an existing geographic system survives), and all of the organism's levels of organization. This influence is going to be countered by a series of local "ascending" reactions, which regroup themselves to adapt, more or less effectively, to what the planet offers. This ascending chain was constructed, mostly phylogenetically, to protect the exigencies of the internal environment. We now know that these bottom/up demands can influence the planetary system.

Psyche and Organism in Biology. Laborit does not spend much time situating the psyche in his model because it is not a topic that he studied.[85] However, he needs to situate psychological dynamics in his general system. He situates them in a particularly complex part of the organizational system of the organism. In the previous section, we have determined the necessity to coordinate two axes:

1. The coordination of organism/environment.
2. The coordination of the ascending and descending causal chains of the organism.

The psyche is situated somewhere at the intersection of these two axes. It participates in the mechanisms that coordinate the inside and outside of the global organism with the demands the ascending and descending chains impose on behavior.

To negotiate with the environment, the complex organisms create a social milieu as an intermediary between the organism and the environment presented by the planet. The more this social environment becomes complex, the more the propensities of the organism mobilize the dynamics of the psyche. Indeed, even before considering language, socialization requires that the members of the species have come to a certain agreement concerning what is perceived and on the correlation between a stimulus and behaviors. With ants, most of the individuals react to a stimulus just about the same way. A certain variation already exists because the conformity is different for each "caste" (worker, soldier, queen). It would seem that the development of the psyche allowed for the appearance of socialized species that attempt, with more or less success, to combine cohesion and diversity. The more the mind can intervene in a complex way into the regulation of the organism, the more the species is able to develop a capacity to combine cohesion and diversity. The need to develop a wide variety of individual particularities can be included in such a point of view.

The Servomechanisms of Stress.   Laborit often takes the thermostat as a simple example of a servomechanism. The thermostat makes it possible for an operator to set a goal for a system. Thus, we use a thermostat to regulate the heating system in a building: to set a target temperature. Take the case of a consumer who regulates his thermostat so that an apartment is always at 20°C. The thermostat activates the heating system for as long as the temperature of the apartment is lower than the temperature set by the consumer, and it brings the activity of the heating system to a stop when the temperature of the space exceeds the set goal. For example, the thermostat is set to engage the heating system as soon as the temperature the apartment falls below 15°C and to shut it off as soon as the temperature in the apartment reaches 25°C. The temperature of the apartment therefore *oscillates* between those two points. This oscillating regulatory system is characteristic of biological functioning in which a static equilibrium is tantamount to death. Only the inanimate world can follow linear functioning.[86] In his discussions with Selye, Laborit distinguished two dimensions:[87]

1. *The axis of stress constitutes a system.* Like every other constituted biological system, this one has the tendency to stabilize by embedding itself into organismic regulatory systems to survive for as long as possible.
2. *The servomechanism.* The axis of stress has a servomechanism, which, like the thermostat, can increase or decrease the functioning of the axis of stress, even extinguish it.

In an environment where the axis of stress is activated by a known predator and extinguished by its moving away, the servomechanism of the axis of stress generally functions quite well. We have seen that aggression in humans is often perpetuated by forces that are more difficult to define and localize in time and space. The servomechanism of the axis of stress is too primitive to adapt itself to the details of a situation like mobbing or a tyrannical political regime. For some people, the axis of stress is easily activated, whereas for others it more easily deactivates. Laborit, for example, studied postoperative shock. For certain people, it seems as if the servomechanism of the axis of stress does not detect that the surgery is over and successful. The organism continues to react as if it were still in the operating room.

Even if the mind participates in the dynamics that turn on and shut off the axis of stress, as Lazarus supposed, the connection is manifestly indirect. A relaxation method, psychotherapy, a tranquilizer—all can deactivate an active axis of stress, but none of these strategies work in every case. Laborit assumed that these interventions have an indirect effect. He therefore looked for the specific servomechanism that directly stops the stress reaction. He was convinced that it must be a specific chemical stimulus that can sometimes be activated by one of the interventions I have just mentioned. The relation between deactivation of stress and relaxation, for example, would then be indirect. When relaxation adequately activates the parasympathetic vegetative system, this system puts a certain amount of substances into the circulation of the blood; if the substance is detected by the servomechanism of the axis of stress, it will cut off the systems it controls.

At the time, the available knowledge allowed one to think that such a servomechanism could be situated in the pituitary gland. Laborit looked for a substance that could have such an effect on the pituitary gland. He then analyzed all the hormones produced by the pituitary gland, with the hope that there would be one that deactivates, in a targeted way, the axis of stress. His hunch led him to the discovery of what we today call the *neuroleptics*. These substances and their derivatives have become one of the principal forms of support that psychiatrists propose to their psychotic patients. This type of intervention permits one to think that one of the mechanisms that activates a psychosis has a particularly low threshold, which puts a more complex version of the axis of stress into play. By inhibiting the substances that activate the physiological dynamics of stress and psychosis, and by raising the values of the servomechanism that activates these states, medication can stop the vicious circle of extremely painful anxiety and hallucinations. This is what neuroleptics do, according to Laborit.

Better to Be a Lout than to Be Resigned.   Henri Laborit[88] uses a simple controlled experiment to show that in the case of stress, it is better to be aggressive and active than to be resigned. For this research, he uses a theoretical model that has the same structure as the one he used in his research on the necessity to maintain the cells active in a deregulated environment. The basic situation is composed of two rat cages linked by a door. The floor of the cages has a wire mesh on it so that one can pass an electric current through it. Rats receive an electric shock ten minutes a day, but the cages allow Laborit to vary the *context* in which this is done:

   Situation 1. The floor tips when the rat changes cage. The rocking of the floor shuts off the electricity. Every time an electric current passes through the mesh on the floor, the rat feels pain. But the rat quickly discovers that in changing cage, the pain ceases. This is the situation of *simple avoidance.*

   Situation 2. The situation is the same as the preceding one, but a light flickers four seconds before the electric current passes through the mesh on the floor. The rat thus changes cage as soon as he sees the light turn on. This time, there is *active avoidance* of a painful situation.

   Situation 3. The door between the two cages is now closed. The rat can only undergo the pain of the electric shock. The situation is "hopeless." At first, the rat moves in every direction; then slowly, something will inhibit his will to react, move, and feel. After having lived in this way for a week, the rat has lost weight. He acquires a stable hypertension, which then takes weeks to resolve. The amount of cortisol in his blood is high. The mucous membranes of the intestines develop ulcers. This state of collapse, contraction, resignation is well known by body psychotherapists who speak of *constriction* and resignation. Reich,[89] for example, describes the reaction of a newborn boy who, after circumcision, can no longer cry and scream, ends up contracting himself and becoming mute. Laborit explains that this pathological state (for the body and mind) can become permanent if the situation remains unbearable. A system *of inhibition of action,*[90] similar to the axis of stress described by Selye, is established.

   Situation 4. The situation is the same as the preceding one, except that at the end of a week, the door between the two cages is open. Even though he is now able to change situation, "he will not profit from it and will remain stuck in his inhibition" (Laborit, 1989, X.5, p. 207; translated by Marcel Duclos)

   Situation 5. The situation is the same as the preceding one, except that in the electrified cage there are now *two* rats. In discovering that they cannot flee the pain caused by the electric shock, the will get up on their hind legs, which at least reduces the area of body surface in contact with the electrified floor. They will then fight, up on their hind legs, and attack one other with the upper part of their body. Indirectly, this reaction renders them a service. As each body serves as a support for the other, the rats are able to remain on their back legs much longer. A week later, their bodies are in relatively good shape, and the mechanisms of stress have not been established. This only works if the rats are about of equal strength. This is what often happens in the gang wars of adolescents who live in desperate social situations. In other words, an available aggression makes it possible for them avoid being shut up in a state of resignation.

These experiments suggest a series of measures one can take to help someone who suffers from being in a traumatizing context:

1. If possible, change the milieu.
2. At least avoid the more tense situations.
3. Keep one's creativity, and allow oneself to become aggressive or to sublimate.

Several recent studies[91] confirm that the more a person has an unfavorable position in the social hierarchy, the greater the probability that the axis of stress would be intensely activated. This has been observed in rats, monkeys, and humans. This phenomenon has become sufficiently common for it to become a medical symptom often identified in psychiatry as social anxiety disorder. This body of research demonstrates to what point interactive behaviors can sometimes have a deep impact on affective and metabolic dynamics.

The Methodological Limits of Stress Research.   Recent technological developments allow us to gather a considerable amount of information on the functioning of an individual (neurological, metabolic, behavioral, psychiatric, sociological, etc.). However, the statistical methods presently available to organize this data do not allow us to manage as much information as is necessary to understand individuals without generating false results. By "false results," I mean statistical tests that signal a strong correlation between several sets of data while the research method does not guarantee that this correlation is not due to chance. The crux of the matter is that statistical tests require a large number of subjects to test the impact of only a few variables. The more variables you have, the larger the required number of subjects. Today, technology allows us to gather huge amounts of data on each subject. On the other hand, the expensive machinery used by neurologists only allows them to observe small groups of subjects. Because they are nevertheless understandably eager to explore the information their electronic devices allow them to gather, they collect whatever data they can and then use classical statistics to analyze it. Because they are not always statistically wise, this procedure yields a large number of false results with apparently high statistical significance. There is therefore a lack of adaptation between the current statistical methods and the recent development of technology. The result is that many researchers are showing us that there is probably a great many situations that produce profound stress. We find the same problem with certain research that associates cancer with certain products. The only guarantee against this type of statistical effect is the *replication* of the experiment by different research groups. The more there is replication, the more the observed result of a particular research study becomes *robust*.

For example, take the excellent recent research conducted by Karin Roelofs and his team (2009) that observed an intense interaction between the following variables on groups of approximately twenty subjects:

1. A photo of an angry face.
2. Gestures of the arms and hands going toward the photo or toward oneself.
3. A diagnosis of post-traumatic anxiety disorder, social phobia, and subjects without any discernible psychiatric diagnosis.
4. Blood pressure.
5. The quantity of mobilized cortisol.

The results indicate that there is probably a strong interaction between these variables. However, the preceding remarks make us cautious. All that we can say about studies of this type is that the researchers would like to show that there is an intimate link between all of the variables that they are able to measure: such is the present-day myth that is in vogue. The whole of body psychotherapy uses an analogous model when it reflects on the functioning of an individual and finds clinical reasons to justify its point of view. The practitioners of body psychotherapy consequently identify this type of research as a *proof* of the soundness of their point of view. But these research studies prove nothing at the moment. They add one more example that supports the myth of an intimate relationship between the dimensions of the organism and its environment. This example reinforces the body of clinical and experimental data that goes in this direction; but the statistical problems I have indicated do not provide a sufficient basis to allow us to speak of scientific proof. In other words, it is possible that there is actually a convergence between clinical and experimental data. For the moment, this convergence only has the status of an intellectual way of thinking that is relatively robust. I have not, for the time being, found research studies that invalidate this point of view.

The aim of this analysis is to render the psychotherapeutic practitioner attentive to the fact that the press is actually full of alarming articles showing that a particular food, a behavior, or a context considerably increases the probability that the axis of stress will be activated or cancer will develop. Most of these works are interesting but suffer from a lack of adequate replication to become anything more than an observation that presents a question. Above all, I hope this research will motivate mathematicians to develop statistical theories that will permit a more fruitful analysis of the immense pile of data that the new technologies have made possible.[92] For the moment, there is such a considerable amount of data that reason often drowns in it all.

Uvnäs-Moberg and Oxytocin: The Axis of Affection

> The "motivation systems" are networks of specialized nerve cells that have the capacity to synthesize and to release certain transmitters such as dopamine, endogenous opioids and oxytocin. These transmitters, if acting in common, may create a psychological state that we call motivation, vitality or creativity. Dopamine gives us the feeling of energy; the opioids provide that we feel fine while doing something and oxytocin motivates us to do something for or together with people we like. (Joachim Bauer, 2009, "The Brain Transforms Psychology into Biology," p. 234)

The axis of stress has sometimes been used as a medical tool. In its simplified version it seems to have clear boundaries, forming a well-differentiated subsystem. This simplification was necessary to support the activity of the practitioners who are not researchers. In reality, the axis of stress is not as coherent as it might seem. It remains a good example of how an affective organization can mobilize all the dimensions of the organism for its own purpose. Thus, the dynamics of consciousness are recruited in such a way that they generate a profusion of pessimistic thoughts. When the organism needs to be motivated to run as fast as it can from danger, this may be a useful mood. When the danger persists, pessimism leads to depression. The stressed person believes that they are his thoughts and defends them. He thus defends the perpetuation of his stress. Yet when the stressed response has been deactivated, the person appreciates having another mood. This model can only be confirmed if there exists other affects that have a similar structure because it is rare that biological evolution sustains a mechanism that has only one function. It would be too costly for the organism. Since the 1960s, researchers have shown that the dynamics isolated around the notions of stress and trauma are also mobilized to construct affective systems that support constructive affects. Having discussed the axis of stress, I am now going to talk about the more recent research studies, and consequently less developed ones, on the vegetative management of positive affiliation.

Introduction: Levine's Rats, Affection, and Health

In the 1950s, psychiatrist Seymour Levine (1960) began his research studies on stress using rats. He employed an experimental device common among the behaviorists, which had also inspired Laborit's research. In a first series of experiments, he studied three types of rats.

1. *Handled and stressed rats.* Every day, newborn rats are placed in cages where they are administered a series of very low electric shocks. The experimenter carries the rats to be placed in such a cage in his hands. The same happens when they are returned to their habitual habitat.
2. *Handled rats.* A group of rats serves as the control group. They are placed in the same cage in the same manner but do not receive an electric shock.
3. *Abandoned rats.* A third group of rats also serves as a control group. They stay in the nest in which they habitually live. Nothing is done to them.

This study was conceived to demonstrate that stress, when inflicted at the beginning of life, has a devastating effect on the development of the rats. Levine was surprised to observe that the group that grew up poorly and exhibited worrisome symptoms when they reached adulthood was the third group: the ones that did not receive daily electric shocks nor were placed in the cage for a time each day. The rats of the third group were noticeably less curious and less active.

Seymour Levine then analyzed more closely the growth and development of the rats who participated in situation 1 and 3 up to adulthood. He observed that the group placed under stress "change gears" more rapidly than the group that stayed in its nest. In this last group, the increase in steroids, in the case of stress, is slower; the activation of the organism is longer lasting and decreases more slowly. In other words, the onset of the axis of stress is less rapid, but once it has been activated it becomes more difficult to deactivate.

Levine and his team changed the focus of their research and started to explore the trauma that could follow from an absence of stress in infancy. The organism needs stimuli that oblige it to mobilize itself and to adjust to its environment. This is yet another example that shows the relevance of one of the themes of this book: propensities come about to structure themselves in function of its interactions with the environment. An environment that does not stress an organism does not allow it to develop adequately.[93] Rosenzweig and his team (1972) confirmed this in their study of the neurological development of two groups of rats:

1. Rats that grow up in a cage.
2. Rats that grow up in a garden.

The rats in the second group, having reached adulthood, had a larger and heavier brain. The difference in the nerve mass is especially observable in the neocortex. Other research studies support and clarify this observation: "Rats raised in an enriched environment have larger, more complex brains than those raised without stimulation and challenge. Specifically, they have more neurons, synaptic connections, blood capillaries, and mitochondrial activity" (Cozolino, 2006, III.6, p. 82).

Levine, as does Rosenzweig, concludes that the fact of being hand-carried, being a center of attention, and changing environment suffices to explain the relative well-being of the rats in the first group. Kerstin Uvnäs-Moberg takes this a step further, showing that affection shapes as much as stress does, if not more. But to accommodate to stress is different than to accommodate to an affectionate environment. Uvnäs-Moberg shows that in the second case, another organismic system is activated: one complementary to the axis of stress. It is therefore probable that the two types of experience are stimulating. If one were to add Laborit's research to this collection of research studies, one would notice that all forms of contact, affectionate or hostile, facilitate stress reduction. The goal of Uvnäs-Moberg's research is to show the specific impact of a pleasant and affectionate contact.

Prolactin/Oxytocin

When Kerstin Uvnäs-Moberg had her first child, she experienced a number of physical and mental changes in herself—changes that she observed in most of the mothers that she encountered. The changes induced by motherhood are well documented but were not explained. At that time, she was conducting studies on the physiology of the intestines. [94] She decided to benefit from her research skill to study the psychophysiological causes of these changes.

She began her research with the endocrine factors most commonly associated with childbirth: *oxytocin* and *prolactin*. As for the axis of stress, the pituitary plays a central role in the regulation of these two hormones in the organism. The amount increases in function of various external stimulations, of which the most well-known is the one produced by a newborn who nurses at his mother's breast:

1. *Prolactin* is a hormone secreted by the anterior pituitary. It has a *mammotropic* effect (enlargement of the mammary glands) and a lactogenic effect (stimulation of milk secretion). It equally acts on the secretion of *progesterone* in women and *testosterone* in men. A lack of prolactin creates an absence of lactation and cessation of amenorrhea in women, and sterility and impotence in men.

2. *Oxytocin* is produced at the level of the supraoptic and paraventricular nuclei of the hypothalamus. The most known effect of this hormone is to facilitate childbirth by provoking the contraction of the smooth muscles of the uterus. Oxytocin is indispensable to the reflex that ejects the placenta and allows the uterus to retract after the expulsion so that it might return to its original position. The dilation of the cervix during childbirth activates the production of oxytocin. After childbirth, sucking of the breast brings about the production of oxytocin by the hypothalamus. Oxytocin activates a number of connections between the pituitary and various zones of the central nervous system. This is how an increase of oxytocin stimulates the production of prolactin and the hormones that regulate the growth of the infant's body.

During childbirth, oxytocin links itself to the parasympathetic system to create an inner atmosphere of calm, whereas *vasopressin* links itself to the sympathetic system to stimulate the circuits of fight or flight, which give the woman the necessary combativeness for the strain of childbirth. This observation is important because it attracts our attention to the fact that the sympathetic and parasympathetic systems can be active at the same time.

Having begun with these two hormones, Uvnäs-Moberg finally discovered a web of influences that include the dynamics of oxytocin and prolactin. As with Selye's axis of stress, the ramifications of this system mobilize neurological, hormonal, affective, and behavioral circuits; except that, this time, the function of this axis is to support *affection* and *amiability*. [95] During many years, she and her collaborators in Sweden tried to study the totality of this circuit. One of the reasons this research is interesting is that it is probably the first attempt to understand the entirety of an individual propensity in an integrated research project.

Childbirth and Oxytocin

After the birth of an infant, oxytocin spontaneously proliferates in the organism of most mothers. The activation of oxytocin can be inhibited by certain factors. The following three are examples:

1. An injection of artificial oxytocin.
2. A low temperature in the room.
3. Intensely bright lighting.

Artificial oxytocin (like misoprostol) is nonetheless sometimes necessary to facilitate the delivery of the placenta and prevent a hemorrhage after delivery. The natural oxytocin produced in the neuronal circuits plays an essential role in the attachment between the mammalian female and her newborn. Studies conducted on nonpregnant sheep have showed that an intraventricular (in the brain) injection of oxytocin allows for the artificial production of maternal reflexes. The administration of estrogen and progesterone, plus a vaginocervical (sexual) stimulation produces the same effect. On the other hand, this effect is canceled if the sheep is under an epidural anesthesia. [96]

Nursing mostly stimulates prolactin and the estrogens. Oxytocin facilitates the ejection of the milk by favoring the contraction of the mammary glands.

If a parent (mother or father) frequently carries the baby belly to belly, Uvnäs-Moberg notes an increase of the amount of oxytocin in the parent and a greater expression of affection toward the newborn. There is a marked difference in behavior relative to length of time and intensity of the contact: the parent spends more time with the infant while giving it thoughtful and attentive care.

Oxytocin and the Lowering of Aggressiveness

When injected into certain parts of the mammalian brain, oxytocin activates a lessening of aggressiveness, an increase in sociability, a greater tolerance to pain, a lowering of arteriole pressure, an increase in appetite, and maternal behavior in women. These effects persist, on average, twice as long in females than in males. The effect of this calm is, first, individual. It easily spreads to other persons in the same group. Experience has showed that this transmission is carried out by olfactory pathways, in all likelihood by the pheromones that touch an archaic part of the olfactory system: the vomeronasal organ. [97] These are hormones secreted to have an impact on other organisms, while the classic hormones are secreted to have an impact on the regulation of the organism that secretes them. In other words, there would again be a dual channel of communication:

1. A serene person has a calming effect on her environment by her behavior.
2. A serene person with a lot of oxytocin also has a calming effect because she emits calming pheromones.

There are certainly parallel actions here, situated at the behavioral and physiological level and coordinated by an organismic regulator that is activated by oxytocin. Kosfeld and colleagues (2005) set up an experiment that shows that a nasal injection of oxytocin administered to students of the University of Zurich suffices to increase their confidence. This research demonstrated the effect of oxytocin on social relations independently of a relationship with newborns.

Oxytocin and Blood Pressure
Uvnäs-Moberg (1998) has showed that repeated injections of oxytocin lowers blood pressure and cortisol secretion (produced especially by stress) and provokes weight gain. The beneficial effect of oxytocin establishes itself in the organism only after a series of injections, given regularly for many days. Uvnäs-Moberg (1998) concludes that this shows this effect is not directly induced by oxytocin but that oxytocin sets circuits in motion that gradually form a healing process in the organism. Thus, only after having injected rats for at least five days do we discern, ten days later, a lasting lowering of blood pressure. The effect is not the same for male and female rats. Weight gain, for example, is a characteristic of females taking oxytocin. These repeated injections disinhibit, in a lasting way, the influence of the axis of stress and arrests the excessive secretion of cortisol.

A similar effect can be obtained by stroking the front of a person's trunk for five minutes each day, for ten or so days, at a rate of forty caresses per minute. It consists of light strokes (but not to the point of becoming erotic) that go from the top of the thorax to the lower abdomen without going all the way to the genitals.[98] This research confirms that a relatively permanent psychosomatic change requires the repeated and regular use of an exercise.

Children who received the kind of attention that activates oxytocin have a lesser chance of developing blood pressure problems as they grow older. Studies on this subject are under way and are worthy of close attention.

THE CIRCUITS OF THE BRAIN

Although some circuits organize aspects of conscious awareness, most serve as the background "glue" of our experience, an interwoven network of sensory, motor and affective circuitry. (Louis Cozolino, 2006, *The Neuroscience of Human Relationships,* II.5, p. 73)

The Myth of an Emotional Brain

For the moment, I have mostly associated the affects to the vegetative system. In the axis of stress, brain circuits[99] are components of a more general physiological circuit that also interacts with mind and behavior. Neurologists who work from such a point of view associate psychological function with *circuits* that can coordinate several parts of the brain. They are then recruited to fulfill particular functions. Other neurological theories have gathered evidence supporting the view that most psychological dynamics are produced by specific areas of the brain. In the second set of neurological approaches, it is assumed that a part of the brain *controls* physiological circuits such as those that I have described for the axis of stress. This point of view is close to the top-down notion that already existed when it was thought that the soul (or psyche) could organize somatic dynamics. The first approach is the most compatible with present-day theories of body psychotherapy, as it describes emotional circuits that coordinate physiology, mind, and behavior. However, we shall see (in chapter 9) that consciousness prefers to associate a specific mental dynamic to a specific organismic structure. As this attitude already exists in neurology, many body psychotherapists cannot prevent themselves from adopting neurological models that localize emotions in the limbic system, as proposed already by Lamarck.[100] You will notice that I am talking here of a preference for neurological theories that are compatible with some phenomena observed in body psychotherapy and of the comfort of our conscious dynamics. Empirical research often follows a different route. I now describe particular research studies on the brain that illustrate this debate. I begin with Cannon's thoughts on the matter.

Emotions and the Brain: The Limbic System of Emotion and the Neocortex of Reason

Cannon approached the brain as a structure that can be recruited by homeostatic circuits. This implies that homeostasis and the affects act on what goes on in the brain and what goes on in the brain has an impact on the vegetative dynamics. This strategy allowed for the isolation of the mechanisms that are situated in the brain and have a close link to the affective dynamics. There were two pitfalls to avoid:

1. The idea that everything that happens in the organism is governed by the brain and that the dynamics of the organism are at the beck and call of the brain.
2. The idea that the vegetative system and the brain form an undifferentiated whole.

Canon, if I understand him correctly, wanted to show that the vegetative system and the brain each have a particular mode of functioning but that there are interfaces (like the pituitary gland) that allow them to communicate. He tried to define the boundaries and the functions of these interfaces and what they coordinate. To try to understand how all of this is organized, Cannon undertook research studies on the *hypothalamus and the thalamus*, which are situated in the limbic system.[101]

Cannon explored the emotional circuit with neurologists Gerard J. Britton and Philip Bard.[102] They anesthetized the neocortex of cats to study their behavior when the neocortex is offline. They noticed that the cats without a functioning cortex entered into a huge rage that mobilized the entire body. These "sham rages" could be unleashed by almost any kind of stimuli. They no longer had a pertinent function. They had become a standard mode of response of the organism that inhibits other forms of possible responses. This body of research showed that an emotion is calibrated by several nervous structures. Cannon defended a theory of emotions that coordinates three types of mechanisms:

1. A stimulus activates parts of the limbic system,[103] which mobilizes the physiological resources necessary for the expression of an emotion like anger. The mobilization of the physiological resources that are needed requires the participation of the vegetative system.

2. During this time, the thalamus stimulates certain parts of the neocortex that mobilize the psychological resources (especially the representations) necessary to experience anger and define its function in a specific context.

3. Setting up the coordinated motion of the physiological and psychological circuits then allows for the emergence of a mobilization of the organism's systems of regulation that support the construction of a particular way to be angry (inhibited anger, impulsive anger, hot or cold anger, etc.). This construction leads to a behavior that not only expresses an emotion but seeks mostly to act on the stimuli that activate that emotion.

This model makes it possible to account for the impulsive aspect of the emotions and the rich complexity of the real-life experiences they create. The fact that the stimulation of the emotional activity is situated in the limbic system makes this phenomenon more archaic than the ones unleashed by the neocortex. However, the fact that it necessarily recruits the neocortex does make the emotional system more complex than a reflex. This kind of description often gives the impression of a precise function, while in fact the limbic circuits can contain zones that are linked to many affects in a small cerebral region. The thalamus is close to the amygdala; we can find pleasure centers in this region as well as anger and fear. The mix of affects is already complex within the limbic system. A person can experience a form of pleasure and fear when they are angry. This is independent of the systems of guilt or of sadistic fantasies that establish themselves with the introduction of social representations. In similar fashion, many people feel a mixture of pleasure and anxiety during coitus.

These studies are often mentioned by researchers who have attempted to confirm a simplified (or simplistic) version of Lamarck's hypothesis, according to which the limbic system is the emotional brain and the neocortex is the rational brain.[104] For them, the limbic system is the neurological center of the emotions. They have presented Cannon as a precursor, while criticizing his conclusions. Today, some neurologists are again getting closer to Cannon's point of view. Thus, Damasio freely takes up the idea that an emotion is, first, activated in the limbic system. This initial activation must then pass through neocortical circuits to associate with representations and information on what happens outside of the organism. Then he clarifies that the coordination between an evoked affect, representations, and the circumstances necessitate a participation of certain zones of the frontal lobe of the neocortex. The frontal neocortex also makes it possible to relate an affect to forms of expressions and the management of emotions that are specific to a culture.[105] This hypothesis remains prevalent: the limbic system and the brainstem activate standardized affective behaviors; the prefrontal cortex allows for the regulation of feelings and affective behaviors. This emotional system is regulated by a web of connections. The complexity of these connections varies from one neurological theory to another. There seems to be few direct routes between the front of the limbic system and the neocortex but, rather, many indirect routes. The theoretical variations seem to be based on how much importance these indirect routes have. Today, there seems to be an agreement that the affects are mostly *activated* by the centers of the limbic system, and are then *regulated* by the centers of the neocortex. This view is susceptible to change in the future.

Neurological Metaphors and Lobotomy

Setting up a dichotomy between the limbic system (= emotions of the mammals) and the neocortex (= the development of intelligence in mammals and humans) became a way to reformulate in a neurological language a debate that opposes the reason of the soul to the diabolic and animal forces of the body. This confusion between metaphor and neurology attained its apex in popularity in 1949 when Antonio Caetano de Abreu Freire Egas Moniz received the Nobel Prize in Medicine for having developed the surgical method for a lobotomy.[106] The procedure consisted of a perfunctory operation, often poorly controlled (the insertion of a scalpel via a nostril, sometimes performed by a nurse) to sever the region of the brain that links the front of the limbic system to the frontal lobes of the cortex. The basic model, proposed by Moniz, inspired by Lamarck, and then supported by MacLean's reformulations, was that the connections between the limbic system and neocortex are rare and are regrouped in the frontal part of the brain. In cutting the connections between the limbic system and the frontal neocortex, Moniz hoped to prevent the limbic system from disorganizing the functioning of the frontal lobe and from having too easy access to the motor system. The lobotomy disorganized a large number of the dynamics of the brain in a nonspecific way, which explains the general dysfunctions that it provoked.

This polarization of the neurological dynamics of the mind is still a current position defended by some neurologists.[107] This model is also used by psychiatrists like Bessel Van der Kolk to establish forms of psychophysical interventions that are used to help persons who suffer from post-traumatic stress disorder (PTSD). Thus, Van der Kolk (2006) mentions some observations that show that in the case of stress, an increase of limbic activity and a decrease of neocortical activity has been observed. This observation is certainly correct; however, there are a number of ways to understand it. The therapeutic approaches and techniques proposed by Van der Kolk and his team are respectful of patients, contrary to a lobotomy, but they do not always take into account the complexity of the mechanisms activated by the trauma. Van der Kolk has collaborated with a number of body psychotherapists to establish forms of intervention often useful at times of humanitarian crises.[108]

This simplistic vision (it dates from Lamarck!) is currently being reformulated by neurologists who propose a more refined version of Cannon's model[109] to show that several brain centers, several physiological mechanisms, and several mental mechanisms coordinate to form a real-life emotional experience. It is impossible for them to reduce such complex phenomena to a few zones of the brain or to a conflict between two zones. Nonetheless, these authors do not abandon Lamarck's and MacLean's model of the triune brain because it remains useful, especially for practitioners who only need a rough sketch of certain emotional mechanisms to support certain forms of intervention. Some neurologists[110] are presently attempting to show that there exist a great number of nerve and chemical connections between the neocortex and the limbic system. Other researchers show that different emotions can be related to different parts of the neocortex. Thus, Ekman and Davidson (1993) show that different smiles can be associated with different forms of activation in the lateral and medial parts of the frontal lobe and the anterior temporal lobe. Davidson and his colleagues (2002) show that depression can be related to a circuit that passes especially through the amygdala and the hippocampus of the limbic system and the prefrontal region of the neocortex. Sanjay J. Mathew and his team (2004) have also associated anxiety with the activity of the prefrontal region of the neocortex. This analysis conforms to the idea that the prefrontal cortex coordinates information on how an organism autoregulates and how it interacts with its environment.[111]

Is a Lesion in the Brain the Direct Cause of Behavioral Disorders?

The theory of cerebral localization has its point of departure from the observation that when a region of the brain is destroyed, a behavior ceases to exist. Even if no one denies this statement, there have been extensive debates on the ways to explain this observation. Traditionally, neurologists estimated that *the region that correlates with the disappearance of a behavior is the site that con-*

trols this behavior. In the 1930s, several neurologists criticized this "linear" way of thinking. For example Kurt Goldstein (in Germany) found it more efficient to use a holistic systemic approach, and Alexander Luria (in the Soviet Union) found some advantages in being forced to justify his argumentations in a Marxist dialectical language. For them, observing that a mechanism necessarily *passes* through a zone of the brain does not mean that this zone of the brain *organizes* this mechanism.[112] For example, the fact that a lesion in Broca's area (often called the language area of the brain) creates language problems (like aphasia) does not mean that the organization of the ability to speak is situated in this area of the brain.

This critique of the theory of cerebral localization is again found in Cannon's school. His student, Edmund Jacobson (1967)[113] prefers to situate the material foundation of a behavior in the *circuits* that link several zones: circuits that are situated in the brain (central nervous system) and at the periphery of the body (peripheral nervous system). Even though Jacobson had not studied language, he could have thought that the physiological circuits that make it possible for language to exist pass not only through the regions of Broca and Wernicke but also through the peripheral nerves that allow for the fine motor coordination of the vocal cords. Jacobson was looking for neurological models that could help him explain the impact of relaxation techniques. Closer to Cannon than to Goldstein and Luria, he nevertheless used a systemic model that also criticized linear causal models. He summarized his views on the matter with the following metaphor:

> Vignette on the metaphor of the central office that manages the exchange between telephones in a region. *You pick up the phone, and dial a friend's number. The central switchboard answers that it is broken, and consequently, it cannot connect you to your friend. In this example, there is a dysfunction in the switchboard (associated to a region of the brain) that prevents you from speaking to your friend (a behavior associated to a peripheral action of the organism). Are we able to deduce from this analysis that the switchboard decides when your friend picks up the telephone?*

We know that thoughts are often activated by the dynamics of our organism, but this does not mean that a particular area of the brain is the only one responsible for what emerges in our consciousness. For Jacobson, the brain is mostly a translator, a transformer that coordinates the dimensions of the organism and knows how to translate a mental operation into an operation that another dimension can activate. Thus, the representation of a gesture is "translated" into sensorimotor instructions that make it possible to activate an appropriate gesture. According to Jacobson, a propensity is organized like an electric circuit. Any device that is connected to the circuit can influence the rest of the circuit or even blow the fuses. The fuse box is a central location with regard to the circuit because I can use it to disconnect the whole circuit. Thus, there are zones in a circuit that can activate it or disconnect it, but that does not mean that these zones control everything that is going on in the other parts of the circuit. These zones have a function close to the notion of a servomechanism used by Laborit. I now describe a few examples of nerve centers that are used as a servomechanism for an affective circuit.

The Biological Roots of the Sensation of Pleasure and Addiction

While Selye and Laborit sought to find the chemical servomechanisms of stress, other researchers were looking to localize other servomechanisms situated in the brain. James Old (Montreal), Rudolf Hess (Zurich), and Jose Manual Rodriguez Delgado (United States) are among those. They were exploring ways of using the new technologies that facilitated the implantation of an electrode in a specific zone of the brain to see what would happen when that zone was stimulated. These researchers concentrated on the limbic system, which was then reputed to be the center of emotions.[114]

OLDS AND THE PLEASURE CIRCUIT

James Olds (1922–1976) completed his doctoral research in psychology with Peter Milner at McGill University in Montreal. Their professor, Donald Olding Hebb (1904–1985),[115] asked them to see if they could find, outside of the thalamus and the hypothalamus, limbic zones associated to affective responses. They explored the zone situated around the thalamus, between the pituitary (the bottom of the limbic system) and the septum (the top of the limbic system). These two centers form an axis that passes vertically by the thalamus. By chance, Olds and his collaborators found a zone of the rhinencephalic structures, strongly associated to the sense of smell, that created a sensation of pleasure each time it was stimulated. It became possible to condition rats by activating this zone, as Pavlov and Skinner did by giving food as a reward. For example, Olds activated the electrode every time the rat walked in a corner of its cage. After a while, the rat visited that corner of the cage more and more frequently.

To deepen his understanding of this phenomenon, Olds connected the electrode to a lever that could be activated by the rat. The rat could freely press on this lever at any time. Most of the rats developed an addiction to this behavior. They pressed on the lever more than 500 times per hour. If the experimenter disconnected the electrode, after half an hour, the rat pressed on the lever for a moment and then fell asleep, exhausted. If the experimenter did not disconnect the electrode, the rat ignored his basic needs (hunger and thirst) and pressed on the lever up to 2,000 times per hour for 24 hours. Some rats pressed on the lever until they died.

The same technique was used to help patients who were seriously troubled (schizophrenia, epilepsy). The behaviorist point of view regarding these treatments was to be able to teach patients to execute certain tasks with pleasure. These patients used words like *relaxing, joy,* or *ecstasy* to describe what they felt but were unable to explain why they felt the compulsive need to press the button.

These results show several interesting things relative to internal propensities:

1. It is possible to distinguish the difference between the need to eat and the pleasure in eating. Olds observes that when a rat feels pleasure, it no longer has to eat. The pleasure in eating connects two distinct mechanisms:
   1a. A propensity, when it is activated, becomes "imperialistic." Not only does it mobilize the whole of the resources of the organism, but it also inhibits the other propensities.
   1b. The pleasure principle does not by itself ensure the survival of the organism.
2. The impact of conditioning varies from one individual to another, even among rats. Certain individuals let themselves "be had" more easily than others.
3. Some human adults with whom Olds used this device can perceive themselves as having pleasure in pushing a lever, but they are not aware that they have *conditioned* themselves to press the button. They always have the impression that they make the decision to act. This shows that *conditioning remains nonconscious, even when the behavior* that *it unleashes can be detected consciously.* This observation is close to that described by hypnotists.

At the beginning, Olds was still influenced by the notion of cerebral localization, given that he speaks of the "pleasure center." But after ten years of research,[116] he shows that the septum is part of a circuit of pleasure that connects a center situated in front of the neocortex (prefrontal cortex) to other zones of the limbic system like the amygdala and the ventral tegmental area (VTA). This neurological circuit is also associated to the dopaminergic system. It plays an important role in conditioning.[117] The pleasure circuit is also associated to hormones of the catecholamine family, like norepinephrine.[118] Olds thus rejoins the point of view concerning the circuits defended by some of Cannon's students.

THE PLEASURE OF ADDICTION AS THE DRIVING FORCE OF SOCIAL RELATIONS

Once these results are associated to a network composed of neural, hormonal, behavioral, and psychological components, it becomes possible to understand how Olds's observations correspond quite precisely to what is observed when a servomechanism is activated not by the electrodes but by social phenomena. Thus, certain forms of social manipulation can create important and profitable dependencies. The most notable cases are the following:

1. *Addiction to drugs* such as heroin and alcohol.
2. *Addiction to computer games.* Dependence on computer games (e.g., solitaire, mahjong, or minesweeper) shows that money is not the chief

motivator of such a dependency, even though it does enrich casinos. One can become addicted to games that do not provide a financial gain, but only various forms of pleasurable *dissociation*. We are, in fact, closer to Olds's model, which shows that once activated, certain pleasurable propensities inhibit the other instincts.

3. Addiction to pornographic Internet sites.[119] Psychotherapists have more and more patients who are caught by perverse compulsive urges by landing on sites containing hard-core pornography. They then become dependent on sadistic, homosexual, or pedophilic urges that were not spontaneously part of their fantasies, nor were they part of their previous life. It is as if a latent side, probably unconscious, took hold of the person in a way that cannot be integrated by his or her conscious capacities. In most of the cases I have seen, they were weak personalities who had not grown up in a positive environment. These cases confirm the dangers, well known to psychotherapists, of going beyond a defense system without first analyzing it. In these cases, we observe a sudden and traumatizing accommodation that is difficult to reverse.

These are examples of cases where an intra-organic propensity becomes embedded in a social circuit without the person being aware of what is happening. The whole world of marketing and publicity plays explicitly on such possibilities. In this case, I use the notion of *external propensities*, which, for me, are different from internal propensities, which are mostly activated by organismic homeostatic dynamics.

Other neurologists have also found centers of *"punishment"* a bit lower in the same region of the brain. If a rat or a monkey presses on a lever that activates an electrode planted in one of these centers, "it will scream, try to flee, become aggressive, and will not do it again" (Laborit, 1989, X.6, p. 208; translated by Marcel Duclos). Acetylcholine is the principal neurotransmitter of this circuit.

For Norwegian philosopher Jon Elster (1999), the mechanisms that regulate the affects also participate in establishing the addiction to drugs, alcohol, cosmetic surgery, and so on. Joachim Bauer (2009, 2010) explains this intimate interconnection between affective organizations and the environment as being due to the need of an organism to socialize. This need would be so profound that it is associated already to the regulators of the genes, which calibrate their dynamics in function of the particularities of the environment.[120] The genes exist to organize the way the dynamics of the organism adapt to the environment. A human organism would not be able to survive without its social environment; and this social environment would not even exist if the human organism had no need of it. Environment and organisms mutually influence each other to such a point that one could nearly say that they are addicted to each other:

That is why Thomas Insel, director of the NIMH [National Institute of Mental Health in Bethesda, Maryland], asked with an ironic smile, 'whether it was an addiction to be socially attached to someone?' The answer is yes. However, it is not a problem; for that is why nature has made us (Joachim Bauer, 2009, "The Brain Transforms Psychology into Biology," p. 235)

Every propensity creates a form of dependence by becoming an obsessive habit. It is because they are based on mechanisms necessary for the affective life that the addictions become installed so easily and lastingly in the dynamics of the organism. The principal difference between an instinct and an addiction is that in the case of an addiction the object is socially constructed (e.g., a photograph) and reinforced by cultural and intellectual constructions. Sexuality and hunger are at the periphery of all these categories of intimate interactions between organismic and social dynamics. In these cases, a way of *perceiving* is the functional goal of an instinct that may transform need into an addiction. As in all forms of perversion, one notices a reversal of function: now the object creates the intensity of a need. This effect acquires even more intensity when it also allows one to participate in social rituals. Thus, for many people, in becoming dependent on erotic sites, they became computer literate. We see in this example the power of these cases that are at the border between satisfying a need and becoming dependent: the fuzziness of this border often allows organisms to rapidly acquire forms of social skills that have a deep impact on the development of new cultural rituals. These mechanisms have probably had a deep influence on how devices such as computers and mobile phones have so rapidly become embedded in the cogwheels of our cultural habits. The time spent in front of a monitor to satisfy one's fantasies or to facilitate the meeting of sexual and intimate partners develops a way to integrate the affects into institutionally constructed channels (Mafia-like, ideological, commercial, etc.). As Hume's model foreshadows,[121] easily accessible images give greater intensity to some fantasies, which are reinforced by becoming a motoric practice (typing on a keyboard and using a mouse to choose certain pictures on the screen).

Once the user spends most of his time in front of a screen, he has less time to learn how to interact with others in the here and now. He does not have the time to develop or maintain the skills that allow him to live with other persons in an intimate way. Thus, interactions that last for months through the intermediary of a computer monitor can disappear in ten minutes when direct behavioral interactive contingencies are activated. These behavioral contingencies are particularly intense among lovers. When they do not have enough time to co-construct themselves, intimate forms of communication cannot find a space in which they can exist.

Like many other thinkers discussed in this volume, Jon Elster situates the affects between physiology and psyche and shows how addictive behaviors influence conscious thoughts unbeknownst to them. The partners of addicted persons have a difficult time understanding that such a person does not explicitly understand his or her conditioning to a drug, to gaming, and so on. They often think that the dependent person lies—denies the evidence. When I explain to a psychotherapist in supervision or to a partner of an addicted person in psycho-therapy that an alcoholic person cannot perceive his or her addiction, some-thing changes in them. Here we are no longer at the level of the defenses described by Freud but at the level of nonconscious connections, woven in the vegetative system and in the brain, which the thoughts of the person concerned are unable to grasp. There can be some denial and insincerity, but mostly there is a sort of *internal psychological blind spot* that prevents the person from per-ceiving what drives him or her to act in such a manner. When one talks with an addicted person, one quickly notices that the dependence cannot be discussed in a rational manner. One gradually realizes that the individual cannot really grasp what is happening to him—something that can be incredibly frustrating for those who try to help. He must be helped, supported, deconditioned until he can take hold of himself, with a continuous support like the kind proposed by Weight Watchers or Alcoholics Anonymous. If this analysis permits a dependent person's circle of family and friends to better understand the communication problems induced by the addiction, it also shows the violence of the social mechanisms that sustain setting up these problems.

Dominance and Aggression

In this section, I give an account of a series of works that describe the existence of servomechanisms that connect social structure, behavior, and individual bio-chemical dynamics.

DOMINANCE AMONG MONKEYS: THE ONE AT THE BOTTOM

In the 1960s at Yale University, neurophysiologist Jose Manuel Rodriguez Del-gado[122] studied the way that certain nerve centers participated in the hierarchical organization in a tribe of baboons. At the time, the hierarchy among baboons was perceived in a relatively caricatured fashion. The rigidity of the mechanisms observed can be partially explained by the fact that numerous studies were based on the observation of animals in captivity. A tribe of monkeys is seen as having a dominant male when he has all of the rights to the food and the avail-able females, whereas at the other extreme, some males content themselves with leftovers and masturbation.[123] The other males find themselves between these extremes. The hierarchical position is determined by one's ability to win a fight against other members. In this game, the chief is the strongest. The females were rarely studied.

Delgado benefited from the use of wireless electrodes, which could be con-trolled from afar. Delgado placed a painless electrode in an area of the brain of a male that allows for the regulation of the amount of aggression.[124] The lever that controls this electrode was placed in the cage in which this baboon lives. One of the females who also lives in this cage learned to use the lever to reduce the aggression and dominance of this male. Certain behavioral signs associated with dominance (or lack of dominance) in this male are stereotypical (always the same). For example, when he can use all of his aggression, he threatens and often bites those around him. When the female presses down on the lever, the male accosts her in a friendlier manner.

Delgado also placed electrodes in dominated monkeys. When their aggression had been stimulated, they used more dominating behaviors, gained respect more often, but they did not become the leaders of the tribe. In these observations, two facts indicate that it does not consist of a simple direct relationship between nerve centers, aggression and social dominance:

1. There are several nerve centers that can be stimulated to obtain this effect. This brings us back to the notion of circuits.
2. The reinforcement of aggression by an electrode does not make it possible for a monkey to have the know-how necessary to acquire the status of a dominant monkey. This implies that the circuit passes through other mechanisms of the body and the mind and by social circuits, like those that lead another to accept an aggressive monkey as the dominant one.

DOMINANCE AMONG HUMANS

The first studies conducted in human ethology shows that there exists hierarchical structures in offices that are relatively similar to those observed among monkeys. A dominant person easily places his feet on the office furniture (table, chair, etc.), easily touches what belongs to others, leaves his belongings everywhere as a way to mark his territory, and ostensibly occupies a colleague's space (the other's chair, for example).[125] Hubert Montagner (1978) shows that there exist two extreme types of connection between aggression and dominance among the children he observed in a child-care center and in school:

1. A child who easily become angry and hits without ever being the strongest in a fight. *This child is at the bottom of the hierarchical ladder;* he has the reputation of being a "problem child" and having temper tantrums.
2. *The dominant child* who mostly carries out conciliatory and calming gestures but who often wins the fights when he is provoked.

This distinction is already evident in a day care center:

> Vignette on aggression and dominance in a day care center. *The leaders express relational and appeasing behaviors much more often than the dominant-aggressive ones. In that way, they stir up closeness and the giving of gifts to others in such a way that it is not possible to conclude that their behavior is displayed with the intention of attracting and leading them along. A child of two to three years of age is all the more attractive, imitated, and followed if the frequency of the child's appeasing behaviors are more numerous than the frequency of his aggression. (Montagner, 1978, p. 161; translated by Marcel Duclos)*

Nadel-Brulfert, Baudonnière, and Fontaine (1983) show that the aggression among children can be regulated by situational factors, almost as easily as Delgado did with his electrodes. In the situations studied by Montagner, there were few toys for many children. He then observes a large amount of aggressive behaviors linked to manifest behaviors of dominance. On the other hand, if the researchers place as many toys as there are children in the room, the amount of aggression and the use of dominance are spectacularly lowered. Even if there were an innate predisposition to include some effects of dominance in the human social interactions, this predisposition would not necessarily be activated in all situations. In other words, certain social configurations are part of the circuit that activates the propensity to situate oneself on the dominance scale. It seems that *the more that the goods are unequally distributed, the more the behaviors are related to the notion of dominance.*

Another type of research shows that the serotonin that circulates in the cerebrospinal fluids[126] makes it possible to *contain* aggression. Certain studies, insufficiently replicated to be considered robust, suggest that the amount varies, especially in function of the quantity of respectful behaviors directed toward a person.

To present this point of view, Buck summarizes an experiment by McGuire, Raleigh, and Brammer (1994) in his textbook on the psychophysiology of affects:

> Vignette on dominance and serotonin. *[This study] demonstrated an interesting similarity in the levels of serotonin in dominant male monkeys and dominant male humans. They found that the level of serotonin in the blood of dominant male rhesus monkeys is twice as high as the level in other male members of the group. When the dominant male is removed from the group, his level of serotonin falls to normal, whereas the level of serotonin in the newly dominant male rises. According to the evidence, the rise of the leader's serotonin level is induced by the submissive behavior he receives from the followers. A similar phenomenon was found in the blood serotonin levels of members of a fraternity at the University of California at Los Angeles: the fraternity officers had higher levels than other members. Whether shifts in leadership status affect the serotonin levels of male humans remains to be investigates. (Buck, 1988, p. 213)*

SUICIDE AND SEROTONIN

The psychiatrists of the 1990s, especially those inspired by Freud,[127] think that suicide and depression are a form of aggression turned against oneself. A considerable amount of research studies have showed that depression is linked to a lowering of the amount of serotonin in the cerebrospinal fluids and that suicide is associated to an even lower amount.[128] Research has also showed that there is a connection between depression and the circulation of serotonin in the brain, but this link is more complex.[129] It is nonetheless on this second network that the antidepressants act, because it is more difficult to act on the cerebrospinal fluids which can only be analyzed after a painful lumbar puncture. Psychiatrists also observed a connection between the lowering of serotonin and the increase in aggression.[130] For example, a very low amount of serotonin in the cerebrospinal fluids can be observed in persons who, all of a sudden, shoot at the inhabitants of a village or become violent toward friends and family, without any of this being predictable. These observations confirm the idea that there is a circuit that connects (a) the amount of serotonin, (b) the containment of aggression, and (c) the need to be respected. This connection is not linear because, as we have seen, the amount of serotonin also depends on other factors like eating habits.

Stress and the Cognitive Approach Proposed by Fradin

> But no one, to my knowledge, has determined the nature and powers of the affects, nor what, on the other hand, the mind can do to moderate them. . . . The affects, therefore, of hate, anger, envy, and the like, considered in themselves, follow the same necessity and force of nature as the other singular things. And therefore they acknowledge certain causes, through which they are understood, and have certain properties, as worthy of our knowledge as the properties of any other thing, by the mere contemplation of which we are pleased. (Spinoza, 1677a, *Ethics*, III. Preface, p. 69)

Anxiety As an Intelligent Indicator of Certain Divergences between Organismic Mechanisms

Frenchman Jacques Fradin (2008, I),[131] who worked with Laborit,[132] developed certain aspects of Laborit's neurological model to create an interesting form of coaching inspired by cognitive therapy. It is true that this neurological metaphor eliminates the social and hormonal dimensions that are part of the model of homeostasis for Laborit, but it has been very useful to me with some patients.

THE COMPLEX NONCONSCIOUS OPERATIONS OF THE BRAIN

Fradin takes up MacLean's framework but also takes into account recent neurological formulations.[133] In a document for the general public, he develops the following points:

1. He situates the *basic regulators of consciousness* between the *upper part* of the limbic system and the sensorimotor cortex. The limbic zone of the cingulate gyrus, for example, is especially related to automatic linguistic behaviors linked to phonology, the articulation of words, and even certain forms of semantic processing.
2. The *prefrontal cortex* manages the nonconscious functions that coordinate the auto-regulation of the organism and interpersonal regulation.[134] The information managed by this area is often more complex than what consciousness can manage. This zone integrates the messages coming from the brainstem (reptilian brain) and from the limbic system (paleomammalian brain) into the dynamics of the neocortex.

3. One of the main functions of the *limbic system* is to manage the standardized and habitual behaviors in association with the mechanisms situated in the brainstem (the reptilian brain in Lamarck's and Mac-Lean's model). In the case of stress, the region of the thalamus and of the amygdala[135] can activate the behaviors of flight, fight, and freeze. Its reactions are standardized, simple, and rapidly influence behavioral responses.

This analysis shows that the limbic system is as cognitive as it is affective, while the neocortex is as affective as it is cognitive. Here we have yet another example of an author who cannot reduce the dichotomy of affective and cognitive procedures to the particularities of these two regions of the brain. Damasio (1999), for example, clearly shows that the different forms of consciousness are constructed from the associations of the neurological dynamics situated in almost all of the parts of the brain. Different combinations permit different forms of conscious thoughts. He also confirms, as do Edelman and Tononi (2000), that certain dynamics of the brain manage a network of information of greater complexity than consciousness could manage and that they regulate the dynamics that end up being a conscious perception. The particularly complex forms of data management that become possible once the brain has a well-developed neocortex is not due to a particular function of a zone but to the fact that the more complex circuits (or networks) can be constructed when there is a greater quantity of structurally and functionally varied zones. Thus, the onset of a movement of flight unleashed in the brainstem is more rapid but simpler than a movement of flight unleashed by a coordination between the brainstem and the inferior limbic system (thalamus and amygdala). When this circuit also passes through the prefrontal regions of the neocortex, the organism is able to handle more sophisticated behaviors of flight that take additional time to mobilize the motor functions.[136] The cortex is mostly composed of association areas. These areas can process all kinds of information, support primary neurological systems (those that have specifically set functions), and enable the brain to produce behaviors requiring the coordination of many areas.

To summarize, consciousness is directly influenced by rapid automatic responses, and indirectly influenced by the processes that use particularly complex forms of data management.

CONSCIOUSNESS WEDGED IN BETWEEN THE SPEED OF THE AUTOMATIC RESPONSES AND THE PROCESSING OF COMPLEX INFORMATION

It is now possible for me to refine the model of the affective systems discussed in the preceding sections. It is such that the limbic system and the prefrontal cortex can end up with a different set of analysis about what should be done. This is often the case, as the neocortex analyzes a larger amount of information using more complex and lengthier procedures. But the dynamics of the limbic system access behavior more easily, especially via the sensorimotor cortex. This speed is possible because the analysis of the sensory signals occurring at the level of the limbic system is rudimentary and the envisaged motor responses are automatic. We have seen that these stereotypical behaviors sometimes had relevance in certain animals but are not necessarily relevant for a human being living in a sophisticated social milieu.

It sometimes happens that a standardized reaction has already been activated, while more complex forms of management are beginning to realize that this action is counter-productive. Nonconscious procedures must now alert conscious procedures that a different course of action must be found. However, there is a difficulty, because the frontal neocortex needs to recruit limbic structures to influence conscious procedures, as it cannot do this directly. Even if Fradin's neurology is arguable, the result of this analysis is known by all teachers: the student, whatever his age or intelligence, first needs to grasp simple ideas close to his automatic thinking. Only subsequently can intelligence elaborate more complex connections, starting from simple ideas that initiate a reflection or a dialogue with another. We have here an example of a sound psychological model that tries to look respectable by presenting itself as a neurological model. However, as the neurological model Fradin uses has become obsolete, the psychological model based on it loses some of its strength.

Fradin's neurological metaphor assumes that when the information processing systems of the neocortex detect that the body and consciousness are about to take a wrong road, it must pass through the limbic system's standardized reactions to alert the ongoing conscious processes. If there is an emergency, its only recourse is to activate a state of crisis in the limbic system, which is experienced as stress. A state of panic ensues that impedes the motor functions from having a coherent behavior and thus slows down the course of action that had been activated. This procedure is about the same as the one that alerts consciousness with pain when the body is sick or wounded. A feeling of anxiety invades consciousness, more and more explicitly, as if to incite it to concentrate more thoroughly on a new course of action. As for the circuits of stress described by Selye and Laborit, this salutary action does not always have the means to succeed because the organism grows in complex social environments that do not always allow a relevant calibration. Anxiety, for example, puts the mind on alert but just as often prevents an appropriate reflection. That is why individuals who are anxious, depressed, or stressed spontaneously seek an environment that could help them escape a vicious circle created by the limits of their organism's systems of auto-reparation and the destructive aspect of their social environment (the link between harassment and stress is an unfortunate current example). Often, an individual does not have the means to know which social environment fosters an adequate social support.

In his therapeutic recommendations,[137] Fradin (2008, I) shows that the understanding of the expressive behaviors activated by the limbic system is not always crucial. What is important is to help the conscious subject contact the internal contradictions and escape from the hold of the automatic procedures.

It seems to me that one of the problems of the standardized reactions activated by the limbic system is that they function mostly through *assimilation*. The anxious reaction must be taken as a signal of a profound dysfunction, unleashed by the prefrontal cortex to impose the necessity to reflect and to arrive at a new form of *accommodation* to the events that the organism's current habitual procedures cannot handle. Fradin shows that when the anxiety is approached as a signal of an inadequacy that necessitates a reflection and a behavior more complex than usual, it becomes possible to reduce the anxiety. The exercises proposed by his team encourage an enhanced attention to the multisensory perceptions that accompany these moments of crises as much as a more subtle analysis of what is happening. Briefly, as the Taoists and Spinoza already suggested, Fradin shows that to incorporate the nonconscious wisdom of one's brain permits everyone to auto-regulate more effectively and efficiently. This an example of why cognitive therapists often appreciate approaches derived from Buddhist mindfulness.

Affects and Organismic Regulations

I now attempt to extract a model of the affective dynamics from the discussions that are developed in other parts of this book (Spinoza, Hume, Darwin, and Downing) that focus on the needs of a practicing psychotherapist:

1. Thought is founded mostly on the relatively simple, schematic, and predictable impressions.
2. The more complex elaborations of the mind have a poorly understood impact on organismic dynamics. The impact of complex conscious thoughts is then nonconscious.
3. If the neurological data entering consciousness are composed mostly of relatively standardized sensorimotor reactions, this confirms the impression that the blockage of feelings and of emotional expressions can block systems of organismic regulation. Working on the expression of blocked emotions is often not enough, because the blockages *signaled* by the inhibition of the standardized expressive systems are situated in deeper organismic structures than those that elicit emotional responses. The bridge between the standardized emotional reactions and the complex elaborations (conscious and nonconscious) are crucial once again. Neo-Reichian psychotherapies have also shown that, in some cases, the exploration of what is activated when a person expresses the depths of his emotions is also what allows a therapist to contact these deep underlying mechanisms.
4. Even in the domain of the affective regulations, the standardized expressive systems are often inadequate. A relevant affective regulation necessitates an accommodating coordination of many types of psychic dynamics (fine motor control and sensory modulation, intelligence, memory, imagination, etc.).[138]

For me, the usefulness of a model such as Fradin's[139] is that it helps the therapist to understand the affective reaction as an alert reaction of the organism, and also helps him not follow automatically all of the signs produced by the symptoms of this reaction. If angry feelings erupt, it is not always necessary to express them. Fradin above all recommends to his patient to better understand and feel in a more detailed way what activates an affect. That often allows a person to find new resources within. He will then become able to approach a situation that is difficult to manage in a more constructive manner.

This section concludes my attempt to show that situating intelligence in the neocortex and affects in the limbic system was just a projection onto the brain of the old opposition between civilized rationality and animal passions.

DISCUSSION: HUME'S PROPENSITY REVISITED

The notion (not the term) of "propensity" has become a theme of this text since it was expressed by Hume and then taken up to discuss the thoughts of several authors who use a similar notion but not always with the same vocabulary. That is why it seems useful to me to specify the meaning of this word and summarize the relevance of this term in biology before approaching its utilization in psychotherapy.

Interacting with One's Environment, Calibrating a Propensity, and Calibrating the Self

> It is easy to see that the habit of exercising an organ, in all living beings that have not yet suffered the reduction of their faculties, not only perfects that organ but even causes it to acquire developments and dimensions which change it imperceptibly; so that with time, it renders it quite different than the same organ considered in another living being that does not exercise it or does so rarely. It is also very easy to prove that the constant lack of exercise of an organ gradually impoverishes it and ends up annihilating it. (Lamarck, 1802, *L'Organisation des Corps Vivants*, I, p. 46)

Our discussion on psychophysiology confirms Hume's intuition that the propensions of an individual are structured by innate mechanisms that require external information to complete their development. This model is compatible with the robust observation that the nervous connections of the brain are calibrated by habitual modes of functioning. However, the adaptations to the environment do not always "improve" the coherence of organismic dynamics. In some cases the adaptations required by the environment generate pathological modes of functioning. Contradictory requirements may activate damaging forms of calibration that the organism cannot integrate and that are not necessarily in accord with the needs of the individual. An example is when the adaptation to sitting on chairs creates varicose veins.[140]

The model of the internal propensities that inserts itself in lifestyles proposed by the theory of evolution often requires multidisciplinary studies to be understood. Indeed, propensities that integrate elements as varied as cellular dynamics and a society's politics of urbanization demand the formation of teams that allow for a varied set of interventions.[141] If the propensity is well understood in its entirety, sometimes it is possible to find an element of the circuit that makes it possible to restore the system's mechanisms of repair. Sometimes the administration of an antidepressant suffices to allow a person to find ways of associating with a milieu of supportive people who will allow him to feel more comfortable. Sometimes individual psychotherapy makes it possible to modify inadequate representations and find a lifestyle that allows the organism to regain a more adequate amount of serotonin. Similarly, a systemic intervention on the network in which a person lives sometimes allows for the creation of new forms of alliances that support the auto-regulation of each member of the group when they are together.[142]

When a therapist meets a patient for the first time, he cannot know which types of intervention are required and which aspect of a propensity especially needs attention. He must have received an education and training that makes it possible for him to localize the places of a propensity that are in most need of attention and to be capable of referring the patient to colleagues when the work is not part of the interventions he competently practices. Sadly, this form of training does not yet exist!

This discussion opens up onto two great present-day theories of the self in the domain of psychotherapy, which are well summarized by Brazilian body psychotherapists Gilberto Safra and Jose Alberto Madeira Cotta (2009):

1. *Society traumatizes the citizens.* Safra and Cotta attribute to Freud, Reich, and Lowen the idea that there would be, on one hand, the instinctual drives, and on the other hand, a social capacity to integrate these instincts. The way society integrates these drives determine the character of a person and lead to psychopathology when social support is poor or does not respect basic instinctual needs. A constructive environment supports the framework for the satisfactory discharge of a drive, implying that the drive can find its object. The environment is then a "vicissitude of the drives themselves."

2. *Individuals and society mutually form (traumatize) each other.* In this model that the authors associate with psychoanalysts like Winnicott, it is not the drives but the relation to others that "constitute the fundamental building blocks of mental life." A self is not an independent construction. It is the interaction between selves that structure a self. "The creation, or re-creation, of specific modes of relatedness with others replaces drive discharge as force motivating human behavior."

The self is the impression that something in us is the agent of one's thoughts and behaviors. This notion was originally introduced in psychotherapeutic literature by Jung, who defined the self as what "thrusts the ego aside and makes room for a supraordinate factor, the totality of a person, which consists of conscious and unconscious and consequently extends far beyond the ego" (Jung, 1950, p. 304). The term was introduced in the psychoanalytical literature by Winnicott (1960) and Kohut (1971), and then became a fashionable concept in experimental psychology.[143] In psychodynamic psychology, the experience of the self constructs itself through interactions with others. It therefore depends on the physiological and body mechanisms that support the interaction between the self of an individual and the self of those with whom he interacts.

The Parallelistic Dynamics of Mood Disorders

It is difficult to engage a therapeutic intervention on dysfunctional propensities because the mechanism on which the therapist intervenes is included in such a complicated network of distinct causal chains. It is consequently impossible to foresee all of the effects of a course of treatment. We have seen that certain aspects of a propensity functions in parallel fashion, following distinct causal chains. For example, I can use George Downing's (1996) proposal, and distinguish between at least two parallel levels: a level that follows mostly a physiological causality, and another that deals with conscious representations. We have seen that for many affective difficulties, there exists a dual causal system (physiological and mental) that creates a global mood state. Thus, a diet is sometimes indicated to reduce an individual's high blood pressure due to an excess of cholesterol, but such a diet could also inhibit the uptake of serotonin. A person will then feel depressed for reasons that are not mental. The common-sense and "trite and banal" handling of the matter by the general practitioner, typical in these cases ("No need to become depressed! A diet, after all, is not the end of the world!"), is therefore sometimes inappropriate. The battle that the individual engages in with regard to his health becomes more difficult if the two causal systems are not explicitly identified, given that he often loses himself in the maze of his affects, his thoughts and his physiology. It is not rare that patients end up by feeling guilty, incompetent, disempowered, and resigned.

The connection between cholesterol and depression also opens up some discussions on the fact that most of the organismic phenomena are modular, that is, multimodal. This implies that cholesterol has different functions in different systems of regulation. Lowering cholesterol can be, at the same time, good for one's health and bad for one's mood. Once again, we must guard against linear causality that considers only one causal chain (less cholesterol = better health = greater happiness).

PART IV

Hypnosis, Relaxation, and Gymnastics at the Birth of Body Psychotherapy: How to Mobilize the Forces of the Organism

For an event to happen, it requires multiple causes that made it possible. The more we seek to find the origins of the relatively simple techniques of body psychotherapy, the more we find that they arose at many crossroads at several moments in history. Body psychotherapy is a kind of "reduction" (in the sense of the culinary arts) of many elements that have found their place as sediments in the spirit of an epoch. This plethora of notions was like dust suspended in air, which everyone breathes without knowing it. It is in this mindset that I will now situate a few movements that developed between the second half of the nineteenth century and the first half of the twentieth. They are part of the particles of knowledge breathed in quite automatically by the insatiable curiosity of the first psychoanalysts, like Freud and Jung, as well as the first psychotherapists who were intrigued by the relation between mind and movement, especially Ferenczi, Groddeck, Fenichel, and Reich.

I already reviewed the grand theories that served as the frame for the emergence of psychotherapy. There also exist myriad movements that left a mark on a generation of practitioners without leaving lasting traces in history. It is impossible to understand the literature on mind and body discussed in this volume without opening a discussion on the apparently peripheral movements and issues that nevertheless had an important influence on the practices that form a kind of geological layer on which other layers arose. Many ideas and methods presently used in psychotherapy were formed in this incubator. As an example, I take the ones that marked the emergence of the body psychotherapies, but today's psychotherapists are inspired by more recent analogous theories. Thus, the first decade of the twenty-first century is distinguished by the use of the Buddhist notion of mindfulness in cognitive therapy (see Kabat-Zinn, 1990, and

Siegel, 2007; examples of practitioners who integrate a similar approach in body psychotherapy are Rytz, 2009, and Weiss, 2009).

The spectacular advances in science in the European civilization during the nineteenth century also upended the intellectual movements that were not scientific. Up until the first French Revolution, the philosophers of the Renaissance and of the Age of Enlightenment defended the existence of science while battling against religion and political prejudice, both hostile to science. With Hegel's proposition at the time of Napoleon and Lamarck, spiritual and scientific visions interact more with each other. An increasing number of researchers tried to synthesize beliefs, spiritual traditions, and knowledge. This context supported the emergence of diverse ideologies (notably certain forms of colonialism, communism, eugenics, and fascism), which then influenced the development of certain scientific theories. This was particularly true for the research that focused on the relation between the body and the mind. For example, it is impossible to take up the development of these disciplines that emerged parallel to psychoanalysis without clarifying the new forms of racism and spirituality that came about during this period. Being unable to treat such a vast topic in this book, I content myself to mention its importance. I will focus on those subjects that had a more explicit impact on the literature of body psychotherapy.

These approaches remain structured as schools which defend a particular vision. The quality of the education and training provided by such schools depends mostly on a genealogy of masters that have led to the creation of such schools (see Comba and Fleury, 1987).

9

Physiognomy, Phrenology, Emotional Expressions, and Character Analysis

A Discussion of Theories Based on the Idea that There Exists a Direct Linear Relation between a Mental and a Psychological Function

In the domain of mind–body, the necessity to mix scientific technical knowledge (anatomy and psychophysiology) and the knowledge derived from the spiritual research disciplines like yoga is particularly strong. This is due to the fact that the disciplines of body psychotherapy have not yet become a center of interest for systematic scientific research. Thus, scientific medicine has set its priority as the detailed anatomical description of the organism. These charts are used by gymnasts, but that discipline only interests the medical faculties as an area in which their knowledge can be applied, not one that deserves to be explored in a systematic way. This explains why the grand syntheses in the domain of the mind–body continue to dip into all the available forms of knowledge. This double-sided knowledge was introduced into psychotherapy by Freud (mesmerism and hypnosis, for example), and then developed by Jung (European and Oriental alchemy). In what follows, I present a few examples of the way that spirituality and science are intermingled in the field of the mind–body approaches.

THE SHAPE OF THE BODY = THE SHAPE OF THE SOUL

Since the beginning of this book, I have insisted on the fact that I *exclude* from my way of thinking the notion that mind and body are connected by direct links. This position is difficult to defend when it is adopted in an absolute fashion, but it is helpful to adopt it as a default position when we do not possess robust data to demonstrate a direct link between a psychological function and a body trait. In the mind–body domain, it is useful to take a clear stand in the face of numerous extremely popular and lucrative approaches that postulate direct links between the dimensions of the organism, psychology, behavior, and the shape of the body. Not only are these theories not supported by available data, they also provoke important ideological and ethical risks. This debate entered especially into the scientific and philosophical literature after the argument between Lamarck and his contemporary, German neurologist Franz Josef Gall. Here I explicitly discuss some of the arguments from these two positions. They can be summarized in this way:

1. The approaches that suppose that there exists *a quasi-unequivocal connection between bodily signs and psychological functions.* These approaches postulate that there are connections between the soul and the body that would be as direct as those associating a word with its meaning. A word is generally associated to a relatively restricted number of meanings that can be listed in a dictionary. The link between the signifier and the signified can be qualified as *relatively* direct. Only in the most simplistic theories can a gesture only be associated to one single meaning, or a facial "expression" associated to only one emotion. However, this is the direction taken by most of the theories I discuss. One of the implications for psychology promoted by these approaches is the need to divide the psychological domain into categories (intelligence, memory, sentiments, etc.) that can be correlated to body categories (areas of the brain, emotional expressions, shape of the body, etc.) in an unequivocal way (Fodor, 1983). In these theories body, behavior, physiology, and organism are not differentiated.

2. In this textbook, I propose and defend systemic theories that postulate *a fuzzier and more indirect type of connections between the body and the mind,* as in the theories of Descartes, Spinoza, Lamarck, and Darwin. For these authors, the mechanisms of the mind are not constructed like the mechanisms of the body. Therefore, they cannot correspond to each other in a simple way. Every bodily event can influence psychological dynamics, and every gesture can have an impact on thoughts; the interface between these two dimensions is necessarily complex, as each dimension has its own independent set of procedures. For these theories, the systems that connect thought and gesture are more *active and complex* than in the theories I refer to as linear.

In other words, the two approaches foresee strong links between the psyche and the body. The difference resides in the way each approach explains these connections. In the field of body psychotherapy, a number of schools use a more or less strong dose of those models that postulate direct links between the soul and the body. This justifies a detailed discussion on the subject.

Dictionaries

We respond to gestures with an extreme alertness and, one might almost say, in accordance with an elaborate and secret code that is written nowhere, known by none, and understood by all. (Edward Sapir, 1927, "The Unconscious Patterning of Behavior in Society," p. 556)

Since time immemorial, there were persons who refused to accept that the thoughts of others were inaccessible to them. The linear theories acquired their popularity by exploiting this frustration, in giving people the hope that by reading the signs produced by the body, they would be able to discover what was hidden in the soul of another. One of the forms that is regularly taken up in the publications of authors who adopt this way of thinking is that of a dictionary: one that permits a person to say that if a bodily configuration or gesture X is observed, it can be expected that with a great probability feeling Y is experienced by an individual.

When a person consults a dictionary of dreams[1] to discover the meaning of an episode or a symbol in a dream, he is consulting a book that postulates a direct link (or nearly so) between a dream and Ideas. These dictionaries often suggest that each dream image has a meaning: each image is a *signifier,* which is associated to a *signified*, to take up the language of linguistics. This link between signifier and signified would be innate and transpersonal. According to this point of view, the link between a dream image and its latent content is rarely accessible, but it exists. Thus, Freud was tempted to see a phallic symbol in every sign, and Jung largely contributed, with his concept of the archetype, to reinforcing the idea that there existed direct transpersonal connections between dream images and the forces that create myths. In similar fashion, we find a great number of works that describe the meaning of gestures and postures, like Desmond Morris's *Manwatching* (1978), Paul Ekman's *The Face of Man* (1980a), Joseph Messinger's *The Gestures that Betray You* (2005), and so on. The meaning of a gesture is presented as a transpersonal and univocal construction because it is independent of an individual's journey and circumstances. The relationship between the signifier and the signified is hard-wired.

As the quote from the anthropologist Sapir so aptly indicates, the body signs always exercise their influence but mostly in a nonconscious manner. It is often unwittingly that our gestures evoke a particular reaction in others.[2] To achieve a certain mastery over these permanent exchanges, cultures have often imposed a strict and explicit etiquette with the hope that these conscious practices might diminish the impact of the regulations brought about by the body in a nonconscious way. In this way of thinking, the individual is as afraid of the hostility he might unknowingly activate in another as of the seduction that others could exercise over him with a manipulative intent.

The Beauty of the Body = The Beauty of the Soul

Many artists (at least since Homer) assume it is possible to guess that a person comes from an illustrious family if his traits are particularly regular and marked. The fundamental argument from this perspective of the rapport between the soul and the body is that of coherence and harmony. The exceptions are rare and often influenced by powerful maleficent forces, like Lucifer, who was the most beautiful of the archangels.

This way to approach the relationship between body and soul seems particularly developed when one falls in love. Lovers often have the tendency to suppose that the loved one is beautiful and that the beauty expresses the beauty of her feelings. On the other hand, at the occasion of a break-up, the other is sometimes suddenly perceived as ugly, stupid, and evil.

The Physiognomy of the Shape of the Body and Soul

If Lamarck is the first to conceptualize in a clear and explicit fashion that the species came about from a common history, there already existed numerous propositions suggesting connections between particular human traits and the characteristics of animals.[3] These models do not postulate an evolution but a creator spirit who used the same creative strategies many times over. I have, for example, indicated in the sections on the martial arts in China, that there exists a chi-kong of the animals.

In Europe, reputable books show by dint of arguments and of illustrations that the shape of the head makes it possible to foresee the characteristics of the workings of the psyche. This tradition came about in the Middle Ages, based on writings attributed to Aristotle. Here are some of the main titles of this movement that are still discussed to this day:[4]

> *De humana physiognomonia,* by Giovanni Battista della Porta (1586)
>
> *A method to learn how to draw the passions,* by Charles Le Brun (1698)
>
> *Essays on Physiognomy,* by Johann Kaspar Lavater (1778)

Le Brun's volumes[5] are full of beautiful and compelling illustrations showing that every shape of the face can be related to the face of an animal, and that this association betrays an animal predisposition of the soul. There are persons who have the face and soul of an eagle, a fox, a wolf, a weasel, a camel, a goat, and so on. Le Brun also proposes beautiful drawings that represent the expressions of the face corresponding to "passions" such as tranquility, anger, desire, horror, and fear.[6] This work inspired many attempts to propose catalogs of emotional expressions through drawings, busts, photos, and films.[7]

The work of Lavater, in Switzerland, shows that in analyzing the shadow of a profile, especially the measurement of the forehead, it would be possible to understand the characteristics and the inclinations of a human being.[8] This system was presented in magnificent volumes edited between 1775 and 1778. They were read in all of the courts of Europe.

The Phrenology of Gall

Lamarck begins his discussion of phrenology[9] with a formal attack against a presentation given by Franz Jozeph Gall (1758–1828) and Johann Spurzheim in front of the elite French researchers of the time. It probably consisted of a presentation of a volume on neurology that these authors were about to publish.[10] Their theory can be understood as an attempt to generalize Descartes's hypothesis related to the H gland to the entire brain[11]:

1. The brain transmits the impressions of the senses to the psyche.
2. It remembers these impressions, and reproduces them "with more or less speed, clarity and abundance when the psyche has need of them for its operations."
3. It transmits "the orders of the will" to the muscles.

This part of Gall's work had a profound influence on the neurology of the nineteenth century and of the first half of the twentieth century. It is often called the theory of *cerebral localization,*[12] which is based on two assumptions:

1. The *theory of cerebral localization* establishes a direct link between psychological faculties and regions of the brain.
2. The *theory of psychological faculties* assumes that there exist distinct psychological functions, quasi-independent from one another. Some of these distinctions have been taken up by psychologists as the distinction between perception, memory, intelligence, intuition, and emotion.

The theory of cerebral localization was still discussed in neurology courses in medical faculties up to the 1970s. In an often quoted work, philosopher Jerry Alan Fodor (1983) shows Gall's influence on the notion of modularity, such as it is used in the domain of the neurosciences and artificial intelligence.

Gall's hypothesis is parallelistic when he argues that the soul and body are not of the same nature and the connection between them cannot be analyzed by scientific methods. However, this parallelism is more simplistic than the one proposed by seventeenth-century philosophers. Spinoza postulates indirect interactions between the dimensions of the organism (global organismic regulations coordinate the body and the mind), whereas Gall postulates direct connections between a particular thought and a particular region of the brain and then between a region of the brain and a gesture.

Gall also developed a series of hypotheses that relate each zone of the brain to "bumps" on the cranium. The more a region of the brain develops, the more it is in need of space. This need for space would create the bumps on the cranium. Once this idea is accepted, it is possible to think that the contours of the skull allow us to know which regions of the brain are particularly well developed. This theory, known as *phrenology,* is notably put forth in a work in six volumes published between 1822 and 1825 with a title that aptly summarizes his proposition: "On the functions of the brain and of each of its parts: with observations on the possibility of determining the instincts, propensities, and talents, or the moral and intellectual dispositions of men and animals, by the configuration of the brain and head."[13]

Phrenology takes up the association between the zones of the brain and psychological faculties. Gall distinguishes twenty-seven mental faculties that may be more or less developed in an individual. He then shows that a phrenologist can analyze the bumps on the cranium and discover if a person has a marked predisposition to trickery, robbery, arrogance, family life, mathematics, murder, foresight, and so on. Gall and his students supported their arguments with the help of statistics showing (a) the importance of distinguishing the faculties, and (b) the significant statistical correlation between a faculty and a bump on the head. An example of the way phrenology conceptualizes the linear rapport between body and emotion is given to us by Alfred Russel Wallace in his autobiography.[14]

> Summary of Wallace's position on phrenology. *In 1844, Wallace, who was then a schoolteacher, went to a conference on mesmerism.[15] He learned that nearly anyone could place nearly anyone else in a hypnotic trance, but some individuals are more susceptible to this type of influence than others. As he explored the art of hypnosis with his students, he read works on phrenology showing that certain bumps on the cranium corresponded to particular emotions. To examine this phenomenon, he put some of his students under hypnosis. On each one's cranium, he then massaged a bump described by Gall. Even under hypnosis, pupils incapable of making a voluntary gesture activated the expression that Gall had associated with this bump. When massaging the bump of anger, their faces spontaneously mimicked the expressions Le Brun and Gall associated with anger. This apparently direct connection between the bump and anger was apparent only in those students who allowed themselves to be easily hypnotized.*

Linear Approaches to Emotional Expressions

The notion of emotional expression has been used in very different ways in the philosophical and scientific literature. Some approaches, like Darwin's, postulate few direct and necessary links between expressions and emotions. Others, on the contrary, try to show that there are direct links between some emotions and certain behaviors that form distinct entities. Once again, those who assume the existence of direct links between feelings and body need to create compatible categories in the dimension of the mind and of the body.

The Coding of Facial Expressions according to Ekman and Friesen

Paul Ekman and Wallace V. Friesen published a manual in 1978 that permitted researchers to code every movement of the face. This coding system is called the *Facial Action Coding System* (FACS).[16] It was first established after a lengthy work carried out in front of a mirror, with precise drawings of the anatomy of the face. They then observed their colleagues and refined their system after multiple observations carried out in many cultures. The coding system facilitates the description of two types of facial activity:

1. *The basic units* of facial activity are activated by a restricted and specific group of muscles. These units have a number, a name, and levels of intensity. For example, stretching the corner of the mouth, which is used for a smile, is number 12 and can have an intensity that varies from X to Z (between A and E for some researchers). The difficulty in establishing this code was to find facial movements that—when possible—corresponded to a single motoric action.

2. *Complex facial expressions or mimics.* A facial expression corresponds to a mimicked configuration at a given moment as visible on a photo. It is a global configuration composed of one or several basic units. Ekman and Friesen reported two difficulties. The first was to explain what was happening when many basic units were activated at the same time. Thus, a person could smile (the corners of the lips rise toward the temples) and at the same time activate the unit that makes the corners of the lips come down (unit 15). In such a case, it must be decided if there is nonetheless a smile, what nuance is brought by this second unit, and how to evaluate the intensity of each unit—not all of which is always evident. The second difficulty is that sometimes certain units commence after another is already fully activated. The researcher must be able to evaluate if this second unit is a nuance brought forth to the first expression or if it creates a second, overlapping expression. Wally Friesen had hoped to be able to codify all of that with a computer program so that researchers would be able to adopt the same criteria. The data gathered in many laboratories resist the desire that every facial phenomenon be situated in a distinct facial expression. Facial activity is, in fact, relatively fluid and only sometimes gives the impression that the face constructs an expression that sends a particular message (Heller and Haynal-Reymond, 1997). This fluidity is hidden when a face is shown in a photograph. The viewer has the impression that what he sees forms a coherent gestalt. This impression is rare in real life or even when one analyzes filmed behavior.

Once they had taught their coding system, many laboratories used it. Ekman and Friesen did an enormous amount of coordination work using the FACS to be able to create a database on facial expressions as complete as possible: a database that integrates the evolution of methodologies (strongly related to the evolution of the computer) used for these studies. This led to a new version of the coding manual (published in 2002). As a coding system of facial expressions, the FACS remains the most efficient known today. I have used it for more than ten years.[17]

This coding system is relatively independent of Paul Ekman's position on the theory of emotions, about which I now speak. This research tried to apply the distinction between basic units and complex expressions to the domain of the emotional expressions of the face. He attacked theories that assume that the affective dynamics, even more than the activity of the face, cannot be reduced to distinct basic emotions that form a succession of distinct expressions (or messages).

THE BASIC EMOTIONAL EXPRESSIONS

In this section, I use Ekman's (1980a) theory and his research as an example of an approach that supposes a direct link between a felt emotion and an emotional expression.[18] This choice imposes itself, given the extent to which Ekman and Friesen's work is often quoted and considered as a reference by colleagues who are not specialists in the domain of emotions. Emotional expressions are behaviors that associate, in a recurrent fashion, (1) an affective mobilization of the organism with (2) an affective impact on other persons. It is possible to distinguish, in Ekman's writings, a *general theory* and a *specific theory* of emotional behavior. Here are a few elements of the general theory:

1. Ekman postulates an emotional dimension distinct from the other psychological functions. He then divides the emotional domains into distinct subcategories, each having a particular function. Sadness is a sort of coordination between feelings, physiology, behavior, and the impact on another that is distinct from what is set about by anger.[19]
2. All these connections are innate and prewired.[20]
3. Consequently, every person who perceives an expression attributes the same emotional system to it. This system is thus transpersonal and universal. This implies that the way an individual reads the expressions of others is also prewired. The other's expression will therefore activate, in the one who perceives it, an automatic psychophysiological reaction.[21]

Even if we are already in a theory that postulates relatively direct links between distinct emotions and motor functions, a large part of this model can be integrated into a more systemic approach, such as Lamarck's and Darwin's. The foregoing three points are taken up in a number of theories of emotions.[22] Other aspects of Ekman's theory form his specific theory. This second group of hypotheses do not necessarily follow from the general theory:[23]

1. Each emotion is a brief reaction lasting, at the maximum, only a few minutes. A mechanism that has an emotional flavor but lasts for hours is not an emotion. This restriction is necessary to support the connection between the emotion that is experienced and the corresponding emotional expression, because a particular facial expression is necessarily brief. The case of chronic muscular tension that forms a kind of permanent mask,[24] quite similar to an emotional expression, consequently is not part of what Ekman defines as an emotion. For him, this restriction applies to the whole of the emotional behaviors. What Ekman calls emo-

tional expressions, I call *emotional reactions*, which would be a sub-grouping of *emotional phenomena*.

2. Ekman rejoins the theories that suppose there are *basic emotions*. In combining with each other, they form *complex emotions*.[25] Thus, it would be possible to distinguish from among the facial expressions contempt (a basic emotion), joy (a basic emotion), and a smile that masks an expression of contempt (a complex emotion).[26] This way to approach the emotions was well known by philosophers like Spinoza and Hume. They applied the theory of color[27] to the emotions, which showed that we can make any color by mixing different amounts of the three basic colors. The basic emotions identified by Ekman (1980a) are anger, disgust, fear, happiness, sadness, and surprise.

In the theory of optics, it is possible to show that the idea of basic colors is robust; in mixing them, we can effectively re-create all the colors distinguishable by the human eye. The most bizarre aspect of Ekman's theory is his insistence on calling it Darwinian. He even goes so far as to become the editor of Darwin's 1872 volume on the emotional expressions. As you read Darwin's text, Ekman inserts comments each time he and Darwin say the same thing. He nevertheless seems blind to the manifest differences between his theory and that of Darwin's.[28] Having said this, Darwin could also have been wrong. It is not because Ekman's theory is incompatible with certain aspects of Darwin's that it is in error. The real connection between Ekman's and Darwin's work is found on the observational plane. Like Darwin, Ekman published incredibly detailed descriptions of emotional expressions that are effectively complementary.

To become robust, the theories centered on the notion that there are basic emotions must justify why a particular affect is a basic emotion and not a complex one. The theories built around a linear understanding of the basic emotional expression are incapable of meeting the conditions they have imposed on themselves. For example, each theory of this type proposes a different list of basic emotions. This notion is therefore in no way robust.[29] Here are three discussions concerning the basic emotions:

1. *Pride.* For Hume,[30] pride is the most basic emotion (he speaks of "simple emotions"). Related to honor, pride was effectively an emotion commonly mentioned at the time. An affront to one's pride justified many forms of violence, such as the murder of a member of the family who would have acted against the code of honor currently in place: duels and sometimes war. This conception of honor is still alive in many cultures, but it is not approved of in the West.[31] In the present theories of emotions, honor is rarely mentioned, indicating that what some considered a central, innate emotion is not so in other cultures.

2. *Fear.* Fear is sometimes included in the list of basic emotions and sometimes not. Ekman and his team[32] observed that the onset of a startle

reaction always occurs more rapidly than an emotion (which is a half-second slower), and it is always followed by a classic emotional reaction. No actor, even after a lot of training, can express alarm as rapidly as an actual outburst of fear, although he can convincingly imitate all of the other emotional expressions. Thus, a startle reflex is not an emotion, if one accepts Ekman's definition of the term. But there are other expressions of fear that come closer to current definitions of emotional dynamics. Here are examples of different forms of fear: (a) the fear associated to a startle reflex, (b) the fear activated in the face of a predator that mobilizes diverse forms of reactions like flight and freezing,[33] and (c) a fear of mental origin such as is felt in a nightmare, close to anxiety. These three forms of fear are related to distinct physiological and psychological systems.[34] The second type of fear can be associated to the notion of basic emotions; but that leaves two other types of fear that are difficult to situate in a linear theory of emotional expressions.

3. For Ed Tronick,[35] an infant often expresses the following emotions: joy, curiosity, sadness, anger, fear, surprise, and distress. Less interested in an eventual direct link between expressions and emotions, Tronick describes these categories without requiring that these emotions be discrete events or limited in time. Also, he does not claim that this list is exhaustive.

Just as the notion of cerebral localization has been thoroughly explored by scientists for more than a century, research is now testing the value of the hypothesis that there exists direct links between emotions and expressions. If this hypothesis were proven to be true, one could assume that there are (a) a certain number of basic emotions clearly distinct from one another, and (b) somatic and behavioral dynamics that would be linearly connected to these basic emotions. As in phrenology, there is a necessity to postulate fixed psychological categories so that there might be a correspondence between the psychic and somatic categories. Although this type of theory is widely accepted, I am not sure that it could withstand a close scrutiny. Despite the fact that Ekman and Friesen's "dictionary of emotions"[36] has been used by numerous researchers,[37] they were never able to publish it in its entirety or defend its validity. Some photographic examples are as convincing as Le Brun's drawings, but this dictionary cannot describe all forms of emotional expressions that can be seen on a film. Having used this dictionary for several years, I noticed that the emotional dictionary can be useful as a first procedure to scan the data, but it cannot support a reliable evaluation of what is expressed.

Several theories criticize this way of describing emotions as discrete prototypical forms of reactions to equally prototypical stimuli. For example, appraisal theories assume "that people respond with different emotions to the same situation depending on how they interpret, or appraise, the situation" (Siemer et al., 2007).[38] One of the implications of this position is "that emotional experience is typically a process that changes over the course of an episode, sometimes very rapidly, sometimes more gradually—in line with additions and revisions in the appraisal" (Ellsworth and Tong, 2006, p. 574).[39] Although appraisal theory allows for a good description of the fluidity of emotional expression that can often be observed, I do not think this fluidity is based only on cognitive factors.

THE RELEVANCE OF EKMAN AND FRIESEN'S DICTIONARY OF EMOTIONS IN PSYCHOTHERAPY

> It has often struck me as a curious fact that so many shades of expressions are instantly recognized without any conscious process of analysis of our part. . . . I have endeavored to show in considerable detail that all the chief expressions[40] exhibited by man are the same throughout the world. This fact is interesting, as it affords a new argument in favor of the several races being descended from a single parent-stock. (Darwin, 1872, *The Expression of the Emotions in Man and Animals*, XIV, p. 359)

For Darwin and Ekman, emotional expression is a particularly nuanced innate transpersonal system. The fact that parts of the mechanisms implied in the communication of the affects are innate is difficult to contest today. I would now like to open a discussion on the use of this type of information in psychotherapy.

The first direct implication concerns the handling of countertransference. Let us detail this reasoning based on the premise that Darwin and those who succeeded him were correct.

1. The expression of the patient has an automatic impact on the other.
2. The psychotherapist is like everyone else. He can feel a part of himself react automatically to the impact of the patient's emotional expression.
3. Therefore, in being attentive to one's reaction, the therapist inevitably feels something that resonates with the intimate affective life of the patient. This interior "burst" provoked by a patient's expression then allows a therapist, who is attentive to this kind of phenomena, to really feel from the inside a possible connection with the patient's inner experience.

It seems to me that it is dangerous to tell a patient something as assertively as: "I feel that you are angry!" as if this automatically implies that the patient is angry even if he is not aware of it.[41] This entire book points out that it is almost impossible for a feeling to be accurate. Feelings (even gut feelings) are like thoughts: they tend to be sometimes relatively correct, and at other times can be completely wrong. Representations and emotions are different forms of data managements. Sometimes thoughts can be wrong and feelings relevant, or both can be relevant for different reasons, and so on. Having the impression that a patient is angry is therefore not necessarily a reliable information concerning what is experienced by the patient, but it can open up a useful inquiry. The therapist can try to understand why he suddenly got the impression that the patient is angry. He may even ask the patient if he feels angry, and then see if this question helps the patient.

Using a tool like Ekman and Friesen's dictionary is even more complex in psychotherapy. I distinguish between two possible strategies. This distinction is based on the idea that without being robust and reliable, this dictionary is the fruit of serious research:

1. *The direct interpretation.* Ekman, in his interventions, gives the impression that when he observes a facial expression, he can know what is felt and whether a person is lying.[42]
2. *The indirect interpretation with inquiry.* Paul Ekman is also an experienced clinician. His publications describe a slightly more flexible vision of the relations between expressions and emotions. The dictionary of emotions is content to propose hypotheses about a set of emotions that can often be associated to specific emotions. It is in that spirit that I sometimes use it. I have, for example, noticed that some patients chronically do not wrinkle their noses (unit 9 has been blocked for many years). According to Ekman's dictionary, that "could mean" that the patient is not able to express disgust. I therefore used this hypothesis as a starting point for an inquiry. I sometimes ask a patient to try to move his nose and to feel what is going on within when he does it. The wording is that of an open question that does not suggest this unit could be associated with a specific emotion. It happens sometimes that I fall on some associations that lead to a feeling of disgust or other negative affects. This method has allowed some of my patients to be able to finally speak about certain layers of their being about which they have so much shame that they did not dare mention it, even in psychotherapy. In certain cases, I have been able to observe that a patient is once again able to wrinkle his nose voluntarily, only after having explored these negative zones that are sometimes related to disgust. Some of these patients began to talk of experiences in which sex and disgust are associated. In other cases, work on wrinkling the nose does not lead to disgust or even feelings of rejection. Sometimes this kind of exploration leads nowhere. This is another example of the necessity of exploring the relevance of a hypothesis with the patient before relying on it. Another useful technique is to ask patients what they experience when I wrinkle my nose.

In psychotherapy, all forms of direct interpretation can be felt as being intrusive and can even lead certain weak personalities to various forms of dependence on therapy or the therapist. Such patients can, for example, believe that a therapist, capable of reading their feelings, is also capable of knowing what they should feel and think. This kind of intervention is to be avoided, even if Ekman's theory were robust. I recommend the same attitude to people who talk about therapists who pretend that every person who crosses his or her arms and legs is necessarily psychologically *closed*, whereas they would be necessarily psychologically *open* if their arms and legs were not touching. This type of intervention seems to be common, according to some of my patients and students, in approaches inspired by Neurolinguistic programming (NLP).[43]

Body and Character in Bioenergetics

Ekman's general theory on the somatic expressions of emotions is close to and contemporary of that which Alexander Lowen developed and included in his Bioenergetics. This proposition is developed from two themes:

1. Closer to Darwin than Ekman, Lowen does not distinguish basic emotions and works with the forms of expression that mobilize the whole body. Thus, sadness[44] is associated with tears but also with the desire to hold someone in one's arms and a loss of strength in one's feet. As with Ekman, these links are direct and necessary. For Lowen, an incomplete or inhibited form of emotional expression destabilizes the organismic mechanisms of regulation and consequently all of the dimensions of the organism (mind, behavior, language, body, and metabolism).[45] What is linear in this proposition is the idea that an emotion can only mobilize and express itself in one way (or in using a restricted repertoire of behaviors). For Lowen, there is a functional identity between body and mind.

2. Lowen (1975) and Keleman (1985) also associate the shape of the body and the character. Their argumentation is that when the organism of an infant grows up, it calibrates itself according to its environment. If some of its emotional expressions are rejected by its social environment, the infant will tense the muscles mobilized by the inhibited expression to impede the expression which is felt. If this form of repression of the emotional expression repeats itself, these tensions become permanent and inhibit the capacity to feel those emotions. These tensions then influence the way the dimensions of the organism will develop, which includes the shape of the skeleton and the quality of the tissues. This form of argumentation is close to Gall's phrenology, but applied to muscles and emotions.

Most of the psychotherapists who follow Alexander Lowen's recommendations diagnose a form of psychopathology in every individual who does not use the expected emotional repertoire. To modify a patient's character structure, one must soften the chronic muscular tensions, which have become rigid to repress certain emotions that have now become unconscious. The patient attends conditioning sessions where he *must* learn to yell when he feels anger, cry when he is sad, and open his mouth when he is happy. These expressions are presented to the patient as necessary forms of the organism's auto-regulation and the only way to communicate what is felt to another. Lowen thus rejoins the theories that presuppose a direct link between feeling and emotional expression that would be innate and necessary for a sound development of body and mind. An individual cannot diminish his sadness if he does not cry with another.[46] If a patient behaves as these theories foresee, it often happens that the therapist gratifies his patient by finding him more "authentic," more "spontaneous," and more "real" than he is. If the patient's affects use other forms of expression, the patient is considered to be a slave to his defense mechanisms and, consequently, subject to a psychopathology.

Another more recent model of this type used in body psychotherapy is that of the *action systems* proposed by Pat Ogden, Kekuni Minton, and Clare Pain (2006, 6). These action systems combine somatic mechanisms, feelings, emotions, and imagery. Each action system is linked to a series of emotions that are the only ones that can allow the system to function adequately. According to these authors, there would be eight basic action systems: defenses, attachment, exploration, regulation of energy, compassion for others, socialization, play, and sexuality. This system is more flexible than either Ekman's and Lowen's systems, which make it easier to use in psychotherapy. An action system includes more than the face and does not necessarily require the mobilization of particular muscles as a function of an emotion whose mental contours are clearly defined. This model is sufficiently systemic as to allow a mixture of direct and indirect relations between the different mechanisms associated with the action system. Nonetheless, the customary critique applies to this list. Why this list and not another?

An example of the most extreme formulation of this type is the Bodynamic manual written by Lisbeth Marcher and Sonja Fich (2010), in which they relate precise muscles and connective tissues with psychological functions such as to feel alive, autonomous, romantic, sexually alive, solitary, or to be in contact with one's needs. The tone of the muscles also allows for the evaluation of a person's will and opinions. Having said this, each psychological faculty distinguished by the authors is associated to such a large number of particular muscles that the apparently linear aspects of this model loses some of its strength.

The weak points in these types of propositions are:

1. It is not possible to propose a robust list of basic affects.
2. There is no theory that can identify specific affects with sufficiently clear boundaries as to be able to relate them to a unique and necessary sensorimotor schema.
3. If one accepts the hypothesis that every innate propensity needs to be calibrated, it is not possible to thinks that every human being needs to calibrate in the same way.

A CRITIQUE OF MODELS BASED ON THE ASSUMPTION
THAT THERE EXISTS A LINEAR AND DIRECT CONNECTION
BETWEEN PSYCHOLOGICAL AND BODILY DYNAMICS

I have already begun a critique of the linear model of the body–spirit relationship. I now try to detail this critique. The basis of this critique is close to the one I proposed concerning Idealism: the conscious mind loves to find linear connections; it treats this type of connection in a particularly comfortable way. What consciousness manages with comfort is felt as true. Science prefers empirical and logical arguments. There is no reason why the dynamics of the universe should be compatible with the comfort of the mind.

A Human Being Needs to Hope that What He Perceives
Has a Meaning He Can Understand

The infatuation for Lavater's physiognomy deflated like an over-baked soufflé after the publication of an article by German philosopher Georg Christoph Lichtenberg (1778). For Lichtenberg, physiognomy does not demonstrate a connection between a shape of the face and a content of the soul; instead, it reflects a spontaneous tendency of the human being to associate faces to some attributes of the soul. In other words, the connection between a physical and a mental trait is in the eyes of the beholder, not necessarily in the mechanisms that associate psychological and physiological dynamics in an organism.

Lichtenberg starts from a model of the mind close to the one of the English empiricists like Hume. The need to guess what another thinks probably created the tendency to attribute to the soul of others a personal experience that associates itself automatically to the other's bodily appearance.[47] An individual conscious system cannot perceive what emerges from the outward manifestation of its organism; it cannot know how others perceive us. To reassure itself, it would like to have, at its disposal, a system that lets it know what aspects of its bodily appearance irritates or seduces those with whom we associate. As soon as an apparently brilliant scientist pretends to be able to propose such a system of readings, each of us experience an inclination to believe that such a system is pertinent and hopes that it can quell a permanent source of anxiety.[48]

> An example of attributing mental traits to a physical appearance. *It comes about that I cross paths with a person who resembles a woman that I loved a long time ago. I sometimes spontaneously attribute mental characteristics to that person that are like those of my friend of yesteryear. If I meet this person a little later and hear that person speak, I notice just as spontaneously that this person thinks and feels differently than my old friend.*

Lichtenberg wanted to denounce certain physiognomists who exploited this propensity to think in a linear fashion to make money. He feared that physiognomy could be used to hang children to whom one would attribute criminal traits before they even had the time to commit a crime.[49] A way to summarize certain of Lichtenberg's arguments is to ask how a man could discover all of his wife's secret feelings by analyzing her profile for a few minutes, when he doesn't get close to understanding her after having scrutinized her body and living with her for decades. Lichtenberg's formula is more succinct: "This incomprehensible being that we are and which would be even more incomprehensible if we were able to approach it even more closely; we ought not to want to find this incomprehensible being on a forehead" (Lichtenberg, 1778).[50]

The Lures of Ethology

In his research studies, German psychologist Siegfried Frey (1999) took up Lichtenberg's hypothesis, according to which humans automatically associate psychological propensities to body traits, even when there is no basis for such an attribution. As in Hume's theory, this tendency to attribute is automatically triggered in the background of the mind every time a body trait is perceived. This trait is automatically associated to any material stored in the memory that has some formal resemblance, such as the shape of someone we knew. For example, when we observe an actor imitate an emotional expression, we automatically conclude that the character played by the actor experiences the emotion corresponding to this expression. The same phenomenon occurs in the drawing of a cartoon, where a few lines allow us to believe that there is a character who feels a violent emotion.

Here, we enter into the realm of the *lures* of the ethologists. Certain parts of the brain seem preprogrammed to make rapid decisions from very few clues, especially at the level of the limbic system.[51] The startle response and the flight-or-fight responses are often cited as examples of this kind of behavior. Given the speed of these responses, they are activated by a rapid and simplified analysis of the sensory material that enters into the organism. Frey shows that the same type of rapid information processing is mobilized by an individual watching a TV news program. Each time a personality appears on the screen, often only for a few seconds, the viewer reacts by mobilizing internal psychophysiological mechanisms that generate an affective impression (cardiac and respiratory rhythms, galvanic skin response, and the size of the pupils). This impression then activates inferences which support an attribution process. This is how, in less than a second,[52] a viewer attributes character traits to personalities he does not know. This process, once set in motion, often creates persistent impressions that are difficult to modify.

Sexual arousal follows a similar process when a drawing, a silhouette, or a brief video clip suffices to activate it. To choose a woman who meets the marketing or pornographic norms of beauty has led many a man to be gravely deceived. In this case, the man has difficulty recognizing the person who is behind a physical shape that meets the aesthetic norms extolled by society. It is common to say that the woman is then perceived as a sexual object instead of as a person. The force of the social stakes that play with this effect shows the power of the phenomena described by Lichtenberg and Frey.

The tendency to associate somatic and mental traits as if they form a coherent functional unity explains the impact of television on politics. The viewers in front of the television speak with each other in such a way as to permit themselves to infer psychological characteristics pertaining to a person based only on perceived appearance (here is a caring person, she seems to be right, we feel that she wants our good, etc.). This system of attribution stabilizes itself and is remembered independently from what is elaborated in a more complex way in other layers of the mind.[53] People seems to prefer to vote for a presidential candidate who "looks good" on television than for a person who has an understanding of important issues.[54]

The Relative Robustness of Results Confirming the Relevance of Linear Models of Emotional Expression

There is something to the idea that certain forms of expression can be associated with more or less probability to certain affective states. However, this formulation is far from confirming a direct link. The first problem is that of the notion of psychological faculties. It is intuitively possible, thanks to some striking examples, to distinguish experiences of memory, intellectual analysis, and emotional reactions, but it is more difficult to make these examples correspond to distinct physiological and psychological mechanisms. I do not know of a theory that proposes a useful way to differentiate terms such as affects, emotions, feelings, passions, and so on. In fact, we do not even know if terms such as *emotion* or *intelligence* correspond to real mechanisms, to existing subsystems of organismic dynamics.[55] For example, the data collected by Paul Ekman (1980a) to demonstrate the existence of emotions proved to be disappointing. The analysis of his results, above all, points to four things:

1. It seems that most of the people who see photos of certain facial expressions associate them to the same emotion. This seems true in most cultures and social milieus. The human mind certainly has a tendency to make a particular kind of inference faced with certain photos, even certain expressions. This confirms Lichtenberg's and Frey's hypotheses. For the moment, until more robust information on such matters becomes available, it is safer to assume that there is no direct link between behavior and personality.
2. The connection between photographs of basic emotions and their impact on viewers has a statistically significant positive correlation, but varies between 63 percent and 97 percent among the individuals interviewed.

A smile with crow's feet at the corner of the eyes[56] is related to joy by more than 87 percent of the people interviewed in Japan, Brazil, Chile, Argentina, and the United States. Ekman does not explain why 13 percent of the subjects did not spontaneously associate the smile with joy. He is satisfied to conjecture that there are always exceptions. These numbers correspond to what we can expect from such a research strategy if the relationship between expression and the felt emotion is a direct universal one for the person who activates and the person who perceives the expression. We discover the same profile for the expressions of disgust and surprise. Sadness, anger, and fear yield less convincing results. The recognition of photos of individuals expressing anger, according to Ekman, varies from 82 percent for Brazilian subjects to 63 percent for the Japanese. The connection does exist, but it is relatively fuzzy, as predicted by systemic hypotheses.[57]

3. An expression can be associated to feelings other than those foreseen by Ekman's theory of emotions. This is particularly evident in the case of actors who want to encourage the audience to infer feelings that the actor does not especially feel, or in the case of singers who make facial expressions to form sounds that do not necessarily have a connection to emotions. This last effect is so well known that Ekman and Friesen recommend that the emotional expressions should not be coded when someone is vocalizing.

4. In analyzing lengthy sample of films (one hour long) instead of photos, the researcher often observes repetitive facial expressions that appear without having been activated by any particular event.[58] Some of them have the configuration of an emotional expression, defined by Ekman and Friesen, when the image on the video is paused. When someone takes a photo, the face is artificially immobilized. What seems to form an expressive configuration on a photo does not necessarily give the same impression when the image is reviewed on film. It seems to me that the press often uses this artifact when they want to make the public believe that a personality has expressed a precise emotion at a key moment. The status of apparently emotional expressions that are transitory (they often last less than a half a second) and are as repetitive as a tic, without a clear stimulus, cannot be defined in the framework of Ekman's specific theory.

Eva Bänninger-Huber and Doris Peham (2010a) mention that in most of the studies that use FACS to study emotional expressions, researchers only code the facial units that are often used for emotional expressions and do not take other units into consideration. They tend to use procedures that are so simplistic that most of these studies are "inappropriate for the study of the various facets of facial behavior" and are therefore "often very limited."

This type of analysis encourages more complex thinking about the connections between affects and behaviors, especially on the way to distinguish different kinds of affective functions. It is now possible for us to appreciate the soundness of Lamarck's attack against linear parallelistic theories such as Gall's: "The essential point to consider is that in every system of animal organization, nature cannot have only one method to make the various organs perform their appropriate functions" (Lamarck, 1809, III, introduction, p. 464).[59]

10
Spirituality, Hypnosis, and Energy

The nineteenth century in Europe was an epoch in which inventiveness manifested itself in all domains, even in what is sometimes referred to as the esoteric sciences. One of the central moving forces of the innovations in this domain is the Freemason movement, which can boast of having influenced the creation of the United States of America,[1] the beginnings of the French Revolution, the women's liberation movement, some non-Marxist socialistic movements, and the need for a secular government.[2] Another important development at the time is formed by the Protestant spiritualist movements that support the impression that one can communicate with the dead and that faith can heal. The whole of the ancient esoteric systems, like tarot and astrology, were entirely revised. Up until the seventeenth century, astrologists were astronomers who drew their charts from the observations of the stars.[3] The illustrious Kepler is one of the last examples of this long tradition, which goes back to the city of Babylon in ancient Mesopotamia. Since the nineteenth century, the astrologists possess printed charts that invent an approximation of the sky whose harmony and logic make easy calculations possible and for conclusions compatible with divination using the symbolic language of tarot.[4]

The filiation that is often mentioned between Mesmer and Freud passes through a series of trends that participate in this immense reconstruction of the field consisting of schools with spiritual orientations. Because I am not a specialist in this matter, I only briefly touch on it. It merits development because it remains powerfully influential in the world of psychotherapy. Some psychotherapists integrate, in innovative ways, approaches developed by the yogi and the alchemists of China and Europe. Jung's name is often used to support this way of thinking.

FROM MESMERISM TO HYPNOSIS

Franz Mesmer (1734–1815) became fashionable in the eighteenth century in various mundane settings that appreciated his healing methods. His theory was that certain magnetic animal fluids could heal illnesses. He presented methods that allowed him to facilitate the passage of these fluids in the organism of an individual who wanted to be cured by him and his followers. He encouraged scientists to undertake research on the phenomena that he brought about with his patients.[5] Researchers often contented themselves to relate Mesmer's magnetism to a *placebo effect*, defined as a mobilization of the patient's hope that can sometimes unleash a cure. Independent of the explanations proposed by Mesmer, many testimonials attest to the efficacy of his practices. To my knowledge, we do not always know today how this placebo effect really functions.[6] Materialistic minds evoke it to disqualify this type of approach, but no serious scientific research demonstrates that Mesmer's fluids are effectively without results or can only be explained by a patient's belief. The scientific point of view developed by Descartes determines that a scientist can only approach a research subject that is close to something that has already been studied and for which he has adequate methodological tools. There are manifestly many subjects that cannot yet be studied scientifically.

Armand Marie Jacques de Chastenet, Marquis de Puysegur, was an influential student of Mesmer. He developed a form of hypnosis that made the subject fall into a state that is close to sleep and trance state and that created an artificial state of somnambulism.

> The effects of hypnosis as described by de Puysegur. *This state activates mechanisms of auto-reparation in the organism. It also permits obtaining information about the subject that the subject ignores in a waking state. Certain types of habits can be eliminated through suggestion. De Puysegur shows that the subject can, under hypnosis, recover memories that are not available in a waking state and that this remembering can treat certain disturbances. This allows him to affirm that the function of memory and consciousness sometimes has an impact on the functioning of the organism without the person knowing it. He also shows that he can suggest something to a person under hypnosis that she will not be able to avoid doing once awake (she strokes her chin every time she hears the word* cat, *for example), while she is unable to recall the suggestions of the hypnotist. When we were to ask why she strokes her chin, she would invent false explanations, as do certain patients who suffer from neurological problems.*

These techniques were gradually integrated into the practice of Mesmer's students, who in turn influenced Freud. The hypnotic methods recommended free association long before Freud did, the exploration of free writing (stream of consciousness), free drawing and free movement, to explore the dimensions of the being that make us move, draw, and write. The basic idea is that mental functioning is part of the equilibrium established by the organism. When a person allows his mental functioning to change, the organism must accommodate to these changes. The methods developed by the hypnotists had the goal of inducing a global change of the organism starting from a functional change of the mind.

John Elliotson introduced hypnosis to medicine around 1840. He was also the first English physician to use the stethoscope. He was particularly interested in the possible anesthetizing effect of hypnosis. In spite of vociferous critics, hypnosis entered into certain medical practices in a lasting way.

THEOSOPHY AND SPIRITUALITY

In the 1850s, a form of mesmerism was assimilated by spiritualistic movements inspired by the visions of the Swede, Emmanuel Swedenborg.[7] This movement also connected with the spiritualism developed by some Protestants in the United States, with which Alfred Russel Wallace associated himself.

Mesmerism and spiritualism joined the theosophical movement founded by Helena Petrova Blavatsky. Influenced by Plato and the Renaissance mystic Jakob Boehme, she integrated into this movement formulations that she discovered in India and China. Theosophy especially makes the idea of *deism* fashionable. Yahweh, Jesus, and Mohammed would be three representations of the same force. The proposal to synthesize all of the forms of spirituality in the world inspired—and inspires—numerous movements.

Theosophy, which is close to some movements of Freemasonry, is associated to a different form of colonialism than the one influenced by eugenics and racism. It consisted in integrating into a grand European synthesis the profound wisdom of every civilization, with the idea that in some domains diverse cultures had developed important forms of knowledge ignored by European philosophers. Having said this, we again find the idea that only the Idealism developed in Europe permits the integration of the entirety of the knowledge on the planet.

ENERGY = THE QUANTITY OF ACTIVITY

The notion of energy used in the European spiritual movements will synthesize, in a poorly differentiated way, three trends of thought:

1. The notion of *soul* as a spiritual force that animates and sometimes shapes matter.[8]
2. The notion of *natural forces* that give direction to the transformations of nature, understood as a systemic totality that animates everything that is happening. This notion is close to what Spinoza called the power of nature. We find a similar notion with philosophers like Henri Bergson, who speak of the life force (*élan vital*).
3. We have already seen that personalities like Mesmer thought that their

formulations had scientific status. To reinforce this impression, schools of spirituality used the new scientific concept of *energy* to designate all that animates the organism and increases the feeling of vitality.

Newton: I Need Theoretical Variables to Describe the Dynamics of the Universe

Sir Isaac Newton (1643–1727) is known for having proposed so powerful a physics of mechanics that it permitted industry to develop its capacity to create machines. He transformed a science that was struggling to find its way into a major social force. One of the aspects of Newton's genius was to have found a way to reduce the immense variety of what exists to a few variables that could be included in mathematical formula, and as such, were capable of predicting certain behaviors of theoretical objects (spheres, cubes, etc.). My understanding of physics is rudimentary. Yet because the notion of energy is so often used by body psychotherapists, I think it can be useful to revisit the basic laws that most of us have learned in school. We need to distinguish between what is *experienced* as energy moving in the organism and what we can reasonably call "energy." I begin this discussion by distinguishing two types of variables:

1. A first series of *variables correlate with what can be perceived*. Weight is something that I can feel when I hold an object in my hands; speed corresponds to information decoded by my eyes; and so on. These variables are reduced to *measurements* that can be examined with instruments.
2. A second level of variables corresponds to some *constant mathematical relations* between measurements. The fact that there is constant rapport between measurements allows us to think that there are laws of the universe that govern what we perceive; but to observe a constant rapport does not permit us to know the nature and the functioning of these *underlying* and unobservable mechanisms. One of the achievements of twentieth-century physics has been to improve our understanding of these phenomena.

The notions of force and gravity do not designate existing phenomena but a constant mathematical ratio between measurements. The classic expression is "everything happens as if" a ratio corresponded to something that exists. Even so, no one to this day has observed a cause, an effect, a force, or gravity. This point is made particularly clear by David Hume, who loved Newton's physics, when he considers the laws of *cause and effect*. He takes two objects and pushes one against the other. It is generally assumed that the movement is the cause of the movement of the second object:

> Let us therefore cast our eyes on any two objects, which we call cause and effect, and turn them on all sides, in order to find that impression, which produces an idea of such prodigious consequence. At first sight I perceive, that I must not search

for it in any of the particular *qualities* of the objects; since, which-ever of these
qualities I pitch on, I find some object, that is not possest of it, and yet falls under
the demonstration of cause and effect. And indeed there is nothing existent, either
externally or internally, which is not consider'd either as a cause or an effect; tho'
'tis plain there is no one quality, which universally belongs to all beings, and gives
a title to that demonstration.

The idea, then, must be deriv'd from some *relation* among objects; and that
relation we must now endeavour to discover. (Hume, 1740, 1.3.2.5–6, p. 53f)

The ratio between mass, distance, and weight furnishes a variable *g* that is gravity or gravitation. Gravity allows us to describe with precision the fall of a body
to the Earth, or the attraction of a planet to another (as the play between the
moon and the Earth, and the influence of this interplay on the tides). We do not
perceive gravitation, but we perceive phenomena that can be elegantly handled
with a model that uses the notions concerning gravity.

An analogous understanding makes it possible to describe the use of the
term *energy* in the physics of the nineteenth century. The notion of energy was
proposed by physicists at the start of the nineteenth century. In 1807, Thomas
Young (1773–1829) proposed a formula to calculate the *kinetic energy* of the
body. The status of energy in contemporary physics is more complex,[9] but it
brings us to the same conclusions. Energy is a measurement that designates the
dynamics of the activity of matter. This activity can manifest itself under the
guise of sound, heat, motion, or light to the human senses; in every case, it is
impossible to isolate an energetic "substance" that engenders this activity. In his
famous formula, $E = mc^2$, Albert Einstein shows that there is a constant rapport
between mass (m) and the energy (E) of an object (c = the speed of light, a constant). The more the mass of the object increases, the more the value of *e* increases. It is the same with gravity. The farther a body is from a planet (an
object of great mass), the weaker the impact of gravity. The organism behaves as
if it were lighter.

It is probable that all of these activities follow laws that are proper to them
due to some mechanisms that are particular in each instance. Nevertheless, it is
useful to have a form of measurement (energy) that makes it possible to show
how a form of activity can engender another: how motion produces heat or
heat produces light.

Imagination and Intellection in Newton's Day

As a blind man has no idea of colours, so we have no idea of the manner by which
the all-wise God perceives and understands all things. He is utterly void of all body
and bodily figure, and can therefore neither be seen, nor heard, nor touched; nor
ought he to be worshiped under the representation of any corporeal thing. We
have no idea of his attributes, but what the real substance of any thing is we know
not. In bodies we see only their figures and colours, we hear only the sounds, we

touch only outward surfaces, we smell only the smells and taste de savours; but their inward substances are not to be known either by our senses, or by any reflex act of our minds. (Newton, 1686, *The principia*, III, p. 441f)

To clarify the difference between a concept such as gravity or energy, and what we are capable of representing to ourselves by using sensory analogies, Newton distinguishes between what can be "imagined" and that about which we can only have an "intellection" (Newton, 1670, 126).[10] Humans can imagine an immense space, and they can imagine that a space can always become a bit bigger, but they cannot have a representation of a limitless space. On the other hand, humans can have a form of precise intuition that can be represented by a mathematical formula Newton calls an *intellection*. The imagination fashions notions that are possible to associate to a mental image or to a gesture, but this type of representation cannot sustain a true reflection on notions such as infinity, gravity, or energy. Mathematics and words are a form of socially constructed representations that can be associated to what an individual can only have an intellection about, be it an idea that cannot manifest itself in a form of representation furnished by the individual psyche. The capacity that certain individuals have to handle this type of notion characterizes intellectual practices. Because humans have the tendency to want to associate an intellection to something that they can imagine, they often deform what they have an intellection about so that the notion might be assimilated into an image.

The Taoists of antiquity feel unendingly obliged to remind everyone that the Tao is an intellection and every representation of it is by definition only an approximation. The Muslims do not cease fighting against all who would like to present an image of God. The human need to represent everything with the same format as the data of the senses corresponds to a need that suits the comfort of the procedures of individual consciousness. Taoist philosophers, Muslims, and scientists engage in the same battle when they ask everyone why they absolutely want the forces that created the universe to resemble an angry old man with a beard.

Fradin's model can be of some help to us in this instance when he shows that consciousness links, above all, data engendered by the circuits of the limbic system and feels surpassed by the nonconscious sophistications of the frontal cortex. The intellections could be similar to nonconscious refinements and often have need of an institutional support (like mathematics or meditation) to maintain themselves in the dynamics of an individual's consciousness.

Energy and Psychological Representations

The physicist conceives of one energy in the sense that there exists but one mathematical definition of energy. This energy is above all distinguished in function of criteria like those that I enumerate here:

1. *The field of application.* Energy can be qualitatively identified in function of its field of application, as that of movement, sound, or light. We speak, for example, of acoustic, radiant, and motor energy.
2. *Mode of production.* Certain machinery produces a form of energy, like steam engines (steam energy), water mills and dams (hydraulic energy), nuclear power plants (nuclear energy), and the solar panels (solar energy).
3. *Mode of utilization.* Certain substances (petroleum fuels) or modes of functioning (electricity) connected to modes of production are also called energy. These modes of utilization can be stored and/or transported.
4. *The consumer.* We also identify energy by its consumer, as in expressions such as "biological energy" or "muscular energy."

This nonexhaustive list of the ways to use the term *energy* in its strict sense does not correspond to a single qualifying statement as to what energy is. Electrical energy is a certain type of activity of matter, but it is not necessarily a particular energy. It is not yet possible to know if there exists a single energetic mechanism that manifests in various ways or myriad mechanisms that we are not yet able to describe.

The theoretical physicists of the nineteenth century quickly stimulated the imagination of people who associated this fashionable term, supported by science, to a kind of mysterious fluid that circulates in and animates nature. They assimilated this term to ancient notions in circulation in the so-called esoteric schools. As we saw while speaking of the soul, vital energy is often nothing other than a transfer of the properties of Plato's soul to a term that has become more respectable. This is how an imagination of Christian inspiration assimilated the notion of energy to a known mythology instead of accommodating itself to what the physicists were discovering. If the same energy can manifest itself in many different ways (vapor, heat, light, wind, etc.), it is then possible to think that a fundamental energy is the force that actively animates the universe. Spiritual movements, like theosophy, developed this way of thinking. These movements wanted to validate this notion by anchoring it in the greatest possible number of ancient traditions. Not only did they associate the respiratory forces of antiquity (prana, chi, and pneuma) to the notion of vital energy, but in return, they influenced the schools in a colonized Far East by explaining to them that they would become scientifically acceptable if they adapted their ancient models to the notion of vital energy.[11] This is particularly evident in the literature on relatively recent disciplines like tai chi chuan and aikido.[12] The teachers of these disciplines give demonstrations showing the chi is what makes the body breathe and the limbs move, anchors the organism in the Earth, and makes it possible to repel the enemy. For them, neither will nor force nor skill can be as effective as the right utilization of chi. Their demonstrations are often spectacular. Designating the chi as whatever produces these capacities does not give any information about the mechanisms at play.

The notion of vital energy developed in a Christian context that associates itself to some simplistic opposition between energy and matter that resembles the opposition between soul and body. These oppositions are not part of the ancient philosophies of the Far East. The notion of vital energy spread out into the world mostly by being associated with Protestant healing movements, born in the United States, and then disseminated in the Philippines, Africa, and South America. Their techniques assimilated the healing methods of the local culture and spirituality.

11

The First Methods of Relaxation

SCHULTZ AND AUTOGENIC TRAINING

Johann Heinrich Schultz (1884–1970) was a German psychiatrist who studied hypnosis and psychoanalysis. He developed a method of relaxation, the Autogenic training (Schultz, 1932), after having been a physician in the German army during World War I. He is part of the immense network of therapists who were trained by the disastrous psychological ravages brought about by that war. His method is based primarily on autohypnosis and yoga. He was a Nazi sympathizer during the World War II, which probably explains why his therapeutic thought finds limited expression, mostly in schools that were influenced by him, like Sophrology.[1]

The Link between Thoughts and Body Are Nonconscious but Manageable

Like the hypnotists, Schultz uses a parallelistic model that presumes a nonconscious power of spirit over matter. An individual cannot, through introspection, know how his thoughts influence the body; but he can learn techniques that increase the control of thoughts on the body. He proposes some simple techniques of autohypnotic relaxation that allow an individual to place himself in a state that reinforces the organism's systems of auto-reparation. Schultz's system also incorporated the medical knowledge of his time, for example when he uses the following principles:

1. The *heavier* the object that a hand holds, the more the extensor muscles of the arm have a tendency to elongate. Shultz therefore supposes that when a person experiences the sensation of heaviness in a part of the

body, the extensor muscles of that part of the body have elongated while relaxing.[2]

2. The link between blood and *warmth* is more direct because a greater flow of blood necessarily brings warmth.

A Practical Introduction to Autogenic Training

Various developments of Autogenic training, like Sophrology, are still used in hospital and psychiatric settings and by many athletes. Besides the many exercises, the quality of a relaxation endeavor depends on the way the therapist integrates what is happening. A few introductory exercises to this method permits the reader to personally become aware of what is referred to as a body–mind experience.

Type of exercise: *my body is heavy.*

1. *Preliminaries.* The individual is in a pleasant space, the light is subdued, the temperature is pleasant. He is lying down comfortably. He closes his eyes with the intention to relax.

2. *General instructions.* The individual repeats a phrase with his internal voice in a calm and regular rhythm, which may become hypnotic. He observes what is happening in his inner space such as he experiences it. He does not try to willfully apply the instruction that he pronounces over and over again internally. Typically, the first phrase is "I am totally calm." The individual repeats this, whether he is calm or not, without having to become calm. He contents himself to observe the sensations, feelings, images, thoughts, and sensations that arise in his interior space while he repeats this phrase.

3. *Specific instructions.* In this exercise, the central variable is the sensation of heaviness. In other words, the sought-after goal is essentially muscular relaxation. The individual runs through all of the parts of the body while saying slowly for about twenty times "my head is heavy," then "my jaw is heavy," then "my arms are heavy," and so on. It is often recommended to journey down the arms before the torso. At the end of about twelve minutes or less, the individual ends this central part of the exercise by repeating "my body is heavy."

4. *Final phase.* This phase is important, because when it is skipped a person may feel more anxious than before. The individual does nothing for a few minutes. His attention is "floating" and has no precise goals. After about thirty breaths, the individual moves his fingers and his toes, slowly opens his eyes, and slowly gets up. If his head turns when he stands, it is often a sign that he arose too quickly.

These exercises are particularly effective when they are practiced several times per week for at least fifteen minutes. The regulatory systems of the organism are especially sensitive to habitual practices. After a while, it suffices to think of the exercise for a certain relaxation to come about.

In these exercises, a parallelistic vision of the organism allows one to enter into the spirit of the exercise. The individual does not try to make his arm heavy while he repeats the phrase "my arm is heavy." For example, the person can feel that the more he repeats the phrase, the more his arms feel light, or that it is his feet that become heavy or warm. Sometimes his attention is mostly drawn to a sensation of anxiety or pleasure.

What I have described is a typical exercise. Schultz developed many variations. Each one focuses on particular dynamics of the organism (muscles, the cardiovascular system, etc.). The aim is to help an individual's consciousness become familiar with and aware of the nonconscious connections between his thoughts and his physiology. The limitation of these exercises is a bit like that of all psychotherapeutic methods: they are useful only to those who like them. In the same way that it is impossible to hypnotize some people, some people are deeply irritated by such immobility. It is because people are so different that so many methods exist. It is rare that an individual who does not favor relaxation can be forced to appreciate it. On the other hand, it does happen that years later the same individual will value this kind of exercise. If the subject is resistant, it can be dangerous to insist, for sometimes hyperactivity is a defense against depression or even an incipient psychosis.

> Vignette on the fear of immobility: *In a training group, a therapist asks a woman to remain lying down for ten minutes without doing anything. In spite of the patient's resistance, the therapist insists; the patient ends up doing what she is told. She then falls into a deep depression. As a result, this woman lost her job, was unable to find employment in her field, and had to change profession (she became a yoga teacher). This crisis lasted three years due to a ten-minute exercise. This anecdote may seem unbelievable, but it is sadly true. Human frailties are sometimes unforeseeable.*

This method can sometimes become very useful for persons who suffer from anxieties with recurrent thoughts. Repeating thoughts on parts of the body may protect the person from the usual obsessional themes.

JACOBSON: PROGRESSIVE RELAXATION

Most of the recent relaxation methods were developed by integrating diverse methods inspired from the Hindu and Chinese approaches[3] with discoveries in psychophysiology and psychotherapeutic techniques. Edmund Jacobson (1888–1983) participated in this development by integrating, in a particularly targeted way, the methods of experimental psychophysiology that make it possible to understand what happens in a relaxation session.

Edmund Jacobson was educated at Harvard University at the beginning of the twentieth century, where he was influenced by psychologist William James and physiologist Walter Bradford Cannon. He undertook his research on relaxation in the Laboratory for Clinical Physiology at the University of Chicago and the Jacobson Clinic. His research relates studies in psychophysiology to clinical studies that take into account the experiences of patients.

The Consciousness of the Gesture according to James

> It is a general principle in Psychology that consciousness deserts all processes where it can no longer be of use. (William James, 1890, *The Principles of Psychology*, XXVI, Will, p. 1107)

> Mental states occasion also changes in the caliber of blood vessels, or alteration in the heart-beats, or processes more subtle still, in glands and viscera. If these are taken into account, as well as acts which follow at some *remote period* because the mental state was once there, it will be safe to lay down the general law that *no mental modification ever occurs which is not accompanied or followed by a bodily change.* (William James, 1890, *The Principles of Psychology*, I, The scope of psychology, p. 19)

William James (1842–1910) was the brother of the equally famous novelist Henry James. He is known as one of the founders of theoretical and experimental psychology, which he taught at Harvard. His often referenced book, *The Principles of Psychology* was published in 1890. This bible of the pioneers in psychology cannot be summarized here, even though many chapters continue to inspire psychologists. I content myself in extracting from the chapter on the will some analyses that permit me to situate the relationship between consciousness and motor functions that inspired Jacobson's theory of relaxation.

For James, consciousness does not have the means to understand or even apprehend the complexity that sets sensations and actions in motion, or even a concerted action, often referred to as voluntary. It is therefore out of the question that an activity of the organism might be launched consciously. Consciousness does not even have the means to know which innervations can be launched by the thought of moving a hand in a certain way.

As an example, consider a painter in the act of painting. His organism moves about the canvas. Consciousness perceives certain forms and colors on the canvas and perceives the movements that create them. For James, this activity is set about without asking of consciousness anything more than some forms of support that render it possible to refine the behavior of the painter. It is only once that an action system is set in place that consciousness can and must intervene. It takes note of the effect of certain acquired gestures and sets in place the necessary systems that modulate the action. In this example, we have three "psychological currents"[4] of the psyche:

1. A sensory-motor activity whose sources and effects can be perceived by consciousness.
2. A nonconscious organizing activity.
3. Consciousness as a system of support that permits the refinement of what is going on.

Many authors quote James as the one who thinks that we feel happy because we smile or we feel sad because we cry.[5] In so doing, the commentators often forget that in James's theory, there are not only tears and conscious feelings but also a nonconscious underlying system that animates and associates both consciousness and behavior. In this, we again find the idea that the affects are regulated outside of the psyche, that they are one of the nonconscious instances that regulate psyche, physiology, body, and behavior, all the while being influenced by each of these dimensions.

The Brain and the Hand

Every representation of a movement awakens in some degree the actual movement which is its object. Every pulse of feeling which we have is the correlate of some neural activity that is already on its way to instigate a movement. Our sensations and thoughts are but cross-sections. (William James, 1890, *The Principles of Psychology*, II, will, p. 1135)

In his studies on the psychophysiology of relaxation, Jacobson corroborates the idea that the architecture of the organism coordinates thoughts and gestures.

The research that I summarize analyzes the temporal rapport between the brain and the muscles of the right hand when a therapist asks a patient to extend his right hand. To study this, Jacobson placed electroencephalograms (EEGs) on the head and electromyograms (EMGs) on the hand. The EEG allows for the detection of the regions of the brain where there is activity, and the EMG allows for the detections of small muscular contractions, indiscernible to the naked eye, to touch, or by introspection.[6]

Typically, people expect that the instruction to move the hand first activates the brain (activity detected by the EEG) and then the muscles of the hand (detected by the EMG). This sequence is often observed in an experimental situation in a laboratory where all the interventions have been prepared in advance with the subject. It is reversed when there is a sensory irritation (excitation of the retina, pain caused by a flame, etc.). Jacobson quotes a few neurological studies of his time (before 1967) that show cases where an instruction given to a subject activates the brain and the hand of the patient *simultaneously*. He concludes that there are circuits that integrate the *peripheral* activity (linked to the muscles and to the skin) and the *central* (brain) nervous system.

Jacobson confirms this hypothesis with studies that tested the temporal coordination between the activity of the hand and the brain at the occasion of a voluntary act. The experimenter asks his subjects to feel their right hand. He observes that in the situations he has created to control this variable, the EEG and the EMG begin plotting simultaneously. These results confirm the hypothesis that the coordination between voluntary movements and thoughts is regulated by organismic circuits, but these studies have not been sufficiently replicated to be considered robust. To my knowledge, they have never been invalidated, even if Jacobson's instruments use a temporal scale somewhat too large to be conclusive.

Jacobson also shows that even with subjects experienced in relaxation, it is impossible to think of a hand movement without generating a slight mobilization of the muscles involved in the movement. This confirms the hypothesis that *a thought is part of a mechanism of organismic regulation, and is never an isolated event.* Jacobson distinguishes (1) thought, (2) the mobilization of the hand, and (3) the mechanisms that coordinate hand and thoughts.

Progressive Muscular Relaxation

Jacobson's research enabled him to describe several mechanisms that associate muscular tension and anxiety. Above all, he uses the *contrast between mobilization and reflux*[7] to allow an individual to refine his awareness of what is happening in a relaxation session. Jacobson's mobilizations are organized mostly around the flexion and extension of the muscles, with attention on the way a gesture coordinates with respiration. I bend the arm, feeling what is happening in the mobilized muscles; then I extend the arm, feeling what is happening gradually as the arms extends further and then relaxes. I can also feel what the movements evoke in me when I change the speed of the movement (slow, fast, etc.). A more subtle exercise is to observe what the movement activates in other parts of the body. An arm movement can have an impact on the muscular chains, on respiration, on the jaw, the feet, and so on. It often happens that an individual cannot clench a fist without tensing other parts of the body at the same time. By using the EEG and EMG, Jacobson can draw a patient's attention to a tension in a part of the body of which the individual was not aware. It then becomes possible to calibrate the consciousness of a subject with regard to minuscule measurable tensions that the patient had not hitherto been able to feel. This method has since been developed to refine the awareness of the mechanisms that associate a thought to any other physiological activity (cardiac, digestive, etc.). It is now mostly known under the name of *biofeedback.*

Chronic Muscular Tensions and Chronic Anxiety

The notion that tense muscles are often related to states of psychic tension is already robust clinical knowledge in yoga. It has henceforth been observed in all of the techniques that use relaxation. It entered into medical thought through many avenues, but it became something that could not be overlooked ever since Edmund Jacobson described this association with the tools of psychophysiology. Jacobson cited a large number of research studies of his day showing that the variations of muscle tone influences certain dynamics of the brain.[8] The maintenance of muscular tension is very costly for the organism, in terms of resources. This maintenance is justifiable when it helps contain anxiety, but it partly explains the recurring fatigue of individuals who are anxious.[9]

Jacobson shows that from the point of view of consciousness, a person can have a representation of a movement, but has trouble identifying which muscles were mobilized and is incapable of determining the innervation that activated the movement. It requires a certain education (relaxation, gymnastics, dance, etc.) to acquire a refined consciousness of the variables of a movement that can become accessible to consciousness.[10]

Jacobson had a profound influence on a number of body psychotherapists, like Braatøy, Waal, and Lowen.[11] Probably through the influence of Jacobson, a number of physical therapists and psychotherapists integrated Cannon's psychophysiology without ever having read one of the great physiologist's works.

DYNAMIC RELAXATION IN PSYCHOTHERAPY

Relaxation has much too specific a goal to pretend to be a form of psychotherapy. But its techniques are often used by different forms of psychotherapy such as Psychoanalysis, Gestalt therapy, Transactional analysis, and others. It can have many functions:

1. Relaxation exercises can be recommended to patients so that they have a way to control their anxiety. The goal here is a bit the same as that of an antianxiety medication (for example, benzodiazepines). Relaxation is then not truly integrated into the psychotherapeutic process.
2. Relaxation exercises can be used as a way to become conscious of the body or certain mental states. In providing a patient an experience of a state of relaxation, it sometimes becomes possible to help the patient feel, by contrast, an anxiety he attempts to ignore.
3. What is experienced in a state of relaxation can relax the defenses against an emotion, increase respiration, and feed dreams.
4. Relaxation can also be used in psychotherapy to help the patient achieve a more refined sensation of the limits between the interior and exterior of the body, or between body and thought. In this kind of utilization, the patient can acquire a tangible impression of self-mastery.

This type of intervention can have psychotherapeutic functions to the extent that the material brought up by the relaxation is *integrated* into a psychotherapeutic process. In the Latin countries of Europe, the integration of relaxation into psychoanalytical psychotherapy has been elaborated in a particularly interesting way by Julian de Ajuriaguerra.[12] This approach was initially developed to tackle issues that cannot be dealt with in a strict psychoanalytic frame, such as those that can be experienced with borderline and narcissist patients, behavior problems, character disorders, and psychoses. It was also conceived to refine the representations linked to psychosomatic problems.

Body psychotherapists like Gerda Boyesen (1970) and Mona-Lisa Boyesen (1980) have developed methods of relaxation conceived for psychotherapeutic work. These methods are often more dynamic and less mental. They sometimes propose that patient move, jump, and cry before collapsing to the ground and feeling the relaxation induced by the reflux that occurs after a strong physiological mobilization. This makes it possible to involve impatient individuals in the work of relaxation. Gerda and Mona-Lisa Boyesen also use breathing and massage, as well as techniques of guided imagery, to induce a state of relaxation and letting go. What is at stake in these methods is to avoid those forms of relaxation that could be used to reinforce the defenses against the emotions, or the voluntary defenses of the super-ego. The use of relaxation can also allow for the refinement of the perception of vegetative sensations that are an issue for a patient.

> Vignette concerning diabetes and relaxation. *I see a patient who is a brittle diabetic. He complains of often being tense, overexcited, and unable to relax, and consequently exhausted. I discover soon enough that he is unable to distinguish between the sensations of relaxation and the sensations that are activated when he is in a hyperglycemic crisis. Every time he relaxes, he has the impression that he has low blood sugar. Consequently, the feeling of relaxation makes him anxious. I therefore use relaxation and his glucometer to measure the amount of insulin needed to teach him to better distinguish between the two effects.*

The effectiveness of relaxation resides especially in the fact that it often proposes to act at the junction between will and bodily sensations in such a way that the exercise influences the regulators of the organism. This point of entry is central, because it makes it possible to reach, in an intuitive (for the patient) and reassuring way, the profound dynamics of the organism.

12

Organismic Gymnastics: From Elsa Gindler to Moshe Feldenkrais

It is perhaps not too bold to introduce here the idea of thinking in terms of movement as contrasted with thinking in words. Movement-thinking could be considered as a gathering of impressions of happenings in one's own mind, for which nomenclature is lacking. (Rudolf Laban, 1950, *The Mastery of Movement*, Introduction, p. 15)

INTRODUCTION: GYMNASTICS AND ORGANISMIC SYSTEM

The primary goal of gymnastics is the development, maintenance, and care of all of the resources of the body.[1] It consists above all of working on the muscle tone, the fascia and tendons, and the skeletal alignment and the coordination of the segments of the body. But in the background, gymnastics also tries to create exercises that allow the whole of the organism to support the healthy functioning of the body. This generally implies the mobilization of the global physiological systems, behavior (as in throwing a javelin), and psychic resources. This endeavor implies that each dimension of the organism is analyzed and evaluated in terms of its capacity to sustain the activity of the body. This endeavor conflicts with the goals of the psychotherapist when the psychic and behavioral dynamics that enter into a conflict with the exigencies of the body are automatically seen as pathological. There is then, in effect, a reduction in the needs of each dimension of the organism in favor of the needs of a single dimension. That is what often happens in methods that require the soul to harmonize itself with the laws of the body. This enterprise opposes itself to certain ascetic movements that want to reduce the needs of the organism to the exigencies of a spiritual inquiry.

Like the other techniques discussed in this part of the book, all kinds of gymnastics have existed since time out of memory. In Europe, gymnastics was already a refined practice in ancient Greece, closely related to medicine and sports (hallowed today in the Olympic Games). It was part of what the Greek and Roman elite called a complete education: one that related the development of philosophy and the body, according to the adage "mens sana in corpore sano" (a sound mind in a sound body). This relationship is evidently important

290

in those warring nations in which superior military officers had to be skilled tacticians and able combatants.

Even when a gymnast holds a respectful view of the demands of each dimension of the organism, and has engaged in a course of psychotherapy, he necessarily has the atlases of anatomy as his reference model. Alignment, the strengthening of the musculature of the back, the flexibility of the joints, the respiratory movement remain his first goal. It is often useful to consult an expert who knows how to analyze this aspect of the organism. The difficulty lies in situating the impact of this bodily endeavor on the organism. As we have already seen many times, approaching the body necessarily has an impact on all the dimensions of the organism, but evaluating the nature of the impact on the dimensions is complex and varies from one individual to another.

In the following sections, I focus on certain gymnasts and psychotherapists who have particularly influenced the first body psychotherapists. My principal examples are Elsa Gindler and Moshe Feldenkrais. In both cases, we see that their understanding synthesizes a European discussion of their time, concerning the body, with important contributions from Asia. It would seem that in these professions, Asia is revisited differently in each generation. Consequently, students have the impression of learning a technique conceived by the pioneer, when such an individual had a particularly interesting way of synthesizing heterogeneous practices he had learned when young. An analogous phenomenon is found in the schools of psychotherapy. I have chosen two particularly important examples, but the history of the domain of body psychotherapy contains many others that would be interesting to discuss.

The Swedish Gymnastics

In the eighteenth century, Swede Per Henrik Ling (1776–1839) imported from the Turkish Empire (which extended to the China of today, Persia, and Egypt) a new form of gymnastics that had an important influence on the development of European gymnastics. He is generally considered the founder of gymnastics compatible with the goals of orthopedic scientific medicine. This contribution was manifestly part of a new style in the Christian world, greatly influenced by the philosophers of the Age of Enlightenment, who openly integrated Asian knowledge. Its method is inspired by two trends:

1. The methods of the Far East, such as the Turkish gymnastics and Chinese acupuncture.
2. The gymnastics such as it was initially conceived in ancient Greece.

Ling integrated these two trends by relating them to the laws of Galileo's and Newton's mechanics. This analysis from physics of the postural dynamic forms the basis of the *biomechanics* of the physical therapists of today. It consists above all of understanding the influence of muscular contractions and extensions on the skeleton in the gravity field.

Ling shows that it is necessary to have a tight abdomen and an open chest to help the spinal column carry its daily load.[2] His approach relates gymnastics, massage, and diverse forms of mobilization that are used by physical therapists. He also introduced gymnastic equipment, like the ladder. One of his students, Georg Mezger (1838–1909), detailed the massage methods used by Ling that constitute the bases of what became the Swedish massage: *effleurage, kneading, percussion, and vibration.*

Also in Sweden, this movement was pursued by Gustav Zander (1835–1920) who developed methods based on the use of weights and springs capable of making the mobilization of certain bodily structures even more precise.[3] The Swedish gymnastics of that time was principally centered on a differentiated development of the large masses of the body (for example, the thorax, the abdomen, and the back are developed with the use of different exercises), equilibrium and mobility of the segments of the body in the gravity field, straightening the spinal column, and full use of external respiration.

The Organism Reduced to the Needs of Gymnastics

> Psychology works with words. Breathing is a physical experience. Also psychology often elucidates the past, while breath therapy takes place exclusively in the present, because it is grounded in sensory perception. Breath work originates in the physical and influences the soul, whereas in psychology it is the other way around. . . . Breath work and psychology can overlap and be similar, yet they can also interfere with each other. (Ilse Middendorf, 1998, quoted and translated by Thea Rytz, 2009, p. 351f)

From this chapter onward, I approach more directly the way a dimension of the organism mobilizes the other dimensions of the individual system. I distinguish two types of interventions:

1. An intervention that aims mostly at one dimension. This type of gymnastics mostly seeks the development of the musculature.
2. An intervention that intervenes mostly on one dimension to influence the functioning of the organism. I then speak of an organismic endeavor. In the case of gymnastics, I speak of organismic gymnastics.

There are many variations between these two poles. There are, for example, few gymnastics that are not also interested in the external respiration, such that it can be apprehended by the mobilization of the thoracic cage and abdominal muscles. Hatha yoga is not really an organismic gymnastics in the sense that it consists of an approach to the body that is conjointly used with other methods (pranayama, meditation, etc.) that aim at other dimensions of the organism.

Organismic gymnastics attempts to influence the rest of the organism in a direct way. It is thus possible to say that the more a form of gymnastics tries to influence all the dimensions of the organism, without seeking to ally itself with other disciplines, the more it has an organismic ambition.

We can now specify the advantage and the limits of approaching a dimension in an organismic perspective. The advantage of focusing on a single dimension is that it is easier to acquire an expertise on a specific aspect of reality. However, the organism is approached only from one point of view. An organismic gymnastic allows one to study the ways the body interacts with the other dimensions and which contributions from the other dimensions are necessary for its proper functioning. But even an organismic gymnast does not always understand why a person smokes, why certain professions and occupations require postures that are detrimental to the back, and so on. In other words, he has difficulty understanding that the other dimensions have demands that are markedly incompatible with the needs of the body. Here is a summary (somewhat of a caricature but still useful) of the way a classical gymnast situates his work with regard to the organismic dimensions:

1. *Respiration:* It is impossible to move without taking note of the impact of gestures and postures on respiration. Furthermore, a prolonged practice of physical exercises requires managing the tendency to become winded. It is therefore necessary to put gymnastic strategies in place to develop a more powerful respiration. This necessarily implies the rapport between internal respiration and metabolism and certain rules of conduct (to not smoke, to not drink alcohol, to eat healthily, etc.).

2. *The psyche:* A gymnastic exercise requires regular practice to become effective, because it is only at that cost that the tissues of the organism will accept developing as required. Moreover, like the other systems of the organism, only a regular and targeted practice allows for the maintenance of an acquired level. It therefore implies being able to count on the *will* for the regularity of the exercises. A certain degree of attention is also required to ensure that the exercises are carried out correctly. Most of the exercises are only effective if they are carried out in a particular manner; otherwise, they can become dangerous. An exercise practiced too violently can damage the musculature, create some tendinitis, or abuse the spinal column. Finally, to the extent that an exercise must be done a certain number of times, the attention must also be able to count and memorize instructions. Also, a certain capacity to carry out the gestures by imitating a teacher is often needed, which requires a form of discipline and the ability to *listen*.

3. The *affects:* Gymnastics does not seek to satisfy affective needs, but certainly the pleasure of movement and a motivation to exercise are necessary to help the psyche fulfill its role. One of the benefits of gymnastics is to sustain a reinforcement of the feeling of vitality, well-being, and a

tonic relaxation that strengthen the motivation to practice a discipline. A well-carried-out gymnastics session can even induce a euphoric state (notably due to a moderate hyper-oxygenation). This benefit is one of the reasons certain individuals become dependent on their gymnastics sessions like others become dependent on substances. Certain hormonal mobilizations that accompany athletic activities can bring about various forms of dissociation and mobilize neurotransmitters, which can reduce the sensations of anxiety and depression.

4. The *behavioral* dimension: Certain trends in gymnastics insist on the quality (the beauty) of the movements and the way to coordinate the segments of the body, as in dance. Many gymnastic sports, like climbing a rope or high jumping, requires work on the sensory-motor coordination, which implies a capacity to put in place diverse forms of relatively complex coordination.

5. *Physiology:* Finally, many people do gymnastics because it promotes better health and fights obesity. These motives show that gymnastics necessarily has an impact on the physiological regulators and the cleansing of the tissues.

The advantage of this point of view allows others to be able to understand the demands that bodywork imposes on the dimensions of the organism. The psychotherapist can then differentiate the demands the body would like to impose on the psyche from the demands of the psyche.

GINDLER'S BERLIN: HOW TO FIND THE GYMNASTIC ONE NEEDS

Gindler was greatly impressed by Isadora Duncan, the only dancer at that time who was consciously feeling out the effect of gravity on movement—so different from all the other dancers who were fighting the pull of the earth. Isadora Duncan worked with gravity in dance as Gindler did in everyday life. (Charlotte Selver, 1978, letter)

Introduction

Having summarized a few bases of the world of gymnastics, I now jump into the world of Berlin gymnast Elsa Gindler (1885–1961).[4] I use Gindler as a concrete example to open up a discussion about gymnastics and psychotherapy.

Gindler influenced many body psychotherapists either directly or indirectly. By indirectly, I mean that some students learned exercises from an instructor who had learned them from one of Gindler's students. As practitioners often have little historical understanding, they rarely know the origin and the course of what they are learning in a series of programs. For example, an exercise taught by Elsa Gindler was taught to Moshe Feldenkrais, who taught it to one of George Downing's teachers, who then taught it to a student who is today trained in body psychotherapy. This exercise was probably transformed on such a journey, and the last colleague in this chain rarely knows that he does exercise originally designed by Gindler.

An Aestheticization of the Liberation of the Expression of the Soul

One of the great tendencies of European art is to represent gods and heroes as having perfectly balanced bodies. In the nineteenth century, this aesthetic perspective went to extremes in the schools of the academic painters such as Albert Joseph Moore (1841–1893) or Hans Makart (1840–1884), who was one of Gustav Klimt's teachers. In Vienna, different movements influenced by the Academic painters try to represent forms of eroticism, which put into question the habits of the period while remaining extremely stylized. They created a movement called *Jugendstil* (the style of the young), which mixes ideas inspired by Rousseau, Romanticism, and "revolutionary" ideas on society.[5] It was one of the first *youth movements*. For these painters, youth had all the rights because in them the recklessness and genius of nature manifested itself in the most spontaneous way. Like nature, the young want to create without being preoccupied with social conventions.

This new way of speaking of creativity opened up an aesthetic change that above all defended the beautiful and sexually attractive bodies, which guaranteed a part of the commercial success of this movement. The Austrian painter Gustav Klimt, French sculptor Auguste Rodin, and the Californian dancer Isadora Duncan[6] are today the most known representatives of this movement, which began in the 1880s.

Around 1900, this movement became fashionable and influenced *Art Nouveau*, which invaded the world of objects as well as the facades of buildings and graphic design in advertising posters. In dance, Isadora Duncan wore thin veils and ran barefoot on the scene, making apparently natural and spontaneous movements. She left behind the tutus and the classical ballet slippers. Her dance was felt to express a form of beauty associated with *joie de vivre*. This trend rapidly spread into the world of fashion. Already in 1905 in Berlin, women no longer felt obliged to wear corsets. They suddenly dared to publicly wear cotton and linen clothing. Nature, such as it is understood by these movements, is Idealistic to the extent that it is necessarily good and beautiful, healthy and creative. Everything happens as if individuals who are ugly, prudish, or stupid have little contact with this profound nature and inadequately express it. All would have an urgent need to support the only form of existing vitality in a society: youth.

The contact between the forces of nature and social creativity necessarily passes through the flesh, which is situated at the intersection between the appearance of the organism and a form of philosophical depth that permits it to root itself in the dynamics of nature. Richard Shusterman (2008) summarizes this thought well when he speaks of a consciousness born of the flesh, a way of thinking with the flesh, which he calls *somaesthetic*. From this thought rooted in the flesh,the data from the senses, intellectual capacities, and needs of the soul can bloom into new rituals that promote a need to feel alive.[7] This consciousness, nourished by the dynamics of the soma, would permit a form of thought distinct from the intellect and reasoning. This ideology favored the coming of schools centered on the body and the psyche, like Gurdjieff's schools and the Eurhythmy of the Anthroposophy of Rudolf Steiner, the gymnastics like those of Jacques Dalcroze or Elsa Gindler, the dancers of the Russian ballet of Sergei Diaghilev (especially dancer Vaslav Nijinsky), students of choreographer Rudolf Laban, and many others.[8] A leading center for this movement was the Monte Verita school for art, near Ascona, Switzerland, which promoted an ideology that believed in harmonization of spirit, mind, body, sexual genders, and nature.[9] This way of associating flesh, aesthetics, revolutionary politics and spirit form a glowing cloud of representations that manifestly influenced the pioneers who participated in the birth of body psychotherapy. Reich's impression that each one of us is animated by the energy of the galaxies takes up this aesthetic. Similarly, for Alexander Lowen,[10] student of Wilhelm Reich, the consciousness of the body dynamics is the basis on which other forms of consciousness are constructed. It is the consciousness of the respiratory rhythms, the muscular vibrations, the spontaneous involuntary actions, the tingling, and the pulsations of the cardiovascular system. This level of the psyche only becomes explicitly conscious in moments of ecstasy and crisis. An individual then has the impression of being able to identify with the living forces of nature.

The Youth Groups

The age of sexual maturity varies according to the cultures and the epochs. In most of the cultures and in most of the periods in Europe, a person is considered sexually mature as soon as he or she is biologically capable of fathering or giving birth to a child. This was, in most cases, true in the cultures in which the couple was part of an *extended* family that structured the behavior of the adolescents. A well-known example is what the mother of Juliet Capulet says to her thirteen-year-old daughter: "Younger than you here in Verona, ladies of esteem, are made already mothers. By my count I was your mother much upon these years" (Shakespeare, 1595, Romeo and Juliette, I.3.70–80, p. 549). In Europe, only in the nineteenth century was the advent of sexuality clearly dissociated from the idea of adulthood. It is therefore not astonishing that a series of youth movements arose that refused to be disempowered by the emergence of the cultural reforms (often qualified as "bourgeois").[11] After the Viennese *Jugendstill*, analogous movements appeared a bit everywhere in Europe. One of the first to establish itself in Berlin was the group *Wandervogel* (migrating birds). This group was founded by Hermann Hoffmann and was taken up by Karl Fischer in Steglitz, near Berlin. They proposed an education close to nature and as far away as possible from the rigidities of the bourgeoisie and the mannerisms of elegance. This organized movement created youth hostels. Also in 1901, the first

German "Light-Air-Swimming-Bath" opened in Berlin, in which visitors went swimming without bathing suits. Young people aimed to free their body from the stiffness of the Wilhelminian[12] (Victorian) society and from the constraints of industrialization. While the electric train conquered Berlin in the last two decades of the nineteenth century, these people wanted to live in the natural surroundings of fields and woods, which then still separated Berlin from Steglitz.[13] The discipline of this movement wanted to be as far away as possible from military discipline, which was not the case of the Scouts movement, founded in England a few years later by Robert Baden-Powell. In Austria, there were numerous and varied youth movements. Adults who directed these movements were close to psychoanalysis, like Siegfried Benfeld. This connection structured itself especially around projects to improve the sexual education of the young.

These youth movements had a marked influence on a number of intellectuals, like the psychoanalysts Otto Fenichel and Wilhelm Reich, and on some of Gindler's gymnastics students, like Clare Nathansonhn-Fenichel.

The Harmonic Gymnastics

In this tumultuous atmosphere, a movement of reform in gymnastics developed—one that sought to liberate the truth of the soul, emotions, and movement by oscillating between anarchic, socialistic, and spiritual tendencies. This trend aimed to develop a gymnastic compatible with the new principles proposed by artists like Isadora Duncan. These gymnasts refused to use the gymnastic apparatus like those developed by the Swedes. The goal of the approach was to help the students find the gestures they need in accordance with the profound rhythms of their being.

They were invited to undertake this exploration by making felt gestures in a slow and gentle fashion. Even if both men and women attended these courses, this gymnastics aimed at forces that were often associated with women. Emile Jacques-Dalcroze (1865–1950), born in Vienna, had created in Geneva, Switzerland, the Eurythmic method.[14] This gymnastics was less ideologically engaged than others, but it already had the explicit goal of harmonizing the dimensions of the organism by proposing harmonious gestures, while being respectful of the needs of the body, the physiological vitality, and the beauty of the soul. He taught his method in Germany, Russia, and France and collaborated with famous artists of the period, especially in the French-speaking areas of Europe who epitomized what followed Art Nouveau.[15] He worked with Rudolf Laban in Germany. Some students educated in this method joined Elsa Gindler in Berlin.[16] Alexander Lowen, the founder of Bioenergetic analysis, was also educated in the eurythmic method.

In 1911, Elsa Gindler came across a book by Hedwig Kallmeyer on harmonizing gymnastics. Kallmeyer was a German gymnastics teacher who had studied with Genevieve Stebbins in New York and had also studied Calisthenics in England.[17] She discovered in Kallmeyer's book the alpha and the omega of all beautiful movements.[18] She started to study at the Seminar fur Harmonische

Gymanistik (school for harmonizing gymnastics) with Hedwig Kallmeyer in the little village of Steglitz, which later became part of Berlin. It was also the village of the Wandervogel. In spite of the apparent freedom of this work, the teachers were obliged to follow a full-time three-year training program before being recognized.[19] More extremist than Jacques-Dalcroze, these gymnasts refused to impose an exterior rhythm on the students (like a teacher who counts for everyone or imposes some music). Each person had to learn to move by following the rhythm that emanated from her organic depth.

Hanish

The specialists associated with the mind-body axis in the 1930s were influenced by the traditional methods of the Far East (yoga, judo, etc.) but also by masters more difficult to situate, like Ottoman Zar-Abdusht Hanish (1844–1936)[20] and George Ivanovitch Gurdjieff. Their knowledge surpasses what is taught in European yoga schools because they would have been trained by the masters of the Far East, who had taught them knowledge rarely disseminated because it was profound, secret, and delicate to handle. As Europeans, they set about to adapt this knowledge according to what a European or an American is able to integrate. Hanish's influence is above all due to his way of coordinating postural work and breathing exercises. He was a reference not only for gymnasts like Elsa Gindler but also for physical therapists and orthopedists like Andre de Sambucy, in France.

Hanish would have been initiated in Iran into a sort of yoga inspired by two sources:

1. *The sculptures of ancient Egypt.* For Hanish, the positions of the statues of the pharaohs are a model of orthopedically healthy behavior, useful to all those who would take the time to explore them. He relates the postures and the gestures of the Egyptian statues to precise breathing exercises which develop the body as well as its coordination with the development of certain mental faculties.
2. *The wisdom of Zoroaster.* Hanish's teaching claims to resurrect the wisdom of the ancient mazdeen religion of the Persians and the teachings of Zoroaster.

For Hanish, the organism is a complex mix of indirect and direct links between the centers of the organism. This explains in part how his system was able to influence so many schools of mind–body work. Each school could take what was convenient. Here are a few examples:

1. Hanish teaches a list of a few *direct links* between parts of the organism, like the following:

a. There would be some direct links between the feet and the ears that would render the massage of the feet useful for the development of hearing.[21]

b. Thoracic breathing develops the intellect and spirituality, while abdominal breathing develops the body and instinctual impulses. Superficial respiration generates superficial thoughts and deep respiration, deep thoughts.[22]

c. There is a "relationship between supple fingers and a supple mind."[23] Every time that I attended a course in a body/mind discipline, I had access to a list of this type: whether it was in acupuncture, in tai chi chuan, in the Mathias Alexander method, or in Biodynamic psychology. Every time, the list is different, and sometimes contradictory.[24] Every time, the link mentioned seems to have a certain relevance that becomes increasingly vague as soon as I try to organize and define these connections in an explicit way.

2. *The harmonization of the rhythms of the organism.* Hanish systematizes the usefulness of coordinating gesture and respiration. This principle had already been introduced from Turkey by Ling; the description proposed by Hanish is more detailed and explicit.[25] This way to associate gestures to respiratory schemas, as if they form a necessary system for the proper unfolding of an activity, is found in tai chi chuan. We find traces of this way of exploring gesture and breathing in Gindler's and Reich's methods. In all these cases, the association between gesture and breathing is considered a building block to create a rhythm that harmonizes all the dimensions of the organism, which then functions in sync with a profound rhythm of the organism taken as a whole.

3. *The complex particularities of each organism and the necessity to learn to experience oneself from the inside.*[26] For Hanish, the organism is an infinitely complex organization that particularizes itself and draws out numerous intricate associations in the course of a lifetime. As all of the gestures, thoughts, and affects that we carry out have an impact on the general functioning of the organism, no one specialist can understand the exact needs of an organism. It is therefore imperative that each individual develop the feeling that permits him or her to experience the organism from the inside. This "sixth sense" allows us to feel what we are doing and how our internal and external actions relate to one other. It also allows a person to understand how his or her particularities form a particular whole that is one of the many possible manifestations of the living. Therefore, only by learning how to explore oneself from this point of view in a detailed manner can an individual learn to appreciate who he is and develop what can only exist in him. Only in becoming sharply aware of the extraordinary richness of our complexity are we able to begin to appreciate the particularities of others.

The way to feel from the inside is a common aspect among most schools of body psychotherapy and of the humanistic ones, such as Gestalt therapy. It was often transmitted to these schools by some of Elsa Gindler's students.

The Organismic Gymnastic of Gindler

> In the 1920s, the gymnastics teacher Elsa Gindler observed how important proprioceptive awareness training is for well-rounded personal development. The German educator pioneered a paradigm shift, without which many of the approaches that focus on awareness of the body and the mind would be inconceivable today. (Thea Rytz, 2009, *Centered and Connected*, p. 30)

From the Beautiful Gesture to the Gesture That Educates Thought and the Dynamics of the Soul

Elsa Gindler opened her school in Berlin in 1917.[27] She called it Seminar fur Harmonische Korperausbildung (School for the Harmonizing of Body Training). The students and the collaborators of this school were, first, all women. Later on, she conducted courses with men and had male collaborators, of whom the most famous is Heinrich Jacoby (1983). Jacoby explored different forms of music associated to various ways of moving as an educational device.[28] Their collaboration developed into a way to work that is sometimes designated as the Jacoby-Gindler work. Jacoby was greatly interested in psychoanalysis. This was also the case for other students of Gindler, like Clare Nathansohn, who was living with psychoanalyst Otto Fenichel at the time. By 1925,[29] they attract several psychoanalysts to the courses given by Gindler or by some of her students like Laura Perls and Annie Reich.

Gindler became interested in psychoanalysis and advised some of her students to follow a psychoanalytic treatment.[30] But neither Gindler nor her principal students tried to integrate psychoanalysis into Gindler's method or Gindler's method to psychoanalytic work. Elsa Gindler did not interest herself, for example, in the psychoanalytical discourse on the symbolic aspect of muscular tension. For example, she did not take up the analysis of Otto Fenichel (1928), according to which muscular tension is often associated to the retention of anal pleasure or the sensation of an erection.[31] She preferred to concentrate on the analysis of the dysfunctional motor aspects of a movement so that it might be carried out in a more relaxed manner or on the internal sensations activated by a gesture. However, I notice that Gindler gradually included more talking in her courses. She now asks that her students learn to speak of their inner sensations, and tends to spend more time giving verbal explanations. She would have become long-winded at the end of her life. I again take up the discussion on the interaction between her students and psychoanalysis once I have presented the other protagonists related to this encounter.[32]

Elsa Gindler's encounter with Heinrich Jacoby and the young psychoanalysts of the 1920s seems to have helped her refine her teaching. One of the long-term goals of this school was to help the students build themselves up as human beings by taking bodywork as a starting point or a lever to harmonize the dimensions of the organism. It consisted mostly about learning how to feel. A gesture is like a stone that creates circles of waves on the water. By noticing the waves propagating themselves in the organism by a movement, the student learns to discover the gestures that are personally agreeable. An admirer of Hanish, Gindler advised her students to seek first the gesture that liberates their breathing, and then observe what this liberation opens up in the world of their sensations and of their thoughts. When a student is suffering from some illness, the same method is used to discover the chain of gestures, respiration, and sensations that allow for relief. Many of Gindler's students have used her method to relieve various forms of infirmities: invalids, persons with communication problems, children with severe motor problems (going all the way to paralysis), children crippled by polio, and so on.[33]

At the beginning, Gindler's work focused on the beauty of the students' gestures.[34] In 1917, she would demonstrate a gesture and the students would try to make the same gesture. These gestures were beautiful, close to those we could reconstruct by observing the statues of ancient Greece. They ought not only to appear beautiful; it had to be felt as beautiful and evoke feelings of beauty in the student's sensations. Everything a student could experience ought to animate and be animated by this gesture.

At the time of her encounter with psychoanalysts, Elsa Gindler left aesthetics aside and focused on the real organism. She integrated into her approach the parts of the body she had not dared to take on, such as the tensions of the anus. She set about asking her students to discover ways of relaxing it. She also worked on the fork between the legs. After meeting Jacoby, she deepened her way of integrating voice into her work.

Gradually, Gindler began the work of training individuals capable of teaching her work. This more focused work obliged her to be more attentive to the strengths and limits of each person. She began to reflect on what such an individual needed to develop to be able to teach the Gindler method well. She became more demanding and wanted that her future collaborators learn to feel, in as precise a manner as possible, who they were and who they could become. She then focused on what a person can do, what she can conceive of being able to do, and what she refuses to imagine or want. In this teaching process, Elsa Gindler gradually distanced herself from a demand for somatoesthetic experiences to interest herself in a more direct way in the mind–body dynamics of a real person, while continuing to demand that the gestures express an interior truth. This expression of the deep sensation of the being is, for her, necessarily a precise coordination between the qualities of movement, respiration, and body sensations. At the end of a long life, a student could learn to use her sensations as a hand that moves with the glove it wears. A student could have the inner impression of a greater and greater expansion while the members of her body unfolded.

A Gymnastics for Busy Persons

The world of bodywork and psychotherapy is full of brilliant and competent individuals who do not publish, publish little, or write poorly.[35] Their knowledge is transmitted through practice. On the other hand, those who write much and well are not always those who are the best practitioners. Writing demands of them a time to explore the expressions of a practice and thus takes away the very time necessary to continue to explore in practice. Elsa Gindler was one of those practitioners who had many students who were particularly brilliant personalities. She did not publicize her work, but she was recognized by most of the gymnasts and some psychotherapists as a particularly brilliant professional. Her classes were full (between thirty and forty people in her Berlin school before World War II). She only wrote one small article, published in 1926 in the *Journal of the German Federation of Gymnastics,* "Gymnastics for Busy Persons." Wanting absolutely that her students learn to feel what they were doing and discover the gestures that fit, Gindler was wary of manuals or books that imposed a technique.

PERCEIVING A GESTURE FROM THE INSIDE (*TASTEN*)

> Penetration into the mysteries of life is intimately connected with the acquisition of well-defined qualities of the feel of movement. (Laban, *The Mastery of Movement,* 1950, VI, p. 143)

> We see to it that our students do not learn an exercise: rather, the *Gymnastic* exercises are a means by which we attempt to increase intelligence. (Gindler, Gymnastik for People Whose Lives Are Full of Activity, 1926, p. 37)

In her article, Elsa Gindler insists on the fact that her objective is not especially learning gestures but the type of concentration the learning permits. In this way, Gindler hoped to develop a form of intelligence that can only come when movements and thoughts are coordinated in a particular way.[36] The student self-explores when he learns new ways of moving.[37] The student thus develops Hanish's "sixth sense": a way of feeling a movement from the inside and letting movements generate inner sensations. This form of exploration (*tasten* in German) allows for the development of the ability to listen to oneself and others. Body sensations, an imaginative form of curiosity, and a need to discover all that exists within one's organismic space are the building blocks of a particular form of intelligence.

In body psychotherapy, the therapist, for example, asks the patient to associate a feeling to parts of the body and use the movement of these body parts to define the boundaries of this affect.[38] Thus, when the patient complains of feeling a ball of anxiety in the belly, the body psychotherapist may ask him to explore this ball by moving it with his breath or movements of the belly. The therapist may also place his hand on that part of the abdomen and ask the patient to feel from the inside the impact of this touch on the belly and on the ball of anxiety. It often occurs, for example, that this anxiety seems to move to the thoracic region or the throat. The patient learns to follow these internal movements and follow the sensations, images, thoughts (eventually memories), breathing, and movements activated at the occasion of this exploration. This exploration is carried out by associating the awareness of what happens inside the organism with what the teacher perceives from the outside.

Some use a Gindler type of work in psychiatric milieus. Thea Rytz (2009, p. 18f), for example, had a student of Elsa Gindler (Sophie Ludwig) as one of her teachers. She proposes a form of "therapeutic approach to mind-body awareness" to patients who are treated for eating disorders at the University Hospital in Bern, Switzerland.[39] The relevance of this approach is evident as soon as we admit that patients who suffer from eating disorders may have an impoverished awareness of their body. They often need to build up psychological tools for themselves that would permit them to better integrate their body sensations. Thea Rytz's approach has a manifest therapeutic impact on her patients. Yet a number of psychotherapeutic associations ask themselves whether a body–mind therapy can ever be assimilated into the notion of psychotherapy. We are here in an undefined zone of body psychotherapy that would benefit from acquiring a more explicit delineation and institutional recognition.

WORK ON BREATHING

To Each His Own Way of Breathing. Gindler's approach to breathing exercises is a good example of exploration from the inside. She does not teach breathing exercises that everyone must learn. She asks each one to explore their own way of breathing when they hold their breath or release an artificially induced tension. It consists, for example, in becoming conscious that a tension in the shoulders inhibits certain forms of respiration. Once this is felt, the gymnast explores gestures and sensations that make it possible to release this tension in such a way that the previously blocked breath might almost spontaneously find a new space for itself. This work is accompanied with a course in anatomy, on the way the muscles and bones of the shoulders are linked. The student compares the movements a skeleton can make to those that he can carry out. Often, people cannot execute the movements the skeleton can. Gindler continues this work by blindfolding the student and asks the gymnast to explore from the inside what stops her from making certain gestures and to notice the impact this blockage has on her breathing. From the moment when all the members of the class are blindfolded, no one can see how the others are carrying on their exploration, and each must seek his own solution by following a path that is often the only one the gymnast can imagine. The teacher, on the other hand, is able to compare the methods of the students and see which ones have the tendency to seek out the most complicated solutions possible to solve a relatively simple biomechanical problem. The teacher and the students discuss all of this after the exercise.

The Effect of Constriction.   Gindler thinks that there is an automatic connection between gesture and breath that flows from the biomechanics of the body. With most mammals and the young human infant, this connection is activated automatically. But with adult humans, these connections are often inhibited. Education and social customs break up the biological unity of the organism. The gestures lose their spontaneous connections with respiration, and consciousness inserts itself with difficulty into the dynamics of the organism. In this, there is an analogy between two analyses:

1. The muscular tensions stop the joints from making all the movements they are able to make when the musculature is relaxed.
2. The respiratory restrictions create a sort of condensation in the psyche that impedes it from perceiving the sensations of the body. This mist often disappears once respiration has regained its flexibility.

Elsa Gindler therefore attempts to repair the fragmentation that inhibits the dialogue between the dimensions of the organism so the individual might create, for his awareness, an interior space with volume, density, transparency, and flexibility. She remarks, for example, that most of the time, when individual speaks or wants to make a small precise gesture, he blocks his respiration. Among many people, she observes a neck shortened by muscular tension that is already anchored around the diaphragm. This shortening is not functional because as soon as exercises nullify it, the body functions better, respiration becomes deeper, and the individual feels liberated from a constraint and a weight. Gindler refers to this kind of shortening that influences not only the muscles but also the shape of the spinal column and the circulation of air in the throat as a *constriction.*[40] The effect of constriction is an example of the mechanisms that the behavioral dimension imposes on the rest of the organism to guarantee a reliable and controllable integration into crucial social practices, such as professional demands. In the sections on postural dynamics, we will see other examples where the behaviors necessary for the exercise of a profession can encumber blood circulation in a lasting way.[41]

For Elsa Gindler, the crux of what she calls the effect of constriction is situated in what the lungs need to accomplish in deep breathing. It consists of a mechanical and physiological necessity. The four phases of a complete respiration (pause, inhalation, pause, exhalation) do not happen any old way.[42] An apnea ought not to be without life, but instead be a pause between two notes of music that have a function in the development of harmonics. Gindler distinguishes the large and smaller bronchi of the lungs (she does not speak of bronchioles). The air cannot freely enter the lungs if both types of bronchi are not open. Access to the smaller bronchi "is provided by vessels more delicate than hair."

An abrupt and voluntary (and often rapid) inspiration does not mobilize the bronchioles. When an individual voluntarily breathes, he is not listening to the needs of his lungs. He only thinks of the large bronchi. He does not give the bronchioles the time to open up. Filling the lungs ends up being awkward and uncomfortable. A thick sensation forms itself around the sternum; the air accumulates in the large bronchi while the bronchioles remain folded and empty. There is then a conflict between the large bronchi, which fill up while the bronchioles struggle to empty out. Most of those who learn to breathe deeply complain about this conflict, which engenders the impression of constriction and compression, which leads to hyperventilation. However, if one has learned to be on the lookout for the pleasure of breathing, one feels the need of the pulmonary tissues to fully deploy. At the pause at the end of the expiration, the little bronchioles have the time to empty themselves by contracting. At that moment the air can infiltrate space sometimes as fine as a strand of hair. When this movement is allowed to be, complete respiration can unfold comfortably and naturally.

Gindler remained in Berlin during World War II. She did not like Hitler's regime and spent much energy protecting and hiding her Jewish students who had not emigrated (mostly to Israel and the United States). All those students who stayed were ultimately killed.[43] In these circumstances, Johanna Kulbach, who was finally able to leave for the United States, lived through the following situation, related to the effect of constriction.

> Vignette on constriction and fear.[44] *The effect of the work was that I lost the fear. I was very much afraid. They were terrible times; we had bomb attacks and besides that we never knew when we were going to be put in a concentration camp—you never knew. I learned instead of staying in fear, to live in spite of it. That's what I learned. So I got stronger and healthier, instead of really ill, as so many people did. I remember one time we experimented in making a fist and feeling out what it did to us. It was not only the fist that was tight; my stomach was in knots, my breathing was tight—it was total tightness. If you hold this for a while and are aware how tight you are, you yearn for letting go. Gindler kept us at this until I had a good sensation of what it is to be tight.[45] Then slowly, slowly, the fist came open, and I tried to feel what changes happened. For the first time I experienced what it means to change after being afraid. . . . That is what the work is: that you learn to sense where you hold, where living processes are not permitted to function. And when you are aware of the holding—where you are not allowing yourself to function—then it's possible to let it go. But you have to sense it. . . . "(Kulbach, 1977, p. 15)*

According to Gindler, only when the coordination of the phases of the respiratory cycle respects the laws of deep respiration (the integration of the large and small bronchi in a respiratory movement) can the gestures become alive and graceful. Only in working in this way are we able to help people in a state of constriction. If the coordination between gesture and respiration does not respect this requirement of the organism, the work on a gesture can reinforce the constriction instead of dissolving it.[46] This is what often happens when someone runs. The emphasis is then mostly on the in-breath, which leaves little space for an effective exhalation. Learning to run while maintaining a full respiration was part of the exercises Gindler taught.

In her analysis of respiration and of constriction, Gindler demonstrates the necessity to include in gymnastics the development of different forms of the self-awareness of relaxation while the gymnast carries out an exercise. This form of gymnastics has such a profound impact on the coordination of the dimensions of the organism that Gindler's personal students do not talk of gymnastics. They speak of "the work." They do not see how her way of working at the end of her life could be reduced to the notion of gymnastics.[47]

Deep Voluntary Breathing That Leads to States of Constriction and Retraumatization.   In the first decades of the development of breathing exercises in body psychotherapy, (Holotropic breathing, Rebirthing, Bioenergetics, Primal scream, etc.) and in fashionable tantric schools in the 1970s,[48] some practitioners had observed that deep voluntary breathing could quickly bring about euphoric states, leading to spectacular emotional discharges. The observation remains useful and interesting, but in a number of cases, the practitioners did not sufficiently understand the mechanics of respiration. They used these exercises without having enough knowledge to have other options. Having only this kind of technique in their tool box, which often led to crises of tetany, they were not able to adapt these breathing exercises to the needs of everyone. These techniques often provoked various forms of retraumatization by bringing people into states they were not able to integrate into the dynamics of their psyche. They could reinforced the capacity to engender states of constriction.

The respiratory mechanics are relatively complex.[49] Only a slow and regular respiration, one that is not forced, permits a complete participation of the bronchioles. This requires a relaxed glottis in which air can circulate comfortably. Where Elsa Gindler speaks of constriction, Guy Postiaux speaks of the "sequestration of air" (Postiaux, 2003, 6.1.1b, pp. 135f and 153). These negative effects are particularly striking when deep breathing exercises are conducted with infants less than a year old. When working with the breathing of small children, it is particularly manifest that the forced exhalation mobilizes the fluids in the bronchi, which provoke the coughing that seeks to decongest the bronchi[50] and a closure of the glottis. In yoga as in Gindler's work, the alliance of attention and respiration permits the air to have a global impact on the functioning of the organism. Being on the lookout for the discomfort felt at the occasion of a breathing exercise and by abstaining from encouraging patients to go beyond their psychic and organic limits, the body psychotherapist can prevent the activation of constrictions.

RELAXATION IN GINDLER'S WORK

For Elsa Gindler, relaxation is not one of the disconnections experienced as sleep approaches or of a hypnotic dissociation. On the contrary, a state of apparent internal immobility renders the individual capable of responding to everything that is going on. The mind is transparent, actively trying to perceive all that is happening without any deformation. Gindler had been able to observe this state in individuals who held important responsible positions in business or in politics (the "busy people" in the title of her article)

> It is a stillness within us, a readiness to respond appropriately to any stimulus. . . . We hear that top businessmen often remain utterly motionless for a moment while directing all their senses inward. Then, suddenly, they seem to awaken and make decision that are uniquely right. It is clear that in this moment of being in themselves relaxation has taken place. (Elsa Gindler, 1926, p. 40)

FROM GURDJIEFF TO FELDENKRAIS

The approaches influenced by Isadora Duncan and Elsa Gindler are attempts to increase harmony and coherence. They are influenced by Plato's *Symposium*. For Heraclitus, harmonizing elements mostly creates coherence at the level you are working on. If you want to harmonize deeper levels of reality, you sometimes need to create frictions and dissonances at the level of perceivable phenomena. An example of such an approach was taught in Gurdjieff's school. One can also find traces of this way of thinking in the approach proposed by Feldenkrais, who was inspired by Gindler, martial arts, and contemporary orthopedics. His body–mind approach is yet another way of developing one's mind by helping it refine awareness of postural dynamics.

Gurdjieff: Exploring Gestures that Educate and Calibrate Organismic Regulation Systems

> You have to bake bread. For this you must first of all prepare the dough. But to make dough you must take definite proportions of flour and water. If there is too little water, you will get, instead of dough, something that will crumble at first touch. If you take too much water, you will simply get a mash, such as it is used for feeding cattle. It is the same in either case. You will not get the dough necessary for baking bread.
>
> The same thing occurs in the formation of every substance necessary for the organism. The parts composing these substances must be combined in strict proportions, both qualitatively and quantitatively.
>
> When you breathe in the ordinary way, you breathe mechanically. The organism, without you, takes from the air the quantity of substances that it needs. The lungs are so constructed that they are accustomed to work with a definite amount of air. But if you increase the amount of air, the composition of what passes

through the lungs is changed, and the further inner processes of mixing and balancing must also inevitably be changed.

Without the knowledge of the fundamental laws of breathing in all particulars, the practice of artificial breathing must inevitably lead, very slowly but nonetheless surely, to self-destruction. (Gurdjieff, 1960, *Meetings with Remarkable Men*, VIII. p. 187[51])

Georges Ivanovitch Gurdjieff (1866–1949) (1960, 1978)[52] is one of those masters who is difficult to situate and who influenced the body psychotherapeutic thinking of the twentieth century.[53] Like Hanish, he "translated" the knowledge of the wise men from the Far East into a language available to Westerners. Gurdjieff studied with masters, mostly Sufi, in the regions that extend from China, the Gobi Desert, Russia, and Turkey.[54] He then attempted to create a useful way to teach the knowledge of his masters in Moscow (Russia), Tiflis (Georgia), then France (Fontainebleau and Paris), and the United States. His thought rejoins the movements about which I have just spoken, movements that wanted to create a new man in Europe, liberated from the irrational constraints imposed by the traditional morality of the day. Gurdjieff influenced many personalities who work with the body in disciplines as diverse as dance (from Isadora Duncan to Maurice Bejart), theater (from Arthur Gordon Craig to Bob Wilson and Peter Brook[55]), gymnastics (Jacques Dalcroze and Sophrology[56]), and even fashion (for example, Coco Chanel). His influence on body psychotherapy is mostly indirect.[57] I content myself to extract from the publications of Gurdjieff and Ouspensky a few useful points to understand certain aspects of the organismic gymnastics of the twentieth century that can become useful for body psychotherapists.

Certain of Gurdjieff's students continue to work with personalities from the East (Sufis, Turks, yogi from India, Chinese tai chi chuan masters, etc.).[58] They sometimes spend a lot of time learning what these personalities are willing to teach them with as much meticulousness and respect as possible, all the while questioning themselves on the impact of disciplines heavily anchored in one culture and exported into another cultural context. A European is not able to learn and integrate tai chi chuan as does a Chinese; what is good for one is not good always good for the other. One of the first students, Piotr Demianovitch Ouspensky (1949), developed a particularly clear language with regard to Gurdjieff's first formulations, when he was still teaching in Russia.

Gurdjieff's techniques and models were taught in a school.[59] Only part of his teaching is available for those who do not belong to a Gurdjieff school. Since I have not participated in any Gurdjieff workshop, I limit myself to select notions that I have learned of this movement that may be useful for body psychotherapeutic work. I am not always able to provide clear references, as some writings were discussed with me by members of a Gurdjieff school without being available to the noninitiate. Other aspects are taught through practical exercises that cannot be described in a written text. It is assumed that the exercises can be dangerous when they are not taught in a proper context.[60]

A vignette on the simplistic interventions that sometimes do more harm than good.[61] *It consisted of a beautiful passage in which one of Gurdjieff's Sufi masters, Ekim Bey, ridicules those who follow the schools of yoga that propose eating regimens and obligatory breathing techniques poorly adapted to a European lifestyle. For this master, a vegetarian regime and standard breathing exercises have a profound influence on the coordination between psyche, physiology, and metabolism. When they are not properly utilized, these techniques can have a harmful effect on the organism. In effect, the coordination of the dynamics of the organism is so complex that it requires a prudent approach, particularly adapted to the particular needs of each person. According to this master, an organism is an amalgam of millions of chemical activities. To propose a standard selection of foods or a specific way to breathe necessarily has unforeseeable impact on this complexity. Thus, to fully chew every mouthful before swallowing deprives the muscles of the digestive tract of their necessary exercise. This injunction to chew well is therefore useful for individuals who have some digestive problems, like some elderly people; but if followed by younger people, chewing everything as much as possible prevents a proper calibration of the chemical and physical processes of digestion.*

The Rapport between the Dimensions of the Organism Needs Tension As Well As Harmony

In the sections dedicated to Plato's Idealism, I evoked the idea that a human being ought to seek to harmonize fire and water as well as the whole of the heteroclite mechanisms of the organism. The physician *Eryximachus*, a character in Plato's *Symposium*, thought that all sicknesses came about when a disharmony installed itself into the forces of the organism. I then showed that philosophers like Heraclitus thought differently. For them, the disharmony between the mechanisms of an organism, or between the members of a society, is what permits a system to surpass itself and find a profound harmony. Gurdjieff is one of the rare authors I know who inspires himself as much from Heraclitus as from Plato and Pythagoras in his approach to an individual. Thus, Gurdjieff shows that certain experiences like a shock, startle responses, or friction between centers of the organism, can have the beneficial effect of waking someone up. An incident of panic affecting set modes of functioning sometimes allows for a profound modification of the individual's organism.[62] Gurdjieff's way of speaking about frictions, it seems to me, is a useful metaphor to help readers imagine something other than Plato's proposition and to learn to play, in a creative fashion, with the heterogeneity of the regulators of thought and of the whole organism.[63]

CHARGE, TENSION, AND FRICTION GENERATES AS A SOURCE OF LIFE

In this section, it is my intent to show that working on polarizing heterogeneous mechanisms can be creative. Two metaphors summarize this point:

1. In striking two flint stones against one another, humans changed the course of their history because they learned how to master fire. This dis-

covery, and everything that flows from it, allowed the human species to increase, to a considerable extent, the quantity of energy at their disposal and develop technologies hitherto unimaginable.

2. In electricity, it is the opposition between the positive and the negative pole that allows for the creation of an electric field. The greater the difference in potential, the greater the available electric charge. Once again, the mastery of this phenomenon creates an increase in energetic resources and spectacular technologies.

In the last example, it is evident that a polarization follows laws that should be understood; too great a difference in a polarity can create a short-circuit capable of starting a fire. It is the same when this notion is used for work on oneself. That is why it is always recommended to proceed with caution. This danger exists with all the effective therapeutic techniques. A scalpel must be extremely sharp to be of use to the surgeon. However, when it is used inappropriately, it can create significant damage. The same is true for taking potent medications. Taking more medication than prescribed is a common way of committing suicide. In talking about the physiological bases of stress, we have seen that the mechanisms conceived to promote the survival of the organism could also destroy the organism when they are overstimulated.

THE HETEROGENEITY OF THE CENTERS OF THE ORGANISM
Gurdjieff's teaching is similar to yoga when it proposes work on the organismic system from a reflection on the way the dimensions of the organism differentiate and coordinate. Gurdjieff speaks of *centers* around which a set of automatic reactions organize in a relatively independent fashion.[64] These centers somewhat resemble the Hindu chakras.[65] According to Gurdjieff, for most people, these centers have not received an appropriate education. They are underutilized and poorly used. To develop the latent possibilities that sleep within him, the student attempts to calibrate the functioning of each center by a regular practice that seeks to transform and develop these centers and ameliorate their coordination.

Gurdjieff identifies three main centers: the intellectual, the emotional, and the motor centers. Each one of these centers is composed of subcenters that also function relatively independently from each other. They generally fulfill, somewhat automatically, functions that are proper to them. Most of these centers generally function in association with other centers. For example, to influence the behavior of the organism, the sexual center needs to associate itself to the intellectual, emotional, and motor centers. These centers function like different brains: "The activity of the human machine . . . is regulated, not by one, but by many brains, entirely independent one from the other, having distinct functions, and distinct domains of manifestations" (Ouspensky, 1949, III, p. 89, translated by Marcel Duclos).[66] Each center has a particular functioning, energetic modality, and type of food. The intellect does not nourish itself from the same stimulations as the motor and instinctive centers. The organism thus requires a variety of inputs, such as matter, air, and impressions. Nutritional and sexual activities are associated to different forms of pleasure. There is dysfunction when one center dips into the energy of another. Thus, many centers dip into the energy of the sexual center, which overflows with energy. This creates *useless excitations* in the functioning of the emotional, intellectual, and body dynamics, which impoverishes the sexual center. In a concrete way, this implies that each student learns to recognize, through self-observation, how one of his inner dynamics relates to which centers and which ways of acting are associated to them. He then learns to identify his practices more clearly. Each center functions at a different speed:

1. Imagination passes more rapidly from one impression to another than does the body from one posture to another. It takes less than a second to imagine being on another planet, whereas the body need an epic social process to travel that distance.
2. Once an acquired knowledge has become a set of automatic skills, these skills function much faster and manage more complexity than what consciousness can grasp.
3. An organism can survive days without food, but it cannot withstand being deprived of impressions for one hour.[67]

If the intellect can be experienced as a rapid and incessant flow of impressions, the capacity to understand is something that functions more slowly. To perceive impressions and be able to understand activates different dynamics of the intellect. This is particularly clear if, as I have often showed in this book, the understanding of a phenomenon is a collective work that could have taken thousands of years. This capacity is different than the one that allows for the assimilation of a current thought.

What we find of these ideas in the writings of Moshe Feldenkrais and George Downing, of whom I speak later, is the observation that the motor functions often act without the mind being aware of what is afoot. Everything happens as if the motor, affective, and mental centers were each activated by a different organization. The interaction between the mental and the motor dynamics often seem fortuitous and generally require a particular attention (an exhausting one) to get along. This analysis becomes particularly evident when I describe the video analysis of nonverbal behavior at the end of the book.

Becoming Able to Be Who We Are

Gurdjieff regularly distinguishes between the ordinary man and the man who has given himself the means to become who he "really" is.[68] With the ordinary man, the centers function automatically and are mostly organized by reflex mechanisms. His centers are insufficiently (a) utilized, (b) mobilized, (c) nourished, (d) educated, and (e) poorly integrated into the functioning of the organism. For Gurdjieff, most people do not really know who they are, what they want, and where they are going. They are not within themselves.

Everyone can sing or throw a punch. However, even among the most gifted, these skills must be honed through training if an individual wants to master them and transform them into effective tools. Even a function as instinctive as sexual activity requires a long practice before becoming associated to the dimensions of the organism in such a way as to reach an organismic and relational functioning capable of promoting satisfaction. The goal of Gurdjieff's teaching brings us back to Plato's metaphor of the charioteer.[69]

In Plato's fable, the human soul is the driver of a chariot drawn by a team of two horses: a white one and a black one. This scene describes the soul. The white horse represents that aspect of the soul that wants to rise to the world of Ideas. The black horse represents the aspect that wants to descend into the material world. The chariot is the envelope of the soul—the body—and the driver is the part of the soul that can direct the chariot. A soul can be more or less well integrated in the psyche of the driver. The mind often panics because it is not able to manage both mounts.

Gurdjieff proposes a similar metaphor, but one that details more explicitly the difference between the soul, the intellect, the passions, and the body. His central idea is that his teaching allows a soul to provide an aim to his organism, whereas most of the time it is a pile of disorganized activities of the reflexes. It is the intent of Gurdjieff's program is to give to the psyche the force to gain control over the chaotic structure of the organism and permit a reorganization of the centers and the way they relate. Once this work is accomplished, an individual is able to identify with the forces of his organism and become profoundly who he is. This metaphor can be summarized in the following vignette.[70]

> Vignette on the coach metaphor. *The normal man is like a carriage (the mechanics of the body) drawn by two horses (the feelings) lead by a coachman (the intellect). The coachman is not stupid because he knows how to read and count, and he knows the laws of the country and can find his way to an address. But this mind is a heap of mental habits that allow him to find clients, who all of a sudden, give him a direction, a route. The horses have been ill cared for and poorly fed (only straw from early on in life). They are collapsed in on themselves. Even the coach is badly maintained by a coachman who does not understand his equipment. Described in this manner, the human being is a kind of disarticulated clown and relatively impotent.*

Typically, the coach obeys the orders of the many clients who impose their authority at various moments. Gurdjieff's aim is to form a deeper self that can take care of all the parts of an individual system in a coherent way. In differentiating the intelligence of the coachman from that of the person who stepped into the carriage, Gurdjieff differentiates (more explicitly than Plato) the intellect and the soul. Only the soul can verify the well-being of each center of the organism (well-treated horses, well-oiled carriage, a relevant and well-trained intellect, etc.) and find a direction that promotes the coordination of the centers of the organism. Once the organism is actively inhabited, it can at last potentiate its gifts in a way that makes sense. Like Socrates, this soul is what Gurdjieff attempts to activate with his method. This is an elitist method, like that of Plato's, because it separates those carriages that have an occupant from the others. But this does not prevent it from being relevant.

Gurdjieff, just like Fodor (2000), accepts the theories of Hume and Darwin and their implications for all of the parts of the organism that function automatically. The challenge that the spiritual movements pose to the scientific theories is that it is possible to create a context that permits something to emerge in the middle of this chaotic assemblage that is an organism so that something might emerge and crystallize in the form of what the ancients called a soul. This context requires a collective endeavor in which the particular essence of an individual can blossom like a flower out of its bud.

Movement As a Way to Educate an Individual

> These Movements have a double aim. By requiring a quality of attention on several parts at the same time, they help us to get out of the narrow circle of our automatism. And through a strict succession of attitudes, they lead us to a new possibility of thinking, feeling and action. (Jeanne de Salzmann, 2010, *The Reality of Being*, 57, p. 121f)

THE QUALITY OF ATTENTION

The "normal" man often focuses his attention in a rather hazy and unsustained manner. When an individual observes himself attentively, he inevitably notices that the concentration time rarely lasts more than a few minutes. Gurdjieff used many methods to develop the duration and the quality of attention. They often consisted of exercises or dances[71] that mobilized the relationship between the intellect and the diverse centers of the organism. The pupil then learned to increase the length of time during which he could concentrate, the number of elements on which he could concentrate at the same time, and the precision of awareness. He also learned to clean up his sense of observation of the prejudices and his encumbering expectations. One typical exercise is to walk at a certain speed on a street full of pedestrians and count the number of women who are wearing red. Another is to make a brisk movement with one arm and a slow, gentle one with the other. This second type of exercise is similar to the kind used by a pianist who must play differently with each hand. To be capable of being attentive to several events at the same time and different points of view (cognition, affect, sensations, etc.), is one of the goals sought by Gurdjieff's students. A good pianist plays different notes with each hand, but he can also create a different mood with each hand when it is called for. The student thus learns to feel that each of his centers reacts to a given event with a particular point of view.

Once he really comes to feel this, he can learn to consciously coordinate most of the points of view with which his organism experiences a singular event.

THE QUALITY OF ATTENTION MEASURED BY A GESTURE

Vignette showing how a gesture allows for the observation of the duration of attention. *Take a simple exercise: ask yourself to raise and lower your arms exactly the same way 100 times. Someone in the room can verify the exactness of your count. If your attention is not trained for this type of task, you will not be able to accomplish this gesture exactly 100 times in a row. You will improve if you practice over and over again. Typically, this is what happens: At the beginning you have no problem. But as soon as you perform this gesture for, say, the thirtieth time, you think of something else. You think that you are executing an exercise, which is too easy for you, very well; and the individual suggesting this exercise to you must think you more stupid than you are; or you think of what is waiting for you at home; or you are thinking of the last film you saw, and so on. In short, you forgot to keep on counting. You therefore pick a number at random, forty for example, and you begin to count again. Because of this momentary inattention, you end up having completed this movement approximately but not exactly 100 times. Irritated with yourself, you begin the exercise over; once again, your count will be interrupted at least once by other considerations that will interfere with your consciousness without you really knowing why. You will invent many explanations, for example, that it is impossible to remain attentive when an exercise is so boring or so lacking in motivation. There is also a strong chance you will feel irritated because you were not able to complete such a stupid task. This type of exercise allows us to see that attention is a difficult mental tool to manage. Few people recognize the weakness of their attention when it has not been developed.*

Now consider another example that permits us to go a little further concerning what the observations of an individual's gestures teaches us about his mental attention. For this, I take a typical lesson in tai chi chuan carried out in slow motion. (I have briefly described this discipline in the chapters dedicated to the Chinese martial arts.) The situation I propose is for you to imagine yourself as a beginning student who is observing a tai chi master demonstrating a movement. From the point of view of your conscious perception, the master's gestures are relatively simple and hardly acrobatic. You have the impression of perceiving each element of the moving posture being demonstrated. The master asks you to repeat the movement you have just seen. To help you, he does it with you. If he is a good teacher, he repeats it exactly the same way as many times as you want. Doing this requires a rare quality of attention. Typically, you repeat this exercise, somewhat proud of having done it well, but conscious that your imitation is only a close approximation. If a third person compares what you have just done with the movement of the master, he will see that the difference is, in fact, enormous. If the scene was filmed, you would soon be made aware of the difference. The distance between the hands and the torso, the distribution of the weight on the feet, the fact that the *impulse* of the gesture originates from the feet and from the pelvis are things that, typically, the beginner does not perceive. The student soon notices that he is able to concentrate on only two or three parts of the body at the same time, while there are many variables to integrate to complete a movement correctly. The master knows from experience that it will take years of regular work to be able to imitate, with sufficiently adequate precision, what he has just demonstrated to you. Given that tai chi is a sequence composed of around 100 global body movements, the student is confronted not only by the limits of his attention but also by the limits of his memory.

We have to accept that there exists a kind of memory of the gesture that does not function like memory through visual representation. After having followed many courses and having practiced at home, some gestures and even entire sequences become motor habits. After a certain amount of time (months and even years for some people), the student gains the ability to carry out the entire sequence with relative accuracy on automatic pilot—that is, thinking of other things most of the time, like the driver of an automobile. But the teacher sees this right away because the motor centers deform the gestures to assimilate them. They create automatic dynamics that produce mechanical gestures that do not have the postural structure mobilized by the master. The student must then learn to coordinate his mental memory and his motor memory to execute his form of tai chi with greater precision.

This is an example of the usefulness of the notion of centers such as Gurdjieff conceives them. It consists in training the motor and intellectual centers at the same time and the way they are coordinated. In tai chi, this coordination requires certain coordination between motor activity, respiration, and mental activity. This makes things even more difficult to follow with a mental attention that can incorporate only a few elements at the same time. Furthermore, we must take into account the fact that tai chi is, before anything else, a martial art, and that each position has a function in combat. Finally, mental attention must also integrate a listening to what the Chinese call the chi, which is, according to a rudimentary simplification, the internal force from which all of the centers of the organism are organized. This is just the beginning of tai chi. In effect, tai chi is a martial art. In combat, it is executed with a speed and sense of purpose aimed at vanquishing the opponent.

For many years, I followed such training with Lizelle Reymond and her students. She was often amused by the countless distorted faces we made when we concentrated (tongues licking lips, frowns worthy of a horror film, a strained and pale face, etc.). This is a good example of the *useless stimulations* we ceaselessly mobilize. Films of the great violinist Yehudi Menuhin show us that his face is practically immobile, even when he is playing heartbreaking melodies. Everything that artists like him have to give to us is expressed in the music produced by their handling of the instrument. On the other hand, among excellent musicians of a lesser talent, probably because they must presently accommodate the exigencies of the visual media, emotional expressions burst forth in all directions and their music is often less expressive. Everything happens as if each facial expression takes something away from the attention focused on the violin and its sound.

As we have already seen with Elsa Gindler, these methods aspire to develop the intelligence of each person by integrating different forms of intelligence: like the intelligence that guides movements, the intelligence that guides the affects, the intelligence that guides the senses, and so on. The theories proposed by the schools inspired by Gurdjieff are debatable, but it seems that the few elements I have singled out indicate that many aspects of this approach are worthy of more attention on the part of psychologists and psychotherapists.

Feldenkrais

Moshe Feldenkrais (1904–1984) was born on the May 6, 1904, in Slavuta, Ukraine. He was interested in Japanese martial arts from the age of fourteen. He involved himself in the creation of a Jewish state in Palestine. In 1930, in Paris, he became an engineering student and studied physics. At the same time, he enhanced his practice of judo to treat an injured knee. He joined the English army during World War II. While working as an engineer, he developed his method of bodywork. His central idea seems to be that developing the dynamics of the body necessarily mobilizes the development of the others dimensions of the organism. Only then can a person acquire greater *maturity.*

Feldenkrais's method was established by 1949. It integrates different skills from judo, Matthias Alexander, Gindler, William Bates, and maybe Gurdjieff. He obtained his knowledge of Gindler's method from a meeting with Heinrich Jacoby.[72] He retains from this encounter the necessity to let his students learn to explore, feel, and discover how their organism needs to develop.

Feldenkrais's method includes a particularly refined analysis of the alignment of the body in the gravity field and the automatic habits an organism forges for itself. He uses these automatic procedures like a trampoline, a spring that can take other forms when it loses its tension. The individual can use this force to transform himself and build useful automatic habits he had not yet acquired but needs. Feldenkrais thinks the organism needs habits to function, but once put in place, they are difficult to recalibrate. An individual's innate and acquired habits are not always constructive or synergistically put together in the present context.

Feldenkrais is known mostly for his work on the re-calibration of sensory-motor and respiratory habits. For him, this implies a reconstruction of the way an individual thinks about and experiences his postural alignment, respiration, gestures, and affects. By learning to integrate these forces, the individual can develop his intelligence and acquire greater maturity. Feldenkrais's method is taught all over the world. It has inspired the bodywork of several body psychotherapists in the United States, such as Jerry Kogan, Ron Kurtz,[73] and George Downing.[74] I briefly summarize some aspects of his system, which takes up themes discussed in other parts of this manual.

A Modular Organism That Seeks Its Coherence and Maturity
Feldenkrais situates his method between two poles:[75]

1. The methods showing that the *mind influences the functioning of the organism:* hypnosis, autosuggestion, psychoanalysis, and so on.
2. The methods showing that *bodywork is able to ameliorate mental equilibrium:* yoga, martial arts, relaxation, breathing methods, certain schools of dance, and so on.

According to him, these two types of approaches have helped many people, but neither can help everyone. To combine them, he proposes an organismic approach that sometimes reminds one of Gurdjieff's formulations. For example, when he distinguishes distinct centers:[76]

1. The *vegetative mechanisms.* These are the most ancient mechanisms of the organism from the point of view of the theory of evolution.
2. *Reflexes and automatic habits.* The automatic sensorimotor habits are ancient, and they have a form of reliable and robust calibration when the demands of the environment correspond to what they know to do.
3. *Consciousness.* The mental dynamics are more recent and more subtle but also slower than habitual behaviors and emotional reactions. These dynamics are so flexible that it is often difficult to know in advance to which thoughts and behaviors they will lead.

As in Lamarck's and MacLean's models, these three centers correspond to levels of the nervous system that formed at different moments in the course of evolution, and therefore have distinct modes of functioning. Each center can function in parallel in a relatively independent way. Thus, some automatic behaviors set up without the knowledge of consciousness may automatically recruit certain conscious mechanisms.[77]

Like Gindler, Feldenkrais (1949, p. 13) explores a "sixth sense" that can develop when an individual has refined his ability to perceive his body. For Feldenkrais, the sixth sense organizes itself around the kinesthetic perception, as when one attempts to evaluate the weight of an object without a scale, eyes closed. Another example on the usefulness of developing this sixth sense is his work on certain affects, like fear. According to Feldenkrais,[78] an affect is necessarily a form of nonconscious coordination between the sensory, intellectual, and somatic domains. A readjustment of an individual's affective life therefore necessarily implies work that combines interventions on all these dimensions. He does not believe an individual who is blocked regarding the alignment of the segments, muscle tone, respiration, and intellectual capacities would have the resources required to integrate his affective dynamics. Feldenkrais also thinks an individual must recover the entirety of his fundamental postural repertoire to find a kind of maturity. He voluntarily admits that certain parts of the body are more important than others, that certain forms of connections between the dynamics of the organism are particularly relevant for an individual's maturation. This allows him to accomplish remarkable work with some physically disabled people. Even a person who has lost a leg can mobilize some postural dynamics that lengthen tendons, awaken motor cells, activate rarely used brain circuits, realign available segments of the body, and so on.

In his teaching, Feldenkrais (1980) uses his hands to help an individual feel how the segments of his body ought to be aligned in the gravity field. He begins by coordinating the alignment of the head and the shoulders in coordination with the breath; then he descends toward the feet. When possible, he works with a person thirty to forty times on successive days, in individual or in group sessions, then less frequently according to what is happening in the patient's organism. Once again, we find the idea that the functioning of an organism cannot change unless it learns new practices on a regular basis. An apprenticeship is a matter not only of consciousness but also of motor activity and nervous and physiological systems. It also needs the support of an external expert presence. Doing it alone with a book or a DVD is never enough.

Like Gurdjieff, Feldenkrais became an advocate and practitioner of a modular and parallel approach before this position became fashionable. He freely admitted that each organism is composed of heteroclite mechanisms that simultaneously impose different requirements on each organism. But like most engineers of his generation, he still used the classical causal system. Each center interacts in a direct fashion, like the sequential movements of billiard balls.

The Affective Reactions

To become activated, the readjustments of the body effected by Feldenkrais's method must ally themselves with the mental and affective dynamics of the person. This work can only be accomplished with people who accept opening themselves up to modes of emotional functioning that are relatively spontaneous and expressive.[79] This seems to go on by itself when we admit that a feeling is formed by nonconscious mechanisms that animate the body and the mind. That is why it can happen that a feeling sometimes expresses itself through a motor expression, visible to another, without the individual having any conscious awareness of the event. Once this form of reaction has become coconscious, it can more easily find its place in conscious dynamics.

Like many people who were skilled in gymnastics, Feldenkrais (1980) assumed that there exists only one healthy and normal functioning. This functioning serves as the reference point to evaluate everything that functions differently. A spine should have a certain curvature or it is sickly and deformed. The criterion Feldenkrais adopted to assess the healthy way to move is close to that used in the martial arts: a gesture functions normally when it is executed with the least amount of energy possible. I have already showed that this economy is only observed with people who have followed a regular physical training. For him, an "I" begins to exist only once the individual can clearly differentiate the signals created by the organism from those that come from the environment (space, gravity, and the social dynamics).

One of the things Feldenkrais did remarkably well was to exploit the existing systems of the organism and support their capacity to readjust. Consider the case of a chronic startle reflex, which shortens the extensor muscles.[80] It sometimes suffices to increase this chronic tension and these elastics, which are the muscles, will be inclined to stretch and return to their place of origin. He can thus contact the natural propensions of muscles, and then help them to readjust themselves spontaneously. This is, for example, what he does when he works on the organism's need for orgasm. For Feldenkrais, the orgasm, as a reaction, is composed of different sensorimotor mechanisms and innate affects. Like Reich but with greater finesse, Feldenkrais[81] describes the biomechanics of the orgasm like a type of reaction that constitutes itself spontaneously if the individual only lets the different centers of the organism become activated without inhibiting them. The reflexes that manage the movements of the pelvis, its rhythm, and its coordination with the pelvic movements of the partner function even if the nerves of the spinal column at the dorsal levels are sectioned off. This observation suggests that the relevant centers of the brain are activated in parallel, simultaneously, in a modular fashion during coitus. Some people have the anxious impression of falling when a startle reflex blocks the orgasmic reflex. This feeling would come from the fact that the conflict between the anxiety circuit and the orgasm reaction activates nervous mechanisms that influence the equilibrium centers situated in the ears.[82] Feldenkrais's analysis indicates that an affective act like coitus is a coordination of specific modular practices that are situated in all of the dimensions of the organism. That is why, for Feldenkrais as with Reich, only individuals who are physically mature (muscles and respiration function well), affectively mature (enjoy a sexual relationship), and mentally mature (have a moral framework that permits agreeable sexual relations) are able to live a satisfactory orgasmic sexuality. Feldenkrais shows how frustration causes an impoverishment in the quality of the tissues, the muscles, respiration, and flexibility (and thus of the postural repertoire), while reinforcing the neurological and hormonal circuit that set in place the circuits of stress and anxiety.

The work of Feldenkrais is often used by those body psychotherapists who are not particularly Reichians and who want to have modes of body intervention at their disposal that are more precise and effective than those developed by orthodox Reichians. However, Feldenkrais's vision is different from psychotherapy's vision. Consequently, it is difficult to integrate the two approaches.

13

The Postural Dynamics

The Awareness of my body is not the awareness of an isolated entity or "block," it corresponds instead to the knowledge of a postural schema, it is the perception of my body's position in relation to the vertical, the horizontal, and to certain important axes of the environment's coordinates in which my body is embedded. (Maurice Merleau-Ponty, 1967, *Les relations avec autrui chez l'enfant* [*Relating to Others during Childhood*], p. 23, translated in Rochat, 2010)

INTRODUCTION: THE POSTURE AS AN INTERFACE
BETWEEN THE ORGANISM AND ITS SOCIAL ECOLOGY

Up to now, I have described the organism as a *closed system*, a system of diverse dimensions that interact with each other in different ways. Such an approach of the individual is often useful during a body psychotherapy session. I have already showed in many places that the organism is in fact an *open system*. It is regulated by internal and external exigencies at the same time. The body psychotherapist must often switch from one vision to another. At one moment he needs to focus on how dimensions interact within the organism, and then on how dimensions interact with the external environment of a patient. The postural dynamics model that I describe can be used when one needs to coordinate these points of views.

To open this discussion, I show how three dimensions of the organism can be discussed when they are considered a subsystem of an open system:

1. *Thoughts.* I know of no one who would be able to specify which aspects of his thoughts are uniquely influenced by his system of intra-organismic regulation and which aspects are uniquely influenced by other persons. The mixture is total. Even my dreams can use personages from a film I have seen to convey to my awareness a profound and intimate need.
2. *Behavior.* Ethologists[1] attempt to extract from the behavioral repertoire of human behavior those gestures that would have had their roots in the phylogenetic history; sociologists[2] show how behaviors are structured according to precise cultural variables.

3. *Metabolism.* Even the mechanisms as profoundly anchored in the organism as the metabolic activity is influenced by the quality of the air and food that enters into the organism.

In each of these cases, we observe the following factors:

1. *The influence of the environment on a dimension* then influences the way a dimension interacts with the rest of the organism. Thus, the risk of losing one's job can create thoughts that awaken the physiological circuits of stress.
2. *The functioning of a dimension can influence the functioning of its environment.* Thus, my thoughts and my affects can influence how I am going to vote. My health problems can make me vote for a political party that supports health care facilities that are open to all.
3. Once we admit that each dimension serves as an interface between the organism and the environment, it becomes evident that each dimension has its own way of accomplishing its interface function. It is not the same mechanisms or procedures that mix the thoughts forged by the metabolic exigencies, by society, the phylogenetically built behaviors and behaviors needed for a good social insertion. In these two cases, the mixture is not only possible but also necessary to ensure the survival of the organism in an environment.

I now illustrate the relevance of this model by showing how posture plays its role of interface between the organism and the environment. In gymnastics, the instructor explains to the consciousness of the student what he must do with his body and how he must listen to his body's messages. In other words, the teacher gives instructions to the mind of the student. He then observes how these instructions are played out by the body. In ordinary life, things happen quite differently. The organism accumulates millions of postural habits that are automatically set in place. One way to characterize the social rituals is to indicate the postural repertoire that they create. To conform to a ritual is to accept a certain observable behavior, independently of what we think of the ritual. In the period of slavery, such body dynamics induced by society were inculcated by whippings. Today, the cultures generated by the economic markets have found even more effective ways to oblige everyone's organism to act in certain ways. In all cases, the habitual postural dynamics structures, in parallel fashion, both the environment and the dynamics of the organism. Posture as an interface obeys the laws of modularity and parallelism. I can, in effect, have to adapt myself simultaneously to the customs of an enterprise and the particular requirements of an interaction with a colleague and the exigencies an ambient temperature imposes on me, and so on. At the same time, the dimensions of my organism react differently to all the stimuli that influence my organism and impose their own requirements (my health, my affects, my habits, my skills and particular interests, etc.) on how I act and react. All of these variables, all of these links, have their own proper ways to function and are set in place in a nonsequential manner. My hand does not wait to know what I think of my colleague to wave hello when he sits down in front of me.

The goal of the following sections is to give to the body psychotherapist tools for evaluating the postural behavior of his patients. He will be able to use the tools of the biomechanics of the body to understand its impact on the other dimensions of the organism and the communication strategies to which the posture participates.[3]

THE NOTION OF POSTURE

> Think of throwing a ball. The arm gesture and the body adjustments that carry the arm gesture are generally merged in a well-coordinated athlete. They start and stop together, or flow smoothly into one another. Someone who has never thrown a ball will, at first try, have moments where only gesture or only posture is in motion at a given time. The act looks clumsy. (Daniel Stern, 2010, *Forms of Vitality,* p. 87)

A contemporary way of analyzing a body is to dissect it into segments, and then observe how these segments coordinate within the gravity field. Posture[4] is the organization of the body's segments in the space of gravity. Each cell of the body, each fluttering of an eyelid and the cardiac rhythm, are under the pull of gravity: a force that draws everything that exists on the planet toward its center. Posture allows for the organization of relationship that establishes itself between gravity and subsystems of the organism.

The segmentation of the body varies from one school of thought to another. The division depends on the way that the body is analyzed and the bodywork that is envisioned. Nonetheless, most of the body-focused methods include the following distinctions in their analysis:

1. The segments are differentiated in function of *the large joints of the skeleton*: feet, calves, thighs, pelvis, thorax, shoulders, arms, forearms, hands, neck, and cranium. The great flexibility of the vertebrae at the base of the neck does not form a joint, but it differentiates the neck from the trunk.
2. The ventral and thoracic segments of the trunk are separated by the *diaphragm*. This distinction is especially useful for the analysis of respiratory behavior.
3. The *orientation of the gaze* is included in the postural dynamics at the occasion of a detailed analysis of the orientation of the segments of the body.

Posture and Gravity

> Gravity is a very attractive force, and everybody is constantly exposed to its influence. The pull of this force makes us all stay on the ground. It even tries to pull us under the ground. But fortunately there is another force in us which does not permit that. That is energy. (Charlotte Selver, "Gravity, Energy and the Support of the Ground," 2009)

Rodin's *The Thinker* (figure 13.1), will serve as an example to describe for you how to analyze the architecture of a posture which is comprised of three main subgroups:

1. A *basic posture,* constituted principally by all of the parts of the body that transmit the weight of the organism to the surface that carries the body, which is called the *support surface.*

FIGURE 13.1. Rodin's sculpture *The Thinker. Source:* http://fr.wikipedia.org/wiki/Image: Rodin_le_penseur.JPG.

2. A *posture of auto-contact*, principally constituted by all of the parts of the body that touch each other.
3. A *surface posture*, constituted by the parts of the body that are not used by the first two levels.

In *The Thinker*, all of the segments of the body are in either basic posture or auto-contact posture. There is consequently no other parts of the body to interact with the objects and the persons that surround *The Thinker*.

The Floors of the Postural Construction

The principal functions of the posture are:

1. To *regulate* how each particle of the organism is placed in the gravity field in every moment.
2. To *coordinate* the organism–gravity relationship with the actions an organism needs to execute.
3. To *support* the fine motor skills.

The analysis of a posture distinguishes two types of surfaces that make it possible to *situate* the parts of the body that participate in the construction of a posture:[5]

1. The *support surface* is the surface on which the weight of the body distributes itself. The parts of the body that touch the support surface form the *basic posture*. This postural dimension is characterized by the two following criteria:
   1.1. The parts of the body that transmit the greatest amount of body weight to the *support surface* form the *anchoring point*. When a person is sitting down, the principal anchor point is the pelvis. The anchor point defines how the body's is *grounded* in methods such as Alexander Lowen's Bioenergetic analysis.[6]
   1.2. The *pelvic angle* is the angle formed by the trunk and the thighs. It is a determining factor to differentiate the postures. In the vertical positions, it is at 180°, but in the squatting and sitting positions it oscillates in the vicinity of 90°.
2. All of the parts of the body that touch another part of the body form the auto-contact surface.
   2.1. These parts of the body transmit the weight of one segment of the body to another segment that transmits this weight to the basic posture. This aspect of the auto-contact thus forms a *secondary system in the mechanisms of regulation of the organism in the gravity field*, as is so well illustrated in *The Thinker*. *The Thinker* is sitting

down, leaning forward, both feet on the ground. This is his basic posture. His auto-contact posture includes many segments of the body. The weight of the head is carried by the right fist, which touches the chin. The right elbow transmits the weight of the head and the arm to the left thigh. The left forearm also rests on the left thigh, which makes it such that the weight of the upper body (from the head to the hands) is transmitted to the left thigh and then to the left foot. If *The Thinker* were standing up straight, the weight of the upper body would have been transmitted by the back to the pelvis and from the pelvis to the feet. Here, the work of the back and of the pelvis is lightened.

2.2. The auto-contact surface also participates in the physiological auto-regulation (especially vegetative) of the organism. For example, the posture of Rodin's *Thinker* leaves less space for abdominal breathing than a posture that would maintain his thorax in a vertical position.

The basic posture forms the ground floor of a body structure; the auto-contact surface forms the other floors. The whole of the behaviors that seek to manage objects and persons with fine motor skills forms the surface of the posture, or the *surface posture*. To be able to play the piano for a long time, the musician must first master his basic posture so that his arms and hands might be able to interact with the piano with as much freedom as possible. This freedom supposes two postural functions:

1. As much as is possible, the arms and the hands are free of the task of regulating the relationship between the organism and gravity.
2. The back is sufficiently strong, relaxed, and stable to serve as a mechanical base for the arms.

Musicians know this dynamic between posture and gesture very well. To regulate the postural background of their fine motor activity, they often take courses in proper posture and carriage, which helps them master this dynamic. Violinist Yehudi Menuhin, for example, mostly used yoga, which he learned from the yogi Iyengar who is often quoted in chapter 1 on hatha yoga. Another technique frequently used by musicians is the method created by Australian Mathias Alexander at the beginning of the twentieth century.[7]

Basic Posture and the Setting of Psychotherapy

There is a relationship between the increase of the surface of contact, the increase in the number of centers of gravity, and relaxation. Consider the two most extreme examples, standing and lying down.

1. *Standing,* the surface of contact is small (the feet) and there is just one center of gravity (in the lower abdomen). Most of the muscles of the body participate in the regulation of the impact of gravity on the organism in an important way. Therefore the standing posture demands and mobilizes a *maximum muscle tone.* The ability to act for a very long time in a vertical position is, besides other factors, one of the principal human postural particularities because it allows for a greater differentiation between hands and feet than one sees in monkeys.[8]

2. When *lying down* on the back, all of the body segments are part of the basic surface, and each segment of the body has a different center of gravity. No part of the body carries the weight of another segment. It is thus possible to remain immobile for a long time; to have, on average, *the lowest muscle tone*; and to not think. This is thus the standard position for sleep, which allows for the restoration of the organism. These arguments had been taken up to explain the choice of the couch in Psychoanalysis.[9]

The choice of a basic posture, especially an anchor point, *regulates* two dimensions:

1. The *auto-regulation* of the organism. When one stands on one's feet, gravity favors the descent of the blood toward the feet and slows the rise of the blood toward the head. When one stands on one's head, gravity has the inverse effect.

2. The *regulation of the setting.* Every ritual is notably defined by the disposition of the postural anchor points of individuals who interact with each other in the context of a space. All human ceremonies include decisions concerning the anchoring points of the participants. The basic posture, therefore, participates in the definition of a form of interaction almost independently of the content of the interaction. The fact of putting the weight of one's body in a given space is a fundamental choice (deliberate or not). To have one's weight in a space at a given moment (in prison, in therapy, in love, etc.) necessarily has a number of important implications. In the same therapeutic frame, a great variety of themes can be elaborated. Often in the verbal therapies, *frame and anchor points are not differentiated.* A characteristic of the classical psychoanalytic situation is that the patient lies on a couch while the therapist sits at the head of the couch. The verbal psychotherapies (apart from Psychoanalysis) are characterized by the fact that the patient and the psychotherapists are both sitting down. The positions of the chairs are often identical for every session. On the contrary, in body psychotherapy and other forms of psychotherapy influenced by active techniques (Gestalt, Transactional Analysis, etc.), *the anchorage no longer characterize the setting.* The dynamics of the anchor points can vary in the course of a session, or

from one session to another. In my practice, either we are sitting more or less face to face (we discuss together) or the patient is lying down on a massage table (I engage in massage), lying down on a mattress (we work with free associations, engage in a relaxation session, etc.), or standing in a sufficiently large space to explore various forms of movement. In other words, we explicitly create a postural frame that corresponds to one kind of exploration of the psyche. In Bioenergetic analysis, the decision to work standing is often related to the intent to explore the notion of grounding.[10]

These examples show that even if the basic posture is rarely mentioned in psychotherapeutic writings, it is at the center of the central dynamics that characterize a therapeutic technique.

THE NOTION OF POSTURAL REPERTOIRE

The notion of repertoire is rarely used in the human sciences and body psychotherapy, yet this tool facilitates the characterization of a set of practices in a particularly useful way.

The repertoire of a language is its vocabulary. The vocabulary of the French language is the collection of the terms accepted by the Académie Française. Most other European languages leave it up to dictionaries and custom to decide if a word is part of the language. We can contrast this linguistic definition with a cultural definition: the French vocabulary is the collection of the terms used by at least 50 percent of the people living on French soil.

Similarly, it is possible to distinguish two repertoires of the body associated to the French culture:

1. All the gestures that can be observed on French soil.
2. All the gestures used by all of the persons who have a French passport.

These are two different ways of defining the repertoire of gestures used in France. Some gestures (and a number of persons) are included in both repertoires; others would fit more strongly in one or the other.

Some postures are more often observable in certain countries than in others. Therefore, a postural repertoire is defined in function of two anthropological analyses:

1. A list of postures that have been used at least once in a culture.
2. The probability of being able to observe a particular posture at a given moment in a given population.

We can observe a person who crouches in France and in India, but the probability of seeing a person actually squatting is higher in India than in France. In

France, there is a greater probability of seeing a person crouching in a yoga studio than in a restaurant. Similarly, the postural repertoire that we observe in a school of hatha yoga in India is different from the one we would observe on the streets of Bombay. This time the differences are more subtle, given that the members of the yoga school in Bombay are also part of the population of the city. It is also possible to talk about a person's repertoire of gestures, or of that person's postural repertoire in a given situation. The behavioral repertoire of a child is not always the same with its mother, with its father, or when they are all together. The child uses different behaviors in each of the three situations. Some are used more often with the mother than with the father, and some are used with the father when the mother is not present. These variations in repertoires form the *dynamics of an individual repertoire*.

Some postures are considered universal, but it is not known whether they have the same function when the repertoire of which they are a part varies. Thus, being seated in a chair does not have the same implication in an office, on a throne, in a reception hall, or in a theater.

THE GYMNAST AND THE CITIZEN

The Ideal Type and Muscle Tone

Physical therapists have tried to establish rules to analyze the functioning of a healthy body that are close to the definitions used as guides in orthopedics to repair a broken body. The reference body is the one described in an atlas of anatomy. The spinal columns are impeccable, the tones of each muscle are organized like the strings of a violin at the start of a concert. No deformity comes to trouble the idea that the human body has been planned by an engineer-god. This state of the body is often proposed by the schools of gymnastics.[11] I use the concept of Max Weber's "ideal type"[12] to indicate this way of thinking about a healthy body.

> Vignette on muscle tone. *So Buddha went to the new monk and told him:*
> *"I have heard that when you were a king you were a great musician, you used to play the sitar." "Yes, but that is finished now, I have forgotten about it. That was my only hobby, I used to practice at least eight hours per day and I had become famous for that."*
> *Buddha said: "I have to ask you one question: if the strings of your sitar are too tight, what will happen?" He said: "What will happen? It is simple! The strings will break when you will attempt to play." "Another question," Buddha said. "If they are too loose, what will happen then?" "If they are too loose, no music can be produced on them, because there is no tension," the answer came.*
> *After this Buddha said: "You are an intelligent person—I need not say anything more to you. Remember, life is also a musical instrument. It needs a certain tension, but only a certain one. Less than that and your life is too loose and there is no music. If the tension is too much, you start breaking down, you start going mad. First you lived a very loose life and you missed the inner music; now you are living a very uptight life—you are still missing the music!*[13]

This anecdote is a good way to introduce the notion of muscular tone. Each muscle would have its own degree of appropriate tension, called *tone*. The tone, like the well-tuned sitar, implies a certain stretching of the muscle. The muscles can become *hypertonic* (too hard too short) or *hypotonic* (flaccid and deformed).

Physiotherapists have a full array of models that describe body movements that are automatically (orthopedically) healthy and can be assimilated into ideal types of relations between physiology, body, and behavior. In the appendix dedicated to postures, I give some examples of sitting "correctly" on the ischia bones of the pelvis and the alignment of the body segments of a person standing according to the "plumb-line rule."[14]

The Logic of the Body and the Logic of the Organs: Symmetries and Asymmetries

> Conflicts become an inherent component of the phylogenetic equilibrium of the subject, because it is intrinsic to the "human condition" which determines the functional architecture of a human organism. (Guy Cellérier, 2010, *Postface,* p. 131; translated by Michael C. Heller and Marcel Duclos)

An individual who wants to understand how a skeleton, the muscles, the fascia, and the ligaments are coordinated can easily arrive at the conclusion that symmetry is the basic rule of the organism. On the other hand, as soon as this person includes the functioning of the organs into his observations, he will have to admit that there exists a manifest heterogeneity between the body system and the organ system. Some organs respect the rules of symmetry (the brain, lungs), whereas others are clearly asymmetric (heart and liver). To this, we have to add the functional asymmetry imposed by some organs, like the brain, which makes most of us either right- or left-handed. This differentiation implies a different calibration of the sensory-motor circuits and of the development of the muscular mass. The necessity to create modes of bodily compensation to integrate the asymmetry imposed by the organs is therefore a necessary part of the requirements that the physiologic dimension imposes on the body. The result is that most of the human bodies are more or less asymmetrical while the comfort and the health of the body seek symmetry. The health of the organs also imposes requirements on other dimensions, like the respect of the demands of the metabolism. Here are new conflicts of interest between the dimensions. Especially when the social environment provides for an ample supply of water and nourishment, behavioral and psychological propensions do not respect metabolic needs. They tend to take more. Everything happens as if the homeostatic mechanisms operate according to the following rules:

1. A metabolic disequilibrium can activate the homeostatic mechanisms that influence all of the dimensions of the organism.
2. The mechanisms that permit a homeostatic propensity to recruit the

support of the other dimensions also permits each dimension to activate this propensity for their own ends, which may have nothing to do with metabolic needs (for example, to drink alcohol to drown a sorrow and not because one is thirsty).

3. The psychic and behavioral dimensions have no direct link with the homeostatic equilibrium. Therefore, consciousness does not have the means to explicitly know the metabolic exigencies.

The Citizen's Body

The yogi can only transform himself by remaining at the margin of social life. He would not be able to loosen all his joints in a more stressful environment. The citizen is someone who accepts that his body adapts itself to a lifestyle, to the demands of a culture, a profession, and the role of a parent. It seems that every form of adaptation has a price. The yogi pays a price constructing himself a space which is, in the end, social to the extent that yoga is also a socially constructed approach. The methods that the yogi uses, the position that he occupies at the heart of a culture, had been in development for centuries. The reference on the matter remains the model of *the distinction* by Pierre Bourdieu (1979), when he illustrates that the choice of a lifestyle (a *habitus*[15]) shapes the body and the social identity of an individual. The yogi defines one pole in which the habitus adapts itself to the necessities of anatomy and physiology. At the other extreme, we have the lifestyles in which the body dynamics are submitted to the demands of survival in a society. To have to bend over every day to garden imposes demands on the back that no physiotherapists could recommend. Here is a personal anecdote illustrating this point.

> A vignette concerning Isaac Stern. *Some time ago, in the 1970s, I went to hear violinist Isaac Stern with a friend who is a Rolfer[16] and who was trying to straighten my back. Stern was already an old man. By dint of bending over his violin, he was almost hunchback between the shoulder blades. When he stopped playing, he greeted us with a broad and charming smile, but his back did not straighten and his head remained slightly bent toward the left shoulder on which he usually rested his violin. I asked my friend if Isaac Stern would still be as good a violinist if we straightened his back. It was my impression that we were looking at an adaptation of the body that allowed for an even better playing of the violin, even if it was detrimental from a medical point of view. Not every professional violinist adapts to his instrument in this way, but they are all in a struggle that their way of playing might be less detrimental to their body and allow them to play as well as possible. I recall that at the end of his life, violinist Sándor Végh, who had spent his life playing the violin in a quartet sitting on a chair, was also incapable of completely straightening his legs when he stood up.*

The laws of behavior and the mind follow modes of functioning that force the organism to adapt to those demands of the environment that cannot be managed in a compatible way with the demands of physiology. It is precisely because the human organism is capable of managing dimensions that function differently, the human species was able to adapt to such varied natural and social contexts.[17] This plasticity renders every notion of an ideal body hardly useful in psychotherapy. An examination of the rapport between the returning blood flow in the veins and the sitting posture provides me with the opportunity to develop this point with a few examples.

The Return of the Venous Blood in the Legs: Behavior and Physiology

Posture and Venous Circulation

The interaction between the chair and the return of the blood via the leg veins illustrates how posture participates automatically, without conscious thought, in the way a lifestyle influences the mechanisms of physiological regulation.

In a wide and deep river, the water flows gently. If the river abruptly narrows, and boulders impede its way, the water becomes turbulent and the flow of the rivers is slowed down. This increases the pressure of the water on the boulders. The boulders retain the deposits carried by the water, and the current slowly erodes them. As for the circulation of the blood, each joint is a passage of this type.

A European, accustomed to eating sitting on a chair, soon enters in contact with this particularity when he arrives in Japan and sits on the floor with his buttocks on his heels. Unless his joints are particularly (for a European) flexible, he will soon experience pain in his legs. When he unfolds them to stretch, his legs will be numb and almost without sensation. He then has the impression that his legs and feet have become a formless tingling mass. After having moved his legs, he gradually acquires the impression of reappropriating them. They return to their usual state. This individual suffered from having placed himself in a position for which his venous circulation is not adapted. The folding of his knees and the compression of the muscular tissues of the leg seriously slowed down the venous circulation. Movement, stretching the muscles, opening the joints, breathing deeply, and massage are all ways to stimulate the circulation of the blood so that it might take up its habitual functioning. This example also illustrates that a lifestyle influences the adaptation of circulation to a postural repertoire. The Japanese generally do not have this kind of problem when they eat sitting on the floor, legs folded, feet under the pelvis.

The Return of Venous Blood

Each contraction of the muscles of the feet and of the legs pushes the venous blood upward (see figures 13.2 and 13.3). Valves situated in the veins allow the blood to flow toward the abdomen but stop it from going back to the feet. This mechanism is influenced by social behavior, independently of any cognitive and affective experience.

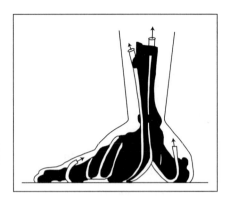

FIGURE 13.2. The venous pump of the muscles of the legs (the effect of walking on the plantar veins). *Source:* Bonnet and Millet (1971, p. 250).

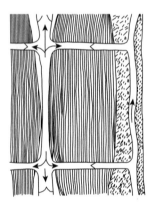 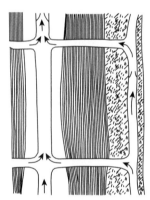

FIGURE 13.3. The muscular pump of the calves. The arrows indicate the direction of the muscular contraction. *Source:* Bonnet and Millet (1971, p. 250).

The relationship between posture and the cardiovascular system is particularly close in the venous circulation of the legs. In most of the common positions, when the arterial blood descends from the heart to the feet, it is pushed by the cardiac pump and gravity. On the other hand, when the venous blood returns from the feet to the heart, it must fight gravity, and it receives no help from the heart because the venous circulation is largely independent of cardiac activity.

The legs are endowed with a device that pushes the blood upward. This engine depends on two fundamental mechanisms: the firmness of the veins and the valves. The valves are like mouths that open only in one direction. They open to let the upward-moving venous blood pass through when the surrounding muscles contract and close when the surrounding muscles relax to stop it from descending. This movement begins in the feet because they contain a thick venous channel that forms a sort of sponge. Every time an individual rests on this "sponge,"[18] the venous blood escapes and rises toward the calves. This is why walking is excellent for the venous circulation. The return of the venous blood is also modulated by the following mechanisms:

1. An *adequate pressure and venous flow* (which is not always the case).
2. The *thoracic pump*, created by the movements of the diaphragm while breathing, also participates in the regulation of the circulation of the venous blood in the lower body.[19]
3. The *heartbeats*. When the heart expulses its content into the arteries, it creates an empty space that sucks up the venous blood. However weak, this effect increases the drawing forth carried out by the diaphragm.

The fact that the venous circulation depends on body movements and regulates the consistency of tissues is well known in hospitals. When a person remains immobile for hours, the tissues are no longer purified by the venous blood because of poor circulation. This causes the formation of ulcers on the skin that are often referred to as bedsores. The lesions of the skin mostly appear on the points of contact between the body and the mattress, like areas on the buttocks or the heels for a patient who is lying on his back. To avoid this, nurses regularly modify the patient's position, rub the patient's skin, and sometime change to a more proper mattress.[20]

Yoga teachers have always integrated recent discoveries into their understanding of the body. I do not know when they first found an explicit mechanical link between exercises and the return of the venous blood, but long ago they observed a correlation between certain exercises and the return of the venous blood.[21] All the positions in which the legs are extended toward the ceiling (the sirsa-asanas) allow gravity to favor the voyage of the venous blood of the legs toward the heart, but these positions do not develop the abilities required during walking. On the other hand, the exercise called the *sponge* supports the development of the muscles–veins relationship. In this exercise, you contract and relax each muscle several times over as if each were a sponge that you wring out. This can be done without paying attention to the respiratory rhythm or done in coordination with it. For example, you inhale every time that you contract a muscle at the same time. Other combinations can be made in function of various refinements. Certain massage techniques enliven this mechanism. The massage therapist takes a regular rhythm marked by the compression of the muscle and its release. Once more, this rhythm can be coordinated with the respiratory rhythm or not.

The basic principle of this exercise is found in most gymnastics and massage methods in the world. This technique has been taken up, for example, by Edmund Jacobson's relaxation. In a course where Gerda Boyesen taught her variation, she suggested that we massage the return of the venous blood from head to foot. She feared that by going from the feet to the head, the massage therapist would create too strong a venous flow, which the heart may not be able to manage.[22] In the case of Europeans who have difficulty sitting as the Japanese do, chronic muscular tension probably inhibits the plasticity required by the interaction between the venous circulation and the muscles of the legs.

Venous Circulation and Social Ritual: The Necessity to Have a Varied Postural Repertoire

The studies on the varicose veins in the legs confirm and increase our knowledge concerning the rapport between posture, cultural behavior, the dynamics of the veins and the state of the tissues. I am thinking of a series of studies that coordinate three dimensions:

1. Professional behavior
2. Postural repertoire
3. Venous circulation

This interaction is notably studied in research[23] that wants to demonstrate the impact of professional behavior on health. It would seem that all of the professions that impose a posture throughout the day considerably increase the probability that employees will have serious venous circulatory problems, like the formation of varicose veins.

Individuals who remain sitting in a chair all day long every day seem to be particularly vulnerable to circulatory problems of the venous return. Japan presents an interesting case. Since the Japanese traditionally does not often use chairs, they use a highly varied postural repertoire in their daily life. Before World War II, varicose veins were rare. On the other hand, ever since the lifestyle from the United States and Europe has increasingly influenced the behavior of the Japanese, they now spend more time sitting on chairs; cases of varicose veins have increased.

Another area of research on this theme studies the ergonomics of chairs.[24] It consists in finding a way to design comfortable chairs that are also beneficial to one's health. Chronic sitting not only has a detrimental effect on the return of venous blood but is also detrimental to the back, the muscle tone of the abdominals, the neck, the shoulders, the arms, and the hands. These studies show that there is no way to sit that is both comfortable in the long run and orthopedically healthy. Comfort and health obey, in this case, different laws that are not possible to coordinate in any harmonious manner.

It is thus possible to conclude that the human organism is poorly adapted to *monopostural* activities. The adaptation to sitting on a chair or a bench is particularly poor. These research studies draw attention to the fact that only recently (within the past few centuries) has sitting on a chair become a common human practice. It probably is not yet part of the mechanisms that have influenced the selection of human genes. It is thus possible that the dichotomies associated with sitting, like the one between comfort and proper orthopedics, are related to the fact that sitting does not figure among the anatomical and physiological innate adaptation mechanisms of the human organism. If sitting embeds itself into the human postural repertoire in centuries to come, and if humanity survives that long, it will be interesting to observe how the organism will adapt itself at the genetic level to the use of this posture.[25]

PART V

The Psyche as Regulator of the Organism

I have discussed the disciplines that do not belong to the realm of psycho-therapy but have had a strong impact on body psychotherapy. I now focus on the field of psychotherapy. This discipline was "in the air" in Europe during the second half of the nineteenth century. Psychiatrists were exploring for ways to use the newborn psychological science and hypnosis to improve their relatively inefficient treatments of mental disorders. Charcot, Breuer, and Bleuer are some of the best known figures of this generation. However, Sigmund Freud was the magnet around which the field of psychotherapy managed to organize itself, even if Pierre Janet was exploring similar ideas in Paris. The strength of Freud's approach was probably his method, which was based on free association.

The concept of the organism as the integration of the body and psyche is more familiar to the biologist than to the psychologist and psychotherapist. It is not for nothing that the first psychologists and psychotherapists who insisted that the psyche was part of the organismic systems of regulation had education and training in biology (like Jean Piaget) or medicine (like Freud). However, we have to wait until the 1930s before psychoanalysts managed to create methods that could tackle the connection between mind, affect, physiology, and the body in a concrete way.

What follows is an attempt to render this recalibration of Freud's proposal more explicit. To understand how body psychotherapy emerged, the easiest route is to begin to understand what was floating in the air at the beginning of Freud's career in Vienna, and then to show how it leads to the discussions among Fenichel, Reich, Gindler, and Lindenberg in Berlin. I use George Makari's brilliant book, *The Creation of Psychoanalysis,* as a reference to travel along this roadway.

Like the schools discussed in the preceding sections, psychotherapy is not an academic discipline. It follows the logic of the proliferation of different schools.

14

The Origins of Psychoanalysis and Freud's First Topography

Von Helmholtz and Wundt

For many, Hermann von Helmholtz (1821–1894) incarnates the birth of German experimental psychology. This philosopher physician intervened in significant ways in several sciences. At the time that Thompson and Maxwell were defining energy, von Helmholtz (1863) described how energy could neither be created nor destroyed but could be transformed. For example, the energy generated by a steam engine can transform itself into a kinetic energy (movement). He invented the ophthalmoscope, which makes possible a detailed observation of the retina. He was the first to find a way to measure the speed of a nerve impulse, and he contributed to the development of the psychophysiology of perception. One of his students, physician and philosopher Wilhelm Maximilian Wundt (1832–1920), established the first official laboratory in psychology in Berlin in 1879. This event is generally considered to be the date of the birth of psychology. Other researchers in the world, like Theodule Ribot[1] in France and William James in the United States, established research laboratories that went in the same direction.

At that time, many neurologists believed that it would one day be possible to explain the behavior of thoughts by studying the brain. This project is still at the center of the neurosciences. Wundt[2] proposed a soft parallelism to define the domain of psychology. His aim was to show that the science of psychology was distinct from neurology. He distinguishes the real world from our representations.[3] Our representations are clearly distinct from what creatures perceive and what they think about. On the one side, we thus have the realm of psychologists, which consists of perceptions and the organization of perceptions, which is called the psyche. The mind is a closed world that functions according to laws regulating the interactions between thoughts, perceptions, intelligence, memory, and so on. Physicists use psychological procedures to try to create psychological representations that become increasingly close to the dynamics of the real world. These procedures rely on tools that enhance the power of the senses. Physicians apply such procedures to intervene with increasing precision on the material aspects of the organism. However, only the psychologist can understand how the psychological dynamics function. His procedures are necessarily adapted to its object (e.g., the realm of thoughts and affects) and the laws that govern its dynamics. The material and the psychological dimensions are part of the same universe. Therefore, there must exist some laws that apply to both domains and allow various forms of connections between the mental and the physical planes. Sensory-motor phenomena are manifest examples of psychophysiological dynamics. Mind and soma gradually differentiated during the evolutionary process described since Lamarck. Wundt's psychological dynamics are thus clearly embodied. We shall soon see that certain arguments used by Wundt to distinguish psychology from other sciences are used by Freud to distinguish psychotherapy from other forms of medical intervention.

At the beginning of his career, Wundt was mostly interested in the development of the psychophysiology of perception. During the last twenty years of his life, he created a social psychology (*Volkerpsychologie*) that studied the psyche as the basis of language (1900), art (1908), myths and religion (1914), society (1918), as well as culture and history (1920). These developments had a profound influence on Freud and Jung, who began to propose a psychoanalytic perspective of these domains. For these first psychologists, thought is part of what the development of the brain has made possible; but thoughts have an emergent dynamic that is specific to them and constitutes itself in a field whose poles are the dynamics of the brain and society.

Introspection and Experimental Psychology

The first psychologists thought that they could establish their science through self-observation by using introspection as the basic tool. In a typical situation of the time, many people, one after the other, sit in the same chair to accomplish a rigorously defined task. They were then asked to explore through introspection what they perceived while doing the task. Other experimental methods, especially physiological ones, were used as a complementary source of information and a control to compensate for the excessive personal and variable aspects of self-exploration.[4] Like the halo that circles above a saint's head, the psyche was thought of as the aura of the brain, an aura capable of forming a virtual world that structures itself by linking everyone's soul and immortalizes itself by influencing the thoughts of the generations to come.

In experimental psychology, methods based on introspection became obsolete with the revolution of the behaviorist. For the founder of this movement, John Broadus Watson (1878–1958), the only way to scientifically understand the psyche is to begin by studying behavior and then infer the algorithms that produce behavior.[5] The psyche then becomes the system of organismic strings that make the body move and generate the behavioral reactions. The analysis of behavior is capable of being objective because it can be observed by many people and can be recorded (filmed). This way of proceeding has since generated video-analysis, especially focused on behavioral communication. Video-analysis, which is discussed in the last sections of this volume,[6] is used both in research and in therapy.

Watson perhaps does not always recognize that he wants to refine the strategy of the viewers of silent movies. Each spectator believes he is able to understand the thoughts of manifestly fictional characters. Most behaviorists commit the error of believing that behavior correlates exactly with the algorithms of the mind because they believe in a direct link between thought and behavior.

In the meantime, psychoanalysis, and then most of the psychotherapeutic modalities it inspired, resisted such a view. They show that in strengthening the ties between therapist and patient, it is possible to continue to use introspection to explore the zones of individual experience inaccessible to the behaviorists.

The Unconscious Inferences of von Helmholtz and Wundt

By astutely correlating physiology and what is consciously perceived, the first psychologists soon discovered strong correlations between physiological dynamics and conscious perceptions that introspection could not detect. Around 1850, von Helmholtz and Wundt each tried, in a secret competition, to find a way to study the sometimes massive impact of physiology on thoughts that unfolds unbeknownst to the subject. To explain the works of this influence, they concentrate on the analysis of optical illusions, which had been already studied in many psychophysiological laboratories. The basic idea is that the nervous system automatically generates models that complete the sensory data and permits the building of conscious perceptions.[7] Von Helmholtz and Wundt called these elaborate constructions in the nervous system of "unconscious inferences" (*unbewusster schluss*). Von Helmholtz also shows that the tendency to attribute psychological traits according to physical traits is a type of unconscious inference. These inferences impose themselves on consciousness like an almost exterior compulsive force to which thoughts are hardly able to escape:[8] "Whatever interpretation the human perceptual apparatus may give to what meets the eye, the resulting impression is, Helmholtz concluded, not open to revision; the human eye, so to speak, cannot doubt" (Frey, 2001, p. 261). After including these notions in their textbooks, the two authors had to admit that they had not been able to find experimental procedures that could allow them to examine this topic with reliability. They abandoned this research and removed the chapters dedicated to this notion in the last editions of their textbooks. Until recently this research project was only known about by a few erudite scholars because today we are only able to find these last editions. This subject is undertaken today with more sophisticated[9] methods of analysis. This neuronal or cerebral unconscious[10] is more often qualified as nonconscious because it is inaccessible to introspection and is not always of a mental nature.

Freud and Cocaine

Having become a physician in Vienna, Sigmund Freud (1856–1939) worked from 1876 to 1882 in von Brücke's research laboratory in physiology. Von Brücke had studied with von Helmholtz. In 1884, under the advisement of his mentor, Freud undertook a study of the effect of cocaine on nerve tissues as his thesis in neurology.[11] At that time, cocaine was legal and fashionable. It was, for example, one of the original ingredients in Coca-Cola and featured in the life of the popular (but fictional) Sherlock Holmes.

Freud published a few articles in which he declared that cocaine is a medicine capable of treating a wide array of illnesses. It is presented as a relaxing agent that increases the force of motor activity, promotes the cessation of dependence on morphine without creating a dependency, and heals certain eye problems. These publications, supported by the students of the illustrious von Helmholtz, were read by numerous physicians in Europe and in the United States. Thus Freud participated in setting in place the idea that substances could contribute to the healing of psychic and somatic ailments. The reactions were negative. Many physicians complained about Freud's article because after having followed his recommendations, they noticed that cocaine created a powerful dependence. Around 1903, the consumption of cocaine was forbidden.

Like many other physicians who had believed cocaine could be useful, Freud had consumed some himself and had become dependent. In his correspondence with his friend and colleague Wilhelm Fliess, he complains several times of the problems it creates in his nostrils (an irritated nose, swollen nostrils, weeping pus, etc.). It is not impossible that his need to hide his nose from his patients was one of the reasons he preferred to sit behind them.

Freud was ambitious. He absolutely wanted to become a genius.[12] Cocaine had brought him to a career impasse. He set out to find other areas of research. He succeeded in having the University of Vienna finance his stay in Paris with the illustrious neurologist Jean-Martin Charcot (1825–1893). During this trip, he acquired knowledge in psychiatry: hysteria (Charcot was the authority on the subject at the time) and hypnosis.[13]

In 1883, having returned to Vienna, Freud was named to the post of researcher and instructor in one of the most famous laboratories in neurology in the world, directed by Theodor Meynert. He then discovered the works of Hyp-polite Bernheim, who taught in Nancy, and he translated some of his writings. Bernheim modified Charcot's theory on the relationship between hypnosis, psyche, and hysteria.[14] Freud takes away from the whole of these studies the hypothesis that in the case of hysteria, mental problems create pathological so-matic functioning.

Freud then specialized in the study of cerebral motor disabilities in chil-dren. In 1886, he directed the neurological service in the public children's hospi-tal and opened a private practice in which he hopes to develop what he has learned about hysteria and hypnosis. His position in the clinic allows him to refine his reflections on the relationship between body and mind and acquire a developmental view of the human being.[15] All of his life, Freud retained the no-tion that what happens in early infancy influences the development of personal-ity. His association with von Helmholtz's students also taught him that the psychophysiological approach had its limits. It became evident that the neuro-logical approach to thought had to be complemented with an approach based on the exploitation of the resources of introspection.

Freud apparently ended his use of cocaine at the time of the death of his father in 1896.[16] It is possible that in his severance from the drug (no one knows how he succeeded or what interior price he paid), Freud became conscious that it could be interesting to relate the impact of cocaine on what he felt to the data that he had collected on this impact as a neurologist. In any case, at this time he set for himself the task of trying to find a formulation that would permit him to describe in what ways the psychological dynamics are different from the physi-ological dynamics. He also discovered what he calls the Oedipal complex.[17] For him, this complex is manifestly a mechanism that only the psyche can generate. A neurologist would never be able to analyze this phenomenon by observing the brain. This period of personal crisis unleashed an intimate and creative convic-tion in Freud that encouraged him to funnel his energies in the systematic explo-ration of psychological therapeutic tools.

Freud did not freely admit that he was influenced by Wundt's ideas on un-conscious processes, but he must have heard of these ideas while he worked with von Brücke. By studying the impact of cocaine on thoughts and physiol-ogy, he was working exactly on the dimension that von Helmholtz and Wundt wanted to analyze. This cocaine episode illustrates an important limit of Freud's scientific ethics: a tendency to generalize hastily on the basis of observations made on a few cases.

This way of doing things is a classic procedure in neurology because most lesions are rare. However, a neurologist can count on colleagues who can verify such an observation on other patients, in other countries. In psychotherapy, this strategy is difficult to manage when there are few colleagues who can verify an observation, such as was the case at the end of the nineteenth century. Going from cocaine to the Oedipal complex, Freud seems to have retained his ten-dency to propose hasty generalizations.

PRINCIPLES OF THE FIRST TOPOGRAPHY

Freud's First Topography: The Unconscious, the Preconscious, and the Conscious

In his book on dreams, Freud (1900) describes the psyche as a distinct system from the physiological dimension. The psyche is a virtual entity distinct from the brain but anchored in it by a symbiotic relationship. It is a kind of parasitic system that exists thanks to the brain. This First Topography had the advantage of imposing onto the medical world the idea that the psyche did not follow the same laws as the physiological dynamics and that it had, of necessity, the need to be treated with interventions that were adapted to it. This is Freud's *First Topography* (unconscious, preconscious, and conscious). This proposition contained a series of intuitions that remain interesting but also posed all sorts of problems, like creating too sharp a distinction between the psychological and physiological dimensions.

Numerous aspects of the First Topography are attempts to give answers to clinical intuitions that remain interesting. These intuitions continue to stimulate the imagination of today's psychotherapists because the questions they raise have not always received satisfying answers. Freud attempted to resolve some of these issues when he proposed a *Second Topography* (id, ego, and super-ego). Even though this Second Topography is also useful, it does not resolve any of the problems posited by the First Topography. Moreover, it is less often referred to outside of the psychoanalytic school.

The Unconscious of the Neurologist and That of Hypnosis

> If we try to imagine an idea as persisting beneath the limen of consciousness, we can as a matter of fact only think of it as still an idea, i.e., as the same process as that which it was so long as we were conscious of it, with the single difference that it is now no longer conscious. But this implies that psychological explanation has here reached a limit similar to that which confronts it in the question as to the ultimate origin of sensations. It is the limit beyond one of the two causal series,—the physical,—can be continued, but where the other, the psychical,—can be continued, but where the attempt to push this latter farther must inevitably lead to the thinking of the psychical in physical—i.e., material,—terms. (Wilhelm Wundt, 1892, *Principles of Psychophysiological Psychology*, 30.V, p. 453)

In the preceding section, we saw that during his studies, Freud learned to recognize two types of phenomena that influence the conscious dynamics unbeknownst to them:

1. *The physiological unconscious.* The studies of von Helmholtz's students demonstrate that it is possible to influence what a person thinks consciously without the person being aware of it by acting on physiological circuits such as the nervous and hormonal systems. Freud had worked on this type of unconscious influences while he was studying the effects

of cocaine. If, in the case of cocaine, the impact of the neurological dynamics is consciously perceived, consciousness cannot understand how this influence acts. Thus, at the start, Freud did not realize that he was becoming dependent.

2. *The psychological unconscious.* In acquiring theoretical and practical knowledge concerning hypnosis, Freud discovered that there were also psychic dynamics momentarily inaccessible to consciousness but which influenced the way a person thought and behaved. The psychic origin of this influence is attested to by the fact that this effect can be triggered by a hypnotist, that the intervention addresses the psyche, and that the effect has the same configuration as a conscious psychic activity, save that the individual does not realize he is acting under hypnosis. Differently than for cocaine, the effect of hypnosis can act integrally outside of the individual's field of consciousness, while recruiting all of the know-how of consciousness. In this case, and only in this case for Freud, there is a manifest and indisputable unconscious psychic activity that is activated in parallel to the conscious activity of the patient. The unconscious activity can mobilize all of the resources of consciousness and link them to the resources of the physiological unconscious. This capacity of the psychological unconscious to join forces with the physiological unconscious will fascinate a great number of people. It was used to explain the impact of the psyche on the physiological dynamics that were observed in hysterical patients.

Even today, most of the physicians who make use of hypnosis combine the models of psychiatry with the formulations of hypnotherapists. One of Freud's most original contributions is to have used his knowledge of hypnosis to create a new form of intervention: *psychotherapy.* It then consisted of getting physicians to admit that there were two types of interventions:[18]

1. *An intervention on the physiological dynamics that influence the psyche.* Freud's study of cocaine is an example of this kind of intervention. More recent examples are the use of tranquilizers, antidepressants, and neuroleptics.

2. *An intervention on the psyche that makes the treatment of psychological problems possible and sometimes treats physical symptoms,* as in the case of hysterics. Freud used hypnosis like a particular case out of a complete set of psychic interventions that can act on the psyche.

The Description of Freud's Psychic System, or ψ System

THE TOPOGRAPHY, THE SEQUENCING, AND THE DYNAMIC
OF FREUD'S PSYCHOLOGICAL SYSTEM

Around this distinction between conscious and unconscious, Freud constructed a model about what the mental apparatus (or ψ system) could be. To impose his point of view, he had to present a sort of anatomical and physiological model of the psyche that could frame the psychotherapeutic cures. The "anatomical" aspect of this model distinguishes the unconscious, the preconscious, and the conscious; the "physiological" aspect describes the dynamic that permits a thought to circulate in the mental domain. The psychic system is described as a sort of geography or *topography* in which there would be the three following regions:

1. *The unconscious* designates a place where there exist thoughts that are not accessible through introspection.[19]
2. *The preconscious* designates a place where thoughts are not consciously perceived at a given moment; but they can easily become conscious in another moment.
3. *The conscious* only contains those thoughts that are perceived explicitly, and which can be organized with explicit procedures like the laws of logic, politeness or morality.

This topography has a *direction*:

1. The unconscious receives all the information that the brain "fabricates" for the mind. Freud is not explicit concerning this fabrication system; but what is postulated is an interface that transforms the *sensory data* into thoughts. The number of thoughts that are poured into the unconscious is enormous but not organized. As in Spinoza's understanding of imagination, here we have to deal with the irruption of a volcano, or with the lava that penetrates the psyche in a mostly disorganized way.
2. Consciousness integrates, as much as possible, the thoughts that arise from the unconscious. This process requires a lot of energy and uses procedures that can only organize a limited amount of information. These procedures are delicate and get disorganized as soon as they are not able to integrate (or digest) the available information.[20]
3. The preconscious is a sort of triage station that receives a large number of thoughts produced in the unconscious and the reactions or conclusions of consciousness. There, thoughts have access to *motor activity*.

This topography has a *dynamic*. The thoughts that enter into the unconscious have a weak intensity, very close to the intensity of the data treated by the nervous system. The psyche also has its own proper energetic system, which is greatly influenced by the affects. This energy will invest the unconscious thoughts and give them a charge. The more a thought is charged, the more it is intense, and the more it will approach consciousness. As the unconscious produces more thoughts than the conscious can manage, it belongs to the preconscious to manage the thoughts that try to become conscious.

The difference between a preconscious and an unconscious representation is that an unconscious representation cannot become conscious once it is repressed, whereas preconscious representations can. Thus, in a dream, unconscious drives activate preconscious material which can be perceived by consciousness.[21]

If all thoughts were necessarily conscious, we would be able to manage so few of them that the psyche would not be able to accomplish its function. It is therefore essential for the survival of the organism that what is perceived does not only depend on consciousness:[22] "Nothing is more natural than to think of consciousness as a kind of stage upon which our ideas are the actors, appearing, withdrawing behind the scenes, and coming on again when their cue is given" (Wundt, 1892, XVI.I, p. 233). In this metaphor of the theater, it is evident that what is happening on the scene in front of the audience (in consciousness) may follow different rules as what is going on backstage (in the preconscious). The observation that there are preconscious phenomena corresponds to everyone's experience, like a memory that we cannot retrieve in one minute and that reappears ten minutes later; or like a nervous movement of the foot of which we only become conscious once that it is pointed out by someone else.

This second example illustrates a preconscious phenomenon. A foot moves incessantly without the individual noticing it. This activity is accessible to consciousness if it directs its attention to the foot, but the activity remains in the preconscious as long as attention is distracted from it by other events. The notion of preconscious situates the fact that at a given moment, our awareness perceives only a part of what could be perceived, and the subject can have the tendency to avoid certain thoughts without having them necessarily maintained in the unconscious.[23]

> Metaphor concerning the preconscious repression. *King Arthur systematically avoids looking at Lancelot ever since his knight had an affair with Queen Guinevere, but he needs Lancelot to continue to be a knight of the Round Table. Arthur's mental barrage is conscious. The problem this poses for the Knights of the Round Table is that it is difficult for them to talk about Lancelot with their king. Moreover, Arthur inhibits himself from taking note of Lancelot's behavior when he is in the royal hall.*

If the distinction unconscious/preconscious is often useful, it becomes a trap for Freud when he claims that all the examples of unconscious mechanisms that were described and that did not correspond to Freud's unconscious were necessarily of the preconscious. Freud then spoke of *two kinds of unconscious:*[24] (1) Freud's unconscious, and (2) the unconscious of others, which would in fact be examples of preconscious thoughts. This remark was challenging. To understand why, let us come back to Wundt's theatrical metaphor. One could distinguish two distinct types of mechanisms behind the stage:

1. Actors and objects that exit and enter the stage. These would be metaphors of preconscious activity.
2. The more administrative and organizational dynamics that shaped the

play. Those who directed the actors, created their costumes, sponsored the costs, cleaned the theater every day can even be far away from the theater when the public is there. But their impact can manifest itself numerous times during the theatrical season.

Distinguishing at least two different types of psychological unconscious, one being more easily accessible conscious processes than the other, was useful. Psychologists and psychotherapists could explore different ways of refining such a distinction. But even today, we do not have the means of knowing exactly how to define the different mechanisms involved and how they interact with consciousness.

The intellectual context of the First Topography is close to the model established by Descartes. This is evident in Freud's original texts.

> *The German language does not have an equivalent of the English word* consciousness. *Freud uses the term* bewusst *to designate a thought of which a person has knowledge, and* unbewusst *for a thought that is active without one knowing it. The terminology is thus the same as the one used by Descartes and Lamarck. Descartes's and Freud's vocabulary allow for a more subtle way of using Freud's First Topography than the rigid categories that are often associated with the conscious/unconscious distinction.*

In Freud's time, a simplified version of Descartes's model was the implicit model that nearly everybody had in their head relative to thoughts. That is why it is useful to remember the similarities between the models of Descartes and Freud—because they can in part explain how so many people immediately grasped the importance of Freud's First Topography. The twentieth-century reader easily follows Freud when he explains that a thought cannot remain in the unconscious but for a *dysfunction* of the mental apparatus.

The topographical aspect of Freud's psychic system is a case of pedagogical shrewdness. Freud was too good of a neurologist to imagine that the unconscious zone and the conscious zone were associated to distinct areas of the brain and that an idea changed properties as it circulated from one area to the other. The degree of consciousness of a thought is a qualitative change, but in becoming conscious, it does not change cerebral location.[25] In other words, even unconscious, a thought already has a configuration that allows it to become conscious. In the language of this book, a thought has a "format" that permits it to become conscious, even when it remains unconscious. Freud's model was conceived to help practitioners classify the often unbelievably complex mental phenomena they observe. He does not claim to describe the real functioning of the psyche. He facilitates the observation of the existence of conscious, preconscious, and unconscious phenomena and the isolation of certain dynamics that regulate the mobility of thoughts. It is therefore recommended not to fall into the well-known trap of taking a useful metaphor for a description of reality.

THE NOTION OF CHARGE

> In mental functions, something is to be distinguished—a quota of affect or sum of
> excitation—which possesses all the characteristics of quantity (though we have no
> means of measuring it), which is capable of increase, diminution, displacement and
> discharge, and which is spread over memory-traces of ideas somewhat as an elec-
> tric charge is spread on the surface of a body. (Freud, 1894, *The Neuro-Psychoses
> of Defense*, p. 60)

Spinoza spoke of power, Hume of intensity, and Freud of excitation. There would
be, for the Freud of the First Topography, a psychic energy that renders the
thoughts more or less intense. This energy follows laws close to nervous energy
but would be purely psychological. Freud has a difficult time proposing a clear
model of what he calls psychic energy. He is content to conjecture, in early writings discovered after his death,[26] that physiological sexual energy "transforms"
itself into psychological sexual energy when the information managed by the
brain transforms into thoughts in the unconscious. In his work, Freud speaks of
this psychic energy as if the notion is self-evident as soon as we admit that the
psyche is distinct from physiology.

Freud does not really succeed in imagining how the psychic system could
regulate the charge of each unconscious thought, even if this regulation plays
an essential role in Freudian psychology. His thoughts on energetic dynamics
were used to create a model of the mechanisms that regulate the behavior of
thoughts by employing the capacity of the German language to create variations around a key word: *besetzung*. James Beaumont Strachey (1887–1967),
who translated Freud's work into English with Freud's permission, translates
besetzung with the Greek term *cathexis*. Reich mostly used the term *charge* to
remain close to notions such as those of intensity and the quantity of energy
associated to a thought.[27] Freud distinguished the following mental energetic
mechanisms:

1. *Cathexis*. The more cathexis there is, the more a representation becomes
   intense, the more there is excitation, the more there is conscious perception, and the more there is a need of discharge.
2. *Decathexis*. Certain mechanisms of the psyche can make it such that a
   representation loses a part of its intensity. In using this possibility, the
   psyche can transform a worrisome representation into a thought that
   can only exit in the unconscious, because it no longer has an intensity
   that can transform it in a conscious perception.
3. *Anticathexis or countercathexis*. Here, a thought is rendered more intense to barrage another thought. This is another strategy to contain a
   troubling thought. We have already encountered this while talking about
   Hume and Darwin; we find it again in Reich's Character analysis.
4. *Hypercathexis*. Sometimes a thought acquires a power such that it captures all the resources of consciousness (like a regiment captures a fort).

It then becomes difficult to introduce other thoughts into consciousness.

There is a *recathexis* when an object remembered from a long time ago regains its intensity while it was hardly present in a person's conscious thoughts. When there is a recathexis that links up with a hypercathexis, Freud often talks of a cathartic regression.[28]

Freud never took a definite position on the questions raised by the notion of psychological energy because he did not have the means to do so. The discussions on this aspect of his First Topography have been unending. Only when Freud indicated his dissatisfaction with the First Topography did analysts like Ferenczi explicitly reintroduce the idea that behind the mental operations there would be physiological dynamics. This idea has traveled far and wide since then without having yet taken a definitive form.[29]

The psychologist of today mostly retains the notions of conscious, preconscious, and unconscious from the First Topography because this categorization remains useful. Even if no one, to this day, has proposed a competing model to that of Freud, it becomes evident that it is more of a useful metaphor than a description of the functioning of the psyche. There are too many loose ends in this model for it to be retained in its entirety.

The Regulatory Systems of the Psyche that Create Psychopathology

> I enjoin you to take this expression to the letter: what is repressed does not disappear, it just does not stay in its place; it is pushed into some corner, where it is not treated justly, where it feels limited and disadvantaged. It then constantly rises up with all of its power to regain the place where it should be, and as soon as it sees a breach in the wall, it attempts to slip through. It may succeed, but when it reaches the foreground, it has expended all of its strength and any kind of attack from any authoritarian power sends it back. This is a very disagreeable situation and you can imagine the leap that such a repressed, crushed, broken being makes when it is finally liberated. (Georg Groddeck, 1923, *The Book of the It*, p. 85f)[30]

Freud called all of the mental operations that regulate the flow of thoughts in the psychic system the "defense mechanisms." He ought to have named them the regulatory system of the psyche when he speaks of the psyche in general. But what interested him was the study of the psychic dysfunctions, and the key clinical elements that he had discovered in his patients was that consciousness is vulnerable, that it cannot deal with all of the information that exits in the unconscious. To ensure the sound functioning of consciousness, the regulatory systems of the psyche must, of necessity, protect and defend consciousness against the intrusion of thoughts that would destabilize it. Only that particular function of the psychological regulatory system should have been associated to "defense mechanisms." Thus, Freud's first patients suffering from hysteria had sexual desires that generated anxious conflict when they penetrated into consciousness and hurled themselves against the conscious moral rules of an individual who wants to be honest and coherent.

> A vignette concerning desire and hysteria. *In the case of one patient, the problem was that she loved her sister's husband. This passion raised a wide variety of issues that threatened the equilibrium of her way of thinking. The first is that the biological sexual needs of the patient do not require that the patient relate to her brother-in law. The patient's psyche has associated the power of her sexual instinct to the image of her brother-in-law. This association does not necessarily satisfy the demands of the instincts, but once this association has been forged, it imposes itself with an unrelenting force. The coupling between an instinctual force and a preconscious representation is what Freud calls a drive. The other difficulty for the patient was that she was reproaching herself so intensely for this desire that the conflict between her guilt and her desire was experienced as painful. It exhausted her. Her attempt to maintain this desire in the preconscious generated terrifying panic attacks. The patient's psychic apparatus then repressed this desire into her unconscious. But to maintain such a powerful thought in the unconscious requires so much energy that the entire functioning of the organism is consequently troubled. Thus, according to Freud, the psychological and somatic symptoms of hysteria are formed. The entire organism, and a part of the patient's entourage, are disturbed by the need to defend consciousness against such an unbearable thought.*[31]

There would therefore be psychopathology every time the conscious procedures are incapable of managing a desire or all other forms of highly charged representations. If the defense system could really repress an undesirable thought effectively, there would be no need for neuroses. This implies that the defense systems also have a blend of capacities and limits. We are now going to see that like the circuit of stress, a massive utilization of the system of defense generates psychopathological functioning.

The defense mechanisms repress the thoughts that destabilize consciousness into the unconscious. A disturbing thought that appears only once in consciousness is not dangerous. The system of defense is mostly conceived to take care of the recurrent thoughts that are constantly resourced. They often become overinvested. Therefore, to push back such overcharged thoughts requires a large amount of energy.

To maintain an overinvested thought in the unconscious contradicts the modes of functioning of the unconscious. The maintenance of charged thoughts in a zone that can only manage thoughts that have a weak excitation creates dysfunctions (1) in the unconscious procedures, (2) in the interaction between the unconscious and the preconscious, and (3) in the interfaces that allow the psyche to interact with the physiological dimension (sensory in the case of the unconscious and motoric in the case of the preconscious). This explains why the necessity to repress, in a persistent fashion, creates psychopathology. In effect, charged psychic material unceasingly tries to rise to consciousness. This is inevitable if we suppose that the more a thought is charged, the more it inserts itself into the conscious dynamics. A repressed drive is a bit like a balloon a child tries to keep under water. Even if the child succeeds temporarily, the balloon tries to resurface. The child must be unceasingly stronger than the thrust of the balloon. If the child loses concentration, the balloon will surface. This is how an unconscious content animates a dream when the organism relaxes to sleep.

The Nonconscious and the Unconscious

An Unending Debate

One of the strengths of Freud's psychological theory is to have helped all of humanity to speak of the unconscious forces of the psyche in a more explicit way. It is also true that at the beginning, Freudians had to learn how to battle against a well-organized opposition. But they then benefited from their immense media success when they argued that their unconscious was the only plausible approach to the psychological unconscious. When psychologists defined the conscious and unconscious dynamics of the psyche differently than Freud had, numerous psychoanalysts accused their colleagues of adopting an intellectual strategy that permitted them to avoid the content they were repressing into their unconscious. This attitude was vehemently criticized by philosophers such as Wittgenstein, who admitted that Freud had indubitably something interesting to say,[32] but that the psychoanalytical community defended itself more like a sect than like scientists who defend their theory. The violence of the blackmail exercised by this style of intellectual pursuit rendered every attempt to distinguish between many different types of psychic unconscious difficult. The situations were made even more complicated by the fact that many intellectuals had undergone psychoanalysis or were at least sympathetic toward psychoanalysis (like Wittgenstein, Vygotsky, Lévi-Strauss and Bourdieu). Inspired by Freud, they set about finding other forms of psychic unconscious—that is, a psychic mechanism that was activated independently of consciousness but which did not necessarily correspond to Freud's unconscious. Up until the 1970s, when I began my studies, it was impossible to present a talk concerning the psychological unconscious without having some psychoanalysts tell you that you were not talking about the *true* unconscious. The Freudians refused to admit that their unconscious dynamic was not the only form of unconscious used by the psyche. Even so, the discussion can easily be divided into two types of issues that refer to distinct forms of knowledge:

1. *The unconscious of the practitioner.*[33] My psychotherapists had enough clinical experience to sense when something in me refused to perceive a particular content in my memory, or when I used a form of rationalization to defend myself against an unfulfilled wish. They could have every reason to think that I was in conflict with an unconscious part of myself. It was also interesting to take into consideration what is repressed as a force which biases the reflection of the "psy." But then this argument is

also valid for psychoanalysts, as it is well known that even after a lengthy psychoanalysis, the resistances may have softened, but they are always present and active.

2. *The unconscious of the theoretician.* Freud's model was able to impose the idea that there is a psychic unconscious, but this does not mean that his theory is correct or that it accurately describes the whole of the unconscious phenomena of the psyche. It would not be surprising if the future allows us to show that the unconscious, such as it is perceived by so many clinicians, in fact corresponds to a series of distinct phenomena and that the amalgam Freud made in 1900 was useful but incomplete.

Freud's dynamic unconscious was soon accepted by a great number of researchers in the human sciences, whereas on the contrary the notions of resistance and the defense mechanisms are often ignored. Thus, when I used Ekman and Friesen's FACS coding system of the face, I wanted to code the chronic muscular tensions of the face that, according to Reich and Fenichel, could be the manifestation of the system of defense established around an affect. Ekman insisted that I only code the observable *movements* because these were the only data that could be irrefutable facts. He was not entirely wrong, because there is no robust way to distinguish between chronic muscular tension and the innate traits of the face. In the course of discussions with Ekman's colleagues, I noticed that the notion of defenses against the expression of an emotion is not used in most academic approaches of the emotional expression with the methods taken from ethology. The only exceptions were the psychoanalysts who used FACS to study interactions in psychotherapy.[34]

For 70 years, psychoanalytic and non-psychoanalytic psy unendingly discussed the topic in this way. Since the Freudians had kidnapped the term *unconscious* by depriving it of its natural multiplicity of meanings, the psy no longer knew what to call the unconscious impact of the physiological, relational, and social dynamics on the psyche.[35] Everybody wanted to use the term *unconscious*, fashionable thanks to Freud, but to designate psychic phenomena manifestly unconscious with loose boundaries that did not resemble the dynamics of repressed memories. They did not know what to call the unconscious mechanisms that combine mental regulations and organismic regulations, or mental regulations and social regulations, or a combination of all three (as Bourdieu's *habitus*). Some, like Lévi-Strauss and Bourdieu, could have proposed that the unconscious of the social sciences form another layer of the psyche that functions differently than the one described by Freud; but they did not dare take this step.[36] It is the same with Vygotsky (1927) with regard to certain layers of the psyche which develop by synthesizing the mechanisms of thoughts and the impact of the learning of a language. All of these emerging entities that form themselves in the individual thought have a complexity that an individual conscious thought cannot apprehend.[37]

In body psychotherapy, no one dared affirm that a massage acted simultaneously on the unconscious in two ways:

1. The fantasies of the patient's Freudian unconscious assimilate the actions of the massage therapist in their own way.
2. The massage acts on the physiology, which itself has an influence on the psyche. This influence probably mobilizes other mechanisms than those described by Freud.

Psychoanalysts often speak of the first effect and counsel against the massage of hysterical patients.[38] Their argument is that whatever the expressed conscious reactions are, hysterical patients experience the massage unconsciously as a sexual intrusion, a form of imposed recathexis that often leads to hypercathexis. Body psychotherapists do not often observe this, when they massage hysterical patients. In many cases, an approach with a touch that takes into account the anxieties of the patient can be beneficial. This discussion continues to this day.[39] Clinical practice (based on a discussion of real-life cases) has not permitted the closure of this discussion. As with all these methods, including psychoanalysis, massage is useful for some patients, but not for all. I see patients who were retraumatized by the silent distance of a psychoanalyst, and psychoanalysts see patients who were retraumatized by the intrusive methods of body psychotherapists. The ideal solution would be to exchange our observations to improve the calibration of our respective methods, instead of using the data to compete. This could be a debate that illustrates the difference between the unconscious impact of the physiological and the Freudian unconscious, but body psychotherapy was created around the idea that these two sometimes form an emerging entity in the psyche.

These hypotheses remain plausible, but we lack analyses based on empirical observations (clinical and experimental) that allow for drawing them. The difficulty is that it is not even possible to reliably demonstrate the existence of conscious thoughts. It is consequently even more difficult to discern the shape of unconscious thoughts. The Freudian unconscious can at least claim for itself that its unconscious thoughts can become conscious again. Thanks to that fact, emerging repressed thoughts can be studied in a relatively robust way. What we do not know how to analyze reliably are the unconscious dynamics of the psyche, which never become conscious. Nevertheless, a series of robust inferences obliges us to suppose that there exist unconscious mental dynamics that do not seek to be become conscious.

Since the 1980s, to work in peace, a growing number of biologists, neurologists, and psychologists use the term *nonconscious* to speak of unconscious dynamics that escape introspection.[40] From the point of view of consciousness, a nonconscious event is a fuzzy phenomenon that influences the periphery of our inner atmosphere, but not as something that can be grasped in an explicit way through introspection. This implies that there exists psychological dynamics that can never become conscious. The Freudian unconscious is henceforth one particular chapter in the study of unconscious processes, associated to the notion of the repression of thoughts that had been conscious. This attitude was summarized by the French professor of experimental psychology Paul Fraisse (1992) in the following way:

> I refuse to talk about the unconscious because it is essentially a psychoanalytical concept. . . . For my part, I agree to talk about non-consciousness, which is anyway a manner of speaking. . . . One could say that the unconscious is nonconscious, but I prefer to speak about the non-conscious because I do not want to endorse the psychoanalytic interpretation of these phenomena.
>
> My actual consciousness depends on all that I have been up until now. That is to say, it is an extraordinarily rich non-conscious totality that contains all that I have lived, all that I have been and which defines me today. . . . The non-conscious exceeds by far that which the psychoanalysts call the unconscious. (Paul Fraisse, 1992, "The Non Conscious," pp. 174–175; translated by Marcel Duclos)

A number of psychoanalysts[41] have courageously confronted the fact that the knowledge connected to the term *nonconscious* implies a reformulation of the role of the Freudian unconscious. Given that the Freudian unconscious has found a corresponding place in the theories of the psyche, body psychotherapists can now more explicitly establish the relationship between the nonconscious, unconscious, and consciousness, which they manage every day.

The Systemic and Nonconscious Dimensions of Freud's Psyche

> As much as we would want to count the grains of sand picked up by the wind at the sea shore during a stormy day; it would be equally impossible to enumerate the contradictory ideas that come, one after the other, hatched in the brain of Gorenflot before breakfast. (Alexander Dumas, 1846, *La dame de Monsoreau* [*The Lady of Monsoreau*], III, V, p. 370; translated by Marcel Duclos)

Not having been able to differentiate sufficiently the unconscious from the nonconscious, Freud did not succeed in situating the regulation systems of the psyche and the defense mechanisms. If a thought can be more or less conscious, can the mechanisms that put the defenses in place also function more or less consciously? The only plausible answer, for the moment, is that the content of the thoughts and drives can be more or less conscious, but that the regulation mechanisms that structure the psychic dynamics are mostly nonconscious. It is the same for the energetic dimension of the Freudian theory.

To clarify this discussion, I propose distinguishing two aspects of the defense mechanisms:

1. A *manifestation* (a lapse, a behavioral habit, a trembling of the voice, etc.) that allows a person (as it happens, the psychotherapist) to detect

the existence of a defense. Lacan (1949) distinguishes the "Me" (the aspect of myself I consciously perceive) and the "I" (the aspect of myself I do not perceive, save when I am in front of a mirror, but that everyone who meets me can see). I cannot see my behavior while anybody else can easily see it. Some manifestations (like a foot that moves) can be consciously perceived by another and not be perceived by myself.[42] At a given moment, my "Me" has but a partial and fragmented view of my organism, whereas another person perceives my organism as a totality, as a gestalt, as an apparently coherent whole. There is a permanent rift between these two ways of consciously perceiving the same person that, according to Lacan, tends to generate anxiety.[43]

2. The *mechanisms* that set in place the defense mechanisms and their manifestations. These mechanisms are generally nonconscious. The action of these mechanisms becomes tangible when a therapist and his patient discuss the behavior perceived by the therapist. The therapist sees what is going on better than the patient, although only the patient can know what he perceives while the behavior is occurring. But even here, there is another rift: that between my consciousness and my behavior. The conscious explanation I have for my behavior may not correspond to organismic mechanisms that activated the behavior. In discussing what is going on and by exchanging information, the functioning of a defense slowly becomes perceivable. There is then the construction of what Philip Rochat calls a "co-conscious" thought.[44] This shared construction permits the patient and the therapist to become conscious of the contour of a patient's resistance. The psychotherapist needs a supervisor to perceive the resistances and biases that arise in him when this form of co-consciousness emerges.

Having assimilated the idea that the defense mechanisms are part of the nonconscious dimensions of the psyche, Rene Roussillon proposes a useful reformulation of Freud's psyche. Above all, he shows that every influence of the environment on the organism is necessarily transformed so it can be used by the mechanisms of the organism. Each organ (liver and lungs) and the physiological system (respiration and circulation) have a particular way of functioning. Thus, food is rapidly transformed in the digestive tract into a series of products that can be assimilated by the digestive mechanisms. When indigestible products are regularly ingested, the digestive mechanisms are gradually and profoundly deregulated. It is the same in the psyche. The psyche is not always able to digest all of the information the nervous system transmits to it:

> This "prime matter" of the psyche, mixes and entangles multiple internal and external perceptions, sensations and driven motions.... It is multi-perceptive, multi-sensory, multi-affective, multi-instinctive: it mixes, given its position in the topography, the inside and the outside, the "Me" and the "non-Me." (Roussillon, 2007, p. 341; translated by Marcel Duclos)

This "pandemonium"[45] is digestible for the unconscious but not for consciousness. Each level of the psyche has its mode of functioning, exigencies, and limits. As it is for Spinoza's imagination, coherence is not a requirement of Freud's unconscious. However, consciousness does have this requirement. It is incapable of managing the lava that erupts in the unconscious. It needs to protect itself and reduce what enters into something it can digest or metabolize. The first function of the defense mechanisms is therefore to allow for a triage, a slowing down of the lava, which promotes the construction of a manageable subjective experience. The thoughts necessarily transform everything into representations because thoughts cannot organize themselves except through representations. These can have multiple supports, such as words, images, impressions, sensations, and gestures.[46] When the regulatory systems of the psyche are flooded by the intrusion of powerful affects, consciousness generates an anxiety or a depressive feeling that inhibits the habitual behavioral dynamics and creates a sort of organismic disarray described by the studies on the biology of stress. This is what Freud observes by analyzing his first hysterical patients.

NEUROSIS AS THE CONTENT OF THE FIRST TOPOGRAPHY

Freud was conscious that a relatively coherent global architecture was missing in his theory: architecture in which is it possible to situate all of the components of his model. The Freudian theory has a quasi-postmodern structure composed of constituent parts whose architecture has not yet been clarified.[47] Like Plato, Freud prefers to approach themes about which he has something to say and leave aside—sometimes with regret—that about which he is unable to come to a conclusion.

The Etiology of Neurosis

Etymologically, since the eighteenth century, English and French psychiatrists use the term *neurosis* to designate "nervous" problems without a known physiological basis. It indicates functional problems of the brain that are not due to lesions or hormonal problems. With regard to language, it would have been wise to use the term *psychosis* to indicate the problems that are uniquely due to functional problems of the psyche. However, in Freud's time, the term *psychosis* was already being used in psychiatry to indicate problems associated to symptoms such as hallucinations and delusions of grandeur. A psychotic was a type of patient who justified the existence of psychiatric institutions, while a person suffering from a neurosis could be followed and sometimes treated in the framework of private practice. The term *neurosis* therefore identifies a mixture of functional problems of the brain, the hormonal system, and the psyche. The blending of this mixture varies in function of the theory used, on the one hand, and also because the way a mental problem manifests depends on the constitution and on the life journey of each individual. Anxiety may be treated in part with tranquilizers or psychotherapy. But neither one of these two kinds of treatment can treat every anxious individual in a lasting way.

The discussions on the difference between these two large categories in psychiatry, neuroses and psychoses, continued up to the 1980s. It is impossible to read the writings to which I refer without knowing this distinction. Today, psychiatrists no longer use these terms; they prefer to use more detailed and operational definitions in their diagnostic systems (for example in the *DSM-IV* and the *ICD-10*, or De Lange et al., 2008).

It is difficult to define the word *neurosis* in a more precise way because its meaning changes every ten years, whether in the works of Freud or, generally, in psychiatry textbooks. The relationship between neurosis and psychosis in psychoanalysis only became stabilized after Jung participated in the elaboration of psychoanalytic concepts around 1910.[48] For the following sections, it suffices to relate the term *neurosis* to the notion of behavioral problems that cannot be attributed to physiological dynamics, a psychosis, or depression, and that are associated with severe forms of anxiety. Among these neuroses, Freud first specialized in the study of hysteria, which he differentiates from the other forms of neurosis.

In psychiatry, the mental problems are often defined in function of behavioral problems. The originality of Freud's endeavor was to want to distinguish between psychopathologies in function of the psychic mechanisms that engender behavioral problems. It is therefore possible, in the Freudian system, that a behavioral or affective symptom can be observed in individuals who suffer from distinct psychological illnesses. This endeavor is analogous to that which is followed to categorize the species of animals. Thus, even if they live in the water, biologists do not classify whales in the same category as fish because they have a distinct respiratory system, one that is close to that of other mammals.

Hysteria in Psychiatry Today

The term *hysteria* has at least two meanings:

1. *Popular meaning.* A chauvinistic term referring to all attractive, extroverted, demanding, hypersensitive women who, in the end, are not necessarily "easy to be with" and who are easily treated as "a tease" by many men. Darwin[49] gives an example of hysterical "patients" who rapidly go from laughter to tears to rather infantile fits of anger. This popular meaning is sadly incorporated in some systems of "body reading" and "character analysis" utilized by certain schools of body psychotherapy. The psychoanalyst Otto Fenichel classifies as hysterical persons whose principal crux is a fear of sexuality in conflict with a repressed, intense sexual desire. These internal dynamics generate a tendency to attribute sexual connotations to all forms of behavior. We will see that Fenichel had a profound impact on several psychodynamic and body

psychotherapy schools. No doubt because of this, variations of this definition is found in many schools of body psychotherapy, influenced by
Reich, like the schools founded by Ellsworth Baker, Alexander Lowen,
and Gerda Boyesen.[50] I have even heard some female colleagues in body
psychotherapy assert that the hysterical woman necessarily has a wide
pelvis and ample breasts because it always consists of characters whose
problems are linked to the oedipal structuring, that is, once that the libido begins to associate itself to the sexual organs.[51]

2. *Psychiatric meaning.* There is *conversion* hysteria[52] when there is a physical disability without a discernible physical cause. The proof for it is
that the disability disappears as suddenly as it appeared without a physician being able to explain what triggered the healing. Therefore, we do
not know if the causes of hysteria are in fact mental, because they are
simply unexplainable. Freud thought the cause was mental. For him,
everything happens as if mental awareness dissociates from organismic
activities. Another form of hysteria is characterized by a *convulsive* attack, during which the body of the patient suddenly begins to move in
all directions in a manner that is unexpected both by the patient and by
the entourage. Charcot, with whom Freud studied in Paris, had asked
others to draw or photograph his patients is such a crisis state. These illustrations have often been reproduced.[53] These hysterical convulsive attacks are sometime difficult to distinguish from epileptic convulsions
caused by a grand mal seizure.[54] These cases were frequent enough at the
end of the nineteenth century in Europe. They subsequently became less
frequent and are now rare. This shows that even if there is a link between hysteria and biology, the cultural factors are equally important. In
other forms of hysteria, a person suffers from a *dissociative* fugue or
tends to regularly sleep walk. These manifestations are mostly observed
in women but also appear in men. Hysteria, in the psychiatric sense of
the word, is a serious and rare symptom that is difficult to treat.[55]

These two ways to use the term *hysteria* are only sometimes reconcilable. Having uncovered sexual abuse or intense fantasies of abuse in many of his hysterical patients, Freud proposed a model of hysteria in which sexual conflicts played
a central role. The psychological interpretation of the causes of hysteria, de-
tached from its symptoms, is one of the factors that encouraged several psychotherapists to gradually return to the popular sense of the term.

Today, most psychiatrists use the diagnostic term of *dissociative convulsion*
when they describe Charcot's hysterical attacks. To differentiate these convulsions from an epileptic attack is something that remains difficult. Thanks to
video, it has become possible to isolate the following characteristic traits:[56] balancing movements of the pelvis, lateral movement of the head (as is often done
when one says "no" with a head movement), an arched back with facial grimac-
ing (opisthotonus), a slow start but progressively lengthy duration of the attack,

and closing the eyes. The traits of the epileptic attack are more manifestly convulsive, and its movements often escape every attempt to give them a meaning. On the other hand, the traits of a hysterical discharge are found in many forms of profound emotional discharges. It is possible to assign a functional expression to them, even if they can be explained otherwise. Recent studies show that at least 20 percent of patients who suffer from dissociative convulsions have suffered sexual abuse or emotional and or mental abuse. Balancing the pelvis and the head could be associated with this past, but it is also seen in a population for whom it has not been possible to establish that there has been abuse during childhood. Here again, as soon as we postulate a direct link between behavior and the affects, we are open to simplifications.[57] The research by Karin Roelofs and her collaborators (Spinhoven et al., 2010, and Voon et al., 2010) confirms a strong percentage of sexual abuse either through violent physical abuse during childhood by the father and/or the mother in a population of patients classically considered as hysterics. We also find in the neurosciences the idea that when the parents abuse their children, they create profound problems with the coordination between representation, emotion, and behavior.[58] Today, it is also possible to consider hysteria as a particular form of post-traumatic stress disorder due to abuse that occurred during childhood.

I have allowed myself to emphasize the psychiatric definition of hysteria because it clearly shows that to discuss this condition necessarily requires that we investigate the rapport between the psyche and the organism.

Breuer, the Cathartic Method, and the "Talking Cure"

When Freud returned from Paris, he was still a young physician without significant means who was beginning to acquire a modest reputation. He wanted to establish himself so that he might practice what he had learned relative to the treatment of hysterical patients. He also wanted to earn enough money to marry his fiancée, Martha Bernays. He counted among his acquaintances a renowned generalist, Dr. Joseph Breuer (1842–1925). They had known each other for a dozen years. Breuer, with others, financially supported Freud. Between 1880 and 1882, Breuer had attempted to treat a hysterical patient, known under the name of Anna O. He let her talk, seeking to find in what she said indicators that would permit him to reconstruct her past and understand the particularities of her sentiments. He thus invented what he called the "talking cure" (to heal oneself by talking).[59] During this treatment, Breuer noticed that Anna O. had similar forms of dissociation as the ones associated with hypnotic states.[60] In 1887, Breuer asked Freud to collaborate with him by hypnotizing his hysterical patients. Their collaboration led to the creation of what they called the *cathartic method*. It consisted in blending the talking cure and hypnosis to induce regressive states, during which patients relived the traumatizing moments of their childhood. This form of regression could be sustained by hand pressure on a part of the body, for instance, the forehead. The therapist asks the patient what she experiences when she is touched.[61] Freud sometimes insistently tried to persuade her that she should become aware of the contradictions in her story and that these were probably generated by her mind to hide painful memories she wants to forget. During this work, the physician and the patient establish a particular form of relationship: "intensely emotional, of a suggestive-hypnotic type. . . . Physician and patient join the forces of their efforts to attempt to reconstruct in some way the repressed causes of the illness from disparate fragments of associated material" (Ferenczi, 1930, p. 84).

According to Breuer and Freud, each time these patients were able to recover the repressed situations that had traumatized them, the mind and body symptoms activated by the repression disappeared once and for all, as if the pathogenic effect of the repressed memories were chased out of the patient's organism. This type of remembering is so strong that no possible suggestion by the therapist could induce it; the patient can therefore have but one scene in mind.[62] This work was disclosed and expounded in the famous *Studies on Hysteria* which Breuer and Freud published in 1895.

In his hysterical patients, Freud noticed dysfunctions of consciousness so manifest that he did not need to invoke the notion of the unconscious to talk about them. These patient are haunted by desires that create so many contradictions that what is experienced as a "central conscious me"[63] cannot function anymore. Let us take the case of Elizabeth Von R. to illustrate this mechanism.[64]

Vignette concerning Elizabeth Von R. *When she comes to see Freud in 1892, this young woman, age 24, has been suffering for 2 years from inexplicable pain in her legs; she complains of often being fatigued. She has just come out of a painful period of time during which she had to take care of her father and a sister who died after having been ill, and her mother, who had eye surgery. Apart from her symptom, she seems to function adequately, with intelligence, good humor, and courage. She is even quite lovely. Freud associates this apparent well-being to the* belle indifference *that then characterized hysterical patients. He accepts her as a patient for psychotherapy, while ensuring that she follows a physical therapy treatment for her legs.*

When her father became ill for 18 months, it was mostly Elizabeth who took care of him. She slept in the same room with him. That was when the patient's leg pain began. But the pain was only episodic then. A year after the father's death, once the period of mourning was over, her oldest sister married a man that Freud described as gifted and energetic. His arrival into the family's life occurred in a manner that Elizabeth experienced as disagreeable. She regularly showed him her irritation.

Subsequently, a second sister got married. This new brother-in-law, "though less outstanding, intellectually, was a man 'after the heart' of these cultivated women" (Breuer and Freud, 1895, II.5, p. 209). Then the mother had serious eye problems and had to be cared for in a dark room for months before the operation. Again, it was mostly Elizabeth who took care of her mother's needs. After the operation, two years after the death of the father, Elizabeth's leg pain reoccurs. The second sister became pregnant but did not make it through the pregnancy. She became ill and died.

In the course of her treatment with Freud, Elizabeth ended up talking to him about a young man, known to her family, for whom she held secret romantic feelings. She could not stop herself from thinking about him while she took care of her father, but she did not give herself the right to have these feelings in such circumstances. Then her organism learned to transform her desire into the leg pain for reasons that Freud only vaguely understood. This conflict was nonetheless less serious than when she began secretly to fall in love with her second sister's husband. When this sister, whom she loved very much, died, she could not stop thinking that she could now marry her brother-in-law.

This case shows a scrupulously honest and moral woman who cannot prevent herself from feeling desires incompatible with her moral standards. Her conscious thoughts do not know how to integrate the contradictions set in place between her beliefs and her desires. To protect the coherence of her central conscious me, she feels obliged to repress her romantic needs. This strategy is relatively conscious, but she does not take into account that a desire is not only a thought, it is also a physiological mobilization linked to sexuality. By refusing to become aware of the physiological charge that enlivens her desires, she prevents some physiological propensities from coordinating with her thoughts. Yet such a connection is a necessary part of the mechanism that regulates the propensities of her organism.[65] There is consequently not only a repression of a thought but also an inhibition and a deviation of a physiological dynamic. This deviation, according to Freud, finally lodged in her leg, which became painful, and in the regulatory mechanism of sleep.

The organism does not do well when the dialogue between dimensions and regulators of the organism is interrupted to preserve the apparent good functioning of a single dimension. Here, the organism is sacrificed to secure, for consciousness, a feeling of self-esteem and coherence. The general implication of this case study is that a propensity can only express itself by being able to count on a certain type of collaboration with the conscious dynamics of the psyche. There was healing, according to Freud, as soon as Elizabeth Von R.'s conscious dynamics had a way to integrate the existence of what for her was an incestuous love[66] and the fact that this love was not possible. We also see in this example that what is perceived as a central me can be reinforced and learn to better manage the material that forms in the person; on the other hand, the needs that manifest themselves to the person do so without asking advice of her conscious procedures. To not be able to admit the existence of a need not only weakens what I have momentarily called a "conscious central me" but also handicaps the whole of the organism.

The Causes of Neurosis: Initial Trauma or Blockage of the Accommodation?

This involves some psychological preparation of the patient. We must aim at bringing about two changes in him: an increase in the attention he pays to his own mental perceptions and the elimination of the criticism by which he normally sifts the thoughts that occur to him (Freud, 1900, *The Interpretation of Dreams*, II, p. 101)

To heal analytically signifies above all to recognize the developmental failures, and in the measure possible, to benefit from this understanding to rectify these failures. (Wilhelm Reich, 1927a, *The Impulsive Character*, I, p. 247)

A Myth of Psychotherapy That Many Take for Reality

I still have patients who come to me thinking that the goal of psychotherapy is to recover the memory of an event repressed in the unconscious and then they will be cured. Some even believe that this repressed memory is necessarily that of a sexual abuse that occurred in their childhood. In some cases, these patients are psychologists with a good training in psychodynamic psychotherapy. They attribute this view of psychotherapy to Freud. Such a view was indeed presented by Freud in three articles published in 1896 (1896a; 1896b; 1896c). He speaks of the first thirteen cases of hysteria that would have been healed after being able to recover the memory of "a precocious experience of sexual relations with actual excitement of the genitals, resulting from sexual abuse committed by another person; and the period of life in which this fatal event takes place is the earliest years—the years up to eight or ten, before the child has reached sexual maturity" (Freud, 1896a: 152). If Freud plainly explored this trail, he did not defend it later on—mostly because he did not think that he had enough evidence to prove this hypothesis. For example, the case of Elizabeth Von R. is a manifest exception to this rule, as Freud does not report that she had been abused in her childhood.

On this fragile base is constructed the myth according to which every neurosis is caused by a sexual trauma in childhood and that it suffices to revive the repressed traumatizing memory to be healed. Freud imagined that once repressed, these memories became more intense when the traumatized child became an adult and fell in love. The events of the present resonated with the repressed memories and affects, creating a work overload for the defense system, which destabilized the individual. Every time the person fell in love, a whirlwind of thoughts and feelings arose and rendered him or her so ambivalent and anxious that the organism preferred to organize symptoms that would render the romantic relation less pleasing, or even impossible.

Today, psychiatric institutions and the social services have showed that Freud's first intuition was indeed founded. Sadly, we know that there is much more abuse of children than even Freud could have imagined. Probably because of this fact, some psychoanalysts have questioned themselves about what would have become of Freud's theory if he had supported his first hypothesis.[67]

Genital Sexuality As the Source of Trauma for the Child

Between 1906 and 1908, Freud analyzed a child born in 1903 using a psychoanalytically informed type of intervention adapted to what can be done with a child. It is the case of *Little Hans*. When he was three years old, a little sister was born. His father explained to him that she was a gift from a stork. However, children are not stupid. They know that funny things happen in the parent's bedroom when father is there, because they cannot sleep with mama on those nights. They have seen their mother's belly blow up like a balloon and then deflate as soon as the sister arrived. They have perhaps seen a calf come out from between the legs of a cow or a stallion mount a mare. But they have no tools to explain what they see. Consequently, they invent some fanciful explications. Hans told himself that children come out of the mother's belly like poop and that he is probably a bit of special poop. If he would have seen his father put his penis between his mother's legs, he would have maybe imagined that his father was urinating. In brief, he fabricates for himself an unsavory image of sexual life and his origins, which he prefers to repress to continue to value what goes on in his home and to value himself. Freud analyzes an entire series of events of this type that lead to a manifest phobia when Hans was five years old—a phobia of horses that Freud ends up healing.

Freud then supposed that when the child grows up and falls in love, the present events resonate with what is repressed. The infantile imagery concerning sexuality becomes more intense. The defense system has more work. A whirlwind of ambivalent and anxious thoughts inexplicably invade the consciousness. The individual's behavior becomes increasingly inappropriate. Symptoms arise. The relationship with the loved one becomes less pleasant and sometimes impossible. The individual feels anxious but is able to continue to function as before. Within a conflicted life of this type, a particularly intense one, symptomatic hysteria can come about.[68] In this example, there is no abuse, but there is an inability to manage what is perceived in a constructive fashion. Freud concluded that the best way to prevent a neurosis is a good sexual education. The sexual trauma is thus mostly a psychological phenomenon that constructs itself around a weakness of the mind rather that around real traumatic events.

This new elaboration of the traumatizing aspect of sexual life already began in 1895 when Freud noticed that there is no initial trauma for what he calls the *anxiety neuroses*.[69] This type of neurosis blends (as does hysteria) physical symptoms (excessive cardiac palpitations, respiratory and digestive problems, bodily shaking and trembling, cravings, vertigo, etc.) and mental symptoms (fear and anxiety), but they are caused by other mechanisms. The anxiety neuroses can also have a sexual cause. But it consists this time of *recurring* frustrating behaviors. For example, as there was no reliable form of contraception at the time, a husband would withdraw before ejaculating when he made love, to avoid having a child. This is the model that Freud uses henceforth to analyze most of the neurotic problems.

In his 1900 *The Interpretation of Dreams*, Freud shows that his treatment is always founded on an exploration of the unconscious:

> [For] certain psychopathological structures—hysterical phobias, obsessive ideas, and so on . . . unraveling them coincided with removing them. . . . If a pathological

idea of this sort can be traced back to the elements in the patient's mental life from which it originated, it simultaneously crumbles away and the patient is freed from them. (1900, II, p. 100)

However, it now consists, as the case of Hans so well illustrates, in analyzing the meanderings of the false reasoning that are lodged in destructive ways in the mental life of an individual. It now consists of undertaking a reconstruction of the psyche that permits more lucidity and more self-confidence and confidence in one's surroundings. This exploration fosters the reconstruction of a person's history so as to understand how the inadequate schemata that constituted an imagined personal history came about and stabilized.

FREE ASSOCIATIONS AS THE BASIC METHOD OF THE FIRST TOPOGRAPHY

The Talking Cure of Breuer and Freud

The classic psychoanalytic method is based on a fundamental contract with the patient that is built around two rules:[70]

1. *The respect for the frame* (time schedule, finances, postures). The appointment is fixed in advance, and all sessions booked are paid. The mode of payment is agreed to in advance. The patient sees the therapist at least three times a week for at least 40 minutes. The patient remains lying down on the divan and the therapist sits behind the patient at his head. The therapist guarantees, except in an absolute emergency, that the session will not be interrupted. The patient and the therapist do not touch, save eventually out of politeness when they greet each other at the start and at the end of the session.
2. The patient does his best to say *out loud,* in a language that the therapist understands, *everything that comes to mind.*

The second rule is a technique used by the hypnotists of the nineteenth century. It is the foundation of the psychoanalytic method of *free association.*[71] It consists in associating out loud, not hiding any thought from the therapist at any given moment, even if it seems insignificant and irrelevant: the sound of the street cars, the smell of the room, the internal comments related to the therapist, the ironies concerning the price of the session, the pride in having worn a nice shirt, and so on. When the patient embarks on a *structured* narrative, he avoids associating and he dissociates from these little facts that build what is going on for him in the present moment. The structured discourse is a particularly powerful defense when the patient relates such moving and dramatic memories that the therapist does not dare interrupt.

A structured discourse (a narration, for example) deprives the therapist of a mine of information:

1. The therapist does not know how the patient views him, how he is reacting to the frame. To not say what is being thought in the present moment can be a way to mask the positive and negative transferences.
2. The therapist does not know how the diverse thoughts develop into themes and relate to one another as a function of the patient's varied affects.

When a patient gives an account of a dramatic event, he informs the therapist, and he lets off steam, which is useful, but it draws the attention of the therapist and the patient to something that is not happening here and now. The therapist is certainly interested in knowing that the patient was beaten. But when this complaint is repeated, the therapist would like to know why the patient wants the focus of their attention to revolve around this event. The therapist tries to understand why the patient prefers to talk about the past instead of focusing on his need to complain. The past cannot be changed. The goal of psychotherapy is to help the patient better understand his present behavior so as to prepare for the future. An individual's history explains who he is, but the story that a person tells himself is certainly not all of his history.

Interpretation is the psychoanalyst's second basic tool. Interpretation can be related to context and content.

1. Interpretations of *context* are related to the manner in which the patient associates. The therapist may, for example, notice that certain themes are not often developed. He can then infer that there are zones of timidity and intimacy that are painful to divulge. What an individual chooses to say and not say, to unveil and to veil, reveals not only an individual's diffidence but also his perception of the therapist. The patient is saying to himself that such a fact is useful in therapy and another is useless. This behavior implies an implicit definition of therapy and of the therapist and identifies the way the patient tends to approach situations and persons in his current life. Here, the idea is that an individual has habits, ways of doing things that he has developed in the course of his life that he inevitably uses in his meeting with his psychotherapist. This type of mechanism is what Reich makes explicit in his Character analysis.
2. The analysis of *content* focuses on the themes that are transmitted by dreams, memories, behaviors, and so on. The interpretation distinguishes between the *manifest and* the *latent* content.[72] The manifest content of a dream, for example, is what the patient recounts. The latent content is discovered by following the associations that are organized around the dream by the patient and the therapist. These associations make it possible to free the underlying dynamics that have generated the dream. The repressed unconscious content is a part of the latent content of a dream, a "lapsus," and so on. The manifest content is preconscious material activated by unconscious forces to influence conscious dynamics.

In exploring what is not said, in these twilight zones of the mind, the psychoanalyst not only finds the zones of timidity, affection, and irritation toward oneself and therapy but also the doors that allow the patient to enter anew in contact with the repressed thoughts and the defense mechanisms that structure his functioning.

The Power of the Mind on the Body

The body, according to Freud, combines the physiological and bodily dimensions of the organism, such as I have described them in the System of the Dimensions of the Organism. The organism is still, for him, a coordination between mind and body. He claims that psychoanalysis is a mental treatment that takes its origin in the soul, begins by healing the soul, but can then also influence physiology.[73]

In Freud's time, the soul/matter polarity was becoming increasingly difficult to defend. Scientists were all looking for a new theory concerning the organismic dimensions that could fit the data. Freud's psyche elegantly fit into the spirit of the time as the mind is simultaneously integrated into the regulators of the organism but remains distinct from the other dimensions (body, behavior, physiology, etc.) with which it constantly interacts in an intimate way. His study of hysteria permits him to detail this view. By deciding to center his attention on the analysis of the content of what is being said, Freud focuses his attention on the mind more that on what he calls the body. Like all choices, it implies a gain and a loss. Some analysts go so far as to justify this choice by minimizing bodywork, like La Fontaine's fable on the fox who finds appetizing grapes too sour *because* he cannot jump high enough to eat them. Others maintained the course fixed by Freud. The organism is constantly part of their peripheral vision. This was the case of Otto Fenichel, who reaffirmed in 1945 that "Mental phenomena occur only in living organisms" (Fenichel, 1945a, Introduction, p. 5).

Psychopathology, according to Freud, is certainly a dysfunction of the psyche, caused by a context to which an individual's mind is incapable of accommodating itself other that in creating chronic repression in the unconscious. If a certain dose of chronic unconscious is inevitable, the dose found in Freud's patients is too important to allow the psyche to adequately accomplish its function as an organismic regulator. Now the repressed has an impact not only on the mind but also on the organism; it can, for example, unleash functional problems of physiological and sexual behavior.[74]

Although the organism was part of Breuer's and Freud's thinking, they thought that a trauma, due to one or many events of sexual abuse, could be treated with *psycho*therapy, that is, by working only on mental dynamics (hypnosis, memory, understanding, regression, etc.). In short, the idea is that a woman's body suffers just momentarily from being raped, because the physical wounds heal, whereas the wounds of the soul are often lasting. This analysis rests on some experience of hypnosis in which the unconscious seems to have a total control of the body mechanics, like the soul on the body in healing movements:

> If we put a person into deep hypnosis and suggest the idea to him that he sees nothing with one of his eyes, he will in fact behave as though he has become blind with one of his eyes, like a hysteric who has developed a visual disturbance spontaneously. . . . In a hysteric the idea of being blind arises, not from the prompting of a hypnotist, but spontaneously—by autosuggestion, as people say; and in both cases this idea is so powerful that it turns into reality, exactly like a suggested hallucination, paralysis, etc. (Freud, 1910a, p. 107)

The hysterical revulsions are therefore "nothing else but phantasies translated into the motor sphere, projected on to mobility and portrayed in pantomime" (Freud, 1909a, A, p. 97).[75] The observation that a mental suggestion can have an enormous power over the body is an indisputable fact, but there are many ways to understand it. In the mind of many psychoanalysts, a mental representation can have a *direct* impact on the functioning of the organs. There would then be a direct parallelism. Freud knew enough to sense that this was not a direction to take. We must, in effect, explain the relative efficacy of hypnosis because it is more effective (that is, more powerful, longer lasting, etc.) with some people than with others. Hypnosis is effective when a series of mechanisms (mental, organismic, and bodily) are able to align themselves around a representation. As soon as a representation becomes what activates a schema, it acquires a stunning power. I have the impression that these "sudden cures" can inscribe themselves in the organism if there is already an organismic schema that uses this representation as a stimulus of reference, as in the case of the conditioned reflexes described by Pavlov (1927). This alignment around a representation can sometimes happen all of a sudden, as hypnotists demonstrate;[76] or by a gradual construction as shown by the analysis of the anxiety neuroses that seems to create a mechanism that is close to conditioned reflexes already in place.

For a number of body psychotherapists, trauma often inscribes itself into the organism, in the functioning of the nervous system, in muscular tension, in the tissues that no longer respond as they should.[77] In these cases, the wounding of the soul does not explain all of the suffering that builds up in an abused organism.[78] Since Reich, it is admitted that the orgasm is an organismic conduct, not only a fantasy. The hysterical convulsion, when it resembles a stimulation of the sexual act, certainly would not be the play of an actor that activates the body. A convulsion activates psychophysiological remnants of the orgasm reflex that revives past pains.[79] This vision is close to Descartes's living body, capable of being wounded as profoundly by a physical intrusion (rape, violence) as by what is going on at the level of the representations. I do not believe that the psychoanalysts of today, like Francois Sironi (1999), who has helped people who have been tortured, could entertain a position like the one that Freud held early on. Since the work done on stress and oxytocin, we know that the body reacts as much as the thoughts do to trauma and that healing can rarely be only mental. The disorganizations induced by trauma in the innate reactions of the organism are one of the reasons that render the treatment of serious trauma so difficult and only rarely completely effective. This type of argument justifies the inclusion of interventions on body dynamics in a therapeutic treatment plan for traumatized persons.[80]

From Dream Analysis to Behavior Analysis

> It is not necessarily words that frighten children: certain attitudes, involuntary gestures, a hardly noticeable annoyance may sometimes have much more impact. (Georg Groddeck, 1923, *The Book of the It*, p. 217)[81]

The Analysis of Verbal Associations

> The interview of the patient must be as objective as possible. We limit ourselves to asking the patient to focus attentively on one of the images of the dream and to express the ideas that they evoke as they appear. (Jean Piaget, 1920, *Psychoanalysis and Child Psychology*, p. 20; translated by Marcel Duclos)

In the case of hysterical patients, free association had centers of clear attention because there was a crisis and manifest symptoms. By "center of attention," I mean phenomena around which the associations organize themselves repeatedly and which facilitate the pinpointing of the themes that link the symptoms to the underlying mental dynamics. Each association becomes a note in the musical score of the mental dynamics that the psychoanalyst is then able to apprehend. In the case of neuroses that are not caused by a specific trauma, there are no clear symptoms that serve as a point of departure for the patient's associations. The analyst is then inundated by associations with which he does not always know what to do. No musical form (fugue, sonata, etc.) allows for structuring all the notes that takes hold of the atmosphere in the therapy room, of the soul of the patient and that of the therapist.

Each time a researcher is inundated with data, he follows Descartes's method. He first concentrates on what can be most easily assimilated. There is hope that once the researcher has clarified the more simple mechanisms, he will be able to confront the increasing complexity. To achieve this, the psychoanalyst typically uses a small repertoire of sexual behaviors as a reference point for associations, because at least he has a theory to support this choice. The reference point is then a key instinctual drive for psychoanalysts. This repertoire of sexual metaphors (castration, primal scene, etc.) often activates strong explicit reactions in the patient, which can be used like a symptom, like a reference for a wide range of associations.

Another manifestation that can serve as a center of organization for the associations is a dream. This is even one of the most useful centers, because the dream brings metaphors produced by the patient to the therapist. These metaphors can be used to build a ground of shared associations between the patient and the therapist.[82] This is one of the reasons why I think that dreams remain a "royal road" to the unconscious.[83]

The Basic Freudian Dream Analysis Technique: Latent and Manifest Content

> I proceed *concentrically*, instead of by free association that sort of zigzags away from the dream and lands in some place or another. So the question to the dreamer is: "What comes to mind about X, what do you think of it? And what else comes to mind about X?" Whereas the question in free association is: "What comes to mind about X? And then? And then?". And so on. In this way the associations are about *other associations*, instead of about X. In contrast to this method, I stay with the original image of X. (Karl Gustav Jung, 1940, *Children's Dreams*, 1, p. 26)

Freud uses the method of free association to find the *latent* content of a dream.[84] He first writes down the dream the patient tells him. Then he cuts it up into little "bricks" that contain one or several words.[85] He then presents a first brick to the patient while asking him to say every thought that comes to mind. Freud presents the next brick and again asks for the associations. The first phase of the analysis of the dream is complete when all the pieces have been presented for the spoken associations of the patient and for the internal associations of the therapist. The latent content emerges once all these associations have been heard. These associations form the pieces of a puzzle that can then be perceive as forming a scenario.

> A vignette on dreams. *I had a patient for whom the latent content was always the opposite of the manifest content. For months, she presented frightening nightmares of monsters that attacked her during the night. Through the associations, she rediscovered her love for her father. Afterward, for many months, she came with dreams that made her happy because she saw herself with her lover on a wonderful sandy beach on a Pacific isle. Each time, she rediscovered in her associations the anxiety of loving someone who can disappoint you and even abandon you. The horrible dreams led to the need to love and to the pleasure of being loved: then, having found someone to love, the heavenly dreams led to the anxieties of love.*

An astute technique is to ask the patient what is the first thing that comes to him when he hears the therapist read a brick of the dream, then free associate uniquely on this first association by forgetting the pieces derived from the manifest dream. The difference between the manifest and the latent content is made clearer because we can often reconstruct a "hidden history" by putting the first associations together. For example, the therapist says "beach" and the patient associates "shark." The therapist then asks the patient to free associate on the shark instead of the beach.

The material gathered in this way leads to the second phase of the analysis, which is the integration of the latent content into the mental dynamics of the patient. One of the difficulties when you use this technique is that the latent content has been repressed because it could not be integrated without creating chaos in the mind. In Freud's time, for example, a number of patients followed a religious morality that did not tolerate sexual or violent fantasies. Freud helped his patients reconstruct a moral vision capable of including these fantasies without having the impression of acting immorally. In carrying out this work, psychoanalysis put into question the foundations of the official morality in European countries.

It became necessary to clearly differentiate delusions of the mind from behavior. From the point of view of psychoanalysis, the content of a sadistic dream becomes reprehensible as soon as it acted on, but not before. To dream that we are torturing a sexual partner, rendering him totally submissive, is one thing; *becoming* sadistic is something else. Thus the psychoanalysts showed that to apply the same moral laws to thoughts as to behaviors often leads to deeply rooted neuroses. The neurotic criticizes his thoughts as if they were behaviors. He represses his "unacceptable" thoughts for fear of what others would think of him. He censures these fantasies before they reach awareness. In this way, he need not feel guilty for having them and feels assured that they will not influence his behavior. On the contrary, a pervert is compelled to act out what he imagines and is often incapable of stopping himself. The common element between neurosis and perversion would be a poor differentiation between the requirements of the mind and those of behavior. This lack of differentiation is one of the weak points of certain forms of humanistic psychotherapy, notably certain body psychotherapy approaches, that encourage, in a simplistic way, all manner of self-expression.

One of the recurrent themes in the psychoanalytic literature is that the unconscious dynamics fabricates fantasies, without taking into account the moral requirements of the cultural environment of the individual. This production is submissive to intra-organismic modes of functioning. To want dreams to avoid imagining reprehensible behavior according to the social environment would be to deny that biological needs do not follow the same rules as the legal system of the state. Psychoanalysts want to know all the fantasies produced by the mind so as to understand how the psyche functions and then prevent the patient from acting out the fantasy. Only once the dynamics of an individual's drives are understood, is it possible to approach the inevitable issues posed by the behavior, which, by definition, is a bridge between drives and social practices. This procedure allows one to know what aspects of the individual a society needs to support and what aspects of the individual's inner dynamics cannot be integrated in a type of society that demands the respect of other people. This example, like so many others, shows why it is important to postulate that behavior and mind do not follow the same modes of functioning. In psychoanalytic jargon, when the mental content automatically becomes behavior, there is "acting out."[86] Other forms of psychotherapy, like most body psychotherapies, require that one understands how thoughts and behaviors are related. Some types of coordination between thoughts and behavior are useful and need to be supported, whereas others are destructive. These therapies are therefore against the psychoanalytic stance that all forms of coordination between mind and behavior should be negatively connoted as a form of acting out. Most of the humanistic psychotherapies, in effect, encourage the attempts that the patient makes to explore new ways of coordinating feelings and expressions.

The Analysis of the Verbal and Nonverbal Associations

> In what concerns this patient, we were really able to celebrate, that day when after a session where he had expressed himself in a particularly superficial, insincere and affected way; he said, "During all of this session, I experienced something like a weight on my stomach." It was important at that moment to show him that it was this impression of weight, and not his words, which represented the "associations" that we searched for during this session; in other words, the real offshoots of the unconscious.
>
> "It was not anxiety," he says, "only a sort of vague pressure."
>
> "Like a stomachache?"
>
> "Not like that either. It was something mental but not like anxiety. More like a nightmare when we have the impression that there is someone sitting on your chest." (Otto Fenichel, 1941, *Problems of Psychoanalytic Technique*, pp. 8–9; translated by Marcel Duclos)

Filled with wonder by the effectiveness of this way to combine the free associations and the centers of attention, Freud (1901) used the same method to find the latent content carried by a lapse, mistakes, awkwardness, and failures. The body psychotherapists also use free association to create ways to read body dynamics. These developments allow psychotherapists to include gestures in a chain of associations. To explore a gesture can sometimes generate thoughts and associations[87] as effectively as exploring a dream. A gesture can be associated to another movement, and that movement to a thought and/or an affective dynamic. The fundamental idea is that a gesture can sometime be the center around which is organized an entire series of thoughts; these thoughts are not necessarily those that consciousness spontaneously includes in a verbalized chain of associations. A chain of verbalized associations is necessarily linear (one word at a time), whereas imagination often manages several impressions simultaneously.

> Vignette concerning the associative systems of gestures and words. *Here, I take, as an example of dream analysis, the technique in which I ask the patient to tell me*

the first association *that comes up when I read a brick of his dream to him. The difference with the classic psychoanalytic technique is that a conscious thought or gesture is considered an association. Thus, when I present the brick to a patient, I am attentive to what the body does as much as the first words. If, after a brick, a patient laughs, then gives me a verbal association, I assign to the smile the status of first association. Then, on this smile, I will ask the patient to associate, with gestures and words, to seek the latent content of the dream. Experience has showed me that this method often leads to useful discoveries for the development of the patient and the understanding of his functioning.*

Here is an example of an analysis of the three bricks of a patient's dream for which the first association was a reaction of the body.

> *The text of the dream:* I jump in my car to run away. A man, on the bridge that crosses this small square, shoots at me.
>
> *Piece I: I jump in my car.* While I read this brick, the patient slightly raises her eyebrows. I ask her about what this slight raising of her eyebrows might remind her. The affect associated with it is surprise. Surprise to find herself thinking of her first lover, to the mixture of pleasure and shame with which she was filled the first time she made love, even though it was pleasant enough.
>
> *Piece II: Run away.* As soon as I finished reading these two words, she exhales deeply. She attempts to control a rising anxiety, a feeling of depression, followed by anger against everybody.
>
> *Piece III: A man.* This time she laughs. She sees her father's expression of mockery when he made everyone laugh. She then remembers vacations when she was six years old. The family is about to laugh in an inflatable boat on the sea. At that time, the father took care of the children. It was fun.

This dream analysis was important for the patient because she had pushed away from her thoughts the father who had abandoned her. She gradually rediscovered that this father is not only bad. There had been a happy time between the two of them. Technically, in this example, the first reaction—the *stimulus association*, as we sometimes say—is a body reaction from which the associative chain returns to the verbal level. I chose this example because it is easy to transcribe, but all sorts of combinations are possible. For example, the first association is verbal, which then opens up on the exploration of a gesture that unleashes an affective reaction.

In this precise case, this memory of the pleasure that she had of wonderful vacations with her father did not "cure" the patient, but this memory is part of a process that permitted her to reconstruct a more accurate and helpful image of her father and who she is.

Gestured Thoughts and Spoken Thoughts

Psychoanalysts like Wilma Bucci have recently combined empirical and theoretical research to explore in a particularly detailed way the link between the nonverbal and the verbal expression of a thought. The goal of this study is to propose a psychodynamic view, inspired by the research in the neurosciences, which facilitates the inclusion of movement in the psychoanalytic technique.

The Split Brain According to Sperry and Gazzaniga: The Intermodality

Wilma Bucci is especially inspired by the studies taken up by the neurologist Michael S. Gazzaniga (1985) in the laboratory directed by the Nobel Laureate, Roger Wolcott Sperry.[88] Gazzaniga participated in the research concerning what happens when a surgeon severs the corpus callosum. The corpus callosum is composed of nerve fibers that connect the two lobes of the neocortex. The aim of this surgery was to diminish the impact of violent epileptic attacks of one hemisphere on the rest of the brain. At first, these operations did not seem to have a discernible impact on the mental functioning of the patients. Nevertheless, they complained of difficulties that were difficult to describe. Sperry decided to investigate. The first result of this research was to specify the different functions of each lobe. Sperry confirms, for example, that language is mostly organized by the left brain, even though certain linguistic mechanisms are also associated to the right brain,[89] and images would be mostly dealt with by the right brain. That said, there are neurological pathways that link the two hemispheres of the neocortex through subcortical pathways. These nerves remain intact after the pathways of the corpus callosum have been severed. The right visual field is linked to the left brain, and the left visual field is linked to the right brain.

Michael Gazzaniga joined Sperry's team to explore what is going on at the level of thoughts when the two hemispheres can no longer coordinate with each other. One subject of investigation was to find out how this intervention influences the coordination of images and words. He used different strategies to test combinations between objects and words. For example, a subject must touch an object with one hand. He cannot see the object, given that it is hidden by a screen. The object is easy to describe. It is round or square, big or small:

1. When it is the right hand (the one that communicates with the left brain) that touches the object, the subject can verbally describe the object.
2. When it is the left hand (the one that communicates with the right brain) that touches the object, the subject is not able to verbally describe the object.

Gazzaniga then wanted to know if the movement of the left hand is conscious. He repeats the same experiment as before, except that he asks the subject not to verbally name what he touches. Instead, he presents a drawn picture of all the objects used in the experiment. When the subject touched an object with his left hand, he was able to point to the corresponding image. Even when the subject is right-handed, he can more easily make a drawing of the object that had been touched by his left hand. He can also recognize the object. In short, the subject can perform a series of apparently conscious operations with his left hand, but he is not able to say what he is doing.

I heard about these studies while I was a student. Yet even today, I cannot begin to imagine that I am capable of performing some conscious operation about which I would not be able to speak. There are some feelings that I have difficulty describing in words, like a musical experience, but in this case I am able to say that I had such a musical experience that I am unable to describe in words. Sperry and Gazzaniga's subjects are different. They can remember an object and then point to it, or they can see an image and choose the appropriate object. But if they performed this task without seeing what they were doing with their left hand, they are unable to say that they touched an object, or that they recognized an object. The researcher asks them to take up the same object, and they do so. But they are incapable of saying what they are doing. Here we have a situation that is difficult to grasp; even if we can reason about it. Conscious movements cannot be stored by the type of memory used for speech. Sperry's team, in these cases, speaks of an *intermodal transfer of information.*

In Kant's time, the reference model was that a concept could be expressed in many ways (with words, movements, a painting, etc.) without being modified. The modular models that researchers like Sperry introduced supports another theory. Each sensory modality is linked to distinct dynamics of the brain. This implies that each modality (movement, image, or word as it happens) is associated to a particular form of conceptualization. The representation of a doorknob varies in function of the modality employed. A doorknob touched, looked at, or verbally described would not be represented the same way in the brain. Furthermore, each type of representation inserts itself into different ways of thinking. When I think of the doorknob with my hands, I think of this doorknob differently than when I talk about it. I think differently when I dance than when I write or paint.[90]

Sperry ends up asking himself whether each modality engenders different types of conscious awareness. Each type of consciousness, in combination with others, participates in the formation of a sort of general impression that is multimodal. This form of consciousness allows for structuring what is going on into forms of thought associated to each modality. For body psychotherapy, this research reinforces the necessity to develop a multimodal approach in psychotherapy.

Bucci and Intermodality in Psychotherapy

The notion of intermodality has entered into the domain of psychotherapy above all with *The Interpersonal World of the Infant* by psychoanalyst and researcher Daniel N. Stern (1985). He shows that the newborn poorly differentiates the modalities and only with the advent of speech does the child begin to distinguish clearly and explicitly what is seen from what is heard, felt, or touched. This notion became widespread and is found today in the discourse of many movements in psychotherapy.

Wilma Bucci[91] is a psychoanalyst who has studied how intermodality, as defined by Gazzaniga and Stern, is involved in the relationship between patient and psychoanalyst. With methods different that those used by neurologists, she specifies the following points:

1. What is easily communicated through movement is sometimes harder to be communicated with words. For example, it is well known that it is difficult to teach children to tie their shoes without using gestures.[92]
2. Once this has been accepted, it becomes interesting to ask oneself how the mind can "translate" what is easily conceptualized with words into gestures and vice versa. It often happens, for example, that a parent tries to repeat with words what a child has expressed with movement, like an echo. Bucci created a test that allows her to measure the ease with which such translations occur, and she uses it to analyze what happens in psychoanalytical sessions. She observed that in a psychoanalytical process that is proceeding well,[93] therapist and patient have been able to establish a good *intermodal dialogue*. Each person is able to respond to a gesture with speech, or even repeat the content of a remark with a gesture. The *translation* between modalities of communication has then become easy. In recounting a dream, the patient is better able to use gestures and words to express himself. He then has the impression of being "better" understood.

To draw from the language of computers, everything happens as if a thought expressed with gesture was "formatted" differently than a thought expressed with words. To manage these different forms of thoughts, each person must develop within himself interfaces that permit the association of the constructed content with each modality. Bucci's studies shows that these interfaces are more or less developed, and they can be refined if an individual lives the experiences that allow for the calibration of these interface. Here, Bucci rejoins Bruner (1966 , 1973) who distinguished two modes of representation:

1. Iconic and symbolic modes of representation.
2. An "enactive" mode that manifests as motor skills, such as counting on one's fingers or nailing with a hammer.[94]

For Daniel Stern, when there is an "affect attunement" between mother and child, the mother can respond to the infants' communication in another modality.[95]

May: When Affects and Objects Have Not Formatted in the Same Way

AFFECTS WITHOUT AN OBJECT

In speaking of Kurt Goldstein, I discussed the difficulty of working with affects "without objects." These affects manifest at the level of feelings and behavior, but the representations that can be associated with them either remain in the unconscious or have never been able to establish themselves in the conscious mind. They can influence behavior but do not act on the thoughts, save in a nonconscious fashion. Goldstein's patients were soldiers who had experienced trauma in such a confusing war that they were not able to relate the representation of an aggressor to their fear.

Beatrice Beebe (2005) describes the same kind of phenomenon concerning a patient who had undergone a long series of traumatic events, especially sexual ones, ever since birth. These events had occurred before the formation of her explicit memory. As an adult, this person, a brilliant academic, could not apprehend the crumbling state of her affects.

John May (2006a),[96] a body psychotherapist in the United States, has taken up the hypotheses of Bucci, Beebe, Downing, and Heller to talk about a patient who experiences strong emotions but cannot connect them to any meaning or words.

ARCHAIC BODY/SYMBOLIC LANGUAGE

More and more often, psychoanalysts include the body in their reflections, and they continue to assign to it modes of thought that are archaic, subsymbolic, and infantile. In other words, the body is closer to the vegetative layers, while speech permits the integration of the complex functions of the mind. The body psychotherapist more easily integrates an adult, creative, and intelligent body into his reflections, like the one of the lover, the dancer, the gymnast, and the craftsman. This brings us to a picture with at least two entry points (it is always possible to refine this by adding additional categories):

1. (A) archaic layers and (B) complex layers of the mind.
2. (A) thinking with gestures and (B) thinking with words.

Wilma Bucci's model is centered on the coordination between the cases 1A–2A (the archaic layers elaborated by passing through motor activity) and 1B–2A (the symbolized layers that are elaborated thanks to language), and it leaves the other possibilities aside. John May takes up this discussion by presenting the case of a patient (JL) who suffers from alexithymia.[97] This case makes it possible to illustrate how the 1B–2A axis is built.

> Vignette on JL. *JL is unable to relate the representative aspect of the emotions with the vegetative dimension of the emotions. In the session described in his article, May proposes to the patient that he take a bioenergetic posture[98] that allows him*

to feel the tension that inhibits respiration. He asks the patient not to control what will happen with his mind and to have confidence that the posture that he is proposing will do all of the work. In less than a minute, the patient's diaphragm distends, and the patient begins to cry. The tears gradually transform into a demonic rage. In this session, the patient clearly feels his violent emotions and expresses them in a way that the therapist can have a clear impression of what is experienced, but the patient has no image, no words to describe what has just happened. This does not prevent the patient from feeling better and being more relaxed at the end of the session, as if he had expressed something that had been built up in him. May knows by experience that these emotions will return with force in the weeks to come.

By working this way for several years, the patient could "recognizes somatic sensations and events that he was not aware of previously. He has learned that they sometimes indicate that he is sensing some sort of emotion, and in many cases he can directly experience the emotion." This work of calibration goes on at the level of the body without opening up onto the representations at first. Here, May uses Bucci's notion of "subsymbolism" to explain this work of calibration. He does not try to create a direct link between body feelings and representations. His strategy is to help the patient increasingly feel clear links between his emotions and his expressions, which he could describe verbally. May explicitly works from the notion that an emotion is elaborated by the treatment of different neurological, organismic, and mental circuits that are "formatted" in different "machine languages," most of which do not use representational systems to function.[99] The aim of John May's work is to support different forms of coordination between the subsymbolic systems to create the conditions that will support the emergence of the mechanisms that allow explicit connections between affects and representations. To create a link with the systems of representation, he set about to take the same postures as JL's in front of a mirror. JL is then able to verbally describe what he perceives in his therapist. This technique creates a system of reference between the verbalized representations of the patient, John May's posture, and the patient's posture.[100] This type of mirror play can also awaken circuits from early infancy when the baby rejoiced every time his parents imitated him. With this type of approach and concepts, gradually the rapport between body representations and verbal representations was able to relate anew in JL's mind when he felt an emotion.

15

From the Dynamics of the Libido to the Second Topography and the Death Instinct

LIBIDO DISORDERS CREATE NEUROSIS

It is undeniable that this doctrine of Freud . . . is of great interest. . . . Nonetheless, can we say that the principle which seems to constitute his central theme, but which, in reality is more theory than practice, I am referring here to his pansexualism, would be sufficiently evident to lead to a conviction? It is permissible to doubt it. There is something a bit outrageous to want to bring by stone or by force, certain tendencies to the sexual instinct that somehow seem more primitive, like the revolt of a son against his father, often due to the simple survival instinct. . . . There are no parts in the psychic life that does not nourish some link with the whole of the personality. But to reduce this entire complex to a single fundamental tendency is to expose ourselves to insurmountable difficulties. (Jean Piaget, 1920, *Psychoanalysis and Child Psychology*, p. 34; translated by Marcel Duclos)

The Libido

Observation teaches us that individual human beings realize the general picture of humanity in an almost infinite variety of ways. If we yield to the legitimate needs to distinguish particular types in this multiplicity, we shall first have to choose what characteristics and what points of view we shall take as the bases of our differentiation. For that purpose, physical qualities will no doubt serve as well as mental ones: *the most valuable distinctions will be those which promise to present a regular combination of physical and mental characteristics.* (Freud, 1931, *Libidinal Types,* p. 361; emphasis added)

The Sources of the Libido

The individual is a temporary and transient appendage to the quasi-immortal germ-plasma, which is entrusted to him by the process of generation. (Freud, 1915b, *Metapsychology*, p. 125)

379

Freud's libido is a force that organizes all of the dynamics of the organism and pushes it to maximize its pleasure in general and sexual pleasure in particular. Although it plays a central role in his theoretical proposition, it is managed with reserve. He believes in it, but at the same time he reduced it to an innate hormonal construction selected by the mechanisms of biological evolution. He explains everything with it, but at the same time, its force is like that of the water in a brook, which must go around the boulders that slow down its flow. Without this water, the region it irrigates would become a desert. There is altogether a Viennese reserve in this theory of vital energy, which masks a conviction that is so strong that no one can influence it.[1] When Jung—inspired by the vitalism of Henri Bergson—associated the libido to creative and spiritual energy, Freud so abruptly applied the brakes that Jung was expelled from the psychoanalytic movement. When Reich wanted to transform this brook into a political sexual tide, Freud reacted the same way. When Reich finally transformed the libido into an ocean of pleasure, Freud was deceased, but most of the orthodox psychoanalysts turned their backs on him. To his dying days, Reich was convinced that he was defending the most profound parts of Freud's thought.

The term *libido* appeared very early in Freud's psychoanalytic writings. Right from the start, it is powerful but contained, central but not invasive. Everything that deviated the course of the libido was a source of illness, but not necessarily evil. This conviction is one of the inexplicable drives of Freud's personality that none of his students ever understood.

The complexity of Freud's libido is close enough to what humans come to think about their sexuality: omnipresent and distant, source of pleasure and anxiety, and most of all elusive and incomprehensible. To this day, there is no instructive vision of sexuality, and the traps that sexual politics tend to fall into are unbelievably varied. Its influence does not let itself be cornered by words and theories, but it nonetheless has an unceasing effect in us. Freud especially defended this elusive aspect of sexuality. He therefore distrusted every individual who pretended to understand, situate, and master sexuality. He was not always sufficiently suspicious of the traps in which his way of handling the notion of libido caused him to stumble. This critique is done with great empathy for someone who at least dared to make explicit and undeniable the fact that questioning sexuality is a central preoccupation of every person who wants to understand human nature.

Sexual Appetite

For an *external* frustration to become pathogenic, an *internal* frustration must be added to it. In that case, of course, the external and the internal frustration relate to different paths and objects.[2] The external frustration removes one possibility of satisfaction and the internal frustration seeks to exclude *another* possibility, about which the conflict then breaks out. (Freud, 1916, *Introductory Lectures on Psychoanalysis,* III. 22, p. 395)

If I take up the System of the Dimensions of the Organism that serve as the reference point for this volume, it is possible to distinguish in Freud's analysis (a) physical symptoms, (b) mental symptoms, (c) behavioral symptoms, and (d) a link between these domains. This "link" is the domain of the affects and the vegetative functioning of the organism, which was still not well known at the start of the twentieth century. For Freud, the central regulator of this affective domain is sexuality. He thinks that a person who is without a sexual problem cannot be neurotic. He calls the physiological aspect of sexuality, which activates the *libido*, a sexual appetite.[3] This appetite would be linked to forms of physiological mobilizations distinct from those associated to hunger and thirst. At the time of his First Topography, Freud thinks that psychopathology appears when conscious thought is incapable of integrating the exigencies that sexuality would like to impose. To integrate these demands does not imply accepting them but to remain in dialogue with them.

Frustration

> We can only venture to say so much: that pleasure is in *some way* connected with the diminution, reduction or extinction of the amounts of stimulus prevailing in the mental apparatus, and that similarly un-pleasure is connected with their increase. An examination of the most intense pleasure which is accessible to human beings, the pleasure of accomplishing the sexual act, leaves little doubt on this point. Since in such processes related to pleasure is a question of what happens to *quantities* of mental excitation or energy, we call considerations of this kind economic. It will be noticed that we can describe the tasks and achievements of the mental apparatus in another and more general way than by stressing the acquisition of pleasure. We can say that the mental apparatus serves the purpose of mastering and disposing of the amounts of stimulus and the sums of excitation that impinge on it from the outside and inside. It is immediately obvious that the sexual instincts, from the beginning to end of their development, work towards obtaining pleasure; they retain their original function unaltered. (Freud, 1916, *Introductory Lectures on Psychoanalysis.* III, 22, p. 402)

The idea that there exist propensities with sexual goals, and that they play a fundamental role in the dynamics of the organism and of the mind, is ancient.[4] Freud's innovation lies in his analysis of what happens when a propensity does not attain its objectives. This was new for at least two reasons:

1. The evolutionists were mostly interested in how propensities *insert themselves* in the dynamics of an emerging species. Freud is interested in the *unfolding* of an individual propensity at a given moment.
2. The biologists were especially interested in the resources mobilized by a propensity. Freud is interested in the *dynamics of what is mobilized* in real time. He notably analyzes how a propensity terminates and reabsorbs itself very much before physiologists become interested in this question.

Freud's idea is that a propensity mobilizes resources to achieve a goal. As long as this goal is not reached, the person experiences a disagreeable tension.[5] When the goal is attained, the mechanisms of mobilization diminish and create an impression of pleasure and relaxation.[6] If the goal is not reached, the organism engenders impressions like frustration and anxiety.[7] A libido stasis then forms in the organism and impedes it from having the necessary resources to accomplish other tasks.

A few isolated sexual frustrations reabsorb with time. But if they are repeated, there will be an accumulation of retained metabolic waste products, feelings of frustration, and an excessive recourse to compensatory modes of satisfaction. An individual will feel anguished and will experience cravings, headaches, and so on. In brief, an entire series of behavioral, physiological, and mental mechanisms continue to deregulate until the organism has found a way of surviving more or less adequately in its environment.

This analysis leads to a central point in Freud's theory: the organism cannot comfortably survive if consciousness does not fulfill its role of coordinator in an instinctive propensity. In the case of a dysfunction, the organism's nonconscious mechanisms of regulation cause a splitting of the mind, which will maintain some desires in the unconscious and create the displacements of some propensities. These displacements are dangerous because the sexual desire can be replaced by an excessive activation of other propensities like hunger, aggression, hallucinations, and so on.[8] In this organismic context, consciousness is unable to adequately achieve its role. The notion that the instinct needs to recruit the support of consciousness to be able to fulfill its functions is well summarized in the *Three Essays on Sexuality*:

> The simplest and likeliest assumption as to the nature of instincts would seem to be that in itself an instinct is without quality, and, so far as mental life is concerned, is only to be regarded as a measure of the demand made upon the mind for work. What distinguishes the instincts from one another and endows them with specific qualities is their relation to their somatic sources and to their aims. (Freud, 1905, p. 83)

Object-Oriented Libido and the Libido of Auto-Regulation

> As the libido is predominantly allocated to the provinces of the mental apparatus, we can distinguish three main libidinal types. To give names to these types is not particularly easy: following the lines of our depth-psychology, I should like to call them the *erotic*, the *narcissistic* and the *obsessional* types. (Freud, 1931, *Libidinal Types*, p. 362)[9]

LOVE TO HAVE PLEASURE OR LOVE TO PERPETUATE
AND TRANSFORM A FAMILY TRADITION?
At the start, Freud's insistence to associate anxiety disorders to the inhibition of the libido was perhaps accidental: that is, linked (a) to the particularities of cer-

tain patients, and (b) to his own personal inclinations. But when, as early as 1900,[10] he began to train colleagues, he tried to shore up this association, because some of his students were particularly critical of this aspect of his theory.[11] The argument that Freud forged in his discussions with Jung[12] is that the central role of sexuality is comprehensible if we consider that it is the only innate instinct that exercises a pressure on the totality of the organism to satisfy the needs of the species instead of those of the organism.[13] Let us take up the elements of this argument:

1. There are *homeostatic instincts* that regulate the survival of an individual (hunger, thirst, the need for warmth, etc.). In humans, these homeostatic instincts need a social organization to function, but the center of each instinctive propensity remains a function of the individual organism.
2. *Sexuality* is the only instinct that fulfills, above all, a requirement of the species, and only indirectly a function for the individual. An individual without a sexual life does not die. Such an individual can even get used to living without making love.

Sexuality is a drive that has at least two dimensions:

1. The *mechanisms of procreation* relate a series of propensities that manage what happens once an ovum has been fertilized. These propensities oblige the organism to have a minimum of concern for others. An extreme expression of this drive is the capacity to sacrifice one's life for the survival of the tribe. This form of altruism already exists in the ant.
2. *The dimension of pleasure* related to the sexual act is a sort of innate motivator that increases the probability that two humans of different sexes will make love. This propensity encourages the organism to have a minimum of concern for oneself: for its well-being and its survival.

As in Darwin's proposal, there is not just one instinct that motivates humans to become sexually active for the propagation of descendants.[14] The human sexual instinct gathers distinct instinctual mechanisms that have heterogeneous goals. As I have explained in the sections dedicated to Wallace and Darwin, there is no need for coherence in nature's choices. As it happens, there was no selection of organisms that have both the pleasure in copulating and the desire to have offspring. Practice shows us that these two tendencies coexist in the species, but not always in an individual. There are people who want to have children and like making love but are unable to have children; there are others who like to have intercourse without wanting any children; some who have child after child without caring for them; others who have pleasure only in making love with someone of the same sex and would like to have children; and others who do not enjoy making love but want to have children, and so on. This variety can be seen every day.[15] There would be two types of frustration linked to the libido:

1. A *frustration linked to the auto-regulation of libido*, one linked to the frustration of not having discharged the urge to copulate. We have here that aspect of those individuals who feel well when they have experienced enjoyable sex.
2. A *frustration of the relational aspect of libido*, linked to the frustration of not having had intercourse in an affectively constructed frame, leading not only to a stable relationship but also to the possibility of offering a protective social environment to the desired children. We are considering here the individual who has the need to participate in the future of the species and of a cultural environment.

For Freud, the libido is then the regulator of the organism that promotes the linking of the attachment to the group to oneself. Sexuality would then be "the" instinctual propensity that plays a central role as organizer of the connection of body, mind, behavior, and society.

The Judeo-Christian thought has great difficulty entertaining the right to masturbate, to occupy oneself with one's own comfort. This embarrassment is seen in the table manners of "educated" people who forbid every manifestation of postural comfort like resting one's arms on the dinner table. At the beginning of the nineteenth century, the style of novels is seen as quasi-masturbatory and reprehensible. Freud defended the right to masturbate and auto-regulation all his life, but he chose terms and metaphors that rendered the integration of auto-regulation problematic. Thus, he referred to the necessity to self-regulate as narcissism, conferring to this need an imagery of reprehensible self-admiration; yet he recognized that the organism can only survive if it appreciates the activities that allow it to self-regulate.[16] Later, Freud (1915f, p. 222) associated a restorative auto-regulation that allows for sleep to a regressive and egotistic state that permits the organism to find a nearly fetal state. In short, the parasympathetic activity of the organism cannot truly be considered mature. Fundamentally, Freud is in agreement with those who defend the importance of auto-regulation, but the form that psychoanalysts still often use to speak of this primordial organismic activity remains problematic because the terminology and the metaphors can easily be experienced as negative. That is why I prefer to speak of auto-regulation rather than narcissism. This choice is found in a large part of the body psychotherapy literature.

FROM HOMEOSTASIS TO SOCIABILITY

Like Descartes and Hume, the psychoanalyst's patient sits in his thoughts to observe what is going on. From the point of view of his consciousness, he analyzes his way of thinking and the rapport between thoughts and the rest of the organism. But in psychoanalysis, this practice is carried out in tandem with someone in a relationship; it has as its goal the co-construction of what is perceived by one person. This frame values the fact that the relationship with the other is finally as powerful as the relationship with the self. This strategy makes it possible for the patient to perceive aspects of his internal world he would not have been able to perceive and, above all, explain without his therapist. There is evidently an entire series of mechanisms, in addition to sexuality, that requires a connection to another to function well. Libido is thus only one of the social instincts[17] that compel an organism to interact with other members of his species.

In the theory of transference originally proposed by Freud, interaction was a secondary variable.[18] As the experience of the psychoanalysts trained by Freud gradually developed, they became aware that shared experiences play a central role in the development of a human being. Here are a few examples:

1. *Countertransference:*[19] Freud's first students pointed out to him that the therapist is not able to understand what he perceives pertaining to his patient if he does not also analyze the relationship he establishes with the patient. This understanding requires a clear and stable frame and the support of a supervisor.

2. The studies on *attachment and abandonment* demonstrate that the attempt of the newborn to enter into a relationship with his parents lasts a lifetime, even when a parent has abandoned or abused the child (Bowlby, 1969). Spitz (1945, 1965) demonstrates, for example, that a child can die if he has not received attention and has not been touched. Harlow (1986) demonstrates that a young monkey never heals completely from the deprivations suffered during infancy. Since that time, trauma research confirms that no one completely survives a serious trauma, whatever the age at which it was experienced (Sironi, 1999, VI, p. 121). However, the earlier the trauma the deeper the scar, because the organism has not been able to mature in a coordinated fashion (van der Kolk, 2003).

3. Daniel Stern (1985) analyzes the strategies of attachment between a mother and her baby by showing how a form of constant multimodal intersubjective calibration establishes itself between them. The baby has the capacity to influence his parents from the moment of birth.

4. Beatrice Beebe and colleagues (2005, I, p. 10f.) demonstrate that the system of attachment and auto-regulation forms a whole that calibrates both the formation of the organism and its way to be with another.

These studies show that some important relational problems from the earliest infancy also damage the development of the mechanisms of auto-regulation of the organism. The first article entirely dedicated to countertransference was written by Sándor Ferenczi in 1909. Freud did not publish *The Dynamics of Transference* until 1912. Freud discusses countertransference in only two publications.[20] It is therefore evident that Freud's colleagues added an intersubjective dimension to his intra-organismic view. Psychoanalysis thus rejoins other theories that believe that psychological dynamics are necessarily interpersonal.[21] Besides the body psychotherapists who use a psychodynamic theory as the frame of reference, the notion of transferential dynamics is not always used in body psychotherapy. Others, for example, will use family therapy as a reference to coordinate their work on the dynamics of the organism and relational dynamics.

Freud sets about to distinguish two types of characters:

1. *The object-oriented personalities*. These individuals invest above all in a sexuality that aims at relationships and building a family, but they often forget to invest in their capacity to self-regulate.
2. *The narcissistic personalities*. These individuals often try to have a coherent behavior and auto-regulation, even if this implies difficulty in having a relational life that permits setting up a family and inserting oneself into a cultural network.

An individual centered on his auto-regulation cannot benefit from a psychoanalytical treatment unless he admits that the object-oriented libido is more important than the narcissistic libido. Freud nonetheless admits that the narcissistic personalities have trump cards that make them useful for the whole of society. For example, that is the case for a creative artist like Beethoven. Narcissistic personalities "are especially suited to act as a support for others, to take on the role of leaders and to give a fresh stimulus to cultural development or to damage the established state of affairs" (Freud, 1931, p. 363). The psychodynamics arguments that he gives to support this analysis of the narcissistic type are the following:

> There is no tension between ego and super-ego (indeed on the strength of this type one would scarcely have arrived at the hypothesis of a super-ego), and there is no preponderance of sexual needs. The subject's main interest is directed to self-preservation. The ego has a large amount of aggressiveness at its disposal, which also manifests itself in readiness for activity. In his erotic life, loving is preferred above being loved. People belonging to this type impress others as being "personalities." (Freud, 1931, p. 362f.)

Having a healthy narcissistic libidinal activity and a healthy object libido is evidently advantageous. However it is rare that both develop well in an individual. The practitioner generally knows how to evaluate this equilibrium in an individual. Those that the psys currently qualify as *narcissistic personalities*[22] are individuals who have a narcissistic problem, a deficiency in the narcissistic dynamics that they try to compensate for in different ways. Otto Kernberg (1975) thus speaks of "pathological narcissism." Individuals who suffer from a *deficit* of narcissism desperately try to function close to the libidinal type, but they are only partially successful. They often are afraid to cause harm and be rejected by others. These feelings become a form of central obsession that drains all of their energy and deprives them of sufficient resources to be able to help others, understand points of view other than their own, and coordinate their actions with others constructively. It is to poorly understand the theory of narcissism to believe that an individual can suffer from too much narcissism.

Narcissism was initially introduced by Freud to integrate within a psychoanalytic frame Jung's theory on psychosis, once Jung had left the psychoanalytical association. That may explain why Freud uses a myth to describe a notion. As he called the pathological deviation of object oriented libido "narcissism," he created an enduring semantic confusion between healthy and pathological narcissism. To be precise, Freud distinguishes between narcissistic (healthy) libido and (pathological) narcissism. I prefer to follow Wilhelm Reich's proposition and refer to healthy narcissistic libido as the pleasure of autoregulation. Today, many psychiatrists prefer to use a set of precise descriptive symptoms as suggested by the *DSM-V* and avoid using the term *narcissistic* as a psychiatric diagnosis.[23]

Body Segments and Libido

Freud's Psycho-Organic Circle

In a period when he was still flirting with the spiritualist thoughts of the schools of hypnosis, Freud (1895a) for a moment imagined that the libido was an energy that circulated in the body through particular pathways. He played with the idea of a libido that, as in the circulations described by Taoist alchemists, followed this route:

1. The physiologic mobilization of the libido begins in the pelvis.
2. This mobilization rises in the spinal column by recruiting the necessary physiological forces via the spinal marrow, generating voluptuous feelings.
3. Having reached the head, it activates a mental sexual excitation.
4. This mental arousal seeks "its object" (a sexual partner) in the environment.
5. The mental arousal, sustained by a constant contribution of appropriate physiological mobilization, activates a series of behaviors whose goals are to activate the sexual organs and ensure that the partner be appropriately (psychologically, physiologically, posturally, etc.) favorably disposed. During this phase, the libido activates a wide variety of expressive behaviors (face, arms, genitals, pelvis, legs, etc.) situated mostly on the ventral surface of the body.
6. After the sexual discharge, the sexual tension (physiological and mental) is reabsorbed and activates feelings of relaxation (physiological and mental) and of affection.

Freud uses this schema to explain that in individuals who suffer from "melancholy," the mental libido pushes the physiological libido toward the base of the pelvis. They are afraid of a sexual charge greater than one for which they have the impression of being able to integrate without creating insurmountable conscious conflicts. A way of dealing with this, according to Freud, is to masturbate so that the somatic sexual tension would never be able to acquire the sufficient force to activate an intense mental desire. According to this model, melancholy would be the sadness of having repressed not only the libido but also the desire. In the 1970s, Paul Boyesen proposed almost exactly a same model, which he called the psycho-organic circle.[24] Freud's reflections on this subject interest me for two reasons:

1. *Freud's reasons for thinking about it.* This model details Freud's first theory of the drives in a very useful way by showing how the libido coordinates physiological, mental, and behavioral activation in function of an activity that has a relatively precise relational goal. The fact that Freud would have thought of this model shows to what extent the confusion between the soul, the spiritual forces, the forces of hypnosis, and the linear connections between bodily and mental functions were rampant at the time. It was almost impossible that Freud, like any other cultured person, would not have thought of this type of model. Later on, not only did others think about it, they made it one of the foundations of their approach, like the originators of *Psycho-Organic* analysis.[25]

2. *The reasons Freud so quickly rejected it.* Having developed this model in a private rough draft concerning depression, he never returned to it. Even if he sometimes liked to roam around in the occult sciences, it is evident for him that energy is not a substance independent of matter that would have an independent route in the physiological circuits. Freud takes up the schema of the Taoist alchemists popularized in Europe by movements such as Theosophy, according to which the activation is forcibly linked to the back and the expression to the front of the torso. This schema is found in some neo-Darwinian models (Morris, 1978). It could be considered defensible, but Freud knew that energy does not follow such simple physiological routes. The marrow manages the sensory and motor nerves; the vegetative systems contain a sympathetic and parasympathetic system, and so on. Furthermore, as we have already seen in describing the First Topography and as we will observe in the following sections, Freud spent his life seeking a way to understand this double nature of the drives without ever arriving at a satisfying formulation.[26]

In 1905, Freud took up certain ideas contained in the first model and proposed a *theory of the psychosexual stages* that shows that the libido gradually structures itself by associating different erogenous zones of the body to different psychological and interpersonal functions.

The Psychosexual Stages

> Sexual life includes the functions of obtaining pleasure from zones of the body.
> (Freud, 1938, *Outline of Psychoanalysis*, III, p. 152)

The Freudian psychosexual stages were still commonly used and taught in the 1970s. Since then, for reasons that I have not understood, this theory is rarely mentioned. Some authors still use it to identify a problem linked to a zone of the body, like when psychoanalysts use the term *orality*[27] in a discussion on eating disorders or poor eating habits (Goldsztub and Lévy, 2006).

In 1905, Freud proposed that sexuality develops around the erogenous zones of the body that corresponds to a child's central phases of development. He describes five periods:[28]

1. During *the oral stage* (0–18 months), the libido structures itself around the eroticization of the mouth, which encourages the young organism to have the desire to suck (alimentary pleasure) and explore the mother's nipple (exploratory pleasure). The infant thus learns to accept and refuse, to appreciate positive dependency and refuse (those are the oral rages) what displeases him (like distasteful food). The oral rages are also associated to the intolerance of frustration and the desire to bite.

2. The *anal stage* (18–36 months). The libido continues to constitute itself around various functions accomplished by the mouth, but it concentrates itself especially on the anus. The child thus learns to organize giving and retention not only of feces but also of objects. For example, there would be a possible link between constipation and the tendency to become stingy, or diarrhea and the tendency to be a spendthrift. Maintaining overactive "anal-erotic components" can lead to "character traits" such as "orderliness, parsimony and obstinacy" (Freud, 1917, p. 295).

3. The *phallic stage* (three to seven years old) increases the number of erogenous zones because in addition to the oral and anal zones, the genitals become a major erogenous zone. The penis is susceptible to erections from birth; but only now does it become frankly an erogenous zone. During this stage, children are able to experience pleasure in masturbation, have romantic fantasies (the desire of the boy to become his mother's husband). Also at that age, according to Freud, children become haunted by the fantasies produced by the Oedipal complex (Freud, 1924a).

4. *Latency* (7–11 years old). At the end of infancy, the erogenous desires linked to the mouth, anus, and genitals become latent. They are practically ignored by consciousness, even if they continue to have a subterranean life in the unconscious.

5. *The genital stage* (from puberty until death). From puberty onward (the first menses, the first pubic hair, etc.), the oral, anal, and phallic libido always exist, but the genital libido renders the desire to make sexual contact with the genitals of another person imperative and to establish relationships in which sexuality plays many roles: especially that of establishing a family to have children. The term *genitality* is also used in a less precise way by some psychoanalysts to designate the forms of pleasures related to the sexual organs from birth.

These are approximate ages, indicative of an average that varies in each case. This rough sketch of a genetic model of the drives contains several important points:

1. There is no substitution of one erogenous zone by another. Instead, there is a gradual *differentiation* of the libido in function of the priority of the needs of the *organism* when it interacts with others. The libido is therefore sensitive to the interpersonal dimensions from the very beginning.

2. The organization of a stage of development is so complex that it takes months or even years for it to organize. Each stage develops schemata that can be taken up by other stages. In that way, a child can develop a way of utilizing his orality that will influence the manner with which he will approach his anality. The milieu is also in constant evolution. A mother who likes to nurse is not necessarily a mother who likes to clean dirty bottoms. Some parents are inept with babies but marvelous with adolescents, and so on.

3. Frustration can also partly block this development, which is also dependent on the environment. Consequently, some adults may have an overdeveloped orality and an underdeveloped genitality. It all seems to happen as if the organism possessed a limited amount of libido and too large a mobilization in one zone deprives the other zones.[29]

4. Freud distinguishes *phallic* sexual pleasure (the pleasure of playing with the genitals as erogenous zones) and *genital* sexual pleasure (a relationship in which there is a desire for sexual interaction between the sexes). This distinction is useful to understand certain forms of flighty sexuality between adults, but it probably situates homosexuality too quickly as phallic sexuality. Yet Freud and most psychoanalysts have done much to achieve a better social integration of homosexuality.

5. At the occasion of the analysis of sexual abuse, it is important to take into account the fact that each stage coordinates the erogenous zone, the mental functions, and the interpersonal functions. It is possible that some children would have a certain pleasure playing with the genitals as a sort of game with other children, or when children explore the genitals of their parents in bed or the bath. But the phallic stage does not permit a child to enter into relational contacts that develop during the genital

stage. Freud describes very well the impossibility of having a genital relation, at four years old, because such a relation is situated at all the
levels of a child's being: physiological, psychological, libidinal, behavioral, and relational. At that age, children would have difficulty assimilating the sexual love-making of their parents were they to witness it.[30]

A delicate point of this theory concerns its relationship with the notion of
the Oedipal complex, which plays a central role in Freud's thought. The Oedipal
complex, as discussed by the majority of psychoanalysts, comes about around
the age of three. Many psychoanalysts affirm that the male child entertains a
genital love for his mother.[31] Freud's model is more refined. Around three years
old, the boy has a sensual and erotic behavior toward his mother without a
genital design. He wants to marry her, sleep with her, smell her skin, and sometimes play with her genitals if he is aware of them, but that is where things
stop.[32] At puberty, the genital sexuality enters into a resonance with the ancient
sensuality associated with the mother and transforms the ancient drive into a
genital drive. There then arises a genital Oedipal conflict. The sensual rapport
toward the mother that was established at the age of three is reactivated in the
adolescent by its association to manifest genital sexual drives. The conflict that
develops in the unconscious of the young man can only be resolved if he learns
to detach "his libidinal wishes from his mother and employ them for the choice
of a real outside love-object" (Freud, 1916, III.21, p. 380). That is the only way
he could really reconcile with his father.

The Confusion of Partial Drives

Almost all narcissists and children in particular, are voyeurs. More than others,
they are attracted to ambiguous events. They want to see for the same reason that
they want to be seen. There is in this an interesting complex in the consequences it
has in art or even in metaphysical intuitionism. (Jean Piaget, 1920, *Psychoanalysis
and Child Psychology*, p. 32)

The sadistic relation can only be sustained in so far as the other is on the verge of
still remaining a subject. If he is no longer anything more that reacting flesh, a kind
of mollusk whose edges one titillates and which palpitates, the sadistic relation no
longer exists. (Jacques Lacan, 1954, *The Seminar*, XVII.3, p. 215)

At first, the oral, anal, and phallic drives are identified as pregenital instinctual
"components"[33] that will be coordinated under the primacy of the genital
zone:[34] "What we call genitality is a summation of instinct components, so
called, and of excitations of the erotogenous zones" (Ferenczi, 1929). Subsequently, Freud's theory of the drives became fuzzier for many reasons. It seems
to me that the following are the most interesting ones for the development of
body psychotherapy.

1. In addition to the oral, anal, and phallic drives, Freud admits that other zones of the body can become erogenous zones linked to partial sexual drives, especially the eyes and the skin.[35] This leads to the analyses of partial drives that annul each other, turn each other around, reverse each other, transform each other into their opposites, and so on.[36] A sadistic drive and a masochistic drive can hold each other in check around an erogenous zone and can hamper the proper functioning of that zone. That is how, for example, Freud and Abraham explain hysterical blindness. The idea that the structure of a character is based on the proliferation of partial drives is brilliantly exploited by Wilhelm Reich in his character analysis of the 1930s.
2. In the same articles, Freud and Abraham apply this model of the partial drives not only to the other instincts (hunger and thirst) but also to emotional propensities such as aggression.

Karl Abraham often associated, in direct fashion as in phrenology, the erogenous behaviors of a particular zone of the body to a specific psychological problem. Thus, one of his patients handled light with difficulty because his eyes were central symbolic components of different drives:[37]

1. "He had first expressed this attitude by speaking of his 'ardent respect' for his father."
2. "He identified his father's watchful eye with the sun"
3. "The patient had also transferred to the sun his ambivalent attitude towards his father in a remarkable way. He disliked the light of the sun but he loved its warmth."

From a theoretical point of view, a bizarre mixture begins with Karl Abraham. On the one hand, we have a systemic model "à la Freud" that supposed a great flexibility of the libidinal coordination between the body and the spirit; on the other hand, we find ourselves more and more often left with a rigid, linear link between a mental and a behavioral trait. This mixture is probably what created a manifest hostility toward a Psychoanalysis that reduces the wealth of thoughts to not only simplistic schemata but also poorly supported ones or only supported by few cases.

Sándor Ferenczi, another of Freud's close collaborators, developed similar themes. He proposed a *urethral stage* between the anal and the phallic stages that is linked to the pleasure in urination. He associated a panoply of mental problems to the functioning of the bladder, like enuresis, premature ejaculation, the pleasure of urinating to fight against anxiety, a sexuality based on morning erections, pissing contests between children, and so on.

More recently, psychoanalyst Gerard Bonnet, influenced by Freud, Sartre,[38] and Lacan,[39] took up Abraham's work on a person's gaze and avoided most of the mistakes of the Berlin model. His 1981 publication, titled *Voir et être vu* [To see and to be seen], is a good example of a certain French psychoanalysis that is centered on what they call the "subject."[40] In concentrating on the perceptions of the subject, Bonnet skillfully avoids the necessity to directly relate to the mind, the perceptions, the libidinal stages, and the parts of the body. He details his analysis of the gaze with numerous clinical cases that show how to see and be seen forms a polarity that creates a resonance between the unconscious of a family, or of a group of people, in a certain way. The central issue pointed out by Sartre, which inspired Bonnet, is that seen from the outside, humans perceive each other as objects, but as objects that have a self. Person A cannot perceive the self of person B, but A knows that B is reacting as a subject to A, that B is evaluating A:

> As a temporal-spatial object in the world, as an essential structure of a temporal-spatial situation in the world, I offer myself to the Other's appraisal. This also I apprehend by the pure exercise of the *cogito*. To be looked at is to apprehend oneself as the unknown object of unknowable appraisals—in particular, of value judgments. (Sartre, 1943, III.I.IV, p. 358)

The analysis leans toward a way to integrate and to envision that which we have chosen to see and show. To quickly summarize some of Bonnet's point of view on voyeurism, I evoke the ostrich who believes the enemy has disappeared by sticking its head in the sand. Of course, I am taking a shortcut here because this work speaks mostly of voyeurism and exhibitionism:

1. As soon as individuals interact in a same time-space, the seeing and the being-seen are automatically in place. There is no escaping this.
2. Seeing and expressing have constantly a subjective intentionality composed of conscious, unconscious, and nonconscious heteroclite dynamics.

The body is inevitably present in most of Bonnet's clinical examples, but his interventions remain strictly verbal. Gerard Bonnet insists on the fact that the voyeur is always visible, one way or another; even if he is not seen by the one he looks at.

The beauty of Bonnet's approach is his exploration with the patients of what certain ways of seeing and exhibiting (or hiding) signify to the psyche of the subject while admitting that the libido of viewing and exposing inscribes itself necessarily in a complex and polysemous intra- and interpsychic channel. What is felt by each one enters into a Lacanian frame of an interplay between virtual thoughts that activate, without the subject knowing how, the behaviors and feelings that take place in the consciousness of each implicated individual. None of them can understand or even grasp the stakes of what is being perceived. Here, in summary, is an example from Bonnet:

Vignette on an exhibitionist. *During the first 14 years of his life, the patient slept in the same room with his parents. Even if the patient does not mention it, Bonnet concludes that when it looked as if the boy seemed to be asleep, his parents secretly made love, trying not to wake up their child. In fact, it is possible that his parents no longer made love, or did so elsewhere, in other moments than nighttime. But Bonnet imagines that his patient has often witnessed what the psychoanalysts call the "primitive scene." There would have been a child who sees his parents have intercourse while they were convinced that they were not seen. They did things that they did not have the right to do in the presence of their child. We have, in these few words, a sample of what Bonnet called seeing and being seen. In these first years, the child does not know what is afoot; he does not know what it is to make love. He probably feels that his parents are having an intense encounter, touching and caressing each other while wanting to exclude him. He realizes very well that by feigning not seeing, he is able to observe. If the parents sensed that he was not asleep, their intimate ballet was interrupted. The child would have witnessed events that were not spoken about, that were not possible to talk about. Evidently, if this is how things happened, the pleasure of the parents and the curiosity of the witness was enveloped in shame and with forbidden feelings.*

Bonnet is manifestly a specialist in the dynamics of the partial drives[41] that transform themselves in every which way. Once an adult, the patient becomes an exhibitionist. He stands in front of a woman who is parking her car in the dark of the evening. He is easily visible under the street lights. He opens his overcoat and exposes his genitals. "To the desire to see, to spy what he experienced all of his childhood without ever being able to make sense of it, the desire to expose himself again and again in order to exorcise the vision that obsesses him abruptly succeeds, according to a reversal that is very characteristic in this matter" (Bonnet, 1981, 2.3.3, p. 79; translated by Marcel Duclos).

Bonnet's explanation does not stop there, because he needs to understand his role as the therapist in the transferential dynamic that is constructed between him and his patient. He then begins to reflect on the fact that this exhibitionist pursues his prey, who are always adults and always in populated areas, until such time as he is arrested by the police and convicted. At the occasion of one of these episodes, the patient is referred to Gerard Bonnet by the justice system for a psychiatric evaluation and treatment. Given his status of voyeur, which he established with his parents at the occasion of their love-making, the patient does not know how to exist. The subject that he is has no status, has no permission, no right to exist. In transforming his voyeurism into exhibitionism to the point of attracting the attention of the police, what was traumatizing in the bedroom acquires a status, attracts attention, is discussed and judged. In therapy, the patient is able to speak, express himself, and especially to be heard. It is not only his words that are heard; he is listened to as a subject who is trying to understand himself and exist in the eyes of another. It would therefore be much more the search of a judgment than the need to expose oneself that motivates the behavior of this patient.

Bonnet's analysis is even more interesting than I have been able to express in these few sentences. I encourage you to read what he has to say concerning this case, because it is equally instructive from the point of view of the formation of a psychotherapist. It consists in understanding the frame that the dynamics of the transference builds around what, in the first instance, is felt as an empathic exchange of information between two selves. To speak and be heard is a way to replay the problem of voyeurism.

Freud's Unconscious Becomes "Dynamic"

The idea of the drive is connected, at the same time, to a vegetative and hydraulic metaphor. A drive pushes toward a goal like a tree that grows its branches, leaves, and fruits toward the sun. This drive also pushes like water held back by a dam and like water that carves a river bed to finally reach the ocean. The activity of a drive is first an organic propensity that recruits mental and behavioral energy in function of its needs.[42]

Andre Haynal (1992) reminds his readers that the term *repression* only partially translates the metaphor carried by the term *Verdranung* used by Freud. A defense, according to Freud, is like a boat that splits the waters of a river and displaces it on either side. This water no longer goes where it wanted to go; it forms waves in the water. Once a thought or a drive has been displaced, it no longer manifests in its original form, but the ripples it creates are sometimes perceived by consciousness without knowing what created them. These aquatic displacements put pressure on the river banks (the nonconscious mechanisms). If the displacement of fluids occurs in a cask, the fluids put "pressure on the walls. The repression would be a board that leans on the water, increases the pressure . . . sometimes to the point that the water squirts through the slits" (Haynal, 1992, p. 15; translated by Marcel Duclos).

THE METAPSYCHOLOGY

> A riddle is lurking in the region of affects. (Sigmund Freud in a letter to Wilhelm Fliess, November 7, 1899, in Freud, 1904)

It Is Time to Change!

And then World War I broke out; everything around Freud had changed. He was at the head of a movement that unceasingly asked him to provide guidance on how to practice Psychoanalysis and the recommendations relative to a particular cure. His colleagues were, at the same time, intelligent, dynamic, and often unstable in the sphere of their personal identity. They were on a search; they believed that Freud could give them a frame which, all at the same time, could orient them, support them, and allow them to express everything that they feel and think. Psychoanalysis became a career path, a source of income. Twice already, the psychoanalytic movement split because it was unable to reconcile so many demands. Adler and Jung had supported the creation of the psychoanalytic movement and admired Freud; both wanted him to accept their ideas. But it was not possible. Freud accepted only the formulations that he could understand and integrate. Therefore, they each founded their own psychoanalytic movement. Freud's psychoanalysis nonetheless remained the trunk, the reference point in the field of psychotherapy. A trunk that has branches becomes a tree.

There was suffering and anguish but also satisfaction in all of these adventures. Freudian psychoanalysis became visible in the academic and psychiatric world from the Urals to the Rocky Mountains. Freud, Jung, and Ferenczi were invited by Clark University in the United States to present their thoughts.[43] There, they met the first psychoanalysts who were established in the region and William James of Harvard University. The psychoanalysts had a journal. In entering the marketplace of official theories, psychoanalysis must accept a harsh competition that is sometimes led by powerful personalities. Some of these reactions were ferociously opposed to Freud's formulations. The psychoanalysts developed their own arsenal to confront this opposition.

Then there was war: a horrible, idiotic, and nasty war.[44] Friends and colleagues fought each other in the trenches. He worried about his sons, who were fighting in the Austrian army. There was also less money, fewer patients. Editors had difficulty finding enough paper to publish the writings of the psychoanalysts. Colleagues no longer dared travel. Freud had time on his hands. He reflected. He wrote. He undertook an overall revision of all the models that he had set forth.[45] In editing what was supposed to be a kind of synthesis of his work, he began to nail down the flaws in his theory more explicitly. He vaguely sensed that psychoanalysis must change gear.

He wrote *Metapsychology* to define the questions that he had to answer. He defined and then modified the five models that seem to him to have the greatest need of review and correction: the instincts and their vicissitudes, the notion of repression in the defense system, the unconscious, and his theory of dreams. He also incorporated his understanding of depression into all of this. Depression is not a neurosis, but he was thinking about it already in his correspondence with Fliess. He deeply sensed that Psychoanalysis must address pathologies other than just neurosis if it wanted to become a general theory of psychotherapy. Jung had already discussed this with him by showing that Freud's understanding did not allow an approach to the treatment of those suffering from psychoses. Freud summarized the benefits of this discussion in refining his reflections on narcissism. He must also assimilate all of the discussions on transference and countertransference that his colleagues were about to place at the center of psychoanalytic preoccupations, while he remains mostly interested in an intraorganismic psychology.

Like many practitioners who were establishing themselves, Freud had long hoped to find a solid academic research position that would permit him to practice psychotherapy as a secondary career. He held on to the ambition that one day he would be able to synthesize the neurology, psychology, and philosophy that he had studied in medical school. His First Topography contained many formulations that could easily be used in academic discussions. For example, we have already seen that his psy system included a theory of thought close to that of Descartes. His writings on the relationship between the dynamics of the libido and the mind attempted to be compatible with a certain view of the nervous system.[46]

At almost 60 years old, Freud grieved these ambitions, and resigned himself to the idea that it would be future generations who will fulfill this dream.[47] The researchers who will relate neurology and psychoanalysis will require resources to which the practitioners in Freud's day did not have access.[48] On the other hand, if a practitioner furnishes a precise clinical description, associated to a model that makes explicit the reasoning of the practitioner, he may inspire the researchers of tomorrow and help them know on what to concentrate to relate clinical and experimental research. In other words, Freud continued to want to create explicit and detailed models and to further explicate, as much as possible, the procedures used in Psychoanalysis. From then on, he focused on practical and technical issues that could improve the efficiency of psychotherapy. He had to tinker with models that support a clinical exploration in those areas which scientists have no means to study:

> We know two kinds of things about what we call our psyche (or mental life): firstly its bodily organ and scene of action, the brain (or nervous system) and, on the other hand, our acts of consciousness, which are immediate data and cannot be further explained by any sort of description. Everything that lies in between is unknown to us, and the data do not include any direct relation between these two terminal points of our knowledge.[49] (Freud, 1938, I, p. 144)

Consequently, the regions the psychoanalysts explore are situated in a waste ground, still poorly explored, between consciousness and the brain. It was not possible at the time to propose a coherent theory of the mind. In trying to resolve the contradictions that remain in his theory, Freud initiated a great reformulation of psychoanalytic theory by proposing his Second Topography. This reformulation provides the means for certain psychoanalysts to explore different ways to integrate somatic and behavioral approaches to psychoanalysis. That said, the Second Topography resolves certain problems and creates others. Consequently, the coherence of psychoanalytic theory was not reinforced in the end.

From Thoughts to Drives

Is It Useful to Think about Thoughts?

> I am in fact of the opinion that the antithesis of conscious and unconscious is not applicable to instincts. (Freud, 1915a, *Metapsychology*, III, p. 177)

The psy system of the 1890s describes the circulation of *mental representations.* This is the model that was presented to the general public in Freud's first works and that has so pleased personalities like Jung and Ferenczi. But everyone senses that this model poorly coordinated the dynamics of the drives and the dynamics of the thoughts. Jung leaned toward a global psychophysiological interaction, but he had to admit such generalities were of no help to psychotherapists. He ended up thinking that between the brain and the psy system there was a special interface that produced phenomena like archetypes. The interface between the unconscious and the brain is then perceived *from the point of view of consciousness,*[50] as the mouth of a volcano, like something that is not a complete whole but an aspect of the global organization. Freud thought instead of a sort of necessity on the part of the instincts to recruit a regiment of thoughts that play a particularly useful function in a propensity's army. This is a bit like what Cannon envisioned, in the same period, when he constructed his homeostatic model. For Freud, this axis organizes itself necessarily around pleasure: a biological pleasure and a mental pleasure, the organic pleasure to eat or to make love, and the mental pleasure of eating or of making love. There is also, on the side of the preconscious, another interface that connects the mental pleasure and the organic pleasure of moving, doing things, playing the violin, baking a good bread, hugging one's partner. Seen from this angle, the only *biologically* constructed pleasure that links physiology, representations, and actions built with another is the sexual interaction. That is the center around which all the other pleasures are built. Freud insisted in distinguishing organic pleasure and mental pleasure because they manifestly function differently. The pleasure of eating that turns into a tendency toward bulimia is a prime example. A more complicated example is the one of a union between individuals who like each other but who do not have chemical systems that would promote an active sexual life. It is sad that only rarely does all of the apparatus of the soma and the psyche need the same person and that it be reciprocal.

Since 1905, when Freud defended his model of the libido, he created a kind of dichotomy in psychoanalytical thought. The desire coordinates the physiological dimension and the psychological dimension of a drive. When Freud spoke of the psy system, he clearly distinguished physiology and representations, but this differentiation takes on water as soon as he speaks of libido. The anal libido is attached to a part of the body, a physiological function, affective needs (to be miserly), ways of thinking (to be very rational), behavior patterns (to be very organized), and relationship styles (sadomasochistic relationships). It becomes evident that not only the thought of anger is repressed but so is a particular outburst of anger. The body psychotherapists, right from the Reichian Vegetotherapy, went to the outer limits of the idea that the entire organism is harnessed to repress the composites of anger. Freud did not go as far, but he did take a first step in this direction. Henceforth, he admitted that in repressing the thought of being angry, the propensity and its need to recruit the help of the psyche is disturbed. The defense system acts on the mental dimension and more

indirectly, for Freud, in the physiological dimension of the drive. The First Topography does not achieve a description of this double psychological and physiological activity. Add to that the transferential dynamics described by Ferenczi,
which give a greater importance than before to the interface between the mind
and motor activity. The First Topography made it possible to impose the idea
that the mind must also be treated by mental methods. But this beautiful theory,
this clarity, does not take the fuzzier dynamics of the organism into account.
Another approach had to be adopted.

This change is not just induced by the internal inconsistencies of the Freudian model. Psychoanalysts, even Freud, encounter a key problem in their practice that is linked to the inconsistencies I have just summarized. They had several
cases in which the patient recovered memories of situations repressed in the
unconscious without being relieved of the symptoms that motivated coming to
psychotherapy. The psychoanalysts of the day explained this by telling themselves that these patients had recovered the cognitive memory of the repressed
situation but not the memory of its affective content. The defense system therefore has the capacity to render an analysis ineffective by activating only half the
memory: either its affective content deprived of the associated images, or only
the images. The challenge for the practitioner is to find techniques that will help
resolve this problem. Evidently, asking the patient to free associate and analyze
the mental lapses and dreams does not always suffice. The solution that Freud
envisioned is to propose a system of *interpretation* of the material brought forth
by the associations of the patient that centers more on the coordination between representations and affects. We will see that for others, like Ferenczi and
Reich, the problem could only be resolved by adopting more active methods
that solicit the motor system more directly.

Primary and Secondary Processes

The clinical questions that Freud took up in this period imply that a thought
links three dimensions: the representations, the affects, and the physiologic activity. This transition phase of psychoanalytical thinking is built around the
model of the primary and secondary processes, a distinction that Freud thought
about from 1895 up to the time of his death.[51]

1. *Secondary process.* In the best-case scenario, the three dimensions of a
   mental activity mutually influence each other. The libido is then bound.[52]
   It inserts itself into a transferential type of dynamic that structures itself
   around the following processes: (a) the libido binds itself to a coordination between affects and representations that connect with each other to
   respond to the solicitations of the demands of a real relationship; (b)
   representations and relational experiences mutually influence each other
   to integrate the drives of interacting organisms; and (c) relational experiences and the drives form an alliance so that an individual's psyche
   might forge representations for itself that foster the integration of these

connections. An example of an association between a ritual and a drive that allows a person to forge a constructive representation of her place in the world is the act of nursing or the act of gently rocking a baby in one's arms.

2. *Primary process.* In the worst-case scenario, mind, affects, and relationship are poorly coordinated. Sometimes they even act independently of one another. They are like bits and pieces that drift aimlessly, without any link to each other. The libido has no precise aims. Sometimes it clings to fragments of mental entities. All that can be said of the libido in such a context is that it is *mobile.* This is often caused by a relational system that does not allow the libido to invest constructively in a coordination between drive, representation, and relationship because all the possible combinations generate displeasure. The drives are structured in function of a lack: either a lack of constructive attention, abuse, or an inexistent affective frame. Borderline personalities are generally referred to as examples of individuals who sometimes function this way. In the psychoanalytic approach to this type of problem, the psychotherapist helps his patient bind his libido and create connections between drives, representations, and relational experiences developed with a particular person (e.g., the therapist).[53]

In a psychotherapy practice, it is relatively easy to inventory the needs a patient manifests, the way a patient represents what is going on inside, and his relational experiences. It is therefore possible to list how these three types of phenomena inter-relate for an individual, even if the practitioner does not know the underlying mechanisms that organize this type of coordination.

We see that in this, Psychoanalysis increasingly becomes a collective endeavor because Freud broached notions that he probably would not have been able to discover alone. He would not have dared to move forward in a direction that rendered psychoanalysis irreplaceable and at the same time conceptually difficult to grasp. Spontaneously, and up to the end of his life, Freud liked having ideas as clear as possible.

FREUD'S SECOND TOPOGRAPHY

As I have already remarked,[54] the traumatizing events of World War I had an enormous impact on the development of the treatment for soldiers. In participating in this collective effort, psychoanalysts showed everyone that they could propose useful forms of therapeutic interventions. At the same time, they were placed in direct competition with other approaches like those of Goldstein and Cannon. These initiatives could only propose forms of intervention that were still works in progress. The psychoanalysts had to work with a new clientele that could not be treated in the comfortable and warm-hearted intimacy of an individual private practice. Hospitals became their principal workplace. It was no longer a question of asking the patients to have a session of psychotherapy each workday of the week for at least one hour. The psychoanalysts were obliged to adapt their theory to their practice. This allowed Freud, with the help of his collaborators, to calibrate the changes that he was about to put in place. Here are a few salient traits that characterize this mutation:

1. The end of the Austro-Hungarian Empire and the fall of the Kaiser transformed Austria into a small republic. She retained a radiating artistic and intellectual activity up to World War II, but her glory was already fading. The center of Psychoanalysis was displaced first to Berlin and then to New York. Today, psychoanalysis is a discipline that is firmly planted in many European countries and the Americas. Freud became less and less the center of the developments in Psychoanalysis even if he remains a central reference.

2. The reputation of psychoanalytic work on trauma made it possible for a number of physicians, who were also psychoanalysts, to enter into most of the medical services to treat soldiers.[55] The trauma of war, depression, anxiety, suicidal tendencies, and even various psychoses became the pathologies that required profound transformations on the part of psychoanalysis. An increasing number of psychoanalysts direct psychiatric institutions.

3. Freud responded to this demand (a) by replacing his First Topography (unconscious, preconscious, and conscious) with a Second Topography (id, ego, and super-ego); and (b) by finally admitting that the organism is, sadly, not only enliven by the search for pleasure (*Eros*) but also by destructive inclinations (*Thanatos*).

4. The required changes were not only theoretical but also practical. Some of Freud's students, such as Ernst Simmel, acquired a certain form of independence from psychoanalysis as practiced by Freud by exploring psychotherapeutic techniques less costly in time and involvement on the part of the patient than classical psychoanalysis. There arose a great variety of *psychotherapies of psychoanalytic inspiration*. These explorations of techniques are organized around a theme that Ferenczi calls *the active techniques*. The psychoanalyst is no longer content to listen and interpret, and he often sits more or less facing the patient.

This turn of events permitted a creative proliferation in the area of techniques that encourage an increasing number of psychoanalysts to question themselves about the utility of relating the psychoanalytic approach to body and behavior therapy approaches.

Finally, around 1923, Freud learned that a cancer was growing in his jaw and threatens one of his dearest pleasures: smoking a cigar. He preferred to die rather than stop smoking. This cancer was often brought up as a cause of his growing pessimism, but it could also have obliged him to integrate the notion of corporality more explicitly into his theoretical elaboration.

The Necessity to Create a Second Topography

It is in this context that Freud proposed his Second Topography with the hope that it would allow for a better management of the drives. This theme became a central preoccupation. He was aware that the second model was less precise on certain points, but more flexible and more relevant for the needs of a psychotherapist. The distinction between representation and drive became somewhat blurred but also more complex. It is the same for the distinction between mental energy and physiological energy. This Second Topography of the psyche distinguishes between the id, the ego, and the super-ego:[56]

1. The *id* is close to the physiological dynamics. "It contains everything that is inherited, that is present at birth, that is laid down in the constitution—above all, therefore the instincts, which originate from somatic organization and which find a first psychical expression here, in the Id, in forms unknown to us" (Freud, 1938. I, p. 146). The id brings to the psyche not only the exigencies of the instincts but also their energy.[57] Freud specifies[58] that it consists mostly (but not only) of the libido. In this model, when the defense system prevents a drive from entering the psyche, it also influences the physiological mechanisms that would like to mobilize psychological resources. The dynamics of the id are mostly primary and unconscious. There are few connections between the contents of the id.

2. The *ego* is a mixture of unconscious, preconscious, and conscious mechanisms.

   > The ego has voluntary movement at its command. It has the task of self-preservation. As regards *external* events, it performs the task by becoming aware of a stimuli, by storing up experiences about them (in the memory), by avoiding excessively strong stimuli (through flight), by dealing with moderate stimuli (through adaptation) and finally by learning to bring about expedient changes in the external world to its own advantage (through activity). As regards to *internal* events, in relation to the Id, it performs that task by gaining control over the demands of the instincts, by deciding whether they are to be allowed satisfaction, by postponing that satisfaction to times and circumstances favorable in the external world or by suppression their excitation entirely. (Freud, 1938, I, p. 145f).

   The ego, above all, manages the organism's relations with what is going on in the present.[59] The psyche's defense system is mostly controlled by the ego, which is able to link affects, representations, and relations.

3. The *super-ego* structures itself in function of external influences that the psyche internalizes.[60] It often represents mechanisms built in the past that integrate (with difficulty) the particularities of a situation constructed in the present. Like the internalized directives of the parents, the super-ego tries to give orders to the rest of the psyche and even the rest of the organism. That said, the wishes of the super-ego are rarely effective, and sometime are detrimental to the global equilibrium of the psyche and its way of interacting with the organism.

Notice that there are some common points between Freud's two topographies. Consequently, the id—as the unconscious—is mostly linked to the physiological mobilizations and the sensory data processed by the brain. The ego—like the preconscious—interacts with the memory and mechanisms that regulate movement. On the other hand, unconscious, preconscious, and conscious are now distributed into all of the systems of the Second Topography. The unconscious is, however, preponderant in the id, whereas the super-ego often has a conscious activity.[61]

Each level of the Second Topography generates certain forms of pathology. To be cut off from one's id destabilizes the equilibrium between psyche and organism, while the intrusions of the id can bring about various forms of overinvestment that the psyche is not able to integrate. An ego can be too rigid (it imprisons) or too weak (it does not contain enough).[62] The super-ego is sometimes overdeveloped in individuals with a weak ego, incapable of containing the demands of the drives' dynamics. We then witness the formation of a continual battle between rigorous willfulness and chaotic drives.

In the supervision sessions that I took with him in the 1980s, Willy Pasini distinguished three function of the ego:

1. *Delay* system: The ego, as mentioned by Freud, allows one to choose at which moment it is possible to satisfy a drive. It allows me to wait for the meal when I am hungry.
2. *Cooling* system: When the engine runs hot (overinvestment), the ego allows me to cool the engine.
3. *Sublimation*: When a drive cannot obtain the satisfaction foreseen for it by the biological requirements, its energy can be used to other ends like creativity or social engagement.

For these three functions to become operational, an individual must have a sufficiently structured ego to tolerate a strong dose of frustration without self-destructing (while maintaining a secondary functioning). The repressed unconscious material continues to exist outside of the ego. This implies that it is not submitted to the correction of experience. It remains unchanged while the rest of the personality evolves.[63] The link between the drives and experience allows the ego to build itself up while tolerating a certain amount of frustration. The

First Topography was especially relevant for the treatment of neuroses. The Second Topography adjusts itself to the fact that a growing number of clients suffer from other problems. With neurotics, the patients have a secondary process that is relatively well structured and that, above all, needs to be revised. On the other hand, individuals with a weak ego also have a lot of free energy. Individuals who nowadays we refer to as narcissistic and borderline personalities require active psychotherapeutic strategies that reinforce the ego and allow the libido to connect to forms of thought and constructive relations. In these cases, to permit the unconscious to become conscious does not suffice, for several reasons:

1. What some patients have lived through is truly atrocious. It is possible to help a person to develop constructively in spite of the fact that she has experienced indigestible events, but it is impossible to reinvent a new life for oneself and forget events like regular sexual abuse from the ages of 1 to 13.

2. According to the definitions of the Second Topography, the ego has the ability to activate procedures of repression. This law is clinically relevant because the patients who have a weak ego often remember perfectly well what they have suffered. The problem is therefore not that of remembering but that of taking a distant stance in relation to certain memories still felt as humiliating.

3. Here I take up the same theme as the preceding one but from another angle. Individuals who have a weak ego do not necessarily have the capacity to repress. Yet repressing what cannot be integrated is indispensable if one wants to evolve from a primary to a secondary mode of functioning. Otherwise, the person remains a whirlwind of affects, cognitions, and elusive libidinal charges that float like free electrons. These shredded pieces of psyche express themselves, react, and think chaotically. Lacan therefore speaks of individuals incapable of symbolizing what is going on within; Kohut speaks of a self that is not able to form itself; and others speak of a search for meaning. The truth is that no one can say up to what point the psyche can acquire meaning or coherence, as we have seen in the chapter on Hume; evidently we need a few small islands of internal coherence, which the child can acquire when he experiences moments of coherent support and attention from adults. *These havens of peace are sometimes sufficient to serve as a basis for the building of an internal structure.* Freud's ego is that part of us that has acquired a form of mastery, little islands of secondary organization between thoughts, affects, behaviors, and relation.

In *Instincts and Their Vicissitudes,*[64] Freud attempts to clarify the rapport between psyche and motor activity. He considers consciousness as not having a direct access to the drive. On the other hand, when a drive mobilizes the organism to construct an action that allows it to find a form of satisfaction, the motor system solicits the intervention of consciousness to calibrate the gestures, to accommodate them to the surrounding reality. Consciousness takes notice of an instinct by sensing its impact on motor activity. This regulation of the motor activity imposes on the thoughts the necessity to be able to distinguish between what is inside and what is outside, between a need and what this need is able obtain (the reality principle). In *The Ego and the Id*,[65] Freud situates the ego in the space that links motor activity and consciousness as the container and regulator of the relation between thoughts, motor activity, and drives. This placement is so clear for Freud that he asserts (a) that one part of the functioning of the ego is out of the reach of consciousness; and (b) that "the Ego is, first and foremost a bodily ego" (Freud, 1923a, II, p. 26)!

A fact that is rarely commented on is the rapidity with which some individuals close to Freud seized on these formulations to develop different ways to increase the importance of the body in the reflections of psychoanalysts. In the next chapter, I describe this exploration of the rapport between psyche, body, behavior, and organism carried out by the psychoanalysts during the years between the World Wars.

Why Does an Organism Need Nightmares?

The individuals traumatized by war responded only moderately well to psychoanalytical treatment. The psychoanalysts had an especially difficult time understanding why some horrible nightmares regularly haunted the soldiers after the war once the organism was no longer menaced. They had the impression that their patients latched on to these images that intruded into their psyche, not only at night but sometimes during the day. To answer this clinical question, Freud asked himself if it were possible to explain everything with a deviation of the pleasure principle. This same pleasure principle is also incapable of explaining the horrible drives that were expressed in by the masses during World War I, with no one capable of understanding their usefulness. Because of these observations, as well as others of a similar kind, Freud felt forced to postulate the existence of a destructive instinct (Thanatos) of self and others that is at least as powerful as the need to create pleasurable experiences (Eros).[66] Thanatos creates a compulsion to repeat painful situations.

Before 1914, Freud refused to accept the criticisms of Jung, Adler, and Bleuer, who could not see how one could construct a psychiatric theory by affirming that everything organized itself around the pleasure principle. The destructive human tendencies are evident in psychiatry or as soon as one studies the history of humanity. Jung and Bleuer preferred to adopt a traditional position of vitalism. They believed that all the dimensions of the organism are animated by a basic energy. This energy is then used by a variety of propensions such as the sexual need, domination, aggression, and so on. Jung's vital force contained as much shadow as it did light, as much destructive as constructive creativity. Because they refused to accept the primacy of the libido, Freud engineered their expulsion from the Psychoanalytic Association before World War I.[67]

Behold, in *The Ego and the Id* (1923a), Freud rejoins his old protagonists, at least partially, when he writes that the energy that animates the affects and thoughts is neutral and takes on erotic or destructive aspects. But he refuses to recognize that this reformulation was influenced by his discussions with Jung. In 1912, Sabina Spielrein consulted with Freud with regard to her private and therapeutic relations with Jung. Freud encouraged her to publish, in a psychoanalytic journal, an article on the death impulse. There was probably a thread of thoughts that go from Jung to Spielrein and from readers of Spielrein to Freud's Thanatos. In 1926, in *Inhibitions, Symptoms and Anxiety,* he distinguishes the mechanisms of the repression of the libido on the one hand and the repression of anxiety on the other.[68] This analysis was taken up by Melanie Klein (1955) to explore the destructive human tendencies in "normal" individuals, without any discernible psychopathology, that seem to be already in place in the very young child.

It is useful to clearly distinguish the Second Topography from the vantage point of the Thanatos hypothesis. These two models were developed during the same period but in parallel. Wilhelm Reich adopts the first model and rejects the second, whereas Melanie Klein blends them together. Others, like Otto Fenichel, differentiate them, all the while using them in parallel fashion. In the psychoanalytic literature of the start of the twenty-first century, I still find many discussions based on revised versions of Freud's Second Topography and very few that evoke the innate instinct to destroy. Having said this, the pleasure principle is also less omnipresent. Fenichel (1934) already insisted more on a defense system that protects from the pain of anxiety than on a psyche ready to risk everything to satisfy a desire to maximize the experience of pleasure. Psychoanalysis today, which long ago left the enclosure of neurosis, attempts to integrate the complexity of the violence of abuse, perversion, and dependence without having recourse to simplistic metaphors.[69]

16

Psychoanalysis and the Body

THE FIRST ATTEMPTS TO INCLUDE CONSIDERATIONS OF THE BODY INTO PSYCHOANALYTICAL TREATMENTS

The following sections are dedicated to some personalities of the psychoanalytic world who are generally quoted as having been the precursors of body psychotherapy.

Adler and the Functional Identity of the Body and the Soul

"The Wednesday group," established in Vienna in 1902, was the first psychoanalytical association. It was composed of medical generalists, neurologists, and sympathetic intellectuals without any psychotherapeutic ambitions, who came to hold discussions with Freud. In 1906, the group was expanded to form the *Psychoanalytical Society* of Vienna, under the presidency of Alfred Adler (1870–1973).

Adler was a medical generalist who thought that a few of his patients could benefit from the psychoanalytic vision, even if they did not need to follow a formal psychotherapy like the one proposed by Freud. When he met Freud to discuss this subject, he already had the desire to widen the spectrum of the interventions inspired by the psychoanalytic approach. Like Freud, Adler thought that the soul[1] influences not only behavior but also, sometimes, the physiological mechanisms that create the symptoms that are treated by general medical practitioners. Adler even went so far as to propose that if the thoughts have the power to influence the physiological dynamics, these can also influence the thoughts. He wanted to develop a psychoanalysis in which work on the physiological dimension sometimes permits the treatment of the psyche, and a work on the psyche that can treat somatic problems. Through his consideration of the evolution of biological organisms, he noted that a plant cannot displace itself; that the more an organism is mobile, the more its psyche is complex: "The result is that, in the development of the life of the soul, everything that pertains to movement and everything that can be linked to the difficulties of a simple displacement must be included" (Adler, 1927, 1.1, p. 19; translated by Marcel Duclos).

Alfred Adler pushed the identity body–mind to such an extent that he believed a person who was psychically immature necessarily had immature organs. He deduced from that analysis that only by treating psyche and soma could a physician help a patient become stronger.[2]

Wilhelm Reich would also describe the individual as a biosystem that influences the psychological (treated in psychotherapy) and somatic (treated in medicine) mechanisms.[3] He therefore had to clarify the differences between his approach and that of Adler. During his psychoanalytic period, Reich understood the body and the psyche as two subsystems of the organism that have a mutual *dialectic*[4] rapport that he identifies as *antithetic*.[5] The body and the psyche necessarily mutually influence each other because they are part of the same organism; this does not mean that they function in identical ways. On the other hand, there would be *functional identity* between physiological and psychological dimensions that are spontaneously related to one another in a healthy organism: the two dimensions collaborate to achieve a common goal. Reich's commentary on Adler summarizes the position that is the most widespread in body psychotherapy: "While we do take the same problem as our point of departure, namely the purposeful mode of operation of what one calls the 'total personality and character,' we nonetheless make use of a fundamentally different theory and method" (Reich, 1949a, VIII.1, p. 169)

During his psychoanalytic period, Reich did not accept the idea that the dynamics of the psyche and the soma are two faces of the same coin that function in the same way. We have seen how Freud had reflected extensively on the connection between psyche and soma. Like other thinkers, he discovered that it was extremely difficult to define what linked these systems together and what differentiated them. This difficulty, distressing to the specialist, still exists today. This explains why so many thinkers,[6] including medical practitioners like Adler and Groddeck, have a problem stopping themselves from using gross simplifications. At the end of his life, Reich returned to his critique of Adler and Groddeck; conceded that there is a "unity of psychic and somatic function" (Reich, 1949a, XIII.9, p. 340). It is mostly this point of view that was then adopted by the neo-Reichian schools; such is not retained in the options defended in this manual.

Another aspect of Adler's thought that influenced some movements in body psychotherapy is the idea that the needs of the organism are necessarily in conflict with the social demands, because these two systems defend incompatible interests and procedures. For Adler, this conflict alone sufficed to explain the strong prevalence of neuroses in the human species.[7]

Spielrein: Psychoanalysis, Cognitive Psychology, and Nonverbal Communication

Sabina Spielrein (1885–1942) was a Russian who studied medicine in Zurich, Switzerland.[8] There, she became a psychiatrist after having met Jung. In 1911, she became a psychoanalyst under Freud's tutelage. She traveled to Germany and then Russia, where she got married. In 1920, she returned to Switzerland, where she founded the Geneva Society of Psychoanalysis. She became a psychologist while working at the Rousseau Institute of Geneva, founded by Édouard Claparède. This institute was renowned for its studies on the psychological development of children. Claparède married Helen Spir, daughter of a Russian philosopher. He was therefore particularly hospitable to Russian psychologists in exile from the new Soviet Union.[9]

Spielrein psychoanalyzed several members of this institute: not only Claparède but also the young Jean Piaget, who then published articles relating psychoanalysis and the psychology of the child.[10] Spielrein's most representative article of this period shows that the spoken language is composed of verbal and nonverbal signs that frame and nuance the meaning of phrases:

> When we adults speak of language, we only think of the content of the word and we do not see the role that the resources drawn from the rhythmic and melodic domain of language can play, even in written texts, such as exclamation points, interrogation marks, etc. These melodic modes of expression are even more at play in conversation. One can add to this a third factor which one could call a visual language, which consists of phenomena such as mimics and gestures. These, as images, can also play a preeminent role in dreams. We should therefore distinguish verbal language from other aspects of language: the melodic language, the visual language (image), the language of actions, etc. (Spielrein, 1920; translated by Marcel Duclos)

Spielrein thus created a bridge between psychoanalysis and nonverbal communication and between the beginnings of the psychoanalysis of children and developmental cognitive psychotherapy. The contacts between child psychoanalysts and cognitive psychologists that she established continued without her. A manifestation of this influence is seen in the way the notion of regulation systems proposed by developmental psychology influenced child psychoanalysis. Only later did the notion of regulation enter the general theory of psychoanalysis. Child psychoanalysis was then in its infancy with the explorations of Hermine Hug von Hugenstein and Anna Freud (daughter of Sigmund Freud).

Spielrein did not do any psychotherapeutic work with children. She studied children at the Jean-Jacques Rousseau Institute with the methods of experimental psychology; she psychoanalyzed adults in her home. Unlike Anna Freud, she did not fall in the trap of reducing nonverbal language to a kind of mechanism of communication that the human inherited from the monkey and which would be more archaic than language. On the contrary, her contact with the psychologists showed her that intelligence needs to pass through gestures to interact with objects and form itself.[11]

Spielrein returned to Russia in 1923. Vygotsky and Luria, who were part of an eminent school of developmental cognitive psychology in the Soviet Union,[12] were on the verge of founding the Russian School of Psychoanalysis.[13] Like her, they were synthesizing cognitive psychology, affective psychology, and psychoanalysis in their studies of child development. She brought them much information on the recent development of psychoanalysis and of child psychology in Geneva. Both thinkers played an important role in Vygotsky's thinking.[14]

In a 1931 article mentioned by Richebächer (2005), Spielrein describes the following study:

> Spielrein asks a hundred children and twenty adults to draw an object. Half of the subjects are able to see what it is that they are creating; while the others draw blind-folded.
>
> Over all, the drawings, made with open eyes, are certainly more precise. But as pertains to the details, Spielrein observes that certain aspects of the object drawn blind-folded are better drawn; as if sight interfered with the memory and the knowledge contained in the gestures.

According to Richebächer,[15] Spielrein concluded that there existed a particular link between gesture and speech. She was so impressed by this observation that she recommended that work with blindfolds be integrated into the new pedagogical methods that soviet psychologists such as Vygotsky were trying to establish in Russia. She was convinced that such methods could enhance the development of the mind.

Spielrein's publications are seldom mentioned. She did not know how to mobilize the means that allow for intellectual success. The value of her ideas did not become evident until a half-century later. Passionate as she was, she nonetheless played the role of a muse for a number of great psychologists and psychoanalysts because she had the knack of finding herself at the intersections crucial to her discipline and she felt the importance of the connections in which she involved herself. She set into motion ideas that psychoanalysts like Jung, Freud, Fenichel, Reich, Vygotsky, and Luria integrated into their thinking.

She was persecuted by Stalinism, which wanted to destroy the Jews, the psychoanalysts, and all "nonconformists." The Spielreins were related to all three of these categories. It is possible that many of her writings were lost during the chaos caused by the terror that dominated the Soviet Union at that time. Finally, she died, executed by a German army firing squad in 1942.[16]

Groddeck

> Nothing happens to you, and you can do nothing unless a multitude of cells work for you, communicate to you joy or sorrow or every other impression, thinks your thoughts, feels your sensations, regulates your heartbeats, make you breathe, make you live. The mouth that you love is formed of living cells; the hand that you seek or seek to avoid is entirely made up of living cells. Everything that you do, every-

thing that you experience is broken down into an infinite number, a countless number of existences and lives. You have felt it yourself: the contact with another has penetrated out of its flux into your soul and body, this presence, this glance provokes a revolution in your entire being, the sound of but one word has repelled you or brought you peace. But it is not you that this contact, this glance, this sound has touched, but some cells that do not obey your reason, that do with you as it pleased them, that pass a thousand impressions before you, before choosing from among them the one that will affect you. (Georg Groddeck, 1913, *Nasamecu*, p. 9; translated by Marcel Duclos)

Walter Georg Groddeck (1866–1934) was a practitioner of general medicine who, like Adler, wanted to use the psychoanalytical conceptual framework to create an approach adapted to the needs of his patients. Almost the same age as Freud, Groddeck comes in contact with Freud in the 1920s. It is probably Groddeck who most directly confronted Freud relative to the difficulty of integrating the activity of the body into the dynamics of the psyche. Groddeck admired Freud's work. He was particularly impressed by the theory of the unconscious in the Second Topography. But as a physician, he maintained the common sense of a generalist. For many students of body psychotherapy, he is the gentle grandfather of their discipline.

Groddeck (1923) proposed a "psychosomatic" psychotherapy that approaches the patient in his organismic whole. Humans cannot be divided into separate parts and treated, as often happened in the medical disciplines. He explored many ways to take the needs of the patient into account: considered under the angle of both body and psyche, which Marulla Hauswirth summarizes in this way:

> Groddeck allies massage and verbal work. He has developed the notion of body defenses, considering that the tensions at the level of the musculature and the reduction of respiration are the means to repress the psychic content susceptible to act as well at the level of the affects and of the drives than of the thoughts. Moreover, Groddeck laid the bases in favor of a systematic work with the negative transference, and he insisted on the importance of paying attention not only to the explicit content, but also to the form of the expression, of the attitudes and to the body postures as carriers of unconscious messages. (Hauswirth, 2002, 1, p. 180; translated by Marcel Duclos)

Even though Groddeck's propositions remain inspiring, they did not evolve into a psychotherapeutic technique. On the other hand, they influenced the explorations of Ferenczi, Fenichel, Braatøy, and Reich. Ferenczi and Freud regularly corresponded with him. A discussion of his work is always part of training in body psychotherapy. His first work, *Nasamecu* or "Nature Heals," published in 1913, is a title that easily relates to the themes developed by the Idealistic methods of body psychotherapy, in spite of a few eugenistic developments.[17] Wilhelm Reich always acknowledged Groddeck's contribution to his thinking. He associates Groddeck's formulations with Adler's, that is, with one of a generalist who does not sufficiently differentiate the functioning of the body and the psyche. Reich thought that the Groddeck's formulations reinforced a psychoanalytical tendency toward the "psychologizing of the somatic":[18]

> It culminated in unscientific psychologistic *interpretations* of bodily processes with the aid of the theory of the unconscious. If, e.g., a woman skipped her menstrual period without being pregnant, this was taken as expressing her aversion for her husband or child. According to this concept, practically all physical diseases were due to unconscious wishes or fears. Thus, one acquired cancer, "in order to . . . ;" one perished from tuberculosis because one unconsciously wished to, etc. Peculiarly enough, psychoanalytical experience provided a multitude of observations which seems to confirm this view. The observations were undeniable but critical considerations warned against such conclusions. (Reich, 1940, III.3, p. 33)

Georg Groddeck can be recognized as the first person to have developed an approach that regularly combines bodywork and a psychotherapeutic approach in the same session.[19] He especially used different forms of deep massage to influence the system of muscular defense that repressed the expression of emotions. At that time, this way to integrate body and psychotherapy was more widespread than we might think:

> In 1931, the 6th congress of the "Common Medical Society for Psychotherapy" met in the German town of Dresden. Its general topic was "treating the soul from the body." The famous Psychiatrist, Ernst Kretschmer, was the chair of this congress. Psychoanalysts Gustav R. Heyer[20] spoke on "Treating the Psyche starting from the Body" and suggested to include gymnastics, sports, breath work and massage into the psychotherapeutic treatment. Other speakers claimed to see psychic as well as somatic phenomena as functions of the entire organism.[21] One speaker went so far as to state that a combined body-mind-therapy would be the future of psychotherapy. Georg Groddeck gave a presentation on "Massage and Psychotherapy,"[22] which is, according to George Downing, one of his finest papers.[23] (Geuter et al., 2010)

Since then, some body psychotherapists use deep massage in a more systematic way, like those who use the massages of Aadel Bulow-Hansen, Gerda Boyesen, or Ida Rolf.[24]

The Active Psychoanalytic Technique of Ferenczi

> Ferenczi's scientific achievement is impressive above all from its many-sidedness. (Sigmund Freud, 1923b, *Dr. Sandor Ferenczi*, p. 268)

The Microscope of Psychoanalysis
Sándor Ferenczi (1873–1933) was, at the same time, one of Freud's close associates and a person who never ceased seeking ways to improve psychoanalysis.[25] His research was as much due to an insatiable imagination and curiosity than a

difficulty in tolerating constraints and limits. Ferenczi still inspires a number of psychotherapists, but his difficulty in respecting boundaries sometimes renders his arguments questionable. He had as patients a mother and her daughter, and he fell in love with both of them. Freud was never able to have confidence in him on boundary issues (Haynal, 1987; Haynal-Reymond et al., 2005). Nonetheless, up to the end of his life, Ferenczi considered Freud his therapist, his friend, and his colleague. His fluid ethics was also what allowed him to become a sort of microscope of the functioning of the psychotherapist and the way he can use his feelings to capture the intimate workings of his patients. Thanks to this capacity to feel what is at play between him and his patients, he became the first prominent expert on *transferential dynamics*.[26]

Irritated by the limits of psychoanalysis, Ferenczi explored, in the 1920s, the possibility of using an *active psychoanalytic technique*.[27] Ferenczi did not have enough internal discipline for his project to succeed; others took up his formulations, which became the basis of most psychotherapeutic approaches (the psychotherapy of psychoanalytical inspiration established by Otto Kernberg, Gestalt therapy, Transactional analysis, body psychotherapy, family therapy, etc.). Ferenczi included in his research the considerations of Adler, Spielrein, and Groddeck on the importance of including the body in a more explicit fashion in a psychotherapeutic process. Ferenczi was at the front of the exploration of techniques undertaken by psychoanalysts after World War I.

Recover the Repressed Affects by Stimulating Thoughts and Behaviors

Ferenczi tried to create methods that permitted him to help people for whom a "classical" psychoanalytical treatment was not sufficiently adapted to the patient's needs. He set about searching for an active method that permits the analysis not only of the thoughts but also the behaviors. One of the basic ideas of the active technique was that the affects (especially sexual) are situated somewhere between behavior and thoughts. Therefore, they can be influenced by psychological and behavioral exercises.[28] This introduces the notion that behaviors and thoughts are distinct systems that interact through intermediary systems (e.g., emotions). The details of the interaction between acts and representations are poorly understood; the psychotherapist notices that they can influence each other in various ways. A person can laugh when she is sad or cry when she is angry. In that example, we observe not only that the connections between behavior and thoughts are multiple but also that there can be a sort of "resonating" effect between these two dimensions of the organism. Consequently, a person is able to dissociate from her sadness by trying to amuse herself without being aware that the expression on her face conveys sadness to others, even when she laughs. If the therapist becomes a mirror that reflects this image of sadness to the patient, he can then promote an awareness that modifies the way the thoughts of the patient approaches this sadness. The active technique is therefore an attempt to analyze the triangle of thought-affect-behavior that structures a therapeutic interaction.[29] In the example just given, if the patient becomes aware that she often dissociates from a sad mood by trying to behave as if she were a happy person, the whole of the triangle restructures itself. Thoughts, affects, and behavior then coordinate together differently; other working modes of the organism become possible.

In Freud's method of analyzing dreams, the patient tell his dream and free associates with the therapist. In the active technique, *the therapist extracts from the patient's preconscious behavior a trait in which he is interested and draws the attention of the patient to this behavior.* Then the therapist decides to make of this behavior a central theme of exploration in the course of subsequent sessions. This manifest creativity of the psychotherapist in interaction with the patient characterizes Ferenczi's active technique. If his basic argumentation always remains pertinent, his way of justifying his technique is less so. He proposes to give the subject certain "permissions," like the right to extend the session and get up from the divan, and so on. He also gave "prohibitions," like proposing to one of his patients that she explore what might happen when she prevents herself from crossing her legs during the sessions when it has been her habit to do so.[30] This language allowed Ferenczi to act as if his technique were but a variation of the classic psychoanalytic frame.

The Active Psychoanalytic Technique and Behavior

The following example shows how a memory can be explored using the active technique:

> A vignette showing how to self-explore through singing. *Ferenczi*[31] *describes a patient with whom he made little progress until the moment when he asked her to sing a melody that she had mentioned in her associations. It took him two sessions before she dares to sing the song while lounging on the divan. At first she was very shy; but Ferenczi persisted in urging her to self-explore while singing the song. Her voice became progressively more at ease. He suggested that she stand and to sing with her body. The patient then remembered that she sang this song with her sister who made gestures that conveyed daring sexually suggestive undertones. During several sessions, Ferenczi invited her to explore what it was that inhibited her from singing this song with her sister's gestures. The patient eventually sang with delight. In this process, Ferenczi and the patient together became conscious of a whole series of inhibitions that inhibited her capacity to lead a pleasant life. Ferenczi thinks that this content would probably have never appeared if he had followed a classical psychoanalytical approach.*

Ferenczi does not explain why he decided to spend so much time on this song. Today, this type of intervention is often used in body psychotherapy. It implies that the therapist has confidence in his non-conscious know-how which permits him to develop "something more than the interpretation" (Haynal, 2001, 9.5, p. 135). The principal justification for what happened with this patient is that this choice facilitated useful discoveries; and that it made the therapeutic sessions more enjoyable, which is never a bad thing. This is a "post-facto" justification.

The technical problem is that in acting in this way, the therapist does not have a rational argument to support his intervention. This line of action is not consistent with Ferenczi's requirement that a therapist should be able to situate his intervention in an explicit technical context.[32]

In this example, as in many others, we see that Ferenczi's active method focuses on behavior rather than what I call the body. Here is another example of an active technique that will be developed when psychotherapists are able to use film and videos in psychotherapy.[33]

> *A vignette on the beginnings of video analysis. Ferenczi (1921b) discusses a work on the subject of tics written by psychiatrists who do not practice psychoanalysis. He nonetheless cites this example because it illustrates a technique that could be included in his active method. The physicians place the patient in front of a mirror and have him observe his tic while asking him to recount its history. At the same time, they teach the patient exercises that allow for the exploration of different ways of moving the muscles mobilized by the tic. They also ask what is going on when he forces himself to immobilize the particular region of the body under question. Ferenczi used this behavioral method to help his patients become aware of their behavior and of how it interacts with thoughts and affects.*

The Neo-Cathartic Relaxation

In addition to these behavioral techniques, Ferenczi (1930) takes up the cathartic methods used by Breuer and Freud in the 1890s. He induces intense states of relaxation[34] and regression that arouse such powerful emotional discharges that they are also able to carry repressed memories. This emotional experience is profound. It mobilizes the whole organism. The remembering is particularly alive and detailed. The patient gets up feeling healed. From my experience, this result lasts for two or three years at best, and sometimes only a few days. These cathartic experiences are regularly observed in psychotherapy groups. They especially allow a patient to feel that it is possible to transform oneself: to transform one's habitual mode of functioning.

Ferenczi in the 1920s thought that such experiences could be usefully reintegrated in the psychoanalytical toolbox if they were well framed. He thought especially of certain patients who have already had extensive psychoanalysis but whose treatment is now stagnant. In that case, the cathartic method might make it possible to shed light into the shadowy zones that classical analysis has not been able to illuminate. To induce a catharsis, he suggests that patients relax and let movements come up the same way that they let thoughts emerge. Ferenczi[35] therefore speaks of relaxation, but the term is taken very loosely, because he does not use any relaxation techniques. He proposes a form of laissez-faire, of letting come what needs to come. Body psychotherapists know this type of session very well. It unfolds in three stages:

1. A general relaxation of the organism also relaxes the defense systems. This state sometimes activates an intense emotion.

2. The patient feels the emotion express itself by mobilizing all of the dimensions of the organism (psyche, behavior, the body from head to foot,
   and the vegetative system).

3. The patient then experiences a profound relaxation, like the air made
   lighter after a storm.

Here are a few examples of what Ferenczi observes by using this technique:

> *Hysterical body symptoms:* paresthesias[36] and clearly localized cramps, violent ex-
> pressive movements evoking small hysterical crises, sudden variations of the state
> of consciousness, slight vertigo and even loss of consciousness often followed by a
> retroactive amnesia. In certain cases, these hysterical accesses take on the propor-
> tions of a veritable *trance state,* in which fragments of the past were relived; and
> therefore, the person of the physician remained the only bridge between the pa-
> tient and reality. It became possible to ask the patient questions in order to obtain
> important information concerning the dissociated parts of the patient's personal-
> ity. (Ferenczi, 1930, pp. 89–92)

Ferenczi thinks that these states emerge spontaneously, simply because he had
authorized such a bodily laissez-faire to exist in a therapeutic frame. He relates
this permission with what happens when a physician administers a hypnotic
tranquilizer, like sodium pentothal, to a soldier traumatized by combat. The
soldier goes through an emotional phase that mobilizes the dimensions of the
organism. The patient cries, screams, and feels the need to retell the traumatizing situation, over and over again. During this phase, we often observe intense
body reactions, like a muscular tension that takes over the entire body, an arrested breathing, or an opisthotonus crisis (see the Glossary). The psychotherapist sometimes observes the same series of phenomena when a patient relives a
childhood trauma. With his neo-cathartic method, Ferenczi evokes these states.
This requires that the therapist is able to accept what is happening in those circumstances, explore the material that appears, and avoid the dangers that can
arise by mobilizing the intensity of these emotional eruptions.[37]

Henceforth, this type of observation became current in the framework of
different forms of body psychotherapy. Gerda Boyesen[38] observed a similar
technique when she was having psychotherapy with Ola Raknes, one of Reich's
students. He obtained similar results by saying: "Here, you can do whatever you
want. Simply, if you break a window, you will have to pay to have it replaced!"
As a therapist she used the following formula: "You can say or do what you
want. But you are not obliged to do or say anything at all. Simply, do not withhold any speech or any movement. Tell me if there is something that you want
me to do or to say."[39] I have often observed how Gerda Boyesen worked, and I
have seen her work many times. She knew how to create an atmosphere that
permitted the apparently spontaneous emergence of phenomena close to those
described by Ferenczi. But I also observed that this type of permission does not
have the same impact when it is proposed by a less charismatic psychotherapist.
It seems to me that this type of effect is sustained by the rumors that transform

some psychotherapists into stars. For example, I achieve such effects when I am presented in a prestigious manner to a training group. On the other hand, I do not have this impact on my regular patients, who have often selected me from a listing in a phone book or from the Internet without knowing anything of my reputation. We are therefore in a situation close to that of hypnosis, where the specific intervention depends on the quality of the general ambience to acquire its effectiveness.

THE CREATIVE FRIENDSHIP BETWEEN FENICHEL AND REICH

Like Rousseau, Beethoven, and Tolstoy, Wilhelm Reich (1897–1957) was an immense humanist, a charismatic teacher, a virtuoso in his profession, with an inspiring intelligence and a powerful imagination; simultaneously, he could be highly selfish and obnoxious with those that were closest to him. Reich reinforced this image by presenting himself as a solitary genius at war against the stupidity of others. He is generally recognized as the father of body psychotherapy.[40] In the following sections, I show that this title is justified if we admit that a father is part of a family and that he does not always agree to have the children that the social dynamics impose on him. We will see, in effect, that after having had a dazzling career as a psychoanalyst, he turned his back on all forms of psychotherapy to develop a new form of therapy that aims not at the psyche but at the organism. If his organismic therapy has nonetheless favored the advent of body psychotherapy such as we know it today, it is because Reich was part of a large and tumultuous family capable of allying itself to his creativity, and then to create different forms of body psychotherapy that emerged during the 1950s. To understand this process, it is also useful to present Otto Fenichel (1897–1946), who is somewhat of a secret and unappreciated uncle of this domain.

When I began to write this book, I had a specific plan in mind. Fenichel was not part of it.[41] For me, he was a boring orthodox Freudian who had been one of the principal references on the psychoanalytical techniques for many generations of psychoanalysts.[42] He would have done everything possible to have Reich expelled from the International Association of Psychoanalysis by spreading the word that he was psychotic. Such was his reputation in the Reichian literature. Yet the more that I read the writings of those who were part of Reich's entourage, the more I encountered Fenichel's name without knowing why. I therefore set about to inform myself more precisely about him. After some research, I discovered that he had played a central role in the birth of body psychotherapy. This function of uncle was obscured by the Reichians and Freudians for reasons that will gradually become evident.

1. The Reichians wanted to augment their prestige by making the world believe that Reich was a singular genius, persecuted like Socrates by all those who cannot stand the brightness of the truth.

2. The Freudians did not want that one of the founders of their movement would have appreciated Reich's findings to the point that he had played a central role in the birth of body psychotherapy.

A Friendship between Students:
The Seminar on Sexuality

Fenichel was born in 1897 of a Jewish family of lawyers in Vienna.[43] His health prohibited him from becoming a soldier. He enrolled in the school of medicine in 1915.

Like many students of his generation, Fenichel regularly frequented the youth movements. It must be said that the communist propaganda of the period attracted numerous people who had been disillusioned by the war. Ever since the Jugendstil and the Wandervogel (the migrating birds) at the start of the century,[44] these movements had multiplied. All of the political parties (from the extreme left to the extreme right), the religious groups (Catholics, Jews, and Protestants), and the ideological movements had their youth movements. Fenichel was close to the Jewish youth movement of the left. Certain directors of this movement, like Siegfried Bernfeld, became psychoanalysts and created bridges between these movements, especially in the matter of sexual education. Probably because of this influence, Fenichel began to attend seminars given by Freud as early as 1916. He participated regularly in the sessions of the Psycho-analytical Society at the beginning of 1918, during the key period when Freud was creating his Second Topography.

The youth from the left denounced an antisexual morality that prohibited adolescents from obtaining a responsible attitude in sexual matters. These movements wanted an education that integrated their need to be sexually in-formed, supported their right to be sexual human beings, and protected them from perversions in which some forces close to prostitution wanted them to succumb. In this context, the young Fenichel approached the theme of sexual education, especially in Max Hodann's journal,[45] which also enthusiastically welcomed (10 years later) Reich's Sex-Pol initiative. Fenichel frequented the animated gatherings by Alfred Kurella,[46] who related communist thinking, het-erosexual Platonic Idealism, and sexual revolution. Kurella defended "a sexual mysticism or Korperseele [the enfleshed spirit] in Vienna and Berlin" (Russel Jacoby, 1983, 2, p. 71f; translated from the French by Marcel Duclos). This branch of the youth movement defended a moral brand of free love and sexual emancipation. The sexual contact of the "new man" necessarily implies the union of souls as well as that of bodies.

In the momentum inspired by his discovery of the youth movements and psychoanalytic thought, between 1919 and 1921 Fenichel proposed a seminar on sexuality, which he opened in the Faculty of Medicine. At the same time, he underwent analysis with Paul Federn, who was a socialist psychoanalyst close to Freud.

Reich: Student and Then Companion of Fenichel

Wilhelm Reich was born in 1897 of a Jewish family of landowners in Galicia, in Ukraine, which was part of the Austro-Hungarian Empire before World War I. When he was 13, his mother committed suicide. This event affected him profoundly.[47] After completing school in 1915, he became a soldier in the Austrian army during World War I. Lenin's takeover of power is considered by many Europeans the triumph of liberty over tyranny. The Treaty of Versailles dismantled the Austro-Hungarian Empire. Hungary and Czechoslovakia became independent, and Galicia was annexed by Poland. Henceforth, Vienna was but the immense capital of a small country. Former combatants were allowed to try to pass their medical exams in four years. Reich brilliantly undertook this accelerated formation after he completed his military service. The Reich family had lost all of its possessions. In coming to Vienna with his brother, Reich maintained his Austrian nationality, but he had the status of an Austrian of the old colonies. It seems to me, given the choices that he made in his lifetime, that he identified mostly with antebellum Vienna. He felt close to the critical artistic movements like the Jugendstil and the Secession.[48] When he later lived in the United States, he gave to his theory of cosmic energy an aesthetic that makes one think of the apparently natural beauty, such as represented by Gustav Klimt, and to a notion of the natural spontaneity of the gesture incarnated by the dance of Isadora Duncan.

At the end of the war, Reich paid little attention to politics because, above all, he had to fight to provide for his and his brother's needs. He heard about Fenichel's seminar on sexology and registered for it in 1919.

In this seminar, Fenichel helped him discover the following topics:

1. The *youth movements* of the left. Reich felt close to this youth that wanted to live a less anxious and more responsible sexuality than the one that he lived in his daily life. He discovered that the sexual misery[49] he knows is not a personal problem, nor even a fatality; that it is imperative to join together to deeply transform the mores of society to be able to live in an open and radiant fashion.

2. *Psychoanalysis.* Freud would have demonstrated that the existing sexual misery causes mental and somatic problems in many people. Psychoanalysis allows one to understand in a detailed way how the sexual mores of the period deregulate the functioning of the psyche and the organism. Therefore, Freud also proposed a profound revision of the sexual mores for medical reasons. This transformation of social experience can only be accomplished by acting simultaneously at the level of the individual (in psychoanalysis), the level of education, and the level of the institutions (to sustain a transformation of the social rituals and myths related to sexuality). The only country at that time that undertook change on these themes at the level of institutions and education

was the Soviet Union under the direction of Lenin. It was now necessary to relate psychoanalysis to these reforms so that the propositions of the institutions respect the needs of the individuals.

3. *Sexology*. Fenichel also mentioned sexologists often quoted by Freud and described the physiological dimensions of sexuality.

4. A brand of *humanistic Marxism*, influenced by socialism.

In taking this seminar, Reich discovered, with reticence at first, the idea that "sexuality is the center around which gravitates all of social life as well as the spiritual world of the individual" (Reich, 1937, 1.3.1919, p. 109; translated by Marcel Duclos). What Reich discovered in this seminar touched him so deeply that the themes Fenichel conjured up inspired him for the rest of his life.

Reich followed the example of his mentor and became his friend. He started to attend the sessions of the Psychoanalytical Society of Vienna with a passion. Fenichel and Reich became members of the association together in 1920. They were 23 years old. Reich was in two brief psychoanalyses: one with Isodor Isaak Sadger,[50] and then with Paul Federn, who had already analyzed Fenichel.[51] At that time, Freud did not require that the psychoanalysts had to have been psychoanalyzed before practicing.[52] Fenichel often felt like Reich's protective big brother. He helped Reich integrate himself into the Viennese intelligentsia. After 10 difficult years, Reich entered into the happiest period of his life. Each step became a discovery, a new friendship, a new battle, a new theory. With Fenichel, he joined the group of Marxist psychoanalysts, where they met a large number of individuals who were glad to work with them. In this intellectual breeding ground, they finalized a synthesis relating Marxism, the theses of the youth movement, and psychoanalysis. Always together, they are passionately involved in the promotion of Ferenczi's active method. Through the intermediary of Fenichel, Reich met Annie Pink, who became his patient, his spouse, and an eminent psychoanalyst of the left.

Annie was the second patient with whom Reich had an affair.[53] The set-up was always the same. The two young adults fell in love during the psychotherapy sessions. By mutual consent, they ended their therapeutic contract, and the woman continued her therapy with another analyst. Having behaved in an "ethical and responsible manner," they can meet as lovers. If this behavior is considered ethical when this way of acting is accidental, it is no longer considered ethical when it occurs regularly, as was the case for Reich. His first relationship of this type occurred with a friend of Annie who died tragically after a botched abortion, probably after having been impregnated by Reich.[54] Freud scolded Reich for his recurring affairs with former patients.[55] Even so, many analysts of the period had affairs with their patients, like Jung, Gross, and Ferenczi. As if to reassure himself, Reich agreed to marry Annie when she demanded it; he regretted it a few years later. They had two daughters, Eva and Lore. Wilhelm and Annie both had several extramarital affairs but stayed together to care for the children.

Even if both Fenichel and Reich claimed to be communists, they took part in different brands of communism. Reich was mostly interested in the social transformations undertaken by Lenin in the Soviet Union. Fenichel and his colleagues were more sympathetic toward Marxist socialism. Fenichel and Reich spoke very little about communism. Their interest in Marxism was more a hope for change than an understanding of the thinking of Marx and Engel. It appears that they did not read their writings attentively. When Reich became a member of the Communist Party, he started to use all sorts of terms that are part of the jargon of militant communists, without ever giving the impression that he really understood the meaning and implications of the language. However, as we will see, Reich needed the power that can be acquired through the support of a party for his sexual revolution.

Berlin 1923–1929: The Psychoanalytic Clinic of Berlin Meets Gindler's School of Gymnastics

In 1922, Fenichel asked Reich to take over the direction of the seminar on sexology and leaves for Berlin.[56]

Prelude: With Abraham and Nathanson

WITH ABRAHAM: THE CLUB OF THE YOUNG PSYCHOANALYSTS OF TOMORROW
Karl Abraham was first trained by Bleuer and Jung at the Burghölzli psychiatric hospital in Zurich. His unconditional admiration for Freud created sparks that accentuated the tensions between Freud and Jung. He established a psychoanalytical society in Berlin in 1908. After the war, this society grew rapidly. It was joined by personalities such as Ernst Simmel and Max Eitingon. Simmel had developed, during World War I, interventions of psychoanalytic inspiration for traumatized soldiers. Eitingon was a Russian millionaire who had trained in Psychoanalysis with Freud in Vienna, Ferenczi in Budapest, and Jung in Zurich. Eitingon decided to sponsor a psychoanalytical clinic with the support of Simmel and the protective sympathy of Abraham. It was asked of each practitioner to contribute to the existence of the clinic, either by seeing a patient free for a year, or by giving 4 percent of the income from one's practice.[57] The treatments in the clinic were often free. Patients were asked to pay what they could if they were not poor. A section of this clinic, directed by Melanie Klein, treated children.[58]

The project worked so well that Abraham and his colleagues were overwhelmed by the demand for training others in analysis. "Many came to Berlin because the Berlin Poliklinik offered the most rigorous and structured education in psychoanalysis in the world" (Makari, 2008, p. 372). In 1923, the Berlin society and clinic decided to establish "a formal teaching institute with clear requirements" (ibid.). The structure of this first training institute has remained, from then on, the reference for other such training programs around the world. Each individual who wanted to become a psychoanalyst in Berlin was required to have taken courses in psychoanalysis, had personal psychoanalysis with a training analyst, and also individual supervision—something that had not been formally required.[59] This structured formation quickly attracted candidates, not only from Germany (Erich Fromm, Karen Horney, Edith Jacobson) but also from Austria (Melanie Klein and Helen Deutsch), England (Edward and James Glover), Hungary (Michael Balint, Sándor Radó, and Franz Gabriel Alexander), Norway (Nic Waal and Olga Raknes[60]), and even the United States (Trygve Braatøy[61]). All these therapists are discussed today.

The important point here is that Freudians wanted to keep control of their training procedures and refused all advice (from Bleuler, for example) that encouraged them to include their discipline in an academic curriculum.[62] This choice was one of the most explosive positions defended by Freud: creating a liberal profession, based on intellectual skills that cannot be acquired in a university.

When Karl Abraham died in 1925, Eitingon and Simmel ensured the continuation of the institute and the outpatient clinic by recruiting the help of some young colleagues, such as Franz Alexander, Sándor Radó, and Karen Horney.[63] This movement in psychoanalysis, which then developed in the United States, neglected the First Topography (the conscious/unconscious opposition) and focused on the Second Topography.

OTTO FENICHEL ENCOUNTERS CLARE NATHANSON AND DISCOVERS THE GYMNASTICS OF GINDLER

In 1922, Otto Fenichel left Vienna for this Psychoanalytic Institute.[64] He entered into analysis with Sándor Radó. From 1924 onward, he became one of the trainers of the institute.[65]

Otto Fenichel met a pupil of Elsa Gindler named Clare Nathanson.[66] She used Gindler's method with children who suffered from tuberculosis. According to Clare, a mutual friend introduced them to each other: "I thought, 'Poor guy, he does not know it is the body!' And he, of course, thought 'She does not know it is the mind!'" (C. Fenichel, 1981, p. 6). They fell in love and married. Financially, Otto was doing well. He was able to find an apartment sufficiently large for Clare to be able to conduct Gindler gymnastics classes. They had one daughter, whom they named Hanna.[67] During this period, Fenichel began to follow regularly Gindler's course for men to try to rid himself of the terrible migraines that no physician had been able to cure. The Psychoanalytic Institute and Gindler's school were only a 10-minute walk from each other.[68] Gindler's courses treated Fenichel's migraines so well that he became even more interested in her method. He asked Clare to come to the Psychoanalytical Institute to present Gindler's work. These presentations were followed with open discussions. In 1927, Otto gave a presentation at the institute on the way to integrate certain aspects of Gindler's work into psychoanalytical thought.[69]

One of the impacts of these discussions was to further differentiate psyche, physiology, and body. In Vienna, from Freud to Reich, the psychoanalysts did not dare abandon the notion that the psyche is structured by the way it is grounded in the biological dynamics of the drives. This remains true in Berlin, but the discussions concerning Gindler's work and psychoanalysis made it clearer for the two camps that the work on the body mobilizes different organismic resources than the work on the psyche. From the psyche's point of view, the world of thoughts is not the same as the one we perceive starting from the body; reciprocally, the world of body sensations is not the same when we start from the psyche or from real movements. It is as if the psyche imposes a view of the body to function well; the body also imposes a view of the psyche to function well. The same goes for the drives. Different aspects of a drive are mobilized when they are coordinated with the psyche, behavior, or the body. This understanding has clear implications in a practice. According to Fenichel and Gindler, the two approaches can help a person through different means that have a different type of impact. However, each approach has limits and areas of fuzziness. Using both approaches in a single session could increase the area of confusion and diminish the impact each discipline can provide. This practical point of view became clear for Fenichel and for Gindler, who, it seems, never changed their minds thereafter.

On the theoretical plane, these considerations are more difficult to define because clearly the same psyche perceives everything that happens. We had to wait for the modular models to understand that the psyche is a subentity of the organism, and that, like the organism, the psyche is composed of millions of modules that can relate in thousands of ways, in function of the dynamics mobilized in the organism. It is therefore possible that it is not the same organization of the psyche's modules that emerges at the occasion of an introspection that aims at thoughts or at the occasion of an introspection that aims at the coordination between movements and respiration. If this is true, then the mind does not function in exactly the same way during a gymnastic course or during a psychotherapy session.

Fenichel and the Body

"The ego is first and foremost a body-ego," says Freud in *The Ego and the Id*. And he means by this that the distinction between ego and non-ego is first learned by the infant in the discovery of its body in such a way that in its world of ideas its own body begins to be set off from the rest of the environment. (Fenichel, 1938, *The Drive to Amass Wealth*, p. 97)

The epigraph indicates the intellectual environment Fenichel entered when he arrived in Berlin: a refined psychoanalysis about which he was passionate and a gymnast who obliged him to reflect on the contributions of body techniques and their impact on the psyche.

In an unpublished manuscript dating from 1926,[70] Fenichel takes up the possibility of relating gymnastics and psychoanalysis. In 1927, he revealed his thoughts on the subject at the Berlin Psychoanalytic Institute. He proposed a first synthesis of his thoughts on the body and psyche in an article published in 1928, titled "The Libidinization of the Organs." Fenichel preferred this wording, used by Freud,[71] to that of psychosomatic or body–mind. According to this article, the psychological defense system also regulates the way the libido is connected to the physiological regulations. Like almost all of the male physicians of that generation, he mentions neither the nonacademics nor the women who inspired and influenced him (Clare Fenichel and Gindler are not even mentioned in a footnote). He wrote the article as if his thought was a personal discovery, established on academic and psychoanalytic literature. Clearly, well before Reich's arrival in Berlin, the future founders of psychosomatic psychoanalysis, like Radó and Alexander, began to think about the coordination of psychoanalysis, the body, and physiology. I emphasize this because at the end of his life, Reich claimed that all of his Berlin colleagues would have learned everything in this domain from him.

Already at this time, Fenichel intuitively distinguished the physiological dimension from the body of the physical therapists. This body, close to that of Gindler, is a coordination of muscle tone, breathing patterns, postural regulations, and the loops of the sensorimotor nervous system. In this sense, it is possible to say that Fenichel initiated a systematic reflection on the way the body dimension participates in the mechanisms that structure the regulatory system of the psyche. Fenichel (1945a, XIII) did not systematically distinguishing body and physiology, as I do in the System of Dimensions of the Organism. For him, body and physiology both make up the world of the organs. However, on the level of technical interventions, each domain is approached differently, and the body dimension is explicitly discussed.

CORPORALITY AND PSYCHODYNAMICS

> When in their everyday life they have not focused attention on the condition of their musculature, the latter exists in a state of hypertonus, the degree of which varies with the muscle group and with the individual, and which may occasionally reach complete rigidity. Movements may involve not only unnecessary muscle groups (associated movements), but innervations which are unsuitable and of unnecessary intensity. When in a state of rest, we are sometimes inclined to let certain groups become hypotonic, that is, to have an excessively lowered tension, so that their readiness to function is impeded or weakened. . . . In brief, we are dealing here with a defect of varying degree of their "economization and rationalization" of the motor apparatus which is described by Homburger as characteristic of adults. (Fenichel, 1928, "Organ libidinization," I, p. 128f)[72]

For Fenichel, once we admit that the psychological resistances simultaneously influence mind and behavior, it becomes necessary to be able to describe how these resistances structure the gestures and postures mobilized by a behavioral style. The association that Ferenczi and Reich made between behavioral style and defense system had a clinical basis. This observation allowed for an explanation by supposing that this connection had a neurological basis, like Pavlov's conditioned reflexes. But Fenichel was not satisfied with this hypothesis. A behavioral style is often visibly and manifestly influenced by permanent muscular rigidities and sometimes with comical ways of breathing. Specialists in body development show how many children grow up with different forms of scoliosis and lordosis and also respiratory patterns that all gymnastics teachers try to correct. All of this maintains itself "alone" (without permanent interventions by the nervous system) by muscular "dystonia" (hyper- and hypotonus) that have become permanent. Clearly, the neurological and physiological inhibition of movement is based on different mechanisms from those postulated by psychoanalysts for the psychological forms of inhibition.

Muscle tone is influenced not only by the nervous system but also by the quality of the irrigation of the tissues by blood. In becoming rigid, the muscle tissues acquire a particular metabolic quality that will afterward influence the vegetative dynamics and the functioning of the sensorimotor system. It then becomes possible to conceptualize that the defense system which structures the ego is in connection with the systems that structure and inhibit the behavioral repertoire. Fenichel notices that an organism's dystonia cannot be entirely explained by physiologists who try to explain it according to the quality of nutrition, the quantity of athletic activity, and so on. There are clearly, behind all of this, bodily factors interacting with some mental dynamics that psychoanalysts could study. A polite person uses his muscles and joints differently than a quick-tempered person. Fenichel believes that these traits are principally from the character, linked to an individual's psychic structure. The character, such as defined by Abraham and Reich,[73] would then be produced by the interaction between socially constructed bodily practices and the dynamics activated by an organism's drives.

This is how Fenichel arrived at the proposition that analyzing the dynamics of the body and behavior allows a privileged access to the emotional dynamics that regulate thoughts and behavior. He takes up the thesis well known by all body practitioners—that chronic anxiety influences the muscle tone in a lasting way and lifestyle can generate chronic hyper- and hypotension that can last a lifetime.[74] These tensions can also considerably reduce the respiratory repertoire. Thus, many people can only breathe by moving their belly, while others breathe mostly by moving the thorax. These limitations evidently influence the dynamics of the metabolism, which diminishes the energetic resources available to the organism as a whole: motor and behavioral activity, the intensity of experienced affect, and attention.

Fenichel describes patients who tense every muscle in their body to repress an affect that attempts to emerge when the psychological defenses that repress it are dissolving. An example is a patient who complains of feeling nothing but a great void within: her inside was so cramped, her chest and limbs so tense, that they "did not let anything come out" (Fenichel, 1928, p. 131).

THE BODY REGULATORS OF THE PSYCHE

Fenichel's key idea was that the poorly developed bodies the gymnasts attempted to correct and reeducate were probably full of symptoms that psychoanalysts called neuroses.[75] There may be social mechanisms that educate the masses to become easier to handle by creating chronic defense systems that simultaneously structure themselves in the mental and body dimensions of the organism. Around this foundation, the repression of the affects, the reduction of the physiological vitality, and the reduction of the mental imagination can help create behaviors that are compatible with the ideology in power. This key idea for the history of body psychotherapy was set forth by Fenichel as a possibility and then developed by Reich.[76]

Here is a summary of the arguments expressed by Fenichel in 1928.

1. Fenichel associated the lasting restrictions of muscular tone (dystonia) and respiration to the neurotic defense systems. For him, the hypotonus is as pertinent as hypertonus, in the sense that every reduction of the flexibility of the motor system permits the inhibition of the expression of needs and affects. In the last analysis, a restriction of motor activity is a resignation of the ego of the psychoanalysts, an abandonment of the hope that some drives can express themselves and develop with other persons. The connection between muscular tension and the defense system is evident when a patient newly feels repressed drives but does not yet dare to express them. He cited a patient for whom this conflict is experienced as exhausting. The defenses, by definition, mobilize the metabolic resources. These resources must be at least as important as those mobilized by the repressed need. This conflict deprives the organism of the energy mobilized by the repressed need and its repression, which explains the conscious sensation of having fewer resources, of being tired.[77]

2. Fenichel, as a good Marxist, maintains (as does Reich at this time) that the relation between the body and psyche is dialectical. There can be several kinds of relations between body and mind, considered as two distinct subsystems of an organism, which is their emerging synthesis. He assumes that *there are different types of links between the defense system and the muscular tension*,[78] because each of these dimensions is submitted to a distinct causal system. He shows especially that the muscle tone is as much influenced by the brain as by the way the tissues are irrigated.[79] These links would be more thickly packed in hysterical patients than in persons who suffer from compulsions. Given the immense variety of mechanisms that form the context (organic and situational) of an affective dilemma, it is unlikely that the same dilemma inscribed itself in the same fashion in many organisms. This analysis is clearly different from theories like that of Kretschmer, who supposes that there is a *direct* connection between a mental and a body tension.[80]

3. Fenichel proposed a model of the somatic dimension of the ego that constructs itself around not only some inhibitions and motoric activations but also the quality of the body sensations.[81] These sensations can be inhibited (hyposensitivity), felt in an amplified manner (hypersensitivity), or experienced in a relatively integrated way. The construction of the somatic ego would be part of the construction of the psychic ego already defined by Freud.[82]

PSYCHOANALYSIS AND GYMNASTICS

In the following example, Fenichel describes a psychoanalytic intervention with a patient engaged in gymnastics. The gymnastics teacher[83] detects a chronic muscular tension, which is taken up by Fenichel as if it were a symptom produced by Freud's psychological defense system. He shows that in this case, the psychoanalyst resolves a problem that the gymnastics teacher was not able to resolve. In his article, he does not mention that there were also some problems for which the psychoanalysts had no resolution but teachers of gymnastics could treat. We have already seen such an example: Fenichel's headaches, which were successfully treated by Gindler, whereas Fenichel had already followed an analysis with one of Freud's close associates (Federn).

> Vignette of a patient who takes gymnastic courses and undergoes psychoanalysis. *A patient reported that her gymnastics teacher continually called her attention to the intensity with which she kept her neck and throat musculature in a constant spastic tension. Attempts to loosen this tension only increased it. The analysis showed that as a child the patient saw a pigeon's head being torn off and the headless pigeon still moving its wings a few feet away. This experience lent her castration complex a lasting form: she had an unconscious fear of being beheaded, and this fear also manifested itself in numerous other symptoms, modes of behavior, and directions of interest. (Fenichel, 1928, I, p. 133)*

In this example, the gymnastics teacher detects a bodily manifestation of an unconscious fear with sufficient clarity that this manifestation could become a center around which it is possible to organize the associations of the patient. Because the psychoanalyst respects the observation of the gymnast, he succeeds in following an associative chain that leads her to the repressed traumatic memory. This is a first example of how a gymnast and a psychoanalyst are able to collaborate. In this case, the transferential relationship from the patient to her gymnastics teacher made it impossible to treat her via the body, for the teacher was perceived as the equivalent of the forces that had cut off the head of the pigeon, and the patient identified with the pigeon. Probably in the course of the analysis of this patient, Fenichel discovered that the relation between these forces and the pigeon had been taken as a metaphor of an older problem connected to the relationship between this patient and a member of her family.

Later, Charlotte Selver summarized how a "Gindlerian" therapist would tackle a neurotic trait. As you will see, it is complementary to what Fenichel did with his patient:

> The sensory cortex in our brain no only registers sensations as they occur, but is also the storeroom of past impressions, which can be reactivated. The consequence is that a new sensation can be charged with a relation to something perhaps altogether remote. This is the basis of neurotic behavior, and so we sometimes see persons protect themselves from a friendly touch or we see a dog recoil from a friendly greeting. This is a reaction, not to the actual sensation, but to the *memory* of a cruel experience in the past. So in our work, the mere invitation to quiet is often not enough, and we must devise simple means of inviting sensations in a context of peace and security so that the actual perception may be recognized and distinguished from the irrelevant or neurotic component. (Selver and Brooks, 1980, p. 120)

Fenichel used actual body sensations to find repressed associations, whereas Selver and Gindler taught their pupils to differentiate actual sensations from old associations, and then focus on actual sensations.

Reich in Vienna (1920–1930)

After Fenichel's departure, Reich conducted the seminar on sexuality for one year. After his studies, he launched a career as a psychoanalyst that was as brilliant as that of Fenichel.

Prelude: The Compulsion to Do House Cleaning

To help you understand how Reich's character was problematic, I propose an imaginary anecdote in which Reich would have become Freud's housekeeper.

> The Freuds look for a new housekeeper for their family apartment and for the apartment above in which Sigmund works. They accept, for a three-month trial period, a Mrs. Reich, who appears competent. The first month, the Freuds are impressed by the meticulous manner with which each corner, each angle, each object in the apartment are impeccably cleaned. They congratulate Mrs. Reich, who begins to grow more confident. While always appreciating the meticulous work of their housekeeper, the Freuds notice that she permits herself to move objects from their original place. Mrs. Reich explains to them that she has taken the liberty to propose certain rearrangements that she finds useful. Certain changes are effectively an improvement with regard to their usual habit of doing things; but the Freuds, without discussing it with her, return some objects to their original places when they do not appreciate Mrs. Reich's propositions. At the start of the third month, the Freuds leave on vacation. They confide the apartment to Mrs. Reich and ask her to profit from their absence and do a thorough cleaning.
> On their return, the Freuds try to imagine what new changes their housekeeper will have made; they chatter pleasantly about it. Upon opening the door, they discover, with fright, what happens when Mrs. Reich's meticulous creativity is

not contained. Everything is impeccably clean and in order, but everything has been changed place. Where there had been a kitchen, there is now a bathroom. The Freuds' bedroom has become the children's bedroom, and so on. Mrs. Reich feels proud for having totally rethought the apartment, and to have found a solution for all the inconsistencies she had detected. The Freuds dismiss her on the spot and refuse to pay her for the self-appointed work. They call movers to put everything back in their place but retain, in spite of everything, a few of Mrs. Reich's propositions.

This anecdote illustrates many of Reich's striking personality traits. First, there is the rapidity with which he engages himself in a mission and the intensity of his engagement. In his clinical writings, Reich (1927a) identified this type of behavior as *impulsive compulsivity.* The object of attachment is chosen impulsively, and then totally invested (or overinvested) with all the resources of his genius. Each time Reich focused on an issue, he took on a personal contractual obligation to organize everything his colleagues say and do and create a solution for every existing problem. He did not understand that his colleagues did not always appreciate his propositions. He explained to them what they ought to think and do, but he never negotiated or collaborated *with* them. He soon discerned resistance, which he always attributed to the defense of questionable personal interests; he was stunned to be finally rejected by the community for whom he had worked so much. The advantage of this strategy has been that of being able to move forward creatively, without being continually held back by the fears and the disagreements of one and all. The disadvantage was to have avoided the collegial discussions necessary for scientific endeavors. This strategy[84] led Reich to a dead end on the personal and theoretical plane. His propositions also contained inconsistencies that almost everyone noticed at first glance; he was incapable of integrating these criticisms.

Sexology and Psychoanalysis

BIOLOGY AND PANTHEISM

There was a domain in medicine about which Reich was passionate and which had nothing to do with what he discovered with Fenichel: the biology that seeks to describe the functioning of the organism.[85] Reich was passionate about a theory of evolution that wants to understand the secret forces that animate nature and its creatures. Cellular biology creates the energy of the individual organism: it is a manifestation of the profound forces that animate the universe at the core of the individual. This thinking allowed Reich to shape a deep and imperative need to feel what links him to the forces of nature. He always refused to associate this need to spiritual needs.[86] The difficulty for Reich, who was then influenced by a form of diffused Platonism, was to differentiate this profound impression of being animated by nature from the notion of a spiritual quest. The difference between what can be experienced during a meditation session and the impression of being animated by a spirit is always a current topic. Several body psychotherapists influenced by Reich (David Boadella, Gerda Boyesen, Malcolm Brown, or John Pierrakos) took a step in the direction of thinking that Reich's impression was in fact a spiritual quest that he did not dare name. Personally, I agree with Lowen and Reich that it is not necessary to believe in the existence of a spirit to experience the impression of wholeness that can be felt in meditation. It perhaps consists in a necessary illusion, but not an experiential proof that a spiritual force exists. For Reich and Lowen, the capacity to *experience* being in communion with the forces of nature is a human capacity that ought to be able to be described in a framework of scientific thought someday.

At the age of 20, Reich did not have the intellectual means to differentiate what he felt from that of a spiritual quest. Wanting to be more Freudian and more Marxist than Fenichel, he could not be anything other than a profound atheist. In the psychotherapeutic milieu, Jung integrates spirituality and the theories of vitalism. However, Jung was the great dissident. The positions that he advocated during the 1930s, close to those of the Nazi Party in some cases, rendered any appearance of sympathy for Jung even more difficult for a member of the leftist group of psychoanalysts. Reich could not express his need of an internal communion with the forces of nature without accepting becoming the worst student in Fenichel's seminar. On the other hand, biology and the theory of the Freudian libido were, in this context, eminently respectable and legitimate passions.

To try to situate his intimate questions on this issue, Reich published (in 1922) an article in which he renounced his temptation to think like Jung or to adopt the vitalism of Forel and Bergson. This article indicates that he has read these authors with passion, even if he finishes by separating himself from them for the time being. At the same time, he defended the necessity to anchor the libido in the biological thinking of the period. When, in 1934, Reich abandoned psychoanalysis and Marxism, the forces he had built within himself to distinguish his need to unite science and pantheism diminished. Slowly but surely, he began to want to demonstrate that the forces of nature animate each one of us. He then found a thought, near to that of Spinoza, attributing to nature the forces that others associate with a spiritual force, all while remaining resolutely an atheist.

To understand the relationship that Reich establishes with the forces of nature during his studies, it is useful to recall the dominant view in medicine and biology at the time. I summarize a few notions (described in greater detail in the sections devoted to the biologists) to show which aspects of this thinking influenced the young Reich.

THE NOTION OF ORGANISM AMONG THE VIENNESE BIOLOGISTS

During evolution, approach and withdrawal emerged from the general capacity to move. The different emotions then differentiated out from approach and withdrawal. Bodily concepts and then, progressively, language evolved from this movement base (Daniel Stern, 2010, *Forms of Vitality*, I.2, p. 20)

It is useful to recall that genetics was founded in the Austro-Hungarian Empire by Johann Gregor Mendel (1822–1884). He was a Catholic monk. Like Darwin, who was an Anglican priest, Mendel became a genius of an amateur biologist. He conducted research on the reproduction of small peas, which led him to think that there existed, in every organism, genes capable of mutation that permitted the transmission of the basic characteristics of an organism from one generation to another. He published a first series of the laws of genetics in 1865 in Vienna, during the period when the English were discovering the thought of Darwin and Wallace. As I have already indicated, only after World War I did biologists began to create a synthesis of the two movements, which became the modern Darwinism. If the English integrated genetics with Darwinism, the Austrians of the time integrated Darwinism to the research inspired by Mendel. There was, therefore, in the Vienna of the day, an important and lively movement in biological research that also had a great influence in the German universities. These discussions fascinated the students of the time, notably Reich.

Darwin's organism (1871) is more a pile of mechanisms than a coherent whole.[87] The biologists of the 1920s preferred to represent the organism as a system that functions as a totality. One way to understand the function of the genes was to suppose that the information they transmit gives a meaning, direction, and coherence to biological evolution, even if their combination follows the laws of chance and necessity. Thus, the cells of the eyes provide for the sensation of seeing red due to the same electromagnetic waves in all of the animal species sensitive to color. This constant would be due to the fact that the same genes regulate the structure of the rods and cones of the retina. While reinforcing a certain coherence of the building that is an organism, the genes also create a kind of flexibility that permits the system to adapt as much as possible to its natural and social environment. Reich (1940, I, p. 77) remained faithful to this global view of the organism.

During his studies, Reich (1940, I, pp. 1–7) was passionately interested in different ways to exploit the notion of organism. With *Werden des Organismen* (The Becoming of Organisms) by Oscar Hertwig, Reich learned to situate diverse physiological systems and their coordination. Through his writings, Reich discovered a form of biological functionalism that supposes that all that survives has a function. The cell was supposed to have a membrane to better protect itself against external stimuli. The male animals were bigger and stronger than the females, or more beautifully colored, to be more attractive to the females, or they had horns to beat off their rivals. This kind of simplistic finalism, which he associated to certain forms of spirituality like Buddhism and the Anthroposophy of Rudolph Reiner, irritated Reich.[88] In reading *Philosophie des Organischen* (Philosophy of the Organic) by Driesch, Reich became aware of the forces that *animate* the living world. He pursued this theme with enthusiasm for the theory of vitalism of French philosopher Henri Bergson on the relation between consciousness and the evolution of matter (*Matter and Memory*, 1896; *Time and Free Will: Essay on the Immediate Data of Consciousness*, 1889; and *Creative Evolution*, 1907).

Another famous Viennese student of this period, Konrad Zacharias Lorenz (1903–1989), was inspired by this approach to understand the motivations of living organisms. He received the Nobel Prize in Medicine with Nikolaas Tinbergen and Karl von Frisch in 1973. All three were rewarded for having contributed to the founding of ethology. The goal of this science is the study of the innate behaviors of the species and the way those behaviors permitted the evolution of communication strategies. This research had begun with the study of animal behavior (communication among bees, graylag geese, and stickleback fish). It consisted of studying the innate behaviors of many species to then be able to discover the laws of the evolution of behaviors, starting with that of unicellular animals and ending up with humans.[89] Lorenz was born in Vienna, but he studied medicine in New York and Konigsberg (Germany). Once again, politics made it impossible for Reich and Lorenz to appreciate each other's discoveries.[90] It is possible that Lorenz was not a convinced Nazi, but his biological views were compatible with certain Nazi theses.[91]

Nevertheless, Reich and Lorenz had common views on certain aspects of evolution theory. For example, they both thought that the amoeba already contained basic sensorimotor mechanisms that were developed by all of the species.[92] This mechanism is a perfectly functional coordination of core metabolic requirements, the physiological dynamics of an organism, and the regulation of behavior in function of external variables. Reich and Lorenz thought that the social forces of their time destroyed this deep, natural coordination, because they wanted to use the resources of nature for economic ends. For both of them, this was an unacceptable corruption of natural dynamics. Reich's Spinozian idealism could never admit that biological activity would be anything but good, coherent, and constructive. For Lorenz, natural selection was a cruel and merciless competition between organisms, but some routes were more humane than others.

BECOMING A SEXOLOGIST

After his studies, Reich established himself as a psychoanalytically oriented sexologist and psychiatrist. Being particularly attracted by the sexual dimension of psychoanalysis, he began by wanting to establish some order in the theory of the libido.[93] The libido theory was also the only domain of psychoanalysis that had a deep resonance with his interests for the impact of biological dynamics on the psyche.

The Sexual Behavior of People.   Reich had a private practice at the time. With Annie, he participated in the foundation of a clinic called the Psychoanalytic Dispensary. This dispensary, directed by the psychoanalyst Hitschmann, was created in the image of the Berlin Psychoanalytic Clinic.[94] Most patients who frequented this dispensary were in need of psychological support, as Freud's theory foresaw. They often did not have what it takes (not enough time, not enough money, or not the necessary intellectual curiosity) for psychoanalytical treatment.[95] Gradually, Reich became the chief of this dispensary. Patients often came to resolve problems tied to sexuality (sexual problems, methods of contraception, etc.). These were the patients who made it possible for Reich to discover the great variety of sexual behaviors among the Viennese, and this was in a time when he was having his first sexual experiences. He observed that most of the individuals he saw had a sexual behavior incompatible with the morality they were attempting to follow. He was no exception. Reich had difficulty reconciling his visits to prostitutes with what he called "the (idealizing) platonic side of my sexuality" (Reich, 1937, p. 61).

With his psychoanalytic patients, he explored, in great detail, how intimate thoughts and sexual behavior are related. For example, he published an article on the way people masturbate and on their fantasies during masturbation. He is astonished to discover the immense variety of practices. His male patients do not necessarily have an erection when they masturbate. Even those who have a regular heterosexual relationship have difficulty representing, in their dreams, a situation in which they are having vaginal intercourse with their fantasized partner.[96] In another study on coitus and the sexes, Reich (1922b) (a) noticed that the sexual arousal of men often follows a profile a bit different than that of women, and (b) discerned more problems of impotence in men than frigidity in women.[97]

The Curve of an Orgasm.

The orgastic excitation takes hold of the whole body and results in *lively contractions of the whole body musculature*. Self-observations of healthy individuals of both sexes, as well as the analysis of certain disturbances of orgasm, show that we call the release of tension and experience as a motor discharge (descending portion of the orgasm curve) is predominantly the result of a *flowing back of the excitation from the genital to the body*. This flowing back is experienced as a *sudden decrease* of the tension. (Reich, 1940, *The Function of the Orgasm*, IV.3, p.62)

According to Freud, neurosis is nourished by the mobilized sexual energy which the organism fails to express and which is not reabsorbed. Reich attempted to further explain this formula. He asked himself how he might describe what the sexual arousal mobilizes in the organism and how this arousal can express itself in a sufficiently satisfying manner so that there would not be a build-up of a neurosis. The term *orgasm* therefore designates a sexual behavior that does not leave any *sexual stasis*.[98] For Reich, *genital sexuality* always includes a capacity to have an orgasm. He distinguished between an *organic impotence* (frigidity or erectile dysfunction) from an *orgastic impotence* (the impossibility of achieving a vegetative and affective satisfaction). He ends up with the formula of the orgasm which is composed of three main phases:[99]

1. *The intensification.* There is a charge when a sexual propension mobilizes the resources of the organism in such a way as to increase the sympathetic vegetative activity of the organism to create a feeling of sexual arousal. This phase is characterized by a *quantitative and qualitative dimension.* The quantitative dimension is an increase of organismic energy (physiological and mental) mobilized for this propension. This phase initiates the orgasm by activating involuntary movements that take over the organism, independently of the thoughts a person could have at that moment. The person gradually loses control over what is going on. If thoughts welcome somatic arousal, the *propension guides the behavior and the thoughts.*[100]

2. *The climax.* A climax can become orgastic, according to Reich,[101] only if there is an activation of the involuntary movements that take hold of the organism at the end of the intensification phase. These movements organize the felt arousal. There is coordination of the segments of the body that move like waves from feet to head and the physiological mobilization (respiration, circulation of the blood, hormones, etc.) that allows this activity to happen. The movements of the segments of the body coordinate not only *in* each organism but also *between* the organisms involved. If the psyche receives the experience that is built in the organism at that moment, this phase relates to a particularly pleasant sensation. An interruption of the sexual act during orgasm is always experienced as extremely unpleasant.

3. *Evanescence, or the relaxation after coitus.* This phase produces new forms of pleasure. It begins with a phase of detumescence during which the man ejaculates, and after which men and women can "have convulsive spasms of the abdomen that can spread through the entire body" (Reich, 1919, p. 101).[102] After these spasms the phase of evanescence really begins. Later, Reich referred to this phase as a *reflux.* The organism returns to a state of relaxation that permits the evacuation of metabolic wastes generated by motor activity by toppling it over into a parasympathetic vegetative mode of functioning. It thereby finds a basic equilibrium, close to a deep relaxation, that allows for metabolizing the physiological and affective charge mobilized by the act. This moment is often filled with tender and loving images of self and the other. This feeling has reparative functions, for each person and for the couple, which operate in depth. Any limitation of the loving feeling that arises at this moment prevents the phase of evanescence from accomplishing its function of cleaning the tissues and the intensification of the love relationship.

During his Viennese period, it is only when he describes sexual behavior that Reich talks of the body. This body is mostly the visible surface of physiological arousal. It is not yet a distinct dimension of the organism. The interruption of the last two phases of the orgastic reaction can bring about a variety of disagreeable psychophysiological events: palpitations, cardiac irregularities, sweating, back pain, headaches, acute anxiety attacks, general irritability, problems with attention, and so on.[103] There is a circular relation between the intensification and the evanescence.

1. Pleasurable sensations experienced during the evanescence phase are often memorized in association with tender and loving sentiments.
2. Often the pleasure experienced during the reflux can be spoiled by a variety of anxious thoughts, such as guilt, the fear of falling in love or having a child, the lack of time, and so on.[104]
3. Later, when the intensification phase is activated, these loving and pleasurable memories will be associated with the pleasure of excitation. If anxious thoughts have also been stored during the reflux phase, that will come with the pleasurable memories and can then spoil the pleasure experienced during the intensification phase. That explains why many sexual problems observed during the arousal phase originate during the evanescence.[105]

Reich represents the intensity of the sexual charge by a curve that was used by sexologists at the beginning of the twentieth century (see Figure 16.1). He reconstructed with his patients the profile of the curve of a real sexual encounter. The entirety of the curve designates a propension that becomes pleasant in its realization. For Reich, there is no pleasure "that exists *here* and seeks pleasure *there*"; but there is a pleasure brought about by the sensorimotor act and that animates this act (Reich, 1940, III.1, p. 24).

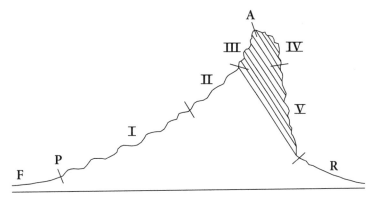

FIGURE 16.1. The curve of the orgasm. F: foreplay, P: penetration, I: Voluntary increase of excitation, II: phase of involuntary increase of excitation. III: Sudden ascent to the acme. A: acme. IV: orgasm. The shaded part represents the phase of involuntary body contractions. V: steep "drop" of excitation. R: relaxation (from 5 to 20 minutes). *Source:* Reich (1940, p. 60).

For Alexander Lowen,[106] the description of the orgasm proposed by Reich is relevant but overevaluated in its importance:

1. To have the *capacity* to have an orgasm does not imply that a person has an orgasm each time that he or she makes love. This only means that when an individual is in an adequate situation, where both partners have a desire to make love, there is the capacity to experience a "Reichian" orgasm. These moments are more or less frequent in the course of a lifetime. According to Lowen, it is rare that all of the components of this situation converge more than a dozen times in a lifetime.
2. Having an orgasm does not necessarily dissolve a neurosis, but it helps.

Having defined the contours of a particular sexual act in a sketch, it becomes easier to analyze the connection between sexual functioning and certain aspects of the theory of the libido. Reich takes up the theme of the intensity of the thoughts in the same way Hume and Freud do, but he links it more explicitly to the vegetative mobilization of the propension that influence the thoughts. He observes that the sexual fantasies are intense before the climax and tend to become milder with the evanescence. He also notices that when the thoughts linked to the genital sexual act are maintained in the unconscious, the vegetative energy is then diverted toward secondary drives, or even in directions still further away from sexuality. In certain cases, the diversion is so important that problems in the sexual mechanics are observable, such as impotence or frigidity. In this, we find once again the idea that a human propension needs to mobilize a certain type of coordination between psychological and physiological systems to become actualized.[107]

As we can see, Reich integrates Freud's drive theory but proposes a simplified analysis of the psychological dynamics. The unconscious contains everything that is repressed (representations and drives), and he already supposes that there is just one energy in the organism: a kind of vegetative libido that can be influenced by behavior and thoughts. The psychological dimension is reduced to mental representations. Even in his psychoanalytic period, *the analytical therapy is conceived as a therapy of the drives more than as psychotherapy.* The only psychological dimension that seems to interest Reich is the ideology or morality adopted by a person. If someone adopts a morality that accepts that affects express themselves by following their own proper procedures, the psyche is healthy; if someone adopts a morality that does not support the regulation of the drives, such an individual would necessarily become ill. The capacity to feel body sensations and remember what happened in one's childhood is also sought by Reich's work at that time.

Reich the Psychoanalyst

The Reichian orgasm is a form of reaction that requires participation from all the dimensions of the organism. When Reich studies the components of an orgastic reactions and their coordination, he inevitably ends up with a systemic view of the individual. In this sense Reich always considered that his formula of the orgasm had been his principal source of inspiration. He consequently detailed this global organismic view in his activity as a psychotherapist. The psychoanalysts of the day sometimes had a systemic intuition (especially Ferenczi), but it remained implicit. The work of systemization of the psychoanalytic techniques was the direction Reich took to put some order in the plethora of local models which the psychoanalysts of the time had to take into account in their practices.

THE "VIENNA SEMINAR FOR PSYCHOANALYTIC THERAPY" SERVES
AS THE BASIS FOR THE ELABORATION OF CHARACTER ANALYSIS

In 1923, Eduard Hitschmann created a training seminar for the psychoanalytic technique. Having become a training analyst, Reich was again Hitschmann's assistant.[108] Freud asked Reich to direct this seminar starting in 1924. He remained in this position until 1930. In the letters addressed to Reich, Freud expressed admiration for his enthusiasm and creativity, while asking him not to transform the seminar into a platform for his particular points of view.[109] In his correspondence with others, Freud makes sarcastic remarks about the orgasm theory that seem exaggeratedly absolute, but he defended Reich against diverse attacks.

Character, Defense System, and Partial Drives.   To understand what follows, recall certain points that were previously discussed:

1. The theoretical context of the Viennese psychoanalytic seminar is that of Freud's Second Topography. Thanks to this seminar the young Viennese psychoanalysts of that day developed the practical implications of this Second Topography and refined the outline Freud had proposed.
2. Given Reich's personal interests, this seminar probably avoided the purely psychological subjects, in order to focus on the drives. At the time, Reich was one of those who had the most refined view of the partial drives and the way they interact.
3. This orientation implies a great attention to the *economy* of a drive (the way in which it manages the libido) and its objects.
4. Reich's originality lies in having showed how partial drives and the defense system are mutually structured. Each link of the defense system is a unit that manages and constructs a partial drive.

This refinement in the analysis of the defense system led Reich to propose a particularly interesting definition of a person's *character*. Every link in the defense system is composed of the gathering of the following forces:

1. When the investment of an object is transformed, the charge of this investment is partially redirected toward another object.[110] This turning

away also diminishes the intensity of the initial drive. The object is a goal, like the love felt for one's mother. The drive is a particular form of love, like the desire to suck at the mother's breast. The investment of the object is the intensity of this drive, such as the quantity of libido mobilized by this micro-drive, defined in purely operational language. This invested object unfolds automatically into a behavior, on an expression that seeks to satisfy this drive.

2. To the extent that this drive cannot achieve its initial aim, it is transformed by the defense system to find a less frustrating goal. For example, at the age of five, the desire to suck at the mother's breast generates frustration when the child lives in a family in which the mother's breast can be suckled only during the first months of an infant's life.

3. To avoid the problems of frustration, a part of the drive that cannot express itself in a given milieu will then be used by the defense system to transform the initial drive into a less intense drive, like the desire to bite into the clothing of a little sister. In this example, the original drive is partially disinvested and repressed to become a new micro-drive.[111] The parents will thus be surprised to note that their child has suddenly started to bite and tear the clothing of his little sister. In certain cases, this replacement drive (or substitute) can be overinvested so as to camouflage what is being repressed. Often, the parents try to suppress this new tendency and the child will, in turn, construct a new link in his character which will be even further away than the original drive.

Content and Manner.   Reich asked the participants of the technical seminar to present cases in which they were experiencing difficulties. The members then detailed the technical aspect of the process engaged in by the therapist. Reich focused the discussion around one of Freud's and Ferenczi's predominant preoccupations at that time:[112] the necessity to relive a repressed situation conjointly on the cognitive and affective plane so that healing might occur.[113] Reich came to the conclusion that no one is able to explain which one of all the techniques makes it possible to achieve this goal.[114] This clinical research soon allowed Reich to propose a series of explicit technical recommendations, such as the following:

1. To refuse to analyze, especially to interpret, material that remains disassociated from the related affects. A patient can remember that he has long wished to suck his mother's breast without having this memory evoke any tangible feelings. The therapist takes note of this memory like something that must be elaborated later on, but does not interpret it or encourage the patient to explore it. He prefers to follow the other associations that develop after recalling the memory.

2. To observe not only the *content* of the thoughts but also the *manner* in which they are presented.

The *content* on which Reich focused is mostly verbal, whereas the *manner* is mostly nonverbal. This distinction is close to what Sabina Spielrein suggested. He concentrated on the tone of voice, the posture, and the gestures that accompany a memory to evaluate the way a patient presents his verbal associations. A voice that is too flat, a chin that tends downward toward the throat can, for example, indicate a holding back of affects. Returning to the previous example, Reich noticed that his patient continuously held back his chin. This bodily trait is a kind of tic that everyone can see. It is found at the visible surface of the behavioral dynamics of the patient. Reich then asked his patient to explore what goes on within him if he moves his chin forward. He then discovered that the muscular tension that maintains the chin so close to the Adam's apple is part of the link that the patient has built to inhibit the desire to bite his little sister's clothing.

In this example, we see that Reich was inspired by Ferenczi's active method. The psychoanalysts, trained in this circle of influence inspired by Ferenczi, ask their patients to associate on the way they present their thoughts. Reich confirmed Ferenczi's observations when he noticed that by focusing on a patient's specific behavioral trait, sometimes the patient strongly experienced repressed emotions, which suddenly erupt into consciousness and the expressive motor system. This emotion captures the organism; even a habitually polite patient can suddenly begin to scream, cry, tremble with fear, or bite a piece of fabric.

Reich eventually proposed a systematic way to approach these resistances (Reich, 1940, V.3, p. 90), which he calls *Character analysis*. It consists in *beginning with the resistances close to consciousness, which would also be close to the surface,*[115] *and concluding with the deepest ones.* In Character analysis, the therapist first analyzes a trait that is particularly easy to approach in the context of the therapeutic relationship. It is often the trait (mental, behavioral, affective, bodily, or physiological) that is most obvious, but not always. It can happen that the therapist discovers two layers in a dream: an aggressive layer and a homosexual one. Reich proposed that in this case, the therapist concentrate on the layer that is more easily accessible to the patient and analyze the second layer later. For example, he can analyze the aggressive dimension of a dream but not the unconscious homosexual desire that generates this aggression. If the patient is knowingly homosexual, it is possible the therapist would begin by analyzing the homosexual dimension of the dream. Everything depends on what the patient is capable of integrating at that moment on the plane of representations and of affects.

This aspect of Character analysis is also part of the strategies explored by Fenichel (1927). In this article, Fenichel gives an example of the way in which the Freudian therapists approached dreams at that time. In his analysis, he uses the model of the layers without referring to Reich, as if this model was also his own. He discovers in his patient an anxious urge to suck his father's penis, which covers up the need—and perhaps the memory—of sucking his mother's breast.

THE ORGANIZATION OF THE DEFENSES STRUCTURES THE LIBIDO
AND THE WAY THE LIBIDO STRUCTURES THE PSYCHE

The Organization of the Characterological Layers.   This way to approach
the defense system led Reich to propose a model of the *character structure* that
would be the organization of the partial drives and the way they are put together by the defense system of an organism. This definition has several implications:

1. By starting with the analysis of the defenses closer to the surface, the
   therapist already activates a slight increase in the quantity of libido that
   is available and an elaboration of the anxiety-provoking materials that
   allows the ego to strengthen itself by going forward. This approach
   therefore prepares the patient to become capable of confronting psychic
   material that hitherto could have activated such a powerful anxiety that
   he would have been weakened instead of strengthened.
2. Another pedagogical advantage of this strategy is that the patient learns
   to accept that his mental life is influenced by his unconscious, his vegetative system (the libido and the affects), and his behavior (which participates in the regulation of the defense system).
3. This approach takes up the notion of the associative chains composed of
   nonverbal and verbal behaviors.
4. It then becomes possible to define a character type by the manner in
   which a person's defenses are organized. The defenses build themselves
   up progressively. Each layer represses the material that the previous
   layer allows through.

Reich eventually conceptualized the character as a series of zones with the
structure of an onion. Each layer contains many links of the defense system,
such as the ones just described. Let us take up this model in greater detail.[116]

1. A drive.
2. A kind of shield that retains a part of the energy of the drive. This shield
   needs as much energy as what it represses. Therefore, there is in each
   layer a dual waste of energy: (a) the repressed energy and (b) the energy
   to repress. The denser the character structure, the less energy remains to
   animate a person's life.
3. A defense filters the repressed drive. In passing through this filter, it also
   changes the content. Thus, a repressed anger can become an irresistible
   desire to bite into food, associated to the sensation of hunger. This new
   drive is a new association between the drives, the vegetative system, and
   behaviors. The urge to hit has become a way to bite into the bread, images of violence become images of meals, and the vegetative system is
   now mobilized to eat instead of hit.

4. The next layer of the defense system manages this urge to bite into a meal in a localized manner without having information concerning what is repressed by the other layers (the anger, in this case).[117]

Reich gives the following example. A child loves his mother, toward whom he has genital fantasies. There is then a split in the energy contained in the love drive that divides into four functions:

1. A part of the energy remains the original drive, which is repressed into the unconscious while unceasingly trying to find a way to penetrate anew into the consciousness of the patient.
2. Another part of the energy is "filtered" and transformed into sadistic (anger and pleasure) thoughts.
3. The sadistic thoughts become a fear of annihilation by the authority of the father.
4. The remainder of the energy creates a surface behavior that participates in setting this defense in place—as it happens, the exaggerated politeness that was so appreciated by a part of the Viennese population of the day.

In this model, we have on one hand a splitting of different parts of the Oedipus complex (love of the mother and conflict with the father), and on the other hand, a dispersion of the energy (disinvestment) that maintains the representation of a drive in the unconscious. This is, of course, a metaphorical model of what really happens, as it is impossible to analyze with precision how these processes function. Furthermore, as Gurdjieff's model shows very well,[118] it is possible that a defense also mobilizes energy coming from sources other than the energy of the repressed drive. The summary I propose is thus a pedagogical simplification of a more fluid and more complex system. That said, whatever might be the real operation put in place, there will be a reduction in the quantity of energy available to the organism and, consequently, a loss of vitality.

The previous example summarizes what has been analyzed in a case having a character Reich[119] identified as "passive-feminine"; a case that can be broken down as follows:

Genital drive: The object-related genital[120] love toward the mother.
• Defense 1. A child is disappointed by a mother who is not totally available to his desires. Not wanting to feel a need that painfully frustrates him many times during the day, he defends himself by developing terrifying fantasies concerning the mother's vagina and by becoming sadistic toward her. The genital love is transformed into a negative phallic drive associated to an urge to pierce the mother's body.
• Defense 2. To repress the sadistic manifestations that are unacceptable by his entourage, the child develops a fear of becoming a woman, a fear of being castrated. He also develops a passive feminine attitude toward his father. The drive then becomes anal, which was the current association of

the psychoanalysts of the time for everything that leads to an exaggerated politeness.

- Defense 3. In the face of an excessively authoritarian father, the fear of castration because of his love for his mother becomes more intense; at the same time, his hostility toward his father increases. He begins to dream of castrating his father.
- Defense 4. While all of this construction is based on the fear of his incestuous drive toward the mother, the patient now only has the awareness of his urge to castrate his father. He begins to be afraid that his father will destroy him because of his hostility. His urge to castrate his father becomes an urge to kill him.
- Defense 5. The intensity of his hostility leads him to have a generalized fear of being assaulted.
- Defense 6. The child then has aggressive fantasies against all forms of authority, which he represses with a somewhat ridiculous suspicious attitude. This ridiculous side renders the suspiciousness more acceptable to others.
- Defense 7. Finally, by dint of being suspicious and ridiculous, the child begins to be afraid of losing the love and protection of his parents. He thus becomes particularly polite. This politeness is a lid that represses an intense anxiety.

The establishment of this seven-layered system implies such an expenditure of energy that the patient is now sexually impotent.

Reich's proposition is that this structuring of the drives was produced in the order just given and that the analysis, as much as possible, ought to proceed in the reverse order. With some experience, the analyst who encounters a person having a passive-feminine character will assume that his extreme politeness masks an urge to kill. But if the therapist begins to talk about murderous drives from the start of the analysis, the patient will either reinforce his defense system or experience an anxiety attack, which he will not be able to integrate. The other possibility is that, frightened, the patient stops the therapy and renounces the project of understanding himself better. Reich used such examples to demonstrate that it will never be useful to analyze a deep layer early on in therapy. In body psychotherapy, there are no absolute rules. Each therapist knows of a few cases when an analysis of the deeper layers at the start of therapy was useful. But these cases are rare. By default, the rules that Reich proposes in Character analysis are recommendations that are often best to follow.

Remember that a thought is maintained in the unconscious because if it rose to consciousness it could to generate a general dysfunction of conscious dynamics. This implies that above all we must carry out work that permits consciousness to acquire the capacity to integrate the repressed drives. Character analysis is one way to make this integration possible. Reich begins by asking the patient to talk about his symptom (sexual impotence) and associate his need to be polite (the most manifest defense for the therapist and the patient). Gradually, the patient speaks of his past awkwardness and the mockery he suffered due to his clumsy way of criticizing the various forms of authority that surrounded him (the school, the church, morality, etc.). These associations explain next to nothing. There is a danger to believe that to bring the cause of the seventh layer to the light of day is enough to explain the patient's neurosis. Nonetheless, the analysis of this first layer will allow the patient to have a bit more energy. He gives himself the right to be critical; he learns to better experience and appreciate who he is. For most psychoanalysts, this result only brings transitory benefits if it is not consolidated by the analysis of the other layers. However, many psychotherapists are content with a positive result of this type. The idea is that the patient will be able to follow a more profound treatment once he has appreciated the momentary benefits of this first layer. The advantage of this approach is that the therapist abandons the belief that it is possible and desirable to understand all the details of a patient's mental and affective life. The patient can be content to analyze only those layers that prevent him from having a relatively pleasant life. This result is often preferable to an interminable analysis. I have had many patients who came to see me several times in their lives. What had hitherto been analyzed had been integrated into the life of the patient, and he was then ready to explore a new aspect of his personality: one that is particularly relevant to his life at the time of seeking me out.

Character analysis began with the analysis of individual processes. It was used to discover what had been put in place in the course of an individual's development. It then became possible to detect similar character traits that often require similar forms of intervention. The treatment can then be carried out more quickly, because the therapist will no longer be obliged to feel his way along when he encounters a certain type of character structure.

Each layer of a character constitutes a sort of module that forms "a character trait." The same character trait can be found in several character structures but may fulfill, in each case, a different set of functions.[121] We again find ourselves in a rough sketch of a systemic model where an element potentiates itself differently in function of the construction that contains it. The characters that Reich identifies are the following: compulsive, impulsive, hysteric, masochistic, obsessive, passive-feminine, phallic-narcissistic, rigid, and schizoid. This list is not presented as exhaustive. It represents Reich's clientele. Terms like *oral, anal, genital*, are henceforth a characteristic of certain character traits.

Character and Psychoanalysis. The attempt to define global configurations of behavior and their underlying dynamics was a clinical research that gradually imposed itself on many analysts when the clients became more numerous and consequently more varied. When the psychoanalysts met with each other, they had a sufficient number of cases to attempt to group some of them together and develop strategies in function of these groupings. The first proposition was put forth by Freud around the sexual stages (oral, anal, phallic, and genital). Abraham (1925) had already proposed another characterological system based on different forms of organization of secondary drives.

In the clinics of Berlin and Vienna, Franz Alexander (1923) and Wilhelm Reich (1927a) used the notion of character to describe the personality of the young people at odds with the norms and the laws, antisocial, sometimes violent against others as well as against themselves. Reich categorized these patients as impulsive characters.[122] This work does not concern this textbook; it is noteworthy to the extent that it will serve as a basis (probably through the intermediary of Annie Reich) for Otto Friedmann Kernberg's (1984) notion of "borderline personality organization." Alexander and Reich draw inspiration from the works of Viennese pedagogue and social worker August Aichhorn (1925) who worked with this type of youth. Aichhorn recommended for them an active method of psychotherapy particularly adapted to their problems: one that could contain them, correspond to them, and protect them. The character analysis of "impulsive characters" inspired Reich to pursue methods much more active than Ferenczi had imagined.

Reich in Berlin (1930–1933): Communism and Sexual Liberation, Character Analysis and the Body

From Vienna to Berlin in 1930

Reich left for Berlin just before being dismissed from his positions as director of the seminar and the polyclinic. His Viennese colleagues appreciated his creativity, inventiveness, and intelligence, but they suffered from his intransigent authoritarianism and the fact that he used his institutional power to promote his own theories. Also, they were not pleased to have communist jargon thrown at them at any given moment. They were hoping for a more pedagogical attitude, like that of the Berlin Institute, which allowed each one to find a "personal style" while remaining within the psychoanalytic frame of thinking. In Vienna, only Reich had the right to a personal style. Freud would have said of Reich that "the one who wants unceasingly to be placed at the front of the scene shows that he wants to be right at whatever price."[123]

In Berlin, the sponsor of the institute, Max Eitingon, had lost a large portion of his fortune in the financial crash of 1929. Some members of the board of directors were afraid of the rising power of anti-Semitism that was manifest in all of Europe and especially in the German-speaking countries. For these reasons, many eminent members of the Berlin Psychoanalytic Institute accepted positions outside of Europe. This was the case for Alexander, who obtained a position in Chicago in 1930. This state of anxiety and concern dominating the psychoanalytic community in Berlin explains in part why the community was so happy to be able to count Annie and Wilhelm among them as new members. They brought with them the most recent discussions that animated Freud's entourage. Reich was known for his work in sexology, his chairing of the seminar on psychoanalytic technique, and his propositions concerning character analysis. The Reichs joined Fenichel's technical seminar, which had become a meeting place for the psychoanalysts of the left. The practice they opened in Berlin was quickly filled.

Psychiatric Diagnostics and Psychotherapy: Is Reich Schizophrenic?

Given the numerous negative commentaries on his character, Reich began psychoanalysis with Sándor Radó, who had been Fenichel's analyst. This process was interrupted when Radó immigrated to New York in 1931. This was Reich's only attempt to undergo a serious psychoanalysis. Years later, Radó would have told Annie Reich that Wilhelm suffered from an "insidious psychotic process." A rumor circulated, affirming that Radó would have had diagnosed schizophrenia in Reich.[124] This rumor hurt Reich immensely. He thought it had been spread by Fenichel. This rumor probably influenced Fenichel when he questioned himself concerning the mental stability of his friend. If the expression "insidious psychotic process" attributed to Radó is a plausible diagnosis, the one of schizophrenia is so inappropriate that it illustrates two aspects of the mores of psychotherapists, which persists to this day, in all of the schools:

1. Psychotherapists often have insufficient knowledge of psychiatric diagnoses. They generally learn the diagnostic categories defined according to the models used by the school in which they were trained. Thus, the psychoanalysts of the 1920s easily used categories such as orality, genitality, castration complex, and so on. Most of the psychotherapists did not work in psychiatry, or did so only during their internship. Today, psychiatric institutions often encourage a specialization in certain pathologies. Thus, even an individual who works in psychiatry can be knowledgeable about depression but not schizophrenia, of borderline personality disorder but not paranoid psychosis. Another element to add to this discussion is the phobia that certain psychotherapists have toward psychiatric diagnoses or all other forms of classification. They want to build their understanding of the patient on what they have experienced with him, on a sort of empathy based on the transferential dynamics that guide their understanding of the patient. The categories that emanate from a psychotherapeutic technique they use can be integrated by the psychotherapist because they are a part of the approach. Once the diagnostic categories of a school have been made explicit, psychotherapists often try to reduce the psychiatric categories to the categories they know how to treat. This leads to speculative discussions on the nature of psychosis, of neurosis, and so on—often without end. These discussions are frequently confusing because a psychotherapist who works in a private practice has rarely met a psychotic person. Reich was part of this category of psychiatrists who used psychiatric labels by redefining them ac-

cording to the categories of his school. Like many of his colleagues, he redefined psychosis, depression, schizoid personality, or hysteria according to the psychoanalytic diagnostics of the day and then according to the categories of character analysis. This way of proceeding is probably the worst because it does not permit a clear distinction between the categories generated by a form of practice and the psychiatric categories that allow institutions to categorize mental disorders for research or for various forms of social support like health insurance. In other words, most of the psychoanalysts of the time only had a fuzzy understanding of schizophrenia. Among them, only Jung (1907) and Abraham (1907, 1908) had at least worked with schizophrenics early in their careers. A deeper collaboration between psychoanalysis and psychiatry was in the making; even then, many psychoanalysts defended their categories in the face of those proposed by psychiatry.

2. It is not unusual that psychoanalysts refer to a serious psychiatric diagnosis to explain the faults of a colleague, to express their annoyance. To the extent that many psychotherapists suffer from mental disorders that, nonetheless, do not impede them from doing good work, many colleagues believe in the relative pertinence of the usage of these diagnoses to sully the reputation of others. The term *schizophrenia* designated the irritating, intrusive, quick-tempered, sometimes manic, and sometimes suspicious side of Reich, which worsened over time.

We will see shortly how this rumor influenced the relationship between Fenichel and Reich. I do not know what Radó really said about Reich. It is ethically recommended to ignore all manner of diagnosis that is not founded on an appropriate assessment. Even in this case, it is common to notice that the same individual receives different diagnoses in the course of his life. If we imagine the hope with which Reich finally entered psychoanalysis and the sadness he must have felt to be abandoned by Radó, we can only imagine the wound and rancor that was created in him when he heard that his analyst would have circulated such a rumor.

Until the end of his life Otto Fenichel would discuss Reich's psychoanalytical contribution to psychotherapy, but would not say a word on orgone and other exotic considerations.[125] This silence is expressive, coming from someone who was probably informed by mutual friends on Reich's explorations. It certainly expresses embarrassment, maybe the thought that Reich was mad, but also the will not to attack, publically at least, someone he had loved and admired.

The Reichs Discover Gindler's Method
According to Clare Fenichel (1981), Otto presented Reich to everyone as his best friend. On Sundays, the Fenichels regularly walked with the Reichs in the

forests near Berlin. Annie and Eva Reich studied Gindler's method by taking courses with Clare Fenichel.

Years later, in 1984, Judyth O. Weaver, trained in Reichian orgonomy, became friends with Eva Reich.[126] Judyth once told Eva that she had also been trained by Charlotte Selver, one of Gindler's students. Eva replied that her father Reich would have been happy to know that some of his students had followed a Gindlerian training. Eva was convinced that the methods her father established in Oslo and then in the United States were deeply influenced by Gindler. She did not think her father would have set about to work on the body and respiration if his friends had not explained to him how Gindler worked. She also described the gymnastics courses given by Clare Fenichel to children. "Eva Reich recalls liking the school very much because they got to crawl under, around, and over all sorts of things, and she had a very good time. She said that she loved the ways she was encouraged to use her body and be active and creative" (Geuter et al., 2010).

Wilhelm Reich probably never attended one of Elsa Gindler's or Clare Fenichel's courses. He might have come one or two times, but that is not certain. He had other fish to fry, but he listened a lot and learned quickly. What others told him awakened his curiosity. He was forever asking Annie and Eva what went on in their classes. I assume that he also discussed the Gindler approach with the Fenichels.

As a child, Reich had probably suffered from certain secrets concerning his mother's love life.[127] From then on, he wanted everything to be public. He was incapable of respecting the need to have private intimacy, be it for himself or for others. This complex was associated to a silent rage that was palpable by everyone: a silent fury against all those who requested some form of exclusive attachment from him and against all those who refused to attach themselves to him exclusively. This rage was so strong that one of the more famous of Reich's biographers, Myron Sharaf (1983), made it the title of the biography: *Fury on Earth*.

Psychoanalysts tend to differentiate the inside from the outside, what happens in a practice from family and social life. Typically, Annie Reich was not necessarily rigid on such matters, but she appreciated such a differentiation. She could not sympathize with Reich's compulsion to publicly mix therapy, militancy, and his private life.[128]

Fenichel had introduced Annie to Wilhelm in Vienna. He now met his next great love while associating with the friends of the Fenichels: Elsa Lindenberg.[129] Lindenberg was one of four communist star dancers in the Berlin State Opera. She had probably taken a few lessons with Gindler,[130] but she was mostly influenced by lessons taken with choreographer Rudolf Laban, who is still well known today.[131] Laban is often quoted in the literature concerning nonverbal communication as one of the founders of the systems of the modern coding of gestures.[132] He had developed a system that made it possible to record choreography and the dynamics of movements in a detailed way. He is also often mentioned in the literature dedicated to dance therapy.[133] He created his school at Monte Verità near Ascona at the beginning of World War I. In 1930 he was asked to direct dancers at the Berlin State Opera.[134]

Wilhelm Reich left Annie in a particularly visible and public manner by making his relationship with Elsa Lindenberg an example for all those who fought for sexual revolution and against marriage. Without really noticing it, Reich brought his psychoanalytic adventure to an end when, intoxicated by the whirlwind that animated life in Berlin at the time, he left his wife. She kept the surname Reich for the rest of her life. It appears that she would have wanted to stay with Wilhelm, even if their life as a couple was complicated. In 1932, she wrote to Elsa Lindenberg that the new couple's happiness was built on her tears. Annie preferred to return to Vienna, where she divorced Reich.[135] Reich did not abandon his role as a father. He joined Annie to have "family" vacations.[136]

Otto Fenichel and Annie created lasting friendly and professional ties. This probably explains Wilhelm Reich's growing hostility toward Fenichel. Fenichel wanted to remain on friendly terms with Annie and Elsa. I am convinced that this lasting friendship was something that Reich never accepted. He felt excluded from the "group" of which he was a part before betraying her so openly. It is bizarre that this possible cause of the conflict between the two friends is not mentioned in the biographies of either Reich or Fenichel.

Character Structure: The Coordination of Muscular and Mental Tensions
In the 1933 version of *Character Analysis*, Reich insists on the fact that he uses the analysis of *behavior* to bring forth the *mental* defense system of a patient.[137] Only in passing does he relate the character armor to muscular tension: "All the muscles of the body, but especially those of the pelvic floor and pelvis, the muscles of the shoulders and those of the face (c.f. the "hard," almost mask-like physiognomy of compulsive characters), are in a state of hypertonia" (Reich, 1949a, IV.2, p. 214). Reich speaks here of hypertonic muscles and not hypotonic muscles, as Fenichel does. We will see that the Oslo School of Body Psychotherapy speaks as much about the hypotonic as the hypertonic muscles, as Fenichel did. Generally, the Reichians know how to work with the hypertonic muscles and have no techniques to approach the hypotonic muscles.

Reich quickly developed this line of thought by focusing on the vegetative system, which would be the link between Fenichel's motor activity and Freud's psyche. He progressed very fast in this direction. At the 1934 Psychoanalytic Congress in Lucerne, he discussed his thoughts on the matter in a presentation titled "Psychic Contact and Vegetative Currents." He already spoke of awareness of body and vegetative sensations, such as tingling and warmth, as a way to get in touch with one's libido. This change of direction shows how the seeds sowed by the Fenichels and Elsa Lindenberg[138] regarding the work of Gindler and Laban began to grow in the fertile soil of Reich's imagination and intelligence. It took him less than a year to accommodate his theory and his practice to these new perspectives, which he then developed in Oslo.[139] Given that his point of view was sharpened by his increased familiarity with the techniques of dance and gymnastics, more and more, Reich left the psychoanalytic reserve behind to directly approach the behavioral attitudes and bodily tensions of his patients. He imitated them and encouraged them to modify their habitual behaviors. He observed their breathing and made comments on whether it was too ventral or thoracic; he invited them to explore different ways of breathing. He began to analyze the way the segments of the body are coordinated with each other and breathing. He palpated the muscles. He explored what is going on when he massages them while asking the patient to explore the movement or the expression blocked by a chronic muscular tension. He asked some patients to explore the feelings associated with a particular kind of chronic restriction in their breathing. Briefly, instead of respecting the limits that psychoanalysts and Gindleriens set for themselves, Reich explored possibilities that were considered dangerous for the patient and for the therapist. He thus began to perceive that the muscular dimension of the defense system that regulated the drives has an organization all its own. It is sometimes structured like a "corset" or "armor."[140] These technical explorations far exceeded what psychoanalysts like Ferenczi and Fenichel dared undertake. He now utilized more explicitly a brand of introspection close to that used by Gindler. He asked his patients to feel their body from the inside, insisting mostly on the sensation and the affects that are related to the parts of the body being explored. This Reich is the father of body psychotherapy.

Up to this point, Fenichel and Reich assumed that the chronic tensions organized themselves around specific behaviors (the urge to cry, hit, be caressed, etc.). By consulting the body specialists, Reich became aware that *a local muscular tension inserts itself into the muscular chains* that coordinate the muscles from head to foot. He confirmed Fenichel's hypothesis that each dimension has its own particular functioning by discovering that the body has a particular coherence, linked to the postural organization within the gravity field. This implies that a chronic local muscular tension influences the whole of the functioning of the muscular chains from head to foot. The inhibition of the urge to strike out with one's fist is rapidly associated to an inhibition of the breath, voice, gaze, and support taken by the feet to reinforce the back, and so on. This is how what Reich called the *character armor* gradually formed itself. The notion of armor proposed by Reich is nothing more than the result of an entire series of tensions—each one associated to a partial drive. It gradually becomes a kind of pathological organization of the musculature and of the equilibrium of somatic dynamics:

1. It stiffens the coordination of the segments of the body,
2. reduces the postural repertoire,
3. inhibits the respiration,
4. diminishes the perception of what goes on in the body, and

5. represses the libido and reabsorbs the anxiety generated by this repression.

The armor is first formed through its participation in the repression of specific affects and their expression. However, gradually, these tensions also influence other muscles, and cause general compensating postural disturbances. It thus creates a structure of tensions that follow bodily causal chains, are built parallel to the mental defenses, and then influence the way the mind inhabits the body and what surrounds it.

Because of these formulations and his way of working, Reich became known as the one who dared to introduce bodywork into the psychoanalytic frame. Fenichel approached the subject only on the plane of psychoanalytic theory. Reich wanted his psychoanalyst colleagues to do like him and intervene on the body during sessions of psychoanalysis or of psychoanalytic psychotherapy. He asked them to approach the mind in its interaction with somatic dynamics. The mind passes necessarily through the body to encounter others. The body is therefore part of the transferential relationship.[141]

Social Sexology

> The influence of the character structure of the masses determines the state form, no matter whether it expresses itself by passivity or by activity.... Only this mass structure is capable of implanting in itself the true democratic tendencies of a state administration, by taking over, piece by piece, the administration "above it." (Reich, 1946, *Mass Psychology of Fascism*, IX.8, p. 242f)[142]

A SEXUAL REVOLUTION FOR THE MASSES AND FOR FAMILY PLANNING

Given that neurosis is a widespread and socially constructed illness, Reich proposed an epidemiological approach to sexual problems. A recent example of this medical approach is the strategy put in place, these past 20 or so years, to understand and to treat AIDS. Institutions like the World Health Organization have supported actions that gather the analyses of the cells of an organism, analyses of sexual behaviors, the high stakes of industry (research for a vaccine and condom manufacturing), the recruiting of political support, educators, and advertising capable of teaching people about the necessity of wearing a condom when having sex, and so on. In acting on such a heterogeneous set of institutions, the prevalence of AIDS was reduced. With far fewer means, Reich tried to mobilize a similar strategy to undertake a preventive action against neurosis by helping people ameliorate their way of approaching sexuality.

What was new was the recommendation of an epidemiological approach to modify the way that people behaved sexually; for many, their behavior conformed to current usage. The difficulty of this position was to convince physicians and authorities that their habitual sexual behavior was often neurotic. An epidemiological endeavor inevitably necessitates relations with political institutions. Reich found the support he needed for this in the Communist Party. He was thus able to mobilize an important institutional support but also the individual militancy of the communists to discuss intimate behavior in public debates. This type of militancy had already been proposed by the feminist movements of the nineteenth century and is taken up today by ecologists to save the planet from the effects of overpopulation and pollution.

That Austrian Communist Party of 1928 was a small organization in which Reich intervened, as always, wanting to give it some structure. He made financial contributions for the establishment of a Socialist Society of Sexual Information and Research. He expanded this activity when he moved to Berlin in 1930, where he became part of the executive committee of the German Communist Party which was in direct competition with the National Socialist Party (Nazi), directed by Adolf Hitler. The society for sexual education founded by Reich in the Communist Party was called the Association for a Proletarian Sexual Policy. This association proposed encounters between individuals who desire to share their sexual experiences, as well as a support and consultation service. The association had at least 30,000 active members[143] and reached far greater number of sympathizers through its conferences and journal. Many themes are taken up, and almost all have been incorporated into various institutions, like the family planning movement that became influential in the 1960s. Some of the proposed reforms also entered into the lives of many families around the world, especially in urban centers. Here are a few examples:

1. An explanation of the sexual and reproduction mechanism.
2. A sound instruction on the prevention and termination of pregnancies.
3. The right of adolescents to sleep in their own room, instead of common rooms. At the time, many families slept in a single bedroom. Reich showed that it created untenable psychological situations and impeded all sorts of satisfying sexual activity for the parents and the children (e.g., masturbation).
4. Showing that a desire and a variety of sexual practices are healthy needs that do not merit the sanction of a shaming discourse.
5. Encouraging the creation of nurseries to allow women to work outside the home.

Reich (1932) even wrote a pamphlet that directly addressed the adolescents, proposing that they engage in a militant activity to protect their right to a sexual life. This publication would have fit in well with the thinking of the youth movements of the left, if it were not written in the jargon of Leninists. A language with less of a leftist connotation would probably have had a larger impact. The developed themes, on the other hand, would remain the same when Reich discovered that the communist movement was about to become a form of "red fascism."[144] Only in the second edition of *Mass Psychology of Fascism* did Reich describe in an explicit fashion how he discovered that Stalin was establishing the same laws pertaining to sexuality and the family in the Soviet Union as Hitler was in Germany. This family policy contradicted all of Lenin's laws on education.

> Vignette on sexual liberation and Gustav Marlock. *In a conference,*[145] *Gustav Marlock commented on the Reichian sexual revolution, from 1930 to 2006, and on what differentiated it from the proposition of the psychoanalysts. He underscored that it was conceived as a reform of the sexuality of families and the education of children.*[146] *It is also in this sense that the Reichian theme was taken up by the youth movements at the end of the 1960s in the United States and Europe. Only in the 1970s was the movement gradually taken up by various types of homosexual militancy to become a movement of liberation for all forms of sexuality. This liberation of sexual behavior is closer to psychoanalytic propositions*[147] *than to Reichian propositions. It seems to me that it is useful to distinguish between these two movements of sexual liberation because they have different goals. Reich was defending the sexual life of heterosexual families. Like most psychiatrists of his day, he considered homosexuality to be a perversion. This homophobic position has not been retained by the neo-Reichian movements.*

SEXUALITY AS AN EXTERNAL PROPENSION

The libido expresses itself in the sexual encounter and in the encounter between colleagues. "The biological center and its libido need to express themselves sexually and professionally" (Reich, 1940, V.5, p. 146f).

Reich's social work showed how diverse types of social services are necessary for the development of the instincts. He is one of the few who dared to follow the trajectory of an instinctive propension on its journey within the center of individual organisms and within the maze of the regulations in social systems. He thus explored all the articulations of an instinct and showed that most of these articulations are not accessible within a psychotherapeutic frame. The establishment of systemic therapy, centered on the functioning of the family, has henceforth reinforced this demonstration. The action of the psychotherapist is thus situated as a kind of social action, capable of supporting certain conditions of a propension, but not of all of them.

In terms of a goal for psychotherapy, this implies that the therapist and his patient are able to evaluate what changes are possible in a given situation. A married patient may discover that at the heart of his couple relationship, there are no longer any sexual relations possible and may prefer, to remain in the relationship nonetheless. This choice implies the analysis of high stakes that are not all of a sexual nature. Again, nonetheless, if the rapport between libido and sexuality remain unchanged, it will remain pathogenic even if it is accepted.

This brings us back to Guy Cellérier's impossible agenda. Even if choices are inevitable, they always have a price. It would seem that human organisms can survive with an impossible agenda, but they do not have the resources to manage their complexity. For Reich, this analysis expresses a form of resignation. He believed that this complexity could be mastered in a coherent way.

Reich told his patients that the developments that were not able to be accomplished by them today because of the political situation would have to be undertaken by their children. For Reich, a patient who really understood his message would necessarily became a militant for life, someone who wants that the humanity of tomorrow become more human than the one of today. This was already the gamble of the women's liberation movements. Some social changes are at least as important for the well-being of everyone as the change that can be accomplished by psychotherapy.

CHARACTER AND POLITICS

When Hitler was elected in 1933, Reich published *The Mass Psychology of Fascism*, in which he denounces on the one hand the huge danger that Nazism represents, but also the limits of the communist strategy that the election revealed.[148] The goal of his book is to explain why a number of proletarian communists ended up electing Hitler. Reich blamed the communists for having only understood the economic structure of a society. Then he showed, by quoting *Mein Kampf,* that Hitler manipulated another social dimension: the psychology of the masses, or the value system of the people. Hitler, like religious institutions, manipulated the people's fear, their attachment to the notion of the family and to the cultural values of their nation, their more or less explicit racism, and their sexual mores. For Reich, this dimension is, from the point of view of sociology, as important as the economic dimension. It would be harmful, according to him, if only the movements of the extreme right proposed political means to regulate what is for Reich an important regulator of social life and the motives that influence the vote of the population.

In 1946, Reich understood that the soviet regime had become as horrible as that of the Germans. His analysis of communism gradually became the following. When Lenin took power, he believed that changing the laws would suffice to change a society. These laws clearly foresaw a change in education (divorce, nurseries, etc.), but he did not expect that the masses would remain loyal to a tyrannical power structure. Reich's reasoning was that the laws can change in one day, whereas the *character structures* require generations to be transformed. Not taking this variable into account leads to social disasters. In Germany and in Russia, everybody, outside of the intellectual and marginal milieus, had developed in function of a kind of power built into the educational systems for centuries. The citizens consequently have a character structure that does not function unless there is a strong central power. The elimination of the Kaiser and the Tsar did not modify this state of affairs, which explains in part the enthusiasm of the masses for setting up pseudo-kaisers like Stalin and Hitler. Reich noticed that Stalin decreed the same laws as Hitler concerning the cohesion of the family, the official prudery, and sexual repression. All of Lenin's innovative laws on the matter were abolished. For Reich, this confirms the hypothesis that to strengthen itself, tyranny needs to create a psychology of the masses that develops individual character traits for its own ends.

For the future, he recommended cohesion between the modifications of the laws and the manner in which individuals function. This proposition is also compatible with Marx's position that perceives the social development as a slow process that needs to advance one small step at a time. This analysis is close to the Darwinian theory. In Marxism and in Darwinism, the main argument is that what needs to be changed is so complex, and has so many ramifications, that it requires a slow process to regulate what is happening. Once genetics became a central metaphor, one could envisage small abrupt changes; but even then, a follow-up is still needed. Marx so admired Darwin that he asked him if he could dedicate *Das Capital* to him (Berlin, 1963, X, p. 247f).

The social regulation of sexuality would be the link between economic regulation and the regulation of each individual's character. In other words, the anthropological dimension would be the interface that coordinates economic power and the needs of individuals. In a tyranny or in capitalism the anthropological dimension serves to enslave the masses. Thus, getting the people to believe that the family is a sacred notion or that sexual pleasure was created by the devil generates various forms of neurosis. Citizens are then easily manipulated. We find in this analysis the idea that all social dimensions are linked to each other and, at the same time, that they each have a particular function. From the point of view of individual consciousness, to believe that the family is sacred and to have a secret shame about one's sexuality is one issue. To want to fight for the improvement of the elite is another. There are no direct explicit links between these two kinds of preoccupations. Reich shows that Hitler's genius lies in leading the masses to believe that he defends only a limited number of cultural values that have no link with the power of money or an eventual warrior spirit. Once this value system became the center of attention of the masses, it became evident that Hitler and his entourage had selected some themes that indirectly led to the enslavement of the masses and the installation of a regime that we can, in retrospect, identify as horrible. Reich's genius was to have detected this danger as soon as Hitler was elected. The tool that allowed him to do so is his flexible systems analysis, inherited from psychoanalysis and Marxism, which made it possible to coordinate the apparently heterogenic logic of the dimensions of a system. To summarize, the citizen believes he has voted for someone who will protect his family from the perverse mores advanced by the media and the world market; he finally finds himself imprisoned in a still more dangerous imperialism, without knowing how this turn of events came about.

This analysis can still be used today without referring to its original Marxist theoretical context. It can also be used to reframe the aims of psychotherapy, by stressing that one of the functions of psychotherapy is to allow people to feel their own needs and want to participate in building a social environment that respects their deepest needs. Reich also sought to promote policies that could respond to these exigencies without each and every citizen having to undergo psychotherapy. For him, it consisted of finding kinds of social support (institutions, laws, education, etc.) that permit the promotion of changes in mores that individuals need to integrate to participate in a functioning democracy. Here, he rejoins Freud's analysis. The internal repression of sexual drives, advanced by some religious movements (especially Christians, Muslims, and Jews), is incompatible with the notion of mental health. The message that Reich addressed to the political forces of the left was the following: teaching people to defend the cultural values compatible with their profound needs is a crucial necessity. To defend only the economic advantages is insufficient. The denial of the importance of the cultural dimension that has become prevalent in the nations with large economies can only lead, for a Reichian, to social disasters.

AN INDIGESTIBLE POLICY

After the publication of the *Mass Psychology of Fascism* in 1934, Reich was thrown out of the Communist Party because he excessively focused the debate on sexuality and began to be suspicious of the turn taken by Stalinism. He was also thrown out of Germany because he was (a) Jewish and (b) a communist. A year later, Reich was excluded from the International Association of Psychoanalysis for reasons that seem mostly political. Briefly, I describe the complex situation by distinguishing two extreme positions within the International Psychoanalytical Association (IPA):

1. A group of Jewish psychoanalysts who feel threatened by the rise of Nazism but who want to be able to continue to live at home. This was notably the case for Freud, who was 75 years old. This group's strategy was to use the non-Jewish psychoanalysts, led by Ernest Jones, to find a compromise with the Nazis. It was probably mostly because he was not Jewish that Jones had just been elected president of the International Association of Psychoanalysis. This political strategy required that psychoanalysis present, above all, its "scientific" profile: neutral on the political and religious plane.
2. A group of Jewish psychoanalysts of the left which is divided into (a) a group of Marxist socialists led by Fenichel and (b) a group of Leninist communists led by Reich. Realizing the rapprochement of some of Jones's allies with the Nazis, Reich proposed resigning from the association and establishing a new and more honorable psychoanalytic association. Fenichel objected to this proposition, knowing that Freud had always had comfortable and friendly relationships with friends and colleagues of the left.

Reich had become such a prominent figure of the Leninist movement in Germany that it became difficult to include him in the group of leftist psychoanalysts in Berlin who had Marxist leanings but were less involved in the immediate politics. Reich referred to his colleagues as cowards, and they warned him that he was becoming foolhardy. Around this discussion a conflict erupted between those who followed Reich and those who followed Fenichel. In 1934, at the congress in Lucerne, prudently held in Switzerland, the International Association of Psychoanalysis expelled Reich. Reich's friends were asking themselves if it was the fellow, the politician, or his positions on sexuality, the body, and psychoanalysis that the association was expelling. At the time, it was assumed that it consisted of a bit of everything. Today, we know that it was mostly the politician who was expelled.

If I understood correctly, the technicalities of this situation are a bit more complicated. According to the rules of the IPA, an analyst joins his *national* association and is then automatically a member of the *international* association. Reich, having been excluded from the German association, could not, consequently, belong to the international association. When Fenichel and Reich lived in Oslo, Reich could have joined the national psychoanalytic association of Norway. Therefore, he would have been automatically a member of the international association. It is mostly Reich, who rendered this solution impossible, while everyone in his entourage, Fenichel included, encouraged him to take this step.

In his correspondence with Ferenczi, Freud demanded Reich's expulsion because of his "bolshevisms," while adding, with a bit of bad faith, that it was probably this nonscientific doctrine that pushed Reich to reject his concept of the death drive, "Thanatos."[149] For Ferenczi and Freud, Reich's theory on masochism, which opposed the necessity to invoke a death instinct, is just an ideological position.[150] Freud also reproached Fenichel for having remained too loyal to Reich and deprived him of his position as editor of the *Internationale Zeitschrift für Psychoanalyse*.[151] He explicitly complained about the "part played by Fenichel in favor of Reich's bolshevism and other tactless behavior" (letter to Ferenczi of June 13, 1932; translated by Marcel Duclos). Notice that the term selected is "bolshevism" and not "communist"; otherwise, Freud would have had to exclude the entire group of psychoanalysts of the left, which would have angered a great number of psychoanalysts. Freud asks the editors of books written by psychoanalysts not to publish Reich's book on character analysis.[152] Reich published this masterpiece out of his own pocket.

Purely intellectual motives were given to explain Reich's expulsion. It follows that his positions on the body, emotions, behavior, and the right to touch was then considered incompatible with the psychoanalytic approach.[153] For at least 30 years, most psychoanalysts avoided exploring the possibility of including the emotional expression and the touch of the body in the psychoanalytic frame. We will see that a certain number among them could not restrain themselves from having an interest in the subject. But they had an awareness that they were entering into somewhat of an "exotic" domain in the eyes of their psychoanalytic colleagues.

Reich's expulsion was nonetheless useless, since Freud finally had to exile himself.[154] This exclusion is an example of the way movements like the Nazi government divide to conquer.[155] They divided the psychoanalysts by letting them believe that most of them would be spared if they chased away the black sheep; yet in the end, the Nazis led the entire herd to the slaughterhouse.

Reich was convinced that Fenichel and his friends had supported the decision of the central committee of the International Psychoanalytic Association. The fact that Fenichel did not leave the association to establish another association with him was proof enough, for Reich, that his interpretation was correct. Fenichel considered his disagreement with Reich as a passionate discussion between friends and allies. He did not want to separate himself from Reich, whom he admired.[156] According to Reich,[157] Fenichel was so saddened by his expulsion that he had a "nervous breakdown," which necessitated that he spend three weeks in a rest home. Reich understood this depression as the result of a tumultuous ambivalence toward him. Fenichel was probably deeply wounded by the impression that everyone asked him to choose between his friendship with Reich and his passion for psychoanalysis. For him, Reich remained a great psychoanalyst. He refused to choose.

The Berlin Students of Fenichel, Gindler, and Reich

Before World War II, Fenichel, Gindler, and Reich had many students. They created, among them, a network of knowledge that then developed in the United States.[158] They animated what we now call humanistic psychotherapy. In the 1960s, one of its most representative centers was Esalen, on the coast of California. This center combined new forms of psychotherapy like Fritz Perls's Gestalt therapy and an assortment of body–mind approaches:[159]

1. Students trained by Gindler or Jacoby: principally Laura Perls, Charlotte Selver, and Magda Proskauer.
2. Body disciplines developed in the United States: Ida Rolf (Rolfing), Ilse Middendorf (like Gindler, she had been influenced by Hanish's breathing exercises), Illana Rubenfeld (Rubenfeld synergy method) and Pierre Pannetier (Polarization).
3. Different students of Moshe Feldenkrais and Mathias Alexander.
4. Different teachers of yoga, tai chi chuan, and meditation (like Alan Watts).
5. Dance therapy.

Many body psychotherapists in the United States had spent time in Esalen or were trained by a person who had taught in this center. These personalities in the world of body psychotherapy refined body–mind methods and developed new ways of approaching psychological dynamics. The "awareness exercises" developed by Fritz Perls and his colleagues (1951) are examples of these new techniques. These exercises were probably inspired by "the exploration of the gesture from the inside" (*tasten*) developed by Gindler. It allowed a certain number of psychotherapists to develop new forms of introspection and dream analysis (e.g., "directed daydream" or "waking dreams" techniques developed by Desoille, 1966).

The popularity of awareness exercises that developed in California during the 1950s and 1960s had several sources. The three most important ones are probably a renewed interest for Far Eastern meditation, an interest in Reichian Orgonomy, and the popularity of body–mind techniques such as those derived from Moshe Feldenkrais and Elsa Gindler. One of the key figures of this development was Charlotte Selver (1901–2003), who had studied with a student of Jacques Dalcroze (Rudolf Bode[160]) and Elsa Gindler. Even if Selver[161] had worked at Esalen with students who were in psychotherapy, her workshops did not have psychotherapeutic goals. She developed a method that she called sensory awareness, which, above all, sought to develop the capacity to be aware of what is going on in the space that is a body. To allow her students to enter into the world of body sensations, she used a form of internal exploration that has been taken up by many body psychotherapists of today.

Here is a sample of what Selver asked her pupils once they were able to enter into conscious contact with what was going on in them:

> You may feel how easy it would be for gravity to become overwhelming, pulling you down to the ground and how the earth even wants to swallow you. But no, there is something under you which supports you—and something inside you which reconditions you from moment to moment.
>
> Could you be open in your bones and other tissues for that which supports you? Be grateful for that support—grateful in every cell, grateful in your skin, and in your bones! (Selver, 2007, p. 44)

Having experienced many exercises that use this type of mental technique, I know that it is possible to have the impression of feeling our tissues breathe; when this type of awareness becomes intense, it can activate a type of relaxation that gives the impression of being whole. I also know that introspection does not have the capacity to feel what is really going on in the tissues in such an explicit way.[162] Thus, Selver solicits not only a state of exaltation in her students but also a type of introspection open to suggestion.

This is not what I am referring to when I speak of an exploration of the inside of a movement. These very precise "awareness exercises" in Gestalt therapy allowed many people to sharpen their contact with body sensations, first through suggestions, then in a more refined and precise manner. Selver influenced many body psychotherapists like Judith E. Weaver and Malcolm Brown. Brown was the first to have developed a form of body psychotherapy that is explicitly organismic. His school, founded in 1977, is called Organismic psychotherapy.[163]

Another student of Gindler was Laura Posener, who married Fritz Perls. Laura Perls was one of these women of this generation who were less well known than the man she married and inspired but who is probably at least as competent. She was part of the Berlin Psychoanalytic Institute in the 1930s. She was in supervision with Otto Fenichel, while Fritz Perls went to Reich for his psychotherapy.[164] Fritz trained in psychiatry under Kurt Goldstein in Frankfort. Laura studied phenomenology in Frankfort. She also studied with Gindler.[165] Fritz and Laura both completed training in Gestalt psychology. The synthesis of Gestalt psychology and phenomenology, which is at the heart of Gestalt therapy, combines the knowledge of Laura and Fritz Perls. Laura and Fritz Perls left Germany for South Africa after Hitler's election in 1933.

I have taken Esalen as a point of reference, but the influence of Gestalt therapy and Gindler's students developed in many different parts of the United States. Thus, after her divorce from Otto Fenichel, Clare Fenichel taught mostly in New York. In what follows, we will see that henceforth there will be two types of body psychotherapy:

1. A combination between a psychotherapy treatment and bodywork carried out by a team. This is the Fenichel/Gindler solution, which was often adopted, for example, in Esalen.
2. A method where body and psychological processes are combined by a single therapist, with a psychotherapeutic aim. This is the solution adopted after World War II by neo-Reichian body psychotherapists like David Boadella, Malcolm Brown, and Alexander Lowen. We also find this option in some movements that were not influenced by Reich, like the Ajuriaguerra relaxation.[166]

Other schools oscillate between these two possibilities, like the Biodynamic psychology of Gerda Boyesen, who was explicitly influenced by the two movements. I was trained in this third movement.

PART VI

The Organismic Approach of Wilhelm Reich and the Systemic Psychosomatics of Otto Fenichel

17

Vegetotherapy

In the following sections, dedicated to Reich's Scandinavian period, I am going to situate the first of his organismic approaches: Vegetotherapy.

TRANSITION PHASE

The exodus of the Jewish psychoanalysts from Germany accelerated with Hitler's coming to power in 1933. Otto Fenichel left for Oslo (Norway), Reich left for Copenhagen (Denmark), and Annie Reich went to Prague (Czechoslovakia). Otto Fenichel joined her when Reich made his life too complicated in Oslo.

His demonic reputation pursued Reich wherever he went. He was Mr. Sexual Liberation, Mr. Orgasm, Mr. Revolutionary Communist, and expert psychoanalyst. He was, for some, the incarnation of dangerous and perverse thoughts disseminated by Jewish intellectuals. After his arrival in Denmark, attacks engineered by the press forced him to leave for Sweden. The same pressures from Nazi Germany and the same attacks from the media of the right obliged him to go to Norway. There, Otto Fenichel organized a warm and solid welcome for his friend and colleague.

I have already showed that even when he was a psychoanalyst, Reich was more interested in the domain of the drives than that of the psyche. Now that he was no longer held by a group discipline, he gradually focused on what I call an *organismic therapy*.[1] The reference model remains the Reichian model of the orgasm, that is, a type of interaction with other persons that is built on an unceasing modulation of the dynamics of the organism. Psyche, affects, and behaviors are henceforth approached as dimensions of the organism that participate in the way the organism self-regulates while interacting with its environment. Reich's expulsion from psychoanalysis, communism, and German culture created a void that was quickly filled by the repressed organismic vision that had

inspired Reich in his studies in biology. Having lost every reliable external reference point, he also anchored himself in Idealism, which had been, up until then,
a sort of powerful but private leaning: one that he had not dared develop when
he was a psychoanalyst and a communist. This direction solidified itself in his
creation of *Vegetotherapy* in Oslo and then *Orgone* therapy in the United States.

His old friends failed to understand this complete change in direction.
Fenichel believed he was helping his friend when he persisted in presenting him
as a talented psychoanalyst unjustly persecuted for his political positions. For
Reich, at that moment in his life, such friends were useful because they introduced him into Norway; but they were also a hindrance to what he was in the
process of developing. He therefore preferred to surround himself with individuals who know little of him as an icon of Marxist psychoanalysis, and who appreciate the organismic direction of his thinking.

OSLO: REICH CREATES A NEW FORM OF THERAPY

Reich was first received in Oslo (where he stayed from 1934 to 1939) by professor Harald Schjelderrup, director of the Institute of Psychology at the University
of Oslo.[2] In Oslo, he found psychoanalysts he had known in Berlin, like Trygve
Braatøy, Ola Raknes, and Nic Waal.[3] Reich had been one of their principal trainers in psychoanalysis. Some of them took courses and underwent therapy with
Reich. The groups following Fenichel and Reich were then in discussions to try to
establish common ground. Fenichel, for example, helped Reich create a journal.[4]

Reich's formulations and his body–mind techniques were well received by
the psy milieu in Oslo. In Scandinavia the work on the body has, for a long
time, been part of the culture. Reich attracted a group of colleagues who were
interested in his work. Many came from psychoanalytic circles. Others were
mostly interested in his more recent formulations, such as his epidemiological
approach and his Vegetotherapy. This was the case of educator Alexander
Sutherland Neill,[5] who began to travel regularly from Scotland to Scandinavia
for psychotherapy sessions. It was mostly with these newcomers that Reich
formed a new circle of friends and colleagues who sustained his need to treat a
psyche integrated in its organismic and social environment. Neill became Reich's
close friend. After having immigrated to the United States, Reich stayed in close
contact with some of his Oslo friends.

Reich Turns His Back on Psychotherapy to Help
the Organism Find Its Pulsation

A First Discussion of Vegetotherapy: Pulling Back the Veils that Hide the
Manifestations of the Vegetative Experience of an Organism

> Let us also remember why magic is a constant enemy of analysis. "The surprise
> performs the cure." This statement is used unwisely by many patients who, given

their resistance, count on magic. And in the mind of analysis, a dangerous element cooperates with this hope placed on magic. The temptation to play the prophet is largely widespread. (Fenichel, 1941, *Psychoanalytic Technique*, Introduction, p. 12f; translated by Marcel Duclos)

If Reich regretted the network of his psychoanalyst friends with whom he had been close, he did not have the impression of being an Adam, chased out of Paradise! In Berlin, his attempts to blend body and mind in a psychoanalytic frame had not appeared conclusive to him. He was finally in agreement with Fenichel and Gindler that it was not easy to relate these two dimensions of the organism into a single treatment. He did not have the time to occupy himself with such a complex problem, because he felt that he finally had the freedom to concentrate on what really interested him. He was, in fact, interested in neither the psychology of the psychoanalysts nor in the body of the gymnasts. His creativity was focused on the implications of his theory on the orgasm, on that zone that *spontaneously* coordinates mind, body, and behavior. At first, he associated this zone to the sympathetic and parasympathetic vegetative systems. For him, it consisted in going beyond Freud's psyche and Gindler's body so as to work on what animates and links these two dimensions. His strategy was to focus on the large regulators of the organism to heal the organism as a whole. He "is essentially a *biotherapist*, and no longer merely a psychotherapist" (Reich, 1949a, second introduction: xvii).[6]

Reich started with the idea that the theory of the libido is the core of Freud's thought. He therefore had the impression that he is more faithful to Freud's thought than the psychoanalysts because, by focusing on the vegetative dimension, he could clarify Freud's model of the libido and drives. Reich left to the psychoanalysts the task of exploring the representations in detail. We saw that at the beginning, psychoanalysts had a tendency to think that the body could imitate the fantasies. Reich contended that thoughts are but the marionettes of the affects.[7] For this research, he focused on the following components of the orgastic reflex:

1. The emotion and the instincts.
2. Respiration.
3. The coordination of the segments of the body.
4. The capacity of the psyche to integrate the impact of the vegetative system.

Two of his technical innovations are particularly difficult for his psychoanalytic colleagues:[8]

1. More and more, Reich touches his patients.
2. He asks his patients to undress. Influenced by the nudist movements, he and Ola Raknes often asked their male patients to be completely naked

(the women could keep their underwear).[9] They do this to be able to observe, in a detailed fashion, the dynamics of respiration, the muscular masses, and the changes in the quality of the skin. To be naked was also for them proof that the Christian morality and the taboos it imposed had been abandoned.

After the war, when some of Reich's students wanted to create a form of body psychotherapy based on his organismic approach, this second technique was abandoned. The shyness and the protection of the private and intimate life are henceforth considered as some healthy and useful feelings. Most of Reich's students, like Alexander Lowen, required that his patients at least wear their undergarments. In a conference in Geneva, Lowen explained that total nudity had too large an impact on the transference of the therapist. He is not able to manage such an impact in the psychotherapeutic frame. For him, an individual who likes to present in the nude to strangers lacks a necessary defense, has a weak ego, and lacks maturity. In our cultures (Europe and North America), only little children walk around naked without any embarrassment. From puberty onward, to act as if one believes that nudity has no sexual impact on others is a form of apparent innocence that hides a serious lacuna in the structure of the identity, the sexual body, and the relationship to others.

Having said this, it remains useful, in certain cases, to ask a patient in body psychotherapy to strip down to their underwear to observe the impact of the vegetative system on the body. Today, this is done by elaborating on the embarrassment (or the lack of it) felt by some patients when this is asked of them. A patient who is not certain if he can have confidence in a therapist who requests this disrobing is not necessarily neurotic, because the press occasionally publishes articles pertaining to therapists for whom this request is a first step to eventual abuse. On the other hand, it is useful to note that therapists who abuse their patients are found in all schools of psychotherapy, including the verbal therapies. There is therefore no cause-and-effect connection between asking that the patient wear only underclothing when it is relevant to the treatment and the abuse that occurs in therapy. By default, the recommended rule, in this case, is to respect everyone's shyness and be attentive to the lack of modesty. Generally, this request is only justifiable when the work is centered on the vegetative reactions of the skin, the details of muscle tone and respiration, and the use of massage. Within the frame of body psychotherapy, it is rare that all of the sessions require this focus.

Reich had an intrusive side that did not always respect the defenses of his patients. For him, all forms of defenses were pathological. Only when a strategy required it, did he approach a defense with apparent respect. Even when he was a psychoanalyst, he had the tendency to think that the defense system was necessarily a neurotic introject of social oppression. Once he began to practice Vegetotherapy, this position became even more explicit. The patient must be able to live without a defense system, without false modesty, seeking a total transparency in his relationships with others. The capacity to be naked and candid, at the level of one's being, as at the level of the body, was for Reich proof of good health. Here, he applies, in extreme fashion, the foundational rule of the psychoanalytic method,[10] which requires that the patient say everything. Freud had also recommended that the therapist have the necessary tact for this rule to be used constructively. This is a nuance that has important implications: *saying* everything that one feels is not the same thing as *expressing* everything with one's body and vegetative system. What is possible in purely verbal therapies may need to be reformulated in approaches that work with bodily expression.

Like Ferenczi, Reich revisited Freud's early notion of catharsis as soon as he looked for ways of mobilizing affects that connect conscious and unconscious dynamics, vegetative regulation, and the body. He kept the traditional notion that catharsis mobilizes powerful tragic affects until the organism can get rid of them and acquire the impression that it is been cleaned, like the summer air that becomes transparent after a storm. However, he preferred to use the term *discharge* instead of *catharsis*. In most schools inspired by Reich, a full emotional discharge is a way of helping the organism to throw away all forms of toxins, repressed emotions, and negative impressions. In other words, discharge is a form of abreaction that can clean all the tissues of the organism, and bring clarity to the psyche.

Lindenberg and Vegetotherapy

When she arrived in Oslo, Elsa Lindenberg became a choreographer at the National Theater in Oslo.[11] The relationship between Elsa Lindenberg and Reich was a succession of break-ups and reconciliations. She nonetheless stayed with him up until his departure in August 1939, when the war exploded. In New York, he fell in love with Ilse Ollendorf, with whom he had a son, Peter.[12] Reich and Elsa wrote to each other into 1940 and maintained a great affection for one another; I do not know if they saw each other again after the war. After Reich's departure, Elsa continued to practice Vegetotherapy, and she founded a school of dance psychotherapy in which she was able to take advantage of her in-depth knowledge of the dynamics of the body. In effect, in creating his Vegetotherapy, Reich included only a small part of Elsa Lindenberg's knowledge. After the war, she renewed her contact with Gindler to improve her mode of dance therapy. Her method is still taught in Oslo today.[13]

Most of the individuals[14] who looked into the development of the Reichian approach have difficulty seeing how Reich could have developed the bodily dimension of Vegetotherapy without the help of Elsa Lindenberg, who provided him with a large number of body techniques. Upon his arrival in Oslo, incidentally, he asked Elsa Lindenberg to take courses with Clare Fenichel so that she might better understand what Gindler's work might bring him.[15] It is difficult to understand how Reich, who did not know the body techniques, could have established the notion of the coordination of the segments of the body that characterizes Vegetotherapy without the help of Elsa Lindenberg, who allowed him to integrate certain aspects of Laban's and Gindler's.[16] For example, Reich's interest in the spontaneous gesture and his ability to analyze such gestures would have been inspired by Laban. Reich was also assisted by his Scandinavian colleagues, like Ola Raknes and Nic Waal, who knew the Swedish massage and gymnastics methods, and Edmund Jacobson's relaxation method. It would seem that Reich never followed courses on how to work on the body, yet it is impossible to acquire an exquisite know-how of body techniques without having properly worked on one's own body.

We are far from the myth according to which Reich created Vegetotherapy all by himself. This does not diminish the importance of his genius, because in this milieu, he was the only one to create a way of working that can be considered the foundation of body psychotherapy. Where the others had good ideas on how psychoanalysis and body techniques could influence one another, Reich created the necessary and useful first steps. To decide to aim directly at the vegetative dimension instead of trying to blend the impossible was a brilliant strategy. It was only later that several generations of body psychotherapists had the time to reflect on the technical difficulties brought up by every attempt to relate body and psyche in psychotherapy. Their response required a refinement of Reich's organismic approach. Reich's task was to create a therapeutic approach for the large regulators of the organism. He advanced so rapidly that his work became, even to his own admission, a series of discoveries: a first exploration of an unknown continent. He intermingled all sorts of models in this adventure, some more relevant than others. He had confidence in the generations to come to make the necessary revisions when they would explore, in a more systematic fashion, the continent he had discovered.

The Vegetative Dimension Animates and Coordinates the Psyche and the Body

Having defined his theory of the psychological (character) and muscular defenses (armor), Reich deepened his understanding of what is inhibited by the defense systems. He tries to define how the vegetative mechanisms of the organism shape the affects and the libido and, therefore, the way the affective and sexual functioning of an individual influences the mechanisms of vegetative regulations.

A New Approach to the Organism: Touch the Body and Activate the Organism

In deciding to tackle the vegetative dimension directly, Reich explored a domain for which he was not really properly trained. He asked people to breathe deeply, massaged tense muscles, encouraged global movements of the body, became attentive to the itinerant sensations that the physiology creates in the psyche which he calls the "vegetative currents" (Reich, 1949a, XIII), and encouraged folks to self-explore through movement. He had the impression of working on what Descartes was looking for: the *active* connection between thoughts and the body. He used thoughts and the body to modulate the vegetative activity, and thus explore the system of which the thoughts and the gestures are a part.

The phenomenon that Reich calls the vegetative currents becomes salient as soon as a person becomes sensitive to the vegetative dimension of one's own being. It consists in sensations such as hot and cold, tingling or prickling, the impression of being more or less full or dense. From the point of view of consciousness, these sensations seem to move without following any anatomical pathway. This observation is so robust that it was already one of the reasons the Chinese sought to define the meridians for their acupuncture. These sensations are born of a kind of association between physiology and consciousness that is still poorly understood. Thus, in relaxation, it is customary to conjecture that the impression of pleasant warmth diffused throughout the body is related to a better blood circulation. From the point of view of consciousness, this impression resembles more a diffusion of a colored liquid in transparent water than to a sensation that follows arterial pathways.

Another striking phenomenon for all those who discover this dimension of one's being is that the simple fact of becoming conscious of these sensations seems to have a particular effect on the psychophysiology. To listen to one's breathing automatically modifies the respiratory schema. Often (but not always), when an individual focuses his attention on the warmth that appears in his hand, the sensation of warmth spreads throughout the organism. This diffusion can occur in many different ways:

1. *Diffusion in isolated parts:* There is first warmth in a hand, then in a foot, then on the cheeks, and so on. This form of diffusion is not continuous. It seems to jump from one island of sensation to another.
2. *Continuous diffusion:* The warmth fills the hand, the arm, the thorax, and finally the entire space of the body. This diffusion can be *ascending* (moves up toward the head), *descending* (moving toward the feet), or *radiating* (the individual has the impression of radiating sensations).[17]

The therapist sometimes places a hand on the skin to see if this impression of the diffusion of warmth is only psychological (the skin remains cold) or vegetative (the warmth is really diffused in the skin, following the path described by the patient). In some cases, as the warmth is diffused, it can transform into a sensation of density, tingling, and so on. When this phenomenon of diffusion contours a part of the anatomy or stops at a specific point, the therapist, by default, thinks that there is a "blockage" of the energetic dynamics of the organism that must be explored and understood.

One of the difficulties encountered in this work is to distinguish between the vegetative dynamics linked to relaxation and the vegetative dynamics generated by problems that are usually treated by a physician. Most of the time, a physician relates this type of sensation to physical symptoms. For example, I have helped a diabetic patient differentiate what he feels when he relaxes and when he is in hypoglycemic crisis. He had not been able to differentiate the sensations of relaxation and hypoglycemia. Consequently, he was afraid to relax.[18] These sensations are caused by different dynamics. By sharpening his perception of the vegetative sensations, this patient was able to dare to relax. Nonetheless, the proximity of these sensations to consciousness only allows for a partial relaxation. Here, as elsewhere, hurried generalizations can sometimes become dangerous for certain patients while remaining useful for many others.[19]

Like many people who explore this world of vegetative sensations, Reich began to think in terms of *energy*. These vegetative activities are related by following a logic of their own that can make one think of electric energy that transforms itself into kinetic, caloric, or acoustic energy. To learn to feel these sensations was therefore, for Reich, to learn to feel the manifestations of the biological energy that animates us. This position is explicitly used in numerous body–mind approaches that are based on an energetic model. The popularity of this model in the mind–body domain rendered Reich's position reasonable. He had the impression that it would be possible to create a scientific theory that would describe what all the body specialists do not always dare to think out loud. The problem, in this type of analysis, is that we must not forget that every mental perception is an approximate reconstruction of what happens in reality. We again have a demonstration that introspection does not permit a particularly faithful reconstruction of what happens on the physiological plane.

For Reich, this view of energy, like for most of his contemporaries, was a reality discovered by science rather than a metaphor. The idea that there exists a strong link between emotional arousal and electrogalvanic activity was a familiar hypothesis for most psychologists during the first half of the twentieth century.[20] Reich followed this line of research when he attempted to measure the electrical dynamics of the body to see if they correlate with the vegetative sensations. In discovering the vegetative sensations, Reich, as always, felt the need to bring order to this domain, which seemed to him to be at the heart of the Freudian theory of the libido (Reich, 1940, chapters VII and IX). Reich was then in line with the thoughts of psychologists who based themselves on Helmholtz's notion of energy to study how affects transformed metabolic energy into thoughts and behavior. This interest encouraged Reich to transform himself into a self-taught chemist and physicist. He created a laboratory to isolate the mechanics and thermodynamics of vital energy. The difficulty for his colleagues came when Reich used these studies to show that the energetic dynamics described by Helmholtz and most other psychophysiologists all take root in a single form of vital energy. Reich's psychoanalysts friends, like Fenichel, related this watershed moment to a sudden delirium. But some of his other friends, trained in other intellectual movements, perceived this turn of events as a manifestation of his genius. Personally, I recognize the existence of these phenomena that I have often observed, but I am wary of those explanatory models that exist in spiritually or scientifically inspired schools, because they are extremely varied and hardly robust. The danger, from the point of view of body psychotherapy techniques, is to believe that these signs necessarily designate a potential healing, relaxation, and pleasure.

The Orgastic Reflex

THE EARTHWORM: THE ORGASM AS THE GLOBAL REACTION OF THE ORGANISM
Faithful to his sexological point of view, Reich attacked this new series of clinical research by identifying the status of the orgastic reaction in the organism. He had many good reasons to begin from there:

1. There are already many experiments in this domain.
2. According to Freud, the libido is the watershed plate of the vegetative dynamics and the bridge between the thoughts, behavior, and metabolism.
3. He can identify the vegetative dynamics around this theme in the individual and social functioning.

The sexual satisfaction appeases vegetative demands first and then the psychic ones. Consequently, it consists of finding a model of sexual behavior that satisfies the neurological and chemical exigencies of the vegetative system. Inspired by dance and Gindler's method, Reich tackled the orgasm as vegetative discharge that manifests itself by coordinating the movements and the breathing of two partners.[21] He tried to identify the coordination of the body segments during the orgasm, as well as the involuntary dimension that takes hold of the lovers during climax: something which sexologists briefly describe. Reich goes from the idea, close to that of the ethologists, that there must be an innate organization that is unleashed during coitus, and its core mechanisms are consequently universal. The shape of this spontaneous reaction therefore does not depend on what the mind imagines. The conscious mind can only follow or inhibit the orgasm. This is what Reich calls the *orgastic reflex.*

To describe an uninhibited orgastic reflex of a person stretched out on his or her back, Reich thinks of a movements of a snake or an earthworm, of a "fluid undulation which involves the whole body" (Reich, 1940, VIII.4, p. 227), going through the head, the neck, the chest, the belly, the pelvis, the legs, and the feet. This engages the heteroclite mechanism of the body in a movement that has a coherence that functions "as a whole." This apparently fluid movement is made up of a rhythmic, pulsating succession of expansion and contraction of each segment.

OPENING THE SPONTANEOUS EXHALATION
The blockage of a segment of the body impedes the propagation of the fluid movement of the earthworm. On each side of the blockage, two independent

fluid movements are created without any coordination between them. The case of an alcoholic, about which I speak later, shows what happens when the segment of the abdomen is blocked. Reich observed two spontaneous movements:

1. An upward movement that links the diaphragm to the head.
2. A downward movement that links the pelvis to the feet.

Each of these movements is activated independently and in a nonsynchronistic fashion. According to Reich,[22] the same thing happens when a thread is attached around one of the rings of the earthworm: on each side of the thread, a different movement is activated. In humans, a muscular block breaks up the global orgastic reflex and the sensations it generates.

The senses only perceive modifications, changes, variations of a stimulus. The individual cannot perceive the parts of his organism that have become static. To make it possible for an individual to perceive his armor requires not only the intervention of an external view but also that the individual introduce some modifications in what is frozen. One of Reich's strategies was to increase the tensions so that they become even more salient and their shape can be more easily grasped, not only by the patient's consciousness but also by that of the vegetotherapist.

Breathing is one of the principal links between armor and vegetative currents on which Reich works. He noticed that most of his patients have a partial and shallow breathing. They are often incapable of having an ongoing respiration, in a continuous fashion, from the throat to the lower abdomen in breathing out and from the abdomen to the throat in breathing in:[23]

1. There is either a thoracic mobility or an abdominal mobility.
2. The passage of the respiratory movement from one segment to another (for example, from the thorax to the abdomen) is disjointed.
3. The respiratory movement jumps over a segment (for example, the respiratory movement is perceivable only at the top of the thorax and at the bottom of the abdomen).
4. The movement mobilizes all of the segments at the front of the trunk, but not the muscles of the back.
5. There is no lateral respiration (the right and left flanks do not separate in breathing in).
6. There is a full respiration of the entire trunk, but a reduction in amplitude. This schema would be particularly frequent in psychotic and prepsychotic patients (especially what we today call borderline personality disorders).[24]

In the view of the segments of the body as proposed by Reich, a mobilization necessarily activates the entire segment (front/back, left/right). The lateral dimension (left/right) is often forgotten in practice because it is not so easy to perceive, but it has importance. For example, working on breathing in a lateral fashion often helps a patient experience a form of comfortable embodiment. These blocks impede inspiration and expiration, but it is the breathings out that Reich is most interested in. One of the reasons motivating this interest is its link to the orgastic reflex. Breathing out spontaneously rocks the pelvis in such a way as to move the genitals toward the front. This is particularly and easily evident when the patient is lying on his back, knees bent, feet flat on the floor. In this position expiration necessarily mobilizes the spinal column and therefore the muscular chains that connect the head to the feet. Reich tries to open up the respiration in ways that do not require voluntary respiration exercises.[25] This strategy tries, above all, to deactivate a too strong a connection between the super-ego and a spontaneous respiration.

To deepen exhalation without soliciting too much willfulness on the part of the patient, Reich placed his hand on the upper abdomen, between the navel and the sternum. He asked the patient to simply breathe. Using his hand to press on the abdomen, Reich accentuated the expiration movement of the abdomen. At first, he pressed gently; he progressively increased the pressure, which sometimes becomes important.[26] It was therefore his will, and not that of the patient, that modulated the behavior of the external respiration. Working in this manner, Reich noticed the type of interaction that establishes itself between the movement of his hand and the bodily reactions of the patient, on the one hand, and the emotional rapport that establishes itself between the patient and himself, on the other hand. He remarked that very few patients tolerate a pressure on their solar plexus. Some of them show a hint of a countermovement by arching the back.[27] Others appreciate this exercise that then opens up onto "wavelike contractions in the abdomen," which sometimes induce the "orgastic reflex" (Reich, 1940, VIII.4, p. 230).

Working in this way, Reich unleashed a kind of *facsimile of the orgastic reflex,* or "therapeutic orgastic reflex." The goal is to confirm whether the patient has the *bodily capacity* to move like an earthworm and if he has the *psychic capacity* to accept and integrate this kind of spontaneous reaction. There can then be a simultaneous pleasure in all of the dimensions of the organism. The automatic activation in therapy is a form of global reaction of the organism that is *especially* used in an orgasm. This reaction can also be unleashed by dancing or by trance techniques. I have already described this type of mobilization when I spoke of the kundalini yoga,[28] which relates the movements of the spinal column to a serpent that coordinate the body segments (the chakras). Reich thought that the complete orgastic reflex cannot come about other than between two sexual partners, because part of the reflex is an automatic reaction to the movements and the scent of the other.[29]

Ethically, it is important that the body psychotherapist be clear about the reasons for which he focuses on the therapeutic orgastic reflexes in his sessions and then analyze the way the patient includes this reaction in the context of a real relationship.

The Segmentation of the Character Armor

THE SEVEN SEGMENTS OF VEGETOTHERAPY

In following the metaphor of the earthworm, Reich divided the body into seven *segments*. This division is convenient to his work, for practical reasons. He also identified two *dimensions* when the individual is stretched out on his back:[30]

1. A *horizontal* dimension relates one segment to the neighboring ones (the thoracic segment relates to the neck, the arms, and the abdomen). The greater the number of relaxed adjacent segments, the longer the horizontal vegetative movement.
2. The dynamics of a segment are mostly *vertical*. The mobilization of a segment implies a volume of mechanisms, a body mass that would form a coherent subsystem of functions. Thus, the movement of the eyes mobilizes the muscles of the forehead, the temples, the base of the back of the cranium, and even the top of the nape of the neck. The ocular movements are also associated to the tear glands and the nervous system. They sometimes influence the organs of equilibrium situated in the ears. For the repression of the urge to cry, there is necessarily constriction of the lips, jaw, throat, and respiration.[31] To work on the ocular segment is therefore to work not only on the eyes but also on everything that is related in the upper area of the head.

For each segment Reich asked the patient to explore what is going on when he tries to move the tense muscles. Reich identified the following segments:[32]

1. The *ocular* segment goes from the eyes to the base in the back of the cranium passing through the top of the cranium. It included the ears and the top of the nose. A block of this segment can manifest with a blank stare and a frozen forehead, the impossibility of crying, chronically shrunken eyes, and vision problems (myopia and astigmatism). The work concerning this segment was especially deepened by Charles Kelley (1971), a student of Reich. He incorporated into the Reichian work, Bates's (1920) relaxation techniques of the eyes. Some researchers associate the blockage of the ocular segment to schizophrenia and autism, but Abraham relates it also to hysteria and to voyeurism,[33] and Shapiro associates it to types of dissociation caused by a traumatic experience.[34] Francine Shapiro (2001) developed methods close to those of Kelley and Bates, called EMDR (Eye Movement Desensitization and Reprocessing). Her approach is not directly inspired by Reich's work. The remarkable results of EMDR shows to what point stimulating the eyes can influence certain coordination between the nervous system, affects, and representations. In spite of the neurological research conducted on EMDR, the phenomenon remains unexplained, a fact that does not in any way deny

the robust nature of the psychotherapeutic results obtained by working with the ocular segment. These techniques can also be used to induce hypnotic states. With people who have an addiction to pornographic websites, exploring the eyes often leads to interesting and useful information and experiences.

2. The *oral* segment relates the chin, jaw, lips, and top of the nape of the neck. According to Reich, it allows for the repression of the urge to cry, bite, and suck. Paul Ekman shows that tightening the lips can also be related to joy, anger, and sadness.[35] Reich sometimes stimulates the vomiting reflex to provoke tearfulness. He only has recourse to this method after having opened the ocular segment.

3. The *cervical* segment is mostly associated to any form of respiratory, swallowing, or vocal discomfort that is situated in the throat. Muscular tensions or chronic illnesses in that part of the body are also of interest. For Reich, the structure of the muscles justify that the tongue is included in this segment. The vomiting reflex is also used to mobilize the connections between swallowing and the diaphragm.

4. The *thoracic* segment allows for the modulation of respiration. Reich relates the mobility of this region to the intercostal muscles, the large pectorals, the deltoids, and the subclavicles. In Reich's time, many individuals maintained a puffed-out chest to inhibit exhalation. This defense is less frequently used today.[36] It became important to work on this position and the mobility of the scapula (shoulder blade) in association with the stiffness of the nape of the neck and the position of the thorax. This segment is also the basis of the movements of the arms and hands, and consequently of the gestures like taking, giving, rejecting, and creating.

5. The *diaphragmatic* segment encompasses the diaphragm, the organs beneath the diaphragm, the epigastria, the inferior part of the sternum, and the line of the inferior ribs. Reich also mobilized the vomiting reflex to relax this zone. This segment is one of the most difficult to approach because the diaphragm is difficult to reach. Consequently, it is important to approach it lightly so as not to create tension in the tissues that are then difficult to attain by techniques such as massage. Mechanical modes of intervention, particularly in this zone, are not recommended. A way to approach these muscles is to encourage yawning, sighs, and stretching. This can be done especially by using movements that mobilize the connections between the large dorsal muscles and the diaphragm. For example, Thornquist and Bunkan[37] propose that patients lift their arms during inhalation and then to let the chest and the arms fall like a stone during expiration. The liberation of the diaphragm also requires particular knowledge about postural dynamics. A correct alignment of the position of the pelvis and the nape of the neck relaxes the diaphragm almost automatically. There are many methods, but the effective methods all have the same characteristic: they only solicit the diaphragm *indirectly*.

For example, in the exercise where we ask the patient to let his arms drop while exhaling, the therapist does not speak about the diaphragm, and the patient concentrates on the rapport between the arms and thoracic respiration.

6. The *abdominal* segment contains the vertical, horizontal, and transverse muscles of the lower back and the abdominal muscles that link the lower ribs to the pelvis. The horizontal and transverse muscles also mobilize the lower back. With these muscles (and others situated more deeply, like the psoas), the spontaneous movements of the upper and lower body are coordinated. The orgastic reflex globalizes itself, and an automatic colonic movement commandeers the muscles of the abdomen and the diaphragm. This segment also mobilizes the organs and physiological dynamics that participate in the functioning of digestion. This segment is relatively easy to access through massage and movement. It is therefore one of the segments on which Reich worked the most.

7. The *pelvic* segment. Reich includes the legs in this segment because the pelvis is the basis of the connection between the legs and the torso. Here, he follows the same logic that makes him include the arms in the thoracic segment. The habitual position of the pelvis—in the standing, sitting, and lying down position—permits the easy detection of the principal muscular tension if we know our anatomy. The different physiological manifestations that end up in this segment often prolong the dynamics of the abdominal segment. Physical therapists[38] know that the tensions of the inferior limbs and the pelvis have an impact on the entire mechanical, physiological and affective functioning. At the mechanical level, the pelvis plays a central role in the functioning of posture. A problem of the joints of the hips disturbs the functioning of the postural mechanics that is visible to anyone. It is the same for the menstrual problems that manifestly influence vegetative dynamics and, consequently, a woman's mood each month. The digestive problems that manifest at this level also play a preponderant role in the Freudian theory of the libido (anal and urethral stages). Reich observes some types of anxiety and anger that cannot be expressed except by movements of the pelvis. The anal manifestations of the affects are in part common to both sexes, while the genital expressions are necessarily different. Thus, the urge to pierce the other with the front of the pelvis or the fear of melting in the other is built differently for each sex. For example, this urge is manifest with some women who like to use a dildo with other women.

Reich and his colleagues developed a clinical knowledge on how the affects relate to different types of movements. With Reich, it consists mostly of clinical examples that do not imply a necessary link between a gesture and an affect, while with some of his students, the connection becomes more linear.

The basic therapeutic strategy is to begin with the ocular segment and descend gradually toward the lower body. This strategy, inspired by Character analysis, contends that the more the segment is situated toward the lower end of the body, the more it is related to genital sexuality, and the more it mobilizes a deep level of the being. By showing the links between ocular blocks and psychosis, Reich partially weakens this reasoning. Baker, Kelley, and Lowen showed that sometimes work on the eyes can also mobilize extremely deep levels in one's being. Fenichel[39] therefore had reason to think that the organism is not necessarily organized as Reich thought because the depth is sometimes already totally engaged by dealing with the eyes.

At first, the approach to the patient's vegetative dimension is done gently with open-ended questions (what do you feel when you concentrate on the movement of your eyes?). It consists mostly in helping the patient pedagogically understand a body–mind exploration of his vegetative dimension. In becoming more systematic, the therapist asks the patient to explore the three superior segments (eyes, jaw, and neck). As soon as the therapist notices that the thoracic segment becomes more enlivened, he proposes new exercises for the segments of the upper body that are now related more explicitly to respiration. These exercises then have as their goal to begin work on the way the segments are coordinated:

> Example I. *On the coordination of eyes-jaw-hands-thorax.* The therapist asks the patient to open the eyes and mouth as much as possible during inspiration and then totally let go. In this example, at least three segments are coordinated. We can also associate the opening of the eyes to the opening of the hands and feet.
>
> Example II. *Stimulation of the vomiting reflex.* The use of the vomiting reflex in Vegetotherapy and Bioenergetic analysis is also a good example of this strategy. Typically, the therapist asks the patient to explore what is going on when he makes himself vomit in a receptacle. At first, mostly the eyes are discussed. When this goes well, these relax and water.[40] Then everything that is related to the jaw, tongue, and swallowing comes up. Subsequently, the moment arrives when the patient feels the contractions of the gut and an automatic spasm that starts in the belly and mobilizes the diaphragm. In this exploration, respiration and the voice also play a role. This work can also activate diverse types of resistance, like disgust, the impression of being a filthy person, and so on.

A basic rule for the orthodox Reichians, in this comings-and-goings, is not to proceed downward until the patient achieves a spontaneous partial coordination of the movements of the upper segments. There are sometimes affects, linked to the eyes, that do not become constructively and therapeutically acces-

sible until the pelvis and legs relax. This is how, gradually, the repressed dynamics of a segment do not become clear until it is possible to understand the integration of a segment in the global organismic system.

THE ORAL ORGASM AND THE HEALING OF AN ALCOHOLIC

Having anchored his reflection in the vegetative dimension, Reich abandoned
every attempt to find connections between a muscular tension and a set of specific psychic issues. Let us take up the case of a patient who suffered from alcoholism. Reich describes a process that allows the unconscious to become
conscious again, but whose line of work is mostly vegetative. He goes from the
head and the tension of the mouth and then frees the movement of the "earthworm" by moving downward from segment to segment and opening the way
for a more complete coordination of the segments of the body. Reich observed a
particular orgastic movement in this patient because it seems to go from the
mouth and spread itself to the entire body. This is characteristic of what Reich
calls an *oral orgasm*.[41]

First vignette of Vegetotherapy with an alcoholic patient. *The more Reich extends
his analysis to all the segments of the upper body, the more the muscles of the
lower thorax and upper abdomen become as hard as a board. When these tensions
soften, "It looked as if some inner force were lifting the upper part of his body,
against his will, off the couch and were keeping it in that position" (Reich, 1940.
VIII.3, p. 218). This tension is then reinforced in the lower abdomen, pelvis, and
legs. The tension in the legs is experienced by the patient as "extremely pleasurable" (ibid., p. 218). Reich then set about analyzing the ways the patient expresses
his anger with his fists. The fist forms, rises, but never strikes the couch. Something
in the patient stops him from completing the gesture, even in a mechanical manner.
That is when he remembers events that occurred when he was five years old. He
was playing quietly at the edge of a sea cliff. His mother saw him and thought that
she absolutely had to get her son away from such a dangerous place. "She beckons
him to her with the kindest of words, promising to give him a candy. Then as he
went to her, she gave him a terrible beating" (ibid., p. 219). This memory allows
him to remember his mother's unpredictable tendencies to go from gentleness to
anger, at the time. He associates that with his ambivalence toward women. The
muscular tension of the upper body relaxes, but those of the belly strengthen. As
this tension gradually relaxes, his movements become increasingly coordinated.
The patient feels like a fish caught in a net from which he is trying to escape. Reich
then has the impression that his patient's basic defense, apparently so amicable, is
a suspicion, a fear, and a refusal to be caught. Gradually, the patient feels vegetative currents flowing through his body. He has the sensuous impression of melting.
The only ring that is now truly tense is the pelvis. Vegetative currents invade his
genitals. A global orgastic reflex takes hold of his organism. He now remembers
of a night, on the sea shore, when he looked at his mother while she was asleep.
The memories of tender contacts with his mother, when he was a little child, return to consciousness. He experiences profoundly pleasurable feelings without*

any distrust. Then more complex memories arise, during which he relives moments of conflict around his need to suckle. Reich was then able to quickly broach conflicts linked to the father.

The Vegetative Dynamics of the Body–Mind Coordination

The hormonal dynamics of the mechanism of the vegetative and affective regulation apply pressure on the dimensions of the organism to create an instinctive or emotional global mobilization. This pressure would be blocked or transformed in the vegetative system by the armor, even before it could insert itself into the unconscious. Consciousness would then receive (a) information about a deformed drive, and (b) an impression of anxiety that allows consciousness to know that the affective representations it receives do not correspond to the initial vegetative pressure. When the vegetative mobilization is totally blocked, consciousness only receives an impression of anxiety.

For Reich, an anxiety-ridden sexual experience would be caused by a partially repressed sexual arousal.[42] This anxiety can be caused by psychic mechanisms of repression like a conscious moral rule, or by a chronically inhibited vegetative system that has not developed a capacity to support comfortable sexual activity. For example the muscles and breathing patterns required during coitus may lack exercise, which implies that the required sensorimotor organization, cardiovascular dynamics, muscular strength, and flexibility of the joints may be insufficiently developed.

The muscular armor is built not only to inhibit the drives but also to reabsorb the sensation of anxiety it generates. In reducing respiration, the muscular tension reduces the supply of oxygen to the metabolic activity. This lowering of metabolic activity diminishes the quantity of energy available for a vegetative mobilization of the affects. The defect in this defense system against anxiety is that the smallest relaxation (like sleep, a good meal, or a concert) or an incidental pleasure that provokes a relaxation (like an orgasm) will lift the cover that represses the anxiety. This explanatory system of certain neurotic symptoms is, for the moment, conceived by Reich as complementary to Freud's theory. The armor can be more or less flexible according to each case. The greater the flexibility, the healthier the person. Some persons can relax in agreeable situations and reactivate the armor in distressing situations.

The notion that the armor represses global vegetative reactions of the organism comes from concrete observations of what is going on when chronic muscular tensions relax. The therapist and the patient are sometimes surprised to see an emotion or a sexual arousal[43] take over the whole organism. A person starts to have the urge to cry or yell in such a way that it mobilizes all the resources of the organism. As Ferenczi proposed, Reich researches moments of this type that make old repressed affects resurface and that are linked to a series of situations maintained in the unconscious. One phase of the therapy of Reich's alcoholic patient illustrates this phenomenon:

Second vignette of Vegetotherapy with an alcoholic patient. *This patient was seen almost daily for six and a half months. Reich first concentrates on his face, which appears empty, has glistening and tender skin, and even more particularly small and tight lips that move as little as possible. To understand what is repressed by the tightness of the lips, Reich asks the patient to mentally explore what is happening inside his lips and let the associations come up from within. After a while, the patient feels some small rhythmic movements take over his lips, like an automatic mechanism that is activated independently of the patient's volition. One day, these movements are accentuated and lead Reich to think of a crisis of repressed tears. But finally, these movements are associated to anger.[44] In the course of an exploration that lasted several weeks, the expression of anger is made clear. The mouth twists, the jaw juts out pronouncedly, the teeth grind. Reich decided to conclude "the experiment of destroying the defensive forces consistently from the muscular side, and not from the psychic side." The patient tightens his fists then falls back on the couch. The patient experiences the rise of an impotent rage within him, which he associates to what he felt when his older brother "used to bully and maltreat him badly when he was a child." (Reich, 1940, VIII.3, pp. 213–216)*

These body movements that animate themselves and lead to memories that emerge without requiring that the therapist propose an interpretation, are known to all who have used this kind of approach, at least since Ferenczi. Reich thus discovered the *imperative* and *imperialistic* force of certain drives through clinical observation, 25 years before neurologists like Olds observed this phenomenon using more rigorous experimental procedures. During the same period, ethologists were making similar observation in animals.[45]

At the beginning, Reich's character structures were an organization of internalized conflicts in the psyche that mobilized the body in a particular ways. Reich modified this model when he found a way to describe how these conflicts, experienced by an individual, also structured the organism. In the structuring process, the character structure influences all of the dimensions. It is therefore possible to begin the analysis of a character starting with the global feelings. Here are two examples of global conscious feelings linked to a character structure.

1. *The fear of exploding*, of losing control of what one feels is experienced by almost everyone who feels that their character structure is crumbling. This fear is also often related to an impression of intrusion. It is, according to Reich and his students,[46] particularly intense in masochistic personalities.

2. *The constriction.* At the end of his life, Reich speaks of anorgonia[47] to describe a state in which everything happens as if there were a narrowing, a shrinkage, a strangulation, a cramp, a contraction, a tightening, pangs of anguish, tension, even a retraction of life and fluids from all levels of the organism. Neo-Reichian therapists, like Clover Southwell

(1980), use the term *constriction* to designate such a shrinkage of the organism that the individual has the impression that a vampire has sucked all of his energy. Reich relates this notion to that of life strangling itself at the vegetative level, like in the case of patients who suffer from cancer or schizophrenia.[48] The term has since been taken up by Austrian psychiatrist Erwin Ringel (1976) to identify a presuicidal syndrome in which a person has the impression that all doors are closing and the field of possibilities is narrowing: no more possibilities of work, no more possibilities of future romance, no more available friends, and a loss of internal resources. This impression of the constriction of life's field would lead these individuals to get closer to the only door that forever remains open: death.[49]

Around 1945, Reich distanced himself from his hypothesis on the antithetical relationship between body and mind to take up an organismic model that resembles evermore to the notion of functional identity between body and mind. These two dimensions are always distinct, but they are organized by the "orgone" in such a way that a feeling, at the psychological level, corresponds to a mode of functioning at the level of the physiological support of the affects.[50] This is particularly clear in his chapter on sexuality and anxiety,[51] in which he assumes that anxiety and pleasure are exactly opposites not only on the feeling and doing level but also at the level of the dynamics of the fluids and the electrical activity. The contraction associated with an anxiety attack would be observable in all dimensions of the organism, as if there were no more real difference in the proper functioning of each dimension.

A Typical Vegetotherapy Session

We have seen that in Freud's theory of the cathexis of drives, a drive can be invested, underinvested, or overinvested. In the context of the psychoanalytic technique, it mostly consists of the psychological sensation of an affect (anger, sadness, need, etc.) and its object (the mother, the brother, one's children, a colleague, etc.) when a drive has a secondary structure.[52] Reich takes up this model to analyze the vegetative dynamics. A partial drive builds itself from the vegetative dynamic structures, which are overinvested or underinvested:

1. *Overinvested* physiological mechanisms: Strong muscular tensions, rapid respiration, very warm skin, red skin and greasy hair, sweat, constant useless movements, expressions that are more intense than is appropriate, loud voice, recurring thoughts, and so on.
2. *Underinvested* physiological mechanisms are characterized by the impression that there is a withdrawal of vitality: weak muscles, poor respiration, cold skin, pale skin, dry skin and hair, persistent functionless immobility, lack of expression, weak voice, penury of thoughts, and so on.

A typical session therefore begins with an inspection of the distribution of the energetic charge in the patient's organism and the impact of this charge on the organism of the therapist. Then, if the patient is not already in an extreme state of overinvestment or underinvestment, the Vegetotherapy of the 1930s increases the charge of the patient's organism by having him move (for example, hitting the mattress with hands and feet) and by mobilizing deep breathing. Once the vegetative charge of the organism has become more intense, the therapist looks for what this increase has provokes as a counter-reaction: which parts of the organism react by becoming overinvested and which react by becoming under-invested. Having detected these reactions, the therapist concentrates on those that are nearest to the cranium, while avoiding making requests that would awaken thoughts and affects the patient is not able to integrate. For example, if the fists are extended with a furious urge to hit, but the patient does not have an image of the person whom he has the urge to hit, the therapist can change to a more verbal style of exploration, seeking to discover who might be the object of that anger, or focus on another part of the organism.

The goals sought by this session are twofold:

1. To have repressed memories and feelings return to the surface in its entirety. That implies that a repressed affect finally take its place in the dynamics of the organism and coordinates the dimensions of the organism in such a way as to be able to express itself fully and completely. The physiological and psychological mobilization is complete.
2. To thus permit a restoration of the organism's mechanisms of auto-regulation: metabolic and physiological auto-regulation on one hand, but affective on the other. The organism learns, by these sessions, to dare to live its emotions in the face of others and of oneself.

Reich Picks the Wrong Enemy: What Fenichel Would Have Liked to Discuss with Reich with Regard to the Body and Psychotherapeutic Technique

> Fenichel never wanted to commit himself unequivocally to my scientific platform. He did not want to be just one of the "Reich group" (Reich, 1994, *Beyond Psychology*, p. 11). Yesterday, Fenichel presented his "criticism" of my technique and everybody was against him, including most of his own analysands (Nic Hoel, Raknes). Did you know he's leaving Oslo? Things have been hard for him lately because the superiority of character analysis had become obvious to all. He's going to Prague. Unfortunately, he believes that this will solve his problems. The whole Norwegian group has sided with me, except for some who doesn't know what it is all about, and two people who are honestly trying but are structurally incapable. (Reich, 1994, *Beyond Psychology*, p. 41)

Reich finally admitted that Fenichel was a loyal friend who was against his expulsion from the International Association of Psychoanalysis.[53] But he could not

stand that Fenichel attempted to defend him against everyone without understanding what was at stake in his endeavor and that he permitted himself to
criticize certain aspects of his work.[54] For Reich, Fenichel became the kind of
friend one prefers to have as an enemy. Fenichel could not accept that Reich had
left psychotherapy to the psychoanalysts and was now passionately involved in
something that was an unknown territory on the continent of therapies. Fenichel
thought he was honoring Reich by guaranteeing his ability as a psychoanalyst,
but he did not want to recognize that Reich's genius went beyond psychology
by following a road that led to regions in which psychoanalysis is part of a distant horizon left far behind.

In Copenhagen in 1933, Reich discussed his theories concerning the vital
energy with Otto Fenichel and Edith Gyömröi. In listening to Reich speak,
Fenichel was worried about Reich's mental health. As if he were following the
logic of denial, Reich asked them if they took him for a schizophrenic about to
become delusional. Annie Reich was also talking about a growing delusional
condition, without necessarily invoking a diagnosis as defined as the one evoked
by Reich himself.[55] Reich transformed the sincere concern of his friends for his
mental health into a persecutory theme. In somewhat of a perverse fashion, he
set about clamoring everywhere that his old psychoanalytic colleagues wanted
to pass him off as a psychotic to eliminate a dissident. It was as if he wanted to
have his psychoanalytic friends seen as a kind of Gestapo, which they certainly
were not. The Reichian legend of the great evil Fenichel who crushed Reich, the
great victim, is false, as evident by the position taken by Lore Reich-Rubin, the
daughter of Wilhelm and Annie Reich, with regard to this conflict.[56]

In 1935, Fenichel summarized his thoughts at the occasion of his discussions with Reich in Oslo in an article titled: "Concerning the Theory of Psychoanalytic Technique." Fenichel wanted to make his respect for Reich public by
engaging in a discussion with him relative to the last propositions of his friend
and colleague. He showed, among other things, that in his estimation, Reich
remained an important personality of the psychoanalytic movement, even if he
had been knocked around by the gloomy events that rocked psychoanalysis
since the election of Hitler. Fenichel thought Reich might be able to rejoin the
Norwegian Association of Psychoanalysts, and thus rejoin the International
Psychoanalytic Association. This was a realistic possibility that Fenichel and his
colleagues wanted to support. The article highlights that Reich had a deep understanding of the work of Freud and that he was, at that time, one of the great
specialists of the psychoanalytic technique, especially with regard to the analysis of the defenses and resistance. Therefore, Fenichel declared publically that
Reich's exclusion has taken nothing away from his competence.

Fenichel distinguished two aspects in Reich's theory:

1. A *general theory* with which he is in agreement. This theory describes
   the way the body and the psyche are mobilized by the construction of
   the defense system that builds an individual's *character*. This theory es-

pecially encourages psychoanalysts to discover new way of working that
develop, in original ways, the propositions of Freud and Ferenczi.

2. Some technical recommendations and particular ways to proceed with
which Fenichel is sometimes in disagreement. Fenichel clarifies that it
consists of criticisms on some details.

Even if this critique contains many interesting points, it is addressed to a Reich
who would be attempting to create a new form of psychoanalysis. It does not
include in the discussion the new direction that Reich's research took. This is
probably the reason this discussion is more interesting for the body psychotherapists of today than for the vegetotherapists of that time. Fenichel concentrated on the questions of techniques used with patients.

For Otto Fenichel, to make the unconscious conscious and explore the resonance of the therapist's unconscious with that of the patient characterizes the
intimate dimension of the psychoanalyst's task. However, this goal is only at-
tainable when it is related to a solid technique that aims above all at the dynamic of the libido and its channeling by the defense system. This second aspect
of the psychoanalytic technique is what Reich would have brilliantly developed
in his Character analysis. Fenichel shows that in dissolving a defense, the therapist can always count on an alliance of the repressed drive, because the repressed drive tries unceasingly to manifest itself. The strategy of beginning with
the more superficial layers of the character is essential if we want to avoid a
flooding that consciousness is incapable of managing without *reinforcing* the
present defense system at the start of therapy. If Character analysis is poorly
managed, it can transform psychotherapy into a retraumatization that will add
new defenses to the old ones or, worse still, replace the old defenses with more
powerfully disrupting ones.[57] He also adhered to the idea that the analysis of
behavior and body blocks (muscular tension and chronic respiratory problems)
does help an affective layer to emerge into the consciousness of the patient and
the therapist, and to ensure that this consciousness contains a maximum of affective and cognitive elements. The idea that loosening up the mind and body
fosters a general softening of the patient's rigid character traits is therefore, for
Fenichel, an important and useful formulation. In broad strokes, these are the
elements of the Reichian proposition that Fenichel retained. His analysis is always useful reading for all those who are influenced by Character analysis.

Fenichel joins those who think that with his Vegetotherapy, Reich approaches the defense system too directly and rigidly. Fenichel detailed his critique by distinguishing the following points:

1. He recalls Freud's phrase, according to which "The patient determines
the theme of the session." According to Fenichel, what Reich brought to
the psychoanalytic technique is the conviction that the patient does not
always know what he needs to experience in a session. The patient may
be conscious of an emotion (sadness) while evidently another (rage) mo-

bilizes the regulatory systems of the organism. This is because the mind is composed of strata of which only the uppermost can become conscious. Certain reactions are expressed muscularly in a manifest fashion for everyone (therefore for the therapist) without being able to be felt consciously by the patient.

2. The authority that Reich often presents in front of a patient is based on the Character analysis, which proposes to approach the defenses in a determined order. For Fenichel, the organization of secondary drives is fuzzier than what Reich imagines.[58] This implies an approach to the defenses that requires a finer touch than what Reich teaches.

3. Fenichel would also like a more imaginative approach toward habitual behavior. Some habits are not only defenses or resistances but also competencies. By showing the connections that certain forms of bodily and behavioral rigidity could have with the defense system, Reich enlightened many colleagues and advanced the psychoanalytic technique. Now that this point is made, it becomes useful to integrate a bit more of the complexity and to admit that many habits are, above all, ways to act that allow an organism to function better. The psychotherapist should approach the habits with more options than what Reich proposes by questioning how they came to be, learning about their function and about their meaning.[59]

4. Consistent with the foregoing, Fenichel criticized the excessively direct manner with which Reich attacked the muscular armor of his patients. The risk is that the patient will strengthen his armor or that it will disintegrate. I have often noticed that Character analysis, used in a persistent fashion, is difficult to digest for the patient's narcissism.[60] Fenichel clearly stated that he was not afraid of the profound emotional discharges that Reich unleashed one after the other, and that some of them can be useful. Once again, Reich enlarged the psychoanalyst's palette of interventions; it is now important to learn how to master this new tool. Fenichel mentioned, as one of the dangers, the case of patients who unconsciously use their vegetotherapists to retraumatize themselves, or therapists who use their patients to relive their own problematic relationship with trauma.

In one of his letters (quoted at the beginning of this section), Reich declared that the psychotherapists in Oslo had unanimously found him more interesting than Fenichel. However, Fenichel's criticism was taken up in Oslo, especially by Trygve Braatøy. This heritage circulated in the schools of body psychotherapy like Biodynamic psychology, Psycho-Organic analysis, the Bodynamic school and Somatic experiencing.[61] These do not always know that what they inherited from Braatøy and Bülow-Hansen[62] had first of all been formulated by Fenichel, whom they generally have not read. Thus, when Gerda Boyesen fervently asks that psychotherapists and their patients learn "to make friends with their defenses,"[63] she is developing—without knowing it—a theme inherited from Fenichel. We discover this relationship when she criticizes the rigidity of Reich's model of the segments: something she finds too "compulsive," and which, according to her, illustrates the rigidity of masculine thought.[64]

The Fenichels left Oslo to rejoin Annie Reich in Prague in 1935 to help their friend Edith Jacobson, who had been imprisoned for two years by the Germans. The decision not to return to Oslo was probably also a way to avoid being confronted by Reich's hateful outbursts of anger. Obsessed by the necessity to make himself known, Reich did nothing to help his amicable colleague from Berlin. In Prague, with his colleagues, Fenichel was able to maintain the circle of Marxist psychoanalysts up until his departure in 1938 for Los Angeles. This group remained in contact in spite of the anti-marxist stance that developed in America.

That said, Otto Fenichel's 1935 article is double-edged, because the second half is a direct critique of a psychoanalyst who is a member of "Reich's group," called Helmuth Kaiser.[65] Later on, as we will see, Fenichel dares to write that certain aspects of Reich's technique can be dangerous and that these aspects are not always minor.

18

Psychosomatics and Orgonomy

The body, that complicated machine, carries out the most complex and refined motor activities under the influence of such psychological phenomena as ideas and wishes. The most specifically human of all bodily functions, speech, is nothing but the expression of ideas through a refined musical instrument, the vocal apparatus. All our emotions we express through physiological processes; sorrow, by weeping; amusement, by laughter; and shame, by blushing. All emotions are accompanied by physiological changes: fear by palpitation of the heart; anger by increased heart activity, elevation of blood pressure and changes in carbohydrate metabolism; despair by a deep inspiration and expiration called sighing. All these physiological phenomena are the results of complex muscular interaction under the influence of nervous impulses, carried to the expressive muscles of the face and to the diaphragm in laughter, to the lacrimal glands in weeping, to the heart in fear, and to the adrenal glands and to the vascular system in rage. The nervous impulses arise in certain emotional situations which in turn originate from our interaction with other people. The originating psychological situations can only be understood . . . as total responses of the organism to its environment. (Franz Alexander, 1950, *Psychosomatic Medicine*, pp. 38–39)

Vienna was invaded by the Nazis in 1938. The totalitarian fascists and communists dominated almost all of Europe. Obliged to leave Europe (only England and Switzerland were still able to resist), the first psychoanalysts were dispersed across other continents. Most of the members of the Berlin institute immigrated to the United States. This country was so immense that they lived relatively far from one another. They only saw each other at the occasion of reunions and at congresses, which changed their relationships as friends to mostly that of colleagues. The competition between them became more evident. The spread of the movement increased after Freud's death in 1939. Everyone was free to define what Freud would have thought or what psychoanalysis ought to become. Several members of the Berlin group continued to reflect on the connection between mental treatment, somatic treatment, and treatment via the body. In spite of the differences on the plane of psychoanalytic theory that was crystallizing, the interest in the body remained as a link from the past, as a memory of friendship and camaraderie.

Thus, Franz Alexander (in Chicago) and Sándor Radó (in New York)[1] tried to integrate the works of Walter Cannon[2] to be able to propose a psychosomatics of psychoanalytic inspiration.[3] Otto Fenichel established himself in Los Angeles in 1938. He reconnected with colleagues like Ernst Simmel and Hanna Heilborn, whom he eventually married.[4] Fenichel (1945a, 1945b) vaguely felt that Alexander's psychosomatics was not going in the right direction because he was remaining too loyal to the classical psychoanalytic view of a psyche that influenced physiology while symbolizing it. Alexander and Radó seemed to underestimate the impact of physiology on the psyche.[5] Fenichel felt that psychoanalysis could and ought to maintain its rigor, but it also ought to integrate the innovations of psychophysiology and the body-focused approaches.

Alexander's and Radó's formulations were, for Reich, pale copies of his theory, which they would have imported from Berlin. Erich Fromm maintained his contact with some of Elsa Gindler's students, such as Charlotte Selver and Clare Fenichel. Laura and Fritz Perls, who were in South Africa during the war, first reunited with Selver in New York and then in California to create what became Gestalt therapy and the mix of psychotherapeutic and body approaches that characterized the activities of the center they established in Esalen. In all of these movements, the body is often solicited while remaining only a chapter in the repertoire of techniques in psychotherapy.

For Otto Fenichel, the following issues were crucial for the survival of psychoanalysis:

1. *Help psychoanalysis survive after the death of Freud.* This consisted of preserving a vision, a technique, and a mode of inquiry. Fenichel's contribution was to have rendered as explicit as possible the principles of psychoanalytic technique.
2. *The market of patients traumatized by war.* We have seen that this therapeutic business opened up on a grand scale at the occasion of World War I. Thanks to this impetus, psychoanalysis took hold of numerous psychiatric institutions. World War II restored importance to this market, which developed still more with the wars undertaken by the United States in the Far-East and in the some Arab nations.

There are two powerful forces behind this second field of interest. The most important is that medicine intends to treat all the ills on the planet. Second, but nonetheless influential, is the idea set forth by Freud that trauma could and ought to be treated by psychoanalysts. Already at the time of World War II, a ferocious competition existed between two camps.

Cannon's psychophysiological position was on the way to making spectacular advances. This was especially due to the works of another Viennese: Hans Selye.[6] The psychophysiological theory of stress was in the process of being formulated. It postulates a profound interaction between behavior and mind that is regulated by neurological circuits and hormones. To the extent that, for Selye, the pertinent mental factors are mostly cognitive, this approach forges an alliance with the cognitive therapies[7] to manage the mental factors of stress.

This trend was followed closely by the introduction of medications that have an effect on the mind as early as 1951 by Henri Laborit and his colleagues.[8]

Given the importance taken on by this trend, Fenichel was not surprised to see all of these psychoanalysts congregated around Cannon's theory like bees around a jar of honey. Fenichel clearly saw that they did not understand what was at stake and they did not really grasp the implications of the psychophysiological approach of the time for psychoanalysis. Reich did not take a position in this competition. His options were not compatible in an institutional enterprise.

FENICHEL'S LAST FORMULATIONS ON THE COORDINATION OF MIND, AFFECTS, PHYSIOLOGY, AND BODY (1939–1946)

Any misuse of an organ is psychogenic too. (Fenichel, 1945a, XIII, p. 236)

In Los Angeles, Otto Fenichel began to write a short book, *Problems of Psychoanalytic Technique,* based on the last courses he had given in Vienna. In this work, which appeared in 1941, he attempted to summarize the essence of the technical questions that preoccupied the clinical psychoanalysts of the 1930s in Europe. It consisted in keeping alive a heritage from Freud in a rapidly changing world.

In this book (chapter VII, p. 122f), Fenichel becomes openly critical of the approach developed by Reich in Oslo and then in the United States. His criticism focuses on Reich's psychotherapeutic techniques. Fenichel again praises the Character analysis and continues to find it useful to approach the mind as one of the cogwheels of the organism. But he finds that in his interventions, Reich approaches the defense system as if it were an illness, whereas for Fenichel, it is somewhat an equivalent of the immune system. According to him, Reich's approach is centered on trauma in a simplistic manner. He encourages his patients to experience, from the start of a process, profound and retraumatizing "theatrical" emotional discharges. Fenichel also points out to his colleagues that Reich has "entirely distanced himself from psychoanalysis" (Fenichel, 1941, p. 122; translated by Marcel Duclos). In short, Fenichel finally dares to express that he disagrees with Reich's recent options and chooses his camp. In Oslo, Fenichel represented an all-powerful psychoanalysis, directed personally by Freud, in the face of a disgraced Reich. Now, the future of psychoanalysis seems more uncertain. The future stakes are too important for Fenichel to lose his remaining energy in a battle with someone who despises everyone. Fenichel quotes Reich to the end of his life, but only what Reich wrote before 1936.[9]

We have seen that Fenichel was also very critical, for other reasons, of the psychosomatics proposed by Alexander and Radó. He felt the need to synthesize his thinking on the relationship between mind, organism, physiology, behavior, and body. He revisited his discussions with Elsa Gindler, Clare Fenichel, Wilhelm Reich, and Trygve Braatøy; and he also took up in a more systematic way the more physiological approaches on the dynamics of the organism, like those of Kurt Goldstein and those of Walter B. Cannon.[10] He published, in 1945, this synthesis in chapter XIII of *The Psychoanalytic Theory of Neurosis*, which was his testament.

A Multiple Parallelism

Fenichel's position is that of a flexible parallelism, like that of Laborit. It differentiates each of the dimensions of the organism: thoughts, drives, physiology, behavior, and body. Each dimension is a distinct causal network. When you throw a stone into the water, ripples form around the stone's point of entry. The same thing happens when a dream generates a fear that creates muscular tension, and a constricted respiration. This respiratory reaction spontaneously activates a physiological causal chain that may have nothing to do with the fear. The lack of oxygen will automatically influence the quality of the blood, the tissues, the metabolic activity, and so on. The same thing happens when a stomach ache is caused by a piece of spoiled meat that creates a pain that activates a dream. This dream inserts itself into a network of mental associations that was already in place before the food was swallowed.

I would take, as an example, the well-known link between anxiety or aggression and stomach ulcers.[11] Anxiety can activate a physiological activity that causes a stomach ulcer. This ulcer will pour stomach acids on the surrounding tissues. Some tissue damage will remain and can last even if a psychoanalytic treatment allows for the reduction of this anxiety. On the other hand, the suffering caused by an ulcer of physiological origin can resonate with unconscious mental content and can activate terrors repressed long ago. These terrors can, in certain cases, continue to develop in the psyche after the ulcer has been treated with medication or a surgical intervention. Even if a psychoanalytic treatment reduces and transforms the initial anxiety, the stomach will continue to attack the tissues in its immediate environment for as long as it is not healed. Fenichel's core argument is that the anxiety may have been activated by the psychological defense system, but not with the intention of causing an ulcer. The ulcer is sometimes an unexpected consequence of the anxious reaction. In other words, psychological defense mechanisms depend on a local causal chain, which cannot integrate all the implications of the strategy that emerged in the psyche.

We will see, a little later on, that in Oslo, psychoanalyst and psychiatrist Trygve Braatøy, one of Fenichel's students, undertook psychoanalytic treatments in collaboration with a physical therapist, Aadel Bulow-Hansen.[12] The same patient could be in psychoanalysis with Braatøy and in a massage therapy that addressed his muscular armor. In this case, body and psyche both received an in-depth treatment in parallel. What remains unclear in this endeavor is the connection between these two dimensions. There are explored on two levels:

1. At the level of the relationship between the psychotherapist and physical therapist, who work as a team.
2. At a more mysterious level that is activated at the core of the patient's organism by this collaboration.

Fenichel and Braatøy know that the interactions between psyche and body are still poorly understood but that they regulate themselves without the help of consciousness. They content themselves with observing with as much accuracy as possible how the various systems of the organism react to what has been elaborated in psychotherapy and how the psyche integrates what has been activated in a massage session.

Integration of the Physiological Dynamics in Psychotherapy

> The modern term "psychosomatic" disturbance has the disadvantage of suggesting a dualism that does not exist. Every disease is "psychosomatic." (Fenichel, 1945a, *The Psychoanalytic Theory of Neurosis*, p. 237)

One of Fenichel's key ideas is that the organism calibrates itself in function of what it does.[13] In other words, the mind can interact with physiological and behavioral dynamics,[14] and behavior can influence physiological and psychological dynamics. By regularly moving in a particular manner, I influence the development of my body, physiology, mind, and relationships with others. The dimensions of the organism mutually influence each other by passing through internal pathways (situated in the organism) and external pathways (passing through the social rituals and relationships with others). This coordination between dimensions can be initiated by any dimension. Being obliged to sit in an uncomfortable chair, an employee can create a series of disagreeable implications at the level of the body, physiology, the emotions, thoughts, and so on. As some habitual behaviors can be acquired without having a conscious process to integrate them, they "may influence organic functions in a physiological way, even if these changes have no psychic 'meaning'" (Fenichel, 1945a, p. 256). In other words, every habitual event of the organism necessarily influences all of the dimensions of the organism to a certain degree, as well as their way of coordinating each other; but these changes are not necessarily functionally related. *Each dimension is animated by a particular set of causal chains.*

For the purpose of situating the interventions on the interfaces that link psyche and soma, Fenichel differentiates the classic conversion neuroses (the psyche influences the physiology) and the neuroses of the organs in the following fashion:

1. The *conversion neurosis* is the one that Freud observes in his hysterical patients. It "is an expression of a fantasy in a 'body language' and is di-

rectly accessible to psychoanalysis in the same way as a dream" (Fenichel, 1945a, p. 236). Here, we are close to the notion that there would be some relatively direct links between thoughts and some physiological mechanisms.

2. *Organ neurosis* "is physical in nature and consists of physiological changes caused by the inappropriate use of the function in question" (Fenichel, 1945a, p. 236). The idea is that a repetitive way of moving necessarily has physiological as well as psychological implications. A way of moving influences the development of the physiological coordination by following rules that are proper to each implicated system (mechanical, toxic, and physical causes). These inappropriate but repeated ways of acting influence "a large field of functional and even anatomical alterations" (ibid., p. 236). He specifies that the multiple impacts these phenomena can have on the psyche are not of the same nature as the influence of what is repressed in the unconscious.[15] Here, we are close to the notion that mostly indirect and multiple links coordinate the dimensions of the organism.

The following are a few points developed in Fenichel's chapter that are still relevant:

1. *Affect equivalents*: For Fenichel, an affect is an automatic behavior that often constructs itself outside of the mental and behavioral fields. To express itself, this affect must recruit the support of conscious mental apparatus or automatic behaviors accessible to consciousness. When certain affects are repressed, when consciousness panics at the sight of them, an affect can express itself by a substitute affect or sensation. Thus, an urge to cry can transform itself into an urge to scream or into a breathing difficulty. Having become habitual, this defective coordination of the dimensions of the organism can induce organic, mental, and behavioral dysfunctions. These shifts of terrain are not only used to repress sexuality, creativity, and the spirit of independence but also to reabsorb the anxiety the repression generates. The muscular spasms of the skeletal muscles are one of the physical signs of anxiety. Sometimes "they may appear as an anxiety equivalent" (ibid., p. 247). The reabsorption of anxiety seems to depend in a particular important fashion on the possibilities that the mechanisms of respiratory inhibition offer (ibid., p. 250).

2. An *instinct* is a propensity that builds itself starting from the hormonal dynamics, and gradually recruits the help of the mind and behavior to be able to become manifest and attain satisfaction. When the unconscious inhibitions stop the *formation* of this integration of the dimensions of the organism, each dimension is also disorganized in a more localized way. There is then not only a malformation of the appropriateness between perception and bodily event but also a gradual organic dysfunc-

tion. These problems can influence the biochemical bases of the dynamics (hormonal and metabolic) that stimulate the instincts. The hormonal dynamics influence the instinctive dynamics, but they also have other independent impacts on the organism. Their functioning can reach some organic functions that may have no connection to the drives, like the quality of the tissues.[16] The trap into which too many psychotherapists fall, is to think that all the heterogeneous events are linked by a coherent organismic goal.

3. The inhibition of motor and mental manifestations activated by hormonal pressure that accompanies a drive, in some cases, leads to periodic emotional outbursts. The mechanism imagined by Fenichel is quite refined. In repressing an emotion, I place myself in situations that render a violent explosion of this inevitable affect: "Everybody knows what a latent rage or a latent anxiety is: a state in which neither rage nor anxiety is felt but where there is a readiness to react with exaggerated rage or exaggerated anxiety to stimuli that would normally provoke a slight anger or a slight anxiety" (ibid., p. 238). However there is no direct link between the situations, the unconscious aim of this anger and what is expressed. This outburst has at least managed to let some of the accumulated steam out of the system for a while.

4. Fenichel also confirms his idea that repression by the body and by the mind follow different paths, because they are ruled by mechanisms that have almost nothing in common. Thus, the use of muscles to repress an affect activates different procedures than those that are used to repress conscious representations of this affect.

5. Fenichel discusses the relations between the psyche and the following physiological phenomena: metabolic activity, hormonal and vegetative regulation, digestive system, muscular tonus (hyper- and hypo-tonic), respiration, heart and the cardiovascular system, skin, and eyes.

Even though this view is close to the one adopted by most of the current schools in body psychotherapy, none make reference to these writings. Everything is carried out as if this analysis had never been heard. It is possible that this view of the rapport between body and mind was orally transmitted to Fenichel's students, who took it up as their own, in Oslo as well as in California.

For example, we find in Fenichel's chapter a critique of the notion of the Reichian emotional discharge that is close to recent critiques of neo-Reichian approaches.[17] A good example is that of Fenichel's idea that a psychoanalysis tries, before anything else, to reactivate all of the repressed experiences. This was also one of Reich's war horses in his Character analysis. According to Fenichel, to content oneself by expressing emotions that are not closely related to repressed situations is to permit these expressions to reinforce the defense system. A patient, tears in his eyes, rage in his fists, tells you a true story that moves him today. Sometimes, the poignant intensity of the account resides in the fact that the emotions draw their strength from other situations that are not yet perceived consciously by the patient. The memory that arises is the first of a whole series of layers of memories quite different from one other. When the therapist becomes hypnotized by this first reminiscence, he may find himself trapped, as if at the foot of a tree that hides his view of the forest. By capturing the attention of the patient and the therapist, this memory, full of touching emotions that evoke empathy from the therapist, plays the same role as that of a manifest dream. It is but a small part of the experience that the patient needs to reexperience to understand and restructure himself. By deeply exploring this memory and its associations, therapy risks reinforcing what separates this memory from the latent experiences that are unconsciously associated to it. The therapist who believes that theatrical emotional expression of dramatic and moving events allows him to understand his patient's deeper feelings is a bit like Christopher Columbus who believed he had reached India when he arrived at the Balearic Islands. He takes a huge step in the right direction, but he will not necessarily succeed in forming a clear vision of what is growing in the patient's unconscious. As you well know, the question is not even that the Balearic Islands are not India, but that, between the two, there was a new continent.

At the death of Fenichel, Reich wrote this in his notes:

20 February, 1946
I found out that Otto Fenichel died of a heart attack three weeks ago.

That man died of his structural cowardice, I cannot judge whether my publication of his misdeed which appeared in April 1945 gave him a push. In his book he plagiarized everything from me and since he was aware of this it must have been a terrible ordeal for him. (Reich, 1999)

FROM NEW YORK TO MAINE (1939–1957): REICH DISCOVERS ORGONE

Hope Is for Tomorrow, When a True Democracy Will Become Possible

There is no way of basically changing people once they have developed the wrong character structure. You cannot make a crooked tree straight again. Therefore lets concentrate on the newborn ones, and lets divert human attention from evil politics towards the child. (Reich to Neill, October 8, 1951)

Reich departed from Oslo on August 20, 1939, for New York. There he was welcomed by colleagues like Theodore P. Wolfe, who translated many of Reich's works into English. He did not seem to have any contact with his old psychoanalytical companions from Berlin, because he now represented a theory that could undermine the foundations of their approach.

Reich's theory was now resolutely "vitalistic." In 1940, he had acquired[18] enough money to be able to isolate himself in the wilds of Maine not far from the Canadian border, on a property he named "Orgonon."[19] There, he pursued his experimental research on the way that cosmic energy, which he called orgone,[20] animates every cell and the global regulators of the organism. This notion is a sort of synthesis between (a) the force of nature described by Spinoza, (b) the vitalism of Jung,[21] and (c) Freud's libido. Reich attempted to analyze this cosmic force scientifically and propose a medical approach based on his observations.[22]

His Vegetotherapy thus becomes Orgone therapy. The principal difference, on the plane of mind–body techniques, is that Reich was less interested in the movements that go from head to foot during an orgasm and focused his attention on the regular pulsations of the organism, which contract and expand unceasingly like a great heart or lungs. To work on a thought or a tense muscle is part of a panoply of methods that make it possible to influence the quality of the pulsation of an organism and its capacity to auto-regulate. During this period he intensifies his research on machinery capable of mastering the dynamics of the orgone like the orgone accumulator.

As early as 1930, the politics in Europe were so disastrous that by contrast, the United States was gradually perceived as a possible haven of peace. When Reich and Fenichel arrived in the United States, they tried to believe that they were landing in what could become a robust democracy. Fenichel, happily for him, died at a time when it was possible to think that he was living among those who defended freedom in the world. Reich quickly discovered that the United States was only a bit better than the Soviet Union. After the euphoria following the victory against Germany, Italy, and Japan, he became increasingly pessimistic about the democratic potential of the United States. At first, there had been the interminable discussion by the armed forces on the use of the atomic bomb. The racial discrimination against blacks was everywhere. And then there was the persecution of the communists. For example, Charlie Chaplin was persecuted as early as 1947 for being a communist sympathizer; he went into exile in Switzerland in 1952. Paradoxically, Western Europe was becoming more democratic than the United States, thanks to the Marshall Plan.

Little by little, the United States developed a "social cancer," the third that Reich had witnessed in his life, called McCarthyism, which lasted from 1950 to around 1956. This movement was certainly less terrible than Stalinism and Nazism, but Reich was surprised to encounter it in the country that exemplified democracy. This time, he was crushed, morally at first, but mostly by being imprisoned where he died. After the advent of Stalinism in the country of the Marxist hope and McCarthyism in the country of democratic hope, Reich definitely lost confidence in the humanity of his day. A good example of the way McCarthyism destroyed individuals like Reich is the film *Lenny*, directed by Bob Fosse with Dustin Hoffman in the lead role.

At first, Reich hoped that once people would lose their armor and the secondary layer of hate that is imbedded in constricted tissues, their Orgonomic core would regulate their organisms and the way they interact with others and with nature. Doubt crept in when he and Neil had children they could raise in homes that promote self-regulation. At first the two fathers thought that in such a supportive context, both children would spontaneously do what they needed. Their organisms would know when to sleep and when to eat. However, in their correspondence, both shared the observation that even their children appreciated being nasty at times, and that self-regulation was not enough:

> Have you considered the sleep angle? Recently our kids have been breaking all bedtime laws. A meeting was strict about them, and for a week they have gone to bed early. Result: most of the bad tempers, destructiveness etc. have lessened greatly. (Neill to Reich, December 12, 1948).

The surrounding political events of the 1950s strengthened their impression that no one could escape having a hateful layer and an armor.

At age fifty, Reich theorized to support the generations to come, to help them to build a less ferocious world and one more respectful of the nature that animates them.[23] Therefore, he undertook, with a few friends like the educator Neill and his daughter, Eva Reich (an obstetrician), a profound reflection on what one could hope for the humanity of the future. He began to study the birthing rituals. For him, the only way to repair a humanity harmed by millennia of tyrannical and religious destructiveness was to begin the work at this level, that is, by studying the social and psychological ways that humans conceive (in every sense of the word) their offspring. For Reich, it was not possible to respect oneself without respecting nature and the universe of which we are an integral part. To detest what we are is to hate the nature that animates us. We will see, in our discussion of Ed Tronick's studies (see chapter 21, p. 623f), that repair systems undoubtedly exist in human organisms. They can be supported to become increasingly efficient. However, even these forms of healthy repair systems do not follow the laws of Idealism and of the orgone. They seem to follow the general laws of the theory of evolution: they are not perfect, they can even generate mechanisms that lead to destructive behaviors.

After launching an anticommunist movement of the left, Wilhelm Reich became one of the precursors of ecological thinking. Reich's vision[24] was in part taken up by the youth movements of the 1960s in America and Europe. Fenichel's and Reich's careers began with youth movements. It is through them that Reich became known again after his thought was banned for a dozen years.

With such preoccupations, Reich was no longer interested in what was at stake in the world of psychotherapy.

Orgonomic Therapy and Psychotherapy

> All psychological manifestations of the schizophrenic process had to be understood in terms of deep *biophysical processes which underlie and determine the*

functions of the mind. Our assumption is that the realm of the psyche is much narrower than the realm of biophysical functioning. (Reich, 1949a, XV.44, p. 433)

Reich's research on vital energy began in Oslo.[25] It is thus one of the topics on which he and his collaborators worked for the longest time. Nonetheless, this research did not go beyond the stage of imaginative studies on interesting speculations. It is not unusual that a creative person is not known for what he has the most passion for; history does not retain his works on the topic. In the same way, we do not study Kepler's astrological thought today. But a certain number of isolated propositions, formulated in the context of the studies on the orgone, have influenced numerous practices and merit a brief description in this book. For example, Reich's interest in the stakes involved in pregnancy and the birth process remains relevant. Eva Reich stayed in touch with the research on childbirth by Frederic Leboyer (1974) and Michel Odent (1976), and she even contributed financially to some of Odent's research to validate his approach.

The hypothesis that affective dynamics participate in the development of some cancers is still not confirmed by scientific research, but it remain a focus of research that reappears periodically in professional journals.[26] This topic presupposes that we imagine the existence of connections between affects and metabolic dynamics (chemical and energetic). Reich explored this connection when he studied the dynamics of the fluids of the organism and the vitality of blood cells.

Other themes from Orgone therapy have their place in a psychotherapy textbook to the extent that they can be integrated in a theoretical context close to actual scientific knowledge.

Sex and Work

According to Reich, the circulation of orgone in the organism gives a sensation of pleasure, like Freud's libido. Those who experience this circulation with anx-

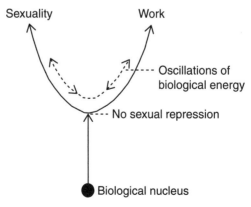

FIGURE 18.1. Libido.

iety have developed, in the course of their lives, a fear of the pleasure of being alive. This statement refers to a pleasure that can become intense. Thus, some people are not afraid of small pleasures but are afraid of an orgasm, or the love that can be created between parent and child. Freud's libido is thus a manifestation of the orgone. Reich ends up proposing that in the organism, the orgone has two basic modes of expression: sexual love and the creativity linked to work. These two creative energies coordinate the internal dynamics and social dynamics and are found in the activity of all the species. Creativity also has its somatic organization (fine motor activity, the brain, etc.). In psychotherapy, this implies that self-expression through one's work is as important as self-expression through sexuality and that the repression of these two basic needs can damage in the vegetative dimension.

The central importance of a professional integration of not only the mental equilibrium but also the health of the organism is confirmed by numerous research studies on the impact of unemployment on mental and physical health. This stream of research began with the works of Austrians Marie Jahoda, Paul Felix Lazarsfeld, and Hans Zeisel at the occasion of the 1929 Great Depression. Reich probably heard of these studies. These first observations have been robustly confirmed since that time.[27] From the point of view of body psychotherapy, the accent is placed on the fact that a profession is one of the principal modes of calibrating behavior and psyche. The gestures develop in function of the needs of a team; the mind is formed by preoccupying itself with the management of the information that allows for a professional or occupational practice that is recognized by economic and cultural networks in which an organism integrates itself. In this perspective, creativity and sexuality are, at the same time, two necessities and two forms of pleasure.

Tissues and Fluids

In becoming increasingly interested in the manifestations of the orgone in the organism, Reich further studied the dynamics and quality of organic fluids. He also observes more closely the quality of the metabolic activity of the tissues. These can be more or less supple, more or less saturated with metabolic wastes or more or less irrigated. In certain body psychotherapy practices, like mine, the quality of the gaze and the skin becomes as pertinent than the analysis of muscular tension (Thornquist and Bunkan, 1991, 5.5.5, p. 55). The idea would be that the tissues reflect in a particularly refined way the nuances of the interaction among affective, metabolic, and vegetative dynamics.

I have the impression, for example, that for some people, the quality of the skin varies in a particularly identifiable way in function of a depressive mood and sexual satisfaction. The skin can be more or less dry, tight, transparent, pink, supple or soft, and with more or less marked wrinkles. At the occasion of an anxiety attack, I sometimes observe that around the mouth the pores of the skin become enlarged or tight, change direction, while the skin is slightly jaundiced or gray. I then put forth the hypothesis that the patient is living a form of anxiety that Freud associates to orality (for example, when there is an unconscious rage against someone on whom one is dependent). Once one knows the phenomenon, it is easily noticed. It usually escapes observation if one is not trained to see it.

This interest in the fluids and the tissues is also a topic explored independently by biologists (Pert, 1997; Vincent, 1986) and by some body psychotherapists (G. Boyesen, 1985a). It is probable that this topic will be explored in an evolving way in the years to come.

Global Organismic Regulation of Vitality and Pulsation

Reich's orgone is, above all, a force that animates everything that exists. Without this force, nothing would exist. It is also *a force that gives itself a shape, a contour, and a dynamic*. The orgone creates and forms the atoms, the cells, the organisms, the planets, and the galaxies. In the human being, the orgone is the metabolic activity of all of the cells, especially those of the blood that transports the oxygen, the nervous systems that transports information, the sexual dynamics that have an impact on genetic dynamics, the skin that regulates the transaction between the internal and external environment, and so on. The intensity of the cellular activity is the basic support of all these functions. The greater the vitality, the more the operations carried out by the organism has the means to accomplish their tasks. For this activity to take shape, the organismic activities must find a dynamic and an appropriate rhythm, a mode of functioning that allows each task to accomplish its functions. For Reich, the basic dynamic of the orgone is *pulsation*. Each and every entity has its own proper pulsation. Pulsation makes it possible to contain mobilized orgone. When there is no pulsation, the energy loses its organizing quality and becomes a destructive energy that leads to *anorgonia* (negative orgone). In pulsating, a system acquires its shape, contour, rhythm, and force—in short, its dynamic properties. The orgone would generate the pulsations of respiration and the heart, the oscillation between wakefulness and sleep, and the feelings of openness and closure toward those around us. Often, social obligations poorly respect the needs of organisms. They thus reduce the amplitude and the rhythmic regularity of the pulsations that structure an organism. This may lead to a pollution of the orgone (e.g., metabolic wastes accumulate in the tissues) that produces various forms of *anorgonia*.

Over a dozen years, Reich imagined that this pulsation of the orgone existed at the *core* of each of us. The repressive evil of the social dynamics create a kind of obscure world around this central kernel of life. This *secondary layer* is full of hate, anger, sadness, and rancor which haunts and animates the history of human societies for past millennia. A third layer forms itself at the surface of the being to create an apparently friendly *mask* that hides from the eyes of others this intolerable hell that proliferates between the mask and the core. This mask draws its inspiration from the forces of the orgone to propose a message of love and gentility, a becoming aesthetic and compassion that resonates with empathy with the repressed depths in the kernel that animates us. There is something quite complex at play in this. Such as:

1. By entering into resonance with our core, this message of compassion and solidarity dips into the depths of our organismic resources like a magnet that attracts iron. We believe in it profoundly and in good faith.
2. But this apparent goodness is in fact activated by the second layer of the being, which transforms the pure waters of our depths into an implacable destructive mechanism.

Reich concluded that healing passes through a strengthening of the core organismic pulsation[28] which requires that the conscious dynamics learn to acknowledge and integrate this force and that the organism learns anew to live as a global pulsation. As early as 1933,[29] Reich sometimes asked his patients to explore a movement that sets the entire body into a pulsation. Lying on his back, the patient oscillates between a phase of extension (the arms and legs are as far as possible from one another) and a phase of condensation (feet, hands, and head as close as possible to each other). This oscillation is done in coordination with respiration (deflating and breathing out, extension and breathing in). Having performed this exercise several times, the patient may experience, after a while, the impression of being a global pulsation that moves the body, the respiration, and the sensations of the body. The organism thus recovers a flexibility that allows its pulsations to animate its systems of auto-reparation. Reich proposes that the patient move like a jellyfish propelling itself in the sea.

The persons who can feel these pulsations in their organism, have, according to Reich, a good organ sensation.[30] Some individuals can feel the pulsation of their brains, which can become especially evident at the occasion of an osteopathic massage of the cranium.[31] Some women can feel when they ovulate, and others do not even notice that they are pregnant by the end of the first trimester.

GLOBAL PULSATION

Most humans have sometimes had the impression of being a global pulsation. It generally consists of pleasurable moments, tied to relaxation after an intense activity (what Reich calls the reflux): after having made love with delight, after a good massage or a relaxation exercise, after having exhausted oneself playing sports. The individuals who appreciate this type of sensation often declare having the impression that "the energy circulates everywhere," that they feel "alive and whole," that they have the feeling of being "one." Others are anxiously troubled by these sensations. For example, they experience the impression of being depersonalized, or they are made anxious by an unfamiliar sensation, by something out of their control. The customary explanation of the Reichians is that the anxious reaction is symptomatic of an organismic constriction, which can be experienced as an identity problem, an impression of being uprooted, whereas the capacity to experience the pleasure of the global pulsation is a sign of health, strength, and maturity.

For Reich, being an immense pulsation is what is experienced when an individual accepts to feel the orgone that circulates within. Even if Reich's *explanation* cannot be maintained, his *description* allows one to grasp certain psychic experiences related to the organism in a particularly explicit fashion. In other words, we would have an example of an erroneous theory that has permitted the observation of a phenomenon that is useful to integrate, especially in a body psychotherapeutic approach.[32] I have experienced this sensation, and some of my patients have also described it. Therefore, clinical experience allows me to confirm that focusing on the experience of being a global pulsation is a useful therapeutic tool, but I have no valid way of explaining it. I have no problem admitting that I cannot explain all that I observe.

THE ATROPHY OF THE PULSATION

Sometimes a patient who comes to a psychotherapist for a consultation describes an impression of "constriction." Everything in him seems to have dwindled. His gestures are weak, the skin sensitive and pale, a dull look, hair in poor condition, weak breathing and voice. I have often used this term[33] to describe what is for Reich one of the basic forms of the discontent that is experienced as soon as forces try to inhibit the spontaneous pulsations of the organism. In the case of an extreme constriction of the organism, most of the therapists, whatever their approach, have the same prudent reaction to want to create a mobility, a pulsation, an internal space that leads to an appearance opposite the one I just described: like radiance, flexibility in the respiratory rhythm, and enhanced mobility.

With the notion of pulsation in mind, the intervention becomes more targeted. It does not consist of proposing to this individual a diametrically different behavior but to gradually augment his repertoire. A constricted individual moves very little but cannot remain immobile. He is tired but sleeps badly. He is trapped in a narrow repertoire of organismic states. The notion of pulsation evokes an analysis that takes the following elements into account:

1. The *variety of repertoires*. It consists in knowing how many different states are still possible in the basic polarities like somnolence/wakefulness, relaxation/excitation, mobility/immobility, a restricted and stereotypical behavioral repertoire/a varied repertoire, and so on.
2. The *amplitude* or *intensity* of the variations: shallow exhalation, profound sleep, hyper-mobility, and so on.
3. The *duration* of each phase: brief sleep, shortness of breath, creativity lasting hours, and so on.
4. *Rhythm of transitions*: the passage from breathing in to breathing out can be more or less rapid or more or less marked. Some people are either hyper-active or sleep. In this case the polarization is extreme.

The same variables can be used to analyze a relationship. In a couple, some individuals have a difficulty finding space to be alone or to be sexually unavailable. The oscillation of states like being at ease with the other/with oneself, intense sexual arousal/being turned off, creativity/laziness are common with most people, but it is rarely tolerated by the other or by oneself. To permit the partners in a couple to mutually authorize each other to have different rhythms and negotiate these transitions is often useful. The important point, which is evident when we consider the notion of vegetative pulsation, is that the two phases cannot occur simultaneously. It is not possible to be fully attentive to oneself and the other at the same time except in particularly intense moments (e.g., when one falls in love). It is not possible to be here and there; but we can be here in one moment and elsewhere in another. To admit to this, and to have it admitted, is an example of relational work based on the notion of pulsation. Theoretically, this point seems evident. In practice, I notice that many people reproach themselves for not being able to be calm and enthusiastic at the same time. With this type of analysis, the therapist can avoid the cliché commonly used, like the notion that a patient is "closed" when he opens himself up to internal sensations, and "open" when he is available to communications from the other. What the Reichian therapist then defends is the possibility *of oscillating* between openness to oneself and openness to another. This pulsation can have different timing. The oscillation can happen in a few seconds or a few months. The state of constriction is a closing off to self and others, like in certain extreme types of depression. Knowing how to pass from one state to the other is vital.

THE CIRCLE OF RESPIRATION IN PULSATION

In analyzing the relationship between pulsation and respiration, we again find the four moments of respiration already described in the sections on the methods from the Far East and gymnastics.[34] Like the Hindus and the Chinese, and like Freud for a brief moment,[35] Reich conceptualizes four phases of mobilization that are also four phases of the circulation of energy. This activation rises up the back, passes through the cranium, and returns down over the ventral surface toward the genitals.[36] This current is associated to the movements of the fluids and respiration.[37] There would be a connection between the *flux* (ascending energy, mobilization, inspiration) and *reflux* (descending energy, an expression leading to relaxation, and exhalation).[38]

The orgasm coordinates intra-organism and inter-organism regulations in an intimate way (see figure 18.2). Orgasm becomes a particularly striking example of the form of reaction that mobilizes all these mechanisms. It creates a profound dynamic of the organism that allows for a deep cleaning of the tissues and fluids, a discharge of emotional tension, and a form of contact with the other that is necessary for someone to be able to let go. Only when two individuals have an orgasm together does such a powerful discharge become possible.[39] In other words, the orgasm is not just a pleasurable reflex unleashed by a

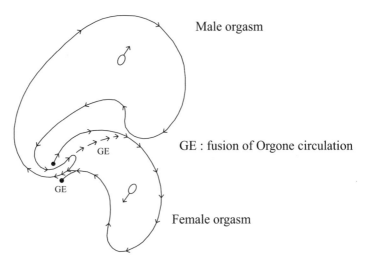

Male orgasm

GE : fusion of Orgone circulation

Female orgasm

FIGURE 18.2. The circulation of energy during orgasm. There would be one pulsation that integrates the two organisms. *Source:* Reich (1951, p. 80).

few nerve centers. It is a profound need that allows an organism to renew itself. In this sense, for Reich, "sexual stasis represents a fundamental disturbance of biological pulsation" (Reich, 1948c, V.1, p. 153f). Having arrived at this stage of his thinking, he has a model in hand that answers all the questions he had asked himself with regard to the orgasm when he was still a student. This model made it possible for the subsequent generations to ask other questions that necessitated other models in the future.

Reich asked his patients to move like a jellyfish but had not, it seems, made of this proposition a structured exercise. It was, for him, more of an astute teaching tool. Judyth O. Weaver told me that most orgonomists in the United States do not know this exercise.[40] It would seem that it was Ola Rakes who started to develop this exercise in Oslo after visiting Reich at his property in Maine. Gerda Boyesen and her students then created an entire series of exercises based on this proposition (Heller, 2007).

JELLYFISH EXERCISES AND AUTO-REGULATION
The jellyfish exercises[41] show how choreographer Rudolf Laban, through the intermediary of Elsa Lindenberg, influenced Reich's bodywork. Laban distinguished two basic movements of the body: "It has been found that bodily attitudes during movement are determined by main action forms. One of these forms goes from the periphery outwards into space, while the other comes from the periphery of the kinesphere inwards towards the center" (Laban, 1950, IV, p. 83). The analysis of this basic movement by Laban is certainly more refined that that of Reich's. He differentiates a global pulsatory movement from a more dynamic differentiated pulsation of body parts: a hand may contract while the

other opens up. Laban sometimes uses global pulsatory movements, but he does not understand these two general movements as being healthier than a dynamic play of tensions between parts of the body. A tensing of one part can serve as a basis to accentuate the opening of another part of the body as when a compressed spring suddenly lets go. He distinguishes between the forms of harmonious dances that impose a global expansion or a contraction on the body and the other forms of dance that exploit a multitude of contractions and expansions in different parts. For Laban, the adoption of either of these is mostly an option between styles and cultures.[42] He refers to every blend of parts of the body in extension and in contraction as "arabesque" and global movements as "attitudes":

> Attitudes show a relationship to all dimensions: high, deep, right, left, forward and backwards. It is as if all the space were raised into one comprehensive dimension giving a similar aesthetic impression to that of an orchid whose intertwining curves create a perfect unity. Attitudes are final poses which cannot well be further developed. (Laban, 1950, IV, p. 86)

Every combination of the parts of the body in extension and in contraction creates a kind of symbolization that would always be, according to Laban, that which creates the necessity to develop the art of movement, like dance:

> Experience of the symbolic content and its significance must be left to the immediate comprehension of the person who watches the movement. Any verbal interpretation of this inner feeling will always be something like a translation of poetry into prose and will remain all the while unsatisfying. (Laban, 1950, IV, p. 86)

To explore the impact of orgone on the organism, Reich worked with global body movements that can help the patient become aware of the deeper dynamics of his being. He focused on the activation of a harmonious and global pulsation. He did not take the time to observe the different types of pulsations that can be generated by the different organismic dimensions. An organ does not necessarily pulsate like a tissue, a fluid, a muscle, and so on. Reich does not explore the dynamics that emerge from the dynamic resonance between Laban's "arabesques." Elsa Lindenberg, who was probably an expert in contrasting arabesques, did not want to wait. I assume that her need to mix dance techniques, such as Laban's arabesques, and Vegetotherapy was one of the reasons that encouraged her to create, at the end of her life, a school of dance therapy.

Introduction to the Jellyfish Exercises.   Here is a simple exercise that permits the introduction of the basic principles of Reich's jellyfish exercises.

> Vignette on orgone sensation. *You relax, eyes closed, sitting on your ischia bones, back straight. You are aware of how you breathe. You then rub the palms of your*

*hands together rapidly from top to bottom for a few minutes. You slowly separate
your hands apart not more than an inch, keeping them parallel, one palm facing
the other.*

At that moment, most everyone with whom I conduct this exercise senses a
dense field between their hands. They have the impression that this field has a
rhythmic pulse that subtly pushes the hands apart and draws them to each
other. It is recommended to verify that the respiration in not inhibited while the
patient is concentrating on the field between their hands.

The foregoing is a typical Reichian exercise. I practiced it with several body
therapists, including Eva Reich in Geneva. A Reichian explains that this field
that you feel between your hands is orgone energy and that the pulse is one of
the properties of this energy. The impression that something pulsates between
the hands is often reported. Typically, when I guide others in this exercise, individuals also feel warmth and tinglingin their hands. These vegetative sensations
sometimes sweeps over the body. An individual may feel a circulation in the
body that gradually becomes an impression of global pulsation. These types of
sensation are often associated to the circulation of the chi, of the orgone, or of
"vital energy." Whatever these mechanisms might be called, this experience is
frequently observed and experienced as beneficial by individuals who are not
afraid of pleasurable sensations that arise in the body. For example Hiroshi
Nozaki taught the same exercise in his courses of Chinese massage, to make us
feel the circulation of the chi.

Brief Description of the Main Jellyfish Exercise.   This exercise is conducted while lying on one's back. It consists in opening, as much as possible
(hands and feet as far away from each other as possible), then closing oneself up
as much as possible (knees and elbows as close as possible to the center of the
thorax). In these exercises, the patient explores different ways of going from one
extreme to the other, at different speeds, in a more or less coordinated fashion
with respiration. It is easy to demonstrate that in these postures, it is impossible
to be curled up and fully expanded at the same time.

Reich's idea, at the time, was that the center of the orgastic reflex organized
itself around the segment of the diaphragm. Genitals, mouth, and arms get close
together in exhaling; they distance themselves somewhat with inhaling. This
movement in pulsation is what organizes and coordinates the movements of the
organism. The body passes alternatively from a C position to an X position.

When a jellyfish moves, both ends of the body get close to and far from one
another, in a rhythmic movement, which can become clonic. Taking this movement as a metaphor, we arrive at the following hypothesis:

The expressive movements in the orgasm reflex are, viewed in terms of identity of
function, the same as those of a living and swimming jellyfish. In both cases, the
end of the body, i.e., the ends of the trunk move towards one another in a rhythmic
motion, as if they wanted to touch one another. When they are close together, we

have the condition of contraction. When they are as far apart as they can be, we have the condition of expansion or relaxation of the orgonotic system. It is a very primitive form of biological pulsation. If this pulsation is accelerated, if it takes on a clonic form, we have the expressive movement of the orgastic convulsion. (Reich, 1949a, XIV.4, p. 396f)

The movements of the jellyfish exercise are carried out by the patient. The therapist intervenes very little, for this work aims at developing the capacity of the patient to auto-regulate. The therapist is content to help the patient learn the movements, then to talk with him about how the segments of the body coordinate themselves and what was experienced. Therefore the patient moves himself, coordinates his gestures with his breathing. The difficulties of coordination are perceived by the patient and the therapist simultaneously. We always find in body exercises the fact that the therapist sees things that the patient cannot see. Thus, the therapist often observes with greater precision the synchrony between gestures and breathing, but he cannot perceive the patient's experience. Patient and therapist each perceive different aspects of the global experience. This technique allows a form a co-construction process, during which what was perceived by each person allows them to create a global vision of the patient's nonconscious and conscious dimensions that were activated in the patient's organism during the jellyfish exercise. Among the Reichians, this co-construction necessitates a straight-talking style. The patient learns to tell the therapist when he has the impression that the therapist has a false view of what is going on within him. The patient also learns to manage similar remarks by the therapist without automatically accepting them. Typically, during these exercises, the Reichian therapist does not interpret. He is content to communicate what he perceives to the patient and asks the patient to do the same. It then becomes possible to ask oneself what sometimes causes a different perception of the same phenomenon.

An Example of the Analysis of the Muscular Chains with the Jellyfish. Here is an example that shows how the jellyfish exercises makes it possible to test the function of the muscular chain that links the back of the cranium to the heels. It consists in oscillating in a continuous fashion between the two extremes (positions A and C):

    A. *Point of departure.* The individual is lying on his back. The legs are folded, the hands are placed on the knees, the knees are as close to the thorax as possible while keeping the arms and hands relaxed.

    B. *Dynamic phase I.* The knees gradually distance themselves as far as possible from the thorax, the hands and arms remain relaxed and are carried by the movements of the legs.

    C. *The point of arrival.* The basic posture is identical (on the back, legs folded, hands on the knees), but this time, the knees are vertical above the pelvis, the hands are on the knees, hands and arms are relaxed.

D. *Dynamic phase II*. The knees gradually approach the thorax. The hands and the arms are relaxed. They are carried by the movements of the legs.

During the whole exercise knees and feet never touch (see figure 18.3).

To regulate the rhythm of the movement, you may ask the patient what he experiences when his knees approach the thorax during exhalation and when he moves away during inhalation. Or you can ask him to perform this gesture very slowly. Relaxation is the mood that is hoped for.

If the muscles of the back are relaxed, each time the knees approach the thorax, the nape of the neck hollows out a bit, and the head tips slightly backward. This movement is subtle. It is passive. It is activated by the lengthening of the muscles on each side of the spinal column and the muscles that link the lower back to the knees. Each time the knees move away from the thorax, the stretching of the back muscles diminishes; the nape of the neck lengthens as it relaxes. If the individual is not relaxed, provide him with a mental exercise (for example, ask him to think of a pleasant vacation) so that the attention does not interrupt the mechanical activation of the motoric chain.

The basic lever of this mobilization is the rocking of the pelvis toward the front and toward the back. If this head–pelvis coordination does not occur, the therapist knows that there is an important tension to be discovered in the back. He may either identify its localization by palpating the muscles or by exploring with the patient what is happening when the patient, tries to feel the coordination between the head and pelvis at the level of the nape of the neck.

Body Defenses with or without the Mobilizations of Hypo- and Hyper-muscular Tensions

A large part of the psychodynamic thought used by psychotherapists of Reichian inspiration takes up, from a particular psychoanalytic trend, the neurosis–psychosis dichotomy in association with the strong ego–weak ego dichotomy.[43]

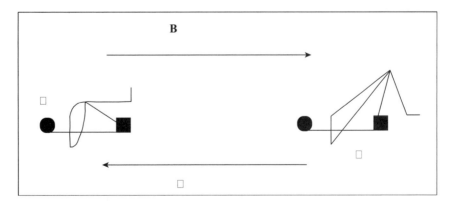

FIGURE 18.3. Sketch of the exercise. *Source:* Heller (1994).

For these Reichian therapists, the mental defense system that is constructed in creating a muscular armor is associated with a strong ego. When the armor becomes too rigid, it associates itself to diverse forms of neuroses. At the other extreme—that of the psychoses—Reich and his students speak of a weak ego, which relates to a defense system that does not include the muscular system in its defense strategy. They are thus like Socrates's soul: particularly fragile oysters without shells.

This polarity was established by Reich basing himself on a series of sessions that he had with a female schizophrenic patient. He noticed that she hardly breathed, even though "her chest appeared soft, not rigid as in the case of compulsion neurosis" (Reich, 1949a, XV.1, p. 406). The respiratory inhibition is therefore not due to a muscular block. Everything happens as if she must continuously inhibit her breathing to control the intensity of her feelings. One of the rare islands of muscular defense (rigidity) that she had was situated in the ocular segment.[44]

Characters that Reich situates midway between neurosis and psychosis have an intermediary configuration. Thus, for certain "the rigidity is paired with flabbiness (hypotonus) of the other muscles areas" (Reich, 1949a, XIII.9, p. 341). These patients, similar to Kernberg's (1984) and Kohut's (1971) narcissistic personalities, have—in my experience—a tendency to fight to preserve, as much as possible, a sensitivity in contact with the deep movements of the organism. Their dilemma is that they can only construct themselves by inhibiting these deep sensations, and this they refuse. A Reichian would say that they have not found a way to pulsate between deep introspection and active contact with others. The transition phases are underdeveloped. They have a muscular armor that is only partially built; it is so full of holes that, in these cases, Reich speaks of "small islets of armor." Some artists who cannot live without destroying themselves (for example, often having recourse to alcohol and other drugs) are often part of this population. Their dilemma is to feel so much and be able to contain so little.

To summarize, the distinction between hyper- and hypoarmored personalities brings together the following traits:

1. A person is said to be *hyper-armored* when the therapist observes a network of muscular tensions that influence all segments of the body. The muscular chains are rigid. There is then an important reduction in a person's postural and respiratory repertoire. The typical analysis is that these individuals are barricaded behind a physical and psychological defense system that reabsorbs the sexual needs and anxieties at the maximum. These individuals are often relatively insensitive to affects and body sensations. In two words: they control. It is mostly for this type of personality that the first methods in body psychotherapy (Reich's Vegetotherapy, the Bülow-Hansen method, Lowen's Bioenergetics) were created.
2. A *hypo-armored* individual has few chronic muscular tensions. They often have a few "small islets" of tension around certain joints. The typ-

ical understanding is that these individuals lack defenses, and that it would be dangerous to relax the few tensions they have left before reinforcing their ego and their defense system. At the level of the body, it consists in beginning by improving their grounding, their muscle tone, the amplitude of their breathing, their capacity to display emotional expressions, and eye contact while they interact with others.[45] This method aims at constructing ego defenses. It requires tact and forms of intervention that are not intrusive because these personalities can overreact or underreact to any kind of stimulation (verbal, behavioral, or bodily). When one uses the jellyfish exercises with these patients, it can be useful to develop what is experienced in the transition phases that lead from one extreme position to the other. The first hypothesis that comes to a body psychotherapist when he observes an insufficiently structured muscular armor is that the patient may suffer from a fragility close to what is observed with psychosis and major depression.[46] Depressive patients often have hypotonic muscles at the junction between the arms and the back. For many neo-Reichian psychotherapists, these hypotonic muscles prevent the force of the back to express itself through the arms. The metaphor is energetic, as it presumes that the tonic energy that rises up the back ought to flow into the arms of someone who needs to grasp or to repel.

If this distinction is a bit simplistic, it remains useful. For example, in a recent study, Berit Bunkan (2003, p. 51) observed that most psychotic patients can have strong chronic muscular tensions in the back, which is compatible with the notion that psychotics can have "islets" of tension. She also observed, like Reich, that psychotic patients modify their respiratory behavior with difficulty. This analysis of psychotic patients forced Reich to change the initial position he developed when he created *Character analysis* and in *Vegetotherapy*, which assumed that a healthy individual would be without defenses. This is perhaps true for yogis, but not for an ordinary citizen.

This change of direction in the Reichian theory brings us back to Otto Fenichel's (1935) notion that the defenses are not necessarily the sign of a pathology. Individuals could not function without a defense system. What Freud designated with his model of defenses in 1900 is today associated with the idea that the defenses often designate ways of structuring the psyche and its relationship with the rest of the organism. As Darwinism suggests, it is improbable that these organizational systems be truly coherent, and in certain cases, it is possible that they adopt a kind of functioning that does not enhance an individual's chances of survival.

The Forms of Vitality According to Stern

Vitality is a theme found here and there in the literature, but it has not yet been explored in a systematic way. We already encountered it in Descartes, when in his fifties and dying, he composed the *Treatise on the Passions* in 1649. We find this theme developed with an even greater passion by Reich as he approached his fifties and his death. In 2010, Daniel N. Stern undertakes this theme anew. It would seem that it takes a mature person to appreciate the importance of vitality. Probably only when it begins to diminish does the mind grasp its importance.

For Stern, the vitality is regulated in the brainstem, which can actively integrate information on metabolic dynamics. In the Reichian theory, metabolism has an active and powerful impact on the brain and mind. The brainstem is only a cog in the dynamics that coordinate mind and metabolism. The interaction established between respiration, blood circulation, and the brain influences the vitality of all brain cells.[47] The interaction between body and brain, and between gesture and thoughts, shape the activity of the brain, respiration. and circulation of the blood. The brain is influenced at least as much as it influences.

However, Daniel Stern describes in a particularly fine manner the impact of vitality on the mind and the necessity of integrating this organismic force in the theory and technique of psychotherapy. He also makes it possible for the contemporary body psychotherapist to discover the neurological mechanisms that shape the dynamics of vitality. For example, he shows that an experience, whether it is perceived by oneself or by another, has a "contour of vitality" that is a sort of gestalt (Stern, 2010, p. 4f). This activity coordinates gestures, thoughts, affects, and behavior around an energetic dynamic that can become more or less conscious. This remains true while we attend a dance event or when we interact with someone. The contour of vitality is also one of the forces that coordinate organisms.

The Idealism of Reich

Psychotherapy and Idealism

The period after Wilhelm Reich's death was problematic for many reasons that are mostly linked to ideological and political issues. Reich had beliefs that were difficult to accept: on Martians and simplistic machines that would control the circulation of cosmic energy. He claimed that he often saw flying saucers. These perceptions were, for Reich, so tangible that he wanted his son to help him save the world by fighting against a Martian invasion.[48] There are so many books on this subject[49] that I need not make any further comments at on this subject. Reich acquired the reputation of a mad hallucinating genius. I content myself to underscore the connections between Reichian theory and Idealism because, it seems to me, this is what the Reichian of today needs to understand. At that time, Reich often used one of Socrates's favorite rhetorical techniques: playing the innocent.[50] It consists in feigning to know nothing, to be like an alien who discovers the human species and seeks to know if it consists of civilized people. This strategy presupposes that humanity ought to be coherent and rational and that each irrational trait merits an ironic comment or even a condemnation. Again, it is striking to notice how Reich uses this caustic tool like a virtuoso without ever using it to critique himself. Socrates at least tried to look as if he were critiquing himself.

It is too easy to throw all of Reich into the garbage just because we do not like Idealists, or an author who has psychiatric symptoms, as Pascal Bruckner and Alain Finkielkraut (1979) proposed. We would lose too much time having to reinvent some indispensable tools for the psychotherapy of tomorrow. Having said this, to disentangle Reich's Idealism from his therapeutic work is still an unfinished task, fifty years after his death.[51] As I had indicated with regard to Plato, Idealism corresponds so well to the comfort needs of consciousness that it is difficult to let it go.

Even though Socrates and Reich do not resemble each other, their trials have some common characteristics. In both cases, they have the impression of being innocent victims of the stupidity of their co-citizens. In both cases, the justice that condemns them is experienced as arbitrary; nothing seems to justify the violence of the legal punishment that they suffered for their offense. Even if their theories were entirely delusional (which is not the case), nothing justifies a death sentence in one case and two years of imprisonment in the other. It was subsequently forbidden for citizens of the United States to own a publication on orgone, written by Reich or his pupils. Law enforcement agencies conducted searches of particular individuals; books that were found were burned in a public place. These persecutions were still going on after the election of John F. Kennedy as president of the United States. I do not advance any explanations on the incredible severity of this repression, and I do not know of any satisfying analysis of the situation. Most of the analysis published by those close to and admirers of Reich defend an Idealistic scenario similar to that used by the pupils of Socrates: the idiots have persecuted a great genius because they could not cope with the luminous truth that he was bringing to the people.[52]

We had to wait until the Italian publisher Giangiacomo Feltrinelli[53] dared to publish one of Reich's works in 1963 and the rising of youth movements in 1966 in Berkeley and May 1968 in Paris for Reich's work to become available in Europe once again. In that context, it was difficult to have a rational discussion relative to his legacy. His work was taken up every which way by all kinds of people for reasons that had nothing to do with Reich's real career.

In this, we find one of the principal symptoms of Idealist movements already discussed with regard to Socrates and his disciples: an inseparable connection between scientific reasoning, political utopia, sexual politics, power over others, and self-exploration. In both cases, it is not appropriate to speak of sects, but surely of Idealism. This inseparable connection is difficult to grasp and master when we do not have a clear understanding of Idealism.[54]

Locked up in prison, Reich was terrified to see the advent of movements that exploited his status as a martyr to the advantage of goals he did not approve. Some ascribed to him the idea that giving birth was an orgasm and that parents ought to initiate their children to sexuality by making love in front of them. The notion that a healthy birth is necessarily orgastic is attributed by

Reich to Paul and Jean Ritter (1975) in letters addressed to Neill (e.g., March 3 and 8, 1956). In his letter to Neill of March 8, 1956, he associates the name of David Boadella. Boadella was trained by Paul Ritter and then collaborated with him. For Reich, Ritter's group was part of extreme left movements who used Reich's name to hide "their ignorance and their quackery." The "Ritter and Company" so upset Reich in the last weeks of his life that he almost ended his deep friendship with Neill, who supported them (letter from Neill to Reich, October 1, 1956). Given the importance of Boadella in the neo-Reichian move-ment, it is perhaps useful to recall that Reich could easily exclude individuals who admired him (e.g., Otto Fenichel) and that Neill supported Boadella, knowing all the while what Reich thought about him. It remains true that Boadella developed a personal view of Reich's thought.

Others made use of the notion of sexual revolution to promote various forms of prostitution. At the end of his life, Reich wanted to disassociate his name explicitly from the insults made against women and their pain in child-birth,[55] from the practices of pedophile parents, and from the pornographic sexual industry conducted by various forms of Mafia organizations.

It is now time to take up Reich's work in such a way as to define the Ideal-istic components of it.

The Orgone of the World of Ideas

The Idealistic properties of the orgone are as follows.

1. Orgone is a creative and coherent force. Its impact on each individual is necessarily constructive, healing, a source of love, and leads to the joy of being alive.[56] One should adapt one's life and the institutions to which one belongs according to the functioning of the orgone, as did the Tao-ists who dreamed of making politics a manifestation of the Tao.
2. The dynamics of the orgone represent a manifest truth that does not allow any other truth to exist. The truth that Reich and the humanity of the future will build is truer than that of the others because it rests on a scientific research conducted by scientists in contact with the circulation of the orgone within themselves. This is close to the description of the philosophers in Plato's *Republic*, who have the advantage over other scientists to be in contact with the Ideas.[57]
3. Orgone manifests in the depths of the organism, far from consciousness. We must therefore attend a Reichian school[58] before our consciousness can acquire the capacity to contact organ sensations and one's pulsation, and to let itself be guided by orgone dynamics in a constructive way.

Although Reich argues against the idea of the state that follows from Plato's theory, their theories share many similarities.[59]

Reich had hoped that scientists like Albert Einstein would have replicated his research; at the same time, he thought that these replications could not be undertaken by anyone other than individuals who accepted the theory of the orgone.[60] Yet it is exactly when individuals want to contradict the results of experimental research that a scientific debate can sometimes lead to confirmations that render a model even more robust.[61]

Society against Nature

Reich and Plato have the same difficulty as most of the religions influenced by Idealism: the explanation of evil. How can a universe made by omnipotent beneficent forces give birth to evil? With Reich, there would be a structuring of political power that intends to concentrate power in the hands of a few. These forces would have created an "emotional plague" (Reich, 1949a, III.XVI; 1946, XIII.1), which weakens the natural links between consciousness and the depths of the organism by inhibiting sexuality. According to Reich, this inner division is at the origin of all illnesses (cancer, neurosis, psychosis, and so on), human malice, and misery.[62] He fought violently against any attempt to associate his orgone to spiritual movements. For him, spirituality and the religions are based on a false perception of the orgone, which engenders emotional plague.

With this way of seeing things, Reich created a feeling of estrangement between himself and others, between the armored "little men"[63] and those who are in contact with their orgone. This may explain why he was unable to engage in a constructive discussion with the great men whom he tried to contact, like Freud and Einstein. Even in these instances, he only wanted them to approve of his endeavors. Reducing most citizens to the category of little men is not so different from the way Plato had to disqualify his colleagues by referring to them as "sophists." In Plato's *Dialogues*, Socrates listens to the other only to impose his own point of view, his own way of formulating a problem.[64]

Socrates and Reich both went to prison mostly because, during their trials, they believed themselves more intelligent and more just than the court before which they stood. In both cases, the court did not have a severe judgment in store for them. Their final decision was provoked by the attitude of the accused. We have more information on the proceedings of Reich's trial than that of Socrates. Reich was hounded because he sold or rented accumulators to patients to cure their illness (e.g., cancer). He was put in prison because he declared that he refused to present himself before a court of justice until scientists could have tested the soundness of his observations.[65] He was finally condemned for contempt of court. Having said this, as for Socrates, the final judgment is particularly severe for an insult to the judicial system.

A striking example of Reich's Idealism is revealed to us in a moving recording that he left for posterity on April 3, 1952, after a severe accident caused by his experiments on orgone and nuclear energy. Clearly depressed, Reich (1952b) gives witness to posterity that he is the only one to have grasped the actual situation and to be able to propose adequate solutions. He is desolate to be surrounded by incompetent persons (too neurotic) to understand, as he did, what was at stake. He is evidently the one through whom cosmic truth can express itself and incarnate itself in this world.

During this period Reich presents himself as a modern Socrates, innocent and pure.[66] He pretends that the authorities are wrong to doubt his uprightness and his ethics, and that it is not because he advances sexual freedom that he sleeps with his female patients. In short, he is persecuted for his ideas and the truths they contain. If the argument and the plea are credible, it does not correspond to the reality. It is not certain that the flying saucers he contends to have seen really existed. It is probable that he was intolerant and that acting out with female patients or ex-patients had occurred on several occasions in his life (from 1920 to 1955). As with Jean-Jacques Rousseau and his theories on the education of children, there is clearly an abyss between what Reich advocates and how he lives. It is apparent in a form of negation or at least denial and also bad faith.[67] Reich claims that only people who are able to have orgasms have a healthy mind and that he is an example of this truth. In fact, if he truly had orgasms, he was the living proof that his theory is false.

This brings us back to the basic position of this book with regard to Reich: we must take from his work what remains worthwhile and avoid personalizing the debate. The problem with the devotees of Reich is that they want to love and believe in what he *claims* to have loved and believed. Today, this is not a defensible position.

Von Helmholtz Reprimands Goethe and Reich in the Name of Science

I have already presented Hermann von Helmholtz as one of the founders of experimental psychology and one of Freud's references in neurology. He was, among other topics, an expert in the psychoneurology of vision. I summarize a lecture Helmholtz (1853) gave on Goethe's theory of perception. This theory is still read today in milieus close to spiritual movements.[68] Goethe considers his theory scientific. Helmholtz wants to show that Goethe's text on perception is interesting but has nothing scientific in it. Helmholtz makes use of this discussion to indicate the characteristics of a scientific discourse on perception.

Science, according to Helmholtz, seeks methods that promote the observation of what is happening while having recourse to human perception as little as possible. Introspection is able to furnish complementary information to the objective observations, but it cannot provide the basis of scientific knowledge in psychology. The mechanisms the scientist attempts to isolate are active in the wings of the theater of life independently of what we think of them. As the marvelous poet that he is, Goethe constructs a theory of perception from what he consciously feels. Given his genius, the theory he proposes is full of fascinating intuitions, some of which are confirmed by scientific research; the whole remains a theory of what the poet perceives and not a scientific theory of perception.

This lecture could have been addressed to Reich, a century later. Parts of Reich's work are relatively robust: those that are based on his experience in psychotherapy and sexual epidemiology, whose clinical validity has been confirmed by numerous colleagues since then. But, like Goethe, Reich too often bases his theory of the orgone on what he and his patients experience.

For Reich, what is perceived by an "unarmored" person must exist. He certainly spent large sums of money to buy sophisticated materials with the intent to scientifically analyze the orgone, but he did not have the means to undertake a reliable research on the subject. I have known many psychotherapists who have attempted to combine clinical and experimental research. Their work, often imaginative, can inspire but never allows for drawing a solid conclusion. Given a psychotherapist's education and training, he can collaborate with research teams, but he wastes his time and that of others when he undertakes research by himself. Reich confirms this analysis.

19

After Reich (1945–2000)

PUTTING THE BODY AND THE PSYCHE
IN THE ORGANISM AGAIN

I have distinguished two principal phases in Wilhelm Reich's career:

1. A career as a psychotherapist and psychiatrist with a psychoanalytic and Marxist orientation.
2. The discovery of organismic therapies, centered on the great regulators of the organism and a political action aiming at improving the articulation between the health of humans and the health of nature. Reich turned his back on psychoanalysis and Marxism to adopt a more utopian and Idealistic attitude, inspired more or less directly by Spinoza, Rousseau, and Tolstoy.

Reich the body psychotherapist only existed in the transition phase between his career as a psychoanalyst and the establishment of Vegetotherapy. Among his collaborators and students, we find at least four different kinds:

1. Those who are mostly influenced by Reich the psychoanalyst, like Otto Fenichel.
2. Those who are mostly influenced by Reich the expert of organismic regulation, like Ellsworth Baker.
3. Those who were mostly influenced by Reich the body psychotherapist, like Fritz Perls.
4. Those who benefited from an organismic treatment with Reich and then needed a more classic psychotherapeutic treatment to digest mentally what they had discovered, like Alexander Lowen and Myron Sharaf.

It is mostly from among the third and fourth groups that we find the founders of body psychotherapy as it existed in 2000. The common goal of these approaches is the creation of a form of psychotherapy that has explicit organismic goals.

The distinction between body psychotherapy and a Reichian organismic psychotherapy is presently a work in progress. The attempt to clarify these forms of intervention is rendered more complex by the fact that psychotherapy is a recognized discipline and often reimbursed, whereas the therapy of the organism remains a field the institutions refuse to recognize. Some Reichians sought to present their work as a form of psychotherapy for political reasons. Thus, numerous schools whose goals are all of the regulatory systems of the organism promise their students a formation in psychotherapy that is not recognized by institutions. It seems to me that a clearer position would permit certain schools to fight to have organismic therapy recognized because they have a real usefulness, instead of wanting to have their approach recognized as a form of body psychotherapy.[1]

This sowed an important confusion in the domain. We find an analogous debate with the behavioral and systemic therapy approaches that treat behavior and not really the psyche. Again, the fact that these approaches are not psychotherapy, in the strict sense of the word, does not take anything away from their relevance.

The problem is as much on the side of the schools that could not survive in the current context without claiming that they are a psychotherapy school, as on the side of the institutions that refuse to recognize the therapies whose goals are the great regulatory systems of the organism, and opt for a fuzzy view of psychotherapy. All share in the confusion. The institutions do not know how to define psychotherapy[2] and do not want to recognize work on the regulators of the organism or on behavior as different forms of intervention. Practitioners are afraid to provide an explicit definition of their field, as it might weaken the chances that their school will be included in the list of reimbursed treatments.

In the following sections, I describe the development of the neo-Reichian therapies that present themselves as having a psychotherapeutic goal by insisting on the difference between forms of treatment that mostly focus on the organism and forms of treatment that mostly focus on the psyche. It is understood that the fact of including the psyche in the dynamics of the organism and interpersonal interaction as a regulator of the organism make a sharp distinction between the two domains impossible.

The Development of Body Psychotherapy

If the legal repression against Reichian thought ceased at the end of the 1960s, it is still difficult to pursue an academic career in the 2000s if we accept some of Reich's ideas.[3] In the 1950s and 1960s, the political and academic repression of Orgonomy generated chaos in the field of body psychotherapy. Only now are we painfully emerging from that chaos. This situation engendered a vicious circle. It was impossible to access a serious formation; therefore, even people who wanted a serious formation were insufficiently trained. It was then easy to disqualify the clinical research on the body–mind dimension inspired by Reich, by assuming that all those who used his theory for their research were poorly trained. There were many traps set by this situation for the next generations. The more visible ones hid the more subtle ones. It is therefore as intellectual adventurers that the students of the 1960s and 1970s entered into the domain of body psychotherapy.

In the following sections, I show how body psychotherapy movement succeeded in restructuring itself without letting go of the most interesting aspects of Reich's proposition. This endeavor required a reformulation that dealt with Reich's Idealistic theses that impeded a serious reflection on body psychotherapy. After all, it is important to distinguish between the sympathy we may have for an individual, however brilliant he might be, and a domain that needs to develop itself for the interest of all: patients and researchers in particular.

The 1960s Attempts to Defend Reich's Proposition

Having showed that Orgone therapy aims at global organismic regulatory systems that are beyond the psyche, Reich demanded that only physicians be authorized to practice his approach. This requirement is not innocent. He suspected that all of the hyenas of the therapeutic marketplace would throw themselves on his carcass after his death. That is why Orgonomy remains a domain reserved, almost hidden, for a few physicians who constitute the membership of the American College of Orgonomy around personalities like Ellsworth Baker (1967). Moreover, there were good reasons for this. I even met, in the 1970s, self-taught "practitioners of Bioenergetics" who asked their patients to explore their inner fantasies on holidays in a "psychotherapy" group. They then sold the content of these fantasies to travel agencies, who wanted to know what images could be efficiently used for publicity. There certainly was a free-for-all that was created around Reich's name after his death.

While the persecution against the Reichian movement was strong, the students of Reich were aware of the medical option. Alexander Lowen, for example, was a teacher of gymnastics and relaxation. Because he was passionate about everything that dealt with the coordination between mind and body, he underwent psychotherapy with Reich. Wanting to continue to work in this domain, he obtained his medical degree before creating *Bioenergetic analysis*.

In Europe, Reich was mostly represented by Ola Raknes, a psychologist in Oslo, and A. S. Neill, a famous educator. There was greater flexibility regarding the association between Orgone therapy and medicine. In autumn 1947, Gerda Boyesen attended a conference by Trygve Braatøy that was an important experience for the development of her thinking. He had then declared that to become a vegetotherapist, "it was necessary to be either a physician or a physical therapist" (Boyesen, 1985b, p. 14). Many years later, Boyesen decided to follow his

advice and complement her training in clinical psychology by becoming a physical therapist. Federico Navarro (1984) is a neuropsychiatrist. He developed his
view of Vegetotherapy after training with Raknes. Reich and Raknes both had
had an excellent formation in Psychoanalysis. This was not the case for most
physicians who were keen about Orgonomy.

The very influential David Boadella[4] did university studies in pedagogy
(which included studies in psychology and in the humanities). He also studied
the biological bases of behavior at the Open University of London. He then
studied for a dozen years with sociologist Paul Ritter, who had been trained in
Vegetotherapy by a student of Reich, Constance Tracey. A personal process in
Vegetotherapy with Paul Ritter (Ritter and Ritter, 1975) was part of his formation. In his writing, Ritter tries to promote a lifestyle and a libertarian and humanistic morality that he identifies as Reichian. This training is discussed in
Ritter's journal, *Orgonomic Functionalism*, which appeared for several years
(40 issues) and in his books. We have seen how angry Reich was with some of
Ritter's propositions. He had asked Neill to warn Ritter and Boadella that they
were no longer to associate his name to their school. Nonetheless, with Neill's
support, David Boadella continued to explore Reich's thinking by undergoing
Vegetotherapy with Ola Raknes (when he was in London) and with Doris Howard. He then went to the Open University to take up his studies in the biological
bases of behavior. It was difficult to obtain a more rigorous course of studies for
body psychotherapy in Great Britain. Boadella (1987) established a school of
body psychotherapy called Biosynthesis,[5] which became one of the principal
neo-Reichian schools in the world (especially in Europe, the United States, Brazil, Australia, and Japan). This school attempts to synthesize, as a coherent
whole, the knowledge developed in the neo-Reichian schools. To accomplish
this, Boadella created the journal *Energy & Character* in 1970. This journal
welcomed all who wanted to express themselves in it. For a long time, it was the
only real intellectual link between the neo-Reichian schools and the only attempt to create a shared intellectual structure.

One of the most well-known Reichians in California was Charles R. Kelley.
He had trained as an experimental psychologist and had been in therapy with
Reich. He then undertook experimental research on the orgone and became an
expert on the analysis of the ocular segment.

From that point forward, the Reichian methods entered into a confusing
march of ideas and methods. The domain was dispersed into small schools,
grouped around teachers who were more or less trained, mostly situated in California, New York, and London. It was a walk through the desert for the domain.
The only place where body psychotherapy was practiced within institutions was
in Scandinavia (mostly Oslo, as we will see).

The 1970s: Body Psychotherapy as Consumer Products

A new conception that concerns man's destiny in the world and is not alien to the
cultural movements of the '60s has given rise to the emergence of an extensive

range of techniques of self-actualization and personal growth. A common radical to all these techniques is the anti-intellectualism that stresses emotional development. Some of these techniques are based on psychoanalysis; others have a strong oriental flavor. Some body-centered techniques have even introduced the use of drugs and sexual contact with the clients. . . . The boundaries of psychotherapy have become blurred. Not only encounter groups, but also jogging, aerobics and even golf could be considered psychotherapies in this context. (Jose Guimón, 1997b, *The Body in Psychotherapy*, p. 3f)

The youth movements that arose as early as 1966 in the United States and then Europe brought Reich's work back into fashion. It was a tidal wave that forced the authorities to moderate their persecution of the Reichian milieus. The academic milieus adopted an attitude that blended a pitiful smile, irony, and disdain. Body psychotherapy has to have recourse to a sort of popular suffrage to resist political and academic repression. This strategy paid off! Body psychotherapy became a social phenomenon. A form of impulsive speculation, often imaginative and rarely well framed, became fashionable with the neo-Reichians of the day.[6] Without an ethical backbone, these movements associated themselves to different fashionable methods, sometimes to drug use (especially hashish and LSD) and to popular gurus.[7] Sexual ethics became as blurred as it was at the beginning of psychoanalysis, because some profited from a reflection on the taboos to promote as an expression of emotional health their perverse sexual attraction for their patients.

Reich could have easily agreed with the youth movements of the '60s but probably not with the "New Age" movements of the '80s. The generation of Gerda Boyesen and Alexander Lowen had just a humanitarian interest for leftist theses and were astonished to see hundreds of long-haired intellectuals enter their training programs. Up until then, they only had had as students a few well-educated individuals, deeply interested in approaches such as those of Reich. There was a bit of everything in this new generation. Some were really interested in the notion of body psychotherapy, while some wanted to earn as much as a psychiatrist by completing just a few workshops a year for training.[8] Gerda Boyesen and Alexander Lowen surfed this wave without really understanding what was happening to them, but they appreciated the fame, admiration, and money this fashion brought them. These students can be grouped into three basic categories:[9]

1. Individuals with university education in physics, biology, chemistry, social sciences, geography, engineering, humanities, general medicine, pedagogy, psychology, philosophy, psychiatry, theology, political science, economics, and so on.
2. Individuals educated in professional schools: accounting, education, ergo therapy, nursing, physical therapy, social work, computer engineering, and so on.
3. Individuals who present themselves as having life experience like political or spiritual militancy, or in the education of their children, and so on.

This list indicates to what extent training programs of the period attracted a heteroclite population. Training was open to anyone who could pay. The courses were good enough to allow some of these students to become excellent psychotherapists. However, the criteria for selection were low.

For some individuals with a university education, the formulations advanced in the schools of body psychotherapy in the 1970s were embarrassing, given to what extent they had become folkloric.[10] However, they admired what could be experienced, thanks to these approaches. The basic strategy of these intellectuals was to learn what there was to learn in the schools of body psychotherapy of the time, while seeking to participate in the new developments in psychology and psychotherapy. One of the reasons the schools of body psychotherapy could not be ignored was the way they approached problems associated with the affects. The permission to experience one's organism and the forces that animate it intensely was far beyond what traditional systems of education allowed one to imagine. Sustained by a spirit of discovery associated to student movements of the 1960s, a number of intellectuals explored these pathways with a creative passion.[11]

In all of this chaos, a new way of approaching psychology begins to emerge in what is known as humanistic psychotherapies. To be trained, students now need to integrate a variety of relevant set of concepts, techniques, and personal experiences. Experiential workshops became a source of information as crucial as books and courses. It is no longer enough to be familiar with one approach, as required by the traditional psychotherapies. Students learn to know their field by participating in experiential workshops given by a variety of schools. They want to integrate in their personal development a combination of habits, theories, and beliefs.

Distressed by the reactions incited by new developments in body psychotherapy, most Scandinavians withdrew into their shell. There, body–mind therapeutic interventions remain anchored in institutions. In Oslo, practitioners abstain from publishing in a language other than their own. Thus, they preserve an island of competence and tranquility. The Danes are more willing to present their work to the world. That is especially the case for the Bodynamic School (MacNaughton, 2004; Marcher and Fich, 2010), founded by Lisbeth Marcher with, among others, Marianne Bentzen, Peter Bernhardt, Erik Jarlnaes, Peter Levine, Ian MacNaughton, and Lennart Ollars.

The 1980s: The Need to Undertake an In-Depth Clinical Research on the Relevance of Body Psychotherapy

In 1980, it became quite evident to some new members of the domain of body psychotherapy that their domain was going to sink if it were not supported by knowledge based on a more robust ethic of knowledge (Heller, 1993d). Numerous individuals attempted to reconstruct a connection between the human sciences of the time and the practices of body psychotherapy. Here are a few representative names of this movement who influenced the thinking in this text:

Maarten Aalberse, Jacqueline and Yves Brault, Christine Caldwell, Jacqueline A. Carlton, George Downing, Alison Duguid, Peter Levine, Mark Ludwig, John May, Gustl Marlock, Pat Ogden, and Luciano Rispoli. This is not an exhaustive list. Most of them published in *Energy & Character*, *Adire*,[12] or *USA Body Psychotherapy Journal*. The expansion of basic references in body psychotherapy that followed developed in two directions: toward science and toward spirituality. The source reference for the second was Jung, for whom all available theories and knowledge can become useful and relevant for the development of psychotherapy.

The founding of the European Association of Body Psychotherapy (EABP) on December 20, 1988, by Bjørn Blumenthal, Malcolm Brown, and Jay Stattman[13] allowed for strengthening this attempt at reformulation by bringing members from most of the schools together to meet and dialogue with each other. A similar association was founded in the United States in 1996: The United States Association for Body Psychotherapy (USABP). Finally, body psychotherapists were able to differentiate the particularities of their approach from what could be considered a common ground of knowledge. This font of knowledge is in fact only partially in common, because most ideas are used differently in several schools, but none by every school.

The 1990s: Body Psychotherapy as an Emerging Field

The authors I have just mentioned continued their work of reconstruction in the 1990s.[14] The strategy that is taken is to establish a dialogue with the different ways of approaching the human being that they learned to appreciate in becoming body psychotherapists and the knowledge established in other approaches. The critics in medical and academic milieus are confronted head on. The standout event of this endeavor was the publication of *Körper und Wort in der Psychotherapie: Leitlinien für der Praxis* [Body and Word in Psychotherapy: Guidelines for a Practice] by George Downing in 1996.[15] The work set in motion by this generation of body psychotherapists is analogous to that undertaken by the generation of Otto Fenichel in Psychoanalysis in the 1930s. They were trying to reformulate the psychoanalytic theory by stripping it of its mystical origins (hypnosis and mesmerism) and creating some bridges between clinical work and the recent formulation from the sciences: "Psychoanalysis as it is now constituted undoubtedly contains mystic elements, the rudiments of its past, as well as natural-scientific elements toward which it is striving" (Fenichel, 1945a, p. 5).

Since the 1990s, the whole world of psychotherapy has been trying to free itself from the constraints of particular schools without losing what makes certain methods so valuable. Such an endeavor is risky, because the methods, spirit, and theory of an approach make up a coherent entity. A psychoanalytic method (e.g., free association) used in another setting may lose or modify its relevance. Nevertheless, the need to go beyond a form of knowledge structured by particular schools became a necessity.

This reflection is supported by setting up diverse ethics committees capable of ruling on complaints made by colleagues or by patients. One of the discoveries made by these committees is that, contrary to what rumors led some to believe,[16] there did not seem to be more sexual boundary violations between psychotherapist and patients among body psychotherapists than in verbal approaches. The phenomenon of patient abuse seems to be a sadly human inclination that is relatively rare but persistent. These ethics committees deal with complaints of patient abuse more directly and publicly than most other therapeutic approaches do. As soon as touch and trust become an important mode of intervention, a particularly rigorous ethic and deontology become indispensable. Setting up these ethical standards is a central issue for the European Association of Body Psychotherapy (EABP).[17]

BACK TO OSLO

Psychotherapy or Body Psychotherapy?

Imagine how it must have been fascinating for a psychotherapist to be in Oslo in 1934. The insatiable Fenichel and Reich delved with pleasure into countless arguments. They discussed not only with colleagues but also mingled with the artistic and intellectual life of the city. I imagine that Clare Fenichel and Elsa Lindenberg sometimes brought the debates back to the use of the body in psychotherapy or to the relevance of Vegetotherapy to understand what is going on for a ballet dancer.

The debate between Fenichel and Reich on the way to include the body in psychotherapy became a subject that could not be overlooked. The Scandinavians have a tradition of body techniques so anchored in the customs of their culture that the subject imposed itself. Reich's and Fenichel's colleagues were certainly interested in Elsa Gindler's and Rudolf Laban's approaches such as they were described by Clare Fenichel and Elsa Lindenberg, but they also incorporated the entirety of the body methods appreciated in these regions. The idea of situating the affects, the thoughts, and gymnastics as different ways of approaching the regulators of the organism was, in any case, fashionable because Cannon's books were representing recent medical developments in the United States for the European medicine of the day. The connection between Cannon's theories and the body–mind approaches was Edmund Jacobson's relaxation. The Autogenic training of German psychiatrist Johann Heinrich Schultz was also often used.

Even if Reich pretended to be interested only in the organism, many in his entourage were psychotherapists and psychiatrists for whom the use of body techniques with their patients one way or another had become an important research topic. For most psys stimulated by this debate, the emerging discipline evoked by the discussions between Fenichel and Reich was important, not necessarily their proposals. Vegetotherapy was a reference because it was the first body–mind technique developed by a psychotherapist; once the interest in inte-

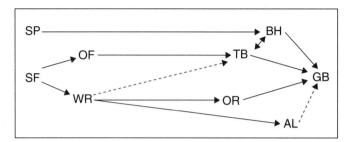

FIGURE 19.1. Affiliations of the Oslo schools in the 1960s. SF = Sigmund Freud; SP = Scandinavian physiotherapy; OF = Otto Fenichel; WR = Wilhelm Reich; TB = Trygve Braatøy; OR = Ola Raknes; BH = Bulow-Hansen; GB = Gerda Boyesen; AL = Alexander Lowen. Dotted arrows indicate indirect influences.

grating body and psyche became manifest, it was this theme (more than Reich's technique) that was explored. It was evident for the people educated in body techniques that Wilhelm Reich was a brilliant beginner. His proposition was convincing, but it had to be refined.

For the protagonists in Oslo in 1950, the technical developments they were making were integrated into a vision focused on the notion of *psychotherapy.* Their work focused on the same clientele as that of the psychiatrists of the day who were psychoanalysts. They considered themselves simply psychotherapists, but ones who explicitly included the psyche in the dynamics of the organism. This new way to approach the individual, fashionable since the work of Kurt Goldstein (1939) on the organism, necessarily opened up a new way to envision psychotherapy. They did not see the necessity to distinguish themselves by calling themselves body psychotherapists. Not all of them considered themselves Reichians. As soon as we admit that the psyche is part of the regulators of the organism, it becomes almost natural to approach the psyche by observing how it relates with the behavioral, bodily, and physiological dimensions.[18] They did not oppose body and verbal therapy, because speech is only one of the behaviors of the human organism.

I illustrate this development by taking a few important personalities as an example—mostly Nic Waal and Trygve Braatøy, who introduced Reich's and Fenichel's points of view to psychiatric institutions to develop modes of interventions that combine different body and psychotherapeutic methods. I then speak of Gerda Boyesen, who introduced a synthesis of the Fenichel-Reich debate, as well as other Scandinavian approaches, in body psychotherapy. That is why she did not like that I referred to her, in my earlier writings, as a representative of the neo-Reichian movement. Gerda Boyesen synthesized what was said and practiced around her without knowing that her proposition was influenced by the teachings of Fenichel in Oslo when she was twelve years old.

After World War II, we witnessed a kind of trench warfare between the psychiatrists who were psychoanalysts in dominant positions and the movements in psychotherapy breaking away from psychoanalysis, like Jungian analysis and Reichian Vegetotherapy. Oslo is one of the rare places where the discussion between Fenichel and Reich concerning the body in psychotherapy could survive within the academic institutions.

Waal

Vegetotherapy Enters Oslo's Psychiatric Institutions

Nic Waal[19] (1905–1960) was a psychiatrist who used body-oriented techniques such as Vegetotherapy in a psychiatric institution. She trained in child psychiatry and became a psychoanalyst in the Berlin Institute, where she also joined communist-oriented psychoanalysts such as Otto Fenichel, Wilhelm Reich and Edith Jacobson. She had worked with Reich in the Berlin psychoanalytic clinic. In Oslo, she actively helped Jewish children escape from Nazi persecution. She became the head of the child psychiatry department at Oslo University. In Copenhagen, she trained child psychiatrists in the state hospital and at the university. At the end of her life, she created a Nic Waal Institute, designed to help handicapped children.[20]

With Ola Raknes, Nic Waal used Vegetotherapy in Gaustad and Ulevaal psychiatric hospitals. They remained in contact with Reich.[21] She also undertook clinical research with other colleagues to demonstrate the utility of using body techniques as a form of psychiatric intervention. Like Trygve Braatøy, she collaborated with research projects in Rappaport's Menninger Clinic, Kansas (USA).[22] In Oslo, some of her research attempted to validate the use of the following forms of intervention in psychiatry:

1. Ways of working with emotions using the working models of Cannon, James, Lange, and Pavlov.
2. Relaxations techniques such as those of Schultz and Jacobson. Waal detailed the differences between relaxation techniques and Vegetotherapy.
3. Body–mind techniques such as dance, gymnastics, physiotherapy, and Gerda Alexander's Eutony.

In the Reichian world, Nic Waal is known mostly for the detailed techniques of body analysis that she developed for Vegetotherapists. Recently, Berit Bunkan[23] has included Waal's system in a synthesis of body analysis techniques created in Oslo.

Passive Movements

Nic Waal also found ways of using the classical technique of passive movements developed by physiotherapists to analyze the psychological state of patients and their way of relating to their therapists. A passive movement occurs when a therapist moves a segment of the patient's body. This technique is mostly used to evaluate the state of joints, tendons, and certain reflexes. Arms, legs, or head are moved relatively slowly to observe how respiration responds to this mobilization. Both the patient and the therapist can observe these reactions simultaneously. It is thus easy, as in Reich's jellyfish exercises, to create a co-conscious experience of the patient's body responses. The patient's reactions allow the therapist to generate a form of diagnosis that captures what is happening during the exercise, and the patient can therefore grasp it as well. This type of "local" operational diagnosis is different from the more global forms of diagnoses that were in use in psychiatry in those days. As an example, I describe different responses that are observable when a patient allows the therapist to move his right arm:

1. *Dissociation.* The patient allows the therapist to move his arm as the therapist wishes, but the patient reduces the volume of his breathing pattern. This is typical of a patient who wants to dissociate from what is happening between his arm and the therapist.
2. *Obedient activity.* The patient cannot prevent himself from helping the therapist, which implies that he is constantly trying to predict what the therapist wants to do and comply. This is often observed in patients who try to control what their therapist is doing.
3. *Self-assertive activity.* The patient cannot prevent his muscles tightening every time the therapist attempts to move the arm. He thus resists being moved. This is often observed in patients who are afraid of losing control.
4. *Impulsive activity.* The patient's movements are jerky, uneven, rough, and strong. The movement changes tempo on the part of the patient independently of the therapist's change of tempo, and the movements have an uncontrolled and involuntary character.
5. Certain patients trigger a *resistance* only when there is an extension or a contraction of the arm.

Probably influenced by Fenichel's remarks on hypotone, Nic Waal, like other Norwegian colleagues working in therapies that combine body techniques with psychotherapeutic intentions, included an analysis of hypotone in her work with passive movements: "one does not find resistance, but a characteristic looseness and slackness. It can vary between lazy, dull, 'dead' or can be recognized by a strange lightness" (Waal et al., 1976, p. 274). When touched, hypotonic muscles feel gelatinous.

Braatøy: The Couch and the Massage Table

A Psychoanalytic Approach that Integrates the Knowledge of Body Techniques

Trygve Braatøy (1904–1953) was born in the Norwegian community of Minneapolis, Minnesota (USA), where his father was a Protestant minister. He studied neurology in Paris and trained as a psychoanalyst in the Berlin Institute, mostly with Fenichel, in the early 1930s. There, he was also influenced by Wilhelm Reich's psychoanalytic ideas and the Gindlerian discussions on the body. In 1933, he went to Oslo, where he worked as a psychoanalytic psychiatrist in the Ulevaal psychiatric hospital. He was actively engaged in combating Norwegian movements that sympathized with the Nazis by publishing his opinions in the "illegal press." With Waal, among others, he also helped people running away from occupied Sweden by giving them a diagnosis that justified their hospitalization until it was safe for them to flee.[24] In 1954, he published *Fundamentals of Psychoanalytic Technique*, which is his testament. Fenichel only mentions Braatøy for his psychoanalytic publications on adolescence and schizophrenia.[25]

In Norway, Trygve Braatøy (1942, 1947, 1948, 1954) tried to develop a way of introducing the body in a psychoanalytic framework that is compatible with Ferenczi and Fenichel's technical propositions. However, he also agreed with Reich that psychoanalysts should find ways of including some "hands-on" work during psychotherapy. After World War II, there were two main groups of body psychotherapists in Oslo:[26]

1. Fenichel's group, which had worked with Braatøy when Fenichel left for Czechoslovakia in 1935.
2. After Reich's departure for the United States, Ola Raknes became the central figure of Norwegian vegetotherapists working in a private practice.

This division lasted for the rest of the century. Fenichel's group was strengthened when Trygve Braatøy became professor of psychiatry and head of Oslo's psychiatric institutions in 1945. One reason for his nomination may have been his capacity to integrate the work of Reichians working in these institutions, such as Nic Waal.[27] Braatøy saw himself as (a) a practitioner with a broad and humanistic approach to patients with (b) a psychoanalytic specialization. For him, patients were more important than theory. He did not participate in the bitter wars between psychoanalytic clans. He explored ways of associating knowledge on body techniques that was available around him, with a classical but flexible psychoanalytical setting. For example, he analyzed the biomechanical implications of having patients lie on a couch. He made explicit descriptions of the influence of this posture on the mind of patients and their way of communicating with a psychotherapist. He would discuss with patients some of their motor patterns; sometimes he would touch a patient who needed comfort. He also included the analysis of patient breathing patterns in his psychoanalytic work. Although Braatøy acknowledged Reich's contribution to discussions on the association of body techniques and psychotherapy, he seldom used Vegetotherapy techniques. He preferred other body–mind approaches:[28] Ferenczi's active technique, yoga, or the relaxation methods of Schultz and Edmund Jacobson.

Like Fenichel (1935), Braatøy admired Reich's Character analysis. He often used it to begin a psychotherapy process. It could help a patient become aware of how he presented himself. The content of the representations was only discussed later. According to Braatøy, it is easier to explore a patient's anger once he has experienced his ways of controlling it. Braatøy was irritated by Reich's constant need to seduce everyone and his need to be every one's boss. After 1933, "he, in his impatience with our slow progress, changed into a trinity of Freud, Einstein, and Wilhelm der Grosse[29] and must be read accordingly" (Braatøy, 1954, p. 101).

Braatøy did not have the time to acquire knowledge of physical therapy. He preferred to collaborate with people who had knowledge of the same caliber as Elsa Gindler. According to him, Reich's Vegetotherapy mixed simplistic body and psychological techniques in an unsophisticated way.[30] Vegetotherapists tend to overestimate the need to support emotional expression and underestimate the need to strengthen the patient's capacity for insight.[31] Braatøy thought that if a patient needs to explore himself using body and psychotherapy techniques, he might get a better treatment if he sees a competent physical therapist and a trained psychotherapist who work as a team. To develop a form of body treatment that could be used as a complement to a psychotherapeutic approach, Braatøy collaborated with an impressive Scandinavian orthopedic physiotherapist, Aadel Bülow-Hansen. She developed forms of massage that could be used in a complementary way with a psychoanalytically oriented psychotherapy. Like Fenichel and Reich before him, Braatøy followed the standard practice of not mentioning his team's body experts. Even Nic Waal does not appear in his references. Like his colleagues, he presents his thoughts and methods as if he had developed them alone.

Although Braatøy had the impression that he was proposing a reasonable way of integrating bodywork in a psychoanalytical process, his synthesis was different from most discussions in psychoanalytic circles. Like other psychoanalysts of his generation, trained in Berlin, he often used notions associated to regulation systems and was less interested by the more fashionable terminology of object-oriented psychoanalysis. He avoided reducing what patients experienced to Freud's second topographical model or too simplistic sexual metaphors. He was of course familiar with Freudian dichotomies (e.g., narcissism/object relation, id/super-ego, Eros/Thanatos.), but they did not strike him as particularly useful for his work with psychiatric patients. This choice led him to pay particular attention to how individuals, such as a patient and a therapist, auto-regulate and regulate each other. This approach is closer to the one recently developed by psychoanalysts such as Daniel Stern and Beatrice Beebe[32] than the one by Melanie Klein.[33] Today, for most psychotherapists, the importance of regulation systems is so obvious that the notion is considered standard professional terminology.

Transference in Psychotherapies that Use Bodywork

Braatøy[34] is also prudently interested in Groddeck's and Reich's need to make the patient's negative transference apparent as soon as possible. It is possible that this urge could be a part of their need to charm patients. For Braatøy, it is obvious that at the end of a successful analysis, a patient should be able to speak his mind, but this does not mean that every disagreement in the course of treatment is necessarily resistance. The patient, who is an adult human being, should be able to express resentment and other reactions directly.[35] However, by entering too quickly into an analysis of negative transference, the therapist may restrain the patient's spontaneity and prevent him from discovering that even positive transference may incorporate critical stances, while negative attitudes are always a "part of one's love" (Braatøy, 1954, p. 304).

Developing a critical form of thinking, respecting one's ambivalence, and even open resistance to some proposals made by one's psychotherapist is part of the psychoanalytical process. Learning to integrate such abilities can have "high survival values" (Braatøy, 1954, p. 304).

TRANSFERENCE AND CHARACTER

Laplanche and Pontalis (1967, p. 492) distinguish a general meaning of transference and countertransference from narrower and more specific uses of the terms. The wider meaning designates everything that is experienced by a patient and a therapist for each other. In its narrower meaning, the term *transference* only designates instances when a patient unconsciously assimilates his therapist into to a scheme constructed with someone else. For example, there is transference when a patient reacts to the therapist with the representations and behaviors he, the patient, developed to deal with his mother. This transference can activate a set of unconscious experiences within the therapist that consists of what he experienced with his own mother. Today, it is well understood that anyone can transfer and countertransfer, even a therapist. The important point is that one person experiences transference, and this triggers a countertransference in another person. The structure of transference is like that of a dream: unconscious material activates preconscious affects and representations. Often, a therapist is aware of the manifest preconscious dimension of his countertransference and forgets that the unconscious is really unconscious. Only during supervision can he become aware of the unconscious dimensions of his countertransference.

Braatøy mostly used the narrower definition of these terms, because he wanted to differentiate transference from other nonconscious relational dynamics that can also occur during a therapeutic interaction. For example, he wants to differentiate transferential dynamics from projections or the impact of character as clearly as possible. An example of an interaction with a communicative strategy, activated by a character structure is that of a patient who has a characteristic tendency to sulk with everyone. He will therefore also sulk with his therapist. Braatøy tries to experience the impact of this sulking behavior on the way he perceives the patient, and then talk about the impression this habitual behavior has on his way of interacting with the patient. For Braatøy, this form of habitual behavior is a character trait but not transference. Braatøy sometime supported various forms of bodily activity during a session, as these could facilitate the analysis of how a patient deals with others, by default. It is not really transference, because the therapist is not identified to another person. It is the patient's standardized form of adaptation.

Character traits, like other patterns observed in studies of nonverbal communication, are mostly regulated by nonconscious mechanisms. Only their manifestation can reach consciousness. On the other hand, transferential phenomena are principally regulated by the unconscious dynamics described by psychodynamic models. For example, every time his patient sulked, Braatøy noticed a characteristic tightening of the lips. This is clearly a form of automatic reflex. This reaction may have a history that might be discovered by looking at photographs or films taken by the family and sometimes by interviewing the parents. Braatøy asked his patient to explore this tightness in various ways—exaggerating it, doing the opposite, and so on. It is only a manifestation of transference when there is evidence to show that this tightening expresses an affect that was constructed in the patient's past within a specific relational scenario.

To summarize, Braatøy thinks that a psychotherapist needs to differentiate at least two types of communication patterns that are triggered by a patient's habitual way of functioning:

1. *Character assimilation.* A character trait is a standardized way of functioning that assimilates reality through a type of regulation pattern that is composed of (a) a way of evaluating reality, (b) a way of understanding what is happening, and (c) a way of reacting. Like ethological patterns, a character trait assimilates certain events in a stereotypic way. This pattern is not personalized, and its organization is nonconscious.

2. *Transferential assimilation.* In transferential communication, the patient tries to re-create with the therapist a relational pattern that has been previously constructed with someone else. The therapist is assimilated into schemas that were constructed in relationship to a particular person. Therapists working with transference will try to help the patient accommodate these schemas to dynamics that are particular to what is happening in the here and now. For example, I may assimilate all angry males smoking a pipe to my father's fits of anger.[36] I then react as if all pipe smokers were my father and try to handle them as I learned to handle him. I can only experience this transference with males who (a) smoke a pipe, like my father, and (b) in whom I can activate the same sort of anger (that is the countertransference). This transferential dynamic cannot emerge when I interact with males who cannot become angry in a way that is similar to my father's form of anger. When my therapist feels that I am activating anger in him, his anger may have different sources than the anger of my father, but my therapist can feel the sort of anger I am expecting. The therapist can thus use his countertransference to understand my expectations. Furthermore, these expectations always have a manifest conscious and an unconscious content. Counter-

transference has the same structure. This is why therapists need a particular type of supervision when they work with transference.

The structure of transference and its analysis is thus more complex than what occurs with character traits. In a study on suicide attempts, carried out with my colleagues of the Laboratory of Affect and Communication (LAC), we[37] isolated behaviors that could differentiate the following two groups of patients, all of whom were interviewed by the same psychiatrist:

1. *Attempters*. Patients who were interviewed after a suicide attempt and who did not make another attempt within the next two years.
2. *Reattempters*. Patients who were interviewed after a suicide attempt and who made another attempt within the next two years.

These behaviors had a systematic impact on their therapists' nonconscious behavior. The therapist was not aware of (a) the patient's behaviors that varied in function of suicidal risk, and (b) the impact of these behaviors on her. We then showed our films to the therapist and pointed out the behaviors of the patient and the therapist that varied in function of the patient's suicidal risk. These behaviors had no apparent meaning for her.[38] Nonconscious processes had probably activated the structure of these behaviors. These behaviors are differentiated in function of a diagnosis and may have been generated by organismic regulation systems.[39] However, it is highly unlikely that all reattempters had a particular type of transference on the therapist and that all attempters had another common transference.

VEGETATIVE IDENTIFICATION OR ORGANIC TRANSFERENCE
Reich describes yet another form of nonconscious interaction between a patient and a therapist:

> The patient's expressive movements involuntarily bring about *an imitation* in our own organism. By imitating these movements, we "sense" and understand the expression in ourselves and, consequently, in the patient. When we use the term "character attitude," what we have in mind is the *total expression* of an organism. This is literally the same as the *total impression* that the organism makes on us. (Wilhelm Reich, 1949a, *Character Analysis*, III.XIV.2, p. 363)

This relational effect was later called *vegetative identification*.[40]

Influenced by studies on nonverbal behavior,[41] Bjørn Blumenthal assumes that a psychotherapist can only perceive a small part of the complex system that regulates his interaction with a patient.[42] Consciousness can only focus on a few, relatively simple, events.[43] It is incapable of perceiving something as complex as a set of communication strategies that often co-occur. We therefore need to distinguish the following forms of data management:

1. First, the nonconscious ways of processing huge amounts of nonverbal information that is being interchanged in a therapeutic relationship. Habitual forms of data management acquired by all the organisms involved already bias this data management.

2. These nonconscious processes interact with what is being processed by unconscious, preconscious, and conscious processes.

3. Conscious processes then single out a few elements of behavior to produce an explanation of what is happening. This explanation is really an attribution process based on a conscious reasoning, influenced by unconscious and nonconscious processes. The information that is used in an explicit way can become a reassuring fiction built on a small percentage of what is really happening.

4. The explanations thus forged by consciousness may then influence preconscious, unconscious, and nonconscious affective processes.

There is thus a bottom-up and a top-down interaction that is constantly occurring. This explains why the conscious explanations provided by a therapist or a patient relative to a given set of behaviors (a) does not have the means to propose a robust analysis of what is happening, but (b) may have a form of relevance that cannot be explained by the explicit rational being used.

For example, a patient's breathing pattern may influence the therapist's breathing pattern. Most of the time, neither the patient nor the therapist is aware that their way of breathing is under some mutual influence. In group therapy, however, sometimes a third person notices the phenomenon. He may share his impression that the breathing of two persons who are interacting with each other has become shallower, in a coordinated manner. The patient and the therapist may then become aware of a form of interpersonal "resonance"[44] between each other's breathing patterns. Body psychotherapists have thus learned to become aware of such moments. They do not understand how this mutual regulation occurs, but they learn to notice it, as if from the outside. It is a bit like a person who notices that his shirt has a spot on it when he passes in front of a mirror. Some vegetotherapists call this type of mutual quasi-physiological interpersonal regulation *vegetative identification*. Having learned to notice these forms of physiological interpersonal impacts, the therapist can also become aware of certain fuzzy variables, like the particular atmosphere of a relationship that may correlate with such adaptations. He then tries to specify some characteristics of this atmosphere, like vocal tone, the rhythm of gestures or affects.[45] David Boadella regularly stresses that these forms of resonance are a form of *contact*. They emerge in the background while conscious dynamics are focusing on an explicit content. For example, I may be discussing a dream with a patient, and in the background a kind of sympathy is emerging.

At the end of his life, Braatøy discovered that he could use films to notice such forms of mutual nonconscious adaptation between therapist and patient: adaptations that could not have been noticed otherwise.[46] What we are dealing with, in such cases, is a form of automatic coordination of numerous organismic skills situated in different dimensions of the organism (mind, affects, behavior, physiology, body). Jay Stattman (1987) also talks of *organic transference.* Here is an example:

> Vignette on organic transference. *A psychotherapist, who is using massage, feels with his hands that his patient's skin is cold. This therapist has a history in which cold skin has played an important role. The therapist has worked on this issue during his personal psychotherapeutic process. He is aware of how he automatically reacts when his hands contact a certain type of cold skin. However, he cannot prevent his hands from moving in ways that convey anxiety. The therapist decides that with this patient, massage is not a tool that he can use. He has a negative organic transference with this patient. However, the patient responds to this decision as a failure, just like the therapist's father experienced failure and rejection when his child began to avoid contact with him. The patient wants the massage to continue. He becomes furious when the therapist insists that he wants to continue the therapy with other methods.*

This is an example in which the therapist is transferring, while the patient is experiencing a countertransference. In such a situation, vegetative identification and psychodynamic transference are both active. To understand this situation, it is useful to have a working model that allows the therapist and his supervisor to distinguish the different mechanisms involved. The difficulty in this situation is that the patient has an affective countertransference triggered by the therapist's organic transference.

Mobility and Therapeutic Setting

The psychoanalyst's automatic fear of "acting out" is a form of rigidity that Braatøy criticizes (Braatøy, 1954, V.4, p. 134). If one assumes that a psychoanalytic cure may influence the dynamics of the organism, one can expect that a patient will develop a more varied and comfortable postural repertoire when the psychotherapy is effective. This modification of the patient's body dynamics are activated by mechanisms that are different from those on which a physical therapist tends to work.[47] When a patient feels better, he *needs* to explore more comfortable and open ways of expressing himself. For Reich and Braatøy, the phrase "acting out" only applies when the therapist can demonstrate that what the patient is doing is a form of resistance against the therapy. For example, they do not consider that making love with one's lover during the psychotherapy process is necessarily a form of "acting out." This analysis is close to Fenichel's (1945a, p. 246), who thought that sensorimotor inhibition could be a part of a defense that protects a psychological incapacity to integrate an emotion. Less interested by the more cognitive aspects of the psychoanalytic technique, Braatøy sometimes forgets that it is difficult simultaneously to (a) integrate all aspects of a person and (b) focus on the delicate and complex intricacies of thoughts and affects.

Psychoanalysis begins its liberating influence by requiring that the patient lie on a couch. This position was used in hypnosis and in relaxation, and it is recommended because it allows maximum relaxation of all the muscles. It minimizes the pull of gravity on posture. The patient can then breathe more easily, his defense system will relax, and his emotions will enter more easily into the realm of thoughts and behavior.[48] The main physiological function of lying on the couch is that this posture supports a process that enhances the coordination among muscles, breathing, guts, and somatic reflexes. "This is the physiological *raison d'être* of the couch in psychotherapy" (Braatøy, 1954, VI.2–3, p. 169). This process is an efficient way of loosening the defense system that may activate a need to move and change position—precisely the sort of spontaneous behavior a psychotherapist may want to support. In clinical approaches, no rule is absolute. There are always cases in which such a development could be harmful.

Another implication of the standard psychoanalytical setting is that lying on the couch may induce more vulnerability in fragile patients. Today, most psychoanalysts use a similar analysis and recommend that fragile patients (e.g., narcissistic and borderline patients) remain seated during therapy. In this way, the back muscles and the muscular defenses remain mobilized. Others work with fragile patients lying on the couch but personalize the contact by using techniques such as Ajuriaguerra's relaxation method.[49] For psychiatric treatment, Braatøy recommends an adaptation of a basic posture (lying, sitting, standing, etc.) to the therapeutic needs of the moment. Here are a few examples:

1. When a patient is particularly confused, Braatøy will ask him to sit down while he collects information on the patient's real situation (financial, professional, family, etc.).
2. "Psychotics cannot be treated with classic psychoanalysis because they don't stay on the couch or they get completely paralyzed or rigid. However, in getting up and walking around, they can more easily control themselves because gravity tenses their postural muscles, and this tension coupled with deliberate motor activity help to control emotional spontaneity. Basically, the patients are not as afraid of the therapist as they are of their own impulses" (Braatøy, 1954, VI.4, p. 177).
3. Not all traumas are unconscious. When the patient is fully aware of past traumatizing situations, direct emotional expression and release in a safe environment is often helpful.[50]
4. From the point of view of psychoanalysts, monotheist religions (Judaism, Christianity, and Islam) have generated cultures in which people are rigidly judgmental and intolerant of instincts and affects. Psychotherapists often considered the Norwegian Protestants of the 1940s a good example of this phenomenon. With those who do not sexualize every gesture,[51] Braatøy would sometimes touch a patient on the shoulder to

see whether physical contact is found acceptable or unacceptable. Thus, touching a patient can yield useful information.

5. Here is an example in which Braatøy will accept to change the psychoanalytic setting to such an extent that he will also use bodywork "resembling direct physical therapy." He will use what is, for the psychoanalyst that he is, a drastic modification with "patients whose general tension is so great that it more or less blocks them completely, including their verbal expressions. In such cases, I immediately comment on this tension and interpret it in terms of fear, anxiety, and embarrassment. I permit the patient to sit up or change the setting in other ways. If these adaptations do not give sufficient help, I change the analytic procedure into something resembling direct physiotherapy. With passive movements[52] and with concentration on local muscular tension, I try to help the patient to relax; and at the same time, release his breathing" (Braatøy, 1954, V.7, p. 144).

What was, in Braatøy's professional environment, daring psychotherapeutic proposals have become relatively standard in contemporary body psychotherapy. Physiotherapists and osteopaths often notice that their work elicits intense emotional reactions, but they do not have a frame of reference that allows them to deal adequately with such events.[53] When Braatøy tried to loosen a jaw, he would use "a firm pressure against the masseter muscles blocking a specific way of conducting the jaw and mouth, or a similar pressure under the chin against persistent tension in the jaw openers" (Braatøy, 1954, V.7, p. 144; VIII.1, p. 235). These interventions, close to the techniques used by Reich in Berlin and Oslo, could release deep respiration and crying, as well as other forms of intense expressions.[54] This analysis was confirmed when he analyzed a film of a psychotherapy session given by Paul Roland to a schizophrenic patient.[55] Braatøy observed that Roland helped the patient by "gently but firmly stroking his back and neck. He asked the patient at the same time to relax and told him he wanted to help him." He noted that a key feature of this intervention was that the therapist spoke with a very low voice, moving close to the patient. In that particular case, the therapist's tone of voice was so soft that the microphones could not record it clearly. Braatøy's comments about this film mentions that Pavlov had also noticed that when a therapist asked his questions "very softly in very quiet surroundings," a frightened schizophrenic patient would answer. He made a similar observation when talking to infants. Finally, he quotes a study published in 1885 by Weir Mitchell, showing that softening one's approach to patients who suffer from anorexia nervosa could also be effective. For Braatøy, it was important to make this point in his textbook for psychoanalysts because it was not the current practice in his day to accommodate one's behavior to the needs of a patient.

Braatøy found ways of analyzing behavior in a more fluid and precise way than Ferenczi. He is sensitive to small variations of the voice, as when a voice becomes irritating once it becomes high pitched and overeager,[56] or when the flow of words becomes particularly rapid. He is attentive to various forms of gazes and to how the patient manages to capture the therapist's visual attention. Quoting one of Reich's cases, Braatøy shows that words and gestures may be indicative of different layers of the patient's character. In such cases, it would be clumsy to attract the patient's attention to both these phenomena, as the patient may then receive more information than he can handle. Often, a high-pitched voice is a sign of defense against emotions, as when an adult woman absolutely wants to maintain a girlish stance, a "good-little-girl eagerness" (Braatøy, 1954, V.6, p. 141). When a female patient passes from high pitch to a lower pitch and develops a "Marlene Dietrich" kind of voice, it is often because her vocal apparatus has relaxed. "A deeper, more adult voice, results in a radical new sort of feedback from her own behavior. The tone of voice may be of basic importance in changing the patient's patterns" (Braatøy, 1954, p. 141).

This analysis was often taught by Gerda Boyesen during the 1970s, in her training courses. It is also close to some of Downing's observations, described in his 1996 book, *The Body and the Word*. These are but two examples showing that Braatøy already explored techniques that became popular during the second half of the century. Once again, I am not saying that Braatøy is at the origin of Downing's formulations, as it is by following different routes that Downing arrived at the conclusion that working on the connection between words and gestures in this way is a particularly useful psychotherapeutic method.

The Yawn and Startle Reflexes in Psychodynamic Psychotherapy

BREATHING, TRANSFERENTIAL DYNAMICS, AND YAWNING

Chronic muscular tensions may repress certain forms of emotional expression in a relatively direct way (e.g., when a person tightens the jaws to inhibit a need to shout or cry) or inhibit emotional dynamics in indirect ways (e.g., by reducing breathing motility):[57]

> When such a person practices *coitus interruptus*, an eager and potent—or non-frigid—person tries to counter an intense sexual excitement with an even more intense holding-back attitude, blocking the panting and the sexual outcry at the height of the acme; that is, his sexual blocking includes an abrupt and intense blocking of respiration. By observing and describing these manifest phenomena, one can connect specific aspects of his sexual behavior with his respiratory tenseness and precordial and shoulder myalgia. (Braatøy, 1954, X.5, p. 326f)

Most psychotherapists, even those who have no training in body dynamics, intuitively perceive that a patient feels better when his breathing becomes more relaxed and variable.[58] For Braatøy, breathing is a part of the regulation system that deals with attention and affects. When a person becomes attentive, she often breathes less; when she cries the breathing becomes intense. Influenced by Edmund Jacobson's progressive relaxation technique,[59] Braatøy was particularly interested in spontaneous respiratory changes, as in the following example of an explicit way of working with breathing:

> When I work in this way with patients, I continually observe their breathing and always fit the suggestion, "Relax!" to the beginning of expiration. By that, I intend to call forth a summation of the local relaxation of the muscle group we work with and the general relaxation that goes with the expiration. If one does not in this way "dance with the rhythm and relaxation of expiration," one risks giving the specific suggestion, "Relax!" at a time when the respiratory muscles tense themselves in inspiration. This produces then an interference. (Wolfgang Kohlrausch 1940, quoted in Braatøy, 1954, p. 166)

Gerda Boyesen often taught this method in her training courses during the 1970s. It is close to Gindler's need to avoid constricted breathing. This same type of analysis may have been introduced in Oslo by Clare Fenichel and Elsa Lindenberg, and/or it may be obvious to any person who knows how to work with the complexity of respiration. This is an example of a technique that Braatøy must have calibrated with experts of bodywork he does not quote.

Braatøy (1954) was also attentive to moments when yawning manifests itself spontaneously, because it can be a "compensatory respiration when opportunity for relaxation arises" (p. 165). In some cases, yawning may become so intense that it will drag "the whole body with it in a global cat-like stretching-yawning movement" (p. 165). When yawning is associated with deep relaxation, it is often accompanied by "rumbling in the abdomen" (p. 169) and stretching.

This is also true for therapists, as attention tends to reduce breathing. The young and eager therapist's continuous attention may become harmful for him. Thus, professional habits may generate harmful chronic forms of tensions (Blumenthal, 2001). This is another reason why the therapist's floating attention, recommended by Freud, is beneficial—not only as a way of listening to what the patient is saying but also to the psychotherapist's own auto-regulation.

One day, Braatøy[60] noticed that a patient's yawning reaction was partially blocked. She had an apparent stretch-and-yawn reaction,[61] but the inspiration was weak: "Charles Darwin . . . said that yawning may appear as a symptom of a slight fright. The slight fear induces alert, watchful attention and thereby restricts breathing; but because it is slight, it permits the oxygen need to break through from time to time in yawning" (Braatøy, 1954, p. 167).

SUDDEN SURPRISE, FEAR, AND RELEASE

Braatøy and Bülow-Hansen opposed the startle reflex to the orgastic reflex, as if they formed a polarity. They gradually constructed a new version of the Reichian expansion (healthy)–contraction (unhealthy) opposition. A startle reaction is mostly connected to fear and anxiety, whereas yawning and stretching is manifestly a way of being more comfortable and alive. Like other colleagues, I have integrated in my clinical work this modification of Reich's rigid way of associating contraction and anxiety.

For Trygve Braatøy, the need to avoid surprise seems to be the nucleus around which a neurotic psychosomatic regulation organizes itself.[62] Surprise is then experienced as the risk of losing control and a general feeling of insecurity. At the age when a child's perception of the world is full of magical notions, the child does not yet have the capacity to master his behavior or hide an expression of surprise when adults display unexpected behaviors. The fear of expressing surprise is particularly strong in a strict environment that does not tolerate uncontrolled childish forms of behavior. Yet children cannot control their behavior when unexpected situations arise.

Gradually, the child develops an anxiety and even a fear of being caught using forms of behavior that adults do not tolerate. He is afraid of not behaving as he should. In such moments of shock, when caught doing what is forbidden, a crucial knot of neurotic regulation is formed. The compulsive neurotic's stubborn behavior, which persists on all levels, including his doubts and objections, expresses his attempt to control all situations. If he does not control the situation, he may run up against a surprise and then—bang—lose control of himself: "Discussing this attitude on the verbal psychological level, to point out that this is 'intellectual resistance' does not get anybody anywhere. The therapist must be able to bring out in a convincing way that it is the *bump*, the surprise, that the patient is afraid of—*and for good reasons!*" (Braatøy, 1954, VIII.3, p. 261). This model is useful to explain the behavior of patients who are apparently in control of everything they do, and then suddenly surprise everyone by becoming dispersed and impulsive, often for irrational reasons.

The startle reaction is the prime archaic reaction when a child is surprised doing something that meets the disapproval of others.[63] The startle is at first so intense that it mobilizes the whole body. Therefore, the vegetative and body dimensions of neurosis structure themselves around this reflex. At first, the child's repeated startle response mobilizes many parts of the body. Gradually, the startle reaction tenses those muscles that are most often used to control its expression: the eyes, the neck muscles, reduction of mobility, and of the postural repertoire are involved in the formation of a more detailed description of what Reich called the neurotic armor. This analysis, which combines neurological, body, and psychological dynamics, led Braatøy to recommend to young psychoanalysts that they should learn to become attentive to the following points when they use character analysis:

1. Being attentive to the relational context in which a character trait appears allows one to specify the contours of this trait. For example, when a patient repeatedly forgets to pay his therapist, he activates a particular form of relationship. Not paying is not necessarily a resistance to the treatment, or not *only* a resistance to treatment. It can also be an unconscious way to bring forth a deep layer of the patient's character in such a

way as to attract the attention of the therapist. The patient puts himself in a dangerous context that will reveal how his fears and anxieties are experienced.[64]

2. When a patient's awareness contacts a forgotten layer of the character, a particular transferential dynamic becomes active. Once the therapist becomes capable of feeling the texture of his patient's fear, he often notices that the relationship issues associated with this fear influences the relational dynamics in the therapy. Suddenly, the therapist is afraid that some of his interventions, mistakes, or unexpected events (e.g., the therapist cannot always arrive at the session or not always on time, for example, because too much snow has fallen during the night) will activate an immense anxiety crisis in the patient. Braatøy[65] quotes Ferenczi's analysis of such moments, where panic creates "a paralysis of all spontaneity." The patient "will turn deadly pale, or fall into a condition, like fainting; or there can be a general increase in muscular tension which may be carried to the point of opisthotonus."[66] Panic attacks become an important part of the relation. Braatøy assumes that these pervasive panic attacks can be associated to preverbal layers, similar to those that can be observed in films of three-year-old children. During this period, the patient is often incapable of integrating the therapist's interpretations.

3. The crisis now becomes a transferential crisis. Braatøy recommends an attitude that addresses both psychological and body dynamics. He often tells the patient that being spontaneous and producing material for the therapist is not the same thing. To remain silent, motionless, and trying not to be polite can sometimes be a form of spontaneity. On the other hand, when the patient's body becomes too rigid, it is important not to leave him alone in this state, and help him get out of it by taking hold of him. The therapist may need to push the body to flatten it out again, if the opisthotonus arch becomes intense. He can thus support a restoration of a normal breathing rhythm and accompany the powerful emotional expressions (rage, sobbing, etc.) that may then emerge. Such forms of support are required until the patient finds some sort of mastery again. These moments sometimes help the patient accept that he has intense emotional needs and become less afraid of expressing them.

During such delicate moments, Braatøy uses his model of the startle reflex to guide his interventions. As the startle shortens most extensors, he tries to counter that effect by seeking to activate a pleasurable stretch-yawn reflex and the affective feelings that tend to associate themselves with this reaction (Braatøy, 1954, VI.2–3, p. 168f). In her courses, Gerda Boyesen mentioned that when such an intervention is efficient, the patient would report that he has the impression of *melting*.

As long as a person stretches without pleasure and without yawning, Braatøy assumes that the startle reaction is still active. Thus, when a patient stretches without pleasure, he can look for already active chronic startle reactions responses. For this, he will use his knowledge of body reading and the patient's introspective powers. For Braatøy, a startle reflex is the somatic part of a more general fear response that also includes affective and psychological regulators.

Bülow-Hansen: A Psychomotor Exploration of Emotional Embodiment

Aadel Bülow-Hansen (1906–2001) was a physical therapist trained to use Scandinavian massage techniques for orthopedic purposes. She was also evidently influenced by the psychophysiology of her day, as she adopted a holistic organismic stance developed by researchers such as Walter B. Cannon (1932) and Kurt Goldstein (1939). The colleagues whom she trained in her school are still highly appreciated in Norwegian hospital services.

Bülow-Hansen collaborated with Braatøy from 1947 to 1953 to develop a massage method as a complement to the psychoanalytic treatments proposed by Braatøy and his team. This treatment was developed within a frame compatible with current scientific and clinical knowledge of the time. Its aim was to support freeing the physiological and body dynamic involved in the regulation and inhibition of emotional experience. It aimed at a relaxation state, induced by reducing muscular tensions and increasing the flexibility of breathing patterns in patients who were characterized as particularly rigid (or armored, to use Reich's terminology).[67] As the method developed, it was gradually able to deal with a wider set of symptoms. The treatment was at first called the Braatøy–Bülow-Hansen therapy, and then Psychomotor therapy.[68]

When Aadel Bülow-Hansen left the psychiatric institutions, she continued to train highly competent physical therapists who, like Berit Heir Bunkan (2003), continued to incorporate this method and its new developments in the Norwegian health system. A third generation of active practitioners is developing the work of Bülow-Hansen in the largest Norwegian towns and institutions. Having participated in a reunion in Oslo in 2005 with presentations given by psychomotor therapists who demonstrated how physiotherapists can become involved in a psychotherapeutic process, I consider it one of the leading massage schools in the world. This was also made possible by therapists who trained in psychology and physiotherapy, like Berit Heir Bunkan and Gerda Boyesen.

The Braatøy-Hansen combination of (a) psychotherapy and (b) bodywork by a team of people specialized in each form of intervention is what I call the Fenichel-Gindler option for body psychotherapy, in opposition to the Reichian option, in which one therapist combines intervention on all of the organismic dimensions. For the moment, only the second option is considered body psychotherapy. However, the Fenichel option is used by many psychiatric services. For example, I have observed it in the Psychosomatic Gynecology and Sexology Unit, in the Geneva Department of Psychiatry, when Willy Pasini directed it in the 1980s.[69] The team combined several approaches, such as psychomotricity[70] and behavior therapy, in association with a type of psychotherapy based on psychodynamic principles and on the Ajuriaguerra psychodynamic relaxation technique.

A Body Approach to a Chronic Startle Reflex

Aadel Bülow-Hansen created an efficient way of working on the dissolutions of tensions that participate in the maintenance of a chronic startle reflex. She found ways of detecting muscular tensions and restrictions in breathing that could be associated with such a reflex. This enabled her to describe and define them with more precision. Most of the time, it is not the whole startle mobilization that is activated in a system of chronic tensions, but only "remnants" (M.-L. Boyesen, 1976). Here are examples of techniques used to find these remnants.

> Vignette on body reading and startle reflex. *The patient lies on his back on a flat firm surface (e.g., a massage table or a couch). Each time there is an empty space, an arch, between a part of the body and the flat surface, analysis begins. The higher the empty space, the more one can suspect shortened extensor muscles that could be associated to a chronic startle reflex. This is most frequently the case under the following parts of the body: neck, shoulders, wrists, shoulder blades, lower back, thigh, knees, ankles, and soles of the feet. The length of an arch (e.g., from hip to shoulder blades) is also a sign of the importance of chronic tensions of the extensors. The suspicion that one is facing a chronic startle reflex increases when these tensions are associated to a mainly thoracic form of breathing. The more the abdominal breathing is inhibited, the more one can suspect fear. A difficulty in having a relaxed deep expiration is also a criterion of the same. Other signs of fear are eyes that are chronically wide open or eyes tensely shut (Brakel, 2006; Hillman et al., 2005).*

There are often several possible causes contributing to a body profile. The practitioner who notices such a configuration must then begin an inquiry to ascertain that a chronic startle reflex is present. He may, for example, ask the patient what is experienced when an arch is artificially amplified or reduced. In such cases, I often ask the patient to explore what happens when he coordinates this movement with his breathing (e.g., what happens when he extends the wrist at each expiration).

Stretching Oneself Out of One's Neurotic Fears

> Separate your lips slightly. Let your lower jaw drop as much as possible. Close your eyes. Slowly tilt your head backwards until it delicately touches the back of the neck. At the same time, gradually open your mouth as much as possible "as if to swallow a peach."
>
> You are yawning. That is the aim of the exercise. . . .
>
> N.B. yawning is the most efficient cure for nervous tension and fatigue. (Wespin, 1973, on tai chi, p. 60; translated by Marcel Duclos)

In collaboration with Braatøy, Bülow-Hansen developed methods that stimulate the pleasure of yawing and stretching oneself out of one's shell of fear: "If you did not feel like stretching, then try another way of releasing respiration and the stretch impulses: wriggle your jaw from side to side, spread your fingers and toes and move your tongue around" (Thornquist and Bunkan, 1991, p. 79).

Bülow-Hansen also welcomes sighs and farts.[71] The aim is to lower the inhibition of the vegetative dynamics of the affects and strengthen their capacity to participate in organismic regulations during an interaction. In other words, these methods attempt to help people experience themselves as an emotional and sexualized being with vegetative needs. When a patient expresses affective arousal during a psychomotor session, the physiotherapist steps back and supports whatever forms of expressions that need to become manifest. For Bülow-Hansen, the psychotherapist is the one who may propose interpretations of the emerging process and help the patient manage whatever complications arise in his mind and his environments. This technical point may seem trivial to some, but it often happens that I must repeatedly emphasize it during supervision. Those who use massage as a way of strengthening affective dynamics often find it difficult not to become psychotherapeutic. The basic rule, in such cases, is to allow affects to appear in the room but resist the urge to provide an interpretation or solicit its expression. Being aware of such limitations is a way of not strengthening emerging transferential processes. As soon as a psychomotor therapist goes beyond this frame, he often finds himself involved in relational dynamics that neither he nor his patients know how to manage (Thornquist and Bunkan, 1991, 9, p. 116f).

A useful ritual is to let a patient alone for a while at the end of each session to decompress. If ever the libido pressure becomes stronger than can be handled in such a setting, the therapists trained in Biodynamic Psychology will say that it is time to employ the decompression ritual and leave the patient alone so that he can regulate his sexuality privately. I do not know how psychomotor therapists manage such moments, which are not frequent but nonetheless exist. The aim of such treatments is to help a patient express the released emotional and libidinous impulses outside of the massage sessions. These issues can be processed in psychotherapy sessions if they become problematic. When such events repeat themselves during massage sessions, massage is not presently a recommended approach for this patient.

Bülow-Hansen Refuses to Use Reich's Notion of Cosmic Energy

For Braatøy and Bülow-Hansen, Reich's use of cosmic energy made no sense. The only bioenergy that exists for them is that produced by metabolic biochemical processes. Body sensations, like circulating warmth, can always be explained by mechanisms such as the dynamics of body fluids (e.g., cardiovascular system). Even when there is no adequate explanation for such a sensation, this does not imply that a reference to cosmic energy is relevant or useful. Many sensations that are activated by a breathing exercise, associated by Reichians to orgone, can be more easily understood as the activated metabolic dynamic consequences of internal breathing. This analysis is the same as that proposed by body psychotherapists such as Downing (1996, I.4).

A Massage Session Must Always Integrate a Symptom in the Global Dynamics of the Body

Bülow-Hansen believed that a treatment only acquires a lasting effect if the masseur integrates the symptomatic part of the body in the global postural dynamics. When one focuses on a scoliosis, one should also take into account the fact that this symptom creates disturbances in the global alignment of the body. When a masseur works on the tensions that maintain a scoliosis, he also influences the muscular dorsal chains, from head to toe.[72] This is why Aadel Bülow-Hansen taught her pupils to always massage the whole body and integrate in each session some direct work on the symptomatic part of the body that justifies the session. This principle, which was followed by Gerda Boyesen and adopted by her students, is different from the Reichian tendency to focus on a single body block during several sessions.

> Vignette on a massage demonstration given by Bülow-Hansen.[73] *Bülow-Hansen's way of dealing with the "whole body" is not necessarily that of dealing with every muscle. She tackles a general postural issue and analyzes a muscular chain from several angles, focusing on key points. In the case of a woman who could not touch her feet, she massages the muscles behind the legs, some muscles of the belly, and then the throat. She then coordinates the massage of the throat with the breathing behavior of the upper half of the thoracic cage. From that point, she supports the abdominal breathing. Having loosened the muscular chain and the corresponding breathing pattern, she asks the patient to explore how her belly muscles and breathing are integrated when she tries to bend her body again. Finally, she discusses with the patient what she experiences when the patient stands. For example, she asks the patient to become aware of how the tone of certain body parts is integrated in the global posture.*

This technique emphasizes *connections* between different parts of the body and tries to avoid the impression that the body is a construction of disconnected parts. Body reading is usually conducted with the patient standing, so that the connection between body parts can be situated in relation to the pressure of gravity. This strategy helps the therapist be clearly aware that loosening one part of the body may create tensions in other parts.[74] Sometimes a tension may move from an easily accessible part, situated on the surface of the body (e.g., the shoulders), to a less accessible part (e.g., the diaphragm or the psoas). This must be avoided, for one would then be creating a greater problem than the one the patient originally presented. A typical example is that of a patient who is submitted to a painful muscular massage. The masseur may soften the original tension, but to bear the pain of the massage, the patient may have tensed other parts of the body (sometimes most of the body). In the 1970s, Gerda Boyesen regularly used this argument in her criticism of methods developed in the United States, such as Orgonomy, Rolfing, and Bioenergetics.

A holistic approach to body tensions, such as the ones proposed by Rolfing and Bülow-Hansen's method, often creates a modification of postural dynamics and therefore of the body's alignment in the field of gravity.[75] The neck, back, and legs may become longer, the shoulder may move backward, and the feet may then need bigger shoes. These modifications are not only muscular. They also influence the fascia[76] and postural sensorimotor circuits. Technically, this means that the physiotherapist will focus on how the tone of several muscles interacts, rather than on a single muscle.[77] For example, Bülow-Hansen focused on the capacity muscles have to not only initiate movement but also inhibit them.[78]

Always Observe the Impact of an Action on Breathing

Aadel Bülow-Hansen often observed how a body movement or a behavior (even verbal) interacts with vegetative dynamics.[79] Breathing is the most visible part of vegetative dynamics. An individual's breathing pattern can vary at any moment in a visible way. These modifications influence the rhythm, amplitude, and shape of external breathing patterns. If the patient has a rapid shallow breathing movement at the beginning of a session, the therapist can observe if his interventions have an impact that creates an even stronger inhibition of the breathing pattern, or on the contrary, creates more amplitude (a) in the thorax, belly, or diaphragm; and (b) mostly on the front, side, or back of the torso. At each moment, the therapist can modify his way of touching, in support of these modifications of the breathing pattern, and thus learn what helps a person or frightens her. Some therapists (like Gerald Kogan and Jay Stattman, trained in Gestalt therapy), modify their verbal interventions in function of such modifications.

According to Thornquist and Bunkan, Braatøy distinguished "breathing in fear" and "breathing to prevent fear" in his work on the startle reflex:

> The person who is "*breathing to prevent the fear*," who does not accept his feelings, has a breathing pattern characterized by active use of muscles and steering throughout the respiratory cycle. There is no exchange between tension and relaxation; there is constant, if varying muscular control. Breathing is restrained. Respiratory movement is mainly abdominal. In this "stomach breathing", expansion takes place in the sagittal plane only. Respiratory frequency is low with an even rhythm. The pause at the end of expiration is longer than normal, and there is little ability to adapt to either physical or psychological stress. Breathing does not change spontaneously but is controlled the whole time. This way of breathing shows that feelings are shut off. Fear is held outside the consciousness and is not allowed in the open to become an experience.
>
> The person who is "*breathing in fear*" has superficial rapid respiration. Movement is taking place primarily in the upper chest, with neck and shoulder muscles taking an active part in the work of respiration. Breathing is rapid and often uneven. This way of breathing tells us that this person is in contact with and experiences fear. (Thornquist and Bunkan 1991, 3, p. 25)

Some of Aadel Bülow-Hansen's pupils further developed her work in collaboration with body psychotherapists. Lillemor Johnsen (1976a, 1976b, 1979) has taught her work to founders of the Danish body psychotherapy school called Bodynamic (MacNaughton, 2004). Their work has been widespread in the United States by therapists such as Peter Levine (2004) and Babette Rothschild (2000), who have developed particularly efficient ways of working with trauma using body psychotherapy techniques. Gerda Boyesen is another pupil of Bülow-Hansen who integrated psychomotoric work in body psychotherapy. (I say more about her work in the following sections.)

Gerda Boyesen

A Clinical Psychologist Studies Physiotherapy

Gerda Boyesen (1922–2005)[80] is often acclaimed as one of the important European body psychotherapist of the 1970s. Roz Carroll presents her as "the mother of body psychotherapy" (Carroll, 2002, p. 87). Although she mostly focused on the vegetative dynamics and how they are experienced, she approached the phenomenon from several points of view, developed in psychology, physiotherapy, and schools of spirituality. This type of synthesis is not only a good example of the theories in body psychotherapy that emerged in the 1970s, but also an example of why it so difficult to characterize this discipline.

She first trained as clinical psychologist in Oslo in the late 1940s. She then worked in psychiatric institutions that were still influenced by Trygve Braatøy. The content of the courses she followed can be situated somewhere between Freud and Jung, Pavlov and Cannon. Boyesen was manifestly interested by some psychological dynamics, but not in psychology as a field. For example, she was not interested in the issues raised by cognitive psychology pertaining to the dynamics of representations. The only aspect of Piaget's theory that might have interested her was the idea that children learn most efficiently when they can become active, playful participants in their learning process. On the other hand, she was constantly working with an individual's capacity to visualize body sensations and situations. This interest kept her close to the techniques of Jungian dream analysis and Gestalt therapy. In her classes, she often mentioned Freud's two topical models, but she did so in a rather simplistic way. She began her career as a clinical psychologist in psychiatric institutions.

Ola Raknes was Gerda Boyesen's principal psychotherapist. At the first session, he asked her to say a few words about her life history; then he asked her to explore Reich's jellyfish exercise:[81]

> Then it was breathing: imagine you are a jellyfish. Moreover, it is with this simple proposal that the dynamic began. Imagine you are a jellyfish . . . let movement and breathing move freely. . . . I had read books on psychoanalysis, but I had never imagined that a psychotherapy treatment could become something like that. I thus let my body move with my breathing: as I exhaled, my head would advance for-

ward, and my chest would sink. It was a pulsation movement of the whole body.
An extremely intense dynamic process began. (Gerda Boyesen, 1985a, I.2, p. 16f;
translated by Michael Heller)

Raknes had an ambivalent relationship with Boyesen. He never recognized her
as fully trained in the Reichian method he taught; however, when he left London, he asked her to replace him in his English practice. After this relatively
psychological phase of her life, she focused on the vegetative dimensions of affective dynamics.

Fascinated by Reich's proposal, she remembered a conference given by
Braatøy in 1947, when she was a student.[82] During this conference, he said that
to become a vegetotherapist, one had to be a medical doctor or at least trained
in physiotherapy. It is impossible to become a body psychotherapist without
having a good understanding of how a body functions. Because she did not have
the courage to begin medical studies at her age, she trained in physiotherapy
and chose the Bülow-Hansen Institute for her specialization in this domain.
Bülow-Hansen required therapy of the students in her method of training;
Boyesen received psychomotor treatment. During this process she acquired deep
experiences of what Reich called the vegetative process. Bülow-Hansen's work
on her activated powerful emotional and bodily mobilizations and discharges.
This experience was crucial. She not only received an excellent training in physiotherapy, she also felt an urge to explore and understand the vegetative dynamics of the self. She associated these dynamics with various theories of life energy
such as Reich's Orgonomy taught by Raknes. One of the reasons Gerda Boyesen became so famous is that she spent her life transmitting to others her hypnotic fascination for the vegetative dimensions of affective experience. For her,
as for Lowen, identity is rooted in these vegetative dynamics. Influenced by
other Scandinavian teachers, Boyesen also integrated work on the fluids of the
organism, mostly venous blood and the moisture of the skin. She talks of "energetic fluids," where, in Cannon's style, I would be content with "biologically
regulated fluids."

Biodynamic Psychology

Biodynamic psychotherapists work in a variety of physical positions, each suitable
for a different kind and level of interaction and each furthering in the client different levels of consciousness and exploration. Whether we are working with words,
touch or in silence, we are reaching to the whole person and expecting our work to
affect body and psyche together. (Clover Southwell, 2010, "Levels of Consciousness and Contact in Biodynamic Psychology," p. 10)

Having taken over Ola Raknes's practice in London, Gerda Boyesen now worked
alone. She needed to learn how to combine body and psychological techniques
in a treatment. Her reference for that was Vegetotherapy. However, Reichian

body techniques are simplistic, so she also looked for ways to combine Vegeto-therapy with what she had learned from Bülow-Hansen. The method she gradu-ally developed in this context maintained clear distinctions between bodywork (mainly Psychomotor and Alexander Lowen's postures), psychological approaches to the organism (mainly Freudian, Jungian, and Gestalt), and approaches to the organismic regulation systems (mainly Vegetotherapy and Orgonomy). Like Reich in his later years, she used psychological approaches and bodywork mostly to have an impact on the vegetative dimension of experience; she also did so to obtain information on how her work on organismic regulatory sys-tems was experienced and assimilated by her patients. For example, she would use techniques like imagery work and guided exploration of fantasies to in-crease awareness of feelings and body sensations. This way of placing explicit perception and affects in resonance is an effective way of soliciting emotions. She developed her work in collaboration with other London colleagues, like David Boadella (1987) and Malcolm Brown (2001). Boyesen's work can be identified as a particular way of combining vegetative, body, and psychological work with the aim of strengthening an organism's auto-regulation systems.

As she began to teach, her three children joined her: Ebba (1985), Mona-Lisa (1976), and Paul (1993). Together, they created Biodynamic psychology as a way of combining what each family member and their colleagues were discov-ering. Other often-quoted names in that school are Jeff Barlow, Robin Lee (1977), Peg Nunnely (2000), Francis Pope, Clover Southwell (1980), and the members of the Biodynamic School of Montpellier, founded by Christiane and François Lewin.

As soon as her school was large enough, Gerda Boyesen created a clinic in which bodywork (which she called *physiatry*) and psychotherapy were often carried out by different persons. That choice highlights two practical points:

1. The underlying assumption for separating bodywork and psychotherapy is that these are two dimensions, animated by distinct mechanisms, that require distinct forms of training (e.g., physiotherapy and psychology) to be adequately managed. This helps the patient have a clear under-standing of this distinction, instead of giving the patient the impression that they form a sort of "fruit salad."[83]

2. It is not always the same person who can offer good psychotherapy and good bodywork. There are exceptions, but they are, in the final analysis, relatively rare. Body psychotherapy had no institutional support, and training was financed by what students were able to pay, and they some-times wanted recognition more than competence. When I was a Boyesen trainer, I often saw Gerda annoyed at pupils (including myself) who lacked specific knowledge on certain topics. For example, certain train-ees offered massage with a good sensitivity for global "energetic" im-pressions but did not know which muscle they were touching, or the psychophysiological implications of loosening such a muscle. She trained

them to acknowledge their limits and develop their therapeutic potential within the limits that such awareness created.

Boyesen was trained to use methods (psychomotor and Reichian) designed to treat rigid persons. Rigidity (muscular and psychological) was highly praised quality during a first half of the twentieth century, a period that had been massively influenced by military and religious discipline. Two world wars strengthened this traditional trait. However, rigidity became a huge issue in the 1960s in North America as well as in Europe. In the 1970s psychotherapists observed an increasing number of patients who suffered from a lack of rigidity and weak defense systems. This cultural change required important changes of strategy in all forms of psychotherapy. Gerda Boyesen was one of the first body psychotherapists to sense this change and look for methods that could help patients with poor defense systems. Her method was sometimes referred to as a form of "soft Bioenergetics," different from the more confrontational approach developed by Alexander Lowen. Most body techniques try to relax hypertonic muscles. She was original when she developed ways of focusing on hypotonic muscles as way of constructing psychophysiological defense systems.[84] This area of work, already suggested by Otto Fenichel (1928), was also being developed by other pupils of Bülow-Hansen, mostly Lillemor Johnsen and Berit Bunkan. Gerda Boyesen also developed *active* relaxation techniques and massage that helped people experience their body as something that could contain their feelings.[85]

Gerda Boyesen's attempts at producing a theoretical framework for her method followed paths developed by neo-Reichian Idealism. A central theme in her thinking was to help the organism restore its capacity to repair itself. That requires that a person becomes capable of integrating the experience that there is an "ocean of cosmic energy" (Boyesen, 1985a, II.12, p. 89f) animating the organism.

Once Boyesen's colleagues began to have their own theories, Biodynamic psychology lost its grounding in the Oslo tradition. It became an agglomeration of personal visions, loosely connected to Gerda Boyesen's initial proposals. Wanting to keep a form of coherence in this dispersion of models and techniques, she focused on what her creativity was elaborating, and she increasingly set aside her attempt to develop what she had learned in Oslo. For her last years of work, she wanted to focus on her main interests at the time: a sort of alchemy, or spiritually oriented psychophysiology. Her courageous fight against aging and illness strengthened this trend. From then on, Biodynamic psychology lost its impact on the development of body psychotherapy, and it dissolved its creativity into schools that mostly defended the whims, fantasies, and skills of individuals and a certain humanistic stance that is a part of Boyesen's legacy. Her approach finally became a fascinating New Age movement, which had lost contact with psychotherapy. David Boadella's Biosynthesis may be taking a similar direction.

Psychoperistalsis

Following a rationale that remains close to Cannon's theory on how visceral activity is included in the homeostatic regulatory system, Gerda Boyesen assumed that peristaltic movements played a central role in the regulation of fluids. Fluid dynamics also play a central role in the regulation of sexuality and other affects (Vincent, 1986). She began to use a stethoscope to explore the correlation between peristaltic activities, self-reports of patients, and visible changes in the body. She observed interesting regularities between these three layers of the organism. For example, certain forms of touch and verbal intervention often activated peristaltic activity in certain ways, whereas other interventions would inhibit it. Like Cannon, she observed that these correlations were complex. Anxiety often inhibits peristaltic activity but can also activate extreme forms of it. Sometimes deep forms of relaxation, which also inhibit emotional feelings, can slow down peristaltic activity. Theoretically, these variations between affective states and peristaltism make sense if one thinks of what is known pertaining to the relation between affects and vegetative arousal. Once again, one notices that different psychophysiological dynamics can produce identical signals. It is therefore impossible to rely only on such correlations, but following them can be useful in many situations, if the association is considered with clinical intelligence.

Boyesen is credited with continuing to explore the relationship between affects and gastrointestinal movements at a time when neither Reich nor psychophysiologists found the topic important. These were days when psychophysiology was increasingly being absorbed by neuropsychology. She coined the term *psychoperistalsis* to designate peristaltic activity that was not triggered by the assimilation of food. Her clinical investigation of the phenomenon showed that the relation between affects and bowel activity deserved further investigation.[86]

A Practitioner's Theory

Most of Gerda Boyesen's theorizing was a form of intellectual activity related to her clinical practice and courses. She spent little time reading what her colleagues wrote or going to congresses to understand how her field developed. She satisfied her appetite for theoretical models by inventing "theories" in function of immediate needs. She thus taught a wide variety of models that are often exotic (G. Boyesen, 2001). Nevertheless, they are useful as metaphorical ways of intellectualizing highly relevant clinical intuitions. As an example of this way of thinking, I summarize her distinction among stone, warrior, sunshine, and the princess and the pea.

1. *Stone.* A patient is like a stone when a masseur can press with all his weight on his tense muscles without activating any sensations. Such a patient often reacts to deep or soft massage by saying that he feels nothing special. In such a case, a Reichian therapist refers to a rigid personality or a strong armor.

2. *Warrior*. As soon as a patient is touched, he begins to explore a movement or talks about his relationships with others; he feels angry; he
wants to hit somebody and shout; he needs to enter into a conflict with
someone. These patients often need to improve their awareness of aggressive feelings and their capacity to ground and contain them. They
also need accept their anger as something that they may allow themselves to feel and express and that others can also be warriors. This implies that the patient learns (a) that the others are capable of protecting
themselves when he is angry, and (b) that he can defend himself against
their anger. Today, body psychotherapists tend to talk of "grounded
anger," "embodied anger," or "contained but not repressed" anger. This
attitude is different from a child's temper tantrum, the violence that is
often expressed by brothers and sisters, or the fear of a violent parent
when one is a child. This brings us back to the notion that humans have
to learn ways of dealing with their emotions. We have innate emotions
and an innate need to express them, but not an innate capacity to deal
with our emotions. This capacity needs to be calibrated by culture and
by the psyche.

3. *Sunshine*. This person is so open she becomes hypersensitive. She reacts
to everything that is presented to her with such an abundance of associations and sensations that the therapist often feels drowned by the quantity of information that emerges during a session.

4. *Princess and the pea*. This person (male or female) often overreacts to
any event in an extreme way. Any form of body intervention becomes
impossible, but she refuses to be deprived of body interventions if she
comes to see a body psychotherapist. Any attempt to massage such a
patient will allow him to criticize each proposal, while at the same time
he demands a massage that will contact him in a way he determines appropriate. There is no way a therapist can confront or criticize a patient
who is in such a state of mind. The only thing a body psychotherapist
can do in such a situation is to remain patient and provide containment.
This metaphoric state of the princess and the pea can be activated by a
style of bodywork that lowers the patient's defenses too much. In such
states, a patient can be simultaneously completely open to himself and
his environment and in fear of this state or how others may perceive it.
Extreme activation of the startle reflex and extreme relaxation are often
simultaneously observable when a patient is in this state. In this, we are
close to those models of stress that assume that the parasympathetic
and sympathetic vegetative systems are strongly aroused simultaneously.

By default, a therapist trained by Gerda Boyesen will proceed in the following
way: he will help a stone become a warrior, a warrior become sunshine, and
sunshine become a stone. The important part of the model is that everyone

should learn to pass from one state to another, in function of what he needs to experience at a given moment. A "princess of the small pea"[87] may at first need to descend this path backward, becoming sunshine first, than a warrior, and finally a stone. Being as opened as when one shares orgasm with a lover may be traumatizing in a professional environment.

The foregoing example allows the reader to understand a particular way of producing metaphoric models that is widespread in the field of psychotherapies and in most methods that work on mind and body. Such models can be useful during a session, but they are difficult to explain to colleagues who have trained in other schools of psychotherapy or to scientists.

Individual or Social Ethical Rules?

> Filomena: . . . so I but live honestly, my conscience gives me no disquietude; if others asperse me, God and the truth will take arms in my defense. (Boccaccio, 1353, *The Decameron*, Proem: Kindle 524–43)[88]

For Gerda Boyesen, psychotherapy should help a person find a state of independent well-being. This implies allowing a person to find a form of ethical guidelines that are compatible with who she is, with what she really believes. Like others who grew up during World War II, Boyesen did not trust the ideologies of the masses or official positions, such as those of communism and fascism. In those regimes, professional deontological standards are often influenced by ideology. She even mistrusted the deontology of professional associations created by democratic states that supported colonialism and World War I. In that, she was close to Reich. For her generation, it was more important to develop a personal ethic, compatible with Idealistic notions such as truth and goodness. In her courses, she encouraged her pupils to be "faithful to who we are" or "true to oneself and one's deeper being."[89] Because of the historical circumstances that reinforced her Idealistic inclinations, she was suspicious of official professional ethical standards. The ideological movements that spread during the 1960s and 1970s reinforced this spirit. Her life shows the vulnerability of persons who reject all forms of collegiality. Those who have adopted such positions tend to fall into all sorts of traps set by social reality and personal drives, even when their intentions are honorable. This issue can be summarized by the following question: Can one adopt professional ethical standards when one knows that these standards are subject to manipulation by ideological movements?[90]

There are no satisfying answers to this question. I will let each reader find his own answers to the question. This book defends the ethical notion that collaboration with colleagues is an essential feature of scientific ethics, but it cannot be denied that this requirement is often polluted by the more negative dynamics of the human condition.

Faithful to her individualism, Gerda Boyesen (2001) proposed many concepts that only she could understand. If her theoretical approach was not one that could be used by others, her ideas have nevertheless inspired many body psychotherapists. They integrated her thoughts in their own processes rather than attempting to follow in her footsteps.

From Organismic Therapy to Body Psychotherapy

I believe that this is the first book that proposes a clear and expanded distinction between psychotherapy and the organismic therapies. I propose this distinction with the hope that it will help clarify issues that have created a series of misunderstandings within body psychotherapy and between body psychotherapy and colleagues from other approaches. Primarily, psychotherapy is a recognized "paramedical" domain, whereas the organismic therapies are not. The organismic therapies have had to navigate between Charybdis (their identity) and Scylla (the social recognition of being seen as psychotherapy). Boyesen, like several of her colleagues, said that she practiced and taught her method and conceded (only on the tip of her tongue) that it did consist of psychotherapy.[91] In fact, she freely admitted that her work could be a complement to Freudian or Jungian psychotherapy. It was a regular occurrence to have her say that a patient who had benefited from a treatment with her may now need to undergo an analysis. She saw herself as someone who opens consciousness to the organismic space, but she did not always master the integration of this opening with the patient's mind.

The difficulty with this position is that we find, in a somewhat displaced manner, the ancient split between psyche and soma, save that now, the rift is between organismic therapy and psychotherapy. The division is nonetheless profound. It encouraged personalities like Lowen to create a form of body psychotherapy that integrates the organismic, behavioral, and mental processes. If the proposition of the first generation of body psychotherapists, like Lowen, had great difficulty reconciling Freud and Reich (often going through Jung), the second generation made it possible to put forth a more creditable proposition, which is less dependent on the old analytic psychotherapies and integrates recent formulations from systemic, cognitive, and behavioral therapies.

Reflexes and Reactions

Today, as I read the body psychotherapy literature written between 1940 and 1960 in Oslo, I notice that it could be useful to clarify the difference between *reflexes* and *reactions*. Up to now, I have used these terms as most practitioners use them, which is to say, like two words that mean nearly the same thing. However, it may be useful to distinguish these terms more clearly. What Reich called the orgastic reflex is a more complex entity than the reflexes described by Pavlov.[92] It would be more adequate to speak of a *global organismic reaction* based on a set of innate mechanisms. A reaction is more complex than a reflex, but less flexible than a propension. A reaction can express itself in different ways: it can be more or less intense, recruit a variable proportion of organismic regulation systems, and more or less fully express itself. At a given moment, the orgastic reaction can be particularly active in the legs and the pelvis, but less so in the upper segments of the body. At another moment, it can manifest itself in a different way. A reaction can also acquire individual properties and styles as it accommodates to the particularities of an organism (shape of the body, emotional and cognitive profile, etc.). Some persons are afraid of the impersonal dimension of their orgasm. By "impersonal," I mean those aspects of an orgasm that impose innate urges and modes of functioning to all the dimensions of the organism and to the organism that is one's partner. These fearful persons tend to inhibit their orgastic urges. One way to do this is to associate one's sexual needs to a wide range of acquired requirements to which one identifies (e.g., my orgastic reflex must be elegant, or sexy, or tender, or aristocratic, or cool).

Thelen and Smith (1994) and Downing (1996) have shown that reactions are based on sensorimotor systems that can function in different ways. Thelen and Smith use walking as an example of a sensorimotor system.[93] If one puts the body of a newborn infant in water, his legs move as if he were walking, but the walking sensorimotor system needs a year before it can be integrated by the organism in such a way that walking becomes possible. Thelen and Smith's model allows us to reformulate the relation between Braatøy's startle reflex and Reich's orgastic reflex. As we shall see, one could assume that they are two ways of using the same sensorimotor system.

Reich followed Darwin's notion of *antithesis*[94] to define a reaction designed to inhibit what he calls an orgasm reflex. He calls this antiorgastic reflex *sympathecotonia*: "The basic characteristic of sympathicotonia is the chronic inspiratory attitude of the thorax and the limitation of full (parasympathetic) expiration" (Reich, 1946, VIII.6, p. 247).[95] According to Reich, this chronic counterbody attitude is the resulting construct of social education. He[96] assumed that for most citizens, education had associated their innate experience of pleasure to fear. In Christian and Jewish cultures, every time a pleasurable sexual impression would try to enter a person's mind, it would be replaced by a terrifying image of the devil.[97] Since Boyesen, at least, it has become customary in Norwegian body psychotherapy to equate Reich's sympathecotonia to Braatøy's startle reflex. The association was considered a refinement of Reich's analysis, in the direction of what Otto Fenichel recommended.

What Braatøy calls a startle reflex is a reaction that integrates the reflex in a more complex system of reactions.

Ebba Boyesen (1985) explored the possibility that the movements used by an infant as he comes out of the mother's womb and the orgastic reaction may use the same sensorimotor system. The orgastic reaction could be a new way of using an innate motor pattern that is no longer required once the organism is born. Ebba Boyesen repeatedly demonstrated in her training groups how the same coordination of movements from head to feet is used by these two motor patterns. However, there are also differences: at birth, an infant's head is pushed out of the birth canal, while the orgasmic reflex tends to support pelvic movements. Her analysis is based on the observation that as a girl develops physically, the tilt of the pelvis changes.[98] This shift occurs spontaneously most of the time, but in some cases, the change does not occur or is insufficient to guarantee a comfortable postural coordination during orgasm. This may cause disturbances in the establishment of the orgasmic reflex during puberty. While a woman with this disturbance makes love, she continues to push with the head more than with the pelvis.

Wilhelm Reich,[99] Alexander Lowen, Gerda Boyesen and many others used methods which activate the vomiting reflex (or emesis), when they want to work on the spontaneous coordination of the segments of the upper half of the body. They believed that vomiting mobilize parts of the sensorimotor system used by the orgasmic reflex. When they ask a patient to explore what happens when he vomits, they ask him to focus on the pleasure that can be experienced during and after emesis. The eyes are often wet, there is an experience of inner cleansing like the air after a storm, and one can observe a flowing movement that arises mostly from the diaphragm. Patients who suffer from alcoholism or bulimia know this pleasure and use it to strengthen their symptoms. Asking patients to explore what they experience when they vomit also helps a psychotherapist spot various forms of anxiety associated with disgust. This anxiety may be associated with a disgust at seeing digested food but also with a fear of certain forms of pleasure activated by emesis. This may lead to discovering a fear of certain forms of bodily sensations of pleasure activated during and after orgasm.

We have thus dealt with two mechanisms:

1. *Reflex.* A relatively local and stereotyped action that can be activated by a variety of stimuli: a finger in the throat, food poisoning, brain tumor, etc. The variety of stimuli designates a more complex form of reflex than those described by Pavlov or in a medical textbook. Nevertheless, it could be argued that it is the same type of mechanism.
2. *Reaction.* This type of action automatically creates a certain form of interaction between all the dimensions of the organism. One of its impacts is the activation of affective feelings and expressions such as pleasure, fear, disgust, or anxiety. A reaction may incorporate one (startle reflex, vomiting reflex, etc.) or several reflexes, but these reflexes are now associated to other innate and acquired forms of physiological, bodily, behavioral, and psychological dynamics.

LOWEN AND BIOENERGETIC ANALYSIS

Reich had several patients/students/collaborators/friends in the United States. In his school, we find the same confusion of roles that existed in the early years of the psychoanalytic movement.[100] This confusion situates a school of psychotherapy close to the schools of philosophy like those of Heraclites and Socrates.[101] This type of collaboration associated with a personal process often leads to a kind of cult of personality. A well-documented example is Myron Sharaf (1983). He was Reich's patient, worked in his research laboratory on the orgone. Sharaf believed that Reich was a friend, while Reich was only on friendly terms with him. Sharaf established himself as Reich's biographer. He had the unpleasant surprise of discovering that his wife had an affair with Reich while they were both his patients. Others, like Theodore P. Wolfe, translated Reich's works after having done everything they could to influence U.S. officials to allow Reich entry into the country. Another one of Reich's unexplained traits was his ability to find important financial support, whether in Norway or the United States. It is possible that he knew how to motivate sponsors, but I have never found any information on this topic. The Reichians are silent on the source of his revenues.

For the group of Reichians, Reich was a being without armor and without any neurosis, in contact with the orgone, who was trying to save them. They were fascinated by what they discovered in themselves in Orgone therapy sessions and admired the ideal professed by Reich. Several among them, like Sharaf, nonetheless found it difficult to mentally digest what arose within them when they were freed of their armor. They felt the need to undertake a psychoanalytic psychotherapy to understand what they had experienced in the orgonomy sessions . . . and in their relationship with Reich. It must be said that Reich no longer concerned himself with the dynamics of transference and countertransference.

The Establishment of Bioenergetic Analysis

Alexander Lowen (1910–2008) was born in New York City into a Jewish family that had emigrated from Russia.[102] He received a bachelor's degree in science and business, completed his doctoral studies in the sciences of law, and obtained a law degree. At the same time, he became a sports instructor, then studied diverse body-centered approaches, like Calisthenics (a method to strengthen the muscles), yoga, and the Eurhythmic gymnastic of Emile Jacques-Dalcroze.

Lowen gradually became interested in the interaction between gymnastics and the psyche. He trained in Edmund Jacobson's Progressive relaxation. In 1940, he met Reich in New York City. At that time, Reich was mostly teaching Vegetotherapy and Character analysis. He spoke very little about orgone. Lowen was enthralled by Reich's theory because it made it possible to situate the relationship between the body, the soma, and the psyche in the dynamics of the organism, with a theory that opened up onto a practice. This approach went much further than what Lowen had learned in his training in Jacobson's method. He began his training with Reich in 1941; he went into therapy with him in 1942.

Increasingly, Reich required a medical degree to have the right to open up a practice in orgonomy. Too old to be accepted in a medical school in the United

States,[103] Lowen entered the Geneva University Faculty of Medicine in 1947. When he returned from New York, Lowen kept a positive image of Reich all of his life, without losing his critical eye. Furthermore, he discovered that the experiences activated during his sessions with Reich could not always be integrated by his psyche in an adequate way.

On his return to New York City, Lowen incorporated Reich's new approaches to the body, but he concluded that his patients also needed to be able to cope in a conscious way with what emerged after having relaxed their muscles and breathing. Lowen also remarked that without a psychological integration, the openness achieved by softening a patient's armor lasts only a few months. In 1952, Reich had moved to Maine. He rarely gave individual sessions anymore. He focused on his Orgonomy. The orgonomists defended Reich's change of direction with a fanaticism that Lowen did not share. Lowen associated himself with John Pierrakos and William B. Walling, who were both physicians and Reichians. They decided to work on each other to discover a better way to connect the work on the organism, energy, and the psyche. This exploration lasted three years; it evolved into a form of therapy that they made public in creating, as early as 1956, The Institute for Bioenergetic Analysis.

Bioenergetic analysis integrates two trends:

1. Like many others, Lowen was not satisfied with Reich's relatively simplistic body techniques. He therefore integrated his own knowledge of body techniques into Bioenergetics.
2. For Lowen's generation, the split between Vegetotherapy and Psychoanalysis was unproductive and irrational. They did not want to inherit what they considered to be a split caused by personal power games between prewar clans. He therefore sought to create a synthesis out of what he considered to be two interesting and complementary ways of helping patients. This aspect of the method justifies the use of the term *analysis*. I do not know if he ever undertook a psychoanalytic psychotherapy.

Even though others sought a way to coordinate Vegetotherapy and psychotherapy, Alexander Lowen's proposal was the first to present a coherent method of body psychotherapy. Although Bioenergetics was founded by three individuals, this method was developed, above all, by Lowen. Pierrakos maintained close ties with the development of Orgonomy which he associated with the forces described in spiritual movements. In 1970, Pierrakos founded his own school, Core energetics.

Bioenergetics and Psychotherapy
Initially, the term *bioenergy* had the same meaning as the term *orgone* for Lowen. Lowen and his colleagues solely introduce the term because, in the

United States, it was forbidden by law to use the term *orgone* in a publication or in a public conference.[104] Gradually, Lowen situated his "bioenergy" halfway between orgone and the energy produced by metabolic activity. One could criticize him for using a recognized scientific term to designate cosmic energy, but I think he also wanted to send the message that orgone can only animate the organism by activating biomechanical metabolic dynamics.

To clarify the difference between a vitalistic option and a materialistic energy, I propose the following distinction:

1. Vital energy is a force that animates matter. It structures the material mechanisms that use it.
2. The energy of the chemists (since the work of Claude Bernard on metabolic activity) is a production without a goal. It is like the oil produced beneath the Earth's crust, without the intention of helping humans power their cars. The metabolic dynamics have survived because they can be used for the survival of living creatures, but that does not imply that they produce energy with a specific aim. The mechanisms that use the energy transform it in something that manages to survive. Within organisms, the laws of chance and of necessity lead to a certain form of concordance between the mechanisms that produce energy and the mechanisms that consume it.

Lowen's bioenergy is a creative energy that forms a coherent field, and that field structures the dynamics of the organism. This field surrounds the organism with an aura that some, like Lowen, can see. To be able to sense the dynamics of this field in oneself and in others is, for Lowen, one of the keys of his therapeutic proposition. At the same time, he thinks that one cannot influence the quality of this field without mobilizing metabolic dynamics. Lowen's body and breathing exercises have the primary goal of reinforcing the metabolic activity of the patient, thus permitting a quantitative increase in his vitality and qualitative modifications of the aura. The health and creativity of all the dimensions of the organism are dependent on this vitality: physical health, emotional health, mental health, and so on. As early as in the 1970s, this analysis became more central in his therapeutic activity, probably because it corresponded more to his expertise than to the psychodynamic dimension that was developed mostly by some of his students.

The Reichian armor is understood as an inhibitor of metabolic energy. The mental defenses described by psychoanalysts inhibit the dynamics between the psyche and the metabolism; they create ways of thinking that reinforces behaviors and body practices that inhibit somatic activity. Once somatic dynamics are inhibited, the metabolic activity is no longer sufficiently nourished to support an appropriate organismic activity. To thwart this type of strangling of the organism's dynamics, Lowen seeks above all to mobilize the individual's vegetative vitality by asking him to breathe deeply, express himself emotionally as intensely and explicitly as possible, and hold postures that emphasize muscular tension. The goal of these techniques is to create a global mobilization of the organism that renders the gaze bright and the feet steady, the skin and muscles supple, and stimulate a dynamic and enterprising spirit. Only in making it possible for individuals to attain this vitality that is potentially innate, can each person feel his needs and find the means to become creative in a personal way. The postures that Lowen proposes allow for the precise discovery of the blocks in the body that inhibit a person's vitality. These blocks are explored physically, sometimes with deep and painful massage, and mentally by exploring their history in the life of the patient. For example, a patient who avoids looking at his therapist perhaps has a history in which avoiding looking played a role. As the vitality of an organism becomes increasingly liberated and is able to express itself in the form of "emotional discharges," repressed memories emerge in the patient's consciousness. Lowen therefore establishes new body techniques that complement those used by Reich to "unblock" the acquired inhibitions of the vegetative and affective dynamics. These exercises and this view were integrated in several body psychotherapy schools that developed at the end of the 1960s.

Bioenergetics and Psychodynamic Analysis

The term *analysis* is associated to Bioenergetics to indicate clearly that in his method, Lowen incorporated the psychodynamic thought (but not the method). Reich believed that in ameliorating the organismic auto-regulation he automatically ameliorated what was happening in *all* the dimensions of the organism (metabolism, body, behavior, and thoughts).[105] Practice shows that Reichian work on the regulatory mechanisms of the organism positively influences the global functioning of the psyche but does not always make for the reconstruction of a person's specific habitual psychological functioning. Reichian work has an analogous influence on the cognitive practices of the mind as that of antidepressant medication. It permits certain clarifications and ameliorations that are sometimes spectacular, but it never replaces a detailed analysis of the way a person understands what is happening within oneself and around oneself. Medications aim at physiological and chemical dynamics that can have a positive effect on the behavior of the genes, while bodywork places the emphasis on the coordination between the body, behavior, and soma. The advantage of bodywork over medications is that it allows for a more refined and explicit coordination between vegetative and mental practices.

Lowen mostly focused on the coordination of the following dimensions:

1. The vegetative dynamics.
2. The psychophysiological defense system that structures the functioning of consciousness and the dynamics of the drives.
3. The functioning of the mental, behavioral, and body dynamics.

Without the ambition to propose a psychology that would be compatible with an organismic approach, Lowen adds to his body and energy model a simplified rereading of Freud's Second Topology (id/ego/super-ego) which plays a central role in Reich's psychoanalytic model.[106] Above all, he draws his inspiration from the Ego psychology developed by Heinz Hartmann (1939) in New York, and the writings of Otto Fenichel (1945a), who remained a psychoanalytic reference for Reich's students. His vision of the Second Topic can be summarized in the following way:

1. The *id* is associated with the vegetative, instinctive, and emotional mechanisms and with bioenergy.
2. The *ego* is associated with the psychomuscular defense systems and the notion of grounding.
3. The *super-ego* is associated to all of the forms of cultural influences that create conscious and preconscious ways of adapting to one's environment (body, behavioral, and psychological schemas).

In this type of model, only a strong ego can create a framework of negotiations between the biological needs and social structures. For André Haynal (1967), a "strong" ego, as defined in Ego Psychology, is a well-structured and flexible ego, not a rigid, barricaded, and armored ego.

Approached from the point of view of the psychodynamic defense systems, the relation between armor and vitality is described a bit differently than in the preceding sections on Oslo. In many families, a child has more energy than what the parents can handle. The child has intense needs that cannot always be satisfied. In finding ways to diminish the quantity of energy produced by the metabolic dynamics, the child's organism diminishes the intensity of its needs and consequently reduces the assault of the frustrations that are felt when the environment can no longer satisfy his needs. Moreover, he can thus protect his parents, who feel guilty for not being able to satisfy his demands. This last point is particularly relevant in a period during which three new cultural phenomena are being firmly established:

1. The small family. Immigration is becoming part of the norm. An increasing number of parents live too far away from the rest of their family to receive help from them to care for the children.
2. Since the mother often has time-consuming professional and occupational activities, the child spends much time alone. A family is not always able to ensure that an adult will provide supervision of the child. The new fashion of video games and computers is an arguable way to manage the problem, but it is becoming more widespread each day in the North American and European cultures.[107]
3. Psychoanalysis is used to blame the parents for traumatizing their children for life.

Functional Identity

Lowen refined the Reichian organismic approach, by highlighting specific inter-actions among bioenergy, body,[108] and psyche. This implies the necessity to use techniques with greater specificity to influence, with greater precision, the dy-namics of each dimension. For Lowen, the functional identity between the psyche and the body implies that an organismic function can be approached from the angle of either the psyche or the body, because they share the same underlying dynamics. This implies that in Lowen's theory there are *direct* con-nections between the dimensions of the organism. A particular mental dynamic corresponds to a particular body dynamic and a particular vegetative (or ener-getic) dynamic:[109] the impact of a particular psychic trauma on the body and the health is the same for everyone. This direct link between body and psyche is epitomized in slogans such as "you are your body," "your body is you," or "you are somebody." If mind and body are two facets of a single mechanism, then body or verbal psychotherapy are equally efficient ways of supporting organis-mic regulations. In Bioenergetics, one will therefore (a) use methods to repair failures in body or psychological dynamics, with (b) the aim of restoring a bet-ter organismic coordination of the two dimensions. This strategy is an advan-tage for at least two reasons:

1. This therapeutic flexibility allows for shorter treatments. Body psycho-therapy can last several years, but it requires only one or two sessions per week.
2. This flexibility makes it possible to find an adequate strategy with pa-tients who would tolerate neither a psychoanalytic approach nor Or-gonomy. It becomes possible to measure out the quantity of verbal and bodywork used with a patient in function of what the patient is able to tolerate without reinforcing his defense system.

For Marulla Hauswirth,[110] who was trained in Bioenergetic analysis in Switzer-land, the functional identity hypothesis implies that what is going on in one dimension is necessarily going on in the other dimension. She is part of a gen-eration of Bioenergetic analysts who consider that this vision is too simplistic. It happens too often that in practice, the connections, considered direct, between a type of childhood trauma and body traits are not confirmed.[111] The notions of functional identity and of direct links between psyche and body are the basis of Lowen's *characterology*. These types are illustrated with excellent clinical ex-amples that are often useful. Because the individual cases are so well described, the associated diagnostic system has had a deep impact on the whole of the neo-Reichian community for more than 20 years. I have often taught this diagnostic system but will not summarize it here, because I have found that (a) it does not provide a useful approach to a patient's complexity, and (b) it can even be mis-leading.[112] However, when I see a patient that closely resembles one of Lowen's cases, I have found his case study extremely useful. In other words, Lowen's case analyses are often interesting, but the generalization that he constructs on these cases is arguable. The most contentious generalization is the assumption that the following factors always have the same configuration when they are associated to a specific psychological problem:

1. The shape of the body.
2. A network of muscular tension.
3. A way of breathing.
4. A way to manage metabolic energy.

As always,[113] the hope that one could find such simple relations between the dimensions of the organism easily becomes popular. The popularity of Bioenergetics is yet another example of this observation. However, this argument should not be used to ignore other aspects of Lowen's propositions that are interesting and useful. Here is an example that comes from my own observations, which shows the type of problems to which this kind of diagnostics can lead.

> Vignette on the masochist. *For Lowen, all masochists have the same basic conflict with their parents; they all have the same huge fear of their explosive rage. To stop themselves from exploding, they tighten their lips and shorten the segments of the neck and abdomen. Therefore, they all have a thick and condensed shape.*
>
> *I have treated several patients for whom Lowen's analysis has served me well. Evidently, he generalizes on the basis of the patients he has known. On the other hand, I have also encountered masochistic personalities who had a long and thin neck.*

Alexander Lowen's way of using the notion of functional identity is just one example that shows that the dialectic rapport (or antithetic) between body and mind, proposed by Reich in Berlin has, for the time being, disappeared from the world of body psychotherapy.

Grounding

Lowen's technique that is the most used in other schools of psychotherapy is that of grounding.[114] Grounding is at the same time a notion, an intentionality (a way to approach body sensations), and a type of exercise that already existed in the approaches of the Far East.[115] Grounding is perceived above all as an "earthing" of the organism's energy: "Grounding serves the same function for the organism's energy system that it does for a high-tension electrical circuit. It provides a safety valve for the discharge of excess excitation" (Lowen, 1975, VI: 196). Lowen reformulates this notion in such a way that it can also be used in psychotherapy to strengthen the ego in the following ways:

1. To increase the metabolic vitality in an explicit way.[116] Lowen uses grounding exercises when he treats individuals who suffer from depression.
2. To confront the coordination of the psyche, the vegetative sensations, and the body explicitly.
3. To improve the anchoring of the psyche in the affects and the body. Grounding exercises can be used as ways of helping a patient discover how refining his body awareness can help him contain emotions when his vitality increases.[117] For example, Lowen uses this aspect of grounding when he treats what he calls schizoid character structures.[118]

In the foregoing, I use the expression *explicit* by design to underscore that Lowen uses grounding to promote a certain number of conscious elaborations. It consists in knowing, feeling, and understanding, with as much clarity as possible, the stakes that connect the dimensions of the organism and to discover the inner shadow that impedes the establishment of the fluid relations between psyche and organism. These inner shadowy areas make it possible to localize territories that are susceptible to being occupied by the unconscious stakes.

The Basic Position of Grounding

> We practiced how to stand. He aligned his feet. He unlocked his knees. He leveled his pelvis; brought his pelvis forward; relaxed his buttocks, anus, and entire perineum. We practiced bending over and letting his hands, arms, and torso hang over while breathing deeply. He felt the solidity of his lower back holding him steady: knees slightly bent, each foot planted like a tripod, large muscles vibrating to the flow of energy and consciousness vivifying his stance. (Marcel A. Duclos, 2001, *Keeping It Up*, p. 46)

The notion of grounding[119] is associated with all parts of the body that serve as an anchor point. Such a contact point can be the head when an individual is standing on his head, the pelvis when he is sitting, and the feet when he walks. Being aware of one's grounding can be related to two basic issues:

1. Being of aware of our anchoring points and the way they are anchored.
2. Becoming aware of the stability of a posture.

Individuals who are well grounded are not always aware of their bodily anchoring, but when they direct their attention toward those parts of the body, they can quickly evaluate what is happening with precision. The posture of reference (standing, feet parallel and slightly apart, knees bent) is detailed in the appendix on postures. When an individual no longer has chronic muscular tension, the reference grounding posture is experienced as relaxing and invigorating, as all those who practice the martial arts have come to recognize. However, for the majority of patients in psychotherapy, this position is at first painful if it is held without moving for more than five minutes. Lowen begins by proposing to his patient, at the start of therapy, to hold this position at least 10 minutes, keeping the toes slightly pointed inward and the knees unlocked and slightly bent. If the patient experiences any pain, Lowen invites him to express the pain with his voice and the upper part of the body. Patients quickly discover that the more they hold their breath, the more they tense up, the more this position rapidly becomes painful, but the more that they let go of their breathing, the more they relax, the more this position leads to several interesting experiences.

There are many ways to use this exercise in psychotherapy. To let you sample a taste of these possibilities, I describe a few typical examples.

Grounding and Vibrations

One of the effects of the grounding position is to create vibrations that often rise from the feet to the head. Even though I have not found any satisfying explanations for these vibrations, I observe them regularly. They appear in all sorts of exercises that begin with maintaining tension in the musculature for several minutes. The argument that they would be induced by a muscular fatigue does not hold water because when a person can remain comfortably in this posture for more than 10 minutes, she experiences a form of tonic relaxation that can be beneficial to the body, metabolism and respiration, blood circulation, and moods. This skill is often observed in schools of martial art or among dancers. In medicine, these vibrations are generally related to pathological symptoms like nervous problems and fevers that create antagonistic mobilizations of the limbs. To my knowledge, their activation through bodywork has not been systematically studied. Yet this effect can easily be mobilized and therefore can easily be studied in a laboratory.[120]

Most likely, Lowen first became interested in the vibrations induced by certain postures because they are close to those that he experienced with Reich pertaining to the orgastic reflex or while making love. As I have already indicated when speaking about Reich, these vibrations are part of the typical reactions of an orgasm at its apex or immediately thereafter. It is also possible that Lowen experienced these vibrations while doing gymnastic and yoga exercises. He thought that the exploration of these vibrations promoted well-being.

It would then seem that these vibrations are one of the innate organismic reactions. They are spontaneously related to certain vegetative reactions. Holding the muscles in tension is not the only way to activate these vibrations in the body. They can also be set in motion through breathing exercises,[121] or carrying out the following jellyfish exercise:[122]

Vignette on a jellyfish exercise. *Lie down on your back, bend your knees, place your feet flat on the floor.*[123] *The feet are parallel but apart; they do not change the contact point during the entire exercise (they change position, but always on the same part of the support surface). You slowly open your legs by separating your knees up until your thighs can no longer get any closer to the floor. You remain in this position while relaxing for two breaths. Always slowly, you bring the knees together just to the point where they nearly touch. You stay in this position, relaxing the length of two breaths. You carry out this exercise for at least 10 minutes, letting a slow, regular rhythm establish itself.*

This exercise is also used in some sex therapies.[124] It often promotes on the inside of the thighs, after some time, some soft vibrations. Their activation is less frequent and less spectacular than with the mobilization of antagonist muscles. In her courses, Gerda Boyesen[125] would point out that these exercises activated vibrations only in individuals whose muscular armor was already supple.

Lowen, as do most of the neo-Reichian psychotherapists, considers these vibrations as manifestations of an increased circulation of bioenergy or orgone.

A Typical Use of the Grounding Exercise

A rather common way to work with vibrations with a patient who is not familiar with this type of exercise is the following.[126]

1. The therapist suggests that the patient remain standing with bended knees for at least 10 minutes.
2. At the start, nothing special happens. It is important to let the organism "simmer" in this position for the mechanisms that manifest as vibrations to have the time to happen.
3. After a few minutes, the patient complains of painful tension in his legs. The therapist suggests that he remain in that position while expressing what he feels with the upper part of the body.
4. It is typical for the patient to eventually feel some vibrations in his calves, but to say nothing about it. He experiences this phenomenon as a sign of weakness of some unknown origin for which he is ashamed.
5. Once the therapist observes one or two minutes of vibrations, he asks the patient if he feels the vibrations in his legs. He then asks him how he experiences these vibrations. The therapist gradually explains that they are provoked by this exercise in almost everyone, and one of the goals is to let these vibrations rise into the entire body. He also explains that, as the patient lets his breathing fully expand, the more he relaxes, the more ample the vibrations become, and the muscles will hurt less. It is important that the patient knows that he may stop the exercise at any time by sitting down, stretching out on a mattress, or walking.
6. If the shaking of the calves stops below the knees, the therapist suggests to the patient that he act as if he were able to breathe into this tense area by trying to mentally relax the knees. This suggestion will be used for each area of the body that limits the spreading out of the vibrations.

7. If this mental exercise suffices, the trembling rises to the top of the thighs. The therapist then asks the patient to relax this area, and the vibrations then rise up to the lower abdomen. Typically, at this stage of the exercise, the trembling has descended to the feet. The therapist only proceeds with the exercise if the feet remain stable on the floor. If the patient begins to lose equilibrium, the therapist sees that the patient's grounding is weak, that he easily loses his equilibrium, and that it is best to cease the exercise for this session to explore and understand what is happening. Also at this moment, it becomes possible to see if a patient sets unrealistic goals for himself. For example, some patients who have difficulty keeping their balance nonetheless stubbornly insist on continuing.

8. With a patient who remains solidly anchored while standing, the same procedure is taken up when the trembling stops at the diaphragm, under the shoulder blades, at the throat, at the jaw, and at the eyes.

9. When the body is vibrating from head to toe, it is important to find an appropriate way to end the exercise. For example, we may ask the individual to stretch out on a mattress after a few minutes, or move about the room, and feel what is going on within. Often, the session ends by suggesting to the patient to stretch out on a mattress and let all movements, feelings, and images occur.

This use of the vibrations activated by this basic grounding exercise illustrates a way to approach the organism's vegetative activity as well as the segmental defenses that inhibit this type of mobilization. I have described this exercise without using the word *energy* to illustrate that it is possible to do this work without using this word. Most of the body psychotherapists who use this exercise spontaneously relate the vibrations to an amplification of the circulation of the vital energy. A body psychotherapist will typically assume that tense abdominal muscles block the circulation of vital energy when the trembling only rises to the level of the abdomen. As long as the therapist does not refer to "cosmic energy," the metaphor of an energy block is practical because individuals who have already encountered this way of speaking in the media easily understand it.

For some individuals, this exercise does not go beyond just being painful. In that case it is often recommended to take up the exercise later and discover what is hidden behind this difficulty by using other methods. Sometimes, for reasons based on experience, the therapist concludes that it is useful to insist that the patient continue. There is a whole series of varied postures that are available in this case.[127] If the patient is only able to survive the exercise by tensing up as much as possible, it is then useful to consider conducting relaxation exercises and other techniques to open up the respiration before resuming the grounding exercise. If the patient has already been standing for 10 minutes, minor alterations in the posture can help, as in the following example.

Vignette on vibrations. The trembling is greatly facilitated when the weight of the body is shifted to the front of the feet. At times, Lowen asks an individual to touch the floor with his hands, relax the nape of the neck, and stretch the legs as much as possible without totally eliminating the flexion of the knees (at the maximum, the legs achieve an angle of 170°). This position often accelerates the advent of vibrations in the bottom half of the body.

An Active Body

I often use the grounding exercise and the vibrations it activates to help an individual accept that his body can stimulate global organismic dynamics, without asking the mind for permission.[128] I join with the patient in being curious by admitting that it consists of a puzzling but interesting well-known phenomenon that is easily triggered and not dangerous. With the patient, I rediscover that the trembling seems to be related to an excessive muscular fatigue, but by pursuing the experience, the trembling often allows the discovery of new ways of experiencing one's body, one's organism, and the content of one's mind. We marvel together over the fact that it suffices to take freely a certain type of posture for the body to manifest itself actively in ways that the thoughts had not imagined. In the face of this trembling, the thoughts are manifestly spectators instead of participants.

It then becomes possible to explore together how an individual makes sense out of the fact that the body has means of expression that the mind does not control directly (in taking up a posture, for example). Some people are frightened by this notion; others appreciate it; still others dream about it later on. One of the interesting questions raised by this exercise is the fact that nobody knows how taking a particular posture can activate this phenomenon.

A certain amount of caution is advised when soliciting the vibrations. The trembling does not necessarily stop when an individual ends the exercise. It is therefore useful to stop the exercise around 15 minutes before the end of the session so that patient and therapist are able to discuss and understand the impact of the exercise for the patient.

The Grounding of a Hypo-armored Individual

A PATIENT IMMEDIATELY EXPERIENCES STRONG GLOBAL VIBRATIONS
THE FIRST TIME HE DOES THE GROUNDING EXERCISE
After having bent the knees, a hypo-armored[129] individual often begins to tremble from head to toe in two or three minutes, sometimes sooner. When the therapist sees this, he begins to question whether this individual has hysterical tendencies or a "false-self"[130] (to satisfy the expectations of the therapist with his behavior), or if he has previously worked with another therapist relative to opening the body in another context. If this is not the case, the therapist assumes the patient has a weak ego. He then inquires to check this hypothesis.

In the case of a defense system that is insufficiently organized, the default strategy is to develop the feeling of grounding in homeopathic doses—for example, for only a few minutes in each session with soft exercises, feeling how the weight of the body is distributed on a mattress when the patient is stretched out on it, learning to sit on the ischia, using the stool[131] exercise to facilitate abdominal breathing, and so on. There are often two traps to avoid:

1. Nourishing an overdeveloped super-ego by allowing the patient to imagine how he "ought" to behave.
2. Acting in such a way as to activate more feelings than the patient is able to contain and understand.

When a therapist uses the grounding exercise with a hypo-armored individual, he has, by default, the following ideas in mind.

> Vignette on grounding and ego strength. *The patient does not have a defense system that automatically limits the trembling, which can indicate a lack of grounding. For Reich (1927a), there is a connection between impulsivity and compulsion. Compulsion is often a defense against impulsivity. The patients who suffer from impulsivity have a tendency to persist in voluntarily increasing the strength of their vibrations, even when the trembling is stronger than what they are able to cope with (the grounding then becomes fragile). For such individuals, trembling then sometimes becomes a narcissistic goal, a self-destructive conditioning acquired in therapy.*

ENDO-, MESO-, AND ECTODERM: A DISTINCTION USED BY THE SCHOOLS INFLUENCED BY BIOENERGETICS

Embryology identifies, principally, three types of tissues:

1. The *endoderm* generates mostly the tissues of the organs.
2. The *mesoderm* engenders the tissues of the muscles, the fascia, the cardiovascular system, and the bones.
3. The *ectoderm* especially engenders the skin and the nervous system.[132]

William Herbert Sheldon (1898–1977), a famous psychologist in the United States, asked himself if the histological stages influenced the development of temperament in individuals. He began to photograph thousands of people who had been the subject of aptitude testing he had conducted. The statistical analysis of his results lead to a distinction between three types of temperaments associated to three types of body configurations, called "somatotypes":

1. The *endomorph* is especially influenced by the endoderm, especially the tissues of the digestive tract, which would be particularly developed in him. This is someone who is gregarious and appreciates good food. He is consequently often corpulent and extroverted.

2. The *mesomorph* has a particularly well-developed mesoderm. He likes to use his strength and vitality by getting involved in dynamic and risky activities that require great competence and authority. He therefore has an athletic body.

3. The ectoderm (skin and nerves) is mostly developed in the *ectomorph*. He is a thin, nervous, sensitive, and introverted intellectual.

For Sheldon (1954), we are all inevitably a mixture of these three types because we have all of these three kinds of tissues; but certain individuals more easily develop particular "body types" than others.

In the 1970s, in London, David Boadella, Gerda Boyesen, and Malcolm Brown[133] and then Jerome Liss used a model inspired by Sheldon's work. They had the idea that each layer of tissues (endoderm, mesoderm, and ectoderm) has a particular connection to the psyche. They explored various methods based on the hypothesis that by massaging the skin, the muscles, or the organs, the therapist enters into contact with three distinct layers of the psyche. Yet they do not use the body types as a global description of a personality type. For that, they rather refer to the notion of character, such as it was developed by Lowen.

The idea that different tissues relate differently with the psyche can be useful as a teaching tool to sensitize a person in training to the multiple connections that exist between the diverse organic mechanisms and the psyche. On the other hand, I do not know if this model is uniquely a useful metaphor or if it corresponds to existing psychophysiological mechanisms. This model became influential in body psychotherapy in the 1980s because it provided a formulation that was easily handled and tended to confirm the differentiation between hyper- and hypo-armored individuals, as in the following examples.

1. When an individual does not express his emotions with his muscles, there is a deficit in the explicit emotional expression he produces. The facial expressions, as described by Ekman, are not used; the external breathing does not support the expressive gestures.

2. Some individuals do not use their muscles to express themselves, but the quality of the skin and the gaze can be correlated to emotions and mood disorders. Becoming red-faced or pale is a well-known example. In the case of depression, the skin and/or hair may become extremely and palpably dry or greasy. A dull or burning gaze, dead or alive, may also vary in function of the affective life.

3. In the case of a schizophrenic patient described by Reich,[134] the relationship between the muscles and the moods seem to be deactivated. The mesoderm moves the bones but does not participate in the expression in any other way; the blood does not irrigate the periphery of the organism when the sympathetic system is activated. The mesoderm and the ectoderm are only active in the ocular region. The emotion is expressed mostly by the postures (curling up in a ball in a corner), the quality of

the skin (a pale and colorless skin), the quality of the gaze, and so on. This is, at the same time, an example of a poorly armored individual and one who does not mobilize his mesoderm to construct a defense system.

4. A complementary analysis associates fear and schizophrenia. We have seen, when speaking of Braatøy, that the muscular armor incorporates some residues from the startle reflex. Thus, with certain psychotic patients, seen from the neo-Reichian perspective, the startle reflex could have influenced the endo- and ectodermal layers of the organism, but not the mesodermal levels. Therefore, there may be huge fears that are difficult for the therapist to perceive. These can only be expressed by the armored parts of the body, like the eyes, because there is at least an affective mobilization of the muscles in that region. Fear will then manifest itself in the schizophrenic in the form of a "constriction" of the organism, described in the sections on the Reichian orgonomy. This constriction, which can lead to catatonic attacks, is mostly perceptible when it is related to a restrained respiration, even in the case of physical exertion, and to a skin that is manifestly insufficiently irrigated.

In such cases, the general therapeutic recommendation is to allow a person without endodermic defenses to discover a way to use his musculature in a differentiated manner while increasing his grounding. This necessarily implies that the person would become able to learn how to contain, and sometimes repress, his emotions by using his musculature.

A General Critique of Lowen's Bioenergetics

Traditionally, from Freud to Lowen, psychotherapists thought that the three following stages allowed for the healing of the residuals of trauma:

1. To recover the memory of the traumatic event.
2. To be able to express to someone the emotions experienced at the occasion of the traumatic event and the utter confusion that ensued.
3. To assimilate what happened mentally.

In the body psychotherapy of Reichian inspiration developed in the United States, such as Bioenergetic analysis, this position was developed to the extreme. The emphasis was especially on the first two phases. The therapist not only encouraged the patient to express his emotions but also stimulated the breathing by mobilizing the posture and muscles so that this expression would be as intense as possible. The progress was often spectacular in the short term. Both the patient and the therapist had the impression that a huge weight had been lifted. Intense emotional discharges lead to physiological mobilizations (especially of respiration and blood circulation). Once this charge has expressed itself, it dissolves and often produces a deep relaxation, as well as an impression that the skin is clean and the eyes have acquired a new brightness. These effects are somewhat like what happens when we pleasurably make love, except that in the aforementioned instance, the change may occur without a sexual arousal. Lowen thus speaks of a vitality that can also support an awakening of the libido.

On the other hand, the third phase, which pertains to mental integration, is often treated superficially.[135] Because of this, the benefits of the treatment can be temporary, and in some cases the condition of the individual may subsequently disintegrate. Psychoanalysis was first to provide a series of criticisms of this approach thinking that the intense respiration creates an overinvestment of the libido, which inundates the defense system. Everything happens like a volcano that awakens and then rarely goes back to sleep without having caused terrible damage.[136]

This type of intervention was first criticized by personalities trained in Scandinavia who had the advantage of having been influenced by the critiques that Fenichel addressed with Reich. Already in his 1975 book on bioenergetics, Lowen mostly focused on the energetic and bodily aspects of his work and only had sporadic fits of interest for an in-depth psychodynamic analysis. I have the impression that even if some of Lowen's pupils tried to refine the body techniques in Bioenergetics, most preferred to find psychodynamic formulations that could integrate somatic and body reactions. This second trend of trainers in Bioenergetics developed formulations that often take up (without knowing it) Fenichel's criticisms of Reich.

For the time being, it seems that the members of the school of Bioenergetic analysis are actively looking for new formulations that are compatible with contemporary clinical knowledge. We shall see in the near future how Bioenergetic analysis will manage this transition phase. This may prove interesting, because several brilliant practitioners animate this school. It seems to me that a crucial point will be if they can continue to integrate body dynamics as well as they integrate recent psychodynamic formulations.

A FEW EXAMPLES OF ISSUES REGULARLY RAISED BY BODY PSYCHOTHERAPISTS IN 2010

Attempts to integrate Reichian orgonomy into the field of psychotherapy have evidently reached its limits. Other movements have integrated themselves into the development of body psychotherapy along the way, like the latest developments in systems, psychodynamic, behavioral, and cognitive therapy. This last movement brings a certain way to use yoga and Buddhist meditation techniques, often called "mindfulness." The new formulations in the neurosciences are also often discussed. Furthermore, the psychotherapy market has been profoundly redesigned by the politics of health and health insurance. Today's body psychotherapists are gradually integrating these new approaches and policies.

Psychotherapy is a field composed of many schools. In its early romantic phase, its creativity influenced people from all over the world in many disciplines. It is now becoming an institutionalized form of treatment. This requires that the field accept the need to coordinate the knowledge that has developed in a variety of approaches and that it accept losing some of the particularities that were needed in its early existence. The whole field is being restructured; nobody really knows where this process will lead. I hope that the psychotherapy of tomorrow will rediscover the scope it is about to lose by trying to accommodate itself to the larger social forces. Its prime ethical goal remains the defense and support of individual psychological uniqueness.

The hope of most body psychotherapists is that their methods will become standard methods of psychotherapy. This ongoing process is structured by several debates. For example, as we have seen, some are looking for ways of creating a synthesis between psychodynamic and Reichian approaches. This accommodation to the needs of the psyche often leads to an impoverishment of the knowledge in the domain of body techniques. Here are three examples of what is developing in Europe:

1. Coming from the Bioenergetics of the 1980s, Sander Kirsch and his colleagues created a Belgian school of psychoanalytic body psychotherapy called Psycorps. This school wants to assimilate certain tools from Bioenergetics in an approach that would like to be, above all else, Freudian psychodynamic.
2. Coming from Biodynamic psychology at the end of the decade of the 1970s, Paul Boyesen and his colleagues try to create a "bridge" between psychoanalysis (especially Lacanian) and the organismic approach of Gerda Boyesen. Their journal, *Adire*, provides a regular account of their thinking.
3. The Analytische Korperpsychotherapie (Analytical Body Psychotherapy), was founded by Peter Geissler and his colleagues in Austria and in Germany.[137] This group takes up the work started by Ferenczi in the light of the discoveries made in Bioenergetics and other Reichian movements. They are now synthesizing their endeavor with recent psychoanalytic formulations.[138]

It seems to me that this is a way of stepping back that will not necessarily allow us to jump further ahead. Reich's organismic approach is not the only one that needs a reformulation. The psychoanalytical approach, even when one considers recent developments, can only incorporate a small part of recent research in psychology. Fenichel's intuition that the psychodynamic psychosomatic model cannot integrate recent psychophysiological findings seems to have been correct. The thesis defended in this book is that future developments in psychotherapy will have to find *organismic psychological models*. This is not a personal thesis, but one that has been strengthened by generations of clinicians working on the coordination between mind and matter.

Fenichel and Gindler immediately understood that approaching the body and the mind required different techniques, because these dimensions impose different requirements. An organismic psychology must meet at least two requirements:

1. It must describe a psyche that is part of the organism and explain the relationship between the psyche and the other dimensions of the organism.
2. It must recognize the heterogeneity of the dimensions of the organism. It is not because there are interfaces that permit many interactions between the dimensions of the organism that all the dimensions will be able, one day, to be approached by a unique mode of intervention.

It seems to me more useful to fight for the emergence of this new psychology instead of losing time putting together different psychologies and body modalities that have incompatible views with an organismic approach.

Fenichel's criticisms on the Reichian therapeutic approach are taken up again today by a nonpsychoanalytic movement based on the recent development of the ways to intervene in trauma that developed in the 1990s around the personality of Bessel van der Kolk. Van der Kolk is a Dutch psychiatrist who is established in Boston. He shows how trauma installs itself in the organism by associating itself to the stress circuits, thus forming a negative vicious circle that reinforces itself as soon as it is reactivated.[139] Numerous psychotherapists, including body psychotherapists, have associated themselves with Bessel Van der Kolk to establish forms of treatment that are inspired by this point of view.[140] These approaches are inspired by the psychodynamic, behavioral, and cognitive therapies and the neurosciences.

These body psychotherapists generally favor less intrusive approaches than the neo-Reichian approaches. In the end, the trend is to admit that it is necessary to have a repertoire of varied approaches, eclectic in their way of proceeding, to face all of what the patients present. This eclecticism goes as far as to suggest that most of the psychotherapeutic approaches have a cultural bias that does not allow them to be useful in all the cultures in the world.[141]

PART VII

Nonverbal Communication Research and Psychotherapy

20

Filmed Interactions: The Behavior of an Invisible Visible Body

INTRODUCTION: A NEW WAY TO APPROACH THE ORGANISM

Behavior Can Adapt Itself Simultaneously to a Multitude of Heterogeneous Stimulations

Behavior is often reduced to a body phenomenon or the functioning of the psyche. In the following sections, I show that the study of behavior requires particular methods and theories that are well differentiated from those used to study the psyche or the body. It is useful to clarify the epistemological status of behavior for all forms of psychotherapy because their dynamics are ceaselessly solicited by psychotherapists. In body psychotherapy, the nonverbal behavior is permanently related not only to what is being said but also to the reactions of the body and the vegetative system.

The field of nonverbal communication studies organized itself around the theoretical formulations of Gregory Bateson (1972). One of the first discoveries in Bateson's generation is that an event does not convey a particular meaning, or does not have a particular function, but it is almost always polysemous and multifunctional:

A vignette on a hand that takes a cup of tea.
1. The integration between gesture and physiology. *By taking up a cup of tea, my hand is included in a series of dynamics that coordinate various parts of my nervous system, cardiovascular system, respiration, and the rapport of my body with gravity. This gesture may sometimes be activated by a thirst, itself activated by metabolic activity. The style of this movement may also convey an impression of tension or relaxation to another person.*

2. The gesture as an indicator of personal dynamics. *The particularities of my gesture also depends on my sex, age, cultural origins, mood, way of analyzing what is going on around me, and the impression I want to make on others. I can take the cup politely, by its handle, while holding the saucer under the cup; or I can grab the cup as if it were a bowl to warm my hands. My hand may tremble because I am nervous or because of my age. I can set the cup on the table loudly to express my displeasure, and so on.*

3. The gesture as a stimulus for the other. *A gesture may be carried out with a particular intention and have an unforeseen impact on the other. The typical example is that of intercultural interactions where one gesture changes meaning from one culture to another. An Arab may embrace a U.S. citizen out of politeness while the latter receives it an excess of familiarity.[1] The way the other reacts to the gesture can also define its meaning and function. The others decide whether my way of handling the cup of tea appears to be relaxed, elegant, insulting, irritating or amusing.*

4. The gesture as an object of attribution. *Those who see me take the cup of tea and drink will apply an index of possible readings to my way of behaving that have been constructed in their organism. If several individuals are present, they could each have a different index of possible meanings. One individual may find my gesture sexy, another find it disgraceful, and another still polite.*

You may have noticed that my hand, in this example, can participate in a large number of heterogeneous personal and interpersonal regulations at the same time. I have only mentioned a few of the many possible ways of analyzing what my hand does when it lifts a cup of tea. This movement is influenced by a set of inner dynamics that are often relatively independent from how others perceived it. In this last example, nothing I do or want to do will change anything because it is in the mind of the other that some details of my hand take on a particular meaning. It is also possible that everybody is talking about a painting hanging on a wall and no one notices what I am doing with my hands. This last remark raises the following question: are all of the particularities of the hand gesture necessarily perceived by the nervous system of my protagonists? The answer is probably that many are, but not all. The items selected by a given conscious system may vary from one second to another, but this requires a sustained attention that mobilizes a great quantity of energy. Most of the time, a conscious system prefers to handle the first items that hit it for as long as possible. Only in the case of disequilibrium or a crisis in the interaction does a conscious system feel obliged to look at complementary information.

To scientifically study this type of phenomenon, it is useful to begin by making a list of the concrete options that present themselves. As it happens, we are only at the beginning of a long list that shows that at any given moment, a gesture may be part of a great variety of regulatory systems qualitatively different one from the other. It sometimes happens that a gesture inserts itself into a specific mode of functioning and then acquires a standardized semiotic function within a species or a particular cultural environment. Only in these cases (relatively few with regard to the entirety of mechanisms that can animate a gesture) does it become possible to relate a gesture to a meaning or a particular function. However, even in these cases, a body position can also have a multitude of other functions.

The researchers who analyzed nonverbal behavior in the 1950s where astonished when they observed that almost each *item* of behavior can simultaneously participate in a variety of regulatory systems. This is what allows the body to adapt itself simultaneously to a multitude of more or less heterogeneous stimulations. In the previous examples, we have seen that the movements of a hand can be simultaneously associated to a variety of phenomena, such as furniture, the shape of objects, one's sex, age, etiquette, character, health, weather forecast, and more. These causal systems have not necessarily adapted to each other before influencing the organism. An individual system must continuously react to a multitude of solicitations that have their particular exigencies. It is this multiplicity of behavioral dimensions that allows the human organism to accommodate itself in such a refined way to such a large number of environments and of variables. This particularity of human behavior partly explains the adaptive potential of our species. Once this analysis is understood, it becomes easier to understand why I had emphasized the following quotes by Spinoza:

> In proportion as a body is more capable than others of doing many things at once, or being acted on in many ways at once, so its mind is more capable than others of perceiving many things at once. (Spinoza, 1677a, II, Proposition XIII, scholium, p. 40)

> The human mind is capable of perceiving a great many things, and is the more capable, the more its body can be disposed in a great many ways. (Spinoza, 1677a, II. proposition XIV, p. 44)

Some think that nonverbal communication is too young a science to be able to contradict what is evident to human perception. We will see that they are not entirely wrong. This science has not yet been able to produce a methodology and theory sufficiently robust to be convincing. Many times, in this volume, we have seen that a science often needs centuries to establish itself. Psychology is about 130 years old, and the study of nonverbal communication is barely 60 years of age. Nevertheless, we saw that this discipline has already demonstrated that most gestures cannot be explained by a single causal chain, such as a conscious intention or an emotion. As this thesis is central to my analysis of how human organisms function, I will now try to give tangible and concrete examples to support it. Because this field has not yet been able to discover precise general laws, I have to become a bit more technical than elsewhere to make my point.

The first researchers in nonverbal communication research, like Ray L. Birdwhistell, Edward T. Hall, and Adam Kendon, thought that there was a *body language*. They believed that gestures could be perceived, like words, as signs that represent a meaning. They explicitly referred to diverse linguistic theories, which they attempted to apply to the analysis of movements. However, as soon as they tried to analyze gestures with well-conceived experimental plans, they experienced a deluge of problems. They did not succeed in finding reliable methods that would allow them to describe a body event, analyze what had been observed, and gather the data into a theoretical whole. As gestures are spontaneously managed by all humans, they thought that analysis of them would be relatively easy. They were surprised to discover all the methodological difficulties raised by their project. These difficulties are a mine of challenging information. This is what I focus on in this chapter.

By definition, nonverbal communication studies everything that can be discerned by the nose, ears, and eyes. I concentrate on the study of bodily behavior because it is the visual modality that has been studied the most up to this day and I know this domain particularly well.

A Systemic View of Interaction

> Interest in Ballet becomes more comprehensible if we realize that the most deeply moving moments of our lives usually leave us speechless, and in such moments our body carriage may well be able to express what otherwise would be incomprehensible. (Rudolf Laban, 1950, *The Mastery of Movement*, IV, p. 87)

> Single movements are, of course, only like the words or letters of language; they do not give a definitive impression or a coherent flow of ideas. (Rudolf Laban, 1950, *The Mastery of Movement*, IV, p. 87)

For Thelen and Smith,[2] reality is observed with a microscope that can be adjusted to provide a broad general view of reality. The researcher then perceives a relatively coherent form of reality with large patterns and clearly delineated rhythms. "As we turn up the magnification of our microscope, we see that our vision of linearity, uniformity, inevitable sequencing and even irreversibility break down" (Thelen and Smith, 1994, Introduction, p. xvi). Once the details become increasingly apparent, reality appears so varied and disparate, that it is impossible to categorize into great schemes (e.g., all fingerprints are different). The organization of causal chains now appears to be messy, heterogeneous, and fuzzy. Thus, psychologists situate the distinction between organism, body, and psyche in some global schemes, which they forget as soon as they observe a specific behavior. The researcher and the practitioner prefer to remain as close as possible to the details of what is perceived and measured instead of blinding oneself by following a theory that is only partially relevant.

This change of perspective often trivializes the notion of a global well-organized organism, as described by the System of Dimensions of the Organism. It becomes a meeting place within which heteroclite mechanisms pile up. When a researcher analyses the details of an event, he does not preoccupy himself too much with their status within the organism. The typical researcher will study different aspects of a dancer's gesture without knowing what is psychological, of the body, behavioral or physiological. Certain variables will be collected at all these levels to find some interesting correlations. The questions regarding the way these variables interact are left aside for the day when we have a more consistent theory of the organism. For the moment, researchers tend to assume that there must be a web of connecting interfaces that allow for the multiple correlations that can be observed.

Psychologists often study an interaction between a patient and his therapist by using three kinds of data:

1. What is going on inside the patient's organism.
2. What is going on inside the therapist's organism.
3. The impact of each one's behavior on their interior world and on that of the other.

To coordinate these three pieces of data, researchers in nonverbal behavior tend to use three types of data that can be simultaneously viewed on three screens. The first shows the physiological functioning of an individual. The second films the two interacting organisms. The third shows the physiological functioning of the other individual. These screens give information on what is going on inside and on the surface of each organism in the interaction.

The psyche is situated somewhere in this frame. By following the procedures of artificial intelligence, psychologists then research algorithms that may be able to explain in an economical fashion the way the inside of an organism coordinates with the external surface. They then reduce their definition of the psyche to these hypothetical algorithms. An experimental psychologist can observe three types of phenomena:

1. The way the behaviors of several organisms coordinate to accomplish common tasks (like piloting a sailboat).
2. The way the behavior of an organism influences its physiological functioning and that of other organisms.
3. Individual thoughts.

The content and form of a communicated intention are experienced as being shared material. This aspect is often discussed when members of a family expect that their qualities and efforts would be recognized and appreciated by everyone.

This impression that there exists shared content between humans is exquisitely described by Daniel Stern (1990) in *Diary of a Baby*. In his more rigorous research, Stern (1985) tries to associate a description of behavior and a more intuitive attempt to grasp the intimate sentiments of the subjects. He demands of the experimental psychologist not only a rigorous analysis of behavior but also an attempt to construct for oneself an intuitive impression of the intimate experience of the subjects in interaction. In other words, for Stern, psychologists need to keep an eye on the *psychological* dynamics of organisms in interaction. Thus, in his studies of the interactions between infants and their mothers, Stern sometimes uses an experimental design with two phases:

Phase 1. The researchers film an interaction between the mother and the infant following a research protocol.

Phase 2. The researcher reviews this film with the mother and asks her what she was feeling at each moment and what she is feeling viewing the film. He also asks her what her infant was feeling according to her. Sometimes this second interaction is also filmed and analyzed.

The proposition organized around Gregory Bateson is commonly known as *systemic therapy*. It is one of the foundations of family therapy. This type of therapy assumes the behaviors that bring a patient to a psychotherapist are the symptoms of group dynamics rather than only those of an individual. Therefore the group is the focus of the team of psychotherapists. Systemic therapy functions particularly well when other colleagues observe the interactions between the psychotherapist and the family. In the 1960s, the rest of the team observed the session hidden behind a one-way mirror. Today, the teams often use video recordings. As soon as several organisms are perceived on an image, they form an aesthetic whole for the viewer. He rarely differentiates the verbal from the nonverbal or the roles that each one plays. The looks, words, gestures, and postures blend in his mind in many different ways. A hand relates to the words of one and to the crossing of the legs of another. The mind of the viewer seems to isolate some items in the image, without really understanding how, and explores all sorts of combinations that often seem to have some meaning to him, when he does not analyze the details of what he perceives too closely. The impression that the gestures of others speak to us is a *necessary illusion* of communication, which, as we will see, can never resist the probing analysis of a film.

NONVERBAL COMMUNICATION, OR
THE BODY IN COMMUNICATION

> The positions of the head and of the arms being countless, I will not try to state any rule. (Da Vinci, 1942, *The Notebooks II*, p. 265; translated by Marcel Duclos)

Nonverbal communication designates all forms of behavior that do not require the analysis of the content of words. This definition implies that all behavior can have (but not necessarily will have) a communication function. The difficulty with this definition is to accept that the organism which activates a behavior, even consciously, is not able to know ahead of time how its behavior will be perceived. The writer often admits with difficulty that his readers perceive some thoughts in his work that he never had and that they will never be able to know the intellectual and affective forces that pushed him to write.[3]

Bodily nonverbal communication studies analyze all parts of the organism that appear on a visual recording. Such a recording may use all sorts of support, like a film, a video tape, a DVD. Because these distinctions are not important for the following sections, I will use the term *film* to designate a visual recording capable of capturing the contours of the body and the visible aspects of its texture, whatever the technology that is used. From the point of view of the large categories of this textbook, this means that body and behavior are not always differentiated. On the other hand, it is clear to all researchers that it consists of a partial approach of a whole that is the organism.

An Invisible Visible Body

Structuring How We Look

The individual who can draw knows that the viewer has the impression of seeing everything, but that is not the case. It suffices to try to draw a tree without leaves in winter to discover this. The beginner may try, but he soon discovers a discrepancy between what he sees and what he creates. In the case of the branches of a tree, an art teacher often teaches the student to draw the shape of the space *between* the branches to be able to situate them. The student is then able to pencil a more realistic drawing. This is an example of why we all need to *learn* how to look as soon as we need to integrate what we see in a precise motor action.

The study of how eyes scan a visual field is called pupillometrics. This field analyzes pupil size and movement (Hess, 1965). For example, researchers who wanted to understand how children learn to look asked them to count the number of windows on a photo of a large building. The very young child focuses on one window, then on another, and then another. His eyes jump from one window that attracts his attention to another, but he does not have a strategy. After a while, he no longer knows which window has already been counted and which has not. Most of the older children have acquired an automatic scanning procedure—for example, counting by going from the highest to the lowest row, or going from left to right in each column. This type of strategy allows one to know immediately which windows remain to be counted. In this example, we see that the cognitive performance depends on sensorimotor strategies used by the movements that allow the retina to sweep across a surface (movement of the eyes, of the head, sometime of the bust, etc.).[4]

Necessary Illusion: I See Everything

Researchers like Eckhard H. Hess[5] have established a device that allows one to know what an eye is looking at, at an exact moment. He has shown that pupils scan just a small percentage of the surface of an object. Yet a human has, in every instance, the impression of perceiving a continuous visual field. There are therefore *editing* mechanisms between the retina and a conscious visual perception. They fill in the visual field with information that did not enter through the retina. Francis Crick calls this editing process a form of *filling in* that is based on "unconscious inferences."[6] This effect becomes tangible when a person discovers some new details by concentrating longer and more attentively on an object. The implication of this finding is that a large part of our conscious thoughts are *fabrications:* sensory data is so partial that it requires considerable editing before it can form a conscious perception.[7] This filling-in plays an important role in conscious perception. Imagine that you could only perceive those parts of the surface swept by the central fovea of your retina. You would only see a few pieces of the surface surrounded by empty space, which would be troubling and would stop you from running when it was necessary.

Pierre Bourdieu (1997) describes another illusion that he calls *knowing by body.*[8] This illusion functions in two steps:

1. Our organism (which Bourdieu calls *body*) is part of the physical, biological, and social world, but the mind has the impression that it understands (and includes) the world (pp. 156f and 162f).
2. Our perceptions construct themselves inside the cranium, but we have the impression that they exist outside of the body where the perceived objects are thought to be. This illusion has already been described by Kant: "By means of the external sense (a property of the mind), we represent to ourselves objects as without us, and these all in space" (Kant, 1787, I.I.1.2, p. 43)

These phenomena have a well-known clinical relevance because they allow for the activations of not only projections but also the variants, such as the *expulsion of conflicts* observed by Racamier in psychotics and perverse narcissists:[9] The notion of *expulsion* which thus appears will reveal itself to be central in the discovery of the concept of *narcissistic perversion.* It signals a kind of falling-out of a perspective centered on a suffering individual who dumps his suffering on another. In these mechanisms, there are forms of pouring out from the inside to the outside that allow an individual to have the illusion that he can become a parasite to the soul of the other, settle in there, and feed on it. To the extent that this conscious illusion is accompanied by a nonconscious know-how on the prowl, the perverse narcissist can develop a capacity to manipulate and destroy the other that can become terrifying.[10]

Constructing a Representation of Body Communication

In the previous section, I showed that the perception of the other is not a simple registration of reality. It is at least as complex as what happens in a movie theater. The spectator has the impression of seeing a succession of images, whereas sometimes, between two images, there were months of reflection and crises in the filming crews.

I have already mentioned that the first researchers[11] in nonverbal communication believed that to describe the movements of people would be easy. They thought it would suffice to find a system to note the gestures to describe what everybody sees.[12] An arm displaces itself in a geometric space; a smile is more or less lengthy, and so on. They even hoped to have found a low-cost way to obtain crucial scientific data on human functioning. They were quickly disillusioned. By reviewing the difficulties they encountered, we are able to begin to question ourselves, in a more precise manner, about the way a perceptual system resolves these problems.

How Does a Brain Record Visual Information?

The first practical challenge that a researcher in bodily nonverbal communication must deal with is to obtain images that he can work with. Even when one only studies an interaction between two people (a dyad), it is horribly complicated, if only for the following reasons:

1. *The number of cameras:* There must be cameras that film each body face and profile, from head to toe; and a camera that films, from further away, how bodies are situated in relationship to each other; and sometimes, cameras that film parts of the body that one wants to study in greater detail (e.g., the face and the hands).
2. *The coordination of the cameras:* The cinema has shown that human perception needs at least 25 images per second to be comfortable with a film. The disjointed movements of the early films of Charlie Chaplin used fewer than 20 images per second. To study an individual with several cameras, the images must be coordinated with a precision of at least one one-hundredth of a second. Again, the solutions to this problem require technical means and competent personnel.
3. *The quality of the film:* To observe the large movements of the body does not require high-performance films. On the other hand, as soon as a researcher wants to analyze the varied muscles of the face, he needs to be able to see each muscle. This requires good lighting, the right angle, excellent recording equipment (equivalent to that used by TV cameras). Finally, certain visible body indices are difficult to perceive on film, even when the best equipment is at the disposal of the researcher. I think of the splendor of a glance and the skin, which, after my experience, has an important impact on the way that a person is intuitively perceived. It is rare that a researcher in nonverbal communication can afford equipment that meets these criteria because the opinion persists that studying nonverbal communication is inexpensive. Nobody wants to believe that what he perceives every day in an apparently comfortable manner needs a refined technology to be rigorously analyzed.

These issues highlight the exquisite refinement of sensorimotor circuits, which can deal with such issues rapidly and more efficiently than the most sophisticated laboratories. For the moment, we do not know how nonconscious processes manage this type of information.

How Does the Brain Code Visual Information?

As soon as researchers began to look at a sequence of images many times over, they discovered a lot of things going on in all parts of the body—much more than they thought. They then set about to find ways of codifying everything that could be distinguished in a film. One of the first series of studies was dedicated to the analysis of a film 18 seconds long that showed a family therapy session by Bateson. In this sequence, Bateson lights the cigarette of his female patient.[13] Several researchers (e.g., Birdwhistell) studied this sequence in the course of 12 years. They collected so much material that they were never able to publish all of their observations.[14] Their system of notation often consisted of written and sketched descriptions of what they had observed, all of which generated an enormous pile of unmanageable data.

This problem is partially resolved since the propositions of Ekman and Friesen (1978) relative to the face and Frey (1985) with regard to the whole body. Their solution is to assign a number to each body part and a number for each possible position of that body part and note the position of a body item (the corner of the lips or a hand) in each image.[15] This allows for the completion of a matrix[16] in which each line is a moment and each column, a body item. At the intersection of a line and a column, we have a value that localizes the behavior of a part of the body in space and time. Here is an example.

> Vignette on smiles. *A smile: has a moment t1, the corners of the lips stretch a bit. In Ekman and Friesen's system, a smile is unit 12, and a weak intensity that is barely discernible has an intensity of A. Thus, at the moment t1, the face being analyzed has a 12A.*

With this system, it becomes possible (a) to know exactly how many distinctions a coding grid can distinguish, and (b) to deal with this information with a computer program.

The *basic matrix* contains the data coded by looking at films image by image. This is the coded reality. From there, a series of variables can be defined. Table 20.1 shows a matrix that isolates the coordination between eyebrows and a smile observed on one of the subjects filmed in the Affect and Communication Laboratory (LAC) of Geneva.

An individual who perceives this smile for the first time rarely notices the following details:

1. Only three facial units are mobilized.
2. The *temporal profile* of the expression begins by a mobilization of the eyebrows, then the smile.
3. These details are discerned by the nervous system in a nonconscious

TABLE 20.1. Coordination between Smile and Movement of the Eyebrows

Time	Unit 1	Unit 4	Unit 12
Moment 1	SB	SB	
Moment 2	SB	SD	SC
Moment 3	SD	SD	SC
Moment 4	SB	SB	SB
Moment 5	SB	SB	SB
Moment 6	SB		SA
Moment 7	SA		
Moment 8			

Notes: The time scale is of 20/100th of a second. This table describes how eyebrows and smiles were coordinated over eight frames. The units are coded following the FACS of Ekman and Friesen: 1: rising of the internal eyebrow, 4: narrowing of the eyebrows, and 12: spreading of the corners of the lips. S indicates that the movement is symmetrical. The second letter indicates the intensity of the movement, going from A (a hardly visible activity) to E (maximum intensity).

way, but are often too detailed to be perceived consciously. Brevity is one of the criteria that permit us to affirm that an activity is nonconscious. If the details of the temporal profile of a facial expression correlate with an aspect of the behavior of other persons present, the researcher assumes it is highly probable these details have had an impact on the perceiver's nervous system.

A researcher who applies this type of descriptive system to each part of the body in every film image of two persons in an interaction soon discovers that he needs a matrix capable of distinguishing between millions of possibilities. Only some of these possibilities are used in a particular interaction, but in comparing several interactions, the researcher soon finds himself with more data than he can consciously manage. Such a coding procedure allows a researcher to analyze the density of information exchange between interacting organisms in the course of a one-hour psychotherapy session between two persons.

Statistical Issues

After having discussed issues that relate to data gathering, I now say a few words about the difficulty of managing data on nonverbal behavior. My examples continue to be the analysis of how a psychotherapist interacts with a patient in individual sessions.

Once it became possible to introduce data into computers (in the 1970s), researchers were able to generate two types of matrixes of descriptive data.

1. A *basic matrix*, conceptualized like the smile, contains everything that has been coded.

2. *Derived matrixes* calculate the variables starting from the basic matrix.

For some psychotherapists, the statistical issues I address now may be difficult to grasp. However, I do not have any other means to demonstrate what I must explain. All I can do is to assume that some of my readers have not studied statistics.

THE BASIC MATRIXES

The Structure of the Basic Matrixes. We have just seen a basic matrix of the behavior of an individual. There are as many columns as there are body items, which can be distinguished in a reliable[17] way by anybody who has learned how to code body items. It is evident that some individuals perceive a behavior in greater detail than others. Only what can be reliably perceived by most trained coders can be integrated in the research protocols. This implies that small nuances which may be detected only by some cannot be included in this procedure.

In spite of certain inevitable simplification, the researcher is thus able to gather a considerable amount of data and distinctions. Utilizing Ekman and Friesen's FACS, the analysis of the face allows one to distinguish at least 50 items. If I distinguish everything that is going on in the body with as much detail as I have just described with regard to the movements of the hand, I easily find myself confronted with 103 identified body items. This accounts for the number of columns in a matrix of individual data for one person.

In what pertains to an image by image analysis, every 5/100th of a second, we have 20 lines per second, 1,200 for a second, 720,000 for a minute, up to 43,200,000 for an hour. With 200 columns, that gives us a matrix of 8,640,000,000 cells[18] to describe in a detailed way the behavior of one person during a psychotherapy session. If we analyze an interaction between two individuals, we have at least tripled the number of cases:

1. 8,640,000,000 cells to describe the behavior of the second person.
2. At least as many to describe the relationship between the two persons for each body item (same position, different position, etc.). But this can be done by a computer.

Nonetheless, this gives us 25,920,000,000 cells to form the basic matrix of a body psychotherapy session. Take a study that wants to compare individual psychotherapy sessions with depressed patients and those with nondepressed patients (I will discuss some of these studies in a moment). Statistically, it would require at least 1,000 examples of each type of therapy to be able to complete an analysis that would have a minimum of statistical validity. The researcher would then have 51,840,000,000,000 cells of raw data to analyze.

No research as thorough as this has been carried out in the last decades. I believe I am one of the last to try to carry out a detailed coding of a complete interaction. I had focused on posture, that is, an aspect of behavior that moves relatively little. Before I detail what I have to say on the data management of coded behavior, I need to define *derived data matrixes*.

The Content of the Basic Matrix. I content myself in this section with evoking what happens when a researcher wants to analyze all the aspects of a body behavior of his patient during a one-hour psychotherapy session. There are then 43,200,000 cells to complete. For the moment, the difficulty is that every cell of a basic data matrix must be typed in manually. To continue with the hand movement example, one has to study each dimension of the movement of the hand, image by image.[19] Here are some of the dimensions distinguished to analyze the position taken by a hand at a given moment:

1. *Sagittal.* A hand can go up or down in space. It can, for example, be above the head, at the level of the face, near the knees, or on the floor.
2. *Lateral.* A hand can move from right to left. It can touch a wall at the right of the body, be in front of the torso, or touch an object at the left of the body.
3. *Depth.* The hand can be in front of the torso, can touch the torso, or find itself behind the torso.
4. *Rotation.* The palm of the hand can be oriented toward the ceiling, toward a wall, or toward the floor.
5. *Closure.* The palm of the hand can be more or less open.
6. *Touch.* The hand can touch another part of the body, a part of another's body, an object, the sofa, or nothing at all.
7. *Details difficult to include in one of the preceding* categories, like knowing if the hand is trembling or still.

In other words, there would be seven columns in our matrix to identify the behavior of the hand. The coder codes what he sees, one dimension at a time. He codes the position of the hand in the sagittal dimension at the beginning of the film, and waits until there is another movement of the hand in the sagittal dimension. He then stops the image, and notes the new position on the line that corresponds to the moment inscribed on a timer which has been set on each image (e.g., line 10 for the tenth image). When an individual moves very little, the work is quickly done; when he moves his hand all the time, the work of coding can last a week, doing it part-time (no one can code full-time because the work demands too much attention).

A coder thus develops an impression that a person who moves all the parts of the body all the time will require much more work than a person who moves very little. This creates an impression that a person who moves a lot is necessarily tiring for all the brains that perceive his behavior and for the brain that emits all of these gestures. Because of this impression, he ventures the hypothesis that to move all the time is therefore necessarily a mobilization of the attention of all those concerned. In real life, we notice that, faced with an individual who moves all the time, most people distance themselves and quiet their senses to protect themselves, or they are obliged to be completely awake, as happens sometimes with a clown or a comedian. These relational issues are independent of the content transmitted by the gestures.

The first robust conclusions that his type of research allows is that *there is so much more going on at the level of behavior than is consciously detected.* This is the daily experience of someone who codes films. Each day, he has to concentrate on a few behavioral dimensions; each day he discovers other manifest aspects in the gestures of his subjects that he has not previously perceived.

Today, the researchers hope that new technologies will make it possible to complete these analyses automatically. While waiting for this technology, most researchers focus on a few body dimensions a few moments at a time (typically during a few minutes), selecting samples in a film that seems crucial in a given theoretical frame.

THE MATRIXES DERIVED FROM THE BEHAVIOR OF AN INDIVIDUAL

We are not at the end of our troubles. We must, in effect, construct some *derived matrixes*[20] that will permit us to obtain a set of useful variables that can be extracted by a computer program from the basic matrixes. Here are a few derived variables that are currently being used:

1. *Mobility*: The software counts the number of position changes for each item of the body (in each column). It will, for example, count the number of times that there was a change in the sagittal position of the hand. The derived matrix will then furnish this result for each subject and show that some individuals have moved their hands from high to low more often than others. It is also possible to generate compound variables, like knowing how many times there was a change in at least one of the dimensions used to described the behavior of the hand, or how many times at least one item of the body moved.

2. *Thickness*: The software counts how many parts of the body change position simultaneously. For example, when an individual only moves his hands, the thickness of his behavior is 1; when he moves, at the same time, the hand + the head + a foot + his back, the thickness of his movement has a score of 4. The programs can register in the derived matrix the average thickness of an individual's mobility. A program may also provide a curve that shows the variations of thickness in time. If I want to analyze an interaction between a therapist and a patient, I can ask the program to produce two curves: the variations in the thickness of the gestures of the patient and the variations in the thickness of the gestures of the therapist.

3. *Complexity*: The software counts, for each part of the body, how many

dimensions of one part of the body are mobilized. In the preceding section, I identified seven dimensions of the movement of the hand in space (high/low, right/left, in front/in back, etc.). When the movement of the hand is carried out in a dimension (moving upward, for example), the movement has a complexity of 1. If in moving the hand upward, the palm of the hand closes and turns toward the floor, the movement has three dimensions.

4. *Time spent in motion (TSM)*: The program computes how much time there is a movement in a set of body items (e.g., the activity of the top of the body, of the hand, of the eyes, etc.).

5. *Rhythm.* This variable is defined as the computation of the average length of time between two actions. In these studies, *rhythm* is defined less rigorously than in music. It is defined as the *average* duration during which no movement occurs.

6. *Individual contingencies*: The correlations between the parts of the body of an individual. For example, the software allows one to discover that each time a person smiles, he moves the hand in a certain way in the minute following the smile.

7. *Interpersonal contingencies*: The correlations between the body parts of two individuals. For example, the software discovers that nearly every time that a patient smiles the therapist taps his fingers on the chair.

THE ANALYSIS OF THE DERIVED MATRIXES

The Statistical Analysis of the Derived Matrixes.   Once a researcher has a series of derived matrixes at his disposal, he finds himself faced with an enormous quantity of data, which his consciousness is incapable of managing. He therefore uses statistical programs that try to extract, in function of certain rules of research, particularly characteristic schemas that correlate with known variables. By "known variables," I mean variables obtained independently of the films. For example, some relatively reliable tests allow one to determine a patient's degree of depression and of anxiety. Some software can then search out which behaviors, in the patient and therapist, correlate with the results of the tests of depression and anxiety of the patient.[21]

The difficulty (not yet resolved) is that the current statistics have been constructed to find significant correlations and differences when the researcher has, at his disposal, a small sample of data on a large number of subjects. In nonverbal communication, we have the opposite situation: an enormous amount of data obtained on a ridiculously little cohort of subjects. Therefore, when one asks a statistical program to find correlations and differences, it often finds a great quantity of highly significant results. The only problem is that the mathematical bases foresee that when the statistical tests analyze a great amount of data obtained on small samples, it will find a large number of *apparently* very significant results that are, in fact, due to chance.

We find this difficulty in many domains that manipulate a large amount of data. This is the case in the new explorations in the neurosciences that generate photos of brain activity or of the research that finds correlations between cancer and just about anything. Evidently, new technologies allow us to scan reality in a more refined and automatic fashion. To deal with this type of data, we need statistical theories and procedures that do not yet exist. This is one more reason not to throw ourselves into immense coding projects of nonverbal behavior. Even if we have the data, we are incapable of using them other than as sources of inspiration that allow us to present apparently convincing beautiful graphics. The same problem is evident in the politics of health care. Some statisticians gather an impressive amount of data from practitioners (by imposing routines that are often a burden). Most of the time, once these data have been gathered, the only thing they can do with it is produce beautiful graphs that confirm the political position of the health systems. These statistics are presented to some political parties and the population as "scientific" proof of the soundness of the stated policies. In fact, this is often nothing other than data manipulation, which shows that with statistics an expert is able to demonstrate many things.

To get out of this bind, the hard sciences rely on the *replication* of specific results to render a finding as robust as possible. Once a computer program has generated a list of "highly significant" results, research laboratories can try to replicate one of these results. They can use only a small portion of these results, using longer film samples and more subjects. This requires the participation of several laboratories that are as independent of one another as possible.

Paranoia.   The research procedures that I have just described can be used as a highly simplified version of what a brain must be able to accomplish before it can generate a conscious representation of what is happening in an interaction. A clinician may also draw inspiration from these procedures to revisit the notion of paranoia. The paranoid individual (with delusions of persecution) is traditionally considered as someone who "hallucinates" connections between events that allow him to think that everybody (or a group of individuals) wants to persecute him. However, the statistical procedures we have just taken into consideration show that relatively coherent procedures make it possible to lead one to believe that there are coherent schemas that are actually products of the mind. There is no need to project or hallucinate to find schemas that feed the fear of being persecuted. It suffices to take as fact some rationally constructed observations. Furthermore, it is also true that some groups do try to persecute or manipulate other groups.

A true researcher is someone who knows all that and is not content to find some facts that seem convincing. That is why the ethics of science has developed a series of procedures (like having the replication of one's experiments conducted by somebody one does not necessarily agree with) to try to find, in the plethora of "truths" produced by the human imagination, a few islands of formulations that are as robust as possible. The notion of objectivity implies that a formulation is confirmed by heterogeneous procedures, one different from the others.

Situations and Dyads

Social psychology, at the beginning of the 1950s, sought to show that a group of interacting persons will generate behaviors that the individual members would not have if they were in another group. In other words, "groups have properties different from those of their parts taken separately" (Asch, 1952, p. 141).[22] This type of research showed that the dynamics and organization of a group could influence the behavior of a member independently of the specific traits and conscious will of the individual.

THE SITUATION: AN INTERPERSONAL SPACE

> We start with the bare observation that a number of persons will, in a given situation, perceive objects and happenings within it in a similar way; and that modes of action in the situation will also have a basic similarity. The tree that I see others see too; what I hear they hear. Indeed, to every change and gradation of my perception there correspond similar changes in the perception of others. (Solomon Eliot Asch, 1952, "The Individual and the Group," p. 146)

Imagine that you want to film five persons about to have tea together, and you have no impact on what is going on because you and your cameras are invisible to them. You will nonetheless have to take the shape of the room, the lighting, and the objects present into account. When we later view what you have filmed, we notice a variety of events. Some objects are touched but do not move (like the carpet on which the individuals have their feet and the chairs on which they are sitting). This forms the world of the *support* and *basic postures*.[23] Other objects move, like the door and the windows when they are opened or closed, the tea cups and the sugar, the cigarettes (if there are any). Then there is the visible and audible surface of the behaviors, as well as clothing. After having coded an hour's worth of interactions, frame by frame, taking into account all the visual and auditory information, you would have acquired tens of millions pieces of information. Some of the gestures and postures you observe are easily understood: like the fact of putting or not putting sugar in one's tea, certain gestures that emphasize what is being said, the orientation of the gaze toward the person to whom one speaks, to stand up to air out the room, and certain expressions that ostensibly express a feeling. Other data are more difficult to identify but are perceived intuitively by all who look at the film, such as behavior styles. Some hold the saucer with the cup on it; others take hold of the cup directly. Some are more extroverted than others; some interrupt more often; some agree with what is being said while others prefer to contradict.[24] Then there are all sorts of gestures whose meaning is more difficult to grasp, like habits and gestures that mostly look like random discharges of the nervous system: to scratch, blink, lick one's lip or tap a foot. As I have already explained, you are not able to assign a meaning or a robust function to more than 1 percent of what is coded; and the explicit consciousness of the individuals who participate in the gathering will not have registered more than 1/1000th of what you see and hear in the film. The whole of these phenomena form what we can call an *interpersonal space* or a *situation*.

It then becomes evident that the totality making up the situation is structured relatively independently of the dynamics of each organism. A situation has a bit of the same structure as that of the stage direction of a play: it can be maintained for years on end, even if the actors change. Some actors are better than others, but the nature of the play remains. A situation is animated by a multitude of dynamics quite distinct from the dynamics of the psyche. Psyche and situation interact in a continuous fashion by going through the behavioral dynamics of each one but also by the dynamics induced by the size of the room, the lighting, and the objects. What emerges from all of this (that is, the situation) will also have properties that are more than the sum of each individual behavior. To understand the dynamics of a situation requires more than the analysis of each organismic dynamic.

THE DYADIC DERIVED MATRIXES

Given the cost of conducting a study of a situation, several researchers limit themselves to the study of the situation involving a dialogue between two individuals, currently called *dyads*. I have already indicated that this reduction is essentially due to methodological limitations, like the difficulty of coordinating the filming of several cameras, the limits of statistical methods, and the lack of methods capable of automatically coding all of the variables that can be obtained from the filming of an interaction.

These methodological constraints encouraged the study of the interactions that occur spontaneously in didactic fashion, like individual psychotherapy[25] or the mother–infant interaction.[26] In this context the *derived dyadic variables* were created. The basic notion is quite simple. Consider a typical research issue as an example: the hypothesis that depression creates a decrease in motor activity.[27] The researcher who wants to verify this hypothesis often employs three types of experimental strategies that compare individual psychotherapy with manifestly depressed patients (DP), and individual psychotherapy with patients who are no longer depressed (HP):

1. *Influence of pathology on the patient.* To know whether there are some common points in the behavior of depressed patients, the researchers will, for example, compare the number of movements made by DP patients, and the number of movements made by HP patients. If the first patients move less, the hypothesis that depression slows motor activity is confirmed.

2. *The influence of the patient on others.* The researcher can also study the *impact* of the patient's depression on the behavior of those with which

he interacts. He will then compare the therapists of the DP dyads with those of the HP dyads. If the first therapist moves less than the second one, the researcher is able to speak of some kind of contagion from the depression on the therapist. To understand this contagion, he can then establish more exact correlations between the mobility of the therapist and that of the patient. If he observes that the less a patient moves, the less the therapist moves, the researcher is able to conclude that the therapist has a certain way of reacting to the slowing down of the patient's motor activity. Whereas if he observes that the less a patient moves, the more the therapist moves, the researcher is able to conclude that the therapist has another way of reacting to the slowing down of the patient's motor activity.

3. *The influence of the patient on the structure of the interaction.* Finally, the researcher is able to create some *dyadic variables*, as the sum of the movements made by both protagonists. He then compares the mobility in the DP dyads with those in the HP dyads. Since some researchers[28] have not observed clear differences in making the previous comparisons, they sought to discover if the inhibition of the body mobility influences at least the therapeutic dyad, taken as a whole. They can then see whether there were dyadic differences. If they find a clear difference with these data, they are going to conclude that the depression creates an atmosphere in the room that can slow down the motor activity of the therapist, or of the patient, or of both. The impact may vary from one dyad to another, but in all cases, the dyadic mobility will be lower in the DP dyads than in the HP dyads. This result reinforces the impression that depression influences the emergence of the structure of the dyad as much as the individuals who are part of it. If only the results of the third type are observed, they are difficult to explain by the individual variables alone. There is then necessarily an interaction between the state of the patient and the organization of the interaction.

An example of dyadic data was published by Siegfried Frey and his team.[29] It consists of a study that analyzes the stability of basic postures and hierarchical status. In this study, the researcher compared situations where female students were in a discussion with other female students and situations where the female students were in a discussion with university teaching assistants.[30] In the dyads with the assistants, the postures were somewhat more stable than in the dyads with other students.[31] This difference was not created by the students or assistants, because it was not always the same protagonist who had a particularly unstable posture. An exact formulation would be that in the dyads with the inequality in status, the probability is greater that one of the two protagonists at least would have a stable posture, or that in the dyads with equal status, the protagonists change posture more easily.

Researchers who have been influenced by systems theory have tried to further understand this third type of data by speaking of *dyadic effects*. They hypothesize that the connection between the behaviors of several individuals can be as indirect as the relationships between the dimensions of an organism. A gesture does not always directly influence the other individuals in the group. It primarily influences the structure of an interaction; that change then influences the other person. The difficulty with this type of model is that no one knows if there is a group entity capable of perceiving a gesture. We must then suppose that the protagonists of a group seek to maintain group cohesion, and they will therefore react to a gesture that risks reinforcing or weakening the coherence of the group. Let me be more explicit. I can react to an individual who stands up because he is expressing a feeling while rising (there is then a direct interaction between two organisms) or because he is about to end a discussion (the change of ritual provokes the reactions).

Having specified what is meant by the organization of an interaction, researchers were able to refine their analysis. They are no longer content to simply add up individual behaviors. They move, above all, to analyzing the way an individual behavior inserts itself into the organization of a dyad. I will provide examples in my discussion of Stern, Beebe, and Tronick (chapter 21). Here are two typical dyadic variables:

1. Software is able to compute how many times the protagonists look into each other's eyes.
2. A program is able to calculate the number of times a person interrupts the other.

In these two examples, it is the *relationship* between the two persons that is studied. These data could not have been analyzed if the camera had only filmed one of the two protagonists. Another kind of dyadic data is the *temporal organization* of the behaviors of individuals in interaction. For example, Joseph Jaffe and his collaborators (2002) analyzed the rhythm in the exchange of sounds between newborns and adults. Certain relationships have a faster rhythm than others.

In the case of studies on the relationship between a mother and a newborn, the infant does not have the means to structure the relationship in a conscious way. He reacts in a local manner to each event, without being able to become aware of what constructs itself between him and his close ones. Research shows that even in adults, setting up the organization of an interaction is mostly nonconscious. This organization is structured by a few conscious variables for the adults (e.g., cultural norms) and by a succession of events that organize themselves without anyone really understanding how. Individuals have the tendency to feel that they are making a particular gesture for a conscious reason and another gesture for another reason without being able to understand what is organizing itself (in them and around them) while all of these local actions are taking place. Mary Catherine Bateson (1994) analyzes this type of schema between behaviors and thoughts by showing that people often have the impression that they are improvising. In systemic therapy for couples in crisis, this lack of mastery is particularly striking.

An example of the dyadic variable often used in these studies[32] is called the measure of *contingency* by Beatrice Beebe. It consists in finding what gesture often correlates to another gesture: if we see a body item appear in a given context, can we predict which other body item will appear at the same time? Beebe distinguishes between two types of contingencies:

1. A *self-contingency*: A body item is often associated with another body item in the same body. For example, almost every time a subject smiles at another person, she frowns.
2. An *interpersonal contingency*: A body item of a subject predicts the activation of a body item in another person. For example, it often happens that when a subject smiles, the other also smiles.

This allows for the distinction between self-regulation and interpersonal regulation, but it also describes a type of auto-regulation that may have an impact on those who perceive it. This type of auto-regulation is *ostentatious* to the extent that even if it is activated in a nonconscious way, it is part of the mechanisms that regulate the interaction. The research studies that Beebe et al. (2010) refer to and quote report forms of contingencies between a baby and mother that construct themselves in less than half a second.

The difficulty with the dyadic effects is that they have become central in the current research for purely methodological reasons. We will see, in speaking about Stern, Beebe, and Tronick, that certain researchers believe dyadic interactions are a basic building block of human interaction. There is a kind of theoretical bias in this. It uses the methodological limitations that make the dyad central to promote an ideology according to which the mother is uniquely responsible for the welfare or discontent of the infant. This point of view is not false, but it can be more or less relative. In psychoanalysis, the importance given to the mother–child dyad is special to the researchers in the United States; in Europe, and in Freud's work, the father often predominates: "This father, whom he could not help hating as a rival, was the same father whom he had always loved and was bound to go on loving, who had been his model, had been his first playmate, and had looked after him from his earliest infancy: and this is what gave rise to his first conflict" (Freud, 1909b, III, p. 134).

DOES A DEPRESSED PATIENT MOVE LESS OFTEN?

I now give the example of the correlation between the complexity of movements and depression, which will show the advantage for psychotherapy of distinguishing between behavioral dimensions, such as they are computed to generate derived matrixes. In the preceding section, I described hypothetical studies regarding the connection between depression and mobility. Here, I mention a few studies on this phenomenon to show what research can bring to psychotherapy.

For a century (at least), it has been recognized in psychiatry that patients suffering from a major depressive disorder with melancholic features move less than most other persons, except those in a catatonic crisis. Some psychiatrists think the reduction of motor activity can be observed with most depressive patients,[33] whereas speeding up motor activity is a sign of anxiety or mania. This phenomenon has been effectively observed by some researchers, but not by all. It is therefore possible that depression does not act directly on mobility but on something else.

In a series of research studies on depressive behavior, Heiner Ellgring (1989, 1990) observed a drop of mobility linked to depression, but this drop is often local. Certain parts of the body move less in almost every case, but it is not always the same ones: less smiling (61 percent), smaller number of gazes oriented toward the other (58 percent), less facial activity (31 percent), or less verbal activity (33 percent). Ellgring did not observe systematic differences when he analyzed the variety in the facial repertoire, the expressions used, or the gestures associated to speech. There is a correlation between depression and slowing down in at least two of these dimensions among 70 percent of patients. Consciousness generally seeks some solid associations between behavior and psychopathology. Most psychotherapists would very much like researchers to show that each time a person does not move very much, one can conclude that there is depression. Research confirms that the link between behavior and psychopathology is always fuzzy. For example, a patient perhaps smiles less than usual when he is depressed, but nonetheless he smiles more than other persons. This leads to two types of differences between groups:

1. There is an *absolute difference* when most of the members of a group behave differently than all the other members of another group. This kind of difference is observed more often in the studies on cultural differences than on the differences between psychiatric diagnoses.

2. There is a *relative difference* when it is not possible to differentiate all of the members of one group from the members of another group but that, on average, the difference goes in the same direction. The relationship between athletic performance and gender is a very well-known example. It is possible to state that *on average* men have a more powerful body (e.g., from the point of view of respiratory capacity) than women do. It is also manifest that there are many women who have a more powerful body than that of many men. It is probable that the best male tennis player will always have a more powerful game than the best female tennis player, but I could never compete with a female tennis champion. The difference is relative because in each group, the variance is enormous. In clinical research, the behavioral differences are generally relative, as in Ellgring's study. These relative differences are difficult to grasp con-

sciously, especially when they become as diffused as in the observations I have just summarized.

A similar result to those of Heiner Ellgring was found by Beatrice Beebe et al. (2010) in a study on the interaction between four-month-old babies and their depressed mothers. These results concern the analysis of the contingency of movements. She noticed a polarization between the auto-contingency and the interpersonal contingency, which are both particularly elevated and particularly low in depressed mothers. This observation contradicts the hypothesis that the more there is contingency between a mother and her baby, the more constructive the relationship. The nondepressed mothers that Beebe and her team observed have, on average, a *moderate* variable contingency.

In research by Siegfried Frey and his team[34] on the correlation between the behavior of a patient and the seriousness of the depression, he distinguished the *impression* of a slowing down in the consciousness of the psychotherapist and a *real* slowing down in the patient.[35] The patients observed suffer from a "major depression," which is considered less severe that melancholia. Software generated tables for two distinct variables, computed for each part of the body:

1. The time (TSM) during which at least a part of the body moves.
2. The average *complexity* of the mobility, defined as the number of dimensions mobilized by each part of the body, on average.

For this study, Frey and his team coded the position of the head in function of the following dimensions:[36]

1. *Sagittal.* The head moves vertically upward and downward.
2. *Rotation.* The head moves horizontally toward the right or the left.
3. *Lateral.* The head leans to the right or to the left.

When a movement of the head mobilizes one of these dimensions, its complexity is 1; when a movement of the head simultaneously mobilizes three dimensions, there is a complexity of 3. Someone who uses only one dimension in a continual fashion with each part of the body has an average complexity of movement of 1; a person in whom all the body parts simultaneously use all of the conceivable dimensions has an average complexity of movement of 3. Most subjects displayed behaviors that are situated between these two extremes and displayed a distribution of the complexity of movements that varied for each part of the body.

In distinguishing the duration during which a movement occurred and its complexity, Frey and his team were able to demonstrate that the depressed patient moves about as many times as his physician does, and sometimes as often as after he is healed.[37] On the other hand, when they were depressed, the behavior of the patients was less complex. For Frey and his collaborators (1983), the interest in this observation is twofold. First, they introduce the notion of complexity into the psychiatric clinic and allow for a greater precision in the analysis of what is happening. Second, they show how the consciousness of a psychotherapist simplifies what he observes. Only the experts in the study of movement are able to consciously perceive the degree of complexity in the movements of the body. Even for them, this analysis requires an intense attention that rapidly becomes exhausting. However, the nonconscious processes of the therapist (neurological, for example) seem to be sensitive to this complexity. They transform this information into an impression of slowness for the conscious perception. Thus, even when the whole community of psys agrees that they perceive a motor retardation in most depressed patients, they can be suffering from an identical illusion. It is worth noting that most of the time this impression that there is motor retardation suffices for the current needs of the clinician.

These results show why psychiatrists have had so much trouble identifying the bodily and behavioral contours of a psychopathology without the help of systematic studies such as those mentioned here. This type of result supports the suspicion I have often expressed in this book with regard to the belief that there exists direct connections between style of behavior, body shape, and mental problems. The greater the advances in research, the more it becomes evident that conscious observation is incapable of understanding the details of a motoric (or enacted) pattern. Conscious observation can only content itself with simplified data to elaborate its own reflection.[38] This explains the proliferation and the popularity of simplistic models that make everybody believe they are capable of mastering this complexity. The connections are so complex that today's researchers are only beginning to elaborate a theoretical stance that could allow them to understand the dynamics of nonverbal communication. Other resources are necessary to transform these studies into a domain of robust knowledge. On the other hand, research confirms that the therapist can often have confidence in his intuition that when a person is depressed something is slowing down in him and the interaction he has with depressive patients. This fuzzy impression would be a *summary* of what the brain discovers in a nonconscious way. On the other hand, as soon as the therapist attempts to explicitly identify and explain what causes this impression, he often has recourse to simplifications that do not stand up to rigorous observation.

The Body without Sound

When a researcher shows his films without any sound to a group of people who do not know his research, each one proposes personal observations that could explain the meaning attributed to gestures. Each individual notices immediately that the others are making different associations. As soon as the researcher turns on the sound, the meaning of the words varied much less from one person to another. When the researcher reveals the setting in which the film was shot, these individuals immediately distinguish a series of details that hitherto had meant nothing to them and now give a meaning that allows them to support their representation of the situation. Often, the researcher must then explain why this new series of associations are frequently false, even if all the members of the group had spontaneously agreed with each other.

This typical observation teaches us many things. I isolate three of them for the moment.

Only a Few Highly Standardized Gestures Are Understood by Several Persons the Same Way

Research indicates that the body signals to which it is possible to assign a robust meaning are rare.[39] Perhaps less than 1 percent of the gestures observed in a film during a spontaneous interaction can be included in that category. But they are the gestures that are retained in the conscious thoughts of the observer.

Speech Often Helps One Understand What Is Happening at the Level of Behavior or at Least Makes it Possible to Think that a Motor Behavior Has a Precise Meaning

Video analysis allows us to observe how a mother acts differently when she makes a mechanical gesture with the baby without talking to him compared to when she accompanies her gestures with appropriate words. If she puts a spoon in his mouth while watching television, the gestures are often awkward; the coordination between the movements of the baby and the movements of the mother is poor. If she takes the trouble to speak to him, by describing to him what she is about to do while feeding him (e.g., by saying something like "here is something to eat" or "I am bringing the spoon to your mouth"), she becomes more attentive. By speaking with the baby, something in her is better coordinated. As a conscious thought may be used more or less in a central way by a propensity, a gesture may be related in a more or less intense manner with consciousness. By addressing herself to her child, the mother's behavior acquires a better coordination with the infant's responses.

A striking example of movements that take on a meaning after the sound is added, is the research by Siegfried Frey and his collaborators (1980) on psychotherapy with depressed patients (e.g., in which he analyses the complexity of movements). These researchers analyzed interviews between medical psychiatrists and depressed patients in psychotherapy. Each therapeutic process is filmed twice: at the first and last sessions. Frey, Jorns, and Daw (1980) notice a striking difference between the first and last session. In the first, the patients shake their head in the rotational dimension (side to side) and the physicians mostly shake their head in the sagittal dimension (up and down). At the last session, the effect is inversed. The patients mostly move their head up and down while the physicians move it from right to left. How would you explain this difference? Having asked this question of several persons, the researchers noticed the probability that someone, even an expert, would arrive at the right answer almost by chance. By turning on the sound, everything becomes clear:

1. The *first* session:
   a. The *therapist* does not cease saying "yes" that life is worth living to give hope to the patient.
   b. The *patient* does not cease saying "no" to the encouragements of the therapist by denying that there could be any positive event on this horrible planet dominated by a cruel human species.
2. The *last* session:
   a. The *patient* does not cease saying "yes, you have been successful in treating me" to his therapist. He shows a profound admiration for his therapist, characteristic of a slightly manic state a patient can be in when he comes out of his depression.
   b. The *therapist* does not cease saying "no" to this enthusiasm, emphasizing that he has only carried out his duty.

To show that this apparently insignificant aspect masks profound mechanisms, consider the following:

1. The fact that software programs more easily manage coded behavior than conscious perception has made it possible to demonstrate that these moments have a particularly convincing correlation with the amount of patients getting well. The analysis of coded behavior during the interaction demonstrates that these are key moments.
2. This observation shows very well that these key moments are *dyadic*. We observe a change not only in the patient but also in the therapist. Not only is the patient better, but his impact on the physician is different because the physician reacts automatically, without knowing it, in a relatively standardized manner to this improvement.
3. This observation can be quite useful to demonstrate a well-known phenomenon by clinicians in the training of psychotherapists. The tendency to console depressed patients and to have a fear of compliments is an often mentioned mechanism. Having said that, I must compare two types of observations: (a) the experienced psychotherapist often refuses to console a depressed patient and finds it important to accept compliments, and (b) young therapists often have better results than more experienced ones. It is possible that in falling into some traps, beginners allow some relational mechanisms to establish themselves in such a manner that that they are more effective for reasons that no one yet understands. It would be interesting to take up this experiment by differentiating between experienced therapists and those still in training.

A Gesture Rarely Attempts to Convey a Meaning, but It Often Has an Impact

He who will know fully the vanity of man has only to consider the causes and the effects of love. The cause is a "je ne sais quoi" (Corneille), and the effects are dreadful. This "je ne sais quoi," so small an object that we cannot recognize it, agitates a whole country, princes, armies, the entire world. Cleopatra's nose: had it been shorter, the whole aspect of the world would have been altered. (Blaise Pascal, 1669, "Pensées," 162, Kindle 1083)[40]

To introduce you to the realm of questions I wish to discuss in this section, try to understand the meaning of the gestures displayed in figure 20.1.

The first row of photographs in the figure shows "a small girl sitting in the audience of a theatrical performance." In the second row, "a girl watches a woman with a baby." These gestures seem to make immediate sense. However, if several experts try to explain the need to behave in this way in such circumstances in Bali, they will soon discover that such images are like a Rorschach test. Their spontaneous explanation provides more information on how each expert thinks than about the actual event. For example, as soon as these behav-

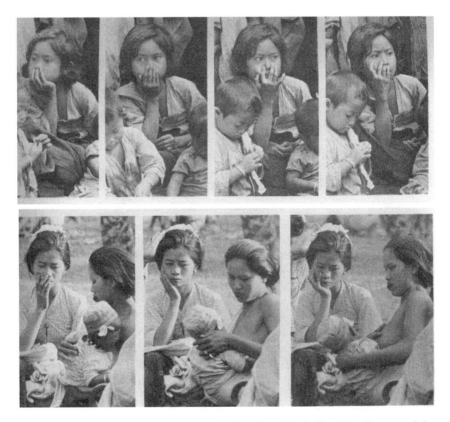

FIGURE 20.1. "The sensory titivation and fidgeting with the hands in the area of the mouth and nose" when observing other people moving, in Bali. *Source:* Bateson and Mead (1947, plate 25, p. 104).

iors are presented as typical in a culture, experts may develop a different set of explanations than if they were asked to explain individual motives.

When one uses video for psychotherapy, one constantly needs information from the patient to understand the gesture. Then one uses a first approximate analysis of the gesture to explore new aspects of the patient's thoughts. Going back and forth between a video, the impressions of the patient, and those of the therapist can become incredibly fruitful, if one is willing to accept that this is a process, an exploration. The threads that move a marionette can be attached to hundreds of different mechanisms. *Balinese Character* (Bateson and Mead, 1947) is an excellent place to begin, if one wants to acquire the type of perception that is required to nonverbal interaction.

GESTURES RARELY "SPEAK" . . .

We have just seen that, isolated from their context, gestures, mimics, and postures rarely have an obvious meaning for conscious thoughts. They mostly serve as support for an associative system that rapidly transforms itself in to an interpretive delirium. The more we question a person concerning the impression a gesture makes on him, the more he discovers that his first impression is nothing other than a "filling in," and this filling in is a mental construction that reinforces the necessary illusion that everything has been seen and understood. Therefore, people who observe a gesture have the tendency to attribute meaning to it that is part of their current beliefs. Let us consider an example.

> Vignette on suicidal behavior. *At the end of the 1990s, most psys believed that the more an individual expressed himself, the healthier he was becoming. At that time, the laboratory where I was working[41] was analyzing the behavior of suicidal patients in the hope of finding behavioral indices that would permit us to predict the risk of future suicide attempts (Heller et al., 2001). When I presented our results to colleagues, they were astonished that the individuals at a high risk of suicide were more expressive than the individuals at low risk. Yet this is easily explainable. These individuals had been brought to the hospital after a suicide attempt and had been filmed during their interview with a psychiatrist in the emergency department. Some felt that their attempt was a mistake and that they would not do it again. This was an episode to forget. They did not feel any need to develop a connection with the psychiatrist. Those who still experienced a need to kill themselves felt that the physician could possibly help them. The patients in the second group therefore had a greater need to interact with the psychiatrist.*

Most of the gestures that are made influence the nonconscious processes of the individual with whom an organisms interacts. This impact can influence the protagonists in less than 250 milliseconds without them realizing it.[42] Even if the subject does not perceive the details of these stimulations, they often create in him a first impression that influences the way he spontaneously reacts. Such a first impression of another person can persist for years.[43] When an individual has the impression of being able to evaluate a candidate for the presidency based on television images, he has the impression of expressing a well-founded personal opinion. Siegfried Frey's research shows that such an intuition is often as strong, powerful, and lasting as it is unreliable.[44] The power of this impression allows citizens to think that there is no need to inquire any further to know the worthiness of a candidate before voting for or against him.

... BUT THEIR IMPACT CAN BE MORE OR LESS PREDICTABLE

An individual is entitled to expect that certain behaviors would have a relatively predictable effect on self and his entourage. For example, recent research has shown that children need to find islands of predictable communication that permit them to have the impression of acquiring a form of mastery over what is happening. Some psychotherapists who defend the notion of a self relate what is predictable to the notion of meaning. This meaning is not necessarily conscious. It may even be nonconscious in the case of automatic interactive exchanges. In the domain of those schools of psychotherapy that take the body into account, this perspective can be found in the writings of psychotherapists such as Beatrice Beebe[45] and Rubens Kignel.[46] In both cases, the idea is that the more contingency there is, the more the impact of a gesture acquires meaning for the mind. It is therefore possible to speak of a fuzzy or soft semiotics for ordinary gestures, in contrast to signs that are explicitly associated to a meaning.

This meaning of a gesture constructs itself in interaction with the person's surroundings.[47] A newborn may produce a reflex movement that the adult (e.g., the mother) perceives as a smile. The newborn then experiences an affective response from the mother that is accompanied by a mimic of what she feels to be a smile. The infant thus learns, by imitation and positive reinforcement, what may happen when he smiles.

Rubens Kignel (2010) refers to Pierce and Ecco to assume that such habits, constructed with an interactive frame, are the basis on which semiotics are co-constructed. As in Piaget's theory of intelligence, these constructions may at first be nonconscious sensorimotor schemas, but the more co-conscious they become the more psychological meaning they generate. This position is not necessarily in contradiction with the notion that some emotional forms of expression have an innate core function. Nevertheless, it imposes the idea that even innate emotional mechanisms must be calibrated in function of contextual, relational, and cultural dynamics. One of the by-products of this calibration process would be the emergence of increasingly meaningful forms of habitual interactive skills, which can sometimes acquire a symbolic configuration.

In his example of the smile, Kignel quotes researchers for whom positive reinforcement is a key motivator for the development of these co-constructed skills. I have noticed with some of my patients that this is not necessarily the case. The prime motivator was, in those cases, a need for predictability. In my experience, this need is deeper than a need for kindness. In some families, the only predictable interactive skills that could be constructed were negative. Because the infant needs to create some form of attachment to his parents and construct an honorable self-image, he will then take these skills as proprieties of his self-image. I have noticed how attached these patients can be, once they are adults, to these predictable interactive co-constructed schemas ... even when they are destructive for themselves as well as for those they live with. The best known example is that of children who had been beaten and then beat their own children.[48] It is then extremely difficult to modify these habitual "meaningful" habits, because they are the unstable sand on which such persons have built their sense of identity. The person grew up investing a huge amount of energy to find ways of surviving in such an environment.

I then observe an internal conflict between (a) an immense aggression against abusive patents, and (b) an attempt to preserve an honorable loyalty to the habits and customs of the abusive family. Having become adults, these individuals may not have enough energy to change their functioning style when they discover that they are able to live in other less hostile environments.

Kignel (2010, p. 18) also discussed gestures produced by a body without any intent to communicate. As soon as they are explicitly perceived by another person, a meaning is often automatically attributed to them. Even when the attributed meaning has no connection to the mechanisms that produced the behavior, it may become one if the entourage begins to incorporate certain repetitive signs into their common communication network. In my research studies on nonverbal communication, I have noticed that most of the bodily activities I coded fit into this category. In our study on the risk of suicidal recidivism (Heller et al., 2001), we observed that patients made a large variety of movements of the lips, which had no discernible communicative relevance. But as soon as our studies demonstrated that there was a correlation between the frequency of these lip movements, very different from each other, and the risk of suicide, we gave them meaning for our psychotherapeutic colleagues. When I perceive them on a video, I think immediately of the person's potential risk of suicidal recidivism. This does not mean that these movements have been generated to communicate a risk of suicide to others. We have been able to establish that the therapists of these patients do not notice these little rapid and often insignificant gestures, that they do not consciously correlate these gestures with suicidal risk.

It often occurs (a) that a patient's familial milieu had contributed a meaning to these multiple gestures that the body ceaselessly produces, and (b) the patient then attributes this meaning each time the gesture happens. There is then a loss of the freedom of mobility. This loss can have a negative effect on the organism when the inhibited gestures are part of the regulatory systems. In other cases, this inhibition permits a calibration of the behavior that allows for a better social integration. Often, as we have already seen, the different dimensions of the organism have some heterogeneous goals that can become contradictory. What is good for social integration is not necessarily good for the health of the organism, and vice versa.[49]

The psychotherapist who is confronted by the "false meanings" the patient has introjected often has the need to sow doubt in the patient, to show him that some of the explanations he attributes to these gestures freeze certain regulatory mechanisms of his organism, notably in the mind. To free consciousness of false explanations about self is as important as showing that some behaviors have an implicit meaning. My patients often have an entire network of false explanations concerning being imprisoned by their body—their weight, their appearance, the grace of their gestures, and so on. To allow them to rediscover their body independently of these aesthetic criteria and of the auto-evaluation that have structured their super-ego is also a task of psychotherapy. One of the strategies used in these cases is to relearn to feel the impact of one's behavior on one's vegetative sensations. The patient is thus able to reflect on the conflicts within him between his somatic needs and those of a social image. He may then search for compromises that he would be better able to take on than before.

This way of defining the meaning of gestures by their predictable impact has a certain but limited usefulness.[50] A gesture may have a function for self, another function for someone else, and a function in dynamic situations. It is only in the case where the three functions are congruent (or at least complementary) that this type of meaning could become useful and constructive. As soon as each one perceives the meaning of a gesture differently, the notion that the function of a gesture can be used to grasp its "meaning" loses its relevance. If the notion of familiarity with certain behaviors and their impact is an important key, it must still be deepened before being able to lead us anywhere. We will see, for example, that it is also possible to take predictable sequences of behavior in a relationship as a relevant functional clue. It is always good to remind ourselves that even a professional actor needs a director to know how his behavior is perceived by others.

In the course of a session, a psychotherapist is bombarded with information. The therapist tends to focus on the behavioral items of the patient that resonate with his affective impressions and clinical preoccupations. He may notice that he experiences sadness when the patient talks in a certain way and anxiety when the patient moves in a certain way. Noticing that the patient is enraged when he mentions certain events of his life is one thing, deciding if exploring this rage is therapeutic is another. By comparing several sessions given by several therapists with numerous patients, research studies make it possible to calibrate the attention of the psychotherapists on the elements that seem truly pertinent. Some of these are not expressive. They belong to the category of apparently meaningless gestures. In the case of our research on suicidal patients, the therapist experienced a variety of emotional impressions, such as anger and sadness, that did not correlate with suicidal risk. We were able to show that the impressions that correlated with suicidal risk were mostly the feelings of comfort and discomfort, self-confidence and lack of confidence.[51] This study needs to be replicated before these findings can be used in a reliable way by psychotherapists.

21

The Mother–Infant Dyads of Stern, Beebe, and Tronick: Self-Regulation and Interaction Regulate Each Other

Body psychotherapists are experts in intra-organismic dynamics. Their publications often include discussions on interpersonal issues in their sessions, but only a few of them have sought to incorporate the issues raised by studies of nonverbal communication. This has slowly changed since the 1990s. An increasing number of body psychotherapists were influenced by systemic therapies and child psychoanalysts who sought ways to incorporate nonconscious processes and nonverbal communication in psychotherapeutic approaches. I present three researchers who have played a key role in this change of perspective. Daniel Stern and Beatrice Beebe are psychoanalysts who have also done a lot of research on mother–infant interaction. Ed Tronick is a researcher, not a psychotherapist, but his studies on mother–infant interaction have had a strong impact on body psychotherapists that have followed this trend.[1] Since then, nonverbal communication between adults and in psychotherapy sessions is also discussed by several body psychotherapists (Heller, 1993a).

THE HISTORICAL BACKGROUND OF THE PSYCHOANALYTIC RESEARCH ON THE BODY IN THE MOTHER–INFANT RELATIONSHIP

In the perception of others, my body and the body of others are coupled, as if performing and acting in concert: this behavior that I only can see in others, I somehow embody it at a distance; I make this behavior becoming mine. I take it over and understand it. Inversely, I know that the gestures I myself execute could become object of intention for others. It is the transfer of my intentions into the body of others, and of other's intentions in to my own body, this alienation of others by me and of me by others that renders possible the perception of others. (Maurice

Merleau-Ponty, 1967, *Les relations avec autrui chez l'enfant* [*Relating to Others during Childhood*], p. 24; translated in Rochat, 2010)

Resigned and at the end of his life, Reich defended the idea that the only way to stop the education systems from generating malice and violence is to take preventive measures at birth.[2]

The research enterprises undertaken on the northeastern seaboard of the United States, a region the aging Reich frequented, greatly influenced the new developments in body psychotherapy. These are especially the experimental and clinical research on post-traumatic stress disorder (PTSD) supported by Bessel Van der Kolk in Boston, mentioned earlier, and the research on infants influenced by Daniel Stern in New York and Boston. I now discuss the second trend. Its impact on the body therapies is not one that Reich anticipated, however it does contribute to develop ways of supporting how an infant grows into the realm of social interactions. This research is influenced by a different trend that blends psychoanalysis, developmental psychology, systemics, and neurosciences.

In the sections dedicated to the body in psychoanalysis, I had touched on this theme in mentioning Sabina Spielrein who had combined two topics:

1. The psychoanalysis of Freud and Jung, and research in developmental psychology inspired by Piaget and Vygotsky.
2. The notion that communication is necessarily verbal and nonverbal.

Even though Spielrein had influenced the first attempts to define the individual as the body–mind entity in Psychoanalysis, her contribution in this area is never referred to by Fenichel and Reich, or the founders of child psychoanalysis. Yet her intuitions already announce a tradition that reinforces itself in Psychoanalysis from Anna Freud to Daniel Stern. In Freud's time, the attempts to include the body by Ferenczi, Groddeck, and especially Reich were considered to be exotic curiosities. However, there was one exception: the Psychoanalysis of the infant. Anna Freud and Melanie Klein developed this field, not together but in a conflictual dialectical relation that became particularly intense in London during World War II. Child psychoanalysis soon developed in a spectacular fashion, thanks to the work of personalities such as Bruno Bettelheim, René Spitz, Margaret Mahler, Françoise Dolto, and several others. It was evident, in that domain, that the interaction with the body and behavior was central because the infant cannot speak.

René Spitz (1965) gave a new impetus to this development by associating clinical psychoanalytic research and the methods of experimental psychology to forge the tools that allow us to better understand and treat infants. Since the work of Bowlby (1969) on attachment, it becomes evident that it was crucial to include the relationship with the mother in all newborn studies. Although the need to include fathers in these studies is discussed, these researchers found it more important to focus on the mother–infant dyad.[3] Ainsworth and Brazelton[4] reinforce the connection between research, psychoanalysis, and studies on nonverbal communication and attachment theory.

STERN AND MUTUAL REGULATION

Daniel Stern undertook an immense research study to identify the bases of relational comfort.[5] He is the psychoanalyst and researcher in psychology most often quoted in the reunions of body psychotherapists during the last decade of the twentieth century. He ended his career as professor of psychopathology in the Faculty of Psychology and of the Sciences of Education in Geneva, Switzerland.

Stern's journey often led him to participate in research groups. The principal ones are:

1. A group of researchers and psychoanalytic clinicians who study the details of communicative bodily behaviors with the help of films and videos. Beatrice Beebe, T. Berry Brazelton, Louis Sander, Colwyn Trevarthen, and Ed Tronick make up this group.
2. He worked with troupes of dancers and actors directed by Jerome Robbins and Robert Wilson. Probably with them he developed his incredible ability to reconstruct the feelings that animate a dialogue of gestures between two individuals.
3. The *Change Process Study Group* in Boston, where he joined Louis Sander and Ed Tronick, as well as Nadia Brunchschweiler-Stern, Alexandra M. Harrison, Karlen Lyons-Ruth, Alexander C. Morgan, and Jeremy P. Nathum.
4. In Switzerland, he also worked at the *Centre d'Études Familiales* (Center of Family Studies), directed by Elizabeth Fivaz-Depeursinge, near Lausanne; and with the Artificial Intelligence and Psychiatry group in Geneva, already mentioned in the sections dedicated to Guy Cellérier (Stern, 2004, acknowledgments).

Each one of these authors published important articles and books on the themes developed in the following sections.

The notions of *affective attunement* and *intersubjectivity* are most often associated with Daniel Stern by body psychotherapists. To be able to describe what these words refer to, first I explain the notion of *contingency* such as it is developed in the psychological studies of infancy.[6] These notions made it possible to frame targeted research on the way that fine motor practices create nuances in intimate relationships. In the case of Stern,[7] it consists in identifying the contour of *affective experiences* that last but a moment, in which a collection of feelings, a way of using one's body, and the perception of the movements of the other form a particular experience, "a world in a grain of sand" (Stern, 2004).

These experiences often have multiple facets that combine so subtly in so little time that they cannot be apprehended explicitly; when they are, it is inevitably in a very partial way. The nonconscious dimension of these experiences become still more tangible when one analyzes filmed interactions that allow one to perceive the exquisite finesse of how these micro-experiences are coordinated during an interactive sequence, touching deep layers in each of the persons involved. The precision, multiplicity, and rapidity of these interpersonal coordinations, as I have already indicated, cannot be fully appreciated without the help of films, from which we extract coded data. This data are then organized by computer programs, while the researcher remains in contact with the experiential dimension that relate to these motor reactions. The way these body–mind units coordinate with each other makes one think of an invisible waltz, a meticulous choreography that the nonconscious mechanisms easily capture but that remain inaccessible to explicit conscious perception.[8]

Contingency

There is contingency when an individual achieves a direct coordination of his gestures with what happens around him.[9] Here is the description of an often-used device to study contingency. The leg of a small infant is connected by a string to a tight cord on which are suspended some objects that make noise, like little bells. The researchers consider that the infant has acquired a feeling of contingency when he moves his leg to shake the objects, and that he manages to modulate the noise of the objects by modulating the movements of his leg. For example, this happens when he moves his leg more rapidly to accelerate the rhythm of the ringing, or when he discovers that the greater the movements of his leg, the louder the sounds.

The capacity to control the contingency between his actions and what is going on around him is central, not only to acquire a skill in the handling of objects but also to calibrate the know-how necessary for a constructive communication.[10]

One of Daniel Stern's major research preoccupations is to understand how all of this know-how constructs itself, and how it can be repaired when it has not received the necessary support to establish itself. This explains the necessity to intervene directly in the educational systems. An adult is only able to assess the damage and learn how to live better with what he has, while improving as much as possible his communication skills; but he is not able to remember what happened in his first year of life.

Attunement

The term *attunement* was a rare word in child psychology until Daniel Stern used it. According to the *New Oxford English Dictionary*, this term designates what a person does so that others become more aware of what is going on with him. Having said that, there is also an intensification of the quality of the communication, as when two musicians tune their instruments so that they might play together. Stern[11] speaks of attunement when a mother accommodates herself to the moods of her baby, calibrating her mental and bodily behavior to support her infant.

This notion of mutual attunement is part of Stern's attempt to identify how a communication should unfold. It consists of being able to tune the behaviors and the affects of each one by following the rules listed here:

1. *Adequate temporal coordination of behaviors.* The necessity of coordinating (a) the way that a parent places a spoon in the mouth of a young child to feed it and (b) the motor skills with which the child eats is already an example of the attunement of behaviors.
2. *Ease of intermodal translation.* I have detailed the notion of intermodality when speaking of Wilma Bucci.[12] It consists of being able to coordinate several communicative modalities (gestures, words, gazes, etc.) at the center of a dialogue between organisms.
3. *Affective resonance.* Stern adds to the two observable requirements, the *intersubjective impression* that these behaviors are part of a shared affective state.[13] That does not necessarily mean that if the child smiles, the adults around him also smile. A relationship can be in accord even if each one retains a personal mood. On the other hand, there can only be attunement if everyone experiences sympathy and empathy for the mood of the other.

Here is an example of an intermodal interaction of this type:

> A ten-month-old girl is seated on the floor facing her mother. She is trying to get a piece of puzzle into the right place. After many failures she finally gets it. She then looks up into her mother's face with delight and an explosion of enthusiasm. She "opens up her face" [her mouths opens, her eyes widen, her eyebrows rise] and then close back down. The time contour of these changes can be described as a smooth arch [a crescendo, a high point, decrescendo]. At the same time her arms rise and fall at her sides. Mother intones by saying "Yeah" with a pitch line that rises and falls as the volume crescendos and decrescendos. "yeeAAAaahh." The mother prosodic contour matches the child's facial-kinetic contour. They also have the same duration. (Stern, 2010, p. 41)

An interesting point in this model is that the goal of such a behavioral attunement is to share an affective dynamic in an interpersonal way. This type of behavior is a way to try to harmonize two souls. Here, Stern distinguishes in a particularly clear manner what is behavioral and what is mental while analyzing how these two dynamics are intertwined: "Affect attunement reflects the mother's attempt to share the infant's subjective experience, not his actions. . . . She wants a matching of internal states" (Stern, 2010, p. 114). For Stern (2010,

p. 41). The vitality form of his mimics the same one the infant can feel in the verbal response of the mother. These behavioral expressions and the impression that he feels correlate. Stern (2010, p. 46) has found some neurological research that describes nerves capable of reacting to nervous reactions coming from different sensory sources. He also quotes the work of Gallese on the *mirror neurons* as being a system that allows for the reconstruction in oneself of certain targeted actions made by others (Stern, 2010, p. 46). He concludes that we are not far away from being able to demonstrate that there are multimodal connections in the brain. These are based in primitive circuits that can treat neurological information independently of the complexity of the information conveyed. These circuits could then become more condensed and capable of coordinating heterogeneous systems of information.

This hypothesis, speculative for the moment, could be extended to the notion of the dimensions of the organism to explain how bodily, behavioral, metabolic, and mental dynamics could coordinate around affective dynamics. This is the thesis that Daniel Stern tries to defend in his 2010 book, *The Forms of Vitality*. He distinguishes the emotional dynamics on the one hand and the dynamics that modulate the vitality of an organism on the other. This hypothesis is close to that of Alexander Lowen (1975).

Intersubjectivity

Intersubjectivity is a need for shared experiences, a desire to be understood and to be able to share experiences with others. Even if it is in fact impossible to share one's experiences with others, the desire is there, it is innate, and it is powerful.[14] It is therefore yet another necessary illusion. This illusion reinforces the need to intensify the exchange of information between two organisms. When this desire constructs itself in a harmonious relationship, it allows each one to better understand oneself and the other. According to Daniel Stern, it is a system of motivation essential for the survival of the species that permits the construction of diverse forms of attachment like those that establish themselves in a love relationship. When a love relationship dies out, the protagonists often discover that the intersubjective impression was mostly an illusion. For example, the parents of a drug-addicted adolescent discover that they never understood him. Most of the time, the extinction of tender feelings and the intersubjective illusion that accompanies it is preceded by a lowering of the intensity of exchanges between the organisms involved.[15]

Even if intersubjectivity is often associated with Daniel Stern's work, other researchers, like Andrew Meltzoff and Colwyn Trevarthen, have also developed the notion in an interesting way.[16]

The Nonconscious Regulations of Muhammad Ali

In 1997, Stern gave an account of what he saw by analyzing, image by image, a boxing match between Mohammed Ali (or Cassius Clay) and Al Mindenberger.[17]

Vignette on Mohammed Ali. *"[Stern] found that 53% of Ali's jab and 36% of Mindenberger's jabs were faster than visual reaction time (180 msec). He concludes that a punch is not the stimulus to which the response is a dodge or a block; that we must look beyond the stimulus and a response to larger sequences. Instead it is more reasonable to assume that a punch or a block is a hypothesis-generating or hypothesis-probing attempt by each person to understand and predict the other person's behavioral sequence in time and space." (Beebe and Lachmann, 2002, p. 97)*

In a brilliant study, Beebe et al. (2008) detail the temporal profile of these non-conscious predictions. She demonstrates that the eagerly awaited behavioral schemas are variations on a theme. The organism awaits not only typical behaviors but also a degree of variety. According to Stern, this type of scenario is established at a "presymbolic" level on a continuum that goes from the reflex to consciousness. This local model implies at least three series of issues:

1. It is probable that communication often unfolds in this way, that is, the interacting protagonists do not truly respond to what the other said or did,[18] but express themselves in function of a foreseen scenario. When the scenario corresponds to what is happening, the protagonists almost have the impression of listening to each other. Real moments of listening do exist, but inevitably require a relatively slow tempo.
2. Stern therefore situates desire and intersubjective illusion at one extreme of the conscious mind; and at the other what is really happening between two organisms in a rapid presymbolic dimension principally managed by nonconscious mechanisms.
3. The faster and more relevant a communication, the more it is constructed before an interaction begins, and the less it takes into account what is going on in the present. This can have a survival value when the essential or daily tasks must be accomplished rapidly and efficiently; but that may also become the cement that kills all constructive listening in a couple or between collaborators.

The more the presymbolic dimension is consciously accepted, the more the protagonists of an interaction can become clear-sighted about what is going on between them. In couples therapy, we often notice that this nonconscious level through which messages are transmitted is poorly integrated in moments of conflict.

Vitality and Cathexis

Stern's last work (2010, p. 107) on vitality allows us to synthesize this theme. The dosage between intensity, form, and relevance is important for the psychotherapist. The more intense a gesture, the more life it carries and more it fascinates (a) if it conserves a relevant shape and (b) if it can be received by the surroundings. This is easily visible in the infant. When he has too much vitality, the infant becomes overexcited and chaotic, bothers everyone, is unable to quiet himself down, and almost always ends up crying even if no one is rejecting him. When the parents present too little stimulation, the infant sometimes calms himself or becomes restless because he is lonely. When parents present an intense and chaotic stimulation, the infant goes away from them as far as is possible.[19] "Babies learn their own special repertoire of behaviors to regulate stimuli that are too intense. They can simply turn their head away from the stimuli, or they can look straight at you but focus on the horizon. Some babies become experts in suddenly falling asleep" (Stern, 2010, p. 107). One of Stern's ideas is that the million pieces of information we receive at every instant group themselves around the contour of vitality. These contours coordinate several meanings, several modalities, and several dimensions in each one of us and in our interaction with another. The management of these contours is explored in the arts like music and dance,[20] which sometime touch the feelings and thoughts of millions of people in similar ways.

BEEBE

Beatrice Beebe is another psychoanalyst who combines psychoanalytical psychotherapy and research on nonverbal communication. Although she does not present herself as a body psychotherapist, her work explicitly incorporates a systemic approach to interaction and the way an individual behaves. Several body–mind therapists, for a long time, have known about her way of regulating her own behavior and that of her patients. Yet the way Beebe (2004) details the dimensions of the patient's experiences establishes her firmly in the psychoanalytic tradition. Daniel Stern guided her thesis. She participates in several research centers at Columbia University in New York City, particularly in the Laboratory of the Communication Sciences under the direction of Joseph Jaffe.

Self-Regulation and the Interactive System

At the start of the 1970s, the eclectic body psychotherapist who was interested in the notion of regulation was torn between two basic models:

1. *The Reichian and physiological models* mostly describe diverse forms of organismic auto-regulation. In this perspective, a behavior mostly regulates internal tensions by expressing them.
2. The *systemic and nonverbal communication models* mostly show how behaviors regulate one another and form networks of regulation between organisms.

The psychodynamic models of the time focused on the analysis of transferential dynamics that explored an intermediary path that did not allow for a satisfactory distinction and coordination of auto-regulation and interpersonal regulation. Most psychotherapists combine the two dimensions in their practice, and some tried to propose explicit ways to coordinate them.[21] To my knowledge, Beebe is the first to integrate these two dimensions explicitly. One of the advantages of her model is that it is based on sophisticated analyses and at the same time comfortably useful in a practice. It is based on the following statistical distinction:

1. *Contingencies with self.* An individual is able to auto-regulate, that is, participate in the regulation of what he thinks and feels. Beebe distinguishes this mental system of auto-regulation from other systems of physiological auto-regulation by speaking of *self-regulation.* In her studies on the way an infant under one year of age interacts with his mother or with other caretakers, she hypothesizes that all the bodily and vocal actions which correlate with each other, participate in self-regulation.
2. *Contingencies with others.* Similarly, there are all sorts of systems of organismic regulation that participate in the construction of the way interacting individuals coordinate with each other. In these studies, she hypothesizes that all of a person's behaviors that correlate with the behavior of other persons form a network of interpersonal contingencies.

In both cases, the definition of the contingencies necessitates the idea that a behavior can be foreseen. Thus, auto-contingency implies that the advent of a behavior made by one person allows for the *anticipation* of the probability that another behavior will appear in that person. Similarly, an interpersonal contingency makes it possible to foresee that if a person behaves in one way there is a certain probability that another person will behave in a predictable way in the following minutes. Beebe remarks that a certain degree of foreseeability makes it possible to render a relationship between several persons more comfortable. This is clinically important for the analysis of narcissistic individuals who are proud when they can be as unpredictable as possible, and then lament because they have been rejected.

Beebe's basic model describes the way interacting individuals auto-regulate, and how these individual processes form the basis from which a relational system emerges.[22] The following shapes the psychotherapeutic relationship between a patient and a therapist:

1. The repertoire of the activities of the patient that correlate with the activities of the patient.
2. The repertoire of the activities of the therapist that correlate with the activities of the therapist.
3. The repertoire of the activities of the patient that correlate with the therapist's behavior.
4. The repertoire of the activities of the therapist that correlate with the patient's behavior.

A repertoire is composed of a set of activities that are more or less probable. This probability can vary in function of (a) personal characteristics, (b) the protagonists, (c) the structure of an interaction, and (d) general situations. In a given therapy session, the repertoire of each participant adapts to the particularities of the relationship. Thus, a patient will have a behavior with his therapist that he also has with other persons, but it will undergo some modifications linked to the frame (chair, sofa, etc.) and the therapist. Similarly, the therapist will have a behavior that he also has in his private life and with other patients, but the particularities of the patient will impose some more or less important modifications. Each of the protagonists will notice that he is more or less comfortable, more or less at ease, more or less anxious, more or less confident, and more or less inspired with certain individuals. This varies from one situation to another, but each one's dreams show that there often exists a series of recurrent expectations. All of these factors influence the quality of a relationship.

Beebe's diagram (see figure 21.1) illustrates what is happening in all kinds of situations by making each arrow in her schema more or less dense in function of the intensity of the activity they represent. I present three crisis situations to illustrate this analysis.[23]

1. The patient is incapable of self-regulation, receiving help, or communicating adequately. It belongs to the therapist to find a way to help him (a) auto-regulate and (b) interact.
2. The patient recalls memories of abuse that are indigestible for him and

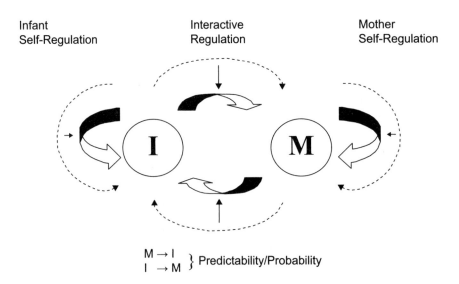

Infant
Self-Regulation

Interactive
Regulation

Mother
Self-Regulation

M → I
I → M } Predictability/Probability

FIGURE 21.1. Systems model of interaction. Arrows indicate predictability ("coordination" or "influence") between partners. Dotted arrows represent the history of the pattern of predictability.

the therapist. The therapist must facilitate a kind of interaction that allows both protagonists to help each other find a minimum of auto-regulation.

3. The patient recalls personal memories that mobilize the memory and conflicting feelings the therapist has experienced in his past. Here, the action of the patient activates the therapist's system of self-regulation. For a moment, the therapist is less active in the relationship and hardly stimulates the patient's auto-regulation. Usually, the therapist does not reveal his countertransference to the patient in this situation.

Actions that Simultaneously Participate in One's Self-Regulation and That of the Other

From the moment a system of self-regulation becomes a behavior that can be perceived by others, it acquires an *ostentatious* status.[24] Let us take the case of the newborn infant who touches himself, turns his gaze, reduces his breathing, and arches his back when he is anxious. These behaviors can help him reduce the disagreeable feelings that are overcoming him, but at the same time, they can inform an attentive adult concerning the type of attention that he needs.[25] It is not necessary that these behaviors have been activated in order to alert the other.[26] These forms of auto-regulation may have been "selected" by evolution-ary dynamics because others can perceive them. The response of adults depends on what catches their attention at that moment and the way they manage to integrate this information.

A more detailed example of the way a behavior participates simultaneously in a form of self-regulation and regulation of the other, which Beebe often quotes, is what happens when two people look into each other's eyes:

1. To look at each other automatically creates in the protagonists an im-pression that the connection is becoming more intense.
2. Both then feel an internal arousal that becomes more intense.
3. There is an increase in cardiac rhythm.

These three points are based on observations of the mother–infant relationship made by Daniel Stern (1971, 1977) and Tiffany Field (1981, 1982). Field dem-onstrates that by avoiding eye contact, the infant automatically reduces his in-ternal tension and cardiac activity. Even if this innate reaction were partially accessible to introspection most of the time, it comes about automatically with-out any conscious involvement.

Transference and Recurrent Regulation

Infants interact with mothers, fathers, and others in unique ways that are mutually created as the infant and the individual engage with each other (Tronick, 1989). These interactions and relational knowing are not generalized but remain specific to specific relationships. . . . Thus, on one side, the reiteration of interactions with others leads to learning general ways of being with others (e.g., "baby small talk"); on the other side, it leads to increasingly specific and particular ways to be with different individuals (e.g., "Only we do this together"). (Ed Tronick, 2001, Commentary on Paper by Frank M. Lachmann)

Beebe's model makes it possible to formulate a series of questions that the practitioner knows well but not always in an explicit way:

1. In the *psychodynamic theory of transference*, the patient has some more or less conscious representations. He assimilates other persons to these representations. The classic definition of transference is that a person has the tendency to assimilate those whom he encounters to the representations he already has. Thus, a patient is in transference when he reacts to a therapist as if he were corresponding to the representation of his mother, his father or a sister.
2. The *behaviorists*[27] speak mostly of *assimilating practices*, of a knowhow that has been built up with a parent, and that become activated later on with other persons who have a few characteristics somewhat like those of the parent. These characteristics can be general or specific. Thus, a woman might have been talkative with her father and becomes talkative with all of the men that she likes (general assimilation) or liked to make coffee for her father when he smoked his pipe and likes to prepare coffee for all the individuals who smoke a pipe (specific assimilation).[28] These practices are not necessarily representations. They can also be habitual sensory-motor or affective schemas.

The first definition refers to a purely mental propension, whereas the behaviorist proposition seems to include the psychodynamic model. The underlying discussion is how clearly psychological dynamics should be differentiated from those of other organismic dimensions. Those that are close to classical psychoanalysis want to associate the term *transference* to mental forms of assimilations. They are afraid that in their practice behaviorists may not spend enough time on psychological dynamics. Others stress that regulation systems tend to coordinate the dimensions of the organism and that purely mental transference is rare.

Regulation of Contingency

The clinical usefulness of the use of the term *contingency* for the correlations between self and other can be illustrated with the analysis of individuals who suffered violent sexual trauma in the first years of life:[29]

> Vignette on hyper-contingency and trauma. *At the occasion of abuse, a young child undergoes an obligation to be intensely in contingency with the abuser. Every part of his organism is abruptly mobilized by the other. In that case, the abuser*

does not allow for any kind of auto-regulation. In each abuse, this child develops a greater aversion to contingency. Later, when he wants to establish an affectionate relationship with someone, he will find it difficult to synchronize his behavior with that of others. The difficulty lies in the fact that affection often activates contingent behavior, and this person has become phobic to contingency. Consequently, he becomes incapable of constructing a lasting relationship with others. In this individual's consciousness, there is no connection between his fear of all kind of attunement and his difficulty in building a loving relationship. The difficulty, in therapy, lies in helping this individual, while helping him self-construct, understand that his trauma has impeded his development of necessary communication skills— something that is difficult to acquire in a few months or even a few years. Even if a certain improvement is possible, some residual damage lasts a lifetime. This is one of the many reasons that sexual abuse during childhood always has devastating consequences. To help an abused person become conscious of his fear of contingency and the connection between contingency and attunement is a way to help him or her assess what can be repaired in the present.[30]

This analysis partially explains why abused patients find it difficult to work with a psychotherapist who associates empathy with contingent behavior. Once this has been understood one has two possibilities. Refer patients to therapists who do not continuously use contingent behavior with patients, or ask psychotherapists to accommodate their behavior to the patient's deep needs. Beebe's studies could help therapists who want to find relevant ways of acquiring the skills that would allow them to follow the second solution without losing their empathy and their need for an intimate self-regulation. This way of associating contingency and abuse is a personal contribution to the discussions of this field (Heller, 2004a). Although I refer to this model several times in the following sections, it is not one that is used by Beebe, Tronick, or Downing.

Beebe and her colleagues noticed that a particularly intense or weak chronic contingency between the behavior of a mother and her child often negatively correlates with the development of the child's capacity for attachment. They conclude that if a high degree of contingency allows for an important exchange of useful information at the occasion of encountering a stranger, it may also be generated by mistrust and insecurity. An example of this type of annoying behavior is the over contingent behavior of mothers who are constantly afraid of "making a mistake" or of being inadequate.[31] A contingency in the "midrange" seems to be, by default,[32] the right quantity of contingency for the development of the capacity to communicate (Beebe, 2011; Beebe et al., 2010). It is experienced as part of a predictable and secure environment. Even if Beatrice Beebe does not speak of this, I think that the variability of the amount of contingency is also an important dimension of a relational pattern.

Beebe finally came to the point of regulating the speed of her movements in function of the speed of those of the patient. She accelerates her movements in front of a patient who is chronically placid, or slows her movements in front of a patient who is relatively excited, and notices that this modulation of her behavior often has a useful impact. Here, she takes up a theme that Braatøy had already begun by observing the film of a therapeutic relationship.[33] He had noticed the extent to which the effectiveness of the therapist can depend on his capacity to modulate his gestures and needs in function of what is going on for the patient. These aspects of the psychotherapist's techniques require filming to grasp, acquire, and master the capacity to accommodate his behavior in ways that allows him to tackle clinical issues.

TRONICK

Edward Z. Tronick is a developmental and clinical experimental psychologist who studies the dysfunctions between mothers and young children by using the research tools of nonverbal communication. His observations highlight mechanisms that are often relevant for psychotherapists. He conducts his research principally in the Child Development Unit at Children's Hospital related to the Faculty of Medicine of Harvard University.

Individual and Dyadic Homeostasis

Tronick's Individual System

> Let me begin with an example of selection from messiness: the infant learning to play peekaboo. The learning of peekaboo emerges through the repetitive operation of coherence on the messiness of the infant's action, intentions and apprehensions in an incremental bit-by-bit and moment-by moment manner. Initially, the infant makes a large number and variety of behaviors and has lots of varying intentions and apprehensions of what is going on. Most of these actions are unrelated to each other or to the adult's game playing actions. (Ed Tronick, 2007, *The Neurobehavioural and Social-Emotional Development of Infants and Children*, 5, 35, p. 493)

Possibly, the influence of Cannon at Harvard partly explains the fact that Tronick (1998) proposes a more "organismic" model of the regulators of the self than do his colleagues Stern, Beebe, and Downing. He is in effect attentive to the fact that when an infant is anxious in front of his mother, it is not only the relational behavior that deregulates but also, often, the whole of the mechanisms of affective and homeostatic regulation of each organism. Tronick does not use the term *organism*. He prefers to use the expression "individual system" (Tronick, 2007, Introduction, p. 2f) which he includes (as do Stern and Beebe) in a dyadic system. Some researchers avoid the term *organism,* because it is too often associated with a form of an idealistic holistic approach that assumes that a biological system is necessarily coherent.

   Like Spinoza, Tronick[34] assumes that when several persons think together, they can process more information than when one is alone. For Tronick, an individual system is mostly regulated by the nonconscious mechanisms that organize themselves in time, in function of practices set in action. It also then consists, like the System of the Dimensions of the Organism, of a systemic ge-netic model in which time plays a central role. Another point in common be-tween the two models is the way Tronick uses the term *messy* to indicate an individual system at birth. Even in adulthood, the individual system is never coherent because the contour of the subsystems of the organism is fuzzy. It is exactly this fuzzy aspect of the subsystems that permits the organism to be in the search of ameliorating its mode of adaptation at every moment. To the ex-tent that the organism is not omniscient, it sometime happens that its attempt to adapt ends up by making choices that damage its functioning in a lasting way. Tronick also presumes that there is not only one mind, one consciousness, one memory, or one perception but a conglomeration of mechanisms that are desig-nated by these terms. This position is shared by other Harvard psychologists, such as Jerome Kagan (1998).

Psychopathology and Reparation

THE CREATIVITY OF IMPERFECTION

Genetically, a person born a million years ago is almost the same as one born today. It is possible that individuals who are particularly adapted to survival in a wild natural environment are less well adapted today, while those that could not survive a million years ago can do so in our modern cities. Over a million years, humans were able to acquire a greater variety of survival and reproduc-tive behaviors and create numerous adaptive devices (buildings, medication, etc.). The human individual system is sufficiently flexible and powerful to be able to calibrate itself in the function of interactions that it establishes with its immediate environment. However, even when they emerged, the most elemen-tary survival functions have need of this mutual calibration, which constructs itself between the newborn and its family circle. The flexibility of the human organism has important constraints and limitations that guarantee its survival and a minimum of coherence to its development. Within this framework, the genetic mechanisms already produce an enormous amount of variations, as we see when we compare fingerprints. The research on nonverbal communication arrives at the same conclusion for almost all the behavioral micro-regulators it has analyzed. At birth, the mechanisms capable of calibrating themselves are more numerous than those that will be solicited by the geographic and social environment. Thus, the infantile vocalizations are more varied than those that will be solicited by a language. The innate phonetic capacities that are not used by the environment will disappear after a while.[35] This explains why so many adults are incapable of acquiring the accent of a new language they are learning. In other words, in growing up, the organism gets rid of some unemployed in-nate capacities to be able to focus its resources on what it needs to develop for survival. This stance is different from the Idealistic position, like that of Reich, which assumes that is poorly developed function is a manifestation of a re-pressed capacity.

In his studies, Tronick tends to focus on the way these choices operate at the core of a mother–child dyad, by distinguishing two factors:

1. The *repertoire*. The repertoire allows us to enumerate which practices are solicited and which are neglected. Here, the criterion is the duration and the frequency of the use of the items in a repertoire.
2. The *virtuosity*. This consists of describing what type of calibration of the action is made possible in a dyadic relationship. Here, the criterion is the quality of a practice, or the virtuosity with which a child becomes capable of mastering a set of practices. A child who has been lovingly caressed and has been able to also caress with pleasure has a greater chance of being able to exchange caresses in a mutually pleasurable fashion as an adult.[36]

For Tronick, this cycle is one of the bases of the creativity of the dynamics of development. A milieu that is too considerate, that almost totally reduces the moments of inadequate coordination can support synergetic strategies, but it could impede the child's ability to learn to recognize dysfunctions and acquire the art of repairing them.[37]

HOMEOSTASIS AND ATTACHMENT

Ed Tronick shows that even the homeostatic mechanisms are dyadic. A nursing infant is not able to provide for himself without the help of his mother. Here we see the limits of a theory based on the notion of the dyad. It is evident that even the mother cannot sufficiently ensure warmth and nourishment for her infant. It seems better to me to situate the interpersonal dimensions of the homeostatic mechanisms in the domain of the external propensities such as they are defined in this volume by Hume, Lamarck, Laborit, and Reich. The heating system that a family uses requires a complex socioeconomic infrastructure.

On the other hand, it is possible to take up Stern's, Beebe's, and Tronick's analyses on the dyads by reminding ourselves that often, for babies, the interface between the organismic propensions and the external propensions has the mother as the intermediary. She is not the center of these regulations but the first relay when the father is often absent. It is therefore possible that the organism of the infant is somewhat conditioned to act *as if* all of its needs depend on the mother.

From the point of view of my practice, I have been struck by the extent to which an abused child remains dependent on his parents for life. The force of the "addiction" has always impressed me. I have had adult patients in psychotherapy who had been abused as children. They complain unceasingly about their parents, preferring to pay me to verify the harm their parents did to them, instead of allowing me to treat them. As soon as the situation presents itself, they seek signs of their parents' repentance, affection, and acknowledgment. Even when this parent is dying, they are there to help him and ask for a final sign that he is sorry for what he did. Therefore, it seems to me that it is quite plausible to think that a certain form of addiction to parents would be one of the natural forms of accommodation between children and parents.[38]

What Laborit and Tronick describe is an association between regulators of the organism and a style of interaction that is set in place in the newborn at birth and probably even before. There would then be a physiologic memory of a state of reference for the systems of regulation of the organism. This state of reference would be felt, *from the point of view of consciousness,* as a profound affective link that mobilizes a feeling of loyalty. Everything happens as if every loving moment developed in adulthood between one's spouse and children is necessarily associated to the state of reference. I do not claim that this is an exact description of what happens when the attachment to the parents of one's early childhood is talked about again in psychotherapy by an adult, but it seems to me we will probably have to go in this direction if we want to explain the dynamics of attachment in the future.

The dynamics of such a state of reference is probably close to imprinting, as observed by Konrad Lorenz at the birth of graylag geese. Breaking out of the egg shell, the gosling attaches itself to the first moving object it sees. There is such a strong imprinting that the gosling continues to maintain the attachment to this object even when they finally meet their biological mother.[39]

THE CYCLE OF "MISMATCHING" AND REPARATION

Tronick approaches this mother–infant dyad by thinking that the newborn is solely an organization of relatively organized behaviors, and the maternal competencies of the mother are only partially developed when she gives birth to her first child. The challenge for both partners in the dyad is to gradually include, in a messy coordination of two messy systems, increasingly coherent and recognizable patterns. The competence to mother an infant mobilizes innate systems of support that are insufficient to teach the mother "what to do." This point of departure in the system inevitably leads to numerous moments when mother and infant coordinate poorly, are "mismatched," and find themselves confused, dysfunctional, and frustrated. Having set this frame, Tronick wants to understand how infants and mothers acquire the ability to coordinate their behavior.[40] To understand this, he focuses his attention on moments during which the behavior of the infant and of the mother seem to "match." Matching is defined and analyzed in two ways (Tronick, 2007, III.15, p. 196):

1. *Behavioral matching.* "The degree to which infant and mother are in the same behavioral state at the same time."
2. *Synchrony.* "How consistently the pair are able to move together over time regardless of the content of their behavior."[41]

Simply put, *matching* describes moments when mother and infant play together in a comfortable way. The apprenticeship of the infant and the mother begins when they become capable of recognizing these moments of relational mismatch and repairing them by establishing greater harmony in their dyadic functioning. The capacity to oscillate between moments of dysfunction and reparation forms one of the nuclei of relational competence that the baby needs to acquire in the first years of life. When the cultural environment does not sustain this type of cycle, the mother's dysfunction is manifest, and that of the infant is almost guaranteed. These remarks concern the repertoire and the virtuosity of the schemas. It consists, in fact, of knowing if the environment solicits a relevant repertoire of behavior and if it permits the development of a certain virtuosity. The infant may thus calibrate in function of a more or less constructive or destructive environment. Some conducts may develop some constructive attitudes in a destructive situation; others may become destructive in a constructive environment, and so on. The destructive aspects seem mostly to develop when the mother is incapable of tolerating the cycle of mismatching and repair. For example, this is the case of mothers who experienced abuse when they were young, who are so afraid that they will also become a bad mother that they become anxious at the least mismatch and become too nervous to allow the mechanisms of reparation to be set up. The positive note in this analysis is that it is no longer the question of isolating traumatizing acts but situating destructive acts into a general context that more or less profoundly supports the possibility of repairing and discovering states of harmony. Some abusive acts are not susceptible to being entirely repaired; but these acts are, in general, extreme. Sadly, in our species, these extreme acts are not so rare.

HOW TO KNOW WHEN ONE'S BABY NO LONGER WANTS TO SUCKLE

A good example of the notion of matching was given to me in films that Martine Zack had taken in Francis Bresson's laboratory. I saw them at the occasion of seminars organized by Siegfried Frey (1985) at the "Maison des Sciences de l'Homme," in Paris. She had filmed nursing mothers. In these films, she sought (among other things) to answer the question: what are the behavioral indicators that permit a mother or a wet nurse to know when a baby no longer desires to suckle?

One of the particularly dramatic dyads presents the following interaction.[42]

> A vignette of nursing. *The mother is clearly anxious about her ability to be a "good mother." Her nursing baby then has the burdensome responsibility to send her reassuring signals. The following example shows what Tronick means by a mismatch, a dyadic relationship that does not become organized. The mother presents a breast to her baby, who sucks with delight. Like many other babies, he pauses, during which he catches his breath and digests. He explores the room with his gaze. He then returns to the breast, looking quite content, to continue to suckle. Yet unexpectedly, in the meantime, the mother concluded that if the nursing baby had so suddenly stopped, it was because he did not like her milk. Offended, she puts away her breast. The baby cries because he cannot find the good breast he was*

expecting. The mother thinks he is crying because she has bad milk, and she does not know what to do. In such situations the mother despairs, but does not know how to repair.

I often refer to this example to point out the danger of leaving a mother alone with her infant too much. It is possible that this mother would not have become demoralized if she had a companion with her who had already nursed a baby herself. The latter would have been able to explain to this new mother that a nursing baby does not drink all at once; because he has the need to auto-regulate, to digest and to breathe. This is also true for the bottle-fed baby.[43]

Beebe and her colleagues (2007) proposed a way of describing these types of mothers. She distinguishes the mother who interprets the fact that the nursing baby who avoids looking at her as the proof that he rejects her (these are the dependent mothers) and the mother who interprets the avoidance of looking as proof of her incompetence (the self-critical mothers). You will notice that in both cases, it is *not* the behavior of the baby that changes the "meaning" of the child's behavior, but the way in which his behavior is perceived.[44] The dependent mother is particularly a person who needs others to auto-regulate her when she experiences negative feelings. The distinction between these two types of mothers is apparently quite small, because in the two cases, there is a lack of confidence in their capacity to become an adequate mother and an excess of aggressiveness (a mixture of annoyance, impatience, discouragement, exasperation, and anxiety that produce ways of acting that are extremely unpleasant for the infant). The clinical difference between these two categories is, on the other hand, evident when we observe the way the behavior of the mother and her infant are coordinated. This coordination structures itself in time in such a complex way that conscious attention is unable to analyze it. But the nonconscious systems of regulation of the protagonists are sensitive to it in a predictable way.[45]

The "Still Face" and Dyadic Disequilibrium

To study the alternation of the phases of mismatch and repair, Ed Tronick creates an experimental situation called the "still-face paradigm,"[46] taken up by several psychologists. In these experimental situations, he films a situation that follows this sequence:[47]

1. A mother plays with her child for ten minutes.
2. A bell rings informing the mother that she must abruptly become immobile, not speak, and especially keep her face completely still for the next two minutes. She can still look at the child. In general, this period is difficult for both the mother and the child. The latter often expresses violent utter confusion. The mother may stop the exercise if the reactions of the child become unbearable for her.

3. A second bell informs the mother that she can now behave as she wants and continue to play. Most of the time, the mother begins by consoling the child and initiates a phase of repair that quickly permits the dyad to return to their play. The phase of repair is a reciprocal accommodation that activates encouraging and stimulating expressions of affection.

The following is an example of the kind of disruption observed during the phase of the immobile face.[48]

> Vignette on the situation with the still face. *A six-month-old girl pleads with her mother to continue playing the game and then throws the toys at her. She then withdraws. Tronick observes a postural collapse and a state of distress. The child then resumes looking at her mother and becomes active. The two types of behavior alternate, but it moves toward the collapse that leads to a sudden rupture in the rhythmic flow of communication.*[49]

The fact that it only takes two minutes to so visibly destabilize the child shows to what extent a child expects certain forms of interaction as early as the first months of life. Ed Tronick associates these mechanisms to the reactions of abandonment Harlow observed in monkeys and in the orphans observed by Spitz.

NORMAL RELATIONSHIPS

Tronick and his colleagues began by studying the situation of the still face with mothers who have no known psychopathology to understand how these alternations between stress and repair unfold. He noticed that during the immobilization of the mother, the children under the age of one follow the sequence below, which may be repeated many times over.[50]

1. The child does not look at the mother.
2. The child looks at what is going on around him (we have just seen an example of this sequence in the vignette concerning breastfeeding).
3. The child begins to interact with an object (a toy, for example).
4. The child looks, at least with a peripheral vision, if the mother is becoming available again.

Phase 3 has particular importance for Tronick because it is the beginning of a personal and independent connection with the world of objects. In this phase, the child learns to auto-regulate by handling toys. Gradually, if the mother persists in her immobility, the fourth phase will transform itself into first an aggressive phase and then into a phase of resignation that leads to the rupture of the cycle. My hypothesis, based on the analysis of adults, is that the pleasure of interacting with objects is probably one of the practices that support the development of the capacity to dissociate. There is then, between the toys and the infant, the formation of a kind of pleasure distinct from narcissism and from the relationship with another. This form of immediate eroticism with objects and media has animated humans since the invention of tools and of solitary creative activities like painting, reading, and writing. Another example is that of people who prefer to spend time on a computer or a mobile phone than to have direct interactions with people. This mechanism is one of the bases of creativity.

Each phase manifests itself through a repertoire of various conducts (around 300 distinct conducts in each observed phase for 54 children) that increase with the age of the child.[51] The phases of destabilization and repair occur repeatedly in a situation where the mother and the child play together with the desire to make each other happy. With children at the age of six months, Tronick and his colleagues observe some micro-phases of repair every three to five seconds.

DYADS WITH DEPRESSIVE MOTHERS

Having observed the way the dialogue organizes itself between children under a year old and their mother who has no known psychopathology, Tronick and his colleagues studied the dyads with depressed mothers. He quotes numerous research studies that demonstrate that depression can have genetic and neurological (especially limbic) causes, or that it can be induced by what occurred in utero. Tronick attempts to describe the disturbances that are added to that during the first year of life.[52]

Tronick confirms Ellgring's analysis when he shows that depressive behavior can manifest in different ways by mobilizing diverse body modalities: face, voice, touch, coordination of movements between themselves or with those of others, and so on. In certain cases, depression does not stop a mother from adequately functioning with her nursing infant. Tronick selects three types from a large variety of depressive behaviors:[53]

1. The *depressed and withdrawn* mothers, who give the impression that they are not present.
2. The *anxious depressed and sometimes hyperactive and intrusive* mothers. These mothers may touch the infant in an abrupt and rough manner, sometimes to the limit that is tolerable, scold the infant, even with a vicious tone of voice, and poke the infant violently with a finger. She may frequently interrupt his play. The mother often has the impression of acting well. She interrupts the infant to propose a "better" game; a minute later, she has another better game to propose. If the infant refuses to stop what he is doing, the mother wants to oblige him to concentrate on what she considers to be the better possible play for him. Some of these films are a horrible testimony to what a desperate desire to do well can activate.
3. The mothers who have an *apparently normal* behavior.

When I view films[54] of an interaction between a "slowed-down" mother and her nursing baby, I am immediately struck by two things:

1. The mother is pleasant and attentive to the needs of her infant
2. The mother initiates few interactions and appears mostly to be carrying out her duties. The interactive game of Ping Pong described by Stern, Beebe, and Tronick is manifestly impoverished.

Tronick and his colleagues detail the dyadic behaviors that create this impression when the mother is hardly expressive. The numbers given pertain to what is visible when the team films a mother and an infant at play:[55]

1. The mother actively plays with the infant 10 percent of the time on average, while other mothers play on average 42 percent of the time.
2. Similarly, the infant only actively plays with his mother 5 percent of the time instead of 13 percent of the time otherwise.
3. There is a strong correlation between the activity of the infant and the mother's invitations to play. This reinforces the impression that depressed mothers are attentive to the basic needs of the infant but are not capable of interacting simply for the *pleasure of interacting*. These mothers also show fewer positive expressions than most mothers.
4. The infants of depressed mothers look at their mothers less often and express more negative feelings.
5. These infants more easily activate the physiological axis of stress. For example, their cardiac activity and their rate of cortisol are elevated.

The small amount of time that a stressed infant spends with his toys when his depressed mother is immobilized is an important point for Tronick. There would then be an inhibition of the infant's capacity to learn to auto-regulate by becoming creative with some objects. These infants sometimes show a developmental delay when they take Piagetian tests on their approach to objects.[56] They sometimes become adults who find it difficult to sublimate their anxiety by engaging in some creative activity. These adults, when there is tension in the family, become incapable of doing anything whatsoever, and they auto-regulate with difficulty.[57]

The type of depression also influences the infants. Thus, with withdrawn mothers, the infants spend more time crying and showing their distress; while the infants of intrusive mothers cry very little, avoid looking at their mother and avoid interacting with her.

The problems of the children of depressed mothers become evident when researchers like Tiffany Field (1995) observe the way they interact with strangers. Because these children are often withdrawn, it is difficult to establish a pleasant and playful contact with them.

This is a good illustration of the idea that a person meets a stranger with the practices at its disposal, and that these practices have multiple impacts that repeat themselves, even in a large variety of situations. With this idea in mind, I analyze the interactive dynamics that develop between my patient and me during the initial sessions.

THE INFANT'S CAPACITY TO "REPAIR" HIS MOTHER

I am now going to summarize an analysis of a case that illustrates the repairing activity of newborns. This case is described by a team of psychiatrists from Heidelberg, who collaborate with George Downing and Ed Tronick.[58] They take into their care mothers who have given birth but suffer from a major mental illness that renders them incapable of assuming their maternal functions without a solid institutional support. They use psychotherapeutic intervention techniques and conduct research using videos analysis techniques developed by George Downing (2003), Mechthild Papousek (2000) and Ed Tronick (2003). The case is one of a 39-year-old mother and her fourth child. As their real names cannot be disclosed, they are referred to as Karen and Diana by the authors of this study. This daughter was conceived in a brief encounter.

Karen and Diana.   To understand the mother, it is useful to recall the vignette of trauma and hyper-contingency. Karen is one of these abused persons who are phobic of contingency.[59] The difficulty for a mother who experiences this type of fear is that a certain contingency is inherent in the affective behavioral dialogue that establishes itself between them. As soon as a tender dialogue sets itself up between the mother and her daughter, the behavioral contingency stimulates memories of past abuse that disorganizes her behavior. This is overwhelmingly painful for Karen, as she has no way to manage these moments of disorganization. Although she wants to create a constructive dialogue with her daughter, the amount of contingency between them is quite low. To protect her 5-month-old daughter from the more impulsive forms of her behavior, she requests help from her psychiatrist.

The video-analysis of Karen and Diana occurred two years after the initial hospitalization. The video recording used for this analysis was 8 minutes long. What follows was observed on a sample of 36 seconds. In viewing the film of the first session, Downing and his colleagues are impressed by the following traits:

1. The mother laughs and moves, taking up the entire space, without feeling when her gestures enter her daughter's intimate space. Her behavior is not one of a joyous person in interactive contact with her daughter, but mostly a sort of basic attitude like role playing.
2. She unceasingly mimics without any real relevance to Diana's behavior. Some gestures express several emotions simultaneously. Aggressiveness, sadness, contempt, affection, and joy are chaotically blended.[60]
3. The mother is unable to prevent herself from becoming intrusive, stringing together one proposal after another in such a rapid rhythm that Diana is incapable of enjoying any one of the proposed games.

Nevertheless, something of the mother's love seems to have been communicated to her daughter, as Diana seems to be doing well, "at least with respect to basic cognitive and motor development" (Downing et al., 2007, p. 284). While her mother is constantly agitated, expressing her affection and her enormous anxiety, which she attempts to control, Diana remains apparently undisturbed. She spends a lot of time looking at her belt and playing with it. Her movements are slow, as if she were exploring what she is touching. She seems to be so concentrated that she appears to ignore what is going on around her. "She is as if in a different temporal universe, one immune to the fast-moving surrounding events" (Ibid.).

Diana's Reparative Potential. For a brief instant, her mother comes out of her chaotic cascade of suggestions for their play. She amuses herself in imitating Diana, who is playing with her belt. She then places her right hand near the child's left hand. Karen's fingers are resting on her daughter's chair, a few centimeters away from Diana's hand. An image-by-image analysis showed that the child reacts in less than a second. With her left hand, with which she was playing with her belt, she takes one of her mother's fingers. Mother and daughter rest in this way for a second. Then Diana slowly approaches her mother's right hand. The mother's movements slow down. Karen and Diana both look toward their joined hands. The mother nonetheless continues to make some abrupt movements of the head and face, but the rest of her body is accommodating to her daughter's slow pace. She lets her daughter lift her hand, and she slowly brings it to her own little chin, and both of them begin to make an O with their lips.[61] The coordination of the lip movements happens in less than a quarter of a second. Diana smiles, her face lights up with pleasure, while she puts her mother's fingers into her mouth. As Karen's head "veers to the left her entire face seems to relax. The brow smoothes out, and the muscles around the eyes and those around the mouth ease some of their holding. She appears to be a different person, straightforward and fresh, for a duration of about three quarters of a second" (Downing et al., 2007, p. 286).

Suddenly, the mother returns to her previous chaotic state. She smiles, while saying, "that does not taste good." In no time at all, the mother begins to move rapidly, and Diana takes her time before concentrating anew on the belt.

Karen and her therapists viewed that moment of peaceful communication several times, wondering how they could gradually become longer:

> A parent who was unable to tolerate the intimacy of a direct, unmediated affect exchanges may do better here, at least for a short while. Starting from a mutual focus upon some physical thing . . . the parent may be able to ease into a certain amount of positive affect exchange as well. Such a pathway probably works because it is less threatening: It is more dosed, more gradual, more controllable.
>
> I call this *the route through the physical object.* (Downing et al., 2007, p. 288)

Karen was able to explore the gestures she observed on the film, and become aware of the deeper emotional issues that generated her chaotic behavior when she tried to play with Diana.

Introducing the Notion of Practices

The researchers on infants that I have briefly summarized will appear, for some, far from the practice of individual adult body psychotherapy that is the central interest of this book. Yet they have allowed us to reconsider the strategies used in adult psychotherapy.[62] One of the principal contributions of the studies on early infancy is to show that straightaway, children are more active than what researchers such as Piaget had expected.[63] The infant already participates in his construction and in modifying the reactions of his parents. Even if several schemas only present themselves in a transitory manner, they already participate in the way the organism calibrates itself by calibrating its environment.

These clinical and experimental studies allow us to describe different kinds of early traumatic forms of interaction that were not available when therapists could only understand childhood through the dreams of adult patients.[64] Now that we know how the baby of a depressed mother tends to behave, we are able to reread adult behavior differently and grasp those aspects of behavior that are remnants of their past. A psychotherapist now is able to note that his adult patient "behaves as if he has had an abusive depressed mother." Or he can notice that the patient "uses types of acceleration of the rhythm of communication described by Beebe." After an inquiry, the therapist may discover that not only did a patient have an intrusive mother, but his wife is also intrusive. It then becomes possible to reflect in a more precise way on all the practices that structure an individual's strategies. This coordination of practices often revises itself in time in function of circumstances; but sometimes some practices form a static nucleus around which others organize themselves.

Quite aware that there is insufficient time to analyze the wealth of practices that gather in an organism (there are millions), the body psychotherapist may use, above and beyond his intuition and know-how, the ongoing research to target his attention. To use these studies, it would be useful if the psychotherapists of today and of tomorrow would take up special studies in video analysis to understand what it can teach them.[65] Here we arrive at the heart of the justification for including skills on the management of the body and behavior in psychotherapy. As soon as the therapist admits that his object is a system of practices produced by the coordination of several dimensions of the organism, he needs to include in his field some professional knowledge on all the dimensions that participate in the regulation of thoughts, affects, and behavior.

A method of following a practice in body psychotherapy is that developed by Ron Kurtz (1990) called "tracking": a term that refers to following the tracks of a prey. According to Ogden and colleagues (2006, 9, p. 189f) "*tracking* refers to the therapist's ability to closely and unobtrusively observe the unfolding of nonverbal components of the client's immediate experience." This technique is designed to follow practices that mobilize several dimensions at the same time (bodily, mental, physiological, etc.) and help the patient become aware of the whole of this experience and its multidimensional contour. The more detailed the description, the more the patient becomes capable of creating co-consciously with the therapist a global and relevant perception of his living experience. It consists of detailing not only the elements of this experience but also of their organization in time, the sequences that can be repeated when the experience is repeated. This analysis of the dynamics of a schema is different from what may be perceived starting from a body reading. Body reading mostly allows for the discovery of what has become encrusted in a lasting and some-times static way in the structure of the muscular and respiratory tensions on the one hand and in the character on the other.

22

Downing and Integrative
Body Psychotherapy in 2001

I would like to conclude this presentation of the issues that animate the field of body psychotherapy around some themes developed by George Downing in his courses and publications. I have the impression that his school best integrates the psychology of today in body psychotherapy. His thoughts can be used as a starting point to open up some discussions that are in the process of elaboration in the congresses and publications in body psychotherapy at the start of the twenty-first century. This will be the occasion to include recent developments in my mapping of what the field of body psychotherapy is becoming.

CALIFORNIA: A GOLDEN AGE FOR
CREATIVE PSYCHOTHERAPISTS

George Downing, a psychologist of American origin, resides in Paris. In the late 1960s Downing lived in California, in the San Francisco area. It had become one of the regions in which one could find the greatest density of Nobel Prize winners. The fabulous creativity of this region was not only manifest in the hard sciences and technology. It also expressed itself by developing psychotherapeutic modes of intervention that are close to the themes developed in this book, such as Gestalt therapy, various modes of intervention centered on body awareness, and systemic approaches. It was then a harbor of intense creativity for those who looked for new modes of intervention that could support the development of not only psychiatric patients but also every citizen who felt a need to enhance the way he or she functioned and understood himself or herself. In such a stimulating context, many wanted to find ways of picking and choosing from different approaches, with the aim of discovering new frames for psychotherapy. Although schools were still the recognizable pillars of this landscape, many hoped to find a form of psychotherapy that could combine in a synergistic way the most efficient psychotherapeutic tools. Downing was one of many searching for such a direction. This stance quickly spread to other areas of America and Europe.

Since 1959, the Mental Research Institute of Palo Alto has been one of the leading sources of innovative models which have influenced interactional and systemic therapies (Watzlawick et al., 1967). It is close to Stanford University, about an hour from San Francisco. This institute was animated by brilliant clinicians and researchers such as Gregory Bateson, Donald Jackson, Jay Haley, and John H. Weakland. Already then, Gregory Bateson was a bridge between systemic approaches, anthropology, and studies on nonverbal communication.

At the time, Downing was teaching both individual and systemic therapy at the California School of Professional Psychology and at a family therapy training institute. He was convinced that all types of therapy could benefit from a more meticulous attention to the concrete specifics of how patients interacted with others. The clinical methods of observation and intervention used in body psychotherapy were one of the tools that could help clinicians to improve the finesse of their approaches.

Downing's initial theoretical formulations drew strongly upon then-current psychodynamic thinking. He had previously written a doctoral dissertation on Freud, participated in a number of psychoanalytic seminars, and thought seriously about becoming a psychoanalyst. He was particularly interested in their sophisticated understanding of transference and countertransference in the therapeutic relationship. In this intellectual context, developing Ferenczi's active technique could become a way of linking bodywork, systemics, and classical psychotherapy.

While he was developing his ideas in systemic and psychodynamic approaches, Downing was involved in the creative interest in the body that developed in California: body re-alignment methods, body awareness, and body psychotherapies (as shown in Kogan, 1980). He went through trainings in a number of them, including the approaches of Stanley Keleman (1970) and Magda Proskauer (1968), as well as Bioenergetic and Reichian therapies. In 1972, he published a reference book on "Californian massage." He was interested in the *modes of intervention* developed in body psychotherapy schools, but was skeptical of their *theoretical formulations* which he found too "esoteric" (Downing, 1980) as well as conceptually lacking in rigor.[1]

Gradually his intent became to develop a synthesis of what he found most useful in each perspective,[2] and create a viable theoretical framework for the more heteroclite vision of psychotherapeutic approaches that was emerging. The shift of paradigm that emerged encouraged *eclectic* or *integrative* psychotherapists to reframe the *methods* discovered by the classical psychotherapy schools into new *modes of intervention*. Methods included techniques (free association, coding nonverbal behavior, or massage) and local models (transferential dynamics, auto-regulation, and interaction). These methods were then redefined in an operational way, in function of current clinical needs, and situated in a viable theoretical framework that could integrate the ongoing development of psychological research. This attempt to find theories that were closer to scientific thinking than what had been produced by psychotherapy schools led to a variety of new outlooks and methods. The term *eclectic* is a slightly pejorative term for psychotherapists who do not follow the tracks proposed by psychotherapy schools. In the future, we should find a more honorable name for colleagues who prefer to follow the cognitive ethics of academia. There have been many highly varied attempts to create such eclectic psychotherapeutic approaches, which are becoming increasingly popular. In all of them, integrating classical methods and models can only be done after a reformulation of what is being assimilated. For Piaget (1985), a new way of integrating old schemas inevitably requires some mutual accommodation and the creation of new schemas to equilibrate the emerging structure. George Downing's proposition is a particular blend that has several characteristic features. One them is his way of integrating body psychotherapeutic approaches. This book follows a complementary path.

The San Francisco Bay area (as well as other parts of California) was the best place, at the time, to accomplish such a synthesis. Far from the East Coast of the United States, it was easier to have some distance from the fanaticism of the Reichians and the rigidity of the Freudians and to profit from the filtering of the Reichian contributions going on at Esalen. Otto Fenichel died in California. It is not impossible that people influenced by Fenichel (e.g., Laura Perls and the Gindlerian group) influenced Downing. However, this influence was probably indirect, as Downing sometimes refers to him, but he does not discuss Fenichel's ideas.

One of Downing's constructive critics of current body psychotherapy was to situate the contributions of Reich in the context of the 1930s and show that he was part of a milieu fighting for a better understanding of the interaction among the mind, the body, and behavior. Thus, Downing takes up the contributions of Groddeck (often underestimated), Ferenczi, and the gymnasts who influenced the first Reichian therapists. Reich is no longer the tree that hides the forest but one of the grand trees in a forest of people who want to improve our understanding of the relation among minds, affects, and body. Downing is probably the first in the field to publish an explicit critical discussion on "Reich's dubious heritage" (Downing, 1996, V.26) that does not lead to a rejection of body psychotherapy.

A BODY PSYCHOTHERAPY THAT SEEKS TO OVERCOME THE CONTROVERSIES BETWEEN SCHOOLS

In 1980, George Downing moved to Paris, where he still lives. Several important changes then took place in the following years. He accepted an invitation to work as a psychologist in a psychiatric unit at Salpêtrière Hospital. This unit, newly created at the time, specialized in the treatment of parent–infant and parent–child relationships from the ages of zero to three years. The body–mental–systemic focus of interest remained, but for each dimension his approach took a new turn:

1. His systemic practice changed considerably when he became involved in research on children, and he began a long collaboration with Beatrice Beebe and Ed Tronick. He learned to spot specific sensorimotor patterns that could be detected with the methods of nonverbal communication and then to integrate them in classical psychotherapy methods. This led him to develop a form of video analysis that could be used by clinicians.
2. He also looked for ways of integrating this detailed analysis of behavior in current body psychotherapy methods. The body psychotherapy methods that he developed from then on could be integrated with systemic and psychodynamic approaches.
3. He remained in contact with new developments in psychodynamic approaches.

The 1980s was the time when many of us, including George Downing, discovered the new psychodynamic approaches developed by Heinz Kohut (1971) and Otto Kernberg (1975, 1976, 1984) to treat patients with narcissistic and borderline personalities. His collaboration with Beatrice Beebe put him contact with *relational psychoanalysis,* such as it was developed by Steven Knoblauch (2000), Joseph D. Lichtenberg (1989), and Thomas Ogden (1990, 2009). This psychoanalytic movement integrates a systemic perspective on behavior and interaction.

As Downing's new job included work with children, he integrated formulations on developmental systemics (Thelen and Smith, 1994; Fogel, Lyra, and Valsiner, 1997). To integrate technics developed in nonverbal communication studies for his video-analysis interventions, he also learned to use strategies developed by cognitive and behavioral therapy (Ryle and Kerr, 2002; Young, Klosko, and Weishaar, 2003; Bateman and Fonagy, 2006). One of the advantages of these new methods is that they are easily adapted to mental health settings.

He therefore needed to create a developmental model in which he could combine the various approaches he was using at the Salpêtrière Hospital. He then developed training in video analysis called *Video Intervention Therapy* (VIT).[3] It is often used to support mothers who have difficulty living with the prospect of an infant coming into their lives (see chapter 21, p. 629f). This method can also be used to analyze other contexts, such as the dynamics of a family or the integration of children who suffer from attention deficit disorder. The work of video analysis makes it possible to analyze, with the patient, the minute behavioral practices he or she uses without noticing. Following the lead of Beebe, Tronick, and several other researchers, he worked out a mode of observational analysis based on what videos allow one to observe in detail. A video would be filmed of a parent and infant, or of an adult couple, or of some other close human relationship. The therapist and the patient or patients would then look at the video together, investigating both outer behavior as well as the inner dynamics driving it. Because so much of interaction depends upon how a participant is using his body, as well as how he is influencing and being influenced by the bodily reactions of the other person, it was for Downing a natural step to draw on body and other experiential techniques in such an intervention.[4]

Once the therapist has isolated some detailed behaviors, he can show these behaviors to the patient and they can discuss them. Such a detailed analysis of their behavior is difficult for many patients to accept and integrate. The patient often has the impression that he is being shamed for something he did not intend to do. He therefore does not feel responsible for it. When the therapist shows the patient the impact of his nonconscious practices on other people, he may feel caught in a trap. The therapist who uses video analysis must therefore find ways of conveying what is visible that can be used constructively and integrated by a patient. For example, a therapist can choose moments when the patient's behavior was relevant for all those concerned, and start with a discussion on why these moments are examples of a useful way of doing things.

Once a patient has a clearer view of problematic aspects of his behavior, he needs to integrate what has been made explicit, so that the underlying organismic regulation systems can find new ways of assimilating what has been observed, and to accommodate by forming new behavioral patterns. This integration is often accomplished with the classical tools of psychotherapy. Downing may also use body psychotherapy techniques to do this. For example, the patient may explore how one of his habitual gestures mobilizes other aspects of the general posture and how it influences respiration. He may also become aware that this exploration triggers new somatic sensations, emotions, and memories. Downing also utilized new ways of using gestures to explore certain aspects of the patient's dreams (Clara Hill, 2004). Bodywork is also used to connect an isolated schema to underlying vegetative mobilizations. For example, a patient may find ways of associating an aggressive facial expression to impressions that have been activated by the autonomic nervous system (Downing, 2000, pp. 251–254). He will then be able to clarify the contour of his anger by putting together what he can feel when his attention explores what is happening in his face, gestures, breathing, heartbeat, and thoughts. Finally, bodywork can help the patient contact lost feelings that formed themselves at a very early time, before memory could be stored in the format of mental representations.

Downing's theoretical framework has also become one of an enhanced cognitive-behavioral therapy. He now works within this tradition, but with the difference that the experiential side includes a substantial amount of focus on the body itself.

Downing teaches video analysis and body psychotherapy in a post-training framework for professionals who are practicing in institutions or in a private setting. He teaches both individual and interactional work in hospitals and universities in several European countries. He is also part of several research teams concerned with parent–infant and parent–child interaction. Many of the persons trained by him are working in mental health institutions: psychiatric hospitals, eating disorders units, substance abuse centers, and home visiting programs for high-risk families. The techniques he teaches can be used in a variety of settings: individual therapy, work with dyadic and triadic[5] interactions, or groups and families.

In 1996, Downing published a first synthesis of his approach, titled *Wort und der Psychotherapy* (*Body and Words in Psychotherapy*).[6] It announces a type of psychotherapy capable of surpassing the formulations elaborated in isolation within each school and at last joining the academic spirit proposed by Plato.

ENERGY AND BODY PSYCHOTHERAPY

Bodily defenses. Amazingly, this aspect has not been researched in experimental psychology. But it is so important I will mention it too. . . . It is familiar ground to many psychotherapists. (George Downing, 2000, "Emotion Theory Reconsidered," p. 255)

One of the first aspects of body psychotherapy theory that George Downing openly disagreed with is the claim that a body psychotherapist needs to believe in cosmic energy to understand how to work. Like Peter Geissler (1997), he thinks that clinicians trained in a neo-Reichian school (e.g., Bioenergetics) will improve their way of working if their energetic models are based on the dynamics of metabolic energy. The practitioner consequently has knowledge at his disposal that is more refined, more precise, and easier to renew.[7]

As the epigraph at the beginning of this section indicates, knowing the academic models in no way stops the practitioner from observing phenomena that the current scientific knowledge cannot explain. For example, I have indicated that the vibrations observed during a grounding exercise or the orgastic reflex are not explained in any satisfactory way by scientific research (see chapter 19, p. 563). To point out those observations that require more research is our duty. To use these observations to justify the use of notions such as cosmic energy or philosophical idealism is another thing altogether. In defining the phenomena that we observe in a comprehensible way for researchers and practitioners, we participate in the universal and collegial adventure that is the development of the human sciences.

When an individual feels a body sensation—like the impression of warmth or pins and needles—circulate in his body, the individual often spontaneously uses the notion of the circulation of energy to express what he feels. This feeling is close enough to what is currently designated by the word *energy*,[8] to the extent that what is felt is a new *activity* in the organism, probably formed by the still poorly understood affective vegetative mechanisms.

This brings us back to an earlier theme[9] that takes up the idea that an impression is a sort of sensory metaphor. These metaphors are ways of informing consciousness that something complex is going on in the organism. They summarize, with an impression accessible to consciousness, a dynamic that is often too complex to be taken up consciously. A perceptional metaphor has the particular ability to vary correlatively with the events described without necessarily corresponding to them. The danger with this type of procedure is to approach a metaphor as an exact representation of what is going on. To feel that something is coming up in me does not necessarily mean that a substance, distinct from physiological mechanisms, is flowing toward my head. What comes up may be a multitude of different activities. A well-known example, brought up when talking about Shultz's Autogenic training (chapter 9, p. 282f), is the association between the sensation of warmth and vascular dynamics, or the sensation of heaviness and muscular relaxation. To feel warmth that spreads in the body while doing an exercise is not feeling the blood being distributed in the arteries. There is a correlation between the two phenomena, but not an identity. Acupuncturists and Reich (probably others also) do not believe that the sensation of warmth always follows vascular dynamics. They may be right when they assume that vegetative sensations often cannot be explained by the current knowledge in anatomy and physiology. That does not necessarily imply that these impressions are caused by a chi or an orgone that remain unexplained phenomena. However, one can argue that these "nonscientific models" support a curiosity and a particular sharp awareness of certain phenomena, while classical physiology may support a form of indifference for the same phenomena. The issue here is why one's attention focuses on some events and not on others. Having a clinical sense of what phenomena should be carefully explored that is as independent as possible from theoretical issues is of utmost importance for patients. They need therapists who are inspired by precise phenomenological descriptions of the dynamics of their sensations. What sometimes happens with these discussions is that future research will come up with a new series of data which will lead to a third solution that is not a synthesis of the previous ones but one that no one imagined.

The role of the psychotherapist is not to believe or refute the explications of the patient who states that he feels his spiritual energy moving upward (see chapter 10, p. 279f). It is to explore more precisely with the patient what he feels and how this feeling is related to his thoughts, his gestures, his affects, and his organism. The fact that what we observe cannot always be described by a reliable scientific model ought not to discourage us; on the contrary, it should encourage us to research more refined descriptions of what is being experienced to define the contours of what we would want scientists to focus on.

THE MICRO-PRACTICES

The neurotic . . . never reacts to the external stimuli in an appropriate manner, but always according to defined reactive schema acquired during infancy. . . . He continuously distorts the present according to the meaning of his unfinished past and as much for his actual instinctual drives as for the actual external reality. . . . The desire experienced by a subject, at a certain moment, to do or to say something, tends to suppress the drives that do not lead to that end. (Otto Fenichel, 1941, *Problems of Psychoanalytic Technique*, III, pp. 36–37; translated from the French by Marcel Duclos)

Organismic Practices

I propose to use the broader expression of *organismic practices* to designate every type of localized standardized functioning of the organism that recruits several dimensions. A practice is a habitual way of accomplishing a task, which may automatically recruit habitual modes of functioning situated in a variety of organismic dimensions. It can, for example, associate a sensorimotor habitual schema with a habitual set of representations and habitual verbal expressions. From the point of view of a person's awareness, a gesture may come to the foreground, while at other moments it is the associated representations that are perceived. In all cases, we are dealing with procedures that can be described. These micro-practices have a limited repertoire that nevertheless sometimes allows subtle modes of adaptation to similar but nonetheless different contexts. Thus, an individual who is accustomed to roasting a chicken may automatically know how to vary the amount of salt and roasting time as a function of the weight of the bird, but the recipe remains the same.

Downing distinguishes the *surface* of a practice (all the variables of a practice) from the *procedural core* of a practice that generates these variables.[10] A "procedural core" is often established during the first two years of life. It forms the infant's basic interactional repertoire. Highly idiosyncratic, each child's procedural core has elements unique to him or her. Later childhood experiences augment and modify the procedural core. Serious body-related trauma, such as physical violence or sexual abuse, can also introduce significant changes in the procedural core. When a psychotherapist aims at a change in a way of doing things, it is mostly the contour of this core that he is trying to identify and change. The reader may have noticed that this formulation implies that a psychotherapist does not focus on a damaging trauma as much as on repairing core modes of functioning. The same can be said of a surgeon who takes care of an organism that has been damaged by a car accident.

For Downing, each practice has a set of aims, intentions, and goals.[11] However, these intentions are not necessarily conscious or coordinated together. We find ourselves in a tradition according to which there may be several intentions from heterogeneous sources in the functioning of a way of accomplishing a task.

Let us now focus on what George Downing calls "micro-practices." When he began to work with researchers on nonverbal communication like Beebe and Tronick, he was fascinated by their capacity to detect short sensorimotor units that seemed to characterize a person's adaptive procedures. Each one of us has particular ways of smiling, looking at others, or of holding a cup of coffee. As soon as one can specify the contour of a way of doing something at a relatively local level, Downing (2001, 2006) speaks of "micro-practices."

> Vignette of a mother who is feeding her baby while watching television. *I have already used the example of a mother who is feeding her baby some food with a spoon while she watches television. The child is sitting beside her on a sofa. While she places the spoon in the baby's mouth with her left hand, her eyes do not leave the television screen. The film shows us the arrival of the spoon to the baby's mouth. Her aim is somewhat on target. She first arrives at the lower region of the face, then to the mouth by feeling her way around without ever looking at what is going on. Here we find ourselves manifestly in the domain of habitual behaviors. The baby does not appreciate this and sometimes spits out the food. Annoyed, the mother finally turns toward the baby to solve the problem and then returns to watching television.*

This vignette poses the problem of the coordination of sensorimotor schemas in the course of an interaction. It is not possible to feed a baby comfortably unless a greater number of activities are coordinated toward the goal. When a mother adds speech to what she is doing, such coordination is often automatically set in place. The very young child does not understand what is being said when the mother moves the spoon to his mouth and says "here is the spoon," but he does notice that the voice, the regard, movement of the torso, and movement of the hand all coordinate in such a way as to bring the spoon comfortably into his mouth. To move while talking coordinates the mother and helps her attend to what she is doing with the baby with greater care. Even if she experiences frustration at that moment because she cannot focus on the television, the relationship between herself and her baby becomes more comfortable. It is a history of choices, of priorities not always easy to establish. In this example, the two practices (feeding the infant and looking at television) are conscious conflicting choices.

We notice, in passing, that in this little family scene, the contingency between the behavior of the mother and that of the infant is weak, especially because she dissociates by looking at the television. We find a mother who, in a more subtle way than in other examples that I have given in the sections dedicated to Beebe and Tronick, seems to avoid too many contingencies in her communication to preserve a private zone for herself.

Micro-practices build themselves up in the organism in function of the needs of auto-regulation and interpersonal regulation. An infant will develop a repertoire that manifests itself differently when he interacts with his father, his mother, or both together (Fivaz-Depeursinge and Corboz-Warnery, 1999). His behavioral repertoire also varies in function of the mood of either one of his parents and of his own mood. The dynamics of an individual's repertoire of micro-practices constitutes his capacity to adapt to his entourage and his drives. I would even say that a practice *is* a regulatory system between certain propensities and certain social practices.

As an adult, an individual comes to psychotherapy with the know-how that constitutes the dynamics of his organism. Downing's approach to psychotherapy is centered on that know-how and with its capacity to accommodate as constructively as possible to a variety of social environments. Once a micro-practice has been observed, he reconstructs, with the patient, the history of this practice in the patient's life and explores different ways of using this practice. The exact mixture of affect, sensorimotor functioning, and representations that characterize this practice gradually establishes itself.[12]

Detecting Micro-Practices

Having characterized what Downing calls micro-procedures, I will now distinguish between apparently *meaningful* and *apparently* meaningless schemas.

Apparently Meaningful Behaviors

Therapists like George Downing and Beatrice Beebe, as well as researchers such as Paul Ekman and Ed Tronick, work on behaviors that have at least one apparent meaning and/or function. Ekman has mostly worked on innate emotional expressions, Tronick looks for gestures that participate in a repair system, and ethologists look for innate forms of communication that regulate rituals such as mating. In the social sciences Kendon (1982, 2004) looks for gestures that frame a conversation and Goffman (1974) for signs that regulate social status. All of the signs are more complex than what can be perceived on photographic or filmed examples, but once they have been detected they are relatively easy to find. These can easily enter in a co-conscious dialogue on the patient's schemas.[13]

Having seen various analyses of this kind in several laboratories, George Downing sensed that this type of phenomenon could have immense clinical implications. Inspired by clinicians who were already using this type of observation in psychotherapy, like Beatrice Beebe (Cohen and Beebe, 2002), he decided look for ways of exploiting this type of intervention with the tools he was already using. He coined the term "micro-practices" to designate behavioral and/ or bodily phenomena that could be detected with this type of procedure. Once one has acquired a habit of observing these sensorimotor patterns, they can often be found without using coding procedures.

A typical way of beginning a video analysis is to look at a sample at normal speed, so as to know what it is about. Often the therapist already has some information on the context of this sample. He may therefore already find a few interesting patterns, which can then be explored with the following simple techniques:

1. *Slow motion.* A picture-by-picture view allows the video analyst to detail the particularities of a micro practice, and observe the coordination of its components. It allows one to follow the coordination between two micro-practices. Those may be situated in one organism, or in two interacting organisms.

2. *Fast motion.* When one accelerates the speed of a film, one can more easily spot recurring events. Some of the oral movements observed on our suicidal patients (see next section) could be assimilated to expressions of despair, sadness, and contempt according to Ekman and Friesen's dictionary. However, as soon we look at the films in fast motion we see that some of these apparently emotional expressions recur at various moments without any manifest relevance. They may therefore be fleeting grimaces shaped by the frequent usage of certain emotional expressions, or they could be emotional leaks. These phenomena have not yet been systematically researched.

3. *Normal speed.* Once one has detected interesting patterns with the preceding procedures, one can return to normal speed to situate them in the ongoing communicative strategies that combine gestures, posture, and conversation. It is often then that one can make sense of the patterns detected at slow or rapid speed.

Once Downing has found ways of detecting clinically relevant micro-practices, he conducts an inquiry on the way the behavior integrates itself into the internal and communicative procedures of the organism. This implies questions on what is experienced by the patient when a practice is activated. Sometimes the patient spontaneously brings forth information, while at other times he is not aware of that behavior, as it was regulated by nonconscious procedures. However, the next time this sensory-schema appears, the therapist can ask the patient what he had experienced at that moment, without even referring to the targeted action. One can also look at a video sample, and ask the patient to associate on what he experiences when he sees himself producing this nonconscious habitual behavior. In doing this work, Downing aims especially at the two subsequent goals I formulate in the language of this book:

1. To influence the way that a particular propensity, or organismic practice, associates the heterogenic mechanisms within the organism

2. To influence the way a schema inserts itself in more general dynamics of the organism and interacts with other propensities.

A focus on micro-practices allows us to extend how we think about working with the body. We can observe how the activation of a micro-practice interacts with muscular tensions, postural alignment, and the coordination of segments; or we can observe how these global regulation systems and practices interact with each other during this action. We also need to take into account the fact that different body systems may have different time frames. For example, the postural dynamics are slow procedures that frame rapidly changing sensorimotor activity (see chapter 13).

We are just at the beginning of learning how to integrate this type of observation into the psychotherapeutic domain. Behavioral work with so-called "social skills training" has of course always touched upon it, but seldom with such detailed descriptions. If one also analyzes how skills insert themselves in the dynamics of the organism, far more is possible however. The aim remains to find techniques that can help a person to find a wider variety of new modes of activating his body, and of finding more creative ways of interacting with others.

Apparently Meaningless Behaviors

Apparently meaningful practices are the ones that attract a therapist's attention, yet they are only a small part of the sensorimotor phenomena that are produced by an organism. Studies of nonverbal behavior also code a wide range of sensorimotor habits that have no apparent function. Conscious attribution devices do not know how to handle them. They tend to ignore them. These actions do not correlate with specific contextual features, they do not correlate in a manifest way with inner affects or health issues, they are not a reaction to a specific stimulation, and they do not have a regular rhythm. It would seem that we constantly generate a multitude of behaviors for no apparent reason. One way of thinking about these actions is that they are part of our personal style. We are then close to theories on social identity such as those of Claude Levy-Strauss (1962) and Pierre Bourdieu (1979). Some of these practices may be an imitation of a person we know, or someone that often appears in the media, or may be the exact opposite of a known practice. They seem to be a form of nonverbal punctuation. One can also think of them as an unconscious lapse or a leak from a repressed emotion. Some of the studies on psychopathology (see chapter 20, p. 601f), suggests that this proliferation is apparently random, but that it can be modulated by moods. Affects can accentuate or inhibit them. If one shows a sample of these gestures to someone, they often try to assimilate it to a familiar pattern. For example, a mimic may appear to be a smile, but is in fact just a grimace.

Here is an example of such behaviors, taken from our suicide study (Heller et al., 2001), that George Downing (2001) and Beatrice Beebe (Beebe and Lachmann, 2002, p. 41; Beebe, 2004b) knows well:

> Vignette on pre-suicidal behavior. *I have already written several times on the study we conducted on the behavior of 23 patients who entered Geneva University Hospital after a suicide attempt (Archinard et al., 2000, and Heller et al., 2001). Their facial behavior was analyzed in its Laboratory of Affect and Communication (LAC) by Véronique Haynal-Reymond, Michael Heller, Christine Lessko, and other collaborators. We coded samples of their behavior using Ekman and Fries-*

en's Facial Action Coding System. We were looking for facial behaviors that could allow us to predict which patients would probably not make a suicide attempt (attempters), and which ones would make another suicide attempt (reattempters) in a two-year follow-up. Once we had coded their behavior, we asked the computer to look for actions that correlated particularly well with the known reattempters. We also compared their behavior with depressive patients with no suicidal risk that we had coded in a previous unpublished study. The correlations that came out drew our attention to a series of mimics none of us had really noticed: oral activity displayed when the subject was not speaking.

Oral activity occurs (a) every time one of the muscles that move the lips without moving the cheeks is activated and (b) when this activation cannot be explained by speech activity. This behavior is displayed 9% of the time on average by patients and the psychiatrist who interviews them. One can therefore not always associate oral activation with suicide reattempt risk. Oral activity groups a wide variety of lip configurations, some of which seemed characteristic of an individual. Some of us could have the impression that an oral activity had a meaningful (e.g., despair or contempt) and relevant function, but then not all the members of our team would attribute the same meaning and/or function to this motor event; at other times, we could not attribute the slightest meaning to these movements. Most of the time these lip movements seemed to appear randomly, in function of inner impulses, or to modulate the general atmosphere of the interview.

Reattempter patients had a systematic tendency to display more oral activation than attempters did, however the interviewer displayed more oral activity than the patients did.

After this finding we looked around us, and saw that some people displayed a lot of oral activity (e.g., President Clinton), while others did not use that type of movement in their current life. For those who did, their mimics where often more intense than those of our patients. We therefore arrived at the conclusion that most of these patients where (a) part of the population that uses oral activity, and (b) that they tried to inhibit that activity. We also observed the same type of oral activity on films of anorexic patients, who often have suicidal intentions.

We have been particularly careful to check with the medical team that medication could not explain this oral activity (e.g., in this hospital service, for such cases, all psychiatric medication was temporarily stopped). The discriminative power of oral activity varied in function of times and circumstances but was often efficient for more than 80% of the patients. The frequency of this activity was particularly strong among reattempters so we could think that certain factors can modulate these patterns, without being their cause. The literature on conversation rules is extensive (Feyereisen and De Lannoy, 1991, pp. 15–20). Nevertheless, high rates of facial mobility when listening remains uncommon (Ellgring, 1990, pp. 390–391) and could have a strong impact on the speaker (Cosnier, 1988). For the moment, the best explanation we may come up with on the function of these lip movements is that they could be representative of an ostentatious way of regulating disagreeable feelings. This implies two steps:

1. *Patient feels a blend of strong feelings such as sadness (or even despair), anger, or contempt.*

2. Patient needs to keep these feelings under control so as not to interrupt the interview by an outburst.

Patients explicitly communicate that they are making a considerable effort to self-regulate such feelings. Both doctor and patients mostly displayed low intensities of oral activation which often barely reach Ekman and Friesen's minimum requirements. This type of behavior could be a universal way of "ostentatious self-regulation." The doctor's behavior changed as a function of the patient's suicide reattempt risk, but we do not know if his nonconscious reactions were guided by these behaviors or other displays that we did not code (see chapter 20, p. 531).

If this type of observation is replicated, then research might show that these apparently meaningless actions are modulated by factors that may have a strong clinical relevance.

To recapitulate: in the history of psychology reviewed in this book, I have distinguished four types of behaviors, all of which have their simple and more complex versions:

1. *Innate* behaviors. The simpler version is that of reflex activity, but ethologists have found innate behaviors that can only be triggered and sequenced by a ritualized interaction. Emotional expressions and orgasm are two forms of reaction that have a strong innate core.[14]

2. *Acquired* behaviors. The simplest version of an acquired behavior is the conditioned reflex described by Pavlov. The core reaction is innate, but it can easily be associated to new stimuli that are not included in the innate reaction. Child psychologists have discovered a wide range of procedures that are not accommodated reflexes, like imitation. The human organism seems to have a spontaneous innate capacity to learn from what others do. The acquisition of professional skills, language, and the management of media are examples of complex acquired behaviors.

3. *Randomly produced* behaviors. We have found examples of spontaneously produced schemas in several chapters of this book: Spinoza's imagination, Hume's associationism, Darwin's theory of emotions, and the basic procedures of Freud's unconscious. Darwin assumes that there are many potentially usable mechanisms that are not developed by the usual innate and acquired behaviors. We have, for example, discussed the theory that assumes that an infant produces a wide variety of sounds. Only those that are required for the language that he learns will be developed, while the capacity to use other sounds is often lost. This was explained by the theory that an organism calibrates in function of what it does. However, it would seem that we have an innate playful jubilation to explore whatever is not used in our organisms. Observing children at play is full of such examples.

4. *Blends*. Hume already showed how different type of behaviors can associate by following relatively arbitrary rules. This vision was confirmed

by Darwin's observations. Piaget shows how simple schemas differenti- ate and proliferate in function of accidental events that often follow a trial-and-error strategy, linked by sketches of logical thinking and some need for coherence. The organization of these accommodative possibili- ties is more complex than Hume's associationism, as it allows emergent mechanisms that create new ways of *structuring* and associating com- plex schemas, and of integrating them in institutional dynamics.

When the noninitiate listens to a Mahler symphony, he will probably focus on the melody and the rhythm. The enlightened amateur will also pay attention to all the instruments that play no melody, that do not support the rhythm, but that are like colored dots that create the texture and the atmosphere of the sym- phony. These apparently useless instruments are a bit like the movements I have just been talking about. We do not know if they have a function, but they do modulate the atmosphere experienced and conveyed by a person. Their action is often quasi-continuous and highly variable. This new type of data brings us back to the observations that motivated Darwin to write a book on emotional expressions that are purposeless (chapter 7, p. 172). Except that we now have more refined observations that bring us beyond the notion of expression. The apparently random motor activity seems to follow a dynamic pattern close to what has been observed on genes and the immune system. I am not assuming that genes regulate the creativity of psychological and behavioral schema, but that each dimension has its particular form of spontaneous creativity. This is a topic that has not yet been explored. It makes us aware of a form of spontane- ous creativity of sounds, gestures, and impressions that seem to proliferate and which sometimes survive. For example, if used by a famous actor, a repetitive behavior may be imitated by millions. The underlying mechanisms of these dy- namics are close to how genes create mutations. Human organisms seem to have a tendency to spontaneously invent new ways of thinking, moving, feeling, and interacting. Some of these proliferations may enhance the capacity of an organism to survive in a given environment, while in other cases they may re- duce the capacity to survive. When a psychotherapist tries to evaluate the adap- tive potential of a patient, he may need to evaluate the impact of these apparently meaningless repetitive activities.

The Analysis of Habits by Merleau-Ponty

> I tried following Tolstoy's advice at one time, and forbade myself to make the sign of the cross. But I can't help it, my hand moves automatically. To not sign myself while praying is like leaving the prayer incomplete. (Alexander Solzhenitsyn, 1984, *November 1916*, V, p. 44)

The French philosopher Maurice Merleau-Ponty is one of the few Western think- ers to claim that our understanding of the world is founded on the body's perception of its surroundings and situations. (Thea Rytz, 2009, *Centered and connected*, p. 20)

In addition to the analyses in the studies of nonverbal communication, it is also useful to introduce into our discussion on micro-practices the analysis of *habitual movements* by French philosopher Maurice Merleau-Ponty (1908–1961).[15] He situates the habitual movements somewhere between a reflex and a conscious behavior: "We have to convey the concepts necessary to convey the fact that the bodily space can be given to me in an intention to hold without being given in an intention to know" (Merleau-Ponty, 1945, I.3, p. 90). Most acquired habits are at first constructed with the support of conscious procedures.[16] Once they have found a relatively satisfactory mode of functioning, they can be activated in more or less nonconscious ways by relatively local organismic systems. A habitual movement has a mobilizing goal (like turning a door handle) for certain bodily and mental activities that lead to a "relaxation" or a deactivation once the intention contained in this behavioral habit is extinguished. A habit is a coherent system, but not an isolated one. Its characteristics are what attracts the attention of the subject or of an observer, while the way it inserts itself in the organism remains in the background of what they perceive. "If I stand in front of my desk and lean on it with both hands, only my hands are stressed and the whole of my body trails behind them like the tail of a comet" (Merleau-Ponty, 1945, I.3, p. 87). Even a reflex inscribes itself in a bodily and mental ecology. There is no purely habitual bodily gesture, as there is no purely mental habitual thought.[17] The connections between a local action and the rest of the organism are partially preconscious, and mostly nonconscious.

Maurice Merleau-Ponty avoids invoking global structures like the organism or the individual system. He admits, nonetheless, that the individual is constituted by distinct dimensions in interaction: "We cannot relate certain movements to bodily mechanism and others to consciousness. The body and consciousness are not mutually limiting. They can only be parallel" (Merleau-Ponty, 1945, I.3, p. 108). From the point of view of consciousness, a gesture is like the visible part of an iceberg. It is a part of an intentional network that coordinates thoughts, nervous networks, muscles, skeleton, respiration, the cardiovascular system, as well as postural support. A specific action can mobilize this network in different ways, generating a variety of motor projects and motor intentionality that guides fine sensory-motor actions. Different actions, such as picking up an object or pointing it out, will mobilize different organismic coordinations.[18]

The chapter by Merleau-Ponty I refer to is built around cases described by neurologist Kurt Goldstein,[19] who introduced the notion of organism in the philosophy of the 1930s. These cases interest Merleau-Ponty because they show that mental disorders are not distinct from physical problems, even in the case of a serious neurological disturbance. There are some necessary ramifications with the way they insert themselves into their organismic ecology.[20] On the other hand, Merleau-Ponty distances himself from the holistic thinking associated with Gestalt psychology that Goldstein proposed when he speaks about the organism.

Micro-Analysis of the Face and Body Psychotherapy

I will now use a set of observations to illustrate how the analysis of a micro-practice can be integrated in classical body psychotherapy. To scan facial micro-practices, I often use Ekman and Friesen's *Facial Action Coding System* (FACS), which I have already presented (see chapter 20, p. 584f). Downing's approach to the analysis of clinical videos has also been influenced by FACS.

Knowing how to work with such methods is an excellent way to learn how to detect micro-practices. Let us now take a concrete example. FACS uses numbers that designate a unit of motor activity, and letters that indicate the intensity of the activation (A = subliminal intensity, D = maximum intensity). I detail this work by using, as an example, the expression 6C + 10C + 12C + 24C:

1. 6 +12 is a classic smile. The 6 designates the crow's feet that form at the corner of the eyes in a complete smile. The 12 designates the pull at the corners of the lips that raise the cheeks.
2. The 10 designates the action of raising the upper lip. This action also creates a descending furrow on each side of the nostrils. According to Ekman and Friesen, it is often related to negative emotions, such as contempt. This action excludes the wrinkling of the nose (which characterizes action unit 9), which Ekman and Friesen relate to disgust.
3. The 24 designates the flattening of the lips that are especially evident when the mouth is open and the lips approach one another.
4. The C designates an average intensity.

Rainer Krause and his team analyzed the interactions between a psychoanalyst (Krause) and a patient.[21] It consisted of filmed sessions of psychodynamic psychotherapy in a face-to-face setting. In examining these films, Krause's team noticed that some of the patient's smiles automatically unleash a reciprocal smile on the part of the therapist; whereas in the face of other smiles, the therapist's expression remains impassive. This is a good example of an interactive micro-practice, to the extent that neither the therapist, however well trained in FACS, nor the patient are conscious of this. In a more detailed analysis of the films, Krause and his colleagues discovered that the (6 + 12) smiles that do not activate a similar behavior in the therapist are in fact (6 + 10 + 12) smiles (see figure 22.1). Following the recommendations of Ekman and Friesen, they interpret this expression as a smile that masks contempt. In the specialized language of psychoanalysis, there would be a negative transference masked by an apparent positive transference. Krause's analysis of the patient, in exploring the patient's associations, confirms the existence of a disguised negative transference.

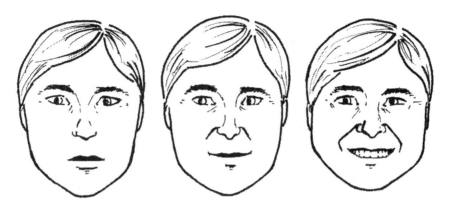

FIGURE 22.1. An example of faces coded with FACS system developed by Ekman and Friesen (1978): neutral face (*left*), face with unit 10 (lifting of the upper lip) and an added mobilization of the unit 06 (crow's feet at the corners of the eyes) (*middle*), and unit 12 (smile) (*right*).

In this example, the therapist's nonconscious processes differentiated between two smiles and triggered a differentiated sensorimotor response. However, neither the difference of smiles nor the correlated responses were perceived conscious processes. All that Krause probably detected is that there was something fishy between him and his patient. Only a coding procedure could have detected these rapid and apparently unconnected events. However, after this observation, Krause was able to pinpoint the masked negative transference of the patient, using classical psychodynamic methods, close to Reich's Character analysis.

Having used FACS for more than a decade, I have learned to recognize some of these patterns without using cameras. I may not be able to detect how my behavior correlates with that of the patients, but I can at least detect phenomena like masked aggression. When patients repetitively used well-defined facial expressions, I looked for ways of integrating this observation with other methods used in psychotherapy. In an initiative similar to that of Krause, the smile cannot be simply presented to the patient. If he is not conscious of his negative transference, there is the risk that he will be wounded and offended by a therapist who attributes feeling to him that he considers shameful and of which he is not aware. If the patient is conscious of his contempt, he risks poorly integrating the "magic" that allows the therapist to "read his thoughts." These difficulties are so real that after a few attempts, I was on the verge of abandoning the possibility of using this type of interpretation in psychotherapy. Discussions with George Downing encouraged me to persevere:

1. It is useful to establish a relational context in which the patient learns to discuss his nonconscious bodily habits without feeling threatened. For example, I begin by pointing out pleasant "macro" behavioral practices

that do not require any expertise to be discovered. In this way, the patient learns to develop a more refined way of perceiving his action system. He can also become less afraid of the fact that only others can see what he does, and that their interpretation may be different from what he feels.

2. Once the therapist has a clear image of the components and the function of a micro-practice, it is necessary to wait for a favorable moment to discuss it with the patient.

Here is an example.

Vignette concerning a young man with a complex smile. *A young man has, from the very first session, a complex smile that is often[22] made of the aforementioned configuration (6C + 10C + 12C + 24C + 26B[23]). After a few months of psychotherapy, we finally get to talk about the fact that the patient is easily self-critical, but he refuses to admit that he might have negative feeling toward those to whom he is close (colleagues, spouse, parents, etc.). With this theme well under way, I finally ask him to explore his smile. During an entire session, I suggest that he take his time to feel what is happening when he lifts his upper lip (AU10); he reports that he feels like a dog that bares his teeth and despises his enemy. I then suggest that he explore what happens when he adds flattening his lips at the same time (AU24) after having opened his jaw (AU26). He feels something that curbs his contempt. I then suggest that he add a smile to this construction, and he suddenly becomes aware that it is close to his habitual smiles. Even at this slow pace, this experience is difficult for him to digest. He is grateful that I have allowed him to become aware of this side of himself that sometimes looks down at his wife, but he is shocked to discover (a) his contempt and (b) that his wife can perceive this. I do not use this technique in the following sessions. Instead, we talk about what he had felt when we explored the details of his smile. An important material emerges that the patient integrates by verbalizing what he feels. Four sessions later, I suggest that he lie down on the mattress and feel in his body what is happening within. He talks again about his smile and his contempt; I do not work on his mimics. I ask him to just feel what is going on inside and localize what these feelings activate in his body. He begins to describe a ball of anxiety that he often feels in his belly, and about which he speaks to no one, not even me, his therapist. He feels his torso taking the shape of a C, with the thorax and the abdomen nearing the spinal column, while throat and pelvis rise upward. He feels the urge to curl up around this ball of anxiety, which he experiences in his belly.*

I wait a minute and notice that he does not turn on to his side to roll up around his pain, as many people do in this case. He stays on his back. Given that the C position is difficult to maintain for a long time, the back relaxes an instant by stretching out and then again takes up the C position. Having taken up this position several times, the movement becomes rhythmic. For a person trained in the Reichian methods, two directions present themselves to the therapist:

1. *The patient needs to go toward this pain slowly.*
2. *The patient is about to be mobilized by what Reich calls the orgastic reflex, and is oriented toward the anxiety of experiencing too much pleasure.*

In both instances, the therapist accompanies and observes, but he has internal questions that keep him curious. As it happens, the work opened up on his fear of love, the fear of losing his identity if he really allows himself to love his wife, body and soul.

This is an example of how a body psychotherapist can begin with a relatively local sensorimotor schema, proceed to explore how it inserts itself into systems of regulation and the dimensions of the organism, which then leads to classic themes for most psychotherapeutic approaches.

Micro-Practices and Representations

It is mostly the nonconscious mechanisms that structure the body's micro-practices. They are often activated outside of conscious thoughts without any awareness on the part of conscious thoughts. Even when a conscious motive expects the appearance of a sensory-motor schema, the mind cannot become aware of how these thoughts managed to activate the relevant habitual behavior. The patient may have to learn how to become conscious of his bodily practices, and accept that he cannot always understand them. Downing gives the following example from the research of psychologist T. G. R. Bower (1978).

> Vignette on a motor evaluation and a conscious evaluation. *Bower gives a child a typical Piagetian test. He presents a clay cylinder to the child. The child takes the cylinder in his hands. Then, in front of the child, Bower transforms the cylinder into a ball and asks the child if the ball weights more than the cylinder. The child answers that it is heavier. Bower hands him the ball.*
> *Bower filmed this interaction. On the film, he notices that the child takes the ball in the same manner that he took the cylinder, as if the spontaneous muscular preparation of the arm expected an identical weight.*

Adam Kendon (2004, p. 81) develops this analysis when he quotes research studies that show that the motor responses of a child who tries to solve a problem, such as those presented by a Piagetian test, seem to envision other strategies than those the child describes verbally. Thus, in observing the options initiated by the gestures, an individual is able to discover other strategies than those that he imagines at the level of the thoughts that can be verbally expressed. (Emmorey and Casey, 2001; Goldin-Meadow, 2003). This research trend confirms the hypothesis that I have previously formulated in other sections, according to which thinking while moving or thinking while talking does not necessarily generate the same strategies.

The notion of automatic preparation of an action has its importance. The organism that initiates a propensity automatically mobilizes the physiological, vegetative, sensorimotor, and affective necessary support. Someone who is going to run experiences a rise of sympathetic activation that increases respiration and the irrigation of the peripheral arteries. This implies evaluating which resources to mobilize and activating what Merleau-Ponty calls a *motor project*. In this sense, psychologists analyze gestures and physiology to evaluate what an organism expects. It then becomes possible to distinguish an automatically activated dimension (getting the arm ready), that Downing simply identifies as bodily, and a conceptual dimension that is animated by different processes (the verbal response of the child). Such a distinction between bodily and conceptual reactions is often pedagogically useful. It highlights the assumption that our organism follows at least two ways of treating information, which follow different algorithms. Each mode has its strong point and its limits. For example, consciousness can only be aware of conscious perceptions. Therefore, it cannot perceive the motoric evaluations of reality and the way they sometimes contradict what is thought.[24] However, a person can learn to develop an intuitive sense of what his nonconscious processes are trying to achieve.

When Downing draws the patient's attention to a small gesture that has many implications, the expression "body micro-practices" immediately speaks for itself. The fact that the reaction is of the body, not of the mind, indicates very well the impression that this type of gesture regulates itself independently from what is thought. The patient may feel relieved to learn that this is a "normal" mode of functioning. The therapist may then co-construct a therapeutic alliance with the patient that permits a better perception and identification of the underlying stakes involved in a habit. Both individuals consciously explore what can be learned concerning a shameful or overvalued practice and what can be done about it. I have often noticed that in this type of work, the patient is afraid the therapist will reproach him for having made a gesture of which he is not aware. The patient concludes that he "ought" to have been conscious of it. It is important not to transform this type of intervention into a way to torture the narcissism of the patient. The spirit in which this type of analysis is carried out is consequently very important. It demands immense tact and sometimes a form of constructive humor.

THE EMOTIONS AS INDICATORS OF CERTAIN MODES OF ORGANISMIC FUNCTIONING

No one, to my knowledge, has determined the nature of powers of the affects, nor what, on the other hand, the mind can do to moderate them. . . . The affects . . . of hate, anger, envy, and the like, considered in themselves, follow with the same necessity and force of Nature as the other singular things. And therefore they acknowledge certain causes, through which they are understood, and have certain properties, as worthy of our knowledge as the properties of any other thing, by the mere contemplation of which we are pleased. (Spinoza, 1677a, *Ethics*, III, Preface, II.1, p. 69)

Whenever we have an emotion our bodily experiences instantly becomes more complex. (Downing, 2000, "Emotion theory reconsidered," p. 255)

According to Downing,[25] an emotion is activated every time an ongoing habitual mode of functioning needs to be questioned.[26] The eruption of an emotion imposes a red light on the current habits. Putting the psyche in a crisis is a way to demand that the mind takes the time to explicitly question the usefulness of what it is about to do. For example, a sudden fear can make me look all around. I could then notice that an animal, detected by nonconscious mechanisms, is roaming in the forest in which I was walking. Furthermore, the emotion already prepares the organism to react by increasing the activation of certain resources that could be needed. In other words, the irruption of an emotion into consciousness obliges the organism to question itself, to try to see if there is—in self or around self—a change that demands a priority accommodation. The emotion also intensifies the collaboration between psychological and physiological mechanisms that it may need to mobilize.[27] Muscles and thoughts are turned away from their current path: "In sum, a paradigm unit of emotion is an extended, complex act. It is simultaneously a bodily sensing; an aligning of the sensing with the relevant situation; and a formation of cognitions" (Downing, 2000, p. 259). This model is used to describe relatively brief emotional reactions (most of the time for only a few minutes), like Paul Ekman's emotional expressions model, which we have already discussed (chapter 9, p. 260f).

The function of the emotions is difficult to determine. Emotions and defenses mobilize independently of what is being thought, on the intimate level as well as on that of an interaction. It often happens that an emotion manifests itself and the individual is unable to relate it to an event. An emotion may arise when it is expected, like at the occasion of the death of a friend, but it may also not manifest itself at such moments, then later surface unexpectedly without any apparent connection with what is happening in the moment. In working on the way that an individual's thoughts and behaviors relate to his affective dynamics, it becomes possible to set about to question the way he functions.

It is sometimes only a few months after a series of interventions that the patient and the therapist are able to notice the changes that emerge into the life of the patient and into the therapeutic relationship. The psychotherapist guides these profound modifications by watching over the *frame* within which these new calibrations are being established, but the nonconscious readjustments that appear during the therapeutic process is not something that he controls. He only knows, by experience, that this type of process may often be set in place when particular conditions are met. For example, instead of fearing his emotions, a person begins to approach them with thoughtful curiosity, like a source of information that is useful but difficult to understand explicitly. They are then no longer perceived as mere manifestations of the archaic animal in us. They also become an alert system that informs consciousness[28] that it should mobilize regulatory mechanisms that are not being activated by the current habitual behavioral process. It is not a question of presupposing, in this model, that the emotions are right more often than the thoughts, but of proposing that different dimensions of the organism can produce different options on how to react in a given situation. The difficulty is to be able to sense what options, or which combination of options, are the most useful in the here and now.

These considerations bring us back to the notion that the affects are strongly influenced by the nonconscious mobilizations that influence behavior and the cognitive dimension without consciousness being able to directly influence this mobilization. We also find this hypothesis in philosophy (Elster, 1999), in some theories on anxiety disorders (Beck and Emery, 1985, p. 188), and in a large part of the literature on trauma, summarized for body psychotherapists by Peter Levine (2004) and Babette Rothschild (2000). These influences are not reciprocal but *asymmetrical*. The influence exercised by the body or the metabolism on the thoughts are not the same kind as those exercised by the thoughts on the rest of the organism.

AN EMERGING MAP OF FUTURE BODY PSYCHOTHERAPY

The preceding discussions bring us to the following list of different way of integrating the analysis of movement in psychotherapy:

1. A behavioral and/or body practice is rendered explicit once the patient and the therapist talk about it. It then becomes possible to analyze, from the point of view of reason and common sense, up to what extent a practice is in accord with the conscious stance of the patient.
2. Once a practice has acquired an explicit contour, it can be submitted to educational procedures, like those used in cognitive and behavior therapy.
3. A practice may be used as a launching pad for a verbalized associative process, as in psychodynamic therapy. There is consequently exploration of the conscious and unconscious implications of this practice for the individual. Here, the focus is on a better psychological integration of the existence of the patient's nonconscious practices and a better understanding of the history of this practice in the patient's life. This work may then activate dreams, memories, and affects and integrate itself in classic psychodynamic process. This, for example, seems to be the route taken by Beebe and her colleagues.[29]
4. For body psychotherapists like Downing, this last development can be associated to light bodywork techniques that extend the verbal associations to what is related at the level of gestures and body sensations.
5. An initiative that is closer to body psychotherapy, such as it is commonly used, would be to explore how a practice integrates itself in the organismic dynamics by using techniques for the exploration of the gesture. Maarten Aalberse (2001) invites the patient to explore the gestures mobilized by a behavior and let them resonate with what is going on in all

the dimensions of the organism.[30] A gesture can influence the cascading of respiration, the affects, the thoughts, the equilibrium of the body, and so on. It is a gathering of phenomena in resonance that then becomes the launching pad from which a micro-practice can be integrated by the patient's organism in an initiative that can lead to new insights.

6. To the extent that a schema has been researched systematically in relation to diverse contexts and psychopathologies, it is also possible to integrate these results in this exploration.

The approaches of Aalberse, Downing, as well as the options I defend in this book integrate all of these possibilities, whereas neo-Reichian body psychotherapy is mostly interested in options 3 and 5. A process that focuses on some of these strategies may have more focused aims and efficiencies, while integrative approaches cover more ground and are more flexible. We already had a similar discussion when I distinguished between a body psychotherapist that works with the body and the mind of the patient (e.g., Lowen and Levine), and a body psychotherapy team in which a body therapist works with the patient's body and a psychotherapist with his representations (e.g., Bülow-Hansen and Braatøy). The more focused work supports more expertise on *certain aspects* of a person, while the broader approach may have more expertise on the *connection* between dimensions. We can now distinguish three types of body psychotherapy:

1. Therapists who can offer deep organismic therapy with some psychotherapeutic integration.
2. Therapists who combine a classical psychotherapeutic approach (e.g., psychodynamic, systemic, cognitive, Gestalt, or Transactional Analysis) with a combination of the six modes of intervention listed above.
3. Integrative approaches include methods created by different schools of psychotherapy in a theoretical framework that should be as close as possible to ongoing research and theoretical propositions. Such approaches may include a combination of the six modes of intervention listed above. Schools like that of George Downing are close to body psychotherapy because (a) he is well informed on modes of intervention that mobilize body and vegetative dynamics, (b) because he often uses these modes of intervention, and (c) they play a central role in the theoretical framework that is used.

George Downing's approach is an example of a *psychotherapeutic* approach of organismic dynamics. The therapist is aware that the mind is a dimension of an organism that interacts with others. However, his key target is the realm of representations. Most humans have the impression that it is something like a core conscious self, or a central me (see chapter 14, p. 362), that initiates what we do and how we perceive or world. This is probably one of the necessary illusions, as I do not think that a person can have an adequate mastery of his actions without having the impression that such a central me exists. Video-analysis shows that most of our actions are activated without the permission of that core conscious self. In some cases our actions and our views are so damaging for our survival that this core conscious self feels disempowered by nonconscious dynamics. I have seen or read about psychiatric patients who cannot prevent themselves from acting in ways that are harmful to others and who are shocked by what they do. This type of dissociation is well known by judges when they ask for a psychiatric expertise to evaluate the responsibility of a person. The patients I am thinking of begged to be maintained in prison or to receive surgical interventions on their brain to prevent them from behaving as they do. These are extreme cases, but for most of us there is a need for a simplistic vision which works on the assumption that *from the point of view of our consciousness* there are events which we can influence and others that proliferate without our knowing how. With tools such as video-analysis we can acquire a better picture of this behavioral proliferation, while the technique of free associations allows us to grasp the spontaneous creativity of our mind. By combining such methods, the subject can be helped to forge for himself a vision of who he is and how others react to his mode of functioning. New ways of evaluating what is happening may help the subject to feel less disempowered by the spontaneous creativity of his organism. I am less optimistic than George Downing, as I do not think that we can change old mental and body habits that have had years to put themselves in place since the first years of one's life. But we can modify the *ecology* of these habits. We can try to live in a more constructive environment, to discover new forms of habitual behaviors and representations. When these become a reality, a patient may discover that with the help of others his core conscious self is less disempowered than he thought. I cannot change the world and my history, but I can initiate new ways of reacting to what is happening. These new mental and behavioral habits change the ecology of old habits. If the old habits have lost the support of that part of us that has the impression of being who one is, they become less powerful, they lose their intensity, and they come less often to the front of the stage. These changes need years before they become well integrated in a global organismic system. In the chapters on evolution I pointed out that changes have unforeseeable implications and ramifications. Those need time to calibrate, because millions of organismic procedures must also calibrate with these new schemas before they can find a comfortable place in the dynamics of the organism. However, in most cases this calibration can continue after psychotherapy has supported important and relevant initial changes, if the patient has enough courage and the support of a constructive social environment. I often warn my patients that they will need to construct, through trial and error, these new forms of functioning. This type of implementation rarely works at the beginning. Success requires small steps and perseverance. Some particularly fragile persons may need a lifelong support, but even in these cases this does not mean that psychotherapists should be consulted all the time. Slices of psychotherapy are often enough. In such cases, the support of social workers and institutions is at least as important as the support of a psychotherapist.

Here is a domain which cries out for new forms of systematic therapeutic attention. Persons familiar with the body psychotherapy tradition would seem especially well positioned to develop new contributions in this respect.

23

Summary: Toward a Form of Psychotherapy that Integrates Nonconscious Practices

The last chapters of this manual describe behavioral and mental practices that unfold outside of the field of consciousness, while shaping it at the same time. These mechanisms are not unconscious (in the Freudian sense), but nonconscious. The therapists of today try to find ways of incorporating these mechanisms into psychotherapeutic methods. To show the problems that the psychotherapeutic community is trying to resolve, I propose that you imagine yourself as the psychotherapist of an adult who had a mother a bit like the ones described by Beebe and Tronick and who presents symptoms that make you think of an adult version of the problems described in their studies of depressed mothers. The fact that there is not an equivalent body of research on the relationship with the father is truly embarrassing for the practitioner. In some cases, it is possible to transpose the data on the dyads with depressive mothers onto a dyad with a depressed father. This solution is sometimes useful and fruitful, but never really satisfying.

The leap between what a patient can recall and the speculations based on research carried out on others are immense. There is the risk of imposing a hypothesis on the patient, of imposing an explanation as a belief that will then grow in his intimate associative system. This is not the aim of body psychotherapists. When they describe an explanatory hypothesis, it is with the hope that it can be explored as a possibility; and that this discussion will integrate itself into the co-conscious experience that structures itself in the process of psychotherapy, by activating insights in the patient. Often the psychotherapeutic process will show that these hypotheses only become partially relevant once they have been modified to fit the patient's experience. In other cases, the therapist and the patient may discover that they are not relevant, or at least that they cannot be integrated by the patient. One should never forget that a hypothesis, even when it is based on robust research, cannot be relevant for everyone.

Even so, it is no longer possible to ignore all of this research. It can be used by a psychotherapist to explore the nonconscious practices of a patient. I take, for example, Beebe's model, which postulates that auto-regulation and interpersonal regulation form a single communication system. An ancient communication system of the patient can find ways of reactualizing itself in a psychotherapeutic process. Once this has occurred in my practice, I can sense the impressions that are associated to this old communication system. I then try to analyze the atmosphere that permeates the room when the patient sits down, our respiratory reactions, the gurgling in our bellies, and I remain attentive to the changes in the quality of the patient's skin and eyes. I use dreams to integrate, with the imagery produced by the patient, what is being woven. Sometimes the patient brings me films or photos with which I shore up my hypotheses. Little by little, a certain common material is constructed with the patient. It allows us to build a network of hypotheses about the way the patient's nonconscious practices constructed themselves in a manner difficult to identify. The infant experienced, reacted; but the infant could not build representation of the grand lines that his organismic development was designing. In hindsight, the adult experiences himself living for decades a certain number of situations that resemble one other. However, the nonconscious mechanisms take such varied forms that it is sometimes difficult to pinpoint what repeats itself. Gradually, this process progresses in resonance with the affective and bodily experience of the patient while the dreams allow the organism to generate more pertinent and illuminating metaphors. Sometimes new memories emerge. Without our truly knowing how, when such a process is pertinent to a given patient at this moment in his life, decisions are made and behaviors fluctuate, and then take on a new equilibrium. These changes also bring their share of information that allows us to calibrate the psychotherapeutic process.

I stop here with regard to these new explorations, for it consists of clinical research in progress, about which it is too early to draw conclusions. We shall see more clearly when more case analyses of this type of approaches are published.

Conclusions

THE LIMITS OF DIVIDING REALITY INTO
DISTINCT REALMS OF KNOWLEDGE

In Europe, science is often taught in the universities by different faculties.[1] Each faculty covers a specific way of studying and understanding the organization of the universe: mathematics, physics, chemistry, biology, psychology, anthropology, sociology, and so on. In the universities, there are also faculties that teach specific competencies, such as the faculties of medicine, law, theology, engineering, and so on. By beginning this book with a discussion on yoga, I wanted to define the development of the human being as a system that is animated by a set of mechanisms so disparate that it would be necessary to take courses taught in each faculty to be able to understand it. The list of courses taught in a faculty of medicine demonstrates this very well. The human is found at the intersection of almost all of the scientific disciplines and practices taught at the university. This is already evident to the yogi. For them, it was impossible to sustain an individual's spiritual development without coordinating different methods that render it possible to make the body supple, reinforce the metabolic activity, stimulate mental activity, acquire a moral sense, and enter into communion with the global dynamics of nature.

Defining the intersection zone of the different bodies of knowledge necessary to create a science of the human is one of the biggest problems I faced when writing this book. One of the original features of body psychotherapy is the will to face this head-on, without worrying about the fact that there is no appropriate definition of such a combination of disciplines and without wanting to re-create a sort of scientific yoga. Body psychotherapy is not a psychotherapy to which an approach to the body is attached. It is a development of psychotherapy that intervenes in the way the psyche inserts itself into its organ-ism.

Yogis admit that an organism forms a coordination of disparate systems that require distinct forms of intervention; they still believe that this disparity can be placed under the yoke of a central will that allows the organism to access the profoundly harmonious core of the human being. I ended this manual with a diametrically different view of the human being by speaking about what is being discovered in the studies on nonverbal communication. If in yoga, the disparity is mostly on the surface of human dynamics, it becomes possible to imagine that it is also situated in its depth. This second path is the one of a syn-thesis between psychology and biology that does not think that there is a central core within an organism. There are no simple solutions to the multiplicity of questions that arise out of the complexity of the organization of nature. There is not one dimension of the organism that creates more truth than another, for each mechanism of the organism approaches what surrounds it with a local competency that is particular to it. The body knows how to do things the mind cannot even imagine, and the organization of the mind is not always more rea-sonable than that of the organism. Staying attuned to what each dimension of the organism can bring about is therefore the beginning of wisdom; staying at-tuned to what each organism, each culture, and each institution can bring may lead to additional wisdom. But in every case, many traps await the practitioner who would like to discover which road to take. I agree with Piaget (1961; Piaget and Weil, 1951) when he hypothesized that the development of intelligence is related to a form of progressive decentering, of the multiplication of different points of view. Most of the schools of body psychotherapy oscillate between the vision proposed by the schools of yoga and those that are developed by the studies on nonverbal communication.

WHAT IS BODY PSYCHOTHERAPY?

The goal of psychotherapy is to intervene on three types of dynamics:

1. The malfunctions of the mind.
2. The malfunctions that are situated in the mechanisms that coordinate the mind and the dynamics of the organism.
3. The malfunctions that are situated at the intersection between mental dynamics and the way an organism inserts itself into its cultural and social environment, and into its biosphere.[2]

In any event, today, it is admitted that these loci of intervention are multiple, even when one mostly takes the psychological dimension into account. There are conscious mechanisms, memories, perceptive modalities, diverse ways of co-ordinating the mind and the other dimensions of the organism, as well as a multitude of cultural and social mechanisms. Body psychotherapist are often interested in these three types of phenomena; but the first one, which focuses on how the psyche is integrated by organismic regulation systems, is manifestly the main focus of most body psychotherapists.

Another central axis of psychotherapy is to think that all biological dynamics are in continuous construction. This plasticity is limited by the properties of the organismic system, but these properties are there to guarantee a flexibility that is one of the characteristics of biological dynamics. A therapist needs to show his patients that this flexibility exists, even if it is limited, and that it is the lever that therapies attempt to exploit.

It has always been that therapy seeks forms of intervention that provide some relief in the relatively short term, even when the mechanisms on which the therapist intervenes are still not well understood. The patient's suffering does not have the time to wait centuries until research can describe all of the mechanisms involved in the cause of these difficulties. On the other hand, every relevant scientific advance is certainly welcomed by psychotherapists and patients. Having said this, it is possible that a recent scientific formulation is unable to satisfy the needs of a therapy because the clinician sometimes perceives practical complexities indicating that the researchers will have to review their formulation in the near future.

The general idea in body psychotherapy is to find the means to sense that an individual needs to be approached from one point of view instead of another at a given moment, while admitting that several forms of interventions (but not all) can lead to constructive solutions. Some memories emerge only when conflicting thoughts are activated by a particular kind of touch, or while the patient associates on a dream; others would have emerged whatever the method used. Seeking what each modality allows one to discover is already part of self-discovery. There are other approaches, like Gestalt therapy, that also use a great diversity of interventions to explore how an individual constructs himself. This is a characteristic of all humanistic psychotherapies. They have all been influenced by Freud, Jung, phenomenology, and Reich. Body psychotherapists have techniques in their tool box that permit explicit intervention on the body such as I define it in this volume, but their approach cannot be limited to this possibility. That is why I have insisted so much on the idea that body psychotherapy, above all else, should be an organismic approach that necessarily includes tools developed in psychotherapy and in mind–body approaches.

As soon as a therapy becomes sensitive to the metabolic activity, it becomes sensitive to the quality of the air, nutrition, and the relationships within which an individual thrives and interacts. That is why the world of body psychotherapy has always been sensitive and open to the notion of an ecological system. A cell is comprehensible only in function of its immediate chemical ecology (this is described in biochemistry), the mind can only be understood if it is situated in its organismic environment (the subject of this volume), and the organism cannot be understood unless one understands how it inserts itself into the relational and cultural network (the ecology of the mind according to Gregory Bateson) that structures itself within an ecosystem, such as the biosphere. There is a central point in this. The psychotherapist is not insensitive to the fact that the mental dynamics are dependent on the support they receive from the economy (the need to have satisfying work), culture (sexual and parental morality), interactions between individuals (nonverbal communication), behavior (appropriate technical competence and the capacity to communicate), the body system (movement and massage), the hormonal system (antidepressants and neuroleptics), the affective dynamics (Vegetotherapy), and so on. In the end, what is important for the psychotherapist is how a person's psyche integrates these multiple systems of necessary support. The therapist cannot require that a patient understand all of this, because neither the therapist nor a gathering of scientists are capable of understanding all of this. The patient needs representations, landmarks, and competencies that permit his psyche to function as constructively as possible in an environment he will never be able to understand. At the occasion of a massage in body psychotherapy, the psychotherapist helps the patient become more explicitly conscious of certain aspects of his relationship with his body. To know how to relax a muscle (this could be done by a physical therapist at another time) is not what is essential for the body psychotherapist. He wants to help the patient develop nonconscious and conscious mental modes of functioning that allow him to refine his perception of the body and be less afraid of interacting with his body from the point of view of his thoughts. The nonconscious mental know-how formed during these sessions can be supported by useful metaphors that allow the patient to find more comfort and efficiency in his organism and in his environment.

THE SYSTEM OF THE DIMENSIONS OF THE ORGANISM: A SUMMARY OF SOME OF THE IMPLICATIONS OF THIS MODEL

I have already described the System of the Dimensions of the Organism in the introduction of this work. This model can be used in different ways. In this book, I have related it to a certain number of positions on the rapport between dimensions within the human organism. I now summarize these issues.

I start with the idea that the universe is made up of interlocking *open systems*. An open system is composed of three basic elements:

1. Characteristic properties of the system without which the system ceases to exist.
2. The capacity to calibrate itself in function of the environmental given to ensure, as much as possible, the survival of the system.
3. The capacity to interact with this environment to be able to make it such

that this environment accommodates itself as much as possible to the needs of the system.

The human organism would be such a system. It is made up of several open subsystems situated at different levels of matter (information exchange, physiology, cellular, chemical, physics, etc.); it can interact with several levels of matter in its environment (physical, chemical, biological, cultural, social, the natural system, etc.). We can imagine two set of quasi-independent causal chains:

1. A subsystem in one individual interacts with a subsystem of another individual.
2. A global organismic regulation interacts with global regulation system of another organism.

In the first scenario, the interaction between subsystems does not mobilize organismic regulation systems, whereas in the second scenario the activity of one subsystem is included in the general organismic system, which has an impact on other organisms and their subsystems.

For example, we have seen that sitting on a chair most of the time may have a deep impact of the venous return mechanisms in the legs. In this case, the influence of the sitting behavior of the person may have an impact on the venous system that is relatively independent from the impact of sitting on behavioral and psychological dynamics. Similarly, the gestures of one individual can influence the dynamics of the brain of another person without influencing the global organismic regulation of these two organisms. Thus, the impact of a gesture on the brain of one individual may unleash a reflex reaction in the other that does not necessarily engage the mind.

One of the particularities of the systemic analysis used in this volume is to insist on the following factors:

1. The variety of the modes of functioning of each system.
2. Given that each subsystem has its own proper exigencies, a group of the subsystems may simultaneously impose contradictory exigencies.
3. It is then necessary to postulate interfaces that permit divergent subsystems to function within a similar system.

In other words, a relative heterogeneity of the modes of functioning of the subsystems of a human organism or of a human society is the norm. Harmony and coherence are possible systemic states, but they are not required and are not always advantageous from the point of view of survival. The interfaces that coordinate the subsystems of an organism have developed in function of the laws of the evolution of the species and a particular organism (phylogenesis and ontogenesis). These interfaces are therefore also heterogeneous and only partially adapted to the subsystems that they coordinate. Here are a few examples of such interfaces:

1. The mechanisms that allow the nervous system and the muscles to interact.
2. The mechanisms that allow thoughts and the dynamics of the brain to interact.
3. The mechanisms that allow individuals to interact within an identical space-time.
4. The mechanisms that allow an individual to interact with institutionalized functions by using tools and the media.

In particular, I have proposed that the affects (instincts, moods, emotions, etc.) are interfaces that actively connect several dimension of the organism (metabolic, physiologic, bodily, behavioral, and mental). Such global interfaces seem to present more flaws than more local interfaces, like the ones that regulate the interaction between a muscle and a few nerves. Concretely, this implies that there are several mental, bodily, behavioral, physiological, and metabolic heterogeneous subsystems. To be explicit, there are, therefore, several heterogeneous psychological functions, and none of them are necessarily more adequate than another. Some are pertinent at certain moments and become dangerous for the survival of the organism in other contexts (e.g., the activation of stress). This explains that a thought can interact, through the intermediary of interfaces, with all the subsystems of the organism, but that it cannot control how these other subsystems are going to react to this impact. My anxieties may eventually unleash a stomach ulcer, but they do not know how this came about and what impact this ulcer will have on my organism and my thoughts. It is even possible that the interaction between ulcer and anxiety would be so indirect that it can be considered fortuitous. For example, my anxieties will create a mobilization of my organism that risk putting all of its weak points to the test. In one individual, anxiety may create an ulcer; in another, an increase in arterial tension; and in another, both. Thoughts do not necessarily master the impact that they inevitably have on the rest of the organism. The inverse is certainly also as true. An ulcer will not necessarily resonate with the mind the same way in different persons. The recognition of this complexity is defended in almost all the chapters of this volume.

A certain number of possibilities can be considered by the practitioner:

1. Whatever the configuration that is contemplated, an apparently direct link between two dimensions (a thought and a gesture, for example), is made up, in fact, of a multitude of mechanisms.
2. There may be more or less direct links between an interface and a dimension. This is the case between affect and physiology in my model. To the extent that an affect has, by definition, a physiological component,

the interaction has direct components even if the multiplicity of the connections mobilized by such an interaction prevents us from thinking that an affect constructs, in any event, the same type of link with a given organ in every body. It is possible, for example, that there is a link between heart and anger; this link builds itself in such a complex and variable organismic ecology that it may manifest differently in each person or at different moments in a person's life. For example, the heart is obviously sensitive to the activity needs associated with an aggressive feeling, but the heart is also sensitive to other variables. Therefore, there is an inevitable network of compensations that relate an affect to the activity of an organ.

3. The connection between two dimensions can pass through an intermediate dimension. Thus, an aggressive feeling may mobilize a certain type of behavior that has a particular link with cardiac activity.

It is useful to speak of association between mechanisms because there are several modes of association possible:

1. A mechanism A influences more or less directly the activation of a mechanism B (when I think of my father, I often want to be alone).
2. A mechanism A is activated by a mechanism B (when I am alone, I often think of my father).
3. A mechanism C activates an association between a mechanism A and a mechanism B (when my respiration becomes superficial, I often have the tendency to want to be alone and to think of my father).

In all three cases, there is an association between wanting to be alone and thinking of my father, but the underlying mechanisms can be completely different.

Therapy is generally considered to be an attempt to use a panoply of interventions more or less targeted, that have the goal of correcting painful modes of functioning that put the survival of an organism in danger. Most of these modes of intervention were initially created by empirical trial and error. Today, some are supported by the development of technology and experimental research. Psychotherapy aims at domains that are still poorly understood (mind, affects, interactive behaviors, social integration, representations of one's identity, etc.).

SPECULATIVE, EMPIRICAL, CLINICAL, AND EXPERIMENTAL SCIENTIFIC RESEARCH

Speaking about the epistemological status of a discipline, I take up Piaget's analysis (1972a), according to which each approach claims to be able to propose a certain form of knowledge concerning an object of study. A form of knowledge is a way of observing, gathering observation, and theorizing about what is happening. It seems useful to me to end this book by identifying why the actual status of psychotherapy is problematic, and why I think this domain ought to at least strive toward a common scientific ethic of knowledge.

The Epistemological Status of Research in Psychotherapy

I broached this discussion in the third part of the introduction of this book when I distinguished between hyphtheses and hypotheses. I called all of the theses that humanity generated, thanks to its imagination, hyphtheses; hypotheses were the most economical theses given the available data. Only the hypotheses are considered scientific at a given moment. Certain hyphtheses (God, cosmic energy, the big bang, etc.) may become hypotheses in the future.

I return to this distinction by taking up four forms of knowledge: speculative, clinical, empirical, and scientific.

1. *Speculative* knowledge seeks to bring order to the human mind by focusing on the hyphtheses. Theology, philosophy, and wisdom (see Piaget, 1965) will try to carry out a triage of these hyphtheses by using diverse forms of thought like logic, dialectics (between yin and yang, for example), common sense, and the beauty of an argument. This strategy also considers scientific hypotheses, but these hypotheses will be organized in function of the analysis of the hyphtheses already in place. An example of this is Reich's attempt to organize available scientific knowledge by assimilating it to his hyphtheses on orgone. It goes without saying that the available hypotheses can sometimes inspire a theory based on speculative research.

2. *Clinical* knowledge is based on the case analyses of individual persons and the way each subject reacts in a relatively standardized setting and set of methods, which allow colleagues to compare their observations. I have discussed two examples, in particular, in this volume to illustrate this type of knowledge: hatha yoga and the free association used by Freud. In hatha yoga, the masters were able to observe numerous individuals who use the same standardized postures (lotus position, standing on one's head, etc.). In psychoanalysis, therapists are able to observe what their patients imagine given certain stimulation (a dream of falling, a dream in which a house burns, etc.). An important part of neurology is based on case analysis and is therefore clinical. One can talk of clinically based scientific research, in contrast to scientific research based on experimental procedures.

3. *Empirical* research tries to find predictable causal chains by collecting standardized data (measures, questionnaires, etc.) on a large number of individuals having some specific traits (anxiety, depression, cancer, race, sex, etc.). This information is then organized with the help of statistics.

4. The *scientific* endeavor is based on two procedures: (a) measures that are as precise as possible, and (b) an attempt to define the invisible

mechanisms that produce the predictable causal chains observed in empirical research.

The history that we know about how aspirin works allows us to illustrate the difference between clinical, empirical, and scientific research.

> *A vignette on the history of aspirin. Over time, clinical experience made it possible to establish that bark from the willow tree had known curative effects for thousands of years. In the nineteenth century, a scientific method in chemistry made it possible to demonstrate that the curative substance contained in willow bark was salicylic acid. This acid was subsequently synthesized, and became the aspirin sold by the Bayer Laboratories since 1899. A combination of clinical and empirical research was able to show that aspirin is often effective for certain problems (flu, headaches, etc.), but not in every case. Up until 1970, no one knew the underlying mechanisms that were activated by aspirin in a human organism. The beginning of a scientific understanding of the impact of aspirin began forty years ago, when researchers like John R. Vane (Nobel Prize in 1982) discovered that aspirin inhibits the production of prostaglandins and thromboxanes.*

Today, all research blends these four forms of knowledge. Even in science, speculative research is an important source of inspiration. In the domain of therapy, the three first forms of research may try to get closer to the demands of science when they respect the following criteria:

1. The reflection is founded uniquely on hypotheses and accepted data by the majority of colleagues.
2. The measures and descriptions are as precise as possible.
3. There is an attempt to understand the mechanisms that generate the symptoms that therapists try to modify.

A school of psychotherapy that follows these three criteria, as much as it is possible, follows the scientific ethical standards on the management of information. It is in the psychotherapist's own interest, in the current political context, to understand this definition of scientific ethics pertaining to knowledge. Psychotherapists also need to understand that the institutions that legislate on health matters tend to present as scientific what is in fact simply empirical research. They often use, mistakenly, the prestigious term *scientific* for empirical findings. To be clear, when the institutions request that schools of psychotherapy scientifically validate their approach, they are, in fact, requiring empirically validated studies. This is problematic for psychotherapy schools that (a) often do not have the means to undertake rigorous empirical studies, while (b) they already have at their disposal clinical observations that are often more scientific then empirical studies. Institutions need to understand that empirical studies are a useful complement to clinical knowledge (based on case studies). These distinctions may help psychotherapy schools fight unreasonable demands from health institutions that defend certain positions for purely political and economic reasons. Clinical issues focus on the health of patients.

The data that the empirical methods produce in psychiatry are often based on partially reliable measures (questionnaires), and the statistics demonstrate relationships that are only partially reliable. These studies are therefore instructive, but in no way scientific. Here is a discussion of well-known empirical studies:

1. *Depression and empirical research.* Zindel V. Segal and his colleagues (2002, I) refer to research that shows that in the United States, 20 percent of women and 7 percent of men suffer from depression in their lifetime, and 80 percent of this population will have several episodes of depression. They quote a report by the World Health Organization which arrives at the conclusion that depression could be the second most frequent illness on the planet. These statistics justify that institutions support the development of increasingly efficient treatments for depression and the possibility of supporting patients between each episode. This analysis is important and interesting. The problem, well known to the clinician, is that these numbers depend on a definition of depression. For some psychiatrists, there is depression as soon as an individual is unhappy and suffers mentally. For others, like Segal and his colleagues, there is depression if the individuals also suffer from sleep problems or poor appetite, absenteeism from work, a lack of motivation, or suicidal ideation. For a clinician, even Segal's definition of depression is too broad. What Segal describes is a tendency of the human temperament (there are also people who are never tired, always motivated, etc.), not a psychopathology. The empirical method does not make it possible to clearly differentiate the tendency to become sad, which is inherent in the human condition, from a pathology that is called depression. Another empirical definition of depression associates this mood to insufficient serotonin (a hormone). Once again, the finding is interesting and useful, as it has supported the industrial fabrication of efficient antidepressant medicine. However these drugs are also used to support difficulties that are experienced by people who would not be diagnosed as depressive by a clinician. These examples show that empirical definitions of depression, even when they are supported by studies of huge samples, (a) do not necessarily lead to a scientific formulation, and (b) are not any closer to the truth than clinical knowledge.

2. *Depression and clinical research.* Clinical observation shows that there are depressive traits in a number of psychiatric disorders (psychoses, borderline personality disorder, phobias, etc.), that suicidal tendencies are found in all of these pathologies, and that certain highly depressive patients can also be highly creative (Beethoven, Tolstoy, etc.).[3] Body psychotherapies are mostly based on clinical research.

Therefore, we have on one side broad lines that can be derived from question-naires answered by a large number of people; and from other quadrants, de-tailed clinical observations showing that the results obtained by an empirical method are interesting, instructive but suffer from lacunae at the level (a) of the measuring instruments and (b) of the reliability of the generalizations proposed by statistical methods. The clinician needs precise categories. So precise that he may lose himself in the nuances that haunt his perception. It is almost impossi-ble to have a significant cohort of subjects that present all of these nuances. Scientific experimental research has financial and technical exigencies that can-not be incorporated into the institutions that occupy themselves with clinical research. The stakes that structure scientific research are different from those that structure clinical and empirical research. We have seen[4] that very probably, the day when scientific research preoccupies itself with what the clinicians ob-serve, it will use an unexpected approach to these phenomena. This unexpected aspect will be based on data that neither clinical research nor empirical research could collect. In some cases they could not even have imagined that such data existed, or that it could be connected to the phenomena they were studying. A scientific approach would therefore inevitable lead to a third form of approach to mental disorders.

For the moment, psychotherapy is focused on a clinical approach that inte-grates, in more or less strong doses, the three forms of knowledge identified (speculative, scientific, and empirical). The problematic status of the epistemo-logical rigor of the psychotherapist seems to me to be partly due to the structure of the schools that prevail in this domain for the time being. The speculative inspiration of the charismatic "master" often has more weight than clinical, empirical, and scientific evidence. For example, a school may only include in its references the evidence that supports their speculative stance. On the other hand, the proliferation of schools is the only form of creativity that seems to be efficient in the field of psychotherapy.

The institutions responsible for the politics of health care may try to im-pose an ethic of knowledge that is as scientific as possible, but the forms of thinking that are useful in science lose most of their relevance in a clinical prac-tice. Today, the general trend is to differentiate *evidence based psychotherapies* (e.g., cognitive and behavioral therapy) from *clinically based psychotherapies* (e.g., psychodynamic, Jungian, Gestalt and body psychotherapies). From the point of view of the practitioner, this distinction is often artificial, as cognitive therapists can be excellent clinicians.

A Robust Ancient Knowledge

The plan of this book is more easily understood at this point because, for the moment, the only true strength of the psychotherapist's knowledge is the ro-bustness of certain themes that support most approaches. Psychotherapists, in most of the schools, have pride in having constructed a unique imaginative and useful knowledge. But they also often have the impression of being the poor parents of the development of knowledge. In spite of a success that has influenced the development of mores in all the cultures and milieus in the world, the social support they have received is relatively weak. One of the causes of this weakness comes from the practitioners themselves. They often have little confidence in the value and originality of their knowledge, while having daily confirmation of the usefulness of their propositions with their patients. I have noticed that, trained in the necessary restricted perspective of one school, practitioners often lack the necessary general culture to recognize that their knowledge has been polished for thousands of years in numerous cultures. In spite of the variety of elaborated approaches, most of them rediscover a certain number of robust practices and concepts that are sadly often drowned in a bizarre conceptualization. This textbook has been written so that in the future, body psychotherapists will be able to face these issues with more confidence.

No one really knows how psychotherapy functions. To take up the metaphor of aspirin, psychotherapy is still at the stage where a clinical knowledge shows that willow bark is therapeutically useful. The few theories about what is therapeutic in psychotherapy are not even at the stage where we know that it is an acid in the bark that heals. Clinicians are only beginning to accept the support of empirical research that describes the circumstances in which psychotherapy is indubitably useful. The theories on the underlying mechanisms of psychotherapy are often closer to speculations than to scientific thought. It seems to me that the few theories on psychotherapy that do exist are more placebo theories created to reassure psychotherapists of their competence. They are not really convincing. The great trump card of psychotherapy is to have cleared a domain that will be approachable by more rigorous thinking tomorrow.

The actual situation of psychotherapy resembles that of physics in Galileo's time. Galileo and his colleagues did not have the scientific proof to support their conviction that the Earth rotates around the sun. Galileo's fight with the Church is therefore the battle of one who wants to have the freedom to presume what he wants; and also to have the time (we are talking of centuries) and the means to seek the proofs necessary to confirm or refute what he and his colleagues have thought about profoundly.[5]

I allow myself this historical digression because the psychotherapy of our time is currently undergoing the same sort of menace that Galileo faced. The enemy is no longer the Church but a sort of scientism sponsored by economic and political stakeholders (the marketplace of health) that want to eliminate clinically based psychotherapies from the marketplace and only support empirically based psychotherapies with the argument that they are more scientific. The reasons certain powerful movements want to eliminate clinically based psychotherapy from the realm of psychotherapy remain unclear to me, but this political and economic trend manifestly exists. The difficulties experienced by psychotherapists in finding the institutional means to demonstrate the value of their approach are similar to those encountered by the scientists of the Renaissance. I hope that in the future, clinical evidence will again be recognized as a necessary complement to empirical evidence.

Like Galileo, I respond that our approach is based on common sense, experience, and a robust tradition. When this enterprise encounters scientific works that deal with subjects that call out to them, psychotherapists often take enthusiastic interest in them. Mostly, research tends to demonstrate the soundness of the global hypotheses of the psychotherapeutic field, instead of invalidating them, while contributing important clarifications. This is truly the spirit of the Renaissance and the Enlightenment that animates psychotherapy.[6]

Today, it is impossible to know what will become of the domain of psychotherapy 100 years from now. The wager taken by the associations of body psychotherapy like the EABP and the USABP is that certain central theses in their domain, such as those I have tried to describe in this volume, will be part of the entire psychotherapeutic endeavor. My secret hope is that the domain will be, from now until then, transformed in such a way that the debate concerning the relationship between mind and organism, and mind and body, will have changed and will develop new issues that permit us to revisit everything that has been said with points of view we have not yet imagined. We will then be able to propose more efficient forms of support than what exists today. This implies that clinical, empirical, and scientific research continues to create a better understanding of the psychological dynamics that animate human organisms.

FINAL REMARKS

At the beginning of this book I promised that I would concentrate on the issues that have structured the field more than on my personal thoughts. However, I also warned the reader that psychotherapy is not a subject on which one can write and remain neutral. Although I have not written much on my personal thoughts, I have taken clear options on each subject, so that the reader who reads this book from beginning to end will notice that some positions are clearly mine. This is why I advised the reader to focus on the issues I raise and then look for personal answers.

Assens (Switzerland), October 2011

Appendix about Postures of Reference

I will now describe a few static positions, used by numerous body psychotherapists as references or positions to use by default. They are compatible with the requirements of orthopedics, physical therapy, and hatha yoga. It is usually asked of the person who is using these postures that he maintains the natural curvature of spine. This requires a tonic balance between the muscular chains that structure the front and back of the body. These are all ideal postures that are promoted by experts.

Some may need to consult a book on anatomy or an online search engine for definitions and illustrations. I do not know of a book that contains all of these notions.

ALIGNMENT OF THE BODY SEGMENTS
WHEN A PERSON IS STANDING

The Reading of the Position with
the Plumb-Line Method

The physical therapists often evaluate a static standing posture with the plumb-line method (see figure A.1).[1] They ask an individual to stand as straight as possible, knees unlocked, with the nape of the neck elongated. The feet are parallel or in the shape of a V (heels touching). In this posture, all of the muscles that permit this stretching (feet, legs, pelvis, back, nape of the neck, cranium, abdominal muscles, etc.) must be toned but not tense. The muscle tone in the front and in the back of the body is in balance. If the required muscle tone is present, and there is no skeletal deviation, the body segments align themselves automatically to provide the best possible balance. Ensuring a minimum of tension in the muscular system in all of the muscles is the criterion.[2]

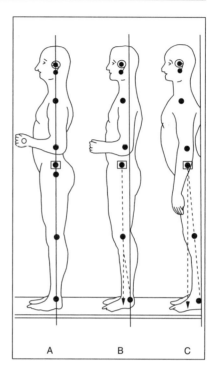

FIGURE A.1. Reading of the posture using the "plumb line" method. (A) An ideal vertical standing position; (B) a restful standing position; (C) a standing-at-attention position. *Source:* Bonnett and Millet (1971, p. 695).

This ideal alignment places the ear, shoulder, pelvis, and middle of the foot on the same axis. A plumb-line that is held up to the side of the body from the profile ought to pass in front of the ear, the shoulder, the articulation of the pelvis, and arrive somewhat in front of the ankle. With practice, the physical therapist abandons the use of the plumb-line, because he has learned to analyze the alignment of the body as if there were a plumb-line. He will mostly use this device so that patients can learn to analyze their alignment when they are standing in front of a mirror.

Most Europeans are aligned toward the back: the plumb-line passes in front of the pelvis, shoulders, and ears. If you place these individuals in an ideal vertical standing position, they generally have the impression of leaning forward; they are afraid of falling. Yet if you test their balance by lightly pushing the chest backward, or the shoulder blades forward, they discover that they are more solidly anchored to the ground in this position. We thus notice that to align an individual also requires a reeducation of bodily sensations.

The "Inner" Axis

The Hindus and the Egyptians of old were already marvelous architects and had mastered geometry. They used the plumb-line to construct their homes.

They imagined that the body balanced itself around an invisible axis that passes through the body's center of gravity while standing. This center is situated in the middle of the abdomen, under the navel (a bit lower for a woman because, on average, her pelvis is heavier than a man's). For the standing position, it therefore consists in aligning the perineum, the belly, and the fontanel, as if a perfectly vertical axis traversed the middle of all these body segments, and planted itself into the ground in between the soles of the feet. This imaginary axis of the vertical body that passes through the body's center of gravity is referred to by the body specialists of almost all cultures, from yoga up to the theories used by the whirling dervishes of Turkey. We encounter this metaphor in several schools of dance that teach the necessity of sensing in oneself an axis that stretches out, in psychomotor schools of scientific inspiration, and in most schools of body–mind aproaches.[3] For example, we ask some people to stand up, eyes closed, and imagine roots coming out of their feet and reaching deep into the earth. To regulate the position of the head, it is often suggested to imagine that a thread ties the fontanel to a star above the fontanel, and this thread tugs in such a way as to elongate the nape of the neck and the spine between the shoulder blades, which induces a lowering of the external part of the clavicles.[4] Ideally, the clavicles form a straight line. It often happens, when we take a workshop in body-work, that the instructors suggest that you feel your feet getting heavy around the axis and your head rising toward the star you were asked to imagine.

In this kind of work, it is often asked of the individual carrying out the exercise to sense the lateral distribution of body weight on the soles of the feet. Does the right or left foot carry more of the weight? Is the weight more on the inside or the outside of the feet? In both cases, it is the balance between the feet that is sought, with a weight that anchors itself at the center of each foot.

The Basic Bioenergetic Grounding Position: Standing with Knees Flexed

With his colleagues, Alexander Lowen established a series of postures that allowed patients to increase their awareness of a series of connections between impressions, breathing and postures (Lowen and Lowen, 1977). The posture that is most often used is called "grounding" (see figure A.2). It was already used in the Chinese martial arts, but Lowen works with it in his own fashion. The basic bioenergetic position is described as follows:

1. The individual is standing.
2. Each foot is beneath the corresponding shoulder. The feet are parallel. Sometimes Lowen requests that the toes point slightly toward each other to increase muscular tension. The weight of the body is halfway between the toes and the ankle, the body's center of gravity is above the space between the feet, in the middle of the right-left axis. To feel the dimension of grounding that Lowen relates to this position, the person who

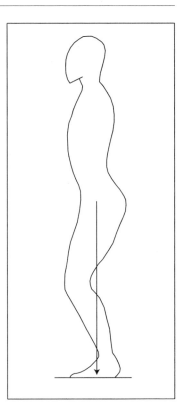

FIGURE A.2. The basic grounding position in bioenergetics.

takes up this position is often asked to imagine that roots are coming out of the soles of his feet, travel through everything that separates the feet from the earth, and then sink into the earth.

3. The knees are bent at about 135°.[5]
4. Feet, pelvis, shoulders, and ears aligned according the rule of the plumb-line.
5. The pelvis is in an orthopedic position. Lowen often asks that the individual move the pelvis forward and backward until he finds the most relaxed position. This movement is often done in coordination with respiration (the lower back is straight in exhaling and arched in inhaling). This position can be taken only if the groin (the junction between the front of the top of the thighs and the lower abdomen, around the genitals) forms a furrow. The mobility of the groin is always an interesting place to work. An image that is currently proposed by some teachers of tai chi chuan and by Lowen is that of the tail of a kangaroo. The virtual tail that extends beyond the coccyx reaches the space between the heels. The individual imagines being able to sit on this tail.
6. The arms are relaxed.

7. The bioenergetic therapists use all of the rules described in the preceding sections.

By default, Lowen asks the patient to be as relaxed as possible, let go of his breathing, and breathe with an open mouth. Breathing through the mouth encourages the advent of vegetative reactions and emotional expressions. Breathing from the nose is a way to diminish these reactions when it is necessary. In tai chi chuan, it is often recommended to breathe in from the nose and to breathe out by the mouth.

SITTING PROPERLY ON THE ISCHIA

There are two basic criteria to characterize sitting:

1. From an orthopedic point of view, one can sit in more or less healthy ways. For example, crossing one's legs is bad for one's health because it inhibits the venous circulation in the legs.
2. Sitting is more or less comfortable. Two criteria measure the comfort: (a) a subjective feeling; (b) the time that a person sits before moving. The longer the time spent in the position, the more comfortable the position.

From an orthopedic point of view, there is only one way to sit. It is roughly the one that is automatically set in place by a person who sits comfortably in a lotus position: the person is sitting on the ground, the right foot high up on top of the left thigh, the left foot high up on top of the right thigh, in such a way the heel of the right foot is near the navel.[6]

The physical therapist[7] typically proposes that an individual sit on a horizontal seat, a bit higher than the knees. The "correct" position of the pelvis is to imagine that the base of the pelvis is a three-legged stool that supports the weight of the upper body. The two "back feet" are the ischia, and the third is an imaginary extension of the perineum when it is as close as possible to the seat. The dorsal face of the pelvis[8] is roughly at a 90° angle to the support surface. The two bones of the pelvis that frame the lower abdomen and the genital region are leaning slightly forward.[9] This position of the pelvis is the best possible base to sustain the flexibility of the spinal column when someone is sitting, and it does not block any ongoing respiratory movements. Furthermore, the vertical position of the hip bone supports the uprightness of the lower back and imposes the necessary curvature. This position also tones up the rectus and obliquus abdominal muscles—just what is needed.

In Europe, many people have difficulty staying in this position for any length of time. In talking with them about their discomfort, it is possible to obtain a lot of information pertaining to their habits and muscular tension. It is sometime useful to recommend an approach to reeducate the relevant muscles and sensory-motor circuits (hatha yoga, the Mathias Alexander technique, Feldenkrais schools, Rolfing, etc.).

THE BASIC REICHIAN POSTURE: LYING ON ONE'S BACK

Going from psychoanalysis to body psychotherapy, Reich kept one constant variable: the patient is, more often than not, lying down on his back on a couch. Yet the therapist is now sitting next to the patient and even sometimes invites a visual contact.

When I speak of the basic Reichian posture (see Figure A.3), I refer to the following position:

1. The patient is stretched out on his back.
2. The patient has bent his legs so that the feet are flat on the support surface.
3. The insides of the legs and feet do not touch.
4. The feet are parallel and separated almost the width of the shoulders.
5. The "correct" distance between the feet and the pelvis is determined in this way: ask the individual lying down to lift and drop the pelvis several times. A proper placement of the feet is the one that facilitates this movement; an improper one inhibits this movement.
6. The position does not aim at comfort. It even seeks to render the tensions of the body perceptible to the patient and the therapist. A dialogue on the location of these tensions is sought. Therefore, the therapist does not immediately ask the patient if he wants a cushion or invite him to choose the position he wants. The slight gap between the legs and the parallel position of the feet may make the tensions on the inside of the thighs more tangible. Reich relates these tensions to the fear of sexual pleasure.

I have not found any text in which Reich describes this position. I have reconstructed it from discussions with individuals who worked with Ola Raknes (e.g., Gerda Boyesen, Bjørn Blumenthal), and with Eva Reich. This posture is also compatible with all of the cases described since 1933. This was Reich's default position; he sometimes observed someone standing or conversed with a patient who was sitting down.

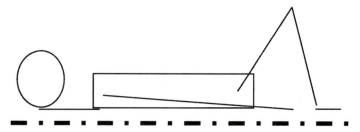

FIGURE A.3.   The basic vegetotherapy position.

Notes

PREFACE

1. Irvin D. Yalom gives stimulating examples of this way of thinking in his novels *The Schopenhauer Cure* and *When Nietzsche Wept.*

INTRODUCTION

1. Luria (1979, 5, p. 81f). Luria and Yudovich (1973), Vygotsky (1934).

2. Heller (1997).

3. The term *robust,* like others, is defined in the Glossary.

4. James (1890, I).

5. At the beginning of the third chapter of *The Origin of Species.*

6. This theory was originally exposed as the general system theory by Ludwig von Bertalanffy (1950, 1968a, 1968b). See also Bateson (1979) or Emery (1981).

7. As in Thelen and Smith (1994) or the Boston Change Process Study Group (2010).

8. See Jean Piaget (1967, 1985).

9. See Henri Laborit (1971, 1974, 1987), who is cited regularly by body psychotherapists who read French (for example, Heller, 2001a, p. 12, or Liss, 2001, p. 177).

10. See Beth and Piaget (1966).

11. Cunningham (2009).

12. Frontier and Picho-Viale (1998), Moessinger (2008, pp. 201–242).

13. Vygotsky (1934, 1, p. 4f).

14. Piaget (1967, p. 20).

15. Piaget used the term *schema* to designate a specific action system, a spontaneous, habitual way of dealing with a task. The same term is used today in certain laboratories (Beebe et al., 2010).

16. See, for example, Jacques Fradin (2008, p. 65), and the section I wrote on him in chapter 8, this volume, p. 246f.

17. Minsky is cofounder of the Artificial Intelligence Laboratory of the Massachusetts Institute of Technology.

18. Main references for this section: Jean Piaget, *Biology and Knowledge* (1967), Ludwig von Bertalanffy, *Organismic Psychology and Systems Theory* (1968).

19. Vaysse (2006, 4.6, p. 178f).

20. For example, Jerome Kagan (1998, p. 83f) and Pierre Moessinger (2000).

21. John Carew Eccles, winner of a Nobel Prize in Medicine (1989, IX.9.8.3, p. 284f) had postulated a neo-neocortex capable of regulating the organism as a whole.

22. Heller (2004c, 2005, and 2006).

23. For example, Myriam Boubli (2009), Jacques Cosnier (1998).

24. See Eva Thompson (2008). The last chapters of this book detail what goes on between the bodies in interaction with each other.

25. This model is described in chapter 14, p. 344f.

26. This model is described in chapter 15, p. 400f.

27. I have organized these dimensions according to their appearance in the evolution of life. Thus, gravity participated in the formation of the Earth's crust, whereas the capacity to participate in institutionalized social behavior came about mostly from the time of the insects.

28. Heller (1991a, 1997).

29. Richard et al. (1998, 9.2, p. 271f).

30. Heller (2006), Leroi-Gourhan (1965).

31. Examples are discussed in chapter 13, p. 328.

32. Wallace (1908, XV, p. 224). This is the same Wallace who, with Darwin, developed the theory of natural selection.

33. For example, different subroutines in software, written by different engineers, may accomplish the same task (e.g., saving text on an external disk).

34. In this book, perception is a form of data management that can be experienced consciously or at least unconsciously. A perception is thus never nonconscious. The same can be said for a thought. For example, a visual perception consists of events detected in a nonconscious way by the eyes, managed by different neurological mechanisms, which then form a perception.

35. Examples of "practice" are given in the last sections of this book, which are dedicated to the analysis of behavior (chapters 21 and 22). The terminology, here as elsewhere, varies. I often use the Piagetian term *schema*, which is still used in cognitive therapy (Young et al., 2003). These mental schemas are studied mostly for their mental dimension; looking at them more closely, they always mobilize other dimensions of the organism (Inhelder and Cellérier, 1992).

36. M. Rochat et al. (2008) demonstrate that the way an eye tracks a gesture is automatically constructed at the sensorimotor level beyond conscious perception. She conducts her research with monkeys, but she shows that these systems of acquisition and collaboration are managed in a perfectly adequate manner by the nervous system.

37. See Newton (1686, III, 320).

38. See Kant's (1776) discussion on a spirit-seer summarized in chapter 8, p. 149f.

PART I

1. Translators of oriental literature use different spellings for the same name. I have used a single current spelling in all cases except in quoted material. I know from experience that whatever choice I take is arguable.

2. Kabat-Zinn (1990); Siegle (2007).

3. Visceglia and Lewis (2011).

CHAPTER 1

I thank Jean-Marie Baron for the advice he gave me when I wrote this chapter.

1. A yogi is a person who regularly practices yoga.

2. Max Weber (1913, chapter X, p. 329).

3. Recommended reading on Hinduism: *Sadhana,* by Rabindranâth Tagore (1913), and the volume on Hinduism edited by Louis Renou (1961).

4. Iyengar (1966, introduction, pp. 31–53). See also Shri Anirvan (2009).

5. I use the term *illumination* to designate this state of enlightenment. The reader can thus immediately know when I refer to a state that can be acquired through Far Eastern meditation techniques (e.g., *Samadhi*) or to the enlightened stance of eighteenth-century European philosophers during the Enlightenment, such as Kant.

6. I follow Iyengar's manual because I can confidently recommend it to you. Other books on yoga are just as interesting. I demanded of myself that I present a Hindu author whose teachings are well received in many countries.

7. Translated in Thich Nhat Hanh(1996).

8. The analysis of this topic is developed in chapter 13, dedicated to postural dynamics. See Heller (1997), Hewes (1955, 1957).

9. This is the "sidd-asana" in yoga (Iyengar, 1966, plate 84). The terminology in this domain is fuzzy. For example, in this case it is the word *position* that designates what I call a posture.

10. We also speak of "setting" or "frame" in psychotherapy.

11. Basic posture and auto-regulation posture are defined in the sections on postural dynamics (chapter 13).

12. The groin is the fold situated between the abdomen and a thigh.

13. The two pointed bones of the pelvis on which one may sit.

14. The tender zone situated at the midpoint between the anus and the genitals called the mulabanda in the language of yoga.

15. Kocer and colleagues (2002) have demonstrated that this technique lowers intraocular pressure. This correlation was strong for men and clearly less so for women. Chen and associates (2004) confirm this result, as well as the influence of this breathing technique on the vegetative nervous system. They specify that this technique, on the other hand, does not markedly influence the regulation of muscle tone.

16. Iyengar (1966, plates 104 and 105).

17. Patanjali (2007, 1.15).

18. Braatøy (1942), Reich (1949a, xiv.1:305f).

19. Iyengar (1966, I Introduction, pp. 20–21).

20. Ibid.

21. Iyengar (1966, plates 363–364).

22. Iyengar (1966, II, Yogasanas, p. 216).

23. We find another example in the chapter on respiration (Iyengar, 1966, Pranayama, Kumi). See section 1.2.

24. Han et al. (2005), Kunik and colleagues (2005). Han's team is Chinese. It consists of researchers who probably know the hypotheses of acupuncturists.

25. I use this term to designate any functioning person. A citizen is not necessarily

someone who is familiar with body techniques or psychotherapy and does not necessarily suffer from a psychiatric disease.

26. The experienced practitioner often utilizes some more refined diagrams.

27. Iyengar (1966, exercise 597, p. 44f.).

28. Iyengar (1966, pranayama, Kumbhakas, p. 435, rule 44).

29. This number is compatible with those proposed in a text on physiology (Bonnet and Millet, 1971, pp. 305–306) for adults. For children, the younger a child the more rapid the respiration (forty-four breaths per minute on an average for newborns).

30. Bunkan (1991).

31. Based on http://www.mamashealth.com/nutrition/anemia.asp retrieved August 2011, and my discussions with Beatrice Bajetta.

32. Oxygen was discovered in Europe in the eighteenth century.

33. West (1975, p. 1365).

34. Ganong (1999, p. 661).

35. Levine and MacNaughton (2004).

36. For David Hume, the English philosopher, faith and the intensity of impressions are related. The more an idea is intense, the more it is experienced as true. See chapter 5, pp. 139–141.

37. See Hedges et al. (1997).

38. In chapter 21, p. 621f, I summarize the result of observations made by Ed Tronick on the impact of a mother's depression on her infants. This is an example of mothers who find it difficult to tolerate too much affective vitality.

39. Bonham (1995).

40. Richerson and colleagues (2005).

41. This geographic detail is not without interest, because I soon speak of the alliance that was made in China between the yoga of postures and the yoga of continuous movement.

42. Certain formulations of bhatia yoga are so close to Sufism that the Bauls from Bengal explicitly integrate these two streams.

43. It is probable that the symbol of the caduceus used by Western physicians, where we see two snakes wrapped around a column, was inspired by the symbol of the kundalini. It would have passed down among the European symbols by becoming associated to the God Hermes (or Mercury). The Germanic word for spine is Wirbelsaute. Wirbel means whirlwind or vertebrae, and Saule means column. Even though this term, in general, designates a column of vertebrae, it denotes literally a whirlwind around the column.

44. Caldwell (1997), Nunnely (2000, 5:85f), Rosenberg and Rand (1985, 5.1, p. 145f), Rubenfeld (1997, p. 210).

45. Iyengar (1966, pranayama, section on the Bandhas, Nadis, and Chakras, p. 439).

CHAPTER 2

Each generation of translators of the Chinese language has modified the spelling of Chinese names in English. I use traditional English spellings that are familiar for most readers.

1. Wilhelm (1924).

2. This proposition is detailed in chapter 5, dedicated to Spinoza, who has a similar thought on this point.

3. The Chinese like to associate a movement to a "founding father." However, these founding fathers have become myths that only partially correspond to existing persons.

4. Logic, mathematics, and program languages are examples of formal languages.

5. Wilhelm (1924, hexagram 31, pp. 122–125).

6. Lowen (1994, II.7, p. 47).

7. Velther and Lamothe (1980).

8. This information was found in Lavier (1973, p. 6), MacDonald (1984, pp. 9, 90–95), and Velther and Lamothe (1980, pp. 55–56).

9. This information was found in Despeux (1979, pp. 83–84), Lavier (1973, pp. 61–74), MacDonald (1984, pp. 9, 96–104), Velther and Lamothe (1980, p. 56), and Yü (1970).

10. MacDonald (1984, p. 30f).

11. Borsarello (1971), Lavier (1973, pp. 237–269), MacDonald (1984, pp. 1–8, 47–48, 84–90), and Velther and Lamothe (1980, pp. 61–66).

12. Lavier (1973, pp. 19–21).

13. Soulié de Morant (1951, III). These historical reconstructions are to be taken as metaphors that have some truth to them but mostly have a goal of helping students get a picture of what they are doing. With authors like Soulié de Morant or Lavier, I have the impression that these writers seek narratives to make acupuncture more digestible for the Western mentality.

14. Tuina in China and shiatsu in Japan.

15. Kaltenmarck (1970).

16. These are approximate dates, particularly so for Lie Tzu.

17. This formulation is a simplification, but I have found such a shortcut useful for teaching purposes as a first approximation.

18. This frame of mind is marvelously illustrated by the poems of Han-shan (end of the sixth century), and other "poetry of the recluse" (Birch 1967, pp. 195–220), written between 200 and 600 BC. These poets are influenced by Buddhism as well as Taoism.

19. In my memory, this image comes from one of the many translations of the *I Ching* I have read, but I have not found this passage while writing this book.

20. Lao-Tseu (1980, LV, p. 209).

21. The works of Kim Tawm (1979) and Rinnie Tang and Gilles Faivre (2003) provide an approximate idea about the exercises of the Taoists.

22. In "Lie Tzu attempts a voyage to Ts'i" (Lie-Tzu, 732, II, XIV), Lie Tzu thinks that when a master has too many sandals in front of his door, he is lost! Once he has become known, he can no longer have any peace, because the words of admirers are a poison.

23. You will find a good example in reading "The student Yin and Lie Tzu" (Lie-Tzu 723, II III). Lie Tzu waits three years before his master even looks at him, five years before his master smiles at him, and seven years before the master invites him to get on the mat.

24. Chuang Tzu (IV, p. 65).

25. For beginners, it is not recommended to do these exercises every day, because they demand too much of the musculature, and they can irritate the tendons of the shoulders. A tangible release of the nape of the neck is often the first benefit.

26. See chapter 19 (p. 555f) for more information on the importance of Alexander Lowen in body psychotherapy.

27. My source here is a demonstration before hundreds of people in Hamburg (Germany) at a congress (July 27–31, 1994) organized by the Milton H. Erickson Foundation around the theme of the evolution of psychotherapy. This demonstration can be regarded as Lowen's typical way of working.

28. Lowen has probably learned to use this posture in yoga courses.

29. Head, nape of the neck, shoulders, arms, and the sole of the feet touch the ground. The rest of the body forms a straight line from neck to knees. The pelvis is as high as possible. Rosenberg and Rand give a useful description (1989, pp. 406–407). They indicate that the muscles mobilized are above all the latissimus dorsi, the psoas, the hinge between the legs and the torso, and the sphincters. We can also find a detailed description in Lowen and Lowen (1977).

30. A chair or a stool does just as well. Gymnasts often use this exercise. For example, it is used in Pilates and is recommended by Sambucy (1973, p. 428).

31. For body psychotherapies, see Aposhyan (1999), Caldwell (1996), Benz-Chartrand (1987), Kurz (1990), Johanson (2006), Ogden et al. (2006), Rytz (2009), and Weiss (2009). Methods such as mindfulness were explicitly integrated in body psychotherapy by the Hakomi School since the 1970s (information supported in March 2011 by Greg Johansson and Halko Weiss). Associating extreme Oriental methods in psychotherapy was thus simultaneously developed by a generation of psychologists who worked in Jungian, cognitive, and body psychotherapies.

32. See Max Weber's 1913 book on India, part III, for a stimulating account of this development.

33. Translated by Richard Wilhelm, who has also translated the *I Ching*.

34. Let us be nonetheless prudent. The Westerners are the ones who compared Buddhism to a religion (Kaltenmark, 1970).

35. They utilized tantric techniques, as do certain Western sects.

36. See Dürkheim (1954).

37. See Lu K'uan Yü (1970, chapters 2 and 11).

38. Baldrian-Hussein (1984, p. 58).

39. Some Taoist schools use a more complicated version of this model. See, for example, Jwing-Ming (1987, 3–2, pp. 52–63).

40. The works of Chinese alchemy sometime mention more centers associated with this circulation; but I have the impression that this is due to the influence of yoga. Thus, Lu K'uan Yü (1970, p. 124) also mentions the center situated behind the solar plexus under the diaphragm (Chung t'u) that plays an important role in yoga. The text translated by Baldrian-Hussein (1984, p. 156) mentions only three centers; but the median field is not the one of the heart but of the solar plexus.

41. Jwing-Ming (1987, 3.3, pp. 53–60).

42. I have not found writings in which this is said, but I have heard it explained by Lowen at conferences in Geneva and Hamburg. This is an example of knowledge that is difficult to find in the literature but is often explained in workshops.

43. In workshops organized by Lizelle Reymond in Cartigny (Switzerland) in July 1976–1979.

44. Despeux (1981).

45. For the images and definitions of postures, I base myself on the manual published by Chen Man Ch'ing and Robert W. Smith (1981) who was suggested to me by Robert C. Fong of San Francisco, my master for a month.

46. The idea that the dynamics of a person's standing posture is built in relation to

the feet and the pelvis is always at play in physical therapy, as Khamis and Yizhar show in their 2007 study.

47. Perlman (2006).

48. This vocabulary is defined in chapter 13. See also Lowen (1975, V.2, pp.146–149).

49. This distinction is taken up by Reich in the jellyfish exercises that I describe in the sections on orgonomy (chapter 18, p. 503f). It is often useful to do an exercise in two different ways and explore what is activated with the patient in each instance.

CHAPTER 3

1. I conform to the practice of capitalizing Plato's Ideas and all the terms derived from it (Truth, Goodness, Beauty, Justice, etc.). The words truth and ideas in lowercase take on the multiple meanings accorded to them in the dictionaries and are no longer associated to philosophical idealism.

2. Jean Piaget developed the notion of natural logic in his works on logic and mathematics (Beth and Piaget, 1966; Piaget, 1972b).

3. English translation by W. E. Leonard found in September 2011 at http://www .gutenberg.org/dirs/7/8/785/785.txt

4. Rey (1973).

5. For example, to quote the authors mentioned in this book, Spinoza, Hume, Darwin, Cellérier, Minsky, Kagan, and Tronick.

6. References: The dialogues of Plato translated by Benjamin Jowett (1937), which can easily be found on the Internet; Châtelet (1989); Gomperz (1905). For quotes, I also used translations published by John M. Cooper (1997), which uses more contemporary formulations. The comments of Theodore Gomperz are often useful for the history of psychotherapy, because Freud discussed Greek philosophy with him. Gomperz was also a reference for Jung. It is useful to have a critic of Plato's political thought before the advent of Soviet communism and Nazism because the relationship between these movements and Plato's thoughts influenced the commentaries of his political philosophy in the writings of the second half of the twentieth century.

7. English translation by W. E. Leonard found in September 2011 at http://www .gutenberg.org/dirs/7/8/785/785.txt

8. Droz (1992), Veyne (1983).

9. I am grateful to Nic Minden for this remark at the occasion of a meeting in Lausanne in June 2007.

10. Plato may have written explicit formulations of his thoughts. But if this is the case, these texts have been lost.

11. Plato, Letter VII, 1950, II, p. 1185.

12. Plato, *Apology* (in Jowett's translation of *The Dialogues of Plato*, 1937, 40f, p. 422).

13. Plato develops this fable in *The Phaedo* or *Concerning the Soul*.

14. Plato, *Phaedrus* (in Jowett's translation of *The Dialogues of Plato*, 1937, 250c, p. 254). This sort of expression attributed to Socrates is to be taken freely. It has a humorous, ironic, and at the same time, a sensual side. We have, in the choice of this metaphor, an example of Socrates' sense of humor.

15. This tale, called *the anamnesis* (Droz, 1992, p. 79), is only suggested by Plato,

never told as such. Its elements are in effect dispersed in three places (Meno 80d–86c, Phaedo 72c–73b, and Phaedrus 249b–255) without ever being explicitly linked.

16. The term *metaphor* is used in this volume in its wider sense, as a sort of symbol that represents a reality in ways that are comfortable for intuitive processes.

17. For a plausible portrait of the real Socrates, see Gomperz (1905, II.III, pp. 66–90).

18. Freud sometimes refers both to Socrates and to Plato. Jung often refers to Plato. But neither proposes Socrates as the archetype of the psychotherapist. Because they both had a solid philosophical education, they knew that Socrates and psychotherapists did not work on the same material, as I am about to demonstrate. I do not know how the relationship between Socrates and the image of the psychotherapist became so intimately linked (Lageman, 1989; Quétier, 2010; Roustang, 2009; Stein, 1991), but I do notice how it is firmly rooted in the discussions with colleagues.

19. Plato, *The Republic*, I, 354b. See Cooper (1997).

20. Roustang (2009), *avant-propos*.

21. Quétier (2010).

22. See Gomperz (1905, II.II.4, p. 49).

23. For Aristotle, the psyche and the soul are synonyms. His text on *Peri psyche* has been translated into Latin as *De anima,* and in English as *On the Soul.*

24. Technically, mathematics and geometry describes conceptual entities that are not Ideas. In his *Metaphysics,* Aristotle (1991, A.6.15, p. 13) writes that, for Plato, numbers are somewhere between sensate things and Ideas. They are different on the one hand from sensate objects, in that they are eternal and immobile, and, on the other hand, from Ideas, in that they are a plurality of similar examples, while the Idea is, in and of itself, a one, individual, and singular reality.

25. See also Plato, *Phaedrus* (in Jowett's translation of *The Dialogues of Plato*, 1937, 249, p. 253f).

26. Jean-Marie Baron helped me formulate, as clearly as possible, what is presented in this section.

27. See the discussion of Jacques Fradin in chapter 8 (p. 246f).

28. We shall see that this project results in the creation of the Academy (p. 104f).

29. Viscount T'ien Ch'eng of Ch'I "was said to have won the support of the people of Ch'I by using a larger-than-standard measure in dolling out grains to people, but the standard measure when collecting taxes in grain" (Chuang Tzu, ~319 X, p. 109).

30. Plato, *The Republic*, V, 506e. See Cooper (1997).

31. Plato, *The Republic*, VII, 507–522. See Cooper (1997).

32. Jung (1960, II.7.417, note 123).

33. Boadella (1987), Boyesen (1985), and Pierrakos (1990).

34. We are not too far off from the formulations of Taoist philosophy.

35. Jansen (1989), Rosenberg and Rand (1985, 9, p. 331f).

36. Jung (1931, p. 182).

37. Heisler (1973), Jung (1954).

38. Laszlo (2004, II.8.1, p. 183f).

39. The point of view that social dynamics can construct ideas that no individual can create is, for example, defended in anthropology by Boyd and Richerson (1996, 2005).

40. Wilber (2000, p. 96f) is a philosopher often mentioned in body psychotherapy conferences. He is particularly appreciated by those psychotherapists who think that their work has an important spiritual dimension, for example, Aalberse (2001) or Marlock and Weiss (2001).

41. See Atran (2010).

42. Laszlo (2004).

43. It is not impossible that Freud had this very discussion in mind when he distinguished the forces of Eros and Thanatos in the libido. In *Beyond the Pleasure Principle,* Freud (1920, p. 57) quotes what Aristophanes recounts in Plato's Symposium. Theodore Gomperz, specialist on the Greek thought of this period, has drawn his attention to this passage.

44. This development announces the notion of emergence, because particular ways to organize high and low notes can give birth to a musical chord. The organization of the elements allows for the creation of an acoustic event that presents to the ear something that is contained in neither the high nor the low note.

45. French psychoanalysts talk of "fusional couples."

46. In his account of Ulysses's sojourn with the Cyrene, Homer provides a good example of what can happen when someone lingers forever in port.

47. As in the first part of *Phaedrus*.

48. It is interesting to see Aristophanes criticize in Socrates what Plato criticizes in the sophists.

49. This position is developed in a fable showing that a ship's pilot cannot be replaced by any other sailor, because to pilot a ship requires a skill that is not made in a ballot box (*The Republic*, VI, 487–490; see Cooper, 1997). This preoccupation is always current, as Bourdieu indicates: In France, "the nineteenth-century reformers expected above all" that education could "ensure the proper function of universal suffrage by producing citizens capable of voting" (Pierre Bourdieu, 1979, 8, p. 414).

50. A recent example is the one of the government of the United States led by President George W. Bush, when he lied about the existence of weapons of mass destruction so that the citizens of his country would accept military involvement against Iraq.

51. Plato, *The Republic*, V, 459, p. 720f. See Jourett (1937).

52. In this text, love grows wings and transforms the young lover into a winged partner.

53. Plato, *The Symposium* (in Jowett's translation of *The Dialogues of Plato*, 1937, 181 a–b, p. 309).

54. Nicole Loraux (2001).

55. Plato, *The Symposium* (in Jowett's translation of *The Dialogues of Plato*, 1937, 179b, p. 307).

56. Plato, *Phaedrus* (in Jowett's translation of *The Dialogues of Plato*, 1937, 250–257). The inclusion of loving a young man in the love of beauty or of being loved as a young man is not explicit and can be more or less hidden by translators such as Jowett.

57. Calame (1992).

58. Loraux (2001, 3.4, p. 75f).

59. Three hundred sixty people voted to have Socrates condemned to death (Gomperz, 1905, II.V.3, p. 100).

60. For more on this Academy, and on idealism, see Sloterdijk (1998, preliminary remarks, pp. 11–15).

CHAPTER 4

Husserl (1936) is the reference for this chapter and the following one. His book is too difficult to read for me to recommend it to everyone.

1. When David Hume visited the College of Fleche in 1735, he discovered a community of Jesuits who defend the thinking of Descartes and his students (Mossner, 1980, I.8, 100f).

2. The painter Vermeer, for example, was Catholic. We shall see, in speaking about Spinoza, that the Jewish community was relatively well integrated in the Protestant United Provinces (Netherlands).

3. Fernand Braudel (1979, II.I, pp. 96–106).

4. Lott (1959): notes on Shakespeare's *Twelfth Night.*

5. Husserl (1936, II.10, 60f).

6. In the traditional perspective, God creates each object and each individual. This is the theory of creationism. In the mind of those scientists who want to preserve a place for God, God would have created the laws that create the objects and would have left a trace of His substance in the souls of beings.

7. Descartes (1649, *Les Passions de l'Âme,* I.30, p. 710).

8. Aristotle (*Of the Soul,* I.2).

9. We will find analogous distinctions in many authors of the twentieth century. For example, in the section dedicated to Henri Laborit's ascending and descending causal chains (chapter 8, p. 223f), I summarize a similar distinction between structural information and circulating information, between information proper to a level of the organism (cells, organs, etc.), or an information that permits the coordination of these levels.

10. The theme of the realm of thoughts is well explained by Alquié (1955, chapter 1).

11. Descartes (1641, *Meditations: Second Responses, Reasons,* p. 390). Most English translations published the main part of the text that Descartes wrote, but not the critiques and the responses to these critiques that the French editions also publish, which are sometimes extremely interesting.

12. Descartes (1649, *Les Passions de l'Âme,* I.17, p. 704).

13. See J. Allan Hobson (1999, p. 11), Rochat (2002).

14. Hobbes is useful to this discussion because he lived between two generations: Descartes's generation that uses the term conscious very rarely, and the generation of Descartes's students, which uses the term more often, to qualify the *reflexive* dimension of thoughts. His writings on thoughts are demonstrably a witness to the changing vocabulary and concepts taking place during that period.

15. Goelzer (1928).

16. Bruner (2008), Heller (2006), Tomasello (1999, 3), Tronick (1998).

17. Rochat (2001, 2009).

18. Rochat (2009).

19. For example, in *The New Oxford Dictionary of English* (1999).

20. According to Alain Rey, *Dictionnaire historique de la langue française: conscience* (*Dictionary of the History of the French Language,* 1992).

21. Perls, Hefferline, and Goodman (1951).

22. Descartes (1646, *Le traité de l'homme*). The relationship between the H gland and the pineal gland is already considered as established by Spinoza (1677a, V, Preface, p. 161f).

23. Crick (1995), Damasio (1999), and Pert (1997).

24. *The Excercitatio Anatomica de Motu Cordiset Sanguinis in Animalibus* by Harvey was published in 1628 in Frankfurt.

25. Descartes does not use this term, and he does not have an equivalent concept. He is content with naming hunger, thirst, appetite, and so on.

26. The same type of mechanisms are described by David Hume and Charles Darwin.

CHAPTER 5

The work of Pierre Macherey (1994) develops the themes that Spinoza only sketched in his *Ethics*.

1. I have added a few references to Buddhist thought to indicate two things: first, to show that the philosophers of the Enlightenment rediscover formulations already found in the writings of Tibetan Buddhists in the Middle Ages and second, to show how a method like introspection through meditation leads to robust results that are found in different cultures. Philosophies and art from the Far East were in vogue. Leibnitz incorporated several aspects of the philosophy of Confucius (Perkins, 2004). Hume may have discussed Buddhist ideas with Jesuit scholars at the Royal College of La Flèche (Gopnick, 2009).

2. This is one of the first analyses of human nature that calls for the necessity of using the most economical hypothesis possible.

3. In both cases, we are in a theory where there exists but one creative force.

4. This term is defined in chapter 10 (p. 278f), in sections dedicated to Newton.

5. This vision has many points in common with those of the Taoist philosophers.

6. Spinoza (1677a, V, Preface, p. 161f, 677a).

7. This notion is quite close to the one that scientists like Cannon and Tronick developed later, which I speak of in chapters 8 (see p. 200f) and 21 (see p. 614f).

8. This point is only valid if, like Spinoza, you believe that Nature is perfect.

9. Spinoza (1677a, III, proposition VII, demonstration, II/146, p. 75).

10. This is what Damasio describes in his book (2003) on Spinoza.

11. Spinoza (1677a, III, definitions, p. 69f). For a more recent analysis of this hypothesis in cognitive therapy, see Beck and Emery (1985, p. 188).

12. This analysis is close to those recently developed by the cognitive movement in psychotherapy and in the theories of emotions. See Solomon (1977).

13. Spinoza (1677a, III, proposition I, p. 70).

14. Contemporary research on ketamine identifies the link between depression and the way the brain makes new permanent cells in itself. According to this research, depression inhibits the mechanisms that renew nerve cells. See http://www.nimh.nih.gov/science-news/2007/faster-acting-antidepressants-closer-to-becoming-a-reality.shtml (accessed May 2010).

15. Here we are in the domains of necessary illusions that I define in chapter 6 (p. 148f).

16. We will see that this is the principal function of the unconscious in Freud's first topography.

17. For Spinoza, physiology is part of what he calls the body.

18. Helmholtz (1853).

19. Roger D. Masters et al. (1991), Siegfried Frey (1999, 2006).

20. Spinoza (1677a, II, propositions 16–17, II.104–106, p. 44f); Heller (2006).

21. This term is used, as always in this book, as it is by Jean Piaget in all of his works. It stresses the need to understand that the way we perceive reality is necessarily a mental and social construction. The same can be said of behavioral patterns and social dynamics.

22. Spinoza's *A Political Treatise* (1677b, II.12, p. 296f).

23. Heller (2006).

24. This argument is based on my clinical observations (Heller, 2006); it is not found in Spinoza's theory. The argumentation is close to that used to explain the effects of sensory deprivation (see Glossary).

25. For example, Reich (1952a, 3, p. 119); Fivaz-Depeursinge (1987); Beebe and colleagues (2005, I, pp. 10–28).

26. Watzlawick et al. (1967), Bateson (1972), Winkin (1981) and Gammer (2005).

CHAPTER 6

References for this section include Mossner (1980) and Husserl (1936, II.23–24, pp. 86–90).

1. Mossner (1980, I.4–9).

2. Quoted in Mossner (1980, I, 6, p. 75).

3. Hume (1737, I.4.2.42, p. 138).

4. We have to wait for the theories of Lamarck and Darwin to show that Hume is probably right. The theory of evolution demonstrates that this functioning acquired a certain relevance, thanks to the natural selection. This is discussed at the beginning of chapter 7 on the theory of evolution. Hume attributed to nature the power to create the mind, all the while knowing that in his time no one could understand how nature functioned. More recently, Rene Roussillon (2007) shows that this position is always a current topic in psychoanalysis and neurology.

5. As quoted by Gopnik (2009). Gopnik is professor of psychology and affiliate professor of philosophy at the University of California at Berkeley.

6. I do not know the connection between Hume's and Freud's thinking, but there are several similarities between their theories. It is possible that Kant is one of the intermediary thinkers, but probably not the only one. The management of the notion of intensity in Freud is close to that of Spinoza (power) and of Hume. It is also true about the way that Freud approaches the notion of truth in science (for example, Freud, 1915b, 210–211, p. 117).

7. Hume (1740, 1.3.2.1–13 p. 52f).

8. I differentiate between (a) what is perceived by a retina situated outside of the organism; (b) what the retina produces in the nervous system; (c) the thought that organize themselves around (b). Hume supposes that (c) is more complex than (b). (a) could be more complex than (c), but not necessarily.

9. Hume (1737, I.3.8.4, p. 70). These are formal rules. They operate notwithstanding the associated content and no matter what content is constructed by an association.

10. I comment on the Freudian notion of catharsis or excitation in the sections dedicated to Freud's first topography (1900, VII. c–f, pp. 550–620). Also see Downing (2000, p. 249f).

11. Hume (1737, I.IV.5.30, p. 162). As Hume develops this theme, we might think that he is near to the thought of the yogis. Unfortunately, it is only a thought made while commenting on the work of Spinoza that will not be taken up again. I mention it only to show that the theories of the eighteenth century could have facilitated the development of the idea of body psychotherapy; however, the philosophers finally developed other themes. Recent research in the neurosciences (De Lange et al., 2008) has found mechanisms that partially support this analysis.

12. Hume (1737, II.1.3. and 4, pp. 384–387).

13. Hume (1737, I.4.6.19, p. 170).

14. Montaigne (1592, I.XXVI, p. 233), for example, speaks of "natural propensity." Also see Elster (1998, IV.2, p. 244).

15. Hume (1737, I.4.2, p. 37f; 2.3.9.3, p. 280f).

16. Hume (1737, 2.2.22, p. 216f).

17. Hume (1737, 1.3.113.10, p. 100f). Also see Heller (2004c, 2005).

18. I make reference here to a letter made public, written by Adam Smith, November 9, 1776, in which he describes in minute detail Hume's dignity in the face of death. Hume was a religious skeptic but not an atheist. See Gaskin's (1993) introduction for a nuanced vision of Hume's views on religion.

19. See, for example, Mossner (1980, 28, pp. 395–402).

20. Cassirer (1932), Kant (1784).

21. Darwin was in a similar state before he discovered Wallace's formulation on the survival of the fittest. See chapter 7 (p. 170).

22. Husserl (1936, II. 23–27, p. 86f).

23. Husserl (1936, II. 25, p. 91f).

24. For example, Fodor (2003).

25. Gregory Bateson (1991).

26. Kant (1787, *Critique of Pure Reason*, II.II, p. 249f).

27. My way of using this term is defined in chapter 10 (p. 278f), in sections dedicated to Newton.

28. Kant (1787, *Critique of Pure Reason*, III–IV, p. 342f).

29. For a summary, see Kant (1783).

30. A perception is a form of intuition that we have of a real object.

31. Kant (1787, *Critique of Pure Reason*, "Of the Paralogisms of Pure Reason," p. 233f).

32. Reduction is used as in phenomenology and cooking, as when a sauce is boiled to become thicker and tastier.

33. That is, for example, the attitude recommended by Gerda Boyesen, Ronnie D. Laing, and James Hillman.

34. See the volume edited by Mark Wrathall and Jeff Malpas (2000) on Hubert L. Dreyfus. Part II of the second volume groups articles of four authors: Daniel Andler, Sean D. Kelly, Harry M. Collins, and Albert Borgmann. They discuss Dreyfus's idea that as thought is embedded in sensory-motor circuits, it cannot exist as a form of "disembodied" computation, as it is carried out by a machine and its neural circuits. Idealists, of course, would not adopt such an argument.

35. As a reminder: in speaking of Plato's cave, I had mentioned that Jung associated these shadows to the mind, and to the uncontrollable power of thoughts.

36. Freud (1900, VII).

37. For example, Kaplan-Solms and Solms (2000), Magistretti and Ansermet (2004), Roussillon (2007).

CHAPTER 7

1. See *The Structure of the Scientific Revolutions* by Thomas Samuel Kuhn (1962) and *The Order of Things: An Archeology of the Human Sciences* by Michel Foucault (1966) explore this theme masterfully.

2. I do not know what causal link related Lamarck's inspiration to that of Hegel's.

3. Hegel (1828). This is the part of Hegel's work that was integrated by Marx.

4. Hegel begins his *Lectures on the History of Philosophy* (1833) by discussing Hindu and Chinese philosophers.

5. Leroi-Gourhan (1964).

6. Our planet formed itself some billions of years ago.

7. Lamarck (1820, I.II.2, p. 36).

8. Lepeltier (2007, 2.2, p. 66f).

9. Jacob (2000).

10. Johann Gregor Mendel was an Austrian monk who discovered the laws of combinatorial genetics in 1865. Wallace and Darwin died without knowing of his works. The synthesis of these two bases for the theory of evolution in the twentieth century was subsequently completed in the 1920s by several biologists (e.g., Mayr, 1942).

11. These remarks forecast some of Reich's positions (1951) at the end of his life. In effect, Reich perceives sexual orgasm as a particular case in the way that vital energy creates what exists.

12. Lamarck (1809, III, p. 213). When discussing the underlying mechanisms of stress in chapter 8, p. 212f, we shall see several examples of constructive biological mechanism that can become destructive in some cases.

13. Buss (2003), Cyrulnik (2006), Masters (1995).

14. Lamarck uses the word body to designate the organism. This usage still persists with some authors (e.g., Bourdieu 1997).

15. Lamarck lived through the time of the royalty, the period of the guillotine, and the Napoleonic Wars.

16. *Hypocephalon* is Lamarck's term for the neocortex.

17. Lamarck (1809, p. 492f). This is the reptilian brain in MacLean's theories (1973).

18. For Lamarck, the brain is under the neo-cortex.

19. For affects Lamarck talks of *sentiments*.

20. See the sections on the myth of an emotional brain in chapter 8, pp. 236f and 246f.

21. This term is often used, for example, in Lamarck (1809, III.I, p. 468f). Lamarck was clearly against theories on the localization of mental functions in zones of the brain as defended by his colleague Gall (see chapter 9, p. 258).

22. Lamarck specifies in this section that he is referring to the organization of an organism that contains a neocortex and not only to the neocortex. See Lamarck (1809, III.I, p. 292).

23. For example, see Eccles (1989) and Lorenz (1973).

24. Damasio (1999), Edelman and Tononi (2000).

25. Koestler (1968, XVI), Liss (2001).

26. Cozolino (2006, p. 24f).

27. This section is based on Lamarck (1820, II.II.1, p. 206f).

28. This principle is found in Descartes, Hume, and Darwin.

29. I notice two camps: (a) Descartes and Hume, for whom the passions are the psychophysiological movements of the affects, and (b) Spinoza and Lamarck, for whom the passions are deregulated affects.

30. See p. 141f on Hume and propensity.

31. Lamarck opposed "su" and "inssu" (known and unknown), which remains the most elegant formulation in French. Jacques Lacan sometimes used this term to discuss Freud's unconscious.

32. Leroi-Gourhan (1964) develops a model that details the way the shape of the body, behaviors, the invention of tools, and the size of the brain mutually influenced each other. These reciprocal interactions participated in the evolution of the human organism for millions of years.

33. The term *schema,* inspired by Kant, is used in the Piagetian literature to designate a system that organizes the mental and bodily mechanisms that allow for the repetition of a way of doing things and to modify it in function of the particularities of an environment (Inhelder and de Caprona, 1992, p. 40f). Piaget defended a typical Swiss neutrality in debates on the respective advantages of the theories inspired by Lamarck and Darwin. He defended the right to use the best of both theories during the cold war, when all who referred to Lamarck where condemned as communists and biased by anti-communist scientists.

34. Downing (1996), Thelen and Smith (1994).

35. Lamarck (1820, II.II.1, p. 209).

36. Lamarck (1815, p. 255f), Lamarck (1820, II.II.1. and III, pp. 218 and 260).

37. I am grateful to Siegfried Frey, who helped me discover the multiple facets of Wallace's theory at the occasion of our many discussions in Duisburg.

38. A proof of the long-standing prejudice against Lamarck in English-speaking nations is that the only English translation of his work that I was able to find is his *Zoological Philosophy,* which is not his most interesting text. Furthermore, the translation has several mistakes (e.g., does not say what Lamarck said). I assume that Darwin read him in French.

39. In this work, Darwin did not write anything on the theory of evolution. He was content to describe only what he had seen.

40. This is the sixth edition of a work that first appeared in 1798.

41. Wallace (1876, 1881).

42. It is Charles Lyell who put forth the idea of the evolution of the Earth's crust.

43. This is where the law of Malthus fits in.

44. These changes are explained when the notion of genes is integrated in evolution theory during the first half of the twentieth century.

45. This form of political "Darwinism" was not developed by Darwin but by his cousin, Francis Galton, founder of eugenics. Neither Wallace nor Darwin were in favor of such developments. Various ways of understanding what is meant by "survival of the fittest" have had dramatic political implications.

46. This meaning was developed by other authors, such as Utilitarian and evolutionist philosopher Herbert Spencer.

47. Berry (2002, pp. 213–214).

48. Wallace (1908, XXI).

49. Wallace (1908, XXIII, p. 381).

50. See Darwin (1871, I.IV, p. 137f).

51. Wallace (1908, XV, p. 224). Here, Wallace speaks of a person who existed and whom he knew.

52. Recommended biography: Desmond and Moore (1991). I am grateful to Christine Caldwell, who forced me to take Darwin's thinking seriously and to love it.

53. The captain adored Lavater's physiognomy.

54. See Desmond and Moore (1991).

55. Frijda (1986, pp. 11–16).

56. Ekman (1979, p. 196), Morris (1978, 26).

57. Boadella (1980, p. 3).

58. Darwin (1872, XIV, p. 359).

59. This argument is mostly developed in *The Descent of Men* (Darwin, 1871, I.IV, p. 153f).

60. I am grateful to Siegfried Frey to have brought my attention to this analysis at the occasion of our many discussions on the theories of emotions.

61. For example, Darwin (1872, I, p. 42; III, pp. 74–76; VI, p. 175; VIII, p. 196; X, p. 239).

62. For example, Darwin (1872, I, pp. 39–42).

63. Darwin (1872, III, p. 67). In this example, as in many others, we see that Darwin regularly invokes Lamarck's second law, even at the end of his life.

64. Darwin (1872, IV, pp. 88–98).

65. Darwin (1872, VI, p. 174f).

66. This is a kind of secondary gain that does not really justify the presence of the trait in the human behavioral repertoire.

67. The reasons I detail this list will become apparent in my discussion of Paul Ekman's theory of emotional expressions in chapter 9, p. 262f.

68. The platysma muscle runs the length of the neck, from the corner of the lips to the shoulder. It is under the control of the facial nerve. It raises the skin of the pectoral and clavicle regions and lowers the interior lip by pulling downward on the corner of the mouth when it contracts.

69. Darwin (1871).

70. Darwin (1872, Introduction, p. 9).

71. Darwin (1872, I, p. 27f).

72. Darwin (1872, I, p. 50).

73. Darwin (1872, Introduction, p. 2).

74. Darwin (1872, VI, p. 158).

75. This analysis by Darwin has been renewed and strengthened by the material brought forth by Zajonc (1985) and colleagues (1989).

76. Chen et al. (2004), Kocer et al. (2002).

77. Darwin (1872, XIV, p. 350f).

78. See, for example, the first pages of Darwin (1871, IV).

79. Darwin's phrase is: "can be transmitted" (Darwin, 1872, I, p. 30). This influence of habits on the nervous system is today largely confirmed by numerous studies that show how experience calibrates the nervous system (for example, Magistretti and Ansermet, 2004). The second half of the argument, on the other hand, has been proven wrong by the study of genes. However, this refutation of Lamarck's law has not found its final formulation.

80. For example, Darwin (1872, I, p. 39, and II, p. 61).

81. See, for example, Jacob (2000).

82. For example, Bateson (1972, V.3, p. 429).

83. Griffiths (1997, p. 65).

84. Kolb (1990).

85. We have here an example of the way that many humans reinforce, without being aware of it, the Idealistic version of a theory that is not Idealist. The formulation I have employed is a compromise between Lamarck's theory and Hegel's.

86. Based principally on the DVD edition (1994–2002) of the Encyclopedia Britannica, Inc.

87. Based principally on the DVD edition (1994–2002) of the Encyclopedia Britannica, Inc.

88. These sections are influenced by several years of discussion in the seminar on artificial intelligence organized by André Haynal at the Geneva Psychiatric University Institutions during the 1990s. The regular participants were Gunther Albers, Guy Cellérier, Jean-Jacques Ducret, André Haynal, Michael Heller, Olivier Real, Daniel Stern, and Richard Vuagniaux. Other joined us for a series of particular discussions, like Bärbel Inhelder.

89. Clark (1997, 2000).

90. Operating systems are the program that appears on the screen when you turn your computer on. It is, like Windows or UNIX, the program that allows other programs (e.g., a word processor) to function in a particular computer.

91. See also the section in chapter 14, p. 374f, on the neurological models developed in Roger W. Sperry's team.

92. Gazzaniga, Bogen, and Sperry (1965), Hubel (1963), Hubel and Wiesel (1963), Sperry (1981). Hubel, Wiesel, and Sperry received the 1981 Nobel Prize for Medicine for their work in neurology.

93. Gazzaniga (1985).

94. In mathematics, the opposition of parallel and sequential corresponds to linear and matrix procedures.

95. See the discussion concerning Johnson-Laird (1988) in Crick (1995, p. 205).

96. I use this term in the same sense Spinoza does, that is, to designate the profusion of perceptions, memories, fantasies, and reflections that ceaselessly inject dynamism into consciousness.

97. Theories like Hume's assumed that this would be enough because they did not take into consideration the complexities required for motor action.

98. See Coppin (2004, 4, pp. 98–115), Newell (1990), and Newell and Simon (1972).

99. See, for example, Pfeifer and Bongard (2006).

100. A similar discussion can be found in Varela (1988, pp. 75–85). Chilean biologist Francisco Javier Varela introduced the notion of embodied mind to many body psychotherapists. They were interested in his way of associating notions developed in artificial intelligence with the Buddhist notion of mindfulness.

101. Cellérier (1968).

102. Cellérier (2010).

103. Anorexia has many variations. This explanation is close to the one developed by Bateson (1972, III, pp. 206–227; pp. 244–270) concerning the double-bind.

104. I am grateful to Alison Duguid for her advice on this section. Above and beyond her academic position and her research in linguistics, Duguid is a body psychotherapist and was the president of the European Association of Body Psychotherapy from 1993 to 1995. She is one of the researchers in the human sciences who found it useful to create bridges between a Reichian body psychotherapy and contemporary research.

105. Fogel, Lyra, and Valsiner (1997), Mann (1973), Thelen and Smith (1994).

106. From the moment that there are several ways to coordinate a thought and a gesture, we remain with the concept of an indirect connection because there necessarily exists one or more switching mechanisms that activate or shut off a form of direct relationship.

107. Kosko (1993), MacNeil and Freiberger (1993).

108. The form is often: If X = A then instruction 1, if X = B then instruction 2, if X = C then instruction 3, or then instruction 4. See MacNeil and Freiberger (1993).

109. Clark (1997, 8.4).

110. Elster (1998, I.2, p. 6; I.4, p. 23). See also the first chapter of Fradin (2008).

111. Clark (1997, 6.2, p. 107).

112. Moessinger (2008) gives several examples of this type of causality.

113. This vision has recently been defended by Theodore Gomperz (1905).

114. Jacob (2000, p. 4f).

115. Bourdieu (1979), Cellérier (1992a, 1992b).

CHAPTER 8

A good general introduction to this domain is *La legende des comportements* (*The legend of the behaviors*). For this period, the English reader can refer to Buck (1988).

1. See the Foreword Philippe Rochat wrote for this book.

2. See Foucault (1996), *The Order of Things: An Archaeology of Human Sciences.*

3. François Jacob (2000).

4. See Gross (1998) for a general presentation of Claude Bernard.

5. The French title refers to biology, not to medicine.

6. Boadella (1980, 1987, 2004), G. Boyesen (1985a, II.12, pp. 88–90), Reich (1951).

7. Lamarck (1809, p. 474f).

8. The pH measures how acidic or basic a solution is. The measure supposes that there exists a correlation between the acidity of a solution and the concentration of positive hydrogen ions (pH= –log [H+]).

9. Bernard (1865, II.I.ii, p. 102).

10. The vitalistic movement thinks that there would be a life energy without which life is not possible. Henri Bergson's theory of the "élan vital" influenced Jung and Reich (Reich, 1919).

11. Lorenz (1973, IV.4, pp. 68–70).

12. The vegetative system is described in the section in this chapter on the system of vegetative regulation and affects, p. 207f.

13. Lorenz (1973, IV.4).

14. Lorenz (1973, IV.4, p. 68f).

15. Levine and Frederick (1997, 1, p. 15f).

16. Reich (1940, VII.5).

17. Cannon wrote an autobiography which he published in 1945. His most referenced work remains *The Wisdom of the Body.*

18. The link between the works of Bernard and Cannon and body psychotherapy is briefly commented on by Levine (1979b).

19. Letter from Neill to Reich dated July 4, 1942 (Reich and Neill, 1982).

20. For example, in his letter to Helen Antipoff, dated February 20, 1931, Édouard Claparède (2010) recommends Cannon's *Bodily Changes in Pain, Hunger, Fear & Rage.*

21. Cannon (1932, p. 24). See also Cannon (1915).

22. Darwin (1872, III, pp. 68–69). Field (1981) has since observed that the cardiac activity increases when two persons look into each other's eyes and that it decreases rapidly as soon as one person breaks the eye contact.

23. Tronick (2007, IV.27, p. 382f).

24. Freud's approach to sexuality, which is similar on these points, is discussed in the first part of chapter 15.

25. This concept is defined in the section in chapter 5 on Spinoza's views on the power of a system, p. 126f.

26. Haynal (1985, I.2, p. 40).

27. Haynal (1985, I.2.3, p. 55).

28. With regard to a psychiatric diagnosis, I often insist on the necessity to isolate marked or ostentatious particularities. This is to avoid labeling a banal character trait or a less intense version of a psychiatric symptom as a psychiatric diagnosis. Misplaced symptomatic attributions are regrettably frequent, even among psychiatrist colleagues as described in chapter 16, p. 445.

29. In such discussions I sometimes take up Yi-King's metaphor that associates consciousness to the captain of a ship discussed in chapter 2, p. 55. He can learn to be a pilot on a river (a mood) if he accepts that he is not able to dominate the river.

30. This is a theoretical example. I am talking of individuals who become obese because of their lifestyle in contrast to those who suffer from manifest innate endocrine problems.

31. Delvaux (2007, 13, p. 63f).

32. Garland et al. (2000).

33. See p. 211 in this chapter. Gershon, who mentions that most of the serotonin of the organism is made from digested carbohydrates. Most antidepressants are conceived from the hypothesis that a lack of serotonin is one of the principal causes of depression and of suicidal tendencies.

34. Golden and Meyer (2003), Wagner et al. (2006).

35. This point touches the issue of the coordination of global and local actions brought up at the end of chapter 7 in the sections dedicated to neo-Darwinism, p. 183f.

36. The term *parentified* is often used to describe children who must protect their parents.

37. Lehninger (1965) is an example of the way biologists of the 1960s approached the word *bioenergy*. See Popp (2001) for a more recent analysis.

38. Reich's orgone and Lowen's bioenergy are vital forces about which I speak in the sections devoted to them in chapters 18 and 19, pp. 499f and 557f, respectively.

39. See Ackernecht (1974), Gershon (1998, I.2, p. 8f). For a recent look at Langley's work, see Nozdrachev (2004).

40. Ackerknecht (1974).

41. Vegetotherapy is described in chapter 17.

42. Levensen et al. (1992).

43. Reich (1940, VII.6, p. 226).

44. Ibid.

45. Cannon and Rosenblueth (1937, III, p. 21).

46. Pert (1997), Uvnäs-Moberg (2003).

47. Cannon (1945, p. 38). See also Cannon (1945, pp. 92f and 109f), Cannon (1911) and Cannon (1936, IV).

48. Cannon (1936, p. 120).

49. Jacobson (1967, 8, pp. 128–131, IX, p. 140).

50. In 1942, Henri Wallon still assumes that the association between the digestive tract and emotions was a common knowledge. See also Braatøy (1954, p. 169).

51. Setekleiv (1980).

52. Braatøy (1954 VI.3, p. 168f).

53. To the left, in the lower abdomen.

54. G. Boyesen (1985a, II.8, pp. 75–82; II.12, pp. 88–90; II.15, pp. 96–98; III.15, pp. 155–162; annex 2, pp. 192–193).

55. Gershon (1998, I.2, pp. 8–36).

56. Nunnely (2000, 6, pp. 127–145).

57. This brings us back to Descartes' intuition, which he tried to illustrate with his famous gland "H."

58. Hobsbawm (1994, 2007).

59. Cocks (1997).

60. Freud 1920 and 1929.

61. See chapter 15, p. 400f, for additional information on this change of theory and on Freud's second topography.

62. I have personally verified this information with Malcolm Brown at the occasion of the 2006 EABP congress.

63. Goldstein (1939, VII.1.1, p. 230).

64. In the sections dedicated to acupuncture (p. 51), I had mentioned that this was already the position of the Chinese physicians.

65. Laborit (1985), Waal (2002).

66. See, for example, Edelman and Tononi (2000) and Vuilleumier (2005).

67. Cannon (1935).

68. A recommended book: *The Stress of Life* (Selye, 1978).

69. This type of sudden modifications is well described by chaos theory. See, for example, Fivaz (1993), Robertson and Combs (1995), and Van Geert (1994).

70. Selye uses the term *adaptation*, but I maintain a vocabulary coherent with the rest of the book.

71. Reich (1949a, III.XV.4, p. 434, Reich (1948b, IX.3, p. 345f).

72. Laborit (1989, 9.5, p. 171f).

73. LeDoux (2002, 8, p. 222f), Van der Kolk (1996a, pp. 293–296).

74. LeDoux (2002, 8, p. 223f).

75. Ibid., p. 281, Czéh et al. (2006), Malberg (2004), Mattson et al. (2004).

76. He signed all his books as Henri Laborit. However, if you want to find Web sites in English on his work, it is best to look for "Henri-Marie Laborit." I have not found English translations of Laborit's publications except *Decoding the Human Message*, which can be a good start, but it is out of print. He received the 1957 Albert Lasker Clinical Medical Research Award (http://www.laskerfoundation.org/awards/1957_c_description.htm#laborit). He is regularly discussed by certain body psychotherapists based in Europe. Apart from a few highly technical papers, the only English text of Laborit that I found is a transcript of a conference he gave in 1963 for the Alfred Korzybski memorial: *The Need for Generalization in Biological Research: Role of the Mathematical Theory of Ensembles.* Available at http://www.generalsemantics.org/misc/akml/akmls/30-31-laborit.pdf (retrieved March 2011).

77. In Laborit (1994), for example.

78. I summarize Laborit's (1989, 7.3) proposition.

79. Laborit (1989, 7.5, p. 108, 8.1, p. 137f).

80. Laborit (1968, 5, pp. 66–75).

81. Laborit (1989, 9.5, p. 171f).

82. See Reich (1946).

83. See Ogden et al. (2006, p. 124) for an example of this form of analysis in body psychotherapy.

84. See also Laborit (1968, 5, pp. 66–75).

85. This does not mean that Laborit was not interested by psychologists such as Piaget, or psychotherapists such as Freud and Reich. The word *psychoanalysis*, used in a wide sense, often appears in his books and conferences.

86. See also Laborit (1968, 5, pp. 66–75).

87. Laborit (1989, 8.1, p. 137f).

88. Laborit (1989, X.3, p. 199f).

89. Reich (1952a, p. 45).

90. Laborit (1989, X.5, p. 203f).

91. See Roelofs et al. (2009).

92. A technical point: the actual formulas focus too much on the comparison of the averages and not enough on the comparison of the variances. For example, a group where everyone does the same thing is different from a group where no one does the same thing. This type of distinction is currently treated poorly by the statistical systems required for publication in an academic journal. See Lemaine and Matalon (1985) for the beginning of a discussion on this topic; also see my discussion on Darwin's theory on the theoretical importance to include the notion of variation in the theories on the biological, psychological, and social mechanisms in chapter 7, p. 176f.

93. In chapter 15 (p. 385), I write about the research on hospitalism (Spitz, 1965) and young monkeys (Harlow, 1986), which goes in the same direction.

94. Uvnäs-Moberg (1989).

95. Uvnäs-Moberg uses the word love, which seems to me to be excessive.

96. Keverne and Kendrick (1994).

97. Pheromones are hormones secreted to have an impact on other organisms, while the classic hormones are secreted to have an impact on the regulation of the organism that secretes them. The vomeronasal organ, or Jacobson's organ, is situated inside the nose. In many mammals, it detects the pheromones. In humans, this detection passes through more complex circuits because they have an atrophied vomeronasal organ.

98. I refer to discussions between Ebba Boyesen, Uvnäs-Moberg, and myself. We were able to verify that these strokes are close to the massage of harmonization and distribution taught by Gerda Boyesen and her colleagues in biodynamic psychology. These discussions took place in the context of the EABP Congresses of 2004 and 2006.

99. The regions of the brain mentioned in this section are easy to find in anatomic drawings. It suffices to type in the name of the zone that interest you in a search engine to find the pertinent illustrations. If you add to the zone the name of the author or the phenomenon mentioned in this text, you will obtain complementary information.

100. See the section on Lamarck's neurology in chapter 7, p. 162.

101. The limbic system corresponds to Lamarck's "brain" (1809, p. 495; 1815, pp. 225–239). It is situated at the center of the brain under the two cortical lobes and above the brainstem.

102. See Bard (1928), Cannon (1927).

103. Cannon talks about the thalamus. But it is possible that other limbic regions are concerned, which does not change much to Cannon's and Bard's 1928 model.

104. The well-known names in this group are Papez (1937), MacLean (1969), Laborit (1979), Delgado (1969), Van der Kolk (1966b, 2006) and LeDoux (1996, 1999). See also Ganong (1999, pp. 248–249). Often, they have not read Lamarck; they do not

know the historical origin of this idea. Nevertheless, this is the hypothesis they work with.

105. Damasio (2003, 2, p. 61).

106. For more information on this event, consult the website on the Nobel Prizes: http://nobelprize.org/nobel_prizes/medicine/laureates/1949/moniz-bio.html

107. Joseph LeDoux (1996), for example, showed that fear is associated to the amygdala, situated in the limbic system, near the thalamus. A few years later, he quoted research that shows connections between the amygdala and the prefrontal cortex. These connections can sometimes modify or even inhibit reactions of fear (LeDoux, 2002, 8, p. 220).

108. Especially Betta de Boer Van der Kolk, Peter Levine, Pat Ogden, and Al Pesso. English articles on the fascinating work of Van der Kolk can be found on the Website http://www.traumacenter.org. See also Levine and Frederick (1997), Ogden et al. (2006), and Rothschild (2000).

109. For example, Panksepp and Smith Pasqualini (2005), Schore (2003), Stern (2010, p. 109), Trevarthen, (2005, p. 67).

110. Edelman and Tononi (2000), Rolls (1999, 4.I, p. 76, 4.5.5.1, and 4.8).

111. For a complementary model of the association between affects and the neocortex, see Cozolino (2006, III), Fradin (2008 p. 51), or Radley and Morrison (2005).

112. Kaplan-Solms and Solms (2000).

113. Also see the section on Edmund Jacobson's relaxation technique in chapter 11, p. 284f.

114. For example, Papez (1937).

115. Donald Hebb is one of the founders of the neurosciences. He is mostly known for his book *The Organization of Behavior* (1949). He details the neuronal circuits and shows that they form complex channels of information. In requiring detailed models of nerve connections associated to a behavior, his proposition is one of the foundations for attempting to construct artificial neural networks (ANN) in a computer which functions like a nervous system.

116. Olds (1965).

117. Boutrel (2006).

118. Laborit (1989, X.6, p. 208).

119. See, for example, Aboujaoude (2011).

120. See Jacob (2000) and Nüsslein-Volhard (2006).

121. See the section in chapter 6 on Spinoza's analysis of complexity, p. 139f.

122. Delgado (1960, 1969), Plotnik, Mir, and Delgado (1971).

123. Delgado (1969).

124. Aggression can be unleashed by electrodes planted in parts of the brain as different as the caudate nucleus (the anterior part of the limbic system) and the red nucleus (under the thalamus toward the top of the brainstem).

125. Henley (1977, p. 127).

126. Cerebrospinal fluids circulate at the center of the spinal column and surround the brain.

127. Freud (1915c, p. 250f).

128. Magistretti (1994), Ringo et al. (1994).

129. See Pandey et al., 2002, Stefulj et al., 2004, and Wasserman, 2006.

130. Moss et al. (1990).

131. I am grateful to Maartin Aalberse for the particularly astute assistance he provided me while I worked on this section. I remain responsible for the finale formulation proposed in this text.

132. Letter from Henri Laborit to Jacques and Fanny Fradin, November 20, 1992, published in Fradin and Fradin (2006).

133. Some of these authors are useful to the body psychotherapist, like Damasio and colleagues (2000), Posner (2005), or Posner and Rothbart (2000), who confirm that the affects are part of the complex systems of the organism's auto-regulation, which includes many zones of the brain, situated in the brainstem, the limbic system, and various zones of the neocortex, and physiological mechanisms situated outside of the brain (like the dynamic of the neurotransmitters). These articles notably confirm the importance of the frontal zones of the neocortex in the affective mechanisms. Posner also proposes a neurological description of certain systems of auto-regulation.

134. Rochat (2010).

135. See LeDoux (1996). Fradin relates these behaviors to certain centers of the reptilian brain. We again find a neurological network that associates neocortex–limbic–brainstem in charitable and altruistic affects (Moll et al., 2006).

136. See Rolls (1999, 9.4, pp. 262–264).

137. The clinical approach of Fradin and his team is an example of a cognitive and behavioral approach that includes somatic methods.

138. This is more or less what Spinoza called imagination and Freud called the unconscious. The notion that neurological data entering the mind could often be of limbic origin is already illustrated in this chapter by a discussion on Cannon's neurological studies, p. 234f. See also Williamson et al. (2000) for simple information on fine sensory-motor practices.

139. George Downing's model, which I describe in chapter 22 (653f), arrives at similar therapeutic propositions but does so for different reasons.

140. See chapter 13, p. 334f.

141. Laborit (1971).

142. See chapter 5, p. 132f, for Spinoza's formulation on the power of groups.

143. See Rochat (1995) for an overview of self psychology in experimental psychology.

CHAPTER 9

1. For example, the work of Chevalier and Gheerbrant (1997).

2. See the section in chapter 20 on the impact of gestures during interactions, p. 575f.

3. Beautiful illustrations on the subject of this section are published in the work in German by Clair, Pichler, and Pircher (1989) on the body and mind in the chapters dedicated to physiognomy (articles by Baltruaitis and Madlener). The commentaries are equally interesting. It consists of a catalog of a magnificent exposition organized in Vienna for Freud's centenary.

4. Clair et al. (1989), Frey (1985).

5. Charles Le Brun was one of the most renowned painters of his time. He decorated many rooms in the Palace of Versailles for King Louis XIV. Examples of his draw-

ings can easily be found on the Web. For example, in September 2011, I found them on http://ia700501.us.archive.org/7/items/caracteresdespas00lebr/caracteresdespas00lebr .pdf and http://catdir.loc.gov/catdir/samples/cam031/00063010.pdf

6. Clair et al. (1989, *Physiognomik*, p. 164).

7. Clair et al. (1989) published several examples. See also Feleky (1924).

8. Dumont (1984).

9. Lamarck (1809, III, introduction, p. 459f).

10. Gall and Spurzheim (1810).

11. Lamarck (1809, III, introduction, p. 459).

12. Ajuriaguerra and Hécaen (1960, Introduction), Kaplan-Solms and Solms (2000, I.1), Luria (1963, I.1).

13. Translation proposed on the following Website, consulted in January 2010: http://www.historyofphrenology.org.uk/biblio.htm#gallsworks

14. Wallace (1908, IX, pp. 124–127). See chapter 7, p. 168f.

15. Mesmer's approach is situated in the sections dedicated to hypnosis in chapter 10, p. 275f.

16. To see concrete examples of the analysis using FACS, see Paul Ekman's site: http://www.paulekman.com (accessed in June 2010).

17. Heller et al. (2001).

18. Other models of the same type are those of Caroll Izard and SilvanSoloman Tomkins (Tomkins and Izard, 1965).

19. Ekman (1980a).

20. Ekman and Davidson (1993), Eibl-Eibesfeldt (1989).

21. Ekman (1980b).

22. Downing (2000), Griffiths (1997). See also Ekman and Davidson (1994), Kagan (2007, *What Is Emotion?*, I, pp. 18–19).

23. For examples of photographs of basic emotional expressions used by Ekman and Friesen, you can download Ekman and Friesen (1986) from http://www.paulekman .com/wp-content/uploads/2009/02/A-New-Pan-Cultural-Facial-Expression-Of-Emotion .pdf (accessed in February 2012).

24. These masks are part of what Reich referred to as a person's *character armor* (chapter 17, p. 479). Clinical experience shows that often (but not always) massaging these muscular facial tensions brings up intense emotions and memories.

25. Fridlund (1994), Izard (1971), Morris (1978), Tomkins and Izard (1965, III, p. 217f).

26. Krause and Lütolf (1988), Steimer-Krause et al. (1990).

27. Spinoza was an optician.

28. See the section in chapter 7 on Darwin and emotions, p. 170f.

29. Elster (1998, IV.1, p. 242f).

30. Hume (1737, 2.1.2, p. 182f).

31. A discourse that relates honor and the right to murder is today called traditional and outmoded. A modern understanding of honor and duels is developed by Elster (1998, III.4, p. 203f).

32. Ekman et al. (1997). See also P. Brown et al. (1991).

33. Ledoux (1996), Levine and Frederick (1997).

34. Heller (2004b).

35. Tronick (2007, III.13, p. 179).

36. Here is a reference given by Ekman (1997, p. 481): P. Ekman and W. Friesen,

Emotional Dictionary (Unpublished manuscript, University of California, San Francisco, 1989).

37. See Ekman and Rosenberg (1997).

38. This analysis is close to that of Spinoza on the interaction between cognition and affects (chapter 5, p. 127).

39. This paragraph is based on a 2010 manuscript written by Susanne Kaiser and Thomas Wehrle.

40. Ekman may have been inspired by such wording when he assumed that his theory of basic emotions was compatible with Darwin's theory of emotions. We have already seen that Darwin could easily change his wording from one page to another.

41. Bateson (1972, III.4, p. 227) has, for example, described the double binds that can develop between the therapist and the patient with this type of intervention.

42. Ekman (1985). The television series *Lie to Me* is a good example of how such direct forms of interpretation can be used by police officers. This series was explicitly presented by Ekman and Fox (the producers) as an illustration of the procedures developed by Ekman for advanced interview training for the police (see, for example, http://www.analyticinterviewing.org/Wordpress/?page_id=148 accessed in February 2012).

43. See Bandler and Grinder (1975) for an introduction to NLP.

44. Lowen (1994, V.3, p. 67f and V.10, p. 84f).

45. Lowen (1975, III.3, p. 89f; 1994, XII.11, p. 363f).

46. Lowen (1975, II.2, p. 49f).

47. Frey (2008) indicates the link between this notion and Helmholtz's unconscious inferences. These are described at the beginning of chapter 14 on the unconscious inferences of von Helmholtz and Wundt, p. 341f.

48. This anxiety is particularly well analyzed by Jacques Lacan's distinction between the Me and the I, summarized in chapter 14, p. 356.

49. See Frey (1993).

50. Translated by Marcel Duclos from a quote published by Frey (1985, p. 9).

51. Ledoux (1996), Tinbergen (1951). See also the section on the myth of the emotional brain in chapter 8, p. 234.

52. Also see Krause (1989).

53. This remark is close to what Spinoza said regarding the perception of the distance of the sun using imagination or reason (see chapter 5, p. 130). Both evaluations coexist even if they are contradictory.

54. Frey (1998, 2006).

55. Santiago-Delfosse (2004).

56. AU6 + AU12 in Ekman and Friesen's coding system. A smile of the mouth without the activity at the external corners of the eyes is not considered a true smile by these authors. The true smile expressed joy, while the other smiles can be simulated, can masque negative feelings, can express a form of sympathy, be a way to control another, and so on.

57. See Russell (1994), Russel and Fernandez-Dols (1997), and Wirth and Kaiser (2010) for a detailed critique of Ekman and Friesen's research methods.

58. Heller et al. (2001).

59. Translated by Michael C. Heller and Marcel Duclos. The published English translation of this paragraph by H. Elliot (p. 288) says the opposite. The French text is the following: "Le point essentiel à considérer, est que, dans tout système d'organisation animale, la nature ne peut avoir un seul moyen à sa disposition, pour faire exécuter aux différents organes les fonctions qui leur sont propres."

CHAPTER 10

1. Their symbols are still on the one-dollar bill.

2. The best introduction to these movements that I know of is the work of Wilson (1982). Even if this is a novel, it gives detailed information in a spirit that takes into account the preoccupations of some schools of body psychotherapy.

3. Koestler (1959).

4. Wirth (1923).

5. The French Academy of science studied Mesmer's theory on fluids and concluded that they did not exist, and that their effect could be explained by the psychological impact of Mesmer and his followers (Badinter and Badinter, 1988, 187ff). Although this commission contained some of the best scientists of this period (Nicolas de Condorcet, Benjamin Franklin, Antoine-Laurent de Lavoisier, etc.), their general attitude was biased against this type of movement.

6. Recent research in neurology has been able to demonstrate that certain beliefs can have specific effects on physiological dynamics (Bingel et al., 2008, Eippert et al., 2009).

7. Swedenborg is presented in a section of chapter 6 dedicated to Kant, p. 149.

8. In body psychotherapy, we find similar formulations in the concepts of orgone and bioenergy presented by the Reichian schools. See also Gomperz (1905, vol. 4, XV.1, p. 175).

9. Physicist Fritz-Albert Popp (2001) wrote an article on the contemporary theories of energy for body psychotherapists.

10. This term is introduced into the language of philosophers mostly by Aristotle. Newton uses it in Latin, but the term is not kept in English translations.

11. For the history of the relationship between Chinese and European thought, see Étiemble (1988).

12. Cauhepe and Kuang (1984), Tohei (1980).

CHAPTER 11

1. Huber (1982, p. 104).

2. Some of my patients experience lightness after a successful relaxation.

3. Huber (1982).

4. This is one of James's expressions (e.g., James 1890, p. 1007).

5. See James (1890), the chapter on the emotions; see also Cannon (1927).

6. Jacobson (1967, VII, p. 99f).

7. Reflux is the relaxation that is spontaneously activated once an effort is ended.

8. See Duffau (2006) and Taub (2004) for a contemporary evaluation of the question.

9. We find this observation in Braatøy (1942), and in the writings of Fenichel and Reich.

10. Braatøy (1942).

11. For more on body psychotherapy in Oslo in the 1950s, see chapter 19, pp. 525f and 554f.

12. Ajuriaguerra and Cahen (1960), Badoni (1997), Dechaud-Ferbus et al. (1994), Roux and Dechaud-Ferbus (1993).

CHAPTER 12

1. In this chapter the body is the one defined in the system of the dimensions of the organism that serves as the basic vocabulary in this manual. The body according to the gymnast is manifestly distinct from the physiologic system that regulates the organism.

2. Sambucy (1973, p. 106). The method of Joseph Hubertus Pilates (1883–1967) has become a popular way of working on this aspect of body dynamics.

3. Illustrations of these devices can be seen on the following site (accessed July 2009): http://yagosweb.blogspot.com/2008/06/gustav-zander-19th-century-gym.html

4. My interest in the importance of Gindler's influence in the history of psychotherapy was brought to my attention by George Downing in 2007, at the occasion of our discussion relative to writing the first edition of this book. This material has been enriched thanks to the comments of colleagues who reacted to my presentation of the French edition of this volume at the Congress on Body Psychotherapy, organized by François Lewin, in Paris, November 2008: David Boadella, Ulfried Geuter, Helen Payne, Judith O. Weaver, Gill Westland, and Courtenay Young. We have exchanged our understanding of this period by email, between the November 19 and 24, 2008, and during the month of June 2009. Not wanting to burden this text with useless references, I refer you to the bibliography of these authors at the end of this volume for more details, and to the article by Geuter et al. (2010).

5. For more information concerning this period, see the publications of Geuter (1996, 2004) and Geuter et al. (2010). Numerous examples of the world of artists mentioned in this section can be found easily with any search engine on the Internet.

6. Isadora Duncan became a part of the culture of Vienna and Berlin at the beginning of the twentieth century.

7. We find here another way to approach the notion of habitus of the phenomenologists of this period.

8. They are still part of today's discussions as we can see by typing their names into a search engine. I talk about some of them in other sections.

9. Kuj Noschis (2011).

10. Lowen (1975, X.1, p. 314).

11. See also Jacoby (1983, p. 61f).

12. Kaiser Wilhelm was the German emperor.

13. Geuter (2004) and Geuter et al. (2010).

14. Rudolf Steiner's method is called the Eurythmy. For pictures, see http://www.rudolfsteinerweb.com/Rudolf_Steiner_and_Eurythmy.php (accessed September 2010).

15. Notably, Adolphe Appia, Diaghilev's Ballets Russes, Bernard Shaw, Arthur Honegger, Ernest Bloch, Le Corbusier, Paul Claudel, Constantin Stanislavski, and Ernest Ansermet.

16. See the interview of Johanna Kulbach by Mary Alice Roche (1978b, p. 14) and Charlotte Selver (1978), who studied with Rudolf Bode, a student of Jacques-Dalcroze. Jacoby was also first educated in a Jacques-Dalcroze school.

17. Lowen also worked with this school. See Steinaecker (2000, p. 165).

18. Ludwig (2002, p. 18).

19. See the interview of Kulbach by Roche (1978b, p. 24).

20. Reference work: *The Power of Breath* (Hanish, 1970). To evaluate Hanish's impact on psychotherapists and gymnasts of today, I based this section on the following two publications: Sambucy, Sambucy, and Laubry (1973, vol. 2) and Roche (1978a), who

speaks of the profound influence of Hanish on Gindler. To the extent that Sambucy and Gindler represent two almost opposite viewpoints concerning gymnastics, these references show the range of influence Hanish had on the history of gymnastics in the twentieth century.

21. Sambucy and Laubry (1973, vol 2, p. 77).

22. Ibid., p. 86.

23. Ibid., p. 88.

24. The most blatant case is massage of the feet. Each technique teaches a chart of points on the feet that would have an effect on a specific other part of the body; but in each technique, the same point has a different effect. It suffices to compare the cartography of foot massage proposed by acupuncturists (especially for shiatsu) and that proposed by a more recent method, such as the reflexology.

25. Sambucy et al. (1973, vol. 2, p. 79).

26. Roche (1978a, p. 4).

27. References for this section: Charlotte Selver Foundation Bulletin 10, I (1978) and Geuter (2000a, 2000b, 2004).

28. This turn of events attracted musicians, like harpsichordist Wanda Landowska, who followed special courses with Gindler (C. Fenichel, 1981).

29. Mühlleitner (2008).

30. Ehrenfried (1991, p. 35).

31. Even if I would speak of a psyche reduced to the exigencies of the body in Gindler, this kind of remark, which is frequent enough among some psychoanalysts, demonstrates a reduction of body sensations to some theoretical psychological clichés that are pertinent only in some very specific cases.

32. See the section on Berlin from 1923 to 1929 in chapter 16, p. 421f.

33. Alice Smith (1978).

34. This paragraph summarizes certain parts of an interview with Clare Fenichel by Richard Lowe in Los Angeles, January 1978.

35. I permitted myself to take up Gindler's article in great depth because it shows very well the somatic foundations that influenced many body psychotherapists from Reich to Downing. This imposes itself even more because this article is not easy to obtain. The title was translated in different ways. I have chosen the one that is the most revealing.

36. Ehrenfried (1991, p. 34).

37. Franzen (1995).

38. Exploring gestures is well described in Aalberse (2001). See also Gendlin (1996, 1998, chapters 6 and 12).

39. Rytz works in the division of endocrinology, diabetology, and clinical nutrition of the Inselspital, one of the most famous Swiss university hospitals.

40. We again find this term in the vocabulary of the Reichian orgone therapy, used to describe a global shortening of all the tissues of the organism and the rigidity of the affects and thought.

41. See the section on postural dynamics and the return of the venous blood in the legs, in chapter 13, p. 331f.

42. See the section on the phases of respiration in the pranayama of yogis in chapter 1, p. 36.

43. Selver (1978).

44. Quoted in Roche (1978a, 1978b).

45. This technique makes explicit a state of diffused tension.

46. This analysis is at the heart of the critique that Otto Fenichel made of Reich's Vegetotherapy in Oslo. When he created his Orgonomic exercises, like the jellyfish exercises, Reich clearly integrated this critique without mentioning Fenichel or Gindler. These remarks will become clearer after having read the sections on Reich's Vegetotherapy in chapter 17.

47. I had this discussion with Judyth Weaver when we were writing an article on Gindler with Ulf Geuter (2010).

48. For example, Rajneesh (1976).

49. See Postiaux (2003, chapter 6) for a detailed visual description of these mechanisms. I thank Urs Daendliker for having helped me in this section.

50. See Postiaux (2003, 6.1.6.C, p. 174).

51. Reference 3145 in the Kindle digital edition. The English translation is not as good as it could be.

52. These are the dates of publication. I was unsuccessful in discovering when these works were actually written.

53. I am grateful to Francois Fleury for his advice on the content of this section.

54. Gurdjieff (1960).

55. We owe a filmed version of Encounters with Remarkable Men by Gurdjieff to Peter Brooke. For the relationship between Brook and Gurdjieff, see the article by Nicolescu (1985), published online at http://www.gurdjieff.org/nicolescu3.htm

56. See Huber (1982, I, p. 105).

57. Young (2010).

58. For example, Reymond (1984).

59. Somewhat a similar model as in Socrates's school of masters.

60. See Fleury and Comba (1987).

61. On this point, Hanish's thought seems close to that of Gurdjieff.

62. Gurdjieff, *Remarkable Men* (1960, chapter VIII).

62. Speaking of harmony in Plato (Plato and Stravinsky's *Rite of Spring*, in chapter 3, pp. 91–95), I had mentioned of a model that plays on the polarities, one taught by Paul Boyesen to explain the dangers of fusion in love.

63. For the illustrations of the mechanisms I summarize, I refer the reader to the books of Ouspensky (1949, 1957, for example).

64. This is a restating of Gurdjieff's thought in the frame of this model.

65. See the section on chakras in chapter 1, p. 45f.

66. We have here a vision that announces the modular and parallelistic models of the neurology at the end of the twentieth century.

67. See the Glossary entry for sensory deprivation.

68. See Gurdjieff (1978).

69. Plato (*Phaedrus*, pp. 246–248).

70. Gurdjieff (1950, 48, p. 382f).

71. De Gaigneron (2010).

72. Feldenkrais (1981), Klinkenberg (2002). Feldenkrais also worked with Lotte Kristelle, who in turn had worked with Gindler (Geuter et al., 2010).

73. Confirmed by an email from Halko Weiss, April 2, 2011.

74. See Downing (1996, pp. 81 and 196).

75. Feldenkrais (1949, p. 4f).

76. Ibid., 2, p. 23f.
77. We find models of this type with Fradin and Downing.
78. Feldenkrais (1949, ch. 15, p. 158).
79. Ibid., ch. 16.
80. Feldenkrais (1949, ch. 10, p. 115).
81. Ibid., ch. 17, p. 174f.
82. Ibid., ch. 10, p. 117.

CHAPTER 13

1. See Eibl-Eibesfeldt (1989).
2. See Bourdieu (1979).
3. Heller (1991a, 1997, 2004a).
4. Rolf (1977).
5. This is a summary of the model of postural dynamics (Heller 1991a, 1997, 2004a).
6. See the sections dedicated to Bioenergetic analysis in chapter 19, p. 555f .
7. Alcantara (1997). Not to be confused with Eutony, created by Gerda Alexander (1981).
8. Leroi-Gourhan (1964, chap, II, pp. 40–89).
9. Braatøy (1954, V.2, p. 117f, VI.4, p. 177).
10. The notion of grounding is also discussed in the sections dedicated to tai chi chuan in chapter 2, p. 65f, and in the section dedicated to Alexander Lowen in chapter 19, p. 561f.
11. For example, Feldenkrais (1949, 12, p. 142f).
12. Weber (1904, p. 90).
13. I quote the version of this tale found online at http://wingchunarnis.wordpress .com/2011/03/16/buddha-and-the-young-king/ (accessed April 2011).
14. See, for example, Sambucy (1973), Feldenkrais (1980), Mézières (1978), and Rolf (1977).
15. Even in the English sociological literature, the Latin word is used. See the Glossary.
16. Rolfing is a very effective physiotherapy conducted through massage, founded by Ida Rolf (1977) that realigns the segments of the body. See also Salveson (1997).
17. Heller (1991a, 1997).
18. An expression by Bonnet and Millet (1971, p. 250).
19. Miller et al. (2005), Willeput et al. (1984).
20. Kozier and Erb (1985, ch. 22).
21. Varicose veins were known fifteen centuries BCE. See Jambon and colleagues (1994).
22. In Gerda Boyesen's approach, this method is called the "orgonomy massage."
23. For example, Bassi (1967, pp. 171–172), Davy (1983), and Kluken (1969).
24. Draganova et al. (1988), Gangloff, Chan Tak Nam, and Lepoutre (1984), Kozier and Erb (1985, pp. 565–566).
25. To understand postural mechanics, it is also useful to understand the notion of muscular chains (see the Glossary).

CHAPTER 14

General reference for this chapter: Makari (2008).

1. For a discussion of the influence of Ribot on Freud, see Makari (2008, I.1, pp. 10–14).

2. Wundt (1874, XVIII; 1892, lecture 30th, V).

3. A similar formulation can be found in James (1890, I, p. 19f).

4. Now that recent technologies can create images of brain activity, this method has become fashionable again.

5. Watson (1919, I.1, p. 1).

6. See the section on nonverbal communication, chapters 20–22.

7. Helmholtz and Wundt refer explicitly to Kant's model.

8. This notion is close to the impact of imagination on reason described by Spinoza. Researchers continue to find examples of automatic inferences of the nervous system that open onto illusions or inadequate adaptations of thoughts and behavior. For example, Povinelli (2000, p. 4), Frey (1998, 2001).

9. Crick (1995, pp. 14, 31, 54–57, 163, 184, 273, 279), Frey (2001), Richards (1980).

10. See Gauchet (1992).

11. I delved into the introduction of the work by Robert Byck (1974) concerning the works of Freud on cocaine to write this section.

12. Letter from Freud to Martha Bernays, February 2, 1886.

13. I will not be speaking of other early forms of psychotherapy such as those of Janet, Adler, and Jung, which have become increasingly important in the field of body psychotherapy since the 1960s. There are two reasons for this choice: (1) I do not know these theories well enough to write on them, and (2) they have not played a central role in the emergence of what can be considered common ground knowledge in body psychotherapy. For Janet's impact on contemporary body psychotherapy, consult the index of Ogden, Minton, and Pain (2006).

14. Makari (2008, p. 29f).

15. Because young infants are not able to speak, infant psychology and psychiatry remains one of the rare domains that oblige psychologists and psychiatrists to take interest in the dimensions of the body and nonverbal communication.

16. Letter to Wilhelm Fliess, October 26, 1896.

17. A first version of the Oedipus complex is mentioned in a letter to Fliess, October 15, 1887.

18. The reader will probably notice that Freud's argumentation is nearly the same as Wundt's.

19. This is what Spinoza called imagination (see chapter 5, p. 130).

20. We have seen, in speaking of Gurdjieff (chapter 12, p. 307f), that some schools of spiritual development propose a teaching that allow for the increase of the power of conscious attention. But the years required to increase the performance of the conscious even just a bit clearly show that these limits are negotiable only with difficulty.

21. Freud (1900, VII.B, p. 537).

22. Freud (1915a, I, p. 208).

23. Freud (1900, VII.6, pp. 522, 524; 1915a, II, pp. 214–215).

24. Ibid., VII.VI, p. 520f.

25. Ibid., VII.F, p. 610; P. Fraisse (1992).

26. Freud (1893, 1895a) and letter to Fliess dated November 2, 1896.

27. The manner in which one defines these terms sometime varies from one author to another. In this instance, I offer definitions that are useful in the framework of this book.

28. See Etchegoyen (1991, sections 1.2–1.3).

29. Fenichel (1928, p. 135f).

30. Quoted in Meylan (2007), translated by Michael C. Heller and Marcel Duclos.

31. I am simplifying the analysis of Elizabeth Von R., which is described in more detail on p. 361, in a section dedicated to Joseph Breuer.

32. Coming from Wittgenstein, this is an enormous compliment.

33. Here, I take up Lacan's (1949) distinction between the I and the Me (see p. 356). What I perceive of myself and what others perceive of me is complementary information concerning my functioning. Nevertheless, as both are biased, they can provide contradictory information.

34. See Krause and Lütolf (1988).

35. In these discussions on psychoanalysis, the philosopher often rejoins Nietzsche, for whom tyranny imposes itself by reducing the multiplicity of meanings of certain terms like the "good" or the "bad" (see Rey, 1973).

36. See Lévi-Strauss (1973, 1), for example.

37. In chapter 8, p. 246f, I show how Fradin approaches this complexity with the means available in cognitive psychotherapy.

38. The male hysterical patients are rarely mentioned in these debates.

39. I have, for example, participated in a discussion on this subject in March 2006 in Geneva, in a day-long conference organized by Francois Ferrero, "Psychotherapy Today: Plurality, Research, Training."

40. Crick (1995), Lewicki (1986), Lewicki et al. (1992).

41. Beebe and Lachmann (2003), Bucci (1997), Pally (2005), Roussillon (2007).

42. This is an example of a preconscious manifestation.

43. See chapter 9, p. 269f. Here, we rejoin, from another angle, the preoccupations of the philosopher Lichtenberg. The anxiety generated by the fact that an individual does not see what others see of him and that which the appearance of the other masks would have been one of the bases of the popularity of the approaches that pretended it is possible to read a person's thoughts by looking at his body.

44. Rochat (2002, 2009, 2011).

45. This is Stern's expression (1995, p. 89); we are close to the imagination as defined by Spinoza.

46. This last aspect of Roussillon's model is taken up in the sections organized around the works of Wilma Bucci.

47. Haynal (1991, 3.I, p. 59; 1992).

48. As we see in *The Loss of Reality in Neurosis and Psychosis* (Freud, 1924b), the distinction between neurosis and psychosis is for Freud a subject about which he has some interesting things to say; mostly his students elaborate a psychoanalytic view pertinent to psychosis during the seconds half of the twentieth century. Freud did not have psychotic patients, but he did have many psychiatrists around him who, especially like Jung and Abraham, worked with psychotic patients. They were both trained by the greatest specialist in the treatment of psychoses of the day: Eugene Bleuler.

49. Darwin (1872, VIII, p. 206).

50. Fenichel (1945a, p. 527), Reich (1949a, X.1, p. 204f), Baker (1967, II.8, p. 134, 140), Lowen (1958, II.12–13, p. 239f).

51. See chapter 15, p. 389f, for more information on the development of the libido in the works of Freud.

52. Today, they are *called dissociative conversion disorders* (category F44) in the ICM-10. See also hysteria in the index of the *DSM-IV-R*. See also de Lange et al. (2008).

53. Certain drawings and photos in the work already cited with regard to physiognomy by Clair et al. (1989, X, pp. 281–294). These images can also be found online (through any search engine).

54. See Berney (2009).

55. Ibid.

56. Ibid.

57. Roelofs and Spinhoven (2007).

58. Vuilleumier (2005).

59. It is in English in the German text. See Breuer and Freud (1895, II.I, p. 83).

60. Breuer and Freud (1895, I.3, p. 63).

61. Ibid., II.3, p. 193.

62. Ibid., IV.3, pp. 375–385.

63. I use this expression uniquely in this section because it allows me to keep it simple. Even if the impression of having a central conscious "me" who decides is quite close to everyone's experience, it does not correspond to the notion that the psychologists eventually formulate.

64. The fifth case in the studies on hysteria by Breuer and Freud (1895a, pp. 202–258).

65. See chapter 15, p. 397f, for a more detailed description on the need to coordinate propensions and thoughts.

66. In some cultures, marrying the husband of a dead sister is not considered as incestuous.

67. Masson (1984).

68. Freud (1909a).

69. Freud (1895b, III, p. 53f).

70. For more on this section's topic, see Etchegoyen (1991, III and IV).

71. Freud (1900, II, pp. 94–96; 1912a), Etchegoyen (1991, I.6.3-4, pp. 64–65).

72. Freud (1900, VII.I, p. 450f).

73. Freud (1890, p. 2). In this article, he uses the German term for soul (Seele). Freud, who was not religious, probably used this term as a common word to designate the mind.

74. I reserve the term *sexology* to designate an approach centered on the functional problems of the sexual organs. These problems can be due to physiological functional issues or organic problems of the hormonal, circulatory, or nervous systems, or to mental problems. Most of the time, these problems are caused by a mixture of two of these three dimensions. I know that certain sexologists (Meignant, 1992, for example) have a more organismic view of their discipline, but we must clearly distinguish psychotherapy and sexology.

75. This position is summarized explicitly in Ferenczi (1919a). Ferenczi (1922) underlines the paradox (a) to think that consciousness is influenced by the drives, and (b) to give so much power to consciousness. He proposes a kind of curve in which he supposes that in recruiting the help of consciousness, the drives arrive at influencing the body in the way Freud described.

76. Sudden healing recoveries are impressive but difficult to explain. Erickson (1982)

furnished many examples of this type of realignments under hypnosis. See also Bourgeois (2003) for a more recent discussion.

77. Levine and Frederick (1997), Ogden et al. (2006), Rothschild (2000), Van der Kolk et al. (1996).

78. For example, Green et al. (1999). See also Poleshuck et al. (2005) for a refinement of this hypothesis.

79. Braatøy's model on the remainder of the fear reflexes that readapt themselves is a variation of the proposition.

80. Van der Kolk (2006).

81. Quoted in Meylan (2007), translated by Marcel Duclos.

82. This explicit common construction is for me one of the centers of the effectiveness of psychotherapy. I generally make reference to it by using the concept of co-consciousness as proposed by Philippe Rochat.

83. Freud (1900, VII.E, p. 608).

84. What I summarize in this section is found mostly in Freud (1900, II).

85. I summarize a basic method here. Once one has become skilled in the art of dream analysis, the psychotherapist can jump from one brick to another by following his clinical intuition. Having said this, even when a therapist has become a brilliant analyst of dreams, it is sometimes useful for the patient to undergo a classic dream analysis, in which the sequencing of the bricks is the one produced by the dream.

86. See Etchegoyen (1991, III and IV, VI.52–54).

87. Aalberse (2001).

88. See Sperry's Nobel Prize speech on the site http://nobelprize.org/nobel_prizes/medicine/laureates/1981/sperry-lecture.html (accessed April 2004).

89. The left/right lateralization of the neurological bases of language varies from one individual to another. Statistically, men would often be more lateralized than women.

90. See the work of Gallagher (2005), *How the Body Shapes the Mind*.

91. Bucci (1997, 2001, and 2002).

92. My example.

93. Bucci uses standardized methods that were already recognized to carry out this evaluation.

94. Personal communication sent to Philippe Rochat by Jerome Bruner on August 3, 2010.

95. Stern (1985, p. 250).

96. May was trained in body psychotherapy at the Radix Institute by Charles Kelley, a student of Wilhelm Reich. He has since developed his own synthesis.

97. Alexithymia is a medical term to designate patients who have a pronounced difficulty recognizing emotional expressions.

98. John May takes a 50-cm–diameter inflated ball that is often used in a gymnasium. The patient places his back at the level of the scapula (the shoulder blades) on the top of the ball. The feet are flat on the floor and parallel, the arms above the head, and the back assumes a concave position that corresponds to the shape of the ball. The patient will feel a mobilization of the thoracic respiration that pulls on the chronic muscular tension that inhibits this breathing. The therapist requests that the patient express the pain felt in this tension instead of quitting the position.

99. See Varela (1988).

100. Reich used this technique with a masochist patient when he was a psychoanalyst. It is still discussed in the psychoanalytic literature (Bonnet, 2005, I.1, pp. 28–32).

CHAPTER 15

1. See Reich (1919).

2. Once again we find the idea that the mental and behavioral dimensions follow different procedures. This difference is often forgotten in the theories of today's body psychotherapists.

3. Freud (1905, I.5, p. 83).

4. This is mentioned in this book in the sections pertaining to the Hindu tantric schools (chapter 1, p. 44f) and by Plato in *Phaedra* (chapter 3, p. 102f).

5. The notion that every intense desire, every strong charge, is necessarily disagreeable remains debatable. The utilitarian part of Freud thinks that if an intense desire was not disagreeable, we would not seek to satisfy a sexual need. Personally, I think this is false trail and that the appetite can be a pleasure in itself.

6. Freud (1920, I).

7. This part of Freud's theory is close to the propositions of the physiologists who studied the stress response. See chapter 8, p. 212f.

8. Freud (1895b, III: 62).

9. This section draws from Freud (1914b).

10. Freud and Adler met in 1895. Together, they founded the Psychoanalytical Society of Vienna.

11. See the first letter from Jung to Freud, dated October 5, 1906, in the correspondence between Freud and Jung, and also Adler (1912, I.I: 14).

12. The correspondence between Jung and Freud summarizes a great part of their discussion on this topic.

13. Freud (1915b).

14. Tinbergen (1952) observes that in the stickleback fish the instinct is already composed of well-differentiated modules.

15. MacDougall (1996).

16. Freud (1914b).

17. Darwin (1871, I.III.1, pp. 79–86).

18. Heller (1987b).

19. Also see Gorkin (1987) and Heller (1993c).

20. Freud (1910b, 1915g). I am indebted to Andre Haynal for this information.

21. For example, Vygotsky (1934) and Rochat (2001).

22. Kohut (1971) and Kernberg (1975), for example.

23. See Ronningstam (2009).

24. Besson and Brault (1999), Fraisse (2002), Heller (1987a).

25. For example, Fraisse (2002).

26. Freud (1923a, IV, p. 44f).

27. *La Revue Francaise de Psychoanalyse* published a special edition on orality in 2001 (vol. 65, no. 5).

28. What follows are approximate ages indicative of an average that varies in each case. Erik Erikson (1950) proposed a continuation of Freud's analysis by describing adult stages up to old age. He also shows how Freud's stages express themselves differently in various cultural contexts.

29. This aspect of Freud's model is close to Gurdjieff's model of the centers discussed in chapter 12, p. 310f.

30. A complementary view is found in Piaget's theory of the stages of the develop-

ment of intelligence (1936). He shows that the child cannot understand certain types of reasoning before having mastered a number of appropriate intellectual tools. The one possible exception is that of cultures in which it is inevitable that the child will witness his parents having sex (Abraham, 1913a). Therefore, there are cultural regulations that allow giving a meaning to love-making (through stories, for examples) that a child can integrate into its age-appropriate understanding.

31. For example, Reich (1940, V.3, p.90f).

32. Freud (1916, III.21, p. 376).

33. Freud (1905, I.5).

34. Ibid., III.1.

35. Abraham (1913b), Freud (1910a).

36. Freud (1915b).

37. Abraham (1913b).

38. See Sartre (1943, III.I.IV, pp. 340–400). This chapter clearly differentiates inter-subjective psychology (as described by Vygotsky and Rochat) from issues on how two intimate subjects communicate.

39. See Lacan (1954, vol. 1, XVII.3, p. 214f).

40. See also Bonnet (2000).

41. Freud (1915b).

42. Ibid.

43. See Makari (2008, p. 234f).

44. Freud (1915e).

45. Freud's *On Psycho-Analysis* (1913) and *On the History of the Psycho-Analytic Movement* (1914a) led to his *Introductory Lectures on Psycho-Analysis* (1916).

46. See Freud's writings between the years 1890 and 1895 listed in the References.

47. Freud (1915b, p. 117f; 1938, IV, p. 28f).

48. This dream is beginning to be realized during the last twelve years. See, for example, Kaplan-Solms and Solms (2000) and Magistretti and Ansermet (2004).

49. This last point shows that like Lamarck (see chapter 9, p. 163), Freud concluded there was no direct link between the regions of the brain and psychological functions.

50. Freud (1915b, p. 125).

51. Freud (1895c, 15, p. 324f, and 1938, IV, p. 37).

52. Freud (1920, 5, p. 34).

53. See chapter 14, p. 377f, where John May shows how primary processes can be managed in body psychotherapy.

54. See chapter 8, p. 212f.

55. Cocks (1997).

56. Freud (1923a).

57. Freud (1938, II, p. 148).

58. Ibid., IV, p. 157.

59. Ibid., I, p. 147.

60. Ibid., I, p.146f.

61. Freud indicates this double organization of the psychical apparatus with a useful sketch in *New Introductory Lectures on Psychoanalysis* (1932, XXXI, p. 108).

62. See Haynal (1967).

63. Fenichel (1941, II, p. 21).

64. Freud (1915b, p. 119f).

65. Freud (1923a, II, p. 25f).
66. Freud (1920, 1929).
67. Makari (2008, II.VII.IV, p. 279f, and III.VIII.IV).
68. Ibid., p. 364).
69. For example, the work of Francoise Sironi (1999) on torture.

CHAPTER 16

1. Adler uses the term *soul* more often than the term *psyche* when he refers to the global psychological system and specific words for specific aspects of the soul. Reference: Adler (1927, 1.1; 1931, 2).
2. Adler (1912, p. 22).
3. Reich (1948b, IV, p. 187f).
4. The choice of this term is manifestly related to Reich's Marxist beliefs.
5. Reich (1938, II.9; 1949a, III.XIII.9, p. 351).
6. See chapter 10 for other examples.
7. Makari (2008, p. 161).
8. This section on Spielrein benefited from the presentations of a congress organized by Kaj Nocis: Who Is Afraid of Sabina Spielrein? These discussions unfolded at the Faculty of Psychology of the University of Lausanne, April 19 and 20, 2007, thanks to the support of Nicholas Duruz. Most speakers recommended Sabine Richebächer's (2005) book on Spielrein. The presentations are published in French, in *Le Coq-Héron*, 197, August 2009.
9. Ruchat (2010).
10. Piaget (1920).
11. This was the theory that Piaget published in 1936. Piaget associated a sensory-motor thought to the birth of intelligence in the newborn. Having never studied adult thought, he does not seem to have understood that what he calls sensory-motor intelligence continues to develop while other, more formal modes of thinking are formed.
12. Van der Veer and Valsiner (1991).
13. Santiago-Delefosse and Delefosse (2002).
14. Ibid., Vygotsky (1934).
15. During this period, Elsa Gindler was already using the blindfolding method to help her students better feel from the inside the functioning of movements. It is therefore very probable that her article was discussed by analysts like Fenichel and Reich, who were exploring, as we later see in greater detail, the possibility of incorporating certain aspects of Gindler's method in psychoanalytic thought and technique. Being communist psychoanalysts, they were naturally aware of the development of psychoanalysis in the Soviet Union and its key promoters, such as Luria. Knowing neither Russian nor German, I base this discussion on the conference that Richebächer gave in English in Lausanne, during the congress organized by Kaj Nocis. The article by Spielrein was published, as most of her articles were, in the Freudian journal *Imago*, in 1931.
16. Santiago-Delefosse and Delefosse (2002).
17. Groddeck (1913, p. 100).
18. Reich (1940, III.3, p. 32f).
19. Downing (1996, V.25, p. 346f, 362).

20. Heyer was a Jungian analyst.

21. We have seen in chapter 8 (p. 214f) that Kurt Goldstein brought this form of thought back into fashion.

22. Groddeck (1977).

23. Downing (1996, p. 362).

24. See chapter 19, pp. 540f and 545f.

25. Recommended reference for this section: Haynal (1987).

26. See the Glossary. I use the expression "transferential dynamic" when the transference and the countertransference are analyzed in a coordinated fashion.

27. Ferenczi (1921a, 1930).

28. Ferenczi (1921a, p. 119).

29. Ferenczi (1921b).

30. Ibid.

31. Ferenczi (1921a, II, p. 120f).

32. Ferenczi and Rank (1924, p. 221).

33. See Ferenczi (1921b). We will see that this technique interests many body psychotherapists, such as Braatøy, Heller, and Downing. The development of the analysis of nonverbal behavior (see part VII) promoted refining the use of this type of intervention in psychotherapy (Beebe, 2004).

34. Ferenczi (1930, p. 89).

35. Ibid.

36. Paresthesia is a form of tingling, disagreeable but not painful, that gives the impression of palpating cotton and creates a loss of sensation.

37. Also see Braatøy (1954, VI.8, p. 193).

38. G. Boyesen (1985a, III.2, pp. 107–108).

39. A technical point: Gerda Boyesen does not say that she will do everything the patient will ask of her.

40. This view is shared by many authors, from Sharaf (1983) to Danto (2005).

41. In this section, I am grateful to Johannes Reichmayr who, at the occasion of our encounter in Vienna in early 2010, helped me correct some false facts I had published concerning Fenichel.

42. Granoff (2004, p. 50).

43. The first half of this section gathers its information from R. Jacoby (1983).

44. See the section in chapter 12, p. 295f, dedicated to Elsa Gindler, for a first discussion of the youth movements at the beginning of the century.

45. See Fenichel (1916).

46. He ended his career as a high official in the Democratic Republic of Germany (communist Germany).

47. It is probable that the first case published by Reich (1920) is what he discovered at the occasion of his first analysis. If this is true, this writing describes the circumstances of this suicide.

48. Clair (1986). See chapter 12, p. 295f.

49. The expression "sexual misery" was proposed by Reich in the 1930s. I use this expression here as a pedagogic shortcut to synthesize what today's reader ought to retain from the discussions that I summarize.

50. Makari (2008, III.9, p. 340).

51. Sharaf (1983, p. 64).

52. Falzeder (2005, p. 141f).

53. Makari (2008, pp. 340–342).

54. Ibid., p. 340.

55. Ibid., p. 346.

56. References for this section: Danto (2005), Fisher (2007), and Makari (2008).

57. Makari (2008, chs. 9 and 10, pp. 325 and 369).

58. Fisher (2007).

59. This was the recommendation that Jung had made while he was the president of the International Psychoanalytical Association between 1911 and 1914.

60. Upon his return to Oslo, Raknes participated in the development of Reich's Vegetotherapy during the 1930s.

61. Mostly trained by Fenichel, Braatøy went to Oslo, where he followed the Reichian adventure up close, without being directly involved.

62. Falzeder (2005), Gougoulis (2010).

63. Makari (2008, p. 379).

64. My principal source for this section is an interview with Clare Fenichel (1981).

65. Makari (2008, p. 387).

66. According to Sharaf (1983, 8, p. 108), she had been one of Fenichel's patients.

67. The daughter of the Fenichels became a political scientist at the University of California. Her full name was Hanna Fenichel Pitkin.

68. Information furnished by Ulf Geuter by phone in August 2010.

69. See Mühlleitner (2008) for more details on the content of this paragraph.

70. Personal communication from Johannes Reichmayr, who studied this text with Elke Mühlleitner.

71. Freud (1915b, p. 125f, p. 138).

72. Fenichel quotes an academically recognized source to describe this phenomenon, but this is an example of what he must have learned from Gindler.

73. See p. 437f for a description of the character analysis that Reich developed in Vienna during the 1920s.

74. See Fenichel (1928, 1931, 1935).

75. This hypothesis is close to the association between a lack of maturity of mind and body as noted by Feldenkrais (see chapter 12, p. 317f).

76. Later, a more subtle version of this theme was developed by sociologists like Bourdieu (1979).

77. See also Fenichel (1945a, XIII, p. 302f).

78. Fenichel, as a good Marxist, maintains (as does Reich at this time) that the relation between the body and psyche is dialectical. There can be several kinds of relations between body and mind considered as two distinct subsystems of an organism, which is their emerging synthesis.

79. Fenichel (1928, p. 129).

80. Ibid., p. 132. According to Downing (1980), Reich was tempted, for a brief time, to incorporate Kretschmer's theories.

81. The importance of being able to feel and identify with finesse the vegetative and bodily sensations is one of the points we find in almost all the schools of body psychotherapy, relaxation, body–mind work, and Gestalt awareness exercises. Fenichel and Reich also stressed the importance of being aware of vegetative and body sensations. Even if they did not quote them, it is probably from Gindler and Lindenberg that they

learned to accord so much importance to the development of this kind of awareness. See also Ogden et al. (2006, I.1.2.4, p.15f).

82. It seems to me that the understanding of the alienation of body sensation in a neurotic person is another example of what Fenichel learned from Gindler. Reich attributed still more importance to this alienation after meeting the dancer Elsa Lindenberg (see chapter 17, p. 467f).

83. Fenichel does not identify the gymnastics teacher to whom he refers. It is probably Gindler or Clare Fenichel.

84. It is a bit similar to Socrates's strategy, even if the style is very different. See chapter 3, p. 104.

85. Reference for this section: Makari (2008).

86. I tend to use words in their narrow sense. In this text, the term *spirituality* designates the belief that there exists a spirit distinct from the dynamics that animate the universe. The wider meaning of the word designates the impression of being a part of forces that permeate and animate everything that exists. This large meaning, which does not imply the hypothesis of a spiritual force, adequately describes what Reich describes. This narrower sense provokes a refusal in Reich to be associated to the notion of spirituality.

87. See chapter 7 on Darwin (p. 171f) and neo-Darwinism (p. 181f).

88. Reich (1940, I, p. 5).

89. Lorenz (1973), Tinbergen (1951).

90. See Heller (1987c).

91. Geuter (1984, p. 73).

92. See chapter 8 on Claude Bernard, p. 197f.

93. Reich (1940, III).

94. See the discussion in the section titled, "With Abraham: The Club of the Young Psychoanalysts of Tomorrow" above, p. 421f.

95. Reich (1940, III.3, p. 39f).

96. Ibid., III.2, p. 25f; Reich (1922a).

97. This observation confirms that of Freud.

98. Reich (1940, III.2, p. 25).

99. Ibid., III.3, Reich (1919, 1927b, I.1, pp. 38–41). Marcel Duclos translated the quotations that come from the French version of the 1919 article.

100. Reich (1927b, I.I.II, p. 41f).

101. To unburden the text, I do not repeat that the definition of the orgasm proposed by Reich is not the current definition of an orgasm. Sexologists take into account certain aspects of the Reichian proposition, but not of all of it. For the moment, we are dealing with rather current notions; gradually, Reich proposed a view of the orgasm that is so normative (things have to occur like this and not like that) that it acquires a status close to the Ideas of the Idealists.

102. Here, Reich summarizes the analysis proposed by Havelock Ellis who was the reference (for Freud among others) on sexology at the time.

103. Reich (1940, IV.2, p. 49).

104. Heller (1987a).

105. This circular dynamic brings Reich in 1951 to take up Freud's psycho-organic circle and redesign it.

106. I heard Lowen speak in detail about this in a conference given in Geneva in the 1980s. See also Lowen (1975, I.2, p. 24).

107. Reich (1940, IV.2, p. 42f).

108. This is the same scenario as the creation of the Psychoanalytic Dispensary. Hitschmann created the institution and Reich directed it.

109. The letters from Freud to Reich date from August 9, 1926, to October 10, 1930. Ernst Falzeder is a historian of psychoanalysis who has notably participated in the publication of the Freud's correspondence with Ferenczi and Abraham. I am grateful to him for having summarized Freud's letters to Reich, letters that he consulted in the Library of Congress in Washington, D.C. These letters cannot yet be published even though they do not contain any private material.

110. In psychoanalytic jargon, the goal of a drive is its object. This object is generally a person.

111. I am taking a shortcut. The desire to bite the little sister's clothing can already be the result of several partial drives: like the rage felt against a sister who gathers the attention of her parents, like the desire to bite the mother's breast, which she gives to the sister but not to the five-year-old boy, and so on.

112. Freud's and Ferenczi's point of view are summarized in Haynal (1987). Here, I present the discussion such as it is presented in Reich (1940, V.1; 1949a, I.I–III).

113. See chapter 15, p. 398.

114. Reich (1949a, I.II, p. 11).

115. The equation "closest to consciousness" = "less deep" is not always true, especially for psychotic, narcissistic, and borderline structures. This is therefore a first approximation that can be used as a procedure by default.

116. Reich (1940, V.3, p. 90).

117. To take up the preceding example, we can suppose that the urge to bite the sister's clothing has become an urge to bite into food, and later, the child started to pull in his chin every time that grown-ups scolded him for being greedy.

118. See chapter 12, p. 310f.

119. Reich (1940, V.3, p. 92).

120. A genital drive toward the mother in a young child is impossible in Freud's first model (see Freud, 1905, and chapter 15, p. 390f). This simplification of Freud's model was quite frequent with psychoanalysts of the time. It is probably also due to the fact that Reich examined, in a rather too superficial fashion at the occasion of one of his brief stages in analysis, his problematic relationship with his mother (see Reich, 1920). The theoretical implication of Reich's position is that the genital drive is in place at birth, but the genital interaction does not become conceivable until puberty. This is an example of Reich's difficulty to integrate the flexibility of sexuality for most psychoanalysts of this time (feminine and masculine, homosexual and heterosexual, etc.).

121. Reich (1949a, I, p. 227f).

122. Reich (1927a, I, p. 252, IV.3, p. 293).

123. Sterba (1982, p. 112). Translated by Marcel Duclos.

124. See Makari (2008, p. 401). See also Sharaf (1983, p. 193).

125. Fenichel wrote "Rundbriefe," letters he duplicated and regularly sent to his psychoanalyst friends of the left. They were published on a CD-ROM by Johannes Reichmayr and Elke Muhlleitner in 1998, but they have not been translated. In an email of November 15, 2010, Johannes Reichmayr sent me a page dated 1933, in which Fenichel criticizes Reich on the technical level, but he does not talk of character problems when he writes about Reich in these letters.

126. Judyth O. Weaver, http://www.judythweaver.com/writings and Geuter et al. (2010).

127. A persistent rumor suggests that the first case published by Reich (1920) summarizes what he discovered about himself during his brief analysis.

128. I once served as an interpreter for Eva Reich when she was in Geneva in the 1990s to give a course at the Ecole du Bon Secours to nurses. She told me that she had been to a Montessori school that she had greatly liked and her father had taken her out to put her in an institution for working-class children, which she hated. Her father also forced her to march in uniform with communist youths, something she also detested. The memories of Peter Reich (1974), a son Reich had in the United States, shows to what extent this mixture of militant life and private life could be at the same time fascinating and destructive. Reich absolutely wanted his private life to demonstrate the rightness of his intellectual position.

129. Sharaf (1983).

130. Information from Ulf Geuter in an email of July 2009.

131. Laban (1920, 1950). We know that Lindenberg studied with Laban and Gindler in the 1930s, but it is possible that others, whom we do not know, could have had a greater influence on her. All of this is a work in progress for the moment.

132. Birdwhistell (1970a), La Barre (2001), Rosenfeld (1982), Stern (2010, 85f). I will not attempt to summarize Laban's proposal, but the reader can use the index to find several quotes and comments that can illustrate his thoughts. For the coding of gestures, see Laban (1950, ch. 2 and 3).

133. Geuter (2004), Payne (2006), Vaysse (2006, 2.6, p. 72).

134. Noschis (2011, chapter 5).

135. Sharaf (1983, p. 195).

136. Ibid., p. 200.

137. Reich (1933; I.IV.2.c, p. 66, and I.IV.2.e, p. 93).

138. Downing (1996, V.26, p. 363f).

139. Ibid.

140. Reich (1949a, III.XIII.9).

141. This is the hypothesis that we have tried to understand more deeply in our research on the relationship of a therapist with suicidal patients (Heller et al., 2001).

142. The quote is taken from Theodore P. Wolfe's 1946 English translation, supervised by Reich, which is available at http://www.whale.to/b/reich.pdf

143. The numbers are difficult to evaluate because the sources I consulted contradict each other. This evaluation has been arrived at with the help of Courtenay Young (email of November 22, 2009). His articles on the history of body psychotherapy can be found on his website: http://www.courtenay-young.co.uk/courtenay/articles

144. See Reich (1946, IX).

145. This conference was given at the 2006 Congress of the European Association of Body Psychotherapy, September 23, in Askov, Denmark.

146. Reich (1945a).

147. MacDougall (1996).

148. This analysis appears in the second edition of the Mass Psychology of Fascism published in 1946 (chapter IX). In the edition of 1933, he mostly attacks the National Socialism Party.

149. Letter of January 24, 1932, from Freud to Ferenczi. The texts Reich wrote in the 1930s used an explicit communist jargon. They have been rewritten since, which explains why this communist idiosyncrasy is not apparent today.

150. Letter of January 26, 1932, from Ferenczi to Eitingon.

151. Makari (2008, p. 450).

152. R. Jacoby (1983, IV, p. 100).

153. See the article by Anzieu (1984) on the twofold prohibition of touching for a summary of the reasons a psychoanalyst ought not to touch a patient. Stern (2010, p. 119f) reminds us that the psychoanalyst's fear of acting out on his patients, something that happened all too often at the beginning of the psychoanalytic adventure, created in the Freudian theory and practice a kind of artificial rupture between verbal and nonverbal behavior.

154. The Nazis exacted a ransom, paid by Princess Marie Bonaparte and important politicians in the United States and in England (Makari, 2008, p. 460).

155. Makari (2008, p. 411).

156. Fisher (1988).

157. Reich (1952a, p. 122).

158. For this section, see Downing (1996, V.25, pp. 344 and 365) for a discussion on the impact of the gymnastic techniques on body psychotherapy.

159. See Kogan (1980).

160. Laeng-Gilliat (1978), Selver (1978).

161. Selver and Brooks (1980).

162. Feldenkrais (1980, p. 73).

163. The phrase *organismic psychology* was explicitly coined by Ludwig von Bertalanffy (1968b), in a talk on Werner's (1957) organismic psychology. My views on organismic psychology (Heller, 1976) were mostly influenced by the works of Piaget and Laborit. We therefore have an example of a parallel elaboration, inspired by the same intellectual fashion. The link between Brown and Selver was pointed out to me by Elizabeth Marshall in an email of September 28, 2010.

164. Perls had several psychoanalysts. The first was Karen Horney. The fourth was Wilhelm Reich.

165. Clarkson and Mackewn (1993).

166. See Ajuriaguerra and Cahen (1960).

CHAPTER 17

This chapter owes much to my discussions with Bjørn Blumenthal and Berit Heir Bunkan.

1. Boadella (1997) speaks of energetic medicine.

2. See Raknes (1970, I.1, p. 20) and Boadella (1997).

3. See the sections in chapter 19 on Oslo, p. 523f.

4. *Zeitschrift für Politische Psychologie und Sexualökonomie* vol. 1, no. 1, 1934.

5. Neill founded the "free" Summerhill School. A correspondence tells the history of their friendship (Reich and Neill, 1982).

6. Also see Reich (1940, IX) and Reich (1994).

7. Reich (1949a, III.XV.5, p. 442). We have seen (chapter 14, p. 367f) that at the beginning psychoanalysts had a tendency toward a passive body and an active mind.

8. Sharaf (1983, p. 234).

9. Sharaf (1983, pp. 234–235, 242).

10. See chapter 14, p. 365f.

11. Ollendorf (1969, p. 45).

12. See P. Reich (1974).

13. In the school of Gro Thorgersbråten and Brit Hammel Malt, for example. I am grateful to Berit Bunkan for this information.

14. Boadella (1990a), Downing (1996, V.26, p. 363f). This point was clarified by David Boadella in an e-mail received on November 24, 2008.

15. C. Fenichel (1981).

16. Downing (1996, V.26, p. 363f).

17. G. Boyesen (1985b).

18. This is an example, among many others, that shows how a body psychotherapy endeavor is often useful for patients who suffer from a problem whose causes are purely physiological or metabolic.

19. The following is an interesting experiment on the subject. Type in on a search engine the following list of words: hot, cold, tingling, stinging, heavy, light. You will first obtain medical sites indicating that these sensations are often symptoms of serious illnesses. Then add the word relaxation to the list and you will find a large number of sites indicating that these are often sensations of relaxation, pleasure, and health.

20. For example Pridaux (1920); letter of Antipoff to Claparède, July 22, 1931 (Claparède, 2010).

21. Feldenkrais (see chapter 12, p. 319) also tried to propose a biomechanical description of the orgastic reaction.

22. Reich (1940, VII.5, p. 191).

23. Ibid., VIII.4, p. 229. I have added a few items that Reich dos not mention but which are very well known today. See also the bottle exercise, described in chapter 2, p. 63. Ebba Boyesen (in Macon, France, in 1977) taught me how to integrate this technique in a workshop on the orgastic reflex.

24. For a less simplistic description of how psychotic patients breathe, see Bunkan (2003, p. 51).

25. See also Thornquist and Bunkan (1991, 6, p. 81f).

26. P. Reich (1974, 5, pp. 136–137).

27. This is the opisthotonus, described in the Glossary.

28. See chapter 1, p. 45f.

29. Reich (1951, 47, p. 80).

30. Reich, still influenced by the psychoanalytic couch, asked his patients to lie down on their backs. When Lowen works on the orgastic reflex with patients who are standing, the horizontal axis becomes the axis of the spinal column.

31. Reich (1940, VIII, p. 208; 1949a, III.XIV.3, p. 312f).

32. The use of an anatomy atlas is recommended to understand the following anatomical references.

33. An example of how psychoanalysts approach gaze is discussed in chapter 15, p. 392f.

34. See Heller (1987c) for a review of the literature on this segment.

35. Here it consists of unit 23 of the coding system of the face (FACS) proposed by Ekman and Friesen (1971, 1978) and in Ekman (1980b).

36. Thornquist and Bunkan (1991, 3.2.1, p. 31) describe individuals who are chronically in a position of expiration.

37. Thornquist and Bunkan (1991, 6, p. 81f). Also see Bunkan (1991).

38. For example, Braddock (1997, p. 222), Rolf (1977), Salveson (1997, p. 42f).

39. See the section "Reich Picks the Wrong Enemy" in this chapter, p. 482.

40. This reflex action is described in chapter 7, p. 155f, dedicated to the way that Darwin analyzes the coming of the tears.

41. I have also noticed this phenomenon in certain alcoholic patients.

42. Reich (1940, V.2, p. 83f, V.4, p. 103f).

43. Reich (1949a, III.XIII.3, p. 304).

44. It is common, in this kind of work, to notice that one emotion covers another.

45. Konrad Lorenz and Nikolaas Tinbergen had already published descriptions of innate behaviors. Lorenz's and Reich's language was quite similar, but they were ideologically so far apart that they refused to quote each other (Heller, 1987c).

46. Baker (1967, II.10, p. 165), Lowen (1967, V.3), Reich (1940, VII.1–2).

47. Reich (1948b, IX, p. 313). See also V.2, p. 154f. Here we have Reich taking up Gindler's term without quoting her.

48. Reich (1948b, IX, p. 313f; 1949a, III.XV).

49. See Salveson (1997) for a fine summary of the way a physical therapist ("a Rolfer") perceives the constriction of an individual.

50. Here we have another variation of Edmund Jacobson's model, which showed that the organism can influence, in a parallel fashion, the psyche and a part of the body (for example, a tension of the hand and the conscious sensation that there is a tension in the hand).

51. Reich (1945b, 3.3, p. 94).

52. See chapters 14, p. 377, and 15, p. 399f. The Reichians do not seem to have retained the distinction between a primary and a secondary structure of the psychoanalysts.

53. References for this section: Alnaes (1980), Jacoby (1983, III and IV), and Reich (1952a, 1994).

54. Reich (1994, p. 7). Letter from Reich to Annie Reich, November 17, 1934.

55. R. Jacoby (1983, IV, p. 99f).

56. Reich-Rubin (2003). The article by Harris and Brock (1992) summarizes the available data on the conflict between Reich and Fenichel.

57. This argument is taken up on the body–mind level by Gerda Boyesen. If a massage therapist loosens the muscular tensions on the surface too quickly, the patient may need to contract the deep muscles, like the diaphragm or the psoas, which are more difficult to loosen manually. There is then a replacement of old tensions by more noxious ones that are more difficult to work with and can create in the patient a fear of future treatments. These criticisms, often formulated by Boyesen in her workshops in the 1970s, were directed against the work of colleagues like Lowen and Rolf.

58. This is well described by Reich in his psychoanalytic model of character analysis (Reich, 1940, V.3.) to which Fenichel remained loyal. It consisted then in modeling the vicissitudes of the libido. This complexity was lost as soon as Reich tried to relate his psychoanalytic model to a body that he had difficulty understanding in a refined way (Reich, 1940, VII.5).

59. In body psychotherapy, this work was taken up in an interesting way by George Downing (1996, 2006).

60. I have often observed the correctness of this analysis.

61. G. Boyesen (1985b), Levine (2008), and Levine and McNaughton (2004).

62. See chapter 19, p. 540f.

63. I am quoting, from memory, phrases heard in her course between 1974 and 1979. See also E. Boyesen (1987).

64. Personal communication in the 1980s in Macon, France. Gerda Boyesen men-

tioned Reich, Lowen, Navarro, and Gurdjieff to me while talking about men's tendency to create unnecessarily rigid distinctions. According to her, the more supple feminine thought makes it possible to better understand the real dynamics.

65. Reich's letter to Elsa Lindenberg, March 1, 1935, in Reich (1994, p. 34).

CHAPTER 18

1. In Berlin, Radó had been Fenichel's analyst and Reich's for a short period (chapter 16, p. 445f).

2. Makari (2008, p. 475f).

3. Alexander (1939, 1950).

4. Hanna Fenichel edited the collected papers of Otto Fenichel.

5. Fenichel (1945a, XIII, p. 238f).

6. See chapter 8, p. 215f.

7. For example, Lazarus and Folkman (1984).

8. See chapter 8, p. 221f.

9. Wilhelm Reich, *Psychischer Kontakt und Vegetative Stroemung. Abhandl, zur personellen Sexualokonomie*, no. 3. (SexpolVerlag, 1935). A rewritten version of the text can be found in Reich (1949a, chapter XIII).

10. Fenichel (1945a, A.I.II, p. 14).

11. Ibid., XIII, p. 246; Haynal et al. (1997, 10, p. 92).

12. See chapter 19, p. 540.

13. In this section, I do not include in my summarization everything included in Fenichel's thinking. Some of his remarks seem uninteresting to me and even, in some cases, implausible. In this textbook, I retain the parts of Fenichel's model that seem to be useful in the body psychotherapy of today.

14. It is mostly this option that is explored by Alexander's psychosomatics.

15. We have here an intuition of the themes developed by body psychotherapists like George Downing (2006) and myself (Heller 2006).

16. This thesis is taken up by the Norwegian school of body psychotherapy.

17. See chapter 19.

18. A part of this money came from donations. It would be interesting to know how Reich collected money.

19. See http://www.wilhelmreichmuseum.org/biography.html

20. Reich (1940, 1948b, 1949a, 1951).

21. Reich (1919).

22. Reich (1948b; 1949a, III.XIII.3; and note in 1945a, p. 254f).

23. Letter from Reich to Neill, December 22, 1950.

24. See Sharaf (1983) for a description of Reich's experience at that time.

25. Reich (1938).

26. Guex (1989), Haynal et al. (1997, 22, 191f), Pert (1997, 9, pp. 191–193), Spiegel et al. (1989).

27. For example, Grove et al. (2005), Prause and Dooley (2001).

28. This model has been taken up by many schools of body psychotherapy, like the core energetics of John Pierrakos and the biodynamic psychology of Gerda Boyesen, when they speak of "primary personality." At the end of his life, Reich no longer believed that each human being has a kernel of pulsating orgone in his core. He believed that this

core ought to exist but that it ought to influence our thoughts and acts. That is why he preferred to promote social reforms rather than new organismic psychotherapies.

29. Reich (1940, VII. 6, p. 197f).

30. This expression is close to Fenichel's 1928 notion of organ libido.

31. See http://www.prohealth.com/library/showarticle.cfm?libid=7747 (accessed in January 2011) for a description of Craniosacral therapy. Eva Reich sometimes used these techniques.

32. See Stern (2010).

33. In his 2010 volume on vitality, Daniel Stern indicates how notions like constriction can be used in psychotherapy independently from vitalistic theories.

34. See chapter 12 on gymnastics, p. 304.

35. See chapter 1, p. 36; chapter 2, p. 65; chapter 15, p. 387.

36. Reich (1951, IV, p. 75).

37. Ibid., p. 61.

38. G. Boyesen (1985b), Heller (1987a).

39. Reich (1951, IV, p. 80).

40. Personal communications from Judyth Weaver, July 26 and 27, 2009.

41. See Heller (1991b, 1993b, and 1994) for a detailed description of these exercises.

42. Laban (1950, IV, p. 120f).

43. The psychoanalytic notion of "ego strength" is well explained by Haynal (1967). In English, see Jacobs et al. (1968).

44. This analysis is taken up by all of Reich's students. For example, Baker (1967, I.4, p. 72f).

45. See Heller (1987c) for a review of the literature on this segment.

46. The diagnostic category of "prepsychotic" has been eliminated from the psychiatric vocabulary some thirty years ago at the time of the introduction of the notion of borderline personality disorder (Kernberg, 1984). This does not settle it for the body psychotherapist, for whom the prepsychotic is not always a borderline personality but a person who is suffering from a latent psychosis that is not yet overtly manifest.

47. Recent research shows that the metabolic activity of the brain cells generates crucial forms of coordination of the brain's activity. Fröhlich and McCormick (2010) say that the brain generates an electrical field: "these results indicate that the electric field generated by the brain facilitates the same neural firing that created the field in the first place" (Ferris Jabr, 2010). Here we have an example of what I mean when I say that often *what is perceived by a mechanism structures the mechanism that produced it.*

48. See the memoires of P. Reich (1974).

49. Boadella (1973), Guasch (2007), Marchi (1973), Sharaf (1983, VIII), Wilson (1987). See also http://www.orgone.org/wr-vs-usa/wr0.htm (accessed in January 2011).

50. Quétier (2010, p. 166). We also discover a systematic critique of the incoherence and the contradictions inherent in all living systems in Spinoza and Marx.

51. Downing (1996, V.26, pp. 366–377) details the difficulties, experienced by several contemporary body psychotherapists, with the theory of the orgone.

52. Dadoun (1976), Marchi (1973), Reich (1953), Sharaf (1983), Wilson (1987).

53. Giangiacomo Feltrinelli is a prestigious publisher who sympathized with the left wing of the Italian Communist Party.

54. See chapter 3 on Plato, p. 100.

55. Letter addressed to Neill on January 3, 1956.

56. See chapter 7, p. 161.

57. See chapter 3 on Plato, p. 100.

58. The only school recognized by Reich's immediate pupils is the American College of Orgonomy (http://www.orgonomy.org/).

59. Reich (1946, IX.7, p. 237).

60. Reich's letter to Ola Raknes, February 13, 1947.

61. Letter of January 13, 1947, from Reich to Raknes.

62. Reich (1952a, 3, p. 119).

63. Reich (1948a).

64. Lyotard, *Le différend, le dialogue*, (1983, p. 42f).

65. The US Food and Drug Administration (FDA) tested Reich's experiment on orgone for several years, before deciding that orgone does not exist. Although biased, their enquiry was serious (Sharaf, 1983, VIII.28).

66. See Reich (1953), *The Murder of Christ*.

67. For a description of Reich's hallucinations, see P. Reich (1974); for the attacks of authoritarianism and his relations with his (former) patients, see Sharaf (1983) and Makari (2008).

68. The translation to an introduction by Rudolph Steiner, which I recommended, shows the relevance of Goethe's text for the movements of theosophical inspiration in the twentieth century.

CHAPTER 19

1. The College of Orgonomy never undertook this kind of endeavor. I have the impression they condemned it.

2. The difficulty is that there is no consensual definition of psychotherapy.

3. Young (2008) offers a complementary view of this history.

4. Boadella provided this information to me via an email on January 19, 2011.

5. For more on Biosynthesis, see Boadella (1987). You could also see http://en.wikipedia.org/wiki/David_Boadella, visited in March 2012.

6. See Boadella (1973) for an overview of the neo-Reichian schools of the 1970s.

7. The most popular guru in the realm of body psychotherapy was probably Bhagwan Shri Rajneesh, who asked to be called Osho when he founded his sect in the United States. His students introduced tantric techniques in Europe and America. See Sloterdijk (1996, p. 105).

8. See Staunton (2002).

9. The categories are based on examples I have known.

10. See, for example, G. Boyesen (2001), Brown (1988), Keleman (1985), or Pierrakos (1990). Their models can be taken as kitschy metaphors that nevertheless express profound clinical intuitions.

11. I am grateful to Angela Belz-Knöferl for having reminded me of the intensity of this avid curiosity that animated the body psychotherapy movements of the 1970s. I am referring to our discussions at the EABP ethics commission near Nuremberg, March 14, 2008.

12. *Adire* was at first the French-language journal of Biodynamic psychology founded by the Boyesen family and their colleagues. It has changed orientation by becoming

the journal of the French School of Psycho-Organic Analysis. I was the first editor-in-chief of this journal.

13. I thank Joop Valstar, then president of the EABP, for providing me with those details (e-mail of July 16, 2007).

14. See also Young (2011).

15. *Körper und Wort in der Psycho-therapie* was written in English, but Downing could not find a publisher who would publish it with acceptable conditions.

16. For example, Duruz and Gennart (2002, p. 179), Guimón (1997a, p. 16). These commentaries make reference mostly to events that happened in the 1970s. These authors claim that the situation is the same today. Having discussed this issue with them, I noticed that they do not really know what is happening today in a field that does not really interest them.

17. The French Psycho-Organic Analysis had put an ethics and deontological committee in place already in the 1980s, which is when it was created.

18. See Boadella (1976) for some examples of the way that this generation thought.

19. Boadella (1976, p. 266).

20. Dadoun (1975, 45, p. 331).

21. See Reich and Raknes (1957).

22. Mostly child psychiatry. See Raknes, letter to Reich, February 16, 1947.

23. Bunkan (2003, 1.2.1, p. 23). Bunkan's general evaluation is that Waal's system of body reading is simplistic if we compare it to other available systems. She included items necessary to Vegetotherapy that are not found in other systems. Bunkan (2003) included these items in her synthesis of Scandinavian systems of body reading.

24. This information is based on an email in which Berit Bunkan reported a conversation she had with Braatøy's wife (October 25, 2006).

25. Fenichel (1945a, pp. 113, 447).

26. Braatøy (1954, p. 55).

27. Braatøy maintained constructive relations with Raknes. See the letters from Raknes to Reich, December 18, 1947, and April 15, 1948.

28. Braatøy (1942; 1954, p. 237).

29. Kaiser Wilhelm II, the last German emperor.

30. I am following Bunkan's memory in a discussion of June 2004.

31. Bunkan (2003, 1.1, p. 22).

32. Beebe (2005), Beebe and Lachmann (2002), Stern (1985). In a discussion I had with Daniel Stern, he confirmed that this was a plausible way of situating his proposal (Geneva, June 13, 2007). See also Braatøy (1954, VIII.1, p. 231).

33. Melanie Klein was one of the most creative psychoanalysts of the 1940s. A more recent development of this way of approaching patients is Otto Kernberg's proposal for narcissistic and borderline patients. One of Klein's most important set of observations is her analysis of human meanness, which she could already detect when working with infants. This theme remains difficult to digest for many of Klein's colleagues but is nonetheless a central issue for all forthcoming theories of human affects. See Edwards (2004), Klein (1923, 1925).

34. Braatøy (1954, VIII.2, p. 104).

35. Ibid., XI.6, p. 363f.

36. This is an imaginary example. My father did not smoke.

37. Heller et al. (2001).

38. See chapter 20, p. 604f, to understand what is meant by habitual behaviors that have no apparent function or meaning.

39. For example, suicide reattempters may have lower levels of serotonin, but this was not tested.

40. Blumenthal (2001), Boadella (1997).

41. Mostly Heller (1998). In this article, I show that probably more than millions of body signs are exchanged in a dyadic psychotherapy session.

42. See chapter 20 on nonverbal communication, p. 581.

43. See chapter 14, p. 346.

44. This is Boadella's term for such phenomena (Boadella, 1987). See also Kignel (2010).

45. Jaffe et al. (2002) and Bucci (1997) give several examples of such forms of interaction. They are psychoanalysts who study how nonconscious interaction patterns participate in a psychoanalytical treatment.

46. Braatøy (1954, VI.1, p. 157), Heller et al. (2001).

47. Braatøy (1954, V.1, p. 117; 1942).

48. Ibid., VIII.1: 237, VI.5, p. 181.

49. Ajuriaguerra and Cahen (1960), Badoni (1997), Dechaud-Ferbus et al. (1994), Roux and Dechaud-Ferbus (1993).

50. Braatøy (1954, III, p. 80f).

51. Ibid., VII.2, pp. 222–225.

52. See p. 525f in this chapter.

53. Braatøy (1954, V.7, p. 144).

54. Ibid., V.7, p. 144, VIII.1, p. 235.

55. Ibid., VI.1, p. 157.

56. Ibid., V.6, p. 141.

57. Ibid., V.5, p. 180s, VI.5, p. 179.

58. Ibid., VI.1, p. 162, VI.4, p. 175f.

59. Jacobson (1938).

60. Braatøy (1954, p. 167).

61. See also Boyesen (1985a, III.11, pp. 133–137), Heller (2004b). For a recent research on the subject of stretch-and-yawn and the startle reflex, see P. Brown et al. (1991) and Van der Linden et al. (2007).

62. Braatøy (1954, VIII.3, p. 261; 1947). Fenichel stresses that the function of the character armor is to avoid the pain of anxiety. The search for pleasure is still a part of the psychoanalytical theory, but it is closer to the horizon than a part of the landscape.

63. Braatøy (1954, V.6–7, p. 142f).

64. Ibid., X.8, p. 373.

65. Ibid., VII.1, p. 233.

66. Opisthotonus is a condition in which, "from a tetanic spasm of the muscles of the back, the head and the lower limbs are bent backward, and the trunk is arched forward" (*Blakiston's New Gould Medical Dictionary*, 1956). See the Glossary for a general definition.

67. Bunkan (2003).

68. See Thornquist and Bunkan (1991) and G. Boyesen (1985a, I.3, p. 23).

69. See Chatton et al. (2001).

70. A French form of psychomotricity that analyzes the biomechanics of movement and does not use massage. Véronique Haynal-Reymond was a member of that team.

71. Bunkan (2003, 11, p. 22).

72. See entry for "muscular chains" in the glossary. Several physiotherapists have taken a similar stand (e.g., Ida Rolf and Françoise Mézières).

73. My information on this topic comes from a DVD of Bülow-Hansen at work, presented by Gudrun Øvreberg, in Norwegian. She kindly sent me a copy in January 2009. See also Øien (2010, p. 24).

74. Braatøy (1954 V.6, p. 143).

75. Boyesen (1985a, I.3, p. 24).

76. Davis (2001), Rolf (1977).

77. Thornquist and Bunkan (1991, 71, pp. 73–85).

78. Andersen (1992, pp. 58–59).

79. See Boyesen (1985a, I.3, p. 25), Thornquist and Bunkan (1991, 9, p. 116f).

80. My information is mostly based on Boyesen (1985a) and on what I learned as one of her students in the 1970s and then as a colleague.

81. See chapter 18, p. 503f.

82. Boyesen (1985a, p. 14).

83. Boyesen's expression in the 1970s, according to my memory.

84. Boyesen (1985a, II.2, p. 46f).

85. Boyesen (1970). Examples of such techniques can be found in the chapter on biodynamic massage, in the 1992 second textbook of the French School of Psycho-Organic Analysis. This volume also contains useful articles written by Jacqueline Besson, Ebba Boyesen, Mona-Lisa Boyesen, Anne Fraisse, and Elsa Vaudaine.

86. See chapter 8, p. 209f.

87. Gerda Boyesen's usual expression.

88. Translated by J. M. Rigg. Downloaded in November 2010 from http://www.gutenberg.org/ebooks/3726

89. This position is, for example, close to some of Simone de Beauvoir's ideas (De Beauvoir (1947).

90. See Geuter (1984) and Cocks (1997) for concrete examples.

91. Boyesen (2001).

92. Konstantin Kornilov, a pupil of Pavlov in the Soviet Union, was developing a theory of reflexes and reactions of the organism. This theory was popular in these days, mostly among researchers and clinicians who sympathized with communism. It was incorporated in the theories of Vygotsky and Luria. This is seldom mentioned today, although it remains interesting. It is probably in this theoretical frame that Reich constructed his theory of reflexes (Van der Veer and Valsiner, 1991, I.6, p. 112f). In Kornilov's "reactology," a reaction is a system of heterogeneous reflexes.

93. Thelen and Smith (1994, I.1, pp. 10–16).

94. See the section in chapter 7 on Darwin, p. 174.

95. See also Reich 1940, VIII.6, p. 281.

96. Reich (1949b).

97. Hugo Heller (1909), Reich (1949b).

98. "Pelvic morphology, as measured by the pelvic incidence angle, tends to increase during childhood and adolescence before stabilizing into adulthood, most likely to maintain an adequate sagittal balance in view of the physiologic and morphologic changes occurring during growth" (Mac-Thiong et al., 2004).

99. See the sections on Vegetotherapy, pp. 475 and 477.

100. See Makari (2008).

101. See chapter 3, p. 93f.

102. The main reference for this section is Lowen (1975, I).

103. In the sections dedicated to Oslo, I have already indicated that Reich required that his students become physicians. The political and judicial repression of the Reichian movement in the United States, at that time, made it indispensable that practitioners be physicians to be socially accepted.

104. For similar reasons, Charles Kelley, another of Reich's students, used the term *radix* when he founded his school.

105. Reich (1949a, III.XV.1, p. 402).

106. Ibid., II.VII.2, p. 155; III.XV.1, p. 400.

107. See Aboujaoude (2011).

108. Lowen distinguishes between the interventions on the body and somatic *interventions*, but he does not distinguish body and physiology in his *theory*.

109. Lowen (1975, II, p. 45f).

110. Hauswirth (2002, p. 183).

111. Hauswirth quotes Schindler (1996) and Downing (1996) as examples of colleagues trained in Bioenergetic analysis who have developed particularly refined body and psychological techniques.

112. See chapter 9, p. 267, for a more explicit critique of this type of character analysis.

113. See chapter 9.

114. Lowen and Lowen (1977, 2, pp. 11–18).

115. See chapter 2, p. 65f.

116. Lowen (1973).

117. Keleman (1970).

118. Lowen (1967), Marlock and Weiss (2006).

119. See chapter 13, p. 324f, and the Appendix.

120. This is an ideal topic for a thesis in a psychophysiology laboratory.

121. You can find a detailed example of this work in Downing (1996, I.3–4. pp. 28–52).

122. Heller (1993b).

123. See, in the appendix on posture, the basic Reichian posture.

124. Veronique Haynal-Reymond told me that she used this exercise when she worked as a psychomotrician in the Department of Sexology at the University Institution of Psychiatry in Geneva.

125. In Geneva in 1977.

126. Such a "typical" example is rarely experienced as such by a real patient; each therapist will use this exercise in his own way.

127. Lowen and Lowen (1977).

128. In this section, for the sake of brevity, I give contemporary clinical indications based on my clinical observations, instead of restricting the analysis to Lowen's hypotheses, which are described in most of his books.

129. The difference between hypo- and hyper-armored was discussed in chapter 18, p. 507f.

130. This is an expression coined by Winnicott (1960) to designate individuals who have a way of behaving that corresponds to an image that they want to give without taking into account what they feel and have the need to express.

131. See chapter 2, p. 60.

132. See Dohmen (1999).

133. In 1999, each one told me that he was the first to use this model. See Boadella's (1990b) clarifying statement on this subject. They did not mention Sheldon's theory.

134. Reich (1949a, XV).

135. See chapter 18 on Fenichel's last formulations on the body, p. 493f.

136. Ogden et al. (2006, 1, p. 4).

137. See Geissler (1996, 1997, 2002, 2005). One of the founders of this school, Jacques Berliner, presently teaches his own method in Belgium.

138. Geissler's journal, *Psychoanalyse und Körper*, develops this point of view since 2002.

139. Van der Kolk et al. (1996).

140. Levine and MacNaughton (2004), Ogden et al. (2006), Pesso (2001), Rothschild (2000).

141. See the authors of Ethnopsychiatry for a defense of this analysis. Kleinman (1986), for example, discusses body symptoms (back and headaches) in China by taking this point of view.

CHAPTER 20

1. Hall (1959, Introduction, p. 11).

2. Thelen and Smith (1994, Introduction). See also Moessinger (2008).

3. Sartre (1947).

4. Vurpillot (1968), Vurpillot and Bullinger (1981).

5. Hess (1965). For a more detailed description, see http://www.muskingum.edu/~psych/psycweb/history/hess.htm

6. This notion is described in the sections dedicated to Von Helmholtz and Wundt (chapter 14, p. 341f). See Crick (1995, pp. 4, 31, 54–57, 163).

7. This position has been brilliantly illustrated by MacEvoy and Epstein (2011).

8. This is a pun on "knowing by heart."

9. Defontaine (2003); Hurni and Stoll (2003, p. 874).

10. Racamier (1992, pp. 280–340).

11. See Winkin (1981).

12. Birdwhistell (1970a).

13. See Birdwhistell (1970a, p. 240f; 1970b) and Bateson (1971).

14. An important issue for such studies is that these researchers did not have the right to publish the film they had analyzed. These legal and ethical constraints prevent us from showing our evidence as often as we would like. In the case of my research, I had to destroy the films once the teams I worked with had finished their analysis.

15. This is the theoretical solution. Practically, the coding is done every 20/100th, 50/100th of a second, or every second.

16. The equivalent of a spreadsheet.

17. For a summary on how to evaluate the reliability of a coding system, see Rosenberg et al. (2008), "Advanced FACS Methodological Issues," http://www.psy.miami.edu/faculty/dmessinger/c_c/rsrcs/rdgs/emot/FACS_conf_methods_workshop_final.ppt%20%5BCompatibility%20Mode.pdf

18. As in a spreadsheet program such as Microsoft Excel, a cell is the intersection between a row and a column.

19. In these sections, I basing the material on the basic system described by Siegfried Frey and his team in the 1980s (Frey et al., 1983) called Time Series Notation (TSN). Dancers like Rudolf Laban make the same kind of distinction, as you are able to discern in the quotes in chapter 18 (p. 504) and chapter 20 (p. 578).

20. This list is mostly based on Frey et al. (1980, 1983) and Heller (1991a).

21. Frey et al. (1980, 1983), Heller et al. (2001).

22. See also Doise (1978). This reasoning is the same as the observation that water has properties (put out a fire) that are not found in its constituent parts (oxygen and hydrogen individually enhance a fire).

23. See chapter 13, p. 323f

24. These behaviors form the frame of an interaction, as described by Goffman (1974). This flux of activities forms the weaving of an interaction.

25. Ekman and Rosenberg (1997), Frey et al. (1980).

26. See Ogden et al. (2006, p. 3) and the section in chapter 21 dedicated to Stern, Beebe, and Tronick.

27. Widlöcher (1983).

28. Frey et al. (1980, 1983).

29. Frey (1984, p. 65).

30. Heller (1991a, 1997).

31. The longer the anchor point of a posture is immobile, the more the posture is referred to as "stable."

32. For example, Haynal-Reymond et al. (2005), Magnusson (2000), Tronick (2007, III.15).

33. Widlöcher (1983).

34. One of the collaborators for this research was Walid Daw, who is now a reputed body psychotherapist in Bern, trained in Core energetics.

35. Frey et al. (1983).

36. Ekman and Friesen also code the depth of the movement—the chin gets closer to the throat without mobilizing the three other dimensions.

37. This study associates healing at the end of a depressive episode, not a healing for life. It therefore consists of amelioration.

38. This brings us back to the analysis of Fradin and his team. (chapter 8, p. 246f).

39. See *Manwatching* by Desmond Morris (1978) for examples.

40. Translation by W. F. Trotte, found online at http://www.gutenberg.org/ebooks/18269

41. The Laboratory of Affect and Communication (see the Glossary).

42. Frey (2008), Krause (1989).

43. Frey (1998, 2001).

44. An example of how the media can use such an effect intentionally is discussed in chapter 7, p. 190f, on "priming."

45. See chapter 21, p. 618f, on contingence.

46. See Kignel (2010).

47. See Kignel (2010, 3, p. 13).

48. For statistics in the United States, see http://www.childhelp.org/pages/statistics

49. See chapter 13, p. 334f, on the postural regulation of venous blood.

50. This is a form of thought at the root of what is called *functionalism* in the social sciences: the function of a phenomenon defines it.

51. Heller et al. (2001).

CHAPTER 21

1. For example, see Downing (1996). Ed Tronick and his team have also presented their findings in several congresses of body psychotherapy.

2. Reich (1948b, IX.3, p. 345f; 1952a, 3, p. 119).

3. The notion that dyads are the basic atom of interaction is also explored by Beebe and Tronick, discussed in this chapter. I have just shown that this theoretical stance can be associated to the methodological difficulties of studying dyads (Fivaz-Depeursinge and Corboz-Warnery, 1999).

4. Brazelton is mostly known for his Neonatal Behavioral Assessment Scale. This scale is based on the coding of 27 items of an infant's behavior and a neurological exam. In 1972, he created the Child Development Unit in the Faculty of Medicine at Harvard: a pediatric research and training center in development. Tronick, of whom I speak later, works in this laboratory.

5. See Rochat (2001 and 2011) for a complementary view of what infants and children need in terms of relational comfort.

6. Gergely and Watson (1999).

7. Stern (1977, 7, p. 128).

8. Ibid., 6, p. 112f. Also see Jaffe et al. (2002).

9. For Stern contingency is mostly an operational term, but some of his research can be used to illustrate my way of using it.

10. Beebe et al. (2007). See Beebe (2004) and Heller (2004a), and the sections dedicated to Beebe, for an example of the problem linked to contingency.

11. Stern (1985, III.9, p. 209f).

12. See chapter 14, the section on Wilma Bucci, p. 375f.

13. Stern (1995).

14. Stern (2004, 6).

15. Heller (2006).

16. See Beebe et al. (2005) for a general discussion on the notion of intersubjectivity.

17. Stern (1977, 6, p. 109f). Also see Beebe and Stern (2002), Beebe and Lachmann (2002, 5, p. 97).

18. On this theme, also see Paul Boyesen (1987).

19. These observations are both confirmed and inspired by the work of Beatrice Beebe and Ed Tronick, discussed in the next sections.

20. We again find the choreographer Laban, who also influenced Reich, as a main reference for Stern. However, we are in a new generation. Stern explicitly mentions in detail and with respect the artists who inspired him.

21. Heller (1991a, 1997), Lichtenberg (1989), Ogden et al. (2006, 3, p. 42), and Sander (1985).

22. Beebe and Lachmann (2002, 7).

23. Beebe et al. (2005, pp. 14–18).

24. Heller et al. (2001), Sperber and Wilson (1986).

25. Beebe and Lachmann (2002, p.156f).

26. Yet many psychotherapists, in all schools, have imposed this type of functional interpretation on their patients.

27. In this discussion, the behaviorist is any psychotherapist who is an expert on behavior. He does not necessarily belong to the behaviorist school of thought inspired by

Watson and Skinner. He can refer to ethology, nonverbal communication, systemics, Gestalt therapy, and body psychotherapy.

28. We are close to the lures described in chapter 9, p. 270f

29. Beebe (2004), Heller (2004a).

30. Also see Heller (2004a). I will soon describe the analysis made by Downing and his colleagues (Downing, Bürgin, Reck, and Ziegenhain, 2008).

31. Beebe et al. (2007).

32. Beebe et al. (2010, 2011). Even if Beebe does not speak of this, I think that the variability of the amount of contingency is also an important dimension of a relational pattern.

33. It consists of a film of a session or psychotherapist Paul Roland with a schizophrenic (Braatøy, 1954, VI, p. 157f.).

34. Tronick (2007, Introduction, pp. 2–4).

35. Hermine Sinclaire de Swart taught this theory in her courses on psycholinguistics at the Jean-Jacques Rousseau Institute in Geneva in the 1970s. See also Werker and Tees (1984).

36. This is an example. I have not found research that attempts to support this hypothesis.

37. This is an example of a hypothesis that we find in Stern and Beebe. It consists of discoveries made in parallel generated by similar research procedures.

38. See chapter 8, p. 241, on the pleasure of dependency as a motivator of social ties.

39. Images of this effect may be seen with a Google search on the phrase "Konrad Lorenz imprinting geese."

40. Tronick (2007, III.15).

41. Tronick bases himself on several sources, among which we find Beatrice Beebe and Colwyn Trevarthen.

42. It consist here of an example of fascinating work that was not developed in a publication. I am therefore referring to what has inscribed in my memory and has since influenced my clinical work with mothers who recently gave birth.

43. M.-L. Boyesen (1985).

44. Frey (2001).

45. See Beebe et al. (2008).

46. Films of these situations can be found with an internet search on Ed Tronick.

47. Tronick (2007, Introduction, p. 11f; IV, 23, p. 325; 25, p. 356f).

48. Tronick (1998).

49. Reich (1952a, p. 44) had also observed the alternating aggression/collapse in the infant during birth rituals.

50. Tronick (2007, III.14, pp. 184–185).

51. The variety of behaviors is a current observation in the studies of nonverbal communication. Heller et al. (2001) used the coding system FACS designed by Ekman and Friesen to analyze the facial behavior of twenty-six depressed patients for twenty seconds. They identified sixty facial expressions. Only ten were used by more than one person, and two by more than three persons. This variety is only accessible through the use of a coding system as refined as FACS.

52. Tronick (2007, III.22. p. 305f).

53. Ibid., III. 22, p. 307; IV. 26, pp. 369–377.

54. Mostly in seminars given by George Downing and Elizabeth Fivaz-Depeursinge.

55. Tronick (2007, III. 14, p. 187f; IV. 22, p. 307; 23, p. 320).

56. This is a case of disturbances that complicate the rapport to an object and not of mental retardation. In his courses, Piaget regularly said that the rapidity of development does not correlate with the final result.

57. This is a speculative example. It corresponds to what I observe in my practice with several adult patients who had a depressed mother. It goes without saying that the mother is not the only determining element in a person's development.

58. Downing et al. (2007). This is my interpretation of the case described by Downing and his collaborators.

59. Heller (2004a).

60. The capacity to discern these multiple expressions by using FACS is discussed in chapter 22, p. 649f dedicated to Downing.

61. This type of common movement of the mouth has been studies in detailed fashion by Papousek and Papousek (1979, 1997).

62. Beebe and Lachmann (2002).

63. Fivaz-Depeursinge and Corboz-Warnery (1999, p. 118), Rochat (2001).

64. As in Jung's work (1940) on what the adult patient's dreams teach us about their childhood.

65. See Beebe and Lachmann (2002), Downing (2006).

CHAPTER 22

1. The interest in the 1980 article is that it addresses itself first to the milieu of body psychotherapists in California and only later to a larger public. The fact that it was published in between an article by David Boadella and another by Eva Reich clearly indicates that he is not the only one to feel the necessity for a reflection of this type. Reich's contribution is known and acknowledged but does not seem to be a central theme in Downing's thoughts on the field of body psychotherapy.

2. See Downing (2001) for an example of the way he sorts out the material proposed by body psychotherapists.

3. Downing (2003). Also see the sections in chapter 21 on the case of Karen and Diana, p. 629f. For other discussions on the analysis of micro-practices with video in psychotherapy, see Cohen and Beebe (2002), Gammer (2005, II.3), M. Papousek (2000).

4. Downing (1980, 1996).

5. For example, he quotes studies on "triads" of Fivaz-Depeursinge and Corboz-Warnery (1999).

6. In Downing's book, body psychotherapy is a set of methods that can be used in various forms of integrative psychotherapy.

7. This section is based on Downing (1996, I.7, pp. 72–99) and on a discussion I had with Downing in Paris on December 9, 2007.

8. See the section in chapter 10 dedicated to issues on energy, p. 277f.

9. See chapter 18, p. 514f, dedicated to von Helmholtz and Goethe.

10. This notion is close to that of *core organizers* proposed by Ron Kurtz (1990, p. 69) and Pat Ogden et al. (2006, II.9, p. 196). See also Chomsky (1980, I.4, p. 144f) for the distinction between base and surface structures in linguistics.

11. I refer to a discussion that I had with Downing on this topic in Paris, December 6, 2009.

12. Downing (1996, 2006).

13. We have seen (chapter 4, p. 260f; chapter 20, p. 112f) that for Hobbes there is a need of at least two for an individual to become conscious of a way of doing things.

14. Papousek and Papousek (1979).

15. For this section, see Merleau-Ponty (1945, I.3, pp. 90–119).

16. Kelly (2000).

17. Merleau-Ponty (1945, I.3, p.116).

18. Ibid.

19. See the sections on Kurt Goldstein in chapter 8, p. 214f.

20. Merleau-Ponty (1945, I.3, p. 116).

21. Krause and Lütolf (1988), Steimer-Krause et al. (1990).

22. The patient's smile was a bit more complicated.

23. Unit 24B is a flattening of the lips against the teeth, and unit 26B indicates a space between the teeth.

24. The distinction between representations of what is done and what is actually put in action is also proposed by Gallagher and Cole (1995), who differentiate body images and body schemas. Gallagher (2005) also uses a distinction of this type. According to him, even on the neurological level, these two types of functioning have fuzzy contours. According to him, these two systems can only be partially differentiated.

25. See Downing (2000, 2006).

26. This aspect of George Downing's model is close to the one that Fradin (2008) and Feldenkrais (1949, 15) describe.

27. Downing quotes, among others, the works of Nico Frijda (1986, 2006) and Keith Oatley (1992), which I can also recommend.

28. See Downing (2000, p. 246f).

29. Beebe and Lachmann (2002), Cohen and Beebe (2002).

30. See also Gendlin (1996, 1998, chapters 6 and 12), Southwell (2010).

CONCLUSIONS

1. In North America "faculties" are often called schools or colleges of science, philosophy, theology, and so on.

2. The notion of *biosphere* was proposed by Viennese geologist Edward Suess (1831–1914). I thank Olivia Heller (email of October 20, 2010) for informing me about this foundational basis of a genetic systemic model that has served as a frame for this book. His theoretical endeavor was constructed to support his research on the evolution of the Earth's crust. It has since inspired the work of psychologists such as Jean Piaget and historians such as Fernand Braudel. Born in London, then professor in Vienna, Suess created the connection between the geology of Charles Lyell, who in turn created a temporal space for the elaboration of Wallace's and Darwin's theory, and the geology that influenced the Viennese philosophers and psychologists.

3. Haynal (1967).

4. In chapter 8, p. 209f, the approaches of Boyesen and Gershon on the connection between peristaltic activity and anxiety are compared.

5. This history is brilliantly told in Koestler (1959).

6. See how Cassirer describes such an ethics of knowledge in *The Philosophy of the Enlightenment* (1932).

APPENDIX

1. Feldenkrais (1949, chapter 12), Perez-Christiaens (1983), Rolf (1977).

2. Nordmark and Rohweder (1967, p. 198).

3. Bullinger (1998, 2004).

4. On this point, also see also Tinbergen (1974).

5. There is an angle of 180° when an individual is standing perfectly straight, and one of 90° when in an orthopedic sitting position.

6. The *padma-asana*, Iyengar (1966, photo 104).

7. Most of the orthopedists and physical therapists know of this way to sit; but they often use more pragmatic strategies to help an individual.

8. The sacrum and the back of the ilium.

9. The posterior superior iliac spine. You can easily feel its extremities protruding on the frontal upper part of the pelvis with your fingers.

Glossary

Accommodation. See *Adaptation.*

Adaptation. The adaptation of a living system is its capacity to find ways of relating to its environment that facilitate its survival. In Piaget's (1967, 1985) theory, this ability to adapt can follow two modes:

1. *Assimilation* permits a system to react appropriately to stimulation with the means available at a given moment. The infant can assimilate milk during its first year but not pieces of meat. A psychologist like Fenichel (1931) uses the terms *introjection* and *identification* to designate primitive forms of assimilation that is experienced as a need to incorporate objects, persons, or skills totally or partially.

2. There is an *accommodation* when an organism modifies an existing schema to adapt itself to a stimulation that it cannot assimilate. An animal organism accommodates its movements to the objects that surround it to use them adequately. Accommodation requires learning and a local modification of one's habitual mode of functioning.

For Piaget, and for most psy, these two modes must develop in a flexible and active way. They structure the dynamics of an organism.

Assimilation. See *Adaptation.*

Chronic. A chronic trait maintains itself over time. A muscular tension is chronic if it lasts at least for a few months, often a lifetime.

Default. I use this term as it is used for computers, to designate a way of functioning that will be used automatically unless other instructions are given.

Dynamic. A mechanism is dynamic when it evolves over time. A system is considered dynamic when it can take on several states or brings about new ones.

Ethics (professional). The French language clearly distinguishes ethics (morality) and deontology (the professional rules of behavior of a profession). In English, ethics often refers to the science and philosophy of morality, and to "a set of moral principles, especially ones relating to or affirming a specified group, field or form of conduct" (*The New Oxford Dictionary of English,* 1999, p. 631). Deontology, as in French, is "the study of the nature of duty and obligation" (*The New Oxford Dictionary of English,* 1999, p. 494). It is only the French professional associations that clearly differentiate between professional moral obligations and professional duties. In most other languages, ethics designates all forms of moral obligations and duty that are required from the members of a profession. The decision of the ethical stance required from the members of a profession is taken in a variety of ways that has changed with time. In some cases experts impose their visions on others in the name of an idealist and/or ideological stance, while in others the decisions follow a democratic procedure. This brings us back to the old issue raised by Plato on whether the vote of the masses can define moral issues.

Being neither solely morality nor solely rules, professional ethics, such as it is conceived by the majority of boards or commissions of professional ethics, is the opposite of individual ethics. The two necessarily have a dialectic dynamic, as there are cases where professional ethics are guided by ideology (as in religious and communist regimes), and cases where individual ethics can lead to behaviors that are condemned by most forms of socially constructed morals and laws. A democratic process such as the ones that have been implemented in the European Association of Body Psychotherapy requires that social and individual ethics enter into a binding dialogue, in which individual ethics can be expressed when professional ethics are being voted, but which may lead to exclusion if a member does not follow the rules that have been implemented. However, a rule can be modified if a strong majority supports this option. The difficulty is that most members adhere to an ethical code by default when they enter the association, but have not followed an in-depth learning process that could allow them to accommodate their inner moral dynamics to professional standards. The ethics of most professionals is therefore a fuzzy compromise which assumes that no one should ignore the law, but that only experts can decide on what is really ethical or not.

Ethics is not simply a game of rules guided by a legal spirit, because above all, it is the pride of a profession and the framework within which it conducts its intellectual and practical life. In the realm of therapies, professional ethics offers protection to the client and the service provider by guaranteeing behaviors that attempt to make the spirit of a profession as explicit as possible. Ethics is more than a set of professional rules. It is an attempt to construct a proactive humanist stance that guarantees that the members of a profession have a moral stance that others can trust. Ethical committees tend to defend principles rather than rules.

Cognitive ethics require that the professional be aware of the theories and techniques that characterize his profession and that colleagues be able to evaluate the practitioner's theories and methods. This implies the capacity to distinguish between personal opinions and beliefs, fashionable ideas, intellectual styles, and the knowledge that supports a form of practice.

FACS. Facial Action Coding System. Ekman and Friesen's (1978, 2002) coding system of facial activity.

Flux and reflux. This term is used by Reich (1951, chapter IV; G. Boyesen, 1985b) and his pupils to describe the dynamics of cosmic energy in the organism. Like the ebb and flow of the tide, the energy rises from the feet to the head (flux) in the dorsal part of the body, and then descends from the face to the feet (reflux) on the front of the body. In Reich's work and in the neo-Reichian schools, the concept of "reflux" describes a global energetic movement that descends from the head toward the feet while mobilizing the organism in a relaxing fashion. The relaxation that occurs after an orgasm is an example of a reflux.

Gestalt. *Gestalt* is the German term for a form. This term designates a German school of experimental psychology that studied the psychology of perception. Their basic assumption is that "one's visual field is structured in terms of 'figure' and 'background'" (Perls et al., 1951, p. 25). A green triangle can be perceived differently if it is painted on a blue or a white background. Gestalt psychology was founded at the beginning of the twentieth century by Max Wertheimer, Wolfgang Kohler, and Kurt Koffka. The movement was centered in Frankfort, where it also found the support of neurologist Kurt Goldstein. Gestalt psychology attained an international reputation during the 1920s. Influenced by phenomenology, it is known for its detailed studies on how the whole influences its parts. This German term is used in most languages to designate a holistic approach to individual systems and shapes. Fritz Perls and his colleagues (1951) created a form of psychotherapy inspired by this psychology. Laura and Fritz Perls had studied with the founders of Gestalt psychology in Frankfurt during the 1930s.

Habitus. This Latin term is used to designate a way of being that interacts reciprocally with a way of doing. This way of being has such deep roots that its manifestations and modes of functioning are nonconscious. This term was originally used by philosophers such as Aristotle, Thomas Aquinas, and Leibniz, but it is mostly Husserl who introduced it in modern literature. His use of the word designates how our past experiences influence our present way of perceiving and reacting to our environment. The term has acquired a slightly different meaning for European sociologists such as Max Weber, Marcel Mauss, and Pierre Bourdieu when they describe an *ethnic habitus*. The habitus is then an acquired mixture of ways of thinking, ways of behaving and of appearance. It is a way of living that is structured by and structures a style of life. Ideology, sports, clothes, and taste can define the habitus of a group or an individual. These manifestations of a lifestyle have such a deep influence on an organism that it can even impact physiological regulatory mechanisms. The example, most often discussed in this textbook, is that of the influence of the ethnic habitus on a person's postural repertoire. For example, I have shown that sitting on chairs has spread throughout the world in the past centuries. This change of the human postural repertoire has generated pathologies such as a loss of the flexibility of the joints, obesity, backaches, and cardiovascular problems. It is probable that body dynamics did not emerge in a world full of chairs and cultural rituals that require that one maintains a posture for hours. "The schemes of the habitus . . . owe their specific efficacy to the fact that they function below the level consciousness and language, beyond the reach of introspective scrutiny or control by the will. Orienting practices practically, they embed what some would mistakenly call *values* in the most automatic gestures or the apparently more insignificant techniques of the body—ways of walking or blowing one's nose, ways of eating and talking—and engage the most fundamental principles of construction an evaluation of the social world" (Bourdieu, 1979, conclusion, p. 466).

Illusions (necessary): Necessary illusions are forms of perception that are generated by the laws that rule mental dynamics. They are *illusions* because they include more than the information provided by the senses; they are *necessary* because without them mental dynamics would cease to function adequately.

Ischia (ischium). The two points (ischial tuberosity) of the pelvis situated on each side of the anus.

LAC. The Laboratory of Affects and Communication, which I directed from 1988 to 1999, was composed of a research team of the Department of Psychiatry of Geneva. My principal collaborators were Christine Lesko, Veronique Haynal-Reymond, and Patricia Claus. The goal of the laboratory was the study of the facial behavior of depressed and suicidal patients, using Ekman and Friesen's FACS procedure.

Latissimi dorsi (the large dorsal muscles). There are two large dorsal muscles, one on each side of the spinal column. The higher end of the muscle is attached under the armpit (axilla). It descends the length of the lumbar vertebrae, all the way to the rhomboid tendons that attach it to the sacrum, slides over the top of the buttocks, and runs along the top of the pelvis. It therefore surrounds the posterior half of the diaphragm. Its elasticity serves as a resistance to and container for the dorsal and lateral respiration of the diaphragm. Finally, these muscles participate in the position of the back and the spinal column. Experimenting with these muscles by moving the spinal column is a way to feel one's strength, not in the sense of violence but in the sense of contained power. What does this mean? First, the activity of the large dorsal is connected to the arms. To stretch the large dorsal muscles by lifting the arms toward the front accentuates the lumbar curvature and makes the pelvis passively back up, while facilitating respiration. By lowering the arms, the lumbar curvature stretches. The coccyx moves forward, the sexual region advances, the abdominal muscles tone up, all of which solicit exhalation. Here, the important little detail is that the rhomboid tendons, situated below the large dorsal muscles (near the spinal column and the pelvis), form a zone that does not *initiate* the movement. The movement is necessarily initiated in the *muscular* zone that supports the armpits. The movement of the large dorsal muscle spreads out toward the trapezoid (toward the top) and the buttocks (toward the bottom), which it coordinates. When you round your back by having the spinal cord take a global concave shape (in a C), which goes from the thighs to the head, the ventral face of the thorax becomes spontaneously convex; if they are relaxed, the arms spontaneously move away from the body toward the front and the side. If you activate such a concave shape of the trunk while standing, you will notice that the pelvis spontaneously moves forward, that you are exhaling, that your knees bend, and that very rapidly you mobilize all of the dorsal chain of the body, from your toes to your ears. To be able to feel this type of movement is often pleasurable, and it can help people become aware of their muscular and mental blocks. A way to explore this mechanical chain is to slowly alternate between a C-shaped (concave) spine and a D-shaped (convex) spine, while coordinating the movement with soft breathing:

> This muscle can function as a strong respiratory inhibitor; due to its position and form it can reduce thorax volume. It can also function as an expiratory muscle. If these muscles are short and tense, dorso-basal and dorso-thoracic expansion is prevented. This muscle can "lock" the back, preventing natural associated movements during different functions. Thus the back and breathing lose important stimuli to maintaining good func-

tion, due to the reduction of trunk rotation. Latissimus dorsi can also "lock" the arms into the thorax, thus preventing and inhibiting free function of arms and scapulae. (Thornquist and Bunkan, 1991, p. 80)

To test the latissimi dorsi, do the following exercise: You are sitting on the edge of a table. The pelvis sits on the ischial tuberocities; the back is straight. The arms rise in front, parallel, until the hands are as high as the skull. The hands are limp. Then, all of a sudden, you let your arms fall while exhaling. Do that a dozen times, taking a few breaths in between each movement. The important detail is to minimally mobilize the space between the shoulder blades.

If you are relaxed, you will be able to feel how lifting the arms arches the lumbar curve a bit, and how it relaxes when the arms come down. Not always, but often, respiration has then been increased at the level of the diaphragm. All of these coordinations are mobilized during orgasm, such as Wilhelm Reich described.

Muscular chains. A muscular chain is a cascade of muscles that link several body segments (Mézières, 1978, 1984). The best known is the dorsal chain that goes from the heels to below the occiput at the top of the neck. It forms a sort of elastic band that, when the body is relaxed, moves the body segments. For example, sit down on the edge of a table, your bottom well placed on the ischial bones, and rock your trunk forward and backward a number of times. You will notice that if you are relaxed, your feet move automatically under the table when you tilt your trunk forward; they move ahead when your trunk tilts backward. When the trunk leans forward, the "elastic" muscular chain extends itself around the pelvis and pulls on the nape of the neck (the head tips lightly backward) as the feet get closer to the bottom. When the trunk tips toward the back, the "elastic" extends itself, the knees stretch out, and the feet go forward. If body segments do not spontaneously coordinate in this way, one can assume that (a) a muscular or psychic tension blocks the elasticity of the muscular chain and/or (b) the pelvis is placed on the coccyx instead of the ischial tuberocities. Wilhelm Reich's orgastic reflex requires a balanced activation of the frontal and dorsal muscular chains.

Nonconscious. I use this term to designate psychological phenomena that influence consciousness but cannot be explicitly perceived through introspection. If it is possible to make the unconscious conscious in approaches such as Psychoanalysis, it is impossible to make the nonconscious conscious, because nonconscious mechanisms do not have a *format* that conscious procedures can grasp (e.g., they are too complex). On the other hand, consciousness is able to infer that what it perceives correlates with a nonconscious phenomenon. The individual may then improve his way of interacting with the nonconscious dynamics.

Opisthotonus. The term *opisthotonus* is a medical term, often used in the nineteenth century. It is a condition in which, "from a tetanic spasm of the muscles of the back, the head and the lower limbs are bent backward, and the trunk is arched forward" (*Blakiston's New Gould Medical Dictionary*, 1956). The body takes on the shape of an arch that renders the dorsal face of the body concave and makes the thorax protrude. This position became known as a sign of suffering by psychoanalysts because it was often associated to hysterical behavior by Charcot. It is a reaction that can be used by a child, when "he tries desperately with his neck and jaw to hold back something which is taken away from him" (Braatøy, 1954, VII.1, p. 233f). It also corresponds to expressions of pain that Reich, Beebe, and Tronick observe in babies who are in a painful crisis. However, it can also be observed in expressions of pleasure in children, or in adults during sexual interactions.

Psys. I use this term so that I not to have to mention psychologists, psychotherapists, and psychoanalysts each time I refer to them as a group.

Psoas. The deep muscles often escape of the analysis of the body psychotherapist, but the psoas is difficult to ignore. It regulates the relationship between the thighs and the spinal column around the pelvis. The psoas goes from the last dorsal vertebrae (that carry the last rib), descends along the inferior part of the spinal column, slides inside the pelvis, and attaches itself to the interior of the thigh (on the top of the femur). It contributes to flexion and external rotation in the hip joint, and is involved in all movements that regulate the angle between the thighs and the trunk.

Regulation. A system of regulation is a circular causal system. It consists in being able to initiate an action and accommodate its dynamic to its goal. There is regulation of respiration when the lungs modify the amplitude of their movements as a function of the oxygen needs of the organism. There is regulation of a population when its demographics vary as a function of its resources. In all of these cases, a causal chain is (a) composed of heteroclite elements that (b) are continuously calibrated in function of how the system inserts itself in its immediate environment. This notion was first developed by biologists such as Lamarck, Bernard, Wallace, and Cannon. It became known in the psychological world in the 1930s, notably in the work of Piaget, Jacobson, and Reich. After Wiener's (1948) presentation of cybernetics, the concept of regulation again finds itself in all disciplines, especially when the theoretical frame is systemic. Internal regulation (or auto-regulation) is the way a system (e.g., an organism) regulates itself in function of its inner requirements, but this system can also be influenced by external procedures produced by other systems (e.g., a group of persons) that contain it. Distinguishing internal and external regulation is often useful, but difficult.

Robust. In statistics, a fact is considered robust when it has been described in a reliable manner by a large number of independent researchers (there has therefore been replication of the observations) who used different methods, even though it cannot yet be explained. A robust fact is therefore a respectable empirical observation that cannot yet acquire the status of being scientific. In theoretical research, a notion only becomes robust when it is used by several different theories. Thus, the correlation between anxiety and respiratory difficulties is robust given that the observation has been made over thousands of years by numerous practitioners who used different approaches. However, for the moment, we do not know which mechanisms connect anxiety and breathing or allow us to treat anxiety in a relatively permanent way using breathing exercises.

Scheme, schema, or schemata. The term *schema,* inspired by Kant, is used in the Piagetian literature to designate a system that organizes local mental and bodily mechanisms that allow a habitual procedure to vary in function of expected modifications of its environment (Inhelder and de Caprona, 1992, p. 40f). It designates any stable strategy that allows an organism to create a relevant way of contacting certain aspects of its environment. In some translations, *schema* and *schemata* are also used. A gesture that allows one to behave in a certain way with an object or a person is a *sensory-motor* scheme. The production of mental strategies to resolve an intellectual problem is a *cognitive* scheme. A scheme is necessarily the product of habits that formed themselves in the past, but which is adapted through a series of assimilation and accommodation to manage a present task. As an organism possesses a large number of schemes, the emergence of a new scheme can activate a general restructuring of the way schemes are coordinated in an organism (Inhelder and de Caprona, 1992, p. 40f). This restructuring is often partial, and rarely coherent. It is constructed through a dialectical dialogue between the constraints of the mechanisms that regulate organismic calibration and a trial-and-error strategy.

Self. The notion of self was introduced by Jung as a psychological equivalent of the soul (in the modern sense defined in this glossary). It refers to a coherent and unified psychological matrix that mostly functions behind the scene of consciousness. This notion was included in modern Freudian psychoanalysis by authors such as Kohut and Winnicott. It is also used in experimental psychologists by authors such as Rochat and Stern.

Sensory deprivation. There is sensory deprivation when senses are prevented, for a certain length of time, from acquiring the information they need. Such an experience may lower the capacity to understand and use information provided after the sensory deprivation experience has ended. This subject has been extensively studied by NASA to understand the difficulties astronauts may experience in space. Sensory deprivation is also a well-known form of torture that can generate lasting forms of mental disorientation and hallucinations (Blouin and Bergeron, 1997, 60; Hebb, 1958; Otterman, 2007; Weinstein, 1967).

Soma and somatic. Soma and somatic therapy schools tend to lump together what I call body, physiology, and metabolism. This can sometimes be a return to the old body/mind duality.

Soul.

1. *Traditional sense.* In the sections of the chapters dedicated to philosophers, I describe several visions of the notion of the soul. Its traditional sense, it seems to me, is that of a force that *structures* the organism in such a way that it becomes capable of organizing itself around conscious thoughts. This approach leads to endless discussions as to which objects and creatures have a soul. This understanding is still alive in those movements that suppose a spirit creates the existence of everything and everyone and consequently is the origin of all souls. The soul "animates" the organism that contains it. In most cases, the psyche is part of the soul (Plato is one of the exceptions).

2. *Modern sense*: the word *soul* is often used to designate all the mechanisms that regulate an individual's thoughts, without distinguishing between affective and cognitive dynamics. In this sense, the term *soul* is sometimes used in this textbook when it is not explicitly associated to a particular school of thought.

Theosophy. The term *theosophy*, as used by certain gnostic and neo-Platonic movements, is associated with great European mystic philosophers like Meister Eckhart, Nicolas de Cusa, and Jacob Boehme. The Theosophical Society was founded in 1875 by Helena Petrova Blavatsky and her companions. Theosophy, inspired by the Free Masons, is based on the notion that all schools of mysticism and religions are different explicit descriptions of a unique spiritual reality.

Thoughts. I use this term, as does Descartes, to designate everything that can be explicitly perceived by consciousness. Therefore, a thought may be a body sensation, a feeling, an idea, a reasoning, a representation, or an ideation.

Transference (or transferential dynamics). Laplanche and Pontalis (1967) distinguish between an extended meaning and a strict meaning of the concept of transference. In its extended sense, transferential dynamics designate any psychological event that occurs in a therapeutic relationship. There is transference, in the strict sense, when the patient expects that the therapist will act like a person he knew in the past. He thus transfers attributes to the therapist that his memory associates with someone else. This transference often awakens repressed material in the therapist. There is then countertransference on his part. The countertransference is unconscious material activated by the transference of the other. The therapist can also initiate a transference. That transference does not depend on the patient's transference. It is activated by the therapist's own associations at the sight of the patient. In this book, I recommend the usage of the word *transference* in its strict sense because therapists today often distinguish relational phenomena that have other properties than those of transference. *Transferential dynamics* describe how transference and countertransference mutually influence each other.

References and Bibliography

Author's Note: The book was originally written in French. To the extent possible, I referred to English translations for key works, but it was not always possible for every reference (e.g., Henri Laborit's books have not been translated into English). Most of the ancient texts mentioned in the book are readily and freely available on the Internet. For recent articles, the abstracts are often available. It suffices to type the reference in a search engine to discover the sources. The advantage of having the text in an online version is to be able to conduct research through words. Create the habit of consulting the sources of what I quote, because they necessarily contain much more information than what I provide in this volume.

The page number is insufficient if you want to find out what I am referring to in another edition than mine. I provide the date of the original publication when it is available in parentheses, and when necessary the date of the edition I consulted at the end. If you consult a work in another language or another translation, the difficulty will even be greater. An asterisk (*) indicates items that can be freely downloaded from the Internet.

Aalberse, M. (2001). Graceful means: Felt gestures and choreographic therapy. In M. Heller (Ed.), *The flesh of the soul: The body we work with*: 101–132. Bern: Peter Lang.

Aboujaoude, E. (2011). *Virtually you: The dangerous powers of the e-personality*. New York: Norton.

Abraham, K. (1907). The experiencing of sexual traumas as a form of sexual activity. In *Selected papers of Karl Abraham*: 47–63. New York: Brunner/Mazel, 1979.

Abraham, K. (1908). The psycho-sexual differences between hysteria and dementia praecox. In *Selected papers*, t.1: 64–79. London: Basic Books, 1954.

Abraham, K. (1913a). Mental after-effects produced in a nine-year-old child by the observation of sexual intercourse between its parents. In *Selected papers*, t.1: 407–417. London: Basic Books, 1954.

Abraham, K. (1913b). Restrictions and transformations of scoptophilia in psychoneurotics; with remarks on analogous phenomena in folk-psychology. In *Selected papers of Karl Abraham*: 201–206. London: Hogarth Press, 1927.

Abraham, K. (1925). Étude psychanalytique de la formation du caractère. In *Selected papers*, t.1: 164–168. London: Basic Books, 1954.

Ackerknecht, E. H. (1974). The history of the discovery of the vegetative (autonomic) nervous system. *Medical History*, 18, 1: 1–8.

Adler, A. (1912). *Le tempérament nerveux* [Nervous character]. Paris: Payot, 1992.

Adler, A. (1927). *Connaissance de l'homme* [Understanding human nature]. Paris: Payot, 1992.

Adler, A. (1931). *What life should mean to you: The psychology of personal development*. Oxford: Oneworld Publications, 1992.*

Aichhorn, A. (1925). *Wayward youth*. London: Imago Publishing, 1951.

Ajuriaguerra, J. de, & Cahen, M. (1960). *La relaxation*. Paris: L'Éxpension.

Ajuriaguerra, J. de, & Hécaen, H. (1964). *Le cortex cérébral. Étude neuro-psycho-pathologique*. Paris: Masson.

Alcantara, P. de (1997). *Indirect procedures: A musician's guide to the Alexander technique*. Oxford: Oxford University Press.

Alexander, F. (1923). The castration complex in the formation of character. In *The scope of psychoanalysis, 1921–1961: Selected papers*: 3–30. New York: Basic Books, 1961.

Alexander, F. (1939). Psychological aspects of medicine. *Psychosomatic Medicine*, 1, 1:7–18.

Alexander, F. (1950). *Psychosomatic medicine: Its principles and applications*. New York: Norton, 1965.

Alexander, F. M. (1932). *The use of the self: Its conscious direction in relation to diagnosis functioning and the control of reaction*. London: Methuen.

Alexander, G. (1981). *Eutony: The holistic discovery of the total person*. New York: Felix Morrow.

Alnaes, R. (1980). The development of psychoanalysis in Norway. *Scandinavian Psychoanalytic Review*, 3:55–101.

Alquié, F. (1955). *Leçons sur Descartes. Science et métaphysique chez Descartes*. Paris: La Table Ronde, 2005.

Andersen, T. (1991). The reflecting team: Dialogues and dialogues about the dialogues. New York: Norton.

Anirvan, S. (2007). *Le yoga intérieur*. Golion: Infolio.

Anzieu, D. (1984). Le double interdit du toucher. *Nouvelle Revue de Psychanalyse*, 29:173–188.

Aposhyan, S. (1999). *Natural intelligence*. Baltimore: Williams & Wilkins.

Archinard, M., Haynal-Reymond, V., & Heller, M. (2000). Doctor's and patient's facial expressions and suicide reattempt risk assessment. *Journal of Psychiatric Research*, 34: 261–262.

Argyle, M., & Kendon, A. (1967). The experimental analysis of social performance. In L. Berkowitz (Ed.), *Advances in experimental social psychology*, 3:55–98. New York: Academic Press.

Aristophanes. (2002). The clouds (A. H. Sommerstein, Trans.). In *Lysistrata and other plays*: 75–132. Harmondsworth: Penguin Books.

Aristotle. *Métaphysique*. Traduit par J. Tricot. Paris: Vrin, 1991.

Aristotle. *Of the soul* (J. A. Smith, Trans.). Available at http://classics.mit.edu/Aristotle/soul.1.i.html

Asch, S. E. (1952). The individual and the group. In F. E. Emery (Ed.), *Systems thinking*, 2:138–156. Harmondsworth: Penguin Books, 1981. (Excerpts from S. E. Asch [1952], *Social Psychology*, 128–137, 257–263. New York: Prentice Hall.)

Atran, S. (2010). The evolution of religion: How cognitive by-products, adaptive learning heuristics, ritual displays, and group competition generate deep commitments to prosocial religions. *Biological Theory*, 5, 1:18–30.*

Bacon, J. (2007). Psyche moving: "Active imagination" and "focusing" in movement based performance and psychotherapy. *Body, Movement and Dance in Psychotherapy*, 2, 1:17–29.

Badoni, M. (1997). Translating the body. In J. Guimón (Ed.), *The body in psychotherapy*: 121–126. Basel: Karger.

Baker, E. F. (1967). *Man in the trap*. New York: Discus Books, Avon, 1974.

Baker, E. F. (1968). Wilhelm Reich. *Journal of Orgonomy*, 1:23–55.

Baldrian-Hussein, F. (1984). *Procédées secrets du joyau magique. Traité d'alchimie taoïste du XIe siècle*. Paris: Les deux océans.

Balestra, C., & Germonpré, P. (2010). EPO and doping. *European Journal of Applied Physiology*: 1001–1002.*

Baltrusaitis, J. (1989) Tierphysiognomik der Menchenseele. In J. Clair, C. Pichler, & P. Wolfgang (Eds.), *Wunderblock. Eine Geschichte des modernen Seele*: 159–179. Vienna: Wiener Festwochen.

Bandler, R., & Grinder, J. (1975). *The structure of magic*. Palo Alto: Science & Behavior Books.*

Bänninger-Huber, E., & Peham, D. (2010a). Current approaches in research on facial behavior: A review. In E. Bänninger-Huber & D. Peham (Eds.), *Current and future perspectives in facial expression research: Topics and methodological questions*. Proceedings of the International Meeting at the Institute of Psychology, University of Innsbruck, Austria: 13–23. Innsbruck: University of Innsbruck Press.

Bänninger-Huber, E., & Peham, D. (2010b). Issues, opportunities and challenges in facial expression research (summary). In E. Bänninger-Huber & D. Peham (Eds.), *Current and future perspectives in facial expression research: Topics and methodological questions*. Proceedings of the International Meeting at the Institute of Psychology, University of Innsbruck, Austria: 99–114. Innsbruck: University of Innsbruck Press.

Bard, P. (1928). A diencephalic mechanism for the expression of rage with special reference to the sympathetic nervous system. *American Journal of Physiology*, 84:490–515.

Baron, J.-M. (2006). *Joseph Kessel: Ami, entends tu…* Paris: La Table Ronde.

Bassi, G. (1967). *Les varices des membres inférieurs*. Paris: Editions Doin.

Batchelor, S. (1997). *Buddhism without beliefs: A contemporary guide to awakening*. New York: Riverhead Books.

Bateman A., & Fonagy, P. (2004). Metalisation based treatment of borderline personality disorder. *Journal of Personality Disorder*. 18:36–51.

Bates, W. H. (1920). *The cure of imperfect sight by treatment without glasses*. New York: Central Fixation.*

Bateson, G. (1971). Communication. In N. A. McQuown (Ed.), *The natural history of an Interview*, 1–40. Microfilm Collection of Manuscripts on Cultural Anthropology,

15th Series. Chicago: University of Chicago, Joseph Regenstein Library, Department of Photoduplication.

Bateson, G. (1972). *Steps to an ecology of mind*. New York: Ballantine Books.

Bateson, G. (1979). *Mind and nature. A necessary unity*. Toronto: Bantam Books, 1988.

Bateson, G. (1991). *A sacred unity: Further steps to an ecology of mind*. New York: HarperCollins Publishers.

Bateson, G., & Mead, M. (1947). *Balinese character. A photographic analysis*. New York: Special publication of the New York Academy of Sciences.

Bateson, M. C. (1994). *Peripheral visions: Learning along the way*. New York: Harper Collins.

Bauer, J. (2009). The brain transforms psychology into biology. *Body, Movement and Dance in Psychotherapy*, 4, 3:231–238.

Bauer, J. (2010). *Das kooperative Gen*. München: Heyne Verlag.

BCPSG (The Boston Change Process Study Group). (2010). *Change in psychotherapy. A unifying paradigm*. New York: Norton.

Beck, A., & Emery, G. (1985). *Anxiety disorders and phobias*. New York: Basic Books.

Beck, A. T., Rush, A. J., Shaw, B. F., & Emery, G. (1979). *Cognitive therapy of depression*. New York: Guilford Press.

Beebe, B. (2004a). A case study. *Psychoanalytic Dialogues*, 13, 6:805–841. (Case published in Beebe et al., 2005.)

Beebe, B. (2004b). Reply to commentaries. *Psychoanalytic Dialogues*, 14, 189–198.

Beebe, B. (2005). Faces-in-relations: Forms of intersubjectivity in adult treatment of early trauma. In B. Beebe, S. Knoblauch, J. Rustin, & D. Sorter (Eds.), *Forms of intersubjectivity in infant research and adult treatment*: 89–144. New York: Other Press.

Beebe, B. (2011). Introduction to mother, infants, and young children of September 11 2011: A primary prevention project. *Journal of Infant, Child & Adolescent Psychotherapy*, 10:145–155.

Beebe, B., Badalamenti, A., Jaffe, J., Feldstein, S., Marquette, L., Helbraun, E., et al. (2008). Distressed mothers and their infants use a less efficient timing mechanism in creating expectancies of each other's looking patterns. *Journal of Psycholinguistic Research*, 37, 5:453–454.

Beebe, B., Jaffe, J., Buck, K., Chen, H., & Cohen, P. (2007). Six-week postpartum maternal self-criticism and dependency and 4-month mother-infant self- and interactive contingencies. *Developmental Psychology*, 43, 6:1360–1376.

Beebe, B., Jaffe, J., Markese, S., Buck, K., Chen, H., Cohen, P., et al. (2010). The origins of 12-month attachment: A microanalysis of 4-month mother-infant interaction. *Attachment & Human Development*, 12, 1:3–141.

Beebe, B., Knoblauch, S., Rustin, J., & Sorter, D. (2005). *Forms of intersubjectivity in infant research and adult treatment*. New York: Other Press.

Beebe, B., & Lachmann, F. (2002). *Infant research and adult treatment: Co-constructing interactions*. Hillsdale, NJ: Analytic Press.

Beebe, B., & Lachmann, F. (2003). The relational turn in psychoanalysis: A dyadic systems view from infant research. *Contemporary Psychoanalysis*, 39, 3:379–409.

Beebe, B., Steele, M., Jaffe, J., Buck, K. A., Chen, H., Cohen, P., et al. (2011). Maternal anxiety symptoms and mother-infant self- and interactive contingency. *Infant Mental Health Journal*, 32, 2:174–206.

Beebe, B., & Stern, D. N. (2002). Engagement-disengagement and early object experience.

In N. Freedman & S. Grand (Eds.), *Communicative structures and psychic structures*: 35–55. New York: Plenum.

Bennett, P. D. C., & Caroll, D. (1994). Cognitive-behavioral interventions in cardiac rehabilitation. *Journal of Psychosomatic Research*, 38:169–182.

Benz-Chartrand, D. (1987). Yoga and Hakomi: Two friends meet. *Hakomi Forum*, 5:38–39.

Bergson, H. (1889). *Time and free will: An essay on the immediate data of consciousness.* Mineola: Dover Publications, 2001.

Bergson, H. (1896). *Matter and memory.* Mineola: Dover Publications, 2004.

Bergson, H. (1907). *Creative evolution.* Mineola: Dover Publications, 1998.

Berlin, I. (1963). *Karl Marx: His life and environment.* London: Oxford University Press, 1965.

Bernard, C. (1865). *Introduction à l'étude de la médecine expérimentale* [Introduction to the Study of Experimental Medicine]. Paris: Flammarion, 1984.

Bernard, C. (1878). *Leçons sur les phénomènes de la vie communs aux animaux et aux végétaux.* Paris: Librairie philosophique J. Vrin, 1966.

Berney, A. (2009). Crises non épileptiques psychogènes: le défi des troubles fonctionnels en neurologie. *Schweizer Archiv für Neurologie und Psychiatire*, 1, §60, 8:347–351.

Berry, A. (2002). Infinite tropics. In *An Alfred Russel Wallace Anthology.* London: Verso.

Bertalanffy, L. von (1950). An outline of general system theory. *British Journal for the Philosophy of Science*, 1, 2:134–165.*

Bertalanffy, L. von (1968a). *General system theory: Foundations, development, applications.* New York: George Braziller.

Bertalanffy, L. von (1968b). *Organismic psychology and systems theory.* Barre: Clark University Press & Barre Publishers.

Besson, J., & Brault, Y. (1991). Le cercle psycho-organique. In J. Besson (Ed.), *Manuel d'enseignement de l'Ecole Française d'Analyse Psycho-organique*, 1:31–85. Gargas: Ecole Française d'Analyse Psycho-organique.

Beth, E. W., & Piaget, J. (1966). *Mathematical epistemology and psychology.* Dordrecht: Reidel.

Bianchi, A., Denavit-Saubie, M., & Champagnat, J. (1995). Central control of breathing in mammals: Neuronal circuitry, membrane properties, and neurotransmitters. *Physiological Reviews*, 75, 1:1–45.

Bichen, Z. (1933). *Traité d'alchimie et de physiologie taoïste.* Paris: Les Deux Océans, 1979.

Birch, C. (1967). *Anthology of Chinese Literature.* Harmonsworth: Penguin Classics.

Birdwhistell, R. (1970a). *Kinesics in context.* Philadelphia: University of Pennsylvania Press.

Birdwhistell, R. (1970b). Un exercice de kinésique et de linguistique: La scène de la cigarette. In Y. Winkin (Ed.), *La nouvelle communication*: 160–190. Paris: Seuil, 1981.

Blouin, M., & Bergeron, C. (1997). *Dictionnaire de la réadaptation, tome 2: Termes d'intervention et d'aides techniques.* Québec: Les Publications du Québec.

Blumenthal, B. (2001). The psychotherapist's body. In M. Heller (Ed.), *The flesh of the soul: The body we work with*: 153–160. Bern: Peter Lang.

Boadella, D. (1972). The atmosphere and the organism. *Energy and Character*, 3, 3:18–37.

Boadella, D. (1973). *Wilhelm Reich, the Evolution of His Work.* Chicago: Henry Regnery.

Boadella, D. (1975). Bioplasma and orgone biophysics. *Energy and Character*, 6, 3:42–47.

Boadella, D. (1976). *In the wake of Reich*. London: Conventure ltd.

Boadella, D. (1980). The language of bio-energy. In J. Kogan (Ed.), *Your body works: A guide to health, energy and balance*: 3–8. Berkeley: And/Or Press and Transformations Press.

Boadella, D. (1987). *Lifestreams: An introduction to biosynthesis*. London: Routledge.

Boadella, D. (1990a). Somatic psychotherapy: Its roots and traditions. *Energy and Character*, 21, 1:2–26.

Boadella, D. (1990b). Embryology and therapy: A historical note on sources. *Energy and Character*, 21, 1:59–60.

Boadella, D. (1997). Wilhelm Reich. From psychoanalysis to energy medicine. *Energy and Character*, 28, 1:13–20.*

Boadella, D. (1999). The bonds of affect: The somatic psychology of Giordano Bruno. *Energy and Character*, 301:121–125.

Boadella, D. (2000a). Shape flow and postures of the soul—the biosynthesis concept of motoric fields. *Energy and Character*, 302:18–21.

Boadella, D. (2000b). The historical development of the concept of motoric fields. *Energy and Character*, 302:7–17.

Boadella, D. (2004). From passions of the body to actions of the soul: Neuroscience, Spinoza and the self. *Energy and Character*, 33:8–12.

Bonham, A. C. (1995). Neurotransmitters in the CNS control of breathing. *Respiration Physiology*, 101, 3:219–230.

Bonnet, G. (1981). *Voir être vu*, vol 1. Paris: Presses Universitaires de France, 2005.

Bonnet, G. (2000). *La violence de voir*. Paris: Presses Universitaires de France, 2005.

Bonnet, G. (2005). *Voir être vu: Figures de l'exhibitionisme aujoud'hui*. Paris: Presses Universitaires de France.

Bonnet, M., & Millet, Y. (1971). *Manuel de physiologie à l'usage des kinésithérapeutes et des professions paramédicales*. Paris: Masson & Cie.

Borsarello, J. (1971). *Le massage dans la médecine chinoise*. Paris: Maisonneuve.

Boubli, M. (2009). *Corps, psyché et language*. Paris: Dunod.

Bourdieu, P. (1979). *Distinction: A social critique of the judgement of taste*. Cambridge, MA: Harvard University Press, 1984.

Bourdieu, P. (1980). *Le sens pratique* [Practical Reason: On the Theory of Action]. Paris: Éditions de Minuit.

Bourdieu, P. (1997). *Méditations pascaliennes* [Pascalian meditations]. Paris: Seuil.

Bourgeois, P. (2003). Les cicatrices invisibles de la chirurgie. *Stress and Trauma*, 3, 4:225–233.

Bourgeois, P. (2008). Les cicatrices invisibles de la chirurgie. *Revue francophone du Stress et du Trauma*, 8, 1:17–23.

Boutrel, B. (2006). Hypocrétines: entre l'envie et le besoin . . . ou l'émergence d'une nouvelle voie d'origine hypothalamique impliquée dans la motivation et l'addiction. *Médecine Sciences*, 22, 6–7:573–575.

Bower, T. (1978). The infant's discovery of objects and mother. In E. Thoman (Ed.), *Origins of the infant's social responsiveness*. Hillsdale, NJ: Erlbaum.

Bowlby, J. (1969). *Attachment and loss*. New York: Basic Books, 1999.

Boyd, R., & Richerson, P. J. (1996). Why culture is common but cultural evolution is rare. *Proceedings of the British Academy*, 88:73–93.*

Boyd, R., & Richerson, P. J. (2005). *The origin and evolution of cultures.* Oxford: Oxford University Press.

Boyer, P., & Liénard, P. (2006). Why ritualized behavior? Precaution systems and action parsing in developmental, pathological and cultural rituals. *Behavioral and Brain Sciences*, 29:1–56.

Boyesen, E. (1985). De la naissance à l'orgasme. Interview de Michel Heller. *Adire*, 1:45–48.

Boyesen, E. (1987). Beyond transference. Interview with Michel Heller. *Adire*, 2–3:229–234.

Boyesen, G. (1970). Experiences with dynamic relaxation and the relationship its discovery to the Reichian bioenergetic view of vegetotherapy. *Energy & Character*, 1, 1–2:21–30.

Boyesen, G. (1985a). *Entre psyché & soma.* Paris: Payot.

Boyesen, G. (1985b). À propos de la psychologie biodynamique. *Adire*, 1:14–44.

Boyesen, G. (1987). Transference in biodynamic psychology. *Adire*, 2–3:171–178.

Boyesen, G. (2001). Body psychotherapy is a psychotherapy. In M. Heller (Ed.), *The flesh of the soul: The body we work with*: 33–44. Bern: Peter Lang.

Boyesen, M.-L. (1976). Psycho-peristaltis, part VII. From libido-theory to cosmic energy. In *The collected papers of biodynamic psychology*. London: Biodynamic Psychology Publications, 1980. (A reprint from *Energy & Character*, 7.2.)

Boyesen, M.-L. (1980). Bio-release. *Energy & Character*, 8, 3:66–69. (A reprint can be obtained at the Ecole d'Analyse Psycho-Organique in France.)

Boyesen, M.-L. (1985). Initiation à la maternité. *Adire*, 1:14–44.

Boyesen, M.-L. (1991). Les concepts de base de la Psychologie Biodynamique. In J. Besson (Ed.), *Manuel d'enseignement de l'École Française d'Analyse Psycho-organique*, tome 1:161–180. Gargas: École Française d'Analyse Psycho-organique.

Boyesen, P. (1987a). Transference and projections. *Adire*, 2–3:221–222.

Boyesen, P. (1987b). Le corps des mots. *Adire*, 2–3:149–168.

Boyesen, P. (1993). *Pour qui je me réveille le matin.* Paris: Editions ADIRE et OPERA.

Boyesen, P. (1999). Les fondamentaux du Cercle Psycho-Dynamique. In J. Besson (Ed.), *Manuel d'enseignement de l'École Française d'Analyse Psycho-organique*, 5:13–40. Gargas: Ecole Française d'Analyse Psycho-organique.

Braatøy, T. (1942). The neuromuscular hypertension and the understanding of nervous conditions. *Journal of Nervous Mental Disease*, 95:550–567. (I thank the *Journal of Nervous and Mental Disease*, who sent me a photocopy of this article.)

Braatøy, T. (1947). De Nervøse sinn. Medicinsk psychologi of psychotherapi. Oslo: Cappelen. (I have discussed the content of this article with my Norwegian colleagues, but have never read it. It has not been translated.)

Braatøy, T. (1948). Indications for shock treatment in psychiatry. *American Journal of Psychiatry*, 104:573–575.

Braatøy, T. (1954). *Fundamentals of psychoanalytic technique.* New York: Wiley.

Braddock, C. (1997). The Braddock body process. In C. Caldwell (Ed.), *Getting in touch: The guide to new body-centered therapies*: 211–226. Wheaton: Quest Books.

Bradley, K. K. (2009). *Rudolf Laban.* Oxon: Taylor & Francis.

Brakel, A. M. L. van. (2006). Eye blink startle responses in behaviorally inhibited and uninhibited children. *International Journal of Behavioral Development*, 30, 5:460–465.

Braudel, F. (1979). *Civilization and capitalism 15th–18th century.* New York: HarperCollins, 1985.

Breuer, J., & Freud, S. (1895). *Studies on hysteria*. Pelican Freud Library, 3. Harmonds-worth: Penguin, 1986.

Brosch, T., & Scherer, K. R. (2009). *Das Komponenten-Prozess-Modell—ein integratives Emotionsmodell [The Component Process Model of Emotion—an integrative model of emotion]*. Göttingen: Hogrefe.*

Brown, M. (1988). *The healing touch: An introduction to organismic psychotherapy*. Mendocino: Life Rhythm, 1989.

Brown, M. (2001). The how is blood-synergy direct touch. In M. Heller (Ed.), *The flesh of the soul: The body we work with*: 45–58. Bern: Peter Lang.

Brown, P., Day, B. L., Rothwell, P. D., & Mardsen, C. D. (1991). The effect of posture on the normal and pathological auditory startle reflex. *Journal of Neurology, Neurosurgery and Psychiatry*, 54:892–897.*

Bruckner, P., & Finkielkraut, A. (1979). *Le nouveau désordre amoureux*. Paris: Seuil.

Brun, J. (1973). *Les présocratiques*. Paris: Presses Universitaires de France.

Bruner, J. S. (1966). *Toward a theory of instruction*. Cambridge, MA: Harvard University Press.

Bruner, J. S. (1973). *Beyond the information given*. New York: Norton.

Bruner, J. S. (2008). Foreword. In P. Rochat, *Others in mind*. Cambridge: Cambridge University Press.

Bucci, W. (1997). *Psychoanalysis and cognitive science: A multiple code theory*. New York: Guilford Press.

Bucci, W. (2001). Pathways of emotional communication. *Psychoanalytic Inquiry*, 21, 1:40–70.

Bucci, W. (2002). The referential process, consciousness, and the sense of self. *Psychoanalytic Inquiry*, 22, 5:766–802.

Buck, R. (1988). *Human motivation and emotion*, 2nd ed. New York: Wiley.

Buddha. *Dhammapada: The sayings of the Buddha* (T. Byron, Trans.). Boston: Shambhala, 1993.

Bullinger, A. (1998). La genèse de l'axe corporel, quelques repères. In A. Bullinger, *Le développement sensori-moteur de l'enfant et ses avatars*: 136–150. Ramonville Saint-Agne: Editions érès, 2004.

Bullinger, A. (Ed.) (2004). *Le développement sensori-moteur de l'enfant et ses avatars*. Ramonville Saint-Agne: Editions érès.

Bunkan, B. H. (1991). The diaphragm—between body and emotions. *Energy & Character*, 22, 2:57–61.

Bunkan, B. H. (2003). *The Comprehensive Body Examination (CBE): A psychometric evaluation*. Oslo: Unipub AS.

Buss, D. (2003). *Evolutionary psychology: The new science of the mind*. Boston: Allyn & Bacon.

Byck, R. (1974). *Cocaine papers*. Hillsboro: Goodwill Books.

Cabrol, C. (1978). *Anatomie*. Paris: Flammarion.

Calame, C. (1992). *The poetics of eros in ancient Greece*. Princeton: Princeton University Press, 1999.

Caldwell, C. (1996). *Getting our bodies back. Recovery, healing, and transformation through body-centered psychotherapy*. Boston: Shambhala.

Caldwell, C. (1997a). The somatic umbrella. In C. Caldwell (Ed.), *Getting in touch: The guide to new body-centered therapies*: 7–28. Wheaton: Quest Books.

Caldwell, C. (1997b). Ethics and techniques for touch in somatic psychotherapy. In C. Caldwell (Ed.), *Getting in touch: The guide to new body-centered therapies*: 227–238. Wheaton: Quest Books.

Caldwell, C. (2001). Addiction as somatic dissociation. In M. Heller (Ed.), *The flesh of the soul: The body we work with*: 213–230. Bern: Peter Lang.

Caldwell, C., & Victoria, H. K. (2011). Breathwork in body psychotherapy: Towards a more unified theory and practice. *Body, Movement and Dance Psychotherapy*, 6, 2:89–102.

Cannon, W. B. (1911). *The mechanical factors of digestion*. Sagamore Beach, MA: Science History Publications/USA, 1986.

Cannon, W. B. (1915). *Bodily changes in pain, hunger, fear and rage*. New York: D. Appleton, 1929.

Cannon, W. B. (1927). The James-Lange theory of emotion: A critical examination and an alternative theory. *American Journal of Psychology*, 39:106–124.

Cannon, W. B. (1932). *The wisdom of the body*. New York: Norton.

Cannon, W. B. (1935). Stresses and strains of homeostasis. *American Journal of Medical Sciences*, 189:1–14.

Cannon, W. B. (1936). *Digestion and health*. New York: Norton, 1960.

Cannon, W. B. (1945). *The way of an investigator*. New York: Norton, 1984.

Cannon, W. B., & Rosenblueth, A. (1937). *Autonomic neuro-effector systems*. New York: Macmillan.

Carotenuto, A., & Trombetta, C. (1981). *Sabina Spielrein: Entre Freud et Jung* [A secret symmetry: Sabina Spielrein between Jung and Freud]. Paris: Aubier Montaigne, 1981.

Carré, P., & Bianu, Z. (1987). *La Montagne vide: Anthologie de la poésie chinoise, 3e-11e siècles*. Paris: Albin-Michel.

Carroll, R. (2002). Biodynamic massage in psychotherapy: Re-integrating, re-owning and re-associating through the body. In T. Staunton (Ed.), *Body psychotherapy*: 78–100. New York: Brunner-Routledge.

Cassirer, E. (1932). *The philosophy of the Enlightenment*. Princeton: Princeton University Press, 1951.

Cauhepe, J.-D., & Kuang, A. (1984). *Le jeu des énergies respiratoires, gestuelles et sonores dans la pratique de l'aïkido*. Paris: Guy Trédaniel.

Cellérier, G. (1968). Modèles cybernétiques et adaptation. In G. Cellérier, S. Papert, & G. Voyat (Eds.), *Cybernétique et épystémologie*: 5–87. Lausanne: Presses Universitaires de France. (Similar content in English can be found in Cellérier's 1983 article, "The historical genesis of cybernetics: Is teleonomy a category of understanding?" *Nature and System*, 5:11–225. Some of Guy Cellérier's English articles can be found in *Piaget Today*, edited by Inhelder and de Caprona.)

Cellérier, G. (1992a). Organisation et fonctionnement des schèmes. In B. Inhelder & G. Cellérier (Eds.), *Le cheminement des découvertes de l'enfant*: 255–302. Lausanne: Delachaux et Niestlé.

Cellérier, G. (1992b). Le constructivisme génétique aujourd'hui. In B. Inhelder & G. Cellérier (Eds.), *Le cheminement des découvertes de l'enfant*: 215–254. Lausanne: Delachaux et Niestlé.

Cellérier, G. (2010). Postface. In O. Real del Sarte, *Le couple coopère-t-il? Perspectives piagétiennes et systémiques*. Toulouse: Erès.

Châtelet, F. (1989). *Platon*. Paris: Gallimard.

Chatton, D., Pause, C., Graf, M., Rossi, L., & Archinard, M. (2001). Activités de formation en sexologie à Genève et en Suisse romande. *Médecine & Hygiène, 59,* 2333: 302–304.

Chen, J. C., Brown, B., & Schmid, K. L. (2004). Effect of unilateral forced nostril breathing on tonic accommodation and intraocular pressure. *Clinical Autonomic Research,* 14, 6:396–400.

Chevalier, J., & Gheerbrant, A. (1996). *The Penguin dictionary of symbols*. New York: Penguin.

Chomsky, N. (1967). A review of B. F. Skinner's *Verbal Behavior*. In L. A. Jakobovits & M. S. Miron (Eds.), *Readings in the psychology of language*: 142–143. Englewood Cliffs, NJ: Prentice-Hall.

Chomsky, N. (1980). *Rules and representations*. Oxford: Basil Blackwell.

Chuang Tzu. (1968). *The complete works of Chuang Tzu* (B. Watson, Trans.). New York: Columbia University Press.

Clair, J. (1986). *Vienne 1880–1938. L'apocalypse joyeuse*. Paris: Editions du Centre Pompidou.

Clair, J. (2005). *Mélancolie. Génie et folie en Occident*. Paris: Gallimard.

Clair, J., Pichler, C., & Pircher, W. (Eds.) (1989). *Wunderblock— Eine Geschichte der modernen Seele*. Wien: Löcker.

Claparède, E. (2010). *Édouard Claparède–Hélène Antipoff: Correspondence (1914–1940)*. Firenze: Leo S. Olschki Editore.

Clark, A. (1997). *Being there: Putting brain, body, and world together again*. Cambridge, MA: MIT Press.*

Clark, A. (2000). *Mindware: An introduction to the philosophy of cognitive science*. Oxford: Oxford University Press.

Clarkin, J. F., Yeomans, F. E., & Kernberg, O. F. (1999). *Psychotherapy for borderline personality*. New York: Wiley.

Clarkson, P., & Mackewn, J. (1993). *Fritz Perls*. London: Sage.

Cocks, G. (1997). *Psychotherapy in the Third Reich*. New Brunswick, NJ: Transaction Publishers.

Cohen, P., & Beebe, B. (2002). Video feedback with a depressed mother and her infant: A collaborative individual psychoanalytic and mother-infant treatment. *Journal of Infant, Child and Adolescent Psychotherapy,* 2, 3:1–55.

Comba, L., & Fleury, F. (1987). Réflexions sur la relation "Maitre et Disciple" dans la transmission d'un savoir traditionnel. *Adire,* 2 & 3:121–140.

Coppin, B. (2004). *Artificial intelligence illuminated*. Sudbury: Jones and Bartlett.

Cornell, W. F. (1997). If Reich had met Winnicott. *Energy and Character,* 28, 2:50–60.

Cornell, W. F. (2000). Transference, desire and vulnerability in body-centered psychotherapy. *Energy and Character,* 302:29–37.

Cosnier, J. (1998). *Le retour de Psyché*. Paris: Desclée de Brouwer.

Cozolino, L. (2006). *The neuroscience of human relationships*. New York: Norton.

Craig, E. G. (1915). "Hamlet" in Moscow: Notes for a short address to the actors of the Moscow Art Theatre. *The Mask,* VII:109–110.

Crick, F. (1995). *The astonishing hypothesis: The scientific search for the soul*. New York: Simon & Schuster.

Cunningham, A. (2009). Memory maintenance. *Scientific American,* 20, 5:10.

Cyrulnik, B. (2004). *Parler d'amour au bord du gouffre*. Paris: Odile Jacob.

Cyrulnik, B. (2006). *De chaire et d'âme*. Paris: Odile Jacob.

Czéh, B., Simon, M., Schmelting, B., Hiemke, C., & Fuchs, E. (2006). Astroglial plasticity in the hippocampus is affected by chronic psychosocial stress and concomitant fluoxetine treatment. *Neuropsychopharmacology* 31:1616–1626.

Dadoun, R. (1976). *Cents fleurs pour Wilhelm Reich*. Payot: Paris, 1999.

Damasio, A. (1994). *Descartes' error*. New York: Penguin Books, 2005.

Damasio, A. (1999). *The feeling of what happens: Body and emotion in the making of consciousness*. New York: Harcourt Brace.

Damasio, A. (2003). *Looking for Spinoza: Joy, sorrow and the feeling brain*. New York: Harcourt.

Damasio, A., Grabowski, T., Bechara, A., Damasio, H., Ponto, L., Parvizi, J., et al. (2000). Subcortical brain activity during the feeling of self-generated emotions. *Nature Neuroscience*, 3, 10:1049–1056.

Danto, E. A. (2005). *Freud's free clinics: Psychoanalysis and social justice*. New York: Columbia University Press.

Darwin, C. (1839). *The voyage of the Beagle*. London: Penguin Books, 1999.*

Darwin, C. (1859). *The origin of species*. London: Penguin Books, 1985.*

Darwin, C. (1871). *The descent of man and selection in relation to sex*. Princeton: Princeton University Press, 1981.*

Darwin, C. (1872). *The expression of the emotions in man and animals*. Chicago: University of Chicago Press, 1965.*

Daumal, R. (1934). *Le mouvement dans l'éducation intégrale de l'Homme*. In R. Daumal, *Essais et notes, I: l'Évidence absurde*: 48–55. Paris: Gallimard.

Davidson, R. J., Pizzagalli, D., Nitschke J. B., & Puttnam, K. (2002). Depression: Perspectives from affective neuroscience. *Annual Review of Psychology*, 53:545–574. (See Richard J. Davidson's website: http://psyphz.psych.wisc.edu/web/personnel/director.html)

Da Vinci, Léonardo. (1942). *Les carnets de Léonard de Vinci*, II [The Notebooks of Leonardo Da Vinci]. Paris: Gallimard.

Davis, W. (2001). Energetics and therapeutic touch. In M. Heller (Ed.), *The flesh of the soul: The body we work with*: 59–80. Bern: Peter Lang.

Davy, A. (1983). Epidémiologie des varices. *Phlébologie* 36, 1:23–26.

De Beauvoir, S. (1947). *The ethics of ambiguity*. New York: Citadel Press, 1949.

Dechaud-Ferbus, M., Roux, M.-L., & Sacco, F. (1994). *Les destins du corps. Psychothérapie de relaxation d'inspiration psychanalytique*. Paris: Erès.

Defontaine, J. (2003). Quelques aspects du transfert dans la perversion narcissique. *Revue Française de Psychanalyse*, 3, 67: 839–855.*

De Gaigneron, M. (1993). Danses sacrées. In J. de Roux (Ed.), *Les dossiers H. Georges Ivanovitch Gurdjieff*: 154–159. Lausanne: l'Âge d'Homme.

De Lange, F. P., Roelofs, K., & Toni, I. (2008). Motor imagery: A window into the mechanisms and alterations of the motor system. *Cortex*, 44, 5:494–506.

Deleuze, G. (1972). Hume. In F. Châtelet, *La philosophie, II*: 226–239. Paris: Librairie Hachette, 1979.

Delgado, J. M. R. (1960). Emotional behavior in animals and humans. In M. B. Arnold (Ed.), *The nature of emotion*: 309–317. Harmondsworth: Penguin.

Delgado, J. M. R. (1969). *Physical control of the mind*. New York: Harper & Row.

Delvaux, G. M. (2007). *A barefoot doctor's guide for women*. Berkeley: North Atlantic Books.

Derrida, J. (1972). La pharmacie de Platon [Plato's pharmacy]. In J. Derrida, *La dissémination*: 77–213. Paris: Éditions du Seuil.

De Salzmann, J. (2010). *The reality of being: The Fourth Way of Gurdjieff.* Boston: Shambhala.

Descartes, R. (1637). Discourse on method. In *Discourse on method and the meditations* (F. E. Sutcliffe, Trans.). Harmondsworth: Penguin, 1985.

Descartes, R. (1641). The meditations. In *Discourse on method and the meditations* (F. E. Sutcliffe, Trans.). Harmondsworth: Penguin, 1985.

Descartes, R. (1644). Letter from the author. In *Discourse on method and the meditations* (F. E. Sutcliffe, Trans.). Harmondsworth: Penguin, 1985.

Descartes, R. (1649). Les passions de l'âme. In R. Descartes, *Oeuvres et lettres* (pp. 691–803). Paris: Editions Gallimard, 1953.

Descartes, R. *Oeuvres. Lettres.* Paris: Editions Gallimard, 1953. (For all references that are not contained in Sutcliff's translations.)

Desmond, A., & Moore J. (1991). *The life of a tormented evolutionist.* New York: Norton, 1994.

Desoille, R. (1966). *The directed daydream.* New York: Psychosynthesis Research Foundation.

Despeux, C. (1979). Introduction au Weisheng Shenglixue Mingshi. In Z. Bichen, *Traité d'alchimie et de physiologie taoïste.* Paris: Les Deux Océans.

Despeux, C. (1981). *Taiji Quan:. Art martial, technique de longue vie.* Paris: Editions de la Maisnie.

Despland, J.-N., Zimmermann, G., & De Roten, Y. (2006). L'évaluation empirique des psychothérapies. *Psychothérapies*, XXVI, 2:91–95.

Diagnostic and Statistical Manual of Mental Disorders (DSM-IV). http://allpsych.com/disorders/dsm.html

Dohmen, B. (1999). La peau et le toucher, instrument de structuration du psychisme. *Psycorps*, 4, 1:87–121.

Doise, W. (1978). *Groups and individuals: Explanations in social psychology.* Cambridge: Cambridge University Press.

Downing, G. (1972). *The massage book.* New York: Random House.

Downing, G. (1980). Psychodiagnosis and the body. In Gerald Kogan (Ed.), *Your body works*: 39–48. Berkeley: And/or Press and Transformations Press.

Downing, G. (1996). *Körper und Wort in der Psychotherapie: Leitlinien für der Praxis.* Munich: Kösel.

Downing, G. (2000). Emotion theory reconsidered. In M. Wrathall & J. Malpas (Eds.), *Heidegger, coping, and cognitive science: Essays in honor of Hubert L. Dreyfus*, 2:245–270. Cambridge, MA: MIT Press.

Downing, G. (2001). Bodies and motion. In M. Heller (Ed.), *The flesh of the soul: The body we work with*: 9–31. Bern: Peter Lang.

Downing, G. (2003). Video Mikroanalyse Therapie: Einige Grundlagen und Prinzipien. In H. Scheuerer-Englisch, G. J. Suess, & W.-K. Pfeifer (Eds.), *Wege zur Sicherheit: Bindungswissen in Diagnostik und Intervention.* Giessen: Psychosozialer Verlag.

Downing, G. (2006). Fruhkinlicher Affektausch une dessen Beziehung zum Korper. In G. Marlock & H. Weiss (Eds.), *Handbuch der Körperpsychotherapie*: 333–350. Gottingen: Hogreve.

Downing, G., Bürgin, D., Reck, C., & Ziegenhain, U. (2008). Interfaces between intersubjectivity and attachment: Three perspectives on a mother-infant inpatient case. *Infant Mental Health Journal*, 29, 3:278–295.

Draganova, N., Tsvetkov, D., Gancheva, P., Armianov, G., & Radneva, R. (1988). Physiological, psychological and ergonomic research on jobs in the manufacture of choc-
olate products. *Probl-Khig*, 13:63–70.

Droz, G. (1992). *Les mythes platoniciens*. Paris: Seuil.

Duclos, M. A. (2001). Keeping it up. In B. J. Brothers (Ed.), *Couples in body psychotherapy*: 43–48. Binghamton, NY: Haworth Press.

Duclos, M. A. (2008). Heller, Michel. Psychotherapies corporelles: Fondements et pra-
tiques [Body psychotherapy: Foundations and practices]. *Keeping in Touch*, 33:8.

Duffau, H. (2006). Brain plasticity: From pathophysiological mechanisms to therapeutic
applications. *Journal of Clinical Neuroscience*, 13, 9:885–897.

Duguid, A. (2008). Men at work: How those at number 10 construct their working identity. In G. Garzone & S. Sarangi (Eds.), *Discourse, ethics and ideology in specialized
communication*: 453–484. Bern: Peter Lang.

Dumas, A. (1846). *La dame de Monsoreau*. Paris: Gallimard, 2008.

Dumont, M. (1984). Le succès mondain d'une fausse science: La physiognomie de Johann
Kaspar Lavater. *Actes de la recherche en sciences sociales*, 54:2–30.

Dürkheim, K.G. (1954). *Hara: The vital centre of man*. London: Unwin, 1988.

Duruz, N., & Gennart, M., Eds. (2002). *Traité de psychothérapie comparée*. Geneva: Éditions Médecine & Hygiène.

Eccles, J.C. (1989). *Évolution du cerveau et création de la conscience:. A la recherche de
la vraie nature de l'homme*. Paris: Flammarion, 1994.

Eckermann, J. P. (1848). *Conversations of Goethe with Eckermann and Soret*, vol. 2 (J.
Oxenford, Trans.). London: Smith, Elder, 1850.*

Edelman, G. M. (1992). *Bright air, brilliant fire. On the matter of the mind*. New York:
Basic Books.

Edelman, G. M., & Tononi, G. (2000). *A universe of consciousness: How matter becomes
imagination*. New York: Basic Books.

Edwards, J. (2004). Making the music visible: Commentary on case study by Beatrice
Beebe. *Psychoanalytic Dialogues*, 14, 1:73–88.

Ehrenfried, L. (1991). Körperliche Erziehung zum seelischen Gleichgewicht. In P. Zeitler
(Ed.), *Erinnerungen an Elsa Gindler*: 34–37. Munich: Uni-Druck.

Eibl-Eibesfeldt, I. (1989). *Human ethology*. New Jersey: Aldine Transaction, 2007.

Eibl-Eibesfeldt, I., & Kemp, S. (1998). *Indoctrinability: Ideology and warfare*. New York:
Berghahn Books.

Einstein, A. (1936). Physics and Reality. *The Journal of the Franklin Institute*, 221: 349–
382.

Einstein, A. (1946). E = MC². In A. Einstein, *Ideas & Opinions*, pp. 238–250. New York:
Modern Library, 1994.

Ekman, P. (1979). About brows. In M. von Cranach, K. Foppa, W. Lepenies, & D. Ploog
(Eds.), *Human ethology: Claims and limits of a new discipline*: 169–202. Cambridge: Cambridge University Press, and Paris: Editions de la Maison des Sciences de
l'Homme.

Ekman, P. (1980a). *The face of man*. New York: Garland STPM Press.

Ekman, P. (1980b). Facial expression and emotion. *La Recherche*, 117:1408–1415.

Ekman, P. (1985). *Telling lies: Clues to deceit in the marketplace, politics, and marriage*.
New York: Norton.

Ekman, P. (1994). Strong evidence for universals in facial expressions: A reply to Russel's
mistaken critique. *Psychological Bulletin*, 115:102–141.

Ekman, P. (1997). What we have learned by measuring facial behavior. In P. Ekman &

E. L. Rosenberg (Eds.), *What the face reveals: Basic and applied studies of spontaneous expression using the Facial Action Coding System (FACS)*: 469–486. Oxford: Oxford University Press.

Ekman, P. (1999). *Basic emotions*. In T. Dalgleish & M. Power (Eds.), *Handbook of Cognition and Emotion*, pp. 45–60. Sussex: Wiley.

Ekman, P., & Davidson, R. J. (1993). Voluntary smiling changes regional brain activity. *American Psychological Society*, 4, 5:342–345.

Ekman, P., & Davidson, R. J. (1994). *The nature of emotion: Fundamental questions*. New York: Oxford University Press.

Ekman, P., Davidson, R. J., & Friesen, W. V. (1990). The Duchenne smile: Emotional expression and brain physiology. *Journal of personality and social psychology*, 58, 2:342–353.

Ekman, P., & Friesen, W. V. (1971). Constants across cultures in the face and emotion. *Journal of Personality and Social Psychology*, 17:124–129.

Ekman, P., & Friesen, W. V. (1978). *Facial Action Coding System*. Palo Alto: Consulting Psychologist Press, Inc. (A CD of the latest version of the manual can be ordered at http://face-and-emotion.com/dataface/facs/description.jsp. Accessed August 2008.)

Ekman, P., & Friesen, W. V. (1986). A new pan-cultural facial expression of emotion. *Motivation and Emotion*, 10, 2:159–168.*

Ekman, P., Friesen, W. V., & Ellsworth, P. (1972). Emotions in the human face: Guidelines for research and an integration of findings. New York: Pergamon Press.

Ekman, P., Friesen, W. V., & Hager, J. C. (2002). Facial Action Coding System (FACS). CD-ROM, E-book. Salt Lake City: Research Nexus.

Ekman, P., Friesen, W. V., & Simons, R. C. (1997). Is the startle reaction an emotion? In P. Ekman & E. L. Rosenberg (Eds.), *What the face reveals*. Oxford: Oxford University Press.

Ekman, P., O'Sullivan, M., Friesen, W. V., & Scherer, K. R. (1991). Face, voice, and body in detecting deception. *Journal of Nonverbal Behavior*, 15:125–135.

Ekman, P., & Rosenberg, E. L. (1997). *What the face reveals: Basic and applied studies of spontaneous expression using the Facial Action Coding System (FACS)*. Oxford: Oxford University Press.

Ellgring, H. (1989). Nonverbal communication in depression. Cambridge: Cambridge University Press, and Paris: Editions de la Maison des Sciences de l'Homme.

Ellgring, H. (1990). Nonverbal expressions of psychological states in psychiatric patients. In P. Ekman. & E. L. Rosenberg (Eds.), *What the face reveals: Basic and applied studies of spontaneous expression using the Facial Action Coding System (FACS)*: 386–398. Oxford: Oxford University Press, 1997.

Ellsworth, P. C., & Tong, E. M.W. (2006). What does it mean to be angry at yourself? Categories, appraisals, and the problem of language. *Emotion*, 6: 572–586.

Elster, J. (1998). *Alchemies of the mind*. Cambridge: Cambridge University Press.

Elster, J. (1999). *Strong feelings: Emotion, addiction, and human behavior*. Cambridge, MA: MIT Press.

Emery, F. E. (1981). *Systems thinking*. Harmondsworth: Penguin.

Emmorey, K., & Casey, S. (2001). Gesture, thought and spatial language. *Gesture*, 1:35–50.

Erickson, M. (1982). *Ta voix t'accompagnera. Milton H. Erickson raconte*. Paris: Hommes et Groupes éditeurs 1986.

Erikson, E. H. (1950). *Childhood and society*. New York: Norton.

Ernst, K. (1921). *Physique and character: An investigation of the nature of constitution and of the theory of temperament*. New York: Harcourt Brace, 1925.

Erwin, E. (2001). *The Freud encyclopedia: Theory, therapy, and culture*. London: Routledge.

Etchegoyen, R. H. (1991). *The fundamentals of psychoanalytic technique*. London: Karnac Books.

Étiemble, R. (1968). *Le mythe de Rimbaud: Genèse du mythe 1869–1949*. Paris: Gallimard.

Étiemble, R. (1988). *L'Europe chinoise*. Paris: Gallimard.

Falzeder, E. (2005). Sigmund Freud et Eugen Bleuler: l'histoire d'une relation ambivalente. In A. Haynal, E. Falzeder, & P. Roazen (Eds.), *Dans les secrets de la psychanalyse et de son histoire*: 131–162. Paris: Presses Universitaires de France. (English version: Falzeder, E. [2007]. The story of an ambivalent relationship: Sigmund Freud and Eugen Bleuler. *Journal of Analytical Psychology*, 52:343–368.)

Feldenkrais, M. (1949). *Body & mature behavior: A study of anxiety, sex, gravitation & learning*. Berkeley: Somatic Ressources.

Feldenkrais, M. (1980). Mind and body. In G. Kogan, *Your body works:. A guide to health, energy and balance*: 72–80. Berkeley: Transformation Press.

Feldenkrais, M. (1981). *The elusive obvious*. Capitola: Meta Publications.

Feleky, A. (1924). *Feelings and emotion*. New York: Pioneer.

Fenichel, C. N. (1981). From the early years of the Gindler work. In Charlotte Selver Foundation Bulletin, *Elsa Gindler, 1885–1961*, 10, 2:4–9.

Fenichel, O. (1916). Sexuelle Aufklärung. In M. Hodann (Ed.), *Schriften zur Jugendbewegung*: 52–60. Berlin: M. Hodann. (In English *History of Modern Morals*.)

Fenichel, O. (1927). Examples of a dream analysis. In H. Fenichel (Ed.), *The collected papers of Otto Fenichel*, First Series: 123–127. New York: Norton, 1953.

Fenichel, O. (1928). Organ libidinization accompanying the defense against drives. In H. Fenichel (Ed.), *The collected papers of Otto Fenichel*, First Series: 128–146. New York: Norton, 1953.

Fenichel, O. (1931). Respiratory introjection. In H. Fenichel (Ed.), *The collected papers of Otto Fenichel*, First Series: 221–240. New York: Norton, 1953.

Fenichel, O. (1934). Defense against anxiety, particularly by libidinization. In H. Fenichel (Ed.), *The collected papers of Otto Fenichel*, First Series: 303–317. New York: Norton, 1953.

Fenichel, O. (1935). Concerning the theory of psychoanalytic technique. In H. Fenichel (Ed.), *The collected papers of Otto Fenichel*, First Series: 89–108. New York: Norton, 1953.

Fenichel, O. (1938). The drive to amass wealth. In H. Fenichel and D. Rapaport (Ed.), *The collected papers of Otto Fenichel*, Second Series: 221–240. New York: Norton, 1954.

Fenichel, O. (1941). *Problèmes de technique psychanalytique* [Problems of psychoanalytic technique]. Paris: Presses Universitaires de France, 1953.

Fenichel, O. (1945a). *The psychoanalytic theory of neurosis*. New York: Norton, 1996.

Fenichel, O. (1945b). Nature and classification of the so-called psychosomatic phenomena. In H. Fenichel and D. Rapaport (Ed.), *The collected papers of Otto Fenichel*, Second Series: 305–323. New York: Norton, 1954.

Fenichel, O. (1998). *119 Rundbriefe. Bd. I. Europa (1934–1938)*. J. Reichmayr & E. Mühlleitner (Eds.). Frankfurt am Main: Stroemfeld Verlag.

Ferenczi, S. (1909). Introjection and transference. In J. Rickman (Ed.), *Further contributions to the theory and technique of psychoanalysis*: 30–79. New York: Brunner/Mazel, 1980.

Ferenczi, S. (1919a). The phenomena of hysterical materialization. In J. Rickman (Ed.), *Further contributions to the theory and technique of psychoanalysis*: 89–104. New York: Brunner/Mazel, 1980.

Ferenczi, S. (1919b). Technical difficulties in the analysis of a case of hysteria: Including observations of larval forms of onanism and onanistic equivalents In J. Rickman (Ed.), *Further contributions to the theory and technique of psychoanalysis* (pp. 291–294). New York: Bruner/Mazel, 1980.

Ferenczi, S. (1921a). Prolongements de la "technique active" en psychanalyse [The further development of the "active technique" in psychoanalysis]. In S. Ferenczi, *Psychanalyse, œuvres complètes*, 3:117–133. Paris: Payot, 1974.

Ferenczi, S. (1921b). Psycho-analytical observations on tic. *International Journal of Psychoanalysis*, 2:1–30.

Ferenczi, S. (1922). La psyché comme organe d'inhibition. In S. Ferenczi, *Psychanalyse, œuvres complètes*, 3:179–182. Paris: Payot, 1974.

Ferenczi, S. (1929). Male and female—psychoanalytic reflections on the "Theory of Genitality," and on secondary and tertiary sex differences. *Psychoanalytic Quarterly*, 1936, 5:249–260.

Ferenczi, S. (1930). Principe de relaxation et néo-catharsis [The principle of relaxation and neocatharsis]. In S. Ferenczi, *Psychanalyse, œuvres complètes*, 4:82–97. Paris: Payot, 1982.

Ferenczi, S., & Rank, O. (1924). *Perspectives de la psychanalyse* [*The development of psychoanalysis*]. In S. Ferenczi (Ed.), *Psychanalyse, oeuvres completes*, 3:220–236. Paris: Payot, 1974.

Feyereisen, P., & De Lannov, J.-D. (1991). *Gestures and speech*. Cambridge, UK, & Paris: Cambridge University Press & Editions de la Maison des Sciences de l'Homme.

Field, T. (1981). Infant gaze aversion and heart rate during face-to face interactions. *Infant Behavior and Development*, 4:307–315.

Field, T. (1982). Infant arousal, attention and affect during early interactions. In L. Lipsitt, (Ed.), *Advances in infant development*, 1:57–100. Norwood: Ablex.

Field, T. (1995). Infants of depressed mothers. *Infant Behavior and Development*, 18:1–13.

Fisher, D. J. (1988). Psychanalyse et engagement: Otto Fenichel et les freudiens politiques. *Revue Internationales d'histoire de la psychanalyse*, 1:375–390.

Fisher, D. J. (2007). Classical psychoanalysis, politics and social engagement in the era between the wars: Reflections on the free clinics. *Psychoanalysis and History*, 9, 2:237–250.

Fivaz, R. (1993). *L'ordre et la volupté*. Lausanne: Presses Polytechniques et Universitaires Romandes.

Fivaz-Depeursinge, E. (1987). *Alliances et mésalliances dans le dialogue entre adulte et bébé. La communication précoce dans la famille*. Paris: Delachaux et Niestlé.

Fivaz-Depeursinge, E., & Corboz-Warnery, A. (1999). *Le triangle primaire. Le père, la mère et le bébé* [The primary triangle: A developmental systems view of mothers, fathers and infants]. Paris: Odile Jacob, 2001.

Fleury, F., & Mahmoud-Shawana, S. (2010). The rupture of links in the context of migration: Open mouthed and sewn mouth. In A. Gautier & A. Sabatini (Eds.), *Bearing witness: Psychoanalytic work with people traumatized by torture and state violence* (pp. 91–112). London: Karnak Books.

Fodor, J. A. (1983). *Modularity of mind: An essay on faculty psychology.* Cambridge, MA: MIT Press.

Fodor, J. A. (1998). *Concepts: Where cognitive science went wrong.* Oxford: Oxford University Press.

Fodor, J. A. (2000). *The mind doesn't work that way: The scope and limits of computational psychology.* Cambridge, MA: MIT Press.

Fodor, J. A. (2003). *Hume variations.* Oxford: Oxford University Press.

Fogel, A., Lyra, M.C.D.P., & Valsiner, J. (1997). *Dynamics and inderterminism in developmental and social processes.* Mahwah, NJ: Lawrence Erlbaum.

Foucault, M. (1966). *The order of things: An archaeology of human sciences.* New York: Vintage.

Fradin, J. (2008). *L'intelligence du stress.* Paris: Eyrolles.

Fradin, J., & Fradin, F. (2006). *La Thérapie Neurocognitive et Comportementale (TNCC). Une nouvelle vision du psychisme issue des sciences du système nerveux et du comportement.* Paris: Éditions Publibook.

Fraisse, A. (2002). Le cercle psycho-organique comme grille de lecture de la relation entre le psychothérapeute et le thérapisant. In J. Besson (Ed.), *Manuel d'enseignement de l'École Française d'Analyse Psycho-Organique*, 6. Toulouse: EFAPO.

Fraisse, A. (2008). *L'Analyse Psycho-Organique.* Manuscrit.

Fraisse, P. (1963). Les émotions. In P. Fraisse & J. Piaget (Eds.), *Traité de psychologie expérimentale, V.: motivation, émotion et personnalité*: 97–182. Paris: Presses Universitaires de France, 1975.

Fraisse, P. (1992). Le non-conscient. Interview avec Anne Fraisse. *Adire*, 7–8:175–182.

Franzen, G. M. (1995). Werden Sie wieder reagierbereit! Elsa Gindler (1885–1961) und ihre Arbeit. *Gestalttherapie*, 9, 2:3–19.

Freud, S. (1890). Traitement psychique (traitement de l'âme) [Psychical (or mental) treatment]. In S. Freud, *Résultats, idées, problèmes*, I, 1890–1920:1–24. Paris: Presses Universitaires de France, 1984.

Freud, S. (1893). Draft E. In J. Strachey (Ed. & Trans.), *The standard edition of the complete psychological works of Sigmund Freud* (Vol. 1, pp. 189–195). London: Hogarth Press, 2001.

Freud, S. (1894). The neuro-psychoses of defense. In J. Strachey (Ed. & Trans.), *The standard edition of the complete psychological works of Sigmund* Freud (Vol. III, pp. 45–61). London: Vintage, 2001.

Freud, S. (1895a). Draft G. In J. Strachey (Ed. & Trans.), *The standard edition of the complete psychological works of Sigmund Freud* (Vol. 1, pp. 200–205). London: Hogarth Press, 2001.

Freud, S. (1895b). *On the grounds for detaching a particular syndrome from neurasthenia under the description "anxiety neurosis"* (Translated under the direction of J. Strachey). *Pelican Freud Library*, 10:31–66. Harmondsworth: Penguin.

Freud, S. (1895c). Project for a scientific psychology. In J. Strachey (Ed. & Trans.), *The standard edition of the complete psychological works of Sigmund Freud* (Vol. 1, pp. 283–346). London: Vintage, 2001.

Freud, S. (1896a). Heredity and the aetiology of the neuroses. In J. Strachey (Ed. & Trans.), *The standard edition of the complete psychological works of Sigmund Freud* (Vol. 3, pp. 141–156). London: Vintage, 2001.

Freud, S. (1896b). Further remarks on the neuro-psychoses of defense. In J. Strachey (Ed. & Trans.), *The standard edition of the complete psychological works of Sigmund Freud* (Vol. 3, pp. 157–185). London: Vintage, 2001.

Freud, S. (1896c). The aetiology of hysteria. In J. Strachey (Ed. & Trans.), *The standard edition of the complete psychological works of Sigmund Freud* (Vol. 3, pp. 189–221). London: Vintage, 2001.

Freud, S. (1900). The interpretation of dreams. In J. Strachey (Ed. & Trans.), *The standard edition of the complete psychological works of Sigmund Freud* (Vol. 5). London: Vintage, 2001.

Freud, S. (1901). The psychopathology of everyday life In J. Strachey (Ed. & Trans.), *The standard edition of the complete psychological works of Sigmund Freud* (Vol. 6). London: Vintage, 2001.

Freud, S. (1904). *The complete letters of Sigmund Freud to Wilhelm Fliess (1887–1904).* Cambridge, MA: Harvard University Press, 1984.

Freud, S. (1905). Three essays on the theory of sexuality. Translated under the direction of James Strachey, in the *Pelican Freud Library*, 7:33–170. Harmondsworth: Penguin, 1976.

Freud, S. (1909a). Some general remarks on hysterical attacks. Translated under the direction of James Strachey, in the *Pelican Freud Library*, 10:95–102. Harmondsworth: Penguin, 1976.

Freud, S. (1909b). Analysis of a phobia in a five-year-old boy. In J. Strachey (Ed. & Trans.), *The standard edition of the complete psychological works of Sigmund Freud* (Vol. 10, 3:152). London: Vintage, 2001.

Freud, S. (1910a). The psychoanalytic view of psychogenic disturbance of vision (Translated under the direction of J. Strachey). *Pelican Freud Library*, 10:103–114. Harmondsworth: Penguin Books, 1976.

Freud, S. (1910b). The future prospects of psychoanalytic therapy. In J. Strachey (Ed. & Trans.), *The standard edition of the complete psychological works of Sigmund Freud* (Vol. 11:139–151. London: Vintage, 2001.

Freud, S. (1912a). Recommendations to physicians practising psycho-analysis. In J. Strachey (Ed. & Trans.), *The standard edition of the complete psychological works of Sigmund Freud* (Vol. 12:109–120). London: Vintage, 2001.

Freud, S. (1912b). The dynamics of transference. In J. Strachey (Ed. & Trans.), *The standard edition of the complete psychological works of Sigmund Freud* (Vol. 12:97–108). London: Vintage, 2001.

Freud, S. (1913). On psycho-analysis. In J. Strachey (Ed. & Trans.), *The standard edition of the complete psychological works of Sigmund Freud* (Vol. 13:205–212). London: Vintage, 2001.

Freud, S. (1914a). On the history of the psycho-analytic movement. In J. Strachey (Ed. & Trans.), *The standard edition of the complete psychological works of Sigmund Freud* (Vol. 14:7–66). London: Vintage, 2001.

Freud, S. (1914b). On narcissism. An introduction. In J. Strachey (Ed. & Trans.), *The standard edition of the complete psychological works of Sigmund Freud* (Vol. 14:67–103. London: Vintage, 2001.

Freud, S. (1915a). Metapsychology. The unconscious. In J. Strachey (Ed. & Trans.), *The standard edition of the complete psychological works of Sigmund Freud* (Vol. 14:159–216. London: Vintage, 2001.

Freud, S. (1915b). Metapsychology. Instincts and their vicissitudes. In J. Strachey (Ed. &

Trans.), *The standard edition of the complete psychological works of Sigmund Freud* (Vol. 14:117–140). London: Vintage, 2001.

Freud, S. (1915c). Metapsychology. Mourning and melancholia. In J. Strachey (Ed. & Trans.), *The standard edition of the complete psychological works of Sigmund Freud* (Vol. 14:237–258). London: Vintage, 2001.

Freud, S. (1915d). Thoughts for the times on war and death. In J. Strachey (Ed. & Trans.), *The standard edition of the complete psychological works of Sigmund Freud* (Vol. 14:275–300). London: Vintage, 2001.

Freud, S. (1915e). Observations on transference-love. In J. Strachey (Ed. & Trans.), *The standard edition of the complete psychological works of Sigmund Freud* (Vol. 14: 157–171). London: Vintage, 2001.

Freud, S. (1915f). A metapsychological supplement to the theory of dreams. In J. Strachey (Ed. & Trans.), *The standard edition of the complete psychological works of Sigmund Freud* (Vol. 14:217–236). London: Vintage, 2001.

Freud, S. (1915g) Observations on transference-love. In J. Strachey (Ed. & Trans.), *The standard edition of the complete psychological works of Sigmund Freud* (Vol. 12: 157–171). London: Vintage, 2001.

Freud, S. (1916). Introductory lectures on psychoanalysis. Translated under the direction of J. Strachey. *Pelican Freud Library*, I. Harmondsworth: Penguin, 1976.

Freud, S. (1917). On transformations of instincts as exemplified in anal erotism. Translated under the direction of J. Strachey. *Pelican Freud Library*, 7:293–302. Harmondsworth: Penguin, 1976.

Freud, S. (1920). Beyond the pleasure principle. In J. Strachey (Ed. & Trans.), *The standard edition of the complete psychological works of Sigmund Freud* (Vol. 18:7–65). London: Vintage, 2001.

Freud, S. (1923a). The Ego and the Id. In J. Strachey (Ed. & Trans.), *The standard edition of the complete psychological works of Sigmund Freud* (Vol. 19:3–67). London: Vintage, 2001.

Freud, S. (1923b). Dr. Sandor Ferenczi (on his 50th birthday). In J. Strachey (Ed. & Trans.), *The standard edition of the complete psychological works of Sigmund Freud* (Vol. 19:262–269). London: Hogarth Press, 2001.

Freud, S. (1924a). The dissolution of the Oedipus complex. In J. Strachey (Ed. & Trans.), *The standard edition of the complete psychological works of Sigmund Freud* (Vol. 19:173–182). London: Vintage, 2001.

Freud, S. (1924b). The loss of reality in neurosis and psychosis. In J. Strachey (Ed. & Trans.), *The standard edition of the complete psychological works of Sigmund Freud* (Vol. 19:183–190). London: Vintage, 2001.

Freud, S. (1925). The resitances to psycho-analysis. In J. Strachey (Ed. & Trans.), *The standard edition of the complete psychological works of Sigmund Freud* (Vol. 19: 213–222). London: Vintage, 2001.

Freud, S. (1926). Inhibitions, symptoms and anxiety. Translated under the direction of J. Strachey. *Pelican Freud Library*, 10:237–315. Harmondsworth: Penguin, 1976.

Freud, S. (1929). *Civilisation and its discontents* (J. Strachey, Trans.). New York: Norton.*

Freud, S. (1931). Libidinal types. Translated under the direction of J. Strachey. *Pelican Freud Library*, 7:359–365. Harmondsworth: Penguin, 1976.

Freud, S. (1932). *Nouvelles conférences d'introduction à la psychanalyse* [New introductory lectures on psycho-analysis]. Paris: Gallimard, 1984.

Freud, S. (1938). An outline of psychoanalysis. In J. Strachey (Ed. & Trans.), *The stan-*

dard edition of the complete psychological works of Sigmund Freud (Vol. 23:141–207). London: Hogarth Press, 2001.

Freud, S. (1975). *The letters of Sigmund Freud*. New York: Basic books.

Freud, S., & Ferenczi, S. (2000). *Correspondance, vol. 3* [The correspondence of Sigmund Freud and Sándor Ferenczi]. Paris: Calmann-Lévy.

Freud, S., & Jung., C. G. (1961). *The Freud/Jung letters*. London: Penguin books, 1991. (This is an abridged version. The complete letters were published by The Hogarth Press and Routledge & Kegan Paul in 1974.)

Frey, S. (1984). *Die non verbale Kommunikation*. Suttgart: SEL-Stiftung für technische und wirtschaftliche Kommunikationsforschung im Stifterverband für die Deutsche Wissenschaft.

Frey, S. (1985). *Décrypter le langage corporel*. Suttgart: SEL-Stiftung für technische und wirtschaftliche Kommunikationsforschung im Stifterverband für die Deutsche Wissenschaft.

Frey, S. (1993). Lavater, Lichtenberg, and the suggestive power of the human face. In E. Shookman (Ed.), *The faces of physiognomy: Interdisciplinary approaches to Johann Caspar Lavater*: 64–103. New York: Camden House.

Frey, S. (1998). Prejudice and inferential communication. In I. Eibl-Eibesfeld & S. Kemp (Eds.), *Indoctrinability: Ideology and warfare*, 189–218. New York: Berghahn Books.

Frey, S. (1999). *Die Macht des Bildes. Der Einfluss der non verbalen Kommunikation auf Kultur und Politik*. Bern: Verlag Hans Huber.

Frey, S. (2001). New directions in communications research: The impact of the human body on the cognitive and affective system of the perceiver. In M. Heller (Ed.), *The flesh of the soul: The body we work with*: 257–282. Bern: Peter Lang.

Frey, S. (2006). The pictorial turn—A shift from reason to instinct? In *Proceedings of the 15th Symposium of the International Design Forum Ulm (IFG Ulm): Form and Sign—Global Communication*. Basel: Birkhäuser.

Frey, S. (2008). Spellbound by images. In A. Zerdick, A. Picot, K. Schrape, J.-C. Burgelman, R. Silverstone, V. Feldmann, C. Wernick, & C. Wolff (Eds.), *European Communication Council report. Emerging media, communication and the media economy of the future*. Berlin: Springer.

Frey, S., Hirsbrunner, H.-P., Florin, A., Daw, W., & Crawford, R. (1983). A unified approach to the investigation of non verbal and verbal behavior in communication research. In W. Doise & S. Moscovici (Eds.), *Current issues in European social psychology*, 1:143–199. Cambridge: Cambridge University Press, and Paris: Éditions de la Maison des Sciences de l'Homme.

Frey, S., Jorns, U., & Daw, W. (1980). A systematic description and analysis of nonverbal interaction between doctors and patients in a psychiatric interview. In S. A. Corson (Ed.), *Ethology and nonverbal communication in mental health*. New York: Pergamon Press.

Frey, S., & Pool, J. (1976). *A new approach to the analysis of visible behaviour*. Research Reports from the Department of Psychology of the University of Bern.

Fridlund, A. (1994). *Human facial expression: An evolutionary view*. San Diego, CA: Academic Press.

Frijda, N. H. (1986). *The emotions*. Cambridge: Cambridge University Press.

Frijda, N. H. (2006). *The laws of emotion*. Mahwah, NJ: Erlbaum.

Fröhlich, F., & McCormick, D. A. (2010). Endogenous electric fields may guide neocortical network activity. *Neuron*, 67:129–143.

Frontier, S., & Pichot-Viale, D. (1998). *Ecosystèmes. Structure, fonctionnement, évolution*. Paris : Dunod.

Fuchs, S. (2004). *Hugo Heller (1870–1923) Buchhändler und Verleger in Wien. Eine Monographie.* Diplomarbeit, Wien 2004.

Galileo, G. (1630). *Dialogue concerning the two chief world systems.* Berkeley: University of California Press, 1967.

Gall, F.-J. (1825). *On the functions of the brain and each of its parts: With observations on the possibility of determining the instincts, propensities and talents, or the moral and intellectual dispositions of men and animals, by the configuration of the head.* Boston: Marsh, Capen & Lyon, 1835.

Gall, F.-J., & Spurzheim, G. (1810). *Anatomie et physiologie du système nerveux en général et du cerveau en particulier, volume 1.* Paris: imprimerie Haussmann et d'Hantel.

Gallagher, S. (2005). *How the body shapes the mind.* Oxford: Clarendon Press.

Gallagher, S., & Cole, J. (1995). Body schema and body image in a deafferented subject. *Journal of Mind and Behavior*, 16:369–390.

Gallese, V. (2005). Embodied simulation: From neurons to phenomenal experience. *Phenomenology and the Cognitive Sciences*, 4, 1:23–48.

Galton, F. (1869). *Hereditary genius: An inquiry into its laws and consequences.* Amherst: Prometheus Books, 2006.

Gammer, C. (2005). *The child's voice in family therapy: A systemic perspective.* New York: Norton, 2009.

Gandt, F. de (1985). Présentation. In I. Newton, *De la gravitation*, suivi de *Du mouvement des corps:* 9–108. Paris: Gallimard, 1995.

Gangloff, B., Chan Tak Nam, J. C., & Lepoutre, F. X. (1984). Étude ergonomique des sièges de secrétariat: Définition d'une problématique. *Le Travail Humain*, 47, 4:329–349.

Ganong, W. F. (1999). *Review of medical physiology*, 19. Stamford: Appleton & Lange.

Garland, M., Hickey, D., Corvin, A., Golden, J., Fitzpatrick, P., Cunningham, S., et al. (2000). Total serum cholesterol in relation to psychological correlates in parasuicide. *British Journal of Psychiatry*, 177:77–83.

Gaskin, J. C. A. (1993). Introduction. In D. Hume, *Dialogues and Natural History of Religion*: ix–xxv. Oxford: Oxford University Press, 2008.

Gauchet, M. (1992). *L'inconscient cérébral.* Paris: Seuil.

Gazzaniga, M. S. (1985). *The social brain.* New York: Basic Books.

Gazzaniga, M. S., Bogen, M. E., & Sperry, R. W. (1965). Observations on visual perception after disconnection of the cerebral hemispheres in man. *Brain*, 88, 2, 22:1–236.

Geissler, P. (1996). *Neue Entwicklungen in der Bioenergetischen Analyse: Materialien zur analytischen körperbezogenen Psychotherapie.* Frankfurt: Peter Lang Verlag.

Geissler, P. (1997). *Analytische Körperpsychotherapie: Bioenergetische und psychoanalytische Grundlagen und aktuelle Trends.* Wien: Facultas Verlag.

Geissler, P. (2002). Following in the footsteps of Ferenczi, Balint and Winnicott: Love and hate in a setting open to body- and action-related interventions. In D. Mann (Ed.), *Love and hate: Psychoanalytic perspectives*: 267–283. London: Brunner-Routledge.

Geissler, P. (2005). *Non verbale Interaktion in der Psychotherapie. Forschung und Relevanz für die Praxis.* Giessen: Psychosozial Verlag.

Gendlin, E. (1996). *Focusing-oriented psychotherapy*. New York: Guilford.

Gendlin, E. (1998). *Focusing-oriented psychotherapy: A manual of the experiential method*. New York: Guilford.

Gergely, G., & Watson, J. S. (1999). Early socio-emotional development: Contingency perception and the social biofeedback model. In P. Rochat (Ed.), *Early social cognition: Understanding others in the first months of life*: 101–137. Mahwah, NJ: Lawrence Erlbaum.

Gershon, M. D. (1998). *The second brain*. New York: Harper Collins.

Geuter, U. (1984). *The professionalization of psychology in Nazi Germany*. Cambridge: Cambridge University Press, 1992.

Geuter, U. (1996). Körperbilder une Körpertechniken in des Psychotherapie. *Psychotherapeut*, 41:99–106.

Geuter, U. (2000a). Wege zum Körper. Zur Geschichte und Theorie des körperbezogenen Ansatzes in der Psychotherapie. *Energie und Charakter*, 22:103–126.

Geuter, U. (2000b). Historischer Abriss zur Entwicklung der körperorientierten Psychotherapie. In F. Röhricht (Ed.), *Körperorientierte Psychotherapie psychischer Störungen*: 53–74. Göttingen: Hogrefe.

Geuter, U. (2004). Die Anfänge der Körperpsychotherapie in Berlin. In T. Müller (Ed.), *Psychotherapie und Körperarbeit in Berlin. Geschichte und Praktiken der Etablierung*: 167–181. Husum: Matthiesen Verlag.

Geuter, U., Heller, M. C., & Weaver, J. O. (2010). Reflections on Elsa Gindler and her influence on Wilhelm Reich and body psychotherapy. *Body, Movement and Dance in Psychotherapy*, 5, 1:59–73.

Gianino, A., & Tronick, E. (1988). The mutual regulation model: Infant's self and interactive regulation and coping and defensive capacities. In T. Field, P. McCabe, & N. Schneiderman (Eds.), *Stress and coping*: 47–60. Hillsdale, NJ: Erlbaum.

Gillham, N. W. (2001). *A life of Sir Francis Galton: From African exploration to the birth of eugenics*. Oxford: Oxford University Press.

Gindler, E. (1926). Gymnastik for people whose lives are full of activity. In D. Johnson (Ed.), *Bone, breath and gesture: Practices of embodiment*: 5–14. Berkeley: North Atlantic Books, 1995.

Goelzer, H. (1928). *Le latin en poche. Dictionnaire Latin-Français*. Paris: Éditions Garnier Frères, 1963.

Goethe, J. W. von (1823). *Theory of colours*. Cambridge, MA: MIT Press, 1982.

Goffman, E. (1974). *Frame analysis: An essay on the organization of experience*. New York: Harper & Row.

Golden, N. H., & Meyer W. (2003). Nutritional rehabilitation of anorexia nervosa: Goals and dangers. *International Journal of Adolescent Medicine and Health*, 16, 2:131–144.*

Goldin-Meadow, S. (2003). Hearing gesture: How our hands help us think. Cambridge, MA: Belknap Press of Harvard University.

Goldstein, K. (1939). *The organism*. New York: Zone Books, 2000.

Goldsztub, L., & Lévy, M. (2006). *Les Dérives de l'oralité*. Paris: Érès.

Gomperz, T. (1905). *The Greek thinkers*. London: John Murray, 1969.

Gopnick, A. (2009). Could David Hume have known about Buddhism? Charles Francois Dolu, the Royal College of la Flèche, and the Global Jesuit Intellectual Network. *Hume Studies*, 35, 1&2:5–28.

Gorkin, M. (1987). *The uses of countertransference*. Northvale, NJ: Jason Aronson.

Gougoulis, N. (2010). Les centres de consultations psychanalytiques dans leur histoire. *Le Coq-héron*, 201:45–52.

Gould, S. J. (1996). *Dinosaur in a haystack*. London: Penguin.

Granoff, W. (2004). *Le désir d'analyse*. Paris: Aubier.

Green, C. R., Flowe-Valencia, H., Rosenblum, L., & Tait, A. R. (1999). Do physical and sexual abuse differentially affect chronic pain states in women? *Journal of Pain and Symptom Management*, 18, 6:420–426.

Griffiths, P. E. (1997). *What emotions really are*. Chicago: University of Chicago Press.

Groddeck, W. G. (1913). *"Nasamecu." La nature guérit* [Nasamecu]. Paris: Aubier Montaigne, 1980.

Groddeck, W. G. (1923). *Le livre du ça* [The book of the it]. Paris: Gallimard, 1963.

Groddeck, W. G. (1931). *Massage in psychotherapy*. In W. G. Groddeck, *The meaning of illness*: 234–240. London: Hogarth Press, 1977.

Groddeck, W. G. (1977). *The meaning of illness*. London: Hogarth Press.

Gross, C. G. (1998). Claude Bernard and the constancy of the internal environment. *Neuroscientist*, 4, 5:380–385.*

Grossinger, R. (1995). *Planet medicine*. Berkeley: North Atlantic Books.

Grove, B., Secker, J., & Seebohm, P. (2005). *New thinking about mental health and employment*. Oxon: Radcliffe Publishing.

Grumberger, B. (1971). *Narcissism*. New York: International Universities Press.

Guasch, G. (2007). *Wilhelm Reich, biographie d'une passion*. Paris: Editions Sully.

Guex, P. (1989). *Psychologie et cancer. Manuel de psycho-oncologie* [An introduction to psycho-oncology]. Lausanne: Editions Payot.

Guimón, J. (1997a). *The body in psychotherapy*. Basel: Karger.

Guimón, J. (1997b). Corporeity and psychotherapy: Some preliminary concepts. In J. Guimón (Ed.), *The body in psychotherapy*: 1–4. Basel: Karger.

Gurdjieff, G. I. (1950). *Beelzebub's tales to his grandson*. London: Arkana, 1985.

Gurdjieff, G. I. (1960). *Meetings with remarkable men*. New York: Penguin Compass, 2002.

Gurdjieff, G. I. (1978). *Life is real only then, when "I am."* London: Routledge & Kegan Paul, 1981.

Haich, E. (1972). *The Wisdom of the Tarot*. Windsor: Mandala Books.

Hall, E. T. (1959). *The silent language*. Greenwich: Facett Premier Book, 1969.

Han, J., Zhu, Y., Li, S., Chen, X., Put, C., Van de Woestijne, K.P., & Van den Bergh, O. (2005). Respiratory complaints in Chinese: Cultural and diagnostic specificities. *Chest*, 127:1942–1951.

Hanish, O. Z. A. (1970). *The power of breath*. Los Angeles: Mazdaznan Press.

Harlow, H. F. (1959). Love in infant monkeys. In S. Coopersmith (Ed.), *Frontiers of psychological research*: 94–100. San Francisco: W. H. Freeman.

Harlow, H. F. (1986). *From Learning to Love: The Selected Papers of H. F. Harlow*. New York: Praeger.

Harris, B., & Brock, A. (1992). Freudian psychopolitics: Rivalry between Wilhelm Reich and Otto Fenichel, 1930–1935. *Bulletin of History of Medicine*, 66:578–612.

Hartmann, H. (1939). *Ego psychology and the problem of adaptation*. New York: International Universities Press.

Hauswirth, M. (2002). De l'analyse bioénergétique aux thérapies psycho-corporelles analytiques. In N. Duruz & M. Gennart (Ed.), *Traité de psychothérapie comparée*: 180–204. Geneva: Éditions Médecine & Hygiène.

Haynal, A. (1967). Contribution à l'étude de la notion de "force du Moi." *L'Évolution Psychiatrique*, 32, 3:617–638.

Haynal, A. (1985). *Dépression et créativité. Le sens du désespoir* [Depression and creativity]. Lyon: Césura Lyon édition, 1987.

Haynal, A. (1987). *The technique at issue. Controversies in psychoanalysis from Freud and Ferenczi to Michael Balint*. London: Karnac Books, 1988.

Haynal, A. (1991). *Psychanalyse et science face à face* [Psychoanalysis and the sciences. Epistemology–History]. Meyzieu: Césura Lyon édition.

Haynal, A. (1992). Au sujet de l'inconscient. Interview avec André Haynal par Michel Heller. *Adire*, 7–8:9–17.

Haynal, A. (2001). *Un psychanalyste pas comme un autre. La renaissance de Sándor Ferenczi* [Disappearing and reviving. Sándor Ferenczi in the history of psychoanalysis]. Lausanne: Delachaux et Niestlé.

Haynal, A. (2005). Dans l'ombre d'une contreverse. Freud et Ferenczi entre 1925 et 1933. In A. Haynal, E. Falzeder, & P. Roazen (Eds.), *Dans les secrets de la Psychanalyse et de son histoire*: 315–326. Paris : Presses Universitaires de France.

Haynal, A., Pasini, W., & Archinard, M. (1997). *Médecine psychosomatique. Aperçus psychosociaux*, 3rd ed. Paris: Masson.

Haynal-Reymond, V., Jonsson, G. K., & Magnusson, M. S. (2005). Nonverbal communication in doctor-suicidal patient interview. In L. Anolli, S. Duncan Jr., M. S. Magnusson, & G. Riva (Eds.), *The hidden structure of interaction: From neurons to culture patterns*. Amsterdam: IOS Press.*

Hebb, D. O. (1958). The motivating effects of exteroceptive stimulation. *American Psychologist*, 3, 3:109–113.

Hecquet, S., & Prokhoris, S. (2007). *Fabriques de la danse*. Paris: Presses Universitaires de France.

Hedges, L. E., Hilton, R., Hilton, W. W., & Caudill, O. B. (1997). *Therapist at risk: Perils of the therapeutic relationship*. Northvale, NJ: Jason Aronson.

Hegel, G. W. F. (1828). *La raison dans l'histoire*. Paris: Librairie Plon.

Hegel, G. W. F. (1833). *Lectures on the history of philosophy*. Lincoln: Bison Books.

Heidegger, M. (1927). *L'être et le temps*. Paris: Gallimard, 1964.

Heisler, V. (1973). The transpersonal in Jungian theory and therapy. *Journal of Religion and Health*, 12, 4:337–341.

Held, R., & Hein, A. (1963). Movement-produced stimulation in the development of visually guided behavior. *Journal of Comparative and Physiological Psychology*, 56, 5, pp. 872–876.

Heller, G. (1988). *Tiens-toi droit. L'enfant à l'école primaire au 19e siècle: espace, morale, santé. L'exemple vaudois*. Lausanne: Éditions d'En Bas.

Heller, H. (1909). Sur l'histoire du diable [On the history of the devil]. In H. Nunberg, H. Federn, & E. Federn (Eds.), *Les premiers psychanalystes. Minutes de la Société psychanalytique de Vienne* [Minutes of the Vienna Psychoanalytic Society], vol. II (1908–1910): 121–127. Paris: Gallimard.

Heller, M. (1976). *La marche à quatre pattes*. PhD diss., University of Geneva.

Heller, M. (1987a). Deflux et contre-transfert. *Adire*, 4:43–82. (A recent version of this text, titled "Ethique et ouverture," is available at www.aqualide.com)

Heller, M. (1987b). Introduction. *Adire*, 4:3–22.

Heller, M. (1987c). The eye block. *Adire*, 4:199–220. (A recent version of this text, titled

"The eye block, schizophrenia and autism: A study on interdisciplinarity," is available at www.aqualide.com)

Heller, M. (1991a). Postural dynamics and social status. PhD diss., 1991. (Can be ordered from the author.)

Heller, M. (1991b). Pratique de la respiration en psychologie biodynamique. In J. Besson (Ed.), *Manuel d'enseignement de l'Ecole Française d'Analyse Psycho-organique*, 1:175–234. Paris: École Française d'Analyse Psycho-organique.

Heller, M. (1993a). Unconscious communication. In B. Maul (Ed.), *Body-psychotherapy or the art of contact*: 155–179. Berlin: Verlag Bernhard Maul.

Heller, M. (1993b). The jellyfish, or the Reichian world of Gerda Boyesen, I. *Energy & Character*, 24, 2:1–27.

Heller, M. (1993c). Le transfert. In J. Besson (Ed.), *Manuel d'enseignement de l'Ecole Française d'Analyse Psycho-organique*, 3:67–122. Paris: École Française d'Analyse Psycho-organique.

Heller, M. (1993d). Wissenschaft & Psychothérapie. *Energy & Character*, 8:191–201.

Heller, M. (1994). The jellyfish, or the Reichian world of Gerda Boyesen, II. *Energy & Character*, 25, 1:18–43.

Heller, M. (1997). Posture as an interface between biology and culture. In U. Segerstrale & P. Molnár (Eds.), *Non-verbal communication: where nature meets culture*: 245–263. Mahwah, NJ: Lawrence Erlbaum.

Heller, M. (1998). La programmation comme microscope du comportement communicatif corporel. *Cahiers Psychiatriques*, 24:101–117.

Heller, M. (1999). Darwin and the animal nature of the humans. *Energy & Character*, 30, 1:67–78. (A recent version of this text entitled *Darwin and the animal nature of the human soul* is available at www.aqualide.com)

Heller, M. (2001). Presentation: The organism as physiology, body flesh and soul. In M. Heller (Ed.), *The flesh of the soul: The body we work with*: 9–32. Bern: Peter Lang.

Heller, M. (2004a). Behind the stage of interacting faces. Commentary on case study by Beatrice Beebe. *Psychoanalytic Dialogues*, 14, 1:53–63.

Heller, M. C. (2004b). Les diverses peurs distinguées en psycho-neurologie, et les dimensions thérapeutiques qui leur correspondent. *Le canard biodynamique, journal de l'Association Professionnelle de Psychologie Biodynamique*, 4:16–21.*

Heller, M. C. (2004c). Ce que le corps nous enseigne sur la topique de l'âme. *Adire*, 20:293–347.

Heller, M. C. (2005). La sexualité en tant que penchant. *Adire*, 21:35–64.

Heller, M. C. (2006). A topography of the mind. *USA Body Psychotherapy Journal*, 5, 2:61–87.

Heller, M. C. (2007). The golden age of body psychotherapy in Oslo I: From gymnastics to psychoanalysis. *Body, Movement and Dance in Psychotherapy*, 2, 1:5–16.*

Heller, M., & Haynal-Reymond, V. (1997a). Depression and suicide faces. In P. Ekman & E. L. Rosenberg (Eds.). *What the face reveals: Basic and applied studies of spontaneous expression using the Facial Action Coding System (FACS)*: 398–407. Oxford: Oxford University Press.

Heller, M., & Haynal-Reymond, V. (1997b). Perspectives for studies of psychopathology and psychotherapy. In P. Ekman & E. L. Rosenberg (Eds.), *What the face reveals. Basic and applied stu-ies of spontaneous expression using the Facial Action Coding System (FACS)*: 408–413. Oxford: Oxford University Press.

Heller, M., & Haynal-Reymond, V. (1997c). The doctor's face: A mirror of his patient's suicidal projects. In J. Guimón (Ed.), *The body in psychotherapy*: 46–50. Basel: Karger.

Heller, M., Haynal-Reymond, V., Haynal, A., & Archinard, M. (2001). Can faces reveal suicide attempt risks? In M. Heller (Ed.), *The flesh of the soul. The body we work with*: 231–256. Bern: Peter Lang.

Helmholtz, H. von. (1853). On Goethe's scientific research. In H. von Helmholtz, *Science and culture: Popular philosophical essays*, 1–17. Chicago: University of Chicago Press, 1995.

Helmholtz, H. von. (1863). On the conservation of force. In H. von Helmholtz (Ed.), *Science and culture: Popular philosophical essays*, 96–126. Chicago: The University of Chicago Press, 1995.

Henley, N. M. (1977). *Body politics: Power, sex and nonverbal communication*. Englewood Cliffs, NJ: Prentice Hall.

Henrich, J., Heine, S. J., & Norenzayan, A. (2010). Most people are not WEIRD. *Nature*, 466, July.

Heraclitus. (2001). *Fragments. The collected wisdom of Heraclitus* (B. Haxton, Trans.). New York: Viking.

Hess, E. H. (1965). Attitude and pupil size. In R. C. Atkinson (Ed.), *Contemporary psychology*: 400–408. San Francisco: Freeman, 1971.

Hewes, G. (1955). World distribution of certain postural habits. *American Anthropologist*, 65:1003–1026.

Hewes, G. (1957). The anthropology of posture. *Scientific American*, 196:122–132.

Hill, C. E. (Ed.). (2004). *Dream work in therapy: Facilitating exploration, insight, and action*. Washington, DC: American Psychological Association.

Hillman, C. H., Hsiao-Weckslerb, E. T., & Rosengren, K. S. (2005). Postural and eyeblink indices of the defensive startle reflex. *International Journal of Psychophysiology*, 55, 1:45–49.

Hillman, J. (1964). *Suicide and the soul*. Dallas: Spring Publications, 1985.

Hobbes, T. (1651) *Leviathan*. Mineola: Dover Publications.*

Hobsbawm, E. J. (1994). *The age of extremes: A history of the world, 1914–1991*. New York: Vintage.

Hobsbawm, E. J. (2007). *Globalisation, democracy and terrorism*. London: Little, Brown.

Hobson, A. J. (1999). *Consciousness*. New York: Scientific American Library.

Hock, R. R. (1992). Forty studies that changed psychology: Explorations into the history of psychological research. Englewood Cliffs, NJ: Prentice-Hall, 1999.

Hoey, M. (2005). *Lexical priming*. London: Routledge.

Hogan, M. J., Staff R. T., Bunting B. P., Murray A. D., Ahearn T. S., Deary I. J., et al. (2011). Cerebellar brain volume accounts for variance in cognitive performance in older adults. *Cortex*. 47, 4:441–450.

Holzman, P. S. (2003). The evolution of my interest in psychoanalysis. *Psychologist-psychoanalyst*, XXIII.1: 9–17.

Hopper, J., Frewen, P., van der Kolk, B., & Lanius, R. (2007). Neural correlates of reexperiencing, avoidance, and dissociation in PTSD: Symptom dimensions and emotion dysregulation in responses to script-driven trauma imagery. *Journal of Traumatic Stress*, 20, 5:713–725.*

Huang, W.-S. (1974). *Fundamentals of Tai Chi Ch'uan*. Hong Kong: South Sky Book Company.

Hubel, D. H. (1963). The visual cortex of the brain. In R. C. Atkinson (Ed.), *Contemporary psychology*: 132–140. San Francisco: Freeman, 1971.

Hubel, D. H., & Wiesel, T. N. (1963). Receptive fields of cells in striate cortex of very young, visually inexperienced kittens. *Journal of Neurophysiology*, 26:944–1002.

Huber, J.-P. (1982). *Traité de sophrologie, I: Origines et développement*. Paris: Le Courrier du Livre.

Hume, D. (1737). *A treatise of human nature*. Oxford: Oxford University Press, 2002.

Hume, D. (1740). My own life. In D. Hume, *Essays moral and political and literary*: xxxi–xlii. Indianapolis: Liberty Fund, 1985.

Hume, D. (1748). *An enquiry concerning human understanding*. Oxford: Oxford University Press, 2002.

Hume, D. (1776). Dialogues concerning natural religion. In D. Hume, *Dialogues and natural history of religion*: 29–132. Oxford: Oxford University Press, 2008.

Hume, D. (1792). *The history of England from the invasion of Julius Ceasar to the revolution in 1688*. Indianapolis: Liberty Fund, 1983.

Hurni, M., & Stoll, G. (2003). Perversions narcissiques dans le couple. *Revue Française de Psychanalyse*, 3, 67:873–893.*

Husserl, E. (1913). *Idées directrices pour une phénoménologie*. Paris: Gallimard, 1989.

Husserl, E. (1936). *The crisis of European sciences and transcendental phenomenology* D. Carr, Trans.). Evanston, IL: Northwestern University Press, 1970.

Inhelder, B., & de Caprona, D. (1992). Vers le constructivisme psychologique: Structures? Procédures? Les deux indissociables. In B. Inhelder & G. Cellérier (Eds.), *Le cheminement des découvertes de l'enfant*: 19–50. Lausanne: Delachaux et Niestlé. (The editors have published a book in English titled *Piaget Today*.)

Inhelder, B., & Cellérier, G. (1992). *Le cheminement des découvertes de l'enfant*. Lausanne: Delachaud et Niestlé. (The editors have published in English a book entitled *Piaget Today*.)

Innes, C. (1983). *Edward Gordon Craig*. Cambridge, UK: Cambridge University Press.

International Classification of Diseases, 10th Edition. World Health Organization. http://apps.who.int/classifications/icd10/browse/2010/en

Iyengar, B. K. S. (1966). *Light on yoga*. London: Unwin Paperbacks, 1984.

Izard, C. E. (1971). *The face of emotion*. New York: Appleton-Century-Crofts.

Jabr, F. (2010). Neural feedback: The brain generates an electric field that influences its own activity. *Scientific American Mind*, 21, 10:42–45.

Jacob, F. (2000). *La souris, la mouche et l'homme* [Of flies, mice and men]. Paris: Odile Jacob.

Jacobson, E. (1938). *Progressive relaxation, a physiological and clinical investigation of muscular states and their significance in psychology and medical practice*. Chicago: University of Chicago Press.

Jacobson, E. (1967). *Biology of emotions: New understanding derived from biological multidisciplinary investigation; first electrophysiological measurements*. Springfield, IL: Charles C Thomas.

Jacoby, H. (1983). *Jenseits von 'Begabt' und 'Unbegabt'. Zweckmäßige Fragestellung und zweckmäßiges Verhalten—Schlüssel für die Entfaltung des Menschen*. Hamburg: Christians.

Jacoby, R. (1983). *Otto Fenichel: Destins de la gauche freudienne* [The Repression of Psychoanalysis: Otto Fenichel and the Political Freudians]. Paris: Presses Universitaires de France, 1986.

Jaffe, J., Beebe, B., Feldstein, S., Crown, C. L., & Jasnow, M. D. (2002). *Rhythms of dialogue in infancy*. Boston: Blackwell.

Jahoda, M., Hans Zeisel, H., & Lazarsfeld, P. (1932). *Marienthal: The sociography of an unemployed community*. Piscataway, NJ: Transaction Publishers, 2009.

Jambon, C., Laborde, J. C., & Quere, I. (1994). Aperçu historique du traitement des varices. *Journal des Maladies Vasculaires*, 19:210–215.

James, W. (1890). *The principles of psychology*. Cambridge, MA: Harvard University Press, 1983.

Janet, P. (1909). *Les névroses* [The neuroses]. Paris: Flammarion.*

Janik, A. S., & Veigl (1998). *Wittgenstein in Vienna: A biographical excursion through the city and its history*. Wien: Springer.

Janov, A. (1973). *The feeling child*. New York: Simon and Schuster.

Jansen, E. M. (1989). Unitive perspective in psychotherapy. In J. Dattman, E. M. Jansen, G. Marlock, M. Aalberse, & H. Stubenrauch (Eds.), *Unitive body-psychotherapy*, vol. 1:15–39. Frankfurt: AFRA.

Johanson, G. J. (2006). A survey of the use of mindfulness in psychotherapy. *Annals of the American Psychotherapy Association*, 9, 2:15–24.

Johnson, L. (1976a). Muscular tonus and integrated respiration. In D. Boadella (Ed.), *In the wake of Reich*: 282–301. London: Conventure.

Johnson, L. (1976b). Integrated respiration therapy. *Energy and Character*, 7, 1:12–22.

Johnson, L. (1979). Developmental steps and centers of growth, 1. *Energy and Character*, 10, 1, pp. 2–12.

Johnson-Laird, P. N. (1988). *The computer and the mind: An introduction to cognitive science*. Cambridge, MA: Harvard University Press.

Jung C. G. (1907). The psychology of dementia praecox. In C. G. Jung, *The collected works of C. G. Jung*, vol. 3:1–151. London: Routledge & Kegan Paul, 1981.

Jung, C. G. (1928). Commentary on The Secret of the Golden Flower. In C. G. Jung, *The collected works of C. G. Jung*, vol. 6:1–57. Princeton: Princeton University Press, 1979.

Jung, C. G. (1931). *Problèmes de l'âme moderne* [Modern man in search of a soul]. Paris: Buchet/Chastel, 1976.

Jung, C. G. (1934). Fonctions et structures du conscient et de l'inconscient. In C. G. Jung, *L'homme à la découverte de son âme*: 85–133. Paris: Payot, 1962.

Jung, C. G. (1939). The meaning of individuation. In C. G. Jung, *The collected works of C. G. Jung*, vol. 9, 1: The archetypes and the collective unconscious: 275–289. London: Routledge & Kegan Paul, 1971.

Jung, C. G. (1940). *Children's dreams. Notes from the seminar given in 1936–1940* (E. Falzeder, Trans.). Princeton: Princeton University Press, 2008.

Jung, C. G. (1950). A study in the process of individuation. In C. G. Jung, *The collected works of C. G. Jung*, vol. 9, 1: The archetypes and the collective unconscious: 182–205. London: Routledge & Kegan Paul, 1971.

Jung, C. G. (1950). The psychological aspects of the Kore. In C. G. Jung, *The collected works of C. G. Jung*, vol. 9, 1: The archetypes and the collective unconscious: 290–353. London: Routledge & Kegan Paul, 1971.

Jung, C. G. (1954). Archetypes of the collective unconscious. In C. G. Jung, *The collected works of C.G. Jung*, vol. 9, 1: The archetypes and the collective unconscious: 3–41. London: Routledge & Kegan Paul, 1971.

Jung, C. G. (1960). *On the nature of the psyche*. London: Ark Paperbacks.

Jung, C. G. (1961). *Essai d'exploration de l'inconscient* [Memories, dreams, reflections]. Paris: Denoël, 1990.

Juslin, P. N., & Scherer, K. R. (2005). Vocal expression of affect. In J. Harrigan, R. Rosenthal, & K. Scherer, (Eds.), *The new handbook of methods in nonverbal behavior research:* 65–135. Oxford: Oxford University Press.

Jwing-Ming, Y. (1987). *Chi kung. Health & marital arts.* Jamaica Plain: Yang's Martial Arts Association.

Kabat-Zinn, J. (1990). *Full catastrophe living: Using the wisdom of the body and mind to face stress, pain and illness.* New York: Delta.

Kagan, J. (1998). *Three seductive ideas.* Cambridge, MA: Harvard University Press.

Kagan, J. (2007). *What is emotion? History, measures, and meanings.* New Haven, CT: Yale University Press.

Kaiser, S., & Wehrle, T. (2010). *Same situation different emotions: Manipulating emotional appraisals with interactive computer games.* Unpublished manuscript.

Kaltenmark, M. (1970). Le taoïsme religieux. In Henri-Charles Puech (Ed.), *Histoire des religions*, I:1219–1248. Paris: Gallimard.

Kant, I. (1776). *Rêves d'un visionnaire expliqués par des rêves métaphysiques* [Dreams of a Spirit-Seer]. Paris: Vrin, 2002.

Kant, I. (1783). *Prolegomena to any future metaphysics* (J. Fieser, Trans.). (1997). http://infomotions.com/etexts/philosophy/1700-1799/kant-prolegomena-752.txt

Kant, I. (1784). *An answer to the question: What is enlightenment?* M. J. Gregor, Trans.). Cambridge: Cambridge University Press, 1996.

Kant, I. (1787). *Critique of pure reason* (J. M. D. Meiklejohn, Trans.). London: Everyman's Library, 1988.

Kaplan, A. (1977). Spinoza and Freud. *Journal of the American Academy of Psychoanalysis, 5,* 3:299–326.

Kaplan-Solms, K., & Solms, M. (2000). *Clinical studies in neuro-psychoanalysis. Introduction to a depth neuropsychology.* London: Karnac Books.

Kappas, A., Hess, U., & Scherer, K. R. (1991). Voice and emotion. In R. S. Feldman, & B. Rimé (Eds.), *Fundamentals of non verbal behavior:* 200–238. Cambridge: Cambridge University Press.

Keleman, S. (1970). Bio-energetic concepts of grounding. In D. Boadella (Ed.), *In the wake of Reich:* 192–209. London: Conventure.

Keleman, S. (1978). A conversation with Stanley Keleman. *Sensory Awareness Newsletter,* Spring: 8–9.

Keleman, S. (1985). *Emotional anatomy: The structure of experience.* Berkeley: Center Press.

Kelley, C. (1971). New techniques in vision improvement. In D. Boadella (Ed.), *In the wake of Reich:* 351–381. London: Conventure, 1976.

Kelley, C. (2004). *Life Force . . . the creative process in man and in nature.* Victoria: Trafford.

Kelly, S. D. (2000). Grasping at straws: Motor intentionality and the cognitive science of skilled behavior. In M. Wrathall & J. Malpas (Eds.), *Heidegger, coping, and cognitive science: Essays in honor of Hubert L. Dreyfus*, vol. 2:161–178. Cambridge, MA: MIT Press.

Kendon, A. (1982). The organization of behavior in face to face interaction: observations on the development of a methodology. In K. R. Scherer & P. Ekman (Eds.), *Hand-*

book of methods in nonverbal behavior research: 440–505. Cambridge & Paris: Cambridge University Press.

Kendon, A. (2004). *Gesture. Visible action as utterance*. Cambridge: Cambridge University Press.

Kernberg, O. (1975). *Borderline conditions and pathological narcissism*. New York: Jason Aronson.

Kernberg, O. (1976). *Object relations theory and clinical psychoanalysis*. Northvale, NJ: Jason Aronson, 1984.

Kernberg, O. (1984). *Severe personality disorders: Psychotherapeutic strategies*. New Haven: Yale University Press.

Keverne, E. B., & Kendrick, K. M. (1994). Maternal-behavior in sheep and its neuroendocrine regulation. *Acta Paediatrica*, 83:47–56.

Khamis, S., & Yizhar, Z. (2007). Effect of feet hyperpronation on pelvic alignment in a standing position. *Gait & Posture*, 25, 1:127–134

Kignel, R. (2010). *Sense development through nonverbal signs: Early infancy and clinical psychotherapy*. Thesis, Universita degli studi di Bologna.

Klein, M. (1923). The development of a child. *International Journal of Psychoanalysis*, 4:419–474.

Klein, M. (1925). A contribution to the psychogenesis of tics. In M. Klein, *Contributions to Psycho-Analysis*: 117–139. London: Hogarth.

Klein, M. (1955). On identification. In M. Klein, P. Heimann, & R. Money-Kyrle (Eds.), *New directions in psycho-analysis*: 309–245. London: Tavistock.

Kleinman, A. (1986). *Social origins of distress and disease: Depression, neurasthenia and pain in modern China*. New Haven: Yale University Press.

Klinkenberg, N. (2002). *Moshé Feldenkrais und Heinrich Jacoby—eine begegnung*. Berlin: Heinrich-Jacoby/Elsa-Gindler-Stiftung.

Kluken, P. (1969). *The bases of social behavior: An approach in terms of order and value*. London: Holt, Rinehart and Winston.

Knoblauch, S. (2000). *The musical edge of therapeutic dialogue*. Hillsdale, NJ: Analytic Press.

Kocer, I., Dane, S., Demirel, S., Demirel, H., & Koylu, H. (2002). Unilateral nostril breathing in intraocular pressure of right-handed healthy subjects. *Perceptual and Motor Skills*, 95, 2:491–496.

Koestler, A. (1959). *Arthur: The sleepwalkers*. Middlesex: Penguin.

Koestler, A. (1968). *The ghost in the machine*. New York: Macmillan.

Kogan, G. (1980). *Your body works. A guide to health energy and balance*. Berkeley: Transformation Press.

Kohut, H. (1971). *The analysis of the self*. New York: International Universities Press.

Kolb, D. (1990). *Postmodern sophistications: Philosophy, architecture, and tradition*. Chicago: University of Chicago Press.

Kornfield, J., & Fronsdal, G. (1993). *Teachings of Buddha*. Boston: Shambhala.

Kosfeld, M., Heinrichs, M., Zak, P. J., Fischbacher, U., & Fer, E. (2005). Letter. *Nature*, 435:673–676.

Kosko, B. (1993). *Fuzzy thinking: The new science of fuzzy logic*. New York: Hyperion.

Koulomzin, M., Beebe, B., Anderson, S., Jaffe, J., Feldstein, S., & Crown, C. (2002). Infant gaze, head, face and self-touch at 4 months differentiate secure vs. avoidant attachment at 1 year: A microanalytic approach. *Attachment & Human Development*, 4, 1:3–24.

Kozier, B., & Erb, G. (1985). *Techniques de soins*. Montréal: Éditions du Renouveau Pédagogique.

Krause, R. (1989). Quand se brouillent les signaux. *Science et Vie*, 168:34–41.

Krause, R., & Lütolf, P. (1988). Facial indicators of transference processes within psychoanalytic treatment. In D.H. Kächele & H. Thomä (Eds.), *Psychoanalytic process research strategies*: 257–273. Heidelberg: Springer.

Kuhn, T. (1962). *The structure of scientific revolutions*. Chicago: University of Chicago Press.

Kulbach, J. (1977). Interviewed by Mary Alice Roche. *Bulletin of the Selver Foundation*, special number on Elsa Gindler, 1978, 10, I: 14–18.

Kunik, M. E., Roundy, K., Veazey, C., Souchek, J., Richardson, P., Wray, N. P., et al. (2005). Surprisingly high prevalence of anxiety and depression in chronic breathing disorders. *Chest*, 127:1205–1211.

Kurtz, R. (1990). *Body-centred psychotherapy: The Hakomy method*. Mendicino, CA: LifeRythm.

Kurtz, R., & Minton, K. (1997). Essentials of Hakomi body-centered psychotherapy. In C. Caldwell (Ed.), *Getting in touch. The guide to new body-centered therapies*: 45–59. Wheaton: Quest Books.

Laban, R. (1920). *Die Welt des Tänzers*. Stuttgart: Seifert.

Laban, R. (1950). *The mastery of movement*. Revised by Lisa Ullmann. Tavistock: Northcote House Publishers, 1988.

La Barre, F. (2001). *On moving and being moved. Nonverbal behavior in clinical practice*. Hillsdale: Analytic Press.

Laborit, H. (1968). *Biologie et structure*. Paris: Gallimard.

Laborit, H. (1970). *L'homme imaginant: Essai de biologie politique*. Paris: Union générale d'éditions, 1981.

Laborit, H. (1971). *L'homme et la ville*. Paris: Flammarion.

Laborit, H. (1974). *La nouvelle grille*. Paris: Flammarion.

Laborit, H. (1979). *L'inhibition de l'action. Biologie, physiologie, psychologie, sociologie*. Paris: Masson.

Laborit, H. (1985). *Eloge de la fuite*. Paris: Gallimard.

Laborit, H. (1987). *Dieu ne joue pas aux dés*. Paris: Bernard Grasset.

Laborit, H. (1989). *La vie antérieure*. Paris: Bernard Grasset.

Laborit, H. (1994). *La légende des comportements*. Paris: Flammarion.

Lacan, J. (1949). The mirror stage as formative of the function of the I as revealed in psychoanalytic experience. In J. Lacan, *Écrits: A Selection*: 1–7. New York: Norton, 1977.

Lacan, J. (1954). *The seminar of Jacques Lacan, book I*. New York: Norton, 1977.

Lachman, R., Lachman, J. L., & Butterfield, E. C. (1979). *Cognitive psychology and information processing: An introduction*. Mahwah, NJ: Erlbaum.

Laeng-Gilliat, S. (1978). Love letters as diary news about the Charlotte Selver oral history and book project. *Sensory Awareness Newsletter*, Spring: 4–5.

Lageman, A. G. (1989). Socrates and psychotherapy. *Journal of Religion and Health*, 28, 3:219–223.

Lamarck, J. B. (1797). Sur les genres de la Seiche, du Calmar et du Poulpe vulgairement nommés polypes de mer. Lu à l'Institut national le 21 floréal an V. *Bulletin de la Société Philomatique*, I:129–131.*

Lamarck, J. B. (1802). *Recherches sur l'organisation des corps vivants*. Paris: Fayard, 1986.*

Lamarck, J. B. (1809). *Philosophie zoologique* [*Zoological philosophy*]. Paris: Flammarian, 1994. T. Elliot's 1914 translation is not reliable.*

Lamarck, J. B. (1815). *Histoire naturelle des animaux sans vertèbres*, vol. 1. Paris: Verdière. (This work, as well as most of Lamarck's publications, can only be consulted in libraries or the Web site of the French National Library [http://gallica.bnf.fr/]).

Lamarck, M. de (1820). *Système analytique des connaissances positives de l'homme* [The analytical system of the positive knowledge about man]. Paris: Presses Universitaires de France, 1988.*

Lancy, D. F. (2007). Accounting for variability in mother–child play. *American Anthropologist*, 109, 2:273–285.

Lancy, D. F. (2008). *Children and culture*. Cambridge, UK: Cambridge University Press.

Langley, J. N. (1899). The sympathetic and other related systems of nerves. In E.A. Schafer (Ed.), *Text-book of physiology*, 2:616–696. Edinburg: Y.J. Pentland.

Lao Tzu. (1949). Tao Tê Ching. In Waley, A. (Trans.), *The way and its power*: 141–245. London: George Allen & Unwin.

Lao Tzu. (~500). *Tao Tö King. Le livre de la voie et de la vertu*. Traduction de J.-J.-L. Duyvendak. Paris: Adrien Maisonneuve, 1975.

Laplanche, J., & Pontalis, J.-B. (1967). *Vocabulaire de la psychanalyse* [The language of psycho-analysis]. Paris: Presses Universitaires de France, 1984.

Laszlo, E. (2004). *Science and the Akashic field: An integral theory of everything*. Rochester: Inner Traditions.

Lavier, J. (1973). *Histoire, doctrine et pratique de l'acupuncture chinoise*. Paris: Edition Henry Veyrier.

Lazarus, R. S. (1991). *Emotion and adaptation*. Oxford: Oxford University Press.

Lazarus, R. S. (1994). *Stress, coping, and development: An integrative perspective*. New York: Guilford Publications.

Lazarus, R. S., & Folkman, S. (1984). *Stress apraisal and coping*. New York: McGraw-Hill.

Leboyer, F. (1974). *Birth without violence*. New York: Knopf, 1984.

LeDoux, J. (1996). *The emotional brain: The mysterious underpinnings of emotional life*. New York: Touchstone Book.

LeDoux, J. (1999). Emotion, memory, and the brain. In *The Scientific American Book of the Brain*: 105–118. New York: Lyons Press.

LeDoux, J. (2002). *Synaptic self: How our brains become who we are*. New York: Viking.

Lee, R. (1977). The scope of energy distribution. *Energy and Character*, 8, 2:119–122.

Lehninger, A. L. (1965). *Bioenergetics*. New York: Benjamin.

Leibnitz, G. W. (1695). *New system of the nature of substances and their communication, and the union of which exists between the soul and the body*. Leibnitz, Philosophical Texts: 143–152. Oxford: Oxford University Press.*

Leibniz, G. W. (1705). *New essays on human understanding* (J. Bennett, Trans.). http://www.struktuur.net/marten/kool/New%20Essays%20on%20Human%20Understanding.pdf Accessed April 2011. (Bennett improves his translation online. For a printed version, see: G. W. Leibniz, *New essays on human understanding* [P. Remnant and J. Bennett, Eds. and Trans.]. New York: Cambridge University Press, 1981.)

Leibniz, G. W. (1714). *Monadology* (J. Bennett, Trans.). http://www.earlymoderntexts.com/pdf/leibmon.pdf

Lemaine, G., & Matalon, B. (1985). *Hommes supérieurs, hommes inférieurs? La controverse sur l'hérédité*. Paris: Armand Colin.

Lepeltier, T. (2007). *Darwin hérétique. L'éternel retour du créationniste.* Paris: Éditions du Seuil.

Leroi-Gourhan, A. (1964). *Gesture and speech.* Cambridge, MA: MIT Press.

Leroi-Gourhan, A. (1965). *Le geste et la parole, II: la mémoire et les rythmes.* Paris: Albin Michel.

Levensen, R. W. (2003). Blood, sweat, and fears: The autonomic architecture of emotion. *Annals of the New York Academy of Sciences,* 1000, 1:348–366.

Levensen, R. W., Ekman, P., Heider, K., & Friesen, W. V. (1992). Emotion and autonomic nervous system activity in the Minangkabau of West Sumatra. *Journal of Personality and Social Psychology,* 62, 6:972–988.

Levine, P. A. (1979a). Autonomic stress and vegetotherapy, I. *Energy and Character,* 10, 2:10–19.

Levine, P. A. (1979b). Autonomic stress and vegetotherapy, II. *Energy and Character,* 10, 3:24–30.

Levine, P. A. (2004). Panic, biology, and reason: Giving the body its due. In I. Macnaughton (Ed.), *Body, breath & consciousness:* 267–286. Berkeley: North Atlantic Books.

Levine, P. A. (2008). Trauma and spirituality. In D. Goleman et al. (Eds.), *The scientific case for spirituality:* 85–100. Berkeley: Sound True.

Levine, P. A., & Frederick, A. (1997). *Walking the tiger: Healing trauma.* Boulder: North Atlantic Books.

Levine, P. A., & MacNaughton, I. (2004). Breath and consciousness: Reconsidering the viability of breathwork in psychological and spiritual interventions in human development. In I. Macnaughton (Ed.), *Body, breath & consciousness:* 367–393. Berkeley: North Atlantic Books.

Levine, S. (1960). Stimulation in infancy. *Scientific American,* 202:81–86.

Lévi-Strauss, C. (1962). *Totemism.* London: Merlin Press, 1964.

Lévi-Strauss, C. (1973). *Structural anthropology,* 1. New York: Doubleday Anchor Books.

Lewicki, P. (1986). *Nonconscious social information processing.* New York: Academic Press.

Lewicki, P., Hill, T., & Czyzewska, M. (1992). Nonconscious acquisition of information. *American Psychologist,* 47:796–801.

Lewis, R. (2006). Frozen transference: Early traumatization and the bodypsychotherapeutic relationship. *The USA Body Psychotherapy Journal,* 5, 2:28–42.

Lichtenberg, G. C. (1778). *Goettinger taschen, Calender von Jahr 1778.* Mainz: Dieterich'sche Verlagsbuhandlung, 1991.

Lichtenberg, J. (1989). *Psychoanalysis and motivation.* Hillsdale, NJ: Analytic Press.

Lie-Tseu. (1980). Le vrai classique du vide parfait [Classic of the perfect emptiness]. In Lio Kia-Hway & Benedykt Grynpas (traducteurs), *Philosophes taoïstes, Lao-Tseu, Chuang Tzu, Lie-Tseu.* Paris: Gallimard.

Linden, M. (1978). Breathing, gravity and evolution. *Energy & Character,* 9, 1:63–71.

Linehan, M. M. (1993). *Cognitive behavioral treatment of borderline personality disorder.* New York: Guilford Press.

Liss, J. (2001). Maps of experience. M. Heller (Ed.), *The flesh of the soul: The body we work with:* 173–186. Bern: Peter Lang.

Liss, J., & Stupiggia, M. (1966). *La thérapie biosystémique.* Paris: Hommes et Perspectives.

Locke, J. (1689). *An essay concerning human understanding.* Oxford: Clarendon Press, 1979.

Loraux, N. (2001). Aspasie [Aspasia], l'étrangère intellectuelle. *CLIO, Histoire Femmes et Sociétés*, 13:17–42.

Lorenz, K. Z. (1973). *L'envers du miroir. Une histoire naturelle de la connaissance* [Behind the mirror: A search for a natural history of human knowledge]. Paris: Flammarion, 1978.

Lott, B. (1959). Edition of Shakespeare's *Twelfth night.* In W. Shakespeare, *Twelfth night.* Edinburg Gate: Longman, 1999.

Lowen, A. (1958). *Language of the body.* New York: Collier Books, 1973.

Lowen, A. (1967). *The betrayal of the body.* New York: Collier Books, 1974.

Lowen, A. (1973). *Depression and the body: The biological basis of faith and reality.* New York: Arkana.

Lowen, A. (1975). *Bioenergetics.* New York: Coward, McCann & Geoghegan.

Lowen, A. (1994). *La joie retrouvée* [Joy. The surrender to the body and to life]. St-Jean-de-Braye: Dangles, 1995.

Lowen, A., & Lowen, L. (1977). *The way to vibrant health: A manual of bioenergetic exercises.* New York. Harper Colophon.

Lucretius. (1998). *De la nature* [On the Nature of Things]. Paris: Flamarion.

Ludwig, S. (2002). *Elsa Gindler—von ihrem Leben und Wirken. "Wahrnehmen, was wir empfinden."* Hamburg: Hans Christians.

Luria, A. R. (1963). *Human brain and psychological processes.* New York: Harper & Row, 1966.

Luria, A. R. (1979). *The making of mind. A personal account of soviet psychology.* Cambridge, MA: Harvard University Press.

Luria, A. R., & Yudovich, F.I. (1973). *Speech and the development of mental processes in the child.* Harmondsworth: Penguin Books.

Lyotard, J. F. (1983). *Le différend, le dialogue.* Paris: Les Éditions de Minuit.

MacDonald, A. (1984). *Acupuncture: From ancient art to modern medicine.* London: Unwin.

MacDougall, J. (1989). *Theatres of the body: A psychoanalytic approach to psychosomatic illness.* London: Free Association.

MacDougall, J. (1996). *The many faces of Eros: A psychoanalytic exploration of human sexuality.* New York: Norton.

MacEvoy, S. P., & Epstein, R. A. (2011). Constructing scenes from objects in human occipitotemporal cortex. *Nature Neuroscience.* DOI: 10.1038/nn.2903. (Available at http://www.nature.com/neuro/journal/vaop/ncurrent/full/nn.2903.html Accessed September 26, 2011).

MacFarland, D. J. (1987). Les fonctions d'organisation des conduites et des données. In J. Piaget, P. Mounoud, & J.-P. Bronckart (Eds.), *Psychologie:* 56–90. Paris: Gallimard.

MacGuire, M. T., Raleigh, M. J., & Brammer, G. L. (1984). Adaptation, selection and benefit-cost balances: Implications of behavioral-physiological studies of social dominance in male vervet monkeys. *Ethology and Sociobiology*, 5:269–277.

Macherey, P. (1994). *Introduction à l'éthique de Spinoza.* Paris: Presses Universitaires de France.

MacLean, P. D. (1969). The paranoid streak in man. In A. Koestler (Ed.), *Beyond reductionism:* 258–278. London: Macmillan.

MacLean, P. D. (1973). *Les trois cerveaux de l'homme.* Paris: Robert Laffont, 1990.

MacNaughton, I. (2004). *Body, breath & consciousness.* Berkeley: North Atlantic Books.

MacNeil, D., & Freiberger, P. (1993). *Fuzzy logic. The revolutionary computer technology that is changing the world.* New York: Touchstone.

Mac-Thiong, J.-M., Labelle, H., Berthonnaud, E., Betz, R. R., & Roussouly, P. (2004). Sagittal spinopelvic balance in norman children and adolescents. *European Spine Journal,* 16, 2:227–234.

Madlener, E. (1989). Die physiognomische Seelenerkundung. J. Clair, C. Pichler, & P. Wolfgang (Eds.), *Wunderblock. Eine Geschichte des modernen Seele*: 159–179. Vienne: Wiener Festwochen.

Magistretti, P J. (1994). Corrélations neurochimiques du suicide: Dosages cherchent désespérément hypothèses. *Cahiers Psychiatriques Genevois,* 16:73–82.

Magistretti, P. J., & Ansermet, F. (2004). *Biology of freedom: Neural plasticity, experience, and the unconscious.* London: Karnac Books, 2007.

Magnusson, M. S. (2000). Discovering hidden patterns in behavior: T-patterns and their detection. *Behaviour Research Methods, Instruments and Computers,* 32, 1:93–110.

Makari, G. (2008). *Revolution in mind: The creation of psychoanalysis.* New York: Harper.

Malberg, J. E. (2004). Implications of adult hippocampal neurogenesis in antidepressant action. *Journal of Psychiatry & Neuroscience,* 29, 3:196–205.

Malthus, T. R. (1826). *An essay on the principle of population.* London: John Murray.*

Man-Ch'ing, C., & Smith, R. W. (1981). *T'ai-chi. The "supreme ultimate" exercise for health, sport and self defense.* Rutland: Charles E. Tuttle.

Mann, W. E. (1973). *Orgone, Reich & eros.* New York: Simon & Schuster.

Marcher, L., & Fich, S. (2010). *Body encyclopedia: A guide to the psychological functions of the muscular system.* Berkeley: North Atlantic Books.

Marchi, L. de. (1973). *Wilhelm Reich, biographie d'une idée.* Paris: Fayard.

Marcuse, H. (1964). *One-dimensional man.* Boston: Beacon.

Marlock, G., & Weiss, H. (2006). In search of the embodied self. In M. Heller (Ed.), *The flesh of the soul: The body we work with*: 133–152. Bern: Peter Lang.

Marty, P. (1980). *L'ordre psychosomatique* [The psychosomatic order]. Paris: Editions Payot.

Masson, J. M. (1984). *The assault on truth: Freud's suppression of the seduction theory.* New York: Farrar Straus & Giroux.

Masters, R. D. (1995). Mechanism and function in evolutionary psychology: Emotion, cognitive neuroscience, and personality. *Psychological Inquiry,* 6, 1:65–68.

Masters, R. D., Frey, S., & Bente, G. (1991). Dominance & attention: Images of leaders in German, French, & American TV news. *Polity,* 23:373–394.

Mathew, S. J., Mao, X., Coplan, J. D., Smith, E. L. P., Sackeim, H. A., Gorman, J. M., et al. (2004). Dorsolateral prefrontal cortical pathology in generalized anxiety disorder: A proton magnetic resonance spectroscopic imaging study. *American Journal of Psychiatry,* 161:1119–1121.

Mattson, M. P., Maudsley, S., & Martin, B. (2004). BDNF and 5-HT: A dynamic duo in age-related neuronal plasticity and neurodegenerative disorders. *Trends in Neurosciences,* 27, 10:589–594

Mauss, M. (1934). Techniques of the body. *Economy and Society,* 1973, 2:70–88.

May, J. (2006a). Subsymbolische Arbeit mit einem alexithymischen Klienten. In G. Marlock & H. Weiss (Eds.), *Handbuch der Körperpsychotherapie*: 871–880. Allemagne: Schattauer Verlag.

May, J. (2006b). Empirical analyses of the character typologies of Alexander Lowen and Charles Kelley. *USA Body Psychotherapy Journal*, 5, 2:97–106.

Mayr, E. (1942). *Systematics and the origin of species from the viewpoint of a zoologist.* New York: Columbia University Press.

Mead, M. (1932). An investigation of the thought of primitive children, with special reference to animism. *Journal of the Royal Anthropological Institute*, LXII:188–190.

Mead, M., & Byers, P. (1968). *The small conference.* The Hague: Mouton.

Mehrabian, A. (1968). Inference of attitudes from the posture, orientation and distance of a communicator. In M. Argyle (Ed.), *Social encounters: Readings in social interaction.* Harmondsworth: Penguin, 1978.

Mehrabian, A. (1969). Significance of posture and position in the communication of attitude and status relationships. *Psychological Bulletin*, 71:359–372.

Mehrabian A. (1981). *Silent messages.* Belmont: Wadsworth.

Meignant, M. (1992). *Amourologue.* Paris: Buchet/Castel.

Meng Chiao. (814). Song of the old man of the hills. In A. C. Graham, *Poems of the late T'ang.* Harmondsworth: Penguin Classics, 1965.

Merker, B. (2007). Consciousness without a cerebral cortex: A challenge for neuroscience and medicine. *Behavioral and Brain Sciences*, 30:63–134.

Merleau-Ponty, M. (1945). *Phenomenology of perception* (C. Smith, Trans.). London: Routledge, 2005.

Merleau-Ponty, M. (1967). *Les relations avec autrui chez l'enfant. Les cours de Sorbonne.* Paris: Centre de Documentation Universitaire.

Messinger, J. (2005). *Ces gestes qui vous trahissent. Découvrez le sens caché de vos gestes.* Paris: Editions Générales First.

Meylan, M. (2007). *Analogie entre les théories de Groddeck et celle de la biodynamique.* Travail remis à l'Ecole Biodynamique de Montpellier, France.

Meyran, R. (2009). Claude Lévi-Straus: Un regard neuf sur l'autre. *Pour la science, les génies de la science*, 38.

Mézières, F. (1978). Retour à l'harmonie morphologique par une rééducation spécialisée. *Kinésithérapie Scientifique*, 157:45–54.

Mézières, F. (1984). *Originalité de la méthode Mézières* [The originality of the Mezieres method]. Paris: Maloine.

Middendorf, I. (1980). The meaning of breathing. In Gerald Kogan (Ed.), *Your body works*: 100–114. Berkeley: And/or Press & Transformations Press.

Middendorf, I. (1998). Die Kraft des Atems. Interview. *A. Vogel's Gesundheits Nachrichten*: 10–12.

Michel, E. (1997). *Bent out of shape.* Alachua: Bioenergetics Press.

Miller, J. D., Pegeflow, D. F., Jacques, A. J., & Dempsey, J. A. (2005). Skeletal muscle pump versus respiratory muscle pump: Modulation of venous return from the locomotor limb in humans. *Journal of Physiology*, 563:925–943.

Minsky, M. (1985). *The society of mind.* New York: Touchstone.

Misrahi, R., (1992). *Le corps et l'esprit dans la philosophie de Spinoza.* Paris: Les Empêcheurs de Penser en Rond.

Moessinger, P. (2000). *Le jeu et l'identité.* Paris: Presses Universitaires de France.

Moessinger, P. (2008). *Voir la société. Le micro et le macro.* Paris: Hermann Editeurs.

Moll, J., Krueger, F., Zahn, R., Pardini, M., Olivera-Souza, R. de, & Grafman, J. (2006).

Human fronto-mesolimbic networks guide decisions about charitable donation. *Procedings of the National Academy of Sciences of the United States of America*, 103, 42:15623–15628.*

Montagner, H. (1978). *L'enfant et la communication*. Paris: Stock.

Montaigne, M. (1592). *Essais I*. Paris: Gallimard, 1965.

Morris, D. (1978). *Man watching: A field guide to human behavior*. St. Albans: Triad Panther.

Moscovici, S. (1981). *The age of the crowd: A historical treatise on mass psychology*. Cambridge, UK: Cambridge University Press, 1985.

Moss, H. B., Yao, J. K., & Panzak G. L. (1990). Serotonergic responsivity and behavioral dimensions in antisocial personality disorder with substance abuse. *Biological Psychiatry*, 28:325–338.

Mossner, E. G. (1980). *The life of David Hume*. Oxford: Clarendon Press, 2001.

Mühlleitner, E. (2008). *Ich—Fenichel. Das Leben eines Psychoanalytikers im 20. Jahrhundert*. Wien: Zsolnay.

Nadel-Brulfert, J., Baudonnière, P.-M., & Fontaine, A.-M. (1983). Les comportements sociaux imitatifs. *Recherches de Psychologie Sociale*, 5:15–29.

Navarro, F. (1984). *Un autre regard sur la pathologie. La somato psychodynamique*. Paris: Éditions de l'Épi.

Newell, A. (1990). *Unified theories of cognition*. Cambridge, MA: Harvard University Press.

Newell, A., & Simon, H. A. (1972). *Human problem solving*. Englewood Cliffs, NJ: Prentice-Hall.

Newton, I. (1670). De Gravitatione. In I. Newton, *Philosophical writings*: 12–39. Cambridge: Cambridge University Press, 2004.

Newton, I. (1686). *The principia. Mathematical principles of natural philosophy*. Snowball Publishing, 2010.

Nicolescu, B. (1985). *Peter Brook et la pensée traditionnelle*. Les Voies de la Création Théâtrale, XIII.

Nicolle, J. (1973). *Structure moléculaire et propriétés biologiques*. Paris: Flammarion.

Nietzsche, F. (1876). *Introduction à la lecture des dialogues de Platon*. Paris: L'éclat, 1991.

Nietzsche, F. (2003). *Writings from late notebooks*. Cambridge, UK: Cambridge University Press.

Nordmark, M. T., & Rohweder, A. W. (1967). *Scientific foundations of nursing*. Philadelphia: Lippincott.

Noschis, K. (2011). *Monte Verità, Ascona et le genie du lieu*. Lausanne: Presses Polytechniques et Universitaires Romandes.

Nozdrachev, A. D. (2004). John Newport Langley and his construction of the autonomic (vegetative) nervous system. *Journal of Evolutionary Biochemistry and Physiology*, 38, 5:2002.

Nunnely, P. (2000). *The biodynamic philosophy and treatment of psychosomatic conditions*. Bern: Peter Lang.

Nüsslein-Volhard, C. (2006). *Coming to life: How genes drive development*. Carlsbad, CA: Kales Press.

Oatley, K. (1992). *Best laid schemes: The psychology of emotions*. New York: Cambridge University Press.*

Odent, M. (1976). *Bien naître*. Paris: Seuil, 1976. (Similar content can be found in Michel Odent, [1994], *Birth reborn*.)

Oganesian, N. (2009). Dance therapy as form of communication activating psychotherapy for schizophrenic patients. *Body, Movement and Dance in Psychotherapy*, 3, 2: 97–106.

Ogden, P. (1997). Hakomi integrative somatics: Hands-on psychotherapy. In C. Caldwell (Ed.), *Getting in touch, the Guide to New Body-Centered Therapies*: 153–178. Wheaton, IL: Quest Books.

Ogden, P., Minton, K., & Pain, C. (2006). *Trauma and the body: A sensorimotor approach to psychotherapy*. New York: Norton.

Ogden, T. H. (1990). *The primitive edge of experience*. Northvale: Jason Aronson.

Ogden, T. H. (2009). *Rediscovering psychoanalysis: Thinking and dreaming, learning and forgetting*. London: Routledge.

Øien, A. M. (2010). *Change and communication: Long-term Norwegian psychomotor physiotherapy treatment for patients with chronic muscle pain*. Doctoral dissertation, Section of Physiotherapy Science, Department of Public Health, Primary Health Care, Faculty of Medicine and Dentistry, University of Bergen. Published online at http://brage.bibsys.no/hsf/bitstream/URN:NBN:no-bibsys_brage_26255/4/Dr .thesis_Aud%20Marie%20Oien.pdf

Olds, J. (1956). Pleasure centers in the brain. In R. C. Atkinson (Ed.), *Contemporary Psychology*: 25–39. San Francisco: Freeman, 1971.

Olds, J. (1965). Pleasure centers in the brain. *Scientific American*, 195:105–116.

Ollendorf, I. (1969). *Wilhelm Reich: A personal biography*. London: Elek.

Ortony, A., & Turner, T. J. (1990). What's basic about basic emotions? *Psychological Review*, 97:315–331.

Otterman, M. (2007). *American torture: From the cold war to Abu Ghraib and beyond*. Melbourne: Melbourne University Press.

Ouspensky, P. D. (1949). *Fragments d'un enseignement inconnu* [In search of the miraculous: Fragments of an unknown teaching]. Paris: Stok, 1974.

Ouspensky, P. D. (1957). *The fourth way:. A record of talks and answers to questions based on the teaching of G. I. Gurdjieff*. London: Routledge & Kegan Paul.

Pally, R. (2005). Non-conscious prediction and a role for consciousness in correcting prediction errors. *Cortex*, 41, 5:643–662.

Pandey, G. N., Dwivedi, Y., Rizavi, H. S., Ren, X., Pandey, S. C., Pesold, C., et al. (2002). Higher expression of serotonin 5-HT2A receptors in the postmortem brains of teenage suicide victims. *American Journal of Psychiatry*, 159:419–429.

Panksepp, J., & Smith Pasqualini, M. (2005). The search for the fundamental brain/mind sources of affective experience. In J. Nadel & D. Muir (Eds.), *Emotional development*: 5–30. Oxford: Oxford University Press.

Papez, J. W. (1937). A proposed mechanism of emotion. *Archives of Neurology and Psychiatry*, 38:725–743.

Papousek, H., & Papousek, M. (1979). Early ontogeny of human social behavior: Its roots and social dimension. In M. von Cranach, K. Foppa, W. Lepenies, & D. Ploog (Eds.), *Human ethology: Claims and limits of a new discipline*. Cambridge: Cambridge University Press, and Paris: Editions de la Maison des Sciences de l'Homme.

Papousek, H., & Papousek, M. (1997). Preverbal communication in humans and the genesis of culture. In U. Segerstrale & P. Molnár (Eds.), *Non-verbal communication: Where nature meets culture*: 87–108. Mahwah, NJ: Lawrence Erlbaum.

Papousek, M. (2000). Einsatz von Vidéo in der Eltern-Säuglings-Beratung und Psychotherapie. *Praxis des Kinderpsychologie und Kinderpsychiatrie*, 23:593–605.

Papousek, M. (2007). Communication in early infancy: An arena of intersubjective learning. *Infant Behavior and Development*, 30, 2:258–266.

Pascal, B. (1669). Pensées. In *Œuvres complètes*. Paris: Gallimard, 1954.

Patanjali. (2007). *The yoga sutras* (Swami Vivekananda, Trans.). London: Watkins.

Pavlov, I. P. (1927). *Conditional reflexes*. New York: Dover Publications, 1960.*

Payne, H. (2006). Tracking the web of interconnectivity. *Body, Movement and Dance in Psychotherapy*, 1, 1:7–15.

Payne, H. (2009). Pilot study to evaluate Dance Movement Psychotherapy (the Body-Mind Approach) in patients with medically unexplained symptoms: Participants and facilitator perceptions and a summary discussion. *Body, Movement and Dance in Psychotherapy*, 4, 2:77–94.

Perez-Christiaens, N. (1983). *Être d'aplomb*. Paris: Institut Supèrieur d'Aplomb.

Perkins, F. (2004). *Leibniz and China: A commerce of light*. Cambridge: Cambridge University Press.

Perlman, S. (2006). *The book of martial art: The universal guide to the combative arts*. New York: Overlook Press.

Perls, F. S., Hefferline R. F., & Goodman P. (1951). *Gestalt therapy: Excitement and growth in the human personality*. London: Souvenir Press.

Pert, C. B. (1997). *Molecules of emotion*. New York: Scribner.

Pesso, A. (2001). The elusvie "I." In M. Heller (Ed.), *The flesh of the soul: The body we work with*: 189–212. Bern: Peter Lang.

Pfeifer, R., & Bongard, J. C. (2006). *How the body shapes the way we think: A new view of intelligence*. Cambridge, MA: MIT Press.

Piaget, J. (1920). La psychanalyse dans ses rapports avec la psychologie de l'enfant. *Bulletin mensuel de la Société Alfred Binet*, 131:18–34.*

Piaget, J. (1936). *Origins of intelligence in the child*. London: Routledge & Kegan Paul, 1953.

Piaget, J. (1961). *The mechanisms of perception*. London: Routledge & Kegan Paul, 1969.

Piaget, J. (1965). *Insights and illusions of philosophy*, W. Mays, trans. London: Routledge and Kegan Paul, 1972.

Piaget, J. (1967). *Biologie et connaissance* [Biology and knowledge]. Paris: Gallimard.

Piaget, J. (1972a). *Psychology and epistemology: Towards a theory of knowledge*. Harmondsworth: Penguin.

Piaget, J. (1972b). *Essai de logique opératoire*. Paris: Dunod.

Piaget, J. (1985). *Equilibration of cognitive structures*. Chicago: University of Chicago Press.

Piaget, J., & Weil, A.-M. (1951). The development in the child of the idea of homeland and of foreign relationships. In J. Piaget, *Sociological studies*: 248–275. London: Routledge

Piattelli-Palmarini, M. (1994). *Inevitable illusions. How mistakes of reason rule our minds*. New York: Wiley.

Pierrakos, J. (1990). *Core energetics: Developing the capacity to love and heal*. Mendocino, CA: Life Rhythm.

Pilates, J. H. (1945). *Your health: A corrective system of exercising that revolutionizes the entire field of physical education*. Incline Village: Presentation Dynamics.

Plato. (1997). *Complete works*. J. M. Cooper (Ed.). Indianapolis & Cambridge: Hackett Publishing.

Plato. (1937). *The dialogues of Plato* (B. Jowett, Trans.). New York: Random House.*

Plato. Letter VII. In *Œuvres complètes: 1184–1207* (L. Robin, Trans.). Paris: Gallimard, 1950.

Plotnik, R., Mir, D., & Delgado, J. M. R. (1971). Aggression, noxiousness and brain stimulation in unrestrained rhesus monkey. In B. E. Eleftherion & J. P. Scott (Eds.), *The physiology of aggression and defeat*. London: Plenum Press.

Plutchik, R. (2002). *Emotions and life: Perspectives from psychology, piology, and evolution*. Washington, DC: American Psychological Association.

Poleshuck, E. L., Dworkin, R. H., Howard, F. M., Foster, D. C., Shields, C. G., Giles, D. E., et al. (2005). Contributions of physical and sexual abuse to women's experiences with chronic pelvic pain. *Journal of Reproductive Medicine*, 50, 2:91–100.

Popp, F.-A. (2001). Biophysical aspects of the psychic situation. M. Heller (Ed.), *The flesh of the soul: The body we work with*: 81–97. Bern: Peter Lang.

Posner, M., & Rothbart, M. K. (2000). Developing mechanisms of self-regulation. *Development and Psychopathology*, 12:195–204.

Posner, M. I. (2005). Commentary on becoming aware of feelings. *Neuro-Psychoanalysis*, 7:55–57.

Postiaux, G. (2003). *Kinésithérapeute respiratoire de l'enfant. Les Techniques de soins guidées par l'auscultation pulmonaire*. Bruxelles: De Boeck.*

Povinelli, D. J. (2000). *Folk physics for apes: The chimpanzee's theory of how the world works*. Oxford: Oxford University Press.

Pradier, J. M. (1997). *La scène et la fabrique des corps. Ethnoscénologie du spectacle vivant en Occident (Ve siècle av. J.-C.—XVIIIe siècle)*. Bordeaux: Presses Universitaires de Bordeaux.*

Prause, J., & Dooley, D. (2001). Favourable employment status change and psychological depression: A two-year follow-up analysis of the National Longitudinal Survey of Youth. *Applied Psychology*, 50, 2:282–304.

Preuschoft, S., & Van Hoof, Jan A.R.A.M. (1997). The social function of "smile" and "laughter": Variations across primate species and societies. In U. Segerstrale & P. Molnár (Eds.), *Non-verbal communication: Where nature meets culture*: 171–190. Mahwah, NJ: Erlbaum.

Pridaux, E. (1920). The psychogalvanic reflex: A review. *Brain*, 43, 1:50–73.

Proskauer, M. (1968). Breathing therapy. In H. Mann & H. Otto (Eds.), *Ways of growth*. New York: Grossman.

Quétier, E. (2010). Peut-on en finir avec Socrate? *Adire*, 24:161–178.

Racamier, P.-C. (1992). *Le génie des origines. Psychanalyse et psychoses*. Paris: Payot.

Radley, J. J., & Morrison, J. H. (2005). Repeated stress and structural plasticity in the brain. *Ageing Research Reviews*, 4:271–287.

Rajneesh, O. B. S (1976). *The hidden harmony (discourses on the fragments of Heraclitus)*. Poona: Rajneesh Foundation.

Rajneesh, O. B. S. (1983). *The book of secrets: 112 keys to the mystery within*. New York: Saint Martin's Press.

Raknes, O. (1970). *Wilhelm Reich et l'orgonomie* [Wilhelm Reich and orgonomy]. Nice: Édition érès—SEDIFOR, 1988.

Reck, C., Hunt, A., Weiss, R., Fuchs, T., Moehler, E., Downing, G., Tronick, E., & Mundt, C. (2004). Interactive regulation of affect in postpartum depressed mothers and their infants: An overview. *Psychopathology* 37:272–280.

Reich, E. (1980). Prevention of neurosis: Self-regulation from birth on. *Journal of Biodynamic Psychology*, 1:18–49.

Reich, P. (1974). *A book of dreams*. London: Picador, 1976.

Reich, W. (1919). De Forel à Jung [The concept of libido from Forel to Jung]. In W. Reich, *Premiers écrits* 1:99–136. Paris: Payot, 1976.

Reich, W. (1920). A propos d'un cas de transgression de l'interdit de l'inceste à la puberté. In W. Reich, *Premiers écrits* 1:78–85. Paris: Payot, 1976.

Reich, W. (1922a). Sur la spécificité des formes d'onanisme. In W. Reich, *Premiers écrits* 1:136–143. Paris: Payot, 1976.

Reich, W. (1922b). Le coït et les sexes. In W. Reich, *Premiers écrits* 1: 86–98. Paris: Payot, 1976.

Reich, W. (1927a). Le caractère impulsif [The impulsive character]. In W. Reich, *Premiers écrits* 1:246–342. Paris: Payot, 1976.

Reich, W. (1927b). La génitalité [genitality]. In W. Reich, *Premiers écrits* 2. Paris: Payot, 1976.

Reich, W. (1932). *La lutte sexuelle des jeunes* [The sexual struggle of youth]. Paris: Maspero, 1972.

Reich, W. (1933). *L'analyse caractérielle*. Nice: Constantin Sinelnikoff, 1971.

Reich, W. (1937). *Passion de jeunesse* [Passion of youth: An autobiography, 1897–1922]. Paris: L'Arche, 1989.

Reich, W. (1938). *The bion experiments on the origin of life*. New York: Farrar, Straus and Giroux, 1979.

Reich, W. (1940). *The function of orgasm: Sex-economic problems of biological energy* (T. P. Wole, Trans.). New York: Bantam Books, 1967.

Reich, W. (1945a). *La révolution sexuelle* [The sexual revolution: Toward a self-governing character structure]. Paris: Christian Bourgois, 1993

Reich, W. (1945b). *The bioelectrical investigation of sexuality and anxiety*. New York: Farrar, Straus and Giroux, 1982.

Reich, W. (1946). *Psychologie de masse du fascisme* [The mass psychology of fascism]. Paris: Payot, 1998. (The original English translation by Theodore P. Wolfe, supervised by Wilhelm Reich, is available at http://www.whale.to/b/reich.pdf)

Reich, W. (1948a). *Ecoute, petit homme* [Listen little man!]. Paris: Payot, 2006.

Reich, W. (1948b). *La biopathie du cancer* [Cancer biopathy]. Paris: Payot, 1976.

Reich, W. (1948c). Cancer biopathy. New York: Farrar, Straus and Giroux, 1982.

Reich, W. (1949a). *Character analysis*, 3rd ed. New York: 1987.

Reich, W. (1949b). *Ether, God and devil*. New York: Farrar, Straus and Giroux, 1972.

Reich, W. (1951). *La superposition cosmique* [Cosmic superimposition]. Paris: Payot, 1974.

Reich, W. (1952a). Interview de Reich par Kurt Eissler. In M. Higgins & C. M. Raphael (Eds.), *Reich parle de Freud* [Reich speaks of Freud]. Paris: Payot, 1972.

Reich, W. (1952b). Alone. Recording available at http://www.orgone.org

Reich, W. (1953). *The murder of Christ*. New York: Farrar, Straus and Giroux.

Reich, W. (1994). *Beyond psychology: Letters and journals, 1934–1939*. New York: Farrar, Straus and Giroux.

Reich, W. (1999). *American odyssey: Letters and journals, 1940–1947*. New York: Farrar, Straus and Giroux.

Reich, W., & Neill, A. S. (1982). *The correspondence of Wilhelm Reich and A. S. Neill*. London: Victor Gollancz.

Reich, W., & Raknes, O. (1957). *The correspondence of Wilhelm Reich and Ola Raknes (1946–1957)* (B. Blumenthal, Trans.). Unpublished.

Reich-Rubin, L. (2003). Wilhelm Reich and Anna Freud: His explusion from psycho-analysis. *International Forum of Psychoanalysis*, 12, 203:109–117.

Renou, L. (1961). *Hinduism*. London: Prentice Hall.

Rey, J.-M. (1973). La généalogie nietzschéenne. In F. Châtelet (Ed.), *La philosophie, III: de Kant à Husserl*: 222–260. Bruxelles: Marabout, 1979.

Reymond, L. (1984). *To live within: A woman's spiritual pilgrimage in a Himalayan hermitage*. New York: Sterling, 1995.

Richard, D., Anselme, B., Baehr, J.-C., Chaffard, J., Méreaux, J., Périlleux, É., et al. (1998). *Physiologie des animaux. Tome 2: Construction de l'organisme, homéostasie et fonctions de relations*. Paris: Nathan.

Richards, R. J. (1980). Wundt's early theories of unconscious inference and cognitive evolution in their relation to Darwinian biopsychology. In W. G. Bringmann & T. Ryan (Eds.), *Wundt studies. A centennial collection*: 42–70. Toronto: C. J. Hogrefe.

Richebächer, S. (2005). *Sabina Spielrein. Eine fast grausame Liebe zur Wissenschaft*. Zürich: Dörlemann.

Richerson, G. B., Wang, W., Hodges, M. R., Dohle, C. I., & Diez-Sampedro, A. (2005). Homing in on the specific phenotype(s) of central respiratory chemoreceptors. *Experimental Physiology*, 90, 3:259–266.

Rilke, R.-M. (1908). *Letters to a young poet* (S. Mitchell, Trans.). New York: Vintage Books, 1984.

Ringel, E. (1976). The pre-suicidal syndrome. *Suicide and Life-Threatening Behavior*, 6:131–149.

Ringo, D. L., Lindley, S. E., Faull, K. F., & Faustman, W. O. (1994). Cholesterol and serotonin: Seeking a possible link between blood cholesterol and CSF 5-HIAA. *Biological Psychiatry*, 35:957–959.

Rispoli, L. (1995). La psychothérapie fonctionnelle. *Diagonales*, I:61–90.

Rispoli, L. (2001). Functional psychology and the basic experience of the self. M. Heller (Ed.), *The flesh of the soul: The body we work with*: 161–173. Bern: Peter Lang.

Rispoli, L. (2004). *The basic experience and the development of the self*. Bern: Peter Lang, 2008.

Rispoli, L., Di Nuovo, S., & Genta, E. (2000). *Misurare lo stress*. Milano: FrancoAngeli.

Ritter, P., & Ritter, J. (1975). *Free family and feedback*. London: Victor Golancz.

Robertson, R., & Combs, A. (1995). *Chaos theory in psychology and the life sciences*. Mawah, NJ: Erlbaum.

Rochat, M., Serra, E., Fadiga, L., & Gallese, V. (2008). The evolution of social cognition: Goal familiarity shapes monkeys' action understanding. *Current Biology*, 1.*

Rochat, P. (1995). *The self in infancy*. Amsterdam: Elsevier.

Rochat, P. (2001). *The infant's world*. Cambridge, MA: Harvard University Press.

Rochat, P. (2002). Naissance de la co-conscience. *Intellectica*, 1, 34:99–123.

Rochat, P. (2009). *Others in mind*. Cambridge: Cambridge University Press.

Rochat, P. (2010). The innate sense of the body develops to become a public affair by 2–3 years. *Neuropsychologia*, 48:738–745.

Rochat, P. (2011). Self-conceptualizing in development. In P. Zelazo (Ed.), *Oxford handbook of developmental psychology*. New York: Oxford University Press.

Roche, M. A. (1978a). Foreword. *Bulletin, Charlotte Selver Foundation*, 10, 1:2–5.

Roche, M.A. (1978b). Interviews with two Gindler students. *Bulletin, Charlotte Selver Foundation*, 10, 1:14–24.

Roelofs, K., & Spinhoven, P. (2007). Trauma and medically unexplained symptoms towards an integration of cognitive and neurobiological accounts. *Clinical Psychology Review*, 27, 7:798–820.

Roelofs, K., van Peer, J., Berretty, E., de Jong, P., Spinhoven, P., & Elzinga, B. M. (2009). Hypothalamus-pituitary-adrenal axis. Hyperresponsiveness is associated with increased social avoidance behavior in social phobia. *Biological Psychiatry*, 64:336–343.

Roland, B. (2004). Les instituts de formation des psychanalystes: Berlin, Vienne, Budapest. *Horizons asiatiques de la Psychanalyse*, 13, 2:133–146.

Rolf, I. P. (1977). *Rolfing: The integration of human structures*. New York: Harper & Row.

Rolls, E. T. (1999). *The brain and emotion*. Oxford: Oxford University Press.

Ronningstam, E. (2009). Narcissistic personality disorder: Facing DSM-V. *Psychiatric Annals*, 39, 3:111–121.*

Rosenberg, J. L., & Rand, M. L. (1985). *Le corps, le soi et l'âme* [Body, self and soul]. Quebec: Les Éditions Québec, 1989.

Rosenfeld, H. M. (1982). Measurement of body motion and orientation. In K. R. Scherer & P. Ekman (Eds.), *Handbook of methods in nonverbal behavior research*: 199–286. Cambridge: Cambridge University Press, and Paris: Editons de la Maison des Sciences de l'Homme.

Rosenschein, S. J. (1999). Intelligent agent architecture. In R. A. Wilson & C. K. Frank (Eds.), *The MIT encyclopedia of the cognitive sciences*: 410–412. Cambridge, MA: MIT Press.

Rosenzweig, M. R., Bennett, E. L., & Diamond, M. C. (1972). Brain changes in response to experience. *Scientific American*, 226, 2:22–29.

Rothschild, B. (2000). *The body remembers*. New York: Norton.

Roussillon, R. (2007). La représentance et l'actualisation pulsionnelle. *Revue Française de Psychanalyse*, 2, 71:339–358.

Roustang, F. (2009). *Le secret de Socrate pour changer la vie*. Paris: Odile Jacob.

Roux, M. L., & Dechaud-Ferbus, M. (1993). *Le corps dans la psyché*. Paris: L'Harmattan. (For an English summary: Déchaud-Ferbus, M. [1996]. The concept of process in relaxation psychotherapy. In J. Guimón [Ed.], *The body in psychotherapy*: 145–154. Basel: Karger.)

Rubenfeld, I. (1997). Healing the emotional/spiritual body: The Rubenfeld synergy method. In C. Caldwell (Ed.), *Getting in touch: The guide to new body-centered therapies*: 179–210. Wheaton: Quest Books.

Ruchat, M. (2010). Présentation. In M. Ruchat, *Édouard Claparède–Hélène Antipoff: Correspondence (1914–1940)*. Firenze: Leo S. Olschki Editore.

Russell, J. A. (1994). Is there universal recognition of emotion in facial expression? A review of cross-cultural studies. *Psychological Bulletin*, 115:102–141.

Russell, J. A., & Fernandez-Dols, J. M. (1997). *The psychology of facial expression*. New York: Cambridge University Press.

Ryle, A., & Kerr, I. (2002). *Introducing cognitive and analytic therapy: Principles and practice*. Chichester, UK: Wiley.

Rytz, T. (2009). *Centered and connected: A therapeutic approach to mind-body awareness*. Berkeley: North Atlantic Books.

Saaresranta, T., & Polo, O. (2002). Hormones and breathing. *Chest*, 122:2165–2182.

Safra, G., & Cotta J. A. M. (2009). Some notions of embodiment and theorizing modes. *Body, Movement and Dance in Psychotherapy*, 4, 3:239–250.

Salveson, M. (1997). Rolfing. In D. H. Johnson (Ed.), *Groundworks: Narratives of embodiment*: 33–37. Berkeley: North Atlantic Books.

Sambucy, A. de (1973). *Gymnastique corrective vertébrale*. Paris: Editions Dangles.

Sambucy, A. de, Sambucy, M. de, & Laubry, J. J. (1973). *Pour comprendre le yoga et les lois brahmaniques*. Paris: Editions Dangles.

Sander, L. (1985). Toward a logic of organization in psycho-biological development. In J. D. Call, E. Galenson, & R. Tyson (Eds.), *Frontiers of infant psychiatry*: 315–327. Washington, DC: Monograph Series, American Psychiatric Press.

Santiago-Delefosse, M. (2004). Activité et émotions. Perspective développementale des émotions comme instruments psychologiques. *Bulletin de Psychologie*, 469: 29–37.

Santiago-Delefosse, M., & Delefosse, J. M. O. (2002). Piaget, Spielrein, Vygotsky: Three positions about child thought and language. *Theory and Psychology*, 12, 6:723–747.

Sapir, E. (1927). The unconscious patterning of behavior in society. In D. G. Mendelbaum (Ed.), *Selected writings of Edward Sapir*: 544–559. Berkeley: University of California Press, 1949.

Sartre, J.-P. (1938). *Nausea*. New York: New Directions Publishing, 1964.

Sartre, J.-P. (1943). *Being and nothingness*. Washington, DC: Washington Square Press, 1992.

Sartre, J.-P. (1947). *What is literature?* London: Routledge, 2001.

Scherer, K. R. (1984). On the nature and function of emotion: A component process approach. In K. R. Scherer & P. Ekman (Eds.), *Approaches to emotion*: 293–317. Hillsdale, NJ: Erlbaum.

Scherer, K. R. (2001). Appraisal considered as a process of multi-level sequential checking. In K. R. Scherer, A. Schorr, & T. Johnstone (Eds.), *Appraisal processes in emotion: Theory, methods, research*: 92–120. Oxford: Oxford University Press.

Scherer, K. R. (2007). Component models of emotion can inform the quest for emotional competence. In G. Matthews, M. Zeidner, and R. D. Roberts (Eds.), *The science of emotional intelligence: Knowns and unknowns*: 101–126. New York: Oxford University Press.

Scherer, K. R., & Zei, B. (1989). La voix comme indice affectif. *Revue Suisse de Médicine*, 109:61–66.

Scherer, K. R., & Ekman, P. (1982). *Handbook of methods in nonverbal behavior research*. Cambridge & Paris: Cambridge University Press & Editons de la Maison des Sciences.

Schermer, M. (2002). *In Darwin's shadow: A biographical study on the psychology of history*. Oxford: Oxford University Press.

Schindler, P. (1996). Woher wir kommen—wohin wir gehen: Zur geschichte und Entwicklung der bioenergetischen analyse. In T. P. Ehrensperger (Ed.), *Körper und Seele, t.5: Zwischen Himmel und Erde: Beiträge zum grounding-concept*: 19–39. Basel: Schwabe Verlag.

Schore, A. N. (2003). *Affect regulation and the repair of the self*. New York: Norton.

Schultz, J. H. (1932) *Autogenic training: A psycho-physiologic approach in psychotherapy*. New York: Grune & Stratton, 1959.

Schünke, M., Schulte, E., Schumacher, U., Voll, M., & Wesker, K. (2005). *Atlas d'anatomie Prométhée: Anatomie générale et système locomoteur*. Paris: Maloine, 2006.

Segal, Z. V., Williams, J. M. G., & Teasdale, J. D. (2002). *Mindfulness-based cognitive therapy for depression: A new approach to preventing relapse*. New York: Guilford Press.

Selver, C. (1978). Letter, Sausalito, USA October, 1977. *Bulletin, Charlotte Selver Foundation*, 10, 1:27–32.

Selver, C. (2007). *Reclaiming vitality and presence*. Berkeley: North Atlantic Books.

Selver, C. (2009). Gravity, energy and the support of the ground. *Sensory Awareness Newsletter*, Spring:3–5.

Selver, C., & Brooks, C. V. W. (1980). Sensory awareness: Theory and practice. In J. Kogan (Ed.), *Your body works:. A guide to health, energy and balance*: 117–125. Berkeley: And/Or Press and Transformations Press.

Selye, H. (1936). A syndrome produced by diverse nocuous agents. *Nature*, 138:32.

Selye, H. (1978). *The stress of life*, 2nd ed. New York: McGraw-Hill.

Setekleiv, J. (1980). The "spontaneous" rhythmical activity in smooth musculature. *Journal of Biodynamic Psychology*, 1:72–81.

Shakespeare, W. (1595). Romeo and Juliette. In *Oeuvres complete*, edition bilingue, *Tragédies* 1: 507–680. Paris: Robert Laffont, 1997.

Shapiro, F. (2001). *Eye movement desensitization and reprocessing: Basic principles, protocols and procedures*, 2nd ed. New York: Guilford Press.

Sharaf, M. R. (1983). *Fury on earth: A biography of Wilhelm Reich*. New York: St. Martin's Press, 1994.

Shearer, A. (1984). Introduction. In Patanjali (Ed.), *Les Yoga Sûtras*. Paris: A.L.T.E.S.S., 1993.

Sheldon, W. (1954). *Atlas of men: A guide for somatotyping the adult male at all ages*. New York: Harper.

Shusterman, R. (2008). *Body consciousnes:. A philosophy of mindfulness and somaesthetics*. Cambridge: Cambridge University Press.

Siegel, A. (2004). *The neurobiology of aggression and rage*. Cleveland, OH: CRC Press.

Siegel, D. J. (1999). *The developing mind: Toward a neurobiology of interpersonal experience*. New York: Norton.

Siegel, D. J. (2007). *The mindful brain: Reflection and attunement in the cultivation of well-being*. New York: Guilford Press.

Siemer, M., Mauss, I., & Gross, J. J. (2007). Same situation—different emotions: How appraisals shape our emotions. *Emotion*, 7, 3:592–600.*

Sinclair, H., Stambak, M., Lezine, I., Rayna, S., & Verba, M. (1989). *Infants and objects: The creativity of cognitive development*. San Diego, CA: Academic Press.

Sing, R. H. & Udupa, K. N. (1982). Physiological and therapeutic studies on yoga. *The Yoga Review*, vol. II, n.4, 185–209.

Sironi, F. (1999). *Bourreaux et victimes. Psychologie de la torture*. Paris: Éditions Odile Jacob. (For an English summary: Sironi, F., & Branche, R. [2002]. Torture and the borders of humanity. *International Social Science Journal*, 54:539–548.)

Sitsen, J. M., Van Ree, J. M., & De Jong, W. (1982). Cardiovascular and respiratory effects of beta-endorphin in anesthetized and conscious rats. *Journal of Cardiovascular Pharmacology*, 4, 6:883–888.

Sloterdijk, P. (1996). *Selbstversuch: Ein gespräch mit Carlos Oliveira*. Munich: Carl Hanser Verlag.

Sloterdijk, P. (1998). *Bulles: Sphères I. [Bubbles: Spheres I]*. Paris: Pluriel, 2010. (An English version came out in 2010.)

Smith, A. (1759). *Théorie des sentiments moraux*. Paris: Presses Universitaires de France, 1999.

Smith, A. (1978). Impressions of the Burg Rothenfels meeting—October 1976. *Bulletin, Charlotte Selver Foundation*, 10, 1:6–8.

Solomon, R. (1977). *The passions*. New York: Anchor.

Solzhenitsyn, A. (1984). *November 1916: The red wheel, knot II* (H. T. Willetts, Trans.). New York: Farrar, Straus and Giroux, 2000.

Soulié de Morant, G. (1951). *Acuponcture (communications 1929–1951)*. Paris: Éditions de la Maisnie.

Southwell, C. (1980). Internal organismic pressure. *Journal of Biodynamic Psychology*, 1:8–13.

Southwell, C. (2010). Levels of consciousness and contact in biodynamic psychotherapy. *Psychotherapist*, 47:10–11.

Spencer, H. (1864). *The principles of biology*, vol. 2. Edinburgh: Williams and Norgate.*

Sperber, D. (1996). *La contagion des idées*. Paris: Odile Jacob.

Sperber, D., & Wilson, D. (1986). *Relevance. Communication and cognition*. Cambridge, MA: Harvard University Press.

Sperber, M. (1976). Malraux et la politique [Malraux and politics]. In M. de Courcel (Ed.), *Malraux. Être et dire*: 198–215 [*Malraux: Life and work*]. Paris: Plon. (Sperber, M. [1976]. *Malraux and politics*. In M. de Courcel (Ed.), *Malraux: Life and work*. New York: Harcourt, Brace, Jovanovich, 1976.)

Sperry, R.W. (1981). Nobel lecture. http://nobelprize.org/nobel_prizes/medicine/laureates/1981/sperry-lecture.html

Spiegel, D., Bloom, J. R., Kraemer, H. C., & Gottheil, E. (1989). Effect of psychosocial treatment on survival of patients with metastatic cancer. *Lancet*, 8668, 2:888–889.

Spielrein, S. (1912). *La destruction comme cause du devenir* [Die Destruktion als Ursache der Werdens]. In A. Carotenuto & C. Trombetta (Eds.), *Sabina Spielrein: Entre Freud et Jung*: 213–255. Paris: Aubier Montaigne, 1981.

Spielrein, S. (1920). La genèse des mots enfantins papa et maman [The origin of the child's words papa and mama]. In A. Carotenuto & C. Trombetta (Eds.), *Sabina Spielrein: Entre Freud et Jung*: 327–342. Paris: Aubier Montaigne, 1981.

Spinhoven, P., Elzinga, B. M., Hovens, J.G.F.M., Karin Roelofs, K., Zitman, F. G., van Oppen, P. et al. (2010). The specificity of childhood adversities and negative life events across the life span to anxiety and depressive disorders. *Journal of Affective Disorders*, 126, 1–2:103–112.*

Spinoza, B. de (1677a). *Ethics* (E. Curley, Trans.). Harmondsworth: Penguin, 1996.

Spinoza, B. de (1677b). *A political treatise* (R. H. M. Elwes, Trans.). New York: Dover Publications, 1951.

Spitz, R. A. (1945). Hospitalism: An inquiry into the genesis of psychiatric conditions. *Early Childhood. Psychoanalytic Study of the Child*, 1:53–74.

Spitz, R. A. (1965). *The first year of life: A psychoanalytic study of normal and deviant development of object relations*. New York: International Universities Press.

Stattman, J. (1987). Organic transference. *Adire*, 2–3:179–198. (Reprinted in Stattman et al., 1989.)

Stattman, J., Jansen, E. M., Marlock, G., Aalberse, M., & Stubenrauch, H. (1989). *Unitive body-psychotherapy. Collected papers*, vol. 1. Frankfurt: AFRA.

Staunton, T. (2002). *Body psychotherapy*. London: Brunner-Routledge.

Stcherbatsky, T. (1930). *Buddhist logic*, vol. I. New York: Dover Publications, 1962.

Stefulj, J., Buttner, A., Skavic, J., Zill, P., Balija, M., Eisenmenger, W., et al. (2004). Serotonin 1B (5HT-1B) receptor polymorphism (G861C) in suicide victims: Association studies in German and Slavic population. *American Journal of Medical Genetics*, 15, 127, 1:48–50.

Steimer-Krause, E., Krause, R., & Wagner, G. (1990). Interaction regulations used by schizophrenic and psychosomatic patients. In P. Ekman. & E. L. Rosenberg (Eds.), *What the face reveals: Basic and applied studies of spontaneous expression using the Facial Action Coding System (FACS)*: 361–380. Oxford: Oxford University Press, 1997.

Stein, H. (1991). Adler and Socrates: Similarities and differences. *Individual Psychology*, 47:241–246.

Steinaecker, K. von. (2000). *Luftsprünge. Anfänge moderner Körpertherapie*. München: Urban & Fischer.

Steiner, R. (1932). *Eurythmy as visible music*. London: Rudolf Steiner Press, 1977.

Sterba, R. F. (1982). *Réminiscences d'un psychanalyste viennois* [Reminiscences of a Viennese psychoanalyst]. Toulouse: Privat.

Stern, D. N. (1971). A microanalysis of the mother infant interaction. *Journal of the American Academy of Child Psychiatry*, 10:501–507.

Stern, D. N. (1974). Mother and infant at play: The dyadic interaction involving facial, vocal and gaze behaviors. In M. Lewis & L. Rosenblum (Eds.), *The effect of the infant on its caregiver*: 187–213. New York: Wiley.

Stern, D. N. (1977). *The first relationship: Infant and mother*. Cambridge, MA: Harvard University Press, 2002.

Stern, D. N. (1985). *Le monde interpersonnel du nourrisson* [The interpersonal world of the infant: A view from psychoanalysis and developmental psychology]. Paris: Presses Universitaires de France, 1989.

Stern, D. N. (1990). *Diary of a baby*. New York: Basic Books.

Stern, D. N. (1995). *La constellation maternelle* [The motherhood constellation]. Paris: Calmann-Lévy, 1997.

Stern, D. N. (2004). *Le moment présent en psychothérapie. Un monde dans un grain de sable* [The present moment in psychotherapy and everyday life]. Paris: Odile Jacob.

Stern, D. N. (2010). *Forms of vitality. Exploring dynamic experience in psychology and the arts*. Oxford: Oxford University Press.

Tagore, R. (1913). *Sadhana: The realization of life*. London: Macmillan.*

Tang, R., & Faivre, G. (2003). *Exercices taoïstes de santé pour les gens pressés*. Paris: Librairie You Feng.

Tarsissi, O., Gaussères, V., Raffray, M., & Helesbeux, S. (2005). Maladie veineuse chronique au travail: À propos d'une série à la Mutualité sociale agricole de la Mayenne. *Archives des maladies professionnelles et de médecine du travail*, 66, 1:37–44.

Taub, E. (2004). Harnessing brain plasticity through behavioral techniques to produce new treatments in neurorehabilitation. *American Psychologist*, 59, 8:692–704.

Tawm, K. (1979). *Les exercices secrets des moines taoïstes*. Paris: Guy Trédaniel.

Thelen, E., & Smith, L. B. (1994). *A dynamic systems approach to the development of cognition and action*. Cambridge, MA: MIT Press.

The Rig Veda (1981). Translated by Wendy Doniger O'Flaherty. Harmondsworth: Penguin Books.

Thich Nhat Hanh. (1996). *Breathe! You are alive: Sutra on the full awareness of breathing*. Berkeley: Parallax Press.

Thompson, E. (2008). *Mind in life*. Cambridge, MA: Harvard University Press.

Thornquist, E., & Bunkan, B. H. (1991). *What is psychomotor therapy?* Oslo: Norwegian University Press.

Tinbergen, N. (1951). *The study of instinct*. Oxford: Oxford University Press, 1969.

Tinbergen N. (1952). The curious behaviour of the stickleback. In S. Coopersmith (Ed.), *Frontiers of psychological research*: 8–12. Sans Francisco: Freeman.

Tinbergen N. (1974). Ethology and stress diseases. *Science*, 185, 4145:20–27.

Tohei, K. (1980). *Le livre du ki. L'unification de l'Esprit et du Corps dans la vie quotidienne*. Paris: Guy Trédaniel, 1982.

Tomasello, M. (1999). *The cultural origins of human cognition*. Cambridge, MA: Harvard University Press.

Tomkins, S. S., & Demos, E. V. (1995). *Exploring affect: The selected writings of Silvan S. Tomkins*. Cambridge & Paris: Cambridge University Press & Éditions de la Maison des Sciences de l'Homme.

Tomkins, S. S., & Izard, C. E. (1965). *Affect, cognition, and personality: Empirical studies*. New York: Springer.

Trevarthen, C. (2005). Action and emotion in development of cultural intelligence: Why infants have feelings like ours. In J. Nadel & D. Muir (Eds.), *Emotional development*: 61–91. Oxford: Oxford University Press.

Tronick, E. Z. (1989). Emotions and emotional communication in infants. *American Psychologist*, 44, 2:112–119.*

Tronick, E. Z. (1998). Dyadically expanded states of consciousness and the processes of therapeutic change. *Infant Mental Health Journal*, 19: 290–299.

Tronick, E. Z. (2001). Emotional connections and dyadic consciousness in infant–mother and patient–therapist interactions. Commentary on paper by Frank M. Lachmann. *Psychoanalytic Dialogues*, 11, 2:187–194.

Tronick, E. Z. (2003). Thoughts on the still-face: Disconnection and dyadic expansion of consciousness. *Infancy*, 4, 4:475–481.

Tronick, E. Z. (2007). *The neurobehavioural and social-emotional development of infants and children*. New York: Norton.

Tronick, E. Z., Als, H., Adamson, L., Wise, S., & Brazelton, T. B. (1978). The infant's response to entrapment between contradictory messages in face-to-face interaction. *Journal of the American Academy of Child Psychiatry*, 17:1–13.

Tudge, C. (2000). *In Mendel's footnotes*. London: Vintage, 2002.

Uvnäs-Moberg, K. (1989). The gastrointestinal tract in growth and reproduction. *Scientific American*, 261:60–65.

Uvnäs-Moberg, K. (1998). Antistress pattern induced by oxytocin. *News in Physiological Sciences*, 13, 1:22–25.

Uvnäs-Moberg, K. (2003). *The oxytocin factor. Tapping the hormone of calm, love, and healing*. Cambridge, MA: Da Capo Press.

Van der Kolk, B. A. (1996a). The body keeps the score: Approaches to the psychobiology of posttraumatic stress disorder. In B. A. van der Kolk, A. C. MacFarlane, & L. Weisaeth (Eds.), *Traumatic stress: The effects of overwhelming experience on mind, body, and society*: 214–241. New York: Guilford Press.

Van der Kolk, B. A. (1996b). Trauma and memory. In B. A. van der Kolk, A. C. MacFarlane, & L. Weisaeth (Eds.), *Traumatic stress: The effects of overwhelming experience on mind, body, and society*: 279–302. New York: Guilford Press.

Van der Kolk, B. A. (1996c). The complexity of adaptation to trauma: Self-regulation, stimulus discrimination, and characterological development. In B. A. van der Kolk, A. C. MacFarlane, & L. Weisaeth (Eds.), *Traumatic stress: The effects of overwhelming experience on mind, body, and society*: 182–213. New York: Guilford Press.

Van der Kolk, B. A. (2002a). In terror's grip: Healing the ravages of trauma. *Cerebrum*, 4:34–50. (Several articles by Bessel van der Kolk can be found at http://www .traumacenter.org)

Van der Kolk, B. A. (2002b). The assessment and treatment of complex PTSD. In R. Yehuda (Ed.), *Treating trauma survivors with PTSD*: 127–156. Washington, DC: American Psychiatric Press.

Van der Kolk, B. A. (2003). The neurobiology of childhood trauma and abuse. *Child and Adolescent Psychiatric Clinics of North America*, 12:293–317.*

Van der Kolk, B. A. (2006). Clinical implications of neuroscience research in PTSD. *Annals of the New York Academy of Sciences*, 1071, 1:1–17.*

Van der Kolk, B. A., McFarlane, A., & Weisaeth, L., eds. (1996). *Traumatic stress:. The effects of overwhelming experience on mind, body, and society*. New York: Guilford Press.

Van der Linden, M. H., Marigold, D. S., Gabreëls, J. M., & Dysens, J. (2007). Muscle reflexes and synergies triggered by an unexpected support surface height during walking. *Journal of Neurophysiology*, 97:3639–3650.*

Van der Veer, R., & Valsiner, J. (1991). *Understanding Vygotsky. A quest for synthesis*. Oxford: Blackwell.

Van Geert, P. (1994). *Dynamic systems of development: Change between complexity and chaos*. New York: Prentice Hall/Harvester Wheatsheaf.

Varela, F. J. (1988). *Connaître les sciences cognitives. Tendances et perspectives*. Paris: Gallimard. (This book has not been translated into English. Similar formulations can be found in F. Varela, E. Thompson, & E. Rosch. [1991]. *The embodied mind: Cognitive science and human experience*. Cambridge, MA: MIT Press.)

Varenne, J. (1970). La religion védique. In H.-C. Puech (Ed.), *Histoire des religions*, 1:578–624. Paris: Gallimard.

Vaysse, J. (2006). *La danse-thérapie. Histoire, technique, théories*. Paris: L'Harmattan.

Velther, A., & Lamothe, M.-J. (1980). *Les outils du corps. Soigner les hommes*. Paris: Denöel/Gonthier.

Verin, L. (1980). The teaching of Moshe Feldenkrais. In G. Kogan (Ed.), *Your body works: A guide to health energy and balance*: 72–80. Berkeley: Transformation Press.

Veyne, P. (1983). *Did the Greeks believe in their myths? An essay on the constitutive imagination*. Chicago: University of Chicago Press, 1988.

Vincent, J.-D. (1986). *Biologie des passions*. Paris: Seuil.

Visceglia, E., & Lewis, S. (2011). Yoga therapy as an adjunctive treatment for schizophrenia: A randomized, controlled pilot study. *Journal of Alternative and Complementary Medicine*, 7, 7:601–607.

Voon, V., Brezing, D., Gallea, D., Rezvan Ameli, R., Roelofs, K., LaFrance, Jr., W. C., et al. (2010). Emotional stimuli and motor conversion disorder. *Brain*, 133: 1526–1536.

Vuilleumier, P. (2005). Hysterical conversion and brain function. *Progress in Brain Research*, 150:309–329.*

Vurpillot, E. (1968). The development of scanning strategies and their relations to visual differentiation. *Journal of Experimental Child Psychology*, 6:622–650.

Vurpillot, E., & Bullinger, A. (1981). Y a-t-il des âges clefs dans la première année de vie de l'enfant? In S. de Schonen (Ed.), *Les débuts du développement*. Paris: Presses Universitaires de France.

Vygotsky, L. S. (1927). The historical meaning of the crisis in psychology: A methodological investigation. In L. S. Vygotsky, *The collected works of L. S. Vygotsky*, vol. 3: *Problems of the theory and history of psychology*: 233–344. New York: Plenum Press, 1997.

Vygotsky, L. S. (1934). *Thought and language*. Cambridge, MA: MIT Press, 1986.

Waal, F. de (1998). *Chimpanzee politics: Power and sex among apes,* rev. ed. Baltimore: Johns Hopkins University Press.

Waal, F. de (2002). *The ape and the sushi master*. London: Penguin.

Waal, N., Grieg, A., & Rasmussen, M. (1976). The psycho-diagnosis of the body. In D. Boadella (Ed.), *In the wake of Reich*: 266–281. London: Conventure.

Wagner, A., Greer, P., Bailer, U. F., Frank, G. D., Henry, S. E., Putnam, K. K., et al. (2006). Normal brain tissue volumes after long-term recovery in anorexia and bulimia nervosa. *Biological Psychiatry*, 59, 3:291–293.*

Wallace, A. R. (1855). On the law which has regulated the introduction of new species. *Annals and Magazine of Natural History*, 16:184–196.

Wallace, A. R. (1858). On the tendency of varieties to depart indefinitely from the original type. In Philip Appleman (Ed.), *Darwin*: 61–64. New York: Norton, 2001.

Wallace, A. R. (1876). *The heographical distribution of animals*. London: Macmillan.

Wallace, A. R. (1881). *Island life*. New York: Prometheus Books, 1998.

Wallace, A. R. (1889). *Darwinism. An exposition of the theory of natural selection with some of its applications*. London: Macmillan.

Wallace, A. R. (1908). *My life. A record of events and opinions*. Whitefish, MT: Kessinger Publishing, 2004.

Wallon, H. (1942). *De l'acte à la pensée. Essai de psychologie comparée* [From action to thought]. Paris: Flammarion (1973).

Wasserman, D. G., Sokolowski, M., Rozanov, V., & Wasserman, J. (2006) The serotonin 1A receptor C(-1019)G polymorphism in relation to suicide attempt. *Behavioral and Brain Functions*, 2:14.*

Watson J. B. (1919). *Psychology from the standpoint of a behaviorist*. Philadelphia: Lippincott.

Watson, J. B., & Rayner, R. (1920). *Little emotional Albert*. Philadelphia: Lippincott.

Watzlawick, P., Beavin, J. H., & Jackson, D. D. (1967). *Pragmatics of human communication: A study of interactional patterns, pathologies, and paradoxes*. New York: Norton.

Waley, A. (1934). *The way and its power*. London: Allen & Unwin, 1949.

Weaver, J. O. (2004). Integrating sensory awareness and somatic psychotherapy. *USA Body Psychotherapy Journal*, 3, 2:56–65.*

Weaver, J. O. (2009). Integrating sensory awareness and somatic psychotherapy. *Sensory Awareness Newsletter*, Spring: 6–8.

Weber, M. (1904). Objectivity in social science and social policy (E. A. Shils & H. A. Finch, Trans.). In M. Weber, *The methodology of the social sciences*: 50–112. New York: Free Press, 1949.

Weber, M. (1913). *The religion of India: The sociology of Hinduism and Buddhism* (H. H. Gerth & D. Martindale, Trans.). Glencoe, IL: Free Press, 1949.

Wegner, D. M. (2002). *The illusions of conscious will*. Cambridge, MA: MIT Press.

Weinstein, S. (1967). *The effects of sensory deprivation on sensory, perceptual, motor, cognitive, and physiological functions*. National Aeronautics and Space Administration.

Weiss, H. (2009). The use of mindfulness in psychodynamic and body oriented psychotherapy. *Body, Movement and Dance in Psychotherapy*, 4, 1:5–16.

Werker, J. F., & Tees, R. C. (1984). Cross-language speech perception: Evidence for perceptual reorganization during the first year of life. *Infant Behavior and Development*, 7:49–63.

Werner, H. (1957). The concept of development from a comparative and organismic point of view. In D. Harris (Ed.), *The concept of development*. Minneapolis: University of Minnesota Press.

Wespin, D. de. (1973). *Relaxation, sérénité, équilibre. Sur les traces du tai ki tchuan*. Verviers: Marabouts, 1975.

West, J. B. (1975). Anamalie de la regulation de la respiration. In T. R. Harrison (Ed.), *Principes de medicine interne* [*Harrison's principles of internal medicine*], 255: 1361–1366. Paris: Flammarion.

Wheatley-Crosbie, J. R. (2006). Healing traumatic reenactment: Psyche's return from soma's underworld. *USA Body Psychotherapy Journal*, 5, 2:4–10.

Widlöcher, D. (1983). *Le ralentissement dépressif*. Paris: Presses Universitaires de France.

Wiener, N. (1948). *Cybernetics or control and communication in the animal and the machine*. Cambridge, MA: MIT Press.

Wilber, K. (2000). *Integral psychology. Consciousness, spirit, psychology, therapy*. Boston: Shambhala.

Wile, D. (1983). *T'ai-chi touchstones: Yang family secret transmissions*. Brooklyn: Sweet Ch'i Press.

Wilhelm, R. (1924). *I Ching or book of changes*. London: Routledge & Kegan Paul, 1984.

Willeput, R., Rondeux, C., & De Troyer, A. (1984). Breathing affects venous return from legs in humans. *Journal of Applied Physiology*, 57:971–976.

Williamson, G. G., Anzzalone, M. E., & Hanft, B. E. (2000). *Assessment of sensory processing, praxis, and motor performance. ICDL clinical practice guidelines*, 155–175. College Park, MD: ICDL Press.*

Wilson R. A. (1982). *The historical illuminatus chronicles*. New York: Bluejay Books, 1984.

Wilson, R. A. (1987). *Wilhelm Reich in hell*. Phoenix: Falcon Press.

Wing Fun, C., & Collet, H. (2010). *Li Po. L'immortel banni sur terre buvant seul sous la lune*. Paris: Albin Michel.

Winkin, Y. (1981). *La nouvelle communication*. Paris: Éditions du Seuil.

Winnicott, D. W. (1960). Distorsions du moi en fonction du vrai et du faux "self." In D. W. Winnicott, *Processus de maturation chez l'enfant. Développement affectif et environnement*: 115–132. Paris: Payot, 1983.

Wirth, O. (1923). *The tarot of the magicians*. York Beach, ME: Samuel Weiser.*

Wirth, S., & Kaiser, S. (2010). Multimodal annotation of emotional signals in social interactions. In E. Bänninger-Huber & D. Peham (Eds.), *Current and future perspectives in facial expression research: Topics and methodological questions*: 66–80. Proceedings of the international meeting of the Institute of Psychology, University of Insbruck, Austria.

Wittgenstein, L. (1967). Conversations on Freud. In C. Barrett (Ed.), *Wittgenstein lectures and conversations on aesthetics, psychology, and religious belief*: 41–52. Berkeley: University of California Press.

Wortmann-Fleischer, S., Hornstein, C., & Downing, G. (2005). *Postpartale psychische Störungen. Ein interaktionszentrierter Therapieleitfaden*. Stuttgart: Kohlhammer.

Wrathall, M., & Malpas, J. (2000). *Heidegger, coping, and cognitive science. Essays in honor of Hubert L. Dreyfus*, vol. 2. Cambridge, MA: MIT Press.

Wundt, W. (1874). Eléments de psychologie physiologique, sixième section: De l'origine de développement intellectuel [Principles of physiological psychology, chapter 23]. In J. Daniel (Ed.), *La psychologie. Les plus grands textes d'Aristote à Freud et Bowlby*: 233–260. Paris: Le Nouvel Observateur & CNRS Editions, 2011.

Wundt, W. (1892). *Lectures on human and animal psychology*. Washington, DC: University Publications of America.

Young, C. (2006). One hundred and fifty years on: The history, significance and scope of body psychotherapy today. *Body, Movement and Dance in Psychotherapy*, 1, 1:17–28.

Young, C. (2008). The history and development of body-psychotherapy. *Body, Movement and Dance in Psychotherapy*, 3, 1:5–18.

Young, C. (2009). On Elsa Lindenberg and Reich. http://www.courtenay-young.co.uk/courtenay/articles/index.htm#B-P%20Articles. (This article will soon be published in a volume edited by Courtney Young: *The historical basis of body psychotherapy*. London: Body Psychotherapy Publications.)

Young, C. (2010). The history and development of body-psychotherapy: European diversity. *Body, Movement and Dance in Psychotherapy*, 5, 1:5–19.

Young, C. (2011). The history and development of body-psychotherapy: European collaboration. *Body, Movement and Dance in Psychotherapy*, 6, 1:57–68.

Young, J. E., Klosko, J. S., & Weishaar, M. E. (2003). *Schema therapy: A practitioner's guide*. New York: Guilford Press.

Yü, L. K. (1970). *Taoist yoga: Alchemy and immortality*. London: Rider.

Zajonc, R. B. (1985). Emotion and facial efference: A theory reclaimed. *Science*, 228:15–21.

Zajonc, R. B., Murphy, S. T., & Inglehart, M. (1989). Feeling and facial efference: Implications of the vascular theory of emotion. *Psychological Review*, 96:395–416.

Name Index

Subject Index

In this index, *f* denotes figure, *n* denotes endnote, and *t* denotes table. Bold page numbers indicate in-depth topic discussion. Please also note that this index is not exhaustive, but covers the major terms of the book.

abandonment, 385, 619
abdomen, 292, 303, 565
   See also diaphragm
abdominal respirations, 299, 472, 473
abdominal segments (Vegetotherapy), 476
absolute versus relative differences, 596–97
abuse, 466
   See also childhood abuse; sexual abuse
Academic painters, 295
Academy (Plato), 105, 688*n*28
accommodation, **6–7**, 167
   See also adaptation; assimilation; general adaptation syndrome; regulatory mechanisms
accumulators, 513
acetylcholine, 241
acquired behaviors, 646
ACTH, 219
acting out, 371–72, 514, 533, 723*n*153
action systems, 268
active psychoanalytic techniques, 401, **413–15**, 420, 439, 634
acupuncture, 50, **52–53**, 469, 685*n*13–85*n*14
acupuncturists, 35
adaptation (Piaget), **3–4**, **6–7**, 621
   See also accommodation; assimilation; general adaptation syndrome; regulatory mechanisms
addictions (Elster), **239–43**, 622–23
   See also cocaine; computer games
Adire, 522, 571, 729*n*12
adolescents, sexual reforms and, 451
adrenal glands, 216, 217, 219
adrenaline, 216, 219
affect attunement, 376, **610–12**
   See also contingency
affect equivalents, 492
affection, axis of, **229–33**
   See also loving sentiments
affective resonance, 611
affects
   activation and regulation of, 236, 249–50
   acupuncture and, 53
   addictions and, 241–42
   behaviors and, 413–14, 465, 484

beliefs influenced by, 146
body segments and, 475, 476–78
definitions of, 118, 202, 492
depressive, 129
exhaustion phase after stress and, 220
Feldenkrais on, 317, 318–19
laws of cause and effect and, 138
moods and, **202–3**
muscular tension and, 33
neurological organization of, 703*n*133
organismic gymnastics and, 293–94
Peripatetic seat of, 108
peristaltic activity and, 549
physiology and, 666–67
power of a system and, 127
primary and secondary processes and, 399–400
reactions and, 554
with or without objects, 377–78
   See also anxiety; emotions and emotional expressions; passions
affiliation. *See* axis of affection
agenda (Cellérier), 189–90
aggression
   ambiguity of predator and, 215
   axis of stress and, 225
   bioenergetic analysis of, 66
   depression as, 128
   expansions and, 200
   FACS and masked, 650
   Laborit's experiments showing, 226–27
   neurological organization of, 702*n*124
   in nursing mothers, 625
   oxytocin and, 232–33
   serotonin and, 246
   social dominance and, 243–45
   ulcers and, 490
   warrior's punch and, 67
   See also anger
agitation, anxiety and, 199–200
AIDS, 450
Ajuriaguerra relaxation method, 459, 534
alchemy, of Taoism, **62–63**, 64*f*
Alcoholics Anonymous, 243
alcoholism, 240, 478–79, 480, 554

instincts
    addictions versus, 242
    definitions of, 174, 202, 382, 383, 492
    drives and, 351
    id as, 402
    Lamarck on, 163
    sexual pleasure as, 381
    soul and, 121
    See also propensities or propensions
Institute for Bioenergetic Analysis (Lowen),
    556
Institute of Psychology (University of Oslo),
    464
institutional organizations, 15–16, 450, 451,
    454–55, 517, 521
    See also culture, social rituals, and tradi-
    tions
intellection, 278–79, 310–11
    See also thoughts
intelligence
    gestures and, 409, 410
    Lamarck on, 163
    Piaget on, 662, 716*n*30, 717*n*11, 737*n*56
    See also artificial intelligence; centers
    (Gurdjieff); embodied intelligence
intensification, before orgasms, 434, 435
intensity
    of body contact, 232
    curve of the orgasm and, 435, 435*f*
    of gestures, 613–14
    of mood swings, 203
    of passions or emotions, 142, 175, 242
    of passion and thoughts, 139-141, 346,
    436
    pulsations and, 501
    recathexis and, 350
    of stress reaction, 219
    See also drives; energy; Facial Action Cod-
    ing System (FACS); vitality
interactions, **578–80**, 586–88, 592–93, 594
    See also mother–child relationships; situa-
    tions and dyads
intermodal dialogues, 376
intermodal transfer of information, 374–76,
    611
internal environment (Bernard), **198–200**
    See also cell ecology (Laborit)
internal propensities, 142–43, 240–41
internal respirations, 34–35, **39–41**, 684*n*32
International Association of Psychoanalysis
    (IPA), 417, 455, 456, 457, 482, 483
interpersonal dynamics, libido and, 390
    See also countertransference; situations
    and dyads; sociability
interpersonal space, 591–92
The Interpersonal World of the Infant
    (Stern), 375–76

The Interpretation of Dreams (Freud), 364–
    65
interpretations, classic psychoanalysis and,
    366–67
intersubjectivity, **612**, 613
    See also attunement, affect; contingency;
    situations and dyads
*Introduction to the Study of Experimental
    Medicine* (Bernard), 197, 698*n*5
Introductory Lectures on Psycho-Analysis
    (Freud), 716*n*45
introjection and identification, 6
introspection
    body sensations and, 449
    definition of, 9
    experimental psychology and, **340–41,**
    342
    meditation and, 691*n*1
    organization of psyche and, 423
    science versus, 514–15
    the unconscious and, 346
    See also body–mind exploration
intuition, **130**
IPA. *See* International Association of
    Psychoanalysis (IPA)
iron, in blood, 40, 684*n*31
ischia, 32, 329, 567, 679–80, 683*n*13

Jacobson's organ, 701*n*97
jellyfish exercises
    auto-regulation and, 503–6, 687*n*49
    Boyesen on, 545–46
    hypoarmored individuals and, 509
    muscular chain analysis and, 506–7, 507*f*
    origin of, 500, 503
    vibrations and, 563–64
Jesuits, 107, 690*n*1
Jewish persecution, 101, 305, 410, 455, 463,
    525
Jugendstil, 295, 296, 418, 419
Justice. *See* Idealism

ketamine, 691*n*14
kinesthetic perceptions, 317
knowledge
    confidence in, 671–72, 673
    forms of, 668–69
    social construction of, 85, 688*n*28
    types of, 376, 582
Korperseele, 418
kundalini, 45, 473, 684*n*43
    See also orgastic reflex

Laboratory of Affect and Communication
    (LAC), 531, 584, 644
Laboratory of the Communication Sciences,
    614

regulatory mechanisms (*continued*)
  rational thought as, 146
  SDO model and, 9, 10, 11–12, 11*f*, 16–17,
    16*f*, 682*n*21
  social dynamics as, **132–33**
  state of reference for, 623
  thoughts as, 287
  See also auto-regulation; homeostasis; in-
    ternal environment (Bernard); meta-
    bolic regulation
Reichians versus Freudians, 417–18
Reich versus Fenichel
relational psychoanalysis, 636
relationships, human, 502, 615–16
  See also dyadic effects; interactions;
    mother–child relationships; situations
    and dyads
relative differences. *See* absolute versus
  relative differences
relaxation
  Ajuriaguerra's methods, 459, 534
  axis of stress and, 225
  Boyesen on, 548
  after coitus, 434
  first methods of, **282–89**
  grounding posture and, 565
  gymnastics and, 306, 307
  as a haven, 95–96, 689*n*46
  hypotonic muscles and, 424
  jellyfish exercises and, 507
  neo-cathartic, 415–17
  peristaltic activity and, 210, 549
  prana and, 41
  princess and the pea (Boyesen) and, 550
  progressive, **284–88**, 555
  respirations and, 537
  sensory awareness method and, 458, 469
  vegetative sensations and, 470, 724*n*19
  See also yawning
release. *See* orgasms; relaxation; stretch-and-
  yawn reaction
religious wars, 107
reminiscence, 83
repair systems (Tronick)
  cosmic energy and, 548
  evolution and, 496
  in mother–child relationships, 624, 626,
    627, 630
  procedural core and, 640
representations
  behaviors and, 165
  co-construction and, 115
  energy and psychological, **279–81**
  hypnosis and, 368
  intermodality and, 375
  micro-practices and, 652–53
  of movements, 286, 288
  as necessary illusions, 656–57

organization of, 139, 146, 150–51
passions and, 143
physiology and, 368
primary and secondary processes and,
  399–400
psychic system and, 10, 346–47, 349–50
symbolic language and body, 377–78
thoughts and, 357
Wundt and, 339
See also false memories; sensory impressions; thoughts
repression
  anger and, 398–99
  body versus mind and, 493
  cathartic method and, 361
  character type and organization of, 440–
    42
  ego and, 404
  emotional outbursts and, 493
  Groddeck on, 411
  latent content and, 366–67
  muscular tension and, 267, 425, 427–28,
    450, 536
  neuroses and, 371
  physiology and, 367
  of sexual drives and mental health, 455
  unconscious thoughts and, 354–55
  Verdrängung and, 395
  vital energy and, 558
  See also defense mechanisms
reproduction, 166–67, 177
  See also procreation, instinct and drive for
reptilian brain, 694*n*17
research
  clinical **31–32**, 106–107
  data collection methods in, 579, 580, 583,
    584–85, 585*t*, 588
  data management during, 369, 584, 586,
    589–91
  definitions of, 32, 196
  empirical, 106–107
  ethics in, 590–91
  forms of knowledge in, 669–71
  imagination stimulated through, 124
  methodological limits of developmental,
    157–58
  methodological limits of nonverbal com-
    munication, 578, 583, 592
  methodological limits of orgone, 515
  methodological limits of stress, 227–28,
    701*n*92
  placebo effect and, 275
  statistical analysis in, 227–229, 589–91,
    701
  See also Facial Action Coding System
    (FACS); *specific names in name index*
resignation, 226, 227
resilience, 194

and the body (Descartes), 109–10, 117–
18, 120–21
and the body (Groddeck), **410–11**
and the body (Gurdjieff), 312
and the body (Plato), **77–79**, 80, 83
and the body (shape of), **255–56**
burial of, 162
energy and, 276
Freud on, 713*n*73
functional identity and, 407
intellect versus, 312–13
Lamarck on, 162
mind versus, **83–88**, 688*n*23
thoughts and, **79–83**
space-time continuum, 109, 139–40, 141,
157–58
See also a priori mechanisms; evolution
speculative knowledge, 668
speech, 238, 376, 410, 535–36, 621, 646
See also communication; language
speed, in video-analysis, 642–43
spinal column, 292, 304, 319, 322
spinal cord (Lamarck), 162
spine, Hindu importance of, 45–46
spiritualist movements, **274, 276**
See also energy
spirituality, 280–81, 299, 429–30, 513,
720*n*86
split-brain surgery, 374
sponge, in venous circulation, 332, 333
spontaneous respirations, 35, 38, 39, 56–
57
sports trainers, 30
squatting, 58, 324, 327
Stalinism, 410, 452, 453
standing, as basic posture, 326, 327
See also grounding
startle reflex
body reading and, 541
breathing in fear and to prevent fear,
544
ecto- and endoderms and, 569
muscular tension and, 319, 541
princess and the pea (Boyesen) and, 550
as a regulatory mechanism, 270, 309
remnants, 541
speed of emotion versus, 263–64
stretch-and-yawn reaction and, 537–40
sympathicotonia and, 553
statistical analysis, of derived matrixes, 589–
91
stethoscopes, 209, 276, 549
still-face paradigm, 625–27
stimulus association, 373
stone (Boyesen), 549
stool exercise, 60–61, 60*f*, 686*n*30
stress, **212–28, 218***f*, 230, 310, 488
stretch-and-yawn reaction, 537, 539

stretching
basic posture and, 32
diaphragmatic segments (Vegetotherapy)
and, 475
relaxation and, 39, 208
to release fear, 542
venous circulation and, 331
yawning and, 537
structured discourse, 365–66
See also talking cure
sublimation, 403
subsymbolism, 378
subsystems, 130, 665–66
See also heteroclite subsystems
suckling indicators, of infants, 624–25
suicide, 245–46, 419, 604, 606, 719*n*47
suicide attempts studies, 531, 602, 644–46,
730*n*39
sunshine (Boyesen), 550
super-ego, 29, 403, 559
See also conscious, the (Freud)
support surfaces, 323, 591
suprarenal glands, 218, 218*f*
surface, of a practice, 640
surface postures, 324
surprise, 538
See also startle reflex
survival, 529, 612, 613, 621
survival of the fittest, 167–68, 171, 172
Swedish gymnastics, **291–92**
Swedish massage, 292
symbolic language, body representations
and, 377–78
See also nonverbal communication
symmetry and asymmetry, of body, 329–30
sympathetic nervous system
cortisol and, 217
fight, flight, or freeze behaviors and, 216
functions of, 207–8
orgasms and, 434
vasopressin and, 231
vegetative system and, 199, 200
sympathicotonia, 553
synchrony, 506, 623
systemic therapy, 452, 580, 595
system of the dimensions of the organism
(SDO)
open systems in, 320–21, 664–65
overview of, **3–21, 11***f*, **13***f*, **14***f*, **16***f*
subsystems in, 665–66
See also I Ching
systems
defined, 4, 7–8
and parts, **5–6**
systems theory, 4–6, 10, **122–34**, 681*n*6

tai chi chuan, 67–70, 188, 299, 314–15,
682*n*1, 686*n*45–87*n*46